University Casebook Series

October, 1993

ACCOUNTING AND THE LAW, Fourth Edition (1978), with Problems Pamphlet (Successor to Dohr, Phillips, Thompson & Warren)

George C. Thompson, Professor, Columbia University Graduate School of Business.

Robert Whitman, Professor of Law, University of Connecticut.

Ellis L. Phillips, Jr., Member of the New York Bar.

William C. Warren, Professor of Law Emeritus, Columbia University.

ACCOUNTING FOR LAWYERS, MATERIALS ON (1980)

David R. Herwitz, Professor of Law, Harvard University.

ADMINISTRATIVE LAW, Eighth Edition (1987), with 1993 Case Supplement and 1983 Problems Supplement (Supplement edited in association with Paul R. Verkuil, Dean and Professor of Law, Tulane University)

Walter Gellhorn, University Professor Emeritus, Columbia University.

Clark Byse, Professor of Law, Harvard University.

Peter L. Strauss, Professor of Law, Columbia University.

Todd D. Rakoff, Professor of Law, Harvard University.

Roy A. Schotland, Professor of Law, Georgetown University.

ADMIRALTY, Third Edition (1987), with 1991 Statute and Rule Supplement

Jo Desha Lucas, Professor of Law, University of Chicago.

ADVOCACY, see also Lawyering Process

AGENCY, see also Enterprise Organization

AGENCY—PARTNERSHIPS, Fourth Edition (1987)

Abridgement from Conard, Knauss & Siegel's Enterprise Organization, Fourth Edition.

AGENCY AND PARTNERSHIPS (1987)

Melvin A. Eisenberg, Professor of Law, University of California, Berkeley.

ANTITRUST: FREE ENTERPRISE AND ECONOMIC ORGANIZATION, Sixth Edition (1983), with 1983 Problems in Antitrust Supplement and 1993 Case Supplement

Louis B. Schwartz, Professor of Law, University of Pennsylvania.

John J. Flynn, Professor of Law, University of Utah.

Harry First, Professor of Law, New York University.

BANKRUPTCY, Third Edition (1993)

Robert L. Jordan, Professor of Law, University of California, Los Angeles.

William D. Warren, Professor of Law, University of California, Los Angeles.

BANKRUPTCY AND DEBTOR–CREDITOR LAW, Second Edition (1988)

Theodore Eisenberg, Professor of Law, Cornell University.

[i]

BUSINESS ASSOCIATIONS, AGENCY, PARTNERSHIPS, AND CORPORATIONS (1991), with 1993 Supplement

William A. Klein, Professor of Law, University of California, Los Angeles.
Mark Ramseyer, Professor of Law, University of California, Los Angeles.

BUSINESS CRIME (1990), with 1993–94 Case Supplement

Harry First, Professor of Law, New York University.

BUSINESS ORGANIZATION, see also Enterprise Organization

BUSINESS PLANNING (1991)

Franklin Gevurtz, Professor of Law, McGeorge School of Law.

BUSINESS PLANNING, Temporary Second Edition (1984)

David R. Herwitz, Professor of Law, Harvard University.

BUSINESS TORTS (1972)

Milton Handler, Professor of Law Emeritus, Columbia University.

CHILDREN IN THE LEGAL SYSTEM (1983), with 1990 Supplement (Supplement edited in association with Elizabeth S. Scott, Professor of Law, University of Virginia)

Walter Wadlington, Professor of Law, University of Virginia.
Charles H. Whitebread, Professor of Law, University of Southern California.
Samuel Davis, Professor of Law, University of Georgia.

CIVIL PROCEDURE, see Procedure

CIVIL RIGHTS ACTIONS (1988), with 1993 Supplement

Peter W. Low, Professor of Law, University of Virginia.
John C. Jeffries, Jr., Professor of Law, University of Virginia.

CLINIC, see also Lawyering Process

COMMERCIAL AND DEBTOR–CREDITOR LAW: SELECTED STATUTES, 1993 EDITION

COMMERCIAL LAW, Third Edition (1992)

Robert L. Jordan, Professor of Law, University of California, Los Angeles.
William D. Warren, Professor of Law, University of California, Los Angeles.

COMMERCIAL LAW, Fifth Edition (1993)

E. Allan Farnsworth, Professor of Law, Columbia University.
John O. Honnold, Professor of Law Emeritus, University of Pennsylvania.
Curtis R. Reitz, Professor of Law, University of Pennsylvania.
Steven L. Harris, Professor of Law, University of Illinois.
Charles Mooney, Jr., Professor of Law, University of Pennsylvania.

COMMERCIAL PAPER, see also Negotiable Instruments

COMMERCIAL PAPER AND BANK DEPOSITS AND COLLECTIONS (1967), with Statutory Supplement

William D. Hawkland, Professor of Law, University of Illinois.

UNIVERSITY CASEBOOK SERIES—Continued

COMMERCIAL TRANSACTIONS—Principles and Policies, Second Edition (1991)

Alan Schwartz, Professor of Law, Yale University.
Robert E. Scott, Professor of Law, University of Virginia.

COMPARATIVE LAW, Fifth Edition (1988)

Rudolf B. Schlesinger, Professor of Law, Hastings College of the Law.
Hans W. Baade, Professor of Law, University of Texas.
Mirjan P. Damaska, Professor of Law, Yale Law School.
Peter E. Herzog, Professor of Law, Syracuse University.

COMPETITIVE PROCESS, LEGAL REGULATION OF THE, Revised Fourth Edition (1991), with 1993 Selected Statutes Supplement

Edmund W. Kitch, Professor of Law, University of Virginia.
Harvey S. Perlman, Dean of the Law School, University of Nebraska.

CONFLICT OF LAWS, Ninth Edition (1990), with Revised 1993 Supplement

Willis L. M. Reese, Professor of Law, Columbia University.
Maurice Rosenberg, Professor of Law, Columbia University.
Peter Hay, Professor of Law, University of Illinois.

CONSTITUTIONAL LAW, CIVIL LIBERTY AND INDIVIDUAL RIGHTS, Second Edition (1982), with 1992 Supplement

William Cohen, Professor of Law, Stanford University.
John Kaplan, Professor of Law, Stanford University.

CONSTITUTIONAL LAW, Ninth Edition (1993), with 1993 Supplement

William Cohen, Professor of Law, Stanford University.
Jonathan D. Varat, Professor of Law, University of California, Los Angeles.

CONSTITUTIONAL LAW, Twelfth Edition (1991), with 1993 Supplement (Supplement edited in association with Frederick F. Schauer, Professor, Harvard University)

Gerald Gunther, Professor of Law, Stanford University.

CONSTITUTIONAL LAW, INDIVIDUAL RIGHTS IN, Fifth Edition (1992) (Reprinted from CONSTITUTIONAL LAW, Twelfth Edition), with 1993 Supplement (Supplement edited in association with Frederick F. Schauer, Professor, Harvard University)

Gerald Gunther, Professor of Law, Stanford University.

CONSUMER TRANSACTIONS, Second Edition (1991), with Selected Statutes and Regulations Supplement

Michael M. Greenfield, Professor of Law, Washington University.

CONTRACT LAW AND ITS APPLICATION, Fourth Edition (1988)

Arthur Rosett, Professor of Law, University of California, Los Angeles.

CONTRACT LAW, STUDIES IN, Fourth Edition (1991)

Edward J. Murphy, Professor of Law, University of Notre Dame.
Richard E. Speidel, Professor of Law, Northwestern University.

[iii]

CONTRACTS, Sixth Edition (1993)

John P. Dawson, late Professor of Law, Harvard University.
William Burnett Harvey, Professor of Law and Political Science, Boston University.
Stanley D. Henderson, Professor of Law, University of Virginia.

CONTRACTS, Fourth Edition (1988)

E. Allan Farnsworth, Professor of Law, Columbia University.
William F. Young, Professor of Law, Columbia University.

CONTRACTS, Selections on (statutory materials) (1992)

CONTRACTS, Second Edition (1978), with Statutory and Administrative Law Supplement (1978)

Ian R. Macneil, Professor of Law, Cornell University.

COPYRIGHT, PATENTS AND TRADEMARKS, see also Competitive Process; see also Selected Statutes and International Agreements

COPYRIGHT, PATENT, TRADEMARK AND RELATED STATE DOCTRINES, Revised Third Edition (1993), with 1993 Selected Statutes Supplement and 1981 Problem Supplement

Paul Goldstein, Professor of Law, Stanford University.

COPYRIGHT, Unfair Competition, and Other Topics Bearing on the Protection of Literary, Musical, and Artistic Works, Fifth Edition (1990), with 1993 Statutory and Case Supplement

Ralph S. Brown, Jr., Professor of Law, Yale University.
Robert C. Denicola, Professor of Law, University of Nebraska.

CORPORATE ACQUISITIONS, The Law and Finance of (1986), with 1993 Supplement

Ronald J. Gilson, Professor of Law, Stanford University.

CORPORATE FINANCE, Brudney and Chirelstein's Fourth Edition (1993)

Victor Brudney, Professor of Law, Harvard University.
William W. Bratton, Jr., Professor of Law, Rutgers University, Newark.

CORPORATION LAW, BASIC, Third Edition (1989), with Documentary Supplement

Detlev F. Vagts, Professor of Law, Harvard University.

CORPORATIONS, see also Enterprise Organization and Business Organization

CORPORATIONS, Sixth Edition—Concise (1988), with 1993 Case Supplement and 1993 Statutory Supplement

William L. Cary, late Professor of Law, Columbia University.
Melvin Aron Eisenberg, Professor of Law, University of California, Berkeley.

CORPORATIONS, Sixth Edition—Unabridged (1988), with 1993 Case Supplement and 1993 Statutory Supplement

William L. Cary, late Professor of Law, Columbia University.
Melvin Aron Eisenberg, Professor of Law, University of California, Berkeley.

CORPORATIONS AND BUSINESS ASSOCIATIONS—STATUTES, RULES, AND FORMS, 1993 Edition

UNIVERSITY CASEBOOK SERIES—Continued

CORRECTIONS, see Sentencing

CREDITORS' RIGHTS, see also Debtor–Creditor Law

CRIMINAL JUSTICE ADMINISTRATION, Fourth Edition (1991), with 1993 Supplement

Frank W. Miller, Professor of Law, Washington University.
Robert O. Dawson, Professor of Law, University of Texas.
George E. Dix, Professor of Law, University of Texas.
Raymond I. Parnas, Professor of Law, University of California, Davis.

CRIMINAL LAW, Fifth Edition (1992)

Andre A. Moenssens, Professor of Law, University of Richmond.
Fred E. Inbau, Professor of Law Emeritus, Northwestern University.
Ronald J. Bacigal, Professor of Law, University of Richmond.

CRIMINAL LAW AND APPROACHES TO THE STUDY OF LAW, Second Edition (1991)

John M. Brumbaugh, Professor of Law, University of Maryland.

CRIMINAL LAW, Second Edition (1986)

Peter W. Low, Professor of Law, University of Virginia.
John C. Jeffries, Jr., Professor of Law, University of Virginia.
Richard C. Bonnie, Professor of Law, University of Virginia.

CRIMINAL LAW, Fifth Edition (1993)

Lloyd L. Weinreb, Professor of Law, Harvard University.

CRIMINAL LAW AND PROCEDURE, Seventh Edition (1989)

Ronald N. Boyce, Professor of Law, University of Utah.
Rollin M. Perkins, Professor of Law Emeritus, University of California, Hastings College of the Law.

CRIMINAL PROCEDURE, Fourth Edition (1992), with 1993 Supplement

James B. Haddad, late Professor of Law, Northwestern University.
James B. Zagel, Chief, Criminal Justice Division, Office of Attorney General of Illinois.
Gary L. Starkman, Assistant U.S. Attorney, Northern District of Illinois.
William J. Bauer, Chief Judge of the U.S. Court of Appeals, Seventh Circuit.

CRIMINAL PROCESS, Fifth Edition (1993), with 1993 Supplement

Lloyd L. Weinreb, Professor of Law, Harvard University.

CRIMINAL PROCESS, PART ONE—INVESTIGATION (1993) (Reprint of Chapters 1–6 of Weinreb's CRIMINAL PROCESS, Fifth Edition), with 1993 Supplement

CRIMINAL PROCESS, PART TWO—PROSECUTION (1993) (Reprint of Chapters 7–18 of Weinreb's CRIMINAL PROCESS, Fifth Edition), with 1993 Supplement

DAMAGES, Second Edition (1952)

Charles T. McCormick, late Professor of Law, University of Texas.
William F. Fritz, late Professor of Law, University of Texas.

DECEDENTS' ESTATES AND TRUSTS, see also Family Property Law

UNIVERSITY CASEBOOK SERIES—Continued

DECEDENTS' ESTATES AND TRUSTS, Eighth Edition (1993)

John Ritchie, late Professor of Law, University of Virginia.
Neill H. Alford, Jr., Professor of Law, University of Virginia.
Richard W. Effland, late Professor of Law, Arizona State University.
Joel C. Dobris, Professor of Law, University of California, Davis.

DISPUTE RESOLUTION, Processes of (1989)

John S. Murray, President and Executive Director of The Conflict Clinic, Inc., George Mason University.
Alan Scott Rau, Professor of Law, University of Texas.
Edward F. Sherman, Professor of Law, University of Texas.

DOMESTIC RELATIONS, see also Family Law

DOMESTIC RELATIONS, Second Edition (1990), with 1993 Supplement

Walter Wadlington, Professor of Law, University of Virginia.

EMPLOYMENT DISCRIMINATION, Third Edition (1993)

Joel W. Friedman, Professor of Law, Tulane University.
George M. Strickler, Professor of Law, Tulane University.

EMPLOYMENT LAW, Second Edition (1991), with 1993 Statutory Supplement and 1993 Case Supplement

Mark A. Rothstein, Professor of Law, University of Houston.
Andria S. Knapp, Visiting Professor of Law, Golden Gate University.
Lance Liebman, Professor of Law, Harvard University.

ENERGY LAW (1983), with 1991 Case Supplement

Donald N. Zillman, Professor of Law, University of Utah.
Laurence Lattman, Dean of Mines and Engineering, University of Utah.

ENTERPRISE ORGANIZATION, Fourth Edition (1987), with 1987 Corporation and Partnership Statutes, Rules and Forms Supplement

Alfred F. Conard, Professor of Law, University of Michigan.
Robert L. Knauss, Dean of the Law School, University of Houston.
Stanley Siegel, Professor of Law, University of California, Los Angeles.

ENVIRONMENTAL POLICY LAW, Second Edition (1991)

Thomas J. Schoenbaum, Professor of Law, University of Georgia.
Ronald H. Rosenberg, Professor of Law, College of William and Mary.

EQUITY, see also Remedies

EQUITY, RESTITUTION AND DAMAGES, Second Edition (1974)

Robert Childres, late Professor of Law, Northwestern University.
William F. Johnson, Jr., Professor of Law, New York University.

ESTATE PLANNING, Second Edition (1982), with 1985 Case, Text and Documentary Supplement

David Westfall, Professor of Law, Harvard University.

ETHICS, see Legal Ethics, Legal Profession, Professional Responsibility, and Social Responsibilities

ETHICS OF LAWYERING, THE LAW AND (1990)

Geoffrey C. Hazard, Jr., Professor of Law, Yale University.
Susan P. Koniak, Professor of Law, University of Pittsburgh.

UNIVERSITY CASEBOOK SERIES—Continued

ETHICS AND PROFESSIONAL RESPONSIBILITY (1981) (Reprinted from THE LAWYERING PROCESS)

Gary Bellow, Professor of Law, Harvard University.
Bea Moulton, Legal Services Corporation.

EVIDENCE, Seventh Edition (1992)

John Kaplan, late Professor of Law, Stanford University.
Jon R. Waltz, Professor of Law, Northwestern University.
Roger C. Park, Professor of Law, University of Minnesota.

EVIDENCE, Eighth Edition (1988), with Rules, Statute and Case Supplement (1993)

Jack B. Weinstein, Chief Judge, United States District Court.
John H. Mansfield, Professor of Law, Harvard University.
Norman Abrams, Professor of Law, University of California, Los Angeles.
Margaret Berger, Professor of Law, Brooklyn Law School.

FAMILY LAW, see also Domestic Relations

FAMILY LAW, Third Edition (1992)

Judith C. Areen, Professor of Law, Georgetown University.

FAMILY LAW AND CHILDREN IN THE LEGAL SYSTEM, STATUTORY MATERIALS (1981)

Walter Wadlington, Professor of Law, University of Virginia.

FAMILY PROPERTY LAW, Cases and Materials on Wills, Trusts and Future Interests, Star Edition (1991)

Lawrence W. Waggoner, Professor of Law, University of Michigan.
Richard V. Wellman, Professor of Law, University of Georgia.
Gregory Alexander, Professor of Law, Cornell Law School.
Mary L. Fellows, Professor of Law, University of Minnesota.

FEDERAL COURTS, Ninth Edition (1992)

Charles T. McCormick, late Professor of Law, University of Texas.
James H. Chadbourn, late Professor of Law, Harvard University.
Charles Alan Wright, Professor of Law, University of Texas, Austin.

FEDERAL COURTS AND THE FEDERAL SYSTEM, Hart and Wechsler's Third Edition (1988), with 1993 Case Supplement, and the Judicial Code and Rules of Procedure in the Federal Courts (1993)

Paul M. Bator, Professor of Law, University of Chicago.
Daniel J. Meltzer, Professor of Law, Harvard University.
Paul J. Mishkin, Professor of Law, University of California, Berkeley.
David L. Shapiro, Professor of Law, Harvard University.

FEDERAL COURTS AND THE LAW OF FEDERAL–STATE RELATIONS, Second Edition (1989), with 1993 Supplement

Peter W. Low, Professor of Law, University of Virginia.
John C. Jeffries, Jr., Professor of Law, University of Virginia.

FEDERAL PUBLIC LAND AND RESOURCES LAW, Third Edition (1993), with 1990 Statutory Supplement

George C. Coggins, Professor of Law, University of Kansas.
Charles F. Wilkinson, Professor of Law, University of Oregon.
John D. Leshy, Professor of Law, Arizona State University.

UNIVERSITY CASEBOOK SERIES—Continued

FEDERAL RULES OF CIVIL PROCEDURE and Selected Other Procedural Provisions, 1993 Edition

FEDERAL TAXATION, see Taxation

FIRST AMENDMENT (1991), with 1993 Supplement

William W. Van Alstyne, Professor of Law, Duke University.

FOOD AND DRUG LAW, Second Edition (1991), with Statutory Supplement

Peter Barton Hutt, Esq.
Richard A. Merrill, Professor of Law, University of Virginia.

FUTURE INTERESTS (1970)

Howard R. Williams, Professor of Law, Stanford University.

FUTURE INTERESTS AND ESTATE PLANNING (1961), with 1962 Supplement

W. Barton Leach, late Professor of Law, Harvard University.
James K. Logan, formerly Dean of the Law School, University of Kansas.

GENDER DISCRIMINATION, see Women and the Law

GOVERNMENT CONTRACTS, FEDERAL, Successor Edition (1985), with 1989 Supplement

John W. Whelan, Professor of Law, Hastings College of the Law.

GOVERNMENT REGULATION: FREE ENTERPRISE AND ECONOMIC ORGANIZATION, Sixth Edition (1985)

Louis B. Schwartz, Professor of Law, Hastings College of the Law.
John J. Flynn, Professor of Law, University of Utah.
Harry First, Professor of Law, New York University.

HEALTH CARE LAW AND POLICY (1988), with 1992 Supplement

Clark C. Havighurst, Professor of Law, Duke University.

HINCKLEY, JOHN W., JR., TRIAL OF: A Case Study of the Insanity Defense (1986)

Peter W. Low, Professor of Law, University of Virginia.
John C. Jeffries, Jr., Professor of Law, University of Virginia.
Richard C. Bonnie, Professor of Law, University of Virginia.

IMMIGRATION LAW AND POLICY (1992)

Stephen H. Legomsky, Professor of Law, Washington University.

INJUNCTIONS, Second Edition (1984)

Owen M. Fiss, Professor of Law, Yale University.
Doug Rendleman, Professor of Law, College of William and Mary.

INSTITUTIONAL INVESTORS (1978)

David L. Ratner, Professor of Law, Cornell University.

INSURANCE, Second Edition (1985)

William F. Young, Professor of Law, Columbia University.
Eric M. Holmes, Professor of Law, University of Georgia.

INSURANCE LAW AND REGULATION (1990)

Kenneth S. Abraham, University of Virginia.

UNIVERSITY CASEBOOK SERIES—Continued

INTERNATIONAL LAW, see also Transnational Legal Problems, Transnational Business Problems, and United Nations Law

INTERNATIONAL LAW IN CONTEMPORARY PERSPECTIVE (1981), with Essay Supplement

Myres S. McDougal, Professor of Law, Yale University.
W. Michael Reisman, Professor of Law, Yale University.

INTERNATIONAL LEGAL SYSTEM, Third Edition (1988), with Documentary Supplement

Joseph Modeste Sweeney, Professor of Law, University of California, Hastings.
Covey T. Oliver, Professor of Law, University of Pennsylvania.
Noyes E. Leech, Professor of Law Emeritus, University of Pennsylvania.

INTRODUCTION TO LAW, see also Legal Method, On Law in Courts, and Dynamics of American Law

INTRODUCTION TO THE STUDY OF LAW (1970)

E. Wayne Thode, late Professor of Law, University of Utah.
Leon Lebowitz, Professor of Law, University of Texas.
Lester J. Mazor, Professor of Law, University of Utah.

JUDICIAL CODE and Rules of Procedure in the Federal Courts, Students' Edition, 1993 Revision

Daniel J. Meltzer, Professor of Law, Harvard University.
David L. Shapiro, Professor of Law, Harvard University.

JURISPRUDENCE (Temporary Edition Hardbound) (1949)

Lon L. Fuller, late Professor of Law, Harvard University.

JUVENILE, see also Children

JUVENILE JUSTICE PROCESS, Third Edition (1985)

Frank W. Miller, Professor of Law, Washington University.
Robert O. Dawson, Professor of Law, University of Texas.
George E. Dix, Professor of Law, University of Texas.
Raymond I. Parnas, Professor of Law, University of California, Davis.

LABOR LAW, Eleventh Edition (1991), with 1993 Statutory Supplement and 1992 Case Supplement

Archibald Cox, Professor of Law, Harvard University.
Derek C. Bok, President, Harvard University.
Robert A. Gorman, Professor of Law, University of Pennsylvania.
Matthew W. Finkin, Professor of Law, University of Illinois.

LABOR LAW, Second Edition (1982), with Statutory Supplement

Clyde W. Summers, Professor of Law, University of Pennsylvania.
Harry H. Wellington, Dean of the Law School, Yale University.
Alan Hyde, Professor of Law, Rutgers University.

LAND FINANCING, Third Edition (1985)

Norman Penney, late Professor of Law, Cornell University.
Richard F. Broude, Member of the California Bar.
Roger Cunningham, Professor of Law, University of Michigan.

UNIVERSITY CASEBOOK SERIES—Continued

LAW AND MEDICINE (1980)

Walter Wadlington, Professor of Law and Professor of Legal Medicine, University of Virginia.

Jon R. Waltz, Professor of Law, Northwestern University.

Roger B. Dworkin, Professor of Law, Indiana University, and Professor of Biomedical History, University of Washington.

LAW, LANGUAGE AND ETHICS (1972)

William R. Bishin, Professor of Law, University of Southern California.

Christopher D. Stone, Professor of Law, University of Southern California.

LAW, SCIENCE AND MEDICINE (1984), with 1989 Supplement

Judith C. Areen, Professor of Law, Georgetown University.

Patricia A. King, Professor of Law, Georgetown University.

Steven P. Goldberg, Professor of Law, Georgetown University.

Alexander M. Capron, Professor of Law, University of Southern California.

LAWYERING PROCESS (1978), with Civil Problem Supplement and Criminal Problem Supplement

Gary Bellow, Professor of Law, Harvard University.

Bea Moulton, Professor of Law, Arizona State University.

LEGAL ETHICS (1992)

Deborah Rhode, Professor of Law, Stanford University.

David Luban, Professor of Law, University of Maryland.

LEGAL METHOD (1980)

Harry W. Jones, Professor of Law Emeritus, Columbia University.

John M. Kernochan, Professor of Law, Columbia University.

Arthur W. Murphy, Professor of Law, Columbia University.

LEGAL METHODS (1969)

Robert N. Covington, Professor of Law, Vanderbilt University.

E. Blythe Stason, late Professor of Law, Vanderbilt University.

John W. Wade, Professor of Law, Vanderbilt University.

Elliott E. Cheatham, late Professor of Law, Vanderbilt University.

Theodore A. Smedley, Professor of Law, Vanderbilt University.

LEGAL PROFESSION, THE, Responsibility and Regulation, Second Edition (1988)

Geoffrey C. Hazard, Jr., Professor of Law, Yale University.

Deborah L. Rhode, Professor of Law, Stanford University.

LEGISLATION (1993)

William D. Popkin, Professor of Law, Indiana University at Bloomington.

LEGISLATION, Fourth Edition (1982) (by Fordham)

Horace E. Read, late Vice President, Dalhousie University.

John W. MacDonald, Professor of Law Emeritus, Cornell Law School.

Jefferson B. Fordham, Professor of Law, University of Utah.

William J. Pierce, Professor of Law, University of Michigan.

UNIVERSITY CASEBOOK SERIES—Continued

LEGISLATIVE AND ADMINISTRATIVE PROCESSES, Second Edition (1981)

Hans A. Linde, Judge, Supreme Court of Oregon.
George Bunn, Professor of Law, University of Wisconsin.
Fredericka Paff, Professor of Law, University of Wisconsin.
W. Lawrence Church, Professor of Law, University of Wisconsin.

LOCAL GOVERNMENT LAW, Second Revised Edition (1986)

Jefferson B. Fordham, Professor of Law, University of Utah.

MASS MEDIA LAW, Fourth Edition (1990), with 1993 Supplement

Marc A. Franklin, Professor of Law, Stanford University.
David A. Anderson, Professor of Law, University of Texas.

MUNICIPAL CORPORATIONS, see Local Government Law

NEGOTIABLE INSTRUMENTS, see Commercial Paper

NEGOTIABLE INSTRUMENTS, Fourth Edition (1993)

E. Allan Farnsworth, Professor of Law, Columbia University.

NEGOTIABLE INSTRUMENTS AND LETTERS OF CREDIT (1992) (Reprinted from Commercial Law), Third Edition (1992)

Robert L. Jordan, Professor of Law, University of California, Los Angeles.
William D. Warren, Professor of Law, University of California, Los Angeles.

NEGOTIATION (1981) (Reprinted from THE LAWYERING PROCESS)

Gary Bellow, Professor of Law, Harvard Law School.
Bea Moulton, Legal Services Corporation.

NEW YORK PRACTICE, Fourth Edition (1978)

Herbert Peterfreund, Professor of Law, New York University.
Joseph M. McLaughlin, Dean of the Law School, Fordham University.

OIL AND GAS, Sixth Edition (1992)

Richard C. Maxwell, Professor of Law, Duke University.
Stephen F. Williams, Judge of the United States Court of Appeals.
Patrick Henry Martin, Professor of Law, Louisiana State University.
Bruce M. Kramer, Professor of Law, Texas Tech University.

ON LAW IN COURTS (1965)

Paul J. Mishkin, Professor of Law, University of California, Berkeley.
Clarence Morris, Professor of Law Emeritus, University of Pennsylvania.

PENSION AND EMPLOYEE BENEFIT LAW (1990), with 1993 Supplement

John H. Langbein, Professor of Law, University of Chicago.
Bruce A. Wolk, Professor of Law, University of California, Davis.

PLEADING AND PROCEDURE, see Procedure, Civil

POLICE FUNCTION, Fifth Edition (1991), with 1993 Supplement

Reprint of Chapters 1–10 of Miller, Dawson, Dix and Parnas's CRIMINAL JUSTICE ADMINISTRATION, Fourth Edition.

PREPARING AND PRESENTING THE CASE (1981) (Reprinted from THE LAWYERING PROCESS)

Gary Bellow, Professor of Law, Harvard Law School.
Bea Moulton, Legal Services Corporation.

UNIVERSITY CASEBOOK SERIES—Continued

PROCEDURE (1988), with Procedure Supplement (1991)

Robert M. Cover, late Professor of Law, Yale Law School.
Owen M. Fiss, Professor of Law, Yale Law School.
Judith Resnik, Professor of Law, University of Southern California Law Center.

PROCEDURE—CIVIL PROCEDURE, Sixth Edition (1990), with 1993 Supplement

Richard H. Field, late Professor of Law, Harvard University.
Benjamin Kaplan, Professor of Law Emeritus, Harvard University.
Kevin M. Clermont, Professor of Law, Cornell University.

PROCEDURE—CIVIL PROCEDURE, Successor Edition (1992)

A. Leo Levin, Professor of Law Emeritus, University of Pennsylvania.
Philip Shuchman, Professor of Law, Rutgers University.
Charles M. Yablon, Professor of Law, Yeshiva University.

PROCEDURE—CIVIL PROCEDURE, Fifth Edition (1990), with 1993 Supplement

Maurice Rosenberg, Professor of Law, Columbia University.
Hans Smit, Professor of Law, Columbia University.
Rochelle C. Dreyfuss, Professor of Law, New York University.

PROCEDURE—PLEADING AND PROCEDURE: State and Federal, Sixth Edition (1989), with 1993 Case Supplement

David W. Louisell, late Professor of Law, University of California, Berkeley.
Geoffrey C. Hazard, Jr., Professor of Law, Yale University.
Colin C. Tait, Professor of Law, University of Connecticut.

PROCEDURE—FEDERAL RULES OF CIVIL PROCEDURE, 1993 Edition

PRODUCTS LIABILITY AND SAFETY, Second Edition (1989), with 1993 Case and Statutory Supplement

W. Page Keeton, Professor of Law, University of Texas.
David G. Owen, Professor of Law, University of South Carolina.
John E. Montgomery, Professor of Law, University of South Carolina.
Michael D. Green, Professor of Law, University of Iowa.

PROFESSIONAL RESPONSIBILITY, Fifth Edition (1991), with 1993 Selected Standards on Professional Responsibility Supplement

Thomas D. Morgan, Professor of Law, George Washington University.
Ronald D. Rotunda, Professor of Law, University of Illinois.

PROPERTY, Sixth Edition (1990)

John E. Cribbet, Professor of Law, University of Illinois.
Corwin W. Johnson, Professor of Law, University of Texas.
Roger W. Findley, Professor of Law, University of Illinois.
Ernest E. Smith, Professor of Law, University of Texas.

PROPERTY—PERSONAL (1953)

S. Kenneth Skolfield, late Professor of Law Emeritus, Boston University.

PROPERTY—PERSONAL, Third Edition (1954)

Everett Fraser, late Dean of the Law School Emeritus, University of Minnesota.
Third Edition by Charles W. Taintor, late Professor of Law, University of Pittsburgh.

UNIVERSITY CASEBOOK SERIES—Continued

PROPERTY—INTRODUCTION, TO REAL PROPERTY, Third Edition (1954)

Everett Fraser, late Dean of the Law School Emeritus, University of Minnesota.

PROPERTY—FUNDAMENTALS OF MODERN REAL PROPERTY, Third Edition (1992)

Edward H. Rabin, Professor of Law, University of California, Davis.
Roberta Rosenthal Kwall, Professor of Law, DePaul University.

PROPERTY, REAL (1984), with 1988 Supplement

Paul Goldstein, Professor of Law, Stanford University.

PROSECUTION AND ADJUDICATION, Fourth Edition (1991), with 1993 Supplement

Reprint of Chapters 11–26 of Miller, Dawson, Dix and Parnas's CRIMINAL JUSTICE ADMINISTRATION, Fourth Edition.

PSYCHIATRY AND LAW, see Mental Health, see also Hinckley, Trial of

PUBLIC UTILITY LAW, see Free Enterprise, also Regulated Industries

REAL ESTATE PLANNING, Third Edition (1989), with Revised Problem and Statutory Supplement (1991)

Norton L. Steuben, Professor of Law, University of Colorado.

REAL ESTATE TRANSACTIONS, Third Edition (1993), with Statute, Form and Problem Supplement (1993)

Paul Goldstein, Professor of Law, Stanford University.
Gerald Korngold, Professor of Law, Case Western Reserve University.

RECEIVERSHIP AND CORPORATE REORGANIZATION, see Creditors' Rights

REGULATED INDUSTRIES, Second Edition (1976)

William K. Jones, Professor of Law, Columbia University.

REMEDIES, Third Edition (1992)

Edward D. Re, Professor of Law, St. John's University.
Stanton D. Krauss, Professor of Law, University of Bridgeport.

REMEDIES (1989)

Elaine W. Shoben, Professor of Law, University of Illinois.
Wm. Murray Tabb, Professor of Law, Baylor University.

SALES, Third Edition (1992)

Marion W. Benfield, Jr., Professor of Law, Wake Forest University.
William D. Hawkland, Professor of Law, Louisiana State Law Center.

SALES (1992) (Reprinted from Commercial Law) Third Edition (1992)

Robert L. Jordan, Professor of Law, University of California, Los Angeles.
William D. Warren, Professor of Law, University of California, Los Angeles.

SALES AND SECURED FINANCING, Sixth Edition (1993)

John Honnold, Professor of Law Emeritus, University of Pennsylvania.
Steven L. Harris, Professor of Law, University of Illinois.
Charles Mooney, Jr., Professor of Law, University of Pennsylvania.
Curtis R. Reitz, Professor of Law, University of Pennsylvania.

UNIVERSITY CASEBOOK SERIES—Continued

SALES LAW AND THE CONTRACTING PROCESS, Second Edition (1991) (Reprinted from Commercial Transactions) Second Edition (1991)

Alan Schwartz, Professor of Law, Yale University.
Robert E. Scott, Professor of Law, University of Virginia.

SALES TRANSACTIONS: DOMESTIC AND INTERNATIONAL LAW (1992)

John Honnold, Professor of Law Emeritus, University of Pennsylvania.
Curtis R. Reitz, Professor of Law, University of Pennsylvania.

SECURED TRANSACTIONS IN PERSONAL PROPERTY, Third Edition (1992) (Reprinted from COMMERCIAL LAW, Third Edition (1992))

Robert L. Jordan, Professor of Law, University of California, Los Angeles.
William D. Warren, Professor of Law, University of California, Los Angeles.

SECURITIES REGULATION, Seventh Edition (1992), with 1993 Selected Statutes, Rules and Forms Supplement, and 1993 Cases and Releases Supplement

Richard W. Jennings, Professor of Law, University of California, Berkeley.
Harold Marsh, Jr., Member of California Bar.
John C. Coffee, Jr., Professor of Law, Columbia University.

SECURITIES REGULATION, Second Edition (1988), with Statute, Rule and Form Supplement (1991)

Larry D. Soderquist, Professor of Law, Vanderbilt University.

SECURITY INTERESTS IN PERSONAL PROPERTY, Second Edition (1987)

Douglas G. Baird, Professor of Law, University of Chicago.
Thomas H. Jackson, Dean of the Law School, University of Virginia.

SECURITY INTERESTS IN PERSONAL PROPERTY, Second Edition (1992)

John Honnold, Professor of Law Emeritus, University of Pennsylvania.
Steven L. Harris, Professor of Law, University of Illinois.
Charles W. Mooney, Jr., Professor of Law, University of Pennsylvania.

SELECTED STANDARDS ON PROFESSIONAL RESPONSIBILITY, 1993 Edition

SELECTED STATUTES AND INTERNATIONAL AGREEMENTS ON UNFAIR COMPETITION, TRADEMARK, COPYRIGHT AND PATENT, 1993 Edition

SELECTED STATUTES ON TRUSTS AND ESTATES, 1992 Edition

SOCIAL RESPONSIBILITIES OF LAWYERS, Case Studies (1988)

Philip B. Heymann, Professor of Law, Harvard University.
Lance Liebman, Professor of Law, Harvard University.

SOCIAL SCIENCE IN LAW, Second Edition (1990)

John Monahan, Professor of Law, University of Virginia.
Laurens Walker, Professor of Law, University of Virginia.

TAXATION, FEDERAL INCOME (1989)

Stephen B. Cohen, Professor of Law, Georgetown University.

TAXATION, FEDERAL INCOME, Second Edition (1988), with 1993 Supplement (Supplement edited in association with Deborah H. Schenk, Professor of Law, New York University)

Michael J. Graetz, Professor of Law, Yale University.

TAXATION, FEDERAL INCOME, Seventh Edition (1991)

James J. Freeland, Professor of Law, University of Florida.

Stephen A. Lind, Professor of Law, University of Florida and University of California, Hastings.

Richard B. Stephens, late Professor of Law Emeritus, University of Florida.

TAXATION, FEDERAL INCOME, Successor Edition (1986), with 1993 Supplement

Stanley S. Surrey, late Professor of Law, Harvard University.

Paul R. McDaniel, Professor of Law, Boston College.

Hugh J. Ault, Professor of Law, Boston College.

Stanley A. Koppelman, Professor of Law, Boston University.

TAXATION, FEDERAL INCOME, OF BUSINESS ORGANIZATIONS (1991), with 1993 Supplement

Paul R. McDaniel, Professor of Law, Boston College.

Hugh J. Ault, Professor of Law, Boston College.

Martin J. McMahon, Jr., Professor of Law, University of Kentucky.

Daniel L. Simmons, Professor of Law, University of California, Davis.

TAXATION, FEDERAL INCOME, OF PARTNERSHIPS AND S CORPORATIONS (1991), with 1993 Supplement

Paul R. McDaniel, Professor of Law, Boston College.

Hugh J. Ault, Professor of Law, Boston College.

Martin J. McMahon, Jr., Professor of Law, University of Kentucky.

Daniel L. Simmons, Professor of Law, University of California, Davis.

TAXATION, FEDERAL INCOME, OIL AND GAS, NATURAL RESOURCES TRANSACTIONS (1990)

Peter C. Maxfield, Professor of Law, University of Wyoming.

James L. Houghton, CPA, Partner, Ernst and Young.

James R. Gaar, CPA, Partner, Ernst and Young.

TAXATION, FEDERAL WEALTH TRANSFER, Successor Edition (1987)

Stanley S. Surrey, late Professor of Law, Harvard University.

Paul R. McDaniel, Professor of Law, Boston College.

Harry L. Gutman, Professor of Law, University of Pennsylvania.

TAXATION, FUNDAMENTALS OF CORPORATE, Third Edition (1991), with 1993 Supplement

Stephen A. Lind, Professor of Law, University of Florida and University of California, Hastings.

Stephen Schwarz, Professor of Law, University of California, Hastings.

Daniel J. Lathrope, Professor of Law, University of California, Hastings.

Joshua Rosenberg, Professor of Law, University of San Francisco.

TAXATION, FUNDAMENTALS OF PARTNERSHIP, Third Edition (1992), with 1993 Supplement

Stephen A. Lind, Professor of Law, University of Florida and University of California, Hastings.

Stephen Schwarz, Professor of Law, University of California, Hastings.

Daniel J. Lathrope, Professor of Law, University of California, Hastings.

Joshua Rosenberg, Professor of Law, University of San Francisco.

UNIVERSITY CASEBOOK SERIES—Continued

TAXATION OF CORPORATIONS AND THEIR SHAREHOLDERS (1991), with 1993 Supplement

David J. Shakow, Professor of Law, University of Pennsylvania.

TAXATION, PROBLEMS IN THE FEDERAL INCOME TAXATION OF PARTNER-SHIPS AND CORPORATIONS, Second Edition (1986)

Norton L. Steuben, Professor of Law, University of Colorado.
William J. Turnier, Professor of Law, University of North Carolina.

TAXATION, PROBLEMS IN THE FUNDAMENTALS OF FEDERAL INCOME, Second Edition (1985)

Norton L. Steuben, Professor of Law, University of Colorado.
William J. Turnier, Professor of Law, University of North Carolina.

TORT LAW AND ALTERNATIVES, Fifth Edition (1992)

Marc A. Franklin, Professor of Law, Stanford University.
Robert L. Rabin, Professor of Law, Stanford University.

TORTS, Eighth Edition (1988)

William L. Prosser, late Professor of Law, University of California, Hastings.
John W. Wade, Professor of Law, Vanderbilt University.
Victor E. Schwartz, Adjunct Professor of Law, Georgetown University.

TORTS, Third Edition (1976)

Harry Shulman, late Dean of the Law School, Yale University.
Fleming James, Jr., Professor of Law Emeritus, Yale University.
Oscar S. Gray, Professor of Law, University of Maryland.

TRADE REGULATION, Third Edition (1990), with 1993 Supplement

Milton Handler, Professor of Law Emeritus, Columbia University.
Harlan M. Blake, Professor of Law, Columbia University.
Robert Pitofsky, Professor of Law, Georgetown University.
Harvey J. Goldschmid, Professor of Law, Columbia University.

TRADE REGULATION, see Antitrust

TRANSNATIONAL BUSINESS PROBLEMS (1986)

Detlev F. Vagts, Professor of Law, Harvard University.

TRANSNATIONAL LEGAL PROBLEMS, Third Edition (1986), with 1991 Revised Edition of Documentary Supplement

Henry J. Steiner, Professor of Law, Harvard University.
Detlev F. Vagts, Professor of Law, Harvard University.

TRIAL, see also Evidence, Making the Record, Lawyering Process and Preparing and Presenting the Case

TRUSTS, Sixth Edition (1991)

George G. Bogert, late Professor of Law Emeritus, University of Chicago.
Dallin H. Oaks, President, Brigham Young University.
H. Reese Hansen, Dean and Professor of Law, Brigham Young University.
Claralyn Martin Hill, J.D., Brigham Young University.

TRUSTS AND ESTATES, SELECTED STATUTES ON, 1992 Edition

TRUSTS AND WILLS, see also Decedents' Estates and Trusts, and Family Property Law

[xvi]

UNIVERSITY CASEBOOK SERIES—Continued

UNFAIR COMPETITION, see Competitive Process and Business Torts

WATER RESOURCE MANAGEMENT, Fourth Edition (1993)

A. Dan Tarlock, Professor of Law, IIT Chicago–Kent College of Law.
James N. Corbridge, Jr., Chancellor, University of Colorado at Boulder, and Professor of Law, University of Colorado.
David H. Getches, Professor of Law, University of Colorado.

WOMEN AND THE LAW (1992)

Mary Joe Frug, late Professor of Law, New England School of Law.

WILLS AND ADMINISTRATION, Fifth Edition (1961)

Philip Mechem, late Professor of Law, University of Pennsylvania.
Thomas E. Atkinson, late Professor of Law, New York University.

WRITING AND ANALYSIS IN THE LAW, Second Edition (1991)

Helene S. Shapo, Professor of Law, Northwestern University.
Marilyn R. Walter, Professor of Law, Brooklyn Law School.
Elizabeth Fajans, Writing Specialist, Brooklyn Law School.

University Casebook Series

EDITORIAL BOARD

INSURANCE LAW
AND REGULATION:
CASES AND MATERIALS

By

KENNETH S. ABRAHAM
Class of 1962 Professor of Law
University of Virginia

Westbury, New York
THE FOUNDATION PRESS, INC.
1990

Library of Congress Cataloging-in-Publication Data

Abraham, Kenneth S., 1946–

    Insurance law and regulation : cases and materials / by Kenneth S. Abraham.

        p.   cm. — (University casebook series)

    ISBN 0–88277–791–2

    1. Insurance law—United States—Cases. I. Title. II. Series.

KF1163.A27 1990

346.73'086'026—dc20

[347.30686026]   90–2805

                                         CIP

Abraham—Ins. Law & Reg. UCB

1st Reprint—1993

PRINTED ON 10% POST
CONSUMER RECYCLED PAPER

For Katherine and Michael

*

PREFACE

The law school curriculum has been slow to recognize the importance of insurance in modern law. Insurance was a staple in the curriculum until thirty years ago, but it was largely a course in advanced contracts and some obscure concepts such as the insurance warranty and insurable interest requirements. At that point interest in even these issues diminished, though efforts by such pioneers as Robert Keeton, Spencer Kimball, and William Young to modernize insurance law kept the subject alive in law schools.

Recently there has been a resurgence of interest that can be ascribed to a number of forces. First, litigation of insurance coverage disputes has burgeoned. As the mass tort and environmental cleanup litigation that began in the 1970's has matured, multi-million dollar liability insurance disputes have followed. Second, modern legal theory employs concepts that are at the very heart of insurance: risk spreading and risk allocation. With the rise of the economic analysis of law and the jurisprudential turn of the last two decades or so, it was almost inevitable that the affinity between insurance and these new ways of looking at law would highlight the importance of insurance in modern law. Finally, the liability insurance "crisis" of the mid-1980's focused public attention on the inner workings of insurance and insurance law, as liability insurance premiums skyrocketed and for a time some people and businesses could not obtain liability insurance at any price. All three of these developments—and probably others as well—have focused attention on insurance and insurance law.

This casebook is an effort to respond to this renewed interest in insurance law in a number of ways:

Equal Emphasis on Commercial and Personal Insurance. Perhaps the most important reflection of this effort is the roughly equal emphasis the casebook places on commercial and personal insurance issues. I believe that the traditional emphasis on personal insurance, and especially on automobile insurance, gives law students a misleading impression of the nature of the subject and of the shape of insurance law doctrines. The consumer-protection motive is much stronger in personal than in commercial insurance law, and nowhere is this motive more evident than in automobile insurance disputes. Consequently, I have tried throughout the casebook to provide a representative mix of personal and commercial insurance issues and cases, and I have chosen to treat automobile insurance issues in a separate Chapter devoted exclusively to the very special problems of this field.

Organization by Type of Insurance. The organization of the casebook is in fact more traditional than many others. The first Chapter takes up doctrines governing applications for insurance and representations made by the applicant, the second Chapter examines the law governing Contract Formation and Meaning, and the third Chapter addresses the Regulation of insurance. Beyond these Chapters, however, the casebook does not address general themes. Although certain themes run through all of insurance law, it is extremely difficult to understand a particular insurance law problem without also understanding the kind of insurance it involves. Consequently, in Chapters Four through Eight the casebook focuses not on general themes but on particular types of insurance: fire, property, life, health, disability, personal and commercial general liability, and automobile insurance. Within each Chapter, of course, a series of themes is developed, but the themes are introduced as part of the examination of the kind of insurance to which the Chapter is devoted.

A Focus on Insurance Policies and Policy Language. The starting point for the study of any contractual relationship should be the terms of the contract itself. In insurance, that contract is the insurance policy. The significance of the individual policy provision that is at the center of any given case cannot be fully appreciated in isolation. Rather, a sense of the entire contractual relationship between the insurer and insured—starting with the insurance policy itself—is necessary. Consequently, at the beginning of the Chapters on Property, Life, Liability, and Automobile Insurance I have set out complete copies of standard-form insurance policies. An entire insurance policy is a forbidding document to the uninitiated; but the ability to read an insurance policy is a skill that every lawyer should have mastered.

At the outset of each Chapter, students should become familiar with the structure and organization of the sample policy it contains: the terms of its Insuring Agreement, the location and general focus of the Exclusions, the nature of the Conditions of coverage, and so forth. Then, as each case or problem is addressed, the individual policy provision at issue in the case or problem should be compared with the analogous provision in the sample policy to determine (among other things) whether the terms of the sample differ and, if so, how this difference in wording would have affected the result in the case under study. In this way, students can become familiar not only with the function of individual policy provisions, but also with the overall structure and purpose of the policies in which they are contained.

A Sustained Examination of Insurance Regulation. Chapter Three is devoted entirely to an examination of the administrative and statutory regulation of insurance. All of insurance law, however, is designed to regulate insurance. Consequently, running through this entire casebook is a concern about the nature of insurance regulation. Since insurance is sold in fairly well-developed markets, the central question to be asked about regulation is whether and when the law should intervene in the insurance markets and for what purpose or purposes.

I believe that this kind of inquiry can be advanced by what has come to be known as the economic analysis of law. I do not believe that economic analysis of law is the only or necessarily the most insightful analytical perspective, or that such analysis must be technical or mathematical in order to be useful. Because the purpose of insurance regulation is to influence insurance activity, however, consideration of the possible impact of different forms of regulation on that activity seems to me an essential component of any study of regulation—and this is the purpose of economic analysis. Throughout the casebook, therefore, I have brought economic analysis to bear on regulatory issues, but I have also raised questions about such analysis in order to suggest alternative, non-economic ways of looking at the issues examined.

The Use of Descriptive Introductions and Essays. One of the best ways to study a legal subject is to know the state of the law at the outset, and then to train one's critical faculties on the law as it stands in order to evaluate its strengths and weaknesses. In order to facilitate this process, materials in the casebook are often preceded or followed by brief essays that describe the state of the law on a particular question, analyze it from a particular point of view, or introduce ideas that students are unlikely to develop on their own. In addition, whenever possible I have included cases that not only resolve difficult questions, but also contain brief discussions of the shape of the law on the set of issues under study, so that students are not kept in the dark about the answers to common and straightforward problems.

Of course, I have not hesitated to ask hard questions—some of which do not have definitive answers, or which are designed to encourage students to think critically about the material they have read before they come to class. Rather, the overall strategy of the casebook has been to provide the easiest possible access to descriptive material, so that the hard work of thinking about what has been described can take priority. In this way, ideally, students will enter class with knowledge of the law governing the issues to be discussed in class, and more class time can be devoted to analysis and evalutaion of these issues.

For convenience, I have heavily edited some cases, often omitting string citations and footnotes, and renumbering the latter in consecutive order without specific notation that I have done so. This approach helps opinions to be read more smoothly and quickly, and allows the reasoning employed by the court to be fully exposed. At a few points where reference to leading cases in the field on a given issue has seemed useful, I have retained string citations.

No work of this scope can be prepared entirely alone, and I wish to acknowledge several debts. I am grateful to Oscar S. Gray for his comments on an earlier draft of the casebook, to Charles Havens and William Marcoux for comments on the reinsurance materials in Chapter Ten, and to three fine research assistants—Mercer Bullard, Thomas

Chapman, and Ann Fort—for their invaluable assistance in the preparation of the casebook.

KENNETH S. ABRAHAM

Charlottesville, Virginia
December, 1989

SUMMARY OF CONTENTS

	Page
PREFACE	v
TABLE OF CASES	xvii

Chapter

1.	Introduction	1
2.	Insurance Contract Formation and Meaning	28
3.	Insurance Regulation	90
4.	Fire and Property Insurance	183
5.	Life, Health, and Disability Insurance	279
6.	Liability Insurance	439
7.	Liability Insurance: Defense and Settlement	540
8.	Automobile Insurance	601
9.	Coordinating Multiple Coverages	677
10.	The Secondary Market	710
Index		741

*

TABLE OF CONTENTS

Page

PREFACE _____ v

TABLE OF CASES _____ xvii

Chapter One. Introduction _____ 1

A. The Nature and Functions of Insurance_____ 1

B. The Problem of Imperfect Information _____ 3

    1. Breach of Warranty_____ 5

        Vlastos v. Sumitomo Marine & Fire Insurance Company   5

    2. Misrepresentation and Concealment _____ 14

        Ward v. Durham Life Insurance Company _____ 17

        The AIDS Problem and the Law of Misrepresentation_____ 22

        MacKenzie v. Prudential Insurance Company of America   24

Chapter Two. Insurance Contract Formation and Meaning _____ 28

A. The Role of Standardized Forms _____ 28

    1. The Policy Drafting Process _____ 28

        Insurance Services Office in a Competitive Marketplace:
        ISO'S Role Within the Property Casualty Industry ___ 29

    2. Construing Ambiguities Against the Insurer _____ 33

        *Vargas v. Insurance Company of North America*_____ 33

        Rusthoven v. Commercial Standard Insurance Company   39

    3. Honoring the Reasonable Expectations of the Insured_____ 42

        Atwood v. Hartford Accident & Indemnity Co. _____ 43

        Atwater Creamery Company v. Western National Mutu-
        al Insurance Company _____ 47

B. The Role of Intermediaries _____ 54

    1. The Authority of the Agent _____ 55

        Elmer Tallant Agency, Inc. v. Bailey Wood Products, Inc.   55

    2. Waiver and Estoppel_____ 60

        Roseth v. St. Paul Property & Liability Insurance Com-
        *pany*_____ 61

    3. Group Insurance _____ 65

        Paulson v. Western Life Insurance Company _____ 65

C. Public Policy Restrictions on Contract Terms _____ 72

    St. Paul Insurance Companies v. Talladega Nursing Home,
    Inc. _____ 72

    First Bank (N.A.)—Billings v. Transamerica Insurance Com-
    pany _____ 75

    Strickland v. Gulf Life Insurance Company _____ 83

Chapter Three. Insurance Regulation _____ 90

A. The Allocation of Powers_____ 90

Page

B. The State Regulatory Response 92
   1. Regulation to Assure Solvency 93
      Insurer Failures: Property/Casualty Insurer Insolvencies and State Guaranty Funds 94
   2. Rate Regulation 99
      Ratemaking and Insurer Profitability 99
      A Hypothetical Rate Case 103
      Forms of Rate Regulation 104
      Massachusetts Automobile Rating and Accident Prevention Bureau v. Commissioner of Insurance 105
      Rate Rollbacks Through Voter Initiatives 114
      Calfarm Insurance Company v. Deukmejian 115
   3. "Unfairly Discriminatory" Rates 127
      The Fairness–Efficiency Tension in Insurance Classification 127
      Hartford Accident and Indemnity Co. v. Insurance Commissioner of the Commonwealth of Pennsylvania 129
C. Residual Federal Regulation 139
   1. What Constitutes the "Business of Insurance"? 140
      Union Labor Life Insurance Co. v. Pireno 140
   2. What Constitutes "Regulation" by the States? 154
   3. What Constitutes "Boycott, Coercion, or Intimidation"? ... 154
      Insurance Crises, the Underwriting Cycle, and Claims–Made Coverage 155
      a. The First Round: Medical Malpractice Insurance in the 1970's 156
        St. Paul Fire & Marine Insurance Co. v. Barry 156
      b. The Second Round: Claims–Made Commercial Liability Insurance in the 1980's and the States' Antitrust Suit Against the Industry 167
        In re Insurance Antitrust Litigation 167
      c. The Third Round: The Effort to Repeal McCarran–Ferguson and the Decline of Collective Rate Preparation 180
D. State Antitrust Prohibitions 181

Chapter Four. Fire and Property Insurance 183
A. Sample Homeowners Policy 183
B. The Requirement of an Insurable Interest 196
   Snethen v. Oklahoma State Union of the Farmers Educational and Cooperative Union of America 196
C. Subrogation 201
   Great Northern Oil Company v. St. Paul Fire and Marine Insurance Company 204
D. Limited Interests 209
   1. Mortgagees 209
      Quincy Mutual Fire Insurance Company v. Jones 210

Page

D. Limited Interests—Continued
    2. Leaseholds _____ 216
        Alaska Insurance Company v. RCA Alaska Communica-
        tions, Inc. _____ 216
    3. Real Estate Sales _____ 221
        Paramount Fire Insurance Company v. Aetna Casualty
        and Surety Company _____ 223
    4. Other Limited Interests _____ 229
        The Home Insurance Company v. Adler _____ 229
        The Folger Coffee Company, Inc. v. The Great American
        Insurance Company _____ 233
E. Exclusions and Exceptions _____ 240
    1. The Problem of Causation _____ 241
        Graham v. Public Employees Mutual Insurance Compa-
        ny _____ 242
    2. The Problem of Increased Risk _____ 248
        Commercial Union Insurance Company v. Taylor ___ 249
        Smith v. Lumbermen's Mutual Insurance Company __ 252
F. The Measure of Recovery _____ 257
    Elberon Bathing Company, Inc. v. Ambassador Insurance
    Company, Inc. _____ 258
    Coinsurance in Fire and Property Coverage _____ 267
G. Business Interruption Insurance _____ 269
    Omaha Paper Stock Co. v. Harbor Insurance Company ___ 269

Chapter Five. Life, Health, and Disability Insurance _____ 279
A. Life Insurance _____ 279
    1. Sample Term Life Insurance Policy _____ 279
    2. The Application _____ 299
        Gaunt v. John Hancock Mutual Life Insurance Company 299
    3. The Requirement of an Insurable Interest _____ 304
        Ryan v. Tickle _____ 305
    4. Change of Beneficiary and Assignment _____ 311
        Keeton v. Cherry _____ 312
        Grigsby v. Russell _____ 318
    5. Limitations on Recovery by Beneficiaries _____ 321
        New England Mutual Life Insurance Company v. Null 321
        State Mutual Life Assurance Company of America v.
        Hampton _____ 326
    6. Incontestability _____ 332
        Simpson v. Phoenix Mutual Life Insurance Company __ 333
    7. Limitations of Risk _____ 338
        Silverstein v. Metropolitan Life Insurance Company ___ 339
        Charney v. Illinois Mutual Life Casualty Company ____ 342
    8. Negligence Actions Against the Insurer _____ 344
        Mauroner v. Massachusetts Indemnity and Life Insur-
        ance Company _____ 344

TABLE OF CONTENTS

A. Life Insurance—Continued
       Bacon v. Federal Kemper Life Assurance Company _____ 349
B. Health and Disability Insurance _____ 356
    1. The Nature and Scope of American Health Insurance _____ 356
        Health Insurance and the Uninsured: Background Data
        and Analysis _____ 356
    2. Medically Necessary Services _____ 361
        Sarchett v. Blue Shield of California _____ 361
    3. Coordination of Coverage _____ 371
        Blue Cross and Blue Shield of Kansas, Inc. v. Riverside
        Hospital_____ 372
        Forms of Coordination_____ 381
        Cody v. Connecticut General Life Insurance Company 382
        Associated Hospital Service of Philadelphia v. Pustilnik 387
    4. The Meaning of "Disability"_____ 394
        Moots v. Bankers Life Company _____ 394
        Heller v. The Equitable Life Assurance Society of the
        United States_____ 398
    5. Preexisting Conditions _____ 407
        Holub v. Holy Family Society_____ 407
C. Liability for Bad–Faith Breach _____ 411
    Kewin v. Massachusetts Mutual Life Insurance Company __ 411
    Silberg v. California Life Insurance Company_____ 416
    Pilot Life Insurance Company v. DeDeaux _____ 428

Chapter Six. Liability Insurance _____ 439
A. Sample Commercial General Liability Policy _____ 439
B. The Insuring Agreement_____ 449
    1. What Is an "Occurrence?" _____ 449
        Honeycomb Systems, Inc. v. Admiral Insurance Compa-
        ny _____ 449
    2. The Number of Occurrences _____ 455
        Transport Insurance Company v. Lee Way Motor
        Freight, Inc._____ 455
        Michigan Chemical Corporation v. American Home As-
        surance Company _____ 462
    3. The Meaning of "Damages" _____ 473
        Continental Insurance Companies v. Northeastern Phar-
        maceutical and Chemical Company, Inc. _____ 473
C. Exclusions and Conditions _____ 483
    1. The Owned–Property Exclusion _____ 483
        Diamond Shamrock Chemicals Company v. Aetna Casu-
        alty and Surety Company _____ 483
    2. The Business Risk Exclusions _____ 493
        Weedo v. Stone–E–Brick, Inc. _____ 493

Page

C. Exclusions and Conditions—Continued
    3. Harm Expected or Intended_____ 505
        *Unigard Mutual Insurance Company v. Argonaut Insur-
        ance Company*_____ 505
    4. The Pollution Exclusion_____ 509
        *Broadwell Realty Services, Inc. v. The Fidelity & Casual-
        ty Company of New York*_____ 509
        Claussen v. Aetna Casualty & Surety Company _____ 515
    5. Notice Conditions_____ 522
        Mighty Midgets, Inc. v. Centennial Insurance Company 522
D. Claims–Made Coverage _____ 528
    *Sparks v. St. Paul Insurance Company*_____ 528

Chapter Seven. Liability Insurance: Defense and Settlement___ 540
A. The Duty to Defend and the Consequences of Breach_____ 540
    1. The Scope of the Duty_____ 540
        *Beckwith Machinery Company v. Travelers Indemnity
        Company*_____ 540
    2. Resolving Conflicts of Interest Over Defense _____ 551
        Burd v. Sussex Mutual Insurance Company _____ 551
        The *Cumis* Controversy _____ 558
        Obligation to Defend Action _____ 559
        *Parsons v. Continental National American Group*_____ 561
B. Settlement _____ 568
    *Crisci v. The Security Insurance Company of New Haven,
    Connecticut*_____ 568
    Mowry v. Badger State Mutual Casualty Company _____ 574
    Bad Faith Liability to a Third–Party: The *Royal Globe* Issue 587
C. Relations Between Primary and Excess Insurers _____ 588
    1. The Duty to Settle_____ 588
        *Commercial Union Assurance Companies v. Safeway
        Stores, Inc.* _____ 588
    2. Drop–Down Liability _____ 595
        *Mission National Insurance Company v. Duke Transpor-
        tation Company* _____ 595

Chapter Eight. Automobile Insurance_____ 601
A. Sample Personal Automobile Insurance Policy _____ 602
B. Liability Insurance_____ 613
    1. Compulsory Insurance Requirements _____ 613
        *State Farm Fire & Casualty Company v. Tringali*_____ 613
    2. The Omnibus Clause _____ 620
        *Curtis v. State Farm Mutual Automobile Insurance
        Company*_____ 620
    3. "Use" of the Vehicle _____ 628
        *Allstate Insurance Company v. Gillespie*_____ 628

B. Liability Insurance—Continued
    4. Notice and Cooperation Conditions ------------------------------ 630
      State Farm Mutual Automobile Insurance Company v.
      Davies -- 631
    5. Restrictions on Suits Against the Insurer-------------------- 638
      In re Honosky -- 638
C. Collision and Comprehensive Coverage------------------------------ 642
    Allison v. Iowa Mutual Insurance Company-------------------- 643
    Rodemich v. State Farm Mutual Automobile Insurance Com-
    pany -- 646
D. Auto No–Fault-- 649
    Montgomery v. Daniels-------------------------------------- 650
E. Uninsured Motorists Coverage------------------------------------- 663
    Allstate Insurance v. Boynton ----------------------------- 663
    Simpson v. Farmers Insurance Company, Inc. --------------- 671

Chapter Nine. Coordinating Multiple Coverages------------------- 677
A. The Trigger of Coverage --- 677
    American Home Products Corporation v. Liberty Mutual
    Insurance Company -- 677
B. "Other Insurance" Clauses--------------------------------------- 691
    Jones v. Medox, Inc. -------------------------------------- 691
    Carriers Insurance Company v. American Policyholders'
    Insurance Company -- 698
C. "Stacking" Uninsured Motorists Coverage----------------------- 705
    Taft v. Cerwonka --- 705

Chapter Ten. The Secondary Market----------------------------- 710
A. Residual Market Mechanisms ------------------------------------ 710
    Overview: Residual Market Mechanisms ------------------- 710
B. Surplus and Excess Lines -------------------------------------- 716
C. Reinsurance --- 717
    1. The Duty of Utmost Good Faith-------------------------- 718
      Old Reliable Fire Insurance Company v. Castle Reinsur-
      ance Company, Limited--------------------------------- 718
    2. "Follow-the-Fortunes" Clauses------------------------- 724
      American Insurance Company v. North American Com-
      pany for Property and Casualty Insurance ------------- 724
    3. Insolvency Clauses----------------------------------- 727
      Ainsworth v. General Reinsurance Corporation --------- 727
    4. Set–Offs in Insolvency ------------------------------ 733
      O'Connor v. Insurance Company of North America----- 733

Index--- 741

TABLE OF CASES

Principal cases are in italic type. Non-principal cases are in roman type. References are to Pages.

Aetna Cas. & Sur. Co. v. Certain Underwriters at Lloyds of London, England, 594

Aetna Casualty and Surety Company v. Hanna, 480

Agra–By–Products, Inc. v. Agway, Inc., 221

Ainsworth v. General Reinsurance Corp., 727, 731, 732

Alaska Ins. Co. v. RCA Alaska Communications, Inc., 216, 221

Allison v. Iowa Mut. Ins. Co., 643

Allstate Ins. Co. v. Boynton, 663, 670

Allstate Ins. Co. v. Gillespie, 628, 630

American Cas. Co. v. Rose, 309

American Council of Life Ins. v. District of Columbia, 22

American Home Products Corp. v. Liberty Mut. Ins. Co., 677

American Ins. Co. v. Freeport Cold Storage, Inc., 240

American Ins. Co. v. North American Co. for Property and Cas. Inc., 724

Anzinger v. O'Connor, 137, 138

Arizona Governing Committee for Tax Deferred Annuity and Deferred Compensation Plans v. Norris, 138

Arrow Trucking Co. v. Continental Ins. Co., 732

Asbestos Insurance Coverage Cases, 508

Associated Hospital Service of Philadelphia v. Pustilnik, 387, 392, 393

Attorney General v. Commissioner of Insurance, 112

Atwater Creamery Co. v. Western Nat. Mut. Ins. Co., 47, 52, 53, 89

Atwood v. Hartford Acc. & Indem. Co., 43, 45, 47, 52

Bacon v. Federal Kemper Life Assur. Co., 349, 355, 356

Bankers Trust Co. v. Hartford Acc. and Indem. Co., 482, 493

Beckwith Machinery Co. v. Travelers Indem. Co., 540, 549, 550

Blue Cross and Blue Shield of Kansas, Inc. v. Riverside Hosp., 372, 379, 381

Blume v. Evans Fur Co., 209

Boyes v. Continental Ins. Co., 89

Broadwell Realty Services, Inc. v. Fidelity & Cas. Co. of New York, 480, 483, 487, 509, 521, 522, 528

Brown–Spaulding & Associates, Inc. v. International Surplus Lines Insurance Company, 539

Brownell v. Board of Education of Inside Tax Dist. of City of Saratoga Springs, 222

Bruener v. Twin City Fire Ins. Co., 247

Bryant v. Nationwide Mut. Fire Ins. Co., 27

Burd v. Sussex Mut. Ins. Co., 551, 557, 558, 559

Burr v. Commercial Travelers Mutual Acc. Ass'n of America, 341

Butler v. Farmers Ins. Co. of Arizona, 201

Calfarm Ins. Co. v. Deukmejian, 115

Cameron Mut. Ins. Co. of Missouri v. Bouse, 60

Carriers Ins. Co. v. American Policyholders' Ins. Co., 698, 705

Charney v. Illinois Mut. Life Cas. Co., 342

Chrestman v. United States Fidelity & Guaranty Co., 550

Cissell v. American Home Assur. Co., 641

City of (see name of city)

Claussen v. Aetna Cas. & Sur. Co., 32, 515, 521, 522

Cody v. Community Loan Corp. of Richmond County, 139

Cody v. Connecticut General Life Ins. Co., 382

Collister v. Nationwide Life Ins. Co., 304

Commercial Union Assur. Companies v. Safeway Stores, Inc., 588

Commercial Union Ins. Co. v. Taylor, 249, 257

Commissioner of Insurance v. North Carolina Rate Bureau, 269 S.E.2d 595, p. 112

Commissioner of Insurance v. North Carolina Rate Bureau, 269 S.E.2d 538, p. 112

Commissioner of Insurance v. North Carolina Rate Bureau, 269 S.E.2d 547, p. 112

Connecticut General Life Ins. Co. v. Gulley, 311

Consolidated Asbestos Coverage Cases, 690

Consolidated Mut. Ins. Co. v. Bankers Ins. Co. of Pa., 696

Constantine, Village of v. Home Ins. Co., 200

Continental Assur. Co. v. Carroll, 21

Continental Casualty Co. v. Reserve Ins. Co., 594

xvii

Continental Ins. Companies v. Northeastern Pharmaceutical & Chemical Co., Inc., 473, 479, 480, 481, 482, 493
Corbitt v. Federal Kemper Ins. Co., 60
Crawford v. American Title Ins. Co., 154
Crawford v. Equitable Life Assur. Society of United States, 338
Crider v. Georgia Life & Health Ins. Guar. Ass'n, 98
Crisci v. Security Ins. Co. of New Haven, Conn., 568, 586, 587
Cunningham v. Metropolitan Life Ins. Co., 392
Curtis v. State Farm Mut. Auto. Ins. Co., 620, 627, 628

Dade County Consumer Advocate's Office v. Department of Ins., 54
Dalrymple v. Royal–Globe Ins. Co., 216
Davis v. Boston Mut. Life Ins. Co., 342
Dayton Independent School Dist. v. National Gypsum Co., 504, 690
De Hahn v. Hartley, 10
Desrochers v. New York Casualty Co., 480
Diamond Shamrock Chemicals Co. v. Aetna Cas. and Sur. Co., 483
Drew v. Life Ins. Co. of Georgia, 342

Eagle–Picher Industries, Inc. v. Liberty Mut. Ins. Co., 688
Elberon Bathing Co., Inc. v. Ambassador Ins. Co., Inc., 258, 266
Elmer Tallant Agency, Inc. v. Bailey Wood Products, Inc., 55, 60
Emons Industries, Inc. v. Liberty Mut. Fire Ins. Co., 690
Employers Mut. Cas. Co. v. Nelson, 637
Estate of (see name of party)

Farm Bureau Mut. Ins. Co., Inc. v. Evans, 630
Farmers Ins. Exchange v. Call, 620
Federal Trade Com'n v. Dixie Finance Co., Inc., 152
Federal Trade Com'n v. National Casualty Co., 154
Fernandez v. Florida Ins. Guaranty Ass'n, Inc., 98
First Bank (N.A.)–Billings v. Transamerica Ins. Co., 75
Florida Farm Bureau Ins. Co. v. Martin, 203
Folger Coffee Co. v. Great American Ins. Co., 233
Fontenot v. Haight, 98
Fontenot v. Marquette Casualty Co., 732
Ford v. Ford, 332
Future Realty, Inc. v. Fireman's Fund Ins. Co., 257

Garvey v. State Farm Fire and Cas. Co., 247

Gaunt v. John Hancock Mut. Life Ins. Co., 299, 303
Gerlach v. Allstate Ins. Co., 140
Gomogda v. Prudential Ins. Co. of America, 16
Good v. Continental Ins. Co., 257
Graham v. Public Employees Mut. Ins. Co., 242, 247, 248
Gray v. Zurich Ins. Co., 46, 557, 558, 559
Great American Insurance Co. v. C. G. Tate Construction Co., 527
Greater Palm Beach Symphony Ass'n, Inc. v. Hughes, 82
Great Northern Oil Co. v. St. Paul Fire & M. Ins. Co., 204, 220
Greenwood Cemetery, Inc. v. Travelers Indem. Co., 82
Grigsby v. Russell, 318, 325
Group Life & Health Ins. Co. v. Royal Drug Co., 152, 153, 154
Gruenberg v. Aetna Ins. Co., 426
Guarantee Abstract & Title Co., Inc. v. Interstate Fire and Cas. Co., Inc., 550

Hadley v. Baxendale, 425
Harr v. Allstate Ins. Co., 64
Hartford Acc. and Indem. Co. v. Insurance Com'r of Commonwealth, 129
Hartford Acc. & Indem. Co. v. Civil Service Emp. Ins. Co., 630
Heller v. Equitable Life Assur. Soc. of United States, 398
Herzog v. National Am. Ins. Co., 54
Hionis v. Northern Mut. Ins. Co., 46
Holub v. Holy Family Soc., 407, 410
Home Indem. Co. v. City of Mobile, 473
Home Indem. Co. v. Reed Equipment Co., Inc., 381
Home Ins. Co. v. Adler, 229, 232
Honeycomb Systems, Inc. v. Admiral Ins. Co., 449, 454
Honosky, In re, 638, 642
Huberman v. John Hancock Mut. Life Ins. Co., 355

In re (see name of party)
Insurance Antitrust Litigation, In re, 167, 179, 537
Insurance Co. of North America v. Forty–Eight Insulations, Inc., 688
Isaacson v. California Ins. Guarantee Ass'n, 98

Jackson, Township of v. American Home Assurance Company, 472
Jackson Tp. Municipal Utilities Authority v. Hartford Acc. and Indem. Co., 32
Jenkins v. J. C. Penney Cas. Ins. Co., 587
Johansen v. California State Auto. Ass'n Inter–Insurance Bureau, 587
Jones v. Medox, Inc., 691, 705
Jostens, Inc. v. Mission Ins. Co., 594

Keene Corp. v. Insurance Co. of North America, 43, 688, 690
Keeton v. Cherry, 312, 317
Kennedy v. Laird, 310
Kentucky Cent. Life Ins. Co. v. Webster, 27
Kewin v. Massachusetts Mut. Life Ins. Co., 411, 425, 426
Klamath–Lake Pharmaceutical Ass'n v. Klamath Medical Service Bureau, 154
Klos v. Mobil Oil Co., 47
Knight v. Metropolitan Life Ins. Co., 341
Knipp v. Arizona Property & Cas. Ins. Guar. Fund, 98
Krauss v. Manhattan Life Ins. Co. of New York, 71

Lachs v. Fidelity & Cas. Co. of New York, 47
Lamb–Weston, Inc. v. Oregon Auto. Ins. Co., 704
Lane v. State Farm Mut. Auto. Ins. Co., 641
Lee v. Aetna Casualty & Surety Co., 549
Liberty Nat. Life Ins. Co. v. Weldon, 304
Liverpool & London & Globe Ins. Co., Ltd., v. Bolling, 200
Los Angeles, Dept. of Water and Power, City of v. Manhart, 138

MacKenzie v. Prudential Ins. Co. of America, 24, 26, 27
Maryland Cas. Co. v. Armco, Inc., 480
Massachusetts Auto. Rating and Acc. Prevention Bureau v. Commissioner of Ins., 105
Matsushita Elec. Indus. Co., Ltd. v. Zenith Radio Corp., 179
Matter of (see name of party)
Mauroner v. Massachusetts Indem. and Life Ins. Co., 344, 355
McGehee v. Farmers Ins. Co., Inc., 200
Metropolitan Life Ins. Co. v. Massachusetts, 380
MFA Mut. Ins. Co. v. Sailors, 637
Michigan Chemical Corp. v. American Home Assur. Co., 462, 471, 472
Mighty Midgets, Inc. v. Centennial Ins. Co., 522, 527
Miller v. Dilts, 527
Mission Nat. Ins. Co. v. Duke Transp. Co., Inc., 595, 600
Moe v. Allemannia Fire Ins. Co. of Pittsburgh, 13
Montgomery v. Daniels, 650
Montgomery v. Reserve Life Ins. Co., 15
Moore v. Provident Life and Acc. Ins. Co., 380
Moots v. Bankers Life Co., 394, 397
Moradi–Shalal v. Fireman's Fund Ins. Companies, 588
Mowry v. Badger State Mut. Cas. Co., 574, 586, 587

Mraz v. Canadian Universal Ins. Co., Ltd., 482
Murray v. Montana Ins. Guaranty Ass'n, 98
Mutual Ben. Life Ins. Co. v. JMR Electronics Corp., 17
Mutual of Enumclaw Ins. Co. v. Wiscomb, 619

New Castle County v. Hartford Acc. and Indem. Co., 480
New England Mut. Life Ins. Co. v. Null, 321, 325
New York Life Ins. Co. v. Kuhlenschmidt, 15
New York Times Co. v. Sullivan, 82
Norby v. Bankers Life Co. of Des Moines, Iowa, 71

O'Connor v. Insurance Co. of North America, 733
Odolecki v. Hartford Acc. & Indem. Co., 627
Old Reliable Fire Ins. Co. v. Castle Reinsurance Co., Ltd., 718, 723, 724
Olson v. Bankers Life Ins. Co. of Neb., 22
Omaha Paper Stock Co. v. Harbor Ins. Co., 269, 277
Ott v. All Star Ins. Corp., 732
Owens v. Aetna Life & Cas. Co., 153

Page Flooring and Const. Co. v. Nationwide Life Ins. Co., 341
Pan Am. World Airways, Inc. v. Aetna Cas. & Sur. Co., 196
Paramount Fire Ins. Co. v. Aetna Cas. & Sur. Co., 223, 228
Parsons v. Continental Nat. Am. Group, 557, 561, 567, 568
Patrons–Oxford Mut. Ins. Co. v. Dodge, 508
Paul v. State of Virginia, 90, 182
Paulson v. Western Life Ins. Co., 65
Penn Mut Life Ins Co v. Mechanics' Savings Bank & Trust Co, 14
Perrine v. Prudential Ins. Co. of America, 341
Pilot Life Ins. Co. v. Dedeaux, 428, 438
Ploe v. International Indemnity Co., 247
Poche v. City of New Orleans, 393
Port of Portland v. Water Quality Ins. Syndicate, 480
Powers v. Travelers' Ins. Co., 644
Public Service Mut. Ins. Co. v. Goldfarb, 82
Puritan Ins. Co. v. Canadian Universal Ins. Co., Ltd., 594
Puritan Life Ins. Co. v. Guess, 304

Quincy Mutual Fire Insurance Company v. Jones, 210

Rawlings v. Apodaca, 426, 427
Reazin v. Blue Cross and Blue Shield of Kansas, Inc., 153

Reserve Ins. Co. v. Pisciotta, 600

Reserve Life Ins. Co. v. Commissioner of Commerce, 93

Rinehart v. Hartford Cas. Ins. Co., 98

Rivera v. Southern American Fire Ins. Co., 98

Robins Dry Dock & Repair Co. v. Flint, 209

Rodemich v. State Farm Mut. Auto. Ins. Co., 646, 649

Roque v. Nationwide Mut. Ins. Co., 341

Roseth v. St. Paul Property and Liability Ins. Co., 61, 64

Rova Farms Resort, Inc. v. Investors Ins. Co. of America, 586

Royal Globe Ins. Co. v. Superior Court of Butte County, 587, 588

Royal Indem. Co. v. Little Joe's Catfish Inn, Inc., 277

Rubenstein v. Mutual Life Ins. Co. of New York, 309, 310

Rusthoven v. Commercial Standard Ins. Co., 39, 42

Ryan v. Tickle, 305, 309, 310

Sadlers Company v. Badcock, 201

Samuel N. Zarpas, Inc. v. Morrow, 530

San Diego Navy Federal Credit Union v. Cumis Ins. Soc., Inc., 558, 559, 567

Sarchett v. Blue Shield of California, 361, 371

Scherer v. Wahlstrom, 311

Schmidt v. County Mutual Insurance Company, 392

Schoolcraft v. Ross, 215

Secor v. Pioneer Foundry Co., 310, 311

Securities and Exchange Commission v. National Securities, Inc., 152

Securities and Exchange Commission v. Variable Annuity Life Ins. Co. of America, 152

Security Mut. Cas. Co. v. Century Cas. Co., 724

Security Mut. Ins. Co. of New York v. Acker–Fitzsimons Corp., 527

Seidler v. Georgetown Life Ins. Co., 26

Sentry Ins. Co. v. Stuart, 203

Silberg v. California Life Ins. Co., 416

Silverstein v. Metropolitan Life Ins. Co., 339

Simpson v. Farmers Ins. Co., Inc., 671

Simpson v. Phoenix Mut. Life Ins. Co., 333, 337, 338

S. L. Rowland Const. Co. v. St. Paul Fire & Mar. Ins. Co., 500

Smith v. Lumbermen's Mut. Ins. Co., 252, 257

Smith v. North American Co. for Life, Acc. & H. Ins., 22

Smith v. Westland Life Ins. Co., 304

Snethen v. Oklahoma State Union of Farmers Educational and Co-op. Union of America, 196, 200, 201

South–Eastern Underwriters Ass'n, United States v., 90, 91, 180

Sovereign Life Ins. Co. of California v. Rewald, 15

Sparks v. Republic Nat. Life Ins. Co., 427

Sparks v. St. Paul Ins. Co., 528, 538

Spirt v. Teachers Ins. and Annuity Ass'n, 139

State, Dept. of Ins. v. Insurance Services Office, 138

State ex rel. v. ___ (see opposing party and relator)

State Farm Fire & Cas. Co. v. Tringali, 613, 618, 619

State Farm Fire & Casualty Company v. Muth, 508

State Farm Mut. Auto. Ins. Co. v. American Community Mut. Ins. Co., 380

State Farm Mut. Auto. Ins. Co. v. Davies, 631, 637

State Farm Mut. Auto. Ins. Co. v. Sewell, 89

State Farm Mut. Auto. Ins. Co. v. Shaffer, 644

State Mut. Life Assur. Co. of America v. Hampton, 326

Steinberg v. Guardian Life Ins. Co. of America, 153

Steven v. Fidelity and Casualty Co. of New York, 47

Stipcich v. Metropolitan Life Ins. Co., 26

St. Paul Fire & Marine Ins. Co. v. Barry, 156, 166

St. Paul Ins. Companies v. Talladega Nursing Home, Inc., 72, 81, 82

Strickland v. Gulf Life Ins. Co., 83, 89

Swedish Crucible Steel Co. v. Travelers Indem. Co., 277

Taft v. Cerwonka, 705, 709

Title Ins. Rating Bureau of Arizona, Inc., United States v., 152

Township of (see name of township)

Transport Ins. Co. v. Lee Way Motor Freight, Inc., 455, 471, 472

Tublitz v. Glens Falls Ins. Co., 201

Unigard Mut. Ins. Co. v. Argonaut Ins. Co., 505, 508, 509

Union Labor Life Ins. Co. v. Pireno, 140, 152, 153, 154

Uniroyal, Inc. v. Home Ins. Co., 690

United States v. ___ (see opposing party)

United States Aviex Co. v. Travelers Ins. Co., 480

United States Fidelity and Guar. Co. v. Thomas Solvent Co., 482

Ursin v. Ins. Guaranty Ass'n, 98

Vargas v. Insurance Co. of North America, 33, 38

Vaughn v. Vaughn, 98

Vencill v. Continental Cas. Co., 594

Village of (see name of village)

Virginia Academy of Clinical Psychologists v. Blue Shield of Virginia, 152

Vlastos v. Sumitomo Marine & Fire Ins. Co. (Europe) Ltd., 5, 12

Vogel v. Northern Assur. Co., 228

Wachovia Park & Trust Co. v. Westchester Fire Ins. Co., 644

Ward v. Durham Life Ins. Co., 17

Waste Management of Carolinas, Inc. v. Peerless Ins. Co., 549

Weaver Bros., Inc. v. Chappel, 527

Weedo v. Stone–E–Brick, Inc., 493

Wells v. John Hancock Mut. Life Ins. Co., 356

Western Mut. Ins. Co. v. Baldwin, 637

Wetzel v. Westinghouse Elec. Corp., 341

Wilburn Boat Co. v. Fireman's Fund Ins. Co., 12

Zachary Trading Inc. v. Northwestern Mut. Life Ins. Co., 23

Zurich Ins. Co. v. Northbrook Excess and Surplus Ins. Co., 550

*

INSURANCE LAW
AND REGULATION:
CASES AND MATERIALS

*

Chapter One

INTRODUCTION

A. THE NATURE AND FUNCTIONS OF INSURANCE

Insurance pervades our society. Premiums paid for private insurance in the United States exceed $500 billion per year. The cost of social insurance provided by various levels of government adds several hundred billion dollars more each year to the total national expenditure on insurance. Insurance protecting individuals and businesses is an essential feature of our economic system, for it helps to provide the security necessary to reduce uncertainty, cushion economic hardship, and encourage productive investment.

The principal sellers of insurance are *stock* and *mutual* companies, *not much* although a few unusual forms of operation such as *reciprocals* and *sig - to* *fraternal benefit societies* that are holdovers from an earlier age still *law* exist. The owners of stock companies are shareholders; the owners of mutual companies are policyholders, or "insureds"—the individuals or institutions that have purchased insurance from the company. Notwithstanding this difference in corporate form and ownership, both stock and mutual companies compete with each other in virtually all markets, the products they sell are identical, and the body of insurance law governing them does not depend on the kind of company involved. Some companies sell exclusively through their own agents, while others sell through independent agents who represent more than one company. Once again, this difference in marketing—except for the law governing the different kinds of agency involved—has little practical significance for the rights of policyholders or for the obligations of insuring companies.

The distinction between *property/casualty* and *life and health* *significan* insurance, however, is of some significance. The two terms represent roughly what they suggest—that insurance against loss of property and against legal liability falls into a category separate from insurance against loss of life, ill health, and disability. In the nineteenth century it was common for insurers to sell one category of coverage or the other. It is now typical for large insurers to sell both, sometimes through subsidiaries owned by a holding company and specializing in a particular category. Thus, it is common to see references to the Aetna "group" of companies and the "American International Group." Many other companies still specialize in one category of coverage or the other, and many specialize in selling only certain forms of coverage, or *lines* of insurance, that fall within a category. Some companies sell only

1

health insurance, for example, and others only auto and homeowners insurance.

In the simplest sense, the function of insurance is to protect the policyholder in the event of a future loss. A more sophisticated description, however, recognizes three separate functions. The first is *risk-transfer* from comparatively risk-averse to less risk-averse or risk-neutral parties. A risk-neutral party is indifferent as between a small risk of suffering a large loss and greater risk of suffering a small loss, when each risk has the same *expected value*—the probability of a loss multiplied by its magnitude if it occurs. In contrast, a risk-averse party would prefer the large risk of suffering a small loss to a smaller risk of suffering the large loss.

3 functions

For example, a 1 percent chance of suffering a $10,000 loss and 10 percent chance of suffering a $1000 loss each have the same expected value—$100. A risk-neutral party is indifferent as between the two risks, but a risk-averse party would tend to prefer the latter. Consequently, the risk-averse party is likely to be willing to pay a sum exceeding the expected value of a given risk in order to transfer that risk to another party. In the above example the party transferring a 1 percent chance of suffering a $10,000 loss might be willing to pay a $105, $110, or even $150 premium to transfer the risk of loss, depending on the degree of risk-aversion involved. In this sense, insurance transforms a small risk of suffering a large loss into a large risk (100 percent) of paying a smaller sum—the insurance premium.

2)

The second function of insurance is *risk-pooling,* or diversification. Insurance companies are not intrinsically risk-neutral. Rather, by insuring a large number of insureds posing homogeneous and independent risks, an insurer can reduce the amount of variance in its expected losses to a very small range. In effect, by pooling risks the insurer takes advantage of the law of large numbers and turns a large number of individually risky undertakings into a highly predictable set of obligations. In insurance, the whole risk is smaller than the sum of its parts. In this sense an insurance company is a vehicle by which risk-averse parties combine to share and thereby reduce their collective risk. The company's profits constitute payment for providing this service to its policyholders and for bearing the residual risk that losses will vary beyond the range predicted.

3)

The third function of insurance is *risk-allocation.* Insurers not only accept the transfer of risks and then pool them. In charging for the coverage they provide, insurers attempt to set a price that is proportional to the degree of risk posed by each insured. Insurers thereby allocate risk to groups of insureds posing similar or identical degrees of risk. Different methods of risk classification measure risk in different ways. But by classifying risks and then pricing coverage in accordance with their classifications, insurers can create incentives for insureds to optimize the degree of risk they pose even when insurance against loss is available.

Any given insurance arrangement accomplishes these three functions in varying degrees. For example, a particular insurance policy will transfer some but by no means all the risks faced by the insured. In addition, because an insurer's effort at risk diversification through pooling is always imperfect, insurers inevitably face a greater or lesser degree of risk themselves. Finally, obtaining the information necessary to classify risks and price accordingly is not cost-free; consequently, risk-allocation normally can proceed only to the point at which further refinement is not worthwhile. Insurance law can help or hinder these functions, sometimes with justification and sometimes without it.

In reading the materials in this Chapter and those that follow, therefore, consider whether and to what extent the individual legal rules, judicial decisions, statutes, and regulations that are examined support or undermine the risk-transfer, risk-pooling, and risk-allocation functions of insurance. Also consider on what basis the positions the law takes can be justified. When and for what reasons should insurance markets be permitted to operate without legal intervention? When and for what reasons should the law intervene to promote or to limit the insurance market's effort to perform the functions of insurance? The answers to these questions hinge not only on technical insurance matters, but also on basic issues of legal and political philosophy. There is no avoiding these issues in studying insurance law. Indeed, in a sense insurance law is nothing less than a set of answers to basic questions about the proper role of law in regulating the sharing of risk among private citizens and the institutions they create to serve their aims.

B. THE PROBLEM OF IMPERFECT INFORMATION

The ideal of the perfectly functioning market is never achieved in practice. One obstacle to perfect competition is imperfect information. Without perfect information, the products sold and the prices charged for them vary from the optimum. Insurance is especially sensitive to this problem, because most of the costs incurred by the seller of insurance in providing the insurance product are not known at the time an insurance policy is sold. In addition, typically there is a disparity in the information available to insurers and insureds about the factors that influence the degree of risk posed by a prospective insured. Insureds have more information than insurers about certain aspects of the risks they pose; insurers have more information about other aspects of these risks. As a result of these informational deficiencies, insurance is subject to two potentially disruptive effects: adverse selection and moral hazard.

1. *Adverse selection.* Other things being equal, a party facing a high risk of loss is more likely to seek insurance than a party facing a

lower risk. If potential policyholders know better than insurers whether they pose comparatively high or comparatively low risk, then adverse selection may occur: When insurers charge each party the same
price for coverage, then high-risk parties elect to be insured in greater
proportion than low-risk parties, and insurers are forced to raise the
price of coverage. As a result, some of the comparatively low-risk
parties that had previously been insured decline to purchase coverage,
the average degree of risk posed by the insurer's policyholders rises,
and the insurer is forced to raise prices again, thus restarting the cycle
of adverse selection.

Eventually the insurer's risk pool either unravels completely, or an
equilibrium is reached in which some low-risk parties purchase less
coverage than they would otherwise desire and others purchase none.
In either case, low-risk parties buy less coverage and high-risk parties
buy more coverage than they would if insurers could distinguish the
two classes of policyholders. For classic expositions of the problem, see
Rothschild and Stiglitz, Equilibrium in Competitive Insurance Markets:
An Essay on the Economics of Imperfect Information, 90 Quart.J.Econ.
629 (1976); Akerloff, The Market for "Lemons": Quality Uncertainty
and the Market Mechanism, 74 Quart.J.Econ. 488 (1970). For an
application to a more recent issue, see Priest, The Current Insurance
Crisis and Modern Tort Law, 96 Yale L.J. 1521 (1987).

2. *Moral hazard.* The term moral hazard originated in insurance
law as a description of the risk that an insured or insurance beneficiary
would deliberately destroy the subject matter insured in order to obtain
payment of an insurance benefit. The term now often refers more
generally to the tendency of any insured party to exercise less care to
avoid an insured loss than would be exercised if the loss were not
insured. If insurers could always monitor the behavior of insureds,
insurance could never be plagued by moral hazard. Because premiums
could be charged in proportion to the level of care actually exercised by
the insured, there would be no incentive for insured parties to exercise
less care than those who were uninsured. But of course insurers
cannot costlessly monitor the levels of care their insureds exercise.
Consequently, moral hazard is to a greater or lesser degree a constant
threat to the functioning of insurance.

Insurers attempt to combat adverse selection and moral hazard
with a variety of devices. They screen and evaluate applications to
determine the degree of risk posed by prospective insureds; they
classify insureds based on the degree of risk posed and set premium
levels accordingly; they experience-rate, or charge premiums for coverage renewals based in part on the insured's loss experience during the
previous policy period; they include deductible, coinsurance, and dollar
limits of coverage in policies so that all losses are not fully insured; and
they fashion the terms of coverage so that unusual risks are not insured
by standard policies and so that the results of inordinately dangerous
behavior are not insured. Each of these devices is examined in various
ways in succeeding Chapters.

Two other devices are examined in the following pages. One device, the insurance warranty, is a creation of the insurance market, but is now subject to legal regulation that limits its effect. The other device, the voiding of a policy because of a misrepresentation by the insured in the application process, is a creation of insurance law.

1. Breach of Warranty

VLASTOS v. SUMITOMO MARINE & FIRE INSURANCE COMPANY

United States Court of Appeals, Third Circuit, 1983.
707 F.2d 775.

ADAMS, Circuit Judge.

Evelyn Vlastos appeals from a judgment denying her recovery on an insurance policy for a fire that occurred in a commercial building that she owned. Applying Pennsylvania law, the district court declared that Vlastos had unambiguously warranted that the third floor of her building was occupied exclusively as a janitor's residence. Based on this ruling by the court, the jury found that Vlastos had breached the warranty, and the court declined to set aside the jury verdict. Inasmuch as we hold that it was error to determine that the warranty clause in question is unambiguous, the order of the district court will be vacated and the case remanded for further proceedings.

I.

Vlastos owned a 20′ × 80′ four-story building at 823 Pennsylvania Avenue, Pittsburgh, Pennsylvania. Prior to a fire on April 23, 1980, Vlastos and her son operated a luncheonette and a bar on the first floor of the building. The second and third floors were leased to Spartacus, Inc., which conducted a massage parlor on the second floor. Evidence was introduced at trial tending to show that the massage parlor also utilized at least a portion of the third floor. At the rear of the third floor there was a section variously described as a padlocked room or a section partitioned off from the remainder of the floor. It was in this area that Philip "Red" Pinkney, Vlastos' handyman and janitor, is alleged to have lived. Vlastos kept supplies on the fourth floor, and maintained a small office there as well. She occasionally remained overnight on the fourth floor rather than return to her residence. Vlastos was not staying there the night of the fire, but two friends of hers were residing there temporarily and were killed. A third person was also killed in the fire.

All of Vlastos' insurance matters were handled by her broker, John Mitchell. Mitchell obtained insurance for Vlastos from a group of European insurance companies through two sub-brokers. The policy in question, dated November 22, 1979, provided $345,000 of fire insurance with a $1,000 deductible provision. It contained a section, Endorsement No. 4, expressly incorporated into the policy, which stated in part: "Warranted that the 3rd floor is occupied as Janitor's residence."

refused to pay claim b/c of alleged breach of warranty

After the building and its contents were destroyed by the fire, the insurers refused to pay the claim, citing an alleged breach of the warranty. Vlastos filed a complaint based on diversity jurisdiction. The jury trial was bifurcated as to liability and damages; the parties agreed that Pennsylvania law is applicable. During the trial on liability, the district court ruled that the insurers were not required to produce evidence that the warranty was material to the risk insured against, holding that materiality was irrelevant. At the conclusion of the evidence, the court denied Vlastos' motion for a directed verdict, and proceeded to charge the jury that the warranty regarding the third floor was breached if a massage parlor occupied any significant portion of the floor, regardless of whether the janitor had a residence there as well. The jury was also instructed that if the third floor was totally unoccupied this too would have constituted a breach of the warranty. The sole question put to the jury was: "Have the defendants proved by a preponderance of the evidence that the plaintiff breached the warranty?" The jury answered affirmatively. Vlastos' motions for judgment notwithstanding the verdict or a new trial were denied in a memorandum opinion and order. Vlastos has appealed, raising numerous points, including the contention that the jury was incorrectly instructed that the warranty was unambiguous.

II.

burden of proof as to materiality of warranty of insurance

Vlastos objects that "no proof was offered that the provision in Endorsement No. 4 actually was a warranty." Reply Br. 1. Although her brief does not specify an alternate characterization of the provision, presumably she means to assert that it was a representation. If, as Vlastos implied, it was a representation, then the insurers would be under an obligation to show that the provision was material to the risk insured against in order for the insurers to avoid their obligations under the contract.

Test

A representation, unlike a warranty, is not part of the insurance contract but is collateral to it. If a representation is not material to the risk, its falsity does not avoid the contract. On the other hand, the materiality of a warranty to the risk insured against is irrelevant; if the fact is not as warranted, the insurer may deny recovery. * * * In case of doubt, courts normally construe a statement in an insurance contract as a representation rather than a warranty. See 12A V. Appleman & J. Appleman, Insurance Law and Practice § 7342 (1981); 43 Am.Jur.2d, *Insurance* §§ 1027, 1028 (1982). But no reason has been advanced for doubting that the provision in question here—which by its terms "warrant[s]" a fact and is part of the insurance contract—is a warranty. Accordingly, we cannot hold that it was improper for the trial judge to read this provision as a warranty. The district court therefore did not err in ruling that evidence of materiality would not have been relevant to the question whether Vlastos can recover on the policy.

The parties agree that the provision in question concerned a state of affairs existing at the time the contract was signed, and was not a promise that a janitor *would* occupy the third floor in the future. In other words, the provision is satisfied if a janitor occupied the floor on Nov. 22, 1979, the date the policy was issued, even if the situation had changed by the time of the fire several months later. The district court erroneously instructed the jury on this issue at two points. It stated that Vlastos agreed that the floor "*would be* occupied as a janitor's residence" (App. 389, emphasis added) and that the warranty was breached if "*at the time of the fire*" a massage parlor occupied any significant portion of the floor (App. 390, emphasis added). If the district court on remand decides that the case must be retried (*see infra* Part III), then it should instruct the jury that the relevant time for purposes of the warranty is the time at which the parties entered into the contract.

relevant time for warranty is at the time the parties enter into K.

III.

Having established that Vlastos did warrant that at the time she entered into the contract "the 3rd floor [was] occupied as Janitor's residence," it must be determined what the language of the warranty should be construed to mean. For the reasons set forth below, the provision must be read in Vlastos' favor, as warranting merely that a janitor occupied some portion of the third floor.

What did language mean.

Under Pennsylvania law, the question "whether a written contract is ambiguous is one for the court to decide as a matter of law. * * * Our review therefore is plenary." *Northbrook Insurance Co. v. Kuljjan Corp.*, 690 F.2d 368, 371 (3d Cir.1982). "[T]he language of the policy may not be tortured to create ambiguities where none exist." *Houghton v. American Life Insurance Co.*, 692 F.2d 289, 291 (3d Cir.1982); see *Northbrook*, 690 F.2d at 372. If any ambiguity exists, however, it is well-settled that the ambiguity "*must* be construed against the insurer, and in a manner which is more favorable to coverage." *Houghton*, 692 F.2d at 291 (quoting *Buntin v. Continental Insurance Co.*, 583 F.2d 1201, 1207) (3d Cir.1978) (emphasis in original).

"A provision of an insurance policy is ambiguous if reasonably intelligent [persons] on considering it in the context of the entire policy would honestly differ as to its meaning." *Northbrook*, 690 F.2d at 372 (quoting *Celley v. Mutual Benefit Health & Accident Association*, 229 Pa.Super. 475, 481–82, 324 A.2d 430, 434 (1974)). * * * In determining whether there is any ambiguity, the court need not confine its attention to the "four corners" of the contract but may consider external evidence. *Northbrook*, 690 F.2d at 371–72. *Celley*, 229 Pa. Super. at 482, 324 A.2d at 434, states that the court may consider "whether alternative or more precise language, if used, would have put the matter beyond reasonable question."

test of ambiguity

Applying Pennsylvania law to the facts of this case, we conclude that the warranty here was ambiguous. Although the view of the insurance companies—that Vlastos stated that the floor was to be the janitor's exclusive province—is a possible construction, a reasonable person could have understood Vlastos to have warranted merely that her janitor lived on the third floor.

Even if one takes the warranty clause in isolation, it is questionable that the reading proffered by the insurance companies is the only plausible one. If Pinkney resided on the third floor, then it is not simply and unambiguously false to say that he occupied that floor, even assuming the existence of a significant competing or concurrent use. In response to the query "does a janitor occupy the third floor?" a categorical "no" surely would be misleading at best, and even a qualified "no" ("no, he occupies only part of it" or "no, a massage parlor occupies it as well") is strained. It seems that the most appropriate reply, making the relevant factual assumptions, would be a qualified affirmative ("yes, although he occupies it along with a massage parlor").

When the relevant language is examined in the context of the remainder of the policy, and in light of the alleged purposes for the insertion of the warranty, it becomes even more difficult to say that Vlastos unambiguously warranted that her janitor alone occupied the third floor.

It is significant that the warranty was not made in the course of a description of the various uses to which the building was being put. The policy did not make any warranties as to any other floors of the building. Thus, it would be reasonable to infer that the warranty evinced a concern that there be a resident janitor rather than an intent that the various floors of the building, such as the third floor, be put to relatively safe uses.

Although the actual reasons for the insertion of the warranty are not clear from the record, the insurers represented at trial that one reason was that a resident janitor decreases the risk of losses due to fire. See App. at 358, 372. This purpose of the provision would be fulfilled if Pinkney lived on the third floor, regardless of the proportion of this floor that was reserved for his sole use. Occupancy of the premises by a janitor might increase the likelihood that fire hazards would be taken care of promptly. It also might mean that there is a good chance that if a fire were to begin a responsible person would be on the scene to put it out or call the fire department, thus minimizing the damage from fires that do occur. A full-time resident janitor might also deter prowlers and vandals from entering the building. For reasons such as these, Vlastos could have assumed that the insurance companies looked kindly upon her having a resident janitor, without understanding that the insurance companies had any interest in whether the janitor occupied all or only part of the floor.

It is true that a second reason has been proposed for the insertion of the warranty. If a janitor occupied all of the third floor, then no occupant more dangerous—as a massage parlor perhaps is—would be there. Viewed in light of this possible motive, the warranty would have been intended to contemplate the occupancy of the entire third floor. Although this suggestion as to the purpose of the warranty is plausible, it is less obvious than the first suggested reasons, especially when it is recalled that the insurers did not request any assurance that extremely dangerous usages were absent from the other three floors of the building.

The conclusion that the warranty is ambiguous is buttressed by the consideration that the insurers easily could have precluded doubt by the addition of one word. Had the provision read: "Warranted that the 3rd Floor is occupied solely as Janitor's residence," then the question whether there would be a breach if a massage parlor operated in some of the space would have been unlikely to arise. *Cf. Celley, supra,* 229 Pa.Super. at 482, 324 A.2d at 430.

Because the provision is ambiguous, under Pennsylvania law it must be construed in a manner favorable to insurance coverage. We therefore hold that Vlastos warranted only that a janitor resided on the third floor, not that there was no other occupancy of the floor.

If any jury issue existed at all, it was simply whether or not a janitor resided on the third floor at the time of the contract. The district court at several points indicated that the insurers had presented no evidence that Pinkney did not live on the third floor, and that it would not let the insurers go to the jury on this question.[1] On the other hand, the district court did instruct the jury that it could find "that nothing occupied the space at all. * * *" App. 391. There also is some uncertainty whether the district court, in considering the sufficiency of the evidence that Pinkney did not occupy the third floor, focused on the time of the fire as distinguished from the time that the parties entered into the contract. *See supra,* Part II. Accordingly, on remand the district court should clarify whether, in its view, there was a jury question whether Pinkney lived on the third floor at the time the contract was made. If it determines that there was sufficient evidence to go to the jury on this issue, then a new trial on the liability issue should be held. If there is no jury question, then under the facts of this case a new trial would be unwarranted, and the district should enter judgment for Vlastos on liability. * * *

1. *See* App. 357 ("You [the insurers] haven't produced any evidence that he [Pinkney] was not there or that he was not a janitor in the ordinary sense of the word * * * [the insurers'] only substantial contention * * * is that there was a massage parlor there"); App. 360 ("The only evidence I think that you've introduced, at least the evidence that I'm letting you go to the Jury on, is that there may have been a massage parlor there."). *See also* App. 358, 359. The insurers have not questioned that they bear the burden of proof.

Notes and Questions

1. *The History of Warranties.* Warranties first became prominent during the 18th century in marine insurance. For over one hundred years it had been the practice of shipowners and men of means to gather at Lloyd's Coffee House in London, to arrange for insurance of ships and the cargo they carried. The shipowner would circulate a statement of the subject of the insurance and the amount of coverage desired on a *slip,* and each individual willing to insure a portion of the total coverage requested would write his name under this statement. Thus the insurers became known as *underwriters.* Often those who sought insurance for one voyage participated as underwriters of other voyages. See generally A. Brown, Hazard Unlimited: The Story of Lloyds of London (1973); Vance, The History of the Development of the Warranty in Insurance Law, 20 Yale L.J. 523 (1911). For a modern polemic against Lloyds, see J. Doroshow and J. Wilkes, Goliath: Lloyds of London in the United States (1988).

As part of these insurance agreements, insureds often made statements or promises about certain characteristics of the ship or voyage in question. In a series of decisions during this period, Lord Mansfield made it clear that the terms of an insurance *warranty*—a statement or promise by the policyholder in the policy itself—must be strictly complied with, or the policy is void:

> There is a material distinction between a warranty and a representation. A representation may be equitably and substantially answered; but a warranty must be strictly complied with. Supposing a warranty to sail on the first of August, and the ship did not sail until the second, the warranty would not be complied with. A warranty in a policy of insurance is a condition or a contingency, and unless that be performed, there is no contract. It is perfectly immaterial for what purpose a warranty is introduced; but being inserted, the contract does not exist unless it be literally complied with. Now, in the present case, the condition was the sailing of the ship with a certain number of men; which not being complied with, the policy is void.

De Hahn v. Hartley, 1 T.R. 323 (1786).

The parties to marine insurance warranties were dealing under these circumstances in an atmosphere of mutual obligation and trust. It would not be surprising, therefore, if complete disclosure of all the risks entailed in a particular voyage were expected, and that any deviation from the facts represented to the underwriters by the policyholder would be considered a breach of obligation. The warranty was apparently one method of stating the level of risk in question—e.g., "warranted copper sheathed, and sailed from Liverpool with sixteen pounders, * * * fifty hands or upwards." *Id.* And, of course, the level of risk in question was critical to the underwriters' decision whether to insure and what premium to charge.

2. *Materiality.* The significance of Mansfield's warranty decisions was that the policyholder's breach of a warranty voided the policy even if that breach did not contribute to the loss in question, and even if it did not increase the risk that a loss would occur. Under the circumstances that gave rise to these warranties, however, the latter would rarely be true. Why? Consequently, the real issue in the cases Mansfield decided was whether breach of warranty voided a policy when, although the breach increased the risk taken by the underwriters, the breach did not in fact contribute to the loss that occurred. For example, suppose that breach of a warranty that a ship be copper sheathed had nothing to do with its loss in a hurricane. Does it seem appropriate to deny coverage in such a case?

Despite the apparent unfairness of depriving a policyholder of coverage for an immaterial breach, there are several arguments supporting the approach Mansfield took. First, the rule may well have reflected the moral code of those who frequented Lloyd's. Mansfield would simply have been honoring their expectations. Second, determining whether the breach of a warranty actually contributed to loss typically would be difficult—the loss often occurred at sea, the damaged subject matter could be unavailable for inspection, and often witnesses would have perished with the ship and cargo. On the other hand, almost any breach of warranty would have increased the risk of loss; why else include the warranty in the policy? The cost of coverage for all would be reduced by a rule that created strong incentives to comply with warranties. Third, for the same reasons, monitoring compliance with warranties would be difficult. A rule requiring strict compliance might therefore have been necessary in order to minimize incentives for the occasional renegade to cheat, especially as the marine insurance business grew and the tight community of Lloyds began to dissolve.

Finally, the rule that warranties must be strictly complied with might have been sensible not only for the reasons noted above. That rule—as opposed to one that required actual contribution to loss before a policy could be voided—might in addition have been a relatively inexpensive method of guarding against adverse selection and moral hazard. For instance, it might be argued that requiring strict compliance with warranties put teeth in the risk classification (i.e., the charging of premiums that depended on the level of risk posed) that the use of warranties facilitated, and thereby discouraged adverse selection. The high-risk policyholder was one who breached a warranty and was therefore denied coverage after-the-fact rather than before. Similarly, the rule that breach voided coverage even if it did not contribute to loss might have discouraged policyholders from reducing safety levels after becoming insured, because such a reduction meant that they were uninsured no matter what caused a loss. In this way the rule may also have helped to combat moral hazard.

As the paragraphs that follow indicate, Mansfield's approach was overturned beginning in the 19th century. At the close of the period when the strict compliance rule governing insurance warranties had been reversed by a century of judicial decisions and legislative action, Professor Vance ended a famous article on the issue with the following conclusion:

> It is a cause for gratification that the total abolition of the warranty, which never had good reason for existence and now has none at all, will tend to enable the courts to apply to insurance policies the same rules of construction that determine the meaning of other contracts.

Vance, The History of the Development of the Warranty in Insurance Law, 20 Yale L.J. 523, 534 (1911). In light of the arguments that can be made in favor of the common law treatment of the insurance warranty, do you share Vance's attitude toward the utility of such warranties?

3. *Judicial and Legislative Regulation of Warranties.* The modern approach praised by Vance very narrowly limits the effect of insurance warranties. Whatever may be said in favor of the strict approach when it is applied to marine insurance, the argument for the strict approach is much weaker in cases where the policyholder is not a sophisticated purchaser, where the expectations of the parties about the significance of the insured's representations differ, or where the breach of warranty does not materially increase the risk of loss. For example, a homeowner who purchases fire insurance and does not read the fine print of his policy might be astounded to learn that he had warranted that smoking would not be permitted on the premises, and that his breach of this warranty voided coverage even though that breach was not responsible for the destruction of his property. His situation is quite different from the shipowner who warrants the condition of his vessel.

Beginning in the nineteenth century, both courts and legislatures took action that mitigated the harsh effect of warranty law in contexts such as this. One approach, exemplified in *Vlastos,* is to hold that a warranty should be strictly construed against the insurer, and then to find that it has been complied with. Another is to interpret warranties that seem to relate to future facts ("promissory warranties") as relating only to present facts ("affirmative warranties"). Under this approach the warranty need only be complied with at the time it is made. For elaboration on these and other judicial strategies of interpretation, see R. Jerry, Understanding Insurance Law 515–19 (1987); R. Keeton and A. Widiss, Insurance Law 665–67 (2d ed. 1988).

Legislative action limiting the effect of warranties has been at least as important as judicial regulation. Virtually every state has enacted a statute governing the effect of insurance warranties. In some states the strict compliance rule still applies in marine insurance, while in others it has been limited even in that field. See, e.g., *Wilburn Boat Company v. Fireman's Fund Insurance Company,* 348 U.S. 310, 75 S.Ct.

368, 99 L.Ed. 337 (1955) (applying the liberal Texas rule rather than the "literal performance" requirement of federal admiralty law). Although the statutes vary, their effect is generally to collapse the distinction between warranties and representations, so that breach of a warranty voids a policy only if the breach is material—a standard requirement in the law of misrepresentation. Some statutes provide that the breach is material if it *increases the risk* of loss. See, e.g., Mich.Comp.Laws Ann. § 500.2218. Others require that the breach actually *contribute to loss.* See, e.g., Kan.Stat.Ann. § 40–418. Still others provide as a ground for voiding coverage that statements by the insured will be considered representations and not warranties unless fraudulently made. See, e.g., Neb.Rev.Stat. § 44–502(4). Some statutes simply require that the breach be "material" without defining that term. See, e.g., Wisc.Stat. Ann. § 633.11. And most (including some just cited) combine one or more of these elements. See, e.g., Mass.Gen.Laws Ann., c. 175, § 186:

> No oral or written misrepresentation or warranty made in the negotiation of a policy of insurance by the insured or in his behalf shall be deemed material or prevent its attaching unless such misrepresentation or warranty is made with actual intent to deceive, or unless the matter misrepresented or made a warranty increased the risk of loss.

Although some warranty statutes apply to all forms of insurance, others limit the forms to which they apply; and some apply only to statements made in applications, while others apply to statements in policies as well as in applications. Similarly, some such statutes apply not only to warranties and representations, but to what are typically referred to as *coverage provisions*—conditions and exclusions that specify the terms of coverage. In a jurisdiction whose statute applies only to warranties and representations, it may therefore still be possible for an insurer to phrase a prerequisite to coverage as a condition or exclusion that achieves the same purpose as a warranty. For example, in *Vlastos,* might the insurer have avoided the warranty issue entirely (though it would not necessarily have prevailed by doing so, given the court's interpretive stance) by providing under a section labelled "exclusions" in the policy, "This policy does not provide coverage for any loss occurring while the third floor is not occupied as a janitor's residence."?

4. *Distinguishing Warranties from Coverage Provisions.* A key question in this circumstance is how to distinguish between warranties and representations on the one hand, and coverage provisions on the other. Unfortunately, that distinction is elusive. Each of these different clauses in some sense state conditions precedent to coverage or constitute descriptions of the risk insured. Some courts therefore look to see whether the provision in question is in the verbal form of a warranty, as distinguished, for example, from a condition precedent, and reach a decision on this basis. See, e.g., *Moe v. Allemannia Fire Insurance Company of Pittsburgh,* 209 Wis. 526, 244 N.W. 593 (1932), construing a policy provision that there was no coverage against loss to insured property while it was "incumbered by a chattel mortgage."

The court held that because this provision contained no warranty it was a coverage provision that fell outside the scope of the Wisconsin statute regulating the effect of warranties.

Apparently dissatisfied with this approach, the late Professor Edwin Patterson argued that warranties relate to *potential causes* of loss, whereas coverage provisions relate to *actual causes*. See E. Patterson, Essentials of Insurance Law 272–83 (2d ed. 1957). Patterson's distinction is embodied in a statute to this effect, N.Y.Ins.Law § 3106.[1] Under this statute, a policy provision that there is no coverage against loss by fire while gasoline is stored on the insured premises would seem to constitute a warranty, no matter how phrased; and a provision that there is no coverage against loss by fire caused by the ignition of gasoline stored on the premises would seem to constitute a coverage provision. In a jurisdiction that has also enacted a statute providing that breach of warranty does not void a policy unless breach increases risk or contributes to loss, does this view of the distinction between warranties and coverage provisions make it impossible for an insurer to void a policy in the event that an immaterial breach coincides with an insured loss? Does room for unfairness remain regarding the difference between breaches of warranty that increase risk and those that actually contribute to loss?

2. Misrepresentation and Concealment

Misrepresentation. Even setting aside the peculiar status of the insurance warranty, a series of issues remains regarding the effect of a misrepresentation by the insured on the coverage provided. Standard rules governing the voiding of a contract because of misrepresentation by one of the parties—in insurance and other fields—require that the representation be false, material, and induce justifiable reliance by the party who suffers damages as a result of the misrepresentation. The courts typically do not require complete accuracy of representations made by the insurance applicant; if a statement is substantially true, there has been no misrepresentation.

As to the closely related elements of materiality and justifiable reliance, two different dimensions of assessment are relevant. First, should the test for these elements be objective or subjective? Since the party allegedly victimized by a misrepresentation is the insurer, the issue here is whether the standard should be the *reasonable insurer* or *this insurer.* In most settings the difference will be negligible, although in some cases the insurer's underwriting standards may be sufficiently more exacting than the norm that the choice will be significant. The classic case on the issue is *Penn Mutual Life Insurance Company v. Mechanics' Savings Bank & Trust Company,* 72 Fed. 413 (6th Cir.1896),

---

1. "The term 'warranty' * * * means any provision of an insurance contract which has the effect of requiring, as a condition of the taking effect of such contract or as a condition precedent of the insurer's liability thereunder, the existence of a fact which tends to diminish, or the nonexistence of a fact which tends to increase, the risk of the occurrence of any loss, damage or injury within the coverage of the contract."

which adopted an objective test in an opinion written by Judge (later President and still later Chief Justice) Taft. See also *New York Life Ins. Co. v. Kuhlenschmidt,* 218 Ind. 404, 33 N.E.2d 340 (1941). If an objective test is adopted, is the insurer treated fairly? On the other hand, if a subjective test is adopted, there may not be much left of the distinction between materiality and reliance.

A second dimension of assessment concerns the degree of materiality and reliance required, regardless of whether the test is objective or subjective. At one extreme, the insurer might be required to show that the risk misrepresented was central to the coverage provided and that under no circumstances would a policy have been issued if the insured had made an accurate disclosure. At the other extreme, the insurer might be required to show merely that the fact misrepresented increased the insurer's risk and that knowledge of that fact would have been relevant to the decision about whether to issue a policy, or whether to issue it on the terms and at the rate offered. Occasionally the issue can be sidestepped with something like a statutory or judicial presumption. For example, many state statutes provide that where the insured has misrepresented his age in an application for life insurance—a situation in which both the materiality and reliance elements probably are satisfied even under the more lenient approach—the policy is not voided, but the beneficiary is entitled only to the benefit that would have been payable if the decedent's age had been accurately stated. See, e.g., Annotated Code of Va. § 38.2–3306.

Issues of materiality and reliance are often more difficult to resolve, however, because underwriting standards governing other aspects of the risk being transferred tend to involve judgment rather than mere reference to a mortality table. But it is well-settled that a few kinds of recurring misrepresentations normally are material. See, e.g., *Sovereign Life Insurance Company of California v. Rewald,* 601 F.Supp. 1489 (D.Hawaii 1985) (misrepresentation of the applicant's net worth on a life insurance application); *Montgomery v. Reserve Life Insurance Company,* 585 S.W.2d 620 (Tenn.App.1979) (applicant denied seeing physician within last five years, although she had suffered seven nervous breakdowns during that period and been under the care of four different psychiatrists).

Concealment. The problem of concealment of material facts, as distinguished from affirmative misrepresentation, poses slightly different issues. The insurer must prove a failure to disclose a fact that the *standard* applicant *knows* is material in order to void a policy on the ground of concealment—except in marine insurance, where a more stringent obligation to disclose material information still tends to prevail. But in all other forms of insurance, a *scienter* element of sorts is thus added when concealment, rather than misrepresentation, is involved. An insurer may be able to sidestep this problem by showing that it inquired about the subject matter concealed, and thereby either elicit a false answer (and therefore an affirmative misrepresentation) or at least put the applicant on notice that the subject of the inquiry is material.

Under the modern practice of asking relatively detailed questions on insurance applications, the difficulty of proving knowing concealment rather than innocent but affirmative misrepresentation can be reduced in this way. This problem cannot be completely eliminated, however, because there may still be gaps between the cracks of questions asked, and material facts may fall into these cracks. Moreover, fashioning applications to produce misrepresentation rather than concealment may require a lengthy, potentially off-putting series of questions on applications. Yet, incomplete answers to open-ended questions may be more easily forgiven than false answers to detailed questions. In close cases the common sense morality of a jury may well be more likely to find an affirmative misrepresentation to be blameworthy than the failure to fully and completely answer a question that the insurer could have phrased to elicit a complete response.

The problem is compounded—though perhaps justifiably—by the rule that if the insured furnishes answers that could lead an insurer to the information it seeks through a diligent search, then there has been no misrepresentation or concealment. See, e.g., *Gomogda v. Prudential Insurance Company of America,* 31 Colo.App. 154, 501 P.2d 756 (1972). How should this result be reached—by a holding that there has been no misrepresentation, or that although there has been, the insurer has not justifiably relied upon it?

Problems

1. An applicant (now deceased) had answered "no" to a question on a life insurance application that asked, "Have you been treated by a physician during the last five years?", when in fact he had been treated for high blood pressure on two occasions during the period. In a jurisdiction with a statute making a misrepresentation material if it "increases the risk assumed by the insurer," as counsel for the insurer how would you go about proving materiality and reliance? As counsel for the insured, how would you attempt to refute the insurer's proofs? What kinds of information would you want to discover from the insurer's files?

2. An applicant (now deceased) had answered "no" to a question on a life insurance application that asked, "Do you smoke cigarettes?", when in fact she smoked two packs of cigarettes per day. The insurer issued a policy at the no-smoker premium rate. A "misrepresentation" is defined by statute in that jurisdiction as a false "statement as to past or present fact, made to the insurer . . . at or before the making of the insurance contract as an inducement to the making thereof." The statute provides that the contract may be rescinded if the misrepresentation is "material," and provides that it is material if "knowledge by the insurer of the facts misrepresented would have led to a refusal by the insurer to make such contract." The insured argues that the

misrepresentation is not material, because the insurer would have issued a policy (for a higher premium) even if the misrepresentation had not been made. See *Mutual Benefit Life Insurance Company v. JMR Electronics Corp.,* 848 F.2d 30 (2d Cir.1988) (recovery denied).

WARD v. DURHAM LIFE INSURANCE COMPANY

Court of Appeals of North Carolina, 1988.
90 N.C.App. 286, 368 S.E.2d 391.

COZORT, Judge.

Plaintiff filed this action to recover benefits under her deceased husband's life insurance policy which was issued by defendant. Defendant denied coverage on the basis of misrepresentations in the application for insurance and moved for summary judgment. From the trial court's order granting summary judgment, plaintiff appeals. We reverse.

On 15 October 1985, defendant issued a life insurance policy to plaintiff's husband, Vernon Ward. Plaintiff, the beneficiary under the policy, sought to recover its proceeds after her husband was killed in an automobile accident on 26 January 1986. Defendant refused to pay the benefits on the grounds that there were material misrepresentations made in the application for insurance.

On 12 July 1986, plaintiff filed suit to collect the insurance proceeds. Defendant answered alleging that the insurance contract was null and void because of the misrepresentations and moved for summary judgment. Defendant filed supporting affidavits which stated that Mr. Ward had failed to report his past treatment for high blood pressure and a prior conviction for driving under the influence in his application and that his application would not have been approved had this information been included.

Plaintiff submitted an opposing affidavit which stated the following:

On 5 October 1985, plaintiff and her husband agreed to apply for a life insurance policy through Brenda Ward, Mr. Ward's first cousin. Ms. Ward advised them on that day that she was an agent for defendant. Ms. Ward asked plaintiff and her husband questions from an application for insurance; and, after they answered the questions orally, she recorded their responses on the application herself. When they reached question 30(d), Ms. Ward asked Mr. Ward if he had ever been convicted of driving under the influence. Plaintiff and her husband informed her that he had been so convicted in October, 1982. Ms. Ward responded that since the conviction was more than two years old it would not prevent him from obtaining insurance with her company. When they reached question 32(d), she asked Mr. Ward if he had ever been treated for high blood pressure. Mr. Ward informed her that he had been treated for high blood pressure in 1983, but had not had any problems since that time. Ms. Ward responded that since the treatment had occurred more than two years ago it would be all right and would not prevent Mr. Ward from obtaining insurance with her company. After she completed marking the application, Mr. Ward signed it and paid the premium requested.

After plaintiff filed her affidavit, defendant moved to strike several portions of it. The trial court granted this motion and subsequently granted defendant's motion for summary judgment. From this judgment, plaintiff appeals. * * *

Plaintiff also argues that the trial court erred in granting defendant's motion for summary judgment. When we consider the two erroneously stricken portions of plaintiff's affidavit along with the other affidavits and pleadings, we agree that summary judgment was erroneously granted. * * *

In the case *sub judice,* plaintiff has shown that there is a genuine issue as to whether the omission of material facts in the application is attributable to the applicant or to the insurer. Although "[a]n insurer's duty under an insurance contract may be avoided by a showing that the insured made representations in his insurance application which were material and false," *Willetts v. Insurance Corp.,* 45 N.C. App. 424, 428, 263 S.E.2d 300, 304, *disc. rev. denied,* 300 N.C. 562, 270 S.E.2d 116 (1980), "'an insurance company cannot avoid liability on a life insurance policy on the basis of facts known to it at the time the policy went into effect.'" *Northern Nat'l Life Ins. v. Miller Machine Co.,* 63 N.C.App. 424, 429, 305 S.E.2d 568, 571 (1983). "[K]nowledge of or notice to an agent of an insurer is imputed to the insurer itself, absent collusion between the agent and the insured." *Id.* at 429, 305 S.E.2d at 571–72. "It is well established that when the evidence raises a question of whether a misrepresentation in an application for insurance is attributable to the insured or to the agent of the insurer alone, the question must be resolved by the finder of fact." *Id.* at 429–30, 305 S.E.2d at 572.

In this case, there is no forecast of evidence of collusion or fraud between plaintiff's husband and defendant's agent. According to plaintiff's affidavit, plaintiff and her husband gave a complete and truthful disclosure of Mr. Ward's prior driving conviction and blood pressure condition. Defendant's agent then informed plaintiff and her husband that since these events occurred more than two years earlier, Mr. Ward would not be prevented from obtaining insurance. Trusting in the assurances by defendant's agent, Mr. Ward signed the application in good faith.

Defendant, relying on *Inman v. Woodmen of the World,* 211 N.C. 179, 189 S.E. 496 (1937), and *McCrimmon v. N.C. Mutual Life Ins. Co.,* 69 N.C.App. 683, 317 S.E.2d 709, *disc. rev. denied,* 312 N.C. 84, 322 S.E.2d 175 (1984), contends that any knowledge by its agent cannot be imputed to it once the insured signed the application. *Inman* and *McCrimmon* provide that an insurer has the right to rely upon the statements and representations contained in an application of insurance, if it is in writing and is signed by the applicant, even if an agent of the insurer filled out the application. Any false statements contained in the application would be imputed to the insured and not the insurer.

We believe that the facts of the present case are distinguishable from those in both *Inman* and *McCrimmon*. In *Inman*, the applicant gave truthful answers about his physical condition to the agent who failed to include this information in the application. The insured signed the application without reading it and when his beneficiary sought to recover the policy proceeds, the trial court dismissed the action. The Supreme Court affirmed and held that the agent's knowledge of the false representation could not be imputed to the insurer. The agent informed the applicant that despite his past medical problems, "I think I can get you by. You don't have to have a medical examination anyhow." This statement should have apprised the insured of the agent's intention to *deceive* the insurance company as to his true physical condition. By signing the application the insured condoned the deception.

In *McCrimmon*, plaintiff purchased life insurance on his son who suffered brain damage at birth. Although plaintiff informed the agent of his son's condition, the agent failed to include this information in the application. Plaintiff, without reading it, signed the completed application which falsely stated that his child did not have a defect or deformity. This Court held that, under *Inman*, the false statements in the application were imputed to plaintiff.

It is important to note that *Inman* did not establish a "bright line" rule that an insurer can avoid coverage every time the application is signed by the insured and the application contains a false answer to a question. The court specifically found that the applicant did not read the application or request that it be read to him and that his failure to do either "was not induced by any fraud on the part of the agent." *Inman*, 211 N.C. at 182, 189 S.E. at 497. Likewise, in the *McCrimmon* case we find no indication that there were any facts to support a theory that the agent fraudulently induced the applicant to sign the application.

The facts here make this case distinguishable. Plaintiff's affidavit clearly raises the factual issue of whether the agent fraudulently induced Mr. Ward to sign the application and whether that action should be imputed to the insurer. Plaintiff's husband signed the application only after the agent assured him that since the events occurred more than two years earlier, it was all right and would not prevent him from obtaining insurance. A jury could reasonably find that Mr. Ward justifiably inferred from the agent's statement that these past events were irrelevant to the insurance company in applying for insurance.

We hold that the pleadings and affidavits present a material issue of fact on whether the knowledge of the misrepresentation should be imputed to the insurer. Therefore, the trial court's judgment granting summary judgment is reversed and the case is remanded for a new trial.

Reversed and remanded.   *   *   *

PARKER, Judge, dissenting.

Believing as I do that the facts of this case are not distinguishable from *Thomas–Yelverton Co. v. Insurance Co.,* 238 N.C. 278, 77 S.E.2d 692 (1953), *Inman v. Woodmen of the World,* 211 N.C. 179, 189 S.E. 496 (1937) and *McCrimmon v. N.C. Mutual Life Ins. Co.,* 69 N.C.App. 683, 317 S.E.2d 709, *disc. rev. denied,* 312 N.C. 84, 322 S.E.2d 175 (1984), I respectfully dissent.

In *Thomas–Yelverton, supra,* the Court stated:

> The rule with respect to the knowledge of an agent being imputable to his principal is well stated *   *   * in the following language: "In the absence of fraud or collusion between the insured and the agent, the knowledge of the agent when acting within the scope of the powers entrusted to him will be imputed to the company, though a direct stipulation to the contrary appears in the policy or the application for the same." However, it is otherwise when it clearly appears that an insurance agent and the insured participated in a fraud by inserting false answers with respect to material facts in an application for insurance. The knowledge of the agent in such instances will not be imputable to his principal. (citing cases).
>
> *   *   *
>
> In the instant case, when the insured signed the application he knew the agent had written the answers to the questions contained in it; and by signing it in the form submitted, he represented that the answers were true.

Id. 238 N.C. at 281–83, 77 S.E.2d at 694–95.

In her brief, plaintiff cites a number of cases beginning with *Fishblate v. Fidelity Co.,* 140 N.C. 589, 53 S.E. 354 (1906) to support the position that the knowledge of the agent is imputed to the insurance carrier. However, *Fishblate, supra* and *Northern Nat'l Life Ins. v. Miller Machine Co.,* 63 N.C.App. 424, 305 S.E.2d 568 (1983), *aff'd,* 311 N.C. 62, 316 S.E.2d 256 (1984), relied upon by the majority, are distinguishable in that in those cases there is either a question or no showing as to the insured's knowledge of the contents of the application. There is no evidence that the insured signed the application. Moreover, it is noteworthy that in *Thomas–Yelverton, supra,* where there was no dispute that insured signed the application after the answers were inserted by the agent, the Court acknowledged *Fishblate* and its progeny, but rejected the plaintiff-appellant's argument. Accordingly, in this case I do not agree with plaintiff's oral argument that this Court in *McCrimmon, supra,* misinterpreted *Inman, supra.*

In the instant case from the uncontradicted evidence, plaintiff would have been uninsurable and rejected for insurance had the questions been answered truthfully. The rule is, and plaintiff does not dispute, that misrepresentations as to questions affecting insurability are material as a matter of law. *Tolbert v. Insurance Co.*, 236 N.C. 416, 72 S.E.2d 915 (1952).

The sole purpose of the application is to obtain accurate information for underwriting purposes. Without the false statement inserted by the agent, the uninsurable applicant would not have received a policy. Plaintiff has made no showing that her husband was prevented or prohibited from reading the application before he signed. When Mr. Ward signed the application, he adopted the statements and represented that they were true. If Mr. Ward had corrected the false statements, he would not have obtained the insurance; by signing, he benefited from the agent's action. Defendant has tendered the return of the premiums with interest thereon, and in my view owes nothing more.

Furthermore, even under the majority's theory of the case, I do not think the evidence is sufficient to raise an inference that insured was induced not to give a truthful application by statements of the agent. According to plaintiff's affidavit, the agent told plaintiff and her husband that because Mr. Ward's conviction and treatment for high blood pressure had occurred more than two years before the date of the application, "this was all right and would not prevent [Mr. Ward] from obtaining insurance with [defendant]." Although this statement may have led plaintiff and her husband to believe that the omitted information was not especially important, the agent did not expressly state that they were not required to report it. Plaintiff did not aver that the agent told them that the questions only required information from the past two years, nor did she aver that the agent advised or suggested that her husband not include the omitted information in the application.

For the foregoing, I vote to affirm.

Notes and Questions

1. *Justified Misrepresentation?* A few states require that the applicant know that a representation is false in order to permit the insurer to rescind a policy for misrepresentation. See, e.g., Conn.Gen. Stat. § 38–169(c). Most courts, however, interpret statutes requiring that misrepresentations be "material" in order to void a policy to apply even if a misrepresentation is made in good faith. See, e.g., *Continental Assurance Company v. Carroll*, 485 So.2d 406 (Fla.1986). For this reason, Ward needed something like a justification or excuse for the misrepresentation. One route would be to argue that disclosure of material facts to the agent constitutes disclosure to the insurer. Would this have been sufficient for the court?

2. *Fraudulent Inducement.* What is added by the court's apparent requirement of proof that the agent "fraudulently induced" Ward to sign the application? Suppose that the agent had elicited the same answers from Ward, but had said nothing in response and then completed the application with the same false answers. If Ward had then signed the application without reading it, would the result in the case have been different? Suppose he had both read and signed the application? Suppose that after reading the application Ward had commented on the false answers and was told by the agent that they were "not important"? See *Olson v. Bankers Life Insurance Company,* 63 Wash. 2d 547, 388 P.2d 136 (1964) (policy valid).

3. *"Entire Contract" Statutes.* Many states have enacted statutes providing that the insurance policy and all documents attached to it shall constitute the "entire contract" between the parties. See, e.g., New York Insurance Law § 3204:

> (a)(1) Every policy of life, accident or health insurance, or contract of annuity, delivered or issued for delivery in this state, shall contain the entire contract between the parties, and nothing shall be incorporated therein by reference to any writing, unless a copy thereof is endorsed upon or attached to the policy or contract when issued.

> (2) No application for the issuance of any such policy or contract shall be admissible in evidence unless a true copy was attached to such policy or contract when issued.

Under such statutes it is axiomatic that statements by the insured in the application may not be introduced in evidence unless the application was attached to the policy. See, e.g., *Smith v. North American Co. For Life, Accident & Health Insurance,* 306 So.2d 751 (La.1975).

THE AIDS PROBLEM AND THE LAW OF MISREPRESENTATION

Life and health insurers have been confronted with a new set of challenges by the spread of Acquired Immune Deficiency Syndrome (AIDS). The most prominent insurance problem associated with AIDS is the effort by insurers to screen out individuals who have been exposed to the Human Immunodeficiency Virus (HIV), which causes AIDS. The most effective current method of detecting individuals who have had such exposure but exhibit no symptoms is the HIV antibody test (there are actually two tests, one more accurate than the other). A positive result on the test identifies an individual as being at extremely high risk for contracting AIDS.

When the AIDS epidemic first surfaced, several states prohibited insurers from using the HIV antibody test to determine insurability. California did so by statute, as did the District of Columbia. See Cal. Health & Safety Code § 192.21(f) (West Supp.1986); D.C.Code Annotated §§ 35–221–229 (Supp.1987). In *American Council of Life Insurance v. District of Columbia,* 645 F.Supp. 84 (D.D.C.1986), the constitutionality of the latter law was upheld. In a few other states regulations promulgated by the Insurance Commissioner have prohibited use of the test. With the continued spread of AIDS and growing recognition of the substantial impact the disease may have on insurance costs, however, the emphasis has shifted to regulating and controlling insurers' use of the HIV antibody test rather than prohibiting it altogether.

The principal approach taken by more recent legislation is to attempt to assure the confidentiality of the results and to preclude the use of sexual orientation as the basis for determining which applicants are required to submit to HIV testing. See, e.g., Cal.Ins.Code §§ 799–799.09 (West Supp.1989); Fla.Stat.Ann. § 627.429 (Supp.1988); N.Y. Public Health Law §§ 2780–87 (Supp.1989). For discussion of the issues related to HIV testing, see Perkins, Prohibiting the Use of Human Immunodeficiency Virus Antibody Test by Employers and Insurers, 25 Harv.J. on Legislation 275 (1988); Note, AIDS Antibody Testing and Health Insurance Underwriting: A Paradigmatic Inquiry, 49 Ohio St.L.J. 1059 (1989).

The major problem AIDS poses for insurers is the threat of adverse selection by AIDS carriers and victims. Although the HIV antibody test is not perfectly effective, it is one important method of combatting this threat. Another method, however, is the combined use of the application questionnaire and the law of misrepresentation. The few cases on the issue make it clear that misleading answers by those applicants who know they have AIDS or AIDS-related diseases are very likely to be considered material misrepresentations. See, e.g., *Zachary Trading, Inc. v. Northwestern Mutual Life Insurance Company,* 668 F.Supp. 343 (S.D.N.Y.1987). A more difficult problem that is likely to arise in future cases, however, involves misrepresentations by those who merely suspect that they have been exposed to AIDS. Consider how effective the following set of questions would be in identifying applicants who fall into the latter category, or in permitting insurers to void policies issued as a result of false answers to these questions.

1. Have you had an HIV antibody test within the last fifteen years?

2. If so, what was the test result?

3. Do you believe or have reason to believe you have been exposed to the HIV virus?

4. Do you believe or have reason to believe you have AIDS?

5. Have you been celibate for the last fifteen years?

6. If not, have you had sexual relations with only one person during the past fifteen years, and are you perfectly assured of his or her sexual fidelity to you?

7. If not, are you perfectly assured of the complete sexual and drug use history of every person with whom you have had sexual relations during that time?

If you were a state Insurance Commissioner with authority to prohibit insurers' use of these questions, which would you prohibit, and why?

MACKENZIE v. PRUDENTIAL INSURANCE COMPANY OF AMERICA

United States Court of Appeals, Sixth Circuit, 1969.
411 F.2d 781.

COMBS, Circuit Judge.

Plaintiff-appellant was beneficiary under an insurance policy written by defendant-appellee on the life of her decedent, Jerome F. MacKenzie. After Mr. MacKenzie's death in August, 1966,[1] Prudential refused to pay over the proceeds of the policy, contending that MacKenzie had in legal effect made material misrepresentations concerning his health when he accepted delivery of the policy. This action was brought in state court in Louisville, Kentucky, but was removed to the United States District Court by reason of diversity of citizenship. The district court granted summary judgment for the defendant, and the plaintiff appeals. We affirm. * * *

On August 10, 1964, MacKenzie made initial application with Prudential for a $40,000 decreasing term life insurance policy. The application was completed and signed by MacKenzie in the presence of Dr. Robert McGrath, who had examined MacKenzie at Prudential's request.

The application called for MacKenzie to disclose whether he had ever been treated for or had any known indication of "heart trouble or murmer, high blood pressure, or abnormal pulse?" To this, he answered, "No." He was also asked to disclose any visits to physicians in the preceding five years. In answering this question, MacKenzie listed three visits to doctors, two of which were for routine physical examinations and the other for removal of a cyst. The application provided that no insurance would take effect unless "all of the answers to the question in Part 1 and Part 2 of the application continue to be true and complete answers as of the date of the delivery of the policy * * *."

So far as is known, the above representations were true when MacKenzie signed the application. Dr. McGrath found his blood pressure to be 140/78 (within normal limits). However, sometime before September 17, 1964, the date the policy was delivered, MacKenzie suffered a chest bruise. This was apparently a minor injury, but he sought medical assistance from another doctor on September 16. Upon examining MacKenzie, the doctor found that his blood pressure was 170/100 (higher than normal). He was given a prescription for Naturetin, a diuretic prescribed to decrease blood pressure, and advised to get a complete check-up.

1. The cause of death was pulmonary embolus which developed after decedent was injured in a fall from a bicycle.

When the policy was delivered to MacKenzie by Prudential's agent on the evening of September 17, he said nothing about his recent visit to a doctor or the increase in his blood pressure. He did have the policy decreased to $20,000 because of anticipated difficulty in paying premiums, but no further statement was made concerning the application.[2]

The affidavits and answers to interrogatories appended to Prudential's motion for summary judgment establish without contradiction that Prudential accepted the risk in reliance upon the truthfulness of the answers in the application and that, if MacKenzie had volunteered the truth about his blood pressure, the policy would not have been delivered. One of Prudential's underwriters stated in interrogatories that, if the change in MacKenzie's condition had been divulged, the company either would have refused to issue the policy or would have increased the premium.

Under Kentucky law, which under the *Erie* doctrine is controlling here, misrepresentations sufficient to prevent recovery on an insurance policy must be material to the risk *or* fraudulently made. Ky.Rev.Stat. § 304.656 (1962); *Mills v. Reserve Life Ins. Co.,* Ky., 335 S.W.2d 955 (1960); *The Maccabees v. Covert,* 302 Ky. 481, 194 S.W.2d 498 (1946); *Prudential Ins. Co. of America v. Lampley,* 297 Ky. 495, 180 S.W.2d 399 (1944). Prudential contends and we hold that, since the increase in the blood pressure reading was obviously material, no fraud need be shown. The Kentucky court held in *Maccabees,* supra, that "[t]he standard by which materiality is to be determined is the action which insurance companies generally would have taken on the application, when acting in accordance with their usual practice and usage, if the truth had been told." See also *Northwestern Mut. Life Ins. Co. v. Yoe's Ex'r,* 283 Ky. 406, 141 S.W.2d 554 (1940); *Commonwealth Life Ins. Co. v. Goodknight's Adm'r,* 212 Ky. 763, 280 S.W.2d 123 (1926).

So, the decisive question is whether MacKenzie had a duty to divulge his change in health the breach of which would amount to a material misrepresentation. The Supreme Court has spoken on this question in *Stipcich v. Metropolitan Life Ins. Co.,* 277 U.S. 311, 316–317, 48 S.Ct. 512, 513, 72 L.Ed. 895 (1928):

> "[E]ven the most unsophisticated person must know that, in answering the questionnaire and submitting it to the insurer, he is furnishing the data on the basis of which the company will decide whether, by issuing a policy, it wishes to insure him. If, while the company deliberates, he discovers facts which make portions of his application no longer true, the most elementary spirit of fair dealing would seem to require him to make a full disclosure. If he fails to do so the company may, despite its acceptance of the application, decline to issue a

2. Prudential's agent who delivered the policy, Irvin G. Walter, said that he asked about health changes, but this was contradicted by Mrs. MacKenzie. For the purpose of this appeal, we construe the facts in favor of appellant.

policy, [cases cited] or, if a policy has been issued, it has a valid defense to a suit upon it." [Citations omitted.]

Although the Kentucky Court of Appeals has not considered this specific issue, the rule of *Stipcich* has received rather universal acceptance—and we have no reason to believe Kentucky would not adhere to it. See *New York Life Ins. Co. v. Gay,* 36 F.2d 634 (6th Cir.1929). Accordingly, Mr. MacKenzie's failure to divulge his high blood pressure reading must be regarded as a material misrepresentation sufficient to void the policy.

Judgment affirmed.

Notes and Questions

1. *A Duty To Disclose?* To what extent should the result in *MacKenzie* turn on the provision in the application that no insurance would take effect unless all of the answers continued to be true and complete as of the date of delivery of the policy? Does this provision, in effect, create a duty to disclose? The Supreme Court asserted in *Stipcich* that if an applicant discovers facts that " * * * make portions of his application no longer true, the most elementary spirit of fair dealing would seem to require him to make full disclosure." Suppose that the applicant expects the policy to arrive by mail. To what lengths should he be required to go in order to make disclosure? Would it matter whether he had applied through an intermediary such as an agent or broker whom he could telephone? Should the applicant be expected to make a materiality determination based on his memory of the questions asked in the application, or based on some other standard?

2. *Alternatives.* Would it be preferable to hold that there is no affirmative duty to disclose changes in health or other material conditions unless the insurer or its agent makes a specific inquiry? In *Seidler v. Georgetown Life Insurance Company,* 82 Ill.App.3d 361, 37 Ill. Dec. 664, 402 N.E.2d 666 (1980), the insured signed an application containing a provision that coverage would not take effect unless the health of the insured remained as described in the application. He submitted to a physical examination, but then (before the policy was issued) suffered a heart attack whose occurrence he did not disclose to the insurer. The practice of the insurer's agent (actually a reinsurer) was to require the insured to complete a special form at the time the policy was delivered indicating whether there had been a change in health; but for some reason the form was not completed in Seidler's case. The court held that the insured's failure to disclose was not dispositive.

A different alternative, at least in life and health insurance, is inclusion of a "good health" clause in the application, providing that the policy is not valid unless delivered to the insured while he is in good health. With the rise of AIDS, this approach may be relied upon more and more frequently, although the difficulty of defining the notion of

"good health" in this context and of determining retrospectively whether this test was satisfied may limit its usefulness. See, e.g., *Kentucky
Central Life Insurance Company v. Webster,* 651 F.Supp. 935 (N.D.Ala.
1986).

3. *The Materiality of Materiality.* Over the long run, should it
make any difference to an insurer whether applicants in MacKenzie's
position disclose the occurrence of new and material facts that develop
during the application period? A rule that imposed no duty to disclose
would merely create insurance against the risk that facts would change
during the application period. Does the answer depend on the nature
of the new facts? For example, in fashioning a rule to govern the issue,
would it make sense to distinguish what happened in *MacKenzie* from
the decision of an applicant for fire insurance to begin storing large
amounts of gasoline in her basement the day after completing an
application? What reasons might there be for ignoring this distinction?

4. *Misrepresentation after Loss.* Although the major function of
the prohibition against misrepresentation is to combat adverse selection, the legislative reluctance to countenance what seems like the
forfeiture of coverage also pervades the field. For example, statutes
governing the effects of warranties and misrepresentations often apply
to misstatements made "before or after" loss. Should the same test for
materiality be applied after loss as is applied before?

The issue arises in cases such as *Bryant v. Nationwide Mutual Fire
Insurance Company,* 67 N.C.App. 616, 313 S.E.2d 803 (1984), in which
the insured house was destroyed by fire. In the course of the insurer's
investigation, the insured misrepresented the size of his debts. Since
the desire to capture the benefit of insurance on mortgaged property
might create moral hazard, some courts hold that a misrepresentation
of the size of the insured's debts on an insurance *application* is material. If such a misrepresentation after loss would discourage an insurer
from conducting an arson investigation, is it material? Should the
answer depend on whether in fact there was arson? If so, is there any
need for a post-loss misrepresentation defense?

Chapter Two

INSURANCE CONTRACT FORMATION AND MEANING

A. THE ROLE OF STANDARDIZED FORMS

1. The Policy Drafting Process

Contract law has long recognized the special problems posed by the standard-form contract. Indeed, an early article on contracts of adhesion used insurance contracts as a principal example. See Kessler, Contracts of Adhesion—Some Thoughts About Freedom of Contract, 43 Colum.L.Rev. 629 (1943). For several generations of scholars and judges, these "take-it-or-leave-it" offers have justified greater judicial and legislative regulation than contracts whose terms are individually negotiated, by parties dealing at arms length, with equal resources and information. More attention seems to have been paid to the advantages and disadvantages of standardized contracts, however, than to the process by which these contracts actually become standard.

Although the fact that insurance policies are contracts of adhesion is important to an understanding of the law governing their operation, it is equally important that the same standard-form policies often are used by many insurance companies. Thus, standardization in insurance not only involves a take-it-or-leave-it offer of the same policy by one company to all its customers, but (in the extreme case) an offer of the same policy, to all customers, by all companies. Competition in insurance markets, therefore, often tends to be over price, quality of service, or reliability, but rarely over the terms of coverage itself.

The earliest standard-form policy was Lloyd's Standard Policy, a marine insurance contract adopted by the Lloyd's brokers in 1779. But the first form of coverage to be widely standardized in the United States was fire insurance. In the last quarter of the nineteenth century a number of companies became insolvent, and other unscrupulous operators marketed policies with fine print clauses that were highly disadvantageous to policyholders. Judicial and legislative regulation of the effect of warranties was one result. In addition, a number of states prescribed the content of fire insurance policies by statute. The process continued until the adoption of the now-dominant New York Fire Insurance Policy in 1943.[1] See Wenck, The Historical Development of Standard Policies, 35 J. of Risk and Ins. 537, 538–44 (1968). Other techniques of standardization include administrative

---

1. That policy is now prescribed by New York Ins. Law § 3404.

prescription of policy forms, administrative approval of forms, and cooperation among insurers in developing policy forms. See R. Keeton and A. Widiss, Insurance Law 123–25 (2d ed. 1988).

This last technique is extremely influential in property/casualty insurance. A very substantial percentage of the standard-form policies that the industry uses are prepared by the Insurance Services Office (ISO), a service organization whose membership is comprised exclusively of property/casualty insurers. The following excerpt from an ISO report describes the drafting process and the benefits that ISO (and through ISO, its member companies) believes accrue from the use of standard-form policies.

Insurance Services Office

INSURANCE SERVICES OFFICE IN A COMPETITIVE MARKETPLACE: ISO'S ROLE WITHIN THE PROPERTY CASUALTY INDUSTRY

6–7 (June 1987).*

How ISO Activities Foster Competition

How does ISO development of standard coverage parts improve competition? * * *

ISO coverage parts—the contractual provisions ISO makes available for insurers to use in developing an insurance contract—are designed to provide an industry standard, a benchmark for comparison. Insurance is necessarily a complex product covering a variety of objects and activities that could potentially be damaged, destroyed or lost or could themselves cause a loss at some time in the future. With standard ISO language and coverage parts providing the baseline for decisionmaking, insurance consumers are more readily able to comparison shop for price, coverage and service.

More than 1400 insurers are competing in the property/casualty insurance market. If standardized coverages did not exist, consumers would be confronted with an unintelligible array of different insurance forms. Standard coverage parts permit comparison shopping by consumers without the added confusion of incomparable coverage provisions.

Insureds benefit from the clarity that the standard benchmark coverage language achieves. Standardized, readable language helps the parties to the insurance contract have a similar understanding of the coverage purchased. The purchaser can shop for the best buy with confidence, knowing that a standard minimum level of coverage is offered by almost all insurers.

Insurers also benefit from the consistency of application achieved for all their operations, including data processing, underwriting and

* Copyright, Insurance Services Office, Inc., 1987.

claims handling, resulting in lower processing costs and time savings. From an insurance underwriting perspective, standard benchmark coverage language helps a huge and complex industry better cope with its day-to-day activities. Underwriters, agents and risk managers are provided with a basis on which to build a policy that meets an insured's particular needs.

Court interpretations of any ambiguous phrases or clauses in standard coverage parts will further assure consistent treatment of claimants. Once a judicial precedent is set regarding a standard coverage part, that precedent has far more meaning and scope than if there were a proliferation of differently worded descriptions of coverages in the market.

In order to develop standard coverage parts for both personal and commercial lines of insurance, ISO monitors changes in the insurance industry and in the law. The staff consults with insurers and others on a number of matters including new and revised products needed in the insurance marketplace. In close cooperation with insurers, ISO staff drafts language to express the intent of the new or revised coverage concept necessary to address such matters as new laws, court interpretations of coverage parts or changed market conditions. Once the new coverage part is developed, ISO staff files the proposed coverage part, where necessary, with state insurance regulators for their approval.

*   *   *

"Standard" coverage parts do not mean identical coverages that cannot be customized to meet the individual policyholder's needs. For example, ISO maintains five basic coverage parts, 73 countrywide endorsements, and 118 state-specific endorsements for the Homeowners line alone. With this variety of standard coverage parts, insurers can write Homeowners insurance for an apartment renter in Brooklyn who owns a large collection of art, a condo owner in Duluth who has installed a sauna and burglar alarm and wants high levels of liability coverage, or a homeowner in Palo Alto who has a swimming pool and tennis courts—all using ISO coverage parts.

In the commercial lines of insurance, the availability of such standard coverage parts is even more critical than in the personal lines. Commercial insureds are far more heterogeneous, requiring coverage flexibility to allow an insurer to write a policy reflecting the individual insured's risks. Given this need to package various commercial property and liability coverages in a variety of ways, the need for a selection of standard coverage parts becomes critical. As a result, for the Commercial General Liability line of insurance ISO maintains 11 basic standardized coverage parts, 147 countrywide endorsements and more than 100 additional endorsements geared to specific states.

So, ISO's development and publication of standard coverage parts provide the advisory benchmarks without which insureds, regulators, producers and consumers could not make meaningful price and coverage comparisons among insurers.

Another advantage of ISO standard coverage parts is that they permit the gathering of meaningful data on the insurance coverages that have been sold in order to develop sound actuarial projections for future costs. This advantage is discussed in the next section of this report. How do standard coverage parts relate to the need for high quality ratemaking data? * * *

The goal of data pooling is useful aggregate statistics for ratemaking and regulatory monitoring. Even the most modern computer technology could not make the reported information usable without reporting requirements that generate high-quality compatible data based on standard coverages.

Mountains of unrelated data are meaningless. Generation of consistent and representative data is critical to the proper pricing of the insurance contract. To be usable for analysis of insurers' costs, data must be related to the underlying risk and to the way that risk coverage is sold and serviced. Standard coverage parts permit the collection of comparable statistics. This provides for a more stable and reliable data base and facilitates analysis, including the more accurate forecasting of future costs of ratemaking.

Comparable data that is not monitored and audited for quality is of little value. A staff of actuaries, statisticians and data processing professionals are needed to assure a high degree of data quality and statistical accuracy and to translate that data into meaningful advisory rate information. Forecasting credible insurance rates requires that actuaries develop meaningful classifications, gather reliable data for each of those classes (groupings of risks with similar loss characteristics), and monitor the relationship of loss experience from class to class to determine that the relationship is fair and reasonable. Standard coverage parts greatly assist in the collection of an accurate data base for risk classes and therefore assist in the actuarial forecasting of insurer loss experience. * * *

Notes and Questions

1. *Uniform Language, Diverse Meaning?* Because insurance policies employing the same language are interpreted by different courts (and in some cases, applied by different juries) in different jurisdictions, the ISO Report may exaggerate the degree to which precedent can help to crystalize the meaning of the language in standard form policies. Consider a provision that was once contained in ISO's Comprehensive General Liability (CGL) policy, known as the *pollution exclusion*:

This policy does not apply

* * * to bodily injury or property damage arising out of the discharge, dispersal, release or escape of smoke, vapors, soot,

fumes, acids, alkalis, toxic chemicals, liquids or gases, waste materials or other irritants, contaminants or pollutants into or upon land, the atmosphere or any water course or body of water; *but this exclusion does not apply if such discharge, dispersal, release or escape is sudden and accidental.* [emphasis added]

Many courts have held that the word "sudden" in the italicized exception to the exclusion has a temporal meaning; virtually as many other courts have held that the word has no temporal component, however, and that the exclusion therefore does not apply to "gradual pollution." Compare *Claussen v. Aetna Casualty & Surety Company,* 676 F.Supp. 1571 (S.D.Ga.1987) ("As commonly understood, the word 'sudden' in the pollution exclusion connotes abruptness.") with *Jackson Township Municipal Utilities Authority v. Hartford Accident and Indemnity Company,* 186 N.J.Super. 156, 451 A.2d 990 (Law Div.1982) (" * * * the act or acts are sudden and accidental * * * although the permeation of pollution into the ground water may have been gradual rather than sudden * * *").

How do differences such as this square with the view expressed by Richard E. Stewart, former Superintendent of Insurance of New York, regarding the virtues of uniformity?

I mean more than just word for word the same. Certainly word for word the same. But I mean a provision that is very carefully drawn by the best people in the industry and widely disseminated and understood and expected and desired and needed by the insurance industry to mean the same thing regardless of who issues it, regardless of whom he issues it to or when or where the claim arises or what the claim is, or when the claim arises and who asserts it. The language means the same thing.

Testimony of Richard E. Stewart, *Asbestos Insurance Coverage Cases,* No. 1072, Super.Ct. of San Francisco City and County, Jan. 21, 1986.

If differences over the meaning of as simple a provision as the word "sudden" in a standard policy can arise, Stewart's view could be an idle hope when more complex provisions are interpreted. Standard policy language actually may function more to narrow the range of disagreement between (and perhaps within) jurisdictions than to achieve real uniformity of meaning. Professors Goetz and Scott argue that, among other things, the adoption of standard interpretations in contract law has great virtues, but that a negative effect of this approach is to discourage innovation in the formulation of terms. See Goetz and Scott, The Limits of Expanded Choice: An Analysis of the Interactions Between Express and Implied Contract Terms, 73 Calif.L.Rev. 261 (1985). In light of this argument, the "play in the joints" that exists in interpreting standard policies may have the positive effect of revealing options for innovation that might not otherwise be apparent.

2. *Price Competition or Coverage Competition?* The ISO Report indicates that the use of standard policy language permits easy price comparison by prospective purchasers of insurance. Other things being equal, however, it would also be preferable for insurance companies to compete over the terms of coverage. One major obstacle, however, would stand in the way of at least some competition over the terms of coverage as well as price. ISO not only drafts standard policies, but also maintains data on claims and losses against these policies and makes this data available to insurers for use in setting premium rates. This data is of little value to an insurer that does not use a standard policy; instead, the insurer must set rates based on the non-standard coverage contained in its own policies—a statistically risky enterprise unless its claims and loss experience under its policies is very substantial. Consequently, the pro-competitive aspects of ISO's activities probably also have anti-competitive effects. From the antitrust or regulatory point of view, the critical issue is the balance between these effects. For discussion of this issue, see Chapter Three, Section C.

3. *Life and Health Insurance Standardization.* It is interesting to note that there is no organization that provides services for life and health insurers equivalent to those that ISO provides property/casualty insurers. Rather, these insurers tend to prepare their own policies and set their own rates. Perhaps this is because for life insurers the insured event is straightforward, and the existence of mortality data (collected by life insurance organizations and governmental sources) makes maintaining industry-wide claim and loss data less important. In health insurance, by contrast, the lion's share of coverage is sold on a group basis, usually as a fringe benefit, and the contract terms are individually negotiated by the group representative. Aggregating claims and loss data under different policies providing different coverage therefore would be misleading. Notwithstanding these differences between property/casualty and life and health insurance, however, the ability of life and health insurers to prosper in the absence of an ISO equivalent may raise questions about strength of the justifications for ISO's role set out in its Report.

2. Construing Ambiguities Against the Insurer

VARGAS v. INSURANCE COMPANY OF NORTH AMERICA

United States Court of Appeals, Second Circuit, 1981.
651 F.2d 838.

Sofaer, District Judge:

This is an appeal from a grant of summary judgment to defendant-appellee Insurance Company of North America ("INA") in a declaratory judgment action brought to determine whether INA is liable under an aviation insurance policy issued to Joseph Khurey for his single-engine Piper Arrow. The policy, issued on December 13, 1977, provided in part that it would apply "only to occurrences, accidents or losses which happen ＊ ＊ ＊ within the United States of America, its territories or possessions, Canada or Mexico." An endorsement, added to the policy on December 14, 1977, extended the territorial limits to include the Bahama Islands.

On December 23, 1977, Khurey, his wife, and his daughter were killed when the plane crashed into the sea approximately twenty-five miles west of Puerto Rico. The family had been traveling from New York to Puerto Rico, and they had stopped in Miami and Haiti to rest and refuel. The crash occurred on the last leg of the trip, while the Khureys were en route from Haiti to Puerto Rico. Puerto Rico is a "territory" of the United States. 48 U.S.C. § 731 (1976).

INA denied insurance coverage on the ground that the loss did not occur "within" the United States, its territories, or its possessions. INA claims that the policy covers losses that occur only in the enumerated areas or in territorial waters within three miles adjacent to the coasts of such areas. Appellants read the language more broadly, to include coverage for losses that occur while the plane is traveling between two points that are both within areas expressly covered.

Under New York law, which governs this case, an ambiguous provision in an insurance policy is construed "most favorably to the insured and most strictly against the insurer." *Index Fund, Inc. v. Insurance Company of North America*, 580 F.2d 1158, 1162 (2d Cir. 1978), *cert. denied*, 440 U.S. 912, 99 S.Ct. 1226, 59 L.Ed.2d 461 (1979). The insurer bears a heavy burden of proof, for it must " 'establish that the words and expressions used [in the insurance policy] not only are susceptible of the construction sought by [the insurer] but that it is the only construction which may fairly be placed on them.' " *Filor, Bullard & Smyth v. Insurance Company of North America*, 605 F.2d 598, 602 (2d Cir.1978), *cert. denied*, 440 U.S. 962, 99 S.Ct. 1506, 59 L.Ed.2d 776 (1979) (quoting *Lachs v. Fidelity & Casualty Co. of New York*, 306 N.Y. 357, 365–66, 118 N.E.2d 555, 559 (1954)). The insurer is "obliged to show (1) that it would be unreasonable for the average man reading the policy to [construe it as the insured does] and (2) that its own construction was the only one that fairly could be placed on the policy." *Sincoff v. Liberty Mutual Fire Insurance Co.*, 11 N.Y.2d 386, 390, 230 N.Y.S.2d 13, 16, 183 N.E.2d 899, 901 (1962). Thus, the question in this case is narrow: is the insurer's interpretation of the contract the only reasonable and fair construction as a matter of law? ＊ ＊ ＊

The policy is readily susceptible of a reasonable and fair interpretation that would cover the flight at issue in this case. The policy was for an airplane, which is not merely an object but also a mode of transportation, capable of long-distance travel over water as well as land. The parties knew that the plane would fly substantial distances as it transported the insured and various passengers to their contemplated destinations. The policy, moreover, provided coverage for losses both within the continental United States and within territories more than three miles beyond the continental United States. It is reasonable to construe this coverage of United States territories (some of which are ocean islands), not as restricted to the airspace immediately above them, but rather as including destinations to and from which the plane could travel without forfeiting coverage. Appellants' construction is more consistent with the realities of airplane travel. So long as the plane is on a reasonably direct course from and to geographic areas covered by the policy, the plane could reasonably be said to be within the contemplated territorial limits. Coverage of "ordinary and customary" routes has frequently been implied in analogous marine insurance contracts. *See, e.g.,* 9 Couch on Insurance, § 37:1476 (2d ed. 1962). If the plane were flown on an unreasonable course between two covered points, coverage could be lost.

Appellants' construction is supported by the language of the policy. The territory clause limits coverage to occurrences "within the United States of America, its territories or possessions, Canada or Mexico." The word "within" can reasonably be construed to mean "inside the borders" of the places specified. On the other hand, the term can also reasonably be construed to mean "inside an area that includes the places specified as well as such area as must be crossed in passing to and from the places specified." The policy's "Extension of Territorial Limits Endorsement" is consistent with the latter construction. The endorsement is phrased, not in terms of specific places, but rather in terms of "geographical limits"; and the controlling clause provides that the "limits set forth in the [c]onditions of this policy * * * are extended to include" the places covered by the endorsement. Thus, the "limits" may be read as describing the outside boundaries of an area within which flights, on reasonable routes, are covered.

Appellee concedes that this construction is appropriate with respect to specific places covered by an Extension of Territorial Endorsement. It acknowledges that the insured "requested an endorsement to cover flights *to* the Bahamas." * * * The extension was not explicitly drafted to include the Bahama Islands *and* the route over which a plane would have to fly to get to and return from the Bahamas. Yet, the addition of "The Bahama Islands" to the covered territory reasonably implied that trips to and from those islands, on reasonable routes, would also be covered. Otherwise, an insured would be forced to ship his plane to and from places covered by the policy, although those places are well within the aircraft's known range and capacity. If inclusion of "The Bahama Islands" carries with it inclusion of any reasonable route to and from those islands, then the policy itself should be construed to include reasonable routes to and from any location covered by the policy's territory clause, and within the aircraft's known capacity.

Appellee argues that the terms of the insurance contract are so clear that the court need not resort to rules of construction. The coverage provision of the contract is in fact ambiguous, and the insurer could have avoided that ambiguity by defining the territorial limits with more precision. Had appellee wished to preclude coverage for trips to and from places included in the territory provision, language to accomplish that objective was readily available. As Judge Frankel stated in *Pan American World Airways, Inc. v. Aetna Casualty & Surety Co.,* 368 F.Supp. 1098 (S.D.N.Y.1973), *aff'd,* 505 F.2d 989 (2d Cir.1974):

> Where the risk is well known and there are terms reasonably apt and precise to describe it, the use of substantially less certain phraseology, upon which dictionaries and common understanding may fairly differ, is likely to result in interpretations favoring coverage rather than exclusion.

368 F.Supp. at 1118. * * *

In support of its position that its construction is the only reasonable one, appellee contended at oral argument that flights over waters beyond the territorial limits pose special dangers, for which insureds should be required to pay extra premiums; and it notes that Khurey had rejected an offer to cover the entire Caribbean. This ostensible appeal to commercial commonsense does not withstand analysis. The fact that coverage of the entire Caribbean, including the ocean areas, cost only an additional fifty dollars undermines the argument that substantial additional risks are involved. Moreover, INA offers no evidence that over-water flights between covered locations are more dangerous than flights over points anywhere within the United States, Canada, Alaska, and Mexico—areas that are expressly covered by the policy and that include vast mountain ranges, lakes, deserts, and urban centers with heavy air traffic. Commonsense and experience contradict INA's assertion that over-water flights add materially to these explicitly covered risks.

In fact, it is appellee's construction that appears unreasonable in terms of aviation practice. If the policy excluded coverage for all flights over waters beyond the territorial limits, then flights between certain points within the continental United States would have to stay within the territorial limits in order to remain covered. Yet the most direct routes between many points within the continental United States pass over waters beyond the territorial limits; for example, the most direct route from New York City to Miami takes aircraft more than three miles beyond the coast. The same is true of many other routes, including routes between points within the territorial United States and points in Mexico, Canada, or Alaska, all of which are areas covered by the policy. Were INA's construction accepted, a pilot would be required to follow a less-direct route to avoid losing coverage, and the economic and air-safety consequences of utilizing indirect routes are likely to be far more significant than the cost of covering routes between areas expressly covered, as suggested by INA's price quotation for coverage for the Caribbean. Moreover, inducing aircraft to fly within three miles of the coast, or to risk losing coverage, might well be inconsistent with air-safety practices and rules. The record is barren of evidence as to the likely effects of INA's construction upon, for example, landing patterns at coastal airports that can take planes more than three miles off the coast. INA's assertion that its construction is supported by the reduced safety of flights beyond the territorial limits must be weighed against safety implications of using indirect routes in lieu of more direct, over-water routes.

Another factor that undermines appellee's case for summary judgment is the intent of the parties. *See, e.g., Lipsky v. Commonwealth United Corp.,* 551 F.2d 887, 896 (2d Cir.1976); *Skandia America Reinsurance Corp. v. Schenck,* 441 F.Supp. 715, 723–24 n. 13 (S.D.N.Y.1977); *Kessler Export Corp. v. Reliance Insurance Co.,* 207 F.Supp. 355, 358 (E.D.N.Y.1962), *aff'd,* 310 F.2d 936 (2d Cir.1962). In this case, Khurey revealed in his original insurance application his intention to fly the insured aircraft outside the United States. He responded affirmatively to a question on the application, "Will aircraft be used outside Continental United States?"; and to the request for details, he replied, "for vacations." It was in fact on a flight outside the continental United States, during a Christmas vacation, that Khurey and his family were killed. In addition, appellants allege that Khurey's wife came from Puerto Rico and that the family expected to vacation there occasionally. Appellants have not had an opportunity to prove this allegation or to establish that INA agents knew of Khurey's intentions. But the purported intention is entirely consistent with a belief on Khurey's part that the insurance policy covered flights between the United States and Puerto Rico.

Because appellee failed to prove that its construction of the insurance policy was the only fair and reasonable one, the decision granting it summary judgment is reversed. On the present record, the appellants, rather than the appellee, are entitled to summary judgment on the coverage issue. INA may, however, raise factual questions that would render summary judgment in appellants' favor inappropriate. This and other issues will be for the trial court to determine on remand. * * *

Notes and Questions

1. *Contra Proferentem.* What are the justifications for the rule that ambiguities in an insurance policy are to be construed against its drafter ("*contra proferentem* ")? Should it matter whether the insured read the policy? Whether she thought that she understood it, and construed it as providing the coverage in question? Whether a reasonable person would have so understood it if she had read it? At one time the rule was used as a tiebreaker after other sources of meaning extrinsic to the policy—e.g., the course of dealing between the parties, trade usage, and so forth—did not provide a definitive interpretation. For an argument that the *contra proferentem* rule now has gained priority over these other sources of meaning and that this priority should be reversed, see Note, Insurance as Contract: The Argument for Abandoning the Ambiguity Doctrine, 88 Colum.L.Rev. 1849 (1988).

2. *A Question of Degree?* Does the New York statement of the rule ("is the insurer's interpretation of the contract the only reasonable and fair construction as a matter of law?") presuppose that there are only two possible interpretations of an ambiguous provision: the insurer's and the insured's? Or is the proper question whether, if the insurer's interpretation is not clearly correct, the insured's is plausible? Does the opinion in *Vargas* lean more toward the former or the latter? Would it be more sensible to think of ambiguity as a question of degree than as half of the bipolar notion of clarity/ambiguity? What implications for the interpretation of insurance policies would the adoption of this approach have?

3. *Plain Language or Oversimplified Coverage?* Obviously it is desirable, other things being equal, for insurance policy language to be easily understandable by laypeople. But in light of the complex nature of the coverage people need and the variety of losses to be covered, this goal appears to be in tension with a rule directing courts to construe ambiguities against insurers. For example, can you draft a provision for the INA policy that is easily understandable, but also provides coverage for trips to Puerto Rico while excluding the loss that actually occurred? Is the problem a matter of drafting technique or a contradiction in what the INA policy purported to cover?

4. *You Get What You Pay For.* INA argued that flights beyond territorial limits pose special dangers for which the insured should pay extra premiums. How persuasive was the court's refutation of this argument? Does the fact that coverage for flights over the entire Caribbean would have cost only an additional fifty dollars tell you anything significant without your knowing the total premium paid? Should courts be in the business of determining the meaning of policy language by reference to the price that was paid for coverage?

* * *

The following case also concerns the construction of "ambiguous" policy provisions. The *uninsured motorist insurance* at issue in the case covers the risk of having a cause of action against a judgment-proof driver. Most policies, however, also cover injury caused by a hit-and-run driver. Coverage is provided not only for each individual but also for each vehicle insured. The question posed by the case, whether policies permit adding together the coverage provided for each vehicle, or *stacking* the limits of liability, often arises. For more discussion of the substance of uninsured motorist coverage, see Chapter Eight. The standard treatise on the subject is A. Widiss, Uninsured and Underinsured Motorist Coverage (1985).

RUSTHOVEN v. COMMERCIAL STANDARD INSURANCE COMPANY

Supreme Court of Minnesota, 1986.
387 N.W.2d 642.

YETKA, Justice.

Andrew Rusthoven, Jr., and Western National Mutual Insurance Company appeal from the court of appeals and district court decisions limiting to $25,000 the liability under the uninsured motorist coverage provided by his employer's insurance policy issued by respondent Commercial Standard Insurance Company. We reverse.

On March 8, 1981, Rusthoven was injured in an accident involving a tractor-trailer unit he was driving in the course of his employment. He asserts that an approaching car crossed over the centerline, forcing him onto the shoulder of the road and causing the tractor-trailer to slide into the adjoining ditch and overturn. The car has not been identified or located. The tractor-trailer was rented by R.E.T.E.N.O. Carriers, Inc., Rusthoven's employer. Rusthoven sustained serious and allegedly permanent injury.

R.E.T.E.N.O. was insured under a truckers' policy issued by Commercial. The policy provided liability insurance, personal injury protection, and uninsured motorist coverage, and covered commercial autos owned or rented by R.E.T.E.N.O. The policy contained no schedule of either owned or rented autos, and the premium was calculated on the basis of R.E.T.E.N.O.'s gross receipts. On the date of Rusthoven's accident, R.E.T.E.N.O. leased all 67 of its vehicles.

The relevant sections of the policy are contained in original endorsements CA 2X 17, CA 21 07, and CA 21 24. CA 2X 17, which provides uninsured motorists insurance, states in part:

> Regardless of the number of covered autos, insureds, claims made or vehicles involved in the accident, the most we will pay for all damages resulting from any one accident is the limit of UNINSURED MOTORISTS INSURANCE shown in the declarations.

The declarations sheet does not set out a dollar limit of liability under uninsured motorists coverage, but refers to endorsement CA 21 07. That endorsement, entitled SPLIT UNINSURED MOTORISTS LIMITS, provides for the following liability limitations:

Bodily Injury	$25,000	Each Person
	$50,000	Each Accident
Property Damage	$	Each Accident

The endorsement further declares that the foregoing provision of CA 2X 17 is changed to read as follows:

> Regardless of the number of covered autos, insureds, claims made or vehicles involved in the accident, our limit of liability is as follows:

    a.   The most we will pay for all damages resulting from bodily injury to any one person caused by any one accident is the limit shown in this endorsement for "each person".

    b.   Subject to the limit for "each person", the most we will pay for all damages results from bodily injury caused by any one accident is the limit shown in this endorsement for "each accident".

Endorsement CA 21 24, entitled CHANGES IN UNINSURED MOTORISTS INSURANCE, sets out three changes, one of which alters the same paragraph of CA 2X 17 so that it reads as follows:

Regardless of the number of insureds, claims made or vehicles involved in the accident, the most we will pay for all damages resulting from any one accident is the limit of UNINSURED MOTORISTS INSURANCE shown in the declarations. *If there is more than one covered auto our limit of liability for any one accident is the sum of the limits applicable to each covered auto.*

(Emphasis added.) The parties disagree about the effect of this endorsement on the limits of the uninsured motorist coverage.

At the time of the accident, Rusthoven was the named insured on a policy covering Rusthoven's three personal vehicles and issued by Western. The stacked limits of the uninsured motorist coverage afforded by this policy amount to $75,000.

Rusthoven brought suit against both Commercial and Western in Kandiyohi County District Court. Before trial, the parties submitted to the court the issues of the limit of the uninsured motorist coverage under the Commercial policy and the order in which the Commercial and Western policies should apply to Rusthoven's claim. The judge ruled that the applicable coverage under the Commercial policy was limited to $25,000 (which Commercial had already paid) and that, the limits of the primary coverage having been exhausted, the stacked limits of the uninsured motorist coverage under the Western policy were applicable to the claim. The court set for trial the issue of the amount recoverable under the Western policy. Western then stipulated to the entry of judgment against it in the amount of $75,000. Rusthoven and Western both appealed.

A divided court of appeals affirmed the district court. *Rusthoven v. Commercial Standard Insurance Co.,* 363 N.W.2d 496 (Minn.App. 1985). The majority concluded that the only reasonable interpretation of the Commercial policy limited the uninsured motorist coverage to $25,000. The dissent, however, found the policy to be ambiguous and argued that it should, therefore, be construed in the way most favorable to the insured.

The source of the difficulty here is, of course, the contradictory endorsements attached to the Commercial policy, each of which bears the exhortation: THIS ENDORSEMENT CHANGES THE POLICY.

PLEASE READ IT CAREFULLY. The declaration sheet refers to endorsement CA 21 07 for limits of uninsured motorist coverage. CA 21 07 unequivocally states that, regardless of the number of covered autos, insureds, claims made or vehicles involved in an accident, the most Commercial will pay for bodily injury to one person in one accident is $25,000. The single split limit—i.e., $25,000 each person and $50,000 each accident—provided by CA 21 07 would be consonant with a premium calculated not on the number of insured vehicles, but on the insured's gross receipts. Endorsement CA 21 24, on the other hand, clearly states: "If there is more than one covered auto our limit of liability for any one accident is the sum of the limits applicable to each covered auto." Rusthoven and Western contend that CA 21 24 just as clearly provides for stacking one $25,000 limit for each vehicle covered at the date of the accident. Nothing in the policy explains the presence of these two apparently discordant endorsements in one policy or expressly provides for harmonizing them. Hence, the appellants argue, if CA 21 24 does not override the other endorsements, at least the endorsements are in conflict, creating an ambiguity which must be interpreted to provide the greater protection to the insured. * * *

Since CA 21 07 and CA 21 24 are irreconcilably inconsistent, the policy is ambiguous and, therefore, is to be strictly interpreted against the insurer. One of the ancient principles of contract law is that an ambiguous contract, especially an adhesion contract, is construed against the drafter. See Restatement (Second) of Contracts § 206 (1982); *ICC Leasing Corp. v. Midwestern Machinery Co.*, 257 N.W.2d 551, 555 (Minn.1977). One of the fundamentals of insurance law, it follows, is that ambiguous language in an insurance policy is to be construed in favor of the insured. *See Nordby v. Atlantic Mutual Insurance Co.*, 329 N.W.2d 820, 822 (Minn.1983) ("When language of an insurance policy is ambiguous or susceptible of two meanings, it must be given the meaning which is favorable to the finding of insurance coverage.") * * * The result of such a construction, however, must not be beyond the reasonable expectations of the insured. *See Atwater Creamery Co. v. Western National Mutual Insurance Co.*, 366 N.W.2d 271 (Minn.1985); *see also* Keeton, *Insurance Law Rights at Variance with Policy Provisions*, 83 Harv.L.Rev. 961, 969 (1970) ("It seems likely, however, that, even though not often expressed, there has always been an implicit understanding that ambiguities, which in most cases might be resolved in more than just one or the other of two ways, would be resolved favorably to the insured's claim only if a reasonable person in his position would have expected coverage."); R. Keeton, *Basic Text on Insurance Law* § 6.3(a) (1971).

We find that liability limitation of the uninsured motorist provision of the Commercial policy is $1,675,000, which we find not to exceed the reasonable expectations of the insured. Therefore, we reverse the decision of the court of appeals.

Reversed and remanded.

Notes and Questions

1. *A Tall Stack.* Did it make sense for the court to rule that the policy provided $1,675,000 of coverage (there were 67 covered autos, yielding coverage of $25,000 per auto multiplied by 67) when the premiums paid were based on the gross receipts of the plaintiff's employer rather than the number of vehicles insured?

2. *Varieties of Ambiguity.* A number of different kinds of ambiguity may appear in an insurance policy (or for that matter, in any other piece of language). Words or phrases may be vague or imprecise; they may be organized in a manner that is unclear or creates several possible meanings; and different words or phrases may be inconsistent with each other. See E. Farnsworth, Contracts 479–80 (1982); R. Jerry, Understanding Insurance Law 95–98 (1987). It seems unlikely that a layperson reading the policy in *Rusthoven* could have determined that the endorsements contradicted each other, and even less likely that Rusthoven's employer expected that it had purchased and paid for over a million dollars worth of uninsured motorist coverage for each of its employees. Should these facts have affected the result in the case? Having determined that the endorsements in the policy were contradictory, did the court have any alternative to allowing the stacking of 67 limits of liability?

3. Honoring the Reasonable Expectations of the Insured

Even when the meaning of an insurance policy or a provision in it is not ambiguous, it may be difficult for the layperson to read, or contain surprising limitations on coverage. Many of the cases finding a policy provision to be ambiguous and then construing it against the insurer may in fact be dealing with one of these problems, rather than a simple ambiguity. Beginning several decades ago, some courts began to be more candid about this phenomenon. By 1971 there were enough cases for Professor (now Judge) Robert Keeton to recognize a principle behind these decisions. He called it "honoring the reasonable expectations of the insured."[1] The courts followed his lead, and over a dozen jurisdictions have now explicitly recognized the expectations principle. The courts in other jurisdictions probably are influenced by the principle even if they have not squarely adopted it. For discussions of the principle, see Rahdert, Reasonable Expectations Reconsidered, 18 Conn. L.Rev. 323 (1986); Mayhew, Reasonable Expectations: Seeking A Principled Application, 13 Pepperdine L.Rev. 267 (1986).

Initially, the expectations principle may have been predominantly a method of making the maxim *contra proferentem* operational—an ambiguity was to be construed in accord with the reasonable expectations of the insured. The decisions quickly went beyond this limitation,

1. See R. Keeton, Insurance Law: Basic Text 351 (1971).

however, by invalidating admittedly unambiguous policy provisions that violated the expectations principle. Although most of the decisions still involve ordinary individuals who have purchased personal insurance, an increasing number invoke the expectations principle even when the insured is a sizeable commercial enterprise. See, e.g., *Keene Corporation v. Insurance Company of North America,* 667 F.2d 1034 (D.C.Cir.1981), cert. denied, 455 U.S. 1007, 102 S.Ct. 1644, 71 L.Ed.2d 875 (1982). The editor of this casebook has described the expectations principle as the vehicle through which "judge made insurance" is created. K. Abraham, Distributing Risk: Insurance, Legal Theory, and Public Policy 100–32 (1986). Do the following two cases support this description or contradict it?

ATWOOD v. HARTFORD ACCIDENT & INDEMNITY CO.

Supreme Court of New Hampshire, 1976.
116 N.H. 636, 365 A.2d 744.

KENISON, Chief Justice.

Action by an insured against his insurer for a declaratory judgment that the insurer is obliged to defend the insured and to pay any damages assessed against him in two pending actions. * * *

The plaintiff insured is a self-employed electrician. He wires outlets and fixtures and occasionally repairs electrical appliances but his trade is primarily the performance of a service rather than the sale of merchandise. On November 6, 1972, the janitor of an apartment house called the plaintiff to repair a thermostat in one apartment. The next day the plaintiff learned that a child had died in the apartment from heat prostration. The plaintiff immediately notified his insurance agent of the potential claim. Subsequently, the administrator of the child's estate brought suit against the plaintiff and against a third party who has sought indemnity from the plaintiff.

The defendant Hartford Accident & Indemnity Co. argues that the actions pending against the plaintiff arise from completed operations, which are excluded from the coverage of the policy. The completed operations exclusion in this policy is a standard provision which has produced considerable litigation in New Hampshire and elsewhere. * * * The question in this case is whether an ordinary person in the shoes of the plaintiff would understand that the policy did not cover claims such as those now pressed against him. *Berkshire Mut. Ins. Co. v. LaChance,* 115 N.H. 487, 343 A.2d 642 (1975). The objectively reasonable expectations of the insured will be honored even though painstaking study of the policy provisions would have negated those expectations. *Magulas v. Travelers Ins. Co.,* 114 N.H. 704, 327 A.2d 608 (1974); R. Keeton, Insurance Law § 6.3 (1971).

The trial court found: "A reasonable person in the position of the plaintiff would have believed that he was covered by the policy for any

claims against him for negligence in his work as an electrician.
* * * There is little in the language and arrangement of this policy
which would lead the ordinary person to believe that he had no
coverage for injury or property damage which arose after he completed
a job." An examination of the policy confirms these findings.

The policy consists of a "Declarations–Coverage Part" and a jacket
comprised of definitions and conditions. The front page of the declara-
tions-coverage part contains four indications of the coverage of the
policy. The top of the page has blanks to be filled in with the name of
the insured, the period of the policy, etc. Then, under the heading
"Summary of Advance Premiums," appear the printed words "Manufacturers' and Contractors' Liability Insurance" followed by the typewritten amount of the premium. The heading for the bottom half of
the page is "Manufacturers' and Contractors' Liability Insurance Coverage Part and Schedule." Under the heading "Coverages" are two
categories: "A—Bodily Injury Liability" and "B—Property Damage
Liability." The plaintiff secured both coverages, and the amount of the
premium and the limits of liability in dollars are typewritten in the
space provided for each coverage. The final section of the page contains the rating classification, premium base, rates and premium. The
rating classification is typed in as follows: "ELECTRICAL WIRING
WITHIN BUILDINGS INCLUDING INSTALLATION OR REPAIR OF
FIXTURES OR APPLIANCES[.] INSTALLATION OF ELECTRICAL
MACHINERY OR AUXILIARY APPARATUS TO BE SEPARATELY
RATED[.]" A reasonable person reading this page could only conclude
that the policy covers the claims being asserted against the plaintiff.

On the back of this page, at the top, is the heading "Manufacturers'
and Contractors' Liability Insurance Coverage Part." Below this is a
smaller heading of critical significance, which is considered in the next
paragraph. The balance of the page is divided into two columns. At
the top of the left-hand column is the heading:

Coverage A—Bodily Injury Liability

Coverage B—Property Damage Liability

The first sentence of text, one hundred twenty-nine words in length,
begins: "The company will pay on behalf of the *insured* all sums which
the *insured* shall become legally obligated to pay as *damages* because of
[bodily injury or property damage] to which this insurance applies
* * * ["]. Following this sentence is a list of exclusions.

The critical heading, which is located between two other headings,
reads as follows: "Coverage for Premises and for the Named Insured's
Operations in Progress." It is possible to look through the document
several times before noticing this reading. Yet this is the only affirmative statement of the coverage of the policy. The defendant also relies
on an exclusion clause which provides: "This insurance does not apply
* * * (m) to *bodily injury* or *property damage* included within the
completed operations hazard or the *products hazard* [.]" The definition
of the completed operations hazard is printed elsewhere. This exclu-

sion clause is buried amidst thirteen others, which are either irrelevant to the plaintiff or expected, as for example the exclusion of obligations imposed by workmen's compensation and unemployment compensation laws. Neither the quoted heading nor the quoted exclusion clause constitutes fair notice to the insured that the policy does not cover the risks defined as the completed operations hazard, which the front page would lead him to believe were covered. * * *

The plaintiff and his insurance agent have known each other for thirty years and have had insurance dealings for nearly twenty years. It could be found that the agent knew the plaintiff's business and that the plaintiff relied on the agent to see that the plaintiff was fully insured. *See* R. Keeton, Insurance Law § 6.4 (1971). Although the agent's testimony was at times conflicting, the trial court could and did make the following finding: "The plaintiff's insurance agent * * * never told the plaintiff that he was not insured once he left the job. It never occurred to [the agent] that the plaintiff was not protected by the policy. He did not believe that the plaintiff had any exposure." If an insurance agent with twenty years of experience thought that Atwood was covered for completed operations, it is unreasonable to expect Atwood, who had no experience with reading insurance policies, to know that he was not so covered.

Exceptions overruled.

Notes and Questions

1. *The Theory Behind the Expectations Principle.* There are a number of ways to justify honoring the reasonable expectations of the insured. One is that the insurer in some way has misrepresented what is in the policy; another is that the insurer is estopped to deny coverage because it has allowed the insured to labor under a misimpression about the policy's contents. For an elaboration of these theories, see K. Abraham, Distributing Risk: Insurance, Legal Theory, and Public Policy 104–09 (1986). Do these theories adequately explain the result in *Atwood?*

Under the *misrepresentation* and *estoppel* theories, some proof of the insured's reliance on his misimpression about coverage would seem to be necessary; yet there does not seem to be any such requirement in *Atwood,* or for that matter in most expectations cases. Possibly something like a presumption of reliance is operating where the kind of coverage the insured reasonably expects is available elsewhere. Atwood could and probably would have purchased completed operations coverage had he known that his policy did not provide it. But such a presumption is a mere fiction in cases where the "expected" coverage simply cannot be purchased. For example, most liability insurance policies provide not only for insurance against liability, but for a defense of a claim that would fall within coverage if it were successful, even if the claim is "groundless, false, or fraudulent." Most such policies also contain an exclusion of coverage, however, for harm that is "either expected or intended from the standpoint of the insured."

Suppose that the insured is sued for battery, but claims self-defense. Would an insured reasonably expect the insurer to defend such a claim? *Gray v. Zurich Insurance Company,* 65 Cal.3d 263, 54 Cal.Rptr. 104, 419 P.2d 168 (1966), holds that he would. Perhaps an insured would expect such a defense precisely because separate insurance against the costs of defending against groundless suits for battery is not available. If this is the rationale for invoking the expectations principle in such cases, however, neither the misrepresentation nor estoppel theories can be called upon for support, for there has been no detrimental reliance. Yet if there is ever to be coverage against such costs, it must be made available under ordinary liability policies, which do not cover liability for battery if it is actually imposed.

Another theory that may underlie the expectations principle is that there is something *unconscionable* about omitting coverage that an insured reasonably expects. Is this an adequate explanation of the result in *Atwood?* That is, is it substantively unfair to provide separate coverage against liability arising out of uncompleted as opposed to completed operations? Does this depend in part on what the insured pays for his coverage? When there is no substantive unfairness inherent in an omission of a particular kind of coverage from a policy, and when the insurer has not created the insured's expectation that the policy does contain that coverage, is it ever appropriate to honor the insured's expectation, even if it is reasonable? Put another way, in such a situation there are two sets of reasonable expectations: a) the insured's, derived independently of anything misleading or unconscionable on the part of the insurer; and b) the insurer's, based on what the policy language states. Which meaning should then be given priority, the one derived from the policy language or the one derived from extrinsic sources?

2. *Reasonable or Actual Expectations?* Are you satisfied that the insured in *Atwood* had the expectations the court thought he had? That these expectations were reasonable? Suppose that the insured testified that he thought he would have coverage against the claim in question, but admitted on cross examination that he would not have been surprised to find a series of "fine print" exclusions that limited his rights. Since virtually *no one* reads his insurance policy, why should a policy's meaning depend on whether a provision excluding coverage is buried in the middle of the policy or set out clearly at the beginning?

The cases are sometimes divided, and sometimes unclear, regarding the role to be played by actual as opposed to reasonable expectations. For example, courts sometimes suggest that provisions which the insured would not expect should be pointed out or made conspicuous. See, e.g., *Hionis v. Northern Mutual Insurance Company,* 230 Pa.Super. 511, 327 A.2d 363 (1974). The implication of this suggestion is that the insured's expectations are no longer reasonable if he is aware of a policy provision negating them. Some of the early expectations cases involved automated marketing or solicitation by mail, where there is no practical way for the insured to inquire as to the scope of coverage, or for the insurer to dispel inaccurate expectations. See, e.g., *Lachs v. Fidelity & Casualty Company,* 306 N.Y. 357, 118 N.E.2d 555 (1954) (flight insurance); *Steven v. Fidelity & Casualty Company,* 58 Cal.2d 862, 27 Cal.Rptr. 172, 377 P.2d 284 (1962) (flight insurance); *Klos v. Mobil Oil Company,* 55 N.J. 117, 259 A.2d 889 (1969) (life insurance solicitation by mail). On the other hand, if the touchstone of a provision's invalidity is the reasonable expectations of the great majority of policyholders, the insured's actual expectations might be considered irrelevant. Should they be? In any event, if the insured is not required to testify about his own expectations there is little if any difference between actual and reasonable expectations.

3. *Redraft or Leave Well Enough Alone?* If you were counsel to the insurer in *Atwood,* would you recommend that the policy be redrafted to avoid the result in that case? Would your answer depend on whether you were using an ISO policy form? What else would you take into account?

4. *The Role of the Agent.* The court found it significant that Atwood's agent, with twenty years of experience, thought that Atwood was covered against liability arising out of completed operations. Yet the completed operations exclusion was a standard provision that was routinely included in most CGL policies of the sort that Atwood apparently purchased. Should Atwood's action properly have been against the agent for negligence in failing to procure necessary coverage?

ATWATER CREAMERY COMPANY v. WESTERN NATIONAL MUTUAL INSURANCE COMPANY

Supreme Court of Minnesota, 1985.
366 N.W.2d 271.

WAHL, Justice.

Atwater Creamery Company (Atwater) sought a declaratory judgment against its insurer, Western National Mutual Insurance Company (Western), seeking coverage for losses sustained during a burglary of the creamery's storage building. * * * The Kandiyohi County District Court granted a directed verdict for Strehlow because Atwater failed to establish an insurance agent's standard of care by expert testimony. The trial court then dismissed the jury for lack of disputed issues of fact and ordered judgment in favor of the insurer, concluding that the burglary insurance policy in effect defined burglary so as to exclude coverage of this burglary. We affirm the directed verdict for Strehlow but reverse as to the policy coverage.

Atwater does business as a creamery and as a supplier of farm chemicals in Atwater, Minnesota. It was insured during the time in question against burglary, up to a ceiling of $20,000, by Western under

Mercantile Open Stock Burglary Policy SC10–1010–12, which contained an "evidence of forcible entry" requirement in its definition of burglary. The creamery had recovered small amounts under this policy for two separate burglaries prior to the events in this case. * * *

Sometime between 9:30 p.m., Saturday, April 9, and 6 a.m., Monday, April 11, 1977, one or more persons made unauthorized entry into the building, took chemicals worth $15,587.40, apparently loading them on the truck that had been parked outside and driving away after loosening the turnbuckles on the east door and closing it. The truck was later found parked near the town dump, with the key still in the ignition.

Larry Poe, the plant manager at the Soil Center, had left at 9:30 p.m. on Saturday, after making sure everything was properly secured. On Monday morning, the north side doors were locked securely, but two of the three doors to the storage bin were ajar. Their padlocks were gone and never found. The turnbuckles had been loosened on the east sliding door so that it could be easily opened or closed.

An investigation by the local police, the Kandiyohi County Sheriff's Department, and the Minnesota Bureau of Criminal Investigation determined that no Atwater Creamery employees, past or present, were involved in the burglary. Suspicion settled on persons wholly unconnected with the creamery or even with the local area, but no one has been apprehended or charged with the crime.

Atwater filed a claim with Western under the burglary policy. Western denied coverage because there were no visible marks of physical damage to the exterior at the point of entrance or to the interior at the point of exit, as required by the definition of burglary in the policy. The creamery then brought suit against Western for the $15,587.40 loss, $7,500 in other directly related business losses and costs, disbursements and reasonable attorney fees.

Charles H. Strehlow, the owner of the Strehlow Insurance Agency in Willmar, Minnesota, and Western's agent, testified that he is certain he mentioned the evidence-of-forcible-entry requirement to Poe and members of the Atwater Board of Directors but was unable to say when the discussion occurred. Poe and the board members examined do not remember any such discussion. None of the board members had read the policy, which is kept in the safe at the main plant, and Poe had not read it in its entirety. He stated that he started to read it but gave up because he could not understand it.

The issues on appeal are

* * *

2. whether the reasonable expectations of the insured as to coverage govern to defeat the literal language of the policy
* * *

2. APPLICATION OF THE POLICY DEFINITION OF BURGLARY.

The definition of burglary in this policy is one used generally in burglary insurance. Courts have construed it in different ways. It has been held ambiguous and construed in favor of coverage in the absence of visible marks of forcible entry or exit. *United States Fidelity & Guaranty Co. v. Woodward,* 118 Ga.App. 591, 164 S.E.2d 878 (1968). We reject this analysis because we view the definition in the policy as clear and precise. It is not ambiguous.

In determining the intent of the parties to the insurance contract, courts have looked to the purpose of the visible-marks-of-forcible-entry requirement. These purposes are two: to protect insurance companies from fraud by way of "inside jobs" and to encourage insureds to reasonably secure the premises. See 5 Appleman § 3176 at 517. As long as the theft involved clearly [is] neither an inside job nor the result of a lack of secured premises, some courts have simply held that the definition does not apply. *Limberis v. Aetna Casualty & Surety Co.,* 263 A.2d 83 (Me.1970); *Kretschmer's House of Appliances, Inc. v. United States Fidelity & Guaranty Co.,* 410 S.W.2d 617 (Ky.1966).

In the instant case, there is no dispute as to whether Atwater is attempting to defraud Western or whether the Soil Center was properly secured. The trial court found that the premises were secured before the robbery and that the law enforcement investigators had determined that it was not an "inside job." To enforce the burglary definition literally against the creamery will in no way effectuate either purpose behind the restrictive definition. We are uncomfortable, however, with this analysis given the right of an insurer to limit the risk against which it will indemnify insureds.

At least three state courts have held that the definition merely provides for one form of evidence which may be used to prove a burglary and that, consequently, other evidence of a burglary will suffice to provide coverage. *Ferguson v. Phoenix Assurance Co. of New York,* 189 Kan. 459, 370 P.2d 379 (1962); *National Surety Co. v. Silberberg Bros.,* 176 S.W. 97 (Tex.Civ.App.1915); *Rosenthal v. American Bonding Co. of Baltimore,* 124 N.Y.S. 905 (N.Y.Sup.Ct.1910). The Nebraska Supreme Court recently rejected this argument in *Cochran v. MFA Mutual Insurance Co.,* 201 Neb. 631, 271 N.W.2d 331 (1978). The *Cochran* court held that the definition is not a rule of evidence but is a limit on liability, is unambiguous and is applied literally to the facts of the case at hand. We, too, reject this view of the definition as merely a form of evidence. The policy attempts to comprehensively define burglaries that are covered by it. In essence, this approach ignores the policy definition altogether and substitutes the court's or the statute's definition of burglary. This we decline to do, either via the conformity clause or by calling the policy definition merely one form of evidence of a burglary.

Some courts and commentators have recognized that the burglary definition at issue in this case constitutes a rather hidden exclusion from coverage. Exclusions in insurance contracts are read narrowly against the insurer. Running through the many court opinions refusing to literally enforce this burglary definition is the concept that the definition is surprisingly restrictive, that no one purchasing something called burglary insurance would expect coverage to exclude skilled burglaries that leave no visible marks of forcible entry or exit. Professor Robert E. Keeton, in analyzing these and other insurance cases where the results often do not follow from the rules stated, found there to be two general principles underlying many decisions. These principles are the reasonable expectations of the insured and the unconscionability of the clause itself or as applied to the facts of a specific case. Keeton, Insurance Law Rights at Variance with Policy Provisions, 83 Harv.L.Rev. 961 (1970). Keeton's article and subsequent book, Basic Text on Insurance Law (1971), have had significant impact on the construction of insurance contracts.

The doctrine of protecting the reasonable expectations of the insured is closely related to the doctrine of contracts of adhesion. Where there is unequal bargaining power between the parties so that one party controls all of the terms and offers the contract on a take-it-or-leave-it basis, the contract will be strictly construed against the party who drafted it. Most courts recognize the great disparity in bargaining power between insurance companies and those who seek insurance. Further, they recognize that, in the majority of cases, a lay person lacks the necessary skills to read and understand insurance policies, which are typically long, set out in very small type and written from a legalistic or insurance expert's perspective. Finally, courts recognize that people purchase insurance relying on others, the agent or company, to provide a policy that meets their needs. The result of the lack of insurance expertise on the part of insureds and the recognized marketing techniques of insurance companies is that "[t]he objectively reasonable expectations of applicants and intended beneficiaries regarding the terms of insurance contracts will be honored even though painstaking study of the policy provisions would have negated those expectations." Keeton, 83 Harv.L.Rev. at 967.

The traditional approach to construction of insurance contracts is to require some kind of ambiguity in the policy before applying the doctrine of reasonable expectations. Several courts, however, have adopted Keeton's view that ambiguity ought not be a condition precedent to the application of the reasonable-expectations doctrine.

As of 1980, approximately ten states had adopted the newer rule of reasonable expectations regardless of ambiguity. *Davenport Peters Co. v. Royal Globe Insurance Co.*, 490 F.Supp. 286, 291 (D.Mass.1980). Other states, such as Missouri and North Dakota, have joined the ten since then.[1] Most courts recognize that insureds seldom see the policy

---

1. Some of the major cases adopting the doctrine are: *Gray v. Zurich Ins. Co.*, 65 Cal. 2d 263, 54 Cal.Rptr. 104, 107, 419 P.2d 168, 171 (1966); *Smith v. Westland Life Ins. Co.*, 15 Cal.3d 111, 123 Cal.Rptr. 649, 539 P.2d 433 (1975); *Corgatelli v. Globe Life & Acc. Ins. Co.*, 96 Idaho 616, 533 P.2d 737 (1975) (overruled, see text); *C & J Fertilizer, Inc. v. Allied*

until the premium is paid, and even if they try to read it, they do not comprehend it. Few courts require insureds to have minutely examined the policy before relying on the terms they expect it to have and for which they have paid.

The burglary definition is a classic example of a policy provision that should be, and has been, interpreted according to the reasonable expectations of the insured. *C & J Fertilizer, Inc. v. Allied Mutual Insurance Co.*, 227 N.W.2d 169 (Iowa 1975). *C & J Fertilizer* involved a burglary definition almost exactly like the one in the instant case as well as a burglary very similar to the Atwater burglary. The court applied the reasonable-expectations-regardless-of-ambiguity doctrine, noting that "[t]he most plaintiff might have reasonably anticipated was a policy requirement of visual evidence (abundant here) indicating the burglary was an 'outside' not an 'inside' job. The exclusion in issue, masking as a definition, makes the insurer's obligation to pay turn on the skill of the burglar, not on the event the parties bargained for: a bona fide third party burglary resulting in loss of plaintiff's chemicals and equipment." *Id.* at 177. The burglary in *C & J Fertilizer* left no visible marks on the exterior of the building, but an interior door was damaged. In the instant case, the facts are very similar except that there was no damage to the interior doors; their padlocks were simply gone. In *C & J Fertilizer*, the police concluded that an "outside" burglary had occurred. The same is true here.

Atwater had a burglary policy with Western for more than 30 years. The creamery relied on Charles Strehlow to procure for it insurance suitable for its needs. There is some factual dispute as to whether Strehlow ever told Poe about the "exclusion," as Strehlow called it. Even if he had said that there was a visible-marks-of-forcible-entry requirement, Poe could reasonably have thought that it meant that there must be clear evidence of a burglary. There are, of course, fidelity bonds which cover employee theft. The creamery had such a policy covering director and manager theft. The fidelity company, however, does not undertake to insure against the risk of third-party burglaries. A business that requests and purchases burglary insurance reasonably is seeking coverage for loss from third-party burglaries whether a break-in is accomplished by an inept burglar or by a highly skilled burglar. Two other burglaries had occurred at the Soil Center, for which Atwater had received insurance proceeds under the policy. Poe and the board of the creamery could reasonably have expected the

Mutual Ins. Co., 227 N.W.2d 169 (Iowa 1975); *Collister v. Nationwide Life Ins. Co.*, 479 Pa. 579, 388 A.2d 1346 (1978).

Missouri has recently adopted it in *Estrin Construction Co. v. Aetna Casualty & Surety Co.*, 612 S.W.2d 413 (Mo.App.1981); and North Dakota, in *Mills v. Agrichemical Aviation, Inc.*, 250 N.W.2d 663 (N.D.1977), showed its similarity to North Dakota's doctrine of contract of adhesion, which was followed in that case. Two of the original ten have overruled earlier cases and have reverted to the traditional rule. *Hallowell v. State Farm Mutual Automobile Insurance Co.*, 443 A.2d 925 (Del.1982), and *Casey v. Highlands Insurance Co.*, 600 P.2d 1387 (Idaho 1979). Both courts saw the new rule as relieving the insured of any responsibility for reading the policy.

burglary policy to cover this burglary where the police, as well as the trial court, found that it was an "outside job."

The reasonable-expectations doctrine gives the court a standard by which to construe insurance contracts without having to rely on arbitrary rules which do not reflect real-life situations and without having to bend and stretch those rules to do justice in individual cases. As Professor Keeton points out, ambiguity in the language of the contract is not irrelevant under this standard but becomes a factor in determining the reasonable expectations of the insured, along with such factors as whether the insured was told of important, but obscure, conditions or exclusions and whether the particular provision in the contract at issue is an item known by the public generally. The doctrine does not automatically remove from the insured a responsibility to read the policy. It does, however, recognize that in certain instances, such as where major exclusions are hidden in the definitions section, the insured should be held only to reasonable knowledge of the literal terms and conditions. The insured may show what actual expectations he or she had, but the factfinder should determine whether those expectations were reasonable under the circumstances. * * *

In our view, the reasonable-expectations doctrine does not automatically mandate either pro-insurer or pro-insured results. It does place a burden on insurance companies to communicate coverage and exclusions of policies accurately and clearly. It does require that expectations of coverage by the insured be reasonable under the circumstances. Neither of those requirements seems overly burdensome. Properly used, the doctrine will result in coverage in some cases and in no coverage in others.

We hold that where the technical definition of burglary in a burglary insurance policy is, in effect, an exclusion from coverage, it will not be interpreted so as to defeat the reasonable expectations of the purchaser of the policy. Under the facts and circumstances of this case, Atwater reasonably expected that its burglary insurance policy with Western would cover the burglary that occurred. Our holding requires reversal as to policy coverage.

Notes and Questions

1. *Language in Context?* The courts in *Atwood* and *Atwater Creamery* merely quoted the policy provisions in question, rather than setting out in full the policies in which these provisions were contained. Would it matter to you whether these provisions were easy or difficult to find, given the physical layout of these policies?

2. *Evidentiary Conditions and Moral Hazard.* The court in *Atwater Creamery* determined that the purposes of the evidence-of-forcible-entry requirement were to prevent fraud by way of inside jobs and to encourage insureds to secure the insured premises. Many courts hold that the requirement is merely an evidentiary condition, and that proof that the burglary was not an inside job may come in other ways

as well. See Holmes, Interpreting an Insurance Policy in Georgia: The Problem of an Evidentiary Condition, 12 Ga.L.Rev. 783 (1978). This approach would seem, however, marginally to reduce the insured's incentive to secure the premises, because he may now have coverage even if the making of visible marks of entry is not necessary for a burglar to gain entry. Does this reduction in incentive seem worth what is gained?

3. *Administrative Cost–Saving and Coverage Preferences.* In addition to combatting moral hazard, evidence-of-forcible-entry requirements also serve (as do all *per se* rules) to reduce administrative and litigation costs—they dispense with an inquiry about whether a burglary was an outside job. If the requirement serves both purposes, it would seem to have the effect of reducing the cost of coverage. Do decisions such as *Atwater Creamery* therefore imply that a) the majority of insureds would prefer to pay the extra cost of having burglary insurance even when there is no evidence of forcible entry, so long as they can prove that (select your own preference) the burglary was not an inside job; the insured had secured the premises; or both of the above? Or do such decisions merely hold that b) if insureds are not being provided with all-purpose burglary insurance, they are entitled to disclosure of this fact?

A weakness in explanation (a) is that it suggests that the courts are making decisions on the basis of wholly unsubstantiated (and quite possibly incorrect) assumptions about consumer preferences. If a significant portion of the insured population would be willing to pay extra for the form of coverage created in *Atwater Creamery,* then why would not some insurers already have found it in their interest to offer such coverage? Perhaps the answer is that the cost of marketing both kinds of burglary insurance—i.e., the cost of having agents explain the two options and the benefits of each—are prohibitively high, given the size of the competitive edge that could be obtained by selling two different forms of coverage.

If this explanation is correct, however, then the weakness in explanation (b) emerges. If it is too costly to explain the choice between the two forms of coverage, it will also be too costly to point out the evidence-of-forcible-entry requirement in policies that contain it, because the explanation in the two situations is the same, even if no choice is provided. Consequently, it will be too costly to dispel the "reasonable" expectation that there is coverage for all burglaries. As a result, the broader form of coverage will in effect be incorporated by law into all burglary policies, even though many (perhaps most) insureds would prefer narrower, less expensive coverage. If there are flaws in this analysis, what are they? Is the analysis a prescription for judicial inaction, or a recognition that judicial action has outpaced the courts' capacity to provide a compelling justification for what they are doing in this field?

4. *Unreasonable Expectations.* Even in jurisdictions that have squarely adopted the expectations principle, there are of course decisions in which the insured's claim that she is entitled to coverage notwithstanding its denial by policy provisions is rejected. Some of these decisions are instructive, for they imply that the availability of the coverage allegedly expected by the insured through another kind of policy contributes to the conclusion that an expectation of coverage in that setting is not reasonable. For example, in *Herzog v. National American Insurance Company,* 2 Cal.3d 192, 84 Cal.Rptr. 705, 465 P.2d 841 (1970), the court held that the insured could not reasonably expect coverage for liability arising out of the operation of a motor bike under the liability provisions of a homeowners policy. Many other decisions, however, honor an insured's expectations even when the coverage expected is separately available elsewhere. Should proof of such availability at least be admissible on the reasonableness issue? Should the unavailability of the expected coverage be admissible in the insured's favor?

B. THE ROLE OF INTERMEDIARIES

With the rare exception of insurance sold from vending machines or by mail, all insurance is sold through intermediaries. The two major types of insurance intermediaries are *agents* and *brokers.* A broker is not the general purpose legal agent of an insurance company. Rather, brokers place orders for insurance with companies designated by their policyholder clients or with companies of their own choice. Sometimes, however, brokers do act on behalf of insurers, most notably by collecting premiums and acting as conduits for transmitting notice of loss suffered by the insured to the insurer. Brokers typically operate in the markets for customized commercial coverage rather than in the high-volume personal insurance markets.

In contrast, insurance *agents* are (at least for many purposes) the representatives of insurance companies. *Independent agents* are representatives of more than one insurance company, and either decide or help their clients—applicants for coverage—decide which company to deal with. Agents of *direct writers* are the agents of one company, which sells through its own offices. Agents often perform claim-processing functions in addition to marketing coverage. Typically agents receive commissions from insurers based on a percentage of the premiums on coverage sold. Most jurisdictions have statutes prohibiting agents from rebating their commissions to insureds in the form of reduced premiums. What justifications might be given for this apparently anti-competitive restriction? For discussion, see Adamec, Premium Rebating: An Unnecessary Evil, 1988 FICC Quart. 3. At least one court, however, has determined that in the absence of any justification for the restriction, it violates the due process clause of its state's constitution. See *Dade County Consumer Advocate's Office v. Department of Insurance,* 457 So.2d 495 (Fla.Dist.Ct.App.1984).

As you study the cases that follow, consider whether the institutional structure of insurance marketing is amenable to the kind of influence that the cases presuppose legal rules can have. How capable do insurance agents need to be in order to avoid the kind of tricky problems that sometimes result in litigation? In light of the percentage-of-premium commission system, do these intermediaries seem to have inherent conflicts of interest, or are conflicts more likely to be aberrations? What incentives are there for intermediaries to avoid stirring up concerns when a policy is purchased that will produce trouble only if the insured later suffers a loss? What incentives run in the other direction?

1. The Authority of the Agent

The standard process for obtaining insurance coverage requires the prospective purchaser to make application for coverage through an agent. The agent helps the purchaser to complete an application for coverage. If the agent is independent, she selects a company with which to file the application. If the agent represents a direct writer, she files the application with her company. Eventually the company may reject the application, or accept it and issue a policy.

In the meantime, the agent may or may not have authority to "bind" the company and provide immediate coverage, sometimes subject to later rejection by the company and sometimes not. The cases and treatises are replete with references to the different levels of authority possessed by different kinds of agents. *General agents* are said to have authority to bind the company (except in life insurance, where the home office alone makes binding decisions), but *solicitating agents* and *local agents* do not. The limitations on authority reflected by these categories may hold as between the company and its agents, but as between the company and the insured, or between the agent and the insured, as often as not they are labels applied to legal conclusions reached for reasons independent of the terms of agency contracts themselves.

ELMER TALLANT AGENCY, INC. v. BAILEY WOOD PRODUCTS, INC.

Supreme Court of Alabama, 1979.
374 So.2d 1312.

BLOODWORTH, Justice.

Plaintiff Bailey Wood Products, Inc., instituted this action for declaratory judgment against J.W. Coleman, Elmer Tallant Agency, Inc., and Zurich American Insurance Company seeking a determination as to whether plaintiff is liable to its employee, J.W. Coleman, under Workmen's Compensation and, in the event that the court finds liability, a declaration that Zurich American Insurance Company or Elmer

Tallant Agency, Inc., or both should indemnify Bailey Products to the extent of its liability.

Zurich Insurance and Tallant Agency entered into an agency contract on October 1, 1976, whereby the agency was empowered to "bind and execute contracts of insurance * * * only as specifically authorized in the Schedule of Binding Authority." The schedule states that certain risks may be bound by the agent only if prior approval has been granted by the company. Among these risks is "[a]ny risk that according to the agent's knowledge has been cancelled, declined, or renewal refused by another insurer within the past three years." In addition, the schedule also specifies that agent's general authority to bind the insurance company is limited in that prior approval is required to bind certain classes of businesses including workmen's compensation coverage for sawmill operations, which was one of plaintiff's business operations.

On March 2, 1977, The Home Insurance Company (which had previously handled coverage for Mr. Bailey's operations), refused to renew insurance on another business, Brantley Gin Company, and stated that it could not handle coverage for Bailey Wood Products. Tallant Agency then submitted the risk to Employers Insurance Company of Alabama, Inc. and on March 15, 1977, Employers declined the risk on both Brantley Gin and Bailey Wood Products. On March 18, 1977, Tallant Agency submitted the Brantley Gin account to Zurich. Zurich rejected the application for coverage because of the hazards associated with the varied operations. The risk for Brantley Gin was ultimately assigned to USF&G through the Assigned Risk Pool for "undesirable risks" but no premium was ever paid to USF&G. Thus the risk was never assumed by USF&G.

On June 14, 1977, Mr. Bailey called Kenneth Tallant, Vice President and Secretary of the Tallant Agency, and requested insurance coverage for Brantley Gin Company, Bailey Hardware Store, and Bailey Wood Products. Mr. Tallant told Mr. Bailey that coverage was bound, prepared an application/binder, and forwarded it to Zurich. Tallant did not attempt to secure prior approval of the risk despite the fact that this was a sawmill risk and that coverage of Brantley Gin had recently been declined by more than one insurance company including Zurich.

On June 21, 1977, J.W. Coleman, employed by Bailey Wood Products as a truck driver, was injured in the line and scope of his employment while driving a truck belonging to Bailey Wood Products. On June 30, 1977, Tallant Agency was notified by telephone that Zurich refused to accept the risk submitted and rejected the claim.

We will first consider the appellee and cross-appellant Zurich's contention that the "only basis for holding against Zurich on the original complaint was *Cincinnati Insurance Co. v. City of Talladega*, [342 So.2d 331 (Ala.1977)]" and that *Cincinnati* can be distinguished from the instant case because, in *Cincinnati*, certain bonds with the insurance company's name on them were delivered to the insured while in the instant case Tallant Agency did not divulge the name of Zurich to Mr. Bailey, who did not know with whom he would be insured. Zurich further contends that it was not effectively bound by Tallant Agency, that Mr. Bailey was not relying on Zurich but rather on the agency, that the agency negligently failed to secure insurance, and therefore should be the only party liable. We cannot agree.

In *Cincinnati*, this Court, quoting from *British General Insurance Co., Ltd. v. Simpson Sales Co., Inc.*, 265 Ala. 683, 93 So.2d 763 (1957), stated:

> " ' * * * The company has the power to determine the conditions of the agency. *It may protect itself as it sees fit by requiring surety bond. It may terminate its contract at the first sign of infidelity. It has within its power the determination of what persons shall represent it.* In short, it has *all* the advantages of selection and must bear the burdens thereof if it has failed to choose one faithful to the agency agreement. On the other hand, we have the public, dealing with the agent of the company. In the public view, the agent is the company.
> * * * ' [Emphasis supplied.]"

While the facts in *Cincinnati* do differ in some respects from those in the instant case, we do not find these differences to be significant, particularly in the light of better reasoned authority in this area.

Generally, an oral contract of insurance is valid if made by an agent acting within the actual or apparent scope of his authority. *State Farm Automobile Insurance Company v. Newell*, 270 Ala. 550, 120 So.2d 390 (1960). Tallant Agency, a licensed general agent of Zurich, had apparent authority to bind Zurich on an oral contract of insurance. Undisclosed, private limitations upon the authority of a general agent do not bind a third party who, being unaware of them, contracts with an agent within the customary scope of the agent's authority. *Mayo v. American Fire and Casualty Company*, 282 N.C. 346, 196 S.E.2d 828 (1972). * * *

Moreover, the fact that there was no agreement between the insured and the agent as to the company with which the risk was placed does not relieve Zurich of liability. Even when there is no agreement between applicant and agent as to the company in which the risk is placed, where the agent has actual or apparent authority and designates the company by some positive act prior to the loss, the company has been held liable. *Julien v. Spring Lake Park Agency, Inc.*, 283 Minn. 101, 166 N.W.2d 355 (1969); *Milwaukee Bedding Co. v. Graebner*, 182 Wis. 171, 196 N.W. 533 (1923); Vance on Insurance (3rd ed.), § 37 at p. 223.

In *Milwaukee Bedding, supra*, defendant Graebner was an insurance agent representing several companies. Mr. Schilling of Milwaukee Bedding called Graebner's office and spoke with Graebner's daughter. A renewal was agreed upon and there was an agreement for an additional $2,000 coverage. No specific company was identified in the conversation; however, Ms. Graebner made a designation on a card and added "$2,000 ad'l in L. & A. Co." The Wisconsin court held that there was a valid oral contract of insurance, stating:

> "* * * It is a general rule that, where an application for insurance is made to an agent who represents several companies, no contract of insurance is engendered between the insured, and any particular company until such company is designated by the agent. [Citations omitted.] But where the company is selected by the agent, and in some manner designated as the company in which the insurance is to be written, a binding contract results. [Citations omitted.] In such case the agent becomes the agent of the insured for the purpose of selecting the company. [Citations omitted.]"

Thus, the mere fact that Mr. Bailey was not informed that Zurich was designated as the insurance company at the time Tallant Agency bound coverage does not release Zurich from liability in view of the fact that Zurich was so designated by the agent prior to the loss. Zurich selected Tallant as its general agent and authorized it to bind the company on contracts of insurance. Because Zurich placed Tallant Agency in a position where others might rely on its statements, Zurich is liable to the insured for the amount of the loss on the policy entered into by its agent within its apparent authority and must rely on its selected agent and its credit for indemnification if the agent exceeded its actual authority. *Cincinnati, supra.*

Next we consider appellant Tallant Agency's contention that the trial court erred in finding that the agency exceeded its actual authority in binding Zurich on the risk and that it should be required to indemnify Zurich. Tallant argues that because it had *actual,* not *apparent* authority, to bind the company, that the insurer should be bound but not the agency.

In support of its position, Tallant Agency relies primarily on *Lewis v. Travelers Insurance Company,* 51 N.J. 244, 239 A.2d 4 (1968), a case in which an agent orally bound Travelers on August 27, the insured suffered a loss on September 5, and Travelers denied the claim on September 6, alleging that the binder was merely an application which Travelers rejected. At trial, Travelers filed a cross-claim against the agent and the trial court found that the agent exceeded his actual authority and was therefore required to indemnify Travelers for the amount of insured's loss. The Supreme Court of New Jersey reversed, finding that while the agent did not have actual *express* authority in writing to orally bind the risk without prior approval, it had actual *implied* authority to do so due to Travelers' admitted practice of backdating all policies of that type submitted by agents as of the date of the application.

The case at bar differs from *Lewis.* In the first place, the scope of review in New Jersey differs from that in Alabama in that issues of fact not determined by jury verdict may be reviewed and new or amended findings of fact may be made by New Jersey appellate courts. *Williams v. DeFabio,* 3 N.J.Super. 182, 65 A.2d 858 (1949).

In Alabama, where a decree is rendered on evidence taken *ore tenus,* or partly so, as here, and the trial court has the advantage of hearing the witnesses and observing their demeanor, the judgment of the trial court is accorded the same weight as a jury verdict, and this Court will not disturb the trial court's conclusions unless plainly and palpably erroneous. *McBrayer v. Smith,* 278 Ala. 247, 177 So.2d 571 (1965); *Wolfe v. Thompson,* 285 Ala. 745, 235 So.2d 878 (1970).

Furthermore, unlike *Lewis,* supra, the record here does not affirmatively and clearly reflect that Zurich customarily back-dated policies as of the date of the application on risks for which prior approval is required. Additionally, Kenneth Tallant conceded that he would not have bound coverage with Zurich had he consulted his agency's file and been made aware of his agency's previous dealing in the matter.

Thus, due to Zurich's express written limitations on Tallant's authority, the latter had no *actual* authority (although he possessed *apparent* authority) to bind Zurich to Bailey, and, thus, having exceeded its actual authority, Tallant is liable to indemnify Zurich for any loss which the insurer sustains. *British General Insurance Co. v. Simpson Sales Co., supra.* * * *

Zurich must afford Workmen's Compensation coverage or its equivalent to insure Bailey Wood Products against liability for injury to its employee, J.W. Coleman, and must provide Bailey Products a legal defense in the lawsuit filed against it by said employee, and Tallant Agency is required to indemnify Zurich for any loss and expenses sustained by the insurer due to the agency's exceeding its actual authority. * * *

We cannot find any basis in the record or from the authorities cited for the trial judge's holding that Tallant Agency is "liable for and obligated to afford Plaintiff Bailey Wood Products, Inc. Workman's Compensation coverage," etc. To that extent the trial judge's finding is erroneous and should be corrected on remandment.

AFFIRMED, ON CROSS–APPEAL.

AFFIRMED IN PART, REVERSED IN PART, AND REMANDED ON APPEAL.

Notes and Questions

1. *Clothed With Authority.* What did Zurich do to clothe Tallant with apparent authority to bind Zurich? In light of the finding that Tallant did have apparent authority, what steps would you advise Zurich to take in the future to avoid being bound by agents who act against express instructions? If most general agents have unrestricted authority to bind coverage, does the custom and practice of the industry make limiting apparent authority impossible? The reports are full of decisions on this issue; the implication of many is that little if anything

can be done in this regard. See, e.g., *Corbitt v. Federal Kemper Insurance Company,* 594 S.W.2d 728 (Tenn.App.1980), in which the court held that the insurer was bound by the representations of the agent's secretary.

2. *Indemnity.* In theory, Zurich is protected by its right to indemnification from Tallant for the liability Zurich incurred because Tallant acted beyond the scope of its actual authority. Zurich's ability to vindicate this right depends on the extent of Tallant's assets, including any liability insurance (Errors and Omissions coverage or a Surety Bond) protecting Tallant.

Suppose that the insurer pays a claim under a binder entered into by an agent who has acted beyond the scope of her actual authority. If the insurer then sues the agent for indemnity, must it prove that the agent had apparent authority to bind the insurer? *Cameron Mutual Insurance Company of Missouri v. Bouse,* 635 S.W.2d 488 (Mo.App.1982), holds that it must. Might the insurer have a cause of action against the agent even where the agent did not have apparent authority—or, more realistically, where the insurer could not prove it?

3. *The Applicant's Action Against the Agent.* In situations where the agent has failed to procure the coverage promised—e.g., where the agent has not specified the company with which she intends to place coverage—many courts hold that the putative insured has a cause of action against the agent for negligence, or for breach of a contract to procure coverage. See R. Jerry, Understanding Insurance Law 163–66 (1987). These causes of action, however, are for negligent failure to procure coverage or for breach of contract to procure it, not for the agent's failure to provide it herself. Thus the last paragraph in the court's opinion in *Tallant.* When would the differences among the three kinds of claims matter?

2. Waiver and Estoppel

In addition to the construction of ambiguities against the insurer and the principle that the reasonable expectations of the insured should be honored, insureds commonly rely on the doctrines of waiver and estoppel to combat the insurer's defense that a claim is not covered by the language of a policy. In contrast to the first two approaches, however, waiver and estoppel tend to turn on actions taken or not taken by an agent of the insurer. Waiver is the voluntary relinquishment of a known right; whether there has been a waiver is normally a question of fact. Estoppel, in contrast, results from a change of position by the insured as a consequence of some representation or act by the insurer. Because this is a somewhat vague notion, claims of estoppel often raise perplexing legal questions.

ROSETH v. ST. PAUL PROPERTY & LIABILITY INSURANCE COMPANY

Supreme Court of South Dakota, 1985.
374 N.W.2d 105.

WOLLMAN, Justice.

This is an appeal by St. Paul Property & Liability Insurance Company (St. Paul) from a judgment entered by the trial court in favor of Jerry Roseth, d/b/a Philip Livestock Express. We reverse.

On November 12, 1979, a livestock trailer owned by Roseth and leased to Richard Miller was involved in an accident on U.S. highway 83 near Mission, South Dakota. Miller was transporting 109 calves for the 720 Cattle Company of Idaho, to a buyer in O'Neill, Nebraska, when the accident occurred. Eleven of the cattle were killed at the scene of the accident and two were missing. Miller immediately contacted Roseth by telephone and informed him of the accident.

Miller was transporting the calves from Idaho to Nebraska pursuant to an agreement with Roseth. Under this agreement, Miller would haul livestock for Philip Livestock Express using Roseth's trailer, with Roseth receiving twenty percent of the trucking charge.

On either the day of the accident or the day after, Roseth reported the accident to the Black Hills Agency (Black Hills). Roseth had purchased a cargo insurance policy from St. Paul through Black Hills' agent David Brinkman in 1977. The policy insured against the risk of livestock mortality only, specifically excluding coverage of "any animal able to walk from the conveyance or able to walk after unloading therefrom."

On November 14, 1979, St. Paul adjuster, James Wattleworth, was notified of the mishap by the Black Hills Agency. Wattleworth called Roseth that same day. Roseth informed Wattleworth that the surviving calves, which had been moved to Philip by Roseth, were generally "stiff," "gaunt," and "in pretty tough shape." Roseth also told Wattleworth that he had an all-risk policy that would cover the injured calves. Wattleworth stated to Roseth that he did not have a copy of the policy before him, but assured Roseth that St. Paul would perform in accordance with the provisions of the policy.

Wattleworth and Roseth then discussed alternatives concerning disposition of the surviving calves. Wattleworth advised Roseth that he had a duty to minimize his loss. Both parties agreed that this could best be accomplished by selling the calves the next day at an auction sale scheduled at Roseth's sale barn. Accordingly, the injured calves were sold the next day for approximately $20.00 to $22.00 per hundred weight less than the amount brought by similar, but uninjured, calves. The difference between the net value of the calves prior to the accident and the net value obtained from the sale was $8,865.98.

St. Paul issued payment under the policy for only fourteen calves, which included the eleven dead at the scene, one that later died, and the two that were missing. St. Paul denied coverage for the injured calves pursuant to the exclusion in the policy. Roseth brought an action against St. Paul and Black Hills Agency for recovery of the loss he sustained ($8,865.98) in selling the injured calves for less than their market value.

[The action against the Agency alleged negligence in failing to procure coverage against the kind of loss suffered. The court held that there could be no such action in this case, because the Agency had procured the maximum coverage available on the market at that time, which limited coverage to livestock mortality.] * * *

Roseth's second claimed basis for recovery was that St. Paul should be estopped from denying coverage on the basis of the exclusion contained in the policy for the reason that Wattleworth had failed to correct his misconception that the policy covered the injured calves. Roseth contended that Wattleworth had reinforced his misconception by instructing him to sell the injured calves immediately, and that he sold the calves on the assumption that St. Paul would reimburse him for the diminishing value of the injured calves. Roseth testified that had he been informed that the injured calves were not covered, he would have nurtured them back to a healthier condition and sold them later to obtain a better price. * * *

With respect to Roseth's claim against St. Paul, the trial court held that St. Paul should be estopped from defending on the basis of the exclusion contained in the policy.

The trial court found that Roseth had told Wattleworth that he believed he had an all-risk policy and that the decrease in value of the livestock would be covered under his policy; that Wattleworth thought at the time that St. Paul did not have an all-risk cargo policy; that Wattleworth nevertheless allowed Roseth to go on thinking that the coverage existed because Wattleworth did not want to antagonize Roseth; and that Wattleworth told Roseth that he thought it was a good idea to sell the cattle the next day to minimize the loss. The trial court held that it would be inequitable to allow St. Paul to claim the exclusion under the policy.

St. Paul contends on appeal that the trial court erred in applying the doctrine of estoppel to provide coverage for a risk not covered by the policy where there was no clear and convincing evidence of any misrepresentation or concealment of material fact by Wattleworth. We need not decide this question. Rather, we hold that the doctrine of equitable estoppel is not applicable under the facts of this case.

In *Farmers Mutual Automobile Ins. Co. v. Bechard*, 80 S.D. 237, 246, 122 N.W.2d 86, 91 (1963), this court held:

> [A]n insurance company which in its policy has written the generally broad coverage may be estopped to defend by reason of an exclusionary clause not within the terms the insured

ordered and coverage which he was led to believe was contained therein.

This holding was followed in *State Automobile Casualty Underwriters v. Ruotsalainen,* 81 S.D. 472, 136 N.W.2d 884 (1965). The *Bechard–Ruotsalainen* rule is contrary to the majority rule, which provides that estoppel is not available to bring within the coverage of a policy those risks not covered by its terms or expressly excluded by the policy.

* * *

In adopting the minority rule, the New Jersey Supreme Court held that

[w]here an insurer or its agent misrepresents, even though innocently, the coverage of an insurance contract, or the exclusions therefrom, to an insured *before or at the inception of the contract,* and the insured reasonably relies thereupon to his ultimate detriment, the insurer is estopped to deny coverage after a loss on a risk from a peril actually not covered by the terms of the policy.

Harr v. Allstate Insurance Co., 54 N.J. 287, 306–307, 255 A.2d 208, 219 (1969) (emphasis added). *See also Darner Motor Sales v. Universal Underwriters,* 140 Ariz. 383, 682 P.2d 388, 400 n. 10 (1984) (adopting rule of *Harr*); *Peninsular Life Ins. Co. v. Wade,* 425 So.2d 1181, 1183 (Fla.App.1983).

The requirement that the estopping conduct occur "before or at the inception of the policy" is consistent with the underlying rationale of the minority rule. The minority rule was born out of the inequities which result where an insured relies to his detriment on an insurer's superior knowledge in purchasing a policy of insurance and consequently is deprived of the opportunity to purchase the desired coverage elsewhere. *Harr, supra.*

In both *Bechard* and *Ruotsalainen,* the insureds sought specific coverage for which they gave consideration based on assurances that such coverage was provided for in the policy. Under the facts of the case before us, Wattleworth at most indirectly perpetuated a misconception held by Roseth concerning the nature of his coverage. We hold that under these facts the remedy of estoppel is not available to expand the terms of the policy.

The judgment is reversed.

Notes and Questions

1. *The Purpose of the Exclusion.* Why do you think the policy contained the exclusion that created Roseth's problem?

2. *Commission or Omission?* Do you agree with the court that "* * * Wattleworth at best indirectly perpetuated a misconception held by Roseth * * *"? In light of the court's rationale, was this language mere dictum, or does it cast doubt on what the holding was? Suppose that Roseth had not said that he thought he was covered, but

had merely asked what Wattleworth thought he should do with the cattle, and Wattleworth had replied that Roseth should minimize his losses? Would any other result in *Roseth* have required Wattleworth to deny any assistance or advice to Roseth until he could inspect Roseth's policy? Would that be a realistic requirement?

3. *Limitations on the Scope of Estoppel.* Two points that figure in the *Roseth* opinion are worth noting. First, the majority rule is that neither waiver nor estoppel can create coverage that was not provided for by the policy to begin with: these doctrines can negate defenses, but cannot create additional coverage. This rule amounts to a rejection of promissory, as distinguished from equitable, estoppel. However, the minority rule originating in *Harr v. Allstate Insurance Company,* cited by the court, is growing in influence. Many courts seem quite willing to ignore this distinction and to allow estoppel not only to prevent the forfeiture of coverage afforded by the policy, but to create coverage not explicitly provided for as well. Second, the hornbook rule is that conduct which occurs before or at the inception of the contract can generate an estoppel but conduct that occurs later cannot do so.

In light of the doctrines of apparent authority and reasonable expectations, the unavailability of pre-contractual promissory estoppel may be of less significance than its unavailability in post-contract cases such as *Roseth.* Yet, given the purposes underlying the parol evidence rule, could precisely the opposite approach—disallowing estoppel for pre-contract conduct, but allowing it for post-contract conduct—be preferable? In any event, is there any reason to reject estoppel in either setting as long as the insured must prove detrimental reliance, as has always been required in both equitable and promissory estoppel? Professor Clarence Morris argued that limitations on the scope of waiver and estoppel in insurance law result from a generalized concern by the courts that these rather flexible notions might otherwise carry the process of favoring consumers too far. See Morris, Waiver and Estoppel in Insurance Policy Litigation, 105 U.Pa.L.Rev. 925 (1957). His insightful comments on this and other subjects are always worth careful attention.

Could another concern be that the words and conduct that may constitute a waiver or estoppel are likely to have been uttered or taken place months or years before loss, and in any event to be unrecorded and therefore highly susceptible to fraudulent proof? How much support for its defense can an insurer expect from the testimony of an agent that he simply "cannot remember" the words or conduct that the insured claims created a waiver or estoppel? What incentives might independent agents have not to remember?

4. *A Double Bind.* Interestingly, if Roseth could have invoked estoppel in his behalf, his required proof of detrimental reliance might have reduced the amount to which he was entitled. He argued that he would have nursed the cattle he sold back to good health if he had known that he had no coverage for them. If this were true, by selling

the cattle immediately was he not violating any duty he had to the insurer to mitigate his damages?

3. Group Insurance

Special circumstances sometimes obtain when the insured's coverage is provided under a policy of group insurance. Typically provided as health or disability insurance free of charge as a fringe benefit of employment, or offered as an option in return for a deduction from the employee's paycheck, group insurance can provide a number of advantages. First, because the group insurer's marketing costs are greatly reduced, it can offer coverage at a lower price. Second, other administrative costs may be reduced by allocating certain record-keeping tasks to the employer, which may be able to perform them less expensively because it has easy access to employees and to records that already are maintained for other purposes. This economy may produce still lower premiums.

Two other advantages depend on the degree to which a plan is contributory, i.e., financed by payroll deductions. Even when a plan is wholly contributory and therefore voluntary, adverse selection may be less severe than in non-group insurance, because the pool from which eligible applicants self-select is comprised of a group of persons healthy enough to be employed. When the plan is non-contributory, of course, adverse selection is greatly reduced (though not eliminated), because it can occur only through the employee's choice of employer. Under these circumstances the employer has an incentive to screen out applicants for employment who may be adversely selecting, since the employer's premiums are likely to be experience-rated. Finally, all the employer's contributions for most forms of coverage are deductible by the employer for federal income tax purposes, but are not taxable to the employee as income. See Internal Revenue Code, 26 U.S.C. §§ 104–06.

Because of the substantial economies that can be achieved by deputizing the employer to perform some of the insurer's functions, the question whether the employer is an agent of the employee or of the insurer often arises. How do the incentives of the employer to serve the interests of insurer and insured in cases like the one that follows differ from those of the ordinary independent agent selling non-group insurance?

PAULSON v. WESTERN LIFE INSURANCE COMPANY

Supreme Court of Oregon, 1981.
292 Or. 38, 636 P.2d 935.

PETERSON, Justice.

The rapid growth of group insurance in the United States has given rise to a number of cases in which the principal issue is whether the employer-policyholder, in the administration of the policy, is the agent of the insurer, of the insured worker, or the agent of neither. That issue, among others, is involved in this case.

THE FACTS

Roof & Floor Components, Inc., (hereinafter referred to as "employer" or as "policyholder") is a Salem concern that, in 1974, applied to the defendant for a "group insurance policy" that would provide its employees life insurance benefits, hospital expense benefits, supplemental accident expense benefits, and major medical expense benefits. The policy was issued and became effective on February 7, 1974. It provided for optional coverage of a worker's spouse and specified unmarried children.

The plan covered different classes of employees. A Class I employee qualified for personal coverage and dependents coverage without proof of insurability if application for coverage was made within 30 days following the first day of employment. Plaintiff was a Class I employee. Defendant issued a brochure, which the plaintiff never saw prior to the dispute which gave rise to this case, but which is nonetheless relevant. It provided:

"When you enroll for benefits for your eligible dependents more than 31 days after you are initially eligible, it is necessary that satisfactory evidence of insurability be furnished to the insurance company. Benefits will be effective when approved by the insurance company. You will be notified as to the effective date."

" * * *

"If you enroll when initially eligible, merely complete an enrollment form authorizing necessary salary/payroll deduction and return it to your supervisor.

"Should you wish to enroll more than 31 days after your initial eligibility date for benefits on your eligible dependents, it is necessary that evidence of insurability satisfactory to the insurance company be furnished. Special forms are available for this purpose. Benefits for you and your dependents will be effective when approved by the insurance company." [1]

The brochure also contained provisions relating to the duties of the insurer and the employer:

1. The brochure contained a provision to the effect that the brochure was "not a part of the insurance contract. Your coverage is fully explained by your certificate. You should read it carefully and then place it in the pocket at the back of this booklet for safekeeping."

Reference is made to the brochure because it, more than the policy itself, sets forth the legal effect of the policy in understandable terms. The brochure also reflects the insurer's opinion as to the legal effect of the policy and it also sets forth some policy practices which, as will be seen below, are relevant.

"The Insurance Company will perform the following functions:

1. Maintain records of all employees and dependents insured by the program.

2. Determine the eligibility of individual claimants for receipt of benefits.

3. Process claims for benefits.

4. Authorize the payment of benefits.

5. Make payments of benefits to beneficiaries.

6. Make determination on appeal of claim denials.

"The Plan administrator [the employer] will perform the following functions:

1. Receive and remit contributions for the program.

2. Maintain records of all employees and dependents insured.

3. Select the Insurance Carrier."

The insurance policy contained these provisions:

"Data Required from Policyholder [the employer]: The Policyholder shall furnish periodically to the Company such information relative to individuals becoming insured, changes in amounts of insurance, and terminations of insurance as the Company may require for the administration of the insurance under this policy. The Company shall have the right to inspect any records of the Policyholder which relate to the insurance under this policy at any reasonable time.

"Clerical Error: The Policyholder's failure, due to clerical error, to report the name of any individual who has qualified for insurance under this policy or to report the name of any individual whose classification has been changed shall not deprive such individual of insurance under this policy or affect the amount of insurance to which he is entitled; nor shall the Policyholder's failure to report the termination of insurance for any individual continue such insurance beyond the date of termination determined in accordance with the provisions of this policy."

The insurer provided the employer with enrollment forms and claim forms which, as necessary, were given to the employees by the employer. Claim forms, after they were filled out, were normally mailed to the insurer by the employee.

The plaintiff came to work for the employer on June 23, 1976. His medical insurance then in effect—with another carrier—remained effective until October 1, 1976. Prior to going to work for the employer, he talked to the owner of the business, a Mr. Largent, about the company health insurance. Mr. Largent told the plaintiff that he could elect coverage for himself and for his dependents any time in the first six months of employment without any evidence of insurability required. Paulson therefore decided to keep his other coverage in effect "until it ran out" and then apply for coverage with the employer's carrier. Accordingly, on September 1, 1976, he received and filled out an application for coverage which was sent to the defendant, with appropriate premiums.

On November 3, 1976, the defendant wrote to the employer advising the employer that because the application was not made " * * * within the eligibility period as specified in your policy, evidence of insurability is required." A form was enclosed for Mr. Paulson to execute and return.

After this letter was received, Mr. Largent went "back and forth for about two weeks" with the company's agent, without resolution of the matter. Plaintiff was then advised of the problem. At about the same time, plaintiff's daughter became ill, and he incurred substantial medical expenses to treat the illness. The plaintiff's claim for payment of these medical expenses was denied on the ground that the policy was not in effect. * * *

On trial, at the conclusion of all the evidence, the defendant moved for a directed verdict on several grounds, one being that " * * * Largent was not acting as [the insurer's] agent * * * and the court should rule as a matter of law that he was not. * * * " * * *

"The evidence shows me that the acts of the employer, in this case, Mr. Largent, are nothing more than keeping a supply of application forms, claim forms, brochures, withholding premiums and terminating coverage when the employment ceases and such. It is merely administerial and nothing indicates to me that Mr. Largent was given any authority, apparent or actual, to actually represent the insurance company as agent in any respect." * * *

After extended argument, the trial court granted defendant's motion for a directed verdict. * * *

The Court of Appeals, 47 Or.App. 376, 613 P.2d 1115 in a two-line per curiam opinion, affirmed, citing *Bowes v. Lakeside Industries, Inc.,* 297 Minn. 86, 209 N.W.2d 900 (1973).

"INSURER–ADMINISTERED PLANS" VIS–A–VIS "EMPLOYER–ADMINISTERED PLANS"

The defendant asserts:

"The majority rule is that the employer-master policyholder is not the agent of the insurer in a group insurance context. *Boseman v. Connecticut General Life Ins. Co.,* 301 U.S. 196, 57 S.Ct. 686, 81 L.Ed. 1036 (1937); *Duvall v. Metropolitan Life Ins. Co.,* 82 N.H. 543, 136 A. 400, 50 A.L.R. 1276 (1927). This longstanding rule is still the majority rule. * * * "

Many courts and commentators also discuss cases such as this in terms of a "majority rule" and "minority rule." See cases cited and discussion in D. Gregg, *Group Insurance: Agency Characterization of the Master Policyholder,* 46 Wash.L.Rev. 377 (1971), and R. Borst, *Group Policyholder as Agent of Insurer or Group Member,* Vol. 14, No. 2, Federation of Insurance Counsel Quarterly 11 (1963). Our analysis of the decisions convinces us that many courts, even though they purport to apply a "majority rule" or a "minority rule," actually base their decision upon the facts relating to the division of functions between the insurer and the employer-policyholder and that any "majority" or "minority" rule is more apparent than real. It is more correct to say that when the plan is exclusively administered by the insurer, as a matter of law no agency relationship exists between the insurer and the employer. But if the employer performs all of the administration of the policy, an agency relationship exists between the insurer and the employer, as a matter of law. Between these two extremes, as the division of functions becomes less separate, or to put it another way, as the employer assumes responsibility for more administrative or sales functions which are customarily performed by an insurer, a question of fact will arise as to the agency relationship between the insurer and the employer. * * *

The essence of the plaintiff's claim herein is that Largent told him that he had six months within which to qualify for coverage for himself and his dependents without proof of insurability; that he relied upon Largent's statements and deferred filing his application for coverage; that had he known the true facts, he would have applied for and been issued coverage for himself and his dependents without proof of insurability, which insurance would have been in effect at the time of his daughter's illness.

In the normal two-party insurance transaction, the insurer performs a variety of tasks such as solicitation of the insured, which often includes discussions with the potential insured as to cost of coverage, the benefits, the exclusions, insurability, and other aspects of the insurance policy; the delivery of an application for insurance, sometimes involving assistance with the preparation of the application itself; the processing of the application; the issuance of the insurance policy or certificate of insurance; collecting premiums; and processing claims, including the delivery of claim forms and the handling of the claim after receipt.

By the defendant's express admission in its brochure, some of these tasks were to be performed by the employer, including the receipt and remittance of contributions for the program, and maintenance of records of all insured employees and dependents. Although the contract between the insurer and the employer is silent as to such things as enrollment forms, claim forms, and the like, there is evidence that the insurer expected the employer to distribute application forms to the employees, to receive and forward the application forms to the carrier, and to deliver claim forms to the employees. In this case, when the carrier wrote to the employer regarding the plaintiff's coverage, the insurer relied upon the employer to assist in obtaining evidence of insurability.

The policy itself contains provisions respecting the employer's responsibility, which include periodically furnishing "such information relative to individuals becoming insured * * * as the company may require for the administration of the insurance under this policy." In addition, the policy expressly provides that the insurer remains liable for the employer's errors, in specified respects.

The plaintiff asserts that there is evidence to support a finding that the employer was the agent of the insurer for other purposes, as well— that if the employer is given the responsibility to deliver application forms to the employees, it is not unlikely that the employee might have questions as to the coverage, particularly when the brochure was not given to the employee at the time the application was delivered. We agree. The trier of fact could well find that the employee reasonably believed that the employer was authorized to answer such questions. See Restatement of Agency (Second) 32 § 8, and *Elfstrom v. New York Life Ins. Co., supra,* 63 Cal.Rptr. 35, 432 P.2d at 738. We very much doubt that the insurer would deny that the employer had no right to correctly answer questions regarding the coverage. If true representations are within the employer's authority or apparent authority, in the absence of notice to the employee, the trier of fact could hold the insurer responsible for innocent misrepresentations made by the employer, such as were apparently made in this case. Restatement of Agency (Second) 384, § 162.

In *Beeson v. Hegstad,* 199 Or. 325, 330, 261 P.2d 381 (1953), it is stated that "[i]t is elementary that express authority given an agent to do certain things carries with it the implied authority to do all other things reasonably incident to and necessary for carrying out the objectives of the agency." The evidence shows that the employer had express authority to perform specified acts, and the defendant, in its policy, expressly made itself liable for the employer's failure to perform some of those acts. In addition, the evidence shows that the employer had other responsibilities in the administration of the program. If an employer is charged with the performance of functions incident to the administration or sales of insurance which are commonly performed by the insurer, it is proper to say that the employer is the insurer's agent for those purposes. If there are other functions for which the employer has no responsibility it is equally logical to say that the employer is not the insurer's agent for those purposes.

Here there is evidence, both direct and indirect, that the employer performed some functions incident to the initiation of coverage by employees, which duties included the distribution, receipt and forwarding of applications for insurance and was expressly charged by the insurer with responsibility for " * * * [furnishing] to the Company * * * information relative to individuals becoming insured * * *."

Specific limitations on the employer's duties and responsibilities are not set forth in the policy.

We cannot say, as a matter of law, that the authority to distribute enrollment forms, applications, and claim forms did not carry with it the implied authority to answer questions regarding deadlines for filing such forms. Nor can we say, as a matter of law, that it was unreasonable for the plaintiff to look to Mr. Largent for such information. The trial court erred in directing a verdict for defendant.[2]

[The court then ruled that the plaintiff was not precluded from asserting an estoppel against the insurer on the basis of the employer's representations.] * * *

Reversed and remanded to the trial court for trial.

Notes and Questions

1. *Other Agency Issues.* The tripartite group insurance contract may generate other issues that turn on the agency status of the employer as well. For example, the employer may fail to forward premiums to the insurer. If the employer is the insurer's agent, however, it can be argued that the premium has been paid nonetheless. In this situation, should it matter whether the plan is contributory or not? See *Norby v. Bankers Life Co.,* 304 Minn. 464, 231 N.W.2d 665 (1975).

2. *Conflicts Between Documents.* One problem that is largely independent of agency questions is how to identify the contract that binds the insurer. The typical group insurance policy—the contract executed by the insurer and the employer—is likely to be much longer and more detailed than a standard individual policy. This *Master Policy* is kept on file by the employer, and each employee is issued a *certificate* of insurance that summarizes the terms of coverage and incorporates the Master Policy by reference. Similarly, often the insurer prepares a promotional *brochure* that describes the terms of coverage in language that is even more simple than the individual certificate of insurance.

When the Master Policy contains limitations on coverage that are not described in the brochure or certificate of insurance, which should control? The hornbook rule is that the mere omission of details from the brochure or certificate does not invalidate limitations in the Master Policy. When the two "sources" of obligation conflict, however, the applicable rule is less clear. See, e.g., *Krauss v. Manhattan Life Insurance Company,* 700 F.2d 870 (2d Cir.1983), in which the court held that a limitation on the amount of coverage available to part-time employees in the Master Policy was ineffective, because that limitation was never brought to the insured's attention. In such situations,

---

2. Whether the employer would be the insurer's agent in answering technical questions as to the nature or extent of coverage is not involved in this case. The insurer, by appropriate language on the application form, may be able to restrict its potential liability for unauthorized statements of others.

should the employee have to show detrimental reliance in order to invalidate a coverage limitation in the Master Policy? If not, what is the theory of recovery?

C. PUBLIC POLICY RESTRICTIONS ON CONTRACT TERMS

In addition to the doctrines that govern the *meaning* of provisions in insurance policies, the *validity* of those provisions is governed by the general public policies of the states in which they are sold, and by specific public policies embodied in the constitutions and legislation of these states. The latter are discussed at various points in this book. See, e.g., Chapter Eight's treatment of the validity of the "family exclusion" in uninsured motorists coverage under state statutes requiring that such coverage be offered to the purchasers of auto insurance.

This Section examines the application of a more diffuse but no less important source of public policy: judicial sensitivity to the difference between good and evil, fairness and unfairness, straight dealing and overreaching. Even when all other tests for the validity of insurance policy provisions have been exhausted, this residual category of restrictions on what may and may not be included in a policy remains. As you study the three following cases, consider whether the principles that lie behind the decisions can be generalized beyond the subjects with which they deal, into a formula that might add predictability and structure to this area of insurance law. Are public policy restrictions on the validity of insurance policy provisions an undefinable and brooding omnipresence, or the result of a set of principles that can be articulated and applied in the same manner as other legal rules?

ST. PAUL INSURANCE COMPANIES v. TALLADEGA NURSING HOME, INC.

United States Court of Appeals, Fifth Circuit, 1979.
606 F.2d 631.

GODBOLD, Circuit Judge:

This case involves the liability of an insurance company, under a comprehensive nursing home liability policy, to indemnify and defend the insured in civil actions alleging slander, interference with business relations, and violations of the federal antitrust laws. The district court held that such allegations constitute intentional wrongs and that it is against Alabama public policy to insure against the consequences of intentional wrongs. We affirm.

Appellants William and Hazel Patterson together own 59 shares out of 60 of the Talladega Nursing Home, Inc., and are directors and administrators of the Nursing Home. Both the Pattersons and the Nursing Home were insured by St. Paul's comprehensive nursing home liability policy. Under this policy, St. Paul agreed to pay "all loss by reason of the liability imposed by law or contract upon the Insured for damages * * * on account of injury. * * *" Injury is defined in the contract as "both bodily and personal injury claims (such as libel, slander, invasion of privacy, false detention, etc.)." St. Paul also agreed to defend the Insured in any suit alleging a covered injury, "even if such suit is groundless, false or fraudulent." In 1975, while the St. Paul insurance contract was in force, Ottis D. Cook initiated a civil action in federal district court in Alabama against the Pattersons and the Nursing Home, alleging, in essence, that appellants had intentionally and unlawfully prevented him from successfully operating a rival nursing home in Talladega.[1] In a nine-count complaint, Cook alleged that appellants' acts had amounted to slander, interference with business relations, and violation of the federal antitrust laws. In their answer appellants denied all the material allegations in the complaint and have claimed before this court that the allegations therein are groundless, false or fraudulent. St. Paul then instituted the instant action in federal district court, seeking a declaratory judgment as to its duty to defend. This appeal is taken from the district court's ruling that St. Paul is not obligated to defend the underlying actions.

Appellants argue, first, that Alabama public policy does not prohibit insuring against all intentional wrongs; second, that the allegations of the underlying complaint do not constitute intentional wrongs; and third, that St. Paul's duty to defend is broader than its indemnification liability, so that even if public policy precludes indemnification, St. Paul must still defend the actions.

In *Fidelity–Phenix Fire Ins. Co. v. Murphy,* 226 Ala. 226, 146 So. 387 (1933), the Alabama Supreme Court, in the context of the willful and deliberate destruction of the insured's ship by the insured, held void as against public policy any insurance coverage protecting against "loss which [the insured] may purposely and willfully create." *Id.* at 230, 146 So. at 390. In *Pruet v. Dugger–Holmes & Assoc.,* 276 Ala. 403, 162 So.2d 613 (1964), this doctrine was extended to include a suit for intentional trespass. These two cases have been interpreted to hold that all contracts insuring against loss from intentional wrongs are void in Alabama as against public policy. *See Industrial Sugars, Inc. v. Standard Accident Ins. Co.,* 338 F.2d 673, 676 (CA7, 1964); *Thomason v. United States Fidelity & Guaranty Co.,* 248 F.2d 417, 420 (CA5, 1957) (Rives, J., dissenting). Appellants' contention that the intentional wrongs doctrine is narrowly circumscribed, and limited to such egregious acts as arson, is without merit; the crucial question, therefore, is whether the acts alleged in the underlying complaint constitute intentional wrongs.

Intentional wrongs are defined in Alabama, in the context of insurance, as including both intentionally causing injury and "inten-

---

1. Cook also initiated a similar action in the Circuit Court of Talladega County, alleging slander and malicious interference with his right to do business. The federal district court held St. Paul had no obligation to defend this action. The same considerations govern St. Paul's liability to defend this state action as apply to Cook's federal suit.

tionally doing some act which reasonable and ordinary prudence" would indicate likely to result in injury. *Hartford Fire Ins. Co. v. Blakeney,* 340 So.2d 754, 756 (Ala.1976); *accord, Transit Casualty Co. v. Snow,* 584 F.2d 97, 99 (CA5, 1978). All of the allegations of the underlying complaint fall within this definition, both as a matter of fact and as a matter of law. A close reading of the complaint demonstrates that appellants are alleged to have committed a series of intentional acts, each of which was calculated to prevent Cook from operating a nursing home in competition with that of appellants. It is also clear from the complaint that the sole purpose of appellants' alleged conduct was to eliminate competition.

Moreover, the elements of each of the underlying causes of action include either an intent to injure or the commission of acts reasonably likely to injure. *See Ceravolo v. Brown,* 364 So.2d 1155, 1156 (Ala.1978) (slander); *Marion v. Davis,* 217 Ala. 16, 18, 114 So. 357, 358 (1927) (slander); [2] *Louisville & Nashville Railroad Co. v. Arrow Transportation Co.,* 170 F.Supp. 597, 600 & n. 3 (N.D.Ala.1959) (interference with business relations); *Broadcast Music, Inc. v. CBS,* 441 U.S. 1, 8 n. 13, 99 S.Ct. 1551, 1556 n. 13, 60 L.Ed.2d 1, 23 n. 13 (1979) (Stevens, J., dissenting) (conspiracy to restrain trade); *Shotkin v. General Electric Co.,* 171 F.2d 236, 238 (CA10, 1948) (conspiracy to restrain trade); *Mabry v. State,* 40 Ala.App. 129, 135, 110 So.2d 250, 255, *cert. dismissed,* 268 Ala. 660, 110 So.2d 260 (1959) (conspiracy); *State v. Cawood,* 2 Stew. 360, 363 (Ala.1830) (conspiracy).

Appellants also argue that the acts of the Pattersons cannot be attributed to the Nursing Home, and that St. Paul is obligated to defend the Nursing Home regardless of the resolution of the issue as to the Pattersons. This contention is without merit. The district court properly found Hazel Patterson to be the alter ego of the corporation,[3] and therefore held that her acts were tantamount to acts of the corporation. This is consistent with Alabama law. *Ex parte City Sales Corp., supra; Williams v. North Alabama Express,* 263 Ala. 581, 584, 83 So.2d 330, 333 (1955).

Finally, appellants contend that St. Paul's duty to defend is broader than its liability for indemnification. The insurer's duty to

2. It may be argued that St. Paul should be estopped from denying its duty to defend a slander action because it specifically agreed to insure against suits for slander. However, where public policy forbids a particular insurance contract, "public policy [also] forbids the accomplishment of the result by an estoppel." *Northwestern National Casualty Co. v. McNulty,* 307 F.2d 432, 442 (CA 5, 1962). Moreover, the slander clause might well refer only to the Nursing Home's vicarious liability for the acts of non-administrative personnel. *Cf. Glens Falls Indemnity Co. v. Atlantic Building Corp.,* 199 F.2d 60, 62 (CA 4, 1952) (drawing same distinction with regard to assault clause); *Armstrong v. Security Insurance Group,* 292 Ala. 27, 288 So.2d 134 (1973) (same).

3. In Alabama, the alter ego of a corporation may be either a sole or controlling owner. *U.S. v. Industrial Crane & Manuf. Corp.,* 492 F.2d 772, 774 (CA 5, 1974); *Ex parte City Sales Co.,* 264 Ala. 637, 639, 88 So.2d 668, 669 (1956). Moreover, the manager of operations may also be the alter ego of a corporation. *Buchanan Contracting Co. v. Denson,* 262 Ala. 592, 594, 80 So.2d 614, 615 (1955). Hazel Patterson is both the controlling owner and a general manager of the Talledega Nursing Home.

defend is not determined solely by the bare allegations of the complaint. *Ladner & Co. v. Southern Guaranty Ins. Co., supra,* 347 So.2d at 103; *Alabama Farm Bureau Mutual Cas. Ins. Co. v. Harris,* 279 Ala. 326, 328, 184 So.2d 837, 838 (1966). However, in this case, as in *Ladner,* "there is nothing in the record * * * to indicate that the plaintiffs . . . are asserting any theory of liability" other than deliberate and intentional wrongs. 347 So.2d at 103. There is no duty to defend the cases in their present posture.

The judgment below is AFFIRMED.

FIRST BANK (N.A.)—BILLINGS v. TRANSAMERICA INSURANCE COMPANY

Supreme Court of Montana, 1984.
209 Mont. 93, 679 P.2d 1217.

GULBRANDSON, Justice.

The United States District Court for the District of Montana has certified two questions to this Court for instructions concerning Montana law.

First Bank Billings has been named a defendant in three wrongful repossession cases, two of which have been filed in the District Court of the Thirteenth Judicial District, Yellowstone County, and one in the United States District Court for the District of Montana. Transamerica has undertaken the defense of First Bank, but has reserved its rights under its insurance contract with the bank and has denied any coverage for punitive damages under this contract. Transamerica argues that the public policy of Montana forbids such coverage. On motion of First Bank, the United States District Court has certified the following questions to this Court:

(1) Does the public policy of Montana permit insurance coverage of punitive damages?

(2) If the public policy of Montana does not *generally* permit insurance coverage of punitive damages, would it nevertheless permit coverage for punitive damages for which a banking corporation is or could be held liable by reasons of the acts of its employees?

For the reasons stated below, we conclude in response to the first question that insurance coverage of punitive damages is not a violation of public policy. Thus, we need not address the substance of the second question.

Counsel for First Bank have presented ten considerations in support of permitting insurance coverage of punitive damages. Transamerica has mounted a strong challenge to all of these considerations. We recognize that there is considerable authority supporting the positions of both parties. See generally Annot., 16 ALR 4th 11 (1982) (comparing and contrasting different views on liability insurance coverage as extending to liability for punitive or exemplary damages). We note, however, that most of the important decisions, as well as the major arguments of the parties, emphasize three primary considerations as ultimately dispositive of the questions before us. These are (1) public policy as expressed in constitutions and statutes; (2) the purpose of punitive damages; and (3) the circumstances under which punitive damages become available to aggrieved plaintiffs. Although we address these matters separately in this opinion, we recognize that they are interrelated to a high degree, and we therefore are careful not to sever the important ties that bind them together. * * *

SOURCES OF PUBLIC POLICY IN MONTANA

"Public policy is that principle of law which holds that no citizen can lawfully do that which has a tendency to be injurious to the public or against public good." *Spauling v. Maillet* (1920), 57 Mont. 318, 323, 188 P. 377, 378–9. Public policy is typically found "in the constitution and the laws and the course of administration." *St. Louis Mining & Milling Co. v. Montana Mining Co.* (1898), 171 U.S. 650, 655, 19 S.Ct. 61, 63, 43 L.Ed. 320, 322. In determining the public policy of this state, legislative enactments must yield to constitutional provisions, and judicial decisions must recognize and yield to constitutional provisions and legislative enactments. *Progressive Life Ins. Co. v. Dean* (1936), 192 Ark. 1152, 97 S.W.2d 62; *Electrical Contractors' Ass'n v. A.S. Schulman Elec. Co.* (1945), 391 Ill. 333, 63 N.E.2d 392. Judicial decisions are a superior repository of statements about public policy only in the absence of constitutional and valid legislative declarations. *State ex rel. Holt v. District Court* (1936), 103 Mont. 438, 446, 63 P.2d 1026; *State v. Gateway Mortuaries, Inc.* (1930), 87 Mont. 225, 235, 287 P. 156, 157.

PUBLIC POLICY AS EXPRESSED IN THE CONSTITUTION AND STATUTES

We find nothing in the Montana Constitution declaring a public policy on the question before us. We therefore turn to relevant statutes and case law construing the same.

Prior to adoption of this state's comprehensive insurance code, Sections 33–1–101 et seq., MCA, the law of Montana provided that "[a]n insurer is not liable for a loss caused by the willful act of the insured; but he is not exonerated by the negligence of the insured, or of his agents or others." Section 40–604, R.C.M. 1947 [repealed 1959]. This statute was based on Cal.Ins.Code Section 533 (West 1972), which has been construed to prohibit insurance coverage of punitive damages in most instances in California. See, e.g., *City Products Corp. v. Globe Indem. Co.* (1979), 88 Cal.App.3d 31, 151 Cal.Rptr. 494. See generally Comment, *Insurance for Punitive Damages: A Reevaluation*, 28 Hastings L.J. 431, 446–58 (1976) (discussion of California public policy against insurance coverage of punitive damages). Section 40–604 is no longer law in Montana, having been repealed upon adoption in 1959 of the insurance code. Transamerica argues that repeal "does not mean that the legislature intended to bless the sins of cheats, frauds, and oppressors, and absolve them from wrongdoing." While there is some truth in this assertion, we conclude that not even Transamerica would argue that a repealed statute has a life beyond the grave. If there is a public policy against permitting coverage, it must flow from an existing statute.

Our attention is also directed to the punitive damages law, Section 27–1–221, MCA, which provides that:

"[i]n any action for a breach of an obligation not arising from contract where the defendant has been guilty of oppression, fraud, or malice, actual or presumed, the jury, in addition to the actual damages, may give damages for the sake of example and by way of punishing the defendant."

There is nothing in this statute amounting to an express statement on the public policy issue before us. Nevertheless, Transamerica reasons syllogistically that, because punishment is an explicit aim of applying punitive damages, and because punishment, to be such, must cause its recipient to suffer, there can be no punishment if a defendant is permitted to, in effect, "shift" the financial burden of the imposed punishment to his or her insurance carrier. Transamerica thus concludes that a public policy against coverage emanates from the concept of punishment as embodied in the statute. This is the conclusion reached by courts in some states with the same or similar punitive damages laws, see, e.g., *City Products, supra* (construing Cal.Civ.Code Section 3294, which contains virtually the same language as Section 27–1–221). Although we are impressed with the reasoning behind Transamerica's argument, we reject it, for reasons discussed *infra,* as an inaccurate expression of the practical consequences of applying punitive damages law in some cases in Montana.

Transamerica also directs our attention to Section 28–11–302, MCA, which provides that "[a]n agreement to indemnify a person against an act thereafter to be done is void if the act be known by such person, at the time of doing it, to be unlawful." Transamerica reasons that, because insurance is a contract of indemnity, Section 28–11–302 operates as an express policy against coverage for tortious acts warranting imposition of punitive damages. We reject this interpretation.

Modern insurance contracts typically provide coverage for a host of tortious activities, with the assurance that the insured will be indemnified at least for compensatory damages arising from unlawful conduct by the insured; e.g., libel and slander, malicious prosecution, etc. Even Transamerica would not argue that Section 28–11–302 erects a bar to liability insurance for compensatory damages, be they awarded for ordinary negligence or malicious, fraudulent or oppressive conduct. The need to reduce financial risks and promote economic stability in modern society has rendered this statute applicable only to conduct defined as criminal.

In summary, we find no express policy by the legislature on the subject of insurance coverage for punitive damages. Although reasoned arguments can be made for reading some kind of prohibition into the language of the punitive damages statute, we decline to do so without first examining judicial construction of that statute and then considering the practical consequences of awarding punitive damages.

PUBLIC POLICY IN LIGHT OF JUDICIAL DECISIONS

As noted above, a major aim of awarding punitive damages is punishment of the defendant for oppressive, fraudulent or malicious conduct. We have also recognized that an award of punitive damages can serve as a deterrent to like conduct by other individuals. *First Security Bank v. Goddard* (1979), 181 Mont. 407, 423, 593 P.2d 1040, 1049; *Butcher v. Petranek* (1979), 181 Mont. 358, 363, 593 P.2d 743, 745. Whether both goals will be served adequately by permitting insurance coverage of punitive damages has been the principal concern of courts that have already addressed the coverage question.

Several courts have followed the lead of the Court of Appeals of the Fifth Circuit and have concluded that the mutual goals of punishment and deterrence are defeated if coverage is permitted. In *Northwestern Nat'l Cas. Co. v. McNulty* (5th Cir.1962), 307 F.2d 432, Circuit Judge John Minor Wisdom made this oft-quoted observation:

> "Where a person is able to insure himself against punishment he gains a freedom of misconduct inconsistent with the establishment of sanctions against such misconduct. It is not disputed that insurance against criminal fines or penalties would be void as violative of public policy. The same public policy should invalidate any contract of insurance against the civil punishment that punitive damages represent.

> "The policy considerations in a state where ＊ ＊ ＊ punitive damages are awarded for punishment and deterrence, would seem to require that the damages rest ultimately as well as nominally on the party actually responsible for the wrong. If that person were permitted to shift the burden to an insurance company, punitive damages would serve no useful purpose. Such damages do not compensate the plaintiff for his injury, since compensatory damages already have made the plaintiff whole. And there is no point in punishing the insurance company; it has done no wrong. In actual fact, of course, and considering the extent to which the public is insured, the burden would ultimately come to rest not on the insurance companies but on the public, since the added liability to the insurance companies would be passed along to the premium payers. Society would then be punishing itself for the wrong committed by the insured."

307 F.2d at 440–41. For similar views, see *City Products Corp., supra*; *Ford Motor Co. v. Home Ins. Co.* (1981), 116 Cal.App.3d 374, 172 Cal. Rptr. 59; *Hartford Acc. & Indem. Co. v. Village of Hempstead* (1979), 48 N.Y.2d 218, 397 N.E.2d 737, 422 N.Y.S.2d 47; *First Nat'l Bank of St. Mary's v. Fidelity & Deposit Co.* (1978), 283 Md. 228, 389 A.2d 359, 367

(Levine J., dissenting); *Harrell v. Travelers Indem. Co.* (1977), 279 Or. 199, 567 P.2d 1013, 1022 (Holman, J., dissenting).

Upon reflection, we grant the intellectual appeal of Judge Wisdom's reasoning, and recognize that it has been both praised and followed in other jurisdictions. Nevertheless, we find that this reasoning does not address the substance of punitive damages law as applied in Montana. To determine public policy concerning insurance coverage of punitive damages solely on deductive conclusions like those articulated by Judge Wisdom "is to lean upon a slender reed." *Missouri v. Holland* (1920), 252 U.S. 416, 434, 40 S.Ct. 382, 384, 64 L.Ed. 641, 648.

Oregon Supreme Court Justice Hans Linde correctly observed in his concurring opinion in *Harrell, supra,* that "[a] court-made public policy against otherwise lawful liability insurance can be defended, not *because* the purpose of punitive damages is always deterrence and *because* insurance will always destroy their deterrent effect, but only *when* these considerations apply." (emphasis his). 279 Or. 199, 567 P.2d at 1029. Empirical observation informs us that many kinds of willful and wanton conduct are never successfully deterred by punitive damage awards. This is especially true in automobile accident cases. See, e.g., the discussion in *Lazenby v. Universal Underwriters Ins. Co.* (1964), 214 Tenn. 639, 383 S.W.2d 1, concerning the failure of civil and criminal sanctions to deter wrongful conduct on the highways. We have few doubts that the deterrent impact is minimal in cases involving other types of tortious conduct. This leaves punishment as perhaps the only effectively realizable goal of awarding punitive damages. However, as will be pointed out in the discussion *infra,* punishment in the context of punitive damages may come as a wholly unanticipated aspect of one's conduct, thus weakening the case against permitting insurance coverage of all punitive damage awards.

In the instant dispute, First Bank fears that its insurance contract with Transamerica will become virtually worthless if it is exposed to punitive damage awards without the possibility of coverage. The Bank also claims that such a fine line exists between conduct justifying imposition of punitive damages and conduct not justifying such damages that permitting coverage is not in violation of public policy. Both arguments warrant serious attention.

The contract issued by Transamerica to First Bank is not unlike many insurance agreements. It includes coverage for false arrest, detention, or imprisonment, malicious prosecution, wrongful entry or eviction, libel and slander, racial or religious discrimination, and wrongful repossession. All of these torts give rise to claims for punitive damages; on this there is no dispute. In many cases involving these torts, actual damages may be minimal, but the punitive damages extremely high. Indeed, many claims for relief are not made financially worthwhile without the prospect of recovering punitive damages. See *Harrel,* supra, 279 Or. 199, 567 P.2d at 1029 (Linde, J., concurring). Assuming that coverage was deemed contrary to public policy, and in the event of minimal, if any compensatory damages, an insured facing a significant award of punitives would receive little solace from what would amount to a worthless insurance policy.

The "fine-line" problem raised by First Bank also suggests that a public policy against coverage would have less than desirable results, especially where the defendant is again assessed a particularly large punitive damage award. A consistent theme running through cases holding that public policy does not forbid insurance coverage is that juries and judges typically award punitives for a broad range of conduct not often described as willful or wanton, but as merely reckless or unjustifiable. When combined with the possibility that different fact finders in similar fact situations may reach differing conclusions as to the availability of punitive damages, the argument for denial of coverage becomes difficult to sustain. See *Skyline Harvestore Systems, Inc. v. Centennial Ins. Co.* (Iowa 1983), 331 N.W.2d 106; *First Nat'l Bank of St. Mary's,* supra; *Harrel,* supra; *Lazenby,* supra. See also Comment, *Insurance Coverage of Punitive Damages,* 84 Dick.L.Rev. 221, 231–33 (1980). First Bank also emphasizes, and not without good reason, that a defendant may be subject to a punitive damage award for conduct not considered or known to be wrongful prior to imposition of the award. See, e.g., *Gates v. Life of Montana Ins. Co.* (Mont.1983), 668 P.2d 213, 40 St.Rep. 1287 (reinstating punitive damage award against defendant for conduct which at time committed was not actionable). In these instances, forbidding coverage after the fact may work an injustice to unsuspecting defendants.

We have recently attempted to come to grips with the problem of uncertainty in the area of punitive damages. In *Owens v. Parker Drilling Co.* (Mont.1984), 676 P.2d 162, 41 St.Rep. 66, this Court acknowledged the expanded availability of punitive damage awards based on concepts like gross negligence, recklessness and unjustifiability. With respect to presumed malice as a ground specified in Section 27–1–221, MCA, for imposing exemplary or punitive damages, this Court adopted the following standard:

> "When a person knows or has reason to know of facts which create a high degree of risk of harm to the substantial interests of another, and either deliberately proceeds to act in conscious disregard of or indifference to that risk, or recklessly proceeds in unreasonable disregard of or indifference to that risk, his conduct meets the standard of willful, wanton, and/or reckless to which the law of this State will allow imposition of punitive damages on the basis of presumed malice."

Owens, supra, 676 P.2d 162, 41 St.Rep. at 69. Although we have described this standard as "more definitive and perhaps more stringent than those of the past," *Owens,* supra, 676 P.2d 162, 41 St.Rep. at 69, we acknowledge that fact-finders may still wrestle with concepts like recklessness and reasonableness, such that defendants may not know that their conduct constituted presumed malice until after trial, and that a defendant in one case may never know the sting of punitive damages while another defendant in a similar case may be faced with financing a sizeable award. Similarly, we have yet to work out a definitive standard for "oppression" within the meaning of Section 27–1–221.

Even though we are further down the road to refining the concept of punitive damages than are many other state courts, the law is still in such a state of flux as to warrant caution on the issue of whether public policy prohibits coverage of punitive damages in all cases. We therefore decline the opportunity to define limits for insurance coverage of punitive damages. Insurance companies are more than capable of evaluating risks and deciding whether they will offer policies to indemnify all or some conduct determined by judges or juries to be malicious, fraudulent or oppressive. A likely response to this opinion by some carriers may be the drafting of specific exclusions of coverage of punitive damages. However, the fact that some individuals may be willing to pay higher premiums for such coverage may convince carriers to extend coverage in some situations. It is conceivable that a combination of different approaches by insurance companies may result in a delineation of the limits of coverage better than anything this Court could establish.

CONCLUSION

We find that providing insurance coverage of punitive damages is not contrary to public policy. Transamerica admittedly has set forth a strong argument in support of an opposite holding, but we find the consequences of adopting that position unacceptable. The problems posed by insurance coverage of punitive damages are unquestionably like those inherent in the Gordian Knot. Unlike Alexander the Great, however, we cannot make a clean slice through our version of the Knot, in order to unravel all the aspects of the question before us, without working an injustice to many policy holders. Alexander dealt only with an inanimate object; we deal with people. Use of the judicial sword therefore is inappropriate in this case. Here, we must "untie" the knot, painstaking as the process may be. Until such time that the law of punitive damages is more certain and predictable, or until the legislature alters the law of punitive damages or expressly declares a policy against coverage in all cases, we leave the decision of whether coverage will be permitted to the insurance carriers and other customers.

Notes and Questions

1. *What Is Intentional?* Many courts hold, as did *Talledega*, that insurance against intentional wrongdoing violates public policy. Most liability and property insurance policies contain express exclusions of coverage (or limitations contained in the insuring agreement itself) for harm that is intentionally caused. The phrasing of these provisions varies; the most common excludes coverage of harm that is "either

expected or intended from the standpoint of the insured." Does the decision in *Talledega* provide any guidance regarding the relation between this sort of an exclusion and the public policy against insuring for intentional harm? Do the two coincide, or is the latter broader than the former?

Even setting aside this problem, other tort and insurance concepts are not completely congruent. Consequently, it may be difficult to know whether the allegations of a complaint state a claim beyond the scope of coverage, whether defined by policy provisions alone or public policy as well. For example, under certain circumstances, as a matter of federal constitutional law, a public official may not recover for a libel or slander without proof that the defamatory statement was made with "actual malice." The U.S. Supreme Court has defined as knowledge that the statement is false or reckless disregard of whether the statement is true or false. See *New York Times Company v. Sullivan,* 376 U.S. 254, 84 S.Ct. 710, 11 L.Ed.2d 686 (1964). How would you determine whether allegations of libel brought by a public official against a newspaper fall within the *Talledega* rule? Cf. *Greater Palm Beach Symphony Ass'n v. Hughes,* 441 So.2d 1171 (Fla.Dist.Ct.App.1983), in which the insurer was required to defend a libel and slander action in which some counts of the complaint contained no allegations of malicious intent.

2. *Does the Policy Provide Coverage?* The courts are divided on the question whether a basic liability insurance policy that covers the insured against liability for "damages" covers liability for punitive damages. The majority of courts hold that the standard policy does provide such coverage. See, e.g., *Public Service Mutual Insurance Company v. Goldfarb,* 53 N.Y.2d 392, 442 N.Y.S.2d 422, 425 N.E.2d 810 (1981); *Greenwood Cemetery, Inc. v. Travelers Indemnity Company,* 238 Ga. 313, 232 S.E.2d 910 (1977). South Carolina apparently *requires* that certain auto liability insurance policies include coverage against liability for punitive damages. S.C.Code § 38–77–30(4). In other states, whether the provision of such coverage violates public policy is a separate question. An express exclusion of coverage against liability for punitive damages will negate the inference that such coverage is intended, but most liability policies do not contain such an exclusion. When ISO attempted to introduce such an exclusion into general liability policies in 1977, it was met with a storm of protest from the insurance industry, and the exclusion was withdrawn. See *Business Insurance,* April 3, 1978, page 1.

3. *The Merits of the Issue.* If a state's public policy already precludes insurance against intentionally-caused harm, what is added by precluding insurance against liability for punitive damages? A rule that punitive damages are not insurable would eliminate case-by-case determination of whether the harm was caused intentionally. But would such a *per se* rule be so overbroad as to preclude coverage of a range of liabilities that should be insurable? The issue has been addressed in detail in the literature. See, e.g., Walden, The Publicly

Held Corporation and the Insurability of Punitive Damages, 53 Fordham L.Rev. 1383 (1985); King, The Insurability of Punitive Damages: A New Solution to an Old Dilemma, 16 Wake Forest L.Rev. 345 (1980).

STRICKLAND v. GULF LIFE INSURANCE COMPANY

Supreme Court of Georgia, 1978.
240 Ga. 723, 242 S.E.2d 148.

UNDERCOFLER, Presiding Justice.

This is a certiorari. *Strickland v. Gulf Life Ins. Co.*, 143 Ga.App. 67, 237 S.E.2d 530 (1977). It involves a life-accident policy issued in 1946 which, among other things, insures against the loss of a leg. The policy provides coverage if within 90 days of the injury there is "dismemberment by severance." Strickland injured his right lower leg. Medical efforts to save the leg continued for 118 days. They proved unsuccessful and the leg was amputated. Gulf Life denied coverage because severance of the leg was beyond the 90 day limitation. The trial court granted Gulf Life's motion for summary judgment. The Court of Appeals affirmed. We reverse in order that the trial court may consider in the light of this opinion Strickland's pleadings that the condition requiring severance within 90 days is contrary to public policy.

The Court of Appeals, in considering Strickland's appeal from the trial court's grant of summary judgment in favor of the insurance company, relied on our case of *State Farm Mutual Automobile Ins. Co. v. Sewell*, 223 Ga. 31, 153 S.E.2d 432 (1967), which it had reluctantly followed earlier in *Travelers Ins. Co. v. Pratt*, 130 Ga.App. 331, 203 S.E.2d 302 (1973) and *Boyes v. Continental Ins. Co.*, 139 Ga.App. 609, 229 S.E.2d 75 (1976).

In *Sewell* and *Boyes*, the issue was whether the loss incurred was the loss covered by the policy. The plaintiff in *Sewell* had suffered partial loss of his vision; he could make out images and colors and retained some peripheral vision. The Court of Appeals, in *State Farm Mutual Ins. Co. v. Sewell*, 114 Ga.App. 331, 151 S.E.2d 231 (1966), and in *Georgia Life & Health Ins. Co. v. Sewell*, 113 Ga.App. 443, 148 S.E.2d 447 (1966), construed the policy language, "the irrecoverable loss of the entire sight," as meaning a loss of sight "for all practical purposes" and affirmed such a charge given in the trial court. This court reversed, holding that the word "entire" had to be construed as meaning entire.

Similarly in *Boyes*, supra, the Court of Appeals, following *Sewell*, 223 Ga. 31, 153 S.E.2d 432, supra, held that the total loss of use of the plaintiff's left arm was not covered by an insurance policy covering only a loss of a member by severance. This court denied certiorari.

A time limitation, as is involved in the case now before us, was presented to the Court of Appeals in *Pratt*, supra. The plaintiff's left foot had been injured in a hunting accident, but was not amputated for eighteen months. During this time he was under constant treatment to avoid the amputation. Although the leg as originally injured was completely useless, there remained the possibility that regeneration might occur. It did not, and amputation was eventually necessary. The policy covered a loss by severance within 90 days of the injury. At that point, the plaintiff's leg was still in a cast. The Court of Appeals, relying on *Sewell,* 223 Ga. 31, 153 S.E.2d 432, supra, held that, since the policy required severance within 90 days, rather than merely loss of use during that time, the insurance company was not liable for the loss. Certiorari was denied by a divided court.

The plaintiff raised the public policy argument regarding the time limitation now before us in *Pratt,* but the Court of Appeals denied the challenge on the authority of *Randall v. State Mutual Ins. Co.,* 112 Ga. App. 268, 145 S.E.2d 41 (1965) (death not within 90 days), *Metropolitan Life Ins. Co. v. Jackson,* 79 Ga.App. 263, 53 S.E.2d 378 (1949) (loss of sight not within 90 days) and *Bennett v. Life & Cas. Ins. Co.,* 60 Ga.App. 228, 3 S.E.2d 794 (1939) (death not within 30 days). In all of these cases, the Court of Appeals had held that time limitations in an insurance policy were "valid." This court has not directly ruled on this issue. However, "[s]tandardized contracts such as insurance policies, drafted by powerful commercial units and put before individuals on the 'accept this or get nothing' basis, are carefully scrutinized by the courts for the purpose of avoiding enforcement of 'unconscionable' clauses." Corbin, Contracts § 1376, p. 21.

Where loss of a limb is involved at an arbitrary point in time, here 90 days, the insured under these cases is confronted with the ugly choice whether to continue treatment and retain hope of regaining the use of his leg or to amputate his leg in order to be eligible for insurance benefits which he would forgo if amputation became necessary at a later time. We find an insurance limitation forcing such a gruesome choice may be unreasonable and thus may be void as against public policy.

Finding such a limitation unreasonable is not without precedent. In *Burne v. Franklin Life Ins. Co.,* 451 Pa. 218, 301 A.2d 799, 801 (1973), a pedestrian had been struck by an automobile and had lain in a vegetative state for 4½ years. The insurance company paid the life policy, but refused to pay the double indemnity accidental death benefits which were "payable only if ' * * * such death occurred * * * within ninety days from the date of the accident.' "

As stated in *Burne,* supra, 301 A.2d at pp. 801–802 [footnote omitted.], "[t]here are strong public policy reasons which militate against the enforceability of the ninety day limitation. The provision has its origins at a much earlier stage of medicine. Accordingly, the leading [Pennsylvania] case construing the provision predates three decades of progress in the field of curative medicine. Advancements made during that period have enabled the medical profession to become startlingly adept at delaying death for indeterminate periods. Physicians and surgeons now stand at the very citadel of death, possessing the awesome responsibility of sometimes deciding whether and what measure should be used to prolong, even though momentarily, an individual's life. The legal and ethical issues attending such deliberations are gravely complex.

"The result reached by the trial court presents a gruesome paradox indeed—it would permit double indemnity recovery for the death of an accident victim who dies instantly or within ninety days of an accident, but would deny such recovery for the death of an accident victim who endures the agony of prolonged illness, suffers longer, and necessitates greater expense by his family in hopes of sustaining life even momentarily beyond the ninety day period. To predicate liability under a life insurance policy upon death occurring only on or prior to a specific date, while denying policy recovery if death occurs after that fixed date, offends the basic concepts and fundamental objectives of life insurance and [is] contrary to public policy. Hence, the ninety day limitation is unenforceable.

"All must recognize the mental anguish that quite naturally accompanies these tragic occurrences. Surely that anguish ought not to be aggravated in cases of this kind with concerns of whether the moment of death permits or defeats the double indemnity claim. So too, the decisions as to what medical treatment should be accorded an accident victim should be unhampered by considerations which might have a tendency to encourage something less than the maximum medical care on penalty of financial loss if such care succeeds in extending life beyond the 90th day. All such factors should, wherever possible, be removed from the antiseptic halls of the hospital. Rejection of the arbitrary ninety day provision does exactly that."

The New Jersey court has also found this reasoning persuasive. "The rule in almost every jurisdiction which has considered the question is that the time limitations set forth in the policy are controlling and that recovery must be denied in a case such as the present one. See Appleman, Insurance Law and Practice (2d ed. 1963), § 612. However, a recent decision by the Supreme Court of Pennsylvania has held that such time limitations are unenforceable and has allowed recovery where death by accident occurred well after the period stipulated in the policy. [Cit. omitted.] Although it is presently very much a minority rule, I am persuaded that the rule announced in Burne is the better rule and should be followed." *Karl v. New York Life Ins. Co.*, 139 N.J. Super. 318, 353 A.2d 564, 565 (1976). The court thus allowed the beneficiary of a man who had sustained a skull injury in a criminal assault to recover under the accidental double indemnity provisions in his two policies, which contained 90 and 120 day limitations, even though he died 11 months after the assault.

We note further that in *Karl, supra,* the court considered the question whether with the minimal cost[1] of the accidental death benefit, it would be unfair to the insurance company to ignore these

---

1. In the case before us, Strickland has already paid more in premiums than the face amount of the policy.

time limitations in light of the company's economic risk calculations. It concluded, however, that the real purpose of the time limitation was to limit disputes concerning the causal connection between the death and the accident rather than because of any economic relationship between the premium and the time limitation. Also, the court observed that the reason the cost of accidental death policies was so low was that relatively few deaths occur because of accidents.[2]

In *INA Insurance Co. v. Commonwealth Ins. Dept.,* 376 A.2d 670 (Pa.Cmwlth.1977), the insurance company also argued that the causation problem was the main reason for these time limitations. That court rejected the argument, observing that the burden was on the claimant[3] to establish the causative relationship, and held that causation was not a weighty enough problem to deny benefits arbitrarily to those surviving beyond the time limitation set out in the policy, who had died as a result of the accident. Following *Burne,* the court upheld the insurance commissioner's ruling[4] that all similar time limitations in accident policies are arbitrary and unreasonable and thus against public policy.

"[I]t may be pointed out that 'liberty of contract' as that term is used by its admirers includes two very different elements. These are the privilege of doing the acts constituting the transaction and the power to make it legally operative. One does not have 'liberty of contract' unless organized society both forbears and enforces, forbears to penalize him for making his bargain and enforces it for him after it is made.

"This is the 'liberty of contract' that has so often been extolled as one of the great boons of modern democratic civilization, as one of the principal causes of prosperity and comfort. And yet the very fact that a chapter on 'legality' of contract must be written shows that we have never had and never shall have unlimited liberty of contract, either in its phase of societal forbearance or in its phase of societal enforcement. There are many contract transactions that are definitely forbidden by the law, forbidden under pains and penalties assessed for crime and tort; and there are many more such transactions that are denied judicial enforcement, even though their makers are not subjected to affirmative pains and penalties." Corbin, Contracts § 1376, p. 20.

Corbin, in his treatise on contracts, also observes that the declaration of public policy is the proper function of the courts, as well as of the legislature. "Constitutions and statutes are declarations of public

---

2. In the opinion, the court quotes that only 6.17% of all deaths in the United States in 1967 resulted from accidents. *Karl v. New York Life Insurance Co., supra,* 353 A.2d p. 569.

3. The court established a clear and convincing standard for providing causation where the death occurs after the time limitation in the policy.

4. We note that in the Georgia Insurance Code, Code Ann. ch. 56, the legislature mandates that "[t]he Commissioner shall disapprove any such form [contract] * * * (5) if it contains provisions which are *unfair or inequitable or contrary to the public policy of this State,* or would, because such provisions are unclear or deceptively worded, encourage misrepresentation." Code Ann. § 56–2411. (Emphasis supplied.)

policy by bodies of men authorized to legislate. It is the function of the courts to interpret and apply these, so far as they go and so far as they are understandable. Some judges have thought that they must look solely to constitutions and statutes and to earlier decisions interpreting and applying them as the sources from which they may determine what public policy requires. This is far from true, even though these are the sources that are first to be considered and that often may be conclusive.[5]

" *   *   *

"In determining what public policy requires, there is no limit whatever to the 'sources' to which the court is permitted to go; and there is no limit to the 'evidence' that the court may cause to be produced, *   *   *" 6A Corbin, Contracts, § 1375, pp. 15–19. Then, the validity of the contract in question is one of law for the court.[6] 17A C.J.S. Contracts § 615 p. 1238.

Although we are impressed by the persuasive reasoning of the above authorities, we do not here reach the question of law whether all such policy limitations are void as against public policy, nor indeed whether the 90 days severance clause before us is unenforceable. The trial court granted summary judgment in favor of the insurance company on the authority of *Sewell, Pratt,* and *Boyes, supra,* and on the basis of the pleadings, the contract of insurance and a stipulation of fact by counsel. The stipulated facts included only the date Strickland had been injured and the date over 90 days later that his right lower leg had been amputated, naming the doctor and place of the amputation. No evidence was produced on the issue, raised in Strickland's pleadings, that the contract was unreasonable, and thus void as against public policy. We are reluctant to make such an important pronouncement without further evidence. For example, medical evidence reported in *Reliance Ins. Co. v. Kinman,* 252 Ark. 1168, 483 S.W.2d 166 (1972), that it takes about 18 months for bone and nerve tissue to regenerate would

5. " 'Public policy is the cornerstone—the foundation of all constitutions, statutes, and judicial decisions, and its latitude and longitude, its height and its depth, greater than any or all of them. If this be not true, whence came the first judicial decision on matter of public policy? There was no precedent for it, else it would not have been the first.' *Pittsburgh, C, C & St. L.R. Co. v. Kinney,* 115 N.E. 505, 507, 95 Ohio St. 64, 67, quoted and applied in *Snyder v. Ridge Hill Memorial Park,* 22 N.E.2d 559, 61 Ohio App. 271 (1938)." Corbin, Contracts, § 1375, p. 15, n. 12. [footnote in original].

6. "When the validity of a contract is in issue before a court, the judge is obliged to make decision whatever the degree of his ignorance or wisdom. Before decision there should be some debate and much evidence; afterwards the decision is subject to criticism, by litigant and lawyer, by juryman and jurist, by the learner and the scholar. It is thus that the mores, the considered notions as to what makes for human welfare and survival are formed, to be constantly verified or altered in new cases, forever hammered on the anvil of life experience.

"The court can not postpone decision until all possible evidence is in. Sometimes the judge may properly take 'judicial notice' of what is common knowledge and generally held opinion. But it is never wise to jump to a conclusion or to disregard experience; and it is never necessary to decide an issue as to public policy without expert briefing of former decisions and without listening to the testimony of those whose interests are at stake and of disinterested and experienced observers." Corbin, Contracts § 1375, pp. 10–11. [Footnotes omitted].

be relevant to the reasonableness of the 90 day clause in this insurance policy. Other information important to the court's decision may include, for example, (1) the present state of medical science on rehabilitation of injured limbs; (2) whether the insured had a choice of other policies with other time limitations; (3) whether the time limitation is related to the economic risk of the insurance company and (4) whether there is a relationship between the time limitation and the difficulty of proving causation.

We reverse the Court of Appeals in order that the trial court may fully consider the public policy issue.

Judgment reversed.   *   *   *

BOWLES, Justice, dissenting.

As I read the opinion of the majority, I find only one conclusion reached—that the opinion of the Court of Appeals is reversed so that the matter may be referred back to the trial court to hear evidence, and *"fully consider"* the public policy issue.

Heretofore in Georgia, where the contract is unambiguous, our courts have been able to decide, without the benefit of evidentiary hearings, whether or not a given contract or clause in a given contract violates the public policy of this state. While I do not contend that it is impermissible for a trial judge to hear evidence to aid him in making such a decision, I conclude that the trial judge in this case made his determination based on his experience, common sense, general knowledge prevailing in his community regarding the habits and customs of his people, and prior decisions of our courts touching the question. He was not required by law to hear evidence.

Now, for the first time, we require the trial judge to receive or hear evidence on whether a given contract clause violates public policy. Having done so, he can again use his experience, common sense and general knowledge, and can again consider prior case law in making a determination as to whether or not the 90 day contract clause in question violates the public policy of this state. Thus, we are forcing him to do what he did not consider necessary in the first instance, in addition to his customary procedure.

The majority opinion does not specifically overrule *Travelers Insurance Co. v. Pratt,* 130 Ga.App. 331, 203 S.E.2d 302, which has heretofore decided the exact question contra to this position. But to support their argument the majority quotes approvingly from two decisions in other states representing the minority view in America and which are without precedent. The majority says, "An insurance limitation forcing such a gruesome choice may be unreasonable and thus may be void as against public policy." It also castigates "powerful commercial units" and suggests that the policy of insurance offered in this case may have been offered to the insured on an "accept this or get nothing basis."

The fundamental right of our citizens to legally contract; the fact that the right to contract is paramount public policy of our state and should not be interfered with lightly; and the fact that our appellate courts have heretofore ruled on the exact question one time, and similar questions many times, are disregarded. Unless there is some compelling reason to do so, we do the citizens of Georgia, the practicing lawyers and the lower courts an injustice when we attempt to overrule precedent without justification. I find no compelling reason, in this case, to deviate from the precedent laid down by this court in earlier cases.

I would affirm the opinion of the Court of Appeals without further ado.

I am authorized to state that Justice JORDAN joins in this dissent.

Notes and Questions

1. *Precedent.* Did the court adequately distinguish the holdings in its previous decisions in the *Sewell* and *Boyes* cases? Can you do so?

2. *An Evidentiary Condition?* Did the court do anything more than hold that under certain circumstances, the 90 day requirement is merely a non-exclusive evidentiary condition? Are you more or less comfortable with this approach in *Strickland* than in *Atwater Creamery,* supra (involving the forcible-entry requirement in a burglary insurance policy)? Why?

3. *Crazy Like a Fox?* At first glance the dissent's criticism of the court's remand in *Strickland* may seem well taken. Consider, however, what might have been entailed in fashioning a rule to govern all future cases. The logic of the opinion suggests that there may not be *any* time limit that is automatically valid, because all such limits may be open to challenge depending on the circumstances. But the opinion does not actually state such a rule. Rather than invalidate all such limits, or openly increase unpredictability by stating that such limits are sometimes valid but can always be questioned, the court sidestepped that issue by remanding. Do you support this approach, or would more candor have been preferable?

4. *Problem.* If you represented a disability insurer after the decision in *Strickland,* how (if at all) would you advise that future policies be drafted?

5. *A General Theory of Public Policy Restrictions?* After examining the cases on the issue in this Section, are you prepared to venture a principle or principles that are at the foundation of this field? Consider the following:

> An insurance policy provision violates public policy when a constitution or statute expressly or impliedly prohibits the aim or effect of the provision, when the provision unduly encourages moral hazard, or when the provision would force the insured to engage in unreasonable behavior in order to preserve coverage.

What are the strengths and weaknesses of this formulation?

Chapter Three

INSURANCE REGULATION

A. THE ALLOCATION OF POWERS

The appropriate starting point for any study of insurance regulation is the constitutional and statutory allocation of power between the federal government and the states. Although almost all authority to regulate insurance is currently allocated to the states, the nature of that allocation is complex. In 1869, the United States Supreme Court held, in *Paul v. Virginia,* 75 U.S. (8 Wall.) 168, 19 L.Ed. 357 (1869), that the issuance of an insurance policy is not a transaction of commerce. The result was that Congress had no authority under the Commerce Clause of the U.S. Constitution to regulate insurance. *Paul* squelched an incipient effort (ironically, as it turns out, by the insurance industry itself) to encourage federal rather than state regulation. When the Sherman Act was enacted in 1890, the case also made it clear that the Act's antitrust prohibitions could not be applied to anticompetitive actions involving insurance.

Authority to regulate insurance continued to rest at the state level for the next three-quarters of a century. Viewed from the present perspective, state regulation during this period was unsystematic. Over half the states established insurance departments and vested them with varying powers. The most prominent regulatory task was the assurance of insurer solvency. Other consumer protection authority was sometimes also established in these departments. For detailed discussions of the history of insurance regulation, see J. Day, Economic Regulation of Insurance in the United States (1970); E. Patterson, The Insurance Commissioner in the United States (1927); Kimball, The Purpose of Insurance Regulation: A Preliminary Inquiry in the Theory of Insurance Law, 45 Minn.L.Rev. 471 (1961).

This period came to an abrupt end with the decision in *United States v. South–Eastern Underwriters Association,* 322 U.S. 533, 64 S.Ct. 1162, 88 L.Ed. 1440 (1944). *South–Eastern Underwriters* overruled *Paul v. Virginia.* The case involved an indictment of a "rating bureau" and its member companies for violating the Sherman Act by agreeing to fix premium rates and boycott non-members. The Court held that insurance transactions such as this agreement are subject to federal regulation under the Commerce Clause. The Supreme Court's decision threw the insurance industry into a near panic, for the Court held not only that Congress has the power to regulate insurance; in addition, the effect of the holding was that Congress had already regulated insurance by enacting the Sherman Act and any number of other statutes

90

governing commerce among the states. Federal antitrust prohibitions therefore applied immediately to the business of insurance.

Nothing in *South–Eastern Underwriters,* however, either compelled Congress to exercise its power to regulate insurance or precluded it from allowing the states to exercise concurrent regulatory jurisdiction. The Court merely held that Congress could exercise this power and that to some extent it already had done so without knowing it with the enactment of the Sherman Act. The insurance industry promptly supported legislation prepared by the National Association of Insurance Commissioners (NAIC) that would return regulatory authority to the states. Enacted by Congress in 1945, this legislation is known as the McCarran–Ferguson Act.

The McCarran–Ferguson Act, 15 U.S.C. §§ 1011–15

§ 1011. Declaration of policy [Section 1.]

Congress declares that the continued regulation and taxation by the several States of the business of insurance is in the public interest, and that silence on the part of the Congress shall not be construed to impose any barrier to the regulation or taxation of such business by the several States.

§ 1012. Regulation by State law; Federal law relating specifically to insurance; applicability of certain Federal laws after June 30, 1948 [Section 2.]

(a) The business of insurance, and every person engaged therein, shall be subject to the laws of the several States which relate to the regulation or taxation of such business.

(b) No Act of Congress shall be construed to invalidate, impair, or supersede any law enacted by any State for the purpose of regulating the business of insurance, or which imposes a fee or tax upon such business, unless such Act specifically relates to the business of insurance: *Provided,* That after June 30, 1948, the Act of July 2, 1890, as amended, known as the Sherman Act, and the Act of October 15, 1914, as amended, known as the Clayton Act, and the Act of September 26, 1914, known as the Federal Trade Commission Act, as amended, shall be applicable to the business of insurance to the extent that such business is not regulated by State law.

§ 1013. Suspension until June 30, 1948, of application of certain Federal laws; Sherman Antitrust Act applicable to agreements to, or acts of, boycott, coercion, or intimidation [Section 3.]

(a) Until June 30, 1948, the Act of July 2, 1890, as amended, known as the Sherman Act, and the Act of October 15, 1914, as amended, known as the Clayton Act, and the Act of September 26, 1914, known as the Federal Trade Commission Act, and the Act of June 19, 1936, known as the Robinson–Patman Anti–Discrimination Act, shall not apply to the business of insurance or to acts in the conduct thereof.

(b) Nothing contained in this chapter shall render the said Sherman Act inapplicable to any agreement to boycott, coerce, or intimidate, or act of boycott, coercion, or intimidation.

Notes and Questions

1. *The Character of the Act.* Important as the McCarran–Ferguson Act is, it merely states some ground rules governing the allocation of federal and state regulatory powers. The Act itself does not regulate, nor does it require regulation by the states. Rather, it performs a quasi-constitutional function, by setting the terms under which legislative and administrative regulation may take place. See Kimball and Heaney, Emasculation of the McCarran–Ferguson Act: A Study in Judicial Activism, 1985 Utah L.Rev. 1.

2. *Questions Answered and Unanswered.* The Act can be understood as achieving this allocation of power through two devices. First, Section 2(b) removes most questions about whether federal legislation that does not specifically relate to the business of insurance impliedly preempts state regulation: it does not. Second, the Act provides that, where the states have exercised the regulatory authority which the removal of any implied preemption accords them, the federal antitrust laws (with the exceptions noted in Section 3) shall not apply to the business of insurance. If you had read the Act in 1945, what questions would you conclude it had left open? The last section of this Chapter addresses the answers the courts have given to the questions left open by the McCarran–Ferguson Act. We turn first, however, to the regulatory response that came very quickly from the states, and that continues to this day.

B. THE STATE REGULATORY RESPONSE

The states wasted no time in accepting the McCarran–Ferguson Act's invitation to regulate. Within several years, every state had enacted rate regulation legislation intended to satisfy the McCarran–Ferguson standard. See R. Jerry, Understanding Insurance Law 54 (1987). In virtually every state this legislation provided, among other things, that the official charged with the regulatory function (usually an "Insurance Commissioner") should assure that rates were not "excessive, inadequate, or unfairly discriminatory." Fine-tuning and elaboration followed over the next few decades. State insurance regulation today is a thriving if often criticized enterprise. The following Sections examine three different components of the process of regulation: the effort to assure insurer solvency, to protect consumers against excessive rates, and to assure that the risk classifications that insurers employ do not result in unfair discrimination. Note that in addition to these aspects of the process, most Insurance Commissioners have other authority—including, for example, to disapprove policy forms or provisions if they are inequitable or deceptive. For discussion of this function, see *Reserve Life Insurance Company v. Commissioner of Commerce,* 402 N.W.2d 631 (Minn.App.1987).

1. Regulation to Assure Solvency

State departments of insurance traditionally have considered assuring the solvency of companies selling insurance in their jurisdictions to be their first mission. Insurance is unlike most tangible products, because the insured receives only the insurer's promise to pay in the event that the insured suffers a future loss. That promise to pay is valuable only so long as the insurer making the promise is financially capable of performing it when an insured loss actually occurs.

Statutes in each jurisdiction therefore authorize Insurance Commissioners to license companies to sell insurance and to make compliance with other regulatory requirements designed to assure solvency a condition of licensure. These requirements include filing an "Annual Statement" containing financial data in a standard format, opening company records for examination by the Commissioner's office, complying with minimum capital and surplus requirements and investment restrictions, and submitting to the supervision of the Commissioner when an insolvent company is liquidated.

The detection and prevention of insurer insolvencies is designed to occur through examination of financial data submitted by each insurer, and through periodic and more detailed financial examinations. State laws usually require examinations every three to five years. The National Association of Insurance Commissioners (NAIC) coordinates "zone" examinations of companies that have a large volume of business in many states in order to avoid duplicate examinations. See United States General Accounting Office, Insurer Failures: Property/Casualty Insurer Insolvencies and State Guaranty Funds 11 (1987).

The NAIC uses an Insurance Regulatory Information System (IRIS) to apply diagnostic tests to the financial data submitted annually by insurance companies. The first phase of the IRIS program involves the development of eleven measures of financial condition based on such data as premiums received, investment yield, reserves, and surplus. For example, the *premium-to-surplus* ratio is a measure of the amount of capital available to an insurer in relation to its coverage obligations. Other things being equal, the higher the ratio, the greater the insurer's exposure. Insurers which do not meet specified standards for these ratios are designated for further review. The second phase of IRIS involves detailed examination of these companies, and further designation (usually on a confidential basis) of those in need of special regulatory attention. In 1986, for example, 590 companies, or 23.55 percent of the 2505 reviewed, fell into this category. Notwithstanding the IRIS system, insolvencies do occur, because of underpricing in order to encourage sales, underreserving of funds to cover losses, inability to collect reinsurance, poor management, fraud, or a combination of these factors. There were 65 insolvencies between 1983 and 1986. *Id.* at 13.

In the economy at large, the creditors of a debtor company bear the risk of its insolvency. Once secured creditors are paid, any remaining assets of the insolvent company normally are divided pro-rata among general creditors, who receive less than 100 percent of the amount due them. In contrast, in a few industries especially affecting the public interest such as banking and insurance, financial guarantees are provided to depositors and policyholders. In insurance a statutory system of insurance guaranty funds has developed, under which other insurers provide a limited guaranty of the insolvent company's obligations to its policyholders. As described below, how may these funds create a kind of moral hazard on the part of policyholders? On the part of insurers themselves?

United States General Accounting Office,

INSURER FAILURES: PROPERTY/CASUALTY INSURER INSOLVENCIES AND STATE GUARANTY FUNDS

26–37 (1987).

Property/casualty insurance guaranty funds exist in all states. Their purpose is to protect policyholders and claimants from the financial losses that could result from the insolvency of an insurance company. Claims against insolvent insurers are paid by the funds from assessments made on licensed companies in their states after a property/casualty insurer fails. * * *

A few states created property/casualty guaranty funds in the 1930s and 1940s because they were concerned that policyholders might be deprived of coverage, especially worker's compensation and auto coverage, if insurers became insolvent. However, the vast majority of states did not establish funds until the late 1960s and early 1970s, in response to the prospect that Congress might create a federal guaranty fund. * * *

State guaranty funds are basically similar in structure and in the way they work and generally parallel the NAIC's Model Act. New York's fund, however, is not patterned on the act and is therefore not included in this report's discussion of the funds except where specifically noted.

A guaranty fund, as envisioned in the Model Act, is administered by licensed insurers under the supervision of a state's insurance department. The Act prescribes that all insurers licensed within a state that write lines of insurance covered by the guaranty fund are automatically members of the guaranty fund. These members elect a board of directors, subject to approval by the insurance commissioner, which governs the fund (in some states, the commissioner of insurance is also a member of the board). Because the level of fund activity varies from state to state, the number and nature of the administrative staff vary. Some state funds have a full-time administrator and/or staff; others do not. A number of state funds combine administration on a regional basis—eight guaranty funds in the East are administered by a firm in Boston, while six funds in the Midwest and West are administered by a similar firm in Denver. Additionally, some funds handle claims by hiring claims people or by hiring the services of an insurance company. No matter how the funds are administered, however, the act provides for paying administrative costs out of insurers' assessments.

Assessments are made only when a property/casualty insurer fails. The definition of "failure," and thus the precise event that triggers operation of the funds, differs among states. Some states regard an insolvency order from a state court as sufficient to trigger a guaranty fund operation, while others require an order of liquidation from a court. There may be a significant length of time between when a company is declared insolvent (and placed in rehabilitation or conservation) and when it is ordered into liquidation. This situation can result in the payment of claims to some claimants, while others may have to wait until the guaranty funds they are covered by are activated.

Once an insurer is put into liquidation, all policies are declared to have terminated, usually 30 days after the date of failure. However, claims on the policy dating from before its termination are still valid. These will be paid out of the guaranty fund of the policyholder's state of residence (assuming that the policyholder does not have another policy to cover the claim) if the insolvent insurer was licensed in the policy-holder's state of residence. Under the Model Act, if the insurer was not licensed in the state, the policyholder or claimant is not entitled to file a claim with a guaranty fund but may seek payment through a claim on the failed insurer's estate, which is handled by a liquidator.

As each insolvency takes place, the guaranty fund estimates how much it will need to pay claims resulting from the insolvency, and then assesses member insurers. If the guaranty fund has underestimated the amount necessary, or if the amount cannot be collected because of limits on how much insurers can be assessed in a year, or if more claims are made after the initial insolvency, the process can be repeated in subsequent years. In most states insurers may recover their assessments at a later time, either through a rate increase or by an offset on premium taxes. All states have a limit on how much insurance companies can be assessed in a single year but this limit varies. In 27 states that limit is 2 percent of a member insurer's net direct premiums for the calendar year preceding the assessment, and 20 states have a limit of 1 percent. According to information provided by the NCIGF, guaranty funds have assessed insurers approximately $1.4 billion from November 1969 through December 1986. The net amount assessed during this period was $1.2 billion after refunds were made to member companies. *   *   *

State guaranty funds vary somewhat in the areas of insurance they cover. No fund covers reinsurance or surplus lines insurance (except in New Jersey). The Model Act recommends fund coverage for all kinds of direct insurance except life, title, surety, disability, credit, mortgage guaranty, and ocean marine insurance. While most states have followed this recommendation, some states provide different coverages. One state, for example, excludes only life and disability insurance and another excludes life, health, and annuities. Several states, on the other hand, have excluded additional types of insurance, such as home warranty, health contracts, and mutual protective insurance.

The NAIC Model Act recommends that state fund laws limit the maximum that can be collected from the fund on any one claim to the lesser of $300,000 or the amount of the insurance policy limit. Thirty-three states and the District of Columbia have followed that recommendation. Of the remainder, 14 funds (including Puerto Rico) have limits lower than $300,000 (5 at $150,000, 7 at $100,000, 2 at $50,000). Two funds have limits set at higher levels (one at $500,000 and one at $1 million). Michigan does not set any dollar figure, but sets the maximum in any 1 year as $\frac{1}{20}$ of 1 percent of premiums written by licensed insurers within the state that year. There is no limit on worker's compensation claims in 32 states and the District of Columbia.

The effect of these limits is that part or all of a claim may be paid, depending on the type of claim and the state of policyholder residence. If, for example, a business with $1 million theft coverage is burglarized and has a $500,000 claim against its insolvent insurer, the business could collect the entire claim if it were located in Rhode Island, more than half of it ($300,000) if it were located in Ohio, and one-tenth of it ($50,000) if located in Colorado. If a worker had a $500,000 worker's compensation claim against an insolvent insurer, he or she could collect the entire amount if a resident of Tennessee, but only $50,000 if a resident of neighboring Kentucky, because the former has no limit on worker's compensation claims and the latter does. * * *

Capacity of the Guaranty Funds

The increasing incidence of large company insolvencies has highlighted concerns about the capacity of the property/casualty guaranty fund system. However, there has been no agreement on how large the fund capacity should be nor on how to increase it.

Studies performed since 1984 by the AAI, the Insurance Services Office, Inc. (ISO), and the Illinois Department of Insurance attempted to determine whether the fund system could cover one or more large insurance company insolvencies. While the studies varied in their approach and implications on the scope of the capacity problem, they agreed that the fund system would have difficulty handling large-scale insolvencies.

- The AAI study, which was substantively based on industry averages, projected that in the first year after the insolvency, 38 assessment accounts in 31 states would not be sufficient to cover all costs. Also, 31 accounts in 29 states would not be sufficient in the second year.

- The Illinois study, which used the Reserve Insurance Company insolvency as its basis, projected fund capacity over a number of years. It found that in the first year after the insolvency, 60 assessment accounts in 37 states would not be sufficient to cover costs, 52 accounts in 34 states in the second year, and 41 accounts in 30 states in the third year.

- The study performed by the ISO used a number of hypothetical insolvencies rather than an actual one. ISO took the largest insurers in the United States and calculated the projected liability if each were to go insolvent. It found that the present system could handle any one large insurer insolvency. For example, an Aetna insolvency would require 97.9 percent of the nationwide total capacity of all state guaranty funds; an Allstate insolvency, 86.8 percent; a Hartford insolvency, 67.8 percent.

* * *

Notes and Questions

1. *Fund Structure.* Apart from the fundamental question whether guaranty funds should exist at all, the issues associated with the guaranty fund system can be divided into four categories: Who contributes? On what basis? Who recovers? On what basis?

Who contributes? Generally, insurers licensed to sell lines of insurance covered by a state's fund are subject to assessment. To what extent is this approach likely to reduce competitive activity among insurers in any given line?

On what basis? Premium volume is the most common basis for assessment. All states except New York assess after an insolvency occurs. That is, there is no "fund" to speak of pre-existing an insolvency. New York's fund is financed by pre-insolvency assessments, which cease when the size of the fund reaches a specified ceiling. Is it appropriate that solvent guarantors are allowed to recover their assessments through rate increases or credits against future state taxes on premiums? If so, which method is preferable?

Who recovers? Virtually all those insured by licensed property/casualty insurers are given claims against the fund. Guaranty fund statutes normally limit claims, however, to those concerning property within the state or made by a resident of the state. See, e.g., Ill.Ins. Code § 534.3; Tex.Ins. Code Ann. Art. 21.28–C § 5(2)(a) & (b). Life and disability insurance are sometimes excluded. Is the availability of social insurance against at least some of the losses covered by these excluded lines a sufficient explanation for the exclusion?

On what basis? Until recently there were very few decisions interpreting guaranty fund statutes. Almost all the growth in the case law now concerns this issue. A few examples follow:

a. The funds usually set a limit on the dollar amount of any one claim. Consequently, the definition of the term "claim" can be critically important. Courts interpreting the term generally hold that to the extent possible the term tracks the limits of liability provisions of the policy whose issuing company has become insolvent. See, e.g., *Fontenot v. Haight*, 764 P.2d 378 (Colo.App.1988); *Knipp v. Arizona Property & Casualty Insurance Guaranty Fund*, 156 Ariz. 137, 750 P.2d 895 (Ariz. App.1987).

b. Claimants generally may not collect from the guaranty fund when there is another solvent insurer available to pay the claim. See, e.g., Cal.Ins. Code Ann. § 1063.1(c)(7): " 'Covered claims' shall not include (a) any claim to the extent it is covered by any other insurance of a class covered by the provisions of this article available to any claimant." The issue then becomes what kinds of insurance fall into the same "class" as that sold by the insolvent company. For example, does a claimant's own uninsured motorist coverage fall into the same class as the liability insurance from which he wishes to collect? The courts are divided, in part because of differences in the provisions of the statutes. Compare *Rhinehart v. Hartford Casualty Insurance Company*, 91 N.C.App. 368, 371 S.E.2d 788 (1988) (set-off of UM coverage against guaranty-fund obligation required), with *Murray v. Montana Insurance Guaranty Association*, 175 Mont. 220, 573 P.2d 196 (1977) (no set-off).

c. Most states prohibit payment by the fund to any insurer, since the purpose of the funds is to protect policyholders alone. For the same reasons, assignments by covered individuals to insurers are apparently not guaranteed by the fund, at least in some states. See, e.g., *Ursin v. Insurance Guaranty Association*, 412 So.2d 1285 (La.1981).

d. Although guaranty funds are often considered to stand in the shoes of the insolvent insurer, they do not have all of the duties of insurers under the law. For example, states which have an Unfair Trade Practices Act regulating insurance companies do not apply it to the guaranty funds. *Isaacson v. California Insurance Guaranty Association*, 44 Cal.3d 775, 244 Cal.Rptr. 655, 750 P.2d 297 (1988); *Fernandez v. Florida Insurance Guaranty Association, Inc.*, 383 So.2d 974 (Fla.Dist. Ct.App.1980); *Vaughn v. Vaughn*, 23 Wash.App. 527, 597 P.2d 932 (1979). The guaranty fund is also not liable for any claim against an insolvent insurer which is not a claim under an insurance policy. *Crider v. Georgia Life & Health Insurance Guaranty Association*, 188 Ga.App. 407, 373 S.E.2d 30 (1988) (guaranty fund was not obligated to satisfy judgment for bad-faith penalties and attorney's fees against an insolvent insurer); *Rivera v. Southern American Fire Insurance Company*, 361 So.2d 193 (Fla.Dist.Ct.App.1978) (guaranty fund not vicariously liable for tortious acts of member insurers).

2. *Possible Reforms.* It seems obvious from the GAO study that the guaranty fund system is not financially capable of handling the simultaneous insolvency of two or more major insurers. A number of reforms have been suggested: raise the ceiling on assessments to 3 or 4

percent of annual premium volume; move to the pre-assessment approach in force in New York and accumulate funds sufficient to deal with the problem if it should occur; establish a state-run or federally operated company to insure individual insurers against the risk of insolvency above the financial capacity of the guaranty fund system. Which approach is most appealing?

3. *Selective Deregulation?* What adverse effects may flow from the American system of solvency assurance regulation and guaranty funds? Consider the following (intentionally) provocative argument:

> At present, when a business purchases insurance it may shop for price, terms of coverage, and service reputation; but the purchaser need not worry about the reliability of the insurer's promise to pay, because solvency is virtually assured. Current regulatory schemes discourage insurers from writing high uncertainty environmental insurance because all the assets of multiple-line insurers are vulnerable if one line suffers a loss. Similarly, non-traditional entrepreneurs are not permitted to enter ordinary insurance markets and compete with regulated insurers because they cannot provide the kind of assurances of solvency and reliability that actually have come to be part of the definition of modern insurance. [footnote omitted]

Abraham, Environmental Liability and the Limits of Insurance, 88 Colum.L.Rev. 942, 986 (1988). What would be the dangers of deregulating high-uncertainty forms of insurance for which the market is thin and, periodically, non-existent?

2. Rate Regulation

RATEMAKING AND INSURER PROFITABILITY

In contrast to regulation for solvency, where *financial data* regarding an insurer's assets and liabilities is used to assess the economic health of the company, in ratemaking *statistical data* on claims and losses takes center stage.[1] Insurance premiums, like prices for most products in imperfectly competitive markets, tend to be set with one eye on cost and profitability, and the other on market share. Unlike most products, however, the lion's share of an insurer's costs are unknown at the time it must set a price for coverage. Admittedly, this difference between insurance and other products is sometimes exaggerated. Companies in other lines of business also must make decisions in the face of uncertainty about the future. For example, General Motors must decide whether to build a new plant, open a new assembly line, hire more employees, or design a new model vehicle before it knows what all of its costs will be and how future economic forces will affect

1. Still another concern, the relative profitability of different insurance companies, requires a different measure—*rate of return on equity*. Because this Section is concerned with ratemaking and profitability within a given line of insurance, we set aside this measure here.

demand for its product. But insurers probably know with certainty a smaller proportion of the costs they will ultimately incur when they set their prices than most businesses that operate in other sectors of the economy.

Operating Profit: Underwriting Results and Investment Income

Both the process of insurance ratemaking and the regulation of that process are somewhat uncertain undertakings. If an insurer is to earn an *operating profit,* then the sum of its *underwriting* and *investment* profit and loss must be positive. The underwriting side of the insurance business is the sale of insurance and the payment of claims. Generally, underwriting profit and loss are expressed as the ratio of claim payouts and expenses to premiums earned. If this *combined ratio* is below 100 (or 1.00, depending on the scale used) then the insurer has earned an underwriting profit. If the combined ratio exceeds 100, the insurer has incurred an underwriting loss. For example, an insurer might find that its payouts ("losses") for a given year in a particular line were $.88 for every dollar of premium earned, and that its expenses (for marketing, administration, claim processing, etc.) per dollar of premium were $.22. Its combined ratio would then be 110. Notice that the combined ratio is the result of a comparison (like any ratio) of two numbers: losses-plus-expenses as compared to premiums. Consequently, this ratio will rise either when losses-plus-expenses increase, or when premiums decline; similarly, the combined ratio will fall either when losses-plus-expenses fall or when premiums rise.

The underwriting experience measured by the combined ratio, however, is only half the story. Because the insurer holds premiums for a period of time before it must pay claims against its policies, it can earn income on those premiums by investing them prior to payout. Positive investment income at least partially offsets underwriting losses, and sometimes more than offsets these losses. The longer the insurer holds premiums, the greater the income it can earn by investing them. In a *long-tail* line (one in which the claims against a single year's policies are not all made and paid until half-a-dozen or more years after a policy is issued) such as medical malpractice or products liability, investment income may be able to offset sizeable underwriting losses. As a consequence, premiums should be lower than they would be for coverage of the same aggregate expected loss with a shorter tail. In contrast, in *short-tail* lines such as automobile collision or fire insurance, most claims are made and paid shortly after the expiration of the policy period, and investment income constitutes a smaller percentage of profit or loss. Thus, in a world where insurance companies compete for business, premiums are inevitably set with potential investment income taken into account. Similarly, once all the results are in, a complete picture of an insurer's profitability cannot be obtained without taking its investment income into account.[2]

Ratemaking

Unfortunately, it is a fact of insurance life that at the time an insurer sets rates—and at the time a regulator scrutinizes them— neither can know for certain whether the level at which rates are set will produce profit or loss. In the absence of certainty about the future, past underwriting results are some evidence of what the future may bring. For two reasons, however, even past underwriting results must be adjusted to take account of the future. First, some differences between past and future results may already be known. Comparative negligence may have been adopted, or a statute requiring the installa- tion of sprinkler systems in all public buildings may have been enacted. Second, unless the past underwriting results used as a ratemaking building block are complete, they may be an inaccurate predictor of the future; and to the extent that these results are complete, they may be older than would be ideal for use as predictors. For example, suppose that in 1991 an insurer wanted to set a rate for products liability insurance in 1992. If it looked at data regarding losses paid under 1991 policies, there would be very little data, because claims would only just be coming in. Data on losses paid under 1984 policies would be much more complete; but that data would also be less relevant, because of changes in the social, economic, and legal environments in the interim.

Consequently, when insurers project the future based on underwrit- ing experience in recent years, the validity of their projections depends heavily on the completeness of the data used. When that data is incomplete, insurers follow accounting conventions for projecting the ultimate magnitude of claims and payouts against a particular year's policies, and then draw conclusions regarding the profitability of that year based on these projections. As a result, conclusions about the profitability of long-tail lines of coverage sold in a recent year are partly historical statements, but these conclusions also are partly predictions.

For example, in 1992 an insurer may attempt to determine how profitable its 1991 products liability insurance was, or (what amounts to almost the same thing) how profitable it ultimately will be. The insurer may know that it has paid $500,000 in claims against 1991 policies, and that claims likely to result in payouts of an additional $1,000,000 have already been reported. It will therefore *reserve* $1,000,000 for these reported claims. Then, on the basis of past

2. Of course, the fact that insurers earn income on invested premiums does not necessarily mean that they have an incentive to delay settling claims. Even a coldly calculating insurance executive who had no concern for public relations would need to predict whether the inflation in claim value (because of economic or legal factors) that resulted from any delay in payment of claims exceeded the investment yield on the sum for which the claim could be settled without delay, plus the legal and other expenses incurred in delaying the claim.

experience, the insurer may also project that claims payouts in the first year after a given year's products liability policies have been issued plus sums reserved for claims already-reported-but-not-yet-paid usually have turned out to constitute only 20 percent of ultimate payouts against that year's policies. The insurer will therefore estimate, based on this past pattern of *loss development,* that it will ultimately incur an additional $6,000,000 in losses against 1991 policies for claims *incurred but not reported* (IBNR). It may also note, however, that each year for the past several years its loss development estimates of this sort have turned out to be low; an additional *loss development factor* may therefore be added. In addition, the insurer will employ a *trend factor* to revise this figure upward, based on the pattern of increases in loss rates that it has observed over the past years.

Notice that this entire exercise involves prediction of the future by projecting past results. On top of these projections of past experience, the insurer may also include a factor to take account of the economic and legal inflation that it predicts for the period during which these 1991 policies still will be exposed to claims. In the aggregate, these estimates of the total losses that ultimately will be paid by 1991 policies produce a projection of ultimate underwriting experience that may be used as part of the basis for setting 1992 rates. As long as everyone involved understands what is going on, statements about the underwriting profitability of recent policy years for particular insurance lines can be understood for what they are: the best estimates that may be available, but estimates nonetheless.

If there were no regulation of insurance rates, all this would merely be a description of some of the factors insurers take into account in setting rates. Any insurer that overestimated its future losses—deliberately or in error—might fool its shareholders for a short time, but ultimately other insurers would make more accurate projections and increase their market shares by underpricing the first insurer. To a great extent that kind of competition can and does occur in the existing insurance markets. For reasons described briefly in Chapter Two, however, in at least some lines of property/casualty insurance a somewhat more collective process of ratemaking is the norm, arguably because of the inability of even the largest companies to make rates based on the limited loss data available to them individually.

Partly for this reason, and partly out of independent concern that certain segments of the insurance market are not completely competitive, insurance rates are subject to regulatory scrutiny. Ostensibly, such regulation has been motivated by the tripartite concern that rates not be "excessive, inadequate, or unfairly discriminatory," to quote the standard provision in almost every state's regulatory legislation. In practice, however, most regulatory scrutiny of rates is not focused on whether they are inadequate (a solvency concern) or unfairly discriminatory, though the latter is receiving increasing emphasis. Rather, the typical Insurance Commissioner in a rate hearing, or in deciding whether to have a hearing, is concerned to assure that rates are not excessive.

J.W. Wilson & Associates

A HYPOTHETICAL RATE CASE
(1988).*

		As Seen By:	
		Insurer	**Consumer**
1.	Earned Premium (Current Rates)	$1,597,265	$1,597,265
2.	Incurred Losses (Current Year)	$1,287,416	$1,287,416
3.	Trend Factor	1.100	1.060
4.	Loss Development Factor	1.150	—
5.	Composite Factor (3 × 4)	1.265	1.060
6.	Ultimate Losses (2 × 5)	$1,628,581	$1,364,661
7.	Loss Adjustment Expense Factor	1.120	1.110
8.	Ultimate Losses & LAE (6 × 7)	$1,824,010	$1,514,774
9.	Current Loss & LAE Ratio (8/1)	1.142	.948
10.	Commission & Expense Factor	1.250	1.10 + $159,727
11.	Profit & Contingency Factor	1.050	.90
12.	Indicated Rate Change Factor (9 × 10 × 11)	1.499	.939 + $143,754
13.	Required Rate Increase	$797,035	$46,321
14.	Percentage Increase (13/1)	+ 49.9%	+ 2.9%

Notes

1. Both parties agree on total premiums earned last year.

2. Both accept the insurer's stated "losses"—which includes those paid and those incurred but not paid.

3.–5. The consumer advocate wants to combine development and trend factors into a single number; more importantly, the consumer's projection of development plus trend is .205 lower than the insurer's. In effect, the consumer advocate argues that the insurer's prediction of future increases in loss payouts is excessive.

6. The result is a substantial difference in future projected costs.

7.–8. Differences between the parties as to the projected increase in loss adjustment expenses (in liability insurance, mainly counsel fees) further separates their estimates.

9. Summarizes this difference in the form of a projected combined ratio for this year.

10. The parties also differ about how to project other expense increases—the consumer advocate uses actual expenses plus a factor for future increases, while the insurer simply uses an increase factor.

* (000) omitted.

11. Because the insurer projects an underwriting loss, see item 9 above, it counts on its investment income to offset it, while the consumer advocate projects an underwriting profit, and wants 10 percent of the insurer's investment income used to reduce premiums.

12.–13. This difference between the parties results in different total rate change factors, and a different dollar increase in rates requested.

14. Because of the differences noted, the percentage increases in rates suggested by the parties are radically different.

At an administrative hearing considering the proposed rate increase, both parties (and/or others, depending on the nature of the proceeding and those granted standing) would present evidence in support of their contentions. Precisely this sort of evidence is illustrated in the Massachusetts case set out below. Normally this testimony will be from experts who have examined the insurer's claims experience, and who have made projections based in part on this experience (or the total claims experience of the companies represented by a rate service bureau such as ISO) and in part on judgments about future trends that are not subject to objective proof. The Commissioner would then rule depending on the nature of his authority under the state's insurance code or statutes.

FORMS OF RATE REGULATION

The methods by which Insurance Commissioners exercise their authority varies from state to state, and the lines of insurance subject to different regulatory requirements are likely to vary within each state. Property/casualty insurance rates tend to be more carefully scrutinized than life and health insurance rates. With these caveats, the received understanding is that these methods fall into four general categories, although there are of course hybrids of the four and slight variations in actual use:

State prescription of rates. This is a relatively rare approach, although it is reflected in the case that follows. In practice, the difference between this and the prior approval method is likely to turn on the burden of going forward with evidence in support of or against a rate increase, since insurers supply data on which state-prepared rates are based, and the rates set by a Commissioner may be challenged in court.

Prior approval. Insurers file proposed rates with the Insurance Commissioner, who must approve them before they may be used. In many states, unless the Commissioner disapproves a rate filing within a statutory period (usually 90 days or less) the filed rate goes automatically into effect, or is "deemed" to be approved.

File and use. Under this approach rates become effective immediately upon filing with the Commissioner, but may be disapproved within a specified period. A hybrid of this and the prior approval approach is *flex-rating*, under which rate changes within a specified band may flex through file and use, but changes beyond the band (usually more than 15 or 25 percent) require prior approval.

Open competition. Insurers need not even file rates in lines where it has been determined that competition can effectively regulate rates, although the Commissioner has residual regulatory authority.

Whatever the form of regulation, a Commissioner's scrutiny of a rate involves consideration of roughly the same issues. Few really informed observers believe that all segments of the insurance market are always fully competitive, and few believe that there is always widespread parallel action by insurers, let alone outright conspiracy. The basic philosophical difference between proponents of regulation and proponents of open competition, therefore, turns on their level of confidence (or lack of it) in the capacity of insurance regulators to make the kinds of pricing decisions that would otherwise be made by market forces.

The process of rate-setting analyzed in the following case illustrates both how much potential there is for rate-setting mistakes to be made, whether by insurers or regulators, and how difficult it is to determine whether mistakes actually have been made until data on claims and losses accumulates in the years after a rate is set. In a setting where there is imperfect competition in the market and imperfect information in the Commissioner's office, it might well be argued that the ultimate issue in rate regulation is where to vest the authority to make mistakes.

MASSACHUSETTS AUTOMOBILE RATING AND ACCIDENT PREVENTION BUREAU v. COMMISSIONER OF INSURANCE

Supreme Judicial Court of Massachusetts, Suffolk, 1983.
389 Mass. 824, 453 N.E.2d 381.

LYNCH, Justice.

This is a reservation and report of two cases by a single justice of this court arising out of the decision by the Commissioner of Insurance (Commissioner) fixing and establishing the 1983 automobile insurance rates. The plaintiffs in the two cases are the Massachusetts Automobile Rating and Accident Prevention Bureau (bureau), together with several named insurance companies in the first case, and Liberty Mutual Insurance Company and Liberty Mutual Fire Insurance Company in the second. The plaintiffs brought complaints under G.L. c. 175, § 113B, and alleged both statutory and constitutional violations by the Commissioner in establishing the 1983 automobile rates. The plaintiffs first contend that the rates are not adequate, just, reasonable, and non-discriminatory, as required by G.L. c. 175, § 113B. Additionally, the plaintiffs allege that the rates are confiscatory and, therefore, unconstitutional.

The Commissioner established the 1983 automobile insurance rates after a hearing in which the bureau, the State Rating Bureau, and the office of the Attorney General, were the primary participants. At the hearing, the bureau recommended a rate increase of 18.5%. The 1983 rates that were established provide for a much smaller increase. The Commissioner determined the total premium for each insurance coverage based on the sum of three separately calculated factors: (1) an allowance for losses, which primarily involves the payment of claims; (2) an allowance for company expenses; and (3) an allowance for underwriting profits. The determination of the allowance for underwriting profits is directly influenced by the Commissioner's calculation of the investment income earned by the industry through its use of policyholder premiums and its own capital.

The central disputes between the parties involve the Commissioner's determination of the allowance for losses and the allowance for underwriting profits. The plaintiffs argue generally that the evidence presented at the hearings was insufficient to support the Commissioner's findings for these provisions and that the Commissioner's findings are inadequate, inconsistent, and erroneous as a matter of law. More specifically, the plaintiffs allege two substantial errors by the Commissioner as to the profits provisions and several errors with regard to the determination of the loss provisions. * * *

We uphold the Commissioner's decision with respect to the allowance for profits, but remand for further consideration of the allowance for losses with respect to the Commissioner's decision on the projected effect of the Hospital Cost Containment Act on bodily injury insurance costs.

1. *Standard of Review.*

The bureau devotes a large portion of its brief positing its theory of the proper standard of our review that we should apply to the issues presented. However, the standard of review for this case has been fully developed and established by our prior decisions in this area. Our statutory review "of the Commissioner's decision is limited to a determination of whether the rates are 'adequate, just, reasonable and nondiscriminatory.' G.L. c. 175, § 113B" (footnote omitted). *Massachusetts Auto. Rating & Accident Prevention Bureau v. Commissioner of Ins.,* 384 Mass. 333, 336, 424 N.E.2d 1127. We have repeatedly stated that under this standard of review, "[j]udicial inquiry is limited to whether the rates set by [the Commissioner] have reasonable support in evidence." 424 N.E.2d 1127. *See Massachusetts Auto. Rating & Accident Prevention Bureau v. Commissioner of Ins.,* 381 Mass. 592, 596, 411 N.E.2d 762 (1980); Attorney Gen. v. Commissioner of Ins., 370 Mass. 791, 795 n. 4, 353 N.E.2d 745 (1976). Since fixing the rates is not a judicial function, *id.,* we do not substitute our judgment for that made by the Commissioner as to the adequacy or reasonableness of the premium charges ultimately set. *Massachusetts Auto. Rating & Accident Prevention Bureau v. Commissioner of Ins.,* 384 Mass. at 336, 424

N.E.2d 1127. The Commissioner must make findings that indicate the over-all basis for his decision. 424 N.E.2d 1127. See G.L. c. 175, § 113B; *Insurance Rating Bd. v. Commissioner of Ins.*, 359 Mass. 111, 118, 268 N.E.2d 144 (1971). However, we review the evidence and the findings based on the established standards and give due weight to the Commissioner's experience, technical competence, and specialized knowledge, as well as the discretionary authority vested in the Commissioner by the Legislature. *Massachusetts Auto. Rating & Accident Prevention Bureau v. Commissioner of Ins.*, 384 Mass. at 337, 424 N.E.2d 1127. *Attorney Gen. v. Commissioner of Ins., supra.*

2. *Allowance for Profit.*

a. The statutory/regulatory company investment model and the appropriate tax rate. In establishing the companies' underwriting profit allowance, the Commissioner's objective is "to fix an allowance for underwriting profit which, when added to investment income, would yield a return on shareholder capital comparable to that of unregulated industries of comparable risk." *Massachusetts Auto. Rating & Accident Prevention Bureau v. Commissioner of Ins.*, 381 Mass. at 604–605, 411 N.E.2d 762. An important component of this calculation is the Commissioner's determination of the potential investment income to be attributed to the industry. The importance of this figure, as we have noted, results from, "[t]he financial facts of life—not unrecognized in the industry * * * that money is made on investments, not on underwriting." *Id.* Typically, the premiums which are collected by the industry are combined with a percentage of capital contributed by shareholders, and used for investment.

Beginning with the decision on the 1976 automobile insurance rates, the Commissioner has employed a hypothetical insurance company, the statutory/regulatory company model (model), as the vehicle for estimating these potential investment returns. The basic theory and purpose of this model have been extensively discussed in our prior decisions. See generally *Attorney Gen. v. Commissioner of Ins., supra*, 370 Mass. at 813–815, 353 N.E.2d 745; *Massachusetts Auto. Rating & Accident Prevention Bureau v. Commissioner of Ins.*, 381 Mass. at 604– 606, 411 N.E.2d 762. Briefly, the Commissioner has assumed that this simplified model company invests all its available funds in Treasury securities with maturity dates selected to meet the model company's actual payment patterns for losses and expenses. This basic, conservative investment assumption was designed for rate-making purposes to establish a minimum, reasonable investment yield standard that companies can meet in actual practice.[1]

---

1. We have noted in past decisions that the rate of investment returns to actual insurers has been greater than the income attributed to them by the model. *Massachusetts Auto. Rating & Accident Prevention Bureau v. Commissioner of Ins.*, 384 Mass. 333, 340, 424 N.E.2d 1127. *Massachusetts Auto. Rating & Accident Prevention Bureau v. Commissioner of Ins.*, 381 Mass. 592, 608, 411 N.E.2d 762 (1980).

In past years, the Commissioner has discounted the resulting investment income by the nominal Federal tax rates on income from such securities, presently 46%, to produce the net investment profit figure. The use of this nominal tax rate has been predicated on the implicit assumption that this model company performs no functions other than earning investment income and paying Federal taxes. However, in this year's decision, the Commissioner expressed dissatisfaction with the model's simplicity and decided to take a first step in making it more sophisticated. Accordingly, he modified the basic model by rejecting this unrealistic tax assumption and using an effective tax rate in the model which more closely approximates actual company experience. The Commissioner concluded that using a 28% effective tax rate in the model would be appropriate and he applied that tax rate to the model's projected investment income.

The plaintiffs assert that the Commissioner's decision to modify the model and his choice of the 28% effective tax rate are the most serious errors in his decision and, consequently, present the most important issues raised in their appeal.[2] * * * The recent substantial rise in interest rates has driven the underwriting profits set by the Commissioner from the small positive value fixed in 1976 to a negative value in this year's decision on the major insurance coverages.[3]

The Commissioner's choice of a new tax rate merely recognizes this previously ignored internal factor, that the model company would, as do real companies, combine its underwriting losses with its expenses to reduce the effective tax rate on its investment income. The Commissioner's use of this tax rate merely involves a rationalization and extension of the theories behind the original model's assumptions, not a rejection or adulteration of the model as the plaintiffs assert. Nor does the adoption of this new tax rate create internal inconsistencies in the model. The Commissioner has not combined "real-world" tax rates with hypothetical investment strategies, but rather has extrapolated from his observation of actual companies' experience to obtain a more detailed understanding of the model company's internal actions. This, in turn, provides a more precise calculation of the companies' investment profits.

The plaintiffs' analysis attempts to treat the model company as if its investment actions occurred in a vacuum. However, it is clear that in the present rate setting circumstances the model company would pay taxes at an effective rate considerably less than the 46% rate because of the projected underwriting losses. Without the rationalization of the model to incorporate this tax effect, the projected investment profits would likely be "a very misleading indication of the actual profit made by the insurer[s]." *Attorney Gen. v. Commissioner of Ins.*, 370 Mass.

2. The plaintiffs assert that this modification of the model results in a change of 5.3% in the over-all rate level which will cost the companies approximately $61,000,000.

3. The parties stipulated that the underwriting profit provisions established for the various coverages are: (1) negative 22.3% for bodily injury coverages, (2) negative 3.6% for property damage liability, and (3) positive .4% for physical damage coverages.

791, 812, 353 N.E.2d 745 (1976). The use of this more realistic tax rate for the model company has the effect of more closely "corresponding to the investment policy [that the Commissioner has] assumed." 353 N.E.2d 745. We conclude that the Commissioner adequately explained his reasons for abandoning the existing assumption about the applicable tax rate and we defer to his experience, expertise, and discretion in this decision. *Massachusetts Auto. Rating & Accident Prevention Bureau v. Commissioner of Ins.,* 384 Mass. 333, 343, 424 N.E.2d 1127 * * *

The plaintiffs also contend that the actual choice of the 28% figure as the proper tax rate to be used in the model does not have reasonable support in the evidence. We disagree. In his testimony at the hearing, Dr. Fairley stated that 28% is a reasonable estimate of the actual effective tax rate. In reaching this conclusion, Dr. Fairley relied specifically upon the calculations and tax rate arguments presented by Dr. Hill and Dr. Modigliani at the 1982 hearing.[4] This estimate was consistent with the actual tax rates of ten insurance companies appearing in the Value Line Investment Survey. Dr. Fairley testified that the effective tax rates for all these companies were 20% or less. The Commissioner expressly relied on the testimony of this expert witness in choosing the 28% tax rate as the highest tax rate the model company would pay. This conclusion has reasonable support in the evidence. Moreover the evidence of the Value Line Investment Survey completely rebuts the plaintiffs' assertion that this assumed tax rate is "fanciful or impossible to match in the real world." *Massachusetts Auto. Rating & Accident Prevention Bureau v. Commissioner of Ins.,* 381 Mass. at 608, 411 N.E.2d 762, quoting *Attorney Gen. v. Commissioner of Ins., supra* 370 Mass. at 822, 353 N.E.2d 745.[5] * * *

3. *Allowance for Losses.*

The second major area of the Commissioner's decision challenged by the plaintiffs involves the Commissioner's provision in the rate for losses. The loss provisions established by the Commissioner are based primarily on the Commissioner's projection of the claim frequency changes and the claim cost changes from 1981 to 1983. A settled and direct methodology for determining claim cost trends has been developed in recent years. As a result, the parties have been in general agreement in this area. This year, the plaintiffs raise only a single cost claim issue: They dispute the validity of the Commissioner's assessment of the effect of the Hospital Cost Containment Act.

The Commissioner's estimation of claim frequency trends, on the other hand, continues to generate considerable controversy. This year

4. The Commissioner agreed to take official notice of the 1982 hearing record to the extent it was referred to by witnesses in this year's hearings.

5. We also note that in the 1980 rate hearing the bureau projected an average tax rate of 22% for its companies, *Massachusetts Auto. Rating & Accident Prevention Bureau v. Commissioner of Ins.,* 381 Mass. at 607–608, 411 N.E.2d 762, and that in the 1981 rate hearing the bureau offered 19.28% as an estimate of the actual investment tax rate for the company in its proposed profit model.

the plaintiffs raise three challenges to this part of the Commissioner's decision. First, the plaintiffs object to the methodology used by the Commissioner for determining property damage liability claim frequency. Next, the plaintiffs dispute the Commissioner's conclusion that the putative "energy effect" on driving will lead to a continuing decline in claim frequency. Finally, the plaintiffs similarly challenge the Commissioner's projection of further claim frequency decline due to the new Massachusetts law focusing on the problem of drunk driving, in combination with changes in the merit rating surcharges for repeat offenders of the law. We turn first to these claim frequency issues.

a. *Property damage liability claim frequency.* In attempting to estimate claim frequency changes, the Commissioner traditionally has relied on analysis of the effect of specified external phenomena that are likely to exert a measurable impact on claim frequency, rather than simply extrapolating from reported internal claim frequency data. We expressed general approval of this practice in our decision reviewing the 1976 rates. See *Attorney Gen. v. Commissioner of Ins.*, 370 Mass. 791, 801, 353 N.E.2d 745 (1976) ("It seems to us significant that the Commissioner did not merely attempt to project the data, as did the parties, rather he reached for the underlying causal phenomena and considered what their continuing influence would be"). The basic assumption for this methodology has been that there is no underlying trend in claim frequency.

However, in determining the change in property damage liability claim frequency, the Commissioner concluded that exclusive use of this approach would be inappropriate. The Commissioner observed contrary to that basic assumption that the underlying trend for property damage liability claim frequency has been one of consistent decline for the past four years. Since, contrary to the methodology's assumption, property damage liability claim frequency has demonstrated an underlying trend, the Commissioner decided to reject the plaintiffs' proposal that he base any adjustments in property damage liability claim frequency exclusively on observable external phenomena. Instead, he accepted the SRB's [the State Rating Board's] recommendation that he consider both internal statistical data and external indications for determining this frequency. He also adopted the projected change in claim frequency calculated by the SRB. * * *

The plaintiffs raise several objections to this procedure and the Commissioner's conclusion. The plaintiffs first contend that in projecting the decrease in property damage liability claim frequency, the Commissioner simply extrapolated from internal claim frequency data and did not provide the necessary causal analysis. However, as noted above, it is clear that the Commissioner, in addition to considering the unique internal trend data on property damage liability claim frequency, focused on two significant external causes for this trend, the change in vehicle-miles travelled and the changes in the merit rating program. * * *

Finally, the plaintiffs dispute the Commissioner's assumption that the increases in the merit surcharges will have an effect on driving behavior and they argue that the evidence presented by the SRB supporting a merit rating effect was insubstantial. However, we do not weigh the evidence de novo. *Massachusetts Auto. Rating & Accident Prevention Bureau v. Commissioner of Ins.*, 384 Mass. at 337, 424 N.E.2d 1127. The Commissioner considered the evidence presented of a deterrent effect resulting from the merit rating surcharges and concluded that a 3% decline for property damage liability claim frequency was reasonable and was consistent with the decrease in claim frequency previously attributed to the merit rating surcharges. There was the requisite substantial support in the evidence for the Commissioner to accept the frequency adjustments suggested by the SRB. See 334 Mass. at 338–39; *Massachusetts Auto. Racing & Accident Prevention Bureau v. Commissioner of Ins.*, 381 Mass. 592, 600–601, 411 N.E.2d 762 (1980).

*   *   *

[The court next concluded that the methodology used by the Commissioner to project the effect of gasoline availability and price on claim frequency was not erroneous, and rejected the plaintiffs' argument that the Commissioner's estimate of the impact of increased sanctions for driving under the influence of alcohol on claim frequency did not have reasonable support in the evidence.]

d. *The effect of the Hospital Cost Containment Act.* The Commissioner accepted the SRB's estimate that the Hospital Cost Containment Act (Act), would result in a 2% reduction in hospital costs over a six-year period. Recognizing that 2% would not be a flat reduction in cost but would start at a lower level, the SRB then reduced its estimate of first-year savings to 1% and reasoned that the effect on automobile coverage for 1983 would be a .7% reduction to the medical care components. Both the SRB and the Commissioner premised their estimates on the estimate of an unidentified sponsor of the Act that it would result in an over-all savings in hospital costs of $500,000,000 over six years. Nowhere in the record do we find an explanation by the Commissioner, the SRB, or the "legislative sponsor" of the basis for this estimate. At the hearings, the Commissioner characterized the estimate as the "best guesstimate" of the author or of the committee as it was prepared in the last moments of the legislative process to expedite the passage of the bill. The actuary who prepared this portion of the study for the SRB testified that he did not know how the sponsor of the legislation derived this estimate, that it was really too early to be able to tell what the full impact of the bill would be, and that he based his opinion exclusively on the bill itself and the summary of the bill apparently prepared by the legislative sponsors. The exhibit he identified as the summary he relied upon does not state that the Act will reduce hospital costs $500,000,000 over the six-year period. It does state the Act will limit the *growth* of hospital costs by 7.5% over six years. The Commissioner in his opinion recognized that the effect of the Act would not immediately become known and in order for him to make this determination it was necessary for him to exercise "some judgment." It is one thing to exercise some judgment, and another to speculate as to the existence of some future fact with no explanation of how the exercise of judgment leads to the conclusion that cost reduction will occur in the future. A mere speculation concerning a matter of fact cannot form an adequate foundation for the Commissioner's decision. *Attorney Gen. v. Commissioner of Ins.,* 370 Mass. 791, 805, 353 N.E.2d 745 (1976). On this record we conclude that reasonable support is lacking for the premise that the Act will result in a 1% reduction of hospital costs in the year 1983.

The record before us does not enable us to say what reduction, if any, will result from the Act. If after remand the Commissioner's decision contains any factor for reduction in rates arising from the Act it must contain an adequate foundation for that decision. * * *

5. *Conclusion.*

These cases are remanded to the single justice who is to enter judgment reversing the decision of the Commissioner and directing him to fix and establish the 1983 automobile insurance rates, redetermining the allowance for losses in accordance with this opinion.

Notes and Questions

1. *The Standard of Review.* As the court indicated, its decision was one in a series that began with *Attorney General v. Commissioner of Insurance,* 370 Mass. 791, 353 N.E.2d 745 (1976). Decisions on ratemaking issues from courts of last resort are not common in most states, however. For an instructive set of three such cases, all decided on the same day, see *Commissioner of Insurance v. North Carolina Rate Bureau,* 300 N.C. 381, 269 S.E.2d 547 (1980), 300 N.C. 460, 269 S.E.2d 538 (1980), and 300 N.C. 474, 269 S.E.2d 595 (1980).

The standard of review employed by the court in the principal case is generally accepted in administrative law. The courts do not decide appeals of administrative action *de novo;* rather, they review the evidence below to assure that it provides reasonable support for the decision, or ascertain whether that the decision was arbitrary or capricious. Although the levels of deference to administrative expertise are described in different ways and probably actually vary from state to state, the requirement of some deference is universal. The rationale for this stance, of course, is not only past precedent and (in some states) a statute governing administrative procedure requiring it, but the expertise of the administrative agency to which the legislature delegated regulatory authority in the first instance.

2. *Rhetoric and Reality.* As a general principle of administrative law, this rationale is still accepted, but it is a bit tattered at the edges. Perhaps the primary reason for the tatters is the increased recognition that regulators are not merely experts divorced from the political process, but part of that process and subject to external influences

similar to those which operate in legislatures and in the executive branch of government. See generally Stewart, The Reform of American Administrative Law, 88 Harv.L.Rev. 1167 (1975). Not only is the influence of lobbying and the possible "capture" of administrative agencies by the enterprises that are the very subjects of regulation a threat to disinterested decision-making; the "revolving door" phenomenon, under which regulators move from the regulated industry to the agency regulating it and back again to the industry may create at least the appearance of conflicts of interest on the part of the regulators.

Insurance Commissioners are probably as susceptible to these influences as other regulators. In addition, in all but the largest states, the assumption of administrative expertise that underlies judicial deference may also be less warranted than might be supposed. For example, state insurance departments are notoriously understaffed, and are especially lacking in the key form of expertise necessary for rate regulation—actuarial analysis. In 1985 the National Insurance Consumer Organization (NICO) surveyed all 50 states plus the District of Columbia and Puerto Rico to determine their preparedness for dealing with crises in insurance availability and affordability. NICO found that of these 52 jurisdictions, only 26 have full time actuaries. Of the 7682 actuaries in the nation, these jurisdictions employed 62. Aetna Life and Casualty Insurance Company alone employs 126 actuaries; Travelers has 100. Testimony of J. Robert Hunter, before the Subcommittee on Commerce, Transportation, and Tourism, U.S. House of Representatives (September 19, 1985), quoted in American Bar Association, Report of the Commission to Improve the Liability Insurance System E–10 (1989).

Given this disparity in resources, it may not be surprising that one very able analyst's systematic review of the literature on the impact of different forms of rate regulation on property and liability insurance prices and underwriting results found no conclusive evidence that strong rate regulation produces lower prices than weak regulation or open competition. See Harrington, The Impact of Rate Regulation on Prices and Underwriting Results in the Property–Liability Insurance Industry: A Survey, 51 J. of Risk and Ins. 577 (1984). This finding may suggest that rate regulation is a bad idea, but it may be instead that regulation has not yet been given a fair chance to work.

3. *Deference by the Commissioner?* Should the typical Insurance Commissioner show the same deference to the rates submitted by insurers that the courts show to the Commissioner's decision? Any deference? If not there may not be much practical difference between the different forms of rate regulation—for example, between state prescription of rates prior-approval or file-and-use. The differences will depend less on the nature of the rate regulation that is formally in place than on the amount of resources a Commissioner decides to allocate to the scrutiny of any given rate increase.

4. *Two Models of Rate Regulation.* On what factors should a Commissioner's resource-allocation decisions be based? Under what might be termed the *public utility* model of insurance rate regulation, priority should be given to rate increases likely to have the most impact on the public. Thus, the absolute size of the increase and the prevalence of the coverage for which premiums are to increase should determine the degree of regulatory attention required. In addition, under this model the Commissioner would consider what level of increase would provide the insurer with a fair level of profit. This seems to be the approach taken by Massachusetts in the principal case.

In contrast, under a *competition* model of insurance rate regulation, the primary concern of the Commissioner should be to assure that competition among insurers is an effective regulator of insurance rates. Proposed rate increases would still have to be scrutinized, because steep increases or sizeable profits might be some evidence that competition is not effectively regulating rates. But direct evidence of the degree of competition should also be relevant. The competition model thus does not necessarily embody a *laissez faire* philosophy; rather, the degree of competition within the line of coverage for which an increase is contemplated should determine the regulatory resources allocated to scrutinize the increase. For a statute resembling the competition model, see Annotated Code of Virginia, § 38.2–1904–1912.

Under the public utility model, a Commissioner may expend resources unnecessarily by scrutinizing rate increases in lines where competition itself is effectively regulating rates. On the other hand, under the competition model the Commissioner may expend scarce resources making competitiveness determinations. Even to those for whom the competition model seems preferable in the abstract, Commissioners and their staffs actually may be more qualified to scrutinize individual rate filings than to assess the nature of the markets they are charged with regulating. The former requires the skills of insurance professionals; the latter demands the expertise of antitrust economists. Thus, the older public utility model, selectively applied, may in fact ask less of the regulator than the newer, sometimes interventionist but sometimes hands-off competition model, since under the latter the regulator is always active, even when not actively regulating. Jurisdictions tend to cycle from one model to the other, and at any given time (and with respect to any given line of insurance) may appear to have adopted a hybrid of the two.

RATE ROLLBACKS THROUGH VOTER INITIATIVES

In the Fall of 1988, the voters of California approved Proposition 103, a referendum that ordered the rollback in liability and certain other insurance rates described in the case that follows. Movements to place similar propositions on the ballots of other states began soon thereafter, and the insurance market in California became the subject of national attention. As you examine the reasoning of the Supreme Court of California in upholding the constitutionality of most of Proposition 103, consider whether the possibility that similar laws may be adopted in the future is a healthy or unhealthy threat to the insurance industry.

CALFARM INSURANCE COMPANY v. DEUKMEJIAN

Supreme Court of California, En Banc, 1989.
48 Cal.3d 805, 258 Cal.Rptr. 161, 771 P.2d 1247.

BROUSSARD, Associate Justice.

In this case we consider various challenges to Proposition 103, an initiative measure enacted November 8, 1988, making numerous fundamental changes in the regulation of automobile and other types of insurance.[1] Petitioners, seven insurers and the Association of California Insurance Companies, have filed an original petition for writ of mandate in this court, contending that Proposition 103 is unconstitutional on its face. They named as respondents Governor George Deukmejian, Attorney General John Van de Kamp, Insurance Commissioner Roxani Gillespie, and the State Board of Equalization. The Access to Justice Foundation and other supporters of Proposition 103 (hereafter proponents) have appeared as real parties in interest to oppose the petition. We have also received numerous amicus curiae briefs.

In view of the obvious importance of the case, and the need for a prompt decision (since certain contested provisions are effective for only one year), we assumed original jurisdiction and issued an alternative writ. (See *Brosnahan v. Brown* (1982) 32 Cal.3d 236, 186 Cal.Rptr. 30, 651 P.2d 274; *Hardie v. Eu* (1976) 18 Cal.3d 371, 134 Cal.Rptr. 201, 556 P.2d 301.) Before addressing individually the issues raised by petitioners, we will summarize the initiative's provisions, the contentions raised in regard to those provisions, and our conclusions.

The initiative begins with a statement of findings and purpose, asserting that "[e]normous increases in the cost of insurance have made it both unaffordable and unavailable to millions of Californians," and that "the existing laws inadequately protect consumers and allow insurance companies to charge excessive, unjustified and arbitrary rates." The initiative's stated purpose is to ensure that "insurance is fair, available, and affordable for all Californians."

Insurance rates are to be immediately reduced to "at least 20 percent less" than those in effect on November 8, 1987 (approximately the date when the initiative was proposed, and one year prior to its

---

1. Proposition 103 applies to "all insurance on risks or on operations in this state, except those listed in Section 1851." Insurance code section 1851 lists reinsurance, life insurance, title insurance, certain types of marine insurance, disability insurance, workers' compensation insurance, mortgage insurance, and insurance transacted by county mutual fire insurers.

enactment). (§ 1861.01, subd. (a); all statutory references are to the Insurance Code, unless otherwise stated.) [2] All rate increases require the approval of the Insurance Commissioner, who may not approve rates which are "excessive, inadequate, unfairly discriminatory or otherwise in violation of [the initiative]." (§ 1861.05.) Prior to November 8, 1989, however, rates may be increased only if the commissioner finds "that an insurer is substantially threatened with insolvency." (§ 1861.01, subd. (b).) Certain procedures are specified for hearing applications for rate approvals. (§§ 1861.04–1861.10.)

The initiative prohibits an insurer from declining to renew a policy except for nonpayment of premium, fraud, or significant increase in the hazard insured against. (§ 1861.03, subd. (c).) Insurers are required to mail notices to policy holders informing them they may join a nonprofit corporation to be formed to represent their interests by persons appointed for this purpose by the Insurance Commissioner. (§ 1861.10.) The Board of Equalization is directed to adjust the tax rate on insurance premiums to avoid any loss of tax revenues as a result of decreases in the rates charged by insurers. (Rev. & Tax. Code, § 12202.1.) Finally, the initiative contains a severance provision stating that the invalidity of any portion of the initiative "shall not affect other provisions or applications of the act which can be given effect without the invalid portion. * * *" [3]

On November 10, 1988, we granted petitioners' request to stay the initiative in its entirety. On December 7, 1988, after deciding to assume jurisdiction of the case, and after further study of the issues presented, we vacated the stay except as to the provisions requiring a rate reduction to 20 percent below 1987 rates, limiting relief to companies substantially threatened with insolvency, and requiring a mailing notifying insureds of the opportunity to join a nonprofit corporation to advocate their interests.

Petitioners contend that the initiative's rate regulation provisions violate the due process clauses of the United States and California Constitutions in that the initial reduction to 20 percent below 1987 levels is arbitrary, discriminatory and confiscatory, the rate adjustment mechanism during the first year does not permit relief from confiscato-

---

2. Section 1861.01 further provides: "(d) For those who apply for an automobile insurance policy for the first time on or after November 8, 1988, the rate shall be 20% less than the rate which was in effect on November 8, 1987, for similarly situated risks. [¶] (e) Any separate affiliate of an insurer, established on or after November 8, 1987, shall be subject to the provisions of this section and shall reduce its charges to levels which are at least 20% less than the insurer's charges in effect on that date." Our discussion of the initiative's rate rollback and reduction provisions applies to subdivisions (d) and (e) as well as to subdivision (a) of section 1861.01.

3. Other provisions of the initiative, not challenged here, require that automobile insurance rates, beginning in November 1989, be based on driving record, number of miles driven, years of driving experience, and other factors approved by the commissioner, that good drivers receive a 20 percent discount on automobile insurance rates, that the insurance industry be subject to the Unruh Civil Rights Acts (Civ.Code, §§ 51–53), antitrust laws and unfair business practice laws, and that the Insurance Commissioner be an elective office beginning with the 1990 election.

ry rates, and adequate procedures have not been provided to ensure prompt rate relief. They challenge the provision limiting insurers' power not to renew policies as impermissibly impairing existing contract rights. * * *

1. *Provisions relating to the reduction and subsequent adjustment of insurance rates.*

The constitutional test for the validity of state price controls was established in *Nebbia v. New York* (1934) 291 U.S. 502, 539, 54 S.Ct. 505, 517, 78 L.Ed. 940: "Price control, like any other form of regulation, is unconstitutional only if arbitrary, discriminatory, or demonstrably irrelevant to the policy the legislature is free to adopt, and hence an unnecessary and unwarranted interference with individual liberty." The United States Supreme Court reaffirmed this test in *Pennell v. City of San Jose* (1988) 485 U.S. 1, 11, 108 S.Ct. 849, 857, 99 L.Ed.2d 1. We followed it in *Birkenfeld v. City of Berkeley* (1976) 17 Cal.3d 129, 130 Cal.Rptr. 465, 550 P.2d 1001, a rent control case, and went on to explain that "[t]he provisions are within the police power if they are reasonably calculated to eliminate excessive rents and at the same time provide landlords with a just and reasonable return on their property." (P. 165, 130 Cal.Rptr. 465, 550 P.2d 1001.)

The state and federal Constitutions are concerned not so much with the way in which the initial rates are set as with whether the rates as finally set are confiscatory.[4] "[I]t is the result reached not the method employed which is controlling." (*Power Comm'n v. Hope Gas Co.* (1944) 320 U.S. 591, 602, 64 S.Ct. 281, 287, 88 L.Ed. 333; see *Duquesne Light Co. v. Barasch* (1989) ___ U.S. ___, 109 S.Ct. 609, 617, 102 L.Ed.2d 646. In *Fisher v. City of Berkeley* (1984) 37 Cal.3d 644, 683, 209 Cal.Rptr. 682, 693 P.2d 261, we reaffirmed the rule that "whether a regulation produces a return that is confiscatory or fair depends ultimately on the result, and * * * we will invalidate an ordinance on its face only if its terms preclude avoidance of confiscatory results." Petitioners must show that the law is "so restrictive as to facially preclude any possibility of a just and reasonable return" (*Hutton, supra,* 350 A.2d 1, 16); that "its terms will not permit those who administer it to avoid confiscatory results" (*Birkenfeld v. City of Berkeley, supra,* 17 Cal.3d 129, 165, 130 Cal.Rptr. 465, 550 P.2d 1001).

Consequently, we focus less on the rate specified in the statute than on the ability of the seller to obtain relief if that rate proves confiscatory. The face of a statute rarely reveals whether the rates it specifies are confiscatory or arbitrary, but necessarily discloses its provisions, if any, for rate adjustment. Recognizing that virtually any law which sets prices may prove confiscatory in practice, courts have carefully

4. The terms "fair and reasonable" and "confiscatory" are antonyms, not separate tests. (See *FPC v. Texaco, Inc.* (1974) 417 U.S. 380, 392, 94 S.Ct. 2315, 2323, 41 L.Ed.2d 141; *Board of Comm'rs v. N.Y. Tel. Co.* (1926) 271 U.S. 23, 31, 46 S.Ct. 363, 366, 70 L.Ed. 808; *Hutton Park Gardens v. Town Council* (1975) 68 N.J. 543, 350 A.2d 1, 15 [hereafter *Hutton*].)

scrutinized such provisions to ensure that the sellers will have an adequate remedy for relief from confiscatory rates. In *Birkenfeld v. City of Berkeley, supra,* 17 Cal.3d 129, 130 Cal.Rptr. 465, 550 P.2d 1001, for example, we struck down a rent control law because its procedures were so cumbersome and time-consuming that landlords could not in reality obtain relief from confiscatory rates.

We therefore begin our discussion by considering the provisions in Proposition 103 which would permit an insurer to seek relief from any rate it considers confiscatory. Section 1861.05 provides that "[e]very insurer which desires to change any rate shall file a complete rate application with the commissioner." Subdivision (a) states that the commissioner may not approve or permit any rate "which is excessive, inadequate, unfairly discriminatory or otherwise in violation of this chapter"—language which makes it clear that the commissioner can grant relief from confiscatory rates. Section 1861.01, subdivision (b), however, qualifies section 1861.05 by limiting rate adjustments prior to November 1989 to insurers substantially threatened with insolvency. Petitioners attack the constitutionality of this limitation.

Section 1861.01, subdivision (b), provides that "[b]etween November 8, 1988, and November 8, 1989, rates and premiums reduced pursuant to subdivision (a) may be only increased if the commissioner finds, after a hearing, that an insurer is substantially threatened with insolvency." [5] "Insolvency" has various meanings, but none will allow us to construe subdivision (b) to conform to the constitutional standard of a fair and reasonable return. A company may be insolvent because it has more liabilities than assets, or because it is unable to pay its obligations as they fall due.[6] (See *Maryland Casualty Co. v. Commis-*

---

5. Taken literally, the word "only" in subdivision (b) modifies "increased" and not the following phrase, so all the subdivision provides is that if an insurer is substantially threatened with insolvency, the commissioner can only increase its rates, not decrease them—and says nothing about companies not threatened with insolvency. We assume, however, as do all parties and amici curiae, that the subdivision was intended to permit a rate increase only if a company was substantially threatened with insolvency.

6. If "insolvency" is defined as "bankruptcy," it is clear that rate relief cannot be confined to companies threatened with insolvency. In *Power Comm'n v. Hope Gas Co., supra,* 320 U.S. 591, 603, 64 S.Ct. 281, 288, 88 L.Ed. 333, the court said that in determining a fair rate of return, one must consider "the financial integrity of the company whose rates are being regulated. * * * [I]t is important that there be enough revenue not only for operating expenses but also for the capital costs of the business. These include service on the debt and dividends on the stock. [Citation.] By that standard the return to the equity owner should be commensurate with returns on investment in other enterprises having corresponding risks. That return, moreover, should be sufficient to assure confidence in the financial integrity of the enterprise, so as to maintain its credit and to attract capital." Consequently when the Federal Energy Regulatory Commission argued that judicial review of rates was limited to companies threatened with bankruptcy, the court replied, "*Hope Natural Gas* talks not of an interest in avoiding bankruptcy, but an interest in maintaining access to capital markets, the ability to pay dividends, and general financial integrity. While companies about to go bankrupt would certainly see such interests threatened, companies less imminently imperiled will sometimes be able to make that claim as well. * * * The contention that no company that is not clearly headed for bankruptcy has a judicially enforceable right to have its financial status considered when its rates are determined must be rejected." (*Jersey Cen. Power & Light Co. v. F.E.R.C.* (D.C.Cir.1987) 810 F.2d 1168, 1180.)

sioner of Insurance (1977) 372 Mass. 554, 363 N.E.2d 1087, 1093–1094.) "Insolvency" is defined in the Insurance Code as "any impairment of minimum 'paid-in capital' * * * as defined in Section 36" (§ 985, subd. (a).) (Section 36 defines "paid-in capital" essentially as the excess of assets over liabilities. The statutory minimum for "paid-in capital" ranges from $500,000 to $1.3 million (§ 700.01).) But under all of these definitions, a rate may be confiscatory even though it does not threaten the insurer's solvency.

The insolvency standard of subdivision (b) refers to the financial position of the company as a whole, not merely to the regulated lines of insurance.[7] Many insurers do substantial business outside of California, or in lines of insurance within this state which are not regulated by Proposition 103. If an insurer had substantial net worth, or significant income from sources unregulated by Proposition 103, it might be able to sustain substantial and continuing losses on regulated insurance without danger of insolvency. In such a case the continued solvency of the insurer could not suffice to demonstrate that the regulated rate constitutes a fair return.[8]

The effect of section 1861.01, subdivision (b), is thus to bar safely solvent insurers from obtaining relief from "inadequate" rates until November 1989. Temporary rates which might be below a fair and reasonable level might compel insurers to return to their customers surpluses exacted through allegedly excessive past rates. But the concept that rates may be set at less than a fair rate of return in order to compel the return of past surpluses is not one supported by precedent. "The just compensation safeguarded to the utility by the Fourteenth Amendment is a reasonable return on the value of the property used at the time that it is being used for the public service. * * * [T]he law does not require the company to give up for the benefit of future subscribers any part of its accumulations from past operations. Profits of the past cannot be used to sustain confiscatory rates for the future." (*Board of Comm'rs v. N.Y. Tel. Co., supra,* 271 U.S. 23, 31–32, 46 S.Ct. 363, 366, 70 L.Ed. 808; accord, *American Toll Bridge Co. v. Railroad Com.* (1938) 12 Cal.2d 184, 203, 83 P.2d 1.) *Hutton, supra,* said that if past rents were excessive an ordinance could refuse to give landlords credit for current cost increases if the diminished rate of return was still just and reasonable. (350 A.2d at p. 16.) But no case supports an unreasonably low rate of return on the ground that past profits were excessive.

7. Proponents point out that rates are generally regulated by considering each line of insurance separately, and suggest that "substantially threatened with insolvency" could be analyzed in a like manner. But subdivision (b) refers to the solvency of an "insurer," not a line of insurance. One can speak of a line of insurance as unprofitable, or causing losses, but it would be strained usage to speak of it as threatened with insolvency.

8. Respondents and proponents point out that subdivision (b) requires only that the insurer be "substantially threatened" with insolvency, not teetering on the brink. We agree that this standard gives the commissioner a measure of discretion, but it does not permit her to raise a confiscatorily low rate for a company in no danger whatever of insolvency.

Proponents urge that the insolvency standard can be sustained as a temporary or emergency measure. They point out that temporary freezes while administrative machinery is set up are commonly approved, even if they lack any method whereby a seller can get relief. (See, e.g., *Trans Alaska Pipeline Rate Cases* (1978) 436 U.S. 631, 98 S.Ct. 2053, 56 L.Ed.2d 591; *United States v. SCRAP* (1973) 412 U.S. 669, 93 S.Ct. 2405, 37 L.Ed.2d 254; *Western States Meat Packers Assn., Inc. v. Dunlop* (T.E.C.A.1973) 482 F.2d 1401.) Most freezes are for periods of much less than one year, but courts have sustained freezes of a year or longer. (See, e.g., *Mass. Med. Society v. Comm'r of Ins.* (1988) 402 Mass. 44, 520 N.E.2d 1288 [two-year freeze on medical malpractice insurance rates].) The cases, however, proceed on the assumption that the frozen prices were those set by a seller in a competitive market, and thus were fair rates, so that the only concern is increased costs during the freeze. (See discussion in *Birkenfeld v. City of Berkeley, supra,* 17 Cal.3d 129, 166, 130 Cal.Rptr. 465, 550 P.2d 1001.) Here we have a law which mandates not maintenance of a rate set by the seller, but a reduction to at least 20 percent less than former rates. The risk that the rate set by the statute is confiscatory as to some insurers from its inception is high enough to require an adequate method for obtaining individualized relief.

Proponents further argue that the insolvency standard in Proposition 103 was inserted to combat an emergency created by unavailable and unaffordable insurance. They assert that between 1983 and 1986 automobile insurance rates doubled, while commercial rates increased over 200 percent. They observe also that in 1984 the Legislature enacted the Robins–McAlister Financial Responsibility Act (Stats.1984, ch. 1322), requiring all motorists to purchase liability insurance and carry proof of financial responsibility.

We recognize that emergency situations may require emergency measures.[9] As the court explained in *Hutton,* a rent control case, "[t]he term 'confiscatory' must be understood in light of the surrounding circumstances. There are undoubtedly times of great public exigency during which landlords may temporarily be required to rent their property at rates which do not permit them to obtain what would ordinarily be considered a fair return." (350 A.2d at p. 13.) Numerous cases confirm that measures enacted to combat an emergency of limited duration may be valid even though they do not guarantee a fair rate of return. (See *Bowles v. Willingham* (1944) 321 U.S. 503, 64 S.Ct. 641, 88 L.Ed. 892 [World War II rent control]; *Block v. Hirsh* (1921) 256 U.S. 135, 41 S.Ct. 458, 65 L.Ed. 865 [rent control after World War I]; *Whitney v. Heckler, supra,* 780 F.2d 963 [freeze on Medicare rates and rates charged non-Medicare patients, pursuant to Deficit Reduction Act

---

9. The doctrine that state price control laws are invalid except in an emergency was repudiated by this court in *Birkenfeld v. City of Berkeley, supra,* 17 Cal.3d 129, 159, 130 Cal.Rptr. 465, 550 P.2d 1001. Hence we do not discuss the question of an "emergency" generally with respect to Proposition 103. That matter does become relevant, however, when the state, as in section 1861.10, subdivision (b), seeks to compel sellers to accept less than fair and reasonable rates.

of 1984]; *Western States Meat Packers Assn., Inc. v. Dunlop, supra,* 482
F.2d 1401 [price and wage controls under Economic Stabilization Act of
1970]; *Wilson v. Brown* (Emer.Ct.App.1943) 137 F.2d 348 [price controls
during World War II].)

To justify a measure which deprives persons of a fair return,
however, "an emergency would have to be a temporary situation of
such enormity that all individuals might reasonably be required to
make sacrifices for the common weal." (*Hutton,* 350 A.2d 1, 14.) We
do not believe that the circumstances which inspired Proposition 103
meet this requirement. Our concern is not with the magnitude of the
problem, but with its character. The asserted rise in insurance rates,
rendering insurance unavailable or unaffordable to many, is not a
temporary problem; it is a long term, chronic situation which will not
be solved by compelling insurers to sell at less than a fair return for a
year. Over the long term the state must permit insurers a fair
return; [10] we do not perceive any short term conditions that would
require depriving them of a fair return. We therefore conclude that
subdivision (b) cannot be sustained as an emergency measure fashioned
to meet a temporary exigency. * * * [The court then concluded that
a remaining provision in the initiative that rates shall not be "excessive, inadequate or unfairly discriminatory" provided the insurers with
sufficient protection against confiscatory rates.]

In summary, we have concluded (a) that section 1861.01, subdivision (b), limiting first-year-rate adjustments to insurers substantially
threatened with insolvency, is facially invalid, but severable, and does
not invalidate the remainder of the initiative; (b) that the procedures
for adjustment of insurance rates—including application to the commissioner, the opportunity to seek interim relief, a hearing in accordance
with the Administrative Procedure Act, and judicial review—meet
constitutional standards; and (c) that in view of the safeguards described in this opinion, the rate rollback and reduction of Proposition
103 is not invalid on its face, but the rates thereby established are
necessarily subject to the right of an insurer to demonstrate that a
particular rate is, as applied to it, a confiscatory rate.

2. Restrictions upon the insurers' right to refuse to renew policies.

Proposition 103, in section 1861.03 subdivision (c) [hereafter nonrenewal provision], provides: "Notwithstanding any other provision of
law, a notice of cancellation or non-renewal of a policy for automobile
insurance shall be effective only if it is based on one or more of the
following reasons: (1) nonpayment of premiums; (2) fraud or material
misrepresentation affected the policy or insured; (3) a substantial
increase in the hazard insured against." Before enactment of Proposition 103 insurers had an unfettered right to refuse to renew policies

---

10. *Hutton* noted that "[t]he existence of a chronic housing shortage of indefinite
duration would not justify depriving property owners of a fair return for an indefinite
period." (350 A.2d 1, 13–14.)

(see *Greene v. Safeco Ins. Co.* (1983) 140 Cal.App.3d 535, 538, 189 Cal. Rptr. 616).[11]

Respondent Attorney General and proponents contend that the nonrenewal provision applies to policies issued before enactment of Proposition 103. Petitioners agree that the provision was intended to apply to policies in force when Proposition 103 was enacted but maintain that the application of this provision to such policies would in effect alter their terms, and thereby violate the constitutional prohibition against a "law impairing the obligation of contracts." (U.S. Const., art. I, § 10; see Cal. Const., art. I, § 9.) They do not contend that this subdivision is invalid as applied to policies voluntarily issued or renewed *after* November 8, 1988.[12] Amicus curiae Travelers Indemnity Company argues that the nonrenewal provision was not intended to apply to policies in force before enactment of Proposition 103, pointing to the well-established principle that regardless of considerations of constitutionality, "statutes are not to be given a retrospective operation unless it is clearly made to appear that such was the legislative intent." (*Evangelatos v. Superior Court* (1988) 44 Cal.3d 1188, 1207, 246 Cal.Rptr. 629, 753 P.2d 585; *Aetna Cas. & Surety Co. v. Ind. Acc. Com.* (1947) 30 Cal.2d 388, 393, 182 P.2d 159.)[13] Amicus curiae also contends that we should apply the well-established principle "that a court, when faced with an ambiguous statute that raises serious constitutional questions, should endeavor to construe the statute in a manner which avoids any doubt concerning its validity." (*Young v. Haines* (1986) 41 Cal.3d 883, 898, 226 Cal.Rptr. 547, 718 P.2d 909; *Carlos v. Superior Court* (1983) 35 Cal.3d 131, 147, 152, 197 Cal.Rptr. 79, 672 P.2d 862; *San Francisco Unified School Dist. v. Johnson* (1971) 3 Cal.3d 937, 948, 92 Cal.Rptr. 309, 479 P.2d 669.) We recognize the validity of these precepts, but conclude that the initiative's nonrenewal provision was intended to

11. "Cancellation," as opposed to "non-renewal," refers to termination of a policy before its expiration date. Insurers' power to cancel policies was severely restricted by section 661 before enactment of Proposition 103. The only effect of Proposition 103 upon this section was to eliminate the 60–day grace period following issuance of a policy during which section 661 placed no limits on cancellation.

12. Provisions similar to section 1861.03, subdivision (c), appear in the laws of many states, and as applied to policies issued after the effective date of the statute, have been sustained against constitutional attack. (See *Prudential Prop. & Cas. Co. v. Ins. Com'n* (D.S.C.1982) 534 F.Supp. 571, 581; *Sheeran v. Nationwide Mut. Ins. Co., Inc.* (1979) 80 N.J. 548, 404 A.2d 625, 628, fn. 2.)

13. Travelers points to section 1861.11, which provides: "In the event that the commissioner finds that (a) insurers have substantially withdrawn from any insurance market covered by this article, including insurance described by section 660 [automobile insurance], and (b) a market assistance plan would not be sufficient to make insurance available, the commissioner shall establish a joint underwriting authority in the manner set forth by Section 11891, without the prior creation of a market assistance plan." Under Proposition 103, however, an insurer retains the right to withdraw from the California market by surrendering its certificate pursuant to sections 1070–1076, as explained later in this opinion. (See *post,* p. 176 of 258 Cal.Rptr., p. 1260 of 771 P.2d.) Thus section 1861.11's reference to the possibility that insurers might withdraw from the market does not necessarily imply any distinction between policies issued before November 8, 1988, and those issued or renewed after that date.

apply to existing contracts and that such application does not raise a substantial doubt respecting its constitutionality.

The nonrenewal provision contains no language limiting its effect to policies issued or renewed after November 8, 1988. The omission is significant, because section 1861.01 (the rate-rollback provision) expressly states that it applies only to policies "issued or renewed on or after November 8, 1988." The necessary inference is that the nonrenewal provision was not so limited.

The evident purpose of the nonrenewal provision, moreover, mandates its application to existing policies. The provision is obviously designed to give policyholders a measure of assurance that their coverage would continue, and to prevent widespread refusals to renew in response to the initiative's enactment. Accordingly, the conclusion is inescapable that the nonrenewal provision was intended to apply to policies in force on the effective date of Proposition 103.

We therefore turn to the question whether section 1861.03, if applied to existing policies, unconstitutionally impairs the obligation of contracts. Three relatively recent United States Supreme Court decisions have considered the impairment-of-contract clause.[14] In *Allied Structural Steel Co. v. Spannaus* (1978) 438 U.S. 234, 98 S.Ct. 2716, 57 L.Ed.2d 727, the court struck down a Minnesota statute which required a company terminating operations in Minnesota to transfer to the state a sum sufficient to fund pension obligations to local workers. (Under prior law the company had the right to terminate the pension by refunding the trust amounts.) The court emphasized the narrow focus of the legislation—it was apparently aimed at only a few companies— and the fact that it concerned a subject not previously regulated.

Energy Reserves Group v. Kansas Power & Light, supra, 459 U.S. 400, 103 S.Ct. 697, 74 L.Ed.2d 569, upheld a Kansas law which established rates for natural gas sales and prohibited rate increases based on certain escalator clauses in existing contracts between gas sellers and public utilities. The court distinguished *Allied Structural Steel, supra,* 438 U.S. 234, 98 S.Ct. 2716, primarily on the ground that the parties were operating in a heavily regulated industry.

The most recent decision, *Exxon Corp. v. Eagerton* (1983) 462 U.S. 176, 103 S.Ct. 2296, 76 L.Ed.2d 497, upheld an Alabama law which imposed a severance tax on oil and gas and prohibited price increases which would pass on the burden of the tax even though some sellers had contracts which expressly authorized such price increases. The decision explained that "[a]lthough the language of the Contract Clause is facially absolute, its prohibition must be accommodated to the inherent police power of the State 'to safeguard the vital interests of its

---

14. A fourth decision, *United States Trust Co. v. New Jersey* (1977) 431 U.S. 1, 21, 97 S.Ct. 1505, 1517, 52 L.Ed.2d 92, involved a state statute repudiating the state's own contractual obligations. As later cases have made clear, such a law is subject to a more severe standard than are laws which primarily affect private obligations. (See *Energy Reserves Group v. Kansas Power & Light* (1983) 459 U.S. 400, 412–413, 103 S.Ct. 697, 704– 705, 74 L.Ed.2d 569.)

people.' [Citations.] This Court has long recognized that a statute does not violate the Contract Clause simply because it has the effect of restricting, or even barring altogether, the performance of duties created by contracts entered into prior to its enactment. [Citation.] * * * Thus, a state prohibition law may be applied to contracts for the sale of beer that were valid when entered into [citation], a law barring lotteries may be applied to lottery tickets that were valid when issued [citation], and workmen's compensation law may be applied to employers and employees operating under pre-existing contracts of employment that made no provision for work-related injuries. [Citation.] [¶] Like the laws upheld in these cases, the pass-through prohibition did not prescribe a rule limited in effect to contractual obligations or remedies, but instead imposed a generally applicable rule of conduct designed to advance 'a broad societal interest,' [citation]: protecting consumers from excessive prices. The prohibition applied to all oil and gas producers, regardless of whether they happened to be parties to sale contracts that contained a provision permitting them to pass tax increases through to their purchasers. The effect of the pass-through prohibition * * * was incidental to its main effect of shielding consumers from the burden of the tax increase." (462 U.S. at pp. 190–192, 103 S.Ct. at pp. 2305–2307).[15]

None of the United State Supreme Court cases has considered the contract clause in connection with insurance regulation, but a number of lower court decisions have discussed this matter. *Hinckley v. Bechtel Corp.* (1974) 41 Cal.App.3d 206, 116 Cal.Rptr. 33 involved a law which limited the period during which a retiring employee could exercise his right to convert a group life insurance policy to an individual policy without proof of insurability. Holding that the law could be applied to existing policies, the Court of Appeal stated: "The cases are legion which hold that the police power of the state to regulate the insurance business cannot be contracted away, and the economic interest of the state may justify the exercise of its continuing protective power notwithstanding interference with existing contracts." (P. 215, 116 Cal. Rptr. 33.)

Decisions of other states also offer an analogy. *Smith v. Department of Insurance, supra,* 507 So.2d 1080, offers something for both sides. Florida passed a law which limited noneconomic tort damages, froze insurance rates, required a partial rebate of premiums on existing policies, and prohibited insurers from cancelling or refusing to renew existing policies in order to avoid the rate freeze or rebate. The court held the rebate provision unconstitutional, applying a Florida rule that "virtually no degree of contract impairment is tolerable in this state." (*Pomponio v. Claridge of Pomponio Condominium, Inc.* (Fla.1979) 378 So.2d 774, 780, cited in *Smith, supra,* 507 So.2d at p. 1094). But it

---

15. Professor Tribe suggests that *Exxon Corp., supra,* 462 U.S. 176, 103 S.Ct. 2296, and *Energy Reserves, supra,* 459 U.S. 400, 103 S.Ct. 697, are inconsistent with, and effectively overrule, *Allied Structural Steel, supra,* 438 U.S. 234, 98 S.Ct. 2716. (Tribe, American Constitutional Law (2d ed. 1988) §§ 9–11.)

upheld without discussion all other provisions relating to insurance policies, including the section limiting the insurers' right to refuse to renew policies.

The State of Massachusetts, after regulating insurance rates for many years, discontinued rate regulation as of January 1, 1977. When insurance rates rose rapidly, the state legislature reimposed regulation retroactive to January 1, directed that all policies written since January 1 be rewritten at reduced rates, and excess premiums rebated. In *American Mfrs. Mut. Ins. Co. v. Comm'r of Ins., supra,* 372 N.E.2d 520, the Supreme Judicial Court of Massachusetts upheld the statute. The court relied on the urgent need for immediate correction of insurance rates, and reasoned that insurers, as part of an intensely regulated industry, "were on notice that the premiums received were not firm against legislative adjustment." (372 N.E.2d at p. 528.)

When New York enacted no-fault insurance in 1973, it required insurers to offer that coverage to existing policyholders, and imposed a three-year restriction on nonrenewal of policies. In *Country–Wide Ins. Co. v. Harnett* (S.D.N.Y.1977) 426 F.Supp. 1030, 1035, a three-judge federal court upheld a law extending the restriction for an additional three years, stating that "[t]he law accomplishes a legitimate public goal and any contract rights must yield to it." [16]

We now apply these principles and precedents to the renewal provision of Proposition 103. We begin by assessing the severity of the impairment, since that assessment "measures the height of the hurdle the state legislation must clear" (*Allied Structural Steel v. Spannaus, supra,* 438 U.S. 234, 245, 98 S.Ct. 2716, 2723) then examine the public interest advanced to justify the impairment.

In the present case the impairment, while not so low as to escape constitutional scrutiny, is relatively moderate and restrained, and the hurdle correspondingly low. The insurer may still refuse to renew policies for nonpayment of premium, fraud or misrepresentation, or substantial increase in the hazard insured against. And when it renews pursuant to Proposition 103 it is guaranteed fair and reasonable rates.

Insurance, moreover, is a highly regulated industry, and one in which further regulation can reasonably be anticipated.[17] As we said in *Carpenter v. Pacific Mut. Life Ins. Co.* (1937) 10 Cal.2d 307, 74 P.2d 761: "It is no longer open to question that the business of insurance is

16. One decision has reached a contrary result. In *Health Ins. Ass'n of America v. Harnett* (1978) 44 N.Y.2d 302, 405 N.Y.S.2d 634, 376 N.E.2d 1280, the court held that a law requiring health insurers to offer maternity coverage could not constitutionally be applied to existing health insurance policies. The decision rests on a view of state power far more limited than appears in the California cases, that "[o]nly on rare occasions and in extreme circumstances do rights fixed by the terms of a contract willingly entered into give way to a greater public need." (405 N.Y.S.2d 634, 641, 376 N.E.2d 1280, 1287.)

17. In *California Auto Assn. v. Maloney* (1951) 341 U.S. 105, 109–110, 71 S.Ct. 601, 603–604, 95 L.Ed. 788, the Supreme Court spoke of the "special relationship" between government and the insurance industry as justifying more extensive regulation than might be permitted for other industries.

affected with a public interest. * * * Neither the company nor a policyholder has the inviolate rights that characterize private contracts. The contract of the policyholder is subject to the reasonable exercise of the state's police power." (P. 329, 74 P.2d 761; see *People v. United National Life Ins. Co.* (1967) 66 Cal.2d 577, 595, 58 Cal.Rptr. 599, 427 P.2d 199 and cases there cited.) Indeed it is clear that during the year prior to November 8, 1988—a year during which almost all automobile insurance policies in effect on that date were issued or renewed— insurers were well aware of the possibility that initiatives or ordinary legislation might be enacted that would affect existing policies.

Finally, Proposition 103 does not prevent an insurer from discontinuing its California business. Sections 1070 through 1076 spell out the procedure by which an insurer may withdraw from California by surrendering its certificate of authority. The initiative did not repeal those sections, and indeed recognizes the possibility that insurers may withdraw from some insurance markets by authorizing the commissioner to establish a joint underwriting authority to serve such markets. (§ 1861.11, quoted in fn. 21, *ante.*)

We turn now to examine the public interest to determine whether it justifies the impairment. As we noted earlier, the drafters and the voters were evidently concerned that the enactment of Proposition 103 might cause some insurers not to renew some or all of their existing policies, an action which would undermine Proposition 103's goal of making insurance "available" for all Californians. Indeed if many insurers refused to renew the state could face a crisis in which many of its residents would be unable to obtain insurance and thus could not legally drive, and others would be forced to accept inadequate protection. We conclude that the public interest in averting this danger, when measured against the relatively low degree of impairment of contract rights involved, is sufficient to justify Proposition 103's nonrenewal provision, and accordingly that this provision can be applied to existing policies without violating the state or federal Constitutions.
* * *

Notes and Questions

1. *The Premise of the Proposition.* California is a massive insurance market, with dozens (if not hundreds) of insurers doing business in many lines. Was the premise of Proposition 103 that because all these markets were insufficiently competitive, rates were 20 percent above what they should have been? If not, on precisely what premise did the Proposition rest?

2. *Closing the Non–Renewal Gap.* Should the provisions governing mandatory renewal of auto insurance policies in Proposition 103 be viewed as directed at a problem independent of the rate-rollback question, or were the mandatory renewal provisions necessary to make the rate-rollback in that line succeed? If the latter, how and why?

3. *Does A Route of Escape Remain?* Given the court's decision that the mandatory rate rollback was unconstitutional, and the remaining provision that rates shall not be "excessive, inadequate, nor unfairly discriminatory"—application of which will be made by the Insurance Commissioner—did the Proposition merely focus all public attention on the election of the Commissioner for which it also provided? In a charged political climate such as this (the Proposition passed by a margin of roughly 51 percent to 49 percent) would you want to run for Insurance Commissioner in California?

3. "Unfairly Discriminatory" Rates

THE FAIRNESS–EFFICIENCY TENSION IN INSURANCE CLASSIFICATION

Apart from malice or prejudice (possible attitudes that should not be ignored, but which we set aside here), why would an insurer ever engage in unfair discrimination? Indeed, why would an insurer bother to engage in any form of "discrimination," i.e., charge different policyholders different rates for the same coverage? The reason, of course, is to combat adverse selection and moral hazard. Even an insurer holding a monopoly would have to risk classify to some extent to avoid these problems. Otherwise, high-risk insureds would adversely select into the insurer's single risk pool and cause it to unravel, as lower-risk insureds continually decided to self-insure all or part of the risks they would otherwise transfer to the insurer. Similarly, any insurer that did not make it a practice to classify and charge insureds based on their potential for suffering losses would find that it continually paid more claims for larger sums than it had predicted it would suffer. Those whom it insured would have less incentive to avoid losses than they would if their future premium levels depended on their current levels of precaution or losses. Claim frequency and severity would reflect this moral hazard.

When the monopoly assumption is relaxed and we suppose that there is even a minimal degree of competition in an insurance market, the advantages of risk classification become even more pronounced. Any insurer that does not risk classify, or whose classifications are insufficiently refined or accurate, will find that the low-risk insureds whom it is overcharging seek coverage from insurers who would charge them less. Simultaneously, high-risk insureds being charged more accurately by other insurers will adversely select into the first insurer's risk pool. Thus, the development of risk classification is to be expected as a natural correlate of the very existence of insurance in a world where there is at least some information available about the risks posed by different parties.

How much risk classification and what kind are to be expected, however, are more difficult questions. Risk classifying is not costless. Information about characteristics correlated with losses must be developed and maintained, and reliable data regarding the characteristics of insureds must be obtained and analyzed. The first axiom of risk classification, therefore, is that classification occurs up to the point where the additional competitive advantage gained from classifying equals its costs, but no further. In addition, no insurer would find it worthwhile in the long run to adopt a classification variable or system that was less refined than would be cost-effective, because it would find itself afflicted by the kind of adverse selection described at the beginning of this note. An insurer that wished to prove itself enlightened by charging police on SWAT teams the same price for life insurance as it charged law professors would find that it was besieged by applications from police, and quickly in danger of losing its low-risk law professor applicants. This approach might be a worthwhile public relations device, but applying the same kind of "enlightened" classification practices across-the-board would threaten the insurer with eventual insolvency.

It does not follow, however, that the risk classifications that are in use at any given time are the most cost-effective that could have been developed. Rather, like any other technology, current risk classifications stand on the shoulders of those that have preceded them. This means that decisions made many decades ago about what data to maintain and what statistical operations to perform on it may still rule the current classification structure from their grave. For example, suppose that insurers had never maintained data on two (hypothetically) useful classification variables: physicians' involvement in continuing medical education, and drivers' involvement in high school sports. These classification variables might have proved to be more cost-effective than others in medical malpractice and automobile liability insurance, provided that data concerning them had been maintained for many years. But employing them now would require incurring start-up and data collection costs that could prove to be prohibitively high.

Moreover, even if developing new classification variables were otherwise cost-effective for an insurer, it could not exclude other insurers from free-riding on its investment in developing these variables. Classification schemes cannot be copyrighted; the first insurer to use a new scheme might be able to gain a competitive edge for only a short time before other insurers also adopted it. This threat also seems likely to discourage the development of new variables, and provides an additional justification for the existence of such organizations as the Insurance Services Office, which can help to overcome this collective action problem by developing classifications available to all insurers.

All this is not to say that regulation of insurance risk classification systems is inappropriate. On the contrary, the implication of these insights is that although the free market may produce cost-effective risk classifications, it will not necessarily produce classifications that are considered fair, except for those observers who consider fairness and efficiency to be synonymous. Consequently, there are several questions that must be asked in evaluating whether and when the regulation of risk classification makes sense: What are the social benefits from such regulation? Will a mandated change in risk classification practices cost policyholders additional premiums? Which policyholders will pay these increases if not all policyholders will pay in equal measure, and how much will they pay?

HARTFORD ACCIDENT AND INDEMNITY CO. v. INSURANCE COMMISSIONER OF THE COMMONWEALTH OF PENNSYLVANIA

Supreme Court of Pennsylvania, 1984.
505 Pa. 571, 482 A.2d 542.

NIX, Chief Justice.

In this appeal we have agreed to review the Commonwealth Court's affirmance of an order of the Insurance Commissioner of Pennsylvania ("Commissioner") rescinding his prior approval of Hartford Accident and Indemnity Company's ("Hartford") gender-based automobile insurance rates on the ground they were "unfairly discriminatory" under section 3(d) of the Casualty and Surety Rate Regulation Act ("Rate Act"), Act of June 11, 1947, P.L. 538, § 3(d), 40 P.S. § 1183(d) (1971). After careful consideration we have concluded that the Commissioner's action was both within his statutory authority and mandated by the Rate Act, and, therefore, affirm.

I.

The instant action was initiated by Philip V. Mattes ("Mattes"), a Hartford automobile policyholder, who filed a complaint with the Commissioner challenging the legality of the Commissioner's earlier approval of Hartford's gender-based rates. Mattes established at an evidentiary hearing that, as a twenty-six year old unmarried male with an unblemished driving record, he was obligated to pay One Hundred Forty-eight Dollars ($148) more in annual premiums than would a similarly situated female insured for identical coverage. Hartford sought to justify its rating plan on the ground that actuarial data indicated that male policyholders in Mattes' age group are more likely to incure accident losses than female policyholders in the same age group. The Commissioner, interpreting the Rate Act's prohibition of "unfairly discriminatory" rates in light of this Commonwealth's public policy against sex discrimination as embodied in the Equal Rights Amendment, concluded that Hartford's gender-based rates were "unfairly discriminatory" and therefore invalid.

Hartford filed a petition for review of the Commissioner's adjudication in the Commonwealth Court; Mattes and the State Farm Mutual Automobile Insurance Company ("State Farm") were permitted to intervene. The Commonwealth Court affirmed *en banc,* finding no basis for disturbing the Commissioner's decision. 65 Pa.Commw. 249,

442 A.2d 382 (1982). Petitions for allowance of appeal filed in this Court by Hartford and State Farm were granted.

II.

In order to place Mattes' complaint and the Commissioner's response thereto in their proper context, an understanding of the statutory scheme which forms the background of this controversy is essential. The legislature's purpose in enacting the Rate Act is clearly set forth in section one:

> The purpose of this Act is *to promote the public welfare by regulating insurance rates to the end that they shall not be excessive, inadequate or unfairly discriminatory;* to enable authorized insurers to meet all requirements of the insuring public of this Commonwealth, and to authorize and regulate cooperative action among insurers in rate making and in other matters within the scope of this Act. Nothing in this Act is intended (1) to prohibit or discourage reasonable competition, or (2) to prohibit or encourage uniformity in insurance rates, rating systems, rating plans or practices. *This Act shall be liberally interpreted to carry into effect its purpose as herein set forth.*

40 P.S. § 1181 (1971) (emphasis supplied).

The Rate Act applies, with certain enumerated exceptions, to "all classes and kinds of insurance which may be written by stock or mutual casualty insurance companies, associations or exchanges, and including fidelity, surety and guaranty bonds and all other forms of motor vehicle insurance, and to title insurance on risks or operations in this Commonwealth. * * *" 40 P.S. § 1182 (1971).

The central provision of the Rate Act is section three, which sets forth the manner in which insurers must formulate their rates, thereby creating an affirmative duty of compliance on the part of insurers wishing to do business in this Commonwealth:

> All rates shall be made in accordance with the following provisions:
>
> (a) Due consideration shall be given to past and prospective loss experience within and outside this Commonwealth, to physical hazards, to safety and loss prevention factors, to underwriting practice and judgment to the extent appropriate, to catastrophe hazards, if any, to a reasonable margin for underwriting profit and contingencies, to dividends, savings or unabsorbed premium deposits allowed or returned by insurers to their policyholders, members or subscribers, to past and prospective expenses both country wide and those specially applicable to this Commonwealth, and to all other relevant factors within and outside this Commonwealth;

(b) The systems of expense provisions included in the rates for use by any insurer or group of insurers may differ from those of other insurers or groups of insurers to reflect the requirements of the operating methods of any such insurer or group with respect to any kind of insurance, or with respect to any subdivision or combination thereof for which subdivision or combination separate expense provisions are applicable;

(c) Risks may be grouped by classifications for the establishment of rates and minimum premiums. Classification rates may be modified to produce rates for individual risks in accordance with rating plans which establish standards for measuring variations in hazards or expense provisions, or both. Such standards may measure any differences among risks that can be demonstrated to have a probable effect upon losses or expenses;

(d) *Rates shall not be excessive, inadequate or unfairly discriminatory.*

40 P.S. § 1183 (1971) (emphasis supplied).

It must be emphasized that subsection (d) of section three limits the powers conferred upon insurance companies under subsections (a), (b) and (c). The overriding consideration is section three's mandate that rates may not be "excessive, inadequate or unfairly discriminatory."

To ensure compliance with the above provisions, section four of the Act requires every insurer to "file with the Commissioner every manual of classifications, rules, and rates, every rating plan and every modification of any of the foregoing which it proposes to use." 40 P.S. § 1184(a) (1971).[1] The Commissioner must "review such of the filings as it may be necessary to carry out the purposes of this Act," 40 P.S. § 1184(c) (1971), and is empowered to disapprove, after a hearing, any filing which fails to meet the requirements of the Rate Act. 40 P.S. § 1185 (1971). Beyond this specific delegation of authority, the legislature has committed to the Commissioner the "full power and authority, . . . [and] duty, to enforce by regulations, orders, or otherwise, . . . the provisions of this Act, *and the full intent thereof.*" 40 P.S. § 1193(d) (1971) (emphasis supplied).

Persons aggrieved by an approved filing which has not taken effect are entitled to file a complaint with and have a hearing before the Commissioner. 40 P.S. § 1197(a) (1971); *Commonwealth, Insurance Department v. Adrid,* 24 Pa.Commw. 270, 355 A.2d 597 (1976). Administrative review is available in appropriate cases even where, as in the instant case, the challenged filing is in effect. Moreover, a party adversely affected by the Commissioner's adjudication of a complaint has a right of appeal to the Commonwealth Court. 40 P.S. § 1197(c) (Supp.1983–84); 42 Pa. C.S. § 763(a).

---

1. This obligation may be satisfied through the medium of a licensed rating organization. Act of June 11, 1947, P.L. 538, § 4(b), 40 P.S. § 1184(b) (1971). Hartford is a member of such an organization.

Several important points emerge from the foregoing discussion. The Rate Act evidences the clear legislative determination that the public welfare requires both statutory channeling of the ratemaking process and administrative scrutiny of the resulting rates. One of the principal justifications for governmental involvement identified by the legislature is the need to prevent "unfairly discriminatory" rates. To achieve that goal, the legislature has directly prohibited insurers from making "unfairly discriminatory" rates, and has entrusted enforcement of that prohibition to the Commissioner, and, if need be, to the courts. Thus the Rate Act, independent of any federal or state constitutional provision, proscribes "unfairly discriminatory" ratemaking by insurers in this Commonwealth and provides administrative and judicial remedies therefor.

III.

The basic issue in this appeal is the proper interpretation of the phrase "unfairly discriminatory" as employed in section 3(d) of the Rate Act, 40 P.S. § 1183(d) (1971). That phrase is not defined in the Rate Act itself. The Commissioner concluded that he was compelled to interpret the statutory prohibition against "unfairly discriminatory" rates in a manner consistent with the strong public policy against gender-based discrimination under law as expressed in Pennsylvania's Equal Rights Amendment. Appellants Hartford and State Farm attack that conclusion arguing in favor of a narrow interpretation of the phrase which would limit the prohibition of section 3(d) to rates which are not "actuarially sound." Under the latter view the Rate Act would not only permit insurers to impose gender-based rates but would also prohibit the Commissioner from denying approval to such rates provided the insurer is able to support them with actuarial data.[2]

In the proceedings before the Commissioner, Mattes established conclusively that Hartford required him to pay a significantly higher premium than a similarly situated woman would be charged for identical Hartford coverage solely on the basis of his gender. There is no attempt to suggest that Mattes was not in fact discriminated against because of his sex. The inquiry must begin by accepting that a gender-based discrimination exists. The question to be resolved is whether such discrimination falls within the parameters of the Rate Act's prohibition against "unfairly discriminatory" rates.

Appellants' basic argument is that "unfair" should be limited in meaning to "*actuarially* unfair". Appellants maintain that the Rate Act's prohibition of "unfairly discriminatory" rates relates only to "variations in prices or rates that have no relationship to costs or the risk of loss". Brief for Hartford at 27. Their proffered construction of the Rate Act must be rejected for several reasons.

2. Under section 5(c) of the Rate Act, 40 P.S. § 1185(c), the Commissioner has no power to disapprove a filing or a modification unless a violation can be established.

Appellants base their argument largely on the legislative history of a model statute on which the Rate Act was based. In any event, the legislative history is unpersuasive. Appellants rely on a 1947 report to the National Association of Insurance Commissioners urging the adoption of a model statute drafted in response to the McCarron–Ferguson [sic—further misspellings corrected—ed.] Act, 15 U.S.C. §§ 1011 *et seq.,* which exempted the insurance business from federal antitrust laws to the extent that it was regulated by state law. They argue that the target of the Rate Act's prohibition, therefore, is the type of price discrimination which would violate the antitrust laws. Even assuming *arguendo* that this proposition logically follows, appellants fail to justify its application to the Pennsylvania Rate Act. There is no evidence that the General Assembly made use of the report or that the Rate Act was enacted in response to the McCarran–Ferguson Act. Thus it cannot be presumed that the report reflects the legislature's intent. To the contrary, the legislative response to the McCarran–Ferguson Act was the original Unfair Insurance Practices Act, Act of June 5, 1947, P.L. 445, § 1, 40 P.S. §§ 1151 *et seq.* (repealed 1974), as is explicitly stated in section 1 thereof, 40 P.S. § 1151. There is no reason to believe that the Rate Act was an additional response as claimed by appellants.

Second, the legislature has directed that the Rate Act "shall be liberally construed to carry into effect its purposes. * * *" 40 P.S. § 1181 (1971). The principal purpose of the Rate Act is "to promote the public welfare by regulating insurance rates to the end that they shall not be excessive, inadequate, or unfairly discriminatory; * * *" *Id.* Appellants' interpretation would be the antithesis of a liberal construction, and would severely limit the ability of the Commissioner to effectuate one of the three principal goals of the Rate Act, the prevention of unfairly discriminatory rates.

Third, "[e]very statute shall be construed, if possible, to give effect to all its provisions". 1 Pa.C.S. § 1921(a). Appellants' interpretation would render the phrase "unfairly discriminatory" mere surplusage. * * * Section 3(c) of the Rate Act, 40 P.S. § 1183(c), establishes the requirement of actuarial fairness by permitting an insurer to vary rates within a class only where the risk insured can be "demonstrated to have a probable effect upon losses or expenses." If actuarial fairness were the only concern of the Rate Act, the proscription of "unfairly discriminatory" rates contained in sections 1 and 3(d) would be redundant and of no independent effect; satisfaction of section 3(c) would be dispositive of the requirement of actuarial soundness. In order to give meaning to that proscription, the "fairness" of rates must be recognized as a legislative concern distinct from and transcending the need for sound actuarial justification. Thus we conclude that section 3(d) manifests separate legislative objectives which represent the recognition that a rate may be justified by the actuarial data offered in its support, yet unfair in its underlying assumptions and its application to the individual. Accordingly, appellants' narrow, technical view of the Rate Act's mandate of "fairness" must be rejected.

We must next consider whether the Commissioner was justified in looking to the Pennsylvania Equal Rights Amendment in his determination of whether Hartford's gender-based rate plan was "unfair." Appellants seek to characterize the Commissioner's disapproval of Hartford's rate plan as an unauthorized attempt to impose his personal theories and perceptions of social policy upon the insurance industry. We disagree. As we have already concluded, it was appropriate for the Commissioner to look beyond actuarial statistics in evaluating the fairness of Hartford's discriminatory rates. Since those rates were based on the gender of the insured, the Equal Rights Amendment was necessarily relevant.

The Equal Rights Amendment was adopted by the voters of this Commonwealth on May 18, 1971. The Amendment provides:

Prohibition against denial or abridgement of equality of rights because of sex

Equality of rights under the law shall not be denied or abridged in the Commonwealth of Pennsylvania because of the sex of the individual.

Pa. Const. Art. I, § 28.

In *Henderson v. Henderson,* 458 Pa. 97, 327 A.2d 60 (1974), this Court explained the purpose and effect of the new constitutional amendment:

The thrust of the Equal Rights Amendment is to insure equality of rights under the law and to eliminate sex as a basis for distinction. The sex of citizens of this Commonwealth is no longer a permissible factor in the determination of their legal rights and responsibilities. The law will not impose different benefits or burdens upon the members of a society based on the fact that they may be man or woman.

Id. at 101, 327 A.2d at 62.

We have not hesitated to effectuate the Equal Rights Amendment's prohibition of sex discrimination by striking down statutes and common law doctrines "predicated upon traditional or stereotypic roles of men and women. * * *" *Commonwealth ex rel. Spriggs v. Carson,* 470 Pa. 290, 299–300, 368 A.2d 635, 639 (1977) (plurality opinion) ("Tender years doctrine" offends concept of equality of the sexes embraced in Equal Rights Amendment.); *see Adoption of Walker,* 468 Pa. 165, 360 A.2d 603 (1976) (Adoption Act's failure to require parental consent of unwed father as well as unwed mother violates Equal Rights Amendment.); *Butler v. Butler,* 464 Pa. 522, 347 A.2d 477 (1975) (Presumption that where husband obtains his wife's property without adequate consideration a trust is created in his wife's favor abolished.); *Commonwealth v. Santiago,* 462 Pa. 216, 340 A.2d 440 (1975) (Doctrine of "coverture" requiring presumption that wife who commits crime in presence of husband was coerced by husband discarded.); *Di Florido v. Di Florido,* 459 Pa. 641, 331 A.2d 174 (1975) (Presumption that husband is owner of household goods used and possessed by both spouses abolished.); *Commonwealth v. Butler,* 458 Pa. 289, 328 A.2d 851 (1974) (Statutory scheme under which women are eligible for parole immediately upon incarceration while men must serve minimum sentence violates Equal Rights Amendment.); *Henderson v. Henderson, supra* (Statute providing for alimony pendente lite, counsel fees and expenses in divorce action for wife but not husband violates Equal Rights Amendment.); *Conway v. Dana,* 456 Pa. 536, 318 A.2d 324 (1974) (Presumption that father must bear principal burden of support of minor children abolished.); *cf. Hopkins v. Blanco,* 457 Pa. 90, 320 A.2d 139 (1974) (Equal Rights Amendment requires that wife as well as husband be permitted to recover for loss of consortium.) Gender-based rates such as Hartford's rely on and perpetuate stereotypes similar to those condemned in the above cases.

The efficacy of such rates is questionable even on the actuarial level.

> In terms of simplicity and consistency (i.e., stability and ease of verification), age, sex, and marital status receive high marks as rating factors. This is not the case from the viewpoint of causality. Causality refers to the actual or implied behavioral relationship between a particular rating factor and loss potential. The longer a vehicle is on the road, for example, the more likely it is that the vehicle may be involved in a random traffic accident; thus, daily or annual total mileage may be viewed as a causal rating factor. To the extent that sex and marital status classifications may be defended on causal grounds, the implied behavioral relationships rely largely on questionable social stereotypes. * * * Given the significant changes in traditional sex roles and social attitudes which have occurred in recent years, justifications for rating plans on the grounds of such implied assumptions are unacceptable.

>   *   *   *

> * * * [P]ublic policy considerations require more adequate justification for rating factors than simple statistical correlation with loss; in this regard, the task force recommends consideration of criteria such as causality, reliability, social acceptability, and incentive value in judging the reasonableness of a classification system. Based on these criteria, the task force concludes that as rating characteristics, sex and marital status are seriously lacking in justification and are subject to strong public opposition, and should therefore be prohibited as classification factors.

National Association of Insurance Commissioners. *Report of the Rates and Rating Procedures Task Force of the Automobile Insurance (D3) Subcommittee, November, 1978* at 5–6 (footnotes omitted).

As a matter of public policy, the Insurance Commissioner found that a rate plan based upon gender is offensive to the spirit of Article I, section 28. Appellants argue that Article I, section 28 is not self-executing. Furthermore, they attempt to employ the state action concept of our federal system and argue that here no such action occurred. These arguments are also misplaced in this context.

First, it is not a question as to whether or not Article I, section 28 is self-executing since we are here concerned with the proper interpretation of a legislative enactment. The question presented, properly phrased, is whether the term "unfairly discriminatory" must be read in light of the Equal Rights Amendment to our Pennsylvania Constitution. Unquestionably, sex discrimination in this Commonwealth is now unfair discrimination. It is a cardinal principle that ambiguous statutes should be read in a manner consonant with the Constitution. To read the term "unfairly discriminatory" as excluding sex discrimination would contradict the plain mandate of the Equal Rights Amendment to our Pennsylvania Constitution. Therefore, we must affirm the decision of the Insurance Commissioner. We must do so because the statute must be interpreted to include sex discrimination as one type of unfair discrimination, and not because the Commissioner has the power to implement the public policy of this Commonwealth in the absence of legislative direction.

Further, the notion that the interpretation of this insurance statute involves the concept of "state action" is incorrect in this context. The "state action" test is applied by the courts in determining whether, in a given case, a state's involvement in private activity is sufficient to justify the application of a federal constitutional prohibition of state action to that conduct. The rationale underlying the "state action" doctrine is irrelevant to the interpretation of the scope of the Pennsylvania Equal Rights Amendment, a state constitutional amendment adopted by the Commonwealth as part of its own organic law. The language of that enactment, not a test used to measure the extent of federal constitutional protections, is controlling.

The text of Article I, section 28 makes clear that its prohibition reaches sex discrimination "*under the law.*" As such it circumscribes the conduct of state and local government entities and officials of all levels in their formulation, interpretation and enforcement of statutes, regulations, ordinances and other legislation as well as decisional law. The decision of the Commissioner in a matter brought pursuant to the Rate Act is not only "under the law" but also, to the extent his adjudication is precedent on the question decided, "the law." The Commissioner, as a public official charged with the execution of the Rate Act and sworn to uphold the Constitution and laws of this Commonwealth, Pa.Const. Art. 6, § 3; Act of June 4, 1879, P.L. 99, § 1, 71 P.S. § 761 (1962), was constrained to conform his analysis of Hartford's rate plan and his interpretation of section 3(d) of the Rate Act to Article I, section 28.

Thus, in light of the Pennsylvania Constitution's clear and unqualified prohibition of discrimination "under the law" based upon gender, we conclude that the Commissioner's disapproval of Hartford's discriminatory sex-based rates on the ground they were "unfair" and contrary to established public policy was in conformity with section 3(d) of the Rate Act and an appropriate exercise of his statutory authority.

Accordingly, the Order of the Commonwealth Court affirming the adjudication of the Insurance Commissioner is affirmed. * * *

Notes and Questions

1. *Causality.* In the absence of a state Equal Rights Amendment, how should an Insurance Commissioner pour content into the state Insurance Code's prohibition against unfair discrimination in insurance rating? If women as a class have better driving records than men, what is unfair about a risk classification that takes this difference into account? The court suggested that the absence of a causal connection between the variable used (gender) and the risk in question made a difference. On this theory, is the use of age as a classification variable in life insurance (indeed, the predominant variable) improper?

In determining whether a classification is unfairly discriminatory, should it make a difference whether everyone pays more for insurance after eliminating the discrimination, or those against whom the discrimination operated pay less and those in favor of whom it operated pay more? For example, suppose that, as the court suggested, gender is merely a proxy for mileage driven per year, but the cost of verifying miles driven per year would raise the average price of auto insurance even for those previously discriminated against. What if (as is not normally the case) before unisex rating is adopted men pay an average of $1200 per year and women pay an average of $1000 per year for auto insurance, but after unisex rating is adopted, all drivers pay an average of $1210 per year—the increase in average premiums being the result of higher mileage-verification costs. Is eliminating the symbolic effect of discrimination worth this extra cost? Should the answer depend on which gender the suspect classification "discriminates" against, or does all discrimination discriminate against both genders? See K. Abraham, Distributing Risk: Insurance, Legal Theory, and Public Policy 64–100 (1986); Wortham, Insurance Classification: Too Important To Be Left To The Actuaries, 2 U.Mich.J.Law Reform 349 (1986); Austin, The Insurance Classification Controversy, 131 U.Pa.L.Rev. 517 (1983). For detailed data on the impact of unisex auto insurance rating on premium levels in Montana, see All–Industry Research Advisory Council, Unisex Auto Insurance Rating (1987).

2. *Actuarial Discrimination.* Although the concept of unfair discrimination may not be limited to what the defendants in the principal case termed "actuarial unfairness," the latter is certainly included in the former. For example, in *Anzinger v. O'Connor,* 109 Ill.App.3d 550, 65 Ill.Dec. 159, 440 N.E.2d 1014 (1982), the court reversed a decision by the Illinois Director of Insurance authorizing separate classification of emergency-room physicians by a physician-owned medical malpractice

insurer, on the ground that the decision was contrary to the manifest weight of the evidence regarding the relative riskiness of this specialty. Perhaps a Commissioner should be more willing to allow an arguably unfair discrimination if there is a reasonable degree of competition in the market. Under this view the fact that physician-owned malpractice insurance companies tend to dominate markets where they exist may help to explain the court's unwillingness to defer to administrative expertise in *Anzinger.*

3. *Other State Legislation.* A number of legislatures have addressed the gender discrimination issue more directly, by mandating unisex rating in some or all insurance sold in the state. See, e.g., West's Ann.Cal.Ins.Code § 790.03(f) (life insurance and annuities sold on an individual basis); N.C.Gen.Stat. § 58–124.19(4) (automobile insurance); Mont.Code Ann. § 49–2–309 (all insurance). In contrast, a Florida court held that its state's Insurance Code does not authorize the Insurance Commissioner to prohibit the use of sex, marital status, and scholastic achievement as automobile insurance rating factors. See *State Department of Insurance v. Insurance Services Office,* 434 So.2d 908 (Fla.Dist.Ct.App.1983).

4. *Federal Law.* At the federal level, Title VII of the Civil Rights Act of 1964 makes it an unlawful employment practice "to discriminate against any individual with respect to his compensation, terms, conditions, or privileges of employment, because of such individual's race, color, religion, sex or national origin." 42 U.S.C. § 2000e–2(a)(1). In two important cases, the U.S. Supreme Court has held that gender-based provisions in employer-sponsored pension programs funded by insurance annuities violate the Act. Each involved the difference between male and female life expectancies, since under gender-based mortality tables, females live on the average several years longer than men.

First, in *Los Angeles Department of Water & Power v. Manhart,* 435 U.S. 702, 98 S.Ct. 1370, 55 L.Ed.2d 657 (1978), the employer required females who elected to participate in a pension plan to make 15 percent higher contributions than males, on the ground that pensions for females exceeded the cost of those for males, because females lived longer. The court ruled that this practice nonetheless discriminated against females, since the Act protects women as individuals and the practice treated them as a group. Then, in *Arizona Governing Committee v. Norris,* 463 U.S. 1073, 103 S.Ct. 3492, 77 L.Ed.2d 1236 (1983), the Court was faced with a retirement program that was financed by equal payments from males and females, but paid men higher monthly benefits upon retirement because of their shorter life expectancy. The Court held that this practice also violated the Act, for essentially the reasons given in *Manhart.*

Note that Title VII applies only to discrimination in employment; the Court held that the *employer's* practices in these cases were unlawful, not that the *insurer's* practices were. A male could still take his unisex pension in a lump sum and purchase an annuity in the private market that would pay him a larger monthly sum than a female of like age and circumstances, assuming there were no state prohibition against such a classification. Under a gender-based system females would be paid the same average amounts as males, though over a longer period. Under a life insurance program, of course, the roles would be reversed, since life insurance for females would cost them less than males, because of females' longer life expectancy.

The literature on the application of Title VII to insurance is voluminous. For one very lively set of exchanges on the issues, see Kimball, Reverse Sex Discrimination: Manhart, 1979 Am.Bar Found. Research J. 83; Brilmayer, Hekeler, Laycock, and Sullivan, Sex Discrimination in Employer–Sponsored Insurance Plans: A Legal and Demographic Analysis, 47 U.Chi.L.Rev. 505 (1980); Benston, The Economics of Gender Discrimination in Employee Fringe Benefits: Manhart Revisited, 49 U.Chi.L.Rev. 489 (1982); Brilmayer, Laycock and Sullivan, The Efficient Use of Group Averages as Nondiscrimination: A Rejoinder to Professor Benston, 50 U.Chi.L.Rev. 222 (1983); Benston, Discrimination and Economic Efficiency in Employee Fringe Benefits: A Clarification of Issues and a Response to Professors Brilmayer, Laycock, and Sullivan, 50 U.Chi.L.Rev. 250 (1983).

5. *Remedies.* Once a risk classification is declared discriminatory, the appropriate remedy is at issue. Should some form of retroactive compensation be paid to those who have paid excessive premiums in the past? Here the problems of identifying victims and determining how retroactive the scope of the decision should be would be immense. On the other hand, altering an existing benefit structure to make it unisex—in life insurance, pensions, or annuities, for example, would be a theoretically clean but possibly quite expensive undertaking. The question here is whether to "top up," i.e., provide the group discriminated against with more generous benefits, to reduce the benefits promised a favored group in order to finance increased benefits to others, or to leave the previously discriminatory system in place for past contributions and begin a unisex system for future contributions and benefits. In a leading case decided after *Norris,* the Second Circuit decided that the second approach was appropriate, and estimated that the effect would be to increase the value of female pensions by 8 percent, and reduce the value of male pensions by roughly the same amount. See *Spirt v. Teachers Insurance and Annuity Association,* 735 F.2d 23 (2d Cir.1984).

C. RESIDUAL FEDERAL REGULATION

Although the states now play a predominant role in the regulation of insurance, some federal regulation is nonetheless contemplated by the McCarran–Ferguson Act and does occur. For example, the applicability of a variety of non-antitrust federal statutes to insurance turns in part on the meaning of certain provisions in the Act. See, e.g., *Cody v.*

Community Loan Corporation of Richmond County, 606 F.2d 499 (5th Cir.1979) (Truth in Lending Act applicable to loans made as part of the sale of insurance); but see *Gerlach v. Allstate Insurance Company,* 338 F.Supp. 642 (S.D.Fla.1972) (contra). By far the most important issues regarding the residue of federal regulation of insurance, however, concern the possible application of the United States antitrust laws to the insurance industry's activities.

Now that you are familiar with the scope of state regulation of insurance, recall three features of the McCarran–Ferguson Act: (1) the "business of insurance" is exempted from the reach of the federal antitrust laws, (2) except that these antitrust laws are applicable "to the extent that such business is not regulated by State law," and (3) regardless of state regulation, McCarran–Ferguson does not render the Sherman Act inapplicable to "any agreement to boycott, coerce, or intimidate, or act of boycott, coercion, or intimidation." 15 U.S.C. §§ 1012–13. Each of these features of the Act raises its own set of difficult questions.

1. What Constitutes the "Business of Insurance"?

UNION LABOR LIFE INSURANCE CO. v. PIRENO

Supreme Court of the United States, 1982.
458 U.S. 119, 102 S.Ct. 3002, 73 L.Ed.2d 647.

Justice BRENNAN delivered the opinion of the Court.

In these cases we consider an alleged conspiracy to eliminate price competition among chiropractors, by means of a "peer review committee" that advised an insurance company whether particular chiropractors' treatments and fees were "necessary" and "reasonable." The question presented is whether the alleged conspiracy is exempt from federal antitrust laws as part of the "business of insurance" within the meaning of the McCarran–Ferguson Act.[1]

I.

Petitioners are the New York State Chiropractic Association (NYS-CA), a professional association of chiropractors, and the Union Labor Life Insurance Co. (ULL), a Maryland insurer doing business in New

---

1. 59 Stat. 33, as amended, 15 U.S.C. §§ 1011–1015. The Act provides in relevant part:

"(a) The business of insurance, and every person engaged therein, shall be subject to the laws of the several States which relate to the regulation or taxation of such business.

"(b) No Act of Congress shall be construed to invalidate, impair, or supersede any law enacted by any State for the purpose of regulating the business of insurance, . . . unless such Act specifically relates to the business of insurance. * * *"
§ 2, 15 U.S.C. §§ 1012(a), (b).

"(c) Nothing contained in this Act shall render the * * * Sherman Act inapplicable to any agreement to boycott, coerce, or intimidate, or act of boycott, coercion, or intimidation." § 3, 15 U.S.C. § 1013(b).

York. As required by New York law, ULL's health insurance policies cover certain policyholder claims for chiropractic treatments. But certain ULL policies limit the company's liability to "the *reasonable* charges" for "*necessary* medical care and services." App. 19a, 22a (emphasis added). Accordingly, when presented with a policyholder claim for reimbursement for chiropractic treatments, ULL must determine whether the treatments were necessary and whether the charges for them were reasonable. In making some of these determinations, ULL has arranged with NYSCA to use the advice of NYSCA's Peer Review Committee.

The Committee was established by NYSCA in 1971, primarily to aid insurers in evaluating claims for chiropractic treatments.[2] It is composed of 10 practicing New York chiropractors, who serve on a voluntary basis. At the request of an insurer, the Committee will examine a chiropractor's treatments and charges in a particular case, and will render an opinion on the necessity for the treatments and the reasonableness of the charges made for them. The opinion will be based upon such considerations as the treating chiropractor's experience and specialty degrees; the location of his office; the number of visits and time spent with the patient; the patient's age, occupation, general physical condition, and history of previous treatment; and X-ray findings.

Respondent is a chiropractor licensed and practicing in the State of New York. On a number of occasions his treatments of ULL policyholders, and his charges for those treatments, have been referred by ULL to the Committee, which has sometimes concluded that his treatments were unnecessary or his charges unreasonable. Petitioners assert that respondent has treated his patients "in a manner calculated to maximize the number of treatments for a particular condition, and that his fees for these treatments are unusually high." 650 F.2d 387, 389 (CA2 1981). Respondent, for his part, contends that the members of the Committee "practice 'antiquated' techniques that they seek to impose on their more innovative competitors." Ibid.

This dispute resulted in the present suit, brought by respondent in the United States District Court for the Southern District of New York. Respondent alleged that the peer review practices of petitioners violated § 1 of the Sherman Act.[3] In particular, he claimed that petitioners and others had used the Committee as the vehicle for a conspiracy to fix the prices that chiropractors, including respondent, would be permitted to charge for their services. He concluded that he had been restrained from providing his chiropractic services to the public freely and fully, and that would-be recipients of chiropractic services had been

---

2. The Committee's advice is also available to patients, governmental agencies, and chiropractors themselves, but insurers are the principal users. 650 F.2d 387, 388 (CA2 1981).

3. 15 U.S.C. § 1, which provides in pertinent part that "[e]very contract, combination in the form of trust or otherwise, or conspiracy, in restraint of trade or commerce among the several States, or with foreign nations, is declared to be illegal. • • •"

deprived of the benefits of competition. Respondent requested, inter alia, declaratory and injunctive relief against ULL's continued use of NYSCA's Peer Review Committee in evaluating policyholders' claims.

After extensive discovery, the District Court granted petitioners' motion for summary judgment dismissing respondent's complaint, concluding that ULL's use of NYSCA's Peer Review Committee was exempted from antitrust scrutiny by the McCarran–Ferguson Act, App. to Pet. for Cert. in No. 81–389, pp. 20a–37a. The court noted that three requirements must be met in order to obtain the McCarran–Ferguson exemption: The challenged practices (1) must constitute the "business of insurance," (2) must be regulated by state law, and (3) must not amount to a "boycott, coercion, or intimidation." Id., at 27a–28a. In the court's view, all three of these requirements were satisfied in the present case. In particular, the court held that petitioners' peer review practices constituted the "business of insurance" because they served "to define the precise extent of ULL's contractual obligations * * * under [its] policies." Id., at 29a–30a. Moreover, the court determined that the peer review practices "involve[d] the spreading of risk, an indispensable element of the 'business of insurance.'" Id., at 30a.[4] Respondents' Sherman Act claim was accordingly dismissed with prejudice.

The Court of Appeals for the Second Circuit reversed. 650 F.2d 387 (1981). Relying upon this Court's recent opinion in *Group Life & Health Ins. Co. v. Royal Drug Co.*, 440 U.S. 205, 99 S.Ct. 1067, 59 L.Ed. 2d 261 (1979) the Court of Appeals concluded that the District Court had erred in holding that ULL's use of NYSCA's Peer Review Committee constituted the "business of insurance." [5] Accordingly, the Court of Appeals remanded the action for further proceedings. We granted certiorari to resolve a conflict among the Courts of Appeals on the question presented.[6] 454 U.S. 1052, 102 S.Ct. 595, 70 L.Ed.2d 587 (1981).

4. The court then turned to the Act's second requirement, that the challenged practices be "regulated by state law." The court held that that requirement had been met, as well, observing that New York had "enacted a pervasive scheme of regulation and supervision of insurance," had prohibited "the unfair settlement of claims," and had proscribed "the conduct alleged in the complaint" in its state antitrust law, the Donnelly Act, which by its terms applied to insurers. App. to Pet. for Cert. in No. 81–389, pp. 31a–32a. Finally, the court determined that respondent had neither alleged a "boycott" on petitioners' part, nor offered evidentiary support for such a claim. Id., at 33a–35a. The court thus concluded that the Act's third requirement was satisfied in the present case, and that petitioners' actions were consequently "exempt from application of the antitrust laws." Id., at 36a.

5. Since it reached this conclusion, the Court of Appeals did not definitively address the other holdings of the District Court. See n. 4, supra. The court did note, however, that petitioner NYSCA did not itself "appear to be regulated by state law in the manner § 2(b) requires." 650 F.2d, at 390, n. 5.

6. As noted by the Court of Appeals, id., at 395, n. 13, the decision below is contrary to that of the Court of Appeals for the Fourth Circuit "in a factually identical case." See *Bartholomew v. Virginia Chiropractors Assn.*, 612 F.2d 812 (1979).

II.

The only issue before us is whether petitioners' peer review practices are exempt from antitrust scrutiny as part of the "business of insurance." "It is axiomatic that conduct which is not exempt from the antitrust laws may nevertheless be perfectly legal." *Group Life & Health Ins. Co. v. Royal Drug Co., supra*, at 210, n. 5, 99 S.Ct., at 1072, n. 5. Thus in deciding these cases we have no occasion to address the merits of respondent's Sherman Act claims. However, the Sherman Act does express a "longstanding congressional commitment to the policy of free markets and open competition." *Community Communications Co. v. Boulder*, 455 U.S. 40, 56, 102 S.Ct. 835, 843, 70 L.Ed.2d 810 (1982); see also *United States v. Topco Associates, Inc.*, 405 U.S. 596, 610, 92 S.Ct. 1126, 1134, 31 L.Ed.2d 515 (1972). Accordingly, our precedents consistently hold that exemptions from the antitrust laws must be construed narrowly. *FMC v. Seatrain Lines, Inc.*, 411 U.S. 726, 733, 93 S.Ct. 1773, 1778, 36 L.Ed.2d 620 (1973). This principle applies not only to implicit exemptions, see *Group Life & Health Ins. Co. v. Royal Drug Co., supra*, at 231, 99 S.Ct., at 1083, but also to express statutory exemptions, see *United States v. McKesson & Robbins, Inc.*, 351 U.S. 305, 316, 76 S.Ct. 937, 943, 100 L.Ed. 1209 (1956). In *Royal Drug, supra*, this Court had occasion to re-examine the scope of the express antitrust exemption provided for the "business of insurance" by § 2(b) of the McCarran–Ferguson Act. We hold that decision of the question before us is controlled by *Royal Drug*.

The principal petitioner in *Royal Drug* was a Texas insurance company, Blue Shield, that offered policies entitling insured persons to purchase prescription drugs for $2 each from any pharmacy participating in a "Pharmacy Agreement" with Blue Shield; policyholders were also allowed to purchase prescription drugs from a nonparticipating pharmacy, but in that event they would have to pay full price for the drugs and would be reimbursed by Blue Shield for only a part of that price. Blue Shield offered Pharmacy Agreements to all licensed pharmacies in Texas, but participating pharmacies were required to sell prescription drugs to Blue Shield's policyholders for $2 each, and were reimbursed only for their cost in acquiring the drugs thus sold. "Thus, only pharmacies that [could] afford to distribute prescription drugs for less than this $2 markup [could] profitably participate in the plan." 440 U.S., at 209, 99 S.Ct., at 1072 (footnote omitted).

Respondents in *Royal Drug* were the owners of nonparticipating pharmacies. They sued Blue Shield and several participating pharmacies under § 1 of the Sherman Act, alleging that the Pharmacy Agreements were the instrument by which Blue Shield had conspired with participating pharmacies to fix the retail prices of prescription drugs. Respondents also alleged that the Agreements encouraged Blue Shield's policyholders to avoid nonparticipating pharmacies, thus constituting an unlawful group boycott. The District Court granted summary judgment to Blue Shield and the other petitioners holding that the challenged Agreements were exempt under § 2(b) of the McCarran–Ferguson Act. But the Court of Appeals disagreed, holding that the Agreements were not the "business of insurance" within the meaning of that Act, and reversed. 440 U.S., at 210, 99 S.Ct., at 1072. This Court affirmed. Looking to "the structure of the Act and its legislative history," id., at 211, 99 S.Ct., at 1073, the Court discussed three characteristics of the business of insurance that Congress had intended to exempt through § 2(b).

First, after noting that one "indispensable characteristic of insurance" is the "spreading and underwriting of a policyholder's risk," id., at 211–212, 99 S.Ct., at 1073,[7] the Court observed that parts of the legislative history of the McCarran–Ferguson Act "strongly suggest that Congress understood the business of insurance to be the underwriting and spreading of risk," id., at 220–221, 99 S.Ct., at 1077–1078. The Court then dismissed Blue Shield's contention that its Pharmacy Agreements involved such activities.

> "The Pharmacy Agreements * * * are merely arrangements for the purchase of goods and services by Blue Shield. By agreeing with pharmacies on the maximum prices it will pay for drugs, Blue Shield effectively reduces the total amount it must pay to its policyholders. The Agreements thus enable Blue Shield to minimize costs and maximize profits. Such cost-savings arrangements may well be sound business practice, and may well inure ultimately to the benefit of policyholders in the form of lower premiums, but they are not the 'business of insurance.'" Id., at 214, 99 S.Ct., at 1074 (footnote omitted).

Second, the Court identified "the contract between the insurer and the insured" as "[a]nother commonly understood aspect of the business of insurance." Id., at 215, 99 S.Ct., at 1075. The Court noted that, in enacting the McCarran–Ferguson Act, Congress had been concerned with the " 'relationship between insurer and insured, the type of policy which could be issued, its reliability, interpretation, and enforcement— these were the core of the "business of insurance." ' " Id., at 215–216, 99 S.Ct., at 1075, quoting *SEC v. National Securities, Inc.*, 393 U.S. 453, 460, 89 S.Ct. 564, 568, 21 L.Ed.2d 668 (1969). The Court then rejected Blue Shield's argument that its Pharmacy Agreements were so closely related to the "reliability, interpretation, and enforcement" of its policies as to fall within the intended scope of § 2(b): "This argument * * * proves too much." 440 U.S., at 216, 99 S.Ct., at 1075.

---

7. As the Court explained:

" 'It is characteristic of insurance that a number of risks are accepted, some of which involve losses, and that such losses are spread over all the risks so as too enable the insurer to accept each risk at a slight fraction of the possible liability upon it.' 1 G. Couch, Cyclopedia of Insurance Law § 1:3 (2d ed. 1959). See also R. Keeton, Insurance Law § 1.2(a) (1971) ('Insurance is an arrangement for transferring and distributing risk'); 1 G. Richards, The Law of Insurance § 2 (W. Freedman 5th ed. 1952)." 440 U.S., at 211, 99 S.Ct., at 1073 (footnote omitted).

"At the most, the petitioners have demonstrated that the Pharmacy Agreements result in cost savings to Blue Shield which may be reflected in lower premiums if the cost savings are passed on to policyholders. But, in that sense, every business decision made by an insurance company has some impact on its reliability, its ratemaking, and its status as a reliable insurer * * * [and thus] could be included in the 'business of insurance.' Such a result would be plainly contrary to the statutory language, which exempts the 'business of insurance' and not the 'business of insurance companies.'" Id., at 216–217, 99 S.Ct., at 1075.

Finally, the Court noted that in enacting the McCarran–Ferguson Act, "the primary concern of both representatives of the insurance industry and the Congress was that cooperative ratemaking efforts be exempt from the antitrust laws." Id., at 221, 99 S.Ct., at 1078. This was so because of "the widespread view that it [was] very difficult to underwrite risks in an informed and responsible way without intra-industry cooperation." Ibid. The Court was thus reluctant to extend the § 2(b) exemption to the case before it, "because the Pharmacy Agreements involve parties wholly outside the insurance industry." Id., at 231, 99 S.Ct., at 1083.

"There is not the slightest suggestion in the legislative history that Congress in any way contemplated that arrangements such as the Pharmacy Agreements in this case, which involve the mass purchase of goods and services from entities outside the insurance industry, are the 'business of insurance.'" Id., at 224, 99 S.Ct., at 1079 (footnote omitted).

In sum, Royal Drug identified three criteria relevant in determining whether a particular practice is part of the "business of insurance" exempted from the antitrust laws by § 2(b): first, whether the practice has the effect of transferring or spreading a policyholder's risk; second, whether the practice is an integral part of the policy relationship between the insurer and the insured; and third, whether the practice is limited to entities within the insurance industry. None of these criteria is necessarily determinative in itself, but examining the arrangement between petitioners NYSCA and ULL with respect to all three criteria, we do not hesitate to conclude that it is not a part of the "business of insurance."

Plainly, ULL's use of NYSCA's Peer Review Committee plays no part in the "spreading and underwriting of a policyholder's risk." *Group Life & Health Ins. Co. v. Royal Drug Co.*, 440 U.S., at 211, 99 S.Ct., at 1072. Both the "spreading" and the "underwriting" of risk refer in this context to the transfer of risk characteristic of insurance. See n. 7, supra. And as the Court of Appeals below observed:

"The risk that an insured will require chiropractic treatment has been transferred from the insured to [ULL] by the very purchase of insurance. Peer review takes place only after the risk has been transferred by means of the policy, and then it functions only to determine whether the risk of the entire loss (the insured's cost of treatment) has been transferred to [ULL]—that is, whether the insured's loss falls within the policy limits." 650 F.2d, at 393.

Petitioner ULL argues that the Court of Appeals' analysis is "semantic and unrealistic." Brief for Petitioner ULL 17. Petitioner reasons that "[i]t is inconceivable that Congress would have included risk transfer within the 'business of insurance' but excluded a device that helps 'determine whether the risk * * * has been transferred' and acts as 'an aid in determining the scope of the transfer.'" Ibid. We find no merit in this argument, because the challenged peer review arrangement is logically and temporally unconnected to the transfer of risk accomplished by ULL's insurance policies. The transfer of risk from insured to insurer is effected by means of the contract between the parties—the insurance policy—and that transfer is complete at the time that the contract is entered. See 9 G. Couch, Cyclopedia of Insurance Law §§ 39:53, 39:63 (2d ed. 1962). If the policy limits coverage to "necessary" treatments and "reasonable" charges for them, then that limitation is the measure of the risk that has actually been transferred to the insurer: To the extent that the insured pays unreasonable charges for unnecessary treatments, he will not be reimbursed, because the risk of incurring such treatments and charges was never transferred to the insurer, but was instead always retained by the insured. Petitioner's argument contains the unspoken premise that the transfer of risk from an insured to his insurer actually takes place not when the contract between those parties is completed, but rather only when the insured's claim is settled. This premise is contrary to the fundamental principle of insurance that the insurance policy defines the scope of risk assumed by the insurer from the insured. See id., § 39:3; R. Keeton, Insurance Law § 5.1(a) (1971).

Turning to the second *Royal Drug* criterion, it is clear that ULL's use of NYSCA's Peer Review Committee is not an integral part of the policy relationship between insurer and insured. In the first place, the challenged arrangement between ULL and NYSCA is obviously distinct from ULL's contracts with its policyholders. In this sense the challenged arrangement resembles the Pharmacy Agreements in *Royal Drug*. There the Court rejected the proposition that the Agreements were " 'between insurer and insured.'" *Group Life & Health Ins. Co. v. Royal Drug Co., supra*, at 215, 99 S.Ct., at 1075, quoting *SEC v. National Securities, Inc.*, 393 U.S., at 460, 89 S.Ct., at 568. Rather, it recognized those Agreements as "separate contractual arrangements between Blue Shield and pharmacies engaged in the sale and distribution of goods and services other than insurance." 440 U.S., at 216, 99 S.Ct., at 1075. Similarly, ULL's use of NYSCA's Peer Review Committee is a separate arrangement between the insurer and third parties not engaged in the business of insurance.

Petitioner ULL argues that the challenged peer review practices satisfy this criterion because peer review "directly involves the 'interpretation' and 'enforcement' of the insurance contract." Brief for Petitioner ULL 16. But this argument is essentially identical to one made and rejected in *Royal Drug*. Blue Shield there contended that its Pharmacy Agreements "so closely affected the 'reliability, interpretation, and enforcement' of the insurance contract * * * as to fall within the exempted area." 440 U.S., at 216, 99 S.Ct., at 1075 (footnote omitted). This Court noted, however:

> "The benefit promised to Blue Shield policyholders is that their premiums will cover the cost of prescription drugs except for a $2 charge for each prescription. So long as that promise is kept, policyholders are basically unconcerned with arrangements made between Blue Shield and participating pharmacies." Id., at 213–214, 99 S.Ct., at 1074 (footnotes omitted).

Similarly, when presented with policyholder claims for reimbursement, ULL must decide whether the claims are covered by its policies. But these decisions are entirely ULL's, and its use of NYSCA's Peer Review Committee as an aid in its decisionmaking process is a matter of indifference to the policyholder, whose only concern is *whether* his claim is paid, not *why* it is paid. As in Royal Drug, petitioners have shown, at the most, that the challenged peer review practices result in "cost savings to [ULL] which may be reflected in lower premiums if the cost savings are passed on to policyholders." Id., at 216, 99 S.Ct., at 1075. To grant the practices a § 2(b) exemption on such a showing "would be plainly contrary to the statutory language, which exempts the 'business of insurance' and not the 'business of insurance companies.'" Id., at 217, 99 S.Ct., at 1076.

Finally, as respects the third *Royal Drug* criterion, it is plain that the challenged peer review practices are not limited to entities within the insurance industry. On the contrary, ULL's use of NYSCA's Peer Review Committee inevitably involves third parties wholly outside the insurance industry—namely, practicing chiropractors. Petitioners do not dispute this fact, but instead deprecate its importance. They argue that we should not conclude "that ULL's use of the peer review process is outside the scope of the 'business of insurance' simply because NYSCA is not an insurance company." Brief for Petitioner ULL 25. In petitioners' view,

> "There is nothing in the McCarran–Ferguson Act that limits the 'business of insurance' to the business of insurance companies. As this Court has stated, '[the Act's] language refers not to the persons or companies who are subject to state regulation, but to laws "regulating the *business* of insurance."'" *National Securities*, 393 U.S., at 459 (89 S.Ct. at 568)." Ibid. (emphasis in original of quoted opinion).

Asserting that "the [New York] Superintendent of Insurance effectively can regulate the peer review process through his authority over the claims adjustment procedures of ULL," id., at 26, petitioners conclude that the process is part of the "business of insurance" despite the necessary involvement of third parties outside the insurance industry.

We may assume that the challenged peer review practices need not be denied the § 2(b) exemption *solely* because they involve parties outside the insurance industry. But the involvement of such parties, even if not dispositive, constitutes part of the inquiry mandated by the *Royal Drug* analysis. As the Court noted there, § 2(b) was intended primarily to protect "*intra*-industry cooperation" in the underwriting of risks. 440 U.S., at 221, 99 S.Ct., at 1078 (emphasis added). Arrangements between insurance companies and parties outside the insurance industry can hardly be said to lie at the center of that legislative concern. More importantly, such arrangements may prove contrary to the spirit as well as the letter of § 2(b), because they have the potential to restrain competition in noninsurance markets. Indeed, the peer review practices challenged in the present cases assertedly realize precisely this potential: Respondent's claim is that the practices restrain competition in a provider market—the market for chiropractic services—rather than in an insurance market. App. 8a. Thus we cannot join petitioners in depreciating the fact that parties outside the insurance industry are intimately involved in the peer review practices at issue in these cases.[8]

III.

In sum, we conclude that ULL's use of NYSCA's Peer Review Committee does not constitute the "business of insurance" within the meaning of § 2(b) of the McCarran–Ferguson Act.[9] The judgment of the Court of Appeals is accordingly affirmed.

Justice REHNQUIST, with whom The CHIEF JUSTICE and Justice O'CONNOR join, dissenting.

Purporting to rely upon our recent decision in *Group Life & Health Ins. Co. v. Royal Drug Co.*, 440 U.S. 205, 99 S.Ct. 1067, 59 L.Ed.2d 261

8. The premise of the dissent is that NYSCA's Peer Review Committee actually constitutes "the claims adjustor" in this case. See post, at 3013. From this premise the dissent reasons that since "claims adjustment is part and parcel of the 'business of insurance' protected by the McCarran–Ferguson Act," post, at 3013, it necessarily follows that the peer review practices at issue in this case must enjoy the Act's exemption. The fatal flaw in this syllogism is that NYSCA's Peer Review Committee is *not* the claims adjustor. As the Court of Appeals noted: "Opinions of the committee are not binding unless the parties agree beforehand that they will be." 650 F.2d, at 388. Thus in a case such as the present one, ULL is perfectly free to disregard the Committee's evaluation. Even if ULL were to act upon the Committee's opinion, the nonbinding nature of the Committee's evaluation means that, at most, peer review is merely ancillary to the claims adjustment process. We see no reason that such ancillary activities must necessarily enjoy the McCarran–Ferguson exemption from the antitrust laws. Unlike activities that occur wholly within the insurance industry—such as the claims adjustment process itself—the ancillary peer review practices at issue in this case "involve parties wholly outside the insurance industry." See *Group Life & Health Ins. Co. v. Royal Drug Co.*, 440 U.S., at 231, 99 S.Ct., at 1083. Thus peer review falls afoul of the third *Royal Drug* criterion in a way in which pure claims adjustment activities cannot.

9. This conclusion renders it unnecessary for us to address the questions whether the conduct challenged in respondent's complaint was "regulated by state law" or constituted a "boycott, coercion, or intimidation." See n. 4, *supra*.

(1979), the Court today exposes to antitrust liability an aspect of the business of insurance designed to promote fair and efficient claims settlement. The Court reaches this conclusion by determining that the peer review process does not spread risk, is not an integral part of the insurance relationship, and is not limited to entities within the insurance industry. Because I find the claims adjustment function of the Peer Review Committee to be at the heart of the relationship between insurance companies and their policyholders, I conclude that such committees are clearly within the sphere of insurance activity which the McCarran–Ferguson Act intended to protect from the effect of the antitrust laws.[1] This conclusion finds support in the legislative history of the Act and in *Royal Drug* and its predecessors.

For many years statutes such as the Sherman Act were thought not applicable to the business of insurance, this Court having held in *Paul v. Virginia,* 8 Wall 168, 183, 19 L.Ed. 357 (1869), that "[i]ssuing a policy of insurance is not a transaction of commerce." When this Court held in *United States v. South–Eastern Underwriters Assn.,* 322 U.S. 533, 64 S.Ct. 1162, 88 L.Ed. 1440 (1944), that the business of insurance was a part of interstate commerce subject to the Sherman Act, Congress responded quickly to reestablish the preeminence of States in regulating such business. Congress' response—the McCarran–Ferguson Act—sought primarily to protect the contractual relationship between the insurer and the insured:

> "Under the regime of *Paul v. Virginia, supra,* States had a free hand in regulating the dealings between insurers and their policyholders. Their negotiations, and the contract which resulted, were not considered commerce and were, therefore, left to state regulation. The *South–Eastern Underwriters* decision threatened the continued supremacy of the States in this area. The McCarran–Ferguson Act was an attempt to turn back the clock, to assure that the activities of insurance companies in dealing with their policyholders would remain subject to state regulation." *SEC v. National Securities, Inc.,* 393 U.S. 453, 459, 89 S.Ct. 564, 568, 21 L.Ed.2d 668 (1969).

We recognized this congressional purpose in *Royal Drug:*

> " 'The relationship between insurer and insured, the type of policy which could be issued, its reliability, interpretation, and enforcement—these were the core of the "business of insurance." Undoubtedly, other activities of insurance companies relate so closely to their status as reliable insurers that they too must be placed in the same class. But whatever the exact scope of the statutory term, it is clear where the focus was—it was on the relationship between the insurance company and the policyholder.' " *Group Life & Health Ins. Co. v. Royal*

---

1. Since the Court declines to reach the question of whether petitioners' Committee is regulated by state law as required by the McCarran–Ferguson Act, I likewise do not discuss it. I note, however, that the District Court found petitioners' Committee to be so regulated. App. to Pet. for Cert. in No. 81–389, pp. 31a–32a.

Drug Co., supra, at 215–216, 99 S.Ct., at 1075, (quoting *SEC v. National Securities, Inc., supra,* at 460, 89 S.Ct., at 568).

Thus, whatever else was said in *Royal Drug* about the indispensable characteristic of risk-spreading, the Court found the contractual relationship between the insurer and the insured to be the essence of the "business of insurance."

Central to this contractual relationship is the process of claims adjustment—the determination of the actual payments to be made to the insured for losses covered by the insurance contract. The key representation of the insurance company and the principal expectation of the policyholder is that prompt payment will be made when the event insured against actually occurs. As one commentator has stated:

> "Up until the time there is a claim and a payment is made, the only tangible evidence of insurance is a piece of paper. In other words, the real product of insurance is the claims proceeds. Selection of the prospect, qualifying him for coverage that suits his needs, delivery of a policy, collecting premiums for perhaps years, making changes in coverage to meet changing situations, all of these are but preambles to the one purpose for which the insurance was secured, namely to collect dollars if and when an unforeseen event takes place." J. Wickman, Evaluating the Health Insurance Risk 57 (1965).

It is the claims adjustor—in this case petitioners' Peer Review Committee—which determines whether and to what extent an insured's losses will be covered. The Court thus plainly errs when it concludes that the role of petitioners' Peer Review Committee "is not an integral part of the policy relationship between insurer and insured," ante, at 3009, and "is a matter of indifference to the policyholder." Ante, at 3010. Few insurance matters could be of greater importance to policyholders than whether their claims will be paid, and it is the Peer Review Committee which in effect makes that determination. Being a critical component of the relationship between an insurer and an insured, claims adjustment is part and parcel of the "business of insurance" protected by the McCarran–Ferguson Act.[2]

This conclusion finds support in a source of guidance completely disregarded by the Court—the legislative history of McCarran–Ferguson. The passage of the Act was preceded by the introduction in the

---

2. Apparently unable to discern the difference between a mere method of paying a claim and the more fundamental process of determining whether a claim is covered by the insurance agreement, the Court finds that petitioners' peer review procedure "resembles the Pharmacy Agreements in *Royal Drug.*" Ante, at 3009. But the Pharmacy Agreement at issue in *Royal Drug* was simply a *method* of reimbursing policyowners for medication expenses. The policyowners could obtain medication from participating pharmacies simply by paying the amount that otherwise would not be covered by the insurance plan. The pharmacies thus constituted nothing more than in-kind dispensers of insurance payments; they played no role whatsoever in the more fundamental process of assessing the validity of a claim and determining the amount to be paid. Peer review committees, which fulfill such a fundamental role, are thus quite unlike the arrangements considered by the Court in *Royal Drug.*

Senate Committee of a report and a bill prepared by the National Association of Insurance Commissioners. "The views of the NAIC are particularly significant, because the Act ultimately passed was based in large part on the NAIC bill." *Group Life & Health Ins. Co. v. Royal Drug Co.,* 440 U.S., at 221, 99 S.Ct., at 1078 (footnote omitted). Included in that bill were seven specific insurance practices to which the Sherman Act was not to apply, and to which the Court in *Royal Drug* looked for guidance as to the meaning of the phrase "business of insurance." See id., at 222. Among those seven protected practices was the process of claims adjustment: "the said Sherman Act shall not apply ∗ ∗ ∗ to any cooperative or joint service, *adjustment, investigation, or inspection agreement* relating to insurance." 90 Cong.Rec. A4406 (1944) (emphasis added). Other statements in the legislative history support the conclusion that claims adjustment was to be protected:

> "[W]e come squarely to the question of whether State regulation is adequate to handle insurance, or whether that business should be subject to the provisions of the antitrust laws. ∗ ∗ ∗ A great number of fire-insurance companies have cooperated in mutual agreement—and of necessity—through the Southeastern Underwriters Association and rating bureaus, adjusting policy rates to risks, classifying insurable property either in co-insurance or in re-insurance, *making appraisals of losses,* and working out systems of inspection to improve protection against fires. All of this has been done with splendid success. It would be a pity indeed, after all these years, to have the government intervene. The business of insurance involves long contracts. The fidelity of performance of those contracts will not brook intervention." Id., at 6530 (remarks of Rep. Satterfield) (emphasis added).

See also id., at 6543 (remarks of Rep. Jennings); id., at 6550–6551 (remarks of Rep. Ploeser).

The role of claims adjustment in the insurance relationship and the legislative history of the Act thus unmistakably demonstrate that claims settlement procedures such as petitioners' Peer Review Committee were to be accorded protection from the antitrust laws as the "business of insurance." Few practices followed by insurance companies today present a fairer or more efficient means of claims resolution than professional peer review committees. Insurance claimants seek reimbursement for virtually every form of medical treatment and care, and determining the reasonableness and necessity of such expenses requires the expertise of a practicing physician. Because the entire spectrum of human ailments are involved, the views of one physician are seldom sufficient; specialists from many fields of medicine must be consulted. Few if any insurance companies can afford to staff their claims settlement departments with such a broad range of physicians. The companies thus must either make less than satisfactory claims determinations, or must turn to an outside group of experts such as petitioners' Committee.

Although the Court protests that its decision says nothing about petitioners' antitrust liability, there can be little doubt that today's decision will vastly curtail the peer review process. Few professionals or companies will be willing to expose themselves to possible antitrust liability through such activity. The Court thus not only misreads the McCarran–Ferguson Act and our prior precedents, but also eliminates an aspect of the American insurance industry which has long redounded to the benefit of insurance companies and policyholders alike.

Notes and Questions

1. *The Contours of the Rule.* Does the three-pronged test the Court articulated in *Royal Drug* and applied in *Pireno* provide sufficient predictability as to the scope of the McCarran–Ferguson exemption? For example, suppose an insurer hired outside consultants to provide advice to its policyholders about safety precautions, and offered reductions in future premiums if policyholders' loss rates declined. Would actions taken as part of that process fall within the exemption?

2. *Alternative Tests.* If this test is unsatisfying, can you devise a preferable alternative? Should the relevant time for the application of the test be the point at which risk was transferred or the point at which the insured's claim against the insurer arose? Should the test be whether the activity had a predominant effect in insurance rather than non-insurance markets? Would the outcome of either *Royal Drug* or *Pireno* have been different under any of these tests? Which of the following aspects of the business of insurance companies, which have failed to satisfy the existing test, would satisfy these alternative tests?

The sale of variable annuities. See *SEC v. Variable Annuity Life Insurance Company of America*, 359 U.S. 65, 79 S.Ct. 618, 3 L.Ed.2d 640 (1959).

The merger of two insurance companies. See *Securities & Exchange Commission v. National Securities, Inc.*, 393 U.S. 453, 89 S.Ct. 564, 21 L.Ed.2d 668 (1969).

Tying the purchase of insurance to another product. See *Federal Trade Commission v. Dixie Finance Co., Inc.*, 695 F.2d 926 (5th Cir. 1983), *cert. denied*, 461 U.S. 928, 103 S.Ct. 2088, 77 L.Ed.2d 299 (1983).

Health insurance limitations on coverage of non-physician services to those recommended by and billed through physicians. See *Virginia Academy of Clinical Psychologists v. Blue Shield (Va.)*, 624 F.2d 476 (4th Cir.1980), *cert. denied*, 450 U.S. 916, 101 S.Ct. 1360, 67 L.Ed.2d 342 (1981).

Agreements among title insurers to fix escrow fees. See *United States v. Title Insurance Rating Bureau of Arizona*, 700 F.2d 1247 (9th Cir.1983).

Providing administrative services to self-insured health programs. See *Reazin v. Blue Cross & Blue Shield of Kansas, Inc.,* 663 F.Supp. 1360 (D.Kan.1987).

Notwithstanding the uncertainty surrounding application of the *Royal Drug/Pireno* test, the lower courts have held certain activities that might not seem to satisfy the test to fall within the McCarran–Ferguson exemption. See, e.g., *Steinberg v. Guardian Life Insurance Company,* 486 F.Supp. 122 (E.D.Pa.1980) (insurer-agent arrangements); *Owens v. Aetna Life & Casualty Company,* 654 F.2d 218 (3d Cir.1981), *cert. denied* 454 U.S. 1092, 102 S.Ct. 657, 70 L.Ed.2d 631 (horizontal agreement among insurers regarding filing of rating schedules).

3. *Dual Meaning?* Is it possible that the term "business of insurance" (used twice in § 1012(b) of the Act) means one thing for purposes of the Act's exemption of the business of insurance from the reach of federal antitrust laws, but something else for purposes of providing immunity from the reach of other federal statutes generally? The answer may depend on what fundamental purpose is ascribed to the McCarran–Ferguson Act itself. One view is that the Act merely allocates power to regulate insurance between the states and the federal government. See Kimball and Heaney, Emasculation of the McCarran–Ferguson Act: A Study in Judicial Activism, 1985 Utah L.Rev. 1. See also Anderson, Insurance and Antitrust Law: The McCarran Act and Beyond, 25 Wm. & Mary L.Rev. 81 (1983). On this view, the meaning that is ascribed to the term "business of insurance" should assure that state regulation of insurance is protected from federal interference, and the *Royal Drug/Pireno* test for what constitutes the "business of insurance" is unduly narrow.

An alternative view, however, is that the Act (at least as its purpose has now evolved) is designed to recognize the unique needs of the insurance business for protection against antitrust and other prohibitions generally applicable to the non-insurance world. On this view, the meaning of the term "business of insurance" in the Act should depend on which source of regulatory authority can most effectively deal with the kind of issue involved. Certain kinds of problems (e.g., the sale of securities) may be handled best by federal agencies with national jurisdiction and special expertise in the field in question; others (e.g., regulation of the relations between insurers and health-care providers) may be handled more effectively by state agencies that can investigate, supervise, and categorize these relations than by courts applying federal antitrust law. Then the test would not be three-pronged, but would hinge on whether the challenged practice predominately affects insurance or non-insurance markets.

This latter view would require a flexible and functional definition of the "business of insurance" that varied with the capabilities of the regulatory institutions with potential jurisdiction over the problem in question. But even if this view is in some sense preferable to the first, it appears to be less faithful to the original purposes and the language of the Act. It turns the Act into an almost trans-statutory source of law and may thereby deprive the Act of even more predictability of meaning than the *Royal Drug/Pireno* test.

2.   What Constitutes "Regulation" by the States?

The McCarran–Ferguson Act denies the business of insurance an exemption from the reach of the federal antitrust laws "to the extent the business of insurance is not regulated" by state law. Although there are few decisions interpreting this provision, rough outlines of its meaning have emerged. Generally, the state must have a statute creating authority to regulate the activity in question, and the regulation must be more than mere pretense. See *Federal Trade Commission v. National Casualty Company*, 357 U.S. 560, 78 S.Ct. 1260, 2 L.Ed.2d 1540 (1958). But the courts seem little concerned with the actual degree of state regulation. See, e.g., *Crawford v. American Title Insurance Company*, 518 F.2d 217 (5th Cir.1975). And state regulation of a general class of activities is apparently sufficient even when the specific activity in question has not been explicitly approved. See, e.g., *Klamath–Lake Pharmaceutical Association v. Klamath Medical Service Bureau*, 701 F.2d 1276 (9th Cir.1983), *cert. denied*, 464 U.S. 822, 104 S.Ct. 88, 78 L.Ed.2d 96:

> Unless the practice amounts to a boycott, the states are free to regulate it or choose not to regulate. They do not have to expressly authorize a specific activity, or proscribe it, for the exemption to apply. * * * It is enough that a detailed overall scheme of regulation exists.

701 F.2d at 1287.

At the risk of oversimplification, then, the bottom line seems to be that there is state "regulation" within the meaning of the Act if the state has enacted a statute authorizing regulation of insurance and regulatory authorities have not totally ignored the general class of activities into which that activity falls. On occasion the courts may require a bit more by way of regulatory action or consideration, but only rarely. Does this state of affairs seem consistent with the original intent of the McCarran–Ferguson Act? If not, what test should be used to determine whether a state has sufficiently regulated an activity to trigger the Act's exemption?

3.   What Constitutes "Boycott, Coercion, or Intimidation"?

The McCarran–Ferguson Act makes one exception to its exemption of the business of insurance from the reach of the federal antitrust laws: any agreement "to boycott, coerce or intimidate, or act of boycott, coercion, or intimidation" is still subject to the prohibitions of the Sherman Act. 42 U.S.C. § 1013(b). The most important litigation over the application of this provision has arisen as a result of periodic "crises" in the availability and affordability of liability insurance, occurring first in the mid–1970's, and then again in the mid–1980's. Some background about these crises is helpful in understanding the setting in which this litigation has occurred.

INSURANCE CRISES, THE UNDERWRITING CYCLE, AND CLAIMS–MADE COVERAGE

The property/casualty insurance market appears to be subject to periodic shortages in the supply of coverage. The causes of this insurance underwriting "cycle," as it is commonly known, are open to debate. Fluctuation in the supply of capital to the industry undoubtedly is a major cause. As capital flows in, premium levels tend to remain constant or decline, even in the face of rising costs. As capital flows out, the supply of coverage contracts (or does not increase at the same rate as demand), and premium levels rise. At the tightest point in this cycle, some forms of coverage may become unavailable at any price.

Part of this fluctuation in the price and supply of coverage is the result of external economic forces; much of it probably results, however, from changes in investors' expectations about the profit and loss levels of the industry itself, which in turn are dependent on investment earnings, on levels of competition, and on conditions in the civil liability system. For different views about the relative responsibility of these different factors for the crisis of the mid–1980's, see Angoff, Insurance Against Competition: How the McCarran–Ferguson Act Raises Prices and Profits in the Property–Casualty Insurance Industry, 5 Yale J.Reg. 397 (1988); Winter, The Liability Crisis and the Dynamics of Competitive Insurance Markets, 5 Yale J.Reg. 455 (1988); Abraham, Making Sense of the Liability Insurance Crisis, 48 Ohio State L.J. 399 (1987); Priest, The Current Insurance Crisis and Modern Tort Law, 96 Yale L.J. 1521 (1987); Stewart, Profit Cycles in Property–Liability Insurance, in E. Randall (ed.) 2 Issues in Insurance 111 (1987); Trebilcock, The Social Insurance–Deterrence Dilemma of Modern North American Tort Law: A Canadian Perspective on the Liability Insurance Crisis, 24 San Diego L.Rev. 929 (1987).

Whatever the causes of the underwriting cycle, it is plain that insurers face the most difficulty in setting premiums for long-tail forms of coverage such as medical malpractice, products liability, and commercial general liability insurance. The reason is that such coverage traditionally has been provided by *occurrence policies,* which cover the insured against liability imposed at any time, arising out of bodily injury or property damage occurring during the policy period. Consider the difficulties an insurer faces in insuring against medical malpractice claims brought as a result of injuries not discovered until years after treatment, or products liability actions involving long-latency diseases. To the extent that such liabilities are covered by occurrence policies issued during the year when treatment or product-use first occurred, an insurer setting a price for coverage must predict the level of economic and legal inflation that will occur between the time coverage is sold and all the claims arising out of injury during the policy period ultimately are brought and paid. Yet this period may extend for ten or more years beyond the date of sale. During points in the underwriting cycle when coverage availability is tight and premiums rise, long-tail forms of coverage may well be the first to become unavailable, since they are the riskiest forms for insurers to write. In the alternative, the price of these forms of coverage may rise dramatically, as supply contracts (or, perhaps more accurately, does not expand quickly enough to keep pace with demand).

One of the reactions of the insurance industry to the problems it faces in writing occurrence coverage against long-tail liabilities has been to try to introduce a different form of coverage: claims-made. *Claims-made policies* insure against liability arising out of claims made during the policy period, regardless of when the damage that is the subject of the claim occurred. Consequently, the insurer selling claims-made coverage must predict only the frequency and severity of losses that it will incur during the policy period in order to set a price for this form of coverage—its task is radically simplified, because under claims-made coverage the insured retains the risk of an uncertain long-term economic and legal future.

The public controversies that arise during the tight portion of the underwriting cycle have generated several legal struggles turning on the scope of the McCarran–Ferguson Act's exemption of the business of insurance from the reach of federal antitrust law. The first involved the effort to introduce claims-made medical malpractice coverage in the 1970's; the second was a broader move in the mid–1980's to introduce claims-made coverage into Commercial General Liability coverage; and the third was the decision of the Insurance Services Office to discontinue the preparation of advisory rates in 1990, largely in reaction to the introduction in Congress of legislation proposing repeal of the McCarran–Ferguson antitrust exemption. Each of these three rounds in what has become an extended public controversy is explored below.

a. The First Round: Medical Malpractice Insurance in the 1970's

ST. PAUL FIRE & MARINE INSURANCE CO. v. BARRY

Supreme Court of the United States, 1978.
438 U.S. 531, 98 S.Ct. 2923, 57 L.Ed.2d 932.

Mr. Justice POWELL delivered the opinion of the Court.

Respondents, licensed physicians practicing in the State of Rhode Island and their patients, brought a class action, in part under the Sherman Act, 26 Stat. 209, as amended, 15 U.S.C. § 1 *et seq.* (1976 ed.), against petitioners, the four insurance companies writing medical malpractice insurance in the State. The complaint alleged a private

conspiracy of the four companies in which three refused to sell respondents insurance of any type as a means of compelling their submission
to new ground rules of coverage set by the fourth. Petitioner insurers
successfully moved in District Court to dismiss the antitrust claim on
the ground that it was barred by the McCarran–Ferguson Act (Act), 59
Stat. 33, as amended, 15 U.S.C. §§ 1011–1015 (1976 ed.). The Court of
Appeals reversed, holding that respondents' complaint stated a claim
within the "boycott" exception in § 3(b) of the Act, which provides that
the Sherman Act shall remain applicable "to any agreement to boycott,
coerce, or intimidate, or act of boycott, coercion, or intimidation," 15
U.S.C. § 1013(b) (1976 ed.). 555 F.2d 3 (CA1 1977). We are required to
decide whether the "boycott" exception applies to disputes between
policyholders and insurers.

I

As this case comes to us from the reversal of a successful motion to
dismiss, we treat the factual allegations of respondents' amended complaint as true. During the period in question, petitioners St. Paul Fire
& Marine Insurance Co. (St. Paul), Aetna Casualty & Surety Co.,
Travelers Indemnity of Rhode Island (and two affiliated companies),
and Hartford Casualty Co. (and an affiliated company) were the only
sellers of medical malpractice insurance in Rhode Island. In April
1975, St. Paul, the largest of the insurers, announced that it would not
renew medical malpractice coverage on an "occurrence" basis, but
would write insurance only on a "claims made" basis.[1] Following St.
Paul's announcement, and in furtherance of the alleged conspiracy, the
other petitioners refused to accept applications for any type of insurance from physicians, hospitals, or other medical personnel whom St.
Paul then insured. The object of the conspiracy was to restrict St.
Paul's policyholders to "claims made" coverage by compelling them to
"purchase medical malpractice insurance from one insurer only, to wit
defendant, St. Paul, and that [such] purchase must be made on terms
dictated by the defendant, St. Paul." App. 25. It is alleged that this
scheme was effectuated by a collective refusal to deal, by unfair rate
discrimination, by agreements not to compete, and by horizontal price
fixing, and that petitioners engaged in "a purposeful course of coercion,
intimidation, boycott and unfair competition with respect to the sale of
medical malpractice insurance in the State of Rhode Island." *Id.,* at
24–27.[2]

---

1. An "occurrence" policy protects the policyholder from liability for any act done
while the policy is in effect, whereas a "claims made" policy protects the holder only
against claims made during the life of the policy. The Court of Appeals noted that "a
doctor who practiced for only one year, say 1972, would need only one 1972 'occurrence'
policy to be fully covered, but he would need several years of 'claims made' policies to
protect himself from claims arising out of his acts in 1972." 555 F.2d 3, 5 n. 1 (CA1 1977).

2. Respondents further assert that "it is virtually impossible for a physician, hospital
or other medical personnel to engage in the practice of medicine or provide medical
services or treatment without medical malpractice insurance," App. 22, and that as a
result of petitioners' conspiracy, they "may be forced to withhold medical services and
disengage from the practice of medicine, except on an emergency basis," *id.,* at 26.

On November 19, 1975, the District Court for the District of Rhode Island granted petitioners' motion to dismiss. The District Court declined to give the "boycott" exception the reading suggested by its "broad wording," declaring instead that "the purpose of the boycott, coercion, and intimidation exception was solely to protect insurance agents or other insurance companies from being 'black-listed' by powerful combinations of insurance companies, not to affect the insurer-insured relationship." *Id.,* at 44.

On May 16, 1977, a divided panel of the Court of Appeals for the First Circuit reversed in pertinent part. The majority reasoned that the "boycott" exception was broadly framed, and that there was no reason to decline to give the term "boycott" its "normal Sherman Act scope." 555 F.2d, at 8. "In antitrust law, a boycott is a 'concerted refusal to deal' with a disfavored purchaser or seller." *Id.,* at 7. The court thought that this reading would not undermine state regulation of the industry. "Regulation by the state would be protected; concerted boycotts against groups of consumers not resting on state authority would have no immunity." *Id.,* at 9.

On August 12, 1977, petitioners sought a writ of certiorari in this Court. To resolve the conflicting interpretations of § 3(b) adopted by several Courts of Appeals,[3] we granted the writ on October 31, 1977. 434 U.S. 919, 98 S.Ct. 391, 54 L.Ed.2d 275. We now affirm. * * *

III

The McCarran–Ferguson Act was passed in reaction to this Court's decision in *United States v. South–Eastern Underwriters Assn.,* 322 U.S. 533, 64 S.Ct. 1162, 88 L.Ed. 1440 (1944). Prior to that decision, it had been assumed, in light of *Paul v. Virginia,* 75 U.S. 168, 8 Wall. 168, 183, 19 L.Ed. 357 (1869), that the issuance of an insurance policy was not a transaction in interstate commerce and that the States enjoyed a virtually exclusive domain over the insurance industry. *South–Eastern Underwriters* held that a fire insurance company which conducted a substantial part of its transactions across state lines is engaged in interstate commerce, and that Congress did not intend to exempt the

---

3. Following the rendition of the legislative history in *Transnational Ins. Co. v. Rosenlund,* 261 F.Supp. 12 (Ore.1966), two Circuits squarely have held that § 3(b) reaches only "blacklists" of insurance companies or agents by other insurance companies or agents. See *Meicler v. Aetna Casualty & Surety Co.,* 506 F.2d 732, 734 (CA5 1975); but cf. *Battle v. Liberty National Life Ins. Co.,* 493 F.2d 39, 51 (CA5 1974), cert. denied, 419 U.S. 1110, 95 S.Ct. 784, 42 L.Ed.2d 807 (1975); *Addrissi v. Equitable Life Assurance Soc.,* 503 F.2d 725, 729 (CA9 1974), cert. denied, 420 U.S. 929, 95 S.Ct. 1129, 43 L.Ed.2d 400 (1975).

Two other Circuits have adopted a broader reading of § 3(b). See *Ballard v. Blue Shield of Southern W. Va., Inc.,* 543 F.2d 1075, 1078 (CA4 1976), cert. denied, 430 U.S. 922, 97 S.Ct. 1341, 51 L.Ed.2d 601 (1977) (alleged conspiracy between insurers and physicians to deny health insurance coverage for chiropractic services); *Proctor v. State Farm Mut. Auto. Ins. Co.,* 182 U.S.App.D.C. 264, 276–277, 561 F.2d 262, 274–275 (1977), cert. pending, No. 77–580 (alleged conspiracy between insurers and automobile repair shops to boycott noncooperative repair shops). See also *Monarch Life Ins. Co. v. Loyal Protective Life Ins. Co.,* 326 F.2d 841, 846 (CA2 1963) (dictum), cert. denied, 376 U.S. 952, 84 S.Ct. 968, 11 L.Ed.2d 971 (1964).

business of insurance from the operation of the Sherman Act.[4] The decision provoked widespread concern that the States would no longer be able to engage in taxation and effective regulation of the insurance industry. Congress moved quickly, enacting the McCarran–Ferguson Act within a year of the decision in *South–Eastern Underwriters.*

As this Court observed shortly afterward, "[o]bviously Congress' purpose was broadly to give support to the existing and future state systems for regulating and taxing the business of insurance." *Prudential Insurance Co. v. Benjamin,* 328 U.S. 408, 429, 66 S.Ct. 1142, 1155, 90 L.Ed. 1342 (1946). Our decisions have given effect to this purpose in construing the operative terms of the § 2(b) proviso, which is the critical provision limiting the general applicability of the federal antitrust laws "to the business of insurance to the extent that such business is not regulated by State Law." See *SEC v. National Securities, Inc.,* 393 U.S. 453, 460, 89 S.Ct. 564, 568, 21 L.Ed.2d 668 (1969); *FTC v. National Casualty Co.,* 357 U.S. 560, 78 S.Ct. 1260, 2 L.Ed.2d 1540 (1958); *infra,* at 550–51. Section 2(b) is not in issue in this case.[5] Rather, we are called upon to interpret, for the first time, the scope of § 3(b), the principal exception to this scheme of pre-emptive state regulation of the "business of insurance."

[handwritten margin note: Exception to state freedom of regulation]

The Court of Appeals in this case determined that the word "boycott" in § 3(b) should be given its ordinary Sherman Act meaning as "a concerted refusal to deal." The "boycott" exception, so read, covered the alleged conspiracy of petitioners, conducted "outside any state-permitted structure or procedure, [to] agree among themselves that customers dissatisfied with the coverage offered by one company shall not be sold any policies by any of the other companies." 555 F.2d, at 9.

Petitioners take strong exception to this reading, arguing that the "boycott" exception "should be limited to cases where concerted refusals to deal are used to exclude or penalize insurance companies or other traders which refuse to conform their competitive practices to terms dictated by the conspiracy." Brief for Petitioners 13. This definition is said to accord with the plain meaning and judicial interpretations of the term "boycott," with the evidence of specific legislative intent, and with the overall structure of the Act. Respondents counter that the language of § 3(b) is sweeping, and that there is no warrant for the

---

4. The Government in that case brought a Sherman Act prosecution against the South–Eastern Underwriters Association (SEUA), its membership of nearly 200 private stock fire insurance companies, and 27 individuals. The indictment alleged conspiracies to maintain arbitrary and noncompetitive premium rates on fire and "allied lines" of insurance in several States, and to monopolize trade and commerce in the same lines of insurance. It was asserted that the conspirators not only fixed rates but also, in the Court's words, "employed boycotts together with other types of coercion and intimidation to force nonmember insurance companies into the conspiracies, and to compel persons who needed insurance to buy only from [SEUA] members on [SEUA] terms." *United States v. South–Eastern Underwriters Assn.,* 322 U.S., at 535, 64 S.Ct., at 1164.

5. Respondents did not contest below "that [petitioners'] acts were related to the business of insurance and that Rhode Island effectively regulates that business." 555 F.2d, at 6. They do not argue to the contrary in this Court.

view that the exception protects insurance companies "or other traders" from anticompetitive practices, but withholds similar protection from policyholders victimized by private, predatory agreements. They urge that this case involves a "traditional boycott," defined as a concerted refusal to deal on any terms, as opposed to a refusal to deal except on specified terms. Brief for Respondents 43.

We consider first petitioners' definition of "boycott" in view of the language, legislative history, and structure of the Act.[6]

IV

A

The starting point in any case involving construction of a statute is the language itself. See *Blue Chip Stamps v. Manor Drug Stores,* 421 U.S. 723, 756, 95 S.Ct. 1917, 1935, 44 L.Ed.2d 539 (1975) (Powell, J., concurring). With economy of expression, Congress provided in § 3(b) for the continued applicability of the Sherman Act to "any agreement to boycott, coerce, or intimidate, or act of boycott, coercion, or intimidation." Congress thus employed terminology that evokes a tradition of meaning, as elaborated in the body of decisions interpreting the Sherman Act. It may be assumed, in the absence of indications to the contrary, that Congress intended this language to be read in light of that tradition.

The generic concept of boycott refers to a method of pressuring a party with whom one has a dispute by withholding, or enlisting others to withhold, patronage or services from the target.[7] The word gained currency in this country largely as a term of opprobrium to describe certain tactics employed by parties to labor disputes. See, *e.g., State v. Glidden,* 55 Conn. 46, 8 A. 890 (1887); Laidler, Boycott, in 2 Encyclopaedia of the Social Sciences 662–666 (1930). Thus it is not surprising that the term first entered the lexicon of antitrust law in decisions involving attempts by labor unions to encourage third parties to cease or suspend doing business with employers unwilling to permit unionization. See, *e.g., Loewe v. Lawlor,* 208 U.S. 274, 28 S.Ct. 301, 52 L.Ed. 488 (1908); *Gompers v. Bucks Stove & Range Co.,* 221 U.S. 418, 31 S.Ct. 492, 55 L.Ed. 797 (1911); *Lawlor v. Loewe,* 235 U.S. 522, 35 S.Ct. 170, 59 L.Ed. 341 (1915); *Duplex Co. v. Deering,* 254 U.S. 443, 41 S.Ct. 172, 65 L.Ed. 349 (1921); *Bedford Stone Co. v. Stone Cutters' Assn.,* 274 U.S. 37, 47 S.Ct. 522, 71 L.Ed. 916 (1927).

Petitioners define "boycott" as embracing only those combinations which target *competitors* of the boycotters as the ultimate objects of a

6. The Court of Appeals' ruling rested on the determination that respondents charged petitioners "with an unlawful boycott," *id.,* at 12. In light of our disposition of this case, we do not decide the scope of the terms "coercion" and "intimidation" in § 3(b).

7. See Bird, Sherman Act Limitations on Noncommercial Concerted Refusals to Deal, 1970 Duke L.J. 247, 248; Webster's New International Dictionary of the English Language 321 (2d ed. 1949); 1 The Oxford English Dictionary 1040 (1933); Black's Law Dictionary 234 (4th ed. 1968).

concerted refusal to deal. They cite commentary that attempts to develop a test for distinguishing the types of restraints that warrant *per se* invalidation from other concerted refusals to deal that are not inherently destructive of competition.[8] But the issue before us is whether the conduct in question involves a boycott, not whether it is *per se* unreasonable. In this regard, we have not been referred to any decision of this Court holding that petitioners' test states the necessary elements of a boycott within the purview of the Sherman Act. Indeed, the decisions reflect a marked lack of uniformity in defining the term.

Petitioners refer to cases stating that "group boycotts" are "concerted refusals by traders to deal with other traders," *Klor's v. Broadway–Hale Stores*, 359 U.S. 207, 212, 79 S.Ct. 705, 709, 3 L.Ed.2d 741 (1959), or are combinations of businessmen "to deprive others of access to merchandise which the latter wish to sell to the public," *United States v. General Motors Corp.*, 384 U.S. 127, 146, 86 S.Ct. 1321, 1331, 16 L.Ed.2d 415 (1966). We note that neither standard in terms excludes respondents—for whom medical malpractice insurance is necessary to ply their "trade" of providing health-care services, see n. 2, *supra*—from the class of cognizable victims. But other verbal formulas also have been used. In *FMC v. Svenska Amerika Linien*, 390 U.S. 238, 250, 88 S.Ct. 1005, 1012, 19 L.Ed.2d 1071 (1968), for example, the Court noted that "[u]nder the Sherman Act, any agreement by a group of competitors to boycott a particular buyer or group of buyers is illegal *per se*." The Court also has stated broadly that "group boycotts, or concerted refusals to deal, clearly run afoul of § 1 [of the Sherman Act]." *Times–Picayune v. United States*, 345 U.S. 594, 625, 73 S.Ct. 872, 889, 97 L.Ed. 1277 (1953). Hence, "boycotts are not a unitary phenomenon." P. Areeda, Antitrust Analysis 381 (2d ed. 1974).

As the labor-boycott cases illustrate, the boycotters and the ultimate target need not be in a competitive relationship with each other. This Court also has held unlawful, concerted refusals to deal in cases where the target is a customer of some or all of the conspirators who is being denied access to desired goods or services because of a refusal to accede to particular terms set by some or all of the sellers. See, *e.g.*, *Paramount Famous Corp. v. United States*, 282 U.S. 30, 51 S.Ct. 42, 75 L.Ed. 145 (1930); *United States v. First Nat. Pictures, Inc.*, 282 U.S. 44, 51 S.Ct. 45, 75 L.Ed. 151 (1930); *Binderup v. Pathe Exchange*, 263 U.S. 291, 44 S.Ct. 96, 68 L.Ed. 308 (1923). See also *Anderson v. Shipowners Assn.*, 272 U.S. 359, 47 S.Ct. 125, 71 L.Ed. 298 (1926). As the Court put it in *Kiefer–Stewart Co. v. Seagram & Sons*, 340 U.S. 211, 214, 71 S.Ct. 259, 261, 95 L.Ed. 219 (1951), "the Sherman Act makes it an offense for

---

8. See L. Sullivan, Handbook of the Law of Antitrust 256–259 (1977). Other commentators have framed a somewhat broader definition for a *per se* offense in this area. See Barber, Refusals to Deal under the Federal Antitrust Laws, 103 U.Pa.L.Rev. 847, 875 (1955) ("group action to coerce third parties to conform to the pattern of conduct desired by the group or to secure their removal from competition"); Kirkpatrick, *supra* n. 12, at 305 ("interference with the relations between a nonmember of the combination and its members or others"). We express no opinion, however, as to the merit of any of these definitions.

[businessmen] to agree among themselves to stop selling to particular customers." [9]

Whatever other characterizations are possible,[10] petitioners' conduct fairly may be viewed as "an organized boycott," *Fashion Guild v. FTC*, 312 U.S. 457, 465, 61 S.Ct. 703, 706, 85 L.Ed. 949 (1941), of St. Paul's policyholders. Solely for the purpose of forcing physicians and hospitals to accede to a substantial curtailment of the coverage previously available, St. Paul induced its competitors to refuse to deal on any terms with its customers. This agreement did not simply fix rates or terms of coverage; it effectively barred St. Paul's policyholders from all access to alternative sources of coverage and even from negotiating for more favorable terms elsewhere in the market. The pact served as a tactical weapon invoked by St. Paul in support of a dispute with its policyholders. The enlistment of third parties in an agreement not to trade, as a means of compelling capitulation by the boycotted group, long has been viewed as conduct supporting a finding of unlawful boycott. *Eastern States Lumber Assn. v. United States*, 234 U.S. 600, 612–613, 34 S.Ct., 951, 954, 58 L.Ed. 1490 (1914), citing *Loewe v. Lawlor, supra;* see *Klor's v. Broadway–Hale Stores, supra*, at 213, 79 S.Ct., at 710; *Anderson v. Shipowners Assn., supra*, at 362–363, 364–365, 47 S.Ct., at 126–127. As in *Binderup v. Pathe Exchange, supra*, 263 U.S., at 312, 44 S.Ct., at 100, where film distributors had conspired to cease dealing with an exhibitor because he had declined to purchase films from some of the distributors, "[t]he illegality consists, not in the separate action of each, but in the conspiracy and combination of all to prevent any of them from dealing with the [target]." [11]

Thus if the statutory language is read in light of the customary understanding of "boycott" at the time of enactment, respondents'

9. *Kiefer–Stewart Co.* involved a horizontal resale price maintenance scheme, see *White Motor Co. v. United States*, 372 U.S. 253, 260, 83 S.Ct. 696, 700, 9 L.Ed.2d 738 (1963), but it has been cited as a "group boycott" case, see *Klor's v. Broadway–Hale Stores*, 359 U.S. 207, 212 n. 5, 79 S.Ct. 705, 709, 3 L.Ed.2d 741 (1959); *Times–Picayune v. United States*, 345 U.S. 594, 625, 73 S.Ct. 872, 889, 97 L.Ed. 1277 (1953). See also *United States v. Frankfort Distilleries*, 324 U.S. 293, 295–296, 65 S.Ct. 661, 662–663, 89 L.Ed. 951 (1945) (alleged conspiracy of producers, wholesalers, and retailers to maintain local retail prices by means of a "boycott program").

See generally Report of the U.S. Attorney General's National Committee to Study the Antitrust Laws 137 (1955) ("approv[ing] the established legal doctrines which condemn group boycotts of customers or suppliers as routine unreasonable restraints forbidden by Section 1 of the Sherman Act").

10. Petitioners suggest that the alleged conspiracy in this case presents a horizontal agreement not to compete, as distinguished from a boycott. See *United States v. Topco Associates*, 405 U.S. 596, 612, 92 S.Ct. 1126, 1135, 31 L.Ed.2d 515 (1972); *United States v. Consolidated Laundries Corp.*, 291 F.2d 563, 573–575 (CA2 1961).

11. As one commentator has noted: "If an individual competitor lacks the bargaining power to get a particular contract term, the courts apparently will not let him join with other competitors and use their collective bargaining power to compel the insertion of such a term in the contract, no matter how desirable." Bird, *supra* n.7, at 263, discussing, *inter alia, Binderup v. Pathe Exchange; Paramount Famous Corp. v. United States*, 282 U.S. 30, 51 S.Ct. 42, 75 L.Ed. 145 (1930).

complaint states a claim under § 3(b).[12]   But, as Mr. Justice Cardozo observed, words or phrases in a statute come "freighted with the meaning imparted to them by the mischief to be remedied and by contemporaneous discussion.   In such conditions history is a teacher that is not to be ignored."   *Duparquet Co. v. Evans,* 297 U.S. 216, 221, 56 S.Ct. 412, 414, 80 L.Ed. 591 (1936) (citation omitted).   We therefore must consider whether Congress intended to attach a special meaning to the word "boycott" in § 3(b).

[The Court concluded that it did not.]   *   *   *

C

Petitioners also contend that the structure of the Act supports their reading of § 3(b).   They note that this Court has interpreted the term "business of insurance" in § 2(b) broadly to encompass "[t]he relationship between insurer and insured, the type of policy which could be issued, its reliability, interpretation, and enforcement," *SEC v. National Securities, Inc.,* 393 U.S. at 460, 89 S.Ct., at 568, and has held that the mere enactment of "prohibitory legislation" and provision for "a scheme of administrative supervision" constitute adequate regulation to satisfy the proviso to § 2(b), *FTC v. National Casualty Co.,* 357 U.S., at 564–565, 78 S.Ct., at 1262.   Thus, petitioners conclude, § 3(b) cannot be interpreted in a fashion that would undermine the congressional judgment expressed in § 2(b) that the protection of policyholders is the primary responsibility of the States and that the state regulation which precludes application of federal law is not limited to regulation specifically authorizing the conduct challenged.

Petitioners rely on a syllogism that is faulty in its premise, for it ignores the fact that § 3(b) is an exception to § 2(b), and that Congress intended in the "boycott" clause to carve out of the overall framework of plenary state regulation an area that would remain subject to Sherman Act scrutiny.   The structure of the Act embraces this exception.   Unless § 3(b) is read to limit somewhat the sweep of § 2(b), it serves no purpose whatever.   Petitioners do not press their argument that far, but they suggest no persuasive reason for engrafting a particular limitation on § 3(b) that is justified neither by its language nor by the legislative history.[13]

12.   We note our disagreement with Mr. Justice Stewart's expression of alarm that a reading of the operative terms of § 3(b), consistent with traditional Sherman Act usage, "would plainly devour the broad antitrust immunity bestowed by § 2(b)."   *Post,* at 2938. Whatever the precise reach of the terms "boycott," "coercion," and "intimidation," the decisions of this Court do not support the dissent's suggestion that they are coextensive with the prohibitions of the Sherman Act.   *See, e.g., Eastern States Lumber Assn. v. United States,* 234 U.S. 600, 611, 34 S.Ct. 951, 954, 58 L.Ed. 1490 (1914), quoting *Gompers v. Bucks Stove & Range Co.,* 221 U.S. 418, 438, 31 S.Ct. 492, 496, 55 L.Ed. 797 (1911).   In this regard, we are not cited to any decision illustrating the assertion, *post,* at 559 n.6, that price fixing, in the absence of any additional enforcement activity, has been treated either as "a boycott" or "coercion."

13.   Even under petitioners' reading, certain cooperative arrangements among insurance companies may constitute a "boycott" under § 3(b) notwithstanding the applicability of § 2(b) to activities that "relate *   *   * closely to their status as reliable insurers," *SEC*

V

We hold that the term "boycott" is not limited to concerted activity against insurance companies or agents or, more generally, against competitors of members of the boycotting group. It remains to consider whether the type of private conduct alleged to have taken place in this case, directed against policyholders, constitutes a "boycott" within the meaning of § 3(b).

A

The conduct in question accords with the common understanding of a boycott. The four insurance companies that control the market in medical malpractice insurance are alleged to have agreed that three of the four would not deal on any terms with the policyholders of the fourth. As a means of ensuring policyholder submission to new, restrictive ground rules of coverage, St. Paul obtained the agreement of the other petitioners, strangers to the immediate dispute, to refuse to sell any insurance to its policyholders. "A valuable service germane to [respondents'] business and important to their effective competition with others was withheld from them by collective action." *Silver v. New York Stock Exchange,* 373 U.S. 341, 348–349, n.5, 83 S.Ct. 1246, 1252, 10 L.Ed.2d 389 (1963).

The agreement binding petitioners erected a barrier between St. Paul's customers and any alternative source of the desired coverage, effectively foreclosing all possibility of competition anywhere in the relevant market. This concerted refusal to deal went well beyond a private agreement to fix rates and terms of coverage, as it denied policyholders the benefits of competition in vital matters such as claims policy and quality of service. Cf. *Continental T.V., Inc. v. GTE Sylvania Inc.,* 433 U.S. 36, 55, 97 S.Ct. 2549, 53 L.Ed.2d 568 (1977). St. Paul's policyholders became the captives of their insurer. In a sense the

---

v. National Securities, Inc., 393 U.S. 453, 460, 89 S.Ct. 564, 568, 21 L.Ed.2d 668 (1969), and the adequacy of state regulation of the industry. Hence, petitioners' line may not be as "bright" as they suggest.

The dissenting opinion of Mr. Justice Stewart also argues that the structure of the Act supports a restrictive reading of § 3(b). We do not think the dissent's restatement of the holding in *FTC v. National Casualty Co.,* 357 U.S. 560, 564, 78 S.Ct. 1260, 1262, 2 L.Ed.2d 1540, (1958), see *post,* at 2938, n.4, furthers resolution of the problem at hand. It is not disputed that Congress intended that certain forms of "regulation by private conbinations and groups," 91 Cong. Rec. 1483 (remarks of Sen. O'Mahoney), remain subject to Sherman Act scrutiny, notwithstanding enactment of the type of "prohibitory legislation," coupled with "enforcement through a scheme of administrative supervision," that was deemed sufficient for § 2(b) purposes in *National Casualty Co.* In that case the Court rejected the Federal Trade Commission's argument that "where a statute, instead of sanctioning a particular type of transaction, prohibits conduct in general terms and provides for enforcement through administrative action, there is realistically, in the absence of such enforcement, no 'regulation' in fact." Brief for Federal Trade Commission, O. T. 1957, Nos. 435 and 436, p. 53. The question that nonetheless remains is whether Congress intended to foreclose *all* Sherman Act protection for policyholders victimized by private conspiracies of insurers when a State has engaged in generally comprehensive regulation under § 2(b). We think the record does not support such a foreclosure.

agreement imposed an even greater restraint on competitive forces than a horizontal pact not to compete with respect to price, coverage, claims policy, and service, since the refusal to deal in any fashion reduced the likelihood that a competitor might have broken ranks as to one or more of the fixed terms.[14] The conduct alleged here is certainly not, in Senator O'Mahoney's terms, within the category of "agreements which can normally be made in the insurance business," 91 Cong.Rec. 1444 (1945), or "agreements and combinations in the public interests [sic] which can safely be permitted," id., at 1486.

B

We emphasize that the conduct with which petitioners are charged appears to have occurred outside of any regulatory or cooperative arrangement established by the laws of Rhode Island. There was no state authorization of the conduct in question. This was the explicit premise of the Court of Appeals' decision, see 555 F.2d, at 9, and petitioners do not aver that state law or regulatory policy can be said to have required or authorized the concerted refusal to deal with St. Paul's customers.[15]

Here the complaint alleges an attempt at "regulation by private combinations and groups," 91 Cong.Rec. 1483 (1945) (remarks of Sen. O'Mahoney). This is not a case where a State has decided that regulatory policy requires that certain categories of risks be allocated in a particular fashion among insurers, or where a State authorizes insurers to decline to insure particular risks because the continued provision of that insurance would undermine certain regulatory goals, such as the maintenance of insurer solvency. In this case, a group of insurers decided to resolve by private action the problem of escalating damages claims and verdicts by coercing the policyholders of St. Paul to accept a severe limitation of coverage essential to the provision of medical services. See n. 4, supra. We conclude that this conduct, as alleged in the complaint, constitutes a "boycott" under § 3(b).

14. "[E]ven where prices are rigidly fixed, the members of a cartel will be able to compete with each other with respect to product quality unless a homogeneous product is involved. Indeed, even if the product is homogeneous there will be room for rivalry in such matters as promptness in filling orders and the provision of ancillary services. An effective division of markets, by contrast, might substantially wash out all opportunity for rivalry." Sullivan, supra n.14, at 224–225.

15. Counsel for petitioners stated at oral argument that he was not sure whether St. Paul had filed the specific policy change in issue with the director of the state insurance division. Tr. of Oral Arg. 8. Even if we assume that such a filing had been made, there is no suggestion that the State, in furtherance of its regulatory policies, authorized the concerted refusal to deal on any terms with St. Paul's policyholders.

Although the dissenting opinion below noted "that Rhode Island has exercised its right to regulate all material aspects of the business of insurance and that the actions complained of relative to withholding malpractice insurance were all part of such regulated business," 555 F.2d, at 14, this statement refers to the requirements of the proviso of § 2(b). The dissent did not argue that the agreement in question was within the contemplation of any state regulatory scheme.

Our ruling does not alter § 2(b)'s protection of state regulatory and tax laws, its recognition of the primacy of state regulation, or the limited applicability of the federal antitrust laws generally "to the extent that" the "business of insurance" is not regulated by state law. Moreover, conduct by individual actors falling short of concerted activity is simply not a "boycott" within § 3(b). Cf. *Times–Picayune v. United States,* 345 U.S., at 625, 73 S.Ct., at 889. Finally, while we give force to the congressional intent to preserve Sherman Act review for certain types of private collaborative activity by insurance companies, we do not hold that all concerted activity violative of the Sherman Act comes within § 3(b). Nor does our decision address insurance practices that are compelled or specifically authorized by state regulatory policy.

The judgment of the Court of Appeals therefore is *Affirmed.*

Notes and Questions

1. *Broad or Narrow Exception?* The Court's understanding of the structure of the McCarran–Ferguson Act was that § 3(b) constitutes an exception to the Act's exemption of "the business of insurance" from the reach of federal antitrust law under § 2(b). But is that exception broad, as the Court found, or narrower, as the insurers argued? The dissent in *Barry* argued that the Court's reading threatened to devour the exemption:

> Most practices condemned by the Sherman Act can be cast as an act or agreement of "boycott, coercion, or intimidation." For example, price fixing can be seen either as a refusal to deal except at a uniform price (*i.e.,* a boycott), or as an agreement to force buyers to accept an offer on the sellers' common terms (*i.e.,* coercion). Yet state-sanctioned price fixing immunized by § 2(b) was plainly not intended to fall within the § 3(b) exception.

Stewart, J., dissenting, 438 U.S., at 559 n. 6, 98 S.Ct., at 2939, n. 6. Does it follow that the majority was in fact according some special meaning to the term "boycott?"

2. *The Merits.* The Court did not hold that the defendants had violated the Sherman Act, but only that the acts alleged would constitute a violation if proved. In the antitrust suit itself, proof of the advantage the defendants stood to gain from a boycott might tend to show their intent to engage in one. If you were counsel for the plaintiffs in *Barry,* what reason would you give to explain the defendants' need to engage in the alleged conspiracy? How would you explain why St. Paul did not simply refuse to renew occurrence coverage on its own—a decision that would not have constituted a boycott?

Whatever the explanation, claims-made medical malpractice insurance became widespread across the country beginning at about the time *Barry* was decided. Some physician-owned mutual companies still write occurrence coverage, but many of these and most commercial companies now write claims-made coverage. The attractiveness of claims-made for insurers writing other lines of long-tail coverage is surely part of what prompted the next round in the controversy.

b. The Second Round: Claims–Made Commercial Liability Insurance in the 1980's and the States' Antitrust Suit Against the Industry

IN RE INSURANCE ANTITRUST LITIGATION

United States District Court, N.D.Cal., 1989.
723 F.Supp. 464.

SCHWARZER, District Judge:

I. INTRODUCTION

Nineteen states and numerous private plaintiffs have brought actions against a group of insurance companies, reinsurance companies, underwriters, brokers, and individuals, and the Insurance Services Office, Inc. ("ISO"), charging them with violations of the federal antitrust laws and state laws. The charges rest on alleged conspiracies, boycotts, threats, intimidation, and other coercive conduct by defendants to restrict the availability of certain coverage under policies for commercial general liability insurance ("CGL") and property insurance. The filing of these complaints followed lengthy investigations conducted by the regulatory agencies of several states.

Defendants have moved to dismiss, for judgment on the pleadings, and for summary judgment, and plaintiffs have made cross-motions. For purposes of these motions, the well-pleaded allegations of the complaints are accepted as true, and any factual disputes and inferences are resolved in plaintiffs' favor. * * *

II. FACTUAL BACKGROUND

CGL insurance protects the insured against the risk of liability to third parties for bodily injury or property damage. It is purchased by businesses, non-profit groups, and governmental entities. Defendants Hartford Fire Insurance Company ("Hartford"), Allstate Insurance Company ("Allstate"), Aetna Casualty and Surety Company ("Aetna"), and CIGNA Corporation ("CIGNA") are primary insurers who are major providers of CGL insurance. CGL insurance is written predominantly on standard policy forms developed by ISO.

ISO is an association of more than one thousand property or casualty insurers, including Hartford, Allstate, Aetna, and CIGNA. It is licensed as a rating, rate service, and advisory organization in all fifty states. One of its primary functions is to develop standardized policy forms for property and casualty insurance that comply with state regulations and will be accepted by state insurance departments. On behalf of its members, ISO files standardized policy forms with state insurance departments. ISO also collects historical loss data, projects future loss trends, and calculates advisory rates for insurance.

In the late 1970s, ISO began to develop a revision of the standard CGL form then in use. In 1984, ISO filed or lodged with state insurance departments two proposed new policy forms for CGL insurance. These forms substantially modified coverage previously available to the insured. One of the forms was a "claims-made" policy under which coverage was limited to claims made during the policy period regardless of when the occurrence out of which the claims arose had taken place. This represented a reduction in the coverage available under the previous CGL policy form which was an "occurrence-based" form; under that form, the insured was covered for claims arising out of occurrences during the policy period, no matter when asserted, thus exposing insurers to so-called "long-tail risks" that could arise long after the policy period. The proposed claims-made form reduced that exposure and shifted the risk of future claims to the insured. The other proposed form was a modified occurrence policy.

These forms became the subject of widespread debate and controversy in the insurance industry. Considerable differences of opinion arose over what should trigger coverage, whether retroactivity of claims-made coverage should be limited, whether the pollution exclusion should be modified, and whether defense costs should be limited by the policy limits.

In their complaint, plaintiffs charge defendants Hartford, CIGNA, Allstate, and Aetna with engaging in a concerted effort to block adoption of the 1984 forms because those forms did not restrict coverage sufficiently. Plaintiffs allege that these defendants entered into conspiracies with certain domestic and foreign defendant reinsurance companies, underwriters, and their representatives to "boycott" the 1984 forms unless a retroactive date was added to the claims-made form and a pollution exclusion and defense cost cap were added to both forms. Plaintiffs allege that as a result of the efforts of Hartford, Allstate, Aetna, and CIGNA, certain domestic and London reinsurers threatened to "boycott" North American CGL risks unless these changes were made in the claims-made form and the occurrence form was eliminated. Also as a result of these efforts the ISO executive committee in September 1984 voted to include a retroactive cut-off date in the claims-made policy form, to exclude pollution coverage from both forms, but to defer until later limiting defense costs, and to offer an occurrence form along with the new claims-made form.

Following this agreement, ISO, Hartford, Aetna, and representatives of the London reinsurers undertook joint efforts to promote the new forms. Reinsurers refused to accept new reinsurance business or renew old business unless the primary carrier agreed to switch to the claims-made form when available. Reinsurers also imposed "sunset dates" in their treaties limiting their exposure to losses on occurrence policies. Reinsurance underwriters also entered into an agreement to exclude pollution liability coverage from reinsurance treaties.

During the period from 1984 through 1986, when these events are alleged to have occurred, ISO lodged or filed the proposed forms with the insurance departments of all states. Departments in thirty-five states held public hearings and the policy terms that are the subjects of the complaints were discussed within the industry and in public forums. As a result ISO filed or lodged several revisions of its proposed forms with the state insurance departments. At the conclusion of the various states' proceedings in 1986, all of the plaintiff states and the two non-plaintiff states in which individual plaintiffs reside had approved the ISO forms with the following exceptions: Massachusetts and New Jersey disapproved them, New York approved only the occurrence form, and California and Colorado, having no procedure for approval, took no action. Thereafter ISO withdrew its data collection and risk estimation support for the pre–1984 CGL form. * * *

III. THE FEDERAL LAW VIOLATIONS CHARGED

The state complaints fall into two groups depending on when they were filed. The First Wave Complaints each contain eight federal claims.[1] The Second Wave Complaints each contain six federal claims.[2] All complaints also contain pendent state law claims. The private complaints track the state complaints.

The First Claim of the Second Wave Complaints alleges a global conspiracy by all defendants in violation of Section One of the Sherman Act, 15 U.S.C. § 1,

> for the purpose and with the effect of shrinking the scope of CGL property/casualty insurance and reinsurance and retrocessional reinsurance, * * * to * * * reduce financial exposure to such risks and to increase underwriting profits therefrom.

Plaintiffs allege that defendants used boycotts, coercion, and intimidation to limit available coverage. No corresponding claim is made in the First Wave Complaints.

The Second Claim of the Second Wave Complaints and the First through Fourth Claims of the First Wave Complaints allege a conspiracy by defendants Hartford, Allstate, Aetna, CIGNA, ISO, and certain others to manipulate the ISO design process for CGL forms to limit the available coverage. Plaintiffs allege that defendants conspired to restrict the terms under which reinsurance coverage would be provided for CGL risks, to refuse to provide reinsurance unless the 1984 form were amended to incorporate defendants' terms, to coerce ISO and its members to adopt the coverage terms and exclusions agreed to by defendants, and to boycott the forms unless amended.

1. First Wave Complaints were filed by Alabama, Arizona, California, Massachusetts, New York, West Virginia, and Wisconsin. [Citations to pleadings are omitted without notation—Ed.].

2. Second Wave Complaints were filed by Alaska, Colorado, Connecticut, Louisiana, Maryland, Michigan, Minnesota, Montana, New Jersey, Ohio, Pennsylvania, and Washington. Citations to Second Wave Complaints are to the Connecticut complaint.

The Third Claim of the Second Wave Complaints and the Fifth Claim for the First Wave Complaints in substance charge certain defendants engaged in the reinsurance business at Lloyd's of London with a conspiracy to restrict the terms under which reinsurance coverage would be provided for CGL risks and to refuse to reinsure CGL risks on occurrence forms by coercion and intimidation of primary insurers, among other things.

The Fourth Claim of the Second Wave Complaints and the Sixth Claim of the First Wave Complaints in substance charge certain defendants engaged in the reinsurance business at Lloyd's of London with a conspiracy to restrict the terms under which casualty reinsurance coverage would be provided for CGL risks and to limit the availability of pollution coverage in primary casualty insurance. No boycott, coercion, or intimidation is alleged. * * *

IV. THE MOTIONS BEFORE THE COURT

Defendants have filed five motions to dismiss or for summary judgment on the following grounds:

A. Asserting antitrust immunity under the McCarran–Ferguson Act, 15 U.S.C. §§ 1011–1015 ("the McCarran Act"), all defendants have moved under Federal Rules of Civil Procedure 12(b)(6) and 56 to dismiss or for summary judgment. * * *

V. DISCUSSION

A. THE McCARRAN–FERGUSON ACT DEFENSE

Defendants have moved for summary judgment on all federal claims on the ground that their conduct is immunized from antitrust liability by the McCarran Act. Although the primary thrust of the motion is said to be directed at those claims which are based on policy form development activities, the controlling principles apply to defendants' underwriting-related actions as well. Stripped of their pejorative allegations, those claims charge a conspiracy to reduce the exposure of defendant insurers and reinsurers under CGL policies. The defendants sought to accomplish their objective by bringing about changes in standard policy language and by avoiding underwriting or reinsuring risks written on disfavored policy terms. All of this they did in large part by collective action, and it may be assumed that plaintiffs could prove a consequent lessening of competition among defendants and a diminution of options available in the market for CGL insurance, resulting in a restraint of trade.

In the absence of the McCarran Act, those allegations may well state a claim for relief under the Sherman Act. The issue raised by these motions is whether plaintiffs could prove a set of facts under those general allegations that would entitle them to relief notwithstanding the McCarran Act.

That Act states:

(a) The business of insurance, and every person engaged therein, shall be subject to the laws of the several States which relate to the regulation or taxation of such business.

(b) No Act of Congress shall be construed to invalidate, impair, or supersede any law enacted by any State for the purpose of regulating the business of insurance * * *: Provided, That * * * the Sherman Act, * * * the Clayton Act, and * * * the Federal Trade Commission Act * * * shall be applicable to the business of insurance to the extent that such business is not regulated by State law.

15 U.S.C. § 1012.

Section 1013(b) of the Act further provides:

Nothing contained in this chapter shall render the * * * Sherman Act inapplicable to any agreement to boycott, coerce, or intimidate, or act of boycott, coercion, or intimidation.

The McCarran Act created limited antitrust immunity for the business of insurance following the Supreme Court's departure in *United States v. South–Eastern Underwriters Association,* 322 U.S. 533, 64 S.Ct. 1162, 88 L.Ed. 1440 (1944), from prior holdings that insurance is not a transaction in interstate commerce. See *St. Paul Fire & Marine Ins. Co. v. Barry,* 438 U.S. 531, 538–39, 98 S.Ct. 2923, 2928–29, 57 L.Ed.2d 932 (1978). It was passed in response to widespread concern that the states should not be precluded from continuing to regulate and tax the insurance industry. It immunizes the business of insurance from the antitrust laws but only to the extent that it is regulated by the states and does not involve boycott, coercion, or intimidation. See *Feinstein v. Nettleship Co.,* 714 F.2d 928, 931 (9th Cir.1983), *cert. denied,* 466 U.S. 972, 104 S.Ct. 2346, 80 L.Ed.2d 820 (1984). Like all antitrust immunities, it must, of course, be narrowly construed. See *Group Life & Health Ins. Co. v. Royal Drug Co.,* 440 U.S. 205, 231, 99 S.Ct. 1067, 1083, 59 L.Ed.2d 261 (1979).

The application of the McCarran Act immunity involves a three step analysis:

(1) Whether the conduct is within the scope of the business of insurance;

(2) Whether that business is regulated by the states; and

(3) Whether the conduct involves boycott, coercion, or intimidation.

(1)   The Business of Insurance

* * *

Plaintiffs do not dispute that the activities of defendants insofar as they relate to the terms and conditions of primary, excess, or umbrella insurance, are the business of insurance within the meaning of the McCarran Act. They contend, however, that reinsurance is not the business of insurance because it relates only indirectly to the spreading of the policyholder's risk and because, they contend, it is not an integral part of the policy relationship between the insurer and the insured.

There is no authority for excluding reinsurance from the business of insurance. On the contrary, reinsurance was specifically referred to as a part of the business of insurance in the legislative history of the McCarran Act. *See* 90 Cong.Rec. A4406 (1944); 89 Cong.Rec. 6528 (1943). The Ninth Circuit applied the McCarran exemption to reinsurers as well as to the primary insurer in *Feinstein.* 714 F.2d at 930.

Plaintiffs urge an unreasonably narrow application of the Pireno test. Their own description establishes that reinsurance is an integral and vital part of the business of insurance. The complaints define reinsurance as "insurance for insurers." They go on to describe reinsurance as

> a transaction whereby one insurance company, the reinsurer, agrees to indemnify another insurance company, the primary (or "ceding") insurer, for a designated portion of the insurance risks underwritten by the primary insurer. Reinsurance protects the primary insurer from catastrophic losses, and is heavily relied upon by prudent primary insurers. It also allows the primary insurer to sell more insurance than its own financial capacity might otherwise permit. Thus, the availability of reinsurance affects the ability and willingness of primary insurers to provide insurance to their customers.

Thus, reinsurance is no less a part of the process of underwriting and spreading risks than primary insurance. Plaintiffs' allegations rest, moreover, on the premise that the terms on which reinsurance is available affect the terms on which primary insurance is written and that the terms and availability of reinsurance directly affect the availability of insurance coverage to consumers. As plaintiffs' brief puts it, "by conspiracy to eliminate reinsurance for the consumer-demanded coverages, the reinsurers acted anticompetitively in reinsurance markets * * * [which] led inexorably to an injury to the States in the interrelated primary insurance markets." Because reinsurance is thus an element of the policy relationship with the insured, it is part of the business of insurance. *See also SEC v. National Sec., Inc.,* 393 U.S. 453, 460, 89 S.Ct. 564, 568, 21 L.Ed.2d 668 (1960) (business of insurance includes "activities of insurance companies [that] relate * * * closely to their status as reliable insurers").

By the same logic, retrocessional insurance, which is "insurance for reinsurers," is part of insurance.[3]

---

3. The argument that the exemption is lost as a result of joint action with non-exempt entities is without merit. *Klamath–Lake Pharmaceutical Association v. Klamath Medical Service Bureau,* 701 F.2d 1276, 1288 n.12 (9th Cir.1983), *cert. denied,* 464 U.S. 822, 104 S.Ct. 88, 78 L.Ed.2d 96 (1983).

(2) Regulation by the States

The condition of state regulation is satisfied by "a state regulatory scheme possess[ing] jurisdiction over the challenged practice." *Feinstein,* 714 F.2d at 933. "It is not necessary to point to a state statute which gives express approval to a particular practice." *Id.;* see *Klamath–Lake Pharmaceutical Ass'n v. Klamath Medical Service Bureau,* 701 F.2d 1276, 1287 (9th Cir.), *cert. denied,* 464 U.S. 822, 104 S.Ct. 88, 78 L.Ed.2d 96 (1983); *Dexter v. Equitable Life Assur. Soc.,* 527 F.2d 233, 236 (2d Cir.1975); *Lawyers Title Co. of Mo. v. St. Paul Title Ins. Co.,* 526 F.2d 795, 797–98 (8th Cir.1975); *Ohio AFL–CIO v. Insurance Rating Bd.,* 451 F.2d 1178, 1181–84 (6th Cir.1971), *cert. denied,* 409 U.S. 917, 93 S.Ct. 215, 34 L.Ed.2d 180 (1972); *see also* P. Areeda & H. Hovenkamp, *Antitrust Law* ¶ 210.1b (Supp.1988) (McCarran immunity distinguished from *Parker v. Brown* immunity; the former requiring only the existence of a state regulatory scheme, without regard to the intensity of state regulation).

This case involves the insurance business in twenty-one states. The Ninth Circuit has held that California's scheme of regulation satisfies the McCarran Act. *Addrisi v. Equitable Assur. Soc. of the United States,* 503 F.2d 725, 728 (9th Cir.1974), *cert. denied,* 429 U.S. 929, 95 S.Ct. 1129, 43 L.Ed.2d 400 (1975). The Court takes judicial notice of the laws of the other jurisdictions. Each state has an insurance department with jurisdiction over policy forms. Sixteen of the plaintiff states and the two nonplaintiff states in which private plaintiffs reside require filing and review of policy forms, including umbrella and excess policies offered by admitted insurers. All of the states have licensed ISO and permit joint action by ISO and insurance companies with respect to policy forms. All of the states have unfair insurance trade practice statutes enabling them to proceed against conduct such as that alleged in the complaints. Although plaintiffs contend that reinsurance and umbrella and excess insurance are not regulated by the states, these statutes are broad enough to apply to any persons in the business of insurance, including reinsurers.[4] These statutory schemes are sufficient to qualify under section 1012(b) of the McCarran Act. See *SEC v. National Securities, Inc.,* 393 U.S. 453, 459–60, 89 S.Ct. 564, 568–69, 21 L.Ed.2d 668 (1969) (state laws protecting or regulating, directly or indirectly, relationship between insurer and policy holder qualify); *FTC v. National Cas. Co.,* 357 U.S. 560, 564–65, 78 S.Ct. 1260, 1262, 2 L.Ed.2d 1540 (1958) (state unfair insurance advertising laws qualify); *Mackey v. Nationwide Ins. Co.,* 724 F.2d 419,

---

4. Cal.Insur.Code § 790.01 is typical:

    This article applies to reciprocal and interinsurance exchanges, Lloyds insurers, fraternal benefit societies, fraternal fire insurers, grants and annuities societies, insurers holding certifications of exemptions, motor clubs, nonprofit hospital associations, agents, brokers, solicitors, surplus line brokers and special lines surplus line brokers as well as *all other persons engaged in the business of insurance.*

(Emphasis added.)

421 (4th Cir.1984) (state unfair insurance practice laws that provide for administrative supervision and enforcement qualify). * * *

(3) The Exclusion of Boycott, Coercion, and Intimidation

The States have submitted a Statement of Material Facts in support of their unified opposition brief. The following facts are material to this section of the opinion.

Twenty of the defendants, including primary insurers, reinsurers, brokers, and underwriters, dissatisfied with the CGL forms approved by ISO in 1984 because those forms failed to eliminate occurrence and pollution coverage, "agreed to and undertook a course of concerted action" to limit the availability of certain CGL coverages, and twelve other defendants ultimately joined in. This course of action included the following activities. To coerce ISO into revising its 1984 CGL forms, defendant reinsurers agreed to and did announce that reinsurance would not be provided for coverage written on the 1984 form. In addition, certain defendants took "coercive action" by agreeing to announce and announcing that they would not provide reinsurance on occurrence policies and would impose sunset clauses in their coverage.[5] Certain defendants took "coercive action" by agreeing to include and including a pollution exclusion in their reinsurance treaties. (*Id.* at 13–14.) Certain defendants made a "coercive statement of intention not to provide reinsurance unless the primary policy excludes all property pollution coverage." Finally, certain defendants agreed to eliminate the same coverage from excess and umbrella policy forms. And ISO withdrew statistical support for its 1973 form.

It will be noted that plaintiffs' statement does not allege a boycott. Nor does it (or the complaints) describe conduct that "accords with the common understanding of a boycott." *St. Paul Fire & Marine Ins. Co. v. Barry,* 438 U.S. 531, 552, 98 S.Ct. 2923, 2935, 57 L.Ed.2d 932 (1978). As the Supreme Court described the conduct there in issue,

> The four insurance companies that control the market in medical malpractice insurance are alleged to have agreed that three of the four *would not deal on any terms with the policyholders* of the fourth. As a means of ensuring policyholder submission to new, restrictive ground rules of coverage, St. Paul obtained the agreement of the other petitioners, strangers to the immediate dispute, *to refuse to sell any insurance to its policyholders.* "A valuable service germane to [respondents'] business and important to their effective competition with others was withheld from them by collective action."
>
> The agreement binding petitioners *erected a barrier between St. Paul's customers and any alternative source* of the desired coverage, effectively foreclosing all possibility of competition anywhere in the relevant market. *This concerted refus-*

5. A "sunset clause" limits the reinsurer's liability to those claims presented to it by the primary insurer prior to a specified date.

al to deal went well beyond a private agreement to fix rates and terms of coverage, as it denied policyholders the benefits of competition in vital matters such as claims policy and quality of service.

Id. at 552–53, 98 S.Ct. at 2935–36 (citation omitted) (emphasis added).

In contrast, plaintiffs here charge no more than an agreement to restrict coverage. But they seek to piggyback this charge on conclusory allegations of pressure and compulsion that echo *Barry*. The decision in *Barry*, however, turned not on the pressure and compulsion directed at policyholders to submit to curtailed coverage, but on the agreement with competitors not to deal with those policyholders on any terms. As the Court said:

> Solely for the purpose of forcing physicians and hospitals to accede to a substantial curtailment of the coverage previously available, St. Paul induced its competitors to refuse to deal on any terms with its customers. *This agreement did not simply fix rates or terms of coverage;* it effectively barred St. Paul's policyholders from all access to alternative sources of coverage and even from negotiating for more favorable terms elsewhere in the market. The pact served as a tactical weapon invoked by St. Paul in support of a dispute with its policyholders. *The enlistment of third parties in an agreement not to trade as a means of compelling capitulation by the boycotted group, long has been viewed as conduct supporting a finding of unlawful boycott.*

Id. at 544–45, 98 S.Ct. at 2931 (emphasis added).

Thus, the issue is not whether defendants used pressure to reduce the coverage available to buyers of insurance. The issue is whether they entered into concerted refusals to deal that denied consumers access to the markets for the desired coverages. The Ninth Circuit explained the meaning of boycott in *Feinstein:* "Because [the agreement] in no way limited the doctors' ability to deal with third parties, the agreement itself is not an agreement to boycott or coerce the plaintiff to purchase the defendants' insurance." 714 F.2d at 933.

The distinction between lawful joint action and prohibited boycott and coercion is also explained in *Proctor v. State Farm Mutual Automobile Insurance Co.*, 561 F.2d 262 (D.C.Cir.1977):

> The facts in *South–Eastern Underwriters* are a useful guidepost. Logically speaking, a simple agreement among insurance companies to charge certain premium rates could be viewed as a boycott agreement, since its observance would result in a collective refusal to deal with policyholders except at a fixed price. But the Supreme Court's opinion in *South–Eastern Underwriters* did not characterize the basic rate-fixing agreement in that case in terms of "boycott, coercion, or intimidation"; those terms were reserved for the additional activities utilized to enforce the agreement. Since the McCar-

ran Act was passed in response to *South–Eastern Underwriters,* and since a construction of the boycott provision to encompass a simple rate-fixing agreement would indeed emasculate the Act's antitrust exemption, it is reasonable to infer that in a rate-setting context something in the way of enforcement activity would be required to make out a claim of "boycott, coercion, or intimidation" within the meaning of the Act.

Id. at 274 (citation omitted).[6]

This interpretation of boycott and coercion has been consistently followed, in the context of coverage as well as rates. See, e.g., *Meicler v. Aetna Cas. and Sur. Co.,* 506 F.2d 732, 734 (5th Cir.1975) (parallel actions of insurance companies to refuse to offer insurance except under rate regulation scheme adopted by state not a boycott); *UNR Indus. Inc. v. Continental Ins. Co.,* 607 F.Supp. 855, 862–63 (N.D.Ill. 1984) (conspiracy among insurance companies to refuse to offer occurrence policies not a boycott); *Grant v. Erie Ins. Exch.,* 542 F.Supp. 457, 464–66 (M.D.Pa.1982) (conspiracy to refuse to offer insurance covering work loss benefits of individuals killed in motor vehicle accidents not a boycott) *aff'd mem.,* 716 F.2d 890 (3d Cir.), *cert. denied,* 464 U.S. 938, 104 S.Ct. 349, 78 L.Ed.2d 314 (1983).

Professors Areeda and Hovenkamp concur with this view and reject the interpretation of *Barry* urged by plaintiffs:

> The implications of *St. Paul* are not clear. On the one hand, a horizontal agreement among competitors to set the terms of insurance policies—for example, price fixing—is a collective agreement not to deal on any other terms; by the agreement, each enlists the aid of the other, a third party, "to compel capitulation by the boycotted group," namely, insurance buyers. In this sense, virtually any horizontal agreement among competitors could be called a "boycott."
>
> However, there are two reasons for supposing that the Supreme Court did not mean to go that far. First, such a reading would eviscerate the immunity for horizontal agreements on the "business of insurance" and thus seems inconsistent with the statute. Second, *St. Paul* itself did not involve an agreement to adopt similar terms. Instead, it was alleged that three insurers withdrew from the market for an anticompetitive purpose.

P. Areeda & H. Hovenkamp, *Antitrust Law* ¶ 210.2, at 107–08 (Supp. 1988).

The gravamen of the cases before the Court is alleged horizontal agreements relating to the terms on which the participants were

---

6. The *Proctor* court referred to the Supreme Court's opinion in *United States v. South–Eastern Underwriters Association,* 322 U.S. 533, 64 S.Ct. 1162, 88 L.Ed. 1440 (1944), which described the conduct of defendants as consisting of coercion and intimidation to force non-member insurance companies into the conspiracies and to compel persons who needed insurance to buy only from South–Eastern Underwriters on its terms.

willing to write insurance and reinsurance. By joint action in the ISO and in the reinsurance and umbrella and excess insurance markets, the various defendants sought to bring about the use of policies that would limit their exposure. There is no charge and no evidence that any defendants conspired to refuse to do business with any person or firm to achieve their objectives, or that by other improper means they enforced their collective decisions against others.[7]

The distinction between prohibited boycott and coercion and immune joint activities is illustrated by *In re Workers' Compensation Insurance Antitrust Litigation,* 867 F.2d 1552 (8th Cir.), *cert. denied,* ___ U.S. ___, 109 S.Ct. 3247, 106 L.Ed.2d 593 (1989). That court held that "the practice of mere price fixing, i.e., a refusal to deal except at a specified price, without more," is not a McCarran Act boycott. *Id.* at 1561. "The crucial element * * * [of a boycott] is an effort to exclude or cause disadvantage to one or more competitors by cutting them off from trade relationships which are necessary to any firm trying to compete." *Id.* at 1561, n. 14 (quotation omitted). In reversing a grant of summary judgment of no boycott, the *Workers' Compensation* court relied on evidence of an agreement to exclude competing insurers from membership in the Minnesota Rating Association; such membership was required by Minnesota law as a condition to writing workers' compensation insurance in the state. *Id.* at 1563. In contrast, in the instant case the allegations are limited to collective refusals to do business except upon terms acceptable to defendants. There is not even a suggestion that any underwriter or reinsurer (or anyone else) was prevented from having free and unimpaired access to any market.

---

7. At the hearing, plaintiffs argued that ISO's withdrawal of statistical support for the 1973 policy forms after regulatory approval had been given by the relevant states to new forms amounted to coercion. The complaints allege in relevant part:

> On July 1, 1987, ISO officially withdrew "support" of the 1973 CGL form. "Support" in this context includes the normal data collection and actuarial services performed by ISO in aid of its member companies. Without such support, most ISO members could not continue to use the 1973 occurrence form, because it is very difficult and expensive for any single company to duplicate the critical ISO support functions. (Cal.Compl't ¶ 99; Conn.Compl't ¶ 103.)

The conduct alleged, termination of statistical support for a superseded policy form, is on its face reasonable conduct that one would expect in the normal course of business. There is nothing inherently coercive or wrongful about it. There is no allegation that any insurer desired to continue to write insurance on the 1973 policy form but was coerced by defendants into not doing so by means of this conduct, and plaintiffs did not offer to amend their complaints or conduct specific discovery on this point. The allegation that "most ISO members" would find it "difficult and expensive . . . to duplicate the ISO support functions" is not sufficient to warrant subjecting these defendants to an antitrust action. *See Ocean State Physicians Health Plan Inc. v. Blue Cross & Blue Shield of Rhode Island,* 883 F.2d 1101, 1109, n. 9 (1st Cir.1989) ("Coercion [under the McCarran Act] has not generally been interpreted to include situations where options have not been entirely closed off to the allegedly coerced parties, even though such options may have been made more expensive"). To hold otherwise would be somewhat ironic, for it is the McCarran Act that allows the insurance industry, including defendants, to provide through ISO the support functions which plaintiffs regard as critical; it makes little sense then to impose antitrust liability on defendants, who are permitted by the McCarran Act to agree to provide the support, for agreeing to discontinue it as to a policy form no longer in use.

The purpose of McCarran Act immunity is to permit joint action by insurers and underwriters within the states' regulatory schemes to formulate policy terms and determine coverage. It follows that an agreement not to underwrite particular risks is a likely corollary to any collective policy form development. It makes no sense, therefore, for the plaintiffs to rest their boycott claim on the allegation of such an agreement. It is also implicit that joint action comprehends efforts to seek agreement by others, including those who might be unwilling to agree were it not for economic exigencies, and again it makes no sense to assert that such efforts constitute non-immune coercion.

What the McCarran Act leaves unprotected is conduct which goes beyond the making and implementation of agreements to do business only on terms acceptable to the participant (even if such agreements would otherwise violate Section 1), such as refusals to deal on any terms and exclusion from alternative sources. See *Barry,* 438 U.S. at 544–45, 98 S.Ct. at 2931. Such conduct is not charged here.

Dismissal of a complaint for failure to state a claim is not proper unless it appears beyond doubt that the plaintiff can prove no set of facts in support of its claim which would entitle it to relief. *Conley v. Gibson,* 355 U.S. 41, 45–46, 78 S.Ct. 99, 101–102, 2 L.Ed.2d 80 (1957). But judgment of dismissal is appropriate if it is clear that no relief could be granted under any set of facts that could be proven consistent with the allegations. *McGlinchy v. Shell Chemical Co.,* 845 F.2d 802, 810 (9th Cir.1988). Conclusory allegations without more are insufficient to defeat a motion to dismiss for failure to state a claim. *Id.*

Under the well-pleaded allegations of these complaints, plaintiffs could prove no boycott or coercion. Plaintiffs do not suggest that their pleadings could be amended to cure their deficiencies.

Nor have plaintiffs come forward with specific facts which raise a triable issue as to boycott or coercion. And this is true though plaintiffs in their capacity as state regulators conducted lengthy investigations under their regulatory laws which gave them extensive access to the files and records at least of the domestic defendants as well as to other sources of relevant information. Plaintiffs have been given the opportunity also to conduct relevant discovery and have not suggested that they needed discovery to be able fairly to meet this motion.

Accordingly, all defendants are entitled to dismissal of the complaints without leave to amend, or in the alternative summary judgment (considering defendants' submissions outside the pleadings), on all federal law claims in the various complaints. * * *

Notes and Questions

1. *Coercion or Intimidation?* Even if the actions of the defendants did not constitute a "boycott," were they "coercion" or "intimidation" within the meaning of Section Three of the McCarran–Ferguson Act?

2. *The Rationale for the Alleged Conspiracy.* The concern that lies behind Section Three is that boycotts, coercion, or intimidation may have anticompetitive effects. Is there an anticompetitive explanation for the defendants' alleged behavior that goes beyond the need to cooperate in policy preparation that is implicitly recognized by the McCarran–Ferguson Act? How would you evaluate the following arguments?

a. The defendants were attempting to gain a competitive advantage over their rivals by forcing the adoption of a form of policy over which the defendants had a comparative advantage. For example, large insurers such as the defendants can afford the startup costs of marketing a new policy more than the defendants' smaller competitors. In addition, the inclusion of a retroactive date in the new claims-made policy makes it more difficult for insureds to switch insurers, because of the risk that a new retroactive date will be adopted by the new insurer. Prospective insureds are therefore more likely to purchase claims-made from large, established insurers than from their less stable, smaller competitors. See Ayers and Siegelman, The Economics of the Insurance Antitrust Suits: Toward an Exclusionary Theory, 63 Tulane L.Rev. 971, 998–91 (1989). For an opposing view, see Priest, The Antitrust Suits and the Public Understanding of Insurance, 63 Tulane L.Rev. 999 (1989).

b. The cutthroat competition of the early 1980s kept premiums extremely low—perhaps lower than was economically sensible. This experience caused the defendants concern that there would be continued competition of this sort that would force the defendants to lose their shares of the market unless they priced below their own costs. The cause of this irrational pricing was small companies' underestimation of the threat of long-tail liabilities, such as pollution-related liability, that they faced under the existing occurrence policy. In order to prevent their competitors from engaging in this kind of suicidal price competition in the future, the defendants agreed to the alleged "boycott," which would have limited coverage of long-tail liabilities if the boycott had succeeded.

3. *Proof of Harm?* In *Matsushita Electric Industrial Company v. Zenith Radio Corporation,* 475 U.S. 574, 106 S.Ct. 1348, 89 L.Ed.2d 538 (1986), the U.S. Supreme Court upheld summary judgment for defendants because there was no proof that an alleged conspiracy to violate the antitrust laws would have decreased competition or increased the defendant's profits. If, under *Matsushita,* the plaintiff States in *In re Insurance Antitrust Litigation* would have been forced to prove this kind of harm had the defendants' motion been denied, how would they have done so?

c. The Third Round: The Effort to Repeal McCarran–Ferguson and the Decline of Collective Rate Preparation

At about the same time that the state antitrust actions were brewing, several Bills were introduced in Congress proposing repeal or limitation of the McCarran–Ferguson Act exemption of the insurance industry from federal antitrust prohibitions. See, e.g., S.1299, 100th Cong., 1st Sess. (1987). These Bills have produced Committee Hearings and considerable ferment within and outside the industry, although none has been approved by Committee and sent to the floor of the House or Senate. The central focus of discussion has been the role played by the Insurance Services Office in the preparation of advisory rates. These rates had been available for use by insurance companies, and in states where authorized to do so ISO had filed them on behalf of participating insurers with state Insurance Commissioners. Insurers could then simply state that they subscribed to ISO Advisory Rates or indicate the points at which they planned to deviate from these rates.

The obvious concern of the sponsors of legislation that would remove antitrust immunity from this practice is its potential for limiting price competition among insurers. Although use of ISO rates was not mandatory, their availability as a focal point for price increases during tight phases of the underwriting cycle was cause for speculation about the possibility of price fixing by insurers. In addition, the antitrust exemption for the industry's rate preparation process was a public relations disadvantage.

Apparently in reaction to criticism from all these quarters, the Insurance Services Office announced on April 3, 1989 that it would cease preparing advisory rates beginning in 1990. ISO would continue, however, to circulate what it called "advisory prospective loss costs"—estimates of future loss payments line-by-line and state-by-state, but without the previously included calculations of insurers' marketing and overhead expenses or underwriting profit and contingencies that are built into rates themselves.

Notes and Questions

1. *Economies of Scale.* One advantage of joint preparation of rates—the issue at the heart of the *South-Eastern Underwriter's* case more than five decades ago—has been continually cited in justification of that practice. Virtually all observers agree that joint collection and dissemination of past claim and loss data is necessary to provide individual companies and the insurance industry as a whole with a reliable statistical basis for setting rates. If ratemaking is then done by individual companies, each company must repeat a process that could be accomplished more soundly and less expensively by a joint organization such as ISO. In addition, state Insurance Commissioners often could achieve economies of scale by scrutinizing ISO rates first, and then evaluating company deviations from these rates. These economies

are lost when several hundred or thousand individual filings must be evaluated.

Since individual companies always were permitted to and often did deviate from ISO rates, however, it could be argued that the economies achieved by the ISO practice have been exaggerated. On the other hand, the ISO rate filings may have provided a cost-saving shortcut, and served as benchmark from which deviations could occur. These are empirical issues about which no persuasive data has yet been produced.

2. *Small Companies.* Another justification given for the joint preparation of rates has been that the costs of preparing rates would be prohibitive for small companies without extensive actuarial staffs. If small companies cannot compete effectively with large companies, should lawmakers be concerned? Does the answer depend on whether the additional competition these small companies provided the industry giants was or was not counterbalanced by the decreased competition that resulted from the availability of ISO-prepared rates?

3. *Tempest in a Teapot?* If ISO continues not only to maintain data on past claims and losses, but to project future losses, does it matter that it no longer prepares final rates that include factors for expenses and profits? If individual insurers followed a "go along to get along" philosophy under the advisory final rate system, will they not do roughly the same thing under the advisory prospective loss cost system? On the other hand, if insurers engaged in serious competition under the advisory final rate system, was the change in ISO procedure necessary at all?

D. STATE ANTITRUST PROHIBITIONS

This is not the proper place for an extended discussion of the rather arcane subject of state antitrust law. It is worth noting, however, that even apart from the exemptions from *federal* antitrust prohibitions provided the insurance industry under McCarran–Ferguson, and apart from any exceptions to these exemptions, the regulatory authority of the states includes the authority to prohibit anticompetitive activity by insurance companies through the use of *state* antitrust law. Indeed, since most states have general purpose antitrust laws on their books, the insurance industry's joint activities are subject to the prohibitions contained in these statutes, except to the extent that the states themselves have enacted "mini–McCarran–Ferguson Acts" that exempt insurers from these prohibitions. For example, under the antitrust laws of many states, the activities of ISO might constitute violations if it were not for specific authorizations for the use of rate service organizations and the like. See, e.g., Annotated Code of Virginia § 38.2–1908. Any state that was unsatisfied with the scope of the McCarran–Ferguson exemptions, or with the interpretations placed on the reach of the boycott exception by the Federal courts, certainly would have the power to prohibit by statute or regulatory order the kind of joint activities that are authorized by federal law.

To some extent this already occurs. For example, prior to ISO's 1989 decision to cease preparing advisory rates, several states prohibited rate service organizations from filing such rates with their Insurance Commissioners. The insurance industry was concerned with precisely this kind of patchwork state-by-state regulation at the time the Supreme Court decided *Paul v. Virginia* over a century ago. It may well be that as individual states become more active on the state antitrust front, at least some of the authority that the McCarran–Ferguson Act has traditionally allocated to the states will be reclaimed by the federal government in order to avoid the disorganization that may result from state-by-state regulation of the industry.

Chapter Four

FIRE AND PROPERTY INSURANCE

This Chapter is the first of four that focus on specific forms of insurance coverage. Although many issues in insurance law arise in connection with several different kinds of insurance, others are peculiar to particular forms of coverage. Even common issues may be raised or resolved in subtly different ways depending on the form of coverage involved. Although studying "general principles" of insurance law often is useful, every lawyer knows that legal decisions normally are made in response to concrete problems rather than general issues. Consequently, this Chapter and those that follow attempt to build insights from the ground up, so to speak, rather than from the top down.

At the outset, the distinction between *first-party* and *third-party* insurance is worth noting. First-party insurance protects the insured against a loss that he (or other insureds such as family members) suffers himself; it is "victim's insurance." Fire, property, life, health, and disability insurance fall into this category. In contrast, third-party insurance protects the insured against legal liability to a third-party resulting from the insured's actions. Third-party, or liability insurance, is "injurer's" insurance. This Chapter and Chapter Five are devoted to the different forms of first-party insurance and the issues they raise. Chapters Six and Seven are devoted to third-party insurance, and Chapter Eight covers both, as they are found in automobile insurance.

A. SAMPLE HOMEOWNERS POLICY

The following is a Sample Homeowners Policy insuring against fire, damage to property, and certain forms of liability. It is a combination of first-party and third-party insurance. Because some of the liability insurance provisions ("Part II" of the policy) are examined in Chapter Six, they are omitted here. Although there are several different homeowners policies in use, and commercial property policies are structured somewhat differently, this Policy is a useful introduction to the art of reading insurance policies. It contains provisions similar to those at issue in the cases in subsequent sections of this Chapter. Reading the policy, understanding how it is structured, and familiarizing yourself with the location of different kinds of provisions within it will assist your study of the nature of fire and property insurance generally.

HOMEOWNERS POLICY
Declarations applicable to all policy forms

Policy Number

Policy Period: 12:01 a.m. Standard time   From: To:
                at the residence premises

Named Insured and mailing address

The residence premises covered by this policy is located at the above address unless otherwise stated:

Coverage is provided where a premium or limit of liability is shown for the coverage.

	Limit of Liability	Premium
SECTION I COVERAGES		
A. Dwelling		
B. Other structures		
C. Personal property		
D. Loss of use		
SECTION II COVERAGES		
E. Personal liability: each occurrence		
F. Medical payments to others: each person		

Total premium for endorsements listed below

Policy Total

Forms and endorsements made part of this policy:
Number   Edition Date   Title   Premium

[Special State Provisions: South Carolina: Valuation Clause (Cov.A) $
                            Minnesota Insurable Value (Cov.A) $
                            New York: Coinsurance Clause Applies ___Yes ___No]

DEDUCTIBLE - Section I: $
In case of a loss under Section I, we cover only that part of the loss over the deductible stated.

Section II: Other insured locations:

[Mortgagee/Lienholder (Name and address)]

Countersignature of agent/date   Signature/title - company officer

Ed.4/84   [F3861]

AGREEMENT

We will provide the insurance described in this policy in return for the premium and compliance with all applicable provisions of this policy.

DEFINITIONS

In this policy, "you" and "your" refer to the "named insured" shown in the Declarations and the spouse if a resident of the same household. "We," "us" and "our" refer to the Company providing this insurance. In addition, certain words and phrases are defined as follows:

1. **"bodily injury"** means bodily harm, sickness or disease, including required care, loss of services and death that results.

2. **"business"** includes trade, profession or occupation.

3. **"insured"** means you and residents of your household who are:

   a. your relatives; or

   b. other persons under the age of 21 and in the care of any person named above.

   Under Section II, **"insured"** also means:

   c. with respect to animals or watercraft to which this policy applies, any person or organization legally responsible for these animals or watercraft which are owned by you or any person included in 3a or 3b above. A person or organization using or having custody of these animals or watercraft in the course of any **business** or without consent of the owner is not an **insured;**

   d. with respect to any vehicle to which this policy applies:

      (1) persons while engaged in your employ or that of any person included in 3a or 3b above; or

      (2) other persons using the vehicle on an **insured location** with your consent.

4. **"insured location"** means:

   a. the **residence premises;**

   b. the part of other premises, other structures and grounds used by you as a residence and:

      (1) which is shown in the Declarations; or

      (2) which is acquired by you during the policy period for your use as a residence;

   c. any premises used by you in connection with a premises in 4a or 4b above;

   d. any part of a premises:

      (1) not owned by an **insured;** and

      (2) where an **insured** is temporarily residing;

   e. vacant land, other than farm land, owned by or rented to an **insured;**

   f. land owned by or rented to an **insured** on which a one or two family dwelling is being built as a residence for an **insured;**

   g. individual or family cemetery plots or burial vaults of an **insured;** or

   h. any part of a premises occasionally rented to an **insured** for other than **business** use.

5. **"occurrence"** means an accident, including exposure to conditions, which results, during the policy period, in:

   a. **bodily injury;** or

   b. **property damage.**

6. **"property damage"** means physical injury to, destruction of, or loss of use of tangible property.

7. **"residence employee"** means:

   a. an employee of an **insured** whose duties are related to the maintenance or use of the **residence premises,** including household or domestic services; or

   b. one who performs similar duties elsewhere not related to the **business** of an **insured.**

---

8. **"residence premises"** means:

    a.   the one family dwelling, other structures, and grounds; or

    b.   that part of any other building;

where you reside and which is shown as the **"residence premises"** in the Declarations.

"Residence premises" also means a two family dwelling where you reside in at least one of the family units and which is shown as the **"residence premises"** in the Declarations.

SECTION I—PROPERTY COVERAGES

COVERAGE A—Dwelling

We cover:

1. the dwelling on the **residence premises** shown in the Declarations, including structures attached to the dwelling; and

2. materials and supplies located on or next to the **residence premises** used to construct, alter or repair the dwelling or other structures on the **residence premises.**

This coverage does not apply to land, including land on which the dwelling is located.

COVERAGE B—Other Structures

We cover other structures on the **residence premises** set apart from the dwelling by clear space. This includes structures connected to the dwelling by only a fence, utility line, or similar connection.

This coverage does not apply to land, including land on which the other structures are located.

We do not cover other structures:

1. used in whole or in part for **business;** or

2. rented or held for rental to any person not a tenant of the dwelling, unless used solely as a private garage.

The limit of liability for this coverage will not be more than 10% of the limit of liability that applies to Coverage A. Use of this coverage does not reduce the Coverage A limit of liability.

COVERAGE C—Personal Property

We cover personal property owned or used by an **insured** while it is anywhere in the world. At your request, we will cover personal property owned by:

1. others while the property is on the part of the **residence premises** occupied by an **insured;**

2. a guest or a **residence employee,** while the property is in any residence occupied by an **insured.**

Our limit of liability for personal property usually located at an **insured's** residence, other than the **residence premises,** is 10% of the limit of liability for Coverage C, or $1000, whichever is greater. Personal property in a newly acquired principal residence is not subject to this limitation for the 30 days from the time you begin to move the property there.

Special Limits of Liability. These limits do not increase the Coverage C limit of liability. The special limit for each numbered category below is the total limit for each loss for all property in that category.

1. $200 on money, bank notes, bullion, gold other than goldware, silver other than silverware, platinum, coins and medals.

2. $1000 on securities, accounts, deeds, evidences of debt, letters of credit, notes other than bank notes, manuscripts, passports, tickets and stamps.

3. $1000 on watercraft, including their trailers, furnishings, equipment and outboard motors.

4. $1000 on trailers not used with watercraft.

5. $1000 on grave markers.

6. $1000 for loss by theft of jewelry, watches, furs, precious and semi-precious stones.

7. $2000 for loss by theft of firearms.

8. $2500 for loss by theft of silverware, silver-plated ware, goldware, gold-plated ware and pewterware. This includes flatware, hollowware, tea sets, trays and trophies made of or including silver, gold or pewter.

9. $2500 on property, on the **residence premises,** used at any time or in any manner for any **business** purpose.

10. $250 on property, away from the **residence premises,** used at any time or in any manner for any **business** purpose.

Property Not Covered. We do not cover:

1. articles separately described and specifically insured in this or other insurance;

2. animals, birds or fish;

3. motor vehicles or all other motorized land conveyances. This includes:

   a. equipment and accessories; or

   b. any device or instrument for the transmitting, recording, receiving or reproduction of sound or pictures which is operated by power from the electrical system of motor vehicles or all other motorized land conveyances, including:

      (1) accessories or antennas; or

      (2) tapes, wires, records, discs or other media for use with any such device or instrument;

   while in or upon the vehicle or conveyance.

   We do cover vehicles or conveyances not subject to motor vehicle registration which are:

   a. used to service an **insured's** residence; or

   b. designed for assisting the handicapped;

4. aircraft and parts. Aircraft means any contrivance used or designed for flight, except model or hobby aircraft not used or designed to carry people or cargo;

5. property of roomers, boarders and other tenants, except property of roomers and boarders related to an **insured;**

6. property in an apartment regularly rented or held for rental to others by an **insured;**

7. property rented or held for rental to others off the **residence premises;**

8. a. books of account, drawings or other paper records; or

   b. electronic data processing tapes, wires, records, discs or other software media;

   containing **business** data. But, we do cover the cost of blank or unexposed records and media;

9. credit cards or fund transfer cards except as provided in Additional Coverages 6.

COVERAGE D—Loss Of Use

The limit of liability for Coverage D is the total limit for all the coverages that follow.

1. If a loss covered under this Section makes that part of the **residence premises** where you reside not fit to live in, we cover, at your choice, either of the following. However, if the **residence premises** is not your principal place of residence, we will not provide the option under paragraph b. below.

   a. **Additional Living Expense,** meaning any necessary increase in living expenses incurred by you so that your household can maintain its normal standard of living; or

   b. **Fair Rental Value,** meaning the fair rental value of that part of the **residence premises** where you reside less any expenses that do not continue while the premises is not fit to live in.

   Payment under a. or b. will be for the shortest time required to repair or replace the damage or, if you permanently relocate, the shortest time required for your household to settle elsewhere.

2. If a loss covered under this Section makes that part of the **residence premises** rented to others or held for rental by you not fit to live in, we cover the:

   Fair Rental Value, meaning the fair rental value of that part of the **residence premises** rented to others or held for rental by you less any expenses that do not continue while the premises is not fit to live in.

   Payment will be for the shortest time required to repair or replace that part of the premises rented or held for rental.

3. If a civil authority prohibits you from use of the **residence premises** as a result of direct damage to neighboring premises by a Peril Insured Against in this policy, we cover the Additional Living Expense or Fair Rental Value loss as provided under 1 and 2 above for no more than two weeks.

The periods of time under 1, 2 and 3 above are not limited by expiration of this policy.

We do not cover loss or expense due to cancellation of a lease or agreement.

ADDITIONAL COVERAGES

1. **Debris Removal.** We will pay your reasonable expense for the removal of:

   a. debris of covered property if a Peril Insured Against causes the loss; or

   b. ash, dust or particles from a volcanic eruption that has caused direct loss to a building or property contained in a building.

   This expense is included in the limit of liability that applies to the damaged property. If the amount to be paid for the actual damage to the property plus the debris removal expense is more than the limit of liability for the damaged property, an additional 5% of that limit of liability is available for debris removal expense.

We will also pay your reasonable expense for the removal of fallen trees from the **residence premises** if:

a. coverage is not afforded under Additional Coverages 3 Trees, Shrubs and Other Plants for the peril causing the loss; or

b. the tree is not covered by this policy;

provided the tree damages covered property and a Peril Insured Against under Coverage C causes the tree to fall. Our limit of liability for this coverage will not be more than $500 in the aggregate for any one loss.

2. **Reasonable Repairs.** We will pay the reasonable cost incurred by you for necessary repairs made solely to protect covered property from further damage if a Peril Insured Against causes the loss. This coverage does not increase the limit of liability that applies to the property being repaired.

3. **Trees, Shrubs and Other Plants.** We cover trees, shrubs, plants or lawns, on the **residence premises,** for loss caused by the following Perils Insured Against: Fire or lightning, Explosion, Riot or civil commotion, Aircraft, Vehicles not owned or operated by a resident of the **residence premises,** Vandalism or malicious mischief or Theft.

The limit of liability for this coverage will not be more than 5% of the limit of liability that applies to the dwelling, or more than $500 for any one tree, shrub or plant. We do not cover property grown for **business** purposes.

This coverage is additional insurance.

4. **Fire Department Service Charge.** We will pay up to $500 for your liability assumed by contract or agreement for fire department charges incurred when the fire department is called to save or protect covered property from a Peril Insured Against. We do not cover fire department service charges if the property is located within the limits of the city, municipality or protection district furnishing the fire department response.

This coverage is additional insurance. No deductible applies to this coverage.

5. **Property Removed.** We insure covered property against direct loss from any cause while being removed from a premises endangered by a Peril Insured Against and for no more than 30 days while removed. This coverage does not change the limit of liability that applies to the property being removed.

6. **Credit Card, Fund Transfer Card, Forgery and Counterfeit Money.**

We will pay up to $500 for:

a. the legal obligation of an **insured** to pay because of the theft or unauthorized use of credit cards issued to or registered in an **insured's** name;

b. loss resulting from theft or unauthorized use of a fund transfer card used for deposit, withdrawal or transfer of funds, issued to or registered in an **insured's** name;

c. loss to an **insured** caused by forgery or alteration of any check or negotiable instrument; and

d. loss to an **insured** through acceptance in good faith of counterfeit United States or Canadian paper currency.

We do not cover use of a credit card or fund transfer card:

a. by a resident of your household;

b. by a person who has been entrusted with either type of card; or

c. if an **insured** has not complied with all terms and conditions under which the cards are issued.

All loss resulting from a series of acts committed by any one person or in which any one person is concerned or implicated is considered to be one loss.

We do not cover loss arising out of **business** use or dishonesty of an **insured.**

This coverage is additional insurance. No deductible applies to this coverage.

Defense:

a. We may investigate and settle any claim or suit that we decide is appropriate. Our duty to defend a claim or suit ends when the amount we pay for the loss equals our limit of liability.

b. If a suit is brought against an **insured** for liability under the Credit Card or Fund Transfer Card coverage, we will provide a defense at our expense by counsel of our choice.

c. We have the option to defend at our expense an **insured** or an **insured's** bank against any suit for the enforcement of payment under the Forgery coverage.

7. **Loss Assessment.** We will pay up to $1000 for your share of any loss assessment charged during the policy period against you by a corporation or association of property owners. This only applies when the assessment is made as a result of each direct loss to the property, owned by all members collectively, caused by a Peril Insured Against under Coverage A—Dwelling, other than earthquake or land shock waves or tremors before, during or after a volcanic eruption.

This coverage applies only to loss assessments charged against you as owner or tenant of the **residence premises.**

We do not cover loss assessments charged against you or a corporation or association of property owners by any governmental body.

8. Collapse. We insure for direct physical loss to covered property involving collapse of a building or any part of a building caused only by one or more of the following:

a. Perils Insured Against in Coverage C—Personal Property. These perils apply to covered building and personal property for loss insured by this additional coverage;

b. hidden decay;

c. hidden insect or vermin damage;

d. weight of contents, equipment, animals or people;

e. weight of rain which collects on a roof; or

f. use of defective material or methods in construction, remodeling or renovation if the collapse occurs during the course of the construction, remodeling or renovation.

Loss to an awning, fence, patio, pavement, swimming pool, underground pipe, flue, drain, cesspool, septic tank, foundation, retaining wall, bulkhead, pier, wharf or dock is not included under items b, c, d, e, and f unless the loss is a direct result of the collapse of a building.

Collapse does not include settling, cracking, shrinking, bulging or expansion.

This coverage does not increase the limit of liability applying to the damaged covered property.

SECTION I—PERILS INSURED AGAINST

COVERAGE A—DWELLING and
COVERAGE B—OTHER STRUCTURES

We insure against risks of direct loss to property described in Coverages A and B only if that loss is a physical loss to property; however, we do not insure loss:

1. involving collapse, other than as provided in Additional Coverage 8;

2. caused by:

a. freezing of a plumbing, heating, air conditioning or automatic fire protective sprinkler system or of a household appliance, or by discharge, leakage or overflow from within the system or appliance caused by freezing. This exclusion applies only while the dwelling is vacant, unoccupied or being constructed unless you have used reasonable care to:

(1) maintain heat in the building; or

(2) shut off the water supply and drain the system and appliances of water;

b. freezing, thawing, pressure or weight of water or ice, whether driven by wind or not, to a:

(1) fence, pavement, patio or swimming pool;

(2) foundation, retaining wall or bulkhead; or

(3) pier, wharf or dock;

c. theft in or to a dwelling under construction, or of materials and supplies for use in the construction until the dwelling is finished and occupied;

d. vandalism and malicious mischief or breakage of glass and safety glazing materials if the dwelling has been vacant for more than 30 consecutive days immediately before the

loss. A dwelling being constructed is not considered vacant;

e. constant or repeated seepage or leakage of water or steam over a period of weeks, months or years from within a plumbing, heating, air conditioning or automatic fire protective sprinkler system or from within a household appliance;

f. (1) wear and tear, marring, deterioration;

(2) inherent vice, latent defect, mechanical breakdown;

(3) smog, rust, mold, wet or dry rot;

(4) smoke from agricultural smudging or industrial operations;

(5) release, discharge or dispersal of contaminants or pollutants;

(6) settling, cracking, shrinking, bulging or expansion of pavements, patios, foundations, walls, floors, roofs or ceilings; or

(7) birds, vermin, rodents, insects or domestic animals.

If any of these cause water damage not otherwise excluded, from a plumbing, heating, air conditioning or automatic fire protective sprinkler system or household appliance, we cover loss caused by the water including the cost of tearing out and replacing any part of a building necessary to repair the system or appliance. We do not cover loss to the system or appliance from which this water escaped.

3. excluded under Section I—Exclusions.

Under items 1 and 2, any ensuing loss to property described in Coverages A and B not excluded or excepted in this policy is covered.

COVERAGE C—PERSONAL PROPERTY

We insure for direct physical loss to the property described in Coverage C caused by a peril listed below unless the loss is excluded in Section I—Exclusions.

1. **Fire or lightning.**

2. **Windstorm or hail.**

    This peril does not include loss to the property contained in a building caused by rain, snow, sleet, sand or dust unless the direct force of wind or hail damages the building causing an opening in a roof or wall and the rain, snow, sleet, sand or dust enters through this opening.

    This peril includes loss to watercraft and their trailers, furnishings, equipment, and outboard motors, only while inside a fully enclosed building.

3. **Explosion.**

4. **Riot or civil commotion.**

5. **Aircraft,** including self-propelled missiles and spacecraft.

6. **Vehicles.**

7. **Smoke,** meaning sudden and accidental damage from smoke.

    This peril does not include loss caused by smoke from agricultural smudging or industrial operations.

8. **Vandalism or malicious mischief.**

9. **Theft,** including attempted theft and loss of property from a known place when it is likely that the property has been stolen.

    This peril does not include loss caused by theft:

    a. committed by an **insured;**

    b. in or to a dwelling under construction, or of materials and supplies for use in the construction until the dwelling is finished and occupied; or

    c. from that part of a **residence premises** rented by an **insured** to other than an **insured.**

    This peril does not include loss caused by theft that occurs off the **residence premises** of:

    a. property while at any other residence owned by, rented to, or occupied by an **insured,** except while an **insured** is temporarily living there. Property of a student who is an **insured** is covered while at a residence away from home if the student has been there at any time during the 45 days immediately before the loss;

    b. watercraft, including their furnishings, equipment and outboard motors; or

    c. trailers and campers.

10. **Falling objects.**

    This peril does not include loss to property contained in a building unless the roof or an outside wall of the building is first damaged by a falling object. Damage to the falling object itself is not included.

11. **Weight of ice, snow or sleet** which causes damage to property contained in a building.

12. **Accidental discharge or overflow of water or steam** from within a plumbing, heating, air conditioning or automatic fire protective sprinkler system or from within a household appliance.

    This peril does not include loss:

    a. to the system or appliance from which the water or steam escaped;

    b. caused by or resulting from freezing except as provided in the peril of freezing below; or

    c. on the **residence premises** caused by accidental discharge or overflow which occurs off the **residence premises.**

13. **Sudden and accidental tearing apart, cracking, burning or bulging** of a steam or hot water heating system, an air conditioning or automatic fire protective sprinkler system, or an appliance for heating water.

    We do not cover loss caused by or resulting from freezing under this peril.

14. **Freezing** of a plumbing, heating, air conditioning or automatic fire protective sprinkler system or of a household appliance.

    This peril does not include loss on the **residence premises** while the dwelling is unoccupied, unless you have used reasonable care to:

    a. maintain heat in the building; or

    b. shut off the water supply and drain the system and appliances of water.

15. **Sudden and accidental damage from artificially generated electrical current.**

    This peril does not include loss to a tube, transistor or similar electronic component.

16. **Damage by glass or safety glazing material** which is part of a building, storm door or storm window.

    This peril does not include loss on the **residence premises** if the dwelling has been vacant for more than 30 consecutive days immediately before the loss. A dwelling being constructed is not considered vacant.

17. **Volcanic Eruption** other than loss caused by earthquake, land shock waves or tremors.

SECTION I—EXCLUSIONS

1. We do not insure for loss caused directly or indirectly by any of the following. Such loss is excluded regardless of any other cause or event contributing concurrently or in any sequence to the loss.

   a. **Ordinance or Law,** meaning enforcement of any ordinance or law regulating the construction, repair, or demolition of a building or other structure, unless specifically provided under this policy.

   b. **Earth Movement,** meaning earthquake including land shock waves or tremors before, during or after a volcanic eruption; landslide; mudflow; earth sinking, rising or shifting; unless direct loss by:

      (1) fire;

      (2) explosion; or

      (3) breakage of glass or safety glazing material which is part of a building, storm door or storm window;

      ensues and then we will pay only for the ensuing loss.

      This exclusion does not apply to loss by theft.

   c. **Water Damage,** meaning:

      (1) flood, surface water, waves, tidal water, overflow of a body of water, or spray from any of these, whether or not driven by wind;

      (2) water which backs up through sewers or drains; or

      (3) water below the surface of the ground, including water which exerts pressure on or seeps or leaks through a building, sidewalk, driveway, foundation, swimming pool or other structure.

      Direct loss by fire, explosion or theft resulting from water damage is covered.

   d. **Power Failure,** meaning the failure of power or other utility service if the failure takes place off the **residence premises.** But, if a Peril Insured Against ensues on the **residence premises,** we will pay only for that ensuing loss.

   e. **Neglect,** meaning neglect of the **insured** to use all reasonable means to save and preserve property at and after the time of a loss.

   f. **War,** including undeclared war, civil war, insurrection, rebellion, revolution, warlike act by a military force or military personnel, destruction or seizure or use for a military purpose, and including any consequence of any of these. Discharge of a nuclear weapon will be deemed a warlike act even if accidental.

   g. **Nuclear Hazard,** to the extent set forth in the Nuclear Hazard Clause of Section I—Conditions.

   h. **Intentional Loss,** meaning any loss arising out of any act committed:

      (1) by or at the direction of an **insured;** and

      (2) with the intent to cause a loss.

2. We do not insure for loss to property described in Coverages A and B caused by any of the following. However, any ensuing loss to property described in Coverages A and B not excluded or excepted in this policy is covered.

   a. **Weather conditions.** However, this exclusion only applies if weather conditions contribute in any way with a cause or event excluded in paragraph 1. above to produce the loss;

   b. **Acts or decisions,** including the failure to act or decide, of any person, group, organization or governmental body;

   c. **Faulty, inadequate or defective:**

      (1) planning, zoning, development, surveying, siting;

      (2) design, specifications, workmanship, repair, construction, renovation, remodeling, grading, compaction;

      (3) materials used in repair, construction, renovation or remodeling; or

      (4) maintenance;

      of part or all of any property whether on or off the **residence premises.**

SECTION I—CONDITIONS

1. **Insurable Interest and Limit of Liability.** Even if more than one person has an insurable interest in the property covered, we will not be liable in any one loss:

   a. to the **Insured** for more than the amount of the **Insured's** interest at the time of loss; or

   b. for more than the applicable limit of liability.

2. **Your Duties After Loss.** In case of a loss to covered property, you must see that the following are done:

   a. give prompt notice to us or our agent;

   b. notify the police in case of loss by theft;

   c. notify the credit card or fund transfer card company in case of loss under Credit Card or Fund Transfer Card coverage;

   d. (1) protect the property from further damage;

   (2) make reasonable and necessary repairs to protect the property; and

   (3) keep an accurate record of repair expenses;

   e. prepare an inventory of damaged personal property showing the quantity, description, actual cash value and amount of loss. Attach all bills, receipts and related documents that justify the figures in the inventory;

   f. as often as we reasonably require:

   (1) show the damaged property;

   (2) provide us with records and documents we request and permit us to make copies; and

   (3) submit to questions under oath and sign and swear to them;

   g. send to us, within 60 days after our request, your signed, sworn proof of loss which sets forth, to the best of your knowledge and belief:

   (1) the time and cause of loss;

   (2) the interest of the **Insured** and all others in the property involved and all liens on the property;

   (3) other insurance which may cover the loss;

   (4) changes in title or occupancy of the property during the term of the policy;

   (5) specifications of damaged buildings and detailed repair estimates;

   (6) the inventory of damaged personal property described in 2e above;

   (7) receipts for additional living expenses incurred and records that support the fair rental value loss; and

   (8) evidence or affidavit that supports a claim under the Credit Card, Fund Transfer Card, Forgery and Counterfeit Money coverage, stating the amount and cause of loss.

3. **Loss Settlement.** Covered property losses are settled as follows:

   a. (1) Personal property;

   (2) Awnings, carpeting, household appliances, outdoor antennas and outdoor equipment, whether or not attached to buildings; and

   (3) Structures that are not buildings;

   at actual cash value at the time of loss but not more than the amount required to repair or replace.

   b. Buildings under Coverage A or B at replacement cost without deduction for depreciation, subject to the following:

   (1) If, at the time of loss, the amount of insurance in this policy on the damaged building is 80% or more of the full replacement cost of the building immediately before the loss, we will pay the cost to repair or replace, after application of deductible and without deduction for depreciation, but not more than the least of the following amounts:

   (a) the limit of liability under this policy that applies to the building;

   (b) the replacement cost of that part of the building damaged for like construction and use on the same premises; or

   (c) the necessary amount actually spent to repair or replace the damaged building.

(2) If, at the time of loss, the amount of insurance in this policy on the damaged building is less than 80% of the full replacement cost of the building immediately before the loss, we will pay the greater of the following amounts, but not more than the limit of liability under this policy that applies to the building:

    (a) the actual cash value of that part of the building damaged; or

    (b) that proportion of the cost to repair or replace, after application of deductible and without deduction for depreciation, that part of the building damaged, which the total amount of insurance in this policy on the damaged building bears to 80% of the replacement cost of the building.

(3) To determine the amount of insurance required to equal 80% of the full replacement cost of the building immediately before the loss, do not include the value of:

    (a) excavations, foundations, piers or any supports which are below the undersurface of the lowest basement floor;

    (b) those supports in (a) above which are below the surface of the ground inside the foundation walls, if there is no basement; and

    (c) underground flues, pipes, wiring and drains.

(4) We will pay no more than the actual cash value of the damage unless:

    (a) actual repair or replacement is complete; or

    (b) the cost to repair or replace the damage is both:

        (i) less than 5% of the amount of insurance in this policy on the building; and

        (ii) less than $1000.

(5) You may disregard the replacement cost loss settlement provisions and make claim under this policy for loss or damage to buildings on an actual cash value basis. You may then make claim within 180 days after loss for any additional liability on a replacement cost basis.

4. **Loss to a Pair or Set.** In case of loss to a pair or set we may elect to:

    a. repair or replace any part to restore the pair or set to its value before the loss; or

    b. pay the difference between actual cash value of the property before and after the loss.

5. **Glass Replacement.** Loss for damage to glass caused by a Peril Insured Against will be settled on the basis of replacement with safety glazing materials when required by ordinance or law.

6. **Appraisal.** If you and we fail to agree on the amount of loss, either may demand an appraisal of the loss. In this event, each party will choose a competent appraiser within 20 days after receiving a written request from the other. The two appraisers will choose an umpire. If they cannot agree upon an umpire within 15 days, you or we may request that the choice be made by a judge of a court of record in the state where the **residence premises** is located. The appraisers will separately set the amount of loss. If the appraisers submit a written report of an agreement to us, the amount agreed upon will be the amount of loss. If they fail to agree, they will submit their differences to the umpire. A decision agreed to by any two will set the amount of loss.

Each party will:

    a. pay its own appraiser; and

    b. bear the other expenses of the appraisal and umpire equally.

7. **Other Insurance.** If a loss covered by this policy is also covered by other insurance, we will pay only the proportion of the loss that the limit of liability that applies under this policy bears to the total amount of insurance covering the loss.

8. **Suit Against Us.** No action can be brought unless the policy provisions have been complied with and the action is started within one year after the date of loss.

9. **Our Option.** If we give you written notice within 30 days after we receive your signed, sworn proof of loss, we may repair or replace any part of the damaged property with like property.

10. **Loss Payment.** We will adjust all losses with you. We will pay you unless some other person is named in the policy or is legally entitled to receive payment. Loss will be payable 60 days after we receive your proof of loss and:

    a. reach an agreement with you;

    b. there is an entry of a final judgment; or

    c. there is a filing of an appraisal award with us.

11. **Abandonment of Property.** We need not accept any property abandoned by an **insured**.

12. Mortgage Clause.

The word "mortgagee" includes trustee.

If a mortgagee is named in this policy, any loss payable under Coverage A or B will be paid to the mortgagee and you, as interests appear. If more than one mortgagee is named, the order of payment will be the same as the order of precedence of the mortgages.

If we deny your claim, that denial will not apply to a valid claim of the mortgagee, if the mortgagee:

a. notifies us of any change in ownership, occupancy or substantial change in risk of which the mortgagee is aware;

b. pays any premium due under this policy on demand if you have neglected to pay the premium; and

c. submits a signed, sworn statement of loss within 60 days after receiving notice from us of your failure to do so. Policy conditions relating to Appraisal, Suit Against Us and Loss Payment apply to the mortgagee.

If the policy is cancelled or not renewed by us, the mortgagee will be notified at least 10 days before the date cancellation or nonrenewal takes effect.

If we pay the mortgagee for any loss and deny payment to you:

a. we are subrogated to all the rights of the mortgagee granted under the mortgage on the property; or

b. at our option, we may pay to the mortgagee the whole principal on the mortgage plus any accrued interest. In this event, we will receive a full assignment and transfer of the mortgage and all securities held as collateral to the mortgage debt.

Subrogation will not impair the right of the mortgagee to recover the full amount of the mortgagee's claim.

13. No Benefit to Bailee. We will not recognize any assignment or grant any coverage that benefits a person or organization holding, storing or moving property for a fee regardless of any other provision of this policy.

14. Nuclear Hazard Clause.

a. "Nuclear Hazard" means any nuclear reaction, radiation, or radioactive contamination, all whether controlled or uncontrolled or however caused, or any consequence of any of these.

b. Loss caused by the nuclear hazard will not be considered loss caused by fire, explosion, or smoke, whether these perils are specifically named in or otherwise included within the Perils Insured Against in Section I.

c. This policy does not apply under Section I to loss caused directly or indirectly by nuclear hazard, except that direct loss by fire resulting from the nuclear hazard is covered.

15. Recovered Property. If you or we recover any property for which we have made payment under this policy, you or we will notify the other of the recovery. At your option, the property will be returned to or retained by you or it will become our property. If the recovered property is returned to or retained by you, the loss payment will be adjusted based on the amount you received for the recovered property.

16. Volcanic Eruption Period. One or more volcanic eruptions that occur within a 72-hour period will be considered as one volcanic eruption.

SECTIONS I AND II—CONDITIONS

1. **Policy Period.** This policy applies only to loss in Section I or **bodily injury** or **property damage** in Section II, which occurs during the policy period.

2. **Concealment or Fraud.** We do not provide coverage for an **insured** who has:

   a. intentionally concealed or misrepresented any material fact or circumstance; or

   b. made false statements or engaged in fraudulent conduct;

   relating to this insurance.

3. **Liberalization Clause.** If we adopt a revision which would broaden the coverage under this policy without additional premium within 60 days prior to or during the policy period, the broadened coverage will immediately apply to this policy.

4. **Waiver or Change of Policy Provisions.**

   A waiver or change of a provision of this policy must be in writing by us to be valid. Our request for an appraisal or examination will not waive any of our rights.

5. **Cancellation.**

   a. You may cancel this policy at any time by returning it to us or by letting us know in writing of the date cancellation is to take effect.

   b. We may cancel this policy only for the reasons stated below by letting you know in writing of the date cancellation takes effect. This cancellation notice may be delivered to you, or mailed to you at your mailing address shown in the Declarations.

   Proof of mailing will be sufficient proof of notice.

   (1) When you have not paid the premium, we may cancel at any time by letting you know at least 10 days before the date cancellation takes effect.

   (2) When this policy has been in effect for less than 60 days and is not a renewal with us, we may cancel for any reason by letting you know at least 10 days before the date cancellation takes effect.

   (3) When this policy has been in effect for 60 days or more, or at any time if it is a renewal with us, we may cancel:

   (a) if there has been a material misrepresentation of fact which if known to us would have caused us not to issue the policy; or

   (b) if the risk has changed substantially since the policy was issued.

   This can be done by letting you know at least 30 days before the date cancellation takes effect.

   (4) When this policy is written for a period of more than one year, we may cancel for any reason at anniversary by letting you know at least 30 days before the date cancellation takes effect.

   c. When this policy is cancelled, the premium for the period from the date of cancellation to the expiration date will be refunded pro rata.

   d. If the return premium is not refunded with the notice of cancellation or when this policy is returned to us, we will refund it within a reasonable time after the date cancellation takes effect.

6. **Non-Renewal.** We may elect not to renew this policy. We may do so by delivering to you, or mailing to you at your mailing address shown in the Declarations, written notice at least 30 days before the expiration date of this policy. Proof of mailing will be sufficient proof of notice.

7. **Assignment.** Assignment of this policy will not be valid unless we give our written consent.

8. **Subrogation.** An **insured** may waive in writing before a loss all rights of recovery against any person. If not waived, we may require an assignment of rights of recovery for a loss to the extent that payment is made by us.

   If an assignment is sought, an **insured** must sign and deliver all related papers and cooperate with us.

   Subrogation does not apply under Section II to Medical Payments to Others or Damage to Property of Others.

9. **Death.** If any person named in the Declarations or the spouse, if a resident of the same household, dies:

   a. we insure the legal representative of the deceased but only with respect to the premises and property of the deceased covered under the policy at the time of death;

   b. **insured** includes:

   (1) any member of your household who is an **insured** at the time of your death, but only while a resident of the **residence premises;** and

   (2) with respect to your property, the person having proper temporary custody of the property until appointment and qualification of a legal representative.

HO-3 Ed. 4-84　　　　Copyright, Insurance Services Office, Inc., 1984　　　　**Page 15 of 15**

Notes and Questions

1. *Organization.* Notice that the policy is comprised of six main parts: the Declarations Page, or "dec-sheet;" Definitions; a statement of the Property Coverages; an indication of the causes of damage to or loss that the policy covers, termed the Perils Insured; a set of Exclusions that would otherwise be within the terms of coverage; and

Conditions precedent to coverage. The policy purports to be in plain language. Is the language "plain"? The organization?

2. *Forms of Coverage.* Two distinctions that are often drawn in the fire and property insurance field should be underscored. The first distinction is between *fire insurance* alone and *fire-and-extended* coverage. Fire insurance alone is typically provided under a version of the 1943 New York Standard Fire Insurance Policy, N.Y.Ins.Law § 3404. Fire-and-extended coverage, in contrast, is provided under homeowners and commercial property insurance policies that protect against damage caused not only by fire, but by other causes as well, and that provide certain ancillary coverage on personal property. Sometimes homeowners policies are accompanied by a standard fire policy, a practice which to some extent supplements coverage but in a few other respects may actually limit it, because of certain exclusions in the fire policy that are sometimes omitted from homeowners policies.

The second distinction is between *all-risk* and *specified-risk* coverage. The terms mean exactly what they imply. An all-risk policy covers all risks of the general sort that are covered by the policy—those not excluded are automatically included. In contrast, a specified-risk policy covers only those risks actually specified in the coverage provisions of the policy, subject to exclusions. The foregoing is of course a description of "pure" types; policies usually are not labelled as all-risk or specified-risk. Rather, the language of the coverage provisions yields a characterization that in turn tends to determine whether the insured or the insurer bears the burden of proving that a loss falls within or outside coverage. See, e.g., *Pan American World Airways, Inc. v. Aetna Casualty & Surety Company,* 505 F.2d 989 (2d Cir.1974), in which the court relied heavily on the all-risk character of the policy in finding that Pan American was covered for the loss resulting from destruction of an airliner by a terrorist group. For a useful collection of essays on the nature of all-risk coverage, see Tort and Insurance Practice Section, American Bar Association, The All–Risk Policy: Its Problems, Perils, and Practical Applications (1986).

B. THE REQUIREMENT OF AN INSURABLE INTEREST

SNETHEN v. OKLAHOMA STATE UNION OF THE FARMERS EDUCATIONAL AND COOPERATIVE UNION OF AMERICA

Supreme Court of Oklahoma, 1983.
664 P.2d 377.

OPALA, Justice:

The dispositive issue on certiorari is whether a good-faith purchaser for value of a stolen motor vehicle has an "insurable interest" in the property within the meaning of 36 O.S.1981 § 3605.[1] We answer in the affirmative.

The insurance company [insurer], defendant below, issued an automobile insurance policy to John O. Snethen [insured], plaintiff below, providing coverage against collision loss for his used 1978 Cadillac automobile. Shortly after the purchase the insured's car was involved in a collision with another vehicle. Before a claim for this damage came to be settled between the insurer and insured, the Oklahoma State Bureau of Investigation [OSBI] discovered that the car was a stolen vehicle. Neither the insured nor the insurer knew this before the accident. The OSBI then seized the car for its return to the rightful owner. The insurer subsequently refused to pay for the loss and the insured pressed his claim under the collision coverage of the policy. The trial court rendered summary judgment for the insurer. The Court of Appeals affirmed based on our opinion in *Ernie Miller Pontiac v. Home Insurance Co.*[2] which holds that a good-faith purchaser for value of a stolen vehicle does not have an insurable interest. We granted certiorari on the petition by the insured to reconsider our holding in *Ernie Miller Pontiac*. We now vacate the Court of Appeals' opinion and reverse the trial court's judgment.

It is well settled that both the validity and enforceability of an insurance contract depend upon the presence of insurable interest in the person who purchased the policy. Considerations underlying the insurable interest concept are generally articulated in terms of policy (1) against allowing wagering contracts under the guise of insurance, (2) against fostering temptation to destroy the insured property in an effort to profit from it and (3) favoring limitation upon the sweep of indemnity contracts.

Most forms of wager agreements were valid at common law. They were deemed enforceable until a series of statutes were passed to outlaw the use of insurance contracts to conduct wagers. Wagering is regarded as detrimental to society. It encourages the wagerer to affect by unnatural means the results of the contingent event and increases the insurer's risk of disproportionate indemnification to an insured who has no relationship to, or pecuniary interest in, the insured subject. The goal of insurance is to indemnify the insured for a loss encountered by the impairment of an interest in the subject. Wagerers suffer no such loss. They actually profit from the occurrence of the contingent

---

1. The terms of 36 O.S.1981 § 3605 provide:

"A. No insurance contract on property or of any interest therein or arising therefrom shall be enforceable as to the insurance except for the benefit of persons having an *insurable interest* in the things insured.

B. '*Insurable interest*' as used in this section means any actual, *lawful*, and substantial economic *interest* in the safety or preservation of the subject of the insurance free from loss, destruction, or pecuniary damage or impairment.

C. The measure of an insurable interest in property is the extent to which the insured might be damnified by loss, injury, or impairment thereof." [Emphasis added].

2. Okl., 534 P.2d 1 [1975].

event. It is for the purpose of placing a limit on the insurer's indemnification duty that the law undertook to require the insured to have an insurable interest.

Public policy which favors suppression of temptation to destroy one's insured property underlies the law's requirement of an insurable interest. If the insured has no interest in the property, he suffers no loss from its destruction but actually profits from it. The insurable interest concept tends to deter the temptation to destroy the property which is covered against the risk of loss.

While American jurisdictions generally agree with the public policy considerations that underlie the necessity for an insurable interest, they stand divided on what constitutes an insurable interest. Two basic theories were evolved for measuring the nexus which must be present between the property and its insured for an insurable interest to attach. The literature refers to one of these as the "legal interest" and to the other as the "factual expectation" theory.

Jurisdictions holding to the view that no insurable interest attaches to a stolen automobile in the hands of a good-faith purchaser found their conclusion upon the legal interest theory. Those states that adhere to this concept require that insurable interest be rested upon a *legally cognizable interest* in the property. This view has its roots in Lord Eldon's opinion in *Lucena v. Craufurd.*[3] It was there stated that an interest is insurable only if it is a *legal* or *equitable* right enforceable either at law or in chancery.[4] This represents the strict approach to insurable interest.

Those jurisdictions which allow the bona fide owner of a stolen vehicle to recover follow the "factual expectation" theory. Under this theory there is an insurable interest in the property if the insured would gain some economic advantage by its continued existence or would suffer some economic detriment in case of its loss or destruction. This theory—contrary as it is to the one espoused by Lord Eldon—also derives from *Lucena v. Craufurd.* It was expressed there in Lord Lawrence's separate opinion.[5] He believed that a person has an insurable interest if he stands in some relation to, or has concern in, the insured property which may be prejudiced by the happening of the events insured against. It was his view that the insured must be so circumstanced with respect to the insured subject-matter as to make him interested in its preservation.

We are inclined to the view articulated by the courts adhering to the "factual expectation" test. An interest held in a stolen vehicle by its good-faith purchaser is by that test regarded as insurable. Once the

---

3. 2 Bos. & Pul. (N.R.) 269, 127 Eng.Rep. 630 [1806].

4. *Lucena v. Craufurd,* supra note 3, 2 Bos. & Pul. (N.R.) at 323, 127 Eng.Rep. at 651. Lord Eldon reasoned further that "[e]xpectation though founded on the highest probability, [is] not interest," and "if moral certainty be a ground of insurable interest, there are hundreds, perhaps thousands, who would be entitled to insure" the same property.

5. 2 Bos. & Pul. (N.R.) 269, 302, 127 Eng.Rep. 630, 643.

relationship between the insured and the property is found to be lawful and to create a substantial economic interest, the underlying criteria which make up an insurable interest are met. The insured does hence have a right to enforce the contract regardless of the property's legal status. In the case at bar, the substantial economic interest was created when the insured paid $6,500 for his car and, additionally, parted with his own vehicle as a trade-in. This pecuniary interest, coupled with the insured's undisputed lack of knowledge of the vehicle's stolen status, is adequately substantial. It suffices to negate any notion or intimation of a wager contract. Moreover, the transfer of such a substantial value cannot be viewed as encouraging the insured to destroy the vehicle in order to collect insurance proceeds. Because of the lost investment, indemnification will not amount here to a "profit".

While the insured doubtless does have substantial economic interest, more than that appears to be required. The terms of § 3605(B) explicitly call for an interest that is "lawful". * * *

For the purpose of determining an insurable interest under § 3605, it is necessary to make a distinction between "legal" and "lawful" interests. A substantial economic interest is insurable if it is "lawful" in the sense that it was not acquired in violation of law. As used in § 3605(B), the word "lawful" is not synonymous with "legal". A legal interest is enforceable against the whole world. A good-faith purchaser for value acquires an interest that is lawful and enforceable against all the world but the legal owner. Although it is only a qualified possessory interest, it is lawful and enforceable to a very large *extent*. Section 3605 allows *any lawful interest* to be insurable if the economic interest is substantial.[6] We hence hold that a good-faith purchaser for value of a stolen automobile has a substantial economic interest in the property which is lawful and must be treated as insurable under § 3605.

The insured established a lawful and substantial economic interest—innocently acquired—and covered it by insurance. His interest, which clearly meets the § 3605(B) criteria, is hence entitled to judicial protection.

Insofar as *Ernie Miller Pontiac* is in conflict with our pronouncement herein, it is no longer to be regarded as a correct exposition of the current law. Neither fairness nor any principle of public policy dictates that we give a purely prospective application to the change effected by today's decision. The insured should be allowed to reap the benefit of his successful challenge to the insurable interest test we now reject by this opinion. Our pronouncement today shall hence be given effect to this case and, prospectively, to all insurance losses occurring after mandate herein is issued.

Summary judgment is reversed and cause remanded with directions to proceed further in a manner not inconsistent with the views expressed herein.

All Justices concur.

6. 36 O.S.1981 § 3605(B), supra note 1.

Notes and Questions

1. *History and Policy: The Principle of Indemnity.* The modern function of the requirement of an insurable interest is to serve the principle of indemnity: the notion that the purpose of insurance is to protect the insured against suffering a loss, not to create the opportunity for gain. The requirement of an insurable interest originated in two English statutes enacted in the middle of the eighteenth century to limit the use of life and marine insurance as methods of gambling. See The Life Assurance Act of 1774, 14 Geo. 3, c. 48; Act of 1746, St. 19 Geo. 2, c. 37. In the United States the requirement of an insurable interest for all forms of insurance was first adopted by the courts, although many states later enacted statutes governing the issue. The predominant justification now given for the requirement is that it combats moral hazard: in the absence of an insurable interest in the party procuring insurance, the incentive to destroy insured property or persons would be considerably greater. The requirement is intended to test for situations in which the insured party is presumed to be better off if the insured subject matter continues to exist.

The policy behind the insurable interest requirement is in fact so strong that most courts hold that an insurer cannot be estopped to assert the insurable interest requirement or be held to have waived it. Is this approach appropriate, or should the courts inquire into the actual conduct and incentives of the insured prior to loss in determining whether the insurer's defense is valid? Compare *Liverpool & London & Globe Insurance Company, Limited v. Bolling,* 176 Va. 182, 10 S.E.2d 518 (1940) (waiver and estoppel not applicable where contract is against public policy) with *McGehee v. Farmers Insurance Co., Inc.,* 734 F.2d 1422 (10th Cir.1984) (knowledge of agent imputed to insurer operates as a waiver of the insurable interest requirement).

2. *Four Tests for Insurable Interest.* As the opinion in *Snethen* indicates, there are a number of different tests for the existence of an insurable interest. A *legal or equitable interest* in property will always suffice, subject sometimes to the condition that the interest have value. In many jurisdictions the *factual expectancy* test that the court described also prevails. A *contract right* that depends on the continued existence of property also will support an insurable interest in that property. Secured creditors, for example, fall into this category. Finally, the potential for suffering *legal liability* for the destruction of property will also support an insurable interest in it. See, e.g., *Village of Constantine v. Home Insurance Company,* 427 F.2d 1338 (6th Cir. 1970) (promise to procure insurance on property sold subject to conditional sales contract and later transferred to third party supports insurable interest in seller). To what extent are the last three tests merely different versions of the factual expectancy test? In a jurisdiction that has adopted all four tests—and many have—would counsel ever have an excuse for failing to situate his client so that the

insurance the client wished to purchase was supported by an insurable interest in the client?

3. *Timing.* Does it make sense to require that there be an insurable interest both at the time the property is first insured and at the time of loss? That is the rule derived from the English case of *Sadlers Company v. Badcock,* 2 Atk. 554, 26 Eng. Rpt. 733 (1743), but most modern courts require that the interest exist only at the time of loss. What are the arguments for each approach?

4. *The Interest Insured.* Should a distinction be drawn between the existence of an insurable interest in the abstract and the interest that was actually insured? For example, when the insured in *Snethen* filed his insurance claim he no longer had an interest in the car he had insured against collision. Does it follow nonetheless that because he had an insurable interest at the time of loss, he was entitled to recover? The problem may seem easier if the loss occurs in a different way. For example, in *Butler v. Farmers Insurance Company of Arizona,* 126 Ariz. 371, 616 P.2d 46 (1980), the court held that repossession by the owner from the innocent purchaser constituted "loss ＊ ＊ ＊ caused by ＊ ＊ ＊ any accidental means ＊ ＊ ＊" under the purchaser's policy. Clearly the insured in *Butler* suffered a loss as a result of the repossession, whereas, arguably, the insured in *Snethen* did not suffer a loss as a result of the collision damage to the car. This difference may make one more comfortable with the result in *Butler* than in *Snethen.*

Does the result in *Butler,* however, unduly subject the insurer to the risk of adverse selection, by encouraging those who have doubts about their title to purchase property insurance on their vehicles? On the other hand, since insurers have the power to specifically exclude coverage of loss caused by repossession from an innocent purchaser, is *Butler's* reading of the policy language in that case nonetheless appropriate? Is this also an appropriate answer in a case in which a building insured under a fire policy is destroyed ten days prior to the time it was scheduled for demolition? See *Tublitz v. Glens Falls Insurance Company,* 179 N.J.Super. 275, 431 A.2d 201 (1981) (insurable interest exists, measure of loss unclear). Which provisions in the Definitions and the Conditions sections of the Sample Homeowners Policy address the issues raised in these cases? How clearly do these provisions resolve these issues?

C. SUBROGATION

Subrogation is the term used for a kind of legal substitution. One party is said to be "subrogated" to the rights of another when the first party steps into the second party's shoes, as it were, and assumes the second party's rights against a third party. A rule central to subrogation law follows almost tautologically from this description: an insurer cannot have subrogation against its own insured. Subrogation is important in a number of fields—suretyship, for example—and figures prominently in property, liability and (in some situations) health insurance. In property insurance, the insurer generally is subrogated to the insured's rights of recovery against any other party for a loss covered by the policy. For example, suppose that the insured's home is destroyed by a fire negligently set by her neighbor, and the insurer pays the insured the amount of the loss. The insurer is then entitled to recover this amount from the neighbor, either directly in a suit against the neighbor, or as the real party in interest in a suit brought by the insured.

Types and Functions of Subrogation

There are two types of subrogation, distinguished by the source of the authority to subrogate. *Equitable subrogation* (sometimes called legal subrogation) arises by operation of law, whereas *contractual subrogation* (sometimes called conventional subrogation) results from an agreement of the parties. Most courts hold that a property insurer has rights of subrogation despite the absence of a subrogation provision in the policy, but modern property insurance policies virtually always specify some right of subrogation. Even contractual subrogation is subject to some judicial regulation, but the terms of the subrogation agreement (a provision in the insurance policy) usually are held to be binding. See, e.g., the subrogation provision in the Sample Homeowners Policy (contained in Sections I and II—Conditions).

Two main functions of subrogation figure in analyses of the doctrine. First, subrogation is a method of implementing the *principle of indemnity* that is at the heart of all insurance. Subrogation prevents the insured from recovering more than the amount of his loss, by vesting the insured's rights of recovery against third parties in the insurer, who has already paid the insured for the loss. This reduces the cost of coverage and avoids what might otherwise be perceived as an unjustified windfall for the insured.

Second, subrogation helps to allocate ultimate financial responsibility for some insured losses to the third parties who cause these losses, without producing the windfalls just noted. The aim of the collateral source rule in torts, for example, is to assure that tortfeasors pay the full cost of the damage they have caused. The rule achieves this aim by making evidence of prior payment by plaintiff's insurers to the plaintiff in a tort suit inadmissible in that suit. Wherever the plaintiff's insurers have rights of subrogation, however, the insured plaintiff does not recover twice—once from his insurer and again from the tortfeasor—because all or part of the recovery from the tortfeasor reimburses the plaintiff's insurer and thereby allocates ultimate responsibility for the costs of the loss to the tortfeasor (or its liability insurer) rather than to the plaintiff's insurer.

Subrogation and Settlement

The general rule is that the insured who interferes with an insurer's rights of subrogation after suffering a loss voids his insurance coverage. Thus, if I release my neighbor from any liability he may have for destroying my house by fire, my insurer is no longer obligated to pay my loss. Is this rule a trap for the unwary? One important exception to the rule is that the third party is not released from subrogation liability to the insurer if the third party has notice of the insurer's right of subrogation. See, e.g., *Sentry Ins. Co. v. Stuart*, 246 Ark. 680, 439 S.W.2d 797 (1969). It follows that an insured signing a release under these circumstances has not interfered with the insurer's subrogation rights. What does this exception suggest about the prudent course of action for insurers to follow when they receive notice of loss from an insured? Given the contours of these subrogation rights and obligations, it might be argued that the fire and property insurer's role more closely resembles that of a guarantor of the insured's rights of recovery against others rather than that of a primary obligor.

The view taken of the role of a subrogated insurer may affect the resolution of subsidiary issues in subrogation cases as well. For example, in *Florida Farm Bureau Insurance Company v. Martin*, 377 So.2d 827 (Fla.D.C.A.1979), the insureds' loss exceeded the total of their recoveries from their insurer and the tortfeasor. The subrogation clause of the policy provided, "This Company may require from the insured an assignment of all right of recovery against any party for loss to the extent that payment therefor is made by the Company." The insurer in *Martin* did not take an assignment as provided by the clause; rather, it brought an action claiming that its right of subrogation entitled it to reimbursement out of the insured's recovery from the tortfeasor. The court acknowledged that the insurer had an equitable right of subrogation independent of the subrogation clause in the policy, but denied the insurer's claim on the ground that the principle underlying equitable subrogation—precluding duplicate recovery by the insured—would not be furthered by allowing subrogation when the amount recovered in tort is less than the insured's loss but is the maximum amount available from the tortfeasor. Should the result be different when the insurer is careful to take an express assignment of the insured's rights against the tortfeasor, as the subrogation clause in *Martin* provided? Can the problem be avoided when there is a potential settlement with the tortfeasor, by involving the insurer in advance and specifying the portion of the settlement to be paid the insurer as reimbursement?

GREAT NORTHERN OIL COMPANY v. ST. PAUL FIRE AND MARINE INSURANCE COMPANY

Supreme Court of Minnesota, 1971.
291 Minn. 97, 189 N.W.2d 404.

ROGOSHESKE, Justice.

* * * The issue presented is whether plaintiff-insured, who, prior to a business-interruption loss and by an exculpatory clause in a construction contract, released the contractor from liability for negligently causing the loss, is precluded from pursuing recovery upon a policy of "all-risk" insurance in force prior to the release on the ground that exculpation defeated defendant insurance companies' subrogation rights against the contractor. We hold that plaintiff is not thereby precluded from recovering under the policy and affirm the trial court's order.

Plaintiff, Great Northern Oil Company, owns and operates an oil refinery at Pine Bend in Dakota County, Minnesota. On August 12, 1964, plaintiff procured from the several defendants a 3–year policy of "all-risk" insurance covering, among other things, losses due to the interruption of plaintiff's business. The aggregate amount of coverage is $3,000,000. The insurance policy provided:

> "(H) SUBROGATION. In the event of any payment under this policy the Company shall be subrogated to all the Insured's rights of recovery therefor against any person or organization and the Insured shall execute and deliver instruments and papers and do whatever else is necessary to secure such rights. The Insured shall do nothing after loss to prejudice such rights."

On February 7, 1967, during the term of the policy, plaintiff-insured entered into an agreement with the Litwin Corporation, Inc., for the construction of catalytic cracking expansion facilities, designed to materially increase plaintiff's production. So far as pertinent to the question presented, the construction agreement limited Litwin's liability for bodily injury and damage to plaintiff's property during construction and, by an exculpatory clause, provided that "Contractor shall not be responsible or held liable for any damages or liability for loss of use of the Work, loss of profits therefrom, or business interruption thereof however the same may be caused."

On June 16, 1967, a crane accident caused damage to the partially completed construction work. Plaintiff brought this action against defendant-insurers, contending that the accident had caused it to suffer a substantial business-interruption loss for which defendants are responsible under the terms of the all-risk insurance policy. The defendants' joint answer generally denied that plaintiff had sustained any loss covered by the policy and further alleged that the insured could not recover under the policy because the insured, by releasing Litwin from liability before the accident occurred, had defeated the insurers' rights of subrogation under the policy. The parties made cross-motions for summary judgment on this latter claim, and the court granted plaintiff's motion, striking the foregoing specific defense. Defendants appeal. We affirm and hold that plaintiff, in the absence of a prohibition in the insurance contract against entering into any exculpatory agreements, is not precluded from pursuing its action to recover its loss under the insurance policy.

Subrogation is a normal incident of a contract of insurance. *Aetna Life Ins. Co. v. Moses,* 287 U.S. 530, 53 S.Ct. 231, 77 L.Ed. 477. Its existence does not necessarily depend on the terms of the contract but on the nature of the contract of insurance and on general principles of equity. *Bacich v. Homeland Ins. Co.,* 212 Minn. 375, 3 N.W.2d 665.

Whether or not the insurance policy expressly reserves subrogation rights, it is the universal rule that upon payment of a loss, an insurer is entitled to pursue those rights which the insured party may have against a third party whose negligence or wrongful act caused the loss. See, *Board of Trustees of First Congregational Church of Austin v. Cream City Mutual Ins. Co.,* 255 Minn. 347, 96 N.W.2d 690. However, the insurer, as the subrogee, is entitled to no greater rights than those which the insured-subrogor possesses at the time the subrogee asserts the claim, as the subrogee merely "steps into the shoes" of the subrogor. *Employers Liability Assur. Corp. v. Morse,* 261 Minn. 259, 263, 111 N.W.2d 620, 624. As an application of this rule, it is thus well established that an insured may defeat the insurance company's rights of subrogation by (1) settling with the wrongdoer after loss but before payment of the insurance (e.g., *Bacich v. Homeland Ins. Co. supra; Harter v. American Eagle Fire Ins. Co.* [6 Cir.] 60 F.2d 245); (2) settling with the wrongdoer after payment under the policy (e.g., *National Union Fire Ins. Co. v. Grimes,* 278 Minn. 45, 153 N.W.2d 152); or (3) entering into an agreement of release with the wrongdoer before the policy is issued (e.g., *Hartford Fire Ins. Co. v. Chicago, M. & St. P. Ry. Co.,* 175 U.S. 91, 20 S.Ct. 33, 44 L.Ed. 84).

Unlike the foregoing examples, here plaintiff, by the construction contract (executed subsequent to the issuance of the policy but prior to loss), exonerated the contractor from any potential liability for damages resulting by way of business interruption, "however the same may be caused." The parties appear in agreement that this broad language includes damages caused by the contractor's own negligence. Cf. *General Mills v. Goldman* (8 Cir.) 184 F.2d 359. Such exculpatory agreements releasing a contracting party from liability caused by his own negligence are not uncommon in modern-day construction contracts. They are designed to distribute the burden or risks inherent in the performance of such contracts in such a way as to eliminate foreseeable disputes and to reduce the cost of construction.[1] Such agreements do

---

1. Although it would not appear to be legally significant since no misrepresentation or fraud is claimed, the purpose of including the exculpatory clause in the construction contract does not appear in the record. Whether it was merely a part of a standard form of construction contract which the parties signed without careful consideration of its

not contravene public policy, are valid, and are enforceable. *Independent School Dist. No. 877 v. Loberg Plumbing & Heating Co.,* 266 Minn. 426, 123 N.W.2d 793.

Although there appears to be no case specifically so holding, we assume, as do the parties, that an unambiguous and broad exculpatory agreement of the type used in this case defeats the subrogation rights of the insurance company against the contractor even though it was made subsequent to the issuance of the policy and prior to loss. Upon the assumption that subrogation rights are defeated by a release made after issuance of the policy and before loss, the question arises as to whether such impairment of subrogation rights should also preclude plaintiff from pursuing recovery under the all-risk insurance policy.

Treatises contain language which states generally that a release of liability given to a tortfeasor by the insured bars the insured's right of action on the policy because it destroys the insurer's right of subrogation. 6 Appleman, Insurance Law and Practice, § 4093; 44 Am.Jur. (2d) Insurance, § 1839. However, analysis of the cases cited in support of the rule reveals that it was derived from cases in which defeat of the insurer's right of subrogation occurs after loss. E.g., *Bacich v. Homeland Ins. Co., supra.* Some of the cited cases have held that the insured is precluded from recovery on a policy where he has defeated the insurer's right of subrogation by an agreement made before loss. However, in all such cases the insurance policies provided expressly that relinquishment of the insured's rights against a potential wrongdoer rendered the policy void. * * *

Defendants vigorously argue that an insured who, without reservation, releases all claims for damages against a potential wrongdoer either after or prior to loss, thereby defeating the right of subrogation accorded an insurer by the terms of an insurance policy, should be precluded from making recovery upon the policy for damage resulting from the wrongdoer's negligence. They argue that the insurer, prior to loss, has no way of preserving a remedy against the tortfeasor, and that common sense suggests no basis for according any different treatment to an insured who has released a wrongdoer from liability before the loss occurs than to an insured who has released the wrongdoer after the loss occurs since, in either event, the insured has, by his own conduct, deprived the insurer of a valuable right afforded by the insurance contract—the right to recoup its loss from the one primarily liable. Defendants argue further that by permitting the contractor to avoid the risk of liability, plaintiff got its new facility at a lower cost, thereby receiving one benefit for relinquishing its claim against the contractor, and that plaintiff now seeks the added benefit of compensation by defendant insurers. They contend that they undertook a defined risk— the indemnification of plaintiff from loss resulting from hazards encountered in the operation of a going refinery—but did not undertake

effect upon coverage under defendants' "all-risk" policy, or whether it was deliberately designed to shift liability for the loss which occurred to defendants under the provisions of the policy, as defendants contend, is not revealed by the record.

the risk by providing liability insurance to third parties, and that plaintiff's action thereby imposed a new and different kind of risk on the insurer. Defendants insist that if Litwin Corporation and plaintiff intended to place the risk of loss from delay in the commencement of the operation of the new facilities on the defendants, they could have secured the consent of defendants to the relinquishment of their subrogation rights, affording them the opportunity to evaluate the risk, to specifically include it in the insurance policy, and to assess any added premium cost to plaintiff.

These arguments are not without merit. While we are not free from doubt as to the resolution of the question presented, we are persuaded that considerations of public policy and equitable principles do not restrict our upholding the trial court's disposition. Surely, the considerations of public policy have been put to rest in the numerous cases upholding the validity of exculpatory provisions exonerating a party from liability for damages resulting from his own negligence. The important considerations are the equities between the parties. We believe on balance they fall on the side of the plaintiff-insured. The all-risk insurance policy, as its characterization implies, insured all real and personal property of plaintiff against all hazards encountered in the operation of a refinery, expressly including loss directly resulting from necessary business interruptions caused by any damage to the plaintiff's property. It contained a number of exclusions for which coverage was not provided as well as limiting provisions, including the subrogation clause quoted above. While exemplary fair dealing should have prompted plaintiff to notify defendants of the increased hazards occasioned by new construction activities on its premises, there appears no persuasive reason why defendants, at the time the policy was written, could not have expressly prohibited plaintiff from entering into any agreements prospectively releasing third parties, whose presence on plaintiff's premises was surely foreseeable, from liability for damage caused by their negligence. Defendants' argument that the policy was not intended to provide liability insurance coverage to negligent third parties is not persuasive, since the hazard of damage to plaintiff's property and resultant business interruption by either its own or a third party's negligence was surely one which was covered and reflected in the premium charged plaintiff.

Upon this record, the argument that a construction company's presence on plaintiff's premises would have increased the risk covered by the policy is speculative; even more speculative is the argument that a greater premium would have been assessed for such specific coverage. Thus, to allow plaintiff to pursue its recovery under the all-risk policy inflicts no injustice on defendants because the insured has paid for the hazard covered by the policy and has, as defendants acknowledge, the right to negotiate for and enter into construction contracts and to promote its business interests by avoiding overlapping insurance coverage against hazards inherent in the operation as well as the repair and expansion of its facilities. Plaintiff is seeking to recover only what it had a right to assume it paid the defendants a premium to insure against. While the action of plaintiff in releasing the contractor may have been unintentional or unwitting, defendants had the greater opportunity to prohibit such action by exercising their right to vary the coverage under the policy by endorsements as they deemed necessary.[2]

Affirmed.

Notes and Questions

1. *An Alternative.* How would you react to a rule premised on what the court suggested would have been "exemplary fair dealing" by Great Northern—a rule obliging the insured to notify the insurer of a proposed exculpatory clause in any contract relating to the insured subject matter, and permitting the insurer to charge an additional premium if such a clause is executed? Consider the following factors:

a. The benefits such a rule would afford insureds who do not enter into exculpatory agreements.

b. The fact that insurers have elected not to include provisions creating such an obligation in the subrogation clauses of their policies.

c. The leverage such a rule would give the insurer over the insured.

d. The additional cost of notification.

e. The difficulty of providing insureds with notice of the judicially-created obligation to notify the insurer or forfeit coverage.

2. *Possible Justifications for the Distinction.* Does the court's distinction between releases of third parties after loss and exculpatory clauses executed prior to loss hold water? The notion that because loss has not yet occurred, the insurer has no subrogation right to be interfered with arguably is fallacious, because the exculpatory clause undoubtedly disadvantages the insurer. On the other hand, is it not also clear that as between such parties as Great Northern and Litwin, exculpatory clauses should generally be valid? Exculpatory clauses both permit the parties to apportion the risk of business interruption to the party in the best position to control and/or insure against that risk, and to avoid duplicate insurance against it.

Nevertheless, at least two justifications for the distinction seem plausible. First, the lion's share of exculpatory clauses probably are not separately negotiated, but are contained in fine print on standard-

2. The action may have been no more deliberate or intentional than that of an owner of an automobile who, as a consideration for renting a garage, exculpates the garage owner from any liability for loss of the automobile, and who, subsequently suffering loss of the vehicle resulting from the garage owner's negligent failure to keep the garage door locked, quite naturally would assume that he would recoup his loss under the insurance policy covering his automobile. Although mindful that the wrongdoer does not escape liability, were we to hold under this hypothetical as defendants urge, we would have to unrealistically assume that exoneration of the garage owner from prospective liability would so increase the risks covered by the policy and the premium therefor as to justify imposing on the automobile owner the burden of informing his insurance carrier of his action or suffer loss of coverage for a risk expressly included in the insurance contract.

form contracts that people bound by them do not read. For example, in *Blume v. Evans Fur Company,* 126 Ill.App.3d 52, 81 Ill.Dec. 564, 466 N.E.2d 1366 (1984), the insured stored her fur coat and received a receipt limiting the storage company's liability to $100. Would it be realistic to expect people in Blume's position to identify and appreciate the insurance implications of similar exculpatory or liability-limiting clauses in dry cleaner receipts, storage contracts, garage rental agreements and the like? Does this theory help to explain the difference in the treatment of pre- and post-loss exculpatory clauses?

Second, perhaps property insurers can more precisely risk-classify their insureds than liability insurers of construction contractors can risk-classify their insureds. Property insurers know the value of the property they insure, the potential economic loss if business is interrupted, etc. In contrast, liability insurers in general may have less information about those whom their insureds may injure in the course of their activities, and therefore less information on which to differentiate premium rates from insured to insured. If this were true, then a rule that allows property insurance to stand in the face of pre-loss exculpatory clauses would allocate coverage responsibility to the property insurer rather than the liability insurer, and thereby allows risk classification, over the long run, to have more substantial effect. How great would the differences between the refinement of risk classification in property and liability insurance have to be for this rationale to be satisfactory? Consider also the old tort law rule that there is no liability in negligence for pure economic loss. See, e.g., *Robins Dry Dock & Repair v. Flint,* 275 U.S. 303, 48 S.Ct. 134, 72 L.Ed. 290 (1927). This rule may have had the effect of allocating coverage responsibility to property insurers in a better position to risk-classify their insureds than liability insurers.

Despite these arguments, did the insurer seem to be speaking the truth in *Great Northern* when it argued that, in effect, its insured and Litwin entered into an advance agreement to shift the cost of Litwin's negligence to St. Paul, without paying St. Paul the additional premium it deserved? Litwin probably paid Great Northern for this coverage (in the form of a lower contract price than would have been charged in the absence of the exculpatory clause), but then Great Northern kept this sum instead of paying it to St. Paul. Under what circumstances should an insurer expect to have additional parties benefit from coverage by virtue of their relationship to the named insured, as Litwin benefited? Consider the cases in the following section.

D. LIMITED INTERESTS

1. Mortgagees

The purchase of most real estate and some personal property is financed by loans requiring that the lender be granted a security interest in the property, that the property be insured against fire and other physical damage, and that the lender's security interest be protected by that insurance. The means of protection usually is a *standard,* or *union mortgage clause* in the property owner's fire and property insurance policy. For an example of such a clause, see the sample Homeowners Policy, Section I—Conditions. The effect of the clause is to render the mortgagee/lender an additional insured party. If the property is destroyed, the insurer pays the mortgagee up to the amount of the outstanding balance of the debt owed by the insured, that debt is extinguished, and the amount of any remaining coverage is paid to the insured.

If the insured breaches his obligations under the policy, however— by breaching a warranty, by making fraudulent misrepresentations, or by knowingly increasing the hazard at the property, for example—the standard mortgage clause provides that under specified circumstances the denial of coverage does not apply to the mortgagee. Rather, the insurer pays the mortgagee and is subrogated to the mortgagee's rights against the mortgagor/policyholder. The entire arrangement in this circumstance works as if the only party insured were the mortgagee, whose policy contained a subrogation clause. The standard rule that an insurer cannot have subrogation against its own insured is considered not to be violated because the insured, having breached an obligation under the policy, is not an "insured" for this purpose. When the dust settles, the mortgagor/policyholder is held ultimately responsible for his debt, which is as it should be if his insurance does not cover the loss in question. The relationship among the parties, however, is not always this clearly and cleanly demarcated.

QUINCY MUTUAL FIRE INSURANCE COMPANY v. JONES

Court of Civil Appeals of Texas, 1972.
486 S.W.2d 126.

CLAUDE WILLIAMS, Chief Justice.

This action originated when Paul C. Jordan, trustee under a deed of trust, sold certain real estate situated in Dallas County and had a surplus of funds from such sale which he paid into the registry of the district court in a bill of interpleader. He alleged that J.W. Jones and B.R. Pritchett, jointly, and Quincy Mutual Fire Insurance Company, were making conflicting claims to the surplus funds amounting to $2,575.99. Jones and Pritchett filed their answer asserting their right to receive the funds because they had purchased the property in question and assumed a mortgage debt which had been discharged by the trustee from the proceeds of the sale. The insurance company filed its answer in which it based its claim to the money on the language of the standard mortgage and subrogation clauses of a fire insurance policy issued by it to one of Jones' and Pritchett's predecessors in title. Both Jones and Pritchett and Quincy Mutual filed their motions for summary judgment. The trial court sustained the motion filed by

Jones and Pritchett and rendered judgment awarding them the funds on deposit. The insurance company appeals.

In its primary point appellant alleges error on the part of the trial court in rendering summary judgment for appellees because appellant was subrogated to all rights of a mortgagee and trustee and should have therefore received the surplus proceeds after the mortgagee had been fully indemnified by the trustee's sale.

The facts are stipulated. On August 25, 1964 appellant insurance company issued its Texas standard fire insurance policy to Walter W. Boyd as "insured" with the provision that the loss on the building items should be payable to "Farm & Home Savings Association", as mortgagee or trustee, as its interest might appear. Farm & Home Savings Association's indebtedness was evidenced by a note in the principal sum of $10,600 payable at the rate of $58.93 per month.

The fire insurance policy issued to Boyd, the then owner of the property, extended from August 25, 1964 to August 25, 1969. Boyd thereafter sold the property to James W. White and by endorsement attached to the policy White was shown as the "named insured as owner of the property". Thereafter White, by warranty deed, conveyed the property to Lonnie H. Taylor and wife. The fire insurance policy contained a standard provision to the effect that the insurance company would not be liable for loss occurring following a change of ownership of the insured property unless such change of ownership was shown by endorsement placed upon the policy. At no time was an endorsement included in the policy to show the ownership of the property had changed from White to Taylor and wife.

On November 29, 1966, the property was damaged by fire. By reason of the change of ownership of the property the appellant insurance company denied liability to White and also to Taylor and wife. Neither White nor the Taylors filed a proof of loss or instituted suit against the insurance company to recover the proceeds of the loss.

On September 7, 1967, Farm & Home executed a proof of loss, pursuant to which it was stated that the whole loss and damage by reason of the fire on November 29, 1966 was $3,494.76. That amount was paid by appellant insurance company to Farm & Home.

The insurance policy contained the following standard provision:

> "This policy, as to the interest of the mortgagee only therein, shall not be invalidated by any act or neglect of the mortgagor or owner of the within described property, * * * nor by any change in the title or ownership of the property * * *."

The policy also contained a mortgage clause in accordance with Article 6.15 of the Texas Insurance Code, V.A.T.S. The pertinent portion of said clause provides:

> "If this Company shall claim that no liability existed as to the mortgagor or owner, it shall, to the extent of payment of

loss to the mortgagee, be subrogated to all the mortgagee's rights of recovery, but without impairing mortgagee's right to sue; or it may pay off the mortgage debt and require the assignment thereof and of the mortgage."

Default having been made in the payments of the note held by Farm & Home it declared the whole debt due, appointed Paul C. Jordan as trustee and said trustee posted such real property for foreclosure sale on Tuesday, October 3, 1967. On or about October 3, 1967, the appellees J.W. Jones and B.R. Pritchett, being real estate brokers, acquired title to the real property in question. In the warranty deed Jones assumed the unpaid balance of the note due Farm & Home. At the foreclosure sale held on Tuesday, October 3, 1967, Jordan, as trustee, sold the real property to James M. Cline and John D. McGowen for the sum of $6,300, being the highest and best bid for the property.

At the time of the sale the balance claimed by Farm & Home Savings Association was the sum of $3,442.66 computed by allowing credit of mortgage payments, payment of fire loss, interest, etc.

Farm & Home returned to the trustee the amount of $2,857.34 overage and out of such sum the trustee expended certain amounts for cost and attorney's fees which left a balance of $2,575.99 which the trustee tendered into court.

Appellees contend that the appellant insurance company's subrogation rights were secondary and inferior to the lien on the premises in question held by Farm & Home and that by virtue of the foreclosure of said lien by the mortgagee any subrogation rights of the insurance company were terminated insofar as the security is concerned.

Appellees do not deny the contention of appellant that because of change of ownership the fire insurance policy became void as to the mortgagor. Being of no force and effect as between the mortgagor and the insurance company, the fire insurance contract then became one solely between the insurance company and the mortgagee.

Appellees argue, however, that when the insurance company paid the mortgagee the amount of the loss, which was less than the total indebtedness due mortgagee, that the insurance company acquired subrogation rights which were given in the alternative. It points to the subrogation clause which provides that (1) the insurance company may, by paying the amount less than the outstanding mortgage debt to the mortgagee for fire damage, be subrogated to the mortgagee's "right of recovery", or (2) by paying off all of the outstanding mortgage debt, it may take an assignment of the mortgagee of the mortgage debt and the lien securing it. Appellees say that when appellant followed the first option and by not electing to pay off the mortgage debt and take an assignment of the mortgage it became subrogated only to the mortgagee's right to bring a personal action against the mortgagor at the time of the damage for the amount that it was forced to pay the mortgagee by virtue of the mortgage clause in the insurance policy but such election does not give rise to cause of action for foreclosure of the mortgage lien. To accept appellee's argument as valid would have the effect of defeating the appellant insurer's right of subrogation and would also result in the mortgagor, and his successor in interest, being rewarded by receiving the beneficial results of payments made on a contract to which neither was a party.

The standard clause in the insurance policy providing for subrogation to the mortgagee's right of recovery has been consistently held to be valid by Texas courts as well as those of other jurisdictions. 16 Couch on Insurance, 2d Edition, p. 427, § 61:364 (1966).

In *British American Assurance Co. v. Mid–Continent Life Insurance Co.*, 37 S.W.2d 742 (Tex.Comm'n App.1931), the court acknowledged the validity of the subrogation clause in the policy and noted the mark of distinction between the liability of the insurance company to the mortgagee and to the insured. The court then said:

> "The payment by the insurance company to the mortgagee under the policy on the mortgagor's indebtedness inured to the latter's benefit to the extent his debt was thereby reduced. It, for all practical purposes, constituted a recovery by him under the policy. To deny the insurance company subrogation, under the circumstances, would allow the assured to obtain the full benefit of a policy which because of the violation of its conditions he is not in good conscience entitled to receive. He should not be permitted to receive indirectly a benefit from the policy which the law, because of his conduct, forbids him from receiving directly."

Of course it is also well recognized that since the object of the insurance is indemnity the mortgagee should be satisfied before the insurance company is reimbursed. Because of the mortgagee's prior right claims by insurance companies to a "pro rata" distribution of the proceeds have been consistently rejected. *Union Assurance Soc. v. Equitable Trust Company*, 127 Tex. 618, 94 S.W.2d 1151 (Tex.Comm'n App.1936), and *National Ben Franklin Fire Ins. Co. v. Praetorians*, 67 S.W.2d 333 (Tex.Civ.App., El Paso 1934, writ ref'd). Although the rights of the mortgagee are admittedly superior to those of the insurance company, until the mortgagee's interest has been extinguished, such does not diminish the insurer's right of subrogation to "all the mortgagee's rights of recovery" and this right obviously refers to the right to enforce the collateral agreement. As stated by the *Commission of Appeals in British American Assurance Co.*, supra:

> " * * * In such event the parties have expressly agreed that, upon payment by the insurance company of the loss to the mortgagee, the former shall be entitled to recover through the collateral to which it may be subrogated, money which, as against the mortgagor, it should not have been compelled to pay."

An excellent in depth study and analysis of the authorities on the question of what rights are actually acquired by the insurer upon payment of a portion of the mortgagee's indebtedness, in a situation where the policy as to the mortgagor has become invalid, is contained in the case of *Savings Bank of Ansonia v. Schancupp,* 108 Conn. 588, 144 A. 36 (Conn.S.Ct. of Errors 1928), 63 A.L.R. 1521, in which the court stated that the effect of the mortgage clause is that, from the time the policy becomes void as to the mortgagor, the insurance is only in favor of the mortgagee on its interest as such, and is not insurance on the property generally, to which the mortgagor, or his successor in interest therein, should be entitled. "That the mortgagee should receive the primary benefit, and the insurers the opportunity for ultimate reimbursement, through such security as the mortgage note and mortgage may afford, accords with the general legal and equitable rights of the parties." "The insurers, through their subrogation, virtually occupy the position of a purchaser from the mortgagee for value. * * * The payment, by them, does not operate to reduce or extinguish the mortgage debt or discharge the mortgage, but to satisfy, pro tanto, the mortgagee's claim and assign it to the insurers, leaving it in full force as against the mortgagor and those claiming under him, with no right, on their part, to claim a reduction by the debt by the payment to the mortgagee." * * *

From these authorities it is evident to us that the subrogation rights acquired by appellant-insurer by its payment of the fire loss to the mortgagee, constituted the same rights in the collateral as had been owned by the mortgagee prior to the payment and the mortgagor, not being privy to the fire insurance contract, was not entitled to receive credit upon his indebtedness to mortgagee or to be relieved of the security obligation to the extent of such payment.

Appellees argue that any right acquired by the insurance company to the mortgaged property is, at the most, an equitable claim of which they had no notice. We cannot agree. When the mortgagor conveyed the property by warranty deed almost simultaneously with the foreclosure sale, Jones expressly and admittedly assumed the mortgage indebtedness which at that time was burdened with the subrogation rights of Quincy Mutual. The law, as above outlined, had expressly given to the insurer paying the loss a right of subrogation to the rights held by the mortgagee. It would be unjust and contrary to all legal principles to allow Jones and Pritchett to step in at the last moment and receive credit for payments made on a mortgage loan which the law had denied the mortgagor, who was the predecessor in title. To say that equity would thereby grant benefits in such an indirect manner, when none could be legally claimed directly, does not seem to us to constitute a proper basis of recovery by appellees.

Under these circumstances, and in view of the authorities above cited, it is our judgment that the appellant insurer was entitled to receive the overage payments received by the trustee from the proceeds of the foreclosure sale. Accordingly the trial court should have denied appellees' motion for summary judgment and sustained the motion filed by appellant.   *   *   *

Reversed and rendered.

Notes and Questions

1. *Between a Rock and a Hard Place?* How persuasive was appellees' argument that because the standard mortgage clause in the *Quincy* policy gave the insurer the option of subrogation to the mortgagee's rights or paying off the entire debt and taking an assignment of the mortgage, the insurer should be limited to those two options? Does this argument amount to an assertion that clauses providing contractual subrogation rights displace all rights to equitable subrogation? Should they do so?

2. *Notice.* Should the fact that the appellees had no notice of Quincy's claim have had more impact on the court's decision? If the appellees had notice of the gross amount of the outstanding debt (prior to deducting the insurance payment received by the mortgagee) is that sufficient? Where would they have received such notice?

3. *Rebuild or Repay?* Suppose that after a building is damaged or destroyed by fire the insured wishes to use the insurance proceeds to repair or rebuild, but the mortgagee wants the proceeds applied to reduce the outstanding balance on the mortgage. Does the standard mortgage clause make provision for this contingency? Is the typical Savings and Loan making home mortgage loans likely to prosper if it refuses homeowners the right to rebuild? Would your answer differ in circumstances where interest rates have risen sharply since the original loan was made? Some state statutes deal with the problem, as do some mortgage agreements. In the absence of these sources of guidance, the majority of courts have ruled in favor of the mortgagee. See R. Jerry, Understanding Insurance Law 244 (1987). Under some circumstances, however, courts have given the insured preference. See, e.g., *Schoolcraft v. Ross*, 81 Cal.App.3d 75, 146 Cal.Rptr. 57 (1978) (residential lender may not refuse to allow rebuilding if security for the loan will not be impaired).

4. *Loss–Payee Problems.* Results quite different from those reached under the standard mortgage clause appear when the mortgagee is listed merely as a loss-payee under what is known as an *open mortgage* clause. The clause omits the standard provision protecting the mortgagee's coverage in the event that the mortgagor voids his own insurance by act or neglect. This kind of clause is rare in real estate mortgages, although it is probably less rare in policies of insurance on personal property such as business inventory. Under such a clause the mortgagee's right to coverage is extinguished whenever the insured commits an act or omission that voids his own coverage.

Conversely, because the mortgagee is not an "insured," the possibility that the insurer may seek subrogation against the *mortgagee* after paying an *insured's* claim may arise. Suppose that Adams builds some apartments for Brown, and names Brown (whom he still owes part of the purchase price) as the loss-payee in a fire insurance policy issued to Adams. After a fire at the apartments, the insurer pays Adams the amount of the loss but refuses to pay Brown. Brown sues the insurer. The insurer defends on the ground that the cause of the fire was defective wiring, for which Brown is liable to Adams in tort. The insurer counterclaims against Brown, claiming a right of recovery in the amount of the payment made to Adams, by virtue of the insurer's right of subrogation under Adams' policy to Adams' rights against Brown. What result? Cf. *Dalrymple v. Royal–Globe Insurance Company,* 280 Ark. 514, 659 S.W.2d 938 (1983). If you were counsel for a fire insurer, under what circumstances would you insist that lenders be listed as loss-payees only, rather than as mortgagees under the standard mortgage clause?

2. Leaseholds

ALASKA INSURANCE COMPANY v. RCA ALASKA COMMUNICATIONS, INC.

Supreme Court of Alaska, 1981.
623 P.2d 1216.

CONNOR, Justice.

In this appeal the question is whether a commercial tenant is an "implied co-insured" under its landlord's fire insurance policy, when a provision in the lease requires the landlord to obtain and keep in effect an insurance policy on the leased premises covering loss because of fire. Under the facts of this case, we hold that the tenant is, by legal implications, a co-insured of the landlord's policy, thereby precluding the landlord's insurer from exercising subrogation rights against the tenant.

Bachner Rental Co., Inc. [hereinafter Bachner], as landlord and RCA Alaska Communications, Inc. [hereinafter RCA], as tenant, entered into a one-year commercial lease for a warehouse on October 1, 1976, with possession commencing December 1, 1976. In May of the previous year, Bachner had purchased a three-year policy for fire and extended coverage from appellant insurer, Alaska Insurance Company [hereinafter AIC], protecting its interest in four commercial warehouses, including the structure in question. RCA did not procure additional fire insurance covering its leased warehouse, nor was RCA's name added along with Bachner as an additional insured on the pre-existing policy with AIC.

During the second week of January, 1977, a fire occurred in the rented structure, causing extensive smoke and water damage, and the building was subsequently demolished. AIC paid Bachner for the fire loss pursuant to the insurance policy, and then commenced an action as subrogee of Bachner, contending that RCA, acting through its employees, had negligently caused the fire. At trial, RCA moved for a partial summary judgment on the theory that, as lessee of Bachner, RCA was an implied insured of AIC, thereby precluding appellant AIC from exercising its subrogation rights. The superior court granted a partial summary judgment for RCA. We affirm.

It is a well established rule that "an insurer cannot recover by means of subrogation against its own insured." *Graham v. Rockman,* 504 P.2d 1351, 1356 (Alaska 1972). Since subrogation is an equitable doctrine, equity principles apply in determining its availability. *Cagle, Inc. v. Sammons,* 198 Neb. 595, 254 N.W.2d 398, 403 (1977); *Rock River Lumber Corp. v. Universal Mortgage Corp.,* 82 Wis.2d 235, 262 N.W.2d 114, 117 (1978). As we recognized in *Baugh–Belarde Construction Co. v. College Utilities Corp.,* 561 P.2d 1211, 1214 (Alaska 1977), *quoting Home Insurance Co. v. Pinski Brothers, Inc.,* 160 Mont. 219, 500 P.2d 945, 949 (1972), "[t]o permit the insurer to sue its own insured for a liability covered by the insurance policy would violate * * * basic equity principles, as well as violate sound public policy."

Therefore, if we find that the tenant in this case can be considered a co-insured of the landlord, the insurer cannot exercise a right of subrogation against the tenant. In recent years a number of courts have denied a cause of action to landlords and the right of subrogation to their insurers, when the landlord covenants to carry fire insurance on the leased premises, and the fire damage is allegedly due to the negligence of the tenant. Absent an express provision in the lease establishing the tenant's liability for loss from negligently started fires, the trend has been to find that the insurance obtained was for the mutual benefit of both parties, and that the tenant "stands in the shoes of the insured landlord for the limited purpose of defeating a subrogation claim." *Rizzuto v. Morris,* 22 Wash.App. 951, 592 P.2d 688, 690 (1976), *citing Rock Springs Realty, Inc. v. Waid,* 392 S.W.2d 270, 278 (Mo.1965); *Monterey Corp. v. Hart,* 216 Va. 843, 224 S.E.2d 142, 146 (1976). We think the reasoning of the foregoing cases is sound.

The central issue is whether the lease contains a provision clearly establishing the tenant's liability for negligently caused fire damage. In the case at bar, the lease between the parties contains the following provisions whose significance and construction is in dispute:

"I. COVENANTS OF THE LESSOR:

c.   Lessor warrants that all facilities and appurtenances are in good condition, and that all repairs required to maintain the premises and buildings in an adequate and suitable condition for the purpose of this lease shall be at Lessor's sole cost and expense * * * [except] those damages arising from the direct negligence on the part of the Lessee to any portion of said Facility. * * *

II. COVENANTS OF THE LESSEE:

* * *

b.   Lessee shall use said premises for lawful business purposes and will leave said premises at the expiration of this lease in as good a condition as received, excepting fair wear and tear and/or loss or damage caused by fire, explosion, earthquake or other casualty; provided that such casualty was not caused by the negligent act of the Lessee, its employees or agents. * * *

c. Lessee agrees to indemnify and hold Lessor harmless from and against loss, damage and liability arising from the negligent act of Lessee, its agents, employees, or clients;

III. MUTUAL COVENANTS OF LESSOR AND LESSEE

b. That this lease shall automatically terminate with no penalty to Lessee in event that the leased space becomes unusable due to fire or other cause;

c. Lessor agrees to pay all taxes and assessments made against and levied upon said property. Lessor shall obtain and keep in force during the term of this lease a policy or policies of insurance covering loss or damages to the premises providing protection against all perils and risks including but not limited to the classifications of fire, extended coverage, vandalism and malicious mischief. Lessee agrees that if its usage of leased premises should increase the insurance hazard of the premises in any way during the term of said lease, the Lessee shall bear the additional cost of insurance realized by the Lessor. Lessor agrees to provide Lessee adequate documentation to verify that any additional insurance premium increase is in fact due to Lessee's use of said leased premises."

AIC contends that the absence of an express exemption for negligent liability and the inclusion of paragraphs I. c., II. b., and II. c. of the lease clearly establish RCA's liability for fire damage caused by its own negligence. In the last analysis the question is whether we should give primacy to the redelivery (II. b.) and indemnity (II. c.) covenants of the lessee, or to the insurance clause of III. c., wherein the lessor promises to obtain insurance covering, *inter alia,* damage to the leased premises caused by fire. In our view, the redelivery and indemnity provisions relied on by AIC, when read in conjunction with the insurance clause of III. c., fail to clearly establish RCA's liability for fire damage caused by its own negligence.[1]

We believe that in a situation of this type it would be undesirable as a matter of public policy to permit the risk of loss from a fire

---

1. AIC correctly notes that a majority of the cases cited in note 1, *supra,* also placed emphasis on the exculpatory portion of a "surrender" or "re-delivery" clause which is distinguishable from the surrender clause in the case at bar. *See generally* Annot., 15 A.L.R.3d 786, § 7 (1967 & Supp.1979). The phrase in II. b., "provided that such casualty was not caused by the negligent act of the Lessee, its agent, employees or clients" does not appear in those cases cited in note 1 which have denied a landlord's insurer the right to subrogate. Nevertheless, we do not find this provision of the lease conclusive on the question of the tenant's liability for fire losses, and we ascribe correspondingly greater significance to the insurance clause of III.c.

negligently caused by a tenant to fall upon the tenant rather than the landlord's insurer.[2] *See* R. Keeton, Insurance Law § 4.4(b), at 210 (1971). Since the ordinary and usual meaning of "loss by fire" includes fires of negligent origin, it would contradict the reasonable expectations of a commercial tenant to allow the landlord's insurer to proceed against it after the landlord had contracted in the lease to provide fire insurance on the leased premises. *Rizzuto v. Morris*, 592 P.2d at 690–91; *Monterey Corp. v. Hart*, 224 S.E.2d at 147. We agree with the court in *Sutton v. Jondahl*, 532 P.2d 478 (Okl.App.1975), which stated:

> "Basic equity and fundamental justice upon which the equitable doctrine of subrogation is established require that when fire insurance is provided for a dwelling it protects the insurable interests of all joint owners including the possessory interests of a tenant absent an express agreement by the latter to the contrary. The company affording such coverage should not be allowed to shift a fire loss to an occupying tenant even if the latter negligently caused it."

532 P.2d at 482.

Therefore, we hold that if the landlord in a commercial lease covenants to maintain fire insurance on the leased premises, and the lease does not otherwise clearly establish the tenant's liability for fire loss caused by its own negligence, by reserving to the landlord's insurer the right to subrogate against the tenant, the tenant is, for the limited purpose of defeating the insurer's subrogation claim, an implied co-insured of its landlord.

Accordingly, the judgment of the superior court is affirmed.

AFFIRMED.

Rabinowitz, Chief Justice, dissenting.

I am in agreement with the general principle set out in the majority opinion—*i.e.*, that, "[a]bsent an express provision in the lease establishing the tenant's liability for loss from negligently started fires, the trend has been to find that the insurance obtained was for the mutual benefit of both parties, and that the tenant 'stands in the shoes of the insured landlord for the limited purpose of defeating a subrogation claim.' "

However, here the parties chose to include an express provision establishing the tenant's liability for fires caused by the tenant's own negligence. The majority cites no opinions in which the court has held that the general principle overrules such an express provision, and I would not allow it to do so here. In my opinion, the public policy

---

2. One policy consideration for not permitting a landlord's insurer to subrogate against the landlord's tenant is reduction of litigation. If a landlord's casualty insurer may seek to recoup its payments for fire loss by alleging the negligence of the tenant, many commercial fire losses will result in costly litigation. For similar reasons, we held in *Baugh–Belarde Constr. Co. v. College Utilities Corp.*, 561 P.2d 1211, 1215 (Alaska 1977), that a builder's risk policy prohibited the insurer from subrogating against sub-contractors of the insured general contractor.

considerations involved here are not so overwhelming that the parties ought not to be allowed to contract for a different result according to their own preferences; but the majority's treatment of the language here makes this well-nigh impossible.[1]

My view might be different were this lease a product of a disparity of bargaining power, or similar to a contract of adhesion; but no such claim is made here, and properly so, as neither party can be characterized as unsophisticated in such matters.

I do not read the provisions of the lease as being inconsistent. However, even if they were, I agree with the *Rizzuto* court in its statement that "[o]ur review of the cases in this area leads us to conclude that the intent of the parties is the primary factor considered by the courts in construing exemption clauses." *Rizzuto v. Morris,* 22 Wash.App. 951, 592 P.2d 688, 691 (1979). *Rizzuto* was decided after trial *id.* 22 Wash.App. 951, 592 P.2d at 689, based upon "the undisputed testimony of all the parties." *Id.,* 22 Wash.App. 951, 592 P.2d at 691. The instant case is on appeal from a summary judgment, and I think there are still genuine issues of material fact regarding the intent of the parties.

Notes and Questions

1. *A Rose by Any Other Name.* What did the court mean when it said that, for the limited purpose of defeating the insurer's subrogation claim, the tenant is an "implied co-insured?" Is this anything other than a holding that the landlord had exculpated the tenant from liability for negligently damaging the premises, in much the same way that the insured in *Great Northern* signed an exculpatory clause releasing Litwin in advance from liability for negligently damaging Great Northern's property? Can this holding be squared with the language of the RCA lease?

2. *Standing the Holding on its Head.* If the parties had intended the tenant to be liable for negligently damaging the premises, then what must they have intended by the inclusion of paragraph III. c. of the RCA lease? That the tenant was an implied co-insured for all

1. "The question whether the desired result (that the lessee be given the benefit of the lessor's insurance) should be reached by judicial imposition of such a rule in the absence of statutory or administrative sanctions is debatable. Probably the courts should not so rule if the lease and insurance provisions together clearly express an agreement that the lessor's insurer shall have the right of subrogation." R. Keeton, Insurance Law § 4.4(b), at 210 (1971).

I think that there are two clear provisions establishing the tenant's liability for loss from fires started by its own negligence: paragraph II(c), which states "[l]essee agrees to indemnify and hold lessor harmless from and against loss, damage and liability arising from the negligent act of lessee, its agents, employees or clients;" and Paragraph II(b), which requires the lessee to "leave said premises at the expiration of this lease in as good a condition as received, excepting fair wear and tear and/or loss or damage caused by fire, explosion, earthquake or other casualty; provided that such casualty was not caused by the negligent act of the Lessee, its employees or agents. ＊ ＊ ＊" In my opinion, the lessee by these provisions clearly and unambiguously covenanted to be responsible for fire damage caused by its own negligence.

purposes *except* regarding losses caused by the tenant's own negligence? Isn't this at least as plausible an interpretation of the provisions of the lease as the court's interpretation? Should it matter whether paragraph III. c. was individually drafted or merely boiler plate that was already on a printed form that the parties used?

3. *Variations on a Theme.* Suppose that a lease contains an insurance clause similar to paragraph III. c. but no provisions governing the tenant's liability for negligence. In a jurisdiction in which the tenant is liable at common law for damage to the leased premises resulting from his negligence, what should be the result on facts otherwise like those in the *RCA* case? Suppose that the damage exceeds the limits of the landlord's insurance. Should the landlord be able to collect the amount of this excess from the tenant even if the insurer has no subrogation rights against the tenant? See *Agra–By–Products, Inc. v. Agway, Inc.,* 347 N.W.2d 142 (N.D.1984).

3. Real Estate Sales

In the typical sale of real estate there is a period of time between execution of the contract of sale and transfer of title to the property. When the property is damaged or destroyed during this period there is a possibility of what Professors Young and Holmes have called "mismatched" insurance. See W. Young and E. Holmes, Cases and Materials on Insurance 445 (2d ed. 1985). The possibility of a mismatch arises because one party bears the risk of loss during this period, but the other party alone may have insurance against the loss. Where the party who bears the risk of loss is insured, insurance and risk are matched. But where the seller bears the risk of loss prior to transfer of title, the purchaser alone may be insured; and where the purchaser bears this risk, the seller alone may be insured. The more common situation is the latter, since the inexperienced or legally unrepresented purchaser is unlikely to know that she bears the risk of loss immediately upon signing a contract of sale, and (unlike the seller) she does not already have insurance on the property.

Some Background Rules

At common law the risk of loss during the contract period (in the absence of a contract provision to the contrary) was on the purchaser. Because equitable title to the property had passed to the purchaser upon execution of the contract of sale, it was thought that the risk of loss should pass as well. Did this rule create unnecessary moral hazard in cases where the purchaser did not take immediate possession? About a dozen states have now altered this rule by statute, but this alteration merely reverses the possibility of mismatched insurance. See, e.g., Uniform Vendor and Purchaser Risk Act, 14 U.L.A. 554 (1980). On the risk of loss in transactions in goods, see Uniform Commercial Code, §§ 2–509–10.

Of course, the contract of sale can allocate the risk of loss, and most real estate contracts allocate it to the seller, at least as long as he retains possession. Moreover, many insurers will "endorse" a policy so as to add the purchaser as an insured under it upon request by the insured seller. If you represented a purchaser, would you recommend that she accept this endorsement from the seller or obtain her own policy covering her interest during the period between contract and transfer of title?

Suppose now that the property is destroyed after execution of the contract of sale, but before transfer of title. Probably the most common of several approaches when the purchaser bears the risk of loss and the seller alone is insured is to hold that the seller is entitled to specific performance of the purchaser's promise to buy, but that the seller holds his insurance in constructive trust for the purchaser. In effect, the purchaser is an implied co-insured under the seller's policy. A less commonly adopted alternative that produces the opposite result is to allow the seller to recover the insurance proceeds, but to subrogate the insurer to the seller's right to the purchase price, to the extent of the insurer's payment to the seller. See R. Jerry, Understanding Insurance Law 250 (1987). On the other hand, when the seller bears the risk of loss, the purchaser is much less likely to succeed in a claim that she is entitled to the benefit of the seller's policy. See, e.g., *Brownell v. Board of Education*, 239 N.Y. 369, 146 N.E. 630 (1925).

The Underlying Structure of Limited–Interest Problems

In the previous cases in this Chapter, some provision in a contract between the insured and an otherwise uninsured third party, or in the insurance policy itself, created the basis for a holding that the third party (a construction contractor, mortgagee, or tenant) was to be treated as if that party were an "additional" insured under the policy. Despite the absence of such a provision in the real estate transfer cases, however, through the background rules described above the courts often create such additional coverage in the purchaser who is uninsured. Does this suggest that an insured's intention that another party benefit from his coverage is not a prerequisite to that party's rights under the policy, that real estate transfers are distinguishable from construction contracts, mortgages, and leaseholds in this respect, or that something else entirely is going on? If the latter, what is it?

The converse of insurance mismatch problems in real estate transfers is double insurance: both purchaser and seller have insurance against a loss that occurs during the period between contract and transfer of title. In the case that follows the court was faced with precisely this embarrassment of riches.

PARAMOUNT FIRE INSURANCE COMPANY v. AETNA CASUALTY AND SURETY COMPANY

Supreme Court of Texas, 1962.
163 Tex. 250, 353 S.W.2d 841.

GREENHILL, Justice.

This case is an appeal from a summary judgment. The question is one of first impression in Texas and involves the liability of two insurance companies, each issuing a policy covering improvements which were destroyed by fire.

On July 17, 1957, the heirs of Mrs. R.L. Cameron entered into a written agreement labeled "Contract of sale and receipt for earnest money," whereby the seller(s) "sells and agrees to convey" and the purchaser(s), Mr. and Mrs. Sterling D. Holmes and Pauline Reece, "agrees to consummate the sale within fifteen days from date title company approves title" of a tract of land upon which were situated the improvements later destroyed. The contract specified the total purchase price, a down-payment, and terms of $125 monthly until the final closing date one year later, July 17, 1958, when the balance was due. Both seller and purchaser were given the right of specific performance. Purchasers had the right to occupy the premises from the inception of the contract, which they did, and had the right to make all desired improvements on the property.

On October 12, 1957, sellers procured from petitioner, Paramount Fire Insurance Company, an insurance policy for $15,000 covering improvements on the contracted land and payable only to sellers. A clause extending protection to purchasers under this policy was specifically rejected by sellers.

The fire involved occurred on July 7, 1958. By this time, the title company had issued the title insurance policy. The sellers had prepared a warranty deed conveying the property to the purchasers. Some, but not all of the sellers had already signed the deed, and it was being sent to the others for their signatures and acknowledgments. Purchasers had made the monthly payments of $125 and had procured a sufficient loan from Richardson Savings and Loan Association to pay the balance of the purchase price. Purchasers had also procured an $18,000 fire insurance policy from respondent, Aetna Casualty & Surety Company, in their favor with loss payable clause to the mortgagee as its interest might appear. This policy was dated June 25, 1958. All these and related papers, including the Aetna policy, were deposited in escrow with National Title & Abstract Company for final closing of the transaction on July 8, 1958. Because of the July 7 fire, this meeting was postponed until September 3, 1958. At the latter date, purchasers paid the contract price and received the warranty deed. Sellers, at the same time, assigned all their rights and claims under the Paramount policy to the purchasers.

Thereafter, purchasers and their mortgagee filed suit against both insurance companies, claiming property loss of $14,000. This suit was settled as to the plaintiffs by each insurance company's contributing a prorata share of the loss based on the amount of its respective policy, reserving its rights against the other. The suit then proceeded between the two insurance companies to determine liability as against each other. The trial court rendered summary judgment against Aetna, awarding Paramount the amount of money it contributed in the settlement with purchasers. Aetna's motion for summary judgment was consequently denied. On appeal, the judgment was reversed and the loss prorated between both companies in proportion to the face amount of the respective policies. 347 S.W.2d 281.

Both companies filed applications for writ of error to this Court. Paramount, of course, seeks to have the trial court's judgment affirmed. Aetna asks that the full loss be imposed upon Paramount, or, alternatively, that the judgment of the Court of Civil Appeals be affirmed. * * *

Aetna being the insurer of purchasers in possession under a contract of sale, it must bear all the loss unless it has a right to require Paramount to bear a prorata share as held by the Court of Civil Appeals.

Paramount's application attacks this proration holding, arguing that the vendors suffered no actual pecuniary loss from the fire and that, therefore, the vendees' insurance company should incur the total liability. Paramount's position is based on the generally accepted principle that:

> "Since a contract for insurance against fire ordinarily is a contract of indemnity * * * insured is entitled to receive the sum necessary to indemnify him, or to be put, as far as practicable, in the same condition pecuniarily in which he would have been had there been no fire; that is, he may recover to the extent of his loss occasioned by the fire, but no more, and he cannot recover if he sustained no loss." 45 C.J.S. Insurance § 915, p. 1010.

Aetna does not challenge this principle. Instead, the controversy is as to whether or not the insureds of Paramount suffered any "loss" in a legal sense.

The Court of Civil Appeals regarded the date of the fire as controlling and found that the vendors did incur a loss, despite the fact that they received the full contract price from the vendees after the fire. There is a line of cases which supports this viewpoint. * * * The rationale of these cases is that an insurance company contracts to protect an insured against destruction by fire of his property and that liability is fixed if such fire occurs, all other contract terms being met. Any compensation to the insured from third parties, such as payment from the vendees here, is regarded as being unrelated to the insurance contract, of no concern to the insurance company, and in the nature of a windfall to the insured.

On the other hand, there is also a line of cases which supports Paramount's argument that its insureds ultimately suffered no pecuniary loss from the fire and are therefore not entitled to recover on their insurance contract. In *Ramsdell v. Insurance Company of North America*, 197 Wis. 136, 221 N.W. 654, it was said:

> "The court looks to the substance of the whole transaction rather than to seek a metaphysical hypothesis upon which to justify a loss that is no loss. This is not a case where a stranger to the transaction, out of charity, or for other reasons, might make good the loss ＊　＊　＊. The loss has been made good out of a related transaction ＊　＊　＊."

Accord, *Tauriello v. Aetna Insurance Co.*, 14 N.J.Super. 530, 82 A.2d 226; *Smith v. Jim Dandy Markets*, 172 F.2d 616 (9th Cir.). We are inclined toward this latter view.

The complexity of the present problem is heightened, however, by another widely accepted principle upon which the Court of Civil Appeals relied in ordering a proration between Paramount and Aetna. In 64 A.L.R.2d 1406, § 4, it is said:

> "Where the purchaser as equitable owner will bear the loss occasioned by a destruction of the property pending completion of the sale, and the contract is silent as to insurance, the rule quite generally followed is that the proceeds of the vendor's insurance policies, even though the purchaser did not contribute to their maintenance, constitute a trust fund for the benefit of the purchaser to be credited on the purchase price of the destroyed property, the theory being that the vendor is a trustee of the property for the purchaser."

The difficulty is that in some jurisdictions, even where the vendor is regarded as having suffered no loss from a fire, he is allowed to collect on his insurance policy subject to a constructive trust for the vendee's benefit. E.g., *Wm. Skinner & Sons' Ship–Building and Dry–Dock Co. v. Houghton*, 92 Md. 68, 48 A. 85. Obviously, this result does violence to the indemnity theory of insurance, but as one commentator observed, it represents an attempt by the courts to "accommodate the contract to lay expectation without tarnishing the ideal of freedom of contract." Young, Some "Windfall Coverages" in Property and Liability Insurance, 60 Colum.L.Rev. 1063. The rationale is that if a vendee pays the full contract price for property which has been damaged or destroyed by fire, it is only equitable to allow him the benefit of any insurance proceeds rather than to give the vendor both the insurance proceeds and the proceeds of sale.

Paramount concedes that it is difficult to quarrel with the equity of this rule, but strenuously argues that the rule should have no application when the vendees have secured their own insurance policy. We agree.

Although none of the decisions applying the constructive trust theory purport to base the result on the fact that the vendee had no insurance, yet it appears that such was the situation in all but two cases. The two exceptions are *Vogel v. Northern Assurance Co.*, 219 F.2d 409 (3rd Cir.), and *Insurance Company of North America v. Alberstadt*, 383 Pa. 556, 119 A.2d 83. In these cases, the vendee was allowed to benefit from both his and the vendor's policies, even to the extent of being allowed to profit from the fire in the *Vogel* case. It must be observed, however, that both cases applied Pennsylvania law that an insured's loss is determined as of the date of the fire regardless of any subsequent developments. See *Dubin Paper Co. v. Insurance Company of North America* and *State Mutual Fire Insurance Co. v. Updegraff*, supra.

We believe the better result to be that if a vendor is entitled to specific performance under a contract of sale and thereby collects the full purchase price despite fire damage to improvements, he has suffered no legal loss. As it is not before us here, we leave open the question of whether, where the vendee has no insurance, there can be recovery on the vendor's policy subject to a constructive trust for the vendee, who is often ignorant of his legal liability in such a situation. We believe that there is nothing in the present case, however, which would require such an exception to the principle that an insurance policy is basically a personal, indemnity contract.

Here we are not dealing with an unwitting risk bearer, but rather with vendees who are protected by their own insurance. Also, we do not have a situation where the vendors originally intended for their policy to protect the vendees, for they specifically rejected such a provision. Further we note that in the vendors' own policy there is a provision that Paramount's liability should not exceed "the interest of the insured." After the contract of sale, the interest of Paramount's insured became the amount of the unpaid purchase price and, as to that interest, they suffered no loss. Accordingly, there is no liability under the Paramount policy, and Paramount's insureds had no rights to assign to the vendees. * * *

For the reasons stated herein, the judgment of the Court of Civil Appeals is reversed and the judgment of the trial court is affirmed. * * *

GRIFFIN, Justice (dissenting).

I do not agree that all of the loss from the destruction of the improvements by fire should fall on Aetna. I believe the law requires that the loss be prorated between Aetna and Paramount as decreed by the Court of Civil Appeals.

The majority opinion recognizes that Paramount's insured had an insurable interest in the property at the time of the issuance of that policy. The majority reasons that the liability of Paramount to the insurer is to be determined by events happening after the loss by fire has occurred. The majority say "we note that in the vendors' own policy there is a provision that Paramount's liability should not exceed 'the interest of the insured.' After the contract of sale, the interest of Paramount's insured became the amount of the unpaid purchase price and, as to that interest, they suffered no loss." This statement is based upon the theory that the vendors' debt was paid by the purchaser after the fire.

Such a holding is in direct violation of and contrary to the language of the policy. The policy provides: "Loss on building items shall be payable to ASSURED address _____ as Mortgagee or Trustee, as their *interest may appear at time of loss,* subject to Mortgage Clause (without contribution) printed elsewhere in this policy." (Emphasis mine.) Clearly the loss of the building and the time of the fire are contemporary and simultaneous. The mortgage clause referred to above has no application to our cause. Further, the policy also contained a provision that the liability of the company "shall not exceed the actual cash value of the property *at the time of loss.*" (Emphasis mine.) Thus again this clearly fixes the date of the fire as the date on which liability is to be determined.

Let us apply the majority reasoning that Paramount only insured the vendor for the unpaid balance of his purchase price to the fact situation in this cause. Take the date fixed by the policy for determining this interest—which is the "time of loss"—we find that on the date of the loss, which is the date of the fire, the purchaser owed the vendor $12,675.00, plus the contract interest. This figure is computed by subtracting from the total contract price of $15,250.00 the sum of $1,200.00 paid at the time the contract was signed, less eleven monthly payments of $125.00 each totalling $1,375.00. By the terms of the policy contract between the vendor and Paramount, Paramount's liability became fixed to vendor for this sum of $12,675.00. Purchasers hold an assignment from vendor of all his rights against Paramount. Paramount has never paid this liability. Therefore, I maintain that Paramount is still liable on its policy to the assignees of vendor, and its liability is to be prorated in accordance with the terms of the policy.

No public policy is violated; no statute is offended by the parties to the insurance contract making the contract which they did make. Suppose the vendor and purchaser had entered into a contract providing for $5,000.00 cash payment, the balance to be paid in monthly instalments of $125.00 each due on the 10th day of each successive succeeding month. This would require 82 months, or approximately seven years, to pay the deferred payments. Vendor could not be forced to take his balance in one lump sum. He could insist on the monthly payments as set out in the contract in order to earn the interest. Under the majority holding Paramount's liability would not be known until the last payment had been made. This example illustrates very clearly the fallacy of the reasoning of the majority opinion.

The interests of the vendors and the purchasers were separate and distinct interests. Appleman, Insurance Law and Practice, Vol. 5,

§ 3057 at p. 180, et seq. The assignee of a claim under the policy after a loss stands in the same position as the assignor. Id., § 3462 at p. 643; Id., Vol. 4, § 2181 at p. 53. The vendor, under the contract of sale herein, had an insurable interest in the property destroyed. 24B Tex. Jur. 234, § 95. Vendor retained the legal title to the property until the purchase price was paid. 43A Tex.Jur. 290, § 253, and authorities there cited.

There is an exhaustive annotation entitled "Rights of vendor and purchaser, as between themselves, in insurance proceeds" in 64 A.L.R. 2d, pp. 1402–1420. Section 4 therein states the general rule to be that "where the purchaser as equitable owner will bear the loss occasioned by a destruction of the property pending completion of the sale, and the contract of sale is silent as to insurance [as our contract here is], * * * the proceeds of the vendor's insurance policies, even though the purchaser did not contribute to their maintenance, constitute a trust fund for the benefit of the purchaser to be credited on the purchase price of the destroyed property, the theory being that the vendor is a trustee of the property for the purchaser." Supporting this rule cases are cited from Alabama, California, Georgia, Iowa, Kentucky, Maryland, Missouri, Nebraska, New Jersey, New York, North Dakota, Ohio, Pennsylvania, South Dakota, Washington and Canada. For this result to be reached, the vendor's policy must be valid as of the date of the fire. We have been cited to no Texas cases in point, nor have we found any in our research.

I would affirm the judgment of the Court of Civil Appeals.

Walker and Norvell, JJ., join in this dissent.

Notes and Questions

1. *Double Recovery?* The classic case on this issue, cited by the court, is *Vogel v. Northern Assurance Company,* 219 F.2d 409 (3d Cir. 1955). *Vogel* held that the purchaser could recover a sum from both insurers that in total exceeded the amount of his loss. Is there any justification for this result?

2. *Prorate?* Even if the seller in a case like *Paramount* has suffered no loss, would it not be appropriate to prorate coverage responsibility in proportion to the value of the interests of the purchaser and seller at the date of the fire, as the dissent suggested? Do the cost and difficulty of valuation in the typical case (in which the seller's interest is minimal) argue against taking the trouble to fine-tune the obligations of the two insurers in this fashion?

3. *Let the Chips Fall Where They May?* Now that the rules governing mismatched insurance in real estate sales are well established, should there be any concern for the interests of insurers who have not attempted to displace these rules by contract?

4. Other Limited Interests

THE HOME INSURANCE COMPANY v. ADLER

Court of Appeals of Maryland, 1973.
269 Md. 715, 309 A.2d 751.

MURPHY, Chief Judge.

On August 14, 1966, a fire partially destroyed the house located at 3010 Manhattan Avenue in Baltimore City. The property was insured against direct loss by fire for $17,500 under a Homeowner's policy issued by the appellant, Home Insurance Company (the insurer), to Gertrude Becker (Becker), the sole insured named in the policy. Becker died in the fire, approximately nineteen minutes after it had begun. The insurer paid Abraham Adler (Adler), Becker's Executor and the appellee herein, for personal property lost in the fire; it refused, however, to pay Adler's claim for fire damage to the house, maintaining that Becker had only a life estate therein, that her insurable interest terminated by operation of law at the moment of her death, and that consequently neither Becker nor Adler suffered any pecuniary loss from the damage to the building caused by the fire. Adler sued the insurer, claiming $7,691.06 as the amount of Becker's loss caused by fire damage to the building; he maintained that Becker survived the fire and damage to the property (by nineteen minutes) and thus did sustain loss as a result of the fire. From a judgment of the Superior Court of Baltimore City (Carter, J.) in favor of Adler, the insurer appealed.

The facts are not in dispute. The property was conveyed sometime prior to January 2, 1963, to Lillian Clark for life, remainder to Becker; on January 2, 1963, Clark died, thereby vesting title to the property in fee in Becker. Subsequently, on December 18, 1963, Becker caused the property to be conveyed to herself, as life tenant, with full life powers,[1] remainder in fee simple to Alfred Lee Scheinberg and Diana Sue Scheinberg (the remaindermen). Thereafter, Becker insured the property with the insurer against direct loss by fire for a three year period beginning October 6, 1964. By the terms of the policy, the insurer:

> " * * * insure[d] the Insured named in the declarations above [Gertrude Becker] and legal representatives, to the extent of the actual cash value of the property at the time of loss, but not exceeding the amount which it would cost to repair or replace the property with material of like kind and quality within a reasonable time after such loss . . . nor in any event

1. The deed provided in pertinent part:

" * * * to the proper use and benefit of the said Gertrude Becker, for and during the term of her natural life, with full powers in the said Gertrude Becker, to sell, grant, lease, convey, mortgage, transfer, assign and otherwise dispose of the property hereinabove described, except by her Last Will and Testament, and from and after the death of the said Gertrude Becker, without having exercised the powers of disposition then unto the use and benefit of the said Alfred Lee Scheinberg and Diana Sue Scheinberg, as joint tenants, absolutely in fee simple."

for more than the interest of the insured, against all Direct Loss by fire. * * * "

Neither the Executor nor the remaindermen made any repairs to the house after the fire. No demand was made upon the Executor by the remaindermen to repair the property and he was under no legal obligation to do so. The property was eventually sold on an "as is basis" for $8,825. The remaindermen were not made parties to the present litigation.

The lower court held, on authority of Rogge v. Menard County Mutual Fire Insurance Co., 184 F.Supp. 289 (S.D.Ill.1960), that since Becker died after, and not before, the fire began, the insurer was liable under the policy. The court found that the insurer was not aware of Becker's limited interest in the property prior to the fire; that since all premiums paid by Becker were based on the value of the property being insured, and not on the value of her interest in the property, Adler, as Becker's Executor, was entitled to reimbursement in the full amount of the loss under the insurance contract. The court concluded:

> "Admittedly, a contract of insurance is a personal contract and recovery is based on the actual loss to the insured. Miss Becker was alive after the fire and her actual loss at that time was the damage to both real and personal property caused by the fire, no matter how long she lived thereafter. 'A life tenant has an insurable interest in property to the full value thereof.' 44 C.J.S. Insurance, Sec. 190, p. 891. Under the facts of this case, the limitation in the insurance policy to coverage of only insured's interest, is only applicable if Miss Becker had died prior to the fire, as there would no longer be an interest to be insured."

Relying upon *Glens Falls Insurance Co. v. Sterling*, 219 Md. 217, 148 A.2d 453 (1959), the insurer contends on appeal that a fire insurance policy is a contract of personal indemnity requiring proof of actual pecuniary loss as a prerequisite to the right to recover the policy proceeds. The insurer agrees that $7,691.06 fire damage was done to the property, but maintains that the loss fell upon the remaindermen who are not parties to the suit. The insurer concedes that the fact that Becker lived for approximately nineteen minutes after the fire began "would technically give her and her Personal Representative, Abraham L. Adler, a possible right to recover *provided* the Appellee could show or prove that Gertrude Becker, or her estate, had suffered a *pecuniary loss*," but maintains that the pecuniary loss, if any, is *de minimis*.

Appellee contends that liability under the policy attached the moment the fire started, citing *Rogge v. Menard County Mutual Fire Insurance Co., supra* and *Western Coal & Dock Co. v. Traders Insurance Co.*, 122 Ill.App. 138, 140 (1905); consequently, he maintains that Becker did sustain a loss in her lifetime constituting a debt now payable to her estate by the insurer. He urges that the recovery cannot be limited to Becker's life interest as: (1) the premiums were paid on the fee value of the property; (2) but for Becker's death during the fire, the insurer would not so limit the recovery; and (3) events subsequent to the attaching of liability should not be considered.

In *Glens Falls Insurance Co. v. Sterling, supra,* the question before us was whether there could be a recovery under a fire and windstorm insurance policy when the insured property owner of a building under construction failed to offer any proof that he had sustained an actual pecuniary loss from the damage to the insured property. There was evidence in the case showing that damage had been done to the property of over $5,000, but that the loss was borne by the contractor under his construction contract with the insured. It was against this background that we referred with approval to the holding in *Edlin v. Security Insurance Co.,* 160 F.Supp. 487 (S.D.Ill.1957) that "a fire insurance contract is one of indemnity against such loss as the *insured* may sustain by reason of the damage to the property (not the amount of damage to the *property*) and where no financial or pecuniary loss has been sustained by virtue of the damage to the property, there can be no recovery under such an insurance policy." 219 Md. at 221, 148 A.2d at 456. We said, 219 Md. at 222, 148 A.2d at 456, "that fire insurance * * * is a contract of personal indemnity, not one from which a profit is to be realized," and that the right to recover must be commensurate with the loss actually sustained by the insured. We concluded that the insured had failed to prove an actual pecuniary loss and was not entitled to payment under the policy.

Since a fire insurance policy is a contract of indemnity, it may be that the insured may recover only to the extent of his interest in the property. See 6 Appleman, Insurance Law and Practice § 3867 (1972); 51 Am.Jur.2d, Life Tenants and Remaindermen § 158. It is, however, the rule in many jurisdictions, including Maryland, that a life tenant who insures the property in his own name in the whole value of the fee is not precluded from recovering the full amount of the policy proceeds. See *Forbes v. American International Insurance Co.,* 260 Md. 181, 271 A.2d 684 (1970).[2]

The *Rogge* case, *supra,* upon which the lower court based its decision awarding the insurance proceeds to the appellee, is factually similar to the instant case. There, one Stout owned a life estate, the remainder in fee simple being vested in Rogge. The defendant insurer issued a fire policy to Stout, the house was destroyed by fire, smoke and explosion, and Stout died during the fire. In the course of denying a motion to dismiss, the court held, 184 F.Supp. at 293–294:

"This allegation in plain language says that the fire started before Andrew J. Stout was injured; that thereafter Andrew J.

---

2. During the oral argument before us, counsel for the insurer stated that the premium rate on its "interest policy" is calculated on the building and the risk irrespective of the interest of the insured (*i.e.,* that the same premium is paid by an insured with a fee interest as by an insured with a life interest), and that if Becker had survived the fire and suffered a loss, she would have been paid the full damage within the policy limit rather than the actuarial equivalent of the damage to her life interest.

Stout was injured in some way by the fire after it started, and as a result of the injuries, died. If this allegation be true and the court must take it on its face, the liability under the policy attached the very second that the fire started at a time when Andrew J. Stout was alive.

* * *

Thus the liability attached in favor of Andrew J. Stout in his lifetime. Thus the cause of action * * * [citing the Probate Act of Illinois] survived in favor of the executor of his estate and is not in plaintiff [the remainderman] and the proceeds of the policy must be paid to the executor."

We think the lower court was manifestly correct in concluding, on authority of the *Rogge* case, that the insurer's liability attached under its policy with Becker the moment the fire started. Becker insured the property in the full amount of its value against loss by fire during her lifetime, and when that contingent event occurred prior to her death, resulting in $7,691.06 in damage to the insured property, that loss necessarily accrued in Becker's favor prior to her demise, without regard to the length of time she lived after the fire began. Compare *Pruitt v. Hardware Dealers Mutual Fire Ins. Co.*, 112 F.2d 140 (5th Cir., 1940) and *Pfeiffer v. General Insurance Corp.*, 185 F.Supp. 605 (N.D.Cal., S.C., 1960). The maxim *de minimis non curat lex* ("[T]he law does not care for, or take notice of, very small or trifling matters," Black's Law Dictionary, Revised Fourth Edition) is, in view of our conclusion, plainly without application in the circumstances of this case as a defense to payment of the policy proceeds to Becker's Executor.

Judgment affirmed; costs to be paid by the appellant.

Notes and Questions

1. *Length of Survival.* Was any other solution in *Adler* practical, given that Becker did survive the fire, if only for nineteen minutes? Does this approach place a premium on testimony about minutes of survival, or should the rule apply as long as the insured is alive when the fire begins to destroy the property?

2. *The Rationale for the Rule.* As the court in *Adler* noted, the accepted rule is that a life tenant may insure the full value of the property in which he or she holds that interest. What practical reasons might have given rise to this rule when the creation of life estates in real property was more common than it is today?

3. *Protection of the Remainder Interest.* Should the insured in such a situation be required either to rebuild the property or to hold the insurance proceeds in trust for the remainderman? Is an alternative to hold that a life tenant who pays premiums on the full value of the property is only insured to the extent of her interest, but that the holder of the remainder interest is an implied co-insured for the balance? What if the negligence of the holder of the remainder interest caused the fire?

THE FOLGER COFFEE COMPANY, INC. v. THE GREAT AMERICAN INSURANCE COMPANY

United States District Court, Western District of Missouri, 1971.
333 F.Supp. 1272.

WILLIAM H. BECKER, Chief Judge.

This is an action on a contract of insurance under the diversity statute, § 1332, Title 28, United States Code. Plaintiff's complaint is in two counts. In the first count, it is alleged that $120,448.97 worth of plaintiff's property which was in the possession of defendant's insured Ar–Ka–Mo Sporting Goods, Inc., was, on or about the 26th day of June 1969, while insured's policy with defendant was in force "was totally destroyed or damaged by risks insured against by said policy, and said destruction or damage did not happen from any of the causes excepted in said policy"; that plaintiff "performed all the conditions of said insurance on its part, and on the 7th day of January, 1970, made and delivered to the defendant a claim and demand under said policy which was then and still is due and payable, however, defendant refused and still refuses to consider or pay said claim." Count two alleges destruction of property possessed by the insured on July 7, 1969. A sum of $117,498.56 is demanded in that count. * * *

According to the true copy of the insurance policy attached to the complaint herein, the following is the clause which is relied upon by plaintiff as bringing its losses within the coverage of the policy:

"III. Property covered

The policy covers:

A. Personal property usual to the conduct of the Insured's business, consisting principally of Premiums for Prizes, the property of the Insured, or similar property of others held by the insured *for which the insured is liable,* except as provided elsewhere in this policy." (Emphasis added.)

Defendant relies on the emphasized language, contending that the word "liable" in the provision means "legally liable" and that plaintiff must therefore show the negligence of the bailee Ar–Ka–Mo Sporting Goods, Inc., before it can recover under the policy.

In cases like that at bar, however, the courts have almost uniformly held that if, from the contract construed in its entirety, the fair interpretation and construction of the insurance contract is that it was intended primarily to cover the property held by the insured, then "liable," as used within the policy, does not refer to any fixed legal liability of the insured to respond in damages, but should be construed more broadly to mean "responsible." This view is well developed in the leading cases of *Penn v. Commercial Union Fire Ins. Co.,* 233 Miss. 178, 101 So.2d 535, 67 A.L.R.2d 1238, and *United States v. Globe & Rutgers Fire Ins. Co.* (N.D.Tex.) 104 F.Supp. 632, affirmed (C.A.5) 202 F.2d 696. See also *Michigan Fire & Marine Ins. Co. v. National Sur. Corp.* (C.A.8)

156 F.2d 329. *Penn v. Commercial Union Fire Ins. Co., supra,* expresses the prevailing rule precisely that the insurance covers property in possession of the bailee for which he is responsible, and does not cover the legal liability of the bailee to respond in damages. See also Anno., 67 A.L.R.2d 1241 at pages 1254 and 1255, subparagraph (c); 4 Appleman, Insurance Law and Practice § 2345, p. 341, note 53.75. Missouri law is applicable in this case. From all materials available, including Homan v. Employers Reinsurance Corporation, 345 Mo. 650, 136 S.W.2d 289, it is concluded that the Missouri courts would follow the prevailing view and construe the word "liable" in the policy in the case at bar to be synonymous with "responsible." See definitions in 136 S.W.2d at page 298.

In the *Globe & Rutgers case, supra,* the Government sued the defendant insurance companies for the loss of certain cotton seed which was destroyed by fire at the premises of the McCoy Gin Company, Inc., on November 18, 1949. The policies sued upon all contained the following provision, concerning the property insured:

> "On cotton, ginned and unginned, baled and unbaled, seed cotton, cotton seed, supplies of sacks and other packaging material containing or to contain cotton seed, and bagging and ties, their own, and provided the insured is legally liable therefor, this policy shall also cover such property sold but not delivered, held in trust, or on consignment or for storage."

The Government sued for the loss of cotton seed which it had contracted to buy under price support programs and which was destroyed by fire. In holding that the Government could recover without any showing of negligence on the part of the McCoy Gin Company, Inc., the Court stated as follows:

> "The contention of the defendants is that the plaintiff cannot recover under the present policies without showing that the insured is legally liable for the fire loss of the cotton seed. That view is quite arguable. The pertinent provision of the policies has been quoted in full above and the central phrase thereof reads 'provided the insured is legally liable therefor.' The words 'liability' and 'liable' have manifold meanings in law and that nuance makes 'liable' fit as well in respect to one bound to respond in duty as to one bound to respond in damages. The gin company under its caretaker duty as bailee for hire certainly was responsible for the cotton seed and obligated to keep and deliver same safely, subject to exoneration only if performance be prevented without negligence on its part. That was a present and positive liability, and in fact no other liability ever supervened. In other words that liability in being was complete, and adequately answers the terms of the policy provision. In the typical instance of bailment relationship a proper delivery of the property thereupon satisfies the right of the bailor and discharges the liability of the bailee,

but that does not gainsay the fact that the bailee bore a legal liability during the period of the bailment.

"Of course when construing flexible language the best key usually is the context. The entire language of the relevant policy provision in its ordinary sense consistently points to insurance on *property,* not on the insured's *liability* for a fire loss on such property. A strained construction is required to say that 'legally liable therefor' in the central phrase defines a selective condition on the thing being insured. A simpler statement perhaps is that said central phrase is really some of the descriptive language identifying the property insured. This viewpoint may draw question on the theory that it renders such phrase sterile, presupposing the insured would necessarily and without more be legally liable in the sense herein stressed for all property 'held in trust or on consignment or for storage,' but for one thing that contention would overlook the frequent tendency of bailees to attempt contractual stipulations against their common law liability. [Emphasis in original.]

"If the policy provision in fact read 'on the liability' of the insured then to be sure it could only mean liability for fire loss of the property, and the plaintiff would fail in the suit. This is true for the simple reason that a fire insurance policy, like many forms of insurance, is a contract of pecuniary indemnity. Its subject matter must have a money measure. Such insurance on *liability* cannot become payable apart from an incurred liability of the insured for money damages or at least a pecuniary obligation. The present policies however plainly purport to insure *property,* not only property of the specified kinds belonging to the insured, but also property of like kind, for which insured is liable, belonging to another owner, and the reasonable construction of the insurance contract is that the central phrase of the policy provisions means liability of the insured already present and not contingent liability ushered in by a fortuitous fire. If the contrary meaning had been intended it would have been easy to state same in unmistakable terms. This construction makes for certainty instead of contingency. The protection of the bailor is on a dependable footing. Bailor and bailee are spared the vexation of controversy as to liability of the bailee for the fire loss. No violence is done to the language of the policies. Even any fair doubt should be resolved in favor of the insured. The plaintiff has a good claim under the policies." [Emphasis in original.] 104 F.Supp. at 634–635.

In affirming the judgment, the United States Court of Appeals for the Fifth Circuit held as follows:

"In applying the policy provisions, the Trial Court properly gave weight to the fact that the entire tenor and effect of the contracts was insurance against property loss by fire and not insurance only against the legal liability of the named insured for the fire loss. The policies provide property insurance,—not indemnity or liability insurance. Whether the described commodities were owned by the insured, or 'held in trust or on consignment or for storage,' in either and all events it is provided that the policy shall cover 'property.' It was likewise correctly determined by the Trial Court that the phrase 'provided the insured is legally liable therefor,' when considered in connection with these policy provisions providing insurance on property, should be considered to refer to the present and existing liability of the custodian generally and not restricted to liability which was the consequence alone of a fire." 202 F.2d at 697.

* * *

Defendant relies on the cases of *Millers' Mutual Fire Insurance Association v. Warroad Potato Growers Ass'n* (C.A.8) 94 F.2d 741; *Michigan Fire & Marine Ins. Co. v. National Sur. Corp., supra*; *McCoy v. Home Ins. Co.,* 170 Pa.Super. 38, 84 A.2d 249; *In re Podolsky* (C.A.3) 115 F.2d 965; and *Orient Insurance Co. v. Skellet Co.* (C.A.8) 28 F.2d 968. But those cases either applied the minority view recognized in Minnesota or involved contracts of insurance which specifically and precisely covered only the legal *liability* of the insured to respond in damages. In *Orient Ins. Co. v. Skellet Co., supra*, the insurance contract contained a provision insuring the owners of the public storage warehouse against loss on merchandise not owned by the insured "for which they may be *legally* liable" (emphasis added), as in *United States v. Globe & Rutgers Fire Ins. Co., supra,* but as the Court in the latter case noted, 104 F.Supp. at 635:

"This [*Orient Ins. Co. v. Skellet Co., supra*] would be a formidable decision in behalf of the present defendant, but for the fact that the court also said that if the policy had recited that the goods were held in trust, or in similar custody then there could be no doubt that the insurance was for the benefit of the real owners." [1]

Similarly, the contract involved in *In re Podolsky, supra,* (applying Minnesota law, following the minority view) insured only the insured's *"legal interest in* and * * * legal liability for * * * property held by

---

1. In the *Orient* case, the Court was very explicit on this point, saying:

"Concededly, Skellet Co.'s relation to the owners of the stored goods and its interest in them was such as entitled it to take out insurance for their protection. Any expression in an insurance contract signifying that intent and purpose is sufficient. To that end the clause 'for which they may be legally liable' should have been omitted, or there should have been a statement that the goods described were held in trust, or a similar expression of like import should have been used,—and then there could be no doubt that the contract was made in the name of Skellet Co. for the benefit of the real owners." 28 F.2d at 970.

him." (Emphasis added.) And, in *Millers' Mutual Fire Insurance Association v. Warroad Potato Growers Ass'n, supra* (applying Minnesota law, following the minority view), the policy again purported only to cover legal liability on the loss of the property. The policy was written to make "liability" modify only the word "loss" by making liability contingent upon loss.[2] All of these cases, therefore, are consistent with the theory of *United States v. Globe & Rutgers Fire Ins. Co., supra,* insofar as that case recognized that if the policy provision expressly reads or otherwise indicates that the insurance is "on the liability," then a recovery cannot be had by the "real owners" of the property without a showing of negligence of the bailee. Thus, the contract must be interpreted and construed to determine whether it was intended to cover the liability of the insured to respond in damages or his responsibility for the property. With this proposition, none of the cases are in conflict. See the following analysis in Anno., Fire Insurance—Insured's Bailor, 67 A.L.R.2d at 1244:

> "At one extreme are the decisions in which clauses covering property contained in specific places and for which the insured 'is,' 'are,' 'may be,' or 'shall be' liable, used independently of trust and commission provisions, have been held to insure the property of others while in the insured's custody and control, the courts stating that the word 'liable,' as used in the provision, refers not to a particular fixed legal liability to respond in pecuniary damages, but may instead be equated with 'responsibility,' since a bailee is 'responsible' for the goods of the bailor. Thus, they have held that it is not necessary that there be a showing of the insured's contractual or tort liability to the owner in order to recover the full value of customers' or bailors' property when it is damaged or destroyed by fire while in the insured's building, warehouse, or other location specified in or covered by the policy.

> "At the other extreme are decisions in which the fire policy covered insured's 'interest in and legal liability for' property of others, or property held in trust, on commission, on storage, or otherwise. Here the courts have generally held that the policy was one of indemnity only, that it insured not property but only the liability of the insured with respect to property, and that there could be no recovery from the insurer for customers' or bailors' goods unless the insured himself had incurred legal liability, or at least a pecuniary obligation, because the loss was due to negligence for which he was responsible or because he had contractually assumed liability for loss of the property.

---

2. Again, following *Orient Ins. Co. v. Skellet Co.* (C.A.8) 28 F.2d 968, the *Warroad* case recognized that provisions covering the property would bring about a different result. The Court cited *California Insurance Co. v. Union Compress Co.,* 133 U.S. 387, 10 S.Ct. 365, 33 L.Ed. 730, wherein it was held that the language of a policy "insuring cotton 'their own or held by them in trust or on commission'" insures "all the cotton which was placed in the hands of the plaintiff" by other companies. 133 U.S. at 409, 10 S.Ct. at 369, 33 L.Ed. at 736.

> "*Both of these views would seem to be correct, for it is apparent-
> ly recognized as a rule of construction that if the primary
> intention of the policy is to insure property, then the property of
> others will be included, but that when the intent is only to
> insure against liability, and not to insure property, then only
> the legal liability of the insured with respect to the property
> will be covered.*"   (Emphasis added.)

To the same effect, see *Home Insurance Company of New York v.
Baltimore Warehouse Company,* 93 U.S. 527, 23 L.Ed. 868. See also the
cases distinguished in *United States v. Globe & Rutgers Fire Ins. Co.,
supra,* 202 F.2d at 697, n. 1, and in *Texas City Terminal Ry. Co. v.
American Equitable Assur. Co.* (S.D.Tex.) 130 F.Supp. 843, 855. The
general applicability of the principle is recognized in 43 Am.Jur.2d
Insurance § 311, where it is noted that:

> "Policies are frequently issued to persons holding, storing,
> repairing, or selling property for others, and the question has
> frequently arisen as to what property is covered by policies
> issued to such persons. Where policy provisions show an
> intention to insure for the benefit of owners other than the
> insured, property conforming to the description in the policy
> although owned by bailors or customers of the insured has
> been held covered. Courts have found that an intention to
> insure property of others was shown by the fact that it was
> well known in the community that the insured was in the
> business of handling property belonging to others and was
> under a duty to insure it, or the fact that the description of
> types of property insured by definition was understood to
> include property belonging to others." pp. 373–374.

Further, the Missouri cases which have been decided generally on
the subject of the meaning of "liable" have also concluded that the
word must be interpreted and construed according to the manifest
intent of the parties. *   *   *

The parties have agreed that Missouri law applied to the interpretation
and construction of the contract in this case, and it appears that the
contract of insurance was made in Missouri and that Missouri law
applies. Applying the rule that the meaning of the word "liable" must
be construed according to "its true intent and purpose from the terms
used in the contract" to the case at bar leads to the firm conclusion that
the policy was intended to insure property for which Ar–Ka–Mo Sporting Goods, Inc., was responsible, rather than legal liability of Ar–Ka–
Mo to plaintiff. The opening paragraph of the policy provides that:

> "In consideration of the provisions and stipulations herein or
> added hereto and of the premium above specified, this Compa-
> ny, for the term of years specified from inception date shown
> above at Noon (Standard Time) to expiration date shown above
> at Noon (Standard Time) at location of *property* involved, to an
> amount not exceeding the amount(s) above specified, does in-

sure the insured named above and legal representatives, to the extent of the actual cash value of the *property* at the time of loss, but not exceeding the amount which it would cost to repair or replace the property with material of like kind and quality within a reasonable time after such loss, without allowance for any increased cost of repair or reconstruction by reason of any ordinance or law regulating construction or repair, *and without compensation for loss resulting from interruption of business or manufacture,* nor in any event for more than the interest of the insured, against all direct loss by fire, lightning and by removal from premises insured against in this policy, except as hereinafter provided, to the *property* described herein while located or contained as described in this policy * * *." (Emphasis added.)

An endorsement attached to the policy insures the insured "against all risks of direct physical loss of or to the *property* covered" (emphasis added) including, to a limit of $200,000.00, to "*[p]roperty* at locations owned, leased, operated, regularly used or specifically declared by the Insured" at "1531 Vernon, North Kansas City, Missouri." (Emphasis added.) Then, the policy goes on to cover the *personal property* of the type which plaintiff had bailed with Ar–Ka–Mo Sporting Goods, Inc. From the words and phrases used in the contract, viewed in its entirety, including its repeated use of the word "property" to define the subject matter of the insurance and specifically excluding business interruption and other insurance, the conclusion is that the policy in this case was meant to insure property rather than legal liability. The provisions of the contract, considered in the light of the whole contract, are unambiguous and clearly cover the losses pleaded in the first two counts of plaintiff's complaint. Judgment on the issue of liability only should therefore be entered on the first two counts in favor of plaintiff. It is admitted in the amended Standard Pretrial Order No. 2 that the particular risk is insured against; that the loss was suffered (although the amount thereof appears not to be admitted); and that demand for payment has been made and refused. Because the meaning of the contract, properly construed, is clear and certain, this cause is ripe for summary judgment on the issue of liability. See *Cepeda v. Swift & Co.* (C.A.8) 415 F.2d 1205. * * *

It is therefore

Adjudged that judgment be, and it is hereby, entered for plaintiff and against defendant on the issue of defendant's liability to plaintiff on the insurance policy of defendant numbered 1–00–19–31. * * *

Notes and Questions

1. *Reasonable Expectations.* Which approach is more faithful to the policy language? To the expectations of the bailor? Does the answer to the latter question depend so heavily on the factual context that there can be no "rule" about what the policy provision means?

2. *Duplicate Coverage?* If most bailors are likely to have some form of insurance coverage against losses occuring while property is in a bailee's possession, is there any need for the coverage the court in *Folger* found was provided? On the other hand, since insurers have been made aware of the arguable ambiguity in the phrase "legally liable," if they do not amend it do they have any cause for complaint when this phrase is interpreted against them? The issue continues to be litigated. See, e.g., *American Insurance Company v. Freeport Cold Storage Company,* 703 F.Supp. 1475 (D.Utah 1987).

E. EXCLUSIONS AND EXCEPTIONS

Standard fire and property insurance policies are structured in an unusual manner. They first contain a section describing the kinds of property and interests covered, including the dwelling or building that is the principal subject of coverage, any appurtenant structures, certain personal property, and limited damages resulting from loss of use of the property; they then indicate the "perils insured against"—essentially a list of the causes of damage to the insured property or interests that are or are not covered; and they also contain lists of "exclusions" and "conditions" that further limit coverage. The limitations on coverage contained in these different sections are many and varied; it would be an exercise in oversimplification to try to fit them all into a neat set of functional or conceptual categories. Moreover, a few exclusions, such as the "friendly-fire" exception that precludes coverage of damage caused by "friendly" as opposed to "hostile" fires, are implied rather than expressed. See R. Jerry, Understanding Insurance Law 354–59 (1987). In the case of homeowners coverage, an appreciation of the overall limitations on the coverage otherwise extended by the policy can best be gained by a careful reading of the Sample Homeowners Policy set out in Section A of this Chapter.

Consequently, this Section does not attempt a comprehensive analysis of the typical exclusions of coverage contained in fire and property insurance policies. Rather, the two issues that arise most frequently when these exclusions come into play are addressed. The first is the *problem of causation* in fire and property insurance: when is there coverage of a loss that has more than one cause, if losses resulting from one cause are excluded from coverage and losses resulting from the other cause are not excluded? The second is the *problem of increased risk:* what is the interplay between the effort to combat moral hazard that is at the heart of many of the common fire and property insurance exclusions, and the insured's legitimate expectation that even losses caused by ordinary carelessness or negligence are covered by the standard policy?

1. The Problem of Causation

When property insurance policies limit coverage because an otherwise covered loss results from an excluded cause, they create a problem that has troubled insurance law for decades. The problem is not only the substantive one of whether the loss is covered; it is how to think about the issue itself. Generations of lawyers and law students have engaged in the mental gymnastics necessary to grapple with causation problems in insurance, often without profit. Professor Patterson thought that it would be useful to distinguish excluded causes, excluded events, and excluded results. He proposed that the terms "exception," "exclusion," and "consequence" should be used to refer to these limitations, and that each should automatically carry its own legal effect. Thus, an insurer could assure that a limitation did or did not preclude coverage of all losses falling within its terms by designating it as an exception, exclusion, or consequence. See E. Patterson, Essentials of Insurance Law 226–71 (2d ed. 1957). Perhaps in part because of the great difficulty in practice of distinguishing causes, from events, from results, Patterson's proposal for use of uniform terminology carrying uniform legal effect never gained much support.

One method of at least thinking clearly about causation is to adopt Professor (now Judge) Keeton's distinction between *conclusive* and *inconclusive* exclusions. Keeton suggested that the issue in each case is whether the policy excludes coverage of losses resulting from a specified cause regardless of what other causes concur to produce the loss (a conclusive exclusion), or excludes coverage only if the loss does not also result from a cause that is covered (an inconclusive exclusion). For an updated version of Keeton's original formulation, see R. Keeton and A. Widiss, Insurance Law 547 (2d ed. 1988). Posing the question in this way does not take one any closer to an answer to any specific problem—that is, Keeton's distinction does not include a test for determining when an exclusion is conclusive or inconclusive—but articulating the distinction does help to clarify what is at issue in addressing causation problems.

A method of employing Keeton's distinction that is sometimes (caution: not always) helpful is to ask whether an exclusion of coverage has any exceptions to it. If there are no exceptions to the exclusion (either within the exclusion itself or in another part of the policy) then it is conclusive against coverage—any loss resulting from an excluded cause, and any excluded event or result, are outside coverage. On the other hand, if the exclusion is subject to exceptions, then it is inconclusive, and the question is whether the loss falls within one of the cause, event, or result exceptions to the exclusion. All this is unfortunately only a prelude to the harder work of grappling with actual exclusions and exceptions.

GRAHAM v. PUBLIC EMPLOYEES MUTUAL INSURANCE COMPANY

Supreme Court of Washington, 1983.
98 Wash.2d 533, 656 P.2d 1077.

DORE, Justice.

This appeal arises from a dispute which erupted between two insurance companies and their insureds following the May 18, 1980 explosion of Mt. St. Helens. The early pyroclastic flows from the eruption, along with hot ash and debris, began melting the snow and ice flanking the mountain and the broken glacial ice blocks within the Toutle River valley. This water, combined with torrential rains from the eruption cloud, existing ground water, water displaced from Spirit Lake, and ash and debris, created mudflows which began moving down the valley shortly after the eruption began. This process continued throughout the day of May 18.

At some point, a large mudflow developed in the upper reaches of the south fork of the valley from the Toutle and Talus glaciers. The mudflow gouged and filled the land into new forms as it moved, damaging or destroying many homes within its path. Approximately 10 hours after the eruption began, the appellants' homes, 20–25 miles away from Mt. St. Helens, were destroyed by a mudflow or a combination of mudflows preceded by water damage from flooding.

At the time of the eruption, homeowners insurance policies issued by Public Employees Mutual Insurance Company (hereafter PEMCO) to appellants Graham and Campbell, and a policy issued by Pennsylvania General Insurance Company (hereafter PGI) to appellants Fotheringill were in effect. All three policies provided in pertinent part as follows:

SECTION 1—EXCLUSIONS

We do not cover loss resulting directly or indirectly from:

2. Earth Movement. Direct loss by fire, explosion, theft, or breakage of glass or safety glazing materials resulting from earth movement is covered.

3. Water damage, meaning:

a. flood, * * *

Of the seven exclusions listed in the PEMCO policy, "earth movement" is the only one not specifically defined in the policy.

Prior to March 1980, PEMCO utilized insurance forms containing this exclusionary language:

This policy does not insure against loss:

* * *

2. caused by, resulting from, contributed to or aggravated by any earth movement, including but not limited to earthquake, volcanic eruption, landslide, mudflow, earth sinking, rising or shifting; unless loss by fire, explosion or breakage of glass constituting a part of the

building(s) covered hereunder, including glass in storm doors and storm windows, ensues, and this Company shall then be liable only for such ensuing loss, but this exclusion does not apply to loss by theft;

This language was deleted by PEMCO in an overall effort to simplify the policy language.

The homeowners filed claims against the insurance companies under their homeowners policies, but the insurance companies rejected their claims on the basis that the damage was excludable as "earth movement" in the form of mudflows or a combination of earth movement and water damage. The Grahams and Campbells then commenced this action against PEMCO in Cowlitz County Superior Court. On April 10, 1981, the trial court granted PEMCO's motion for summary judgment, dismissing the homeowners' complaint. Meanwhile, the Fotheringills instituted a suit against PGI in the same court. On April 29, 1981, the trial court, after hearing argument virtually identical to that of the Graham case, granted PGI's motion for summary judgment, dismissing the Fotheringills' complaint.

For the purpose of ruling on the summary judgment motion, the trial court assumed the movement of Mt. St. Helens to be an "explosion" within the terms of the insurance policies. The trial court noted this issue was a factual issue to be determined by a jury. We agree, as the true meaning of "explosion" in each case must be settled by the common experience of jurors. *Oroville Cordell Fruit Growers, Inc. v. Minneapolis Fire & Marine Ins. Co.*, 68 Wash.2d 117, 122, 411 P.2d 873 (1966). Because direct loss from an explosion resulting from earth movement is not excluded from coverage, the jury must also determine the factual issue of whether the earth movements were caused by the earthquakes and harmonic tremors which preceded the eruption.

If the jury determines the volcanic eruption was an explosion resulting from earth movement, it will then be necessary to reach the issue of whether the loss was a direct result of the eruption. The trial court held that the causation analysis of *Bruener v. Twin City Fire Ins. Co.*, 37 Wash.2d 181, 222 P.2d 833 (1950) precluded the plaintiffs' claims.

In *Bruener*, the insured's vehicle skidded on icy pavement and collided with an embankment. The insurance policy contained a collision exclusion to the comprehensive coverage. This court held that the loss was a "collision" for insurance purposes, reasoning as follows at 183–84, 222 P.2d 833:

> In tort cases, the rules of proximate cause are applied for the single purpose of fixing culpability, with which insurance cases are not concerned. For that purpose, the tort rules of proximate cause reach back of both the injury and the physical cause to fix the blame on those who created the situation in which the physical laws of nature operated. The happening of an accident does not, in itself, establish negligence and tort liability. The question is always, why did the injury occur.

Insurance cases are not concerned with why the injury occurred or the question of culpability, but only with the nature of the injury and how it happened.

The *Bruener* court expressly overruled *Ploe v. International Indem. Co.*, 128 Wash. 480, 223 P. 327 (1924), a case involving a driver who lost control of an automobile while rounding a curve on a mountain road. The car left the highway and traveled 25 feet before striking a stump along the road. Holding that the insurer was not liable, the court characterized the proximate cause of the accident to be the skidding of the car and not the collision with the stump. *Ploe*, at 483, 223 p. 327. The court reasoned that the destruction of the car was imminent from the time it left the highway, whether it struck the stump or not. In overruling the *Ploe* decision, the *Bruener* court, 37 Wash.2d at 185, 222 P.2d 833, replaced this proximate cause analysis with one of "direct, violent and efficient cause".

In *Dickson v. United States Fidelity & Guar. Co.*, 77 Wash.2d 785, 466 P.2d 515 (1970), the plaintiff's boom crane was insured under a policy which excluded coverage for latent defects. The boom crane was damaged when earth, collapsing onto an "H" beam that was being removed, caused a sudden stoppage of the hoist. This stoppage put an increase in load on the boom structure, causing a defective weld to break and the boom to collapse. This court affirmed the trial court's ruling that the earth collapse was the external and responsible cause of the failure of the weld and the collapse of the boom, stating at 793, 466 P.2d 515:

> The trial court regarded the collapsing earth as the external and responsible cause of the failure of the weld and the collapse of the boom. He did not thereby rule in contradiction to our rule on insurance causation, as set forth in *Bruener v. Twin City Fire Ins. Co.*, [37 Wash.2d 181, 222 P.2d 833 (1950)] wherein we stated that, for the purposes of insurance litigation, the responsible cause of a loss is that which is the "direct, violent and efficient cause of the damage."

In reviewing the foregoing cases, we conclude the immediate physical cause analysis is no longer appropriate and should be discarded. The *Bruener* rule is an anomaly, inconsistent with the rule in the majority of other jurisdictions.[1] We have defined "proximate cause" as that cause "which, in a natural and continuous sequence, unbroken by any new, independent cause, produces the event, and without which that event would not have occurred". *Stoneman v. Wick Constr. Co.*, 55 Wash.2d 639, 643, 349 P.2d 215 (1960). Where a peril specifically insured against sets other causes in motion which, in an unbroken sequence and connection between the act and final loss, produce the

1. 18 G. Couch, *Insurance* § 74:693 (2d ed. 1968) states the majority rule as:

"When loss is sustained by the insured it is necessary that the loss be proximately, rather than remotely, caused by the peril insured against."

result for which recovery is sought, the insured peril is regarded as the "proximate cause" of the entire loss.   *   *   *

It is the efficient or predominant cause which sets into motion the chain of events producing the loss which is regarded as the proximate cause, not necessarily the last act in a chain of events. *Dickson, supra,* 77 Wash.2d at 794, 466 P.2d 515; 5 J. Appleman, *supra,* at 309–11; *Frontis v. Milwaukee Ins. Co.,* 156 Conn. 492, 242 A.2d 749, 753 (1968); 43 Am.Jur.2d, *supra,* at § 1182. The mechanical simplicity of the *Bruener* rule does not allow inquiry into the intent and expectations of the parties to the insurance contract. *Sears, Roebuck & Co. v. Hartford Accident & Indem. Co.,* 50 Wash.2d 443, 313 P.2d 347 (1957). We now specifically overrule the *Bruener* case.[2]

The determination of proximate cause is well established in this state. As a general rule, the question of proximate cause is for the jury, and it is only when the facts are undisputed and the inferences therefrom are plain and incapable of reasonable doubt or difference of opinion that it may be a question of law for the court. *Bordynoski v. Bergner,* 97 Wash.2d 335, 644 P.2d 1173 (1982); *Smith v. Acme Paving Co.,* 16 Wash.App. 389, 558 P.2d 811 (1976); *Mathers v. Stephens,* 22 Wash.2d 364, 370, 156 P.2d 227 (1945).

In the present case, the mudflows which destroyed the appellants' homes would not have occurred without the eruption of Mt. St. Helens. The eruption displaced water from Spirit Lake, and set into motion the melting of the snow and ice flanking the mountain. A jury could reasonably determine the water displacement, melting snow and ice and mudflows were mere manifestations of the eruption, finding that the eruption of Mt. St. Helens was the proximate cause of the damage to appellants' homes. This issue is not a question of law but a question of fact, to be determined by the trier of facts.

CONCLUSION

The *Bruener* decision is hereby overruled. We remand to the trial court for a jury determination of whether the movement of Mt. St. Helens was an "explosion" within the terms of the insurance policies; whether that "explosion" was preceded by earth movement, and whether appellants' damages were proximately caused by the eruption of Mt. St. Helens on May 18, 1980.   *   *   *

BRACHTENBACH, Chief Justice (dissenting).

In its ardour to explain the relationship of proximate cause to insurance law the majority strays from the basic issues presented by this case. First, what are the express terms of the policy? Second, are

---

2. In *Frontier Lanes v Canadian Indem. Co.,* 26 Wash.App. 342, 346, 613 P.2d 166 (1980), the Court of Appeals read *Bruener v. Twin City Fire Ins. Co.,* 37 Wash.2d 181, 222 P.2d 833 (1950) to require that a loss could be attributed to vandalism or malicious mischief only if "the immediate physical cause of that loss was the vandalistic or malicious act itself or an instrumentality employed directly by the wrongdoer to carry out that act". We decline to follow the *Frontier* analysis insofar as it is inconsistent with our holding in the present case.

any of those terms ambiguous? Third, if the terms of the policy are unambiguous, would application of those terms result in coverage? The majority fails to apply such a step by step analysis. Consequently, it neglects a clear provision of the policy that requires that we affirm the trial court's grant of summary judgment. I therefore dissent.

This court has long recognized that insurance policies are private contracts. *See Sears, Roebuck & Co. v. Hartford Accident & Indem. Co.,* 50 Wash.2d 443, 449, 313 P.2d 347 (1957). As a private contractor, the insurer is ordinarily permitted to limit its liability unless inconsistent with public policy or some statutory provision. *Mutual of Enumclaw Ins. Co. v. Wiscomb,* 97 Wash.2d 203, 210, 643 P.2d 441 (1982). Thus the court's initial task here is to identify fully the terms of this contract. Here the homeowner's policy provided for coverage, against *inter alia,* fire and explosion. In addition, however, the policy contained an exclusion for earth movement which in turn contained its own exception. That exclusion and exception provide:

We do not cover loss resulting directly or indirectly from:

> 2. Earth movement. Direct loss by fire, explosion, theft, or breakage of glass or safety glazing materials resulting from earth movement is covered.

The next step is to determine whether any of these provisions are ambiguous. Although this issue was raised by the parties the majority chooses to ignore it and proceeds instead to analyze the case as if it were a question of proximate cause. It then determines that that issue is a question of fact for the jury and reverses summary judgment.

The obvious flaw in the majority's opinion is that it improperly applies the term of the policy to the chain of events. The facts of this case reveal the following possible chain of events which should result in a denial of coverage regardless of proximate cause analysis. As suggested by the majority, on May 18, 1980, earthquakes and moving lava caused earth to move, which caused an eruption (explosion?), which caused earth movement in the form of mudflows. The majority concludes that the explosion operates to exclude the initial earth movement which preceded the eruption but that the exception for explosion contained in the exclusion brings the incident back within the potential terms of the policy. But if that result is correct, the majority neglects a necessary additional inquiry—that is—should the earth movement exclusion be applied a second time to exclude coverage for mudflows? This last question presents strictly a legal issue involving the proper interpretation of policy terms. I submit that the only logical resolution of this issue is that the earth movement exclusion must be considered a second time. This answer requires, unfortunately, that we deny coverage. To do otherwise, however, would be to use proximate cause analysis to circumvent the clear terms of the policy. In addition, the majority appears to stop its inquiry at a point on the causation chain where coverage would be provided. The majority's analysis requires

that we ignore clear provisions in the insurance contract. This we
cannot do. As we have said in the past:

> Since an insurance policy is merely a written contract between
> an insurer and the insured, courts cannot rule out of the
> contract any language which the parties thereto have put into
> it; cannot revise the contract under the theory of construing it;
> and neither abstract justice nor any rule of construction can
> create a contract for the parties which they did not make for
> themselves.

Sears, Roebuck & Co. v. Hartford Accident & Indem. Co., 50 Wash.2d
443, 449, 313 P.2d 347 (1957).

The interpretation I suggest is necessary to give effect to the
expectations that the parties had at the time they contracted for
insurance coverage. I would therefore deny coverage and affirm the
trial court.

Notes and Questions

1. *Difference of Opinion.* Note that the court believed the insured's claim posed three questions: a) whether the eruption was
caused by earth movement; b) if so, whether the eruption nonetheless
constituted an explosion; and c) if so, whether the plaintiff's loss
qualified as "[d]irect loss by * * * explosion * * * resulting from
earth movement * * *" Did the court hold that the exclusion of
coverage for losses resulting from earth movement was, in effect,
conclusive or inconclusive? Did the dissent disagree with this conclusion? If not, exactly what was its disagreement with the majority? Do
you think that the last step in the *Ploe-to-Bruener-to-Graham* sequence
merely reflects yet another change of the judicial mind, or the exigency
of the problems the State of Washington faced after the Mt. St. Helens
disaster?

2. *Proximate Cause.* Given the complexity of insurance policy
language (even the so-called simplified language at issue in *Graham*),
how sensible is it to devise rules of interpretation that require factual
findings from juries regarding such issues as proximate cause? If the
central issue in the case was whether the proximate cause of the
destruction of plaintiffs' homes was an explosion or a mudflow, why
wasn't the insurer entitled to a directed verdict? In *Garvey v. State
Farm Fire & Casualty Company,* 48 Cal.3d 395, 257 Cal.Rptr. 292, 770
P.2d 704 (1989), the Supreme Court of California agreed with the
Graham court that a proximate cause test was appropriate, but held
that for purposes of first-party property insurance there can be only
one proximate cause of a loss. If there can be more than one proximate
cause of a loss, does a proximate cause test for causation have the effect
of discarding the "directly or indirectly" language of the exclusion in
the *Graham* policy?

3. *The Purpose of the Exclusion.* In order to interpret the policy
in *Graham,* would it have been helpful to know why the Earth Move-

ment exclusion was included in the policy? If (as seems likely) the explanation is the insurer's desire to combat adverse selection and moral hazard, but that the phrasing of the exceptions to the exclusion is essentially an exercise in line-drawing, has this explanation advanced the inquiry any?

4. *Solving the Problem.* Consider the language of Section I— Exclusions, paragraphs 1 and 1(b) in the Sample Homeowners Policy. Does this language solve the problem facing the court in *Graham?*

5. *Causation in Auto Insurance.* The other major area in which causation issues arise involves insurance on another kind of property— motor vehicles. There are two different but to a limited extent overlapping forms of such automobile property insurance: *collision* and *comprehensive* coverage. Collision insurance covers losses caused by collision, with certain specified causes of collision such as fire, theft, and windstorm excluded. Comprehensive insurance covers loss other than by collision. Ordinarily an insured is covered by both forms of insurance. But when she is covered by only one, the kinds of causation questions the court in *Graham* referred to tend to arise.

For example, suppose that insured has collision but no comprehensive coverage, her vehicle catches fire, and (as a result) collides with a tree. If the exclusion of coverage for loss caused by fire is conclusive, and the fire is the (direct, indirect, or proximate cause—depending on rule governing causation in force in the jurisdiction) then there is no coverage. Similarly, if the exclusion is inconclusive, then there is coverage. Finally, even if the exclusion of coverage of loss by fire is conclusive, under the *Graham* rule it is probably a jury question whether fire was the proximate cause of the loss. Note once again, however, that this method of analysis does not move the inquiry any closer to a determination of whether there is coverage for this hypothetical loss; it merely describes a (comparatively) clear way to start asking questions that will lead to that determination. The nature of collision and comprehensive coverage for damage to motor vehicles is addressed in more detail in Chapter Eight.

2. The Problem of Increased Risk

The standard fire or property insurance policy is intended not only to cover purely fortuitous losses, but also in some measure to cover those resulting from the insured's own failure to protect the insured property as carefully as might have been possible. The clearest evidence of this intention is the absence of any general exclusion in standard policies of coverage for harm caused by the insured's own negligence. There are, however, exclusions of coverage for harm caused intentionally by the insured, and for harm that results from the failure of the insured to use reasonable means to protect the property once loss has begun. See, e.g., Sample Homeowners Policy, Section I— Exclusions, paragraphs 1(e) and (h). Thus, although the insured is covered even if he negligently starts a fire that destroys his property, neither the results of the insured's arson nor of fiddling while his home burns are covered.

There is an irreducible minimum of tension, however, between the desire of the insurer to combat moral hazard and the ordinary insured's desire to purchase coverage against certain losses caused by his own insufficient care. The insurance solution has been to place no general limitation on coverage of losses caused in whole or in part by such insufficient care, but to exclude losses caused by or occurring during certain specified risk-increasing actions. Two of the most common such exclusions figure in the following two cases.

COMMERCIAL UNION INSURANCE COMPANY v. TAYLOR

Court of Appeals of Georgia, 1983.
169 Ga.App. 177, 312 S.E.2d 177.

QUILLIAN, Presiding Judge.

This appeal is from judgment for the insureds—Huey and Larry Taylor, d/b/a Taylor's Farm Supply, against their insurer—Commercial Union Insurance Company, for recovery of a loss sustained by fire. The Taylors, father and son, were the owners of Taylor's Farm Supply—a partnership which sold various merchandise used by farmers. Huey—the father, was retired and did not work at the store. Larry ran the business with the help of Steve Taylor—his nephew, and two other employees who loaded and unloaded merchandise.

Larry Taylor was absent from the warehouse one day on a selling trip when the fire sprinkler began leaking and damaged some feed. Steve turned off the master valve in the basement to prevent further damage but did not tell Larry or Huey Taylor what he had done. About two weeks later a fire occurred and Steve recalled that he had turned off the sprinkler system and told Larry. Commercial Union denied the Taylors' claim for damages as a result of the fire on the basis that the insurance policy provided the insurer would not be liable for a loss where "the hazard was increased by any means within the control or knowledge of the insured * * *" The Taylors were also given a reduced rate because of the fire sprinkler system, and in consideration for such rate were required to exercise due diligence in maintaining all equipment installed for detection, prevention and extinguishment of fire, and notice of any impairment in or suspension of such protective services, within the knowledge of the named insured.

This action was tried before the trial judge, without a jury, and Commercial Union appeals judgment for the insureds. *Held:*

1. The appellant alleges the trial court failed to make a sufficient finding of fact on whether the loss resulted because the hazard was increased by a means within the control and knowledge of the insureds. We cannot agree. In *Commercial Union Fire Ins. Co. v. Capouano*, 55 Ga.App. 566, 190 S.E. 815, this Court construed the term "control and

knowledge" and held that "control" presupposes knowledge and that it would be unreasonable to hold that a person had control of a thing of which he had no knowledge. Thus, in effect, finding that there could be no "control" without "knowledge." The trial court found that "[n]either named insured [Huey or Larry Taylor] knew the sprinkler had been turned off until after the fire had started." "There was no evidence that the employee turned the sprinkler off with the authority of any named insured ∗ ∗ ∗ One of the named insureds visually inspected the sprinkler system on a periodic basis. There is absolutely no indication of any wrongdoing on the part of any named insured. The Court finds that the insureds have acted with due diligence in maintaining the sprinkler system." We hold that these findings of fact on the issue of the increase in hazard being within the control and knowledge of the insureds to be sufficient for a determination of this issue.

2. It is contended that the court's finding that the insureds acted with due diligence in maintaining the sprinkler system is not supported by the evidence. Larry Taylor testified that he examined the sprinkler system "every two or three days ∗ ∗ ∗" He had a service contract on the sprinkler system but his insurance agent let the contract expire about a year prior to the fire. The issue of due diligence is for the finder of fact. *R.L. Kimsey Cotton Co. v. Pacific Ins. Co.*, 224 Ga. 249, 161 S.E.2d 315. The trial court's finding is authorized by the evidence and was not clearly erroneous. *Allen v. Cobb Heating, etc. Co.*, 158 Ga. App. 209, 211, 279 S.E.2d 505.

3. The third enumeration of error argues that the conclusion of the trial court that the insureds had no knowledge that the sprinkler system was turned off was contrary to Georgia law and was based on an erroneous legal theory. Appellant argues that Steve Taylor was "the general agent for his employer since he was authorized to run the store while the employers were out," and that knowledge of the agent is knowledge of the principal—the named insureds. Hence, since Steve Taylor turned off the master valve in the fire sprinkler system, this knowledge was imputed to his principal as a matter of law (OCGA § 10–6–58; formerly Code Ann. § 4–309), and knowledge of the lack of a sprinkler system increased the hazard and with the concomitant failure to notify the insurer of the impaired sprinkler system suspended the policy.

Appellant's law is correct but his conclusion is without factual foundation in the record. Steve Taylor testified: "I was a clerk; just waiting on customers mostly." He was one of several employees. The store was divided up into three warehouses, and a retail section in which Steve Taylor was the sole employee other than Larry Taylor when he was there. Larry Taylor said that one of their drivers worked some in the retail store when he was not driving. The other employees worked in the warehouse section of the store.

Larry Taylor described Steve's duties as "when a customer came in to wait on them * * *" However, he maintained two bank accounts for the store and "when I was out somebody would come by and want a bill paid and he had the authority to pay it. Q. So, he did have authority to pay bills, and take in money, and generally to run the store while you were out? A. Yes, sir." The record shows that Larry and Steve were the two who ran the retail section of the store and when Larry was out Steve was left to run the store and if someone had a bill that needed immediate payment—Steve could write a check to pay that bill. This does not show general agency—at most it shows a special agency to pay a store bill when presented in the absence of the owner. See 1 EGL 449–450, Agency, §§ 4, 5; 2A C.J.S. 587, Agency, § 21. In speaking of the distinction between master-servant and principal-agent, Mechem found the "distinguishing characteristic of the agent is that he represents his principal contractually." Mechem, Outlines of the Law of Agency (4th Ed. § 12). Appellant, in claiming general agency, is attempting to show that Steve Taylor had the authority to manage the store in the absence of the owner. Mechem stated that the authority "to manage [a] business" presumptively "will include the authority to do all things which are necessary and proper to be done in carrying on the business in the usual and accustomed way and which the principal would usually do if he were managing the affair in person." Mechem, Outlines of the Law of Agency (4th Ed. § 67). We should note that the present case illustrates no delegated authority to act for the business except to pay bills presented in the absence of the owner. There was no authorization to purchase, to contract, to hire or fire, or even supervise other personnel.

Steve Taylor was asked by appellant's counsel: "So, you were, in essence, in charge of the hands in the back? A. No, I wasn't in charge of them * * * Q. But you directed them as to what to do? A. Well, I handed them the order." His deposition showed he was "[n]ot actually in charge * * * I was the only one there * * * As far as the business in general being in charge, I wasn't in charge of the business; no, sir." A general allegation of agency must yield to specific facts which in themselves negative the agency. *Community Theatres Co. v. Bentley,* 88 Ga.App. 303, 305, 76 S.E.2d 632. As pointed out in *Stewart v. Ga. Mutual Ins. Co.,* 159 Ga.App. 91, 92, 282 S.E.2d 728, "proof of agency can be shown * * * by circumstantial evidence, apparent relations, and conduct of the parties." However, "[i]t has long been the Georgia rule that one who is a party to the [alleged] relationship (the principal or agent) may testify as a fact as to the existence or nonexistence of the relationship and that such testimony would not be subject to the objection that the statement was a conclusion or the ultimate fact." *Salters v. Pugmire Lincoln–Mercury,* 124 Ga.App. 414, 415, 184 S.E.2d 56 * * * The court found Steve Taylor to be an employee, and both named insureds to be without knowledge that the sprinkler system had been turned off. These findings are supported by the evidence of record.

In *Queens Ins. Co. v. Van Giesen,* 136 Ga. 741, 72 S.E. 41, the Supreme Court found that an insurance policy was not voided when an employee brought a can of gasoline onto the premises without the knowledge of the insured even though the policy contained a provision that "it should be void if gasoline were kept, used, or allowed on the premises * * *" The knowledge of the employee was not imputed to the insured where the prohibited act was done without his knowledge or complicity—directly or indirectly. The same facts obtain in the instant case. Accord: *Commercial Union Fire Ins. Co. v. Capouano,* 55 Ga.App. 566, 190 S.E. 815, supra. This enumeration is without merit.

4. The remaining enumerations of error contend the evidence admitted at trial does not support the findings of the court. We do not agree. The trial court found that there was no violation of the policy's Fire Protection Clause and Protective Safeguard Clause. Those findings are supported by the evidence of record.

Judgment affirmed.

SMITH v. LUMBERMEN'S MUTUAL INSURANCE COMPANY

Court of Appeals of Michigan, 1980.
101 Mich.App. 78, 300 N.W.2d 457.

QUINNELL, Judge.

Plaintiff filed a complaint and moved for a declaratory judgment that defendant Lumbermen's Mutual Insurance Company (hereinafter Lumbermen's) was liable to him under an insurance policy for damages to a dwelling caused by the freezing of boiler and water pipes. Lumbermen's denied liability and also moved for declaratory judgment. The trial court granted plaintiff's motion for declaratory judgment. Lumbermen's now appeals as of right.

This case comes to this Court on stipulated facts. Defendant Lynas, the land contract vendor of the subject dwelling, agreed to tender possession to plaintiff on or before January 9, 1977. As part of the agreement, Lynas was permitted to remain in possession of the subject premises for 60 days after closing or until tender of possession was accomplished by turning over the keys to the premises. An appropriate proration of the occupancy charges was made. Also, as part of the agreement, plaintiff was to obtain insurance coverage on the subject property. Plaintiff obtained a policy of insurance from Lumbermen's naming both himself and Lynas as insureds. The premium was paid entirely by the plaintiff.

The closing of the deal took place at the hospital where defendant Lynas was then a patient. In late November, 1976, Lynas returned to the subject premises. Sometime during the first week of December, Lynas moved into an apartment for which he had taken out a lease. However, many of his household items and personal possessions remained within the subject dwelling. On December 6, 1976, Lynas notified the Marathon Oil Company that "the house has been sold, please discontinue service."

In mid-December, 1976, plaintiff's mother was informed by the realtor handling the sale of the possibility that plaintiff could move into the dwelling prior to January 10, 1977. However, no tender of possession by turning over the keys was accomplished.

On December 22, 1976, Lynas fell in his apartment and was admitted again to a hospital for treatment. Between December 25, 1976, and January 9, 1977, while Lynas was in the hospital, the supply of oil to the premises became depleted, rendering no heat to the dwelling and resulting in the water pipes freezing and bursting, causing extensive damage. On January 9, 1977, plaintiff entered the premises after Lynas tendered the keys to the premises. The damage had been discovered earlier that day by Lynas' daughter when she was there to remove Lynas' remaining property.

On January 11, 1977, plaintiff received $1,200, being the total amount escrowed for rent at the time of the closing. Following plaintiff's notification of loss, Lumbermen's denied coverage for the damages, maintaining that the premises were "vacant or unoccupied" within the meaning of the insurance policy.

The portion of the insurance policy upon which Lumbermen's relies provided under the general heading of "PERILS INSURED AGAINST" that:

> "This policy insures against direct loss to the property covered by the following perils as defined and limited herein:
>
>   *   *   *
>
> "17. *Freezing of plumbing, heating and air conditioning systems and domestic appliances,* but excluding loss caused by and resulting from freezing while the building covered is vacant or unoccupied, unless the insured shall have exercised due diligence with respect to maintaining heat in the building, or unless the plumbing and heating systems and domestic appliances have been drained and the water supply shut off during such vacancy or unoccupancy."

The trial court found that this provision was ambiguous and resorted to rules of construction in resolving the matter against Lumbermen's. We agree with the lower court that the provision in question is ambiguous. Neither "vacant" nor "unoccupied" is defined in the insurance policy. There exists a continuum of possible uses between the two obvious points at which we can say that the clause in the policy does and does not apply. On the one hand, where residents of a house are physically inside the dwelling at the very moment of the incident resulting in the loss, it is apparent that the building is not "vacant or unoccupied". On the other hand, where the building stands totally vacant, devoid of all signs of human habitation when the loss is suffered, it is equally clear that the building is "vacant or unoccupied". A plethora of other possible uses is manifest, however, and the quality or extent of any given use may not readily lend itself to categorization as either vacant or full, occupied or unoccupied.

If there is any doubt or ambiguity in a contract of insurance which has been drafted by the insurer, it must be construed most favorably to the insured. *Gorham v. Peerless Life Ins. Co.,* 368 Mich. 335, 118 N.W.2d 306 (1962); *Foremost Life Ins. Co. v. Waters,* 88 Mich.App. 599, 604, 278 N.W.2d 688 (1979). This rule of construction has particular force where contract exclusions and exceptions are under consideration. *Whittaker Corp. v. Michigan Mutual Liability Co.,* 58 Mich.App. 34, 36, 227 N.W.2d 1 (1975); *Kalamazoo Aviation, Inc. v. Royal Globe Ins. Co.,* 70 Mich.App. 267, 270, 245 N.W.2d 754 (1976), *lv. den.* 399 Mich. 871 (1977). This does not mean, however, that the insured must always prevail if there is an ambiguity. It is still the duty of the courts to determine the true intent of the parties insofar as this is possible. A patently unreasonable interpretation of a contractual ambiguity will not be employed merely to allow the insured to recover his losses. *American Fellowship Mutual Ins. Co. v. Ins. Co. of North America,* 90 Mich.App. 633, 636, 282 N.W.2d 425 (1979).

Lumbermen's contends that past decisions of the Michigan Supreme Court preclude the possibility of our construing the clause in dispute in plaintiff's favor. In *Bonenfant v. American Fire Ins. Co.,* 76 Mich. 653, 659, 43 N.W. 682 (1889), the Supreme Court held that: "Occupancy implies an actual use of the house as a dwelling place." Lumbermen's points to the fact that nobody was using the house as a dwelling at the time the pipes froze and burst and concludes that it was not occupied. We disagree. The proposition that occupancy implies an actual use of the premises as a dwelling house first found its way into Michigan jurisprudence in *Shackelton v. Sun Fire Office of London, England,* 55 Mich. 288, 292, 21 N.W. 343 (1884). However, in *Shackelton,* as in the instant case, the house in question was not being used as a dwelling as this term is normally used at the time of the loss. In *Shackelton,* the insured had rented the premises to tenants who had moved out of the house. She decided to occupy the premises herself. Toward this end, she moved furniture and goods into the building and readied it by cleaning. As her husband was ill and could only be left alone for short periods of time, the insured did not stay any nights at the house. The house ultimately burned while the insured was on business in northeastern Michigan before she ever began actually living in the house. Nonetheless, the Supreme Court ruled that the policy was still in force. Although occupancy may imply an actual use of the house as a dwelling place, circumstances may arise in which an insured can be said to be "occupying" a building without continuous possession.

Lumbermen's also relies on *Richards v. Continental Ins. Co. of the City of New York,* 83 Mich. 508, 47 N.W. 350 (1890). In *Richards,* however, the insured had instructed his tenant to vacate the house, which the tenant did. Neither the landlord nor any other person was moving in to take his place. This is not the situation here where plaintiff intended to move into the house when defendant Lynas completely vacated it.

The lower court relied upon *Krajenke v. Preferred Mutual Ins. Co.*, 68 Mich.App. 211, 242 N.W.2d 70 (1976), in reaching its conclusion that the policy remained in full force and effect. In *Krajenke,* the insured's loss came at a time when she was on one of her numerous extended vacations. We held that her temporary physical absence from the residence did not render the house "vacant or unoccupied". As Lumbermen's notes, *Krajenke* can be distinguished from the case at bar. However, in our opinion the similarities between the cases are more important than the differences.

Although defendant Lynas did not intend to return and live in the subject dwelling, plaintiff most assuredly did. Thus, at all times there was a mere temporary physical absence from the house which did not render it unoccupied. Lumbermen's knew at the time that it issued the policy that the subject dwelling was being sold under land contract and that the individuals who occupied the house would change. In many respects, what occurred here is just what happens when rental property is [transferred] between tenants. As 43 Am.Jur.2d, Insurance, § 951, p. 900 states:

> "The great majority of courts have adopted, as to rented property, a liberal construction of provisions against the property becoming vacant and unoccupied. They hold that it is impliedly contemplated by the parties to the contract that any temporary vacancy caused by or incident to a change or removal of tenants is not within the vacancy or unoccupancy clause, and that a reasonable time will be allowed the insured to obtain other tenants before the forfeiture of the policy may be effected. Following this principle, it has been held that a provision avoiding a policy of insurance if the buildings become unoccupied does not apply where a tenant has commenced moving and part of his goods have been taken away and part remain on the insured premises, or where the buildings are vacant for a few days pending a change of tenants. It has likewise been held that where an outgoing tenant has partially removed from the insured premises and the incoming tenant has partially occupied such premises, or where the owner has commenced renovating the premises for the incoming tenant, the premises are not vacant or unoccupied." (Footnotes omitted.)

By analogy, it seems to us that, where the insurer is aware that the dwelling is being sold on a land contract, it is "impliedly contemplated by the parties to the (insurance) contract that any temporary vacancy caused by or incident to a change" to allow the old residents to leave the premises and the new residents to arrive is not within the vacancy clause, absent a clear expression of this intent in the insurance policy.

Having concluded that the premises were not "vacant or unoccupied", we need not address the "due diligence" question.

We review actions in the nature of declaratory judgments *de novo* on the record. We will not reverse the findings of the lower court unless they are clearly erroneous. *McComb v. McComb,* 9 Mich.App. 70, 74, 155 N.W.2d 860 (1967). In the case at bar, no error was committed.

Affirmed.

BASHARA, Presiding Judge (dissenting).

I respectfully dissent. As stated in the majority opinion, "occupancy implies an actual use of the house as a dwelling place". *Bonenfant v. American Fire Ins. Co.,* 76 Mich. 653, 659, 43 N.W. 682 (1889). Although the courts have held that a temporary absence for business, vacation, or illness does not render the premises "unoccupied", the case at bar is distinguishable. There was clearly a permanent discontinuance of residence by Mr. Lynas without tender of possession to the plaintiff. Until possession was given to plaintiff, the home was "vacant" and "unoccupied" within the meaning of the insurance contract. *Richards v. Continental Ins. Co. of the City of New York,* 83 Mich. 508, 47 N.W. 350 (1890).

However, my conclusion is not based on the occupancy requirement alone. Another provision of the insurance agreement reads:

"Conditions suspending or restricting insurance. Unless otherwise provided writing added hereto this Company shall not be liable for loss occurring

"(a) while the hazard is increased by any means within the control or knowledge of the insured * * *."

Mr. Lynas, a named insured, deliberately informed the fuel supplier to discontinue service in the dead of winter. Such action on the part of the insured, which surely caused the pipes to freeze and the resulting damages, acted to relieve the defendant from liability. Therefore, even if the premises were "occupied", it is my feeling that the trial court should have rejected plaintiff's motion for declaratory judgment. Plaintiff's recourse is properly against Mr. Lynas.

I would reverse and remand for entry of judgment in favor of defendant.

Notes and Questions

1. *The Modern Version of Warranties?* Both the increase-of-hazard and vacancy clauses are designed to deal with problems that would once have involved warranties. In what ways is the modern approach superior to the use of warranties? In what ways would the use of warranties, as modified by statutes requiring that breach increase the risk insured, be superior?

2. *Vacant or Vacated?* The freezing clause in the policy at issue in *Smith* excluded loss while the building was vacant *or* unoccupied. The implication of the clause is that the occurrence of either condition suffices to avoid coverage. Are the two conditions merely proxies for the same problem—the absence of a party who will protect the premises from damage or something more? Suppose that the insured removes all furnishings and moves into another apartment, forgetting to close his windows. That evening the temperature drops and the pipes freeze. Is coverage excluded?

3. *Increase-of-Hazard.* Even if the premises are not vacant or unoccupied within the meaning of the freezing clause—on the facts of *Smith* or the above hypothetical—should the increase-of-hazard clause quoted by the dissent apply? Can you construct an analysis of these two exclusions which reads them as modern-day warranties that automatically incorporate an increase-of-risk requirement into them? Should they be read to require not only increase of risk, but contribution to loss?

4. *Fire Plus Homeowners.* Did the court in *Taylor* convert the word "or" in the phrase "within the control or knowledge" of the insured into the word "and?" In view of the purpose of the clause, do you think that this interpretation was appropriate? The increase-of-hazard clause is standard in basic fire insurance. The clause is notably absent from the Sample Homeowners Policy, but the basic fire insurance policy often is attached to a Homeowners Policy. The result may be that, at least for some purposes, an additional policy produces less coverage. The increase-of-hazard clause generally is interpreted according to a rule of reason. Minor and temporary increases that might be expected as part of normal uses of the property do not trigger the clause; prolonged increases that pose more than minimal hazard usually do trigger it. See, e.g., *Good v. Continental Insurance Company,* 277 S.C. 569, 291 S.E.2d 198 (1982), in which the court held that installation of an illegal still in a false closet constituted an increase-of-hazard.

5. *Temporary Suspension during Vacancy.* In addition to the vacancy exclusion in the freezing clause, many policies contain a general condition suspending coverage while the property is "vacant or unoccupied beyond a period of sixty consecutive days * * *." See, e.g., *Future Realty, Inc. v. Fireman's Fund Insurance Company,* 315 F.Supp. 1109 (S.D.Miss.1970). Should such a clause and the increase-of-hazard clause be read together so that no vacancy of less than sixty days suspends coverage under the latter?

F. THE MEASURE OF RECOVERY

The principle of indemnity, together with the insurer's own interest in combating moral hazard, requires that recovery for a loss to property not produce a net gain for the insured who suffers the loss. A number of limitations on recovery are directed at this goal. All policies contain a limit on the amount insured, set with an eye toward the value of the insured property. In addition, standard policies indicate that coverage is provided only to the extent of an insured's interest, and that there is coverage only for the actual cash value of the property damaged or destroyed at the time of loss. See R. Jerry, Understanding Insurance Law 438 (1987). For provisions governing these points, see the Sample Homeowners Policy, Section I—Conditions, paragraphs (1) and (3). The meaning of the phrase *actual cash value* that figures prominently in the measure of recovery has been the subject of considerable judicial interpretation.

ELBERON BATHING COMPANY, INC. v. AMBASSADOR INSURANCE COMPANY, INC.

Supreme Court of New Jersey, 1978.
77 N.J. 1, 389 A.2d 439.

CONFORD, P.J.A.D. (temporarily assigned).

The principal question on this appeal concerns the valuation methods to be used in ascertaining the "actual cash value" of a partial loss under the Standard Form Fire Insurance Policy, *N.J.S.A.* 17:36–5.15 *et seq.* We are also required to determine whether failure to apply the appropriate standard is sufficient cause to set aside an appraisal award. The appeal arises in the context of a judgment in the Law Division in favor of the insured plaintiffs in the amount of $52,000 for excess coverage based on a $77,000 appraisement minus $25,000 primary coverage (on another policy) for a loss due to fire. The Appellate Division affirmed in an unreported opinion.

Defendant, Ambassador Insurance Company, issued a fire insurance policy to plaintiffs, Elberon Bathing Co., Inc. and Elberon Bathing Club, to indemnify them against loss by fire to club facilities and contents situated in Long Branch. The $125,000 policy represented excess coverage over a $25,000 primary policy issued plaintiffs by Great Southwest Fire Insurance Company.

On January 8, 1975, while the policy was in effect, plaintiff's bathing club was damaged by fire to an amount "greatly in excess of $25,000." Great Southwest promptly paid Elberon the $25,000. However, plaintiffs and defendant were unable to adjust plaintiffs' covered loss under the excess policy. Pursuant to the terms of the policy and an "agreement for submission to appraisers," plaintiffs and defendant each appointed an appraiser. The appraisers were, in turn, to select a disinterested umpire. However, they were unable to reach agreement thereon. Plaintiffs then filed a complaint and an order to show cause requesting the court to appoint an umpire pursuant to the terms of the policy.[1] The court appointed an umpire.

---

1. The complaint requested appointment of an umpire "in accordance with the provisions of *N.J.S.A.* 2A:24–5," the Arbitration and Award Act. The appropriate statute governing the appointment of the umpire under a fire policy is *N.J.S.A.* 17:36–5.20.

Shortly thereafter the appraisers and umpire were to inspect the insured premises which had already been repaired. According to affidavits of the umpire and defendant's appraiser, the umpire and plaintiffs' appraiser believed that their role was merely to determine the replacement cost of the damaged property. The umpire and plaintiffs' appraiser determined the actual cash value of the entire property to be $180,000 and the amount of fire loss to the property to total $77,000. This consisted of $8,500 for damage to personal property and $68,500 for pure replacement cost of the realty destroyed. Defendant's appraiser refused to sign the award.

Plaintiffs sought entry of judgment on the appraisement. Defendant answered, denying the finality of the award on the basis of its contention that the umpire had not heard all the evidence nor considered all matters submitted to him. It further disclaimed liability because of Elberon's alleged fraud in submitting a claim which it knew was substantially in excess of the actual cost to it to repair the damage. Defendant demanded that the award be vacated, and requested a jury trial on all the issues. In addition, defendant separately sought discovery of various "loss estimates" prepared by plaintiffs' appraiser and gave notice, pursuant to the policy, of defendant's desire to examine plaintiff's documents and representatives.

The trial judge heard oral argument and reviewed the pleadings and affidavits. He stated that the appraisers could properly determine the replacement cost was the appropriate measure of the actual loss recoverable under the policy. He also found that there was no manifest mistake justifying setting aside the award. After deduction for the primary insurance coverage judgment was entered for plaintiff for $52,000. The Appellate Division, agreeing with the trial judge that under the appropriate narrow standard of review "the facts in the case do not dictate a basis for vacating the award * * *," affirmed. We granted certification. 74 N.J. 284, 377 A.2d 688 (1977).

I.

Defendant argues that an award based on replacement cost without deduction for depreciation contravenes the measure of recovery provided for in the policy, that being "actual cash value." We agree.

N.J.S.A. 17:36–5.15 *et seq.* regulates the subject of fire insurance. As required by *N.J.S.A.* 17:36–5.19, the policy before us insured Elberon " * * * to the extent of the actual cash value of the property at the time of the loss, but not exceeding the amount which it would cost to repair or replace the property with material of like kind and quality * * *." This appeal calls for a determination of the meaning of "actual cash value." That phrase is also found in the appraisal provision of the Standard Form Policy which conforms to the statute.

> In case the insured and this Company shall fail to agree as to the actual cash value or the amount of loss, then, on the written demand of either, each shall select a competent and

disinterested appraiser and notify the other of the appraiser selected within twenty days of such demand. The appraisers shall first select a competent and disinterested umpire; and failing for fifteen days to agree upon such umpire, then, on request of the insured or this Company, such umpire shall be selected by a judge of a court of record in the State in which the property covered is located. *The appraisers shall then appraise the loss, stating separately actual cash value and loss to each item;* and, failing to agree, shall submit their differences, only, to the umpire. An award in writing, so itemized, of any two when filed with this Company shall *determine the amount of actual cash value and loss.* * * * (emphasis added) *N.J.S.A.* 17:36–5.20

The appraisal award here under review purported to follow the stated procedure.

A review of the record indicates that the appraisal was based on replacement cost without consideration of the element of depreciation. Plaintiffs argue that straight replacement cost is a permissible standard. We reject this contention. A standard of replacement without depreciation is inconsistent with the intent and the language of the statute which, as noted above, provides for insurance to the extent of the actual cash value of the property at the time of loss but not to exceed the amount it would cost to repair or replace the property with material of like kind and quality. Repair or replacement costs constitutes an upper limit on, not the absolute measure of, the insurer's liability. See *Riegel & Miller, Fire Insurance from Insurance Principles and Practices,* 360 (3d ed. 1947). To equate "actual cash value" with replacement cost alone would render the limiting phrase meaningless. If actual cash value is less than replacement cost in a particular case the former controls.

Rejection of pure replacement cost is further consonant with the legislative provision permitting insurers to provide for extended coverage to include replacement cost under an extended coverage endorsement. *N.J.S.A.* 17:36–5.22 provides that under such an endorsement the insurer may agree "to reimburse and indemnify the insured for the difference between the actual value of the insured property at the time any loss or damage occurs and the amount actually expended to repair, rebuild or replace with new materials of like size, kind and quality * * *." Such an endorsement specifically precludes deduction for depreciation. See *Ruter v. Northwestern Fire and Marine Ins. Co.,* 72 N.J.Super. 467, 471–473, 178 A.2d 640 (App.Div.), certif. den. 37 N.J. 229, 181 A.2d 12 (1962). It seems clear that if a specific provision is required to reimburse for pure replacement cost then the basic policy should not be so construed.

Finally, allowing pure replacement cost would violate the principle of indemnity by providing a windfall to the insured:

To allow the insured to recover the original value of real estate that has depreciated, * * * would be for the insurance company to pay for losses that were not caused by fire. Such prodigality would simply furnish an incentive for the destruction of property, because more could be recovered as insurance than the undamaged property was worth. Even under present conditions it is found that business depressions, which reduce the values of buildings and stocks of goods, are sometimes accompanied by large increases in the fire losses. Such conditions furnish an incentive for a fire. *Riegel & Miller, supra,* at 358–359.

See Bonbright & Katz, "Valuation of Property to Measure Fire Insurance Losses," 29 *Colum.L.Rev.* 857, 878–879 (1929). * * *

We thus conclude that an appraisal based on replacement cost without consideration of depreciation does not measure "actual cash value" under our statute and is therefore improper.

This appeal constitutes an appropriate vehicle for stating the principles which should guide appraisers in determining "actual cash value." The matter of correct standards has been widely litigated elsewhere.[2] Case law reflects three general categories for measuring "actual cash value": (1) market value, (2) replacement cost less depreciation, and (3) the "broad evidence" rule. See Note, "Valuation and Measure of Recovery Under Fire Insurance Policies," 49 *Colum.L.Rev.* 818, 820–823 (1949); Cozen, *op. cit., supra,* 12 *Forum* at 648–658; Hinkle, "The Meaning of 'Actual Cash Value,'" 1967 *Ins.L.J.* 711. See generally Annot., 61 *A.L.R.2d* 711 (1958).

Market value is generally defined as the price a willing buyer would pay a willing seller, at a fair and *bona fide* sale by private contract, neither being under any compulsion. See *Bartindale v. Aetna Ins. Co.,* 7 *N.J.Misc.* 399, 400, 145 A. 633 (Supp.Ct.1929). But there is a problem in that a building ordinarily has no recognized market value independent of the parcel of property in entirety, land and building together. See Note, *op. cit., supra,* 49 *Colum.L.Rev.* at 820, where it is observed that the majority of courts have rejected market value as the sole criterion or standard of "actual cash value" although they have allowed the fact-finder to consider it as a factor in computing the actual cash value of a building.[3] It is common practice for a valuation expert to develop a residual market value for a structure by deducting from the market value of the whole parcel the appraised market value of the land. In case of a partial loss, the market value approach looks to determination of the difference between the respective market values of the structure before and after the fire. Note, *op. cit., supra,* 49 *Colum. L.Rev.* at 825–826.

2. Every state has some statutorily prescribed fire insurance policy. Most states, like New Jersey, follow the New York Standard form. *Riegel & Miller, supra,* at 351–352.

3. California follows the market value rule. *Jefferson Insurance Co. of N.Y. v. Superior Court,* 3 Cal.3d 398, 90 *Cal.Rptr.* 608, 475 P.2d 880 (Sup.Ct.1970), as does Maine. *Forer v. Quincy Mutual Fire Ins. Co.,* 295 A.2d 247 (Maine Sup.Ct.1972).

Replacement cost less depreciation has the advantage of relative definiteness. It is also easily ascertained. However, it is inflexible, and this characteristic often results in excessive recovery. Many structures today have a high replacement value because of the inflated cost of building materials even though their true commercial value—represented by rentals, prospective profits, usefulness to the present owner, location and age—is considerably less. *Id.* at 821. See *Harper v. Penn Mut. Fire Ins. Co.,* 199 *F.Supp.* 663, 664–665 (E.D.Va.1966).

The problem of excessive recovery under the replacement cost less depreciation rule together with the occasional uncertainty of market value prompted development of what is now the most widely accepted rule, generally denominated as the "broad evidence rule." That rule was well explained by the New York Court of Appeals in *McAnarney v. Newark Fire Insurance Co.,* 247 N.Y. 176, 159 *N.E.* 902 (Ct.App.1928).

In *McAnarney* the insured built a brewery just before Prohibition. The brewery burned down shortly thereafter (arson was not proven). The insured claimed replacement cost minus depreciation, which because of impending Prohibition was more than the building was worth. The insurer was willing to allow market value, which, for the same reason, was probably less than the building would ordinarily have been worth. The Court of Appeals rejected both of these fixed standards of recovery and held that:

> Where insured buildings have been destroyed, the trier of fact may, and should, call to its aid, in order to effectuate complete indemnity, every fact and circumstance which would logically tend to the formation of a correct estimate of the loss. It may consider original cost and cost of reproduction; the opinions upon value given by qualified witnesses; the declarations against interest which may have been made by the assured; the gainful uses to which the buildings might have been put; as well as any other fact reasonably tending to throw light upon the subject. 159 *N.E.* at 905.

McAnarney was intended to assure application of the principle of indemnity (*i.e.,* to make the measure of recovery for fire insurance losses correspond to the actual pecuniary loss sustained by the insured). *Id.* at 904–905. See Bonbright & Katz, *op. cit., supra,* 29 *Colum.L.Rev.* at 899. Under-valuation denies the insured the indemnification due him under the policy. Over-valuation tempts the insured to cause the very loss covered, or at least, to provide inadequate safeguards against the loss. *Id.* at 863.

The commentators generally view the broad evidence rule with approval. See *id.* at 898–899 (a flexible test which can be modified in such a way as to accord more nearly with the principle of indemnity); Cozen, *op. cit., supra,* 12 *Forum* at 657 (sacrificing an easily applied standard for a far more equitable result). It has been adopted in numerous jurisdictions. *   *   *

We find the rationale of the broad evidence rule to be compelling. It requires the fact-finder to consider all evidence an expert would consider relevant to an evaluation, and particularly both fair market value and replacement cost less depreciation. If the appraiser finds it appropriate under the particular circumstances he may, after weighing both factors, settle on either alone. See *Doelger & Kirsten, Inc. v. National Union Fire Ins. Co., supra,* 167 *N.W.*2d at 200; *Schreiber v. Pacific Coast Fire Ins. Co., supra,* 75 A.2d at 111. Normally, replacement cost minus depreciation can be significant evidence of value but it is not necessarily conclusive. See *id.;* Bonbright & Katz, *op. cit., supra,* 29 *Colum.L.Rev.* at 896. Thus under the broad evidence rule the two stated criteria do not bind the fact-finder but instead become guidelines, along with other relevant evidence. No evidence is *per se* exclusive of other evidence; any evidence may be used jointly or alternatively according to the circumstances and the property to be evaluated. See *Pinet v. New Hampshire Fire Ins. Co., supra,* 126 A.2d at 265. *Cf. New Brunswick v. State of N.J. Div. of Tax Appeals,* 39 *N.J.* 537, 542–551, 189 A.2d 702 (1963) (Weintraub, C.J.) (while capitalization of income is an acceptable approach to tax assessment valuation it should not lightly be accepted as the single guide to such; there can be no rigid rule; generally it is well to measure its results against other known data).

The broad evidence rule is consistent with the narrow standard of judicial review generally accorded to appraisal awards. See *Igoe Bros. Inc. v. National Ben Franklin Fire Ins. Co.,* 110 *N.J.Eq.* 373, 160 A. 382 (E. & A.1932). The wider the range of evidence considered by the fact-finder, the more reasonable it is for a court to accept his conclusions. A result reached under the broad evidence rule is more likely to be reliable than one based on either of the other standards alone. See p. 444, *supra.* If the appraiser gives reasonable consideration to all relevant evidence, his award should ordinarily stand.

We thus hold that the proper standard for evaluating "actual cash value" under the New Jersey Standard Form Policy is the broad evidence rule.[4]

II.

There is an alternative justification for setting aside the award. During discussions among the appraisers as to the amount of loss, Thomas, defendant's appraiser, attempted to ascertain such factors as the actual cost to Elberon of effecting the repairs, the actual extent of repairs made, the age of the building, depreciation, the use to which the

---

4. We perceive no reason for distinguishing between the standard of evaluation for a total loss and that for a partial loss. *N.J.S.A.* 17:36–5.19 makes no such distinction; it specifies but one measure of recovery, "actual cash value." Any such distinction may lead to anomalous results. See Note, *supra,* 49 *Colum.L.Rev.* at 826, n. 60 (insured might recover more for a partial loss than a total loss). It is realized, however, that where an appraisal is made after a partial loss there may be difficult proof problems in arriving at the putative market value of the portion of the structure destroyed as distinguished from the entirety.

building had been put and the condition of the building prior to the fire. However, the umpire and the other appraiser refused to attempt to elicit or consider such information.

We have held above that "actual cash value" is to be ascertained by consideration of all relevant evidence. The courts of California and New York have vacated appraisals where the appraisers failed to comply with the applicable standard for ascertaining loss. In *Jefferson Insurance Co. of N.Y. v. Superior Court, supra,* 90 *Cal.Rptr.* at 611, 475 P.2d at 883, the California Supreme Court vacated an appraisal where the appraisers had considered only replacement cost minus depreciation whereas the California standard was market value. In *Gervant v. New England Fire Ins. Co.,* 306 *N.Y.* 393, 118 *N.E.2d* 574 (Ct.App.1954), it was legal misconduct for an appraiser to consider only evidence as to replacement cost minus depreciation because New York follows the broad evidence rule. *Id.* at 577.

We consequently conclude that the refusal of these appraisers even to consider such factors as those listed above constituted legal misconduct and of itself justifies vacation of the award.[5] Compare *N.J.S.A.* 2A:24–8(c), which provides that where arbitrators refuse to hear evidence pertinent and material to the controversy, the court shall vacate the award.

III.

Defendant raises the question whether the trial court was required to proceed in this matter under and pursuant to the Arbitration Act, *N.J.S.A.* 2A:24–1 *et seq.* It asserts that if the act was applicable, the award should be vacated because the procedures followed by the appraisers did not conform thereto. We have concluded that the Arbitration Act is not applicable.

A comparison of appraisal and arbitration will be helpful. The purposes of both are the same: to submit disputes to third parties and effect their speedy and efficient resolution without recourse to the courts. To assure minimum judicial intervention, the scope of judicial review of both types of recourse is narrow. See *Melton Bros. v. Phila. Fire & Marine Ins. Co., supra,* 104 *N.J.Eq.* at 158, 144 A. 726 (appraisal); *Collingswood Hosiery Mills, Inc. v. American Fed'n of Hosiery Workers, supra,* 31 *N.J.Super.* at 471–473, 107 A.2d 43 (arbitration).

The distinctions are significant. An agreement for arbitration ordinarily encompasses the disposition of the entire controversy between the parties, and judgment may be entered upon the award, whereas an appraisal establishes only the amount of loss and not liability. *Lakewood Tp. Mun. Util. v. S. Lakewood Water Co.,* 129 *N.J. Super.* 462, 471, 324 A.2d 78 (App.Div.1974) (citing 5 *Am.Jur., Arbitra-*

---

5. In some cases a refusal to consider relevant evidence, while improper, might not in itself be cause to set aside an award if the result reached appeared reasonable. Here, however, exclusion of depreciation while applying replacement cost new prevents the result from being reasonable.

tion and Award, § 3 at 520, 521). Arbitration is conducted as a quasi-judicial proceeding, with hearings, notice of hearings, oaths of arbitrators and oaths of witnesses. Appraisers act on their own skill and knowledge, need not be sworn and need hold no formal hearings so long as both sides are given an opportunity to state their positions. Note, "Arbitration or Appraisement?," 8 *Syracuse L.Rev.* 205, 206 (1957).

The instant policy provision clearly called for an appraisal. That the procedures mandated by the Arbitration Act, *see, e.g., N.J.S.A.* 2A:24–6, were not followed and that there was no finding with respect to liability tends to indicate that the fact-finders purported to conduct an appraisal. This was entirely proper.

Nothing in the Arbitration Act requires that fire insurance comply with that statute. Indeed, the word "appraisal" is not found in the act. See *In re Delmar Box Co.,* 309 *N.Y.* 60, 127 *N.E.2d* 808, 810–811 (Ct.App. 1955), where the New York court noted the long-prevailing distinctions between appraisals and arbitration, and concluded that any determination that the formal requirements under the arbitration act should apply to fire loss appraisals should come from the Legislature. *Id.* at 813. Compare *Jefferson Insurance Company of N.Y. v. Superior Court, supra,* 90 Cal.Rptr. at 610, n. 41, 475 P.2d at 882, n. 41 (under the California Code of Civil Procedure, enforcement procedures respecting arbitration have been made applicable to appraisals). The intention to change a long-established rule or principle is not to be imputed to the Legislature in the absence of a clear manifestation thereof. *State v. Western Union Tel. Co.,* 12 *N.J.* 468, 486, 97 A.2d 480 (1953).

Furthermore, since application of the broad evidence rule to appraisals will promote the interchange of information between the appraisers and the parties, one may expect enhancement of the fairness of the procedure without burdening the appraisal with the formalities of arbitration (*e.g.,* oaths, notice of hearings, etc.).

Finally, since arbitrators are entrusted with the broader obligation to determine liability as well as the amount of the award, it is reasonable to require broader procedural safeguards in arbitration. The subject-matter responsibility of appraisers being less, the procedural safeguards attending an appraisal may be fewer. However, the Court must correct any erroneous exercise of jurisdiction by an appraiser. * * *

The judgment is reversed and the cause is remanded to the Law Division for further proceedings conforming to this opinion.

Notes and Questions

1. *Two Views of Indemnity.* What is the purpose of the measure of recovery the court held was embodied in the fire policy at issue? On one view, the purpose is to assure that the insured's net worth before and after loss remains the same. This might be termed the *economic conception* of the measure of recovery. In contrast, the purpose of a measure of recovery could be to return the insured to roughly the same

style of life as he or she occupied before loss. This *functional conception* of the measure of recovery might yield a different payment for the same loss. Indeed, payment of full replacement cost without deduction for depreciation might not violate this conception of indemnity at all. For example, the failure to deduct depreciation from the measure of recovery the appraisers used in *Elberon Bathing* seems an obvious mistake, because this would have provided an essentially commercial operation with an asset worth more after payment of the fire insurance proceeds than it was worth before the fire. On the other hand, a homeowner whose twenty-year old garage is destroyed by fire needs a new garage. If he recovers only the market value of the garage, he has the same net-worth before and after loss, but he is worse off nevertheless—because he either has no garage, or must take money out of his pocket in order to build a new one.

Does the condition that actual cash value may not exceed the cost to repair or replace that is included in most policies provide any guidance as to which conception is appropriate? If the economic conception of the measure of recovery in fire and property insurance seems more appropriate for commercial losses, but the functional conception seems more appropriate for personal losses, is the notion of "actual cash value" flexible enough to accommodate both, with the help of the broad evidence rule, or is express policy language that differentiates between commercial and personal losses necessary?

2. *Express Replacement–Cost Coverage.* Necessary or not, when such language is present it can virtually eliminate the dilemma over the proper measure of recovery. Many commercial property and homeowners policies, as well as the collision and comprehensive coverage in many automobile policies, now provide insurance for the cost of replacement without deduction for depreciation. See the Sample Homeowners Policy, *Section I—Conditions,* paragraph 3(b). What moral hazard is associated with providing this kind of coverage and how does the sample policy combat it?

3. *Valued Policies.* Some states have attempted to sidestep one aspect of the measure-of-recovery problem by enacting valued policy statutes. These statutes provide that in the case of total loss of the insured property (the kind of property subject to the statutes varies) the measure of recovery is the face amount of the policy, regardless of its actual cash value at the time of loss. See, e.g., Ark.Stat.Ann. § 23–88–101. The conventional wisdom has been that these statutes are ill-conceived, because they generate unnecessary moral hazard. See, e.g., R. Jerry, Understanding Insurance Law 446 (1987); R. Keeton, Insurance Law 140–42 (1971). One purpose of valued policy statutes may be to protect insurers from their own agents' attempts to earn high commissions by selling policies with face amounts exceeding the actual value of the property insured. Since such statutes merely give insurers an additional reason for doing what they already have reason to do—police their agents' misbehavior—this justification is weak.

Another purpose of the statutes is to encourage insurers to investigate the values insureds place on insured property at the time of an application for coverage, in order to avoid valuation disputes at the time of loss. This has been the explanation for the common, voluntary use of valued policies in marine insurance, where the location of property to be insured at a distance from the underwriter and its subsequent disappearance at sea make avoidance of valuation disputes worthwhile. But it takes only a moment to understand that only a small percentage of all properties insured by fire and property insurers is ever the subject of a claim. The cost to insurers of appraising all insured property prior to loss is likely to far exceed the cost of valuation disputes respecting a fraction of the (already small) fraction of all insured properties that do actually suffer loss. Consequently, because insurers are unlikely to appraise more than a small portion of all the properties they insure, the use of valued policies seems likely to cost more by way of increased moral hazard than it saves by way of reduction in the cost of valuation after loss.

Nonetheless, there may be a kind of rough restitutionary equity at the core of the valued policy idea. The typical homeowner, for example, has paid premiums to his insurer over a period of years prior to suffering a loss. The amount of these premiums is based on the face amount of the policy, not on the actual cash value of the property insured. Without a valued policy, if an insured pays premiums for $100,000 of coverage for ten years even though the actual cash value of the property is only $90,000, then the insurer has been receiving premiums for $10,000 worth of insurance that it has never in fact provided. A valued policy forces the insurer to provide the coverage for which the insured has paid with many years' worth of premiums. Valued policy statutes may simply embody the view that any moral hazard they create is worth tolerating in return for achieving this restitutionary equity.

COINSURANCE IN FIRE AND PROPERTY COVERAGE

One of the burdens that has been shouldered by generations of insurance law students is mastering coinsurance provisions in fire and property insurance. Such provisions are contained in most policies, including the Sample Homeowners Policy at *Section I—Conditions*, paragraph 3(b), which reads in pertinent part:

(2) If, at the time of loss the amount of insurance in this policy on the damaged building is less than 80% of the full replacement cost of the building immediately before the loss, we will pay the greater of the following amount, but not more than the limit of liability under this policy that applies to the building:

(a) the actual cash value of the building damaged; or

(b) *that proportion of the cost to repair or replace* * * *
which the total amount of insurance in this policy on the
damaged building bears to 80% of the replacement cost of the
building. [emphasis added]

1. *The Mechanics.* There are two ways to master this coinsurance
clause. One is to learn the algebraic formula for the measure of
recovery and to apply it mechanically. That formula is as follows,
where x equals the percentage of the loss for which the insured is
covered under the coinsurance clause:

$$x = \frac{\text{face amount policy}}{.8 \text{ multiplied by the replacement cost of property}}$$

Thus, if the insured has insured her $100,000 home for $60,000 and the
replacement cost of her loss is $30,000, she receives:

$$x = \frac{\$60,000}{.8 \text{ multiplied by } \$100,000}$$

$$= \frac{\$60,000}{\$80,000}$$

$= .75$ of her loss of $30,000, or $22,500

Recalculation of this formula on the assumption that the face
amount of the policy was $80,000 will demonstrate that by insuring for
80 percent of the actual cash value of her property, the insured can
assure that she is covered for 100 percent of the value of her partial
losses. Some policies provide for a different coinsurance percentage.
In such cases that percentage must be substituted for the .8 in the
above formula.

2. *The Fundamental Idea.* The preferable way to master coinsurance is to understand its aim. The key is to see two points: 1) total loss
of property is much less likely than partial loss; and 2) property
insurance is priced per $1000 of property value, and premium rates do
not decline the more coverage that is purchased. For example, the
insured who purchases $50,000 of coverage pays half of what she would
pay for $100,000. Without a coinsurance requirement, therefore, in-
sureds might have an incentive to insure for much less than the full
value of their property, and to gamble that they would suffer partial
losses (which would tend to be fully insured) rather than total losses
(which would be fully insured up to the face amount of the policy, and
completely uninsured beyond that amount). This would be a "good"
gamble, since the insured would get more protection for partial losses
(given their higher probability) per dollar of premium than for total
losses.

The aim of coinsurance requirements in fire and property insurance is to neutralize this incentive to insure against partial losses only.
Under the standard coinsurance provision applied above, partial losses
are only partially insured unless the face amount of the policy is equal
to at least 80 percent of the replacement cost of the property (or its
actual cash value, if that is what has been insured). Another way of

avoiding this problem would be to vary premiums with the percentage of cash value or absolute dollar value insured, on the analogy to liability insurance. The insured purchasing $100,000 of coverage would then pay a premium less than twice what the insured purchasing $50,000 of coverage would pay. Would the latter make more sense?

G. BUSINESS INTERRUPTION INSURANCE

OMAHA PAPER STOCK CO. v. HARBOR INSURANCE COMPANY

United States Court of Appeals, Eighth Circuit, 1979.
596 F.2d 283.

STEPHENSON, Circuit Judge.

Defendant-appellant Harbor Insurance Company appeals from the trial court's interpretation of and consequential ruling on a use and occupancy-business interruption insurance contract with the insured, plaintiff-appellee Omaha Paper Stock Company. Harbor contends (1) that the trial court failed to consider Omaha's increased use of and output at a second plant after the fire at the insured plant; (2) that as a result of the use of the second plant, Omaha did not suffer a total suspension of business as defined by the contract; (3) that therefore Omaha did not qualify for the full "valued" per diem payment of $3260 to be paid in the event of a total suspension of business; (4) and that the attorney fee awarded to Omaha's counsel by the trial court is excessive. Harbor cross-appeals on the trial court's denial of prejudgment interest. We hold there was a total suspension of business as defined by the insurance contract and thus affirm the trial court's decision.

Omaha Paper Stock was in the scrap paper processing business. It had two plants in Omaha; a plant located at 1401 Laird Street which handled low-grade scrap paper, and a plant located at 846 South 18th Street, which handled high-grade scrap paper. The record indicates that there is a significant difference between the methods of processing low-grade scrap paper and high-grade scrap paper. High-grade scrap paper processing requires a substantial amount of manual handling; low-grade paper processing can largely be accomplished with little manual handling.

The business at the Laird Street address (the business with which we are primarily concerned) consisted of buying, sorting, bailing, shipping and selling the low-grade scrap paper, i.e., newspapers collected by public service groups. There is also some evidence in the record suggesting that Omaha Paper Stock would occasionally act as a broker; it would find a seller who sorted and bailed its own paper and match that seller with a buyer. When this occurs it is not necessary for the paper to pass through either of the Omaha plants.

The relevant portions of the contract are as follows:

Insured's Name   OMAHA PAPER STOCK COMPANY
  and Address: 846 SOUTH 18TH STREET
                  OMAHA, NEBRASKA

Type of Coverage: VALUED BUSINESS INTERRUPTION

* * *

Assured: OMAHA PAPER STOCK COMPANY

$586,800 on the use and occupancy of all buildings and/or structures and/or machinery and/or equipment and/or raw stock or stock in process contained therein upon the premises owned and/or leased and/or occupied by the Assured, and situated at

1401 LAIRD STREET
OMAHA, NEBRASKA

and operated by the Assured principally as

SCRAP PAPER PROCESSING [Clause A]

INSURING CLAUSE

TOTAL SUSPENSION: The conditions of this contract of insurance are that if the said buildings and/or structures and/or machinery and/or equipment and/or raw stock or stock in process contained therein shall be destroyed or damaged by Fire, Lightning, Explosion, Aircraft, Vehicles, Windstorm, Strikers, Riot(er)s, or Smoke, as hereinafter defined, occurring during the term of this Certificate so as to necessitate a total suspension of business then this insurance shall be liable at a rate of $3,260 per working day/xxxxxxx for such total suspension. [Clause B]

PARTIAL SUSPENSION: If the property damage due to perils insured against results in partial suspension of business then this insurance shall be liable for such proportion of $3,260 per working day/xxxxxxx which the proportion of reduction in output bears to the total production which would, but for such partial suspension, have been obtained during the period of partial suspension. [Clause C]

CONDITIONS

It is a condition of this contract that the length of time or suspension for which loss may be claimed hereunder shall not exceed 180 days at any one location, and shall commence on the eighth day following the date of damage to the property insured hereunder, but loss shall not be claimed for days on which the operations of the assured are not normally performed. The length of time for which suspension may be claimed shall not be limited by the date of expiration of this contract. [Clause D]

* * *

It is a condition of this insurance that buildings, surplus machinery or duplicate parts thereof, equipment, raw stock or stock in process which may be owned, controlled or used by the Assured, shall in the event of loss be used to expedite the continuance of resumption of business. [Clause E]

* * *

In the event of a loss as defined in the Total Suspension Clause herein it is understood and agreed that should the Assured be provided other suitable facilities with which to operate, then upon resumption of operations with such other facilities such loss if any shall be adjusted as defined in the Partial Suspension Clause of this Certificate. [Clause F]

In consideration of the premium charged hereunder it is understood and agreed that this Certificate also covers such extraordinary expenses as are necessarily incurred (with the consent and approval of Underwriters or their representatives hereon) for the purpose of reducing any loss under this Certificate (except expenses incurred to extinguish the fire) not exceeding, however, the amount by which the loss under this Certificate is reduced thereby. [Clause G]

In the event of the described property being so destroyed or damaged as to give rise to a claim hereunder, Underwriters agree that this insurance may be reinstated (subject to prior agreement by Underwriters) without additional premium, but this shall not be construed to increase the daily/weekly/or monthly indemnity specified in the total or partial suspension clauses nor extend the period of indemnity specified in this certificate. [Clause H]

* * *

DUE DILIGENCE CLAUSE: The Assured shall use due diligence and do and concur in doing all things reasonably practicable, namely (1) to avoid the happening of any peril insured against and (2) to resume full operation of their business as early as practicable after any interruption.

It is understood and agreed that loss, if any, hereunder shall be computed on the basis of the time of actual interruption but in no event exceeding the time which it would take with ordinary diligence and dispatch to repair and/or replace the property herein described, nor shall Underwriters be liable as regards the replacement of raw stock or stock in process for a longer period of time than that during which damaged or destroyed raw stock or stock in process would have made operations possible. The indemnity period shall not be limited by the date of expiration named in this Certificate. [Clause I]

The Laird Street plant was destroyed by fire on April 20, 1975.

The problem with which we are confronted is the effect of the increased production at the 18th Street plant of low-grade paper processing (which took place as a result of the fire destroying the Laird Street plant's capacity for production)[1] on the liability of Harbor Insurance Company. Specifically, we are concerned with Clause E which provides, as a condition of the insurance, that Omaha shall use, in the event of a loss, any "buildings, surplus machinery or duplicate parts thereof, equipment, raw stock or stock in process which may be owned, controlled or used" by Omaha to "expedite the continuance or resumption of business."

The trial court interpreted this clause to mean that any such surplus buildings or machinery, etc. must be used to expedite or continue the production of low grades of paper "at the Laird Street plant itself." "[S]urplus production capacity at another and different plant * * * would have no effect upon the resumption or continuance of the plant covered by the insurance policy." *Omaha Paper Stock Co. v. Harbor Ins. Co.*, 445 F.Supp. 179, 184–85 (D.Neb.1978). Consequently, the production at the 18th Street plant of some low-grade scrap paper processing does not affect the necessary determination of whether there was a total suspension of business as the term is used in Clause B. *Id.* at 183–85.

The trial court consequently found that there were 152 working days lost as a result of the fire. Inasmuch as Omaha contributed to the delay of repairing the business, Harbor Insurance Company was found liable for only 130 of the days. Neither party appeals on the basis of this finding.

We agree with the trial court that Clause E is not a mitigation of damages clause; it is a condition of the insurance which requires Omaha, in continuing or resuming business at the Laird Street plant, to use any buildings or equipment that it has which will expedite that process.

At the outset, it is necessary to define the contract terms. The first rule of contract construction is that contracts should be viewed as a whole. *Kansas–Nebraska Natural Gas Co. v. Hawkeye Security Ins. Co.*, 195 Neb. 658, 240 N.W.2d 28, 30 (1976). While an ambiguous contract is to be interpreted in favor of the insured, should the ambiguity allow such an interpretation, "[c]onstruction ought not to be employed to make a plain agreement ambiguous," in order to construe it against the insurer. *Wyatt v. Woodmen Accident & Life Co.*, 194 Neb.

---

1. The trial court found that the Laird Street business utilized the surplus production capacity at the 18th Street plant. *Omaha Paper Stock Co. v. Harbor Ins. Co.*, 445 F.Supp. 179, 184 (D.Neb.1978).

The record before us does not reflect with certainty what proportion of the Laird Street business was continued at the 18th Street plant as a result of the fire destruction, but the trial court found that "the record indicates that 18th Street began to process a small percentage of the total production of lower grades of paper (newspaper and corrugated paper) which had been processed at Laird Street." *Id.* at 184.

614, 618, 234 N.W.2d 217, 220 (1975); *Cordes v. Prudential Ins. Co.,* 181 Neb. 794, 150 N.W.2d 905 (1967). Thus, limitations and exceptions in regard to liability of the insurer, if plainly expressed should be enforced. *Wyatt v. Woodmen Accident & Life Co., supra,* 234 N.W.2d at 219. And finally, an insurance contract should be read and "given effect according to the ordinary sense of the terms used" just as any other contract. *Pettid v. Edwards,* 195 Neb. 713, 240 N.W.2d 344, 346 (1976); *Cordes v. Prudential Ins. Co., supra,* 150 N.W.2d at 908.

We do not find the Omaha–Harbor insurance contract ambiguous. In any event, ambiguities are to be interpreted against the insurer.

We note that this insurance contract is a valued insurance policy. A valued insurance policy does not look to the profits, losses, or real value of the property at the time of casualty; instead, the parties agree to a value of the property or ongoing business as a part of the contract.[2]

The valued policy, more often than not, is designed to cover total losses; it can also be used, however, to cover partial losses, as the contract involved here allowed. R.E. Keeton, Insurance Law Basic Text 140–42 (West 1971). The parties stipulated to a value of the ongoing business at the Laird Street address of $3260 per day (with a limit of 180 working days ($586,000) total loss allowed to be claimed). The partial suspension clause provides that the valued policy also covers necessary partial suspensions of business, and allows a daily valued payment to be made—the payment to be in proportion to the reduction in output of goods.

The term "use and occupancy" is generally used interchangeably with the term "business interruption." Appelman, 4 Ins.L. & Prac. § 2329, p. 323 (West 1968)—indeed, they are both used somewhat interchangeably in this contract. The terms both go to coverage of losses sustained when for one reason or another the operation of the business is interrupted. Business interruption insurance generally puts the insured into the monetary position it would have been in but for the interruption of its business. Use and occupancy insurance provides the same type of coverage, but tends to focus on the business use which the property was capable of prior to the loss.

A case in which a definition of use and occupancy arises out of a factually similar situation is *Michael v. Prussian Nat'l Ins. Co.,* 171 N.Y. 25, 63 N.E. 810 (1902). In *Michael,* the policy read "on the use and occupancy of their property and elevator building, with boiler and engine houses attached, situate * * * in Buffalo, New York, and known as the 'Dakota Elevator.'" *Id.,* 63 N.E. at 811.

Consequently, when the elevator was destroyed by fire so as to prevent use and occupancy, the insurance company was liable for the

---

2. *See* R. Keeton, Insurance Law Basic Text, 141–42 (West 1971). The origination of this type of "valued" policy appears to be in marine insurance, where, in writing the insurance contract at the commencement of the voyage, the insurer and insured stipulated a value of the cargo; this obviated the problem of later, after mid-voyage loss, trying to determine the value at the time of loss. *Id.* at 140.

agreed-upon (valued) per diem for the length of time (with ordinary due diligence and dispatch) it would take to rebuild the elevator to its former capacity.

The insurance company had argued that the term "use and occupancy" required a determination of the loss of profits and earnings resulting from the loss of the use and occupancy of the elevator, as opposed to the mere fact of whether the elevator was capable of being used and occupied by the insured. Thus if, in spite of the loss of use and occupancy, profits and earnings were not lost, the policy would be inapplicable.[3]

The insured argued that the policy did not relate to earnings and profits, but rather, it related to a fixed sum to be paid when loss of use and occupancy occurred as a result of fire. Thus, even if the insured gained from the loss of use and occupancy, the value agreed upon was still owed by the insurance company. The court agreed with the insured.

That the policy in question here was a "valued" use and occupancy policy indicates that the parties wished to avoid post-fire determination of the value of the ongoing business which the use and occupancy of the buildings and machinery at the Laird Street address made capable.

The trial court's analysis of this contract includes reference to *City Tailors, Ltd. v. Evans,* 126 L.T.N.S. 439 (1921), and *Hartford Fire Ins. Co. v. Wilson & Toomer Fertilizer Co.,* 4 F.2d 835 (5th Cir.), *cert. denied,* 268 U.S. 704, 45 S.Ct. 639, 69 L.Ed. 1167 (1925).

In *City Tailors,* the use and occupancy policy covered the business of a clothing factory. The insurance policy provided a stipulated per diem payment to be made each day the work at the factory was prevented due to fire damage. The policy also contained a "due diligence" clause which required the insured to do "all things reasonably practicable to minimize" the loss. *City Tailors, Ltd. v. Evans, supra,* 126 L.T.N.S. at 440.

Following the fire, the insured continued the business of clothing production at a temporary location. The court held that the insured was entitled to keep the profits from the temporary location in addition to recovering the full per diem for the total suspension of production at the insured's factory. The trial court quotes from Lord Judge Scrutton's opinion in *City Tailors:*

> If the assured cannot by reasonable exertions produce an output at [the original factory] there is a total loss; to the extent to which, acting reasonably, his output at [the original factory] is diminished there is a partial loss. In other words, the subject matter of insurance is limited locally; it is profits at [the original factory] derived from output at [the original factory]. The insurance is on a business carried on at [the original factory], not elsewhere; and it is interruption of, or

3. This could occur if a business were operating at a loss prior to the fire.

interference with, that business at [the original factory] by fire which causes the loss.

City Tailors, Ltd. v. Evans, supra, 126 L.T.N.S. at 443, *quoted in Omaha Paper Stock Co. v. Harbor Ins. Co., supra,* 445 F.Supp. at 184. * * *

To further support its conclusion that the extra processing of low-grade scrap paper at the 18th Street address is not relevant to a determination of total or partial suspension of business as defined by the Omaha–Harbor insurance contract, the district court relies upon *Beautytuft, Inc. v. Factory Ins. Assoc.,* 431 F.2d 1122 (6th Cir.1970), and *Hawkinson Tread Tire Serv. Co. v. Indiana Lumbermens Mut. Ins. Co.,* 362 Mo. 823, 245 S.W.2d 24 (1951). In both of these cases the plants were destroyed by fire and the insureds established operations shortly thereafter at other locations.

The *Beautytuft* contract provided for recovery due to business interruption for "the ACTUAL LOSS SUSTAINED * * * *for only such length of time as would be required with the exercise of due diligence * * * to rebuild, repair or replace such described property * * *.*" *Beautytuft, Inc. v. Factory Ins. Assoc., supra,* 431 F.2d at 1124. This is similar to the due diligence clause in the instant contract (Clause I). It was a condition of the contract that if the insured could "reduce the loss resulting from the interruption of business, * * * by making use of other property * * * described herein or elsewhere * * * such reduction shall be taken into account in arriving at the amount of loss hereunder." *Id.*

The insurance company argued that plaintiff was in full production at the new location within approximately three and one-half months after the fire—thus, there was no longer any "business interruption" and the insurance company should not be required to make further payments for any losses sustained beyond that date. Holding the contract language "repair, rebuild or replace" to mean to do those things on the described premises, the Sixth Circuit held that plaintiff should recover for the *theoretical* time period it would have taken to rebuild the plant, adjusted in accord with the contract provision requiring the plaintiff to make use of other property. Thus, plaintiff recovered the actual loss due to business interruption resulting from the fire—the loss per day on the theoretical time period offset by any gains made at the second plant.

In *Hawkinson,* the contract was almost identical, in relevant parts, to the contract in the instant case, except that the *Hawkinson* contract provided for indemnification for the "actual loss sustained" as opposed to a valued loss. The *Hawkinson* contract was identified by the Supreme Court of Missouri as one "indemnifying plaintiff for damage or destruction by fire of the 'use and occupancy' of the described property necessitating an interruption of business[;]" the contract provided that payment of the loss sustained would continue for the length of time that, with due diligence, it would take to rebuild, repair or replace the destroyed property. It also provided that the insured should "make use of other property, if obtainable, if by so doing the amount of loss hereunder will be reduced, and in [such event] * * * such reduction shall be taken into account in arriving at the amount of the loss hereunder." *Hawkinson Tread Tire Serv. Co. v. Indiana Lumbermens Mut. Ins. Co., supra,* 245 S.W.2d at 26.

Thus, as in *Beautytuft,* the court in *Hawkinson* found that:

There was no applicable provision of the policy limiting the extent of defendant's liability to a resumption of normal operations in some "obtainable" property other than that of the Twelfth Street address. We bear in mind the liability under the policy was expressly the actual loss sustained for the "length of time" which would be required to rebuild, repair or replace the property destroyed.

Id. at 29.

Insofar as the use of the second plant was concerned, the Supreme Court of Missouri added:

However, under the "resumption of operations and use of other property" clause, * * * the actual profit and loss experience thereafter at the Market Street address was necessarily and properly taken into account in any *reduction* of the loss sustained.

Id.

On the basis of the contract and these cases, the district court's analysis focused upon the fact that the Laird Street business was the one covered in the contract, and that the resumption or continuance of the business requirement (Clause E) referred to assuming or continuing operations *at the Laird Street address.* Thus the due diligence clause referred to rebuilding or repairing the Laird Street plant, and as in *Beautytuft* and *Hawkinson,* it was that time period for which the indemnification was to be paid (here, a valued sum). Because the surplus production capacity of the 18th Street plant did not affect, nor could it help, the resumption or continuance of business at the Laird Street address, such surplus production was not taken into consideration in determining whether there had been total or partial suspension of the business. *Omaha Paper Stock Co. v. Harbor Ins. Co., supra,* 445 F.Supp. at 184–85. Thus, Harbor was liable under the total suspension of business clause (Clause B). The only manner in which operations at another plant could be considered would be in mitigation of the loss— i.e., in *Beautytuft* and *Hawkinson,* the policies had mitigation of loss provisions. Harbor contends that Clause E is such a clause, but Clause E does not require any mitigation of loss.[4] It only requires that Omaha

4. Appellants cite *Northwestern States Portland Cement Co. v. Hartford Fire Ins. Co.,* 360 F.2d 531 (8th Cir.1966), *modifying and affirming,* 243 F.Supp. 386 (D.Iowa 1965) and *Steel Products Co. v. Millers Nat'l Ins. Co.,* 209 N.W.2d 32 (Iowa 1973), as analogous cases. Both of the contracts in those cases had specific reduction of loss clauses requiring the insured, "if [it] could reduce the loss resulting from the interruption of business," to make use of other property. *Northwestern States Portland Cement Co. v. Hartford Fire Ins. Co.,* 243 F.Supp. 386, 387 (D.Iowa 1965), and *Steel Products Co. v. Millers Nat'l Ins. Co., supra,*

use all available facilities to resume or continue its business at the Laird Street address.

Appellant also contends that some of the Laird Street brokerage business was continued following the fire. At a minimum, to carry on the brokerage business at the Laird Street address, an office would be needed, and the record reflects that the office at the Laird Street plant was destroyed. Further, if the business was not carried on from the Laird Street address, it is not applicable to the question of whether there was a total suspension of business. Finally, the brokerage business prior to the fire did not require the "use and occupancy" of the plant, so the brokerage business was not within the terms of the contract. Thus, there is not sufficient evidence to show that brokerage business, even if carried on, resulted in only a "partial suspension of business" under the terms of the contract. * * *

AFFIRMED.

Notes and Questions

1. *The Basics.* Business interruption insurance provides coverage against economic losses resulting from the damage or destruction of described property owned by the insured. The importance of the designation of the property in question cannot be overstated, for normally the coverage is against loss resulting from damage or destruction of that property only. See, e.g., *Swedish Crucible Steel Company v. Travelers Indemnity Company,* 387 F.Supp. 231 (E.D.Mich.1974). Contingent business interruption insurance provides coverage against such losses resulting from the damage or destruction of specified, non-owned property—for example, the factory of an important supplier of component parts to a manufacturer.

2. *The Issues.* Three major issues tend to arise in cases involving business interruption insurance. Each turns on the cause of the losses claimed. First, the period during which losses are sustained must be determined. This requires a finding as to the point at which the damaged property has been repaired and the business restarted. Second, the gross amount of loss must be determined. The use of a valued policy in *Omaha Paper Stock* avoided this problem, except for the total/partial loss determination. In most cases, however, the problem must be faced head on. Third, the expenses and other costs that continue must be separated from costs (salary, supplies) that do not continue and therefore need not be counted in determining the actual loss sustained. For discussion of this last issue, see *Royal Indemnity Company v. Little Joe's Catfish Inn,* 636 S.W.2d 530 (Texas App.1982).

3. *Due diligence and the duty to mitigate.* The court in *Omaha Paper Stock* understood the insured's obligation (under Clause E) to make use of its own property to expedite resumption of the business to

209 N.W.2d at 34–35. The clause in the Harbor–Omaha contract does not refer to reduction of loss by use of other property. It refers to continuing or resuming the business at the Laird Street address by use of other property.

apply only to property at the Laird Street site. Whether that interpretation was correct or not, it points to a difficult issue in the construction of business interruption policies: if the insured has other property that could be used to continue or resume operations, must that other property be employed? Two questions arise here: does the policy require such use, and how is the cost of such use to be taken into account?

Regarding the first question, some policies contain clauses resembling Clause E. Other policies, however, contain separate clauses imposing a duty to mitigate loss on the insured. Should the presence or absence of the latter clause be dispositive? Regarding the second question, some property which could be used to continue or resume operations may be surplus; should its cost be considered a reimbursable expense? On the other hand, some property may be available only if its use in other operations is discontinued. Should the insured be obligated to make the most valuable use of that property, or should only surplus property be considered available for mitigation of loss? For an excellent survey of these and other issues, see Tort and Insurance Practice Section, American Bar Association, Business Interruption Coverage: A Basic Primer (1984).

Chapter Five

LIFE, HEALTH, AND DISABILITY INSURANCE

A. LIFE INSURANCE

There are two major forms of life insurance: *term* and *whole life.* There are numerous variations on these two themes. The difference between the two is the inclusion of an investment feature in whole life. Term life insurance provides life insurance alone; whole life insurance provides life insurance plus accumulation of a cash-value that permits the insured to surrender the policy for that value, and sometimes to borrow against it without surrender. Because of this investment feature the insured obtains less pure insurance for a given premium under whole life than under term insurance.

The typical policy, whether term or whole life, contains an insuring agreement plus a set of provisions governing premium payment and lapse of coverage for non-payment, ownership of the policy, change of beneficiary and assignment, settlement options (i.e., methods of paying the proceeds of the policy upon the insured's death), the insured's access to or use of the cash-value (if it is a whole life policy), or conversion to whole life (if it is term insurance). A Sample Term Life Insurance Policy is set out below.

1. Sample Term Life Insurance Policy

Source: American Council of Life Insurance and Health Insurance Association of America, Life and Health Insurance: A Teaching Manual. Reprinted with the permission of the American Council of Life Insurance.

SAMPLE POLICY

Sample Term Life Insurance Policy

TO THE READER:

There are no "standard" life insurance policies, and the contracts vary in wording and appearance from company to company. Sometimes there are also significant differences in policy provisions. This policy is generally representative of term life insurance contracts issued in the United States.

Source: LIFE AND HEALTH INSURANCE: A TEACHING MANUAL
Washington, DC: American Council of Life Insurance Health Insurance Association of America

SAMPLE

COUNCIL LIFE INSURANCE COMPANY
WASHINGTON, D.C.

INSURED	DENNIS SMITH	$40,000 SUM INSURED
ORIGINAL TERM EXPIRY DATE	AUG 09, 1983	
POLICY DATE	AUG 09, 1982	062201 0000001 POLICY NUMBER

TERM LIFE INSURANCE POLICY

OUR INSURING AGREEMENT

If the Insured dies while this policy is in full force and prior to the Original Term Expiry Date or prior to any Term Expiry Date after that, we will pay the Sum Insured to the Beneficiary.

We, Council Life Insurance Company, issue this policy in consideration of your application and the payment of premiums.

Our Company and you, the Owner, are bound by the conditions and provisions of the policy.

YOUR RIGHT TO RETURN YOUR POLICY

We want you to be satisifed with your policy. If you aren't, return it to us within 10 days of the date you receive it. Return it to our Home Office or to your agent. We will refund any premium you have paid. We will consider your policy as if it had never existed.

If you have any questions or problems with your policy, we will be ready to help you. You may call upon your agent or our Home Office for assistance at any time.

Signed at our Home Office, Washington, D.C.

Secretary

W. Prescott Smith

President

John E. Wells II

POLICY HIGHLIGHTS:

- ■ YEARLY RENEWABLE LEVEL TERM LIFE INSURANCE TO AGE 98

- ■ CONVERTIBLE

- ■ CONVERSION PRIVILEGE TERMINATES AT AGE 80

- ■ PREMIUMS PAYABLE DURING INSURED'S LIFETIME TO END OF PREMIUM PAYMENT PERIOD

- ■ NONPARTICIPATING— NO DIVIDENDS PAID

1

Source: LIFE AND HEALTH INSURANCE, A TEACHING MANUAL, Washington, DC, American Council of Life Insurance/Health Insurance Association of America

POLICY INDEX

Page

THE CONTRACT 7

- The Entire Contract
- Incontestability
- Misstatement of Age or Sex
- Policy Settlement
- Suicide

CONVERSION 11

- Conditions of Conversion
- Conversion Credit
- Conversion Election
- Issue Age of New Policy

DECREASING TERM INSURANCE
OPTION 12

- Election of Option
- TABLE FOR DECREASING TERM
  OPTION 13

DEFINITIONS 6

- Beneficiary
- Date of Issue
- In Full Force
- Insured
- Issue Age and Attained Age
- Policy Date
- Policy Specifications
- Sum Insured
- We
- Written Notice
- You

OWNERSHIP AND BENEFICIARY 9

- Assignment and Assignee
- Beneficiary
- Change of Ownership or Beneficiary
- Ownership

POLICY SPECIFICATIONS 3

- Benefit and Premium Schedule
- Total Premium on Policy Date
- TABLE OF RENEWAL
  PREMIUMS 4

PREMIUMS 8

- Default
- Frequency
- Grace Period
- Payment
- Reinstatement

RENEWAL 10

- Effect of Total Disability on Renewal
- When Renewal Premium Due
- Yearly Renewal

SETTLEMENT OPTIONS 14

Additional Benefit Provisions, if any, Election of Settlement Options and a copy of the application follow Page 14.

ENDORSEMENTS

2

POLICY SPECIFICATIONS

PLAN OF INSURANCE—YEARLY RENEWABLE AND CONVERTIBLE TERM

INSURED— DENNIS SMITH $40,000 —SUM INSURED

ORIGINAL TERM—
  EXPIRY DATE— AUG 09, 1983

  POLICY DATE— AUG 09, 1982   062201 0000001 —POLICY NUMBER

DATE OF ISSUE— AUG 09, 1982   29—MALE —ISSUE AGE AND SEX

PREMIUM CLASS— STANDARD   MONTHLY —PREMIUM INTERVAL

OWNER, BENEFICIARY—AS DESIGNATED IN THE APPLICATION SUBJECT TO THE PROVISIONS OF THIS POLICY

BENEFIT AND PREMIUM SCHEDULE

FORM NO.	BENEFIT	PREMIUM	PAYMENT PERIOD
BC38F	TERM LIFE INSURANCE FOR 1 YEAR, RENEWABLE EVERY YEAR AS SHOWN IN THE TABLE OF RENEWAL PREMIUMS. CONVERTIBLE ON OR BEFORE AUG 08, 2033. CONVERSION CREDIT OF UP TO $90.00 AVAILABLE IF CONVERTED ON OR BEFORE AUG 08, 1987.	$9.50	1 YEAR
BC63F	PREMIUM WAIVER	$.40	1 YEAR

TOTAL PREMIUM ON POLICY DATE

ANNUAL	SEMIANNUAL	QUARTERLY	B-O-M MONTHLY
$109.80	$56.40	$29.80	$9.90

3

Source: LIFE AND HEALTH INSURANCE: A TEACHING MANUAL. Washington DC: American Council of Life Insurance/Health Insurance Association of America

062201 0000001—POLICY NUMBER

TABLE OF RENEWAL PREMIUMS

POLICY YEAR	ATTAINED AGE	MONTHLY PREMIUMS		
		LIFE INSURANCE	PREMIUM WAIVER	TOTAL
2	30	$ 9.50	$ .40	$ 9.90
3	31	9.50	.40	9.90
4	32	9.90	.40	10.30
5	33	9.90	.40	10.30
6	34	10.30	.40	10.70
7	35	10.30	.40	10.70
8	36	10.70	.40	11.10
9	37	11.50	.80	12.30
10	38	11.90	.80	12.70
11	39	12.70	.80	13.50
12	40	13.90	.80	14.70
13	41	14.70	.80	15.50
14	42	15.90	.80	16.70
15	43	16.70	1.20	17.90
16	44	17.90	1.20	19.10
17	45	19.50	1.20	20.70
18	46	21.10	1.60	22.70
19	47	22.70	1.60	24.30
20	48	24.70	2.00	26.70
21	49	26.70	2.00	28.70
22	50	28.70	2.80	31.50
23	51	31.50	3.20	34.70
24	52	33.90	4.00	37.90
25	53	37.10	5.20	42.30
26	54	40.30	6.00	46.30
27	55	43.90	7.20	51.10
28	56	47.50	8.40	55.90
29	57	51.90	10.00	61.90
30	58	56.70	11.20	67.90
31	59	61.90	12.40	74.30
32	60	67.50	4.40	71.90
33	61	73.90	4.00	77.90
34	62	80.70	3.60	84.30
35	63	88.30	3.20	91.50
36	64	97.10	3.60	100.70
37	65	106.70		106.70
38	66	117.50		117.50
39	67	129.90		129.90
40	68	143.50		143.50

4

062201   0000001—POLICY NUMBER

TABLE OF RENEWAL PREMIUMS

POLICY YEAR	ATTAINED AGE	MONTHLY PREMIUMS		
		LIFE INSURANCE	PREMIUM WAIVER	TOTAL
41	69	158.30		158.30
42	70	174.70		174.70
43	71	191.90		191.90
44	72	209.90		209.90
45	73	229.50		229.50
46	74	250.70		250.70
47	75	273.90		273.90
48	76	300.70		300.70
49	77	330.70		330.70
50	78	365.10		365.10
51	79	402.70		402.70
52	80	443.90		443.90
53	81	487.50		487.50
54	82	533.90		533.90
55	83	581.90		581.90
56	84	631.90		631.90
57	85	683.90		683.90
58	86	737.50		737.50
59	87	793.50		793.50
60	88	852.30		852.30
61	89	915.90		915.90
62	90	985.90		985.90
63	91	1,063.90		1,063.90
64	92	1,153.50		1,153.50
65	93	1,257.50		1,257.50
66	94	1,383.50		1,383.50
67	95	1,509.10		1,509.10
68	96	1,635.10		1,635.10
69	97	1,760.70		1,760.70

5

Source: THE AMERICAN LIFE INSURANCE FACTS: A TEACHING MANUAL. Washington, DC. American Council of Life Insurance/Health Insurance Association of America

DEFINITIONS

This section contains the standard meaning of terms used in your policy.

You

"You" means the Owner of this policy. "Your" and "yours" also refer to the Owner.

We

"We" means our company. "Us," "our" and "ours" also refer to our company.

Insured

"The Insured" is the person whose life is covered by this insurance policy.

Beneficiary

"The Beneficiary" is the person or persons to whom this policy's Sum Insured is paid when the Insured dies.

Sum Insured

"The Sum Insured" is the amount payable under your policy when the Insured dies. It may also be thought of as the death benefit or the face amount.

In Full Force

"In full force" means that each premium has been paid either by its Due Date or within the grace period.

Issue Age and Attained Age

"Issue Age" is the Insured's age on the last birthday before the Policy Date. It is shown on the Policy Specifications Page. We use it for each benefit of your policy, unless a different age is stated. "Attained Age" is the Issue Age plus the number of years and months since your policy was issued.

Written Notice

"Written Notice" is a request or notice in writing by you to us at our Home Office. It is how you let us know any requests you have, or changes you want to make to your policy.

Policy Date

The Policy Date is shown on the Policy Specifications Page. We use it to set premium Due Dates, policy years and policy anniversaries.

Date of Issue

The Date of Issue is shown on the Policy Specifications Page. We use it to interpret the Incontestability and Suicide provisions.

Policy Specifications Page

The Policy Specifications Page starts on Page 3 of your policy and gives basic information about your policy. This includes important items such as Date of Issue and Table of Renewal Premiums.

6

THE CONTRACT

Your insurance policy is a legal contract between you and us. Certain provisions are standard. This section gives these provisions and explains how they can affect your policy.

The Entire Contract

The entire contract is made up of this policy and your written application. We attached a copy of your application at issue.

All statements you made in the application, in the absence of fraud, are considered representations and not warranties. Only the statements made in your written application can be used by us to defend a claim or void this policy.

Changes to this policy are not valid unless we make them in writing. They must be signed by one of our Executive Officers.

Incontestability

We cannot contest your policy after it has been in force during the Insured's lifetime for two years from its Date of Issue, except for nonpayment of premiums.

Suicide

We will not pay the Sum Insured if the Insured commits suicide while sane or insane within two years after the Date of Issue. Instead, we will pay a sum equal to the total amount of premiums paid to that date.

Misstatement of Age or Sex

We will make adjustments if the Insured's age or sex was misstated in the application. The Sum Insured, and any other benefits, will be what the premiums paid would have bought at the correct age and sex.

Policy Settlement

We will pay the Sum Insured to the Beneficiary when we receive proof of the Insured's death. We will refund the part of any premium which has been paid for a period beyond the policy month in which the Insured died.

We may ask that this policy be returned to us at the time of settlement.

Nonparticipating

Your policy is nonparticipating. The premium does not include a charge for participating in surplus. This means we do not pay dividends on your policy.

7

PREMIUMS

You must pay your premiums on time to keep your policy in full force. You have certain rights if you do not. This section explains how and when your premiums are to be paid. It also gives some of your rights if a premium is not paid.

Payment

Your first premium is due on the Policy Date. It must be paid on or before delivery of your policy.

All premiums are to be paid in advance either at our Home Office or to one of our agents authorized to collect premiums. The amount of premium is shown on the Policy Specifications Page. If you request a receipt, we will give you one. It will be signed by an Executive Officer and countersigned by the agent.

Frequency

Premiums are to be paid on the first day of each Premium Interval. This is the "Due Date" of a premium. The Premium Interval is shown on the Policy Specifications Page.

You may change the Premium Interval by Written Notice. The change has to be made in accordance with our published rates and payment rules. No change to a less frequent Premium Interval can be made during the first policy year.

Grace Period

You have 31 days from Due Date to pay a premium. This is called "the grace period." The policy will continue in full force. No interest will be charged. But, if the Insured dies during the grace period, we will subtract the unpaid premium for those 31 days. (There is no grace period for the first premium.)

Default

If a premium is not paid by the end of the grace period, your policy will be in default. It will cease to be in full force. It will have no futher value. The date of default is the Due Date of the unpaid premium.

Reinstatement

You have the right to put your policy back in full force any time within five years of the date of default. You would then resume paying premiums.

We will require you to:

1. Give us evidence the Insured is still insurable according to our rules;

2. Pay the applicable renewal premium for the term period from the date of reinstatement to the next Term Expiry Date; and

3. Pay the unpaid premium for the 31-day grace period following the Due Date of the last premium in default, with compound interest at 6% per year from that Due Date.

8

OWNERSHIP AND BENEFICIARY

This section describes the Owner and the Beneficiary: who they are and what their rights in this policy are.

Ownership

You, the Owner, are named in the application. You may make use of all rights of this policy while the Insured is living. These rights are subject to the rights of any assignee or living irrevocable beneficiary. "Irrevocable" means that you have given up your right to change the Beneficiary named.

If you die, the Contingent Owner, if one is named, will become the Owner. If there is no named Owner then living, the rights of ownership will vest in the executors, administrators or assigns of the Owner.

Beneficiary

The Beneficiary is named in the application. More than one beneficiary may be named. The rights of any beneficiary who dies before the Insured will pass to the surviving beneficiary or beneficiaries unless you provide otherwise.

If no beneficiary is living at the Insured's death, we will pay the Sum Insured to you, your legal representatives or assigns.

The rights of any beneficiary will be subject to all the provisions of this policy. You may impose other limitations with our consent.

Change of Ownership or Beneficiary

You may change the Owner or the Beneficiary, unless an irrevocable one has been named, while the Insured is living. Change is made by Written Notice. The change takes effect on the date the notice was signed, if we acknowledge receipt of your notice in writing.

Any change is subject to any of our actions made before the date your notice was acknowledged. We may require return of this policy for endorsement before making a change.

Assignment and Assignee

Only you may make an assignment of this policy. You must notify us if you assign this policy. We are not responsible for the validity or effect of an assignment. Any change you make is subject to any action we made before the date the notice was received.

9

RENEWAL

Your policy is renewable each year. This section explains what you have to do.

Yearly Renewal

You may renew your policy each year, without evidence of insurability, until the policy anniversary at the Insured's Attained Age 98. A Table of Renewal Premiums showing the premium payable for each policy year is on the Policy Specifications Page. You must pay the renewal premium shown when due to keep your policy in full force. The renewal of your policy becomes effective when we receive the renewal premium, subject to the grace period provision.

When Renewal Premium Due

Your policy has an Original Term Expiry Date which is the end of the first term period. This is the first policy anniversary. Your first renewal premium is due on this date. Each time you renew your policy, you establish a new Term Expiry Date which will be the policy anniversary following the previous expiry date. Your renewal premium for the next term period is due on this new Term Expiry Date.

Effect of Total Disability on Renewal

We will waive any premium coming due and automatically renew your policy for you if:

1. A Premium Waiver Benefit is in your policy:

2. The Insured meets the conditions to qualify for waiver of premiums:

3. The Insured is disabled on any Term Expiry Date; and

4. You have not converted this policy.

10

CONVERSION

You may convert this policy to a different type of life insurance policy. This section explains how this is done.

Conversion Election

You may convert this policy, without evidence of insurability, to a nonparticipating life insurance policy. You must make this election prior to the date shown on the Policy Specifications Page for this and while your policy is in full force. The Sum Insured of the new policy may not be greater than the Sum Insured of this policy on the date of conversion. However, it may be less, subject to our then minimum amount requirements.

Conditions of Conversion

We will issue your new policy subject to the following conditions:

1. The premium during the first year must be as great as the premium for a Whole Life insurance policy with the same initial death benefit.

2. The Sum Insured must be level.

3. Your new policy will be issued on a restricted basis or in a class other than standard if we issued this policy in that way.

4. Your new policy may have a Premium Waiver Benefit if this policy has one. It will be the one we are then issuing. However, you cannot enlarge the Premium Waiver Benefit in this policy, and you must give us proof that the Insured is not disabled on the date of conversion.

   You may do this without evidence of insurability if this term insurance is converted to a Whole Life policy. But, you must have our consent if the Premium Waiver Benefit is to be included in a policy that is not Whole Life.

5. Your new policy may include benefits for loss from accident if these benefits are in this policy. The benefits will be those we are then issuing. However, you cannot enlarge the benefits in this policy.

6. Your new policy may include a Guaranteed Insurability Benefit if this policy has one. It will be the one we are then issuing.

7. You may have our consent to continue any other benefits which are part of this policy.

Issue Age of New Policy

The Issue Age of the new policy may be:

(a) The Insured's Attained Age on the date of conversion; or

(b) The Issue Age of the Insured on the Policy Date of this policy.

If you choose (a), the premium rate will be the one we are using on the date of conversion. Your new policy will become effective when we receive your application and first premium payment.

If you choose (b), the premium rate will be the one we were using on the Policy Date of this policy. Your new policy will become effective when you pay the greater of:

(1) The difference between the premiums you have paid for this policy and the premiums you would have paid for the new policy, plus 6% interest compounded annually; and

(2) The Cash Value of the new policy on the date of conversion.

Conversion Credit

A Conversion Credit is available to you if you convert this policy before the date shown on the Policy Specifications Page for this. The amount of Conversion Credit is also shown there. This amount is multiplied by the ratio of (a) the amount of insurance converted to (b) the Sum Insured on the Date of Issue.

If you convert during the first policy year, the Conversion Credit will be the amount determined above further multiplied by the ratio of (1) the premiums you have paid for this policy to (2) the premiums you would have paid for the new policy.

11

DECREASING TERM INSURANCE OPTION

Your policy is a level term insurance policy. This means the Sum Insured remains the same but the amount of your premium increases each policy year. You may change this and pay the same premium each year and have the Sum Insured decrease. This section explains how this is done.

Election of Option

You may elect this Decreasing Term Insurance Option on any policy anniversary prior to the Insured's Attained Age 80.

You must make this election by Written Notice.

If you do this, you would continue to pay the Life Insurance Premium payable during the prior policy year. You pay this premium instead of the premiums shown in the Table of Renewal Premiums on the Policy Specifications Page.

If you elect this option, the Sum Insured for the next policy year and all policy years after that will be determined from the table on the next page. This amount is based on the premium payable and the Attained Age of the Insured at the beginning of each policy year. Changes in the Sum Insured will occur each year on the policy anniversary.

You determine the Sum Insured from the table by first determining the annual life premium payable. To do this, take the Life Insurance Premium shown on the Policy Specifications Page for the policy year preceding the year in which you elect this option. Then adjust it as follows:

1. If you pay your premiums annually, deduct $15;

2. If you pay your premiums semiannually, multiply by 1.961 and then deduct $15;

3. If you pay your premiums quarterly, multiply by 3.846 and then deduct $15; or

4. If you pay your premiums by Bank-O-Matic (monthly), multiply by 11.494 and then deduct $15.

5. If you pay your premiums by Monthly Account, multiply by 10.417 and then deduct $15.

If your policy has a Premium Waiver Benefit, we will automatically continue the coverage at the premium rate shown on the next page. But, you may terminate this coverage by giving us Written Notice.

You must have our consent to continue any other benefits which are part of your policy.

If you elect this option, your policy must be returned to us for our endorsement. We will return the policy to you with a new Specifications Page showing the Table of Decreasing Sums Insured and the level premium payable.

12

Source: THE AMERICAN INSURANCE I/A TEACHING MANUAL, Washington, DC, American Council of Life Insurance/Health Insurance Association of America.

TABLE FOR DECREASING TERM OPTION

Age Last Birthday Male and Female	Sum Insured Per $100 Annual Life Premium*		Age Last Birthday Male and Female	Sum Insured Per $100 Annual Life Premium*	
	Male	Female		Male	Female
16	45,870	49,260	56	7,540	9,940
17	45,870	49,260	57	6,900	9,100
18	45,870	49,260	58	6,310	8,210
19	45,870	49,260	59	5,770	7,510
20	45,870	49,260	60	5,270	6,860
21	45,870	49,260	61	4,820	6,170
22	45,870	49,260	62	4,400	5,630
23	45,870	49,260	63	4,010	5,130
24	45,870	49,260	64	3,650	4,660
25	45,870	49,260	65	3,310	4,220
26	45,870	49,260	66	3,000	3,820
27	45,660	49,260	67	2,710	3,400
28	45,050	48,780	68	2,450	3,060
29	44,440	48,310	69	2,220	2,760
30	43,860	47,620	70	2,010	2,500
31	43,290	46,950	71	1,830	2,260
32	42,370	46,080	72	1,670	2,030
33	41,490	45,250	73	1,530	1,850
34	40,320	44,440	74	1,400	1,690
35	38,910	43,670	75	1,280	1,540
36	37,170	42,190	76	1,160	1,390
37	35,210	40,490	77	1,060	1,250
38	32,890	38,610	78	960	1,130
39	30,670	37,040	79	870	1,010
40	28,490	34,970	80	790	920
41	26,390	32,890	81	720	830
42	24,450	30,490	82	650	750
43	22,680	28,740	83	600	680
44	21,010	26,670	84	550	620
45	19,420	25,000	85	510	570
46	17,890	23,420	86	470	520
47	16,470	21,880	87	440	480
48	15,130	20,410	88	410	440
49	13,890	19,050	89	380	410
50	12,720	17,480	90	350	380
51	11,660	15,770	91	330	350
52	10,680	14,470	92	300	320
53	9,790	13,090	93	280	290
54	8,980	12,020	94	250	260
55	8,230	10,850	95	230	240
			96	200	210
			97	160	160

ANNUAL PREMIUM FOR PREMIUM WAIVER BENEFIT PER $100 ANNUAL LIFE INSURANCE PREMIUM

Age Last Birthday at Time Option is Selected— Male and Female	Premium**
16-39	$5.00
41-49	7.00
50-59	8.00
60-64	5.00

**Premiums shown will be adjusted for policies in a class other than standard.

*Amounts shown will be adjusted for policies in a class other than standard.

Source: LIFE AND HEALTH INSURANCE: A TEACHING MANUAL. Washington, DC: American Council of Life Insurance/Health Insurance Association of America

13

SETTLEMENT OPTIONS

This section describes the ways the proceeds of this policy can be paid other than in one lump sum payment.

All or any part of the proceeds may be left with us and paid under one of the following options.

Option 1

Interest Income: Proceeds left with us with interest paid at regular times as elected. Interest on each $1,000 of proceeds with be: $30.00 if paid yearly; $14.89 if paid two times a year; $7.42 if paid four times a year; or $2.47 if paid monthly. Payments are made at equal intervals.

Option 2

Installments for Fixed Period: Proceeds paid in equal payments one, two, four or twelve times a year, from one to thirty years. The amount of payment for each $1,000 of proceeds is shown in the Table for Option 2. Payments are made at equal intervals.

Option 3A

Life Income—Guaranteed Period: Proceeds paid in equal payments for as long as the payee lives. This option has guaranteed payment periods of not less than 10 or 20 years as elected.

Option 3B

Life Income—Guaranteed Return of Proceeds: Proceeds paid in equal payments for as long as the payee lives. In addition, a cash refund will be paid at the death of the payee for an amount, if any, equal to the original proceeds less the sum of all installments paid.

The amount of each payment will be in accordance with the Table for Option 3. It will be determined by the payee's sex and age last birthday on the date the first payment is due.

Option 4

Installments for Fixed Amount: Proceeds paid in equal payments one, two, four or twelve times a year. At least 5% of the original proceeds must be paid each year until the entire proceeds and interest are paid. Payments are made at equal intervals.

Option 5

Alternate Life Income: Proceeds paid as a life income. The amount of each payment will be based on our single premium annuity rates on the date of the option. These rates will be furnished on request.

14

Source: LIFE AND HEALTH INSURANCE, A TEACHING MANUAL, Washington, DC: American Council of Life Insurance/Health Insurance Association of America.

ELECTION OF SETTLEMENT OPTIONS

This section tells you how to elect a settlement option.

Election

You may elect a settlement option in the application or by Written Notice. During the Insured's lifetime, only you may make or change any election.

If there is no option in effect when the Insured dies, the payee may elect one. The payee may also name a contingent payee to receive any final payment.

The payee may change an option in effect when the Insured dies only if the option elected does not provide otherwise. However, if a life income option is in effect, that election may not be changed after payments have begun.

Availability

The options are available only with our consent if the payee is other than a natural person acting in his or her own right. Other settlement options can be arranged with our consent.

Guaranteed Interest and Excess Interest

We guarantee an interest rate of 3% per year. compounded yearly, under Options 1, 2 and 4. We will pay or credit additional interest under these options if our Board of Directors votes to do so.

Minimum Amounts

If the proceeds for one payee are less than $1,000, we have the right to pay that amount in a lump sum. No option is available under which the amount of proceeds would not be enough to make payments of at least $25.

Death of Payee

If a payee dies, we will pay any remaining amounts to the payee's legal representatives, unless other arrangements have been made with us. We will pay:

1. Under Options 1 and 4, the unpaid amount plus accrued interest; and

2. Under Options 2 and 3A, the commuted value of the remaining payments.

The commuted value is based on compound interest at 3% per year.

Rights to Commute and Withdraw

Unless other arrangements have been made with us, a payee will have the right to:

1. Withdraw proceeds left under Option 1 or 4; and

2. Withdraw the commuted value of the remaining payments under Option 2.

Proof of Age and Sex

We may require proof of the payee's age and sex before making any payment. If age or sex has been misstated, adjustments will be made.

Operative Date

We put an option into effect on the date the proceeds become payable. or on the date of election, if later. This means the first payment under Option 1 is made at the end of the interest period elected. Under Options 2, 3, 4 and 5, the first payment is made on the date we put the option into effect.

15

TABLE FOR SETTLEMENT OPTIONS

Monthly Payments Per $1000 of Proceeds Applied

OPTION 2			OPTION 3A				OPTION 3B	
			10 Years Certain & Life		20 Years Certain & Life		Cash Refund	
Period of Years	Monthly Payments	Age of Payee	Male	Female	Male	Female	Male	Female
1	$84.47	25 & under	$3.23	$3.09	$3.22	$3.08	$3.19	$3.07
2	42.86	26	3.26	3.11	3.24	3.10	3.22	3.09
3	28.99	27	3.29	3.13	3.27	3.12	3.25	3.11
4	22.06	28	3.32	3.16	3.30	3.15	3.28	3.13
5	17.91	29	3.35	3.18	3.33	3.17	3.30	3.16
6	$15.14	30	3.38	3.21	3.36	3.20	3.33	3.18
7	13.16	31	3.42	3.24	3.40	3.22	3.36	3.21
8	11.68	32	3.46	3.26	3.43	3.25	3.40	3.23
9	10.53	33	3.50	3.30	3.47	3.28	3.43	3.26
10	9.61	34	3.53	3.33	3.50	3.31	3.46	3.29
11	$8.86	35	3.58	3.36	3.54	3.34	3.50	3.32
12	8.24	36	3.62	3.40	3.58	3.38	3.54	3.35
13	7.71	37	3.67	3.43	3.62	3.41	3.58	3.38
14	7.26	38	3.72	3.47	3.66	3.45	3.62	3.42
15	6.87	39	3.77	3.51	3.71	3.48	3.66	3.45
16	$6.53	40	3.82	3.55	3.75	3.52	3.70	3.49
17	6.23	41	3.88	3.60	3.80	3.56	3.75	3.53
18	5.96	42	3.94	3.64	3.85	3.60	3.79	3.57
19	5.73	43	4.00	3.69	3.90	3.65	3.84	3.61
20	5.51	44	4.06	3.74	3.95	3.69	3.89	3.65
21	$5.32	45	4.13	3.79	4.00	3.74	3.94	3.70
22	5.15	46	4.20	3.85	4.05	3.79	4.00	3.75
23	4.99	47	4.27	3.91	4.11	3.84	4.05	3.80
24	4.84	48	4.35	3.97	4.16	3.89	4.11	3.85
25	4.71	49	4.42	4.04	4.22	3.95	4.17	3.90
26	$4.59	50	4.50	4.10	4.28	4.00	4.24	3.96
27	4.47	51	4.59	4.18	4.34	4.06	4.30	4.02
28	4.37	52	4.68	4.25	4.40	4.12	4.37	4.08
29	4.27	53	4.77	4.33	4.46	4.19	4.45	4.15
30	4.18	54	4.87	4.41	4.54	4.25	4.52	4.22
		55	$4.97	$4.50	$4.59	$4.32	$4.60	$4.29
		56	5.07	4.59	4.65	4.39	4.69	4.37
		57	5.18	4.69	4.71	4.46	4.77	4.45
		58	5.30	4.79	4.78	4.53	4.86	4.53
		59	5.41	4.89	4.84	4.60	4.96	4.62
		60	5.54	5.01	4.90	4.67	5.06	4.72
		61	5.67	5.13	4.96	4.74	5.17	4.81
		62	5.81	5.25	5.02	4.82	5.28	4.92
		63	5.95	5.39	5.08	4.89	5.40	5.03
		64	6.10	5.52	5.13	4.96	5.52	5.15
		65	6.25	5.68	5.18	5.03	5.65	5.27
		66	6.41	5.83	5.23	5.09	5.79	5.41
		67	6.57	6.00	5.28	5.15	5.94	5.54
		68	6.75	6.18	5.32	5.21	6.09	5.69
		69	6.93	6.36	5.35	5.26	6.25	5.85
		70	7.10	6.55	5.39	5.31	6.42	6.02
		71	7.28	6.75	5.41	5.35	6.61	6.20
		72	7.47	6.96	5.44	5.38	6.80	6.38
		73	7.65	7.17	5.46	5.41	7.00	6.58
		74	7.84	7.38	5.47	5.43	7.22	6.79
		75	8.02	7.59	5.49	5.45	7.44	7.01
		76	8.20	7.81	5.49	5.47	7.69	7.25
		77	8.38	8.01	5.50	5.48	7.95	7.49
		78	8.54	8.21	5.51	5.49	8.22	7.76
		79	8.70	8.40	5.51	5.49	8.52	8.04
		80	8.85	8.58	5.51	5.50	8.84	8.32
		81	8.99	8.74	5.51	5.50	9.17	8.62
		82	9.12	8.88	5.51	5.51	9.54	8.94
		83	9.23	9.01	5.51	5.51	9.94	9.26
		84	9.31	9.12	5.51	5.51	10.35	9.60
		85 & over	9.39	9.21	5.51	5.51	10.81	9.94

Annual, semiannual or quarterly payments under Option 2 are 11.839, 5.963 and 2.993 respectively times the monthly payments.

16

PART I   Life Insurance Application To *The COUNCIL Life Insurance Company*

IMPORTANT NOTICE—This application is subject to approval by the Company's Home Office. Be sure all questions in all parts of the application are answered completely and accurately, since the application is the basis of the insurance contract and will become part of any policy issued.

1. Insured's Full Name (Please Print-Give title as Mr., Dr., Rev., etc.)

MR. DENNIS SMITH

	Mo., Day, Yr. of Birth	Ins. Age	Sex	Place of Birth	Social Security No.
Single ☑ Married ☐ Widowed ☐ Divorced ☐ Separated ☐	8/25/53	29	M	TULSA OKLA.	0 D1-30-0000

2. Addresses last 5 yrs.

	Number	Street	City	State	Zip Code	County	Yrs.
Mail to ☑ Home: Present	711 SUNSET DRIVE	WASHINGTON DC			20000	USA	3
Former							
☐ Busi-ness: Present							
Former							

3. Occupation

	Title	Describe Exact Duties	Yrs.
Present	COMPUTER SPECIALIST	DEVELOP PROGRAMS FOR CLIENTS	3
Former	COMPUTER ANALYST	DEVELOP SOFTWARE PACKAGES	6

4. a) Employer ABC COMPUTER CONSULTANTS
b) Any change contemplated? Yes ☐ (Explain in Remarks) No ☑

5. Have you ever

	Yes	No
a) been rejected, deferred or discharged by the Armed Forces for medical reasons or applied for a government disability rating?	☐	☑
b) applied for insurance or for reinstatement which was declined, postponed, modified or rated?	☐	☑
c) used LSD, heroin, cocaine or methadone?	☐	☑

6. a) In the past 3 years have you

	Yes	No
(i) had your driver's license suspended or revoked or been convicted of more than one speeding violation?	☐	☑
(ii) operated, been a crew member of, or had any duties aboard any kind of aircraft?	☐	☑
(iii) engaged in underwater diving below 40 feet, parachuting, or motor vehicle racing?	☐	☑
b) In the future, do you intend to engage in any activities mentioned in (ii) and (iii) of a) above? (If "Yes" to 5a or any of 6, complete Supplemental Form 3375)	☐	☑

7. Have you smoked one or more cigarettes within the past 12 months?   ☑ Yes ☐ No

8. Are other insurance applications pending or contemplated?   ☐ Yes ☑ No

9. Do you intend to go to any foreign country?   ☐ Yes ☑ No

10. Will coverage applied for replace or change any life insurance or annuities? (If "Yes", submit Replacement Form)   ☐ Yes ☑ No

11. Total Life Insurance in force $_____ None ☑

12. Face Amount $ 40,000   Plan TERM

Accidental Death ☐   Waiver of Premium ☐
Purchase Option   Regular ☐   Preferred ☐   PEP ☐   GOR ☐
_____ units of Wife's Term   name: _____
$_____ initial amount Decreasing Term, _____ Years
(Joint ☐)   (Mot. Pro. ☐)   (Straight Line ☐)
Children's Term ☐   Other: _____

13. Auto. Prem. Loan provision operative if available? Yes ☑ No ☐

14. Dividend Option

	Additions (for other than Term policies) ☐ Deposits ☐
	Reduce premium, if applicable, otherwise cash ☐
	Supplemental Protection (Keyman only) ☐
	1 Year Term - any balance to ☐
	Deposits ☐ Additions ☐ Reduce prem. (cash if mo.) ☐

15. Beneficiary - for children's, wife's or joint insurance as provided in contract; for other insurance as follows, subject to policy's beneficiary provisions:

	(Name)	(Relationship to Insured)	
1st	KARYN SMITH	MOTHER	if living, if not
2nd	RONALD R. SMITH	FATHER	if living, if not
3rd	JEAN SMITH	SISTER	if living, if not

the executors or administrators of: Insured ☐   Other (use Remarks) ☑
(Joint beneficiaries will receive equally or survivor, unless otherwise specified.)

16. Flexible Plan settlement (personal beneficiary only)   ☑

17. Rights During Insured's lifetime all rights belong to
Insured ☑   Other: _____
Trustee ☐
(attach Trust)
(After Insured's death as provided in contract on wife's insurance.)

18. Premium Frequency MO. Amt. Paid $ 109.80 None ☐
Have you received a Conditional Receipt? Yes ☐   No ☐

REMARKS [Include details (company, date, amt., etc.) for all "Yes" answers to questions 4b, 5b, 5c, 8, 9 and 10]

SMOKES ONE PACK A DAY

I agree that: (1) No one but the Company's President, a Vice-President or Secretary has authority to accept information not contained in the application, to modify or enlarge any contract, or to waive any requirement. (2) Except as otherwise provided in any conditional receipt issued, any policy issued shall take effect upon its delivery and payment of the first premium during the lifetime of each person to be insured. Due dates of later premiums shall be as specified in the policy.

Dated at WASH., D.C.   on AUG 9   19 82   Signature of Insured   *Dennis Smith*

Signature of Applicant (if other than Insured) who agrees to be bound by the representations and agreements in this and any other part of this application   N/A
(Name)

Countersigned by *Michael C. Baker*
Field Underwriter (Licensed Resident Agent)

Source: LIFE AND HEALTH INSURANCE, A TEACHING MANUAL, Washington, DC, American Council of Life Insurance/Health Insurance Association of America

PART 1A	Statements Forming Part Of Application To *The COUNCIL Life Insurance Company* [Complete this Part if any Non-Medical or Family Insurance is Applied For]

1. Name of Insured DENNIS SMITH   Ins. Age **29**   Height **5** ft. **10** in.   Weight **165** lbs.

2. If Family, Children's, Wife's or Joint Insurance desired, other family members proposed for insurance:

Wife (include maiden name)	Ins. Age	Mo., Day, Yr. of Birth	Height ft. in.	Weight lbs.	Life in Force $	Place of Birth

Children	Sex	Ins. Age	Mo., Day, Yr. of Birth	Children	Sex	Ins. Age	Mo., Day, Yr. of Birth

3. Has any eligible dependent (a) been omitted from 2? Yes ☐ No ☑ (b) applied for insurance or for reinstatement which was declined, postponed, modified or rated or had a policy cancelled or renewal refused? Yes ☐ No ☑ (Give name, date, company in 8)

4. Have you or anyone else proposed for insurance, so far as you know, ever been treated for or had indication of (underline applicable item)

		Yes	No
a)	high blood pressure? (If "Yes", list drugs prescribed and dates taken.)	☐	☑
b)	chest pain, heart attack, rheumatic fever, heart murmur, irregular pulse or other disorder of the heart or blood vessels?	☐	☑
c)	cancer, tumor, cyst, or any disorder of the thyroid, skin, or lymph glands?	☐	☑
d)	diabetes or anemia or other blood disorder?	☐	☑
e)	sugar, albumin, blood or pus in the urine, or venereal disease?	☐	☑
f)	any disorder of the kidney, bladder, prostate, breast or reproductive organs?	☐	☑
g)	ulcer, intestinal bleeding, hepatitis, colitis, or other disorder of the stomach, intestine, spleen, pancreas, liver or gall bladder?	☐	☑
h)	asthma, tuberculosis, bronchitis, emphysema or other disorder of the lungs?	☑	☐
i)	fainting, convulsions, migraine headache, paralysis, epilepsy or any mental or nervous disorder?	☐	☑
j)	arthritis, gout, amputation, sciatica, back pain or other disorder of the muscles, bones or joints?	☐	☑
k)	disorder of the eyes, ears, nose, throat or sinuses?	☑	☐
l)	varicose veins, hemorrhoids, hernia or rectal disorder?	☐	☑
m)	alcoholism or drug habit?	☐	☑

5. Have you or anyone else proposed for insurance, so far as you know, (underline applicable item)

		Yes	No
a)	consulted or been **examined** or treated by any physician or practitioner in the past 5 years?	☑	☐
b)	had, or been advised to have, an x-ray, cardiogram, blood or other diagnostic test in the past 5 years?	☐	☑
c)	been a patient in a hospital, clinic, or other medical facility in the past 5 years?	☐	☑
d)	ever had a surgical operation **performed** or advised?	☐	☑
e)	ever made claim for disability or applied for compensation or retirement based on accident or sickness?	☐	☑

6. Are you or any other person proposed for insurance, so far as you know, in impaired physical or mental health, or under any kind of medication? ☐ Yes ☑ No

7. Weight change in last 6 months of adults proposed for insurance.

Name	Gain	Loss	Cause
N/A			

8. Details of all "Yes" answers. For any checkup or routine examination, indicate what symptoms, if any, prompted it and include results of the examination and any special tests. Include clinic number if applicable.

Question No.	Name of Person	Illness & Treatment	No. of Attacks	Dates: Onset-Recovery	Doctor, Clinic or Hospital and Complete Address
4 H	DENNIS SMITH	BRONCHITIS	6	1960-1967	DR. WILLIAM BILLS 29 QUEBEC ST. TULSA OKLA.
4 K	DENNIS SMITH	CONJUNCTIVITIS	1	1981	DR. J.J. MARSHALL
5 B	DENNIS SMITH	CHEST X-RAY – JOB	1		99 ELM ST. WASH, DC.
5 D	DENNIS SMITH	BROKEN KNEECAP	1	1972-1973	DR. WILLIAM BILLS

So far as may be lawful, I waive for myself and all persons claiming an interest in any insurance issued on this application, all provisions of law forbidding any physician or other person who has attended or examined, or who may attend or examine, me or any other person covered by such insurance, from disclosing any knowledge or information which he thereby acquired.

I represent the statements and answers in this and in any other part of this application to be true and complete to the best of my knowledge and belief, and offer them to the Company for the purpose of inducing it to issue the policy or policies and to accept the payment of premiums thereunder. I also agree that payment of the first premium (if after this date) shall be a representation by me that such statements and answers would be the same if made at the time of such payment.

Dated at WASH., DC on AUG. 9 19 82   Signature of Insured *Dennis Smith*

Witnessed by *Michael C. Baker*   Signature of Wife (if insured) N/A
Field Underwriter (Licensed Resident Agent)

AUTHORIZATION

For purposes of determining my eligibility for insurance, I hereby authorize any physician, practitioner, hospital, clinic, institution, insurance company, Medical Information Bureau, or other organization or person that has records or knowledge of me or my health to give any such information to the Council Life Insurance Company.

If application is made to The Council Life Insurance Company for insurance on any member of my family, this authorization also applies to such member. A photostatic copy of this authorization shall be as valid as the original.

Signed on AUG. 9 , 19 82   *Dennis Smith*
                                             Signature of Insured

152

Source: LIFE AND HEALTH INSURANCE: A TEACHING MANUAL. Washington, DC: American Council of Life Insurance Health Insurance Association of America

2. The Application

GAUNT v. JOHN HANCOCK MUTUAL LIFE INSURANCE COMPANY

United States Court of Appeals, Second Circuit, 1947.
160 F.2d 599, cert. denied, 331 U.S. 849, 67 S.Ct. 1736, 91 L.Ed. 1858 (1947).

L. HAND, Circuit Judge.

The plaintiff appeals from a judgment, dismissing her complaint after a trial to the judge, in an action, brought as beneficiary, to recover upon a contract of life insurance upon her son's life. There are only two questions: first, whether the defendant insured the son at all; and second, if so, whether he was intentionally shot, in which event a provision for "double indemnity" did not apply. The judge made detailed findings, the substance of which, so far as they are material to this appeal, is as follows. One, Kelman, a solicitor for the defendant authorized to take applications from prospective customers and to give receipts for first premiums, after two preliminary interviews with Gaunt, the insured, on August 3d, procured from him the signed "application," which is the subject of the action. This was a printed document of considerable length and much detail, the only passage in which here relevant we quote in full in the margin.[1] The important words were: "if the Company is satisfied that on the date of the completion of Part B of this application I was insurable * * * and if this application * * * is, prior to my death, approved by the Company at its Home office, the insurance applied for shall be in force as of the date of completion of said Part B." Number 12 of the answers which the insured was to make in the "application" was in the alternative; it read: "Insurance effective: (Check date desired) Date of Part B ☐ Date of issue of Policy ☐." When Gaunt signed the application he had not checked either of these answers; but after he had delivered it to Kelman, Kelman checked the second, so that, as the "application" read, Gaunt was to be insured only from the issuance of the policy. The judge found that "Both Gaunt and Kelman intended that Gaunt should be covered from the date of the completion of the medical examination"; and that Kelman's checking of the wrong answer "was due to a mutual mistake on the part of Gaunt and Kelman."

At the time of signing the "application" Gaunt paid the full first premium and Kelman gave him a receipt containing the words we have just quoted without substantial change: both the "application" and the receipt were upon forms prepared by the defendant for use by solicitors such as Kelman. On the same day Kelman took Gaunt to the defen-

---

1. "If the first premium or installment thereof above stated was paid when this application was signed, and if the Company is satisfied that on the date of the completion of Part B of this application I was insurable in accordance with the Company's rules for the amount and on the plan applied for without modification, and if this application, including said Part B, is, prior to my death, approved by the Company at its Home Office, the insurance applied for shall be in force as of the date of completion of said Part B, but, if this application so provides, such insurance shall be in force as of the date of issue of the policy."

dant's local examining physician who found him insurable under the rules and who recommended him for acceptance. Kelman delivered the "application" and the premium, and the physician delivered the favorable report, to one, Wholey, the defendant's local agent for Waterbury, Connecticut, who prepared a report recommending acceptance, signed by himself and Kelman, which he sent with the "application" and the physician's report to the "home office," where the documents were received on the 9th. Since it appeared from the papers that Gaunt had been classified as "4F" in the draft because of defective eyesight, the "medical department" at the "home office" required another physical examination in Waterbury. This took place on the 17th; on the same day the local physician wrote to the "home office" again passing Gaunt; and on the 19th "a lay medical examiner" for the "medical department" at the "home office" approved the "application." Nevertheless the "home office" on the 20th wrote to Wholey asking further information as to Gaunt's classification in the draft; Wholey answered satisfactorily on the 24th by a letter received on the 25th; and on the 26th one of the "doctors of the medical department * * * approved" the application from a medical standpoint." The "home office" received news on that day of Gaunt's death, and never finally approved the "application," although the judge found that, if Gaunt had lived, it would have done so. * * *

The first question is whether Gaunt was covered at all at the time of his death. Curiously, neither party has incorporated in the record "Part B," and we do not know what was the date of its "completion." If it was the approval "from a medical standpoint" as "advised by one of the doctors of the medical department," it was not "completed" before Gaunt's death. On the other hand the judge found that "Gaunt was, at the time of the completion of Part B, insurable in accordance with the rules of the defendant company for the plan and the amount applied for," and that is consistent only with the understanding that "completion" was earlier than the 25th. The defendant has not argued to the contrary and we shall so assume. Thus the question becomes whether the words: "if the application, including Part B, is prior to my death, approved by the Company, at its Home Office," must inescapably be read as a condition precedent upon the immediately following promise: "the insurance * * * shall be in force as of the date of the completion of Part B." It is true that if the clause as a whole be read literally, the insured was not covered if he died after "completion of Part B," but before "approval"; and indeed he could not have been because there must always be an insurable interest when the insurance takes effect.[2] Yet what meaning can be given to the words "as of the date of the completion of Part B" if that be true? The defendant suggests six possible "advantages" to the insured which will satisfy the phrase, "the insurance * * * will be in force," (1) The policy would sooner become incontestable. (2) It would earlier reach maturity, with

2. *Griffin v. McCoach*, 5 Cir., 116 F.2d 261; *Starr v. Mutual Life Ins. Co.*, 41 Wash. 228, 83 P. 116.

a corresponding acceleration of dividends and cash surrender. (3) It would cover the period after "approval" and before "issue." (4) If the insured became uninsurable between "completion" and "approval," it would still cover the risk. (5) If the insured's birthday was between "completion" and "approval," the premium would be computed at a lower rate. (6) When the policy covers disability, the coverage dates from "completion." An underwriter might so understand the phrase, when read in its context, but the application was not to be submitted to underwriters; it was to go to persons utterly unacquainted with the niceties of life insurance, who would read it colloquially. It is the understanding of such persons that counts,[3] and not one in a hundred would suppose that he would be covered, not "as of the date of completion of Part B," as the defendant promised, but only as of the date of approval. Had that been what the defendant meant, certainly it was easy to say so; and had it in addition meant to make the policy retroactive for some purposes, certainly it was easy to say that too. To demand that persons wholly unfamiliar with insurance shall spell all this out in the very teeth of the language used, is unpardonable. It does indeed some violence to the words not to make actual "approval" always a condition, and to substitute a prospective approval, however inevitable, when the insured has died before approval. But it does greater violence to make the insurance "in force" only from the date of "approval"; for the ordinary applicant who has paid his first premium and has successfully passed his physical examination, would not by the remotest chance understand the clause as leaving him uncovered until the insurer at its leisure approved the risk; he would assume that he was getting immediate coverage for his money. This is confirmed by the alternatives presented in the twelfth question; the insurance was to be "effective," either when the policy issued, or at the "date of Part B"; there was not an inkling of any other date for the inception of the risk. It is true that in Connecticut as elsewhere the business of writing life insurance is not colored with a public interest; yet in that state, again as elsewhere, the canon contra proferentem is more rigorously applied in insurance than in other contracts, in recognition of the difference between the parties in their acquaintance with the subject matter. A man must indeed read what he signs, and he is charged, if he does not; but insurers who seek to impose upon words of common speech an esoteric significance intelligible only to their craft, must bear the burden of any resulting confusion. We can think of few situations where that canon is more appropriate than in such a case as this.

Situations very close aboard have arisen not infrequently, although the actual words have necessarily varied, so that it is hardly fair to say that any decision is quite on all fours. However, the important question is how far the condition of subsequent approval shall prevail over the promise of immediate coverage as soon as the insured has paid his premium and has passed his physical examination. * * * [The court then discussed a series of cases addressing the issue.] Thus upon a

3. Restatement of Contracts, §§ 230, 233.

preponderance of the decided cases the answer is in doubt, and we cannot be sure how a Connecticut court would decide for the point has never come up in that state. Unaided as we are, we rest our decision upon the reasons which we have tried to set forth.

Judgment reversed; judgment to be entered for plaintiff for $15,000.

CLARK, Circuit Judge (concurring).

I agree that the course of negotiations required and controlled by the insurance company was "unpardonable," and am willing to concur in the decision for that reason. But I do not think we can properly or should rest upon the ambiguity of the company's forms of application and receipt. Had this bargaining occurred between parties with equal knowledge of the business and on equal terms, there could be little difficulty in supporting the condition precedent that the "insurance," i.e., the insurance contract or policy, could not "be in force," i.e., take effect, until approved at the home office, and that then it dated back to an earlier time. Moreover, conditions of this general form are unfortunately still too customary for a court to evince too much surprise at them. There have been acute discussions of the legal problems involved; thus, most helpful is the article, Operation of Binding Receipts in Life Insurance, 44 Yale L.J. 1223.[1] There receipts given for the payment of the first premium were held best divisible in two categories, one requiring approval as a condition precedent to the contract, in substance as here, and the other requiring that the company be satisfied that on the date of the medical examination the applicant was an insurable risk, and that the application was otherwise "acceptable" under the company's regulations for the amount and plan of the policy applied for. The first form, it was said, was generally held to prevent the existence of a contract before acceptance, except with a few courts which found the provision too inequitable to support. The second, however, gave no difficulty where its reasonable requirements were afterwards found to have been met. A questionnaire to insurance officials showed an increasing trend towards the second or fairer form—a development warmly supported by the author. There was further the acute observation that use of the former form resulted in continuous litigation in a field of law where certainty was essentially indispensable, since it stimulated judicial interpretation to resolve the "ambiguity" against the company, followed by the latter's renewed attempts to revise and refine the technical words.

Hence a result placed not squarely upon inequity, but upon interpretation, seems sure to produce continuing uncertainty in the law of insurance contracts. Even though for my part I should feel constrained

---

1. Other references might include Kessler, Contracts of Adhesion—Some Thoughts about Freedom of Contract, 43 Col.L.Rev. 629, 631–635; Patterson, The Delivery of a Life Insurance Policy, 33 Harv.L.Rev. 198; Havighurst, Life Insurance Binding Receipts, 33 Ill.L.Rev. 180.

to concede the weight of judicial authority against our view,[2] I think the considerations stated are persuasive to uphold recovery substantially as would occur under the second form of contract stated above. I am somewhat troubled as to the state of local law in view of the stress in *Swentusky v. Prudential Ins. Co. of America*, 116 Conn. 526, 164 A. 686, upon the absence of unique features to insurance law. But that was actually in another connection, a fact which I think justifies us in not here abdicating our judicial role for that envisioned by Judge Frank in *Richardson v. Commissioner of Internal Revenue*, 2 Cir., 126 F.2d 562, 567, 140 A.L.R. 705, of "ventriloquist's dummy" as to state law.

Notes and Questions

1. *The Function of the Binder.* A document termed a "binder," "binding receipt," or "conditional receipt" usually is issued when the insured pays the first premium upon submitting an application for life insurance. Sometimes it is merely a copy of the application that also contains a set of provisions delineating its effect. Insurers could avoid the problem that arose in *Gaunt* by issuing no binder, or by declining to request payment of the first premium with the application. But the binder gives the impression that the insured is getting something immediately. Payment of a premium both strengthens this impression and makes it less likely the insured will withdraw his application—for then he must attempt to secure a refund of the premium.

2. *The Rationale of the Decision.* Do you agree with Judge Clark's suggestion that Judge Hand's opinion rested on an interpretation of the binder rather than on the inequity of its provisions? Under the insurer's interpretation of the binder, would an applicant's beneficiary ever be entitled to payment if the applicant died before approval of the application? If not, what did it mean to say that the policy would take effect on the date of completion of Part B? Are insurers in such settings guarding themselves against adverse selection or trying to mislead applicants? Even if the latter, do decisions such as *Gaunt* create unmanageable problems of adverse selection or do they merely require more careful supervision of agents by the home office?

3. *Extensions of Hand's Approach.* Many courts have reached the same result as *Gaunt*, sometimes interpreting provisions in applications that purport to make coverage effective "from the date of application" once the conditions specified in the application have been satisfied. The effect of all the decisions seems to be to transform the condition precedent stated in the binder or application (insurability of the insured on some specified date, or actual approval by the company) into a condition subsequent. Why is the practical effect of this transforma-

---

2. Making the distinction between the forms of provision as indicated by my text, I fear I cannot see as much judicial division as my brothers observe; though I do think too far-reaching such statements of annotators with reference to such a conditional receipt: "It is uniformly held that such an instrument is absolutely ineffectual in providing protection to the applicant until the application is approved or accepted." 81 A.L.R. 332, 333; 107 A.L.R. 194, 195.

tion to create immediate "temporary" life insurance for the applicant? The rationale of some of the cases is that the binder is ambiguous. See, e.g., *Puritan Life Insurance Company v. Guess,* 598 P.2d 900 (Alaska 1979). Others conclude that the applicant would reasonably expect immediate coverage upon payment of a premium. See, e.g., *Collister v. Nationwide Life Insurance Company,* 479 Pa. 579, 388 A.2d 1346 (1978), *cert. denied,* 439 U.S. 1089, 99 S.Ct. 871, 59 L.Ed.2d 55 (1979). Do you agree?

Some courts hold that denial of immediate coverage is unconscionable. See, e.g., *Smith v. Westland Life Insurance Company,* 15 Cal.3d 111, 123 Cal.Rptr. 649, 539 P.2d 433 (1975). In *Smith,* the insured was informed that his application had been rejected, but he died one day later, before his premium was returned. The Supreme Court of California held that the temporary insurance created upon payment of the first premium does not terminate until the premium is refunded. What makes denial of coverage under such circumstances unconscionable? For more detailed discussion of *Smith,* see K. Abraham, Distributing Risk: Insurance, Legal Theory, and Public Policy 107–09 (1986).

3. The Requirement of an Insurable Interest

The requirement that the owner of a life insurance policy have an insurable interest in the life of the party insured has existed since the enactment of an anti-wagering insurable interest statute in England in 1774.[1] The moral hazard that would be created if a complete stranger could take out insurance on the life of another is too obvious to require discussion; it is also too obvious for insurers to be misled by such strangers in any but highly unusual circumstances. There are a few cases in which the insurer has been so negligent in failing to detect the policyholder's intention at the time of application to do away with the party whose life is insured that the courts have imposed tort liability on the insurer for that result. Even in these cases, however, there was a pre-existing relationship between the policyholder and the deceased. See, e.g., *Liberty National Life Insurance Company v. Weldon,* 267 Ala. 171, 100 So.2d 696 (1957) in which an aunt-in-law insured and then murdered her two and one-half year old niece. Most of the cases delineating the scope of the insurable interest requirement, in fact, concern parties with at least a colorable claim to having satisfied the insurable interest requirement.

In the United States the insurable interest requirement began as a judicially-imposed doctrine, but many states have enacted statutes codifying or slightly modifying common law rules governing the requirement. The sum and substance of most of these statutes and of decisions in states that have not enacted them is that the requirement is satisfied if (to quote the New York statute) the policyholder has a "substantial interest engendered by love and affection" or a "lawful and substantial economic interest" in the continued existence of the

---

1. The Life Assurance Act of 1774, 14 Geo. 3, c. 48.

person whose life is insured. See New York Ins. Law § 3205. Broad language such as this leaves a good deal of room for judicial backing and filling.

RYAN v. TICKLE

Supreme Court of Nebraska, 1982.
210 Neb. 630, 316 N.W.2d 580.

BRODKEY, J., Retired.

Lois M. Ryan, the plaintiff and appellant herein, is the widow of Eugene Ryan and the executrix of his estate. She commenced this action to recover the proceeds of a life insurance policy which were paid to the decedent's former business partner, appellee Gerald L. Tickle. After a trial in the District Court of Lincoln County, Nebraska, the appellee demurred to the evidence presented by the appellant and moved to dismiss appellant's petition. In its judgment entered on June 4, 1980, the trial court sustained the appellee's motions and dismissed the appellant's petition with prejudice. We affirm.

The facts as revealed in the record disclose that the decedent, Eugene Ryan, was a licensed mortician doing business in North Platte as the manager and president of Ryan Funeral Home, Inc. Tickle was licensed as a mortician doing business in Arnold, Nebraska, as owner of the Quig–Tickle Funeral Home. It appears that the two men had known each other since 1964, and in October 1971 they went into business together. The Ryan Funeral Home, Inc., had 477 outstanding shares of stock distributed among 12 shareholders. Ryan owned 50 shares of the company and Tickle purchased 25 shares. The two men also obtained an option to purchase the remaining outstanding stock in the Ryan Funeral Home from the other shareholders. The 5-year option was to expire on September 2, 1976, and granted Ryan and Tickle, or the survivor of them, the right to exercise the option.

In March 1972 Ryan and Tickle were offered an opportunity to purchase the Mullen Funeral Home located in nearby Mullen, Nebraska. They purchased the funeral home together for $20,000, as equal partners. They borrowed $7,000 for the down-payment and arranged to finance the balance over a period of 5 to 6 years.

Shortly after the purchase of the Mullen Funeral Home, Ryan and Tickle decided to purchase life insurance policies on each other's lives, their ultimate business goal being to acquire ownership of the Ryan and Mullen funeral homes and to provide a fund by which the survivor could purchase the homes upon the death of one of the partners. It was their estimate that if one died, the survivor would need $20,000 to $25,000 to purchase the other's interest in the Mullen Funeral Home and an additional $75,000 to purchase the outstanding stock of the Ryan Funeral Home from the owners thereof under the option agreement.

Ryan and Tickle thereupon purchased decreasing term life insurance policies on their joint lives in the total amount of $100,000. Tickle was designated the owner of one policy which had a face value of $50,000, and Ryan was designated the owner of a second policy, also valued at $50,000. Both policies insured the joint lives of Ryan and Tickle so that the entire proceeds were payable to the survivor of them. The premiums for the insurance were paid by an automatic bank withdrawal arrangement through a partnership bank account maintained for the Mullen Funeral Home.

In early 1973 it was discovered that Ryan had cancer from which he subsequently died on October 25, 1975. Following Ryan's death, Tickle collected a total of $88,000 as the beneficiary of the two life insurance policies. On September 22, 1976, Tickle and the appellant entered into a settlement agreement in which Tickle purchased the decedent's interest in the Mullen Funeral Home for the sum of $15,000. In addition, Tickle agreed to pay an additional $3,000 to the appellant in full and complete distribution of any sum of money claimed to be distributable to the decedent as undistributed earnings from the Mullen partnership. Tickle also agreed to assume and pay the unpaid balance due on the Mullen Funeral Home in the amount of $9,000. He also purchased all the assets of the Ryan Funeral Home from the board of directors and shareholders of the corporation for the sum of $147,000.

On November 7, 1977, the appellant, as executrix of the estate of Eugene Ryan, instituted this action alleging that the estate was entitled to all insurance proceeds paid upon the death of the decedent. In her brief on appeal to this court, appellant makes two principal arguments, to wit: That Tickle did not have an insurable interest in the life of the deceased, Eugene Ryan, and hence was not entitled to receive the proceeds of the insurance policies as the surviving partner of the deceased; and that the proceeds paid under the insurance agreement on decedent's life exceeded by $73,000 the amount of decedent's insurable interest in the Mullen Funeral Home, thus creating a wagering contract which is void as against public policy.

We note at the outset that the evidence in the record clearly indicates that the agreement between the partners had a dual purpose: not only to acquire for the survivor the Mullen Funeral Home but also to acquire the outstanding shares of stock in Ryan Funeral Home, Inc. The trial court found, and we conclude that the record sustains such finding, that the parties made a good faith estimate that the amount of money necessary to accomplish both such purposes would be approximately $100,000. That being so, appellee argues that the insurance contract was not a "wagering" contract but, rather, was a valid and enforceable contract of insurance. Also, with regard to appellant's contention that appellee did not have an insurable interest in the life of the decedent, appellee points out that the term "insurable interest" is defined in Neb.Rev.Stat. § 44–103(13) (Reissue 1978) as follows: "Insurable interest, in the matter of life and health insurance, exists when the beneficiary because of relationship, either pecuniary or from ties of blood or marriage, has reason to expect some benefit from the continuance of the life of the insured." In view of their avowed purpose in obtaining the insurance in question, in addition to the fact that evidence in the record discloses income tax returns showing increased profits from the operation of the funeral homes since the association of the parties as partners, appellee argues that there was clearly an expectation of benefit from the continuance of the life of the insured, and that therefore Tickle had an "insurable interest" in the life of the decedent Ryan.

We conclude, however, that we need not, and indeed may not, decide these issues, for the reason that the appellant herein has no standing or right to bring this lawsuit.

The law is well established throughout the country that only the insurer can raise the objection of want of an insurable interest. "The question of the lack of insurable interest in a life insurance policy may be raised only by the insurance company, and, where the company recognizes the validity of the policy, as by paying the amount thereof to the person named therein or into court, ordinarily adverse claimants to the fund may not raise the objection of lack of insurable interest." 44 C.J.S. *Insurance* § 212 at 915 (1945). See, also, *Poland v. Fisher's Estate,* 329 S.W.2d 768 (Mo.1959); *Ryan v. Andrewski,* 206 Okla. 199, 242 P.2d 448 (1952); *Edgington v. Equitable L. Assur. Soc.,* 236 Iowa 903, 20 N.W.2d 411 (1945). "The heirs of the insured have no cause of action against the insurer upon a policy the proceeds of which have been paid by the insurer to a third person who was the beneficiary designated in the policy, on the ground that the insurer could have refused to make the payment for want of an insurable interest on the part of the beneficiary." 3 Couch on Insurance 2d, Insurable Interest, § 24:6 at 76 (1960).

The above-cited authorities make it clear that only an insurer has standing to complain of a lack of insurable interest and that the heirs of the insured may not proceed on such cause of action against the designated beneficiary. This position was recently discussed in an excellent opinion by the Michigan Court of Appeals in *Secor v. Pioneer Foundry,* 20 Mich.App. 30, 173 N.W.2d 780 (1969). In that case Pioneer Foundry obtained a $50,000 life insurance policy on Secor, who was a 9-year employee of the company. Three years later Secor terminated his employment; however, the company paid the 1964 policy premium 8 months after Secor had terminated his employment. Secor died a month later, and the company collected the proceeds of the insurance. Secor's widow filed suit, alleging that Pioneer Foundry had no insurable interest in Secor's life and sought a constructive trust to be imposed in favor of Secor's estate. The trial court dismissed Mrs. Secor's suit.

On appeal, the Michigan court, citing *Hicks v. Cary,* 332 Mich. 606, 52 N.W.2d 351 (1952), held: " 'We hold to the rule that lack in the beneficiary of an insurable interest equal to the full amount of the insurance policy, to the extent that it thereby renders the policy a wagering contract, constitutes a barrier to the beneficiary's right to receive and retain the full amount of the insurance proceeds, but that *it is one which may be raised by and for the benefit of the insurer alone.'* " *Id.* 20 Mich.App. at 33, 173 N.W.2d at 781. The court concluded that it was the insurer alone who had standing to complain of a lack of insurable interest and noted that the insurance company had paid the proceeds of the policy to Pioneer Foundry without raising the issue. The court affirmed the dismissal of the plaintiff's action based on a lack of standing to complain.

In *Secor* the court at 33, 173 N.W.2d at 782, stated: "The rule that only the insurer can raise the question of lack of insurable interest appears to be well supported in other jurisdictions," and cites in support thereof, 3 Couch on Insurance, *supra;* 2 Appleman, Insurance Law & Practice, § 765 (1966); Vance on Insurance, § 31 at 199 (3d ed. 1951). In the opinion, the court at 34, 173 N.W.2d at 782, states: "In recognition of these considerations the almost universal rule of law in this country is that if the insurable interest requirement is satisfied at the time the policy is issued, the proceeds of the policy must be paid upon the death of the life insured without regard to whether the beneficiary has an insurable interest at the time of death." The court in *Secor* also recognized that there are cases that hold that a creditor who acquires insurance on his debtor's life may not recover more than the amount of the debt and the premiums he paid. In this connection, however, the court at 37, 173 N.W.2d at 784, stated: "This analysis has been rejected in the better-reasoned cases; it is contrary to the principle that the termination of an insurable interest does not affect the rights of an owner-beneficiary in a life policy." The court also noted at 35, 173 N.W.2d at 783: "Life insurance is not meant to assuage grief; its primary function is monetary. It serves fundamentally the same purpose whether the beneficiary is a widow or a business; it seeks to replace with a sum of money the earning capacity of the life insured." The court concluded at 36, 173 N.W.2d at 783: "We also decline to limit Pioneer Foundry's recovery to the amount of its investment in the policy and its financial loss (probably nil) upon Secor's death. Pioneer Foundry's investment in the policy was large both quantitatively and relatively."

The holding and reasoning of the Michigan Court of Appeals is persuasive in the instant case, and we conclude that appellant is without standing to object that no insurable interest existed between the decedent and the appellee, or that the parties had entered into an illegal wagering agreement. The judgment of the District Court dismissing appellant's cause of action must be, and hereby is, affirmed.

AFFIRMED.

Notes and Questions

1. *Wager Nonetheless?* Was the court correct in suggesting that because Ryan and Tickle purchased insurance on each other's lives in

order to help the survivor finance purchase of the other's interest in their business, they were not wagering? What other factors would have to exist for this not to be a wager?

2. *The Creditor's Insurable Interest.* As *Ryan* suggests, the policyholder must not only have an insurable interest in the life of the party insured; he must have an insurable interest at least equal to the amount of the coverage purchased. Where the relationship is between debtor and creditor, the amount of the debt typically is the limit of the creditor's interest, although there are occasional decisions allowing the creditor to insure for a greater amount. See, e.g., *American Casualty Company v. Rose,* 340 F.2d 469 (10th Cir.1964). In other kinds of business relationships there must be some flexibility to the requirement, because the business value of individuals is somewhat subjective, and because both the value of a business and an individual's value to it can fluctuate.

In rare cases, however, reasonable people could not disagree that the amount insured is excessive. One of the most extraordinary cases addressing this issue is *Rubenstein v. The Mutual Life Insurance Company of New York,* 584 F.Supp. 272 (E.D.La.1984). Rubenstein was the owner of a taxi cab when he became interested in starting a "TV Journal" whose revenues would be derived solely from advertising. Connor, who was out of work, was put in touch with Rubenstein by the Louisiana Unemployment Commission. Connor began to work for Rubenstein, and then agreed to purchase a TV Journal "franchise" from him. Connor was 23 years old, had no experience in that line of business, and was at that point earning $100 to $150 per week selling advertising space in the Journal. Given the terms of their agreement, the maximum debt Connor could have owed Rubenstein for the franchise was $2000. They then obtained insurance on Connor's life in the amount of $240,000, naming Rubenstein as beneficiary.

The policy was delivered on October 6. On November 5, Rubenstein, several of his relatives, and a friend of Rubenstein's named Fournier—a convicted felon then on probation—went deer hunting with Connor. According to his mother's testimony, Connor had never been hunting before and was disgusted by the idea of killing animals. "When the party arrived at the location, [Rubenstein] distributed the firearms, ammunition, and orange hunting vest to each member of the group. Thereafter, Kenney locked the car keys inside the car, and the group searched for wire with which to open the door lock. Soon after Connor was able to open the front door on the passenger side, Fournier, who was standing less than 10 feet behind Connor, discharged his gun, a single shot, 12–gauge shotgun. The pellets struck Connor in the back, slightly above the waist. * * *" 584 F.Supp. at 277. Connor died from his wounds, and Rubenstein claimed MONY owed him $240,000. MONY refused to pay, asserting both fraud on Rubenstein's part and the absence of an insurable interest. The court held that where the insurable interest in question is a creditor's interest in repayment of a debt, the beneficiary lacks an insurable interest if the value of the life insurance is grossly disproportionate to the amount actually owed, and the policy is null and void. For this reason Rubenstein had no insurable interest in Connor's life.

3. *Owner and Beneficiary.* Although the court in *Rubenstein* referred to the absence of an insurable interest in a *beneficiary,* its use of that term must be understood in context. Rubenstein's life was not insured; but he was both owner of the policy *and* beneficiary. With the possible exception of Texas, see *Kennedy v. Laird,* 503 S.W.2d 664 (Tex.Civ.App.1973), no modern court has held (and no statute provides) that a beneficiary must have an insurable interest if the owner of the policy insures his own life. But when the owner of the policy insures the life of another—the *cestui que vie*—and designates a third-party as beneficiary, both the owner and that third-party must have an insurable interest in the life of the *cestui que vie.* Some states go further and also require that the *cestui que vie* give consent when insurance is procured on her life. For such a statutory requirement (containing exceptions for spouses and minors), see New York Insurance Law § 3205(c).

4. *Standing.* Is there a justification for the nearly universal rule that only the insurer has standing to question the insurable interest of the owner or beneficiary of a life insurance policy? Can this rule be squared with the purpose underlying the rule that the insurer's prior conduct cannot estop it to question that interest? The argument for the denial of standing to any other party is that normally the policyholder/primary beneficiary may have had no hand in bringing about the death of the *cestui que vie,* in which case the purpose underlying the insurable interest requirement will not have been violated. On the other hand, in the rare cases in which the policyholder is responsible for that death, other rules (discussed below in Subsection 4) can be invoked to preclude his recovery. See R. Jerry, Understanding Insurance Law 200–01 (1987).

5. *Time of Interest.* The insurable interest requirement is said to be satisfied if the interest exists at the time a policy is procured, even if the interest has ceased to exist at the time of the *cestui que vie's* death. The argument supporting this rule is presumably that the central moral hazard in life insurance is the procurement of insurance with intent to murder, rather than the inducement to murder those in whose life one once had but no longer has an insurable interest. Even if the former kind of moral hazard is of principal concern, is the argument convincing? Most of the situations in which an insurable interest exists but later disappears involve business relationships. Aren't these precisely the kind of relationships in which the eventual disappearance of an insurable interest can be anticipated even at the time a policy is procured?

For example, in the *Secor* case cited in *Ryan,* the deceased's employer had purchased "key man" insurance on his life, and continued to pay the premiums after he retired. That the employee might retire rather than die during employment was highly predictable. If moral hazard in principle, rather than in fact, is at stake in insurable interest cases, should the rule that only the insurer has standing to question insurable interest be inapplicable in cases like *Secor*? If moral hazard in fact is what is at stake, is there any way to avoid the kind of individualized inquiry that *per se* rules governing insurable interest are designed to avoid? The court in *Secor* also said that the employer "chose to make the premium payment 8 months after Secor's employment terminated to preserve recovery of its prior expenditures." Would this argument seem to be unavailable if the employer had purchased term rather than whole life insurance, or was the court suggesting that Secor's unanticipated ill-health had become an asset of the employer that it had a right to protect even if it had purchased term insurance only? Should decisions on facts resembling those in *Secor* depend on whether the employer's policy is whole-life rather than term insurance?

4. Change of Beneficiary and Assignment

Designation and change of the beneficiary of a life insurance policy are reasonably straightforward exercises. The applicant indicates on the application whom he designates, and the policy (or a copy of the application attached to the policy) lists the beneficiary. The beneficiary named may be changed by following procedures specified in the policy itself. These procedures may be more or less formal, but always require some form of notification of the company. See the provision governing *Ownership and Beneficiary* in the Sample Life Term Insurance Policy. The former beneficiary normally is not notified of the change by the company.

One much-litigated issue is whether full or only "substantial" compliance with the formalities specified in the policy is required. The obvious differences between courts on this issue in part reflect their greater or lesser emphasis on formality rather than substance. But a reading of a number of the decisions on the issue suggests that the difference in emphasis on compliance with formalities also sometimes masks the courts' concern that the insured have expressed a firm rather than merely tentative intention to make a change of beneficiary. For this reason, expressed intention *plus* the taking of at least some step to make the change seem much more likely to yield a finding that substantial compliance suffices than the former alone. For example, in *Scherer v. Wahlstrom*, 318 S.W.2d 456 (Tex.Civ.App.1958), the insured designated "Mariam Amelia Tatum, Fiancee" as his beneficiary. While he was in the military she sent him a "Dear John" letter and married someone else, but he did not change the beneficiary designation. Six months later he died, and his father claimed the proceeds, but Mariam prevailed, notwithstanding that she had been identified as "Fiancee" in the policy. On the other hand, in *Connecticut General Life Insurance Company v. Gulley*, 668 F.2d 325 (7th Cir.1982), the insured completed a change of beneficiary form and left it with his daughter, indicating that he would return for it. The daughter mailed it after he died. The court held that this constituted substantial compliance with the requirements of the policy.

This general issue has been complicated not only by the courts' understandable sympathy for disappointed (and sometimes quite surprised) relatives of the deceased, but also by the need for rules that provide insurers with a modicum of certainty about the identity of the beneficiaries to whom they are obligated. The less clear the rules, the more incumbent it is upon the insurer to refrain from paying anyone, lest it have to make payment twice: first to a beneficiary named in the policy, and then also to a beneficiary (successful in a suit against the insurer) intended by the insured. Once an insurer becomes aware of a dispute between two putative beneficiaries in any situation of uncertainty, the filing of an interpleader action and the payment of the proceeds into court is the only truly safe action. The clearer the rules governing change of beneficiary, the fewer such interpleader actions there will have to be, and the fewer rightful beneficiaries will have payment delayed and litigation costs imposed on them. But even clear rules will not necessarily suffice, as the case that follows demonstrates.

KEETON v. CHERRY

Missouri Court of Appeals, 1987.
728 S.W.2d 694.

Manford, Judge.

Appellant appeals from the judgment of the Probate Division of the Jackson County Circuit Court which held that appellant, the named beneficiary on life insurance contracts and a retirement fund account owned by her ex-husband (decedent) was not entitled to the proceeds of said contracts and account by virtue of a property settlement agreement executed by appellant and decedent pursuant to the dissolution of their marriage, five years prior to decedent's death.

The judgment is affirmed.

Review of the judgment in this court-tried case is pursuant to *Murphy v. Carron,* 536 S.W.2d 30 (Mo. banc 1976), and the judgment must be affirmed unless it is not supported by substantial evidence, is against the weight of the evidence, or erroneously declares and/or applies the law.

Appellant raises two points and charges, in summary, that the trial court erred in entering judgment in favor of respondent because (1) the court erroneously declared and applied the law because the law is that a named beneficiary is entitled to the proceeds of the contract, and (2) the judgment is not supported by substantial evidence and is against the weight of the evidence because the evidence was that decedent intended that appellant be the beneficiary under the policies up until the time of decedent's death.

The pertinent facts are as follows:

Appellant was divorced from her husband (decedent) on May 21, 1979. Pursuant to the dissolution of their marriage, appellant and decedent entered into a property settlement agreement (hereinafter "agreement") which was found by the court to be reasonable and not unconscionable and was incorporated in the judgment entry of the dissolution. At the time of the dissolution, appellant received custody of the parties' two minor children, Kyle David Keeton and Kyla Denise Keeton.

Among other things, the agreement provided as follows:

8. The parties do each represent that they are now and have been teachers under the Missouri State Teachers Association Retirement Plan, the said husband being so employed for a period of approximately 20 years and the wife being so employed for a period of approximately 16 to 17 years, each having separate retirement accounts with the Missouri State Teachers Association, and they do herewith transfer, relinquish and waive any interest in and to their separate accounts, and all of the right, title, interest and benefit thereto.

* * *

17. It is stipulated and agreed between the parties that husband is the present owner of the following listed life insurance policies and it is agreed between the parties that the wife does transfer any right, title, interest and benefit in and to the said life insurance policies that she may have, relinquishing to husband the full ownership or benefit and control thereto, as follows:

(a) The Northern Life Insurance Company policy No. 507630, effective June 7, 1965, for a face amount of $5,000.00; and

(b) The Northern Life Insurance Company policy No. 489–021, effective September 14, 1961, for a face amount of $5,000.00, and

(c) The Central Life Assurance Company policy No. 91286, effective July 15, 1969, with a face amount of $5,000.00; and

(d) The Central Life Assurance Company, policy No. 1215254, effective February 7, 1972, with a face amount of $10,000.00; and

(e) The Central Life Assurance Company, policy No. 1405567, effective July 27, 1976, with a face amount of $5,000.00.

At the time of the dissolution, appellant was the named beneficiary on the retirement plan and on the three life insurance policies in question.

During the five years following the dissolution, appellant and decedent remained in contact with one another and it appears that they had a friendly relationship. At the time of decedent's death, in May of

1984, appellant was the named beneficiary on the retirement plan and on three of the insurance policies. From the date of dissolution until the date of his death, decedent did not take any affirmative action toward changing the name of the beneficiary on these policies. After the dissolution and prior to his death, decedent purchased a life insurance policy, designating his daughter, Kyla, as beneficiary, and decedent opened an I.R.A. account, designating his son, Kyle, as beneficiary.

After decedent's death, appellant applied for and received the benefit of the three life insurance policies and the retirement plan. Thereafter, the estate, by and through its personal representative, Kyle Keeton, filed a petition to discover assets of the estate, claiming that the estate was entitled to the proceeds of the insurance policies and the retirement plan. The cause was set for hearing in the probate division.

At the hearing, Warren Lathrop, a friend of the decedent's for some thirty-four years, testified that he had told decedent, after decedent's divorce from appellant, of another colleague who divorced his spouse but did not change his retirement beneficiary in case of death. When the colleague died, the former spouse, as named beneficiary, collected the proceeds as opposed to the colleague's widow. Lathrop testified that decedent replied that his (decedent's) teachers' retirement was the way he wanted it and that he (decedent) was not going to change it.

Kyle Keeton testified that he is decedent's son, and that he and decedent had discussed decedent's teachers' retirement plan on two occasions, and that decedent had told him that due to the divorce and the change in appellant's name (she resumed her maiden name after the divorce), that Kyle and Kyla would receive the retirement benefits.

Vicki Ellis testified that she was engaged to decedent at the time of his death, and that she had talked to decedent several times about decedent's retirement plan and insurance policies, and that the decedent was of the belief that the money accrued in these accounts would be left to decedent's children.

Appellant's first point is taken up and, after full consideration, is found to be without merit and is ruled against appellant for the following reasons:

> The rule in Missouri is as follows: [W]here the forms of a separation agreement carried into a divorce decree plainly disclose an intent to remove the named beneficiary in a life insurance policy [or retirement plan] from all rights to the proceeds thereof, such agreement may operate to prevent the named beneficiary from claiming the proceeds upon the death of the insured * * *

Bell v. Garcia, 639 S.W.2d 185, 191 (Mo.App.1982), citing *Cannon v. Hamilton,* 174 Ohio St. 268, 189 N.E.2d 152, 154 (1963).

In the case at bar, the language of the agreement evidences a clear intent of the parties to release or revoke all of appellant's rights to the named insurance policies and retirement plan benefits. *See Bell v. Garcia, supra,* at 191.

The cases cited by appellant in support of her argument do not aid her. None of these cases, save one, deal with a separation or property settlement agreement affecting a change of beneficiary. In the case that does deal with a separation or property settlement agreement, the named beneficiary on a life insurance policy was entitled to the proceeds of said policy notwithstanding a stipulation in a property settlement agreement executed prior to divorce because the court found the situation ambiguous and its meaning unascertainable. *John Hancock Mutual Life Insurance Co. v. Dawson,* 278 S.W.2d 57, 59 (Mo.App.1955). Such is not the case herein where the agreement clearly states that appellant relinquishes all rights, title and interest in specifically designated policies and accounts. The agreement is clear that the parties intended that appellant was to be released as the named beneficiary on the policies and retirement plan.

The trial court did not err in finding that, under the agreement, appellant relinquished all her interests in the accounts, including the right to be named beneficiary.

Appellant's point (2) is taken up and, after full consideration, is found to be without merit and is ruled against appellant for the following reasons:

As this court determined in appellant's point (1), appellant relinquished all rights, title and interest to the policies and retirement plan upon the execution of the agreement, and appellant was bound by the judgment of the trial court which entered the dissolution decree incorporating within said decree the terms of the agreement.

Appellant argues that the probate court's judgment was not supported by substantial evidence and was against the weight of the evidence because the overwhelming evidence was that decedent intended to redesignate or reaffirm appellant as the named beneficiary on the policies and retirement plan. In its entry of judgment, the probate court stated the following:

> The court finds and concludes that the respondent [appellant herein], by the clear and unequivocal words of the property settlement agreement, intended to give up all of her interests in the retirement account and the insurance policy proceeds, including the right to be named beneficiary thereunder. The only evidence before the court is the agreement itself. The court may not speculate as to what the decedent intended, if any at all may be shown, by his failure to change the beneficiaries on the account and the policies.

By stating that "[t]he only evidence before the court is the agreement itself," this court must presume that the probate court found that the testimony of Warren Lathrop, Kyle Keeton, and Vicki Ellis was not probative on the issue of decedent's intent and that the agreement was the only credible evidence introduced at the hearing.

The evidence introduced by appellant was the testimony of Warren Lathrop, who testified that decedent had told him that his (decedent's) retirement plan was the way he (decedent) wanted it, and that he (decedent) wasn't going to change it. Appellant urges this court to draw the conclusion that decedent was aware that appellant was the named beneficiary and that decedent wanted appellant to be beneficiary and that is why decedent did not change the beneficiary on the retirement plan and policies. However, it is equally plausible that by his statement, decedent was acknowledging his understanding that by virtue of the divorce decree, appellant was no longer the beneficiary under the policies and retirement plan and that his failure to designate a new beneficiary would result in the policies' and plan's benefits going to his estate and that Kyle and Kyla would thereby receive the benefits because they were his sole heirs. Therefore, no conclusion can be drawn from Lathrop's testimony.

The evidence introduced by respondent was the testimony of Kyle Keeton and Vicki Ellis. Keeton's testimony reveals decedent's understanding of the effect of the marital property settlement and was not evidence upon the issue of decedent's intent. Ellis' testimony, that decedent told her Kyle and Kyla would receive the money from the policies and retirement plan, also reflects decedent's understanding of the marital property settlement and was not evidence upon the issue of decedent's intent.

Thus, none of the evidence introduced by either appellant or respondent by way of witness Lathrop, Keeton, or Ellis was probative upon the issue of decedent's intent regarding the beneficiary under the insurance policies or the retirement fund account. The trial court, under the facts and circumstances herein, did not err in ignoring this evidence.

This court holds that when a spouse, who has relinquished all rights, title and interest to an insurance policy or retirement plan in a binding dissolution decree, is designated as beneficiary at the time of the insured spouse's death, the spouse-beneficiary is entitled to the proceeds of the policy or plan only if the beneficiary can show, by some affirmative act of the decedent, that the decedent intended to *redesignate* the spouse as beneficiary. Absent some affirmative act of the decedent, the spouse is bound by his or her relinquishment of right, title, and interest in the policy or plan and the spouse is estopped to deny that the decedent intended that the proceeds go to his or her estate.

The judgment is in all respects affirmed.

SHANGLER, J., concurs.

GAITAN, P.J., concurs in separate concurring opinion.

GAITAN, Presiding Judge, concurring.

The factual background which presents us with the legal issue for disposition is not unique. While there may be other methods to eliminate this problem, one seems to be fairly obvious. Here, we have a property settlement agreement which was presumably negotiated by the parties and approved by the court. It provides, in part, that appellant no longer has a legal right of expectancy to the insurance policies as well as the retirement plan in question. That provision was adopted by the court and incorporated into its judgment entry. The attorney or attorneys preparing this settlement agreement could have simply provided for and stated therein a substitute beneficiary. In this case, the children of the decedent could have been named beneficiaries.

While this action may not be enforceable against the insurers, it would provide the court with the clear and unequivocal intention of the insured (decedent). If the insured failed to make those changes to his insurance policy and/or his retirement plan, his intentions in that regard are made clear by the judgment entry. If he has a change of heart, his affirmative act of changing the named beneficiary or reaffirming the former beneficiary also leaves a clear indication of his intention.

Under the majority opinion which appears to be the state of the law in Missouri, the insured would need to take an affirmative step to reaffirm the appellant as his beneficiary. It is not unrealistic for a person to believe that he or she had done that by not changing the beneficiary under the policy or retirement plan.

Notes and Questions

1. *Avoiding Payment by Mistake.* The holding in *Estate of Keeton* is in accord with most decisions on the issue: a divorce decree specifying distribution of life insurance proceeds on the death of one of the spouses may change the designation of one of the spouses as beneficiary without satisfying any requirement in the policy that the insurer be notified before any change will take effect. Some courts require that the decree state specifically the change in the spouse's status as beneficiary; others find a surrender of all interest in the policy sufficient. As between the disappointed spouse and the beneficiary named in the decree, the latter should of course prevail. But suppose the spouse whose rights have been divested by the divorce decree files proof of the other spouse's death and claims the proceeds before the party named in the decree can do so. Is there any way the insurer can protect itself from mistakenly paying the former spouse?

2. *The Purpose of Change of Beneficiary Provisions.* Some courts say that change of beneficiary provisions in life insurance policies are intended to protect insurers from the kind of predicament described in the preceding paragraph. Thus the occasional judicial *ipse dixit* that an insurer who files an interpleader action to determine the rightful beneficiary has "waived" its right to have the formalities for changing

beneficiaries required by the policy followed. But whether the formalities are intended for this purpose alone or not, the interests of beneficiaries still designated in the policy itself—or at least their expectations—nonetheless sometimes elicit judicial concern. The result is a tension between form and substance that is never definitively resolved.

* * *

Ownership of a policy is an issue separate from but related to the designation of beneficiaries. A life insurance policy is an asset that can be sold, or "assigned," as insurance terminology puts it. It is virtually everywhere agreed that an assignment that complies with the notice provisions of a policy automatically makes the assignee the beneficiary, unless and until the assignee himself makes a further change. The question then becomes whether the rules governing insurable interest not only govern purchase of the policy outright, but assignment as well. The closer one comes to death, the more valuable a life insurance policy becomes. Rules restricting assignability therefore also constrain a policyholder's ability to convert the value represented by a policy into capital prior to death.

GRIGSBY v. RUSSELL

Supreme Court of the United States, 1911.
222 U.S. 149, 32 S.Ct. 58, 56 L.Ed. 133.

Mr. Justice HOLMES delivered the opinion of the court.

This is a bill of interpleader brought by an insurance company to determine whether a policy of insurance issued to John C. Burchard, now deceased, upon his life, shall be paid to his administrators or to an assignee, the company having turned the amount into court. The material facts are that after he had paid two premiums and a third was overdue, Burchard, being in want and needing money for a surgical operation, asked Dr. Grigsby to buy the policy and sold it to him in consideration of one hundred dollars and Grigsby's undertaking to pay the premiums due or to become due; and that Grigsby had no interest in the life to be assured. The Circuit Court of Appeals in deference to some intimations of this court held the assignment valid only to the extent of the money actually given for it and the premiums subsequently paid. 168 Fed.Rep. 577, 94 C.C.A. 61.

Of course the ground suggested for denying the validity of an assignment to a person having no interest in the life insured is the public policy that refuses to allow insurance to be taken out by such persons in the first place. A contract of insurance upon a life in which the insured has no interest is a pure wager that gives the insured a sinister counter interest in having the life come to an end. And although that counter interest always exists, as early was emphasized for England in the famous case of Wainewright (Janus Weathercock), the chance that in some cases it may prove a sufficient motive for crime is greatly enhanced if the whole world of the unscrupulous are free to bet on what life they choose. The very meaning of an insurable interest is an interest in having the life continue and so one that is opposed to crime. And, what perhaps is more important, the existence of such an interest makes a roughly selected class of persons who by their general relations with the person whose life is insured are less likely than criminals at large to attempt to compass his death.

But when the question arises upon an assignment it is assumed that the objection to the insurance as a wager is out of the case. In the present instance the policy was perfectly good. There was a faint suggestion in argument that it had become void by the failure of Burchard to pay the third premium *ad diem,* and that when Grigsby paid he was making a new contract. But a condition in a policy that it shall be void if premiums are not paid when due, means only that it shall be voidable at the option of the company. *Knickerbocker Life Insurance Company v. Norton,* 96 U.S. 234, 24 L.Ed. 689; *Oakes v. Manufacturers' Fire & Marine Ins. Co.,* 135 Mass. 248. The company waived the breach, if there was one, and the original contract with Burchard remained on foot. No question as to the character of that contract is before us. It has been performed and the money is in court. But this being so, not only does the objection to wagers disappear, but also the principle of public policy referred to, at least in its most convincing form. The danger that might arise from a general license to all to insure whom they like does not exist. Obviously it is a very different thing from granting such a general license, to allow the holder of a valid insurance upon his own life to transfer it to one whom he, the party most concerned, is not afraid to trust. The law has no universal cynical fear of the temptation opened by a pecuniary benefit accruing upon a death. It shows no prejudice against remainders after life estates, even by the rule in *Shelley's Case.* Indeed, the ground of the objection to life insurance without interest in the earlier English cases was not the temptation to murder but the fact that such wagers came to be regarded as a mischievous kind of gaming. St. 14 George III, c. 48.

On the other hand, life insurance has become in our days one of the best recognized forms of investment and self-compelled saving. So far as reasonable safety permits, it is desirable to give to life policies the ordinary characteristics of property. This is recognized by the Bankruptcy Law, § 70, which provides that unless the cash surrender value of a policy like the one before us is secured to the trustee within thirty days after it has been stated the policy shall pass to the trustee as assets. Of course the trustee may have no interest in the bankrupt's life. To deny the right to sell except to persons having such an interest is to diminish appreciably the value of the contract in the owner's hands. The collateral difficulty that arose from regarding life insurance as a contract of indemnity only, *Godsall v. Boldero,* 9 East, 72, long has disappeared. *Phoenix Mutual Life Ins. Co. v. Bailey,* 13 Wall. 616, 20 L.Ed. 501. And cases in which a person having an interest lends himself to one without any as a cloak to what is in its inception a wager have no similarity to those where an honest contract is sold in good faith.

Coming to the authorities in this court, it is true that there are intimations in favor of the result come to by the Circuit Court of Appeals. But the case in which the strongest of them occur was one of the type just referred to, the policy having been taken out for the purpose of allowing a stranger association to pay the premiums and receive the greater part of the benefit, and having been assigned to it at once. *Warnock v. Davis,* 104 U.S. 775, 26 L.Ed. 924.

On the other hand it has been decided that a valid policy is not avoided by the cessation of the insurable interest, even as against the insurer, unless so provided by the policy itself. *Connecticut Mutual Life Ins. Co. v. Schaefer,* 94 U.S. 457, 24 L.Ed. 251. And expressions more or less in favor of the doctrine that we adopt are to be found also in *Aetna Life Ins. Co. v. France,* 94 U.S. 561, 24 L.Ed. 287; *Mutual Life Ins. Co. v. Armstrong,* 117 U.S. 591, 29 L.Ed. 997, 6 Sup.Ct.Rep. 877. It is enough to say that while the court below might hesitate to decide against the language of *Warnock v. Davis,* there has been no decision that precludes us from exercising our own judgment upon this much debated point. It is at least satisfactory to learn from the decision below that in Tennessee, where this assignment was made, although there has been much division of opinion, the Supreme Court of that State came to the conclusion that we adopt, in an unreported case, *Lewis v. Edwards,* December 14, 1903. The law in England and the preponderance of decisions in our state courts are on the same side.

Some reference was made to a clause in the policy that "any claim against the company arising under any assignment of the policy shall be subject to proof of interest." But it rightly was assumed below that if there was no rule of law to that effect and the company saw fit to pay, the clause did not diminish the rights of Grigsby as against the administrators of Burchard's estate.

Decree reversed.

Notes and Questions

1. *Cui Bono?* The Court distinguished between policies procured as wagers from the inception, and policies assigned some time after they are procured in good faith. Who is entitled to the proceeds of the life insurance in each of the following hypothetical situations, assuming that Burchard dies of natural causes after the facts described?

a. Burchard is examined by Grigsby and is told he needs an operation. A friend gives Burchard the necessary funds; in return, Burchard takes out a policy on his (Burchard's) life, designating the friend as beneficiary.

b. The facts are the same, except that Burchard assigns the policy to the friend immediately after purchase.

c. In return for a free operation, Burchard takes out a policy on his life and names Grigsby his beneficiary.

d. In return for a free operation, Burchard takes out a policy on his life and assigns it to Grigsby.

e. A friend gives Burchard money for the operation, in return for which Burchard takes out a policy on his (Burchard's) life, designates his own estate as beneficiary, and executes a contract with the friend to make a Will naming the friend as a legatee for an amount equal to the face amount of the life insurance. Contracts to make a Will are enforceable in most jurisdictions.

f. Grigsby provides Burchard a free operation, in return for which Burchard takes out a policy on his life, designates his own estate as beneficiary, and agrees to make a Will naming Grigsby a legatee for an amount equal to the face amount of the life insurance.

2. *Problems.* If you were advising a client in Burchard's situation, which of the above alternatives would you prefer? If you represented Grigsby or Burchard's friend, which alternative would you prefer? To what extent do your answers suggest that the rule against wagers in the form of life insurance is merely a trap for the unwary?

5. Limitations on Recovery by Beneficiaries

NEW ENGLAND MUTUAL LIFE INSURANCE COMPANY v. NULL

United States Court of Appeals, Eighth Circuit, 1979.
605 F.2d 421.

HEANEY, Circuit Judge.

Shirley Ann Null appeals from an order of the District Court which declared void a personal insurance policy issued by New England Mutual Life Insurance Company (New England) on the life of Victor Null. Shirley Ann Null contends that the District Court erred in finding that Victor Null contracted for the insurance solely because Ronald and James Calvert required it as security for their investment in the development of Victor Null's invention. The Calverts, however, actually desired the insurance as part of a plan to obtain the proceeds thereof through Victor Null's murder. This finding follows our reversal of a grant of summary judgment in favor of New England, *New England Mut. Life Ins. Co. v. Null,* 554 F.2d 896 (8th Cir.1977). We remanded the case for a plenary trial on the issue

> whether Null executed the application and procured the insurance for his own purposes and thus became the contracting party with the insurer, or instead merely served as an innocent instrumentality in the evil scheming of Ronald Calvert[.]

Id. at 902.

We affirm the District Court's judgment.

The facts giving rise to this action are set out in this Court's prior opinion, id. at 898–899, and we briefly summarize them here. Ronald Calvert planned to obtain several insurance policies on the life of Victor Null, an inventor who sought Calvert's financial backing, and then arrange Null's murder and obtain the insurance proceeds. After an unsuccessful attempt at procuring a $500,000 policy from Prudential Insurance Company, Calvert discussed with New England agents the possibility of obtaining a $500,000 policy on Null's life. New England's underwriter, however, refused to issue more than $150,000 in "business insurance," or insurance for the benefit of Calvert. After consultation with Calvert and Victor Null, the insurance agent requested a $100,000 personal life insurance policy which the company agreed to issue. On Friday, July 21, 1972, Mr. Null executed an application designating as beneficiary the "Estate of Insured." The following Monday, Null and Calvert arrived at New England's St. Louis office and Null executed an "Absolute Assignment and Change of Beneficiary Request" in favor of James Calvert, Ronald Calvert's father and his straw man and agent in the scheme.

Also on Monday, July 24, Calvert paid the premiums for both the $150,000 business policy and the $100,000 personal insurance policy by a check of his father in the amount of $5,616. New England issued the policies and the agent delivered them to Ronald Calvert.

The parties have stipulated that

"The Calverts" at all times pertinent and prior to the issuance of the policy in question, had a preconceived intent to engage in criminal conduct which would and did result in the murder of Victor Null on November 8, 1972, which intent was unknown to Null and the company (plaintiff).

Null contends that the District Court erred in three respects: (1) New England did not meet its burden of proving fraud because it solicited the policy with knowledge of the underlying business transaction and Null's intent to assign the policy to Calvert; (2) the court failed to examine the question whether Null had an independent business purpose in obtaining the insurance but asked only whether Null intended to benefit his estate by obtaining the insurance, thereby incorrectly interpreting our holding in the earlier appeal of this case; and (3) the court misapplied the law because the evidence showed that Null and New England were the real parties to the insurance contract.

The appellant contends that New England could not prove it was defrauded because it had knowledge of the underlying business transaction between Mr. Null and Calvert and specifically solicited the insurance to effectuate that transaction. The evidence shows that New England's agent originally contacted Calvert regarding life insurance for Null after learning of Calvert's unsuccessful application with Prudential. The agent first attempted to obtain a $500,000 policy on Victor Null's life from New England for Calvert's benefit. The company refused to issue more than $150,000 of such insurance. Calvert then told the agent that his business transaction with Null could not go forward with such a small amount of insurance. The agent discussed the situation with several other agents and suggested to Calvert and Victor Null the possibility of obtaining a personal insurance policy which Victor Null would be able to assign to Calvert. The agent, therefore, sought to contravene the company's directive by offering an alternative means of obtaining insurance which would be payable to the Calverts on Victor Null's death. The appellant argues that under these circumstances, New England cannot prove that it was in any way defrauded by the policy application. New England was aware of the business transaction between Calvert and Victor Null. New England, through its agents, supplied Calvert with the incentive to kill Victor Null by issuing insurance in an amount that exceeded Victor Null's worth to Calvert. New England allowed this in spite of its awareness of this risk, which it demonstrated by its refusal to issue more than $150,000 in business insurance. The appellant contends that New England may not show it was defrauded when its eagerness to sell the policy created the risk that resulted in Victor Null's death.

This argument is not unappealing. Historically, the law has looked with disfavor on insurance contracts which create a risk of death to the insured.

> [I]t is contrary to a sound public policy to permit one, having no interest in the continuance of the life of another, to speculate upon that other's life—and it should be added that to permit the same might tend to incite the crime of murder * * * and that the rule is enforced, and the defense permitted, not in the interest of the defendant insurer, but solely for the sake of the law, and in the interest of a sound public policy[.]

Henderson v. Life Ins. Co. of Virginia, 176 S.C. 100, 179 S.E. 680, 692 (1935).

> It is well settled that "to allow the creditor to procure insurance greatly exceeding the amount of the debt might be to tempt him to bring the debtor's life to an unnatural end, and thus contravene the principle of public policy which has been seen to lie at the very basis of the doctrine of insurable interest[.]" (Citation omitted.)

Lakin v. Postal Life and Casualty Insurance Co., 316 S.W.2d 542, 551 (Mo.1958).

The courts have, therefore, voided life insurance policies which have encouraged the murder of the insured. E.g., *Henderson v. Life Ins. Co. of Virginia, supra; Lakin v. Postal Life and Casualty Insurance Co., supra.* These decisions have served the purpose of discouraging beneficiaries who plan a murder, but they do not have the effect of discouraging insurance companies from negligently issuing policies in contravention of the public interest. To reach this problem, the Supreme Courts of Alabama and South Carolina have allowed negligence actions against an insurer who negligently issues a life insurance policy which creates the risk of murder. *Liberty National Life Insurance Company v. Weldon,* 267 Ala. 171, 100 So.2d 696 (1957); *Ramey v. Carolina Life Insurance Company,* 244 S.C. 16, 135 S.E.2d 362 (1964). In *Weldon,* the court allowed a wrongful death action by the father of a minor child against three insurance companies which issued life insurance policies to the insured's aunt. The aunt, who had no insurable interest in the child's life, murdered the child. In *Ramey,* the South Carolina court allowed a suit against an insurance company by an insured who was severely injured by his wife, the owner-beneficiary of a life insurance policy, who attempted to poison him. The insurance company issued the policy without the insured's consent and with knowledge that his wife had forged his signature on the application. In both cases, the courts allowed proof of allegations that the negligent issuance of the policies was the proximate cause of the murders.

We have been unable, however, to find a decision in any state, including Missouri, which has permitted the estate of the insured to recover on the policy itself from an insurer which has negligently issued a policy. In *Lakin v. Postal Life and Casualty Insurance Co., supra,* the Missouri court held a life insurance policy obtained under somewhat similar circumstances void for want of an insurable interest. Although the argument the appellant makes here was not raised in *Lakin,* its facts support an inference that the agent solicited the policy with knowledge of the owner-beneficiary's true relationship with the insured and the lack of any insurable interest. We find no indication in that opinion, or in any other case, that the Missouri court would permit the estate of the insured to recover on the policy itself. In view of the fact that no Missouri decision is precisely on point, we would be prepared to distinguish *Lakin* if persuasive authority for a recovery by the estate on the policy could be discovered elsewhere. Since we find no such authority, we rely on the accepted rule that a life insurance policy is void *ab initio* when it is shown that the beneficiary thereof procured the policy with a present intention to murder the insured. *Mutual Life Ins. Co. v. Armstrong,* 177 U.S. 591, 6 S.Ct. 877, 880–881, 29 L.Ed. 997 (1886); *Colyer's Adm'r v. New York Life Ins. Co.,* 300 Ky. 189, 188 S.W.2d 313, 314 (Ky.App.1945); *Aetna Life Ins. Co. v. Strauch,* 179 Okl. 617, 67 P.2d 452, 453 (1937).

We do not, in this decision, express any opinion on the viability of a wrongful death action under the facts of this case, nor do we express an opinion on whether any limitations period applicable to such an action has been tolled.

As we stated in our disposition of the earlier appeal, the remaining issue is whether the beneficiary or the insured "procured" the insurance policy; i.e., whether Victor Null executed the application for his own purposes or was merely a pawn in the Calverts' plan. The District Court sitting without a jury found from the evidence that he did not execute the application for his own purposes. On appeal, we will not set aside the court's findings of fact unless they are "clearly erroneous."

Fed.R.Civ.P. 52(a).   *   *   * There was no evidence that Victor Null applied for the insurance with a plan to assign it to any backers other than the Calverts, nor was there any evidence that Victor Null intended to obtain such insurance prior to his negotiations with Calvert. The agent testified that at the time of Null's policy application, it was clear to Victor Null that the policy was to be assigned to James Calvert. On this evidence, we must affirm the District Court's factual finding that Victor Null's only reason for obtaining the insurance was because the Calverts deemed it necessary for him to do so. In so doing, we do not imply that Victor Null possessed no motivation for obtaining the insurance, or that he did not believe that he would benefit by so doing. That, however, is not determinative of the question because Victor Null had no motivation other than that supplied by the beneficiary who planned his murder. Victor Null, therefore, was not elevated beyond the status of a "mere instrumentality" in the Calverts' scheme.

The appellant's final contention is that the District Court erred in concluding that Calvert, not Victor Null, was the real party to the contract of insurance with New England. Shirley Ann Null argues that the facts of this case render it so unlike those cases from which the rule was derived that the court could not conclude that it applied so as to void the policy. We have addressed those portions of Shirley Ann Null's argument which attempt to establish that Victor Null applied for the insurance for his own purposes, and have indicated our approval of the District Court's findings on that issue. Because he was no more than an instrumentality in the Calverts' scheme, Victor Null was not the real party to the contract. Shirley Ann Null's reliance on her husband's desire to obtain the policy as a ground for distinguishing this case from *Aetna Life Ins. Co. v. Strauch, supra; Lakin v. Postal Life and Casualty Insurance Co., supra;* and *Colyer's Adm'r v. New York Life Ins. Co., supra,* is misplaced because Victor Null's desire was created by the Calverts for the sole purpose of carrying out their plans.

Notes and Questions

1. *Null and Void?* Are the facts in *Null* distinguishable from any of the hypotheticals in the notes following *Grigsby?*

2. *A "Reverse" Moral Hazard?* Under *Null,* do insurers have anything to lose if they issue policies under suspicious circumstances? Should the result be either that Mrs. Null recovers the proceeds of the policy, or that she has a wrongful death action against the insurer (potentially for considerably more than $100,000) for negligently issuing the policy? What kind of evidence should be required for a finding of negligence, assuming such a cause of action to exist?

STATE MUTUAL LIFE ASSURANCE COMPANY OF AMERICA v. HAMPTON

Supreme Court of Oklahoma, 1985.
696 P.2d 1027.

SIMMS, Chief Justice: * * *

This Court is asked to reverse the findings of the trial court and declare that under 84 O.S.1981, § 231, a beneficiary's right to recover insurance proceeds may be denied only if the beneficiary is convicted of the insured's murder or first-degree manslaughter. Petitioner Sawart Hampton also alleges that the trial court erred in determining that a beneficiary who is acquitted of the insured's murder or first-degree manslaughter is not automatically entitled to recover the insurance proceeds. Petitioner asserts that, contrary to the trial court's findings, the beneficiary's acquittal on criminal charges bars relitigation in a civil proceeding of the issue of whether or not the beneficiary took, or caused to be taken, the life of the insured in such a manner as to constitute murder or first-degree manslaughter.

I.

OPERATIVE FACTS

In 1981, Tony F. Hampton III (husband) entered into a group accidental death and dismemberment policy with State Mutual Life Assurance Company of America (insurance company). Husband named his wife, Sawart Hampton (wife) as beneficiary under the policy.

On or about October 6, 1982, while the policy was in full force and effect, husband died as the result of injuries incurred during a family quarrel.

Wife was arrested and charged with husband's first-degree murder. On June 23, 1983, prior to the final disposition of wife's murder trial, insurance company filed an interpleader action in Tulsa District Court. Named as defendants were wife (named beneficiary), Tony F. Hampton, Jr., (Special Administrator of husband's estate), and State of Oklahoma, ex rel., Department of Human Services, as custodian of the couple's minor children, Maneerat Lalansad and Tull Hampton (children). Guardians ad litem were subsequently appointed to represent children.

Insurance company did not contest its liability under the policy. However, in order to avoid potential conflicting claims by the named beneficiary, children, and special administrator in light of the circumstances surrounding husband's death, insurance company paid the $100,000.00 policy limit into court. The trial court, Judge Jane P. Wiseman, then granted insurance company's motion to be dismissed from further proceedings.

Wife was acquitted on October 21, 1983, of both first-degree murder and the lesser included offense, first-degree manslaughter. Six days thereafter wife filed a motion for summary judgment in the pending interpleader action, asserting that by reason of her acquittal, she was automatically entitled to the insurance proceeds. Wife's motion was overruled by the trial court.

In February, 1984, a pre-trial conference and hearing were held on the interpleader action. Determining the issues that would be litigated at trial, the trial court made the findings and conclusions that were certified for an interlocutory appeal to this Court.

II.

LEGAL ISSUES

In this case, this Court is asked for the first time to determine whether, under 84 O.S.1981, § 231, a named beneficiary under a life insurance policy who is acquitted of the insured's murder or first-degree manslaughter is automatically entitled to recover the insurance proceeds, so that relitigation in a civil proceeding of the issue of the beneficiary's criminal responsibility for the insured's alleged felonious,[1] intentional and unjustified homicide, as distinguished from excusable or justifiable homicide is barred.

Section 231 [2] (commonly known as the "slayer statute") provides in pertinent part:

"No person who is convicted of murder in the first degree, as defined in 21 O.S.1971, Section 701.1, or murder in the second degree, as defined in 21 O.S.1971, Section 701.2, subparagraph 1 or 2, or manslaughter in the first degree, as defined in 21 O.S.1971, Section 711, subparagraph 2, under the laws of this state, or the laws of any other state or foreign country, of having taken, caused, or procured another so to take, the life of an individual, shall inherit from such victim, or receive any interest in the estate of the victim, or take by devise or legacy or as a surviving joint tenant, or descent or distribution, from him, or her, any portion of his or her, estate; *and no beneficiary, of any policy of insurance * * * payable upon the death or disability of any person, who in like manner takes or causes or procures to be taken, the life upon which such policy or*

---

1. Hereinafter, the term "felonious" is used to mean "Proceeding from an evil heart of purpose. Wickedly and against the admonition of the law; unlawfully." Black's Law Dictionary, 5th ed.

2. Section 231 was enacted by the Oklahoma legislature in 1915 (Laws 1915, c. 136 § 1), and was amended in 1963 (Laws 1963, c. 309, § 1) and in 1975 (Laws 1975, c. 356, § 1). In its original form, the first part of the section read: "No person who is convicted of having taken, or causes or procures another so to take, the life of another, shall inherit from such person, * * *" The 1963 amendment added to the beginning of the section the emphasized words: "No person who is convicted of *murder or manslaughter in the first-degree under the laws of this State, or the laws of any other state or Foreign Country,* of having taken, * * *" The 1975 amendment added the statutory definitions of murder in the first-degree, murder in the second degree and first-degree manslaughter, and added the phrase "or as a surviving joint tenant."

The emphasized language in § 231 with regard to beneficiaries of insurance policies has not been amended in any respect.

*certificate is issued, * * * shall take the proceeds of such policy * * *."* [emphasis added]

Wife asserts that under § 231, a beneficiary's right to proceeds under an insurance policy may be denied only if the beneficiary is convicted of the insured's murder or first-degree manslaughter. Thus, wife concludes, she is automatically entitled to recover the proceeds under husband's insurance policy because she has been acquitted of the criminal charges, and the issue of her criminal responsibility for husband's felonious, intentional and unjustified killing may not be relitigated in a civil proceeding.

III.

WHETHER UNDER § 231 A BENEFICIARY'S RIGHT TO RECOVER INSURANCE PROCEEDS MAY BE DENIED ONLY IF THE BENEFICIARY IS CONVICTED OF THE INSURED'S MURDER OR FIRST–DEGREE MANSLAUGHTER.

In *Equitable Life Assurance Society v. Weightman,* 61 Okl. 106, 160 P. 629 (1916), this Court was for the first time asked to determine the rights of a beneficiary who had taken the life of the insured. A wife had been convicted of murdering her husband. This Court held that as a result of her act, the wife forfeited her rights as beneficiary under her husband's insurance policy, and that a constructive trust arose by operation of law in favor of the insured's estate.

Equitable, supra, was based on common law, since the cause of action arose prior to the effective date of Oklahoma's slayer statute. The Court recognized the common law maxim that no person should be permitted to benefit from his own wrongful conduct:

> " * * * Human law is the offspring of divine law. One of the strongest principles of that law is compensation. Every man compensates his own wrong. He cannot claim the benefits of it." 160 P. at 631.

In *Goodwin v. Continental Casualty Co.,* 175 Okl. 469, 53 P.2d 241 (1935), a beneficiary was convicted of manslaughter. Holding that the beneficiary could not recover the proceeds of the insured's life insurance policy, this Court cited *Equitable,* supra, and stated:

> "It may be conceded that a beneficiary in a policy of life insurance who feloniously takes or causes to be taken the life of the assured is thereby barred from collecting the insurance money; and that such rule applies in the absence of statute and is based upon public policy." 53 P.2d at 242.

While in both *Equitable,* supra and *Goodwin,* supra, the beneficiary had been convicted of killing the insured, the holdings in these cases indicate that it was the beneficiary's felonious act rather than the fact of the beneficiary's conviction that this Court found to be determinative.

Neither of these cases, nor the language of § 231 supports wife's conclusion that a conviction is the only basis for denying a beneficiary's right to proceeds under an insurance policy. Had the legislature wished to make a conviction of murder or first-degree manslaughter of the insured the only basis for denying insurance proceeds to a beneficiary, they could easily have inserted language in § 231 restricting disqualification to only those beneficiaries who are convicted. The statute, however, does not declare such a limitation.

A number of states have enacted statutes similar to § 231 which prohibit a beneficiary convicted of killing the insured from recovering the proceeds under the insurance policy.[3] Courts interpreting these statutes have held that the automatic disqualification of a convicted beneficiary is merely an extension of the common law rule that no person should benefit from his own wrongful conduct, and not a limitation or abrogation of that rule.

Prior to its decision in *Harper v. Prudential Ins. Co. of America,* 233 Kan. 358, 662 P.2d 1264 (1983), the Kansas Supreme Court had consistently held that under its slayer statute (KSA § 59–513 (1976)) a conviction was required in order to bar a beneficiary from recovering under the insured's life insurance policy.

In *Harper,* the Kansas court examined its previous decisions construing their statute, which is similar to 84 O.S.1981, § 231, and stated:

> "We have analyzed these cases and concluded that the rule that there must be a conviction of the beneficiary before he may be barred from recovering the proceeds of a life insurance policy was ill-conceived and should no longer be followed in this state and that we should adopt the common-law rule which is almost universally followed in this country and which bars the beneficiary of a life insurance policy who feloniously kills the insured from recovering under the policy *whether convicted or not.*

> " * * * The statute does not preclude judicial application of the common-law rule in cases where the beneficiary killed the insured but *has not been convicted of the crime."* 662 P.2d at 1271. [emphasis added]

Likewise, we find that § 231 bars a beneficiary who has actually been convicted of the insured's murder or first-degree manslaughter from recovering under the insurance policy. However, § 231 does not preclude judicial application of the common law rule expressed in *Equitable Life Assurance Society v. Weightman,* supra, in cases where the beneficiary has not been convicted of the crime.

3. See, e.g., Kan.Stat.Ann. § 59–513 (1983); Ken.Rev.Stat.Ann. § 381.280 (1981); N.C. Gen.Stat. § 31A–3 et seq. (1976); Ohio Rev.Code Ann. § 2105.19 (1976); S.C.Code § 21–1–50 (1976); Va.Code § 64.1–18 (1980); W.Va.Code § 42–4–2 (1982); Utah Code Ann. § 75–2–804 (1975).

Section 231 does not provide that a conviction of the statutorily designated degrees of homicide is the only ground for a beneficiary's disqualification, and we do not choose to construe it so narrowly.

Our construction of § 231 is supported by this Court's holding in *National Life and Accident Ins. Co. v. Reese,* 186 Okl. 133, 96 P.2d 1058 (1939). In *Reese,* there had been no conviction of the beneficiary accused of killing the insured when an action to recover the proceeds of the decedent's life insurance policy was brought by the beneficiary's assignees. This Court, citing its decision in *Equitable,* supra, and *Goodwin,* supra, upheld the trial court's judgment awarding the proceeds to the insured's estate rather than to the beneficiary's assignees.

Thus, we conclude that under § 231, a beneficiary's conviction of the insured's murder or first-degree manslaughter is not required in order to preclude a beneficiary from recovering the proceeds of life insurance.

IV.

"WHETHER UNDER § 231 A BENEFICIARY WHO IS ACQUITTED OF MURDER OR FIRST-DEGREE MANSLAUGHTER OF THE INSURED IS AUTOMATICALLY ENTITLED TO THE INSURANCE PROCEEDS."

Even if § 231 does not require a conviction before a beneficiary's recovery under an insurance policy may be barred, wife argues that her acquittal should still conclusively establish her right to the insurance proceeds, because her criminal responsibility for husband's death has been adjudicated.

Wife suggests that we consider *Wilson v. Wilson,* 78 Cal.App.3d 226, 144 Cal.Rptr. 180 (1978), as persuasive authority. In *Wilson,* a California appellate court held that a wife's acquittal on charges of murdering her husband was conclusive on the wrongfulness of her actions, and that she was therefore entitled to recover the proceeds under her husband's insurance policies. However, unlike § 231, California's slayer statute [Cal.Probate Code Ann. § 258 (West Supp.1984)], expressly gives conclusive effect to an acquittal.

Nor are we persuaded that the Tenth Circuit's interpretation of 84 O.S.1981, § 231 in *Glass v. United States,* 506 F.2d 379 (10th Cir.1974), supports wife's contention that she is entitled to automatically recover the insurance proceeds in light of her acquittal. The court's statement in *Glass* that "[i]t was only after her conviction that [beneficiary], in legal effect, forfeited her right to the policy proceeds * * *" (506 F.2d at 382) only supports the conclusion that because wife was not convicted, she has not forfeited any right she may have to the proceeds of husband's insurance policy.

Wife argues that the issue of her criminal responsibility for husband's death should not be relitigated in a civil proceeding. However, in light of the disparate consequences of a criminal adjudication and a civil proceeding, we find it unlikely that the legislature intended that an acquittal have any effect on the question of a beneficiary's right to insurance proceeds under § 231.

Proof beyond a reasonable doubt is not necessary in order to establish the existence of a crime in a civil proceeding, and an acquittal may merely mean failure to meet the higher standard of proof required in a criminal proceeding. A subsequent civil action based on the same facts could produce a different result since a lesser burden of proof, a preponderance of the evidence, is required.

Moreover, special administrator and children, who are entitled to take under § 231 if wife is barred, were not parties to the criminal case. Due process standards would preclude their being bound by the result of proceedings in which they did not participate. * * *

A number of courts have held that the acquittal of a beneficiary on charges of killing the insured is not conclusive on the issue of the beneficiary's right to insurance proceeds.[4] Likewise, we conclude that a beneficiary's acquittal does not per se entitle that beneficiary to recover proceeds of a decedent's insurance policy. * * *

VI.

CONCLUSION

We agree with the trial court's finding that 84 O.S.1981, § 231 does not require that a beneficiary be convicted of the insured's murder or first-degree manslaughter in order to be disqualified from receiving the proceeds under the insurance policy. We further agree with the trial court that under § 231 an acquittal of these felonies is not conclusive on the issue of whether or not a beneficiary took, or caused to be taken, the life of the insured in such a manner as to constitute a felonious, intentional, unjustifiable homicide, and that this issue may be litigated in a subsequent civil proceeding to determine the rights of claimants to the decedent's insurance proceeds. See, *National Life and Accident Ins. Co. v. Reese,* 186 Okl. 133, 96 P.2d 1058 (1939).

The trial court correctly concluded that wife has the burden of establishing by a preponderance of the evidence the existence of the insurance contract, the death of the insured covered by the policy, and her status as beneficiary under the policy. See, *Metropolitan Life Ins. Co. v. Rosier,* 189 Okl. 448, 117 P.2d 793 (1941).

If wife makes a prima facie showing that she has a right to recover as beneficiary under husband's policy, children and special administrator must be permitted to litigate their affirmative defense, whether or

4. Acquittal based on insanity; see, e.g., *In Re Vadlamudi Estate,* 183 N.J.Super. 342, 443 A.2d 1113 (1982); *California–Western States Life Ins. Co. v. Sanford,* 515 F.Supp. 524 (E.D.La.1981). Acquittal based on self-defense: see, e.g., *United States v. Burns,* 103 F.Supp. 690 (D.Md.1952), aff'd 200 F.2d 106 (4th Cir.1952); *Minnesota Mutual Life Ins. Co. v. James,* 202 F.Supp. 243 (D.C.Mo.1962); *Aetna Life Ins. Co. v. McDuffie,* 273 F.2d 609 (6th Cir.1960).

not wife took, or caused to be taken, the life of husband in such a manner as to constitute a felonious, intentional and unjustified homicide. If they prove this fact by a preponderance of the evidence, wife shall be precluded from recovering the insurance proceeds under husband's policy, and the proceeds shall be distributed according to the provisions set out in 84 O.S.1981, § 231.

The trial court's order is **AFFIRMED,** with directions that the cause proceed to trial in accordance with this opinion. * * *

Notes and Questions

1. *Relitigation.* Does it make sense to relitigate what amounts to the same issue that was tried in the criminal case, even conceding that the burden of proof in the later civil case is different? Is the difficulty of distinguishing an acquittal from a plea-bargain to a lesser charge or from the situation in which the murderer dies before trial always sufficient reason to allow the issue to be relitigated in a later civil action?

2. *Proof of What?* What level of misconduct should Mrs. Hampton's adversaries have to prove in order to defeat her claim? Does the statute provide any guidance? The common law rule is that mere negligence or recklessness is not sufficient; something like intent to kill is required. Thus, a beneficiary who was insane at the time he killed the insured is not necessarily precluded from taking under the insured's Will or an insurance policy. See, e.g., *Ford v. Ford*, 307 Md. 105, 512 A.2d 389 (1986). If the murderer is found to be precluded from taking as a beneficiary, in most jurisdictions he is treated as though he had predeceased the insured; contingent beneficiaries (or the deceased's estate, as a last resort) are then entitled to the proceeds.

6. Incontestability

All life insurance policies issued in this country, and many health and disability insurance policies, contain what is known as an "incontestability clause." The Sample Life Insurance Policy at the beginning of this Chapter, for example, includes such a clause under the heading, "The Contract." Some states require that such a clause conform to specified requirements; others do not. Incontestability clauses create a kind of contractual statute of limitations on certain defenses of the insurer—primarily those involving misstatements by the insured that eventuate in claims of fraud, misrepresentation, concealment, or breach of warranty.

The purpose of incontestability clauses is twofold. First, they provide the insured with assurance that once the period of contestability (almost always two years) passes, his coverage is firm and his beneficiaries are protected. Second, these clauses adjust the balance of advantage that would strongly favor the insurer if it were permitted to raise misstatement defenses after the insured's death made it impossible for him to respond to them. See generally Young, "Incontestable—

As to What?" 1964 Ill.L.Forum 323. Of course, life insurance policies do not become incontestable for all purposes after two years. Otherwise the beneficiary of any person who had purchased a policy more than two years before his death would always automatically be entitled to coverage upon that person's death. Rather, the courts distinguish the kinds of defenses to coverage that must be raised prior to the expiration of the contestability period from those which may be raised thereafter as well. A series of labels has been applied to identify the two categories of defenses, the first in each pair being unavailable after the period of contestability has run: *validity* versus *coverage; conditions* of coverage versus *limitations* on coverage; defenses that render coverage merely *voidable* versus those that make it *void ab initio; conditions* of coverage versus *exceptions* to coverage; and defenses based on *potential causes* of loss versus defenses based on *actual causes.*

Unless one attempts to distinguish these defenses based merely on the *form* of the policy provision generating them, two difficulties can arise. First, in some cases it is impossible to know into which side of the distinction a defense falls without already having a *substantive* theory to explain what should and should not be contestable. Second, even when it is obvious into which side of a distinction a given defense falls, the foreclosure or not of a defense seems arbitrary in the absence of a substantive theory of incontestability. A third problem, unfortunately, is that no substantive theory that is entirely satisfactory has come upon the scene. The best-known is derived in the following case.

SIMPSON v. PHOENIX MUTUAL LIFE INSURANCE COMPANY

Court of Appeals of New York, 1969.
24 N.Y.2d 262, 299 N.Y.S.2d 835, 247 N.E.2d 655.

KEATING, Judge.

Selma Simpson was designated by her husband Leonard as the beneficiary of a group life insurance policy procured by his employer, Lebanon Cemetery Association of Queens, Inc. (hereinafter Lebanon), through the trustees of the Cemetery and Funeral Service and Supply Industry Group Insurance Fund, from Phoenix Mutual Life Insurance Company (hereinafter Phoenix). The master policy issued by Phoenix on January 1, 1963 to Lebanon contained a provision that eligible employees for insurance coverage were all full-time employees regularly working at least 30 hours per week at the employer's usual place of business.

Phoenix supplied enrollment cards to Lebanon to distribute to its eligible employees. The employees filled out the cards designating their beneficiaries.[1] The enrollment card Simpson executed contained

---

1. The policy in dispute was actually a successor policy to one Lebanon had negotiated with Phoenix before it took out the group plan offered by the Association. Phoenix did not require Lebanon to supply new enrollment cards for its employees and simply used the cards already filed.

a printed clause, above the blank left for the applicant's signature, which read: "I request the insurance for which I may become eligible under said Group Policy". Simpson's card along with those of the other employees was forwarded to Phoenix, which then issued individual certificates to each employee. The certificate was a multipage printed form. On the first page of the certificate the employee's name and the amount of insurance coverage he was entitled to under the group policy were inserted. In addition, the first page noted that the terms of the insurance, which were contained in the master policy issued to Lebanon, were set out in the subsequent pages of the document. Simpson received such a certificate and, up until his death, Lebanon paid all the insurance premiums as they became due.

On June 17, 1964 Leonard P. Simpson was killed during a robbery in the elevator of his apartment house. Lebanon filed a notice of claim and proof of death with Phoenix on July 22, 1964 and requested the insurer to transmit the insurance proceeds directly to Mrs. Simpson. Phoenix, after investigating the claim, notified Lebanon that it had discovered that Simpson was not an eligible employee, as defined in the group policy, since he had not been employed 30 hours a week. Therefore, no proceeds would be paid to the employee's beneficiary.

Selma Simpson commenced this action on April 22, 1966 to recover the amount which her husband's certificate indicated his beneficiary was entitled to receive under the group life insurance policy. After issue was joined, plaintiff made a motion of summary judgment. In support of the motion, affidavits were submitted which admitted that Leonard Simpson, though employed by Lebanon, did not work 30 hours a week. Simpson was Lebanon's assistant secretary and his duties required that he devote only a few days a month to the association's business. His yearly remuneration never exceeded $1,000. Simpson's principal vocation was the practice of law. Mrs. Simpson argued that summary judgment was proper, notwithstanding the fact that her husband did not work 30 hours a week, because the policy's incontestable clause barred the insurer from asserting the defense of Simpson's ineligibility at the inception of the group policy as the basis for refusing to pay the insurance proceeds.

In opposing the motion, Phoenix argued that employment eligibility, as established by the group policy, was a limitation of the risk it contracted to insure. Since eligible employment is a limitation rather than a condition, it argues that it was not barred from raising employment eligibility even though the period in which it could contest the validity of the policy had elapsed.

The Supreme Court denied summary judgment. The Appellate Division reversed, one Justice dissenting (30 A.D.2d 265, 291 N.Y.S.2d 532).

The question posed for decision is whether employment, as defined in this group life insurance policy, is a condition of insurance or a limitation of the risk which the insurer contracted to underwrite. If employment is a condition the defense is now barred by the policy's incontestable clause. (See *Piasecki v. Metropolitan Life Ins. Co.*, 243 N.Y. 637, 154 N.E. 637; *Killian v. Metropolitan Life Ins. Co.*, 251 N.Y. 44, 166 N.E. 798, 64 A.L.R. 956; *Romano v. Metropolitan Life Ins. Co.*, 271 N.Y. 288, 2 N.E.2d 661, 105 A.L.R. 989.) If it is a limitation, the beneficiary cannot recover under the policy.

We conclude that employment, as defined in this group policy, is a condition of insurance and, therefore, since the insurer did not contest the employee's eligibility within the period of contestability, it is barred from raising it as a defense to the beneficiary's action (*Eagon v. Union Labor Life Ins. Co.*, 3 N.Y.2d 785, 164 N.Y.S.2d 37, 143 N.E.2d 793).

Our courts in the past have stringently enforced the incontestable provision required by statute to be included in every group and individual life insurance policy because of the important purposes which it is intended to serve. The provision safeguards an insured from excessive litigation many years after a policy has already been enforced and assures him security in financial planning for his family, while providing an insurer a reasonable opportunity to investigate. The troublesome problem in interpreting the precise reach of the incontestable provision is to determine what defenses are barred to the insurer and those which may still be raised after the expiration of the contestable period.

Both parties direct our attention to the identical passage in *Matter of Metropolitan Life Ins. Co. v. Conway*, 252 N.Y. 449, 452, 169 N.E. 642, 643, as controlling the precise question for decision on this appeal. In *Conway*, Chief Judge Cardozo writing for a unanimous court stated, "The provision that a policy shall be incontestable after it has been in force during the lifetime of the insured for a period of two years is not a mandate as to *coverage, a definition of the hazards to be borne by the insurer.* It means only this, that within the limits of the coverage, the policy shall stand, *unaffected by any defense that it was invalid in its inception, or thereafter became invalid by reason of a condition broken.*" (Emphasis added.) Though this passage is instructive, in the context of this appeal it is not dispositive. The quoted passage establishes a frame of reference for decision but does not unequivocally indicate which particular risks are conditions of insurance and thus borne by the insurer, if not discovered and contested within two years of issuance of the policy, and those hazards considered limitations on the risk an insurer is willing to assume and, therefore, not barred by the lapse of time.

In New York the incontestable clause is viewed normally with reference to the manner of death. Risks which are considered limitations are those which could not be ascertained by the insurer by investigation at the time the policy of insurance was issued. (*Matter of Metropolitan Life Ins. Co. v. Conway, supra; Matter of Metropolitan Life Ins. Co. v. Beha*, 226 App.Div. 408, 235 N.Y.S. 501, affd. *sub nom. Matter of Metropolitan Life Ins. Co. v. Conway*, 252 N.Y. 449, 169 N.E.

642, *supra;* *Woodbery v. New York Life Ins. Co.,* 129 Misc. 365, 221
N.Y.S. 357, mod. on another ground 223 App.Div. 272, 227 N.Y.S. 699).
If the additional risk to the insurer of issuing a policy to a particular
applicant could have been discovered at the time the contract was
entered into, the insurer is precluded from raising this fact as a defense
after the period provided for in the incontestable clause had elapsed. It
is only those risks which could not be ascertained at the time of
contracting which can properly be viewed as a limitation on the risk of
insurance. Where the insurer cannot guard against assuming a risk it
does not desire to insure by the simple expedient of investigating, such
as risks of death in noncommercial aviation and while on active
military duty, then the risk is properly classified as a limitation for
purposes of analysis with respect to the incontestable clause (Insurance
Law, Consol.Laws, c. 28 § 155, subd. 2).

The hallmark of the distinction between conditions and limitations
is discoverability. Undoubtedly, eligible employment is ascertainable
when a group policy is issued. Therefore, unless some distinctive
characteristic exists between group life and individual life insurance,
there is no logical reason to find employment a limitation rather than a
condition.

Three major differences emerge when group life insurance is compared with individual life insurance. They are the nature of the
insurance contract, the cost of insurance and the manner of selecting
the risk to be insured. (Gregg, Group Life Insurance [3d ed., 1962], 3–4,
25–49, 172–185; Gregg, Life and Health Insurance Handbook [2d ed.,
1964], 358–368.)

Group life insurance, though contracted for by an employer, is not
indemnity insurance but simply insurance upon the life of employees
for their personal benefit and the protection of those dependent upon
them for financial security. An employee covered by a group life policy
necessarily takes into account the coverage extended by his employer in
determining the amount of coverage he should seek, just as much as a
person who seeks an individual policy. (Gregg, Life and Health Insurance Handbook [2d ed., 1964], 367.) Thus, both group life and individual life insurance have the same ultimate goal—personal security of the
insured's beneficiaries.

Group life insurance is normally offered as a fringe benefit. This
type of insurance coverage is obtained by an employer at favorable
rates because selling and administration costs to the insurer are appreciably smaller than the costs of selling and administering the same
number of individual policies. It is evident that the first two distinctions between group and individual life policies are not critical ones.
The principal difference between group life and individual life insurance is the selection process. It is upon this distinction the insurer
would have us focus.

The major distinction is that under a group insurance policy a
greater number of persons who would not ordinarily procure insurance

are covered because of the requirement, for employer-paid plans, that all employees be included. The population which comprises the employees in a group insurance plan, therefore, constitutes a better insurance risk, taken as a group, from a statistical vantage point, than the same number of persons seeking private policies. It is the process of self-selection in individual life policies which accounts for the greater risk from the point of view of the insurer. Insurers fear that the same possibility of "adverse selection" will exist in group policies if noneligible employees are included because these persons may well be those who are unfavorable insurance risks and who could not procure private insurance except at preferred rates. For example, the private entrepreneur may list his sick son-in-law as an employee.

This problem of adverse selection, however, is not indigenous to group policies but has confronted insurers in individual policies long before group policies came into existence. The same problem has confronted insurers in determining the health status of individuals seeking private insurance. The problem was met in individual policies by requiring physical examinations and investigating medical history. Likewise, it is equally possible to determine employment eligibility by ascertaining employment status at the inception of the plan. Eligible employment can be determined by investigating membership rolls or employment records. The cost of this investigation is appreciably less than medical investigation in private policies and can be undertaken by a nonprofessional staff. The larger the number of persons which comprise the group the more sophisticated will be the accounting system to keep track of the group. The better the record-keeping system, the easier it will be for one to have access to information to determine eligibility. The fact that some insurers in the past have not investigated an employee's eligibility until death cannot be given any weight.

We cannot conclude that the difference in the selection of risks in group as opposed to individual life policies is so significant that it requires a departure from the traditional interpretation of conditions and limitations under New York law. Phoenix had the opportunity at the time it issued the certificates, or within two years of this date, to determine whether in fact the insured was a proper member of the group. The insurer, having failed to investigate, cannot be heard to complain now.

Accordingly, the order of the Appellate Division should be affirmed, with costs.

Notes and Questions

1. *Discoverability.* How satisfactory is the central distinction that does all the court's work in *Simpson?* How would the discoverability test deal with an insurer's defense that the purchaser of a life insurance policy lacked the requisite insurable interest in the life of the *cestui que vie* at the inception of the policy? One of the most critical

issues in life and health insurance today is the impact of the disease AIDS on the application and underwriting processes. As the discussion in Chapter One indicated, a number of states have adopted statutes that regulate insurers' use of blood tests that can help determine whether the applicant has been exposed to the virus associated with AIDS. In such jurisdictions, could a life insurer exclude coverage of death caused by AIDS-related disease, or is the fact that an applicant has been exposed to the HIV virus "discoverable" within the meaning of the *Simpson* test?

2. *Change of Status.* Group insurance poses special problems for incontestability law, because eligibility as such is rarely a question in individual insurance—either the insured has been issued a policy or she has not. Suppose that Leonard Simpson had been eligible for coverage at the time the master policy was issued, but became ineligible more than two years later, after the incontestability period had expired. Should that change in his status be considered discoverable by the insurer for incontestability purposes? If the period of contestability begins to run again from the date of change in status, must insurers continue to monitor eligibility? Does such an approach undercut a major benefit of group insurance—its lower cost because of economies of scale?

3. *Costs and Benefits.* The leading decision contrary to *Simpson, Crawford v. Equitable Life Assurance Society of the United States,* 56 Ill.2d 41, 305 N.E.2d 144 (1973), expressed concern about the potential for fraud that would impose extra costs on other insureds if the *Simpson* rule were adopted. Can insurers avoid these costs (and to a large extent, the kind of fraud with which they are associated) under the *Simpson* approach through contract provisions obligating the employer to indemnify the insurer for any claims resulting from incontestable fraud in which the employer is involved? Is a contract even necessary if the employer participates in the fraud? Which cost is likely to be greater—litigating the incontestability issue on a more individualized basis under *Crawford,* or using a *per se* rule under *Simpson* that avoids litigation but requires more investigation by insurers (or the kind of indemnification by employers suggested above)?

7. Limitations of Risk

However the set of defenses that become incontestable after two years is defined, many limitations on coverage contained in life insurance policies clearly are not subject to the incontestability clause. The following decisions address some of the more prominent of these provisions.

SILVERSTEIN v. METROPOLITAN LIFE INSURANCE COMPANY

Court of Appeals of New York, 1930.
254 N.Y. 81, 171 N.E. 914.

CARDOZO, C.J.

Defendant issued its policy of insurance whereby it insured plaintiff's husband against the results of bodily injuries "caused directly and independently of all other causes by accidental means," the insurance in the event of his death to be payable to his wife. The policy was not to "cover accident, injury, disability, death or other loss caused wholly or partly by disease or bodily or mental infirmity or medical or surgical treatment therefor."

The insured, while lifting a milk can into an ice box, slipped and fell, the can striking him on the abdomen and causing such pain that he was unable to get up. A surgeon, opening the abdomen, found a perforation at the junction of the stomach and the duodenum, through which the contents of the stomach escaped into the peritoneum, causing peritonitis and, later, death. At the point of perforation there had been a duodenal ulcer, about the size of a pea. The existence of this ulcer was unknown to the insured, and, were it not for the blow, would have had no effect upon his health, for it was dormant and not progressive, or so the triers of the facts might find. Even so, there had been a weakening of the wall in some degree, with the result that the impact of the blow was followed by perforation at the point of least resistance. The question is whether death was the result of an accident to the exclusion of other causes.

We think the evidence sustains a finding that the ulcer was not a disease or an infirmity within the meaning of the policy. Left to itself, it would have been as harmless as a pimple or a tiny scratch. Only in the event that it was progressive would it become a source of pain or trouble. If dormant, as it was found to be, it was not only harmless in itself, but incapable of becoming harmful except through catastrophic causes, not commonly to be expected. In a strict or literal sense, any departure from an ideal or perfect norm of health is a disease or an infirmity. Something more, however, must be shown to exclude the effects of accident from the coverage of a policy. The disease or the infirmity must be so considerable or significant that it would be characterized as disease or infirmity in the common speech of men. *Eastern Dist. Piece Dye Works v. Travelers' Ins. Co.*, 234 N.Y. 441, 453, 138 N.E. 401, 26 A.L.R. 1505. "Our guide is the reasonable expectation and purpose of the ordinary business man when making an ordinary business contract." *Bird v. St. Paul Fire & Marine Ins. Co.*, 224 N.Y. 47, 51, 120 N.E. 86, 87, 18 A.L.R. 875; *Goldstein v. Standard Accident Ins. Co.*, 236 N.Y. 178, 183, 140 N.E. 235, 236; *Van Vechten v. American Eagle Fire Ins. Co.*, 239 N.Y. 303, 146 N.E. 432, 38 A.L.R. 1115. A policy of insurance is not accepted with the thought that its coverage is to be restricted to an Apollo or a Hercules.

A distinction, then, is to be drawn between a morbid or abnormal condition of such quality or degree that in its natural and probable development it may be expected to be a source of mischief, in which event it may fairly be described as a disease or an infirmity, and a condition abnormal or unsound when tested by a standard of perfection, yet so remote in its potential mischief that common speech would call it not disease or infirmity, but at most a predisposing tendency. * * * There will be no recovery under a policy so written where an everyday act, involving ordinary exertion, brings death to an insured because he is a sufferer from heart disease. *Allendorf v. Fidelity & Casualty Co. of New York*, 250 N.Y. 529, 166 N.E. 311; *Leland v. Order of United Commercial Travelers of America*, supra. On the other hand, a recovery will not be denied to the sufferer from hernia who has had a predisposition to rupture because the inguinal canal was not closed as it ought to have been (*Collins v. Casualty Co.*, supra), or to one whose hip has been fractured because his bones have become brittle with the advent of old age. Cf. *Taylor v. New York Life Ins. Co.*, supra. "If a man with an abnormally thin skull be struck a blow which would not seriously injure a normal man, but which causes his death, it is perfectly plain that the cause of death is not the thinness of the skull, but the receipt of the blow." *Mutual Life Ins. Co. v. Dodge*, supra, page 489, of 11 F.(2d). An appendix already gangrenous is one thing (*Stanton v. Travelers' Ins. Co.*, 83 Conn. 708, 78 A. 317, 34 L.R.A. (N.S.) 445), and quite another is an appendix, not presently malignant, though a potential source of infection in the future if left within the body. The governing principle has been stated by Rugg, C.J. with clearness and precision: "If there is no active disease, but merely a frail general condition, so that powers of resistance are easily overcome, or merely a tendency to disease which is started up and made operative, whereby death results, then there may be recovery even though the accident would not have caused that effect upon healthy person in a normal state." *Leland v. Order of United Commercial Travelers of America*, supra, at page 564 of 233 Mass., 124 N.E. 517, 520.

An ulcer as trivial and benign as an uninfected pimple is at most a tendency to an infirmity, and not an infirmity itself.

Any different construction would reduce the policy and its coverage to contradiction and absurdity. The infinite interplay of causes makes it impossible to segregate any single cause as operative at any time and place to the exclusion of all others, if cause is to be viewed as a concept of science or philosophy. * * * The courts have set their faces against a view so doctrinaire, an estimate of intention so headed toward futility. "We are to follow the chain of causation so far, and so far only, as the parties meant that we should follow it. 'The causes within their contemplation are the only causes that concern us.'" *Goldstein v. Standard Accident Ins. Co.*, supra.

The judgment should be affirmed, with costs.

Notes and Questions

1. *Means or Results?* Earlier in this century policies covering death caused only by "accidental means" were more common than they are today. Over a period of time many (but by no means all) courts have collapsed the distinction the policies drew between accidental *means* and accidental *results*, holding that there is coverage as long as the cause of death was "accidental" in common parlance. See, e.g., *Burr v. Commercial Travelers Mutual Accident Association of America,* 295 N.Y. 294, 67 N.E.2d 248 (1946) (insured suffered heart attack while shoveling car out of snowdrift on a rural highway after a collision); *Perrine v. Prudential Insurance Company of America,* 56 N.J. 120, 265 A.2d 521 (1970) (insured died from peritonitis caused by intestinal break following heavy lifting). Cf. *Page Flooring and Construction Company v. Nationwide Life Insurance Company,* 840 F.2d 159 (1st Cir. 1988) (death resulting from adverse reaction to dye used in diagnostic medical procedure falls within exclusion of coverage of "death * * * resulting from medical * * * treatment."). In some cases, however, it is self-evident that there is coverage, even apart from the means/results distinction. As the West Publishing Company headnote put it in *Wetzel v. Westinghouse Electric Corporation,* 258 Pa.Super. 500, 393 A.2d 470 (1978), " * * * death of insured was due to 'violent, external and accidental means' within coverage of accidental death policy, and thus innocent beneficiary was entitled to recover benefits, where insured, who was karate expert, grabbed Hawaiian sword and attacked his son, who was also karate expert, in fit of rage over tax return son was preparing for insured, and son killed insured while attempting to subdue him with nanchukas sticks." Aspiring tax lawyers beware.

2. *Dare–Devil Behavior.* The distinction between accidental means and accidental results may be unduly technical when applied to the combination of physical infirmities and external force in cases such as *Silverstein.* Should that distinction retain vitality, however, in the context of physically dangerous activities in which the insured voluntarily engages, such as skydiving, drag racing, or other dare-devil activities? In *Knight v. Metropolitan Life Insurance Company,* 103 Ariz. 100, 437 P.2d 416 (1968), the insured had successfully dived from the top of the Coolidge dam before, but he died in his (needless to say) last attempt. The court held that he was covered by a policy limiting coverage to death caused "solely through violent, external and accidental means." Is this holding correct? Would you apply this clause to death resulting from a gunshot wound incurred in the course of committing a burglary? See *Roque v. Nationwide Mutual Insurance Company,* 502 Pa. 615, 467 A.2d 1128 (1983) (no coverage).

3. *Death While Committing a Crime.* Where the policy in question provides general life insurance rather than coverage for accidental death alone, the meaning of the latter term is not at issue. Some older decisions, however, have held that even general life insurance policies contain implied exceptions for death caused while the insured is en-

gaged in criminal activity. The modern trend is to refuse to create such exceptions. See, e.g., *Davis v. Boston Mutual Life Insurance Company*, 370 Mass. 602, 351 N.E.2d 207 (1976). This is not to say that an express exception of this sort would be inapplicable. See *Drew v. Life Insurance Company of Georgia*, 170 Ga.App. 147, 316 S.E.2d 512 (1984). Did the older approach guard excessively against adverse selection and moral hazard?

CHARNEY v. ILLINOIS MUTUAL LIFE CASUALTY COMPANY

United States Court of Appeals, Eleventh Circuit, 1985.
764 F.2d 1441.

PER CURIAM:

Plaintiffs, the wife and the business partner of the insured, appeal an adverse summary judgment in these consolidated life insurance cases. The district court held that the insured's life insurance policy, which excluded liability for suicide "whether sane or insane" if committed within two years of the policy date, was not ambiguous and that the insured's mental state at the time of his self-inflicted death, allegedly induced by prescribed drugs, was irrelevant to that policy. We affirm.

Dr. Marvin Charney was a Florida veterinarian being treated for hypertension with the medication reserpine. A possible side effect of reserpine is depression. Dr. Charney began showing symptoms of severe depression shortly after being placed on the drug. The evening after Dr. Charney's first visit to a psychiatrist, he went to his office, wrote a note to his family, injected himself with T61 euthanasia solution, and died.

The combined policies at issue here insured Dr. Charney's life in the amount of $500,000 for his wife, and $100,000 for his business partner, Steven Bromberg. Each policy contained the following suicide exclusion:

> SUICIDE. If the Insured, whether sane or insane, shall die by his own hand or act within 2 years after the Date of the Policy, our liability under this Policy shall be limited to the premiums paid hereon.

The insured died within two years of the policy date and defendant tendered the premium paid.

There is no question that Dr. Charney did in fact "die by his own hand." Nor is there any doubt that he "intended" to kill himself in the sense that he knew and understood the physiological effects of injecting himself with T61 euthanasia solution. The sole issue before this Court is whether the suicide exclusionary clause does not apply because Dr. Charney's reserpine-induced depression so diminished his mental capacity that he did not have the requisite intent to commit suicide.

While no Florida case cited to us has discussed this particular issue, there appears to be no reason why the plain and unambiguous language of the policy should not control. Even assuming that the insured was rendered insane by reserpine, there is nothing in the contract that suggests the cause of insanity would make any difference in the policy's coverage. The cause of Dr. Charney's insanity, if he was insane, is simply irrelevant. The following cases have all held that a suicide "sane or insane" clause is to be given effect irrespective of the insured's mental state. *Bigelow v. Berkshire Life Ins. Co.*, 93 U.S. (3 Otto) 284, 287, 23 L.Ed. 918 (1876); *Clarke v. Equitable Life Assur. Soc.*, 118 Fed. 374, 378 (4th Cir.1902); *Johnson v. Metropolitan Life Ins. Co.*, 404 F.2d 1202, 1204 (3d Cir.1968); *Ann Arbor Trust Co. v. North American Co. for Life & Health Ins.*, 527 F.2d 526 (6th Cir.1975), *cert. denied* 425 U.S. 993, 96 S.Ct. 2206, 48 L.Ed.2d 818 (1976).

Plaintiff's argument that the "sane or insane" clause is ambiguous due to the necessity of intent in a suicide is based on *Searle v. Allstate Life Ins. Co.*, 96 Cal.App.3d 614, 616, 158 Cal.Rptr. 5 (1979). That case was recently overturned by the California Supreme Court which held that "we conclude the Court in *Searle I* erred in holding the clause ambiguous and in reasoning that insanity necessarily precludes formation of the intent to commit suicide." *Searle v. Allstate Life Insurance Co.*, 38 Cal.3d 425, 212 Cal.Rptr. 466, 471, 696 P.2d 1308, 1313 (1985). *Searle* is thus now authority for defendant's position.

Florida law requires the intent to achieve self-destruction for suicidal intent to be found. *Gulf Life Ins. Co. v. Nash*, 97 So.2d 4, 6 (Fla.1957). Without the intent of self-destruction there would be no suicide because the death would be accidental. An accidental death would be covered by the instant policy. Plaintiffs have confused felonious intent negated by diminished capacity with the intent to reach an end through a particular means. The only intent *Nash* requires is the intent to cause death, and that is an undisputed fact here.

The three Florida cases relied on by plaintiff to raise an ambiguity in the policy language due to diminished capacity are not on point. Although each dealt with a contractual exclusion held not to apply due to the insured's insanity, *Arkwright–Boston Manufacturers Mutual Ins. Co. v. Dunkel*, 363 So.2d 190 (Fla. 3rd DCA 1978); *Northland Ins. Co. v. Mautino*, 433 So.2d 1225 (Fla. 3d DCA 1983), *pet. for rev. denied*, 447 So. 2d 887 (Fla.1984); *George v. Stone*, 260 So.2d 259 (Fla. 4th DCA 1972), none considered a "sane or insane" clause.

Nor can plaintiff's theory that the insured's death was directly caused by the reserpine-induced depression succeed. Whatever the effect of the reserpine on the insured, the direct cause of his death was the self-injection of T61 euthanasia solution.

The cases cited by plaintiffs, *Travelers Ins. Co. v. Melick*, 65 Fed. 178 (8th Cir.1894) and *Norbeck v. Mutual of Omaha Ins. Co.*, 3 Wash. App. 582, 476 P.2d 546 (1970), both involve ambiguities in the policies themselves. There is no ambiguity in the instant case. Whatever the cause of the insured's mental state, he did in fact intend the result of his act and died by his own hand. That is all Florida law requires.

Notes and Questions

1. *The General Rule.* Absent an express exclusion, recovery for death caused by suicide under a general life insurance policy normally is permitted. Recovery for death caused by suicide is not permitted, however, under a policy insuring only against death by accident or accidental means, or under the accidental death provisions of a general policy. Since the suicide limitation is contained in an exclusion in general purpose policies, the insurer bears the burden of proof on the issue; but the beneficiary apparently bears the burden of proving that death was accidental under an accident policy—a burden that sometimes involves showing that death was not by suicide.

2. *"By His Own Hand".* Standard policy language excludes coverage "If the Insured commits suicide while sane or insane within two years after the Date of Issue." See Sample Life Insurance Policy—The Contract. Might this language sometimes produce different results from the language the policy in *Charney* employed: "If the insured, whether sane or insane, shall die by his own hand or act * * *"? For example, suppose the insured takes a prescription drug that induces hallucinations; he then dies after jumping from a roof, believing that he can fly. Is coverage excluded by either or both of the clauses?

3. *Fatal Illnesses.* The two-year limitation in the typical suicide clause strongly suggests that its objective is to guard against adverse selection. Should the clause therefore be interpreted in light of this objective? For example, suppose that the insured discovers after purchasing a policy that she is suffering from a fatal illness. After her condition has deteriorated, she refuses nourishment while hospitalized and dies within a few days. Uncontested medical testimony indicates that she was within a few weeks of dying from the illness. Does the suicide limitation preclude recovery by her beneficiary?

8. Negligence Actions Against the Insurer

MAURONER v. MASSACHUSETTS INDEMNITY AND LIFE INSURANCE COMPANY

Court of Appeal of Louisiana, 1988.
520 So.2d 451.

CHEHARDY, Chief Judge.

This appeal arises from a judgment awarding plaintiff, Susan Mauroner, the proceeds of a life insurance policy insuring her deceased husband, Milton Mauroner, Jr., who died by suicide. The policy was issued by defendant Massachusetts Indemnity and Life Insurance Company (MILICO) through its agents, defendants Steve Modica and Associates (Modica), a Division of A.L. Williams Company, and Bill Whittle and Associates, Inc. (Whittle). We affirm.

The facts in this case were stipulated to by the parties and show that Modica sold the Mauroners a life insurance policy in the amount of $100,000 covering Milton Mauroner, Jr., with a rider on Susan Mauroner for $10,000. The application was prepared by Steve Modica with information given to him by the applicants. While a medical examination was not required, a medical history was included with the application, along with an authorization for MILICO to consult the doctors and hospital where the Mauroners had previously received treatment or advice. The application was signed and mailed with a check for one month's premium ($60.90) to MILICO on November 6, 1981. Along with the application Modica completed a "MILICO New Business Transmittal Form" describing the coverage sought. It was further stipulated that the normal processing period for acceptance or rejection of these policies was four to eight weeks.

In return for payment of the initial premium, the Mauroners were given a conditional receipt. Under the terms of the receipt, MILICO agreed to provide insurance against any covered loss as of November 6, 1981, if the information in the application was found to be accurate and complete, if the Mauroners were otherwise found qualified and if the policy was thereafter issued.

After receipt of the modification, MILICO notified Modica, through Whittle's office, that a clarification was needed on the coverage for Mr. Mauroner. That letter was dated November 20, 1981 and clarification was needed because Modica erroneously listed on the transmittal form a request for two "MOD 15" base plans for $50,000 each. The correct listing should have been either one "MOD 15" base plan for $100,000 or a "MOD 15" base plan for $50,000 with a companion rider for an additional $50,000.

No further action was taken until January 4, 1982, when someone in Whittle's office telephoned MILICO underwriting in Atlanta, Georgia, to find out the status of the application. After another telephone call the next day, it was determined that a "RVP" (regional vice president) was needed to telephone the correct coverage to MILICO. Upon receipt of the information, MILICO replied on January 7, 1982 that it was forwarding the information to the underwriting section. However, sometime after January 8, but prior to January 25, MILICO sent a copy of its underwriting memo of November 20, 1981, which originally requested the clarification, to the agents stamped "Final Notice". On January 25, 1982, Leslie Whittle of Bill Whittle's office telephoned MILICO again inquiring about the Mauroners' application. On that same day Mrs. Whittle also sent a written memo to MILICO reiterating the correct coverage. MILICO acknowledged receipt of the information the following day. The policy was thereafter issued ten days later on February 4, 1982. It was delivered to the Mauroners on February 28, 1982 at their home by Steve Modica. At that time he discussed the policy contents including the date of issuance (February 11, 1982) and the two-year suicide incontestability clause. In that respect he explained Mr. Mauroner could not "blow his brains out" for at least two years after the issue date of the policy in order for Mrs. Mauroner to collect the proceeds of the life insurance policy.

At the time Steve Modica sold the policy to the Mauroners he was aware that Mr. Mauroner was insured for $100,000 under a policy with State Farm Insurance Company. The Mauroners paid the last premium on that policy in December, 1981 which continued coverage to January 2, 1982. The State Farm coverage thereafter remained in effect through the application of dividends to the payment of premiums until March 2, 1981. From March until August 17, 1982, coverage was continued through the use of the cash surrender value of the policy.

Mr. Mauroner committed suicide on January 13, 1984. Because the death occurred three weeks prior to the end of the two-year suicide exclusion, MILICO refused to pay Mrs. Mauroner the proceeds of the life insurance policy, but refunded the premiums paid ($1,221.21) pursuant to the policy terms. As a result, Mrs. Mauroner filed suit against the above-named defendants.

The case was fixed for trial on February 7, 1987, and at that time was submitted on the record. Judgment was rendered on May 8, 1987 in plaintiff's favor for the full amount of the policy. In his reasons for judgment the trial judge determined the agents of MILICO were negligent in failing to correct the coverage error timely and that the negligent delay caused Mrs. Mauroner's loss of the policy proceeds. He further concluded because of the negligence the policy's issuance date was November 6, 1981 and Mr. Mauroner's suicide occurred after the two-year suicide limitation period.

On appeal, defendants first contend the trial judge erred in finding the negligent delay between the application and the issuance of the policy justified changing the issue date from the actual date of February 4, 1982 to the application date of November 6. Defendants contend the policy issue date controls the commencement of the running of the two years under the suicide clause and that there is neither law nor a factual basis to support the substitution of the application date so as to place the death outside the two-year preclusion of coverage. Defendants secondly assert plaintiff has no cause of action for negligent delay in the issuance of the policy. Alternatively, defendants argue that the trial judge erred in holding the delay in processing the application was negligence or that it caused the plaintiff's damage.

In their first argument, defendants contend the suicide limitation and the incontestability clauses preclude plaintiff's recovery of the policy proceeds, because Milton Mauroner, Jr. committed suicide prior to the expiration of two years from the date the policy was issued. Defendants argue that the trial judge's substitution of the application date for the issue date was legally incorrect and was contrary to the policy and the stipulation of the parties.

The pertinent clauses state as follows: "SUICIDE—If the Insured dies by suicide, while sane or insane, within two years of the date of issue, our only liability will be the amount of premiums paid."

and

"INCONTESTABILITY—This policy will be incontestable after it has been in force for two years. The two years will begin as of the date of issue. This provision does not apply: (1) when any premium is unpaid beyond the grace period; and (2) to any rider for disability benefits or additional insurance specifically for death by accident."

Under these two provisions, it is the date of issue that controls the commencement of the two years and we find no cases which would justify a substitution of the application date for the issue date on the basis of the agent's negligence. However, in rebuttal, plaintiff asserts defendants are estopped from denying liability by the language of the insurance application and receipt. Plaintiff argues that language provides retroactive coverage to the date of application once the policy has been approved and issued.

The application and receipt signed by the parties and dated November 6, 1981 states in pertinent part:

"CONDITIONS OF COVERAGE

I understand and agree that, except as set forth below, I will not be covered for any loss occurring prior to the date on which the Company issues the policy for which I have on this date applied.

However, if all the following conditions are met, I understand and agree that if the Company does issue a policy to me, such policy will cover me in accordance with its provisions, limitations and exceptions for losses on or after the date set forth below:

    1. All the information given by me in my insurance application must be accurate and complete to the best of my knowledge and belief.

    2. The Company must find me qualified for the policy plan and amount applied for in accordance with its normal and customary underwriting standards and practices.

    3. At least one monthly premium for the policy plan and amount applied for must be paid with my insurance application."

It is clear that the policy does provide for retroactive coverage once the conditions have been met and the policy issued. However, the coverage provided is "in accordance with its [the policy's] *provisions, limitations and exceptions.*" Since the two-year suicide clause is a provision or a limitation or an exception, it must be given effect.

Consequently, we find the trial judge erred in substituting the application date for the date the policy was actually issued, although the finding does not per se negate defendants' liability.

In his reasons for judgment the trial judge found the defendants' actions in delaying correction of the error committed by Steve Modica was negligent and caused plaintiff's loss of the policy proceeds. Defendants contend the trial judge erred in this finding in that plaintiff has no cause of action for negligent delay in the issuance of a policy. Further, defendants assert that if a cause of action exists, the delay was not unreasonable and did not cause the loss.

Defendants argue plaintiff has no cause of action because a review of the jurisprudence which has addressed negligent delay has done so only in the context of rejections or cancellations of policies. Since the policy here was issued, defendants conclude there is no cause of action.

Our review of the cases indicate the particular problem we have before us has not been addressed by the courts of this state. The cases, as defendants point out, involve the agents' or brokers' failure to obtain the insurance, the rejection of the applicant, or the cancellation of a policy. In those instances the critical issue was whether the negligent delay prevented the applicant or insured from obtaining coverage elsewhere which would have prevented their loss of particular policy benefits. * * * However, simply because an issue has not been addressed by the courts does not mean a cause of action does not exist. Persons are liable for acts of commission or omission that cause damage to another if a duty imposed by the relationship of the parties is breached by such act or omission. *Smith v. Travelers Ins. Co.*, 430 So. 2d 55 (La.1983); see: LSA–C.C. art. 2315, et seq.; LSA–C.C. art. 2985, et seq.; LSA–C.C. art. 1994, et seq.

In plaintiff's petition she alleges she sustained damage (loss of the insurance proceeds) because of defendants' negligent delay in issuing the policy. Negligence requires a finding that defendants breached a duty to plaintiff and that breach was the legal cause of the damage. In *Davis & Landry v. Guar. Income Life Ins., supra*, the court stated the insurance company has a duty to act upon an application within a reasonable time and a violation of that duty will subject the company to resultant damages for negligence. Although that case involved the death of the applicant before the policy was approved and issued, we find the holding applicable to these facts as well. Thus, we find plaintiff has stated a cause of action for loss of the insurance proceeds.

The next question presented by defendants' appeal is whether the trial judge erred in finding the defendants' delay in correcting its error constituted negligence. In this regard defendants assert the delay in processing the application was reasonable.

It was stipulated by the parties that MILICO normally processed applications within four to eight weeks, or at the maximum, 56 days. In this case the policy was issued 92 days from the date of application, a delay of 36 days. Such a delay was unreasonable in light of the fact that MILICO sought correction of the error in November 1981, but the error was not corrected until January 1982. Our conclusion that this delay was unreasonable is further supported by the fact that once the mistake was corrected, MILICO issued the policy within ten days. Thus, we find the trial judge did not err in finding the defendants were negligent in their handling of plaintiff's application.

Finally, defendants assert that even if their delay in processing the application was negligent, it was not the cause of plaintiff's loss. In this regard defendants contend the damages sustained by plaintiff were caused solely by the deceased's choice in committing suicide three weeks prior to expiration of the two-year preclusion period.

As to this claim by defendants, the evidence shows that had the error not occurred, or had it been corrected promptly, it was more likely than not the suicide would have occurred after the two year period excluding suicide expired. Consequently, the cause of plaintiff's loss was not the deceased's choice in committing suicide on January 13, 1984, but defendants' breach of its duty to the insureds to correct its mistake timely. Thus, we find the trial judge did not err in finding defendants' negligence was the cause of plaintiff's injury and casting them in damages for the amount of the policy ($100,000).

Accordingly, the judgment of the trial court is hereby affirmed. Costs are to be paid by appellant.

AFFIRMED.

BACON v. FEDERAL KEMPER LIFE ASSURANCE COMPANY

Supreme Judicial Court of Massachusetts, 1987.
400 Mass. 850, 512 N.E.2d 941.

NOLAN, Justice.

This appeal arises out of a wrongful death action in which a jury found the defendant, Federal Kemper Life Assurance Company (Kemper) liable for causing the death of Edwin C. Bacon.[1] Adelaide R. Bacon was the wife of Edwin C. Bacon. Kemper is an insurance company which carried a life insurance policy on the life of Bacon. Bacon was found dead in his Boston office on July 30, 1974. In July, 1977, the plaintiff filed a complaint against Kemper alleging both that Kemper's breach of contract and its negligence in accepting and recording a change of beneficiary caused Bacon's murder by his business associate, James Blaikie, Jr. The complaint alleged that Blaikie had forged Bacon's signature on the change of beneficiary form and murdered him in an attempt to collect the proceeds of the life insurance policy.

* * *

1. Adelaide R. Bacon, on behalf of her two daughters, sued as next-of-kin for the decedent's wrongful death and as representative of the decedent's estate for conscious pain and suffering. She also sued individually for her loss of consortium.

2. *Summary of facts.* The life insurance policy, which is central to this case, was issued by Kemper to Edwin C. Bacon on July 1, 1971. The policy carried a face amount of $50,000 and a term of five years. The beneficiary was a trust established by Bacon for his wife and children. In September, 1973, Bacon submitted an application to change the beneficiary of the policy to another but similar trust, known as the Edwin C. Bacon Trust of August 28, 1973. Kemper acknowledged the change of beneficiary by sending Bacon a printed and unsigned form. Bacon was disturbed by Kemper's response. In October, 1973, Bacon's concerns were communicated in a letter to Kemper. Bacon expressed his understanding that Massachusetts law required that the change of beneficiary form be accepted and signed by a company officer. As Bacon put it, this assurance was essential so that both parties knew they were operating from the same facts and because fifty thousand dollars was a considerable sum of money for his family. An officer of Kemper replied (correctly) to Bacon that its legal department's research had not uncovered any such Massachusetts law.

On July 19, 1974, Kemper's home office received another request to change the beneficiary on Bacon's policy. The form, bearing the purported signature of Bacon, requested that the principal beneficiary be designated as James F. Blaikie, Jr., and the Edwin C. Bacon Trust listed as the contingent beneficiary. Bacon's "signature" was witnessed by Blaikie. The application was quickly processed and approved. A letter, dated July 24, 1974, acknowledging the change was sent to Bacon's business address.

Bacon habitually went to his office late in the morning and remained there until very late at night. His wife, in contrast, preferred to arise early in the morning and went to bed before he came home. When she awoke on the morning of July 30, 1974, she realized that her husband had not come home the previous night. She went to his office, arriving there around 7:30 A.M. Mrs. Bacon had to locate the building superintendent because her husband's office door was locked. Upon opening the door they discovered Bacon's body lying face down on the floor next to a water cooler. Shortly afterwards, the police and coroner arrived. When Bacon's body was removed from the office, a note was discovered under his chest. The note, printed in block letters, stated: "I can't stand it anymore." An autopsy was performed later that day. The medical examiner determined that the cause of death was sodium cyanide poisoning.

In August, 1974, Kemper received proof of Bacon's death from Blaikie and a request for the proceeds of the policy. A similar claim was made by Bacon's wife in September. Faced with these conflicting claims, Kemper submitted the last change of beneficiary form to a handwriting expert. The expert concluded that Bacon had not signed that form. Consequently, in December, 1974, Kemper instituted an action of interpleader for an adjudication of the rival policy claims. On June 12, 1975, a judge of the Superior Court entered a judgment, pursuant to Mass.R.Civ.P. 58(a), as amended, 371 Mass. 908 (1977), discharging Kemper "from any and all liability whatsoever on its policy" and enjoining the claimants from making "any further claim or commencing or prosecuting this action or any further action or actions * * * on account of said policy of insurance or anything growing out of the same." Thereafter the judge determined that the proceeds be distributed to the Edwin C. Bacon Trust. Three years later, the plaintiff commenced the present action.

3. *Negligence.* In order to impose liability on Kemper for the death of Edwin Bacon, the plaintiff had the burden of proving by a preponderance of the evidence that (a) Blaikie murdered Bacon; (b) Kemper owed a duty to Bacon; (c) Kemper breached that duty, and (d) Kemper's breach of duty was the proximate cause of Bacon's murder. Kemper contends that it was entitled to the entry of judgment in its favor because the plaintiff's proof was insufficient as a matter of law with respect to each of these issues.

There was sufficient evidence to warrant a finding that Blaikie murdered Bacon and that Kemper owed a duty of care to Bacon in effectuating a change of beneficiary. However, we conclude that there was no evidence to warrant a finding of a breach of duty by Kemper after reviewing the evidence in the light most favorable to the plaintiff and after giving the plaintiff the benefit of every inference favorable to her. *Ferragamo v. Massachusetts Bay Transp. Auth.*, 395 Mass. 581, 591, 481 N.E.2d 477 (1985).

Kemper correctly argues that the evidence was insufficient to justify the jury's finding that its conduct fell below the standard of a reasonably prudent insurance company. Kemper claims that there was not evidence which proved that it knew or should have known that its acceptance and approval of the change of beneficiary request exposed Bacon to an unreasonable risk of harm from criminal conduct by a third party. We agree. The plaintiff contends that Kemper acted unreasonably in approving the beneficiary change because it was not signed by a disinterested witness and because Kemper did not attempt to verify whether Blaikie was actually Bacon's business partner. In addition, the plaintiff claims that the October, 1973, letter Bacon sent to Kemper was further evidence that Kemper should have known that the beneficiary change request was suspicious.

The facts relied on by the plaintiff are simply too innocuous to have aroused Kemper's suspicion that Bacon had not consented to the change of beneficiary. William Jones, a former head of Kemper's policyholder service department, whose deposition was read in evidence by the plaintiff, conceded that it was not unusual for a business partner to be listed as a beneficiary on a policy. Moreover, even though Kemper required a beneficiary to have an insurable interest in an insured's life, and Blaikie would qualify in that respect, there is no such requirement under our law. *Strachan v. Prudential Ins. Co.*, 321 Mass. 507, 509, 73 N.E.2d 840 (1947). Thus, it is immaterial who was listed as the beneficiary. Nor can we say that Blaikie's signature as witness was enough to put Kemper on notice that the request was doubtful. Although Jones testified that he thought the requirement of a disinterested witness had been added as a precaution against fraud or foul play, he did not explain how it could obviate such a possibility. It is conceivable that it could prevent a potential beneficiary from exercising undue influence over an insured, but that obstacle could easily be overcome by a beneficiary forging the witness' signature. An insurance company would have no way of knowing if the witness' signature was forged. At the time the application in this case was received, the disinterested witness requirement was no longer in effect. The woman who assumed Jones' position in April, 1974, testified that she made the decision to eliminate that requirement because the company was receiving too many complaints from agents that it was a hindrance to insureds. Finally, the plaintiff produced no expert testimony that such a requirement was considered good practice in the insurance industry or has any support in law.

The only duty that the law imposes on an insurance company to protect its insured is that the company take reasonable steps to determine whether the insured has consented to the policy or the change of beneficiary. In the cases in which an insurance company has been found liable for harm to its insureds, the company either had actual knowledge that the insured had not consented to the policy, *Life Ins. Co. v. Lopez,* 443 So.2d 947, 948 (Fla.1983) and *Ramey v. Carolina Life Ins. Co.,* 244 S.C. 16, 21, 135 S.E.2d 362 (1964), or should have known that the person who procured the policy did not have an insurable interest in the life of the insured. *Liberty Nat'l Life Ins. Co. v. Weldon,* 267 Ala. 171, 182, 100 So.2d 696 (1957). Here, the Kemper clerk charged with processing change of beneficiary requests compared Bacon's signature on that request with his signature on the original policy application request. Those signatures were identical to the naked eye. Only an expert, after careful examination, was able to conclude that one was a forgery.

4. *Conclusion.* Kemper acted reasonably as a matter of law in approving the request. Therefore, there was no breach of duty. The judgment for the plaintiff is reversed, and judgment is to be entered in favor of Kemper.

So ordered. ∗ ∗ ∗

ABRAMS, Justice (dissenting, with whom LIACOS, J., joins).

The court today departs from its test "whether 'anywhere in the evidence, from whatever source derived, any combination of circumstances could be found from which a reasonable inference could be drawn in favor of the plaintiff.'" *Poirier v. Plymouth,* 374 Mass. 206, 212, 372 N.E.2d 212 (1978), quoting *Raunela v. Hertz Corp.,* 361 Mass. 341, 343, 280 N.E.2d 179 (1972). Because the court departs from its test, I dissent.

I agree with the court that the clerk's [1] comparison of signatures is some evidence that Kemper was not negligent in processing the change of beneficiary form. There was, however, other evidence which indicates negligence on the part of the company. William Jones, the former head of the policyholder service department, said that Kemper required a disinterested third party to witness the signature of the insured. Jones also stated that the beneficiary of a policy would not qualify as a disinterested witness.[2] Jones's successor said that she eliminated Kemper's requirement of a disinterested witness, although there was no evidence she had authority to do so.

The jury could have believed the testimony of Jones that a signature of a disinterested witness was required on a change of beneficiary application and that, because there was no signature of a disinterested witness on the forged application, Kemper had failed to follow its own internal procedures developed to protect against fraud and foul play. The failure of Kemper to follow its company procedures is some evidence of negligence. See *Kushner v. Dravo Corp.*, 339 Mass. 273, 277, 158 N.E.2d 858 (1959); *Kelly v. Boston & Me. R.R.*, 319 Mass. 603, 613, 66 N.E.2d 807 (1946); *Stevens v. Boston Elevated Ry.*, 184 Mass. 476, 478–479, 69 N.E. 338 (1904).

Moreover, the evidence indicates that Bacon had submitted an application to change the beneficiary of his life insurance policy in September, 1973. After this change was processed, Bacon wrote a letter expressing concern to the company regarding the change of beneficiary procedure because the amount of the policy was a significant amount of money to his family.[3] Nine months later, Kemper received a second change of beneficiary application bearing the forged signature of Bacon shifting the proceeds of the policy away from his family. Jones stated that, on the basis of this information alone, he might have been suspicious of the requested change of beneficiary and would have inquired further into the matter before processing the request for a change. Although the Kemper clerk had Bacon's entire file before her in processing the change of beneficiary and could see the prior correspondence regarding the change of beneficiary procedures, she did not investigate this change of beneficiary request. If the jury credited Jones's testimony and rejected the clerk's actions in only comparing the signatures, that was evidence that Kemper violated its

1. I note that there was no evidence that the clerk was trained in handwriting analysis.

2. The court states that Jones did not explain how the requirement of a disinterested witness could protect against fraud or foul play. *Ante* at 944. This observation misses the mark. The jury could use this evidence that Kemper was not following its own internal policies and procedures in determining the issue of negligence. The jury was not asked to assess the appropriateness or effectiveness of Kemper's internal procedures.

3. Bacon's letter to Kemper stated that he thought Massachusetts law required a change of beneficiary form to be accepted in writing by the company and signed by an officer of the company. Bacon stated that this acknowledgement requirement was the only way to assure that both the insured and the company are aware of the change. He stated that he was anxious about this matter because the amount of the policy was "a lot of money to my wife and kids."

duty to act with reasonable care with respect to Bacon. The credibility of the witness is for the jury and it is inappropriate for this court to substitute its judgment on questions of fact. See *Cullen Enterprises, Inc. v. Massachusetts Property Ins. Underwriting Ass'n,* 399 Mass. 886, 897, 507 N.E.2d 717 (1987); *Lupia v. Marino,* 353 Mass. 749, 231 N.E.2d 16 (1967). See also *Foley v. Polaroid Corp.,* 400 Mass. 82, 104, 508 N.E.2d 72 (1987) (Liacos, J., concurring).

Although I believe a per se rule which imposes a duty on insurance companies to verify all change of beneficiary applications is inappropriate, on the basis of the facts of this case, the jury could reasonably have inferred that Kemper had a duty to investigate more fully this change of beneficiary. The insured took extraordinary steps to inform Kemper of his concerns for his family and, only nine months later, the insured seemed to have had a dramatic change of heart, switching the beneficiary away from his family, and this change was witnessed by the new beneficiary. These facts support the jury's determination that Kemper was negligent in handling this particular change of beneficiary application.

In addition, although not required by law, Kemper required a beneficiary to have an insurable interest in an insured's life. While a partner has an insurable interest in the life of another partner, the evidence showed that Kemper made no attempt to ascertain whether Blaikie was, in fact, a partner of Bacon.[4] The clerk simply accepted the application for change of beneficiary without any further investigation. The jury could have found that this failure of the clerk to verify that the company policy concerning insurable interest was adhered to in this application was evidence of negligence.

Finally, there was evidence that the Kemper's clerks responsible for change of beneficiary applications handled ten to twelve requests a day. The jury could reasonably have inferred that the benefit from scrutinizing those few applications which were witnessed by the new beneficiary outweighed the cost of doing so. Kemper's failure to scrutinize those few applications would permit a reasonable inference that Kemper failed to exercise due care in the circumstances.

There was evidence which, if believed, provided a factual basis for an inference that Kemper did not take reasonable steps to determine whether Bacon consented to the change of beneficiary. Instead of adhering to well-established principles of review, the court makes the factual determination that Kemper acted with reasonable care. On the evidence admitted, the jury could have found that Kemper acted reasonably or the jury could have found that Kemper failed to follow its

---

4. As the court states, *ante* at 944, "[I]t is immaterial who was listed as the beneficiary." This statement is far too broad. Pursuant to Kemper's own policies, the beneficiary must be one with an insurable interest in the life of the insured. If the beneficiary named on an application is not such a person, it would be further evidence that Kemper is not following its internal policies and procedures, and evidence which the jury could use to determine whether the defendant was negligent. Although this does not aid the plaintiff here, the court's statement is too broad.

own procedures and exercise a reasonable amount of care in processing the change of beneficiary form. The jury could properly have concluded that Kemper was negligent. "[W]e have no authority to take upon ourselves the duties of a tribunal of fact, and to determine what verdicts should have been rendered by the jury." *Electric Welding Co. v. Prince,* 200 Mass. 386, 392, 86 N.E. 947 (1909).

The court's decision today "trenches on our long-established, consistently applied, and zealously guarded line of demarcation between the respective roles, functions, and responsibilities of the judge and of the jury." *Commonwealth v. Dickerson,* 372 Mass. 783, 802, 364 N.E.2d 1052 (1977) (Quirico, J., concurring). "Jurors saw the witnesses, and their judgment of the credibility of the witnesses, of the comparable strength of the conflicting evidence, and of the factual validity of the contentions put forth by each side should be immune from attack. It is the jurors who decide questions of fact, and who apply the law to the facts, not judges." *Bonin v. Chestnut Hill Towers Realty Corp.,* 392 Mass. 58, 77–78, 466 N.E.2d 90 (1984) (Abrams, J., dissenting). The court's decision deprives the plaintiffs of the right to have the jury decide the facts and usurps the jury's rightful role, thereby "diminishing the extent of citizen participation in the administration of justice and the many benefits which flow from such participation." *Commonwealth v. Canon,* 373 Mass. 494, 516, 368 N.E.2d 1181 (1977), cert. denied, 435 U.S. 933, 98 S.Ct. 1510, 55 L.Ed.2d 531 (1978) (Abrams, J., dissenting).

The facts support a conclusion that "[m]ore than one decision was possible to honest and reasonable [persons], and, therefore, the jury was the tribunal to determine which one." *Hicks v. H.B. Church Truck Serv. Co.,* 259 Mass. 272, 277, 156 N.E. 254 (1927). In sum, the judge correctly denied the motion for directed verdict and the motion for judgment notwithstanding the verdict. I respectfully dissent.

Notes and Questions

1. *Liability for Delay.* It is well-established that an agent or broker may be held liable for negligent failure to procure a policy that would have covered the plaintiff's loss. Similarly, some courts hold that the insurer's negligent delay in processing an application subjects it to liability for damages that proximately result. See e.g., *Huberman v. John Hancock Mutual Life Insurance Company,* 492 So.2d 416 (Fla. Dist.Ct.App.1986). In the latter situation, however, what basis is there for holding that the insurer owes a duty to the applicant? Does the mere furnishing of an application create such a duty? Once such a duty exists, does the holding in *Mauroner* necessarily follow, or might a court properly hold that the delay was not a proximate cause of the loss the plaintiff claimed?

2. *Liability for Negligent Issuance or Misprocessing.* As the court in *Bacon* noted, there are occasional decisions holding life insurers liable for negligently issuing policies to those without an insurable

interest in the life of the *cestui que vie*. The plaintiff's claim in *Bacon* went a step further. Was the court correct in acknowledging that at least in principle the insurer owes the insured a duty to process a change of beneficiary request with due care, or should it have held that there could never be such a duty? Once the duty was acknowledged to exist in principle should the case have gone to the jury on the facts of *Bacon,* in light of the insured's previous communications with the insurer? How persuasive was the dissent's argument that the insurer's failure to follow its own procedures made out a jury question?

3. *A Duty to Former Beneficiaries?* Should insurers be held liable for failing to notify beneficiaries or assignees of changes made in their status? If so, on what legal theory? The courts have proved extremely reluctant to accept any such liability. See, e.g., *Wells v. John Hancock Mutual Life Insurance Company,* 85 Cal.App.3d 66, 149 Cal.Rptr. 171 (1978), in which the court rejected the claim of the holder of an assignment of a policy as security that she had a right to be notified of a lapse in payment of premiums or any additional assignment.

B. HEALTH AND DISABILITY INSURANCE

1. The Nature and Scope of American Health Insurance

Congressional Research Service,

HEALTH INSURANCE AND THE UNINSURED: BACKGROUND DATA AND ANALYSIS

xiii-xvi (1988).

The United States provides health insurance through a combination of private initiatives and public programs. The U.S. health insurance "system" evolved gradually beginning in the late 19th century. Health insurance plans offered by direct providers of health care, such as physicians and hospitals, grew into the Blue Cross/Blue Shield systems in the 1930s. Commercial insurers began offering health insurance policies around the same time. By the end of World War II, increasing numbers of employers were offering health insurance as a fringe benefit, while individuals with the means could buy coverage on their own. Concern that health insurance was still unavailable to many Americans led to a series of Federal attempts to fill the gaps in private coverage, culminating in the 1965 enactment of the Medicare program for the aged (and later the disabled and persons with end-stage renal disease) and the Medicaid program for certain categories of the poor. Still, private insurance, chiefly employment-based, remains the primary source of health coverage for most Americans.

The nature of private coverage has changed as the insurance industry has grown. At one time, the plans offered by Blue Cross/Blue Shield programs differed from those offered by commercial insurers in at least three key respects. First, the Blues offered "service benefits," paying in full for covered services; commercial insurers offered "indemnity" coverage, paying a fixed amount for each service and leaving the enrollee to pay any uncovered balance. Second, the Blues used "community rating," under which premium amounts were based on expected costs for all policyholders; low-cost individuals or groups helped to pay for the participants requiring more expensive services. Commercial insurers used "experience rating," under which the rate for each employer group was based on historic costs for that specific group. Third, most of the Blues practiced a policy of "open enrollment," permitting any individual or group to purchase coverage. Commercial insurers adopted underwriting practices comparable to those traditionally used in their other lines of insurance business, such as life insurance. That is, applicants perceived to be high risk might be charged higher rates, or be denied coverage (temporarily or permanently) for problems already diagnosed at the time the policy took effect. Applicants with costly chronic conditions might be denied coverage altogether.

The differences between the practices of the Blues and commercial insurers have diminished over time. Indemnity coverage is increasingly rare, especially in employment-based plans. Most of the Blues now use experience rating for large employer groups, and many—though not all—have modified their enrollment policies, using underwriting to limit their risks.

Meanwhile, new forms of competition have entered the insurance market. These include health maintenance organizations (HMOs), that directly provide or arrange the services used by their enrollees and seek to reduce unnecessary care, and preferred provider organizations (PPOs), that give their enrollees financial incentives to use the least expensive hospitals and physicians. Traditional insurers are also taking steps to control the use of services and reduce costs; for example, they may require prior authorization or second opinions before certain services are furnished. Finally, many large and medium-sized employers have sought further cost-savings by "self-insuring," covering the costs of their employees' health care directly instead of purchasing insurance from an outside firm.

These changes all have had a potential impact on the ability of individuals and small employer groups to obtain and pay for health insurance.

EXTENT AND ADEQUACY OF HEALTH INSURANCE COVERAGE

As of 1986, 85 percent of all Americans had some form of health insurance coverage during at least part of the year. Of those aged 65 and over, 99 percent were covered, chiefly through Medicare. Of those under 65, 83 percent were covered: and among these nonaged insured persons, over three-quarters were covered through their own employment or that of another family member. The rest were covered by a mix of Medicaid, Medicare, CHAMPUS (the health program for armed services personnel and their dependents), individually purchased private policies, and other health insurance sources.

However, an estimated 37.1 million persons had no coverage at any time during 1986; all but 300,000 were under age 65. More than half of the uninsured were employed during at least part of the year. Younger and lower-paid employees, and those who worked part-time or for only part of the year, were more likely to be without coverage from their own employment. Employer-based coverage was least common for employees in certain sectors of the economy, such as agriculture, personal/household services, and retail trade, and most common for those in manufacturing, mining, or public administration. Small firms were much less likely than larger ones to provide coverage.

The share of the nonaged population lacking health insurance has grown from 14.6% in 1979 to 17.5% in 1986. The most significant change appears to have been in dependent coverage. Fewer people are obtaining insurance through another family member's employment. Two factors appear to have contributed about equally to this change. First, coverage rates for spouses and children have declined. Second, demographic shifts have occurred. For example, children under 18 made up a smaller part of the population in 1986 than in 1979; older children in the household may not be eligible for coverage under their parents' policies. (These findings contradict much "conventional wisdom" about the reasons for the continued large numbers of people without health insurance. Other analysts have speculated that this growth in the uninsured was due to increases in service sector jobs, with relatively low rates of employer-sponsored health insurance, at the expense of manufacturing industries with higher rates. The empirical evidence analyzed here, however, demonstrates that the rise in the uninsured is mainly due to demographic shifts and to lower rates of dependent coverage.)

Those who lack health insurance may face significant financial barriers in obtaining needed health services. According to the 1986 Health Interview Survey, the uninsured see a physician two-thirds as often as the insured, and spend three-fourths as many days in the hospital. They are less likely to obtain care for certain kinds of health problems and are more likely to rely on emergency rooms for routine services. Differences in the use of health services by the insured and uninsured exist even after taking age and income into account.

When the uninsured do obtain services, they must pay for their own care or rely on some form of subsidy. The subsidy may be direct, as when a local government supports the operations of a public hospital, or indirect, as when a provider increases charges for insured patients to help cover the costs of care for patients who cannot pay. There is concern that as the number of uninsured persons grows the ability of providers to spread the costs for their care to other payers declines. Both public and private insurers have become increasingly price-conscious. New forms of insurers, such as HMOs and PPOs, restrict their members to less costly providers or negotiate discounts from the providers' usual charges. The resulting financial pressures may further reduce access to care for the uninsured.

Many persons' health insurance plans leave them at risk for having to pay much of the cost of their own care. Virtually all private health insurance plans require enrollees to make some contribution, in the form of deductibles and coinsurance payments, to the cost of their own care. Most plans have some limit on the cost-sharing amounts an enrollee could be required to pay in the course of a year, but 17 percent of the plans offered by large and medium employers in 1987 had no such limit, and an additional 24 percent had limits in excess of $1,000 for an individual enrollee. Insurance purchased on an individual basis was more likely to have no limitation on an enrollee's potential expenditures for covered services. Enrollees also may be liable for services excluded from a plan (most often prescription drugs or mental health care) or for costs in excess of a lifetime benefit limit imposed by the plan. Fourteen percent of plans offered by medium and large employers had lifetime limits of $250,000 or lower, possibly less than the cost of some kinds of catastrophic episodes. As a result of these coverage limits and enrollee cost-sharing requirements, an estimated 15.3 percent of all insured families had 1987 health expenses (not counting insurance premiums) greater than 5 percent of their family income; 3.7 percent had expenses greater than 25 percent of their family income.

CURRENT REGULATION OF HEALTH INSURANCE AND HEALTH BENEFITS

Responsibility for regulation of health benefits and health insurance is divided between the States and the Federal Government. Regulation of all forms of insurance has traditionally been the province of the States; State primacy in this area was confirmed by the McCarran–Ferguson Act of 1945. However, the right to regulate employee benefits, including health benefits, was reserved by the Federal Government in the Employee Retirement Income Security Act of 1974 (ERISA). ERISA established uniform national standards for employee benefit plans and preempted State regulation of these plans. States can still regulate the companies selling health insurance and the content of the policies they sell. However, States cannot directly regulate the benefit plans offered by employers. An employer that "self-insures" (covers employees' health expenses directly instead of buying insurance from an outside company) is exempt from any State regulation. In part, large employers increasingly choose to self-insure to avoid State regulations, such as mandated coverages in health insurance policies or taxes on insurance premiums.

In comparison to the regulation of pensions and other retirement benefit plans, direct Federal regulation of employee health benefits has been minimal. No employer has been required to furnish health coverage, but employers who do choose to provide coverage have been subjected to certain requirements. The Health Maintenance Organization Act of 1973 requires most employers who provide health benefits to offer employees the option of joining an HMO as an alternative to the employer's basic plan. The Consolidated Omnibus Reconciliation Act of 1985 (COBRA) requires an employer to allow employees and dependents to continue to participate in the employer's health plan, at their own expense, for up to 18 months (or in some cases, 36 months) after an event that would otherwise cause them to be dropped from the plan, such as loss of a job or a change in marital status. Finally, the Tax Reform Act of 1986 requires employers to ensure that their health plans do not discriminate in favor of highly compensated employees. Plans that continue to discriminate will lose the favorable tax treatment given to employee health benefits.

Notes and Questions

1. *Forms of Coverage.* Health insurance is generally subdivided into two categories: medical insurance (covering physician's services) and hospitalization insurance. Typical policies insure against both categories of costs, though often on a different basis. Ordinary physician's services (e.g., office visits) are less likely to be covered, or subject to higher deductible or coinsurance provisions, than the costs of hospitalization and of physicians' services during hospitalization. A third form of health insurance, Major Medical insurance, provides excess coverage (often but not always up to a specified ceiling and subject to its own coverage limitations and coinsurance provisions) over primary health insurance.

2. *Cost Control.* As the CRS study indicates, there are (at least) two burning issues in health insurance today. One is cost control. The pervasive presence of "third-party payors"—mostly insurers—helps to create the problem. In the typical insurance situation, a major risk is that the insured will be less careful to avoid suffering insured losses. This *ex ante* moral hazard may be present to a minimal degree in health insurance, but since most people do not wish to become ill or injured, the problem probably is not great. Once a health insured is ill or injured, however, the availability of insurance benefits to pay for health care may encourage the overconsumption of care. Since health care providers are aware that their patients are insured, their incentive to limit the extent of care provided in order to protect patients' finances probably is also diminished. Insurers have attempted to combat this *ex post* moral hazard by including deductibles and coinsurance provisions in health insurance policies and by limiting coverage to specified sums for specified medical procedures, among other things. As the federal government has come to pay a greater share of the cost of health care in the United States, however, a series of more direct cost-control

measures has been developed. The details of these measures is beyond the scope of a course in insurance; suffice it to say that the insurance industry and government are fast becoming partners in the effort to control health care costs in the United States. See generally, The Legal Implications of Health Care Cost Containment: A Symposium, 36 Case W.Res.L.Rev. 605 (1986).

3. *Uncompensated Care.* The second major issue in health insurance concerns the problem of uncompensated (i.e., uninsured) care. The Congressional Research Service Study indicates that the uninsured receive less health care than the insured; but in fact the uninsured do receive some care, often at a high cost that exhausts their assets and leaves hospitals partially or completely unreimbursed for their costs. Complicated formulas now exist regarding the percentage of uninsured patients hospitals must treat in order to remain eligible for certain federal and state-provided forms of financial support; but whether to create something approaching universal health insurance is now on the agenda of public debate and is likely to remain there during the coming decade. For discussion of approaches to achieving universal health insurance, see Congressional Research Service, Insuring the Uninsured: Options and Analysis (1988); Enthoven and Kronick, A Consumer–Choice Health Plan for the 1990's: Universal Health Insurance in a System Designed to Promote Quality and Economy, 320 New England J. Med. 29 (1989).

2. Medically Necessary Services

SARCHETT v. BLUE SHIELD OF CALIFORNIA
Supreme Court of California, 1987.
43 Cal.3d 1, 233 Cal.Rptr. 76, 729 P.2d 267.

BROUSSARD, Justice.

This dispute arose when defendant Blue Shield of California (Blue Shield) denied plaintiff John Sarchett's claim for hospitalization benefits in the amount of $1,203.05. Sarchett sued Blue Shield for the hospital expenses and also for a breach of the implied covenant of good faith and fair dealing. The trial court directed a verdict for Sarchett on breach of the covenant of good faith and fair dealing, and the jury awarded his hospital costs, $20,000 in compensatory damages and $80,000 in punitive damages. Blue Shield appeals from this verdict.

FACTS AND PROCEDURAL BACKGROUND

In 1966, John Sarchett, a Los Angeles County employee, elected to be insured under a group policy provided by Blue Shield. In January 1976, Sarchett was hospitalized for three days by his family physician, Dr. Bruce Van Vranken, who is a member physician of Blue Shield. Dr. Van Vranken testified that Sarchett, usually a healthy and robust person, reported symptoms during January of fatigue, tremor, disorientation, painful swelling and distension of the stomach and back, changing bowel habits and peculiar stools. His blood test showed low hemoglobin and low white blood cell counts. Sarchett's condition appeared to be deteriorating rapidly during January, and Dr. Van Vranken feared Sarchett might be suffering from a life-threatening bleeding duodenal ulcer or leukemia.

Blue Shield paid Sarchett's medical and diagnostic testing bills, but denied his claim for the hospital stay, amounting to $1,203.05. Its denial was based on two separate provisions of Sarchett's policy: (1) an exclusion for "[s]ervices when hospitalized primarily for *diagnostic purposes* or medical observation, rest or convalescent care * * *" (italics added) and (2) exclusion for services not "medically necessary."[1] The latter exclusion reads as follows: "Medical Necessity: Benefits will be provided under this contract only for such services, whether provided on an Inpatient or Outpatient basis, as are reasonably intended, in the exercise of good medical practice, for the treatment of illness or injury." Blue Shield contended that Dr. Van Vranken's orders for Sarchett's care in the hospital were inconsistent with a belief that Sarchett was seriously ill and hospitalized for medical treatment.[2]

Plaintiff, Dr. Van Vranken, and the hospital utilization review committee protested the denial of coverage. The matter was submitted to arbitration, but the arbitrator's award in favor of plaintiff was vacated by the superior court. The matter was then set for trial de novo in the superior court. * * *

I.

The trial court found that the Blue Shield policy was ambiguous because it did not indicate who would determine when the diagnostic services or medical necessity exclusion barred coverage. Construing that ambiguity in favor of the member, it concluded that he should be able to rely on the judgment of his treating physician as to the purpose and necessity of hospitalization, and that Blue Shield could not question that judgment. Blue Shield contends that the trial court erred in interpreting the policy, and that its right to review claims is inherent in the insurance contract. Sarchett, on the other hand, maintains that only the addition of an explicit statement asserting the insurer's right of retrospective review would cure the ambiguity and, going beyond the

1. Similar exclusions appear in the subscriber's brochure under "Services Not Covered."

2. For instance, Dr. Van Vranken's admitting orders allowed Sarchett to ambulate and to eat the regular house diet, and he did not order serial blood counts, regular monitoring of vital signs, multiple position blood pressure readings, placement of an intravenous line, blood typing and cross-matching in case a blood transfusion became necessary, nasogastric tube insertion to monitor internal bleeding, serial stool checks, or a barium enema—all of which steps Blue Shield claims should have been taken if the admitting physician actually suspected a bleeding duodenal ulcer or leukemia. Blue Shield asserts that Sarchett was suffering only from chronic anemia and a reaction to some "gall bladder pills" ingested in preparation for a gall bladder series, though Sarchett and Dr. Van Vranken claim the symptoms antedate the gall bladder tests.

ruling of the trial judge, argues that regardless of policy language retrospective review should be banned as contrary to public policy.

We begin with the specific language of the policy. The diagnostic exclusion denies coverage for "[s]ervices when hospitalized primarily for diagnostic purposes or medical observation, rest or convalescent care." The "medical necessity" provision provides coverage "only for such services * * * as are reasonably intended, in the exercise of good medical practice, for the treatment of illness or injury." When the two provisions are read together, certain ambiguities appear. In some cases, for example, some diagnostic procedures may be so difficult or hazardous that hospitalization is medically necessary. In others a patient's medical condition may be so serious as to require hospitalization even though the physician is unable to treat that condition without diagnostic tests which ordinarily could be performed on an outpatient basis. Policy coverage for both cases is unclear.

At oral argument, however, counsel for Blue Shield explained that the diagnostic exclusion is intended as a subset of the implied exclusion for unnecessary medical treatment, and that the insurer would cover "medically necessary" hospitalization even if done for diagnostic purposes.[3] Consequently, coverage for plaintiff's hospitalization does not turn on whether he was hospitalized for diagnosis, but simply on whether hospitalization was "medically necessary." Furthermore, strict necessity is not required. The policy language requires only that the services be "reasonably intended * * * for the treatment of illness or injury." The intent in question is apparently that of the treating physician, and "treatment," Blue Shield acknowledges, includes hospitalization required by the subscriber's medical condition even if further diagnosis is essential for further treatment.

Plaintiff's insurance coverage would therefore appear to depend upon three questions of fact: (1) whether Dr. Van Vranken ordered hospitalization with the intention of treating plaintiff's illness or injury, (2) whether the physician's intention was reasonable, and (3) whether that intention conforms to good medical practice. Blue Shield concedes the question of good medical practice, but disputes the other issues, claiming that Dr. Van Vranken did not reasonably believe plaintiff's medical condition called for hospital treatment.

Plaintiff, however, seeks to eliminate even these factual questions, arguing that the policy is ambiguous as to who decides whether hospitalization is medically necessary. As we have noted, the trial court agreed, and directed the jury that Blue Shield violated its duty of good

3. Contrary to the assertion of the dissent, we do not maintain that counsel's concession eliminated ambiguity as to who decides whether a treatment was medically necessary. As we explain later in this opinion, we think the policy unambiguously provides that this decision will ultimately be made by a disinterested third party—a review committee, an arbitrator, or a court. We believe, instead, that counsel's concession resolved an ambiguity concerning the policy's substantive coverage in favor of the insured, thus making it unnecessary for us to employ established rules of construction to reach that same result.

faith and fair dealing by challenging the treating physician's determination of medical necessity.

Upon review of the entire policy, however, we find no ambiguity in this respect. It is true that neither the diagnostic exclusion nor the medical necessity provision provides expressly how coverage disputes will be resolved, but neither does any other exclusionary clause.[4] Instead, Blue Shield has provided a separate provision, entitled "Settlement of Disputes," which applies to all disputes under the policy. That section first provides that "[a] dispute concerning the therapeutic justification for any services rendered to the member shall be resolved by the decision of the appropriate review committee of that medical society * * * for the geographical area in which such services were provided. * * *" It then states that "all other disputes, including disputes with respect to the decisions of the medical society * * * shall be resolved * * * in accordance with the Rules of the American Arbitration Association."

We find no ambiguity in this language relevant to the present case. The dispute between Sarchett and Blue Shield is "a dispute concerning the therapeutic justification" for plaintiff's hospitalization, and even if it were not, it would then be among the "other disputes" governed by the arbitration provision. The point is not that this dispute must be remanded to a medical review committee or an arbitrator—such remedies have been waived or exhausted, and the case was properly in the superior court. It is, instead, that since the policy itself provides unambiguously how disputes are to be resolved, including disputes concerning the "medical necessity" of hospitalization,[5] there is no room for the argument that the policy contains an ambiguity which, construed in plaintiff's favor, would vest the final determination of medical necessity in the treating physician.[6]

Sarchett relies on the decision of the Illinois Court of Appeal in *Van Vactor v. Blue Cross Association* (1977) 50 Ill.App.3d 709, 8 Ill.Dec. 400, 365 N.E.2d 638. *Van Vactor* was a class action by members who had been denied coverage for hospitalization for oral surgery. The policy provided for payment of hospital bills incident to removal of impacted teeth where hospitalization was "medically necessary." The court held that since "nowhere does either the master contract or the

4. Besides the exclusions at issue in this case, the policy also generally excluded coverage for, e.g., mental disorders, routine eye refractions, routine physical examinations, hospitalization for tuberculosis, physical therapy, dental services, organ transplants, and treatment for alcoholism and narcoticism.

5. The wording of the "medical necessity" provision itself supports this analysis. The clause refers to services *reasonably* intended for treatment, yet plaintiff's interpretation would leave the treating physician the sole judge of his own reasonableness. The clause also requires the "exercise of good medical practice," language which suggests an objective standard, not one under which the physician himself decides whether his intentions conform to good medical practice.

6. Plaintiff accused Blue Shield of claiming that it has the final right to determine the "medical necessity" of treatment. But as we understand defendant's position, it is only claiming the right to contest plaintiff's claim, with the ultimate decision confided to an impartial review committee, arbitrator, or court.

brochure provide that a judgment on medical necessity for such inpatient hospitalization is required to be made by anyone other than the duly licensed treating physician as a condition to payment of benefits, there is no justification for the denial of benefits *solely* on the ground that the insurer disagrees with the honest judgment of the treating physician." (365 N.E.2d at p. 642, italics in original.) The court then interpreted the policy to provide that the "determination of whether and to what extent hospital services are medically necessary is 'vested solely and exclusively in the judgment and discretion of the treating physician.' " (P. 647.)

The *Van Vactor* decision, however, stands alone. It has not been followed by any other court.[7] Numerous decisions from other jurisdictions take the position that "medical necessity" or similar policy language is an objective standard to be applied by the trier of fact, not a delegation of power to the treating physician. * * *[8]

We note in particular the last cited case, *Lockshin v. Blue Cross of Northeast Ohio, supra* 434 N.E.2d 754. In that case Blue Cross denied a subscriber's claim for two days of private nursing care following a Cesarean section on the ground that care was ordered to "allay * * * misapprehension" (p. 757) and was not "necessary" within the purview of the insurance policy. "The trial court held that the term 'necessary' was ambiguous, vis-a-vis who must ultimately decide what is 'necessary.' Consequently, the trial court strictly construed the policy against the drafter and found for the claimant (plaintiff)." (P. 755.) The Court of Appeal, however, rejected this view, stating: "[A] function, basic to the insurer, is the right '* * * to determine whether * * * [a] claim should be allowed or rejected.' [Citation.] The function of reviewing claims is obviously reserved by the insurer and implied by the mandatory proces of submitting a proof of claim. [Citations.] Without such a right, an orderly establishment, administration and dispensation of insurance benefits would be virtually impossible." (P. 756.) "While the decision of a physician is both relevant and probative

---

7. Although *Van Vactor* was cited with approval in *Carrao v. Health Care Service Corp.* (1983) 118 Ill.App.3d 417, 73 Ill.Dec. 684, 454 N.E.2d 781, 787–788, that decision rests on different grounds. The policy in *Carrao* contained no medical necessity provision, and the court held only that such a restriction could not be implied from the definition of hospital services or other policy language, nor inserted as a public policy device to protect against rising insurance costs.

8. We note also *Siegal v. Health Care Service Corp.* (1980) 81 Ill.App.3d 784, 36 Ill.Dec. 899, 401 N.E.2d 1037. The *Siegal* court distinguished *Van Vactor* as a case in which the policy explicitly vested the power to determine medical necessity in the treating physician. It then treated the question of medical necessity as a jury question, affirming a verdict finding coverage as supported by substantial evidence.

The court's discussion of *Van Vactor* seems erroneous. The policy in *Van Vactor* did not expressly vest authority in the treating physician; it said nothing about who decided the question of medical necessity, and it was the trial and appellate courts, construing that policy, which held that the good faith judgment of the physician could not be questioned. Nevertheless, in light of *Siegal* it is unclear whether the Illinois courts today would follow *Van Vactor* and direct entry of a judgment for the policyholder in a case in which a jury found lack of medical necessity.

on the issue of necessity, it is not dispositive of the question. * * *"
(*Ibid.*)

In short, we find the policy unambiguous on the question of who decides "medical necessity": in the event of a dispute the decision is made by an impartial review committee, subject to further review through arbitration. Since this is clearly set out in the settlement of disputes section of the policy, it is not necessary for the insurer, to avoid ambiguity, to repeat that language in the diagnostic exclusion or medical necessity clauses. We do not seek to discourage inserting such language into appropriate exclusions; a little judicious repetition may illuminate the meaning of the policy and avert controversy.[9] We hold, however, that the absence of such language does not preclude the insurer from challenging the medical necessity of hospitalization recommended by the treating physician. Thus we conclude that the trial court erred in directing a verdict that Blue Shield violated its duty of good faith and fair dealing by disagreeing with the judgment of the treating physician on retrospective review.

Plaintiff argues, however, even if the policy is not ambiguous upon close reading, it should still be construed in light of the "reasonable expectation of the insured." (*Gray v. Zurich Insurance Co.* (1966) 65 Cal.2d 263, 271, 54 Cal.Rptr. 104, 419 P.2d 168.) The subscriber under a Blue Shield policy, he contends, would reasonably expect to be covered for hospitalization recommended by the treating physician. We do not question this description of the subscriber's expectations, but we doubt that it arises from any belief that Blue Shield will cover all treatment recommended by a physician, however unreasonable the recommendation. Instead, the subscriber expects coverage because he trusts that his physician has recommended a reasonable treatment consistent with good medical practice. Consequently we believe the subscriber's expectations can be best fulfilled not by giving his physician an unreviewable power to determine coverage, but by construing the policy language liberally, so that uncertainties about the reasonableness of treatment will be resolved in favor of coverage.

Finally, plaintiff argues that, entirely apart from the policy language, the courts as a matter of public policy should bar insurers from refusing coverage for hospitalization ordered by the treating physician.[10] He points to the dilemma faced by the subscriber when his

---

9. Some insurers include such language in the policy. For instance, in *Franks v. Louisiana Health Services & Indemnity Co.* (La.App.1980) 382 So.2d 1064, 1066, the policy contained the following provision: "The fact that a physician may prescribe, order, recommend, or approve a service or supply does not, of itself, make it medically necessary or make the charge an allowable expense, even though it is not specifically listed as an exclusion." (Similar language appears in the policies quoted in *Haggard v. Blue Cross–Blue Shield of Alabama* (Ala.Civ.App.1980) 401 So.2d 781, 782, and *Blue Cross and Blue Shield of Kentucky, Inc. v. Smither* (C.A.Ky.1978) 573 S.W.2d 363, 364.)

10. Sarchett cites two decisions to support his contention, *Lopez v. Blue Cross of Louisiana* (La.1981) 397 So.2d 1343, 1345, and *Weissman v. Blue Cross of Western New York, Inc.* (Buffalo City Ct.1982) 116 Misc.2d 1063, 457 N.Y.S.2d 392, revd. (Erie Cty.Ct. 1984) 126 Misc.2d 341, 482 N.Y.S.2d 659. In *Lopez* the Louisiana Supreme Court upheld a judgment for a Blue Cross subscriber whose hospitalization claim for depressive mental

doctor tells him that hospitalization is necessary. Unless a physician himself, the subscriber lacks competence to question his doctor's recommendation. If he follows the recommendation, he takes the risk that the insurer may later deny coverage, leaving the subscriber liable for a hospital bill he cannot afford. Yet if he does not follow the recommendation, he may be foregoing needed treatment. Faced with this dilemma, most subscribers would follow their doctor's recommendation and risk the denial of insurance coverage. Subscribers purchase insurance not only for financial advantage, but to obtain the peace of mind and sense of security that follows from assured payment (cf. *Crisci v. Security Ins. Co.* (1967) 66 Cal.2d 425, 434, 58 Cal.Rptr. 13, 426 P.2d 173), and retrospective review frustrates those objectives.

There are, however, countervailing policy considerations. Sarchett had a choice between the Blue Shield plan, which offered him unlimited selection of physicians but provided for retrospective review, and alternative plans which would require him to choose from among a limited list of physicians but guaranteed payment. A holding that retrospective review is against public policy would narrow the range of choices available to the prospective subscriber, since it is unlikely that any insurer could permit the subscriber free selection of a physician if it were required to accept without question the physician's view of reasonable treatment and good medical practice. If the treating physician makes the final decision whether the treatment he prescribes is covered by the policy, inevitably a few will abuse that power by overutilization of medical procedures, imposing excessive costs on the insurer.

This view finds support in the decision of the Kentucky Supreme Court. In *Blue Cross and Blue Shield of Kentucky, Inc. v. Smither, supra,* 573 S.W.2d 363, the policy covered "medically necessary" hospital services, and warned expressly that the fact that a physician may recommend a service does not of itself make that service medically necessary. Unable to argue ambiguity in the policy, the subscriber nevertheless contended that the decision of the treating physician should always control the question of medical necessity, and that contrary views of nontreating physicians were insufficient to raise a triable issue of fact. The court commended: "Smither's argument is, in

neurosis was denied under a medical necessity clause. The court found that denial of the subscriber's claim based on a mere reading of the records, without examining her, was unreasonable despite the fact that the policy expressly provided that medical necessity would be determined "in the judgment of the Carrier." (*Id.,* at p. 1345.) The court imposed a statutory double penalty for Blue Cross' wrongful denial of the claim.

Weissman found unconscionable a contract clause providing that private nursing services would be covered "only if Blue Cross and Blue Shield, in their sole judgment determine that the medical condition of the member requires private duty nursing care." (*Id.,* 457 N.Y.S.2d at p. 394.) The court found that the health policy was a contract of adhesion and that "no reasonable person would accept these terms unless they had to accept the coverage due to necessity," since "the entire decision [whether the disputed care was necessary] will be based on the review by the party who may be paying for the services." (*Id.,* at p. 396.)

Both cases are distinguishable from the present case. Sarchett's policy did not vest the insurer with final authority to decide questions of medical necessity, but provided for decision by an impartial review committee and arbitration.

essence, that the only medical advice the patient has concerning his hospital stay is that provided by the treating physician, and therefore his opinion should be treated as correct and not be subject to contradiction. We do not believe a treating physician should be placed in this unassailable position. One need only look to the Medicare and Medicaid System for alleged evidence of fraud which may occur on the part of doctors and other persons in the medical care professions, if their decisions are always assumed correct." (P. 365.)

Both the federal Medicare program (42 U.S.C. § 1395y(a)) and the state MediCal program (Welf. & Inst. Code, § 14110, subd. (e)), which permit the patient free choice of physician, also contemplate retrospective review. We cannot declare contrary to public policy a feature found necessary whenever the public, through its representatives, itself sets out the terms of a health insurance program.

In summary, we appreciate the plight of the subscriber, forced to decide whether to follow his doctor's recommendation without assurance that his policy will cover the expense. We do not, however, believe it would be alleviated by requiring the insurer to insert redundant language into the policy to make doubly clear to the subscriber that he really is in a dilemma and cannot count on coverage. And although a judicial ruling that retrospective review violates public policy would protect against retrospective denial of coverage, subscribers would pay the price in reduced insurance alternatives and increased premiums.

The problem of retrospective denial of coverage can be reduced through the growing practice of preadmission screening of nonemergency hospital admissions. When such screening is not feasible, as in the present case, we think the best the courts can do is give the policy every reasonable interpretation in favor of coverage.[11] We trust that, with doubts respecting coverage resolved in favor of the subscriber, there will be few cases in which the physician's judgment is so plainly unreasonable, or contrary to good medical practice, that coverage will be refused. * * *

Mosk, Justice.

I dissent to the conclusion reached in Part I of the majority's opinion. In my view, the policy is ambiguous because, as the trial court found, it does not state that Blue Shield had the right, on the basis of a retrospective review, to disagree with the judgment of the treating physician to hospitalize Sarchett.

The majority admit that the diagnostic exclusion is ambiguous when read in the light of the medical necessity exclusion. However, because of an explanation offered by Blue Shield at oral argument, the majority fail to apply the usual rule of interpreting ambiguous lan-

11. The rule requiring interpretation of insurance policies in favor of coverage applies even if the policy, negotiated on a group basis, is not a contract of adhesion. (*McLaughlin v. Connecticut General Life Ins. Co., supra,* 565 F.Supp. 434, 448 [applying California law]; *Jones v. Crown Life Ins. Co.* (1978) 86 Cal.App.3d 630, 639, fn. 3, 150 Cal.Rptr. 375.)

guage in favor of the insured. But the question of ambiguity cannot be determined from the 11th-hour concession of an insurer before this court as to the meaning of the policy. It must be decided from the terms of the policy itself—terms which the majority concede are ambiguous.

The interpretation now advanced by Blue Shield, i.e., that the diagnostic exclusion is a subset of the implied exclusion for unnecessary medical treatment, and that it would cover medically necessary hospitalization even if done for diagnostic purposes, is not evident from the policy or the subscriber's brochure, which lists 16 categories of "Services Not Covered." The first is the diagnostic exclusion, and the last the "medical necessity" exclusion. There is no indication in the policy that one has any relation to the other. In my view, therefore, the ambiguities in the policy recognized by the majority should be resolved against Blue Shield, in accordance with the usual rule.

Nor do I agree with the majority's second reason for finding that the "medical necessity" exclusion is unambiguous. They conclude because the policy contains a provision that disputes relating to the "therapeutic justification" for services are to be resolved by a review committee, a subscriber is unambiguously notified that Blue Shield may second-guess the subscriber's physician on the issue of medical necessity.

An exclusionary clause in a policy must be "conspicuous, plain and clear." (*State Farm Mut. Auto Ins. Co. v. Jacober* (1973) 10 Cal.3d 193, 202, 110 Cal.Rptr. 1, 514 P.2d 953.) The burden is on the insurer to "phrase exceptions and exclusions in clear and unmistakable language" (*Harris v. Glens Falls Ins. Co.* (1972) 6 Cal.3d 699, 701, 100 Cal.Rptr. 133, 493 P.2d 861), and to "draft its policy to avoid any misinterpretation by the average layman" (*Jacober,* 10 Cal.3d at p. 207, 110 Cal.Rptr. 1, 514 P.2d 953). These rules must be applied with special care in the present case, since the exclusion which Blue Shield seeks to invoke amounts to a "vast, additional exclusionary condition to coverage." (*Van Vactor v. Blue Cross Association* (1977) 50 Ill.App.3d 709, 8 Ill.Dec. 400, 365 N.E.2d 638, 644.)

The provision relating to resolution of disputes does not meet the foregoing standard. It does not state that Blue Shield reserves the right to second-guess the judgment of the subscriber's doctor as to medical necessity. At most, it allows the subscriber, if he ponders the subject at length, to draw an inference that because there exists a right to review of disputes concerning "therapeutic justification" for services, Blue Shield may challenge the judgment of his doctor. On the other hand, the provision relied on by the majority does not even appear on the same page in the subscriber's brochure as the "medical necessity" exclusion. Thus I do not see how it can be said that the power which Blue Shield seeks to exercise is set forth in language clear and unmistakable to the average layman. * * *

Finally, I am unable to concur in the determination of the majority that Sarchett did not have a reasonable expectation of coverage. The opinion states a subscriber could not reasonably expect that Blue Shield would cover all treatment recommended by his physician "however unreasonable the recommendation." A subscriber, unless he is knowledgeable in medical science, is unable to assess the reasonableness of his physician's recommendation for hospitalization. Since in this sense he is controlled by the opinion of his doctor, it is not unreasonable for him to expect that his insurer would likewise be bound by his doctor's judgment regarding the necessity for hospitalization, absent clear notification to the contrary.

The failure of Blue Shield to make clear its claimed right to decide after-the-fact that hospitalization was not a medical necessity deprives a subscriber of his opportunity to make a meaningful selection between various available types of health plans. If the policy and the brochure had made it known to Sarchett that Blue Shield claimed this right, he could have made a meaningful choice between the plan offered by Blue Shield and one with a limited choice of physicians but guaranteed payment. In my view, Sarchett should not be personally burdened with medical expenses which he could have avoided if Blue Shield had fulfilled its duty to make clear the important qualification of coverage which it belatedly advances in this case.

I would affirm the judgment.

BIRD, C.J., and REYNOSO, J., concur.

Notes and Questions

1. *Prepaid Medical Services.* Health Maintenance Organizations (HMOs) and Preferred Provider Organizations (PPOs) are methods of supplying prepaid medical services as an alternative to conventional health insurance. One important difference between these approaches is that the provider of prepaid medical services bears the cost of decisions regarding the necessity of medical treatment, whereas that cost is shared between the patient (who bears the cost of unnecessary services) and the insurer (who pays for necessary services) under conventional health insurance. Should the fact that Sarchett apparently had been given a choice between an insurance plan and prepaid medical services have been as critical to the decision as the court suggested?

2. *The Role of Preadmission Review.* Many health insurers now require preadmission review if services provided during a hospital admission are to be covered. This review can provide the insured some assurance that costs incurred will be covered. But given the complicated schedule of coverages, deductibles, and coinsurance included in most group health insurance, such review at most indicates that the services provided during the hospitalization will be eligible for coverage, but not that all costs incurred actually will be covered. The court may therefore have been a bit disingenuous in suggesting that its holding would

avoid giving patients in Sarchett's position the impossible choice of doing what their physician recommends or acting in a manner that would maximize their coverage. On the other hand, there may not be any real alternative method of controlling *ex post* moral hazard in a system in which health care costs are so heavily financed by private insurance.

3. *Public Policy.* Does the holding in *Sarchett* accord with the proposed rule governing public policy restrictions on the validity of insurance policy provisions proposed at the end of Chapter Two? The rule proposed states:

> An insurance policy provision violates public policy when a constitution or statute expressly or impliedly prohibits the aim or effect of the provision, when the provision unduly encourages moral hazard, or when the provision would force the insured to engage in unreasonable behavior in order to preserve coverage.

Does your answer suggest that the proposed rule should be modified, or that *Sarchett* was incorrectly decided?

3. Coordination of Coverage

One of the most common legal problems encountered in the health insurance field involves the "coordination" of coverage. Because of the patchwork system of health insurance in this country, there not only are gaps in coverage; in some cases insurance provided by more than one source is available to cover a single loss. In addition, sometimes the insured is entitled not only to health insurance benefits, but later recovers a judgment in tort from a party responsible for causing his losses. The method by which overlaps of this sort are coordinated is partly a matter of contract, partly of statute, and partly of judicial decision. Given these different sources of authority, it may not be possible to develop a theory of coordination; the accomodation among different sources of coverage may instead have to remain partly ad hoc. For discussion of issues associated with developing a theory of coordinated coverage, see K. Abraham, Distributing Risk: Insurance, Legal Theory, and Public Policy 133–72 (1986). Notwithstanding the absence of a fully developed theory of coordination, the system confronts certain recurring issues: how to set priorities as between overlapping sources coverage; how far coordination rules should be allowed to reduce the coverage that would otherwise be available to the insured; and how to mesh rules governing subrogation in tort actions with health insurance coordination procedures.

BLUE CROSS AND BLUE SHIELD OF KANSAS, INC. v. RIVERSIDE HOSPITAL

Supreme Court of Kansas, 1985.
237 Kan. 829, 703 P.2d 1384.

McFarland, Justice:

This is a dispute between two employee health care group plans as to which plan has primary coverage and which plan has secondary coverage relative to certain medical expense claims.

BACKGROUND FACTS

The facts are not in dispute and may be summarized as follows. Leslie Stadalman is an employee of defendant Riverside Hospital and, as such, is a "covered person" under that institution's employee health care plan. Leslie Stadalman is the wife of Gregory Stadalman. Mr. Stadalman is employed by the City of Wichita and is covered under his employer's Blue Cross–Blue Shield group health plan. The Blue Cross–Blue Shield plan provides coverage for Mr. Stadalman's dependents. In the Fall of 1982, Leslie Stadalman incurred medical expenses in the amount of $1,963.19. The Riverside plan refused to pay the claims on the basis it provided only secondary coverage. Blue Cross–Blue Shield (plaintiff) initially refused to pay the claims for the same reason—that its plan provided only secondary coverage. Ultimately, Blue Cross–Blue Shield paid the claims, expressly reserving the right to seek contribution and indemnity from Riverside. This action resulted.

BLUE CROSS–BLUE SHIELD PLAN

The Blue Cross–Blue Shield plan contains the following provisions:

NON–DUPLICATION OF BENEFITS.

"M.1 *The Plans will not duplicate benefits for covered health care services for which You are eligible under any of the following Programs:*

Group, blanket, or franchise insurance.

Group practice, individual practice, and other prepayment coverage on a group basis. (This includes group and franchise contracts issued by Blue Cross and Blue Shield Plans.)

Labor-management trusteed plans.

Union welfare plans.

Employee benefit organization programs.

Self-insurance programs providing benefits to employees or members of the self-insurer.

Coverage under government programs (except Medicare; see Part 4, Section A.3) for which the employer must contribute or deduct from his employees' pay, or both.

Individual health insurance contracts are not included as Programs."

"M.2 To avoid duplicate benefit payments, one Program will be 'Primary' and others will be 'Secondary'.

a. *When the Plans are Primary, benefits will be paid without regard to other coverage.*

b. *When the Plans are Secondary, the benefits under this Certificate may be reduced. The benefits for Covered Services will be no more than the balance of charges remaining after the benefits of other Programs are applied to Covered Services.*

A 'Covered Service' is a health care service for which benefits are available to You under this Certificate or at least one Program. When benefits are provided in the form of services, the cash value of these services will be used to determine the amount of benefits You may receive."

"M.3 Under this Certificate, the *Plans are Secondary when:*

a. *You are covered as a dependent under this Certificate but are covered as an employee, union, or association member under another Program; or*

b. You are covered as a dependent of a female under this Certificate but as the dependent of a male under another Program; or

c. The other Program does not have a non-duplication of benefits provision; or

d. The first three rules do not apply and the other Program has been in force for You longer than this Certificate.

In all other instances, the Plans are Primary under this Certificate." (Emphasis supplied.)

RIVERSIDE PLAN

The Riverside Plan contains the following provisions:

"1. ELIGIBILITY FOR COVERED PERSONS: The following persons will be eligible for coverage under the Plan;

(a) All permanent full-time employees in Active Service at their customary place of employment who work a minimum of 30 hours per week for the Employer.

(b) All other persons are excluded."

The term "covered person," only applies to Riverside employees. Coverage to a "covered person" is supplied without cost under the single plan. If family coverage is desired by the "covered person," he or she must contribute thereto. Other family members so covered are referred to as "covered dependents." The plan provides coverage for covered services on a self-insurance basis up to $20,000.00 per incident. Any amount required for covered services in excess of $20,000.00 is covered by a reinsurance contract issued to the health benefit plan.

The Riverside Plan contains the further provision:

NON–DUPLICATION OF BENEFITS

"This *Plan* has been *designed* by specific action of the Board of Directors of Osteopathic Hospital *to coordinate payment of benefits with other plans so as to avoid overpayments. This Plan requires that if any person covered hereunder is also covered under any other plan* (as defined below), *the other plan shall be primary and this Plan shall pay the balance of expenses up to the total eligible charges.* In no event shall the combined payments exceed 100%."

"However, it is the intent of the Plan to be primary as regard to any participant who is not covered under any other Plan as defined below."

"*Plan means any plan providing benefits or services for any health or dental care under any group, franchise, blanket insurance,* health maintenance plan, union welfare, governmental plan, or any coverage required by statute." (Emphasis supplied.)

JUDGMENT OF THE DISTRICT COURT

The district court held the non-duplication of benefits provisions of the two plans to be conflicting and mutually repugnant and directed that the Stadalman claim be paid 50% by each plan. Both Blue Cross–Blue Shield and Riverside were aggrieved by this determination and duly appealed therefrom.

ISSUE NO. 1: WHAT EFFECT DOES THE FACT THAT THE RIVERSIDE PLAN IS AN EMPLOYEE BENEFIT PLAN UNDER THE AUSPICES OF THE EMPLOYMENT RETIREMENT INCOME SECURITY ACT OF 1974, 29 U.S.C. § 1001 *et seq.* (1982), (ERISA) HAVE ON THE ISSUE OF PRIMARY–SECONDARY COVERAGE PRESENTED HEREIN?

The Blue Cross–Blue Shield plan is subject to regulation by the Kansas Commissioner of Insurance. The non-duplication of benefits provision incorporated within its plan is consistent with the requirements of K.A.R. 40–4–34.

The Riverside Plan is not subject to regulation by the Kansas Commissioner of Insurance. Rather, it is governed by the Employment Retirement Income Security Act of 1974, 29 U.S.C. § 1001 *et seq.* (1982). ERISA, as this act is commonly referred to, was enacted to protect the interests of participants and beneficiaries of qualified employee benefit plans by improving "the equitable character and the soundness of such plans," 29 U.S.C. § 1001(c). "The Act was intended to make basic reforms, require certain disclosure and reporting procedures, and establish standards of conduct, responsibility and obligations in the area of employee pensions and other employee benefit programs." *Goben v. Barry,* 237 Kan. 822, 703 P.2d 1378 (1985, this day decided). The non-duplication of benefits provision contained in the Riverside Plan is, apparently, permissible under ERISA. This Riverside contention is not disputed by Blue Cross–Blue Shield.

In 29 U.S.C. § 1144 (1982), ERISA is granted the following preemption:

"(a) Except as provided in subsection (b) of this section, the provisions of this subchapter and subchapter III of this chapter shall supersede any and all State laws insofar as they may now or hereafter relate to any employee benefit plan described in section 1003(a) of this title and not exempt under section 1003(b) of this title. * * *

* * *

"(c) For purposes of this section:

(1) The term 'State law' includes all laws, decisions, rules, regulations, or other State action having the effect of law, of any State. * * *

(2) The term 'State' includes a State, any political subdivisions thereof, or any agency or instrumentality of either, which purports to regulate, directly or indirectly, the terms and conditions of employee benefit plans covered by this subchapter."

Riverside contends, in essence, that by virtue of its plan being rooted in ERISA, it is placed in an unassailable position when challenged by a plan rooted in state law.

The preemption under ERISA is not without limits. The scope of the preemption was discussed in *Goben v. Barry,* wherein we held:

"Where state law has only an indirect effect upon employee benefit plans subject to the provisions of the Employee Retirement Income Security Act of 1974, 29 U.S.C. § 1001 *et seq.* (1982), and where it is one of general application which pertains to an area of important state concern, the federal statutes do not preempt application of state law."

"In making a determination of federal preemption, a court should examine those concerns emphasized by Congress in enacting the legislation. State law should be preempted only to the extent necessary to protect achievement of the purposes of the federal act in question." Syl. ¶¶ 2, 3.

The judgment of the district court herein had the effect of nullifying, at least in part, a provision of the Riverside Plan. This does raise a serious preemption question. We do not believe, however, that resolution of the primary-secondary coverage issue herein requires such action. Rather, we believe the provisions of the plans found by the district court to be mutually repugnant can be harmonized without doing violence to the intentions of, and purposes of, either plan or their respective statutory origins.

The fact that the Riverside plan is rooted in ERISA is not, we believe, a significant factor in the determination of the issue before us. Therefore, the matter of preemption is not involved herein and, even if it were involved, the outcome of the litigation would not be affected as the applicable Kansas and federal rules relative to the interpretation and construction of contracts do not differ.

ISSUE NO. 2. UNDER THE TWO EMPLOYEE HEALTH CARE GROUP PLANS HEREIN, WHICH PLAN IS PRIMARY AND WHICH PLAN IS SECONDARY RELATIVE TO THE STADALMAN CLAIMS?

The case before us involves contract interpretation arising from an uncontroverted factual situation. As stated in *Western Cas. & Surety Co. v. Universal Underwriter Ins. Co.*, 232 Kan. 606, 657 P.2d 576 (1983), quoting *Crestview Bowl, Inc. v. Womer Constr. Co.*, 225 Kan. 335, 592 P.2d 74 (1979):

> " 'When a case is submitted to the trial court on an agreed stipulation of facts and documentary evidence, this court is afforded the same opportunity to consider the evidence as the trial court.'

> " 'Where the controlling facts are based upon written or documentary evidence by way of pleadings, admissions, depositions and stipulations, the trial court has no peculiar opportunity to evaluate the credibility of witnesses. In such situation, this court on appellate review has as good an opportunity to examine and consider the evidence as did the court below, and to determine de novo what the facts establish.' " 232 Kan. at 608, 657 P.2d 576.

As applicable to the narrow issue raised herein, both plans have quite similar purposes. They are group health care plans provided by employers to their employees without cost to the employees where only the employee is covered (single coverage). If the employee desires family coverage, he or she must contribute to the cost of the coverage. These plans seek to provide adequate financially responsible coverage at the lowest cost. In keeping with this goal, benefits should not be duplicated where an individual has coverage under more than one such plan—hence the need for non-duplication of benefits clauses, or as sometimes referred to, "coordination of benefits" clauses. In modern American society, husbands and wives frequently both work outside the home with each being covered by his or her own employee health care group plan. Family coverage, in such circumstances, sets up the potential for duplication of benefits where one or both has family coverage under a plan. Duplication of benefits accomplishes none of the goals of such plans, serving only to run up the cost of the plans. Hassles, such as the one before us, increase the costs of administration of the plans and can delay payment of the medical bills (or reimbursement to the employees who have previously paid the bills). Obviously, litigation of the dispute between plans as to coverage should be avoided wherever possible. For this reason, the Insurance Commissioner of Kansas requires non-duplication of benefits provisions such as included in the Blue Cross–Blue Shield plan. The provisions spell out when the plan is primary and when it is secondary in a variety of foreseeable circumstances. Specifically, K.A.R. 40–4–34 (1982 Supp.) provides:

> "National association of insurance commissioners' coordination of benefit guidelines, June 1980 edition, are hereby adopted by reference subject to the following exceptions: [exceptions not applicable herein]."

The Riverside plan is not in accord with said regulation and guidelines and is not required to be.

If both plans are studied side by side, as equals, it would appear Leslie Stadalman has two secondary coverages and no primary coverage. This is an untenable position to maintain, and this led the district court to hold the plans to be mutually repugnant. This approach was followed (relative to automobile liability policies) in *Western Cas. & Surety Co. v. Universal Underwriters Inc. Co.*, 232 Kan. 606, 657 P.2d 576, wherein we held:

> "The 'other insurance' clauses before us are nearly identical excess coverage provisions. In discussing the general rules relative to this situation, Am.Jur.2d states:
>
> " '[W]here two or more policies provide coverage for the particular event and all the policies in question contain "excess insurance" clauses—it is generally held that such clauses are mutually repugnant and must be disregarded, rendering each company liable for a pro rata share of the judgment or settlement, since, if literal effect were given to both "excess insurance" clauses of the applicable policies, neither policy would cover the loss and such a result would produce an unintended absurdity.' 7A Am.Jur.2d, Automobile Insurance § 434, pp. 87–88."

Authorities in the field of insurance have similarly commented:

> " 'The fact that each insurer has attempted to make his coverage "excess" would not change the result of protecting the insured up to the total of all applicable policies. The courts, which found the insured with two policies, will not leave him with none, but will require the insurers, in the ordinary instance, to prorate the loss.' "

> " 'One of the popular approaches to prorating is to say that where one has conflicting excess clauses, they are mutually "repugnant"—in other words, they cannot be excess to each other, since they are identical. It is a sort of "After you Alphonse; no you, Gaston" act which the courts refuse to countenance.' 8A Appleman, Insurance Law and Practice § 4909 pp. 395–403 (rev. 1981)."

"Conflicting 'other insurance' excess coverage provisions are generally held to be mutually repugnant. Illustrative thereof are: *Blanchard v. Rodrigue*, 340 So.2d 1001, 1008 (La.App.1976); *Carriers Ins. Co. v. Am. Policyholders' Ins. Co.*, 404 A.2d [216] at 220 [Me.1979];

Cosmopolitan Mut. Ins. Co. v. Continental Cas. Co., 28 N.J. [554] at 562 [147 A.2d 529]; and *Harbor Ins. Co. v. United Services Auto. Ass'n,* 114 Ariz. 58, 63, 559 P.2d 178 (Ct.App.1976). See also *Buckeye Union Ins. Co. v. State Auto. Mutl. Ins. Co.,* 49 Ohio St.2d 213, 3 Ohio Op.3d 330, 361 N.E.2d 1052 (1977), and generally Annot., 69 A.L.R.2d 1122.

"We conclude the conflicting 'other insurance' excess coverage provisions herein are mutually repugnant and must be disregarded." 232 Kan. at 611, 657 P.2d 576.

In *Western Cas.,* we concluded:

"[T]he most appropriate method of proration here is to prorate the loss equally up to the limits of the lower policy. Inasmuch as the loss herein was less than the limits of the lower policy, the loss herein should be prorated equally between Western and Universal." 232 Kan. at 613, 657 P.2d 576.

The difficulties of such a proration procedure when applied to employee health care group plans has been pointed out by Blue Cross–Blue Shield—the two plans have different deductibles, covered services, and coinsurance provisions.

Leslie Stadalman is an employee of Riverside and coverage was provided to her as a "covered person" as defined by the plan. Mrs. Stadalman, as a "covered person" (as opposed to a covered dependent), received the coverage as a part of her employment, and, as required by ERISA, was fully advised of the plan in writing. The Riverside Plan was intended to provide her coverage but would not pay duplicate benefits with those she would have under another group employee plan. We believe the logical approach is to look to her own plan first in determining the effect of non-duplication of benefits provisions. The Riverside Plan (repeated for convenience) provides:

"This Plan has been designed by specific action of the Board of Directors of Osteopathic Hospital to *coordinate payment of benefits with other plans so as to avoid overpayments.* This Plan requires that if any person covered hereunder is also covered under any other plan (as defined below), the other plan shall be primary and this Plan shall pay the balance of expenses up to the total eligible charges. In no event shall the combined payments exceed 100%." (Emphasis supplied.)

If Mrs. Stadalman had held two jobs with primary coverage provided by the two respective employers, the Riverside Plan would intend to avoid duplication of benefits by becoming secondary. As a dependent of Gregory Stadalman under his Blue Cross–Blue Shield family plan, Leslie Stadalman has Blue Cross–Blue Shield coverage that is only excess (secondary) in nature. Her own group plan is primary unless another group plan provides primary coverage. The Blue Cross–Blue Shield plan does not provide primary coverage to Mrs. Stadalman by virtue of the fact she is a covered employee in her own group plan. Therefore, there is no potentiality for duplication of benefits or overpayment. In such circumstances, generally, the primary coverage of

Riverside should pay all benefits due thereunder on the claims, and the excess claims should be submitted to Blue Cross–Blue Shield for determination of benefits due under its secondary coverage. On the specific claims involved herein, the parties do not directly address the matter of whether the Riverside plan, as the provider with primary coverage, would provide full coverage therefor. There are inferences that such is the case, but we are not satisfied that the parties have agreed such is true. Therefore, we decline to reverse and enter judgment against Riverside for the entire amount of the claims paid by Blue Cross–Blue Shield. This aspect of the case must be determined by the district court.

We believe the result reached herein holding the Riverside plan provides primary coverage is consistent with the rationale expressed in *Northeast Dept. ILGWU v. Teamsters Local U. No. 229,* 764 F.2d 147 (3d Cir.1985). In *ILGWU* the Third Circuit in considering conflicting coordination of benefits clauses in two ERISA employee health care benefit plans, stated:

> "The general common law rule is that 'the liability of insurers under overlapping coverage policies is to be governed by the intent of the insurers as manifested by the terms of the policies which they have issued.' 16 Couch on Insurance 2d § 62:44, at 480 (rev'd ed. 1983). '(W)here such contractual provisions not inconsistent with public policy, they will be enforced.' 8A Appleman, Insurance Law and Practice § 4907.65, at 367. Under state common law, then, 'the judicial task is first to determine from the contracts themselves what obligations the respective obligors intended to assume and then to determine whether these intentions are compatible not only each with the other but also with the insured's rights and expectations and with the controlling demands of public policy.' *Starks [v. Hospital Service Plan of N.J., Inc.],* 182 N.J. Super. [342] at 351, 440 A.2d [1353] at 1358 [1981]. We believe that this mode of analysis is fundamentally sound. In the ERISA context, courts should give effect to the intent of the trustees of the competing benefit plans, as evidenced by the incorporation of 'other insurance' provisions, if the provisions are compatible; unless doing so results in the enforcement of a provision that conflicts with the provisions and policies of ERISA." 764 F.2d at 159.

The judgment of the district court is reversed and the case is remanded with directions to enter judgment against defendant consistent with this opinion.

Notes and Questions

1. *It Takes Two to Coordinate. Riverside Hospital* illustrates the main obstacle to consistent coordination: unless only one otherwise-applicable policy contains a coordination (or non-duplication of benefits)

clause, or both policies contain consistent clauses, the effort to coordinate by meshing clauses in two separate policies fails. Sometimes insurers selling the same line of coverage agree by treaty to adopt "Guiding Principles" dealing with such issues as coordination. Then the contractual approach is effective not by coincidence, but by design. In addition, regulators ordinarily can impose an obligation on insurers to adopt coordination clauses that will not conflict, as K.A.R. 40–4–34 apparently did, if only by reference to such Guiding Principles. But the court assumed without deciding that the Riverside Plan—which was a self-insurance plan—was not at all subject to state regulation because of the ERISA pre-emption, and therefore was unaffected by the Kansas statutory requirements governing coordination.

Whether that conclusion was correct is not completely clear. ERISA provides that "∗ ∗ ∗ nothing in this subchapter shall be construed to exempt or relieve any person from any law of any State which *regulates insurance* ∗ ∗ ∗ " [emphasis added]. 29 U.S.C. § 1144(b)(2) (A). In *Metropolitan Life Insurance Company v. Commonwealth of Massachusetts,* 471 U.S. 724, 105 S.Ct. 2380, 85 L.Ed.2d 728 (1985), the Supreme Court held that a Massachusetts statute mandating that mental health benefits be included in certain health insurance policies was not pre-empted by ERISA. Similarly, in *State Farm Mutual Automobile Insurance Company v. American Community Mutual Insurance Company,* 659 F.Supp 635 (E.D.Mich.1987), the court held that ERISA did not pre-empt a Michigan law establishing priorities for medical coverage under an employee benefits plan. The plan was self-insured, but the employer was protected by "stop-loss" insurance coverage similar to the reinsurance available to the Riverside Plan, after costs incurred pierced a specified ceiling. However, in *Moore v. Provident Life & Accident Insurance Company,* 786 F.2d 922 (9th Cir.1986), the court held that the California unfair insurance claims statute was pre-empted by ERISA where the employer's stop-loss coverage was not triggered and the former employee in question was ineligible for benefits under the plan. Instead of sidestepping the ERISA issue, could the *Riverside* court have held, based on these decisions, that application of the Kansas coordination statute to the Riverside plan was not pre-empted? What argument could be made in support of this proposition?

2. *The Meaning of "Covered."* How convincing was the court's interpretation of the phrase, "also covered under any other plan" in the Riverside coordination clause? Is there any reason to suppose that Riverside intended the term "covered" to mean covered as a primary insured rather than as a dependent? Since the Blue Cross–Blue Shield provision on this issue was so much clearer, why did it not receive priority?

3. *A Substantive Criterion.* To what extent should the courts take into account the comparative risk-classification capacities of conflicting sources of coverage? For example, if Blue Cross–Blue Shield still engaged in "community rating" but a conflicting source of coverage experience-rated, would it be appropriate to allocate primary coverage

responsibility to the latter? Or would this merely encourage Blue Cross–Blue Shield to continue employing an inefficient classification scheme?

FORMS OF COORDINATION

The court in *Riverside* noted several times that non-duplication of benefits provisions work to the advantage of those insured. These provisions promote the principle of indemnity and thereby (presumably) also limit the cost of coverage. It does not follow from the notion that non-duplication of benefits is desirable, however, that all forms of coordination—of which non-duplication of benefits is only one—are equally worthwhile. The provisions at issue in *Riverside* provided only for non-duplication: Mrs. Stadalman apparently was entitled to the coverage provided by both policies, so long as there was no duplication. That is, although she was not entitled to any more than the amount of her health care costs, she could "stack" the coverage provided by the policies together, if necessary, to cover more of these costs than a single policy alone would cover. If these costs had exceeded the coverage provided by both policies together, there would have been no dispute in this regard. The issue in the case arose because the amount of her total loss did not exceed the total coverage available from both policies. It therefore mattered which policy was primary and which was secondary, because the coverage available from the primary policy would have to be exhausted before the secondary policy would be called upon at all, and the coverage provided by the latter would not be exhausted. There seemed to be no question, however, that she would be fully indemnified (subject to other limitations in the policies) for her loss.

In this situation, the two policies were interpreted so that one was *primary* and the other secondary, or *excess*. Two other kinds of clauses, however, may complicate matters further. A clause may provide that if there is other coverage, it will provide only *pro-rata* coverage, measured in proportion to policy limits or some other criterion. Similarly, an *escape* clause may provide that if there is other available coverage, it provides none. Sometimes there are compounds of these building blocks. A policy may provide, for example, that if there is other available coverage it will contribute on a pro-rata basis, but that the insured should receive no more from both policies than the highest amount available from one policy for a covered loss.

The many possible combinations of such clauses need not be elaborated further, for they are addressed more thoroughly in Chapter Nine. The point worth noting here is that some of these combinations, because they completely or partially bar the stacking of coverage, coordinate overlapping policies in a manner that not only prevents duplication of benefits, but may also deny the insured full indemnification against an otherwise-covered loss. Regulatory oversight and prohibition of such clauses is sometimes possible—although, as *Riverside* suggests, there may not always be sufficient jurisdiction to do so effectively. But are such prohibitions always sensible? For example, how would you assess the argument that those who desire higher levels of coverage than a single policy provides should purchase higher levels of protection from policies expressly designed to provide excess coverage—Major Medical or Excess Major Medical insurance—rather than seek such excess coverage through the back door, so to speak, by stacking together two policies designed to provide primary coverage?

CODY v. CONNECTICUT GENERAL LIFE INSURANCE COMPANY

Supreme Judicial Court of Massachusetts, Middlesex, 1982.
387 Mass. 142, 439 N.E.2d 234.

ABRAMS, Justice.

We granted the parties' applications for direct appellate review to determine whether the public policy of this Commonwealth permits coordination-of-benefits clauses in insurance contracts.[1] We conclude that coordination-of-benefits clauses do not violate the public policy of this Commonwealth unless the company engaged in misleading marketing practices, or the insurance contract as a whole is without substantial economic value.

We summarize the facts. The defendant Connecticut General Life Insurance Co. entered into a group contract of insurance with Sun Oil Company (Sun Oil), effective January 1, 1970. Under the contract, the defendant agreed to pay eligible Sun Oil employees, who become totally disabled, fifty per cent of their base monthly earnings up to $5,000 a month. The contract also contained two coordination-of-benefits clauses. The first clause provided that the benefits under the contract would be reduced by certain other income benefits, including workers' compensation, and fifty per cent of the amount of the employee's primary Social Security benefits.[2] The second clause stated that if the sum of the employee's benefits under the contract, other income benefits,[3] and benefits from Social Security,[4] exceed seventy-five per cent of the employee's base monthly earnings, the benefits under the contract would be reduced until the sum of all benefits equals seventy-five per cent of the employee's base monthly earnings.

1. Coordination-of-benefits clauses allow a company to deduct benefits from other sources from the benefits otherwise provided by the insurance contract.

2. Before a disabled employee can receive any benefits under the contract, he must wait twenty-six weeks. Since the accident in this case occurred on March 1, 1971, the plaintiff was not eligible to receive any benefits before September 1, 1971.

3. Other income benefits include any periodic cash payments on account of the employee's disability under (a) any employee sponsored group insurance coverage, toward which Sun Oil makes contributions, except benefits paid under scheduled injuries or permanent partial awards; (b) any State or Federal government disability or retirement plan; (c) any State or Federal workers' compensation or similar law, except benefits paid under scheduled injuries or permanent partial awards; (d) the maintenance provisions of the Jones Act, as applicable to seamen employed by Sun Oil.

4. These Social Security benefits include benefits payable to the employee's dependents on account of the employee's disability.

The plaintiff William F. Cody, an employee of Sun Oil, elected to purchase the coverage provided by this group contract. Through payroll deductions, the plaintiff paid a portion of the monthly premium for this coverage. The plaintiff never saw a copy of the insurance contract. The defendant did not distribute copies of the insurance contract to the employee-beneficiaries. Instead, the defendant sent a copy of the contract to Sun Oil. Sun Oil then distributed to its employees a booklet describing the benefits provided under the contract. The plaintiff testified that after reading the booklet, he believed that he would receive seventy-five per cent of his base pay in the event of a long term disability.[5]

As an employee, the plaintiff trained new tractor-trailer drivers for Sun Oil. On March 1, 1971, a driver trainee hit an obstruction on Route 95 in Groveland and lost control of the truck he was driving. The plaintiff, a passenger in that truck, was severely injured as a result of this accident. From the date of the accident until April 15, 1981, the date of the trial, the plaintiff has not worked. The plaintiff received no benefits under the contract.

In February, 1977, the plaintiff sued the defendant in the Superior Court. The plaintiff alleged a breach of the insurance contract by the defendant's failure to pay him any benefits. At trial, the parties stipulated that the insurance contract controlled this action. The parties also stipulated that if the judge interpreted the contract to allow the defendant an offset for fifty per cent of the plaintiff's primary Social Security benefits, plus the full amount of workers' compensation payments received between September 1, 1971, and April 15, 1981, the plaintiff would not be entitled to any payments under the contract; if the judge interpreted the contract to allow the defendant to offset only fifty per cent of the plaintiff's primary Social Security benefits, the plaintiff would be entitled to $27,168.05 under the contract; if the judge interpreted the policy to allow no offsets at all, the plaintiff would be entitled to $52,402.70 under the contract. * * *

Over the plaintiff's objection, the judge determined the amount of damages himself. The judge found that under the insurance contract the plaintiff was entitled to recover fifty per cent of his base monthly earnings reduced by his Massachusetts workers' compensation benefits and by fifty per cent of his primary Social Security benefits. Since these offsets reduced the plaintiff's benefits under the insurance contract to nothing, the judge entered judgment for the defendant. We affirm the judgment. We add, however, that coordination-of-benefits clauses will no longer be enforced if they are misleading or if they render the insurance contract as a whole without substantial economic value. * * *

5. The plaintiff may have based this belief on the coordination-of-benefits clause that provided that if benefits from all sources exceed seventy-five per cent of the employee's base monthly earnings, the benefits under the contract will be reduced until benefits from all sources equal seventy-five per cent of the employee's base monthly earnings.

2. *Coordination-of-benefits clauses.* Relying on *Kates v. St. Paul Fire & Marine Ins. Co.*, 509 F.Supp. 477 (D.Mass.1981), the plaintiff claims that the judge erred in enforcing the coordination-of-benefits clauses, because they violate public policy. We agree with the plaintiff that *Kates v. St. Paul Fire & Marine Ins. Co., supra* at 491, correctly states the public policy of this Commonwealth, that insurance contracts may not be misleading, and that coverages may not be "unrealistically limited" or so limited in scope as to be of no "substantial economic value." However, in this case, the insurance contract took effect, and the plaintiff's injury occurred, before the Legislature enacted the statutes that are the source of this public policy. We therefore believe that it would be unfair to apply this public policy in this case.

In the *Kates* case, *supra,* the judge correctly found one source of this public policy in G.L. c. 175, § 110E.[6] Pursuant to G.L. c. 175, § 110E, inserted by St.1973, c. 1081, the Commissioner of Insurance may issue rules and regulations "to establish minimum standards of full and fair disclosure, for the form and content of policies of accident and sickness insurance which provide medical, surgical, or hospital expense benefits. * * *" Among the purposes of these rules and regulations are the "elimination of provisions which may be misleading * * *"; and the "elimination of coverages which are so limited in scope as to be of no substantial economic value." G.L. c. 175, § 110E(b), (e). Although G.L. c. 175, § 110E, expressly does not cover "general" or "blanket" disability insurance contracts like that at issue in this case, the *Kates* decision properly determined that the policies set out in that statute apply to such contracts. Cf. *Mailhot v. Travelers Ins. Co.*, 375 Mass. 342, 348 & n. 7, 377 N.E.2d 681 (1978); *Gaudette v. Webb*, 362 Mass. 60, 70, 284 N.E.2d 222 (1972). Since G.L. c. 175, § 110E, was enacted after the effective date of the insurance contract at issue in this case, and after the injury giving rise to this claim,[7] we believe it would be unfair to apply the public policy set out in that statute.

However, we think it is appropriate to elaborate on this policy for future cases. In the *Kates* case, the insurance contract clearly provided that payments on account of workers' compensation and Social Security would be deducted from the benefits provided by the policy. Nevertheless, the judge concluded that the contract was misleading. "In view of the marketing of this coverage through the workplace, employees electing to participate could reasonably expect to receive lifetime benefits if totally disabled from an injury sustained in their employment. Even though one who has all the relevant information about social

6. There are other statutory sources for this policy. For example, G.L. c. 93A, § 2, inserted by St.1967, c. 813, § 1, prohibits "unfair or deceptive acts or practices in the conduct of any trade or commerce," including insurance. See *Dodd v. Commercial Union Ins. Co.*, 373 Mass. 72, 75–76, 365 N.E.2d 802 (1977). In addition, the Commissioner of Insurance must make sure that insurance policies are readable. See G.L. c. 175, § 2B, inserted by St.1977, c. 801, § 1.

7. The insurance contract in this case took effect in 1970—three years before the enactment of G.L. c. 175, § 110E. The injury on which this claim is based occurred two years prior to the enactment of G.L. c. 175, § 110E.

security and worker compensation benefits could ascertain by close analysis of the coordination-of-benefits provisions that * * * [under the policy he would receive few benefits for on-the-job injuries], it would not be reasonable to expect that this fact would be discovered by a person who was considering whether to apply for participation." [8] *Id.* at 491–492. Thus, the *Kates* case demonstrates that a company's marketing techniques may make even a totally unambiguous insurance contract misleading.[9] Since misleading insurance contracts violate the public policy of this Commonwealth, we believe that courts must limit the enforcement of these contracts to avoid unconscionable results.

* * *

If the insurance contract is not misleading, we think that the court must go on to decide whether the contract as a whole is without substantial economic value.[10] The determination whether the contract is without substantial economic value is similar to an examination of the substantive unconscionability of a contract. A court must determine whether the contract terms are unreasonably favorable to one party. * * * Hence, a court should find that an insurance contract

8. To avoid a claim that an insurance contract like that at issue in this case is misleading, a company should specifically inform the consumer that because of the coordination-of-benefits clauses, he may not be entitled to any benefits under the policy for certain injuries. We emphasize that a clear warning prevents an insurance contract from being misleading.

9. Because of the importance of marketing methods, courts relax the parol evidence rule to admit evidence or oral or written assurances made by the agent who sells the policy. See 7 Williston, Contracts, § 900 at 32–33 (3d ed. 1963), and cases cited. See also K.B. Hughes, Evidence, § 423 (1961), and cases cited; *Adzigian v. WORL Broadcasting Corp.,* 348 Mass. 777, 202 N.E.2d 915 (1964); *Tri–City Concrete Co. v. A.L.A. Constr. Co.,* 343 Mass. 425, 179 N.E.2d 319 (1962).

At trial, the judge did not fully consider the defendant's marketing practices. He excluded the benefits booklet distributed by Sun Oil to its employees. We believe that the booklet is relevant to the issue whether the contract is misleading. But since we have concluded that the policies set out in *Kates* do not apply to this case, we need not decide whether the exclusion of the booklet is an error that requires reversal.

In marketing this contract, the defendant did not make its policies available to the employee-beneficiaries. Instead, the defendant relied on Sun Oil to inform the employees about the benefits under the policy. The defendant chose this marketing technique and is therefore bound by the benefits booklet distributed by Sun Oil. Thus, if the question whether the contract is misleading were an issue in this case, the judge should admit the benefits booklet.

Further, in this case Sun Oil distributed the booklet in 1964, seven years before the plaintiff's disability. The record does not indicate that the defendant ever lodged an objection to the content of the booklet. In addition, the booklet described the policy so precisely, that a reasonable person could conclude that someone from the insurance company prepared it. Since the probability is very high that the defendant at least tacitly approved the benefits booklet distributed by Sun Oil (cf. *Smith v. Ariens Co.,* 375 Mass. 620, 622, 377 N.E.2d 954 [1978]), it would not be unfair to hold the defendant to the terms of the booklet. Unless there were evidence that the defendant asked the employer to withdraw the booklet or to correct it, the judge should assume that the defendant acquiesced in its distribution.

10. In *Kates v. St. Paul Fire & Marine Ins. Co.,* 509 F.Supp. 477, 491–492 (D.Mass. 1981), the judge held that the insurance contract violated public policy, although only one component of the contract, coverage for on-the-job injuries, was without substantial economic value. The judge reached the result because he concluded that the insurance contract was misleading.

like that at issue in this case has substantial economic value as long as the premiums reflect the anticipated effect of any coordination-of-benefits clause.

Finally, we note that coordination-of-benefits clauses serve the public purpose of avoiding duplicate recoveries for the same injuries. *Mailhot v. Travelers Ins. Co.*, 375 Mass. 342, 347–348, 377 N.E.2d 681 (1978). These clauses enable insurance companies to charge lower premiums.[11] See *Lamb v. Connecticut Gen. Life Ins. Co.*, 643 F.2d 108, 109 n. 1 (3d Cir.1981); *Connecticut Gen. Life Ins. Co. v. Craton*, 405 F.2d 41, 47 (5th Cir.1968). We therefore conclude that unless the company engaged in misleading marketing practices, or the insurance contract as a whole is without substantial economic value, coordination-of-benefits clauses do not violate the public policy of this Commonwealth.

Judgment affirmed.

Notes and Questions

1. *The Thin Market for Disability Insurance.* Private disability insurance—coverage against wage loss resulting from illness or injury—is far less prevalent than health insurance. Roughly 25 percent of the American population is covered by private short-term disability insurance, defined as coverage against disability lasting less than two years; and roughly 10 percent of the population is covered by private long-term disability insurance. See Health Insurance Association of America, 1988 Update: Source Book of Health Insurance Data 7. Private disability insurance benefits paid in 1986 totalled $5.6 billion. Id. at 9. Part of the reason for the thin market for private disability insurance is the threat of adverse selection and moral hazard. Both the attractiveness of subsidized unemployment and the difficulty of assessing someone's ability to work or to return to work make these serious threats for disability insurers.

Another major reason for the thin market in private disability insurance, however, is that social insurance against losses resulting from disability already covers large numbers of people for at least subsistence levels of protection. Annual disability benefits paid by public programs in 1986 were almost ten times those paid by private insurers—over $53 billion per year. See U.S. Dep't. of Commerce, Bureau of the Census, Statistical Abstract of the United States 338 (1988). One of the advantages of these forms of social insurance is that because coverage under many of these programs (Social Security Disability, Veteran's Benefits, etc.) is automatic, adverse selection problems are eliminated.

2. *Partial Coverage: A Glass Half–Empty or Half–Full?* Disability insurers typically offer coverage for no more than roughly 60 percent

---

11. The benefits from programs such as workers' compensation and Social Security "can to some extent be actuarially related to the risks the company must take and hence to the premiums it must charge." *Connecticut Gen. Life Ins. Co. v. Craton,* 405 F.2d 41, 47 (5th Cir.1968).

of the insured's after tax income, in order to preserve the insured's incentive to recover from his disability and return to work. What was the predominant effect of the clauses in Cody's policy: minimizing of the cost of coverage, combatting moral hazard, or misleading the insured? Cody could expect to receive about two-thirds of his weekly wage (up to a statutory ceiling) from workers' compensation if he were injured on the job. Social Security disability insurance, for which he apparently was also eligible, covers long-term total disability (up to a statutory ceiling), whether suffered on or off the job. Given the first coordination clause, for what kinds of losses could he expect to be covered under the Connecticut General policy?

3. *Unconscionability: Procedural or Substantive?* The court's two-pronged test for future cases required a decision whether the policy is misleading and, if not, whether it is "without substantial economic value." How can a policy not be misleading if it was without substantial economic value but people have purchased it anyway? What factors should a court consider in deciding whether the contract as a whole is without substantial economic value? How sensible will it be for a court to make inquiry into these factors?

ASSOCIATED HOSPITAL SERVICE OF PHILADELPHIA v. PUSTILNIK

Superior Court of Pennsylvania, 1979.
262 Pa.Super. 600, 396 A.2d 1332.

SPAETH, Judge:

This case arises on cross appeals in an equity action. The issues raised involve the right of subrogation.

On May 27, 1968, Alan Pustilnik was injured when he was struck by a SEPTA subway car in Philadelphia. As a result of the accident, Pustilnik was hospitalized on three separate occasions. Medical bills accruing from these hospitalizations totalled $30,200.87, but Pustilnik was given a credit of $18,960.18 against this amount under the terms of his subscription agreement with Associated Hospital Service of Philadelphia (Blue Cross).

Soon after the accident, Pustilnik instituted suit against SEPTA. During pendency of this suit, Blue Cross notified Pustilnik and his attorney, Malcolm Waldron, of its subrogation interest in any recovery ultimately obtained from SEPTA. Blue Cross also invited Waldron to represent its interest in the suit in return for 25% of any recovery as an attorney's fee, or 33⅓% if the case went to trial. Waldron rejected this offer, demanding 50% of any recovery as a prerequisite for his representation of Blue Cross' interests. Blue Cross did not agree to pay this fee, but nevertheless continued to advise Waldron of its increasing subrogation interest as a result of Pustilnik's second and third hospitalizations.

Pustilnik's suit against SEPTA went to trial in May 1971. After the fifth day of trial, but before a verdict was returned, the parties settled the suit. Pustilnik agreed to take $235,000 in return for his release relieving SEPTA from additional liability. Upon learning of the settlement, Blue Cross, which did not participate in the trial, immediately alerted SEPTA and the trial judge of its subrogation claim. Eventually, when Pustilnik and Blue Cross were unable to agree on the size of Blue Cross' interest, the trial judge placed $30,000 of the settlement monies into an escrow fund. Thereafter, Blue Cross brought the present action in equity to obtain an adjudication governing the disbursement of the escrowed monies.

Trial was held in November 1975. At the close of the evidence, the court ruled that Blue Cross was entitled to subrogation for the amounts it spent on Pustilnik's behalf, but that it had not proved that it had paid $18,960.18, the amount credited against Pustilnik's hospital bills. The court found that although Blue Cross might have paid this sum, its proof failed to show with reasonable certainty that it had expended more than $16,721.64. The court therefore ruled that Blue Cross' subrogation recovery should be limited to this amount. The court further ruled that this amount was subject to the following additional deductions. First, finding that Pustilnik's $235,000 settlement was less than the full value of his personal injury claim, the court reduced Blue Cross' recovery by 50%. Next, the court reduced Blue Cross' recovery by another 40% to reflect its proportionate share of Waldron's attorney's fee. Finally, the court imposed a reduction of $120 to cover Blue Cross' share of the litigation expenses incurred by Waldron in the suit against SEPTA. Judgment was accordingly entered for Blue Cross in the amount of $4,889.49. Both parties filed exceptions to the court's adjudication, which were dismissed by an opinion and order dated February 15, 1977. Pustilnik and Blue Cross cross-appealed (in Nos. 1136 and 1223 October Term, 1977) to this court. The appeals have been consolidated, and will now be decided together.

Pustilnik's Appeal

Pustilnik's principal argument is that Blue Cross erred in bringing its action in equity.[1] Included in Pustilnik's subscription agreement

---

1. Pustilnik makes three other arguments for reversal, which may be disposed of summarily. Pustilnik first argues that Blue Cross waived its subrogation rights when it failed to intervene in his suit against SEPTA or to institute its own separate action. Failure by a subrogee to intervene in a subrogor's suit against a third party tortfeasor has never been construed as a waiver by the subrogee of rights in any settlement or judgment secured by the subrogor from the tortfeasor. *See, e.g., Furia v. Philadelphia,* 180 Pa. Super. 50, 118 A.2d 236 (1955). * * *

Finally, Pustilnik argues that the trial court erred in refusing to condition Blue Cross' recovery upon proof of SEPTA's negligence. This argument is inconsistent with long-standing authority that a subrogee is not required to prove a third party's negligence in a suit to enforce its subrogation rights against the subrogor, when the subrogor brought and settled a previous action against the third party without obtaining a verdict. *Illinois Automobile Insurance Exchange v. Braun,* 280 Pa. 550, 124 A. 691 (1924); *Union Insurance Society, Ltd. v. Saller,* 95 Pa.Super. 41 (1928); *Commercial Casualty Insurance*

with Blue Cross was a provision setting Blue Cross' right to subrogation in any recovery obtained by Pustilnik from a third party on account of his injuries.[2] Pustilnik argues that this provision gave Blue Cross an adequate remedy at law.[3] We do not find these arguments persuasive.

*   *   *

Because Blue Cross' subrogation right existed in equity whether or not that right was recognized in its subscription agreement with Pustilnik, equity could hear Blue Cross' claim. By including a subrogation provision in the agreement, Blue Cross reserved the option to sue in assumpsit to secure subrogation, *See Roberts v. Fireman's Insurance Co. of Newark, New Jersey, supra*, but it did not forfeit its right to sue in equity. Older cases implying that an equitable action in subrogation will not lie when there is an adequate remedy at law are inapposite. *See* P.L.E., *Subrogation § 2* (1958). In *Vogue Co. v. John C. Winston Co.*, 76 Pa.Super. 158 (1921), this court indicated, in *dictum*, that the plaintiff's subrogation was improperly pursued since he possessed a valid breach of warranty claim that would make whole his loss. Here, the only claim Blue Cross possessed was one for subrogation. Since subrogation is an equitable remedy, whether or not contractually declared, Blue Cross' action properly lay in equity.

Blue Cross' Appeal

Blue Cross argues that it was entitled to $18,960.18, less a one third attorney's fee for Waldron, leaving a total recovery of $12,640.12. Blue

Co. v. Leebron, 90 Pa.Super. 201 (1926); *Manley v. Montgomery Bus Co., Inc.*, 82 Pa.Super. 530 (1924).

2. Section XV of the Subscription Agreement entitled "Subrogation" provided:

> In the event any hospital service or benefit is provided or any payment is made to a Subscriber under this Agreement Blue Cross shall be subrogated and succeed to the Subscriber's right of recovery therefor against any person or organization except against insurers on policies of insurance issued to and in the name of the Subscriber, and the Subscriber shall execute and deliver such instruments and take such other action as Blue Cross may require to secure such rights. The Subscriber shall do nothing to prejudice the rights given Blue Cross by this paragraph without its consent.

3. Pustilnik does not argue that Blue Cross' subrogation rights can exist only by virtue of the contractual provision allowing subrogation. Thus, our decision today is based upon the assumption that even in the absence of such a provision, Blue Cross would have a right to subrogation at law. We do not address the interesting issue of whether Blue Cross' subscription agreement was in fact one for the indemnification of medical expenses, and if not, whether Blue Cross had a legal right to subrogation independent of the terms of the subrogation agreement. *See* Annot., 73 A.L.R.3d 1140, 1143 (1976) ("In the few cases that have been found dealing with the subject, no court has recognized the principle of legal subrogation as a basis for recoupment of benefits paid by a hospital or medical service organization * * * "); *see also Morin v. Massachusetts Blue Cross, Inc.*, 365 Mass. 379, 383, 311 N.E.2d 914, 916 (1974) (raising the issue without deciding it); *Michigan Medical Service v. Sharpe*, 339 Mich. 574, 64 N.W.2d 713 (1954) (Blue Cross subscription agreement not contract for indemnity, therefore no right to subrogation exists outside the terms of the contract and suit for subrogation must be brought on law side of court). *But see* Justice Reid's strong dissent in *Michigan Hospital Service v. Sharpe*, 339 Mich. 357, 63 N.W.2d 638, 642 (1954), a companion case to *Michigan Medical Service, supra*, finding Blue Cross subscription agreement sufficiently analogous to indemnity contract to justify application of subrogation at law.

Cross admits that it failed to prove at trial that it paid $18,960.18 on Pustilnik's behalf, but it justified this failure on the ground that its manner of providing medical coverage makes such an exact calculation impossible.

Unlike profit-making insurance carriers, Blue Cross contracts directly with hospitals to provide services to its subscribers.[4] When a hospital under contract with Blue Cross provides services to a subscriber, it credits the subscriber's bill to the extent that it is covered by the subscriber's agreement with Blue Cross. Blue Cross then makes a partial, interim payment to the hospital on the basis of the hospital's bill to the subscriber. Final payment, however, is postponed until Blue Cross conducts its annual audit of the hospital's operations. At that time, all the hospital's costs are totalled, as well as all its charges to Blue Cross. If Blue Cross determines that some of the hospital's costs were unnecessary or resulted from waste, it deducts an appropriate amount from its yearly bill, and pays only the reduced amount. Because of this reimbursement system, which is based on generalized auditing procedures, Blue Cross was unable to isolate the exact amount it paid on account of Pustilnik's hospitalizations.

The trial court reasoned that "no subrogation can rise any higher than what the person paid out," and since Blue Cross did not show that it actually paid out the total amount credited on Pustilnik's bills, it was entitled only to a lesser sum. To illustrate the equity of its holding, the trial court used the following hypothetical example:

> Let us suppose an insurance carrier under its collision policy estimated the damage to a policyholder's car as $500.00 but only paid out $400.00 to a friendly repair shop to fix the car. Should such carrier be able to recover $500.00 because that was the value of the benefits rather than the $400.00 it actually paid out? We think not.

Slip opinion at 11.

The trial court's example does not accurately reflect the facts of the present case; it assumes that it was *Blue Cross* that initially "estimated the damage." However, it was *Pustilnik*, in his suit against SEPTA, who alleged that the face amount of his hospital bills stated the amount of special damages he had suffered as a result of the accident. Therefore, we do not have, as the trial court supposed, a situation where a subrogee sues a tortfeasor for the fair value of the services it provided the subrogor, even though it procured those services at less than fair value. Instead, we have a situation where the subrogor, after recovering from a tortfeasor an amount alleged by the subrogor to be the fair value of services provided by a subrogee, then refuses to hand over that amount to subrogee, assigning as the reason for the refusal the subro-

---

4. Not all hospitals, of course, have contracts with Blue Cross; but since Pustilnik was hospitalized only at hospitals that were under contract, we need not describe the reimbursement procedures used by Blue Cross for services provided hospitals not under contract.

gee's inability to determine whether it actually paid that amount for the services. Equity will not allow such a result. The Restatement of Restitution § 162 states:

> Where property of one person is used in discharging an obligation owed by another * * *, under such circumstances that the other would be unjustly enriched by the retention of the benefit thus conferred, the former is entitled to be subrogated to the position of the obligee. * * *

Cited with approval in Employers Mutual Liability Insurance Co. of Wisconsin v. Melcher, 378 Pa. 598, 601, 107 A.2d 874, 876 (1954). To allow Pustilnik to gain a windfall by taking inconsistent positions in the two lawsuits would result in his unjust enrichment. Once he represented to SEPTA that the $18,960.18 represented the fair value of a part of his special damage, he could not then turn to Blue Cross and claim that the amount was inflated and his special damages were limited to a lesser sum.

The trial court also erred in reducing Blue Cross' recovery by 50% on the ground that Pustilnik had settled with SEPTA for less than the full value of his claim. In *Illinois Automobile Insurance Exchange v. Braun,* 280 Pa. 550, 557–58, 124 A. 691, 693 (1924), the Supreme Court held that when a subrogor settles instead of pressing his suit against an alleged tortfeasor to verdict, he cannot defeat a subrogee's claim by asserting that his loss exceeded the settlement recovery. Sound policy requires this result. It is of course possible that in some cases a subrogor will be well advised to settle for substantially less than his claim because of the tenuous proof establishing the alleged tortfeasor's liability. This possibility, however, does not imply that the subrogor should be permitted to assert against the subrogee that after all, his claim against the tortfeasor really was worth more than he had settled for—which is what the trial court permitted to happen here. Such a procedure would encourage unethical practice, if not perjured testimony: a representation in the court where the suit against the tortfeasor was tried that the case for liability was strong, to obtain a high settlement, followed by a representation in the court where the subrogation claim was tried that the case for liability was weak. Liability should be determined, whenever possible in one proceeding. When a subrogor settles, he waives his right to a judicial determination of his losses, and conclusively establishes the settlement amount as full compensation for his damages.

The final issue concerns the propriety of the trial court's reduction of Blue Cross' recovery to reflect its proportionate share of the attorney's fee and litigation expenses involved in Pustilnik's suit against SEPTA. Pustilnik argues that the reductions were too small, Blue Cross, that they were too large.

In *Furia v. Philadelphia,* 180 Pa.Super. 50, 118 A.2d 236 (1955), we held that when a subrogor's attorney creates a common fund for the benefit of the subrogor and subrogee, the attorney is entitled to reimbursement from the subrogee for its proportionate share of reasonable attorney's fees and litigation expenses. Here, therefore, Waldron is entitled to reimbursement from Blue Cross for a reasonable fee; since the parties failed to agree to a fee themselves, the court must determine what fee is reasonable. [The court then upheld the trial court's reduction of Blue Cross' award by 40 percent to reflect Waldron's counsel fee.] * * *

The judgment is set aside and the case remanded for further disposition in accordance with this opinion.

Notes and Questions

1. *Equitable Versus Contractual Subrogation.* Recall that sources of authority to subrogate fall into two categories: judicially-created authority—known as equitable, or legal subrogation; and authority created by the insurance policy itself, known as conventional, or contractual subrogation. In decades past there was some question whether health insurers were entitled to equitable subrogation. The court in *Pustilnik* rehearsed some of that controversy in footnote 3 of its opinion. An interesting case discussing the distinction is *Cunningham v. Metropolitan Life Insurance Company,* 121 Wis.2d 437, 360 N.W.2d 33 (1985), in which the issue was whether a health insurance policy was designed for indemnity or investment. The court held that if it was the former, then equitable subrogation was to be allowed, in order to further the principle of indemnity. If the latter, however, then subrogation was not to be allowed absent a provision for it in the policy. Does this distinction explain why there has never been equitable subrogation in life insurance? Why have life insurers never included express subrogation provisions in their policies?

Today virtually all health insurance policies contain subrogation provisions, and most courts permit the contractual subrogation for which they provide. Should such a provision entitle an accidental death insurer to subrogation to a wrongful death recovery obtained by the spouse of the insured? See *Schmidt v. Country Mutual Insurance Company,* 79 Ill.App.3d 456, 34 Ill.Dec. 766, 398 N.E.2d 589 (1979). The enactment of statutes modifying the collateral source rule in tort cases by a number of states in the mid–1980's is also likely to shrink the scope of health insurers' subrogation rights. Will the probable insurance effect of such statutes be to shift relative premium volume from liability insurers to health and disability insurers?

2. *Protecting the Insurer.* As in property insurance, a health insured who settles with a tortfeasor after suffering injury has interfered with the insurer's subrogation rights and thereby voids his coverage, unless the tortfeasor has notice of the insurer's interest. The kind of problems addressed in *Pustilnik* arise, however, when settlement of the insured's tort claim occurs after his receipt of health insurance benefits, as it almost always does. Settlements that operate against the insurer's interest cannot be prevented by a rule that

settlement voids coverage, because coverage has already been provided. In this situation the insurer's interest can be protected, if at all, only by rules governing apportionment of the insured's tort recovery between insurer and insured.

Judgments.   Should the insured be heard to complain if the insurer is reimbursed off the top of any recovery awarded at trial?   In theory such a judgment constitutes an award of all the insured's damages; reimbursing the insurer in full out of the recovery therefore does not deny the insured full indemnity.   Suppose, however, that in a comparative negligence jurisdiction the award has been reduced in proportion to the amount of negligence attributed to the insured.   Should the insurer's reimbursement be reduced in that proportion as well?   What role should the insured's counsel fees play in the allocation?

Settlements.   In *Pustilnik* the court devised what amounted to a conclusive presumption that the sum for which an insured settles always constitutes full compensation for all his losses.   Is this an empirical conclusion or a rule designed to force the insured to consider the insurer's interests in reaching settlements?   For example, in *Poche v. City of New Orleans,* 518 So.2d 1137 (La.App.1987) a health insured settled a tort claim which, by stipulation, was intended to exclude past medical expenses paid by the health insurer.   The court held that the subrogation rights of the insurer did not entitle it to recover any of the proceeds of settlement.

The capacity of a rule governing this problem to force consideration of the insurer's interest depends on the method by which the settlement is apportioned between insurer and insured, if it is apportioned at all. One method—adopted by the court in *Pustilnik* —is to pay the insurer *off-the-top* of the settlement.   On the assumption that the settlement constitutes full compensation, this method does not deprive the insured of full indemnity.   But suppose, more realistically, that settlements do not constitute full compensation (after taking into account the insured's uninsured out-of-pocket losses and pain and suffering, for example). Then this method of apportionment prevents the insured from settling (as the insured in *Poche* settled) for a sum that will heavily compensate him while reimbursing the insurer nothing, or only a small portion of the benefits it has already paid the insured.

Two other methods of apportionment protect the insurer's interest less effectively, because they focus more on assuring full (or more nearly full) indemnity for the insured.   A *pro-rata* rule would pay the insurer a portion of the settlement equal to the proportion its payment to the insured bears to the insured's total losses.   For example, if the insured's losses were $100,000, of which the insurer had paid $20,000, and the insured settled with the tortfeasor for $45,000, then the insurer would be reimbursed for twenty percent of the settlement, or $9000.   If not only out-of-pocket losses but also pain and suffering are considered in calculating the insured's total losses, what problems are posed by this approach?   A third method of apportionment would provide *full indemnity for the insured* by reimbursing him first for his uninsured losses. The insurer would then be reimbursed out of any sums remaining, and if a portion of the settlement still remained after such reimbursement, the insured would retain it. Does implementing this rule pose the same kinds of problems that would be encountered by a pro-rata rule? Commentators suggest that this rule has the most support in the precedents. See, e.g., R. Jerry, Understanding Insurance Law 467–68 (1987); R. Keeton and A. Widiss, Insurance Law 236 (2d ed. 1988). But decisions on the issue are sparse enough that perhaps a firm rule really has not yet emerged.

3. *Protecting the Insured.* Is the safest way for an insured to avoid the threat to full indemnity that these apportionment rules pose to bring the insurer into settlement negotiations with the tortfeasor (or its liability insurer)? Will this approach necessarily protect the insured, or will it merely provide the insurer with an opportunity to engage in strategic behavior?

4. The Meaning of "Disability"

MOOTS v. BANKERS LIFE COMPANY
Court of Appeals of Kansas, 1985.
10 Kan.App.2d 640, 707 P.2d 1083.

TERRY L. BULLOCK, District Judge, Assigned:

Bruce Moots was insured under a group policy of disability insurance from Bankers Life Co. Thereafter, Moots suffered disabling back injuries. As a result of these disabilities Bankers paid Moots monthly benefits under the policy for approximately two years. For reasons not fully developed in the record, Bankers then terminated payments to Moots and Moots filed suit seeking both past due and future payments. Bankers moved for summary judgment, contending that Moots was not entitled to any payments for the sole reason that he had taken a job driving a bus *subsequent* to the termination of payments by Bankers. Upon these uncontroverted facts, the trial court granted summary judgment to Bankers. This appeal followed.

We turn first to the relevant portion of the disability contract:

"TOTAL DISABILITY. Total disability, for the purposes of this Policy, means the complete inability of the Person, due to accidental bodily injury or sickness, or both

(a) during the first twenty-four months of such disability, to perform any and every duty pertaining to his own occupation; and

(b) during any continuation of such disability following the first twenty-four months of disability, to engage in any work or occupation for which he is reasonably fitted by education, training or experience; and provided further, that he does not engage in any occupation, work or employment for wage or profit during any such disability."

Bankers concedes that subparagraph (a) provides what is commonly known as "occupational" disability coverage for the first 24 months of disability. Under "occupational" coverage, if an insured is unable, by reason of his disability, to perform the usual and customary duties of his *actual* occupation, disability payments are owing. In the case at bar, Bankers further concedes that Moots was occupationally disabled for the first 24 months after his injuries and was thus entitled to the payments which Bankers paid.

The only question remaining is whether Moots is entitled to further payments under subparagraph (b) of the policy beyond the initial 24–month period of "occupational" disability coverage under subparagraph (a). Subparagraph (b) provides what is commonly described as "general" disability coverage. Under "general" disability coverage, in order to recover the insured must not only be unable to perform the duties of his *actual* occupation, but likewise be unable to "engage in any work or occupation for which he is reasonably fitted by education, training or experience. ∗ ∗ ∗" See 15 Couch on Insurance 2d § 53:45 (rev. ed. 1983), for a similar explanation of the difference between "occupational" and "general" disability coverage. "General," or as is sometimes called "total," disability insurance provisions have been often construed. For many years virtually all courts have held that although the insured must prove inability to perform all jobs for which he is suited by training, education or experience, total helplessness is not required as a condition precedent to recovery for "general" or "total" disability. Specifically, the mere fact that the insured continues to do some compensable work will not alone bar recovery. In *Simmons v. Wilson Employees Mut. Benefit Fund,* 145 Kan. 128, 64 P.2d 50 (1937) an insured was not denied total disability benefits despite the fact that he performed manual labor on relief jobs. The *Simmons* court observed:

> "The fact plaintiff had done work on relief projects would indicate it was imperative he do something to provide food and shelter. He probably thought it was just as well to die trying to work as to starve to death. The fact he did some work at the risk of life did not mean he was not entitled to recover for total permanent disability. [Citations omitted.]" 145 Kan. at 130, 64 P.2d 50.

Although Bankers does not quarrel with these general principles pertaining to usual or typical "general" disability provisions, it argues that the final proviso of subparagraph (b) in the subject policy takes this case outside usual rules and alters the results in its favor. That proviso follows:

> "[P]rovided further, that he does not engage in any occupation, work or employment for wage or profit during any such disability."

Bankers contends that under this so-called "conduct" clause, Moots is barred from all "general" disability benefits because, some four months after they terminated his payments, he accepted limited employment as a school bus driver. Although no Kansas cases have been found construing a similar "conduct" provision in a general disability insurance clause, other courts have done so.

In *Stoner v. New York Life Ins. Co.*, 90 S.W.2d 784 (Mo.App.1936), the policy contained a general clause defining total disability to be when the insured "is so disabled by bodily injury or disease that he is wholly prevented from performing any work, from following any occupation, or from engaging in any business for remuneration or profit. * * *" 90 S.W.2d at 787. The *Stoner* court held that the concluding phrase of the insuring clause did not alter the general insuring clause of the policy. The *Stoner* court held:

> "[T]he insuring clause gives the right to benefits when insured is disabled so as to prevent the doing of certain things. The last clause but negatives his right to benefits when he is not so prevented, but when he is able so to engage and does so engage. They are correlative clauses. Both are to be given the same construction. It would be anomalous that the language employed when found in the insuring clause in one part of the policy should be given one construction and when found in another part of the policy should be given another. In the insuring clause, such language is construed to mean that insured is totally disabled when he cannot perform the material and substantial acts of his occupation [or others for which he is reasonably suited] and is thereupon entitled to benefits; in the last (so-called conduct) clause, it is to be construed as meaning that plaintiff is not totally disabled when he is able to and does perform the substantial and material acts of his occupation [or others for which he is reasonably suited] and is not in such event entitled to benefits. There is then no conflict between the two clauses. The latter has no effect to limit or vary the former. It is but declaratory of the former. It was doubtless inserted in the policies to enable the defendant to review the condition of plaintiff and his disabilities from time to time and to discharge itself of liability under the policies when it is found that plaintiff's disabled condition has so far improved that he is again able substantially to carry on his occupation or substantially to engage in others [for which he is reasonably suited]." 90 S.W.2d at 793.

In *Mutual Life Ins. Co. v. Clark*, 255 Ark. 741, 502 S.W.2d 110 (1973), the policy in issue defined total disability as "disability which wholly and continuously disables the member so that he can perform no duty pertaining to his occupation and during which he is not engaged in any occupation for remuneration or profit." 255 Ark. at 745, 502 S.W.2d 110. The Arkansas court likewise refused to construe the clause literally, holding that the insured was not required to prove that he was not engaged in *any* occupation for remuneration or profit as a condition precedent to recovery. 255 Ark. at 748, 502 S.W.2d 110.

Considerations of policy militate a similar result. It is well known that severely disabled persons, for reasons of physical and mental health, are frequently encouraged by their physicians to take some type of work as therapy. If insureds were able to follow such valuable medical advice only at the peril of losing their only real means of financial survival, we would create for the already disabled a heavy burden indeed. Further, an opposite result would put all insureds at the absolute mercy of their insurers. In such a situation, the insurer could simply terminate disability benefits, wait until the insured is driven by dire necessity to seek *any* kind of employment, and then justify the termination retrospectively based on the subsequent employment. In a society which values work and applauds extraordinary effort by the handicapped such a result would be anomalous, to say the least.

For all of these reasons we hold that a "conduct clause" appended to a general disability insuring agreement, which states, "provided further, that [the insured] does not engage in any occupation, work or employment for wage or profit during any such disability":

(a) does not require a departure from customary rules of construction pertaining to the degree of disability necessary for recovery under general disability insurance policies, and

(b) is construed to be merely the negative or mirror image of the insuring clause; as such, the insured is barred from recovery only if he is *able* to perform "any work or occupation for which he is reasonably fitted by education, training or experience."

Accordingly, we reverse the decision of the trial court and remand with directions to proceed with trial to determine whether Moots can prove he is "generally" disabled in accordance with this opinion.

Notes and Questions

1. *Partial Disability.* Virtually all disability policies provide all or nothing coverage; the insured is either totally disabled, in which case he receives the full amount of coverage afforded by the policy, or he is not totally disabled, in which case he is not covered. Coverage is structured in this manner in order to avoid the problems associated with assessing partial disability. One method of coping indirectly with the partial disability problem is the occupational-disability clause, which treats the partially disabled insured as though he is totally disabled, but only for a specified period. In *Moots* that period was two years; in many policies it is five years. Some insurers offer occupational disability coverage for an unlimited period for an additional premium. See generally R. Soule, Disability Income Insurance: The Unique Risk (1984).

2. *The Scope of the "Conduct" Clause.* Was the court correct to interpret the second clause of paragraph (b) of the general disability provision ("provided further, that he does not engage in any occupation, work or employment for wage or profit during any such disability") as adding nothing to the first clause? In light of the judicial tendency to treat the notion of total disability as flexible, does the second clause not at least imply, "and we really mean *complete inability* to work"? If the second clause does add this meaning, how should the courts make it operational without requiring that the insured be paralyzed from head to toe in order to be totally disabled?

3. *The Function of the Clause.* The additional clause might be viewed as an exclusive evidentiary condition, much like the evidence-of-forcible-entry requirement in a burglary policy. As such the clause may be overbroad, but nonetheless useful as a method of minimizing administrative and litigation costs. On the other hand, unlike the evidence-of-forcible-entry requirement, literal application of the clause would promote rather than reduce moral hazard, because it encourages functionally disabled insureds not to seek even minimal employment. Given this mix of strengths and weaknesses, should the courts or the market decide whether the clause is desirable?

One argument for judicial intervention is that the clause is capable of being invoked selectively in a manner that is difficult for the courts to supervise except by wholesale invalidation. For example, suppose that insurers tend not to enforce the clause literally so long as they believe that the insured is in fact functionally disabled. Suppose further that insurers believe the insured is malingering, they invoke the clause and deny all benefits, instead of proving directly that the insured is not disabled. Selective enforcement of the clause in this manner may constitute a kind of lawlessness. In effect, everyone is entitled to engage in minimal work without becoming ineligible for benefits, except those the insurer suspects but does not want to take the trouble to prove are not functionally disabled. Is the inequity entailed in this stance sufficient justification for a judicial interpretation that transfers decision on this same issue from the insurer to the vagaries of jury decision? Will the treatment of all insureds who engage in minimal work be any more equitable or desirable under the latter approach?

HELLER v. THE EQUITABLE LIFE ASSURANCE SOCIETY OF THE UNITED STATES

United States Court of Appeals, Seventh Circuit, 1987.
833 F.2d 1253.

COFFEY, Circuit Judge.

The Equitable Life Assurance Society, defendant-appellant, appeals from the order of the district court entering a declaratory judgment in favor of Dr. Stanley Heller, plaintiff-appellee, for the defendant's alleged breach of a disability income insurance contract. The district court found that Dr. Heller was entitled to receive $5,880 per month from Equitable on the insurance contract from March 21, 1984, through February 5, 1986, and thereafter for the time period Dr. Heller was totally disabled. Dr. Heller cross-appeals from the district court's order reducing the total amount of disability benefits payable from Equitable, as well as from the district court's refusal to award taxable costs, including attorneys' fees, under Illinois law. We affirm in part, reverse in part, and remand for further proceedings consistent with this opinion.

I

Dr. Stanley Heller, a physician, is licensed to practice medicine in the state of Illinois. Dr. Heller is a board-certified physician in the field of Cardiovascular Diseases and specializes in invasive cardiology. He was also the Director of the Cardiovascular Catheterization Laboratory [1] at St. Joseph's Hospital, Chicago.

In early 1983 Dr. Heller met with Paul Berlin, an agent for the Equitable Life Assurance Society (Equitable) to discuss simplifying his existing professional disability insurance coverage, for at the time he was insured under six or seven different policies issued by at least two different companies. After evaluating Dr. Heller's existing policies, Mr. Berlin informed Dr. Heller that if he decided to purchase the Equitable disability income policy as offered ($7,000 monthly), he would be required to cancel his other disability policies. [2] At the time Dr. Heller applied for disability coverage in March of 1983, he represented on the application that he had no other disability coverage as he intended to cancel his other disability policy at the time Equitable's coverage took effect. Equitable's policy, issued the following month in April of 1983, provided that Dr. Heller would be paid the sum of $7,000 per month, after a 90–day elimination period incorporated therein. Dr.

1. Dr. Heller's practice, for the most part, consisted of performing invasive catheterization procedures:

"Catheterization of the right and left side of the heart and selective injection of contrast media into the coronary arteries and cardiac chambers during exposure of high-speed x-ray motion pictures (cineangiography) remain the most reliable methods for defining the dynamic physiology and anatomy of the heart in the normal state and a variety of cardiac disorders. When performed after the application of noninvasive or atraumatic techniques of cardiac diagnosis, the great majority of disorders of the heart can be accurately and fully defined and a rational decision made for medical or surgical therapy. In addition, in the past half-decade, cardiac catheterization techniques have been developed which provide therapeutic benefit and are not being applied on a broad scale."

Harrison's Principles of Internal Medicine 888 (11th ed. 1987).

2. Equitable sets the amount of disability coverage available to an insured after considering, *inter alia,* the insured's income and the existence of other disability insurance. In order to prevent over-insuring, insurance companies demand that the applicant disclose all other coverage. Dr. Heller's income was $200,000 per year, and in the absence of other disability insurance he would have been eligible for a monthly disability payment of $8,400 to $8,700 on the basic policy. Dr. Heller made application for only $7,000–per–month coverage on the basic policy, representing on the application that he carried no other disability insurance. In addition to the basic $7,000–per–month payment, he also carried an excess coverage as referred to above.

Heller testified that he directed his office manager to cancel all his other disability policies when the Equitable policy became effective, and "to the best of [his] knowledge," she cancelled the policies. He further testified that it was not until November of 1984, some eight months after his withdrawal from practice, that he was informed by an office employee that he still had an American Motorist Insurance Co. (American Motorists) disability policy in full force and effect.[3]

During the latter quarter of 1983 Dr. Heller developed a painful and crippling condition in his left wrist and hand diagnosed as carpal tunnel syndrome.[4] Dr. Heller testified that as he experienced the debilitating symptoms of the condition in his left wrist and into his hand, he was prevented from practicing in his specialty as an invasive cardiologist after March 20, 1984. Dr. Heller applied for benefit payments on his Equitable disability income policy in late March 1984. The policy issued to Dr. Heller defined "total disability" as follows:

> "Total disability means the complete inability of the Insured, because of injury or sickness, to engage in the Insured's regular occupation, * * * provided, however, the total disability will not be considered to exist for any period during which the Insured is not under the regular care and attendance of a physician. * * *"

Dr. Heller claimed that because he was unable to engage in his profession as an invasive cardiologist as a result of the carpal tunnel syndrome condition, and because he was under the regular care of a physician and had made timely premium payments, he was entitled to disability benefits under the policy. Initially, Equitable made payments pursuant to the disability income provisions [5], but terminated these payments after May 5, 1985, because he (Dr. Heller) refused to undergo carpal tunnel surgery upon Equitable's insistence. As a result of Equitable's refusal to continue payments under the contract, Dr. Heller initiated the present action.

Following a trial to the court, the trial judge found that if Dr. Heller were to undergo surgery to decompress the median nerve in his left wrist, he might very well be relieved of the carpal tunnel syndrome

---

3. The office manager, after being directed by Dr. Heller to cancel the American Motorists policy, negligently failed to do so.

4. "Carpal tunnel syndrome * * * results from compression of the median nerve and the volar aspect of the wrist between the longitudinal tendons of forearm muscles that flex the hand and the transverse superficial carpal ligament. This compression produces parasthesias in the radial-palmar aspect of the hand plus pain in the wrist, and the palm, or sometimes proximal to the compression site of the forearm. Sensory deficit in the palmar aspect of the first three digits and/or weakness of the thumb opposition may follow."

The Merck Manual § 11, at 1384 (14th ed. 1982).

5. Equitable made the following payments to Dr. Heller:

12/05/83–03/04/84 $0.00 90–day elimination period.

03/05/84–12/04/84 $8,200 × 9 = $73,800 ($7,000 + $1,200 supplemental provision = $8,200).

12/05/84–05/04/85 $7,000 × 5 = $35,000.

condition, thus allowing him to return to his practice. After reviewing Equitable's disability policy, the trial judge determined that Dr. Heller was not required to submit to elective surgery because Equitable failed to include the surgery requirement in its professional disability contract. The trial court ordered Equitable to reinstate disability payments, but because evidence disclosed that Dr. Heller continued to be insured under an American Motorists policy, the trial court reformed the contract concluding that Equitable would have reduced disability payments to $5,880 per month if Equitable had knowledge of the existence of the other insurance at the time of the issuance of the policy in question.

On appeal Equitable argues that because Dr. Heller refused to submit to surgery to relieve the debilitating and limiting effects of his carpal tunnel syndrome condition, the trial court erred in finding Dr. Heller to be totally disabled under the terms of the policy. Equitable also asserts that because Dr. Heller misrepresented the nonexistence of the American Motorists disability policy on its application form, the insurance contract should have been rescinded under Illinois law [6] rather than reformed. Thus, because Dr. Heller (1) misrepresented the nonexistence of other insurance; and (2) refused to undergo carpal tunnel surgery, Equitable claims that Dr. Heller is not entitled to disability income payments. Dr. Heller cross-appeals, asserting (1) that he is entitled to the full $7,000 per month Equitable disability payments after the expiration of the five-year American Motorists disability policy; (2) that the trial court failed to award him the $1,200 per month supplemental income as required by the terms of the Equitable policy; and (3) that he is entitled to taxable costs, including attorney's fees, as a result of Equitable's unreasonable and vexatious conduct terminating his disability income payments.

II

Illinois law controls this case as Equitable issued the policy to Dr. Heller in Illinois, the state where Dr. Heller resided and practiced medicine. Our research reveals, and both parties agree, that the Illinois courts have not directly addressed the question of whether a disability income policy providing that the claimant must be "under the regular care and attendance of a physician" requires an insured to submit to surgical treatment for the condition causing the total disability in order to receive benefits. Thus, we rely on the traditional principles of insurance and contract law, long recognized by the Illinois

---

6. "No misrepresentation or false warranty made by the insured * * * in the negotiation for a policy of insurance, * * * shall defeat or avoid the policy or prevent its attaching unless such misrepresentation, false warranty or condition shall have been stated in the policy * * *, or in the written application therefor, of which a copy is attached to or indorsed on the policy, and made a part thereof. No such misrepresentation or false warranty shall defeat or avoid the policy unless it shall have been made with actual intent to deceive or materially affects either the acceptance of the risk or the hazard assumed by the company. * * *"

Ill.Rev.Stat. ch. 73 ¶ 766 (1983).

courts as an appropriate basis for resolving whether the clause conditions coverage on the insured's undergoing surgery. Initially, Illinois courts apply the rule that any ambiguities in the provisions of an insurance policy will be construed against the drafter of the instrument, the insurer, and in favor of the insured, *see, e.g., Burton v. Government Employees' Insurance Company,* 135 Ill.App.3d 723, 90 Ill. Dec. 526, 482 N.E.2d 233 (1985); *Dora Twp. v. Indiana Insurance Company,* 78 Ill.2d 376, 36 Ill.Dec. 341, 400 N.E.2d 921 (1980); however, "where * * * there is no ambiguity, [the courts] will not ignore the *very plain language of the policy." Rock Island Bank v. Time Ins. Co.,* 57 Ill.App.3d 220, 14 Ill.Dec. 719, 720, 372 N.E.2d 998, 999 (1978) (emphasis added). Secondly, insurance policy "[e]xceptions to liability must be expressed in unequivocal language so that it is reasonable to assume the insured understood and accepted these limitations." *Garman v. New York Life Insurance Company,* 501 F.Supp. 51, 52 (N.D.Ill. 1980) (citing *Michigan Mutual Liability Company v. Hoover Brothers Inc.,* 96 Ill.App.2d 238, 237 N.E.2d 754 (1968)).

A reading of the Equitable disability policy discloses that it fails to set forth any limitation of coverage requiring an insured to submit to surgery for treatment of the condition causing the total disability. The policy provides coverage where (1) the insured is prevented from engaging in his or her regular occupation because of sickness or injury and is totally disabled; and (2) that the insured be under "the regular care and attendance of a physician." [7] Equitable does not dispute that Dr. Heller is presently unable to practice as an invasive cardiologist but argues that his failure to submit to surgery for his disabling condition as recommended [8] requires a finding by the Court that he is no longer "under the regular care and attendance of a physician." Therefore, Equitable asserts that Dr. Heller is no longer entitled to disability income benefits.

We reject Equitable's arguments because the language in the policy stating that the claimant must be "under the regular care and attendance of a physician" clearly does not include surgical procedures. Although the policy does not define the parameters of the clause "under the regular care and attendance of a physician," we refuse to add to and construe the policy beyond its clear and obvious language, to require the insured to submit to surgery, if and when surgery is recommended by the physician "rendering regular care and [in] attendance." The language is clear on its face to the average citizen and even more so to a member of the medical profession. We are convinced that under Illinois law the clause "under the regular care and attendance" means just what it says, namely, that the insured is obligated to periodically consult and be examined by his or her treating physician at intervals to be determined by the physician. Clearly the language does

7. Physician is defined in the policy: "Physician means a legally qualified physician other than the Insured."

8. Dr. Heller was examined by and consulted with a number of doctors, and at least two recommended surgery.

not condition disability payments on the insured's undergoing surgery if recommended by the physician rendering "regular care and [in] attendance." We refuse to indulge in judicial activism and condition coverage under the contract on the insured's undergoing surgery, when the insurer failed to provide such a conditional clause in the policy.

The clause, "under the regular care and attendance of a physician," was not intended to allow the insurer to scrutinize, determine, and direct the method of treatment the claimant receives. We are convinced that the purpose of the clause requiring the insured to be "under the regular care and attendance of a physician" is to determine that the claimant is actually disabled, *see, e.g., Russell v. Prudential Insurance Company of America*, 437 F.2d 602, 607 (5th Cir.1971), is not malingering, and to prevent fraudulent claims.

The insurance industry by its very nature offers insurance coverage on a non-negotiable basis, and consumers are unable to participate in the drafting of the language or the terms of the policy. Case law and fairness require that ambiguities in insurance policies be construed against the drafter of the policy, the insurance company.

In the absence of a clear, unequivocal and specific contractual requirement that the insured is obligated to undergo surgery to attempt to minimize his disability, we refuse to order the same. To hold otherwise and to impose such a requirement would, in effect, enlarge the terms of the policy beyond those clearly defined in the policy agreed to by the parties. *See, e.g., John Hancock Mutual Life Insurance Company v. Spurgeon*, 175 Tenn. 319, 134 S.W.2d 155 (1939).[9] Thus, under the terms of this disability policy, Dr. Heller is not required to undergo surgery for treatment of his carpal tunnel syndrome condition before he receives disability income payments.

In a feeble attempt for support Equitable reaches out and tries to rely on the Illinois worker's compensation statute for support. The applicable statute, they point out, provides:

9. Equitable asserts that carpal tunnel surgery is "common and of a minor, low-risk variety," and urges this court to apply the reasoning in *Casson v. Nationwide Insurance Co.*, 455 A.2d 361 (Del.Supp.1982), to Dr. Heller's situation. In *Casson*, the court held that the insured must submit to reasonable *medical treatment* if the disability is correctable; thus Equitable asserts that Dr. Heller should be required to undergo minor surgery that, as the district court found, might relieve the disability. But the district court made no finding as to whether the carpal tunnel surgery was "major or minor" and rejected Equitable's argument because the policy did not include an express condition requiring the insured to submit to surgery and noting that surgery is not equivalent to medical treatment, and vice versa. We agree with the district court and direct Equitable's attention to Appleman, Insurance Law and Practice § 656, noting:

"A slightly different situation is presented where the insurer requests the insured to undergo an operation to clear up the difficulty. The better rule is to the effect that the insured, in the absence of a specific policy provision so declaring, is under no obligation whatsoever to the insurer to help it rid itself of its obligations, particularly where an operation is demanded. Accordingly, the insured may refuse to undergo an operation and the insurer must continue to make disability payments to him."

Further, *Casson*, on which Equitable relies, notes that the majority view does not even require the insured to minimize his disability with *medical treatment* absent a specific contractual requirement, much less require an insured to submit to surgery.

> "If any employee * * * shall refuse to submit to such medical, surgical, or hospital treatment as is reasonably essential to promote his recovery, the commission may, in its discretion, reduce or suspend the compensation of any such injured employee."

Ill.Rev.Stat. ch. 48 ¶ 138.19(d) (1985). Equitable, without citing any Illinois authority, requests that we interpret the policy clause "under the regular care and attendance of a physician" to require an insured to submit to surgery and thus incorporate Illinois worker's compensation theories regarding an employee's duty to undergo surgery into this private insurance contract. Equitable simply concludes that "there is no reason to believe Illinois Courts would refuse to imply submission to medical treatment [which in this case is surgery] as part of the requirement to be under the 'care and attendance of a physician.' " App.Br. at 18. We do not agree with Equitable's speculative assertion because the disability policy, unlike the worker's compensation statute, failed to even imply, much less require, that the insured submit to a surgical procedure. We remind Equitable that the policy is not the product of a state-enacted worker's compensation act passed in a legislative arena, the basic purpose of which is to provide prompt relief to injured employees. Rather, Dr. Heller entered into a mutually binding private insurance contract for professional disability insurance with Equitable and obligated himself to pay a substantial bi-annual premium. In the absence of an express provision obligating the insured to undergo surgery, we refuse to place such a requirement upon the insured.[10]

---

10. We will not now consider what might be reasonably essential to promote an insured's recovery where, as here, the insurer fails to include any provision requiring an insured to submit to surgery. But we note that Illinois law "recognizes that consideration must be given to 'divergent personalities, beliefs and fears' in gauging the reasonableness of a claimant's refusal to submit to surgery." *Allied Chemical Corp. v. Industrial Commission of Ill.,* 140 Ill.App.3d 73, 94 Ill.Dec. 604, 607, 488 N.E.2d 603, 606 (1986) (citing *Rockford Clutch v. Industrial Com.,* 34 Ill.2d 240, 215 N.E.2d 209 (1966). In the case at bar, Dr. Perlik, a neurologist at Michael Reese Hospital and the plaintiff's principal treating physician testified as to the possible adverse side effects of the surgery in question as follows:

"Among the complications are as follows: *Number one,* you can cut the palmer cutaneous nerve * * * [and] * * * lose sensation on the palm of your hand. *Number two,* * * * you can develop a thick hypertrophic scar, because you have to go across the wrist. *Number three,* if you are not careful, because there are twenty-nine anatomical [sic] variations of the motor enervation of the median nerve, if a sugeon [sic] is not careful, he can easily cut the motor branch of the median nerve, which goes into the thumb, * * * *[N]umber [four],* and the most common complication associated with carpal tunnel, is incomplete release; and, therefore, people who have gone through surgery and have woken up with the same problem they began with; *[N]umber [five],* you can develop infection; *[N]umber [six],* you can develop adhesions on the synovium, * * *; *[N]umber [seven],* if you explore the carpal tunnel you can develop, because of the nature of the small area that you are working at, if you feel you need to lysis the nerve, you can develop bleeding within the carpal tunnel. If that occurs then you end up right back with the same problem you began with, because that is a median entrapment more distal in the hand. And another uncommon complication is a syndrome known as 'sympathetical reflex distrophy', which is also known as 'causalia', which is a poorly understood but well-known disorder of the nerve, the muscle, the bone and the blood vessel of the hands, which is

Lastly, Equitable argues that the "principle of fairness and good faith, a policy of motivating persons to correct rather than accept physical disabilities," necessitates that an insured suffering from causes that disabled him, avail himself of all reasonable means and remedies to relieve his disability, including surgery. Once again, we reject Equitable's argument. The record clearly establishes that Dr. Heller acted in good faith. Initially, Dr. Heller properly reported his disability to Equitable and consulted with and remained under the regular care of his physician as required under the policy. Further, at Equitable's request, Dr. Heller acquiesced to an examination performed by two specialists selected by Equitable, one a hand surgeon and the other a neurologist, at the Mayo Clinic in Rochester, Minnesota. Additionally, there is nothing in the record to establish that Dr. Heller failed to provide Equitable with any and/or all supplemental information required. The record further demonstrates that after Dr. Heller's condition was diagnosed and before he filed a claim for disability payments, Dr. Heller was forced to reduce his case load beginning in December 1983 to March 1984, and thereafter was forced to withdraw from practice.[11] The trial court found that Dr. Heller fulfilled his obligations under the policy; we agree and hold that Dr. Heller did all that was required of him under the terms of the Equitable disability policy.

However, Equitable insists that the insured, as a party to an insurance contract, has a good faith "duty to cure his disability if he can do so without reasonable risk and pain to himself."[12] Equitable ignores the fact that many insureds like the plaintiff-appellee, choose

characterized by a cold, blue, husky hand, with detractable, persisting pain, that comes about with just the slightest degree of movement; the mechanism for that is very unclear, nevertheless, it is a described complication of that surgery."

Under these circumstances, even if the Equitable policy contained an express term requiring the insured to undergo "reasonably essential" surgery, we seriously doubt that Dr. Heller's refusal to undergo surgery would be unreasonable. This is especially the case because the carpal tunnel syndrome condition can and does frequently reoccur even after the patient undergoes surgery.

11. It is significant to point out that Dr. Heller received treatment for his carpal tunnel syndrome condition. Dr. Lounghran, an orthopedic surgeon at St. Joseph Hospital, injected a steroid into Dr. Heller's wrist, attempting to minimize the disability and allow him to return to practice.

12. Equitable asserts that:

"[t]he person, such as Dr. Heller, who 'clings' to his disability must constantly guard against becoming better. He must always choose the cringing, somewhat masochistic method of dealing with the disability. These are not characteristics the law should encourage and reward." App.Br. at 20. "Masochistic" can be defined as "a tendency to take pleasure in physical or mental suffering inflicted on one by oneself." *Webster's Third New International Dictionary* (1981). The record is barren of evidence that even indicates, much less establishes, that Dr. Heller's method of dealing with his disability was "masochistic," thus Equitable's assertion is necessarily inapt. Furthermore, Equitable never made this outrageous argument to the trial court. We point out that there is a substantial difference between (1) a self-inflicted injury, and (2) a disability not caused by the individual, but who simply refuses to endure the risk, trouble, expense and often trying experiences incident to medical treatment. In the case of a self-inflicted disability, the act itself is contrary to public policy, regardless of the existence of insurance. As we pointed out, Dr. Heller's course of conduct did not exhibit any trace of bad faith, much less indicate the injury was self-inflicted. We caution counsel that in the future it should refrain from

not to undergo surgery because of the accompanying risks of infection, transfusion (hepatitis), bleeding, motor enervation of the median nerve, adhesions, scar tissue, possible anesthetic shock, trauma, anxiety, and even reoccurrence of the carpal tunnel syndrome condition. We are convinced that under Illinois law an insured is not required to undergo these risks in the absence of a specific contractual requirement. Furthermore, it seems very evident that because of these risks and other risks in the majority of surgical procedures, courts have wisely adopted the doctrine of informed consent.

Although we might not choose to follow the same course of conduct and path of reasoning as Dr. Heller,[13] there is no moral, much less legal obligation or compelling reason, to second guess an insured's, and in this case Dr. Heller's, decision to forego surgery. The insurance company seeking to condition coverage on its insureds' acquiescence to undergo surgery to minimize the extent of their disabilities, as well as the financial loss to the insurer, need only incorporate a specific requirement [14] to that effect in the policy, and we would not hesitate to enforce the same. On the other hand, insurers who fail to include this express surgical contractual requirement, and who refuse to cover an insured after entering into a binding and enforceable agreement after accepting substantial premiums, in circumstances such as those before us, cause problems not only for the insured, but for the insurance industry as well. Insurance companies, members of a service industry, must recognize that, like their insureds, they have corresponding duties and obligations under the policy and must conduct themselves accordingly instead of attempting to rely on the courts to correct their own deficiencies in underwriting and/or careless policy drafting. * * *

The judgment of the district court is affirmed in part and reversed in part, and the case is remanded to the district court for further proceedings consistent with this opinion.

Notes and Questions

1. *An Implied Duty to Mitigate?* Would it have been inappropriate for the court to hold that the insured had an implied duty to mitigate his losses? Did the court imply that there might be such a duty when it distinguished the availability of medical treatment for an

inferring such ridiculous and malicious allegations of this nature without one scintilla of support.

13. We note that Dr. Heller has apparently abandoned his profession as a surgeon to pursue a new career in law.

14. For example, an insurance company might include a provision in the policy for submitting claims involving refusals to undergo surgical and medical procedures to a panel of experts. Each party could choose a board-certified specialist in the relevant area of medical expertise required to sit on the panel, and the third panelist, also independent and board-certified, could be chosen by the Dean of a recognized medical school in the area. The specialist would be empaneled to determine the extent and the treatment of the disability and decide whether the insured should submit to surgery. The panel's decision would then be binding on the parties if so written into the contract with specificity.

ailment from the availability of surgical treatment? Are the problems entailed in deciding when it would be reasonable to seek medical (or surgical) treatment too great an obstacle to such an approach, or would they closely resemble tort defendants' frequently raised defense of plaintiffs' failure to mitigate?

2. *Under the Regular Care and Attendance of a Physician.* Under what circumstances should the requirement that an insured be under the regular care of a physician be read as an exclusive evidentiary condition of coverage? Might this clause, like the requirement that the insured be unable to engage in any form of work in *Moots,* create undue moral hazard—but for health insurers, rather than the disability insurers who include it in their policies?

5. Preexisting Conditions

One of the most common provisions in health and disability insurance is an exclusion of coverage of losses resulting from conditions that existed prior to the issuance of the policy. The following illustrates the problems that arise in meshing the language of such exclusions with the concern that lies behind them—the effort to combat adverse selection.

HOLUB v. HOLY FAMILY SOCIETY
Appellate Court of Illinois, 1987.
164 Ill.App.3d 970, 115 Ill.Dec. 894, 518 N.E.2d 419.

Justice LORENZ delivered the opinion of the court:

This is an appeal from an order which granted summary judgment in favor of the plaintiff. The defendant raises the following issues on appeal: (1) whether summary judgment was properly granted; and (2) whether, at the hearing on defendant's motion to reconsider the granting of summary judgment, the trial court tried issues of fact rather than determining if issues of fact existed.

We affirm.

The following facts are pertinent to our disposition. In March 1982, plaintiff filed an application with defendant for health insurance coverage. In this application she disclosed the fact that she had a hypertensive condition, yet she denied that she suffered any other preexisting disorder. The policy excluded coverage of loss resulting from preexisting conditions. Preexisting conditions were defined as,

> "any condition that was diagnosed or treated by a physician within 24 months prior to the effective date of the coverage or produced symptoms within 12 months prior to the effective date of coverage that would have caused an ordinary prudent person to seek medical diagnosis or treatment."

On March 20, 1982, the comprehensive medical coverage policy was issued to plaintiff subject to an exception rider which excluded coverage of loss related to her hypertension.

On October 4, 1982, plaintiff was admitted to Oak Park Hospital complaining of severe abdominal pain. She was diagnosed as having cancer of the rectosigmoid and a colostomy was performed by Dr. William Ashley. Plaintiff remained hospitalized until October 29, 1982.

On November 15, 1982, plaintiff notified defendant of her claim for expenses incurred as a result of her illness. In processing her claim, defendant reviewed a report made by Dr. William Ashley based upon a medical history he had taken from plaintiff prior to the surgery. Plaintiff, at that time, informed Dr. Ashley that she had been under the care of Dr. Edward Klitenick for hypertension and was seen by him every four months for routine examinations. It was during the course of one of those examinations, on October 27, 1980, that plaintiff mentioned that she had experienced blood in her stool but that it had completely subsided without treatment. Dr. Klitenick then performed a rectal examination. The results of that examination were negative and he assured her that there was nothing wrong. Again, on July 27, 1981, in another routine visit to Dr. Klitenick, plaintiff mentioned that since her first check-up, she had had some loose bowel movements. Dr. Klitenick performed a rectal examination, the results of which were negative, and he assured plaintiff that nothing was wrong. He put plaintiff on a bland diet and prescribed combid spansules. According to Dr. Klitenick, he generally prescribed this medication when a patient complained of intestinal disorders such as having the flu.

Based upon a review of plaintiff's medical history and reports, defendant denied coverage under plaintiff's policy and disclaimed all liability on her claim. Defendant claimed that plaintiff failed to disclose a preexisting condition, of which she was aware, on her application for insurance thereby inducing defendant to issue a policy without benefit of a full and complete medical history.

On August 18, 1983, plaintiff filed a complaint to recover these expenses. In response, defendant filed an answer and affirmative defense. On February 27, 1986, plaintiff filed a motion for summary judgment supported by the affidavits of herself and Dr. Klitenick. The motion for summary judgment was granted. Defendant filed a motion to reconsider and plaintiff filed a response. After oral argument, defendant's motion was denied. It is from that order which defendant appeals.

OPINION

Plaintiff's complaint sought to recover payment of her medical expenses relating to her surgery for cancer of the rectum pursuant to her policy with defendant. Defendant denied payment on the grounds that plaintiff knowingly and with the intent to defraud defendant failed to disclose to defendant that she had been "treated for previous abdominal disorders" and failed to disclose this "preexisting condition." The issue, therefore, is whether plaintiff knew or should have known, at the time she filed her application for health insurance, that she had any disease of the rectum.

Defendant asserts that because rectal examinations are not ordinarily part of a routine doctor visit for hypertension, a reasonable person might infer that Dr. Klitenick's conduct amounted to treatment. Defendant notes that while the affidavit of Dr. Klitenick, filed in support of plaintiff's motion for summary judgment, indicates that he never "treated or observed" plaintiff for any disease of the rectum, he fails to acknowledge that he prescribed combid spansules and a bland diet. Specifically, in his deposition testimony, Dr. Klitenick stated that he prescribed medications and advised plaintiff to stay on a bland diet in response to her complaint about an intestinal disorder. Defendant asserts that the statement in his affidavit contradicts his deposition testimony and this, by itself, raises factual questions sufficient to defeat plaintiff's motion for summary judgment.

We disagree. Plaintiff's affidavit unequivocally states that she had no knowledge of any such illness. Also, the affidavit of Dr. Klitenick establishes that prior to October of 1982 he had never informed plaintiff that he was treating or observing her for any disease of the rectum. Defendant has offered nothing to contradict these statements. Summary judgment should be granted if there exists no genuine issue as to any material fact. (*Kolakowski v. Voris* (1980), 83 Ill.2d 388, 47 Ill.Dec. 392, 415 N.E.2d 397.) Issues of fact must be genuine and must be supported by evidentiary facts supporting the position of the opponent of the motion. (*Carruthers v. B.C. Christopher & Co.* (1974), 57 Ill.2d 376, 313 N.E.2d 457.) The purported contradiction in Dr. Klitenick's affidavit and deposition testimony is nothing more than an illustration that plaintiff was unaware of any disease. Whether the doctor "treated" her by prescribing a bland diet and combid spansules is not the issue. At no time prior to her application for insurance did Dr. Klitenick inform the plaintiff that he had diagnosed or was treating her for any disease of the rectum. A rectal examination and the combination of combid spansules and a bland diet do not impute knowledge of the presence of a disease. The issue is, as previously stated, whether plaintiff knew or should have known that she had any such disease.

It has long been the law in this State that an insurance company cannot expect or require an applicant to disclose information concerning her health which is beyond the knowledge of an ordinary layman, when she has not been given such information by her doctor. (*Logan v. Allstate Life Insurance Company* (1974), 19 Ill.App.3d 656, 312 N.E.2d 416.) Here, plaintiff had told her doctor of a single episode of blood in her stool almost 17 months prior to her application. She received no treatment. Again 8 months prior to her application, she reported loose bowel movements to her doctor. On each occasion Dr. Klitenick performed a rectal examination, the results of which were negative. He told her that she had nothing to worry about. In response to her complaint of loose bowel movements he prescribed a bland diet and combid spansules. In the opinion of Dr. Klitenick, he was not treating or observing plaintiff for a disease of the colon or rectum in 1980 or 1981. As such, it cannot be said that she had knowledge of any preexisting condition.

In support of the motion for reconsideration defendant submitted the affidavit of Dr. Gerald Atlas wherein he stated that he had treated many bowel disorders of the type suffered by plaintiff; that the blood in plaintiff's stool and her "chronic" loose bowel movements could constitute a disease of the intestines and other internal organs; and that the prescription of a bland diet and combid spansules in July of 1981 by Dr. Klitenick constituted a medical treatment of such a disorder. Defendant asserts that the Atlas affidavit directly contradicts the affidavit submitted by Dr. Klitenick. Defendant therefore concludes that a material issue of fact exists as to whether plaintiff was aware of the symptoms of the condition for which she ultimately received treatment.

Defendant's argument is illogical. Dr. Atlas cannot testify as to whether plaintiff reasonably relied upon the assurances of her doctor that she was in good health. Whether Dr. Klitenick misdiagnosed plaintiff's condition is not at issue. Consequently, Dr. Atlas's affidavit is wholly irrelevant.

Based on the foregoing we affirm the trial court's granting of summary judgment in favor of plaintiff.

AFFIRMED.

Notes and Questions

1. *The Function of the Exclusion.* An exclusion of coverage for losses resulting from preexisting conditions is very common in both health and disability insurance policies. The obvious function of the exclusion is to combat adverse selection. In light of this function, were the time limits in the policy at issue in *Holub* excessive?

2. *Misrepresentation or Exclusion?* The court in *Holub* seemed more concerned with the insured's knowledge or lack thereof of her preexisting condition than with the exclusion itself. In so doing the court seemed either to be reading an additional pro-insured requirement into the exclusion, or dealing with an independent defense—i.e., that even if the exclusion were inapplicable, the insured had knowingly concealed a material fact when she applied for coverage. Given the language of the exclusion, could the insured in such a situation persuasively argue that it alone establishes which pre-existing exclusions are material?

C. LIABILITY FOR BAD–FAITH BREACH

KEWIN v. MASSACHUSETTS MUTUAL LIFE INSURANCE COMPANY

Supreme Court of Michigan, 1980.
409 Mich. 401, 295 N.W.2d 50.

KAVANAGH, Justice.

This dispute arises out of non-payment of benefits alleged to be due under insurance policies issued to the plaintiff by the defendant. The defendant appealed from a jury verdict rendered on March 29, 1976, in Genesee Circuit Court. The Court of Appeals affirmed in part and reversed in part, 79 Mich.App. 639, 263 N.W.2d 258 (1977). This Court granted leave to appeal and cross appeal limited to the following issues:

"(1) What causes of action and damage remedies are available to an insured who alleges that he has suffered mental anguish as a result of his insurance company's bad-faith refusal to honor a valid claim; [and]

"(2) What causes of action and elements of damage were properly pled by the plaintiff"?

On September 15, 1972, the defendant, Massachusetts Mutual Life Insurance Company, issued two policies of insurance to the plaintiff, Harland Kewin. One policy provided for disability income protection insurance and the other for life insurance. It is the alleged breach of the former policy that is of concern in this appeal. Under the terms of the policy, the plaintiff was entitled to benefits of $500 per month, after a thirty-day waiting period, if he became disabled from performing substantially all of the duties of his usual occupation.

On December 2, 1972, the plaintiff suffered a severe injury to his right knee when he was involved in a motorcycle accident in Florida. After the plaintiff filed a claim for benefits based on this injury, the defendant informed him of the need for a monthly doctor's report substantiating the disability. To facilitate the procedure and to minimize the inconvenience to the plaintiff, it was suggested by Mr. Pemberton, a claims representative employed by the defendant, that the plaintiff visit a local doctor at the defendant's expense. Thereafter, the plaintiff visited Dr. Harris, who forwarded a monthly report to the defendant beginning in March of 1973.

Prior to this conversation between Mr. Pemberton and the plaintiff, the defendant engaged Retail Credit Corporation on January 3, 1973, to do an investigation and report concerning the leg injury claim. That report was received by the defendant on January 15, 1973, and was followed by others which detailed the employment and other activities engaged in by the plaintiff. The report indicated that the plaintiff walked on crutches but was anticipating full-time employment at a Flint realty company as soon as he was able.

The defendant began payment of the monthly benefits due the plaintiff on February 9, 1973, which payment was for the month of January. Late payments for the months of February and March followed. On May 2, 1973, the plaintiff talked on the telephone with Mr. Pemberton and one other representative of the defendant concerning a possible settlement of the plaintiff's claim.

It was agreed during this conversation that the plaintiff would accept $500 for the April benefit payment already due him, plus an advance payment of $1,000, the equivalent of two months' benefits. In exchange the plaintiff agreed to waive any rights to further benefits until October 1, 1973, and further, waive his rights under the policy to forego payment of premiums during that period. Pursuant to this conversation, the defendant prepared two checks, one for $500 and the other for $1,000, and sent them to the plaintiff along with a letter detailing the agreement. The plaintiff negotiated each check.

The plaintiff, in November of 1973, requested and was sent additional claim forms, but never returned them to the defendant. No further correspondence was had between the parties until the plaintiff filed suit in August of 1974.

A jury trial was held, and a verdict in favor of the plaintiff was returned. The jury awarded $16,500 in benefits under the disability insurance contract; $798.40 as agreed cash value of the related life insurance policy; $75,000 for mental or emotional distress; and $50,000 for exemplary damages. The defendant's motions for a new trial, remittitur, and judgment notwithstanding the verdict were denied, and a claim of appeal was filed in the Court of Appeals.

On November 21, 1977, the Court of Appeals held that a disability insurance contract is a contract involving matters of mental concern and solicitude and that, upon proper pleading and proof, mental distress damages are recoverable for breach of the contract. The Court also held that the mental distress damages and exemplary damages awarded by the jury in this case were for the same mental anguish, and accordingly reversed the award of $75,000 for mental or emotional distress. Finally, the Court held that the plaintiff's complaint was insufficiently specific to support either a claim in tort for intentional infliction of emotional distress or a claim in contract for mental anguish damages, but that it did support a recovery of exemplary damages.

The parties do not dispute that a cause of action in contract arises upon a bad-faith breach of a disability insurance contract. Their positions differ sharply, however, on the question of whether and under what circumstances mental distress and exemplary damages are recoverable as a consequence of such a breach.

Under the rule of *Hadley v. Baxendale*, 9 Exch. 341; 156 Eng.Rep. 145 (1854), the damages recoverable for breach of contract are those that arise naturally from the breach or those that were in the contemplation of the parties at the time the contract was made. 5 Corbin,

Contracts, § 1007. Application of this principle in the commercial contract situation generally results in a limitation of damages to the monetary value of the contract had the breaching party fully performed under it. Thus, it is generally held that damages for mental distress cannot be recovered in an action for breach of a contract.

There are exceptions to the general rule limiting the recovery for breach of contract. We are asked to apply an exception recognized in *Stewart v. Rudner,* 349 Mich. 459, 84 N.W.2d 816 (1957), to this case involving disability insurance. The plaintiff in *Stewart* brought suit on a breach of contract theory against the defendant doctor. The defendant had promised to deliver plaintiff's child by Caesarean section, but did not do so. It was asserted that as a result of the breach of the agreement, the plaintiff's child was stillborn.

In writing for four members of this Court, Justice Talbot Smith wrote to allow recovery for mental distress:

> "When we have a contract concerned not with trade and commerce but with life and death, not with profit but with elements of personality, not with pecuniary aggrandizement but with matters of mental concern and solicitude, then a breach of duty with respect to such contracts will inevitably and necessarily result in mental anguish, pain and suffering. In such cases the parties may reasonably be said to have contracted with reference to the payment of damages therefor in event of breach. Far from being outside the contemplation of the parties they are an integral and inseparable part of it."

The nature and object of the agreement justified the treatment accorded it in *Stewart.* A contract to perform a Caesarean section is not a commercial contract in which pecuniary interests are most important. Rather, such a contract involves "rights we cherish, dignities we respect, emotions recognized by all as both sacred and personal." *Stewart,* 469, 84 N.W.2d 823. Where such interests are invaded by breach of a contract meant to secure their protection, mental distress is a particularly likely result. Flowing naturally from the breach, these injuries to the emotions are foreseeable and must be compensated despite the difficulty of monetary estimation.

Insurance contracts for disability income protection do not come within the reach of *Stewart.* Such contracts are commercial in nature; they are agreements to pay a sum of money upon the occurrence of a specific event, *Secor v. Pioneer Foundry Co.,* 20 Mich.App. 30, 35, 173 N.W.2d 780 (1969); 14 Michigan Law & Practice, Insurance, § 71, p. 50. The damage suffered upon the breach of the agreement is capable of adequate compensation by reference to the terms of the contract. We recognize that breach of the insurance contract, as with almost any agreement, results in some annoyance and vexation. But recovery for those consequences is generally not allowed, absent evidence that they were within the contemplation of the parties at the time the contract was made. 22 Am.Jur.2d, Damages, § 64, p. 97. See, also, *Scottish*

Union & National Insurance Co. v. Bejcy, 201 F.2d 163, 166 (CA 6, 1953).

* * *

For the above reasons, we hold that a disability income protection insurance policy contract is a commercial contract, the mere breach of which does not give rise to a right to recover damages for mental distress. The damages recoverable are those damages that arise naturally from the breach, or which can reasonably be said to have been in contemplation of the parties at the time the contract was made. Absent proof of such contemplation, the damages recoverable do not include compensation for mental anguish.

In Michigan, exemplary damages are recoverable as compensation to the plaintiff, not as punishment of the defendant. *Ten Hopen v. Walker,* 96 Mich. 236, 240, 55 N.W. 657 (1893); *McChesney v. Wilson,* 132 Mich. 252, 258, 93 N.W. 627 (1903). Our review of the precedent indicates that those cases which permit recovery of exemplary damages as an element of damages involve tortious conduct on the part of the defendant. See, e.g. *McFadden v. Tate,* 350 Mich. 84, 85 N.W.2d 181 (1957) (assault and battery); *Scripps v. Reilly,* 38 Mich. 10 (1878) (libel); *Welch v. Ware,* 32 Mich. 77 (1875) (assault and battery). An award of exemplary damages is considered proper if it compensates a plaintiff for the "humiliation, sense of outrage, and indignity" resulting from injuries "maliciously, wilfully and wantonly" inflicted by the defendant. *McFadden, supra,* 350 Mich. 89, 85 N.W.2d 181. The theory of these cases is that the reprehensibility of the defendant's conduct both intensifies the injury and justifies the award of exemplary damages as compensation for the harm done the plaintiff's feelings.

In cases involving only a breach of contract, however, the general rule is that exemplary damages are not recoverable. 9 Michigan Law & Practice, Damages, § 91, p. 88; 22 Am.Jur.2d, Damages, § 245, p. 337. Just as with that denying damages for mental distress, the theory underlying the denial of exemplary damages in breach of contract cases is that the plaintiff is adequately compensated when damages are awarded by reference only to the terms of the contract. One exception to the rule was discussed by Professor Corbin in the following terms:

> "The damages that are called punitive in breach of promise cases can generally be properly regarded as *compensatory. They are given as compensation for kinds of harm that cannot easily be estimated in terms of money.* In this respect, the injury caused by breach of promise of marriage has much in common with those injuries that are caused in cases of tort. It is equally obvious that the injuries suffered in breach of promise cases include much that is *not* in common with those that are inflicted by the breach of a commercial bargain. Therefore, the courts have not applied the same measure of recovery; and there is no reason for a supposed rule that would require them to do so." 5 Corbin, *supra,* § 1077, p. 442 (emphasis added).

In the commercial contract situation, unlike the tort and marriage contract actions, the injury which arises under a breach is a financial one, susceptible of accurate pecuniary estimation. The wrong suffered by the plaintiff is the same, whether the breaching party acts with a completely innocent motive or in bad faith. *Durfee v. Newkirk*, 83 Mich. 522, 527, 47 N.W. 351 (1890); *Caradonna v. Thorious*, 17 Mich. App. 41, 169 N.W.2d 179 (1969).

[margin note: Commercial breach is easy to assimilate & assess.]

We hold that, absent allegation and proof of tortious conduct existing independent of the breach, see, e.g., *Harbaugh v. Citizens Telephone Co.*, 190 Mich. 421, 157 N.W. 32 (1916), exemplary damages may not be awarded in common-law actions brought for breach of a commercial contract.[1] * * *

[margin note: exemplary damages may not be awarded in common-law actions]

Plaintiff implies and *amicus curiae* policyholders argue that he has pleaded and this Court should recognize an independent tort based on bad-faith breach of an insurance contract. Plaintiff cites *Harbaugh*, wherein this Court recognized that the same state of facts establishing a breach of contract might also establish a cause of action in tort. *Harbaugh, supra*, 426–427, 157 N.W. 32. *Amicus curiae* policyholders direct our attention to *Gruenberg v. Aetna Insurance Co.*, 9 Cal.3d 566, 108 Cal.Rptr. 480, 510 P.2d 1032 (1973), where the California court recognized a cause of action in tort for the insurer's breach of an implied duty of good faith fair dealing and allowed recovery of emotional distress damages.

Harbaugh involved a breach of a duty imposed by statute upon the defendant. The duty existed independent of and apart from the contractual undertaking. The instant case, in contrast, parallels more closely the situation in *Hart v. Ludwig*, 347 Mich. 559, 79 N.W.2d 895 (1956):

> "We have simply the violation of a promise to perform the agreement. The only duty, other than that voluntarily assumed in the contract to which the defendant was subject, was his duty to perform his promise in a careful and skillful manner without risk of harm to others, the violation of which is not alleged. What we are left with is defendant's failure to complete his contracted-for performance. This is not a duty imposed by the law upon all, the violation of which gives rise to a tort action, but a duty arising out of the intentions of the parties themselves and owed only to those specific individuals to whom the promise runs. A tort action will not lie."

The plaintiff in this case alleged and proved no more than the failure of the defendant to discharge its obligations under the disability insurance contract.

We decline to follow the California court and to declare the mere bad-faith breach of an insurance indemnity contract an independent

[margin note: mere bad faith breach independent tort claim]

---

1. We do not address a question not raised: Whether compensation for attorney's fees or other items of pecuniary loss caused by a breach of the insurer's contractual obligation to process claims in good faith might be recoverable if properly pleaded.

and separately actionable tort and to thereby open the door to recovery for mental pain and suffering caused by breach of a commercial contract.

Accordingly we affirm the decision of the Court of Appeals reversing the award for mental or emotional distress; we reverse the decision affirming the award of exemplary damages and set such award aside; and we affirm the decision of the Court of Appeals affirming the awards of $16,500 for breach of the disability insurance contract and $798.40 for breach of the companion life insurance policy.

No costs, neither party having prevailed in full.

COLEMAN, C.J., FITZGERALD, Deputy C.J., and RYAN, LEVIN and MOODY, JJ., concur.

SILBERG v. CALIFORNIA LIFE INSURANCE COMPANY

Supreme Court of California, 1974.
11 Cal.3d 452, 113 Cal.Rptr. 711, 521 P.2d 1103.

MOSK, Justice.

We are called upon to interpret the provisions of an insurance policy issued to plaintiff by defendant company and the scope of defendant's duty to make payment thereunder. The policy provided that defendant would pay the cost of hospital care, including surgeon's fees, up to a limit of $5,000, with $100 deductible, and there was an exclusion for losses caused by injuries for which compensation was payable under any workmen's compensation law.

In July 1966, while the policy was in effect, plaintiff was seriously injured and as a result ultimately incurred $6,900 in medical charges. Defendant carrier refused to make any payments under the policy because plaintiff had filed a claim for workmen's compensation benefits on account of the injury. The company insisted there could be no final determination as to its liability under the policy until the workmen's compensation proceeding was concluded. At the same time, the workmen's compensation carrier denied liability because of defendant's questionable employment status. The compensation aspect was ultimately determined on April 30, 1968—nearly two years after the injury—when a compromise and release was approved by the Workmen's Compensation Appeals Board, settling the case for $3,700; of this recovery $1,100 was in payment of hospital bills through a lien filed by one hospital, the balance of $5,800 in hospital bills remaining unpaid. Defendant denied liability under the policy on the ground that the $3,700 paid under the compensation settlement rendered the exclusion applicable.

Plaintiff filed this action, alleging two causes of action: the first sought a declaration that defendant was liable under the policy, and the second sought damages for physical and mental distress. It was alleged that defendant was guilty of fraud, bad faith and malicious and oppressive conduct, and that plaintiff was entitled to both compensatory and punitive damages.

Initially, the trial court, sitting without a jury, determined in the declaratory relief count that the policy was ambiguous and that, therefore, defendant was obligated under the policy to pay $4,900 of plaintiff's medical costs (the policy limits minus the $100 deductible). A jury found for plaintiff on the second cause of action, and awarded $75,000 compensatory damages and $500,000 punitive damages. After judgment on the verdict was rendered, the trial court granted defendant's motion for a new trial on the grounds of insufficiency of the evidence to support the verdict, errors in law, and excessive damages. Plaintiff appeals from the order granting the new trial, and defendant cross-appeals from the judgment. (Cal.Rules of Court, rule 3(c).)

The major issues involved in plaintiff's appeal from the order granting a new trial are whether the trial court abused its discretion in concluding that the evidence was insufficient to support a finding defendant was guilty of bad faith justifying an award of compensatory damages, or of fraud or oppression justifying an award of exemplary damages. We determine that the evidence demonstrates as a matter of law that defendant's failure to pay benefits under the policy constituted bad faith but that the trial court did not abuse its discretion in ruling that the evidence was insufficient to support an award of exemplary damages. In defendant's appeal from the judgment, our inquiry focuses primarily upon whether the trial court properly found in the first cause of action that the policy was ambiguous. We conclude the trial court judgment was correct in this regard.

Plaintiff's Appeal

At the time of the accident, plaintiff was 38 years old and the father of two minor children. He owned and operated a dry cleaning business, and earned a monthly income of $500. Plaintiff's landlord owned a laundromat adjacent to the dry cleaning premises. Although not entirely clear from the record, plaintiff apparently agreed with his landlord that, in return for a reduction in rent, he would perform incidental services in connection with the laundromat operation. On July 17, 1966, plaintiff noticed smoke in the laundromat area, and in order to locate its source he climbed onto a washing machine. The glass in the lid of the machine broke; plaintiff's right foot fell into the machine, which was in operation at the time. His foot was severed at the ankle but was surgically restored later that day.

Upon his admission plaintiff advised the hospital that he was insured by defendant, and he notified defendant of the accident within a few days. Defendant immediately sent a routine inquiry to an investigative bureau to determine whether plaintiff had ever previously sought insurance benefits. In the claim forms subsequently filed by plaintiff, he declared that he was self-employed and that he had instituted proceedings to obtain workmen's compensation benefits.

Medical bills for the first hospitalization were received by defendant by early September.

Plaintiff developed an infection in his foot, and further surgery was required. On October 3 he entered another hospital. In his testimony at the trial he claimed that he was unable to return to the hospital where the prior surgery had been performed because its bill remained unpaid. Upon the second admission plaintiff again named defendant as his insurer, and the charges for hospital and surgical services were sent to defendant.

Defendant initially failed to explain to either plaintiff or the hospitals the cause of the delay in making payment, but wrote an adjuster in Los Angeles, requesting him to determine whether plaintiff was covered by workmen's compensation. The letter conceded that workmen's compensation coverage was questionable because plaintiff was the owner-operator of a cleaning plant. The adjuster was also instructed that, in the event workmen's compensation did not cover the injury, he should review plaintiff's medical history for the 10 years prior to the injury. Defendant explained that the purpose of the exhaustive inquiry was to determine if plaintiff might have been uninsurable at the time of the injury. That is, in the event plaintiff had falsified his application in any respect or omitted to mention that he had some prior serious illness such as heart trouble or cancer, defendant could, on the basis of the misrepresentation, rescind the policy, even though such illnesses were not involved in plaintiff's claim.

The adjuster replied in mid-November that the workmen's compensation carrier denied coverage on the ground plaintiff was not an employee at the time of the injury, and that a hearing would be held by the Workmen's Compensation Appeals Board in December to determine the issue. The December hearing was continued to February 1967.

Throughout this period, plaintiff and a representative of the insurance agency through which he had purchased the policy made persistent inquiries regarding his claim, and the hospitals at which he had been treated also expressed impatience with the delay in receiving payment. In November and December defendant informed plaintiff as well as the hospitals that there was a question whether plaintiff was covered by workmen's compensation at the time of the injury, and that until the matter was resolved his benefits under the policy would be withheld.

In April 1967, defendant forwarded its claim file to the Workmen's Compensation Appeals Board in response to a subpoena duces tecum. No further action was taken by defendant until April 1968, when plaintiff's attorney wrote defendant that the workmen's compensation proceeding had been settled by compromise and release because the evidence was in conflict as to whether plaintiff's injury occurred in the course of employment. The attorney stated that since no formal findings of workmen's compensation coverage had been made by the board, defendant was liable under the policy. Defendant denied liability on the ground that the exclusion was applicable because plaintiff had received payment under the workmen's compensation law. It offered to settle the claim for $200 "to avoid litigation." The offer was rejected.

Plaintiff's condition continued to deteriorate after his second hospitalization. In June 1967 he had a third operation, which was performed at the same hospital as the second surgery. The hospital refused to admit him unless he paid $500 of his previous bill. A fourth operation was performed in April 1968, this time at another hospital, since the hospital at which the second and third operations had been performed refused to accept plaintiff as a patient. Plaintiff was also compelled to engage a different surgeon because the surgeon who had previously operated on him had not been paid. In order to obtain the needed surgery plaintiff resorted to a ruse. He entered the hospital on a Saturday, the operation to be performed on Sunday, so that the hospital administrators would not be able to discover over the weekend whether insurance coverage existed. Plaintiff again named defendant as his insurer.[1]

Shortly after his injury defendant borrowed $2,000 to pay business expenses. Ultimately, he lost his business and could not borrow additional funds because unpaid hospital and medical bills established him to be a poor credit risk. He was compelled to change the place of his residence five times during this period because of lack of funds to pay rent. His utilities were turned off several times for nonpayment, his wheelchair was repossessed, and he had difficulty in affording medication to ease his constant pain. Ultimately, in 1969 plaintiff suffered two nervous breakdowns. A psychiatrist testified that plaintiff's concern over inability to meet medical expenses contributed to these episodes.

At the trial, the manager of defendant's claims department testified that defendant refused to pay the medical expenses plaintiff incurred in 1966 because it was awaiting the outcome of the workmen's compensation proceeding in order to determine whether there was liability under the policy.

The evidence was in sharp conflict as to the custom in the insurance industry regarding the payment of a claim for hospital benefits in these circumstances. Several witnesses for defendant testified that during pendency of a workmen's compensation proceeding, it was customary to deny benefits or to suspend judgment on an insured's claim under a hospital care policy until the question of workmen's compensation coverage was finally decided. A witness for plaintiff testified, on the other hand, that the prevailing practice was to pay the

---

1. When the hospital sent the bill for the fourth operation to defendant in April 1968, defendant wrote in response that plaintiff's policy had not been in force for more than a year. As we shall see, defendant took the position that it was not liable for the cost of plaintiff's hospitalization after January 1, 1967, because the policy had lapsed on that date for nonpayment of premiums. This contention will be discussed in the context of defendant's appeal from the judgment on the jury's verdict.

insured's claim if the workmen's compensation carrier denied liability and the insured had suffered severe injuries. Thus, he stated, if no workmen's compensation award was ultimately ordered the payments under the policy would have been properly made, and if benefits were awarded, the insurer could impose a lien on the sums to be paid in the workmen's compensation proceeding.[2]

Compensatory Damages

In its order granting a new trial, the trial court found, for the reasons set forth in the margin, that the evidence was insufficient to justify a finding of bad faith.[3] It is not necessary to analyze these reasons in detail because, in our view, the evidence shows as a matter of law that defendant breached the covenant of good faith and fair dealing implied in every insurance contract by its failure to make payments under the policy and that, therefore, it was liable for the physical and mental distress proximately caused by its conduct.

The principle was firmly established in *Communale v. Traders & General Ins. Co.* (1958) 50 Cal.2d 654, 658–660, 328 P.2d 198, and *Crisci v. Security Ins. Co.* (1967) 66 Cal.2d 425, 429–433, 58 Cal.Rptr. 13, 426 P.2d 173, that the duty of an insurer to accept a reasonable settlement so as to absolve its insured of liability to a third person is implied in the covenant of good faith and fair dealing which exists in every insurance contract. The covenant requires that neither party will do anything to injure the right of the other to receive the benefits of the agreement, and an insurer is obligated to give the interests of the insured at least as much consideration as it gives to its own interests. Violation of the duty of the insurer sounds in tort, we held, and an insured may recover for all detriment resulting from such violation, including mental distress. These principles have been extended to cases in which the insurer unreasonably and in bad faith withholds payment of the claim of the insured. (*Gruenberg v. Aetna Ins. Co.* (1973) 9 Cal.3d 566, 575, 108 Cal.Rptr. 480, 510 P.2d 1032; *Richardson v. Employers Liab. Assur. Corp.* (1972) 25 Cal.App.3d 232, 239, 102 Cal.Rptr. 547 (disapproved on another ground in *Gruenberg v. Aetna Ins. Co., supra,* 9 Cal.3d 566, at

---

2. Another alternative customarily utilized, according to plaintiff's witness, was for the insurer on the hospital benefit policy to attempt to reach an informal agreement for reimbursement with the workmen's compensation carrier.

3. "The evidence was insufficient to support the verdict. The plaintiff was injured in July of 1966. A workmen's compensation claim was filed by him in August of 1966. That matter was pending until April 30, 1968, at which time it was settled by compromise and release. [¶] There was no evidence that at the time the policy was issued the defendant knew or should have known how a Court would rule on this set of facts or that they made any misrepresentation to him on which he relied. In researching the case neither counsel nor the Court found any case specifically on point that they would have been on notice of at the time of issuance of the policy. [¶] Similarly there was insufficient evidence of any custom or usage in the industry at that time to justify any such finding or to impose any duty on the defendant to pay the proceeds of its policy and then assert a lien claim. [¶] There was no sufficient evidence for the jury to determine that the defendant asserted its claim of defense in bad faith, considering the language of the policy, or that the defendant was guilty of oppressive conduct, misrepresentation or bad faith."

fn. 10, pp. 580–581, 108 Cal.Rptr. 480, 510 P.2d 1032); *Fletcher v. Western National Life Ins. Co.* (1970) 10 Cal.App.3d 376, 401, 89 Cal. Rptr. 78.).

In the present case, the company's policy application declared in large, heavy type, "Protect Yourself Against the Medical Bills That Can Ruin You." Plaintiff's application, filed shortly before the accident, indicated that he had no other hospital or disability insurance and, indeed, the manager of defendant's claims department testified that the policy would not have been issued if plaintiff had other hospital insurance. Defendant was aware that plaintiff earned only a modest income and had incurred substantial medical and hospital bills. The company also knew that there was a serious question whether plaintiff would qualify for workmen's compensation benefits, and that the compensation carrier had consistently denied coverage on the ground that plaintiff was not an employee at the time of the accident.

There is no question that if defendant had paid the hospital charges and it was ultimately determined workmen's compensation covered the injury, defendant could have asserted a lien in the workmen's compensation proceeding to recover the payments it had made and it would have been entitled to payment from the proceeds of the award. (Lab.Code, § 4903, subd. (b); *Foremost Dairies v. Industrial Acc. Com.* (1965) 237 Cal.App.2d 560, 579, 47 Cal.Rptr. 173; *Gerson v. Industrial Acc. Com.* (1961) 188 Cal.App.2d 735, 739, 11 Cal.Rptr. 1; see also Rules of Practice & Procedure, Workmen's Comp. App. Bd., art. 15 § 10886.) Indeed, some of the medical bills incurred by plaintiff were paid by the allowance of a lien from the settlement obtained in the workmen's compensation proceeding.

No explanation was advanced by defendant as to why it failed to adopt this course in order to vindicate the promise made in the application that the policy was intended to protect the insured against medical bills which could result in financial ruin. Defendant's attitude toward the payment of plaintiff's claim was expressed in the declaratory relief phase of the case: merely that it was entitled to wait until the pending compensation proceeding was concluded before it paid or denied the claim. The company failed to see a conflict with its express promise to protect against ruinous medical bills.

Although the evidence was in conflict on the issue whether it was customary in the insurance industry to make payments under the policy in these circumstances and the order granting a new trial declared there was insufficient evidence of such a custom, the failure to establish common practice in this regard cannot absolve the insurer. The scope of the duty of an insurer to deal fairly with its insured is prescribed by law and cannot be delineated entirely by customs of the insurance industry.

Under these circumstances defendant's failure to afford relief to its insured against the very eventuality insured against by the policy amounts to a violation as a matter of law of its duty of good faith and fair dealing implied in every policy. Thus, we conclude the trial court abused its discretion in granting a new trial on the ground that the evidence was insufficient to support a finding that plaintiff is entitled to compensatory damages.

In granting a new trial, the court also indicated that the damages were excessive. However, the order failed to state any reason for this ground other than the declaration that the evidence did not justify an award of $75,000 in compensatory damages "for the reasons stated above." Since "the reasons stated above" (see fn. 3, *ante*) did not refer to whether damages awarded by the jury were disproportionate to the injuries suffered by plaintiff but, rather, to whether the evidence justified a finding of bad faith or oppression, the reasons advanced by the trial court for finding the damages to be excessive are clearly inadequate. (See Code Civ.Proc., § 657; *Mercer v. Perez* (1968) 68 Cal. 2d 104, 111 et seq., 65 Cal.Rptr. 315, 436 P.2d 315; *Scala v. Jerry Witt & Sons, Inc.* (1970) 3 Cal.3d 359, 363 et. seq., 90 Cal.Rptr. 592, 475 P.2d 864.) The trial court's order must be reversed insofar as it determines that plaintiff was not entitled to compensatory damages and that an award of $75,000 for such damages was excessive.

Exemplary Damages

It does not follow that because plaintiff is entitled to compensatory damages that he is also entitled to exemplary damages. In order to justify an award of exemplary damages, the defendant must be guilty of oppression, fraud or malice. (Civ.Code, § 3294.) He must act with the intent to vex, injure or annoy, or with a conscious disregard of the plaintiff's rights. (*Wolfsen v. Hathaway* (1948) 32 Cal.2d 632, 647 et seq., 198 P.2d 1 (overruled on another ground in *Florès v. Arroyo* (1961) 56 Cal.2d 492, 497, 15 Cal.Rptr. 87, 364 P.2d 263); *Roth v. Shell Oil Co.* (1960) 185 Cal.App.2d 676, 682, 8 Cal.Rptr. 514.) While we have concluded that defendant violated its duty of good faith and fair dealing, this alone does not necessarily establish that defendant acted with the requisite intent to injure plaintiff.

In granting a new trial the trial court stated that the evidence was insufficient to justify an award of punitive damages because defendant was not put on notice by cases previously decided that its interpretation of the policy was incorrect and because there was insufficient evidence of a practice in the insurance industry to pay a disputed claim and then file a lien in the workmen's compensation proceeding to recover the payments made. The trial court's conclusion that defendant was not guilty of oppressive conduct did not constitute a manifest and unmistakable abuse of discretion. (*Jiminez v. Sears, Roebuck & Co.* (1971) 4 Cal.3d 379, 387, 93 Cal.Rptr. 769, 482 P.2d 681.) Therefore, the order granting a new trial must be affirmed insofar as it determines that the evidence was insufficient to justify the award of punitive damages.

* * *

new trial for suff. of evidence for punitive damages.

Defendant's Appeal

In its appeal from the judgment on the jury's verdict, defendant contends that the trial court erred in the declaratory relief phase of the case in finding the policy to be ambiguous and in awarding plaintiff $4,900 in benefits thereunder.

Two separate clauses of the policy are involved on the issue of liability. The first is the insuring clause. It provides "subject to the exceptions, limitations and provisions of this policy [defendant] promises to pay for loss, except losses covered by any Workmen's Compensation * * * Law * * * covered by this policy and sustained by the insured * * * resulting from injury or sickness; * * * *"

The second relevant provision is the exclusionary clause, which states, "EXCLUSIONS. This policy does not cover any loss caused by or resulting from (1) injury or sickness for which compensation is payable under any Workmen's Compensation * * * Law."

Plaintiff contends, and the trial court found, that the insuring clause could be interpreted to mean that payments would be made under the policy even though plaintiff also recovered workmen's compensation benefits if workmen's compensation did not meet his total medical expenses. That is, defendant was required to pay hospital charges not covered by workmen's compensation payments. Defendant, on the other hand, claims that the insuring clause must be read in conjunction with the exclusionary clause, and that the latter provision makes it plain that if workmen's compensation benefits in any amount are received by the insured, then defendant is not required to make any payments whatever under the policy.

The trial court construed the policy in the light of the familiar rule that any ambiguities in an insurance policy must be read against the insurer. (*Bareno v. Employers Life Ins. Co.* (1972) 7 Cal.3d 875, 878, 103 Cal.Rptr. 865, 500 P.2d 889.) It determined that the word "loss" in the insuring clause could mean compensable expense and, if so, defendant was required to pay hospital expenses not covered by workmen's compensation. The application for the policy declared in large, capital letters, "ALL BENEFITS PAYABLE IN FULL REGARDLESS OF ANY OTHER INSURANCE YOU MAY HAVE." This assurance implies at the very least that the receipt of workmen's compensation payments, comparable to "other insurance" payments, would not entirely vitiate defendant's liability under the policy.

Thus, the provision in the insuring clause that defendant would pay for "loss, except losses covered by * * * Workmen's Compensation" rationally means that defendant promised to pay such hospital expenses incurred by plaintiff as were not paid by workmen's compensation, up to the policy limits.

Defendant relies heavily upon the language of the exclusionary provision, which excludes liability for "any loss caused by or resulting from * * * injury * * * for which compensation is payable under any Workmen's Compensation * * * Law * * *" This provision does not clearly absolve defendant of liability if plaintiff receives any amount in workmen's compensation benefits, particularly since it must be read in conjunction with the insuring clause, which requires defendant to pay expenses not covered by workmen's compensation. At best, even acquiescence in defendant's interpretation of the exclusion would merely result in a conflict between the exclusionary and the insuring clauses. Under prevailing law that conflict must be resolved in plaintiff's favor.[4] Defendant relies upon a number of cases to support its assertion that the policy is not ambiguous. However, with one exception these decisions involved provisions at variance with those in the present case. (E.g., *Laing v. Occidental Life Ins. Co.* (1966) 244 Cal.App. 2d 811, 53 Cal.Rptr. 681; *Wenthe v. Hospital Service, Incorporated, of Iowa* (1960) 251 Iowa 765, 100 N.W.2d 903.) In *Bonney v. Citizens Mut. Auto. Ins. Co.* (1952) 333 Mich. 435, 53 N.W.2d 321, the policy contained a provision similar to the exclusion here. But there was no inconsistency between that provision and another clause of the policy, as in the present case, and the decision merely held that the exclusion applied to persons eligible for workmen's compensation benefits whether or not they had actually received such benefits.

There is a penultimate problem involving the policy provisions: whether defendant's liability terminated as of January 1, 1967, because plaintiff did not pay the premium due on that date. The relevant provision states, "When as the result of injury or sickness and commencing while covered hereunder, any member * * * is necessarily confined in a hospital, the Company will pay, subject to the above limitation, [various specified expenses]." Defendant interprets this provision as meaning that the injury and the hospitalization must both occur while the policy is in effect in order to entitle the insured to benefits and that defendant was not liable for those expenses which were incurred by plaintiff after the policy lapsed for nonpayment of premium on January 1, 1967.

The trial court found that the provision meant that if the insured was injured while the policy was in effect defendant would pay hospital expenses during the term of the policy even though the actual hospitalization or the injury occurred after the policy had been deemed to lapse for nonpayment.[5]

4. The trial court found that the exclusionary clause did not apply where, as here, the workmen's compensation proceeding terminated by compromise and release. Defendant disputes this conclusion, asserting that payments under a compromise and release are "compensation" and are therefore within the ambit of the exclusion. (Citing *Raischell & Cottrell, Inc. v. Workmen's Comp. App. Bd.* (1967) 249 Cal.App.2d 991, 58 Cal.Rptr. 159, and *Aetna Life Ins. Co. v. Ind. Acc. Comm.* (1952) 38 Cal.2d 599, 241 P.2d 530. We need not determine the merits of this claim in view of the conclusions we have reached above.

5. Defendant complains that the trial court misread the provision as though a comma had been printed after the word "When" and as if the word "and" had been deleted. That is, claims defendant, the court rewrote the sentence to read, "When, as the result of injury or sickness commencing while covered hereunder, any member * * * is necessarily confined" etc. The court interpreted the phrase "subject to the above limitations" to include, inter alia, the limitation that the policy was for a two-year term.

At best, the provision is ambiguous. It can reasonably be interpreted to mean that payments would be made if the *injury* commenced during the life of the policy. Under settled rules of construction, the provision must therefore be interpreted against defendant. * * *

The order granting a new trial is reversed insofar as it grants a new trial on defendant's liability for compensatory damages and the amount of compensatory damages, and in all other respects the order is affirmed. On defendant's cross-appeal, the judgment is affirmed insofar as it awards $75,000 in compensatory damages and $4,900 as benefits under the policy. Plaintiff is to recover costs on appeal.

WRIGHT, C.J., and McCOMB, TOBRINER, BURKE and SULLIVAN, JJ., concur.

Notes and Questions

1. *The Rise of the Cause of Action.* Until two decades ago the common law action for bad-faith breach of a first-party insurance policy was virtually unheard of, but it is now accepted in one form or another in about half the states. A number of other states have enacted statutes imposing liability for limited damages (e.g., for counsel fees, or for a multiple of the covered loss) on first-party insurers for bad-faith denial of claims. See, e.g., Ga.Code Ann. § 33–4–6. Many complaints in insurance coverage disputes now routinely include a separate count alleging bad-faith breach of the policy, and bad-faith litigation has become a recognized sub-specialty that has spawned its own professional education programs and practitioners' treatises. See, e.g., W. Shernoff, S. Gage, & H. Levine, Insurance Bad Faith Litigation (1984).

2. *The Underdeterrence Problem.* If, as *Kewin* suggests, in the event of breach the insured is entitled only to the amount of his coverage plus any consequential damages that are contemplated by the parties under *Hadley v. Baxendale,* and the latter category does not include emotional distress, what incentives do insurers have to pay doubtful but legitimate claims?

3. *The Scope of the Action.* Once a cause of action for extra-contractual damages is created, the challenge is to define its contours. Does *Silberg* satisfactorily explain what triggered the insurer's obligation to pay these damages? There are two aspects of the problem—the nature of the cause of action, and the quality of insurer "misbehavior" that triggers it.

The Nature of the Cause of Action

Contract. Some courts consider the action to be in contract, for breach of an implied covenant of good faith. The issue then is, what measure of damages is available? Where the damages are economic, in many cases it is relatively easy to hold that they are within the contemplation of the parties—business disruptions, mortgage foreclosures, etc. If the only damages are noneconomic, however, then a rejection of the *Kewin* holding that emotional distress from breach of a personal insurance contract is not foreseeable is necessary to put teeth in the cause of action.

Independent Tort Necessary. Early in the development of the cause of action, the courts groped for a rationale for what they were doing. Many held then—and some still hold—that extra-contractual damages for breach can be awarded only if the breach also constitutes an independent tort, such as fraud or intentional infliction of emotional distress.

The Tort of Bad Faith. The dominant approach today is to hold that the cause of action sounds in tort, but that an independent tort is not necessary to its existence. Rather, the insurer commits a tort if its breach is in "bad faith." There is then a cause of action in tort for bad-faith breach of contract, and the rules governing recovery of damages in tort apply. Compensatory damages are not limited to those within the contemplation of the parties so long as they are proximately caused by the defendant's tortious action, and punitive damages may be awarded when the misbehavior is sufficiently blameworthy. The key issue then becomes the meaning of "bad faith."

The Insurer Misbehavior Required

Perhaps the most vexing problem in this field is specifying the kind of behavior that triggers the cause of action. Bad faith is not merely the absence of good faith; something more seems to be required. Mere negligence generally is not enough; the fact that the insurer should have known that the insured's claim was covered, or that it was careless in processing a claim, normally does not constitute bad faith. But objective negligence, coupled with evidence that the insurer was probably aware at some point during the claim process that the claim was covered, may constitute bad faith. One court has said that the denial of a claim is in bad faith if it is not "fairly debatable" whether the claim is covered. See *Rawlings v. Apodaca,* 151 Ariz. 149, 726 P.2d 565 (1986).

Beyond this, it may be that each case requires a judgment in context. Certainly many of the decisions in which there is a finding of bad faith involve unconventional situations, in which there is more than the straightforward presentation and denial of a claim. In *Rawlings* the insured's fire insurer also provided liability insurance for the party allegedly responsible for the fire, and refused to supply the insured with an investigation report; in *Silberg* the insurer was aware of the dire circumstances in which its repeated denials of coverage placed the insured.

Many other cases present similarly unusual facts. For example, in one of the earliest, *Gruenberg v. Aetna Insurance Company,* 9 Cal.3d 566, 108 Cal.Rptr. 480, 510 P.2d 1032 (1973), the insured's fire insurers allegedly encouraged the bringing of arson charges against him, and then used his refusal to appear for a civil deposition during the pendency of the criminal action as a pretense for denying his claim. And in *Sparks v. Republic National Life Insurance Company,* 132 Ariz. 529, 647 P.2d 1127 (1982), a health insurer relying on an ambiguous policy provision terminated coverage, and refused to pay the continuing cost of treating injuries that the insured suffered while coverage was in force, because the insured had not paid subsequent premiums—premiums which the insurer might simply have deducted from the several hundred thousand dollars for which it was obligated.

By no means all the decisions involve facts suggesting more by way of bad faith than the mere improper denial of a claim; but the lesson that seems to emerge in the aggregate is that a bad-faith claim has a much greater chance of succeeding where the insurer is guilty of considerably more than a merely unreasonable misinterpretation of the terms of a policy, or has become aware of more facts about the insured's claims than are present in a typical bare-bones claim file.

4. *Punitive Damages.* Punitive damages also may be awarded in a bad-faith claim. If something more than negligence is required to support an action for compensatory damages, is the line dividing these actions from cases in which punitive damages also are available likely to exist more in theory than in practice? The court in *Rawlings v. Apodaca,* 151 Ariz. 149, 726 P.2d 565 (1986), described the difference this way:

> Thus, we establish no new category of punitive damages for bad faith cases. Such damages are recoverable in bad faith tort actions when, *and only when,* the facts establish that defendant's conduct was aggravated, outrageous, malicious or fraudulent. *See Anderson v. Continental Insurance Co.,* 85 Wis.2d 675, 271 N.W.2d 368, 379 (1978). Indifference to facts or failure to investigate are sufficient to establish the tort of bad faith but may not rise to the level required by the punitive damage rule. The difference is no doubt harder to articulate in legalistic terms than it is to differentiate on the facts. To obtain tort damages, for instance, plaintiff must prove only that defendant failed to ascertain the true facts and thus acted without or indifferent to the reasonable basis required for denying the claim. To obtain punitive damages, plaintiff must also show that the evil hand that unjustifiably damaged the objectives sought to be reached by the insurance contract was guided by an evil mind which either consciously sought to damage the insured or acted intentionally, knowing that its conduct was likely to cause unjustified, significant damage to the insured. * * * When defendant's motives are shown to be so improper, *or* its conduct so impressive, outrageous or intolerable that such an "evil mind" may be inferred, punitive damages may be awarded. Restatement (Second) of Torts § 908(2).

PILOT LIFE INSURANCE COMPANY v. DEDEAUX

Supreme Court of the Unites States, 1987.
481 U.S. 41, 107 S.Ct. 1549, 95 L.Ed.2d 39.

Justice O'CONNOR delivered the opinion of the Court.

This case presents the question whether the Employee Retirement Income Security Act of 1974 (ERISA), 88 Stat. 829, as amended, 29 U.S.C. § 1001 *et seq.,* pre-empts state common law tort and contract actions asserting improper processing of a claim for benefits under an insured employee benefit plan.

I

In March 1975, in Gulf Port, Mississippi, respondent Everate W. Dedeaux injured his back in an accident related to his employment for Entex, Inc. (Entex). Entex had at this time a long term disability employee benefit plan established by purchasing a group insurance policy from petitioner, Pilot Life Insurance Co. (Pilot Life). Entex collected and matched its employees' contributions to the plan and forwarded those funds to Pilot Life; the employer also provided forms to its employees for processing disability claims, and forwarded completed forms to Pilot Life. Pilot Life bore the responsibility of determining who would receive disability benefits. Although Dedeaux sought permanent disability benefits following the 1975 accident, Pilot Life terminated his benefits after two years. During the following three years Dedeaux's benefits were reinstated and terminated by Pilot Life several times.

In 1980, Dedeaux instituted a diversity action against Pilot Life in the United States District Court for the Southern District of Mississippi. Dedeaux's complaint contained three counts: "Tortious Breach of Contract"; "Breach of Fiduciary Duties"; and "Fraud in the Inducement." App. 18–23. Dedeaux sought "[d]amages for failure to provide benefits under the insurance policy in a sum to be determined at the time of trial," "[g]eneral damages for mental and emotional distress and other incidental damages in the sum of $250,000.00," and "[p]unitive and exemplary damages in the sum of $500,000.00." *Id.,* at 23–24. Dedeaux did not assert any of the several causes of action available to him under ERISA, see *infra,* at 53.

At the close of discovery, Pilot Life moved for summary judgment, arguing that ERISA pre-empted Dedeaux's common law claim for failure to pay benefits on the group insurance policy. The District Court granted Pilot Life summary judgment, finding all Dedeaux's claims pre-empted. App. to Pet.Cert. 16a.

The Court of Appeals for the Fifth Circuit reversed, primarily on the basis of this Court's decision in *Metropolitan Life Ins. Co. v. Massachusetts,* 471 U.S. 724, 105 S.Ct. 2380, 85 L.Ed.2d 728 (1985). See 770 F.2d 1311 (1985). We granted certiorari, 478 U.S. 1004, 106 S.Ct. 3293, 92 L.Ed.2d 708 (1986), and now reverse.

II

In ERISA, Congress set out to

> "protect * * * participants in employee benefit plans and
> their beneficiaries, by requiring the disclosure and reporting to
> participants and beneficiaries of financial and other informa-
> tion with respect thereto, by establishing standards of conduct,
> responsibility, and obligation for fiduciaries of employee bene-
> fit plans, and by providing for appropriate remedies, sanctions,
> and ready access to the Federal courts." § 2, as set forth in 29
> U.S.C. § 1001(b).

ERISA comprehensively regulates, among other things, employee welfare benefit plans that, "through the purchase of insurance or otherwise," provide medical, surgical, or hospital care, or benefits in the
event of sickness, accident, disability or death. § 3(1), 29 U.S.C.
§ 1002(1).

Congress capped off the massive undertaking of ERISA with three
provisions relating to the pre-emptive effect of the federal legislation:

> "Except as provided in subsection (b) of this section [the
> saving clause], the provisions of this subchapter and sub-
> chapter III of this chapter shall supersede any and all State
> laws insofar as they may now or hereafter relate to any
> employee benefit plan. * * *" § 514(a), as set forth in 29
> U.S.C. § 1144(a) (pre-emption clause).

> "Except as provided in subparagraph (B) [the deemer
> clause], nothing in this subchapter shall be construed to ex-
> empt or relieve any person from any law of any State which
> regulates insurance, banking, or securities." § 514(b)(2)(A), as
> set forth in 29 U.S.C. § 1144(b)(2)(A) (saving clause).

> "Neither an employee benefit plan * * * nor any trust
> established under such a plan, shall be deemed to be an
> insurance company or other insurer, bank, trust company, or
> investment company or to be engaged in the business of insur-
> ance or banking for purposes of any law of any State purport-
> ing to regulate insurance companies, insurance contracts,
> banks, trust companies, or investment companies." Section
> 514(b)(2)(B), 29 U.S.C. § 1144(b)(2)(B) (deemer clause).

To summarize the pure mechanics of the provisions quoted above:
If a state law "relate[s] to * * * employee benefit plan[s]," it is pre-
empted. § 514(a). The saving clause excepts from the pre-emption
clause laws that "regulat[e] insurance." § 514(b)(2)(A). The deemer
clause makes clear that a state law that "purport[s] to regulate insurance" cannot deem an employee benefit plan to be an insurance
company. § 514(b)(2)(B).

"[T]he question whether a certain state action is pre-empted by
federal law is one of congressional intent. ' "The purpose of Congress is

the ultimate touchstone." ' " *Allis–Chalmers Corp. v. Lueck,* 471 U.S. 202, 208, 105 S.Ct. 1904, 1909, 85 L.Ed.2d 206 (1985), quoting *Malone v. White Motor Corp.,* 435 U.S. 497, 504, 98 S.Ct. 1185, 1189, 55 L.Ed.2d 443 (1978), quoting *Retail Clerks v. Schermerhorn,* 375 U.S. 96, 103, 84 S.Ct. 219, 222, 11 L.Ed.2d 179 (1963). We have observed in the past that the express pre-emption provisions of ERISA are deliberately expansive, and designed to "establish pension plan regulation as exclusively a federal concern." *Alessi v. Raybestos–Manhattan, Inc.,* 451 U.S. 504, 523, 101 S.Ct. 1895, 1906, 68 L.Ed.2d 402 (1981). As we explained in *Shaw v. Delta Air Lines, Inc.,* 463 U.S. 85, 98, 103 S.Ct. 2890, 2900, 77 L.Ed.2d 490 (1983):

> "The bill that became ERISA originally contained a limited pre-emption clause, applicable only to state laws relating to the specific subjects covered by ERISA. The Conference Committee rejected those provisions in favor of the present language, and indicated that section's pre-emptive scope was as broad as its language. See H.R.Conf.Rep. No. 93–1280, p. 383 (1974); S.Conf.Rep. No. 93–1090, p. 383 (1974)."

The House and Senate sponsors emphasized both the breadth and importance of the pre-emption provisions. Representative Dent described the "reservation to Federal authority the sole power to regulate the field of employee benefit plans" as ERISA's "crowning achievement." 120 Cong.Rec. 29197 (1974). Senator Williams said:

> "It should be stressed that with the narrow exceptions specified in the bill, the substantive and enforcement provisions of the conference substitute are intended to preempt the field for Federal regulations, thus eliminating the threat of conflicting or inconsistent State and local regulation of employee benefit plans. This principle is intended to apply in its broadest sense to all actions of State or local governments, or any instrumentality thereof, which have the force or effect of law." *Id.,* at 29933.

See also *Shaw v. Delta Air Lines, Inc., supra,* at 99–100, n. 20, 103 S.Ct., at 2901, n. 20 (describing remarks of Sen. Javits).

In *Metropolitan Life,* this Court, noting that the pre-emption and saving clauses "perhaps are not a model of legislative drafting," 471 U.S., at 739, 105 S.Ct., at 2389, interpreted these clauses in relation to a Massachusetts statute that required minimum mental health care benefits to be provided Massachusetts residents covered by general health insurance policies. The appellants in *Metropolitan Life* argued that the state statute, as applied to insurance policies purchased by employee health care plans regulated by ERISA, was pre-empted.

The Court concluded, first, that the Massachusetts statute did "relate to * * * employee benefit plan[s]," thus placing the state statute within the broad sweep of the pre-emption clause, § 514(a). *Metropolitan Life, supra,* at 739, 105 S.Ct., at 2389. However, the Court held that, because the state statute was one that "regulate[d] insurance," the saving clause prevented the state law from being pre-empted. In determining whether the Massachusetts statute regulated insurance, the Court was guided by case law interpreting the phrase "business of insurance" in the McCarran–Ferguson Act, 59 Stat. 33, as amended, 15 U.S.C. § 1011 *et seq.*

Given the "statutory complexity" of ERISA's three pre-emption provisions, *Metropolitan Life, supra,* at 740, 105 S.Ct., at 2389, as well as the wide variety of state statutory and decisional law arguably affected by the federal pre-emption provisions, it is not surprising that we are again called on to interpret these provisions.

III

There is no dispute that the common law causes of action asserted in Dedeaux's complaint "relate to" an employee benefit plan and therefore fall under ERISA's express pre-emption clause, § 514(a). In both *Metropolitan Life, supra,* and *Shaw v. Delta Air Lines, Inc., supra,* 463 U.S., at 96–100, 103 S.Ct., at 2899–2901, we noted the expansive sweep of the pre-emption clause. In both cases "[t]he phrase 'relate to' was given its broad common-sense meaning, such that a state law 'relate[s] to' a benefit plan 'in the normal sense of the phrase, if it has a connection with or reference to such a plan.' " *Metropolitan Life,* 471 U.S., at 739, 105 S.Ct., at 2389, quoting *Shaw v. Delta Air Lines, supra,* 463 U.S., at 97, 103 S.Ct., at 2900. In particular we have emphasized that the pre-emption clause is not limited to "state laws specifically designed to affect employee benefit plans." *Shaw v. Delta Air Lines, supra,* at 98, 103 S.Ct., at 2900. The common law causes of action raised in Dedeaux's complaint, each based on alleged improper processing of a claim for benefits under an employee benefit plan, undoubtedly meet the criteria for pre-emption under § 514(a).

Unless these common law causes of action fall under an exception to § 514(a), therefore, they are expressly pre-empted. Although Dedeaux's complaint pled several state common law causes of action, before this Court Dedeaux has described only one of the three counts— called "tortious breach of contract" in the complaint, and "the Mississippi law of bad faith" in respondent's brief—as protected from the pre-emptive effect of § 514(a). The Mississippi law of bad faith, Dedeaux argues, is a law "which regulates insurance," and thus is saved from pre-emption by § 514(b)(2)(A).[1]

In *Metropolitan Life,* we were guided by several considerations in determining whether a state law falls under the saving clause. First, we took what guidance was available from a "common-sense view" of the language of the saving clause itself. 471 U.S., at 740, 105 S.Ct., at 2390. Second, we made use of the case law interpreting the phrase

---

1. Decisional law that "regulates insurance" may fall under the saving clause. The saving clause, § 514(b)(2)(A), covers "any law of any State." For purposes of § 514, "[t]he term 'State law' includes all laws, decisions, rules, regulations, or other State action having the effect of law, of any State." 29 U.S.C. § 1144(c)(1) and (2).

"business of insurance" under the McCarran–Ferguson Act, 15 U.S.C. § 1011 *et seq.,* in interpreting the saving clause.[2] Three criteria have been used to determine whether a practice falls under the "business of insurance" for purposes of the McCarran–Ferguson Act:

> "*[F]irst,* whether the practice has the effect of transferring or spreading a policyholder's risk; *second,* whether the practice is an integral part of the policy relationship between the insurer and the insured; and *third,* whether the practice is limited to entities within the insurance industry." *Union Labor Life Ins. Co. v. Pireno,* 458 U.S. 119, 129, 102 S.Ct. 3002, 3009, 73 L.Ed. 2d 647 (1982) (emphasis in original).

In the present case, the considerations weighed in *Metropolitan Life* argue against the assertion that the Mississippi law of bad faith is a state law that "regulates insurance."

As early as 1915 the Mississippi Supreme Court had recognized that punitive damages were available in a contract case when "the act or omission constituting the breach of the contract amounts also to the commission of a tort." See *Hood v. Moffett,* 109 Miss. 757, 767, 69 So. 664, 666 (1915) (involving a physician's breach of a contract to attend to a woman at her approaching "accouchement"). In *American Railway Express Co. v. Bailey,* 142 Miss. 622, 631, 107 So. 761, 763 (1926), a case involving a failure of a finance company to deliver to the plaintiff the correct amount of money cabled to the plaintiff through the finance company's offices, the Mississippi Supreme Court explained that punitive damages could be available when the breach of contract was "attended by some intentional wrong, insult, abuse, or gross negligence, which amounts to an independent tort." In *Standard Life Insurance Co. v. Veal,* 354 So.2d 239 (Miss.1977), the Mississippi Supreme Court, citing *D.L. Fair Lumber Co. v. Weems,* 196 Miss. 201, 16 So.2d 770 (1944) (breach of contract was accompanied by "the breaking down and destruction of another's fence"), *American Railway Express Co. v. Bailey, supra,* and *Hood v. Moffett, supra,* upheld an award of punitive damages against a defendant insurance company for failure to pay on a credit life policy. Since *Veal,* the Mississippi Supreme Court has considered a large number of cases in which plaintiffs have sought punitive damages from insurance companies for failure to pay a claim under an insurance contract, and in a great many of these cases the court has used the identical formulation, first stated in *Bailey,* of what must "attend" the breach of contract in order for punitive damages to be recoverable. See, *e.g., Employers Mutual Casualty Co. v. Tompkins,* 490 So.2d 897, 902 (1986); *State Farm Fire & Casualty Co. v. Simpson,* 477 So.2d 242, 248 (1985); *Consolidated American Life Ins. Co. v. Toche,* 410 So.2d 1303, 1304 (1982); *Gulf Guaranty Life Ins. Co. v. Kelley,* 389 So.2d 920, 922 (1980); *State Farm Mutual Automobile Ins. Co. v. Roberts,* 379 So.2d 321, 322 (1980); *New Hampshire Ins. Co. v. Smith,*

---

2. The McCarran–Ferguson Act provides, in relevant part: "The business of insurance, and every person engaged therein, shall be subject to the laws of the several States which relate to the regulation or taxation of such business." 15 U.S.C. § 1012(a).

357 So.2d 119, 121 (1978); *Lincoln National Life Ins. Co. v. Crews,* 341 So.2d 1321, 1322 (1977). Recently the Mississippi Supreme Court stated that "[w]e have come to term an insurance carrier which refuses to pay a claim when there is no reasonably arguable basis to deny it as acting in 'bad faith,' and a lawsuit based upon such an arbitrary refusal as a 'bad faith' cause of action." *Blue Cross & Blue Shield of Mississippi, Inc. v. Campbell,* 466 So.2d 833, 842 (1984).

Certainly a common-sense understanding of the phrase "regulates insurance" does not support the argument that the Mississippi law of bad faith falls under the saving clause. A common-sense view of the word "regulates" would lead to the conclusion that in order to regulate insurance, a law must not just have an impact on the insurance industry, but be specifically directed toward that industry. Even though the Mississippi Supreme Court has identified its law of bad faith with the insurance industry, the roots of this law are firmly planted in the general principles of Mississippi tort and contract law. Any breach of contract, and not merely breach of an insurance contract, may lead to liability for punitive damages under Mississippi law.

Neither do the McCarran–Ferguson Act factors support the assertion that the Mississippi law of bad faith "regulates insurance." Unlike the mandated-benefits law at issue in *Metropolitan Life,* the Mississippi common law of bad faith does not effect a spreading of policyholder risk. The state common law of bad faith may be said to concern "the policy relationship between the insurer and the insured." The connection to the insurer-insured relationship is attenuated at best, however. In contrast to the mandated-benefits law in *Metropolitan Life,* the common law of bad faith does not define the terms of the relationship between the insurer and the insured; it declares only that, whatever terms have been agreed upon in the insurance contract, a breach of that contract may in certain circumstances allow the policyholder to obtain punitive damages. The state common law of bad faith is therefore no more "integral" to the insurer-insured relationship than any state's general contract law is integral to a contract made in that state. Finally, as we have just noted, Mississippi's law of bad faith, even if associated with the insurance industry, has developed from general principles of tort and contract law available in any Mississippi breach of contract case. Cf. *Hart v. Orion Ins. Co.,* 453 F.2d 1358 (CA10 1971) (general state arbitration statutes do not regulate the business of insurance under the McCarran–Ferguson Act); *Hamilton Life Ins. Co. v. Republic National Life Ins. Co.,* 408 F.2d 606 (CA2 1969) (same). Accordingly, the Mississippi common law of bad faith at most meets one of the three criteria used to identify the "business of insurance" under the McCarran–Ferguson Act, and used in *Metropolitan Life* to identify laws that "regulat[e] insurance" under the saving clause.

In the present case, moreover, we are obliged in interpreting the saving clause to consider not only the factors by which we were guided in *Metropolitan Life,* but also the role of the saving clause in ERISA as a whole. On numerous occasions we have noted that " " " '[i]n expounding a statute, we must not be guided by a single sentence or member of a sentence, but look to the provisions of the whole law, and to its object and policy.' " ' " *Kelly v. Robinson,* 479 U.S. 36, 43, 107 S.Ct. 353, 358, 93 L.Ed.2d 216 (1986), quoting *Offshore Logistics, Inc. v. Tallentire,* 477 U.S. 207, 221, 106 S.Ct. 2485, 2494, 91 L.Ed.2d 174 (1986) (quoting *Mastro Plastics Corp. v. NLRB,* 350 U.S. 270, 285, 76 S.Ct. 349, 359, 100 L.Ed. 309 (1956) (in turn quoting *United States v. Heirs of Boisdoré,* 8 How. 113, 122, 12 L.Ed. 1009 (1849))). Because in this case, the state cause of action seeks remedies for the improper processing of a claim for benefits under an ERISA-regulated plan, our understanding of the saving clause must be informed by the legislative intent concerning the civil enforcement provisions provided by ERISA, § 502(a), 29 U.S.C. § 1132(a).

The Solicitor General, for the United States as *amicus curiae,* argues that Congress clearly expressed an intent that the civil enforcement provisions of ERISA § 502(a) be the exclusive vehicle for actions by ERISA-plan participants and beneficiaries asserting improper processing of a claim for benefits, and that varying state causes of action for claims within the scope of § 502(a) would pose an obstacle to the purposes and objectives of Congress. Brief for United States as *Amicus Curiae* 18–19. We agree. The conclusion that § 502(a) was intended to be exclusive is supported, first, by the language and structure of the civil enforcement provisions, and second, by legislative history in which Congress declared that the pre-emptive force of § 502(a) was modeled on the exclusive remedy provided by § 301 of the Labor–Management Relations Act (LMRA), 61 Stat. 156, 29 U.S.C. § 185.

The civil enforcement scheme of § 502(a) is one of the essential tools for accomplishing the stated purposes of ERISA.[3] The civil

---

3. Section 502(a), as set forth in 29 U.S.C. § 1132(a) provides:

"A civil action may be brought—

"(1) by a participant or beneficiary—

"(A) for the relief provided for in subsection (c) of this section [concerning requests to the administrator for information], or

"(B) to recover benefits due to him under the terms of his plan, to enforce his rights under the terms of the plan, or to clarify his rights to future benefits under the terms of the plan;

"(2) by the Secretary, or by a participant, beneficiary or fiduciary for appropriate relief under section 1109 of this title [breach of fiduciary duty];

"(3) by a participant, beneficiary, or fiduciary (A) to enjoin any act or practice which violates any provision of this subchapter or the terms of the plan, or (B) to obtain other appropriate equitable relief (i) to redress such violations or (ii) to enforce any provisions of this subchapter or the terms of the plan;

"(4) by the Secretary, or by a participant, or beneficiary for appropriate relief in the case of a violation of 1025(c) of this title [information to be furnished to participants];

"(5) except as otherwise provided in subsection (b) of this subsection, by the Secretary (A) to enjoin any act or practice which violates any provision of this subchapter, or (B) to obtain other appropriate equitable relief (i) to redress such violation or (ii) to enforce any provision of this subchapter;

enforcement scheme is sandwiched between two other ERISA provisions relevant to enforcement of ERISA and to the processing of a claim for benefits under an employee benefit plan. Section 501, 29 U.S.C. § 1131, authorizes criminal penalties for violations of the reporting and disclosure provisions of ERISA. Section 503, 29 U.S.C. § 1133, requires every employee benefit plan to comply with Department of Labor regulations on giving notice to any participant or beneficiary whose claim for benefits has been denied, and affording a reasonable opportunity for review of the decision denying the claim. Under the civil enforcement provisions of § 502(a), a plan participant or beneficiary may sue to recover benefits due under the plan, to enforce the participant's rights under the plan, or to clarify rights to future benefits. Relief may take the form of accrued benefits due, a declaratory judgment on entitlement to benefits, or an injunction against a plan administrator's improper refusal to pay benefits. A participant or beneficiary may also bring a cause of action for breach of fiduciary duty, and under this cause of action may seek removal of the fiduciary. §§ 502(a)(2), 409. In an action under these civil enforcement provisions, the court in its discretion may allow an award of attorney's fees to either party. § 502(g). See *Massachusetts Mutual Life Ins. Co. v. Russell*, 473 U.S. 134, 147, 105 S.Ct. 3085, 3093, 87 L.Ed.2d 96 (1985). In *Russell*, we concluded that ERISA's breach of fiduciary duty provision, § 409(a), 29 U.S.C. § 1109(a), provided no express authority for an award of punitive damages to a beneficiary. Moreover, we declined to find an implied cause of action for punitive damages in that section, noting that " '[t]he presumption that a remedy was deliberately omitted from a statute is strongest when Congress has enacted a comprehensive legislative scheme including an integrated system of procedures for enforcement.' " *Russell, supra*, at 147, 105 S.Ct., at 3093, quoting *Northwest Airlines, Inc. v. Transport Workers*, 451 U.S. 77, 97, 101 S.Ct. 1571, 1583, 67 L.Ed.2d 750 (1981). Our examination of these provisions made us "reluctant to tamper with an enforcement scheme crafted with such evident care as the one in ERISA." *Russell, supra*, 473 U.S., at 147, 105 S.Ct., at 3093.

In sum, the detailed provisions of § 502(a) set forth a comprehensive civil enforcement scheme that represents a careful balancing of the need for prompt and fair claims settlement procedures against the public interest in encouraging the formation of employee benefit plans. The policy choices reflected in the inclusion of certain remedies and the exclusion of others under the federal scheme would be completely undermined if ERISA–plan participants and beneficiaries were free to obtain remedies under state law that Congress rejected in ERISA. "The six carefully integrated civil enforcement provisions found in § 502(a) of the statute as finally enacted * * * provide strong evidence that Congress did *not* intend to authorize other remedies that it

"(6) by the Secretary to collect any civil penalty under subsection (i) of this section."

simply forgot to incorporate expressly." *Russell, supra,* at 146, 105 S.Ct., at 3093 (emphasis in original).

The deliberate care with which ERISA's civil enforcement remedies were drafted and the balancing of policies embodied in its choice of remedies argue strongly for the conclusion that ERISA's civil enforcement remedies were intended to be exclusive. This conclusion is fully confirmed by the legislative history of the civil enforcement provision. The legislative history demonstrates that the pre-emptive force of § 502(a) was modeled after § 301 of the Labor–Management Relations Act of 1947 (LMRA), 29 U.S.C. § 185.

The Conference Report on ERISA describing the civil enforcement provisions of § 502(a) says:

> "Under the conference agreement, civil actions may be brought by a participant or beneficiary to recover benefits due under the plan, to clarify rights to receive future benefits under the plan, and for relief from breach of fiduciary responsibility. . . . [W]ith respect to suits to enforce benefit rights under the plan or to recover benefits under the plan which do not involve application of the title I provisions, they may be brought not only in U.S. district courts but also in State courts of competent jurisdiction. *All such actions in Federal or State courts are to be regarded as arising under the laws of the United States in similar fashion to those brought under section 301 of the Labor–Management Relations Act of 1947.*" H.R. Conf.Rep. No. 93–1280, p. 327 (1974), U.S.Code Cong. & Admin. News 1974, pp. 4639, 5107 (emphasis added).

Congress was well aware that the powerful pre-emptive force of § 301 of LMRA displaced all state actions for violation of contracts between an employer and a labor organization, even when the state action purported to authorize a remedy unavailable under the federal provision. Section 301 pre-empts any "state-law claim [whose resolution] is substantially dependent upon the analysis of the terms of an agreement made between the parties in a labor contract." *Allis–Chalmers Corp. v. Lueck,* 471 U.S., at 220, 105 S.Ct., at 1916. As we observed in *Allis–Chalmers,* the broad preemptive effect of § 301 was first analyzed in *Teamsters v. Lucas Flour Co.,* 369 U.S. 95, 82 S.Ct. 571, 7 L.Ed.2d 593 (1962). In *Lucas Flour* the Court found that "[t]he dimensions of § 301 require the conclusion that substantive principles of federal labor law must be paramount in the area covered by the statute." *Id.,* at 103, 82 S.Ct., at 576. "[I]n enacting § 301 Congress intended doctrines of federal labor law uniformly to prevail over inconsistent local rules." *Id.,* at 104, 82 S.Ct., at 577. Indeed, for purposes of determining federal jurisdiction, this Court has singled out § 301 of the LMRA as having "pre-emptive force * * * so powerful as to displace entirely any state cause of action 'for violation of contracts between an employer and a labor organization.' Any such suit is purely a creature of federal law." *Franchise Tax Board v. Construction*

Laborers Vacation Trust, 463 U.S. 1, 23, 103 S.Ct. 2841, 2853, 77 L.Ed.2d 420, referring to *Avco Corp. v. Machinists,* 390 U.S. 557, 88 S.Ct. 1235, 20 L.Ed.2d 126 (1968).

Congress' specific reference to § 301 of the LMRA to describe the civil enforcement scheme of ERISA makes clear its intention that all suits brought by beneficiaries or participants asserting improper processing of claims under ERISA–regulated plans be treated as federal questions governed by § 502(a). See also H.R.Rep. No. 93–533, p. 12 (1973), U.S.Code Cong. & Admin.News 1974, p. 4639 reprinted in 2 Senate Committee on Labor and Public Welfare, Legislative History of ERISA 94th Cong., 2d Sess., 2359 (Comm. Print 1976) ("The uniformity of decision which the Act is designed to foster will help administrators, fiduciaries and participants to predict the legality of proposed actions without the necessity of reference to varying state laws"); 120 Cong. Rec. 29933 (1974) (remarks of Sen. Williams) (suits involving claims for benefits "will be regarded as arising under the laws of the United States, in similar fashion to those brought under section 301 of the Labor Management Relations Act"); *id.,* at 29942 (remarks of Sen. Javits) ("[i]t is also intended that a body of Federal substantive law will be developed by the courts to deal with issues involving rights and obligations under private welfare and pension plans"). The expectations that a federal common law of rights and obligations under ERISA–regulated plans would develop, indeed, the entire comparison of ERISA's § 502(a) to § 301 of the LMRA, would make little sense if the remedies available to ERISA participants and beneficiaries under § 502(a) could be supplemented or supplanted by varying state laws.

In *Metropolitan Life Ins. Co. v. Massachusetts,* 471 U.S., at 746, 105 S.Ct., at 2393, this Court rejected an interpretation of the saving clause of ERISA's express pre-emption provisions, § 514(b)(2)(A), 29 U.S.C. § 1144(b)(2)(A), that saved from pre-emption "only state regulations unrelated to the substantive provisions of ERISA," finding that "[n]othing in the language, structure, or legislative history of the Act" supported this reading of the saving clause. *Metropolitan Life,* however, did not involve a state law that conflicted with a substantive provision of ERISA. Therefore the Court's general observation—that state laws related to ERISA may also fall under the saving clause—was not focused on any particular relationship or conflict between a substantive provision of ERISA and a state law. In particular, the Court had no occasion to consider in *Metropolitan Life* the question raised in the present case: whether Congress might clearly express, through the structure and legislative history of a particular substantive provision of ERISA, an intention that the federal remedy provided by that provision displace state causes of action. Our resolution of this different question does not conflict with the Court's earlier general observations in *Metropolitan Life.*

Considering the common-sense understanding of the saving clause, the McCarran–Ferguson Act factors defining the business of insurance, and, most importantly, the clear expression of congressional intent that

ERISA's civil enforcement scheme be exclusive, we conclude that Dedeaux's state law suit asserting improper processing of a claim for benefits under an ERISA–regulated plan is not saved by § 514(b)(2)(A), and therefore is pre-empted by § 514(a).[4] Accordingly, the judgment of the Court of Appeals is

Reversed.

Notes and Questions

1. *Different Rights for Group and Individual Insureds.* It is ironic that a statute which Congress probably believed would expand employees' benefit rights has in some respects contracted them. *Dedeaux* is one example. Does it make sense that, as a result of *Dedeaux,* holders of individual policies have greater rights under state law than holders of group policies provided by employers? Are the ERISA remedies detailed in footnote 3 of the Court's opinion satisfactory substitutes for the bad-faith cause of action?

2. *The Secondary Arguments in Dedeaux.* Even assuming that the intent of Congress to pre-empt such remedies as bad-faith liability were clear, were the other arguments that the Court marshalled persuasive? For example, is there reason to think Congress intended the word "insurance" in the phrase " * * * any law of any State which regulates insurance * * * " in ERISA to have the same meaning as the phrase "the business of insurance" in the McCarran–Ferguson Act? Similarly, if the law governing bad-faith causes of action in Mississippi were now almost exclusively invoked in insurance cases—as it surely is—would the Court's requirement that the state law in question be "specifically directed" at insurance have been satisfied? Finally, if the concern of Congress in mandating preemption was to assure that there is a uniform body of law governing the *lawfulness* of employer actions regarding employment benefits, would that purpose be undermined by varying state rights regarding *remedies* for unlawful denial of benefits by insurers?

4. Because we conclude that Dedeaux's state common law claims fall under the ERISA pre-emption clause and are not rescued by the saving clause, we need not reach petitioner's argument that when an insurance company is engaged in the processing and review of claims for benefits under an employee benefit plan, it is acting in place of the plan's trustees and should be protected from direct state regulation by the deemer clause.

Chapter Six

LIABILITY INSURANCE

A. SAMPLE COMMERCIAL GENERAL LIABILITY POLICY

COMMERCIAL GENERAL LIABILITY DECLARATIONS

POLICY NO. _____

COMPANY NAME AREA	PRODUCER NAME AREA

NAMED INSURED _____

MAILING ADDRESS _____

_____

POLICY PERIOD: From _____to _____at
12:01 A.M. Standard Time at your mailing address shown above.

IN RETURN FOR THE PAYMENT OF THE PREMIUM, AND SUBJECT TO ALL THE TERMS OF THIS POLICY, WE AGREE WITH YOU TO PROVIDE THE INSURANCE AS STATED IN THIS POLICY.

LIMITS OF INSURANCE

GENERAL AGGREGATE LIMIT (Other Than Products—Completed Operations)	$ _____
PRODUCTS-COMPLETED OPERATIONS AGGREGATE LIMIT	$ _____
PERSONAL & ADVERTISING INJURY LIMIT	$ _____
EACH OCCURRENCE LIMIT	$ _____
FIRE DAMAGE LIMIT	$ _____ **ANY ONE FIRE**
MEDICAL EXPENSE LIMIT	$ _____ **ANY ONE PERSON**

RETROACTIVE DATE (CG 00 02 only)

Coverage A of this insurance does not apply to "bodily injury" or "property damage" which occurs before the Retroactive Date, if any, shown below

Retroactive Date: _____
(Enter Date or "None" if no Retroactive Date applies.)

Form of Business:

☐ Individual   ☐ Partnership

☐ Joint Venture   ☐ Organization (Other than Partnership or Joint Venture)

Business Description: _____

Location of All Premises You Own, Rent or Occupy:

_____

_____

CLASSIFICATION	CODE NO.	PREMIUM BASIS	RATE	ADVANCE PREMIUM	
				PR/CO	ALL OTHER
				$	$

TOTAL _____

Premium shown is payable: $_____ at inception.

ENDORSEMENTS ATTACHED TO THIS POLICY: IL 00 21 11 85 — Broad Form Nuclear Exclusion

_____

_____

COUNTERSIGNED _____**BY** _____
(Date)   (Authorized Representative)

NOTE: OFFICERS' FACSIMILE SIGNATURES MAY BE INSERTED HERE, ON THE POLICY COVER OR ELSEWHERE AT THE COMPANY'S OPTION

[F3863]

COMMERCIAL GENERAL LIABILITY COVERAGE FORM

Various provisions in this policy restrict coverage. Read the entire policy carefully to determine rights, duties and what is and is not covered.

Throughout this policy the words "you" and "your" refer to the Named Insured shown in the Declarations. The words "we," "us" and "our" refer to the Company providing this insurance.

The word "insured" means any person or organization qualifying as such under SECTION II — WHO IS AN INSURED.

Other words and phrases that appear in quotation marks have special meaning. Refer to SECTION V — DEFINITIONS.

SECTION I — COVERAGES

COVERAGE A. BODILY INJURY AND PROPERTY DAMAGE LIABILITY

1. Insuring Agreement.

    a. We will pay those sums that the insured becomes legally obligated to pay as damages because of "bodily injury" or "property damage" to which this insurance applies. No other obligation or liability to pay sums or perform acts or services is covered unless explicitly provided for under SUPPLEMENTARY PAYMENTS — COVERAGES A AND B. This insurance applies only to "bodily injury" and "property damage" which occurs during the policy period. The "bodily injury" or "property damage" must be caused by an "occurrence." The "occurrence" must take place in the "coverage territory." We will have the right and duty to defend any "suit" seeking those damages. But:

        (1) The amount we will pay for damages is limited as described in SECTION III — LIMITS OF INSURANCE;

        (2) We may investigate and settle any claim or "suit" at our discretion; and

        (3) Our right and duty to defend end when we have used up the applicable limit of insurance in the payment of judgments or settlements under Coverages A or B or medical expenses under Coverage C.

    b. Damages because of "bodily injury" include damages claimed by any person or organization for care, loss of services or death resulting at any time from the "bodily injury."

    c. "Property damage" that is loss of use of tangible property that is not physically injured shall be deemed to occur at the time of the "occurrence" that caused it.

2. Exclusions.

    This insurance does not apply to:

    a. "Bodily injury" or "property damage" expected or intended from the standpoint of the insured. This exclusion does not apply to "bodily injury" resulting from the use of reasonable force to protect persons or property.

    b. "Bodily injury" or "property damage" for which the insured is obligated to pay damages by reason of the assumption of liability in a contract or agreement. This exclusion does not apply to liability for damages:

        (1) Assumed in a contract or agreement that is an "insured contract;" or

        (2) That the insured would have in the absence of the contract or agreement.

    c. "Bodily injury" or "property damage" for which any insured may be held liable by reason of:

        (1) Causing or contributing to the intoxication of any person;

        (2) The furnishing of alcoholic beverages to a person under the legal drinking age or under the influence of alcohol; or

        (3) Any statute, ordinance or regulation relating to the sale, gift, distribution or use of alcoholic beverages.

    This exclusion applies only if you are in the business of manufacturing, distributing, selling, serving or furnishing alcoholic beverages.

    d. Any obligation of the insured under a workers compensation, disability benefits or unemployment compensation law or any similar law.

    e. "Bodily injury" to:

        (1) An employee of the insured arising out of and in the course of employment by the insured; or

        (2) The spouse, child, parent, brother or sister of that employee as a consequence of (1) above.

    This exclusion applies:

        (1) Whether the insured may be liable as an employer or in any other capacity; and

        (2) To any obligation to share damages with or repay someone else who must pay damages because of the injury.

    This exclusion does not apply to liability assumed by the insured under an "insured contract."

**COMMERCIAL GENERAL LIABILITY
COVERAGE FORM**

f. **(1)** "Bodily injury" or "property damage" arising out of the actual, alleged or threatened discharge, dispersal, release or escape of pollutants:

    (a) At or from premises you own, rent or occupy;

    (b) At or from any site or location used by or for you or others for the handling, storage, disposal, processing or treatment of waste;

    (c) Which are at any time transported, handled, stored, treated, disposed of, or processed as waste by or for you or any person or organization for whom you may be legally responsible; or

    (d) At or from any site or location on which you or any contractors or subcontractors working directly or indirectly on your behalf are performing operations:

        (I) if the pollutants are brought on or to the site or location in connection with such operations; or

        (II) if the operations are to test for, monitor, clean up, remove, contain, treat, detoxify or neutralize the pollutants.

  (2) Any loss, cost, or expense arising out of any governmental direction or request that you test for, monitor, clean up, remove, contain, treat, detoxify or neutralize pollutants.

Pollutants means any solid, liquid, gaseous or thermal irritant or contaminant, including smoke, vapor, soot, fumes, acids, alkalis, chemicals and waste. Waste includes materials to be recycled, reconditioned or reclaimed.

g. "Bodily injury" or "property damage" arising out of the ownership, maintenance, use or entrustment to others of any aircraft, "auto" or watercraft owned or operated by or rented or loaned to any insured. Use includes operation and "loading or unloading."

This exclusion does not apply to:

  (1) A watercraft while ashore on premises you own or rent;

  (2) A watercraft you do not own that is:

    (a) Less than 26 feet long; and

    (b) Not being used to carry persons or property for a charge;

  (3) Parking an "auto" on, or on the ways next to, premises you own or rent, provided the "auto" is not owned by or rented or loaned to you or the insured;

  (4) Liability assumed under any "insured contract" for the ownership, maintenance or use of aircraft or watercraft; or

  (5) "Bodily injury" or "property damage" arising out of the operation of any of the equipment listed in paragraph f.(2) or f.(3) of the definition of "mobile equipment" (Section V.8).

h. "Bodily injury" or "property damage" arising out of:

  (1) The transportation of "mobile equipment" by an "auto" owned or operated by or rented or loaned to any insured; or

  (2) The use of "mobile equipment" in, or while in practice or preparation for, a prearranged racing, speed or demolition contest or in any stunting activity.

i. "Bodily injury" or "property damage" due to war, whether or not declared, or any act or condition incident to war. War includes civil war, insurrection, rebellion or revolution. This exclusion applies only to liability assumed under a contract or agreement.

j. "Property damage" to:

  (1) Property you own, rent, or occupy;

  (2) Premises you sell, give away or abandon, if the "property damage" arises out of any part of those premises;

  (3) Property loaned to you;

  (4) Personal property in your care, custody or control;

  (5) That particular part of real property on which you or any contractors or subcontractors working directly or indirectly on your behalf are performing operations, if the "property damage" arises out of those operations; or

  (6) That particular part of any property that must be restored, repaired or replaced because "your work" was incorrectly performed on it.

Paragraph (2) of this exclusion does not apply if the premises are "your work" and were never occupied, rented or held for rental by you.

Paragraphs (3), (4), (5) and (6) of this exclusion do not apply to liability assumed under a sidetrack agreement.

Paragraph (6) of this exclusion does not apply to "property damage" included in the "products-completed operations hazard."

k. "Property damage" to "your product" arising out of it or any part of it.

l. "Property damage" to "your work" arising out of it or any part of it and included in the "products-completed operations hazard."

This exclusion does not apply if the damaged work or the work out of which the damage arises was performed on your behalf by a subcontractor.

m. "Property damage" to "impaired property" or property that has not been physically injured, arising out of:

(1) A defect, deficiency, inadequacy or dangerous condition in "your product" or "your work;" or

(2) A delay or failure by you or anyone acting on your behalf to perform a contract or agreement in accordance with its terms.

This exclusion does not apply to the loss of use of other property arising out of sudden and accidental physical injury to "your product" or "your work" after it has been put to its intended use.

n. Damages claimed for any loss, cost or expense incurred by you or others for the loss of use, withdrawal, recall, inspection, repair, replacement, adjustment, removal or disposal of:

(1) "Your product;"

(2) "Your work;" or

(3) "Impaired property;"

if such product, work, or property is withdrawn or recalled from the market or from use by any person or organization because of a known or suspected defect, deficiency, inadequacy or dangerous condition in it.

Exclusions c. through n. do not apply to damage by fire to premises rented to you. A separate limit of insurance applies to this coverage as described in SECTION III — LIMITS OF INSURANCE.

COVERAGE B. PERSONAL AND ADVERTISING INJURY LIABILITY

1. **Insuring Agreement.**

a. We will pay those sums that the insured becomes legally obligated to pay as damages because of "personal injury" or "advertising injury" to which this insurance applies. No other obligation or liability to pay sums or perform acts or services is covered unless explicitly provided for under SUPPLEMENTARY PAYMENTS—COVERAGES A AND B. We will have the right and duty to defend any "suit" seeking those damages. But:

(1) The amount we will pay for damages is limited as described in SECTION III — LIMITS OF INSURANCE;

(2) We may investigate and settle any claim or "suit" at our discretion; and

(3) Our right and duty to defend end when we have used up the applicable limit of insurance in the payment of judgments or settlements under Coverages A or B or medical expenses under Coverage C.

b. This insurance applies to "personal injury" only if caused by an offense:

(1) Committed in the "coverage territory" during the policy period; and

(2) Arising out of the conduct of your business, excluding advertising, publishing, broadcasting or telecasting done by or for you.

c. This insurance applies to "advertising injury" only if caused by an offense committed:

(1) In the "coverage territory" during the policy period; and

(2) In the course of advertising your goods, products or services.

2. **Exclusions.**

This insurance does not apply to:

a. "Personal injury" or "advertising injury:"

(1) Arising out of oral or written publication of material, if done by or at the direction of the insured with knowledge of its falsity;

(2) Arising out of oral or written publication of material whose first publication took place before the beginning of the policy period;

(3) Arising out of the willful violation of a penal statute or ordinance committed by or with the consent of the insured; or

(4) For which the insured has assumed liability in a contract or agreement. This exclusion does not apply to liability for damages that the insured would have in the absence of the contract or agreement.

b. "Advertising injury" arising out of:

(1) Breach of contract, other than misappropriation of advertising ideas under an implied contract;

(2) The failure of goods, products or services to conform with advertised quality or performance;

(3) The wrong description of the price of goods, products or services; or

(4) An offense committed by an insured whose business is advertising, broadcasting, publishing or telecasting.

COMMERCIAL GENERAL LIABILITY
COVERAGE FORM

COVERAGE C. MEDICAL PAYMENTS

1. Insuring Agreement.

  a. We will pay medical expenses as described below for "bodily injury" caused by an accident:

    (1) On premises you own or rent;

    (2) On ways next to premises you own or rent; or

    (3) Because of your operations;

    provided that:

    (1) The accident takes place in the "coverage territory" and during the policy period;

    (2) The expenses are incurred and reported to us within one year of the date of the accident; and

    (3) The injured person submits to examination, at our expense, by physicians of our choice as often as we reasonably require.

  b. We will make these payments regardless of fault. These payments will not exceed the applicable limit of insurance. We will pay reasonable expenses for:

    (1) First aid at the time of an accident;

    (2) Necessary medical, surgical, x-ray and dental services, including prosthetic devices; and

    (3) Necessary ambulance, hospital, professional nursing and funeral services.

2. Exclusions.

We will not pay expenses for "bodily injury:"

  a. To any insured.

  b. To a person hired to do work for or on behalf of any insured or a tenant of any insured.

  c. To a person injured on that part of premises you own or rent that the person normally occupies.

  d. To a person, whether or not an employee of any insured, if benefits for the "bodily injury" are payable or must be provided under a workers compensation or disability benefits law or a similar law.

  e. To a person injured while taking part in athletics.

  f. Included within the products-completed operations hazard."

  g. Excluded under Coverage A.

  h. Due to war, whether or not declared, or any act or condition incident to war. War includes civil war, insurrection, rebellion or revolution.

SUPPLEMENTARY PAYMENTS — COVERAGES A AND B

We will pay, with respect to any claim or "suit" we defend:

1. All expenses we incur.

2. Up to $250 for cost of bail bonds required because of accidents or traffic law violations arising out of the use of any vehicle to which the Bodily Injury Liability Coverage applies. We do not have to furnish these bonds.

3. The cost of bonds to release attachments, but only for bond amounts within the applicable limit of insurance. We do not have to furnish these bonds.

4. All reasonable expenses incurred by the insured at our request to assist us in the investigation or defense of the claim or "suit," including actual loss of earnings up to $100 a day because of time off from work.

5. All costs taxed against the insured in the "suit."

6. Pre-judgment interest awarded against the insured on that part of the judgment we pay. If we make an offer to pay the applicable limit of insurance, we will not pay any pre-judgment interest based on that period of time after the offer.

7. All interest on the full amount of any judgment that accrues after entry of the judgment and before we have paid, offered to pay, or deposited in court the part of the judgment that is within the applicable limit of insurance.

These payments will not reduce the limits of insurance.

SECTION II — WHO IS AN INSURED

1. If you are designated in the Declarations as:

  a. An individual, you and your spouse are insureds, but only with respect to the conduct of a business of which you are the sole owner.

  b. A partnership or joint venture, you are an insured. Your members, your partners, and their spouses are also insureds, but only with respect to the conduct of your business.

  c. An organization other than a partnership or joint venture, you are an insured. Your executive officers and directors are insureds, but only with respect to their duties as your officers or directors. Your stockholders are also insureds, but only with respect to their liability as stockholders.

2. Each of the following is also an insured:

  a. Your employees, other than your executive officers, but only for acts within the scope of their employment by you. However, none of these employees is an insured for:

(1) "Bodily injury" or "personal injury" to you or to a co-employee while in the course of his or her employment; or

(2) "Bodily injury" or "personal injury" arising out of his or her providing or failing to provide professional health care services; or

(3) "Property damage" to property owned or occupied by or rented or loaned to that employee, any of your other employees, or any of your partners or members (if you are a partnership or joint venture).

b. Any person (other than your employee), or any organization while acting as your real estate manager.

c. Any person or organization having proper temporary custody of your property if you die, but only:

(1) With respect to liability arising out of the maintenance or use of that property; and

(2) Until your legal representative has been appointed.

d. Your legal representative if you die, but only with respect to duties as such. That representative will have all your rights and duties under this Coverage Part.

3. With respect to "mobile equipment" registered in your name under any motor vehicle registration law, any person is an insured while driving such equipment along a public highway with your permission. Any other person or organization responsible for the conduct of such person is also an insured, but only with respect to liability arising out of the operation of the equipment, and only if no other insurance of any kind is available to that person or organization for this liability. However, no person or organization is an insured with respect to:

a. "Bodily injury" to a co-employee of the person driving the equipment; or

b. "Property damage" to property owned by, rented to, in the charge of or occupied by you or the employer of any person who is an insured under this provision.

4. Any organization you newly acquire or form, other than a partnership or joint venture, and over which you maintain ownership or majority interest, will be deemed to be a Named Insured if there is no other similar insurance available to that organization. However:

a. Coverage under this provision is afforded only until the 90th day after you acquire or form the organization or the end of the policy period, whichever is earlier;

b. Coverage A does not apply to "bodily injury" or "property damage" that occurred before you acquired or formed the organization; and

c. Coverage B does not apply to "personal injury" or "advertising injury" arising out of an offense committed before you acquired or formed the organization.

No person or organization is an insured with respect to the conduct of any current or past partnership or joint venture that is not shown as a Named Insured in the Declarations.

SECTION III — LIMITS OF INSURANCE

1. The Limits of Insurance shown in the Declarations and the rules below fix the most we will pay regardless of the number of:

a. Insureds;

b. Claims made or "suits" brought; or

c. Persons or organizations making claims or bringing "suits."

2. The General Aggregate Limit is the most we will pay for the sum of:

a. Medical expenses under Coverage C; and

b. Damages under Coverage A and Coverage B, except damages because of injury and damage included in the "products-completed operations hazard."

3. The Products-Completed Operations Aggregate Limit is the most we will pay under Coverage A for damages because of injury and damage included in the "products-completed operations hazard."

4. Subject to 2. above, the Personal and Advertising Injury Limit is the most we will pay under Coverage B for the sum of all damages because of all "personal injury" and all "advertising injury" sustained by any one person or organization.

5. Subject to 2. or 3. above, whichever applies, the Each Occurrence Limit is the most we will pay for the sum of:

a. Damages under Coverage A; and

b. Medical expenses under Coverage C

because of all "bodily injury" and "property damage" arising out of any one "occurrence."

6. Subject to 5. above, the Fire Damage Limit is the most we will pay under Coverage A for damages because of "property damage" to premises rented to you arising out of any one fire.

7. Subject to 5. above, the Medical Expense Limit is the most we will pay under Coverage C for all medical expenses because of "bodily injury" sustained by any one person.

COMMERCIAL GENERAL LIABILITY
COVERAGE FORM

The limits of this Coverage Part apply separately to each consecutive annual period and to any remaining period of less than 12 months, starting with the beginning of the policy period shown in the Declarations, unless the policy period is extended after issuance for an additional period of less than 12 months. In that case, the additional period will be deemed part of the last preceding period for purposes of determining the Limits of Insurance.

SECTION IV — COMMERCIAL GENERAL LIABILITY CONDITIONS

1. **Bankruptcy.**

   Bankruptcy or insolvency of the insured or of the insured's estate will not relieve us of our obligations under this Coverage Part.

2. **Duties In The Event Of Occurrence, Claim Or Suit.**

   a. You must see to it that we are notified promptly of an "occurrence" which may result in a claim. Notice should include:

   (1) How, when and where the "occurrence" took place; and

   (2) The names and addresses of any injured persons and witnesses.

   b. If a claim is made or "suit" is brought against any insured, you must see to it that we receive prompt written notice of the claim or "suit."

   c. You and any other involved insured must:

   (1) Immediately send us copies of any demands, notices, summonses or legal papers received in connection with the claim or "suit;"

   (2) Authorize us to obtain records and other information;

   (3) Cooperate with us in the investigation, settlement or defense of the claim or "suit;" and

   (4) Assist us, upon our request, in the enforcement of any right against any person or organization which may be liable to the insured because of injury or damage to which this insurance may also apply.

   d. No insureds will, except at their own cost, voluntarily make a payment, assume any obligation, or incur any expense, other than for first aid, without our consent.

3. **Legal Action Against Us.**

   No person or organization has a right under this Coverage Part:

   a. To join us as a party or otherwise bring us into a "suit" asking for damages from an insured; or

   b. To sue us on this Coverage Part unless all of its terms have been fully complied with.

A person or organization may sue us to recover on an agreed settlement or on a final judgment against an insured obtained after an actual trial; but we will not be liable for damages that are not payable under the terms of this Coverage Part or that are in excess of the applicable limit of insurance. An agreed settlement means a settlement and release of liability signed by us, the insured and the claimant or the claimant's legal representative.

4. **Other Insurance.**

   If other valid and collectible insurance is available to the insured for a loss we cover under Coverages A or B of this Coverage Part, our obligations are limited as follows:

   a. Primary Insurance

   This insurance is primary except when b. below applies. If this insurance is primary, our obligations are not affected unless any of the other insurance is also primary. Then, we will share with all that other insurance by the method described in c. below.

   b. Excess Insurance

   This insurance is excess over any of the other insurance, whether primary, excess, contingent or on any other basis:

   (1) That is Fire, Extended Coverage, Builder's Risk, Installation Risk or similar coverage for "your work;"

   (2) That is Fire insurance for premises rented to you; or

   (3) If the loss arises out of the maintenance or use of aircraft, "autos" or watercraft to the extent not subject to Exclusion g. of Coverage A (Section I).

   When this insurance is excess, we will have no duty under Coverage A or B to defend any claim or "suit" that any other insurer has a duty to defend. If no other insurer defends, we will undertake to do so, but we will be entitled to the insured's rights against all those other insurers.

   When this insurance is excess over other insurance , we will pay only our share of the amount of the loss, if any, that exceeds the sum of:

   (1) The total amount that all such other insurance would pay for the loss in the absence of this insurance; and

   (2) The total of all deductible and self-insured amounts under all that other insurance.

We will share the remaining loss, if any, with any other insurance that is not described in this Excess Insurance provision and was not bought specifically to apply in excess of the Limits of Insurance shown in the Declarations of this Coverage Part.

c. Method of Sharing

If all of the other insurance permits contribution by equal shares, we will follow this method also. Under this approach each insurer contributes equal amounts until it has paid its applicable limit of insurance or none of the loss remains, whichever comes first.

If any of the other insurance does not permit contribution by equal shares, we will contribute by limits. Under this method, each insurer's share is based on the ratio of its applicable limit of insurance to the total applicable limits of insurance of all insurers.

5. Premium Audit.

a. We will compute all premiums for this Coverage Part in accordance with our rules and rates.

b. Premium shown in this Coverage Part as advance premium is a deposit premium only. At the close of each audit period we will compute the earned premium for that period. Audit premiums are due and payable on notice to the first Named Insured. If the sum of the advance and audit premiums paid for the policy term is greater than the earned premium, we will return the excess to the first Named Insured.

c. The first Named Insured must keep records of the information we need for premium computation, and send us copies at such times as we may request.

6. Representations.

By accepting this policy, you agree:

a. The statements in the Declarations are accurate and complete;

b. Those statements are based upon representations you made to us; and

c. We have issued this policy in reliance upon your representations.

7. Separation Of Insureds.

Except with respect to the Limits of Insurance, and any rights or duties specifically assigned in this Coverage Part to the first Named Insured, this insurance applies:

a. As if each Named Insured were the only Named Insured; and

b. Separately to each insured against whom claim is made or "suit" is brought.

8. Transfer Of Rights Of Recovery Against Others To Us.

If the insured has rights to recover all or part of any payment we have made under this Coverage Part, those rights are transferred to us. The insured must do nothing after loss to impair them. At our request, the insured will bring "suit" or transfer those rights to us and help us enforce them.

SECTION V — DEFINITIONS

1. "Advertising injury" means injury arising out of one or more of the following offenses:

a. Oral or written publication of material that slanders or libels a person or organization or disparages a person's or organization's goods, products or services;

b. Oral or written publication of material that violates a person's right of privacy;

c. Misappropriation of advertising ideas or style of doing business; or

d. Infringement of copyright, title or slogan.

2. "Auto" means a land motor vehicle, trailer or semitrailer designed for travel on public roads, including any attached machinery or equipment. But "auto" does not include "mobile equipment."

3. "Bodily injury" means bodily injury, sickness or disease sustained by a person, including death resulting from any of these at any time.

4. "Coverage territory" means:

a. The United States of America (including its territories and possessions), Puerto Rico and Canada;

b. International waters or airspace, provided the injury or damage does not occur in the course of travel or transportation to or from any place not included in a. above; or

c. All parts of the world if:

(1) The injury or damage arises out of:

(a) Goods or products made or sold by you in the territory described in a. above; or

(b) The activities of a person whose home is in the territory described in a. above, but is away for a short time on your business; and

(2) The insured's responsibility to pay damages is determined in a "suit" on the merits, in the territory described in a. above or in a settlement we agree to.

COMMERCIAL GENERAL LIABILITY
COVERAGE FORM

5. "Impaired property" means tangible property, other than "your product" or "your work," that cannot be used or is less useful because:

a. It incorporates "your product" or "your work" that is known or thought to be defective, deficient, inadequate or dangerous; or

b. You have failed to fulfill the terms of a contract or agreement;

if such property can be restored to use by:

a. The repair, replacement, adjustment or removal of "your product" or "your work;" or

b. Your fulfilling the terms of the contract or agreement.

6. "Insured contract" means:

a. A lease of premises;

b. A sidetrack agreement;

c. An easement or license agreement in connection with vehicle or pedestrian private railroad crossings at grade;

d. Any other easement agreement, except in connection with construction or demolition operations on or within 50 feet of a railroad;

e. An indemnification of a municipality as required by ordinance, except in connection with work for a municipality;

f. An elevator maintenance agreement; or

g. That part of any other contract or agreement pertaining to your business under which you assume the tort liability of another to pay damages because of "bodily injury" or "property damage" to a third person or organization, if the contract or agreement is made prior to the "bodily injury" or "property damage." Tort liability means a liability that would be imposed by law in the absence of any contract or agreement.

An "insured contract" does not include that part of any contract or agreement:

a. That indemnifies an architect, engineer or surveyor for injury or damage arising out of:

(1) Preparing, approving or failing to prepare or approve maps, drawings, opinions, reports, surveys, change orders, designs or specifications; or

(2) Giving directions or instructions, or failing to give them, if that is the primary cause of the injury or damage;

b. Under which the insured, if an architect, engineer or surveyor, assumes liability for injury or damage arising out of the insured's rendering or failing to render professional services, including those listed in a. above and supervisory, inspection or engineering services; or

c. That indemnifies any person or organization for damage by fire to premises rented or loaned to you.

7. "Loading or unloading" means the handling of property:

a. After it is moved from the place where it is accepted for movement into or onto an aircraft, watercraft or "auto;"

b. While it is in or on an aircraft, watercraft or "auto;" or

c. While it is being moved from an aircraft, watercraft or "auto" to the place where it is finally delivered;

but "loading or unloading" does not include the movement of property by means of a mechanical device, other than a hand truck, that is not attached to the aircraft, watercraft or "auto."

8. "Mobile equipment" means any of the following types of land vehicles, including any attached machinery or equipment:

a. Bulldozers, farm machinery, forklifts and other vehicles designed for use principally off public roads;

b. Vehicles maintained for use solely on or next to premises you own or rent;

c. Vehicles that travel on crawler treads;

d. Vehicles, whether self-propelled or not, maintained primarily to provide mobility to permanently mounted:

(1) Power cranes, shovels, loaders, diggers or drills; or

(2) Road construction or resurfacing equipment such as graders, scrapers or rollers;

e. Vehicles not described in a., b., c. or d. above that are not self-propelled and are maintained primarily to provide mobility to permanently attached equipment of the following types:

(1) Air compressors, pumps and generators, including spraying, welding, building cleaning, geophysical exploration, lighting and well servicing equipment; or

(2) Cherry pickers and similar devices used to raise or lower workers;

f. Vehicles not described in a., b., c. or d. above maintained primarily for purposes other than the transportation of persons or cargo.

However, self-propelled vehicles with the following types of permanently attached equipment are not "mobile equipment" but will be considered "autos:"

(1) Equipment designed primarily for:

(a) Snow removal;

 CG 00 01 11 85

(b) Road maintenance, but not construction or resurfacing;

(c) Street cleaning;

(2) Cherry pickers and similar devices mounted on automobile or truck chassis and used to raise or lower workers; and

(3) Air compressors, pumps and generators, including spraying, welding, building cleaning, geophysical exploration, lighting and well servicing equipment.

9. "Occurrence" means an accident, including continuous or repeated exposure to substantially the same general harmful conditions.

10. "Personal injury" means injury, other than "bodily injury," arising out of one or more of the following offenses:

a. False arrest, detention or imprisonment;

b. Malicious prosecution;

c. Wrongful entry into, or eviction of a person from, a room, dwelling or premises that the person occupies;

d. Oral or written publication of material that slanders or libels a person or organization or disparages a person's or organization's goods, products or services; or

e. Oral or written publication of material that violates a person's right of privacy.

11. a. "Products-completed operations hazard" includes all "bodily injury" and "property damage" occurring away from premises you own or rent and arising out of "your product" or "your work" except:

(1) Products that are still in your physical possession; or

(2) Work that has not yet been completed or abandoned.

b. "Your work" will be deemed completed at the earliest of the following times:

(1) When all of the work called for in your contract has been completed.

(2) When all of the work to be done at the site has been completed if your contract calls for work at more than one site.

(3) When that part of the work done at a job site has been put to its intended use by any person or organization other than another contractor or subcontractor working on the same project.

Work that may need service, maintenance, correction, repair or replacement, but which is otherwise complete, will be treated as completed.

c. This hazard does not include "bodily injury" or "property damage" arising out of:

(1) The transportation of property, unless the injury or damage arises out of a condition in or on a vehicle created by the "loading or unloading" of it;

(2) The existence of tools, uninstalled equipment or abandoned or unused materials;

(3) Products or operations for which the classification in this Coverage Part or in our manual of rules includes products or completed operations.

12. "Property damage" means:

a. Physical injury to tangible property, including all resulting loss of use of that property; or

b. Loss of use of tangible property that is not physically injured.

13. "Suit" means a civil proceeding in which damages because of "bodily injury," "property damage," "personal injury" or "advertising injury" to which this insurance applies are alleged. "Suit" includes an arbitration proceeding alleging such damages to which you must submit or submit with our consent.

14. "Your product" means:

a. Any goods or products, other than real property, manufactured, sold, handled, distributed or disposed of by:

(1) You;

(2) Others trading under your name; or

(3) A person or organization whose business or assets you have acquired; and

b. Containers (other than vehicles), materials, parts or equipment furnished in connection with such goods or products.

"Your product" includes warranties or representations made at any time with respect to the fitness, quality, durability or performance of any of the items included in a. and b. above.

"Your product" does not include vending machines or other property rented to or located for the use of others but not sold.

15. "Your work" means:

a. Work or operations performed by you or on your behalf; and

b. Materials, parts or equipment furnished in connection with such work or operations.

"Your work" includes warranties or representations made at any time with respect to the fitness, quality, durability or performance of any of the items included in a. or b. above.

Notes and Questions

1. *The New CGL Policy.* The Commercial General Liability (CGL) Policy set out above is the successor to the Comprehensive General Liability (CGL) Policy that was in use (in successive revisions) for several decades. Insurers began marketing the new CGL in the mid-1980's. What does the change of name suggest the drafters were trying to signal?

Many of the cases in this Chapter involve interpretations of older CGL and Excess CGL insurance policy provisions that closely resemble but differ slightly from those contained in the newer CGL Policy. For reasons that will become clearer as you study this Chapter, the provisions of the older policy will remain relevant for years to come, but the new policy will slowly come to dominate legal disputes. As you compare the provisions of the new policy with those at issue in the cases set out below, consider the following questions: Which revisions suggest that the drafters were attempting to reverse the effect of previous judicial decisions? To what extent are the revisions successful? Which revisions have failed to make a difference in the probable outcome of the same dispute under the new policy?

2. *General–Purpose Coverage.* Notice that the CGL provides "general" insurance for businesses. Special-purpose coverage, such as automobile and environmental liability insurance, among others, must be separately purchased.

B. THE INSURING AGREEMENT

Hundreds of millions of dollars have been spent litigating the meaning of several phrases in the standard Insuring Agreement in CGL policies. This section surveys the highlights of this litigation, by addressing the meaning of the key terms and phrases in the Insuring Agreement that, in language identical to or highly similar to the following, promises to pay "all sums the insured becomes *legally obligated* to pay *as damages,* because of *bodily injury or property damage,* caused by an *occurrence.*"

1. What Is an "Occurrence?"

HONEYCOMB SYSTEMS, INC. v. ADMIRAL INSURANCE COMPANY

United States District Court, D. Maine, 1983.
567 F.Supp. 1400.

GIGNOUX, District Judge.

In this declaratory judgment action plaintiff Honeycomb Systems, Inc. ["Honeycomb"] seeks a judgment declaring that certain losses it sustained arising from the 1977 failure of a dryer built by it for Scott Paper Company ["Scott"] are covered by an umbrella liability insurance policy issued to it by defendant Admiral Insurance Company ["Admiral"]. The case is submitted on stipulated facts and cross-motions for summary judgment. The issues have been thoroughly briefed and argued. For the reasons to be stated, Honeycomb's motion for summary judgment is granted and Admiral's motion for summary judgment is denied.

I.

The Stipulated Facts

Honeycomb manufactures, among other products, large dryers that are widely used by paper manufacturers. In the early 1970s Scott, a major manufacturer of paper products, decided to build a new paper machine capable of producing a premium brand of toilet paper. In 1973 two of the senior members of Scott's engineering staff met with Honeycomb's chief engineers to discuss the feasibility of Honeycomb building a dryer with a diameter of 22 feet for incorporation into the new paper machine. Prior to that time the largest dryer ever manufactured by Honeycomb was 12 feet in diameter. Scott and Honeycomb agreed that Honeycomb would perform a feasibility study, the cost of which would be applied to the cost of the new dryer if Scott ordered it. Because proper performance and evaluation of the feasibility study required Scott and Honeycomb to disclose to each other confidential aspects of their respective businesses, they executed an agreement that prohibited disclosure to third parties of each others' trade secrets and that prohibited Honeycomb, for a fixed period of years, from selling to Scott's competitors dryers with diameters greater than 14 feet.

By late 1973 Scott and Honeycomb concluded that the project was feasible, and in November 1973 Scott directed Honeycomb to design and build a 22 foot dryer according to design and operating guidelines provided by Scott. Honeycomb itself designed the dryer and fabricated the "shell," the cylindrical portion of the dryer. It hired Hodge Boiler Works, Inc. ["Hodge"], a well-established firm with long experience in heavy welding and fabrication, to fabricate the "heads," the large circular plates that hold the cylindrical portion of the dryer at each end. In late 1974 the various parts of the dryer were shipped to Scott's plant in Chester, Pennsylvania, where they were assembled and incorporated in the new paper machine. The paper machine was put into operation in May 1975.

In September 1975 Scott inspected the dryer and found that most of the welds around the hub of the front dryer head had failed and that the welds on the back dryer had showed signs of inadequate weld size and quality. The cause of the problem was that Hodge had applied welds that were grossly undersized and of such poor quality that they did not even come close to minimum standards. The dryer was shut down for repair of the welds from September 6 to November 7, 1975. During that time Scott and Honeycomb discovered two other fabrication errors by Hodge affecting the hubs. In boring out the hubs Hodge had bored deeper than specified. In addition, Hodge had erroneously attached a ¾-inch plate closer to the outer end of the flanges on the head than the drawing called for. These two errors greatly increased the stress at the base of the hub flanges.

Scott and Honeycomb each had engineers study the boring and attachment errors to determine whether the errors would significantly impair the integrity of the hub. Each engineer independently concluded that the magnitude of the stress created by these errors was so low as to cause no concern. Honeycomb, however, suggested that Scott continue to monitor the problem using strain gauges.

For two years Scott regularly inspected the welds and monitored the performance of the heads without discovering any problem of significance. The monitoring took the form of visual inspection and, on occasion, the use of x-rays and liquid dye penetrant to detect cracks. It is unclear whether Scott followed Honeycomb's suggestion to use strain gauges. On September 3, 1977, during the routine Labor Day shutdown, Scott discovered a substantial crack in the hub of the back head. The cause of the hub crack was Hodge's boring and attachment errors; it had nothing to do with welding, which had been the cause of the 1975 failure. The crack was a very serious flaw, extending about 35 inches, or through 40% of the hub's circumference. If left unrepaired, the crack would have worsened and caused a severe failure of the dryer. Consequently, Scott shut the machine down until repairs were made, a period of 40 days.

Throughout the period from 1975 through 1978 Honeycomb's primary liability insurer was The Hartford Insurance Co. ["Hartford"]. The Hartford policy afforded property damage liability coverage of $100,000 for each occurrence. At the time of the 1975 failure of the welds, Honeycomb also had an excess ("umbrella") liability policy issued by Aetna Insurance Company ["Aetna"], effective from September 21, 1972 to September 21, 1975. The Aetna policy afforded property damage liability coverage of $2,000,000 for each occurrence, in excess of the Hartford coverage. From September 21, 1975 through July 1, 1977, Federal Insurance Company was the excess liability insurer, providing the same coverage. That policy was succeeded by Admiral's umbrella liability policy, effective from July 1, 1977 to July 1, 1978. Admiral's policy provided $1,000,000 property damage liability coverage for each occurrence, in excess of $100,000.

On September 1, 1978, Scott sued Honeycomb and Hodge in this Court. See *Scott Paper Company v. Honeycomb Systems, Inc.*, Civ. No. 78–177 P (D.Me. filed Sept. 1, 1978). The suit sought recovery of three major elements of damages: the "direct cost" of repairing the 22 foot heads in 1975 and 1977, the lost profits attributable to the interruption of production during each repair period, and the costs of constructing replacement heads. The total claim for damages exceeded $28,000,000.

On September 18, 1981 the Scott suit was settled when Hartford and Aetna between them paid Scott $1,000,000. Honeycomb paid Scott the equivalent of $741,000 in cash by forgiving two Scott debts to Honeycomb, and Honeycomb gave Scott a promissory note for $250,000, payable in three annual installments beginning September 18, 1982, with interest at 8% per year. The parties have stipulated that the $250,000 promissory note represents the amount of the settlement for which Admiral will be liable in this action if Honeycomb establishes

if Honeycomb can
prove this

that Honeycomb's policy with Admiral covers any *one* of the three categories of damages sued for by Scott. The parties have also stipulated that the Court is to add to any award interest on the $250,000 from September 18, 1981, to be computed at a rate of 8% per year, without compounding. Honeycomb also seeks to recover the attorney's fees incurred in bringing this action.

II.

Discussion

lawsuit governed by terms of umbrella liability policy.

standard CGL policy

The parties agree that the present lawsuit is governed by the terms of the umbrella liability policy issued to Honeycomb by Admiral, effective from July 1, 1977 to July 1, 1978. The policy is a standard form comprehensive general liability (CGL) policy.[1] The policy provides that Admiral will indemnify Honeycomb for losses sustained by Honeycomb in excess of $100,000 that Honeycomb is

policy statement

legally obligated to pay as damages because of * * * property damage * * * to which this insurance applies, caused by an occurrence anywhere during the policy period.

Admiral 4 grounds not liable

Admiral disclaims coverage of the 1977 failure on four grounds. Admiral contends (1) that the 1977 hub crack in the dryer did not constitute an "occurrence" within the meaning of the policy, (2) that any "occurrence" that did take place "occurred" before July 1, 1977, (3) that the damages suffered by Honeycomb as a result of the crack do not constitute "damages because of property damage to which this insurance applies," and (4) that the damages suffered by Honeycomb fall within several of the exclusions specified in the policy. The Court finds none of these arguments persuasive.[2]

A. *"Occurrence"*

The Admiral insurance policy defines an "occurrence" as

def. of occurrence in policy

an accident, including continuous or repeated exposure to conditions, which results in * * * property damage * * *

1. The policy in issue here is the fifth generation of a standard form contract that was first promulgated in 1940 and that underwent major revisions in 1943, 1955, 1966 and 1973, *Weedo v. Stone–E–Brick, Inc.,* 81 N.J. 233, 405 A.2d 788, 791 (1979); Tinker, *Comprehensive General Liability Insurance—Perspective and Overview,* 25 Fed'n Ins. Counsel Q. 217, 221 (1975). Provisions in this policy and provisions similar thereto have seen considerable judicial and academic scrutiny.

2. The parties have stipulated that Maine law is the applicable law. As the Maine courts have not interpreted most of the provisions contained in the policy, the Court has had to resort to accepted canons of interpretation of insurance contracts, among which are the canon that ambiguity in an insurance contract is to be construed against the insurer, *Baybutt Construction Corp. v. Commercial Union Insurance Co.,* 455 A.2d 914, 921 (Me.1983); *Farm Bureau Mutual Insurance Co. v. Waugh,* 159 Me. 115, 188 A.2d 889 (1963), and its corollary that exclusions from coverage are to be narrowly construed, *Baybutt Construction Corp., supra,* 455 A.2d at 921; *Travelers Indemnity Co. v. Dingwell,* 414 A.2d 220, 228 (Me.1980). In addition, the Court has referred to decisions in other jurisdictions and the writings of commentators concerning policies similar to the one at issue here.

neither expected nor intended from the standpoint of the insured.

Admiral does not argue that the crack was other than an unintended accident that resulted in property damage.[3] Admiral contends, however, that the 1977 hub crack was "expected from the standpoint of the insured." *Adm. A crack was expected by insured*

Admiral argues that the Court must employ an objective test in determining whether something is "expected." The Supreme Judicial Court of Maine, however, has recently considered and explicitly rejected the contention that application of an objective test is required by the phrase "expected * * * from the standpoint of the insured." In *Patrons–Oxford Mutual Insurance Co. v. Dodge,* 426 A.2d 888, 892 (Me. 1981), the court interpreted the phrase as referring only to injury that the insured "in fact *subjectively foresaw as practically certain.*" (emphasis in original). *Accord City of Virginia Beach v. Aetna Casualty & Surety Co.,* 426 F.Supp. 821, 824–25 (E.D.Va.1976). The record offers no support for the contention that Honeycomb actually foresaw a great likelihood of the crack, and, indeed, Admiral makes no such suggestion. Admiral's argument that the crack was expected therefore fails.

Although the Court perceives no meaningful way to distinguish *Dodge,* even were the Court to adopt an objective standard, defendant's argument would fail. In urging an objective test, Admiral initially suggests that any "reasonably foreseeable" event must be considered expected, citing *Gassaway v. Travelers Insurance Co.,* 222 Tenn. 649, 439 S.W.2d 605, 608–09 (1969). Alternatively, Admiral suggests that the Court adopt the objective test expressed in *City of Carter Lake v. Aetna Casualty & Surety Co.,* 604 F.2d 1052, 1058–59 (8th Cir.1979), which bars recovery for an event if the insured "knew or should have known that there was a substantial probability" of the accident occurring. The *Gassaway* "reasonably foreseeable" test clearly is an erroneous one. Such a test would allow coverage only when the insured is not negligent and hence generally not in need of liability coverage, while the test would disallow coverage when the insured is negligent and hence in need of coverage. As the Eighth Circuit has noted, unless one assumes that insurance companies exist for the sole purpose of receiving premiums, such a construction makes no sense. *City of Carter Lake, supra,* 604 F.2d at 1058. See M. Rhodes, *Couch on Insurance 2d* §§ 44:267, 44:285 (Rev.Ed.1982) (citing cases that hold that the negligence of the insured does not vitiate insurance coverage).

In addition, defendant simply cannot meet the "substantial probability" test announced in *City of Carter Lake.* That test requires a higher degree of expectability than the "reasonably foreseeable" test:

---

3. In passing, Admiral cites two cases that hold that an event that is the result of cumulative effects of exposure to a condition is not an "accident." *See Leggett v. Home Indemnity Co.,* 461 F.2d 257 (10th Cir.1972); *A.D. Irwin Investments, Inc. v. Great American Insurance Co.,* 28 Colo.App. 570, 475 P.2d 633 (1970). Those cases appear to consider pre–1966 CGL policies, which did not contain the phrase "including continuous or repeated exposure to conditions" as part of their definitions of accident. Consequently Admiral quite properly refrains from arguing that these cases control here * * *

> A result is reasonably foreseeable if there are indications which would lead a reasonably prudent man to know that the particular results could follow from his acts. Substantial probability is more than this. The indications must be strong enough to alert a reasonably prudent man not only to the possibility of the results occurring but the indications also must be sufficient to forewarn him that the results are highly likely to occur.

City of Carter Lake, supra, 604 F.2d at 1059 n. 4. In *Carter Lake* the insured suffered equipment failure of a type that clearly indicated a substantial probability of the identical failure recurring. The Court held that five recurrences of the incident during the year subsequent to the original failure were not "unexpected," and hence not covered by the insurance policy. *See also United States Fidelity & Guaranty Co. v. Bonitz Insulation Co. of Alabama,* 424 So.2d 569, 572 (Ala.1982). In this case, by contrast, there was no prior occurrence of the hub crack. Scott and Honeycomb merely discovered deviations from fabrication plans, deviations that engineers for each company independently concluded were no cause for concern. Nothing in the record would permit the Court to find that prior to September 3, 1977 Honeycomb faced indications sufficient to forewarn it that the crack was "highly likely to occur." * * *

Notes and Questions

1. *From "Accident" to "Occurrence."* Prior to 1966, the standard CGL policy provided coverage for damage caused by "accident." Some courts held that the term had a temporal element, and that gradually accumulating damage therefore was not covered; others interpreted the term more broadly. The 1966 revisions adopted the latter approach, by making an "occurrence" the touchstone of coverage. After 1973 CGL policies defined that term in roughly the following language: "An accident, including continuous or repeated exposure to conditions, which results during the policy period in bodily injury or property damage neither expected nor intended from the standpoint of the insured." This definition makes it clear that damage need not occur suddenly in order to be covered, so long as that damage is neither expected nor intended.

2. *Neither Expected Nor Intended.* Most courts follow the *Honeycomb* approach, holding that whether an event is "expected" is a question of degree, but that mere negligence in failing to foresee an event does not constitute expectation. The idea is to combat clear cases of moral hazard while preserving coverage for the kind of carelessness that most tort actions allege. The problem posed by this language, however, is that it is not entirely congruent with the categories employed by tort law—yet it is tort liability against which the policy insures. It is possible, therefore, that there is coverage under the CGL policy against liability for certain intentional torts, and, conversely, no

coverage against certain forms of liability that would not be described by tort law as intentional. Apart from the substance of coverage, notice that this difference in terminology means that the question whether there is coverage will often have to be litigated separately from the question whether the insured is liable in tort. For discussion of this issue, see Chapter Seven.

3. *The Burden of Proof.* The Sample CGL Policy in Section A provides roughly the same coverage as the Insuring Agreement at issue in the *Honeycomb* policy, but transfers the "neither expected nor intended" limitation from the insuring agreement to the list of exclusions. Given that the burden of proving coverage is generally on the insured, and the burden of proving that otherwise-covered events fall within exclusions is generally on the insurer, this might be a significant change. Many of the decisions, however, suggest that whether an event was expected is often a question of law rather than fact. See generally Rynearson, Exclusion of Expected or Intended Personal Injury or Property Damage Under the Occurrence Definition of the Standard Comprehensive General Liability Policy, in A. Liederman (ed.), The Comprehensive General Liability Policy: A Critique of Selected Provisions (1985). And other decisions indicate that because the phrase "neither expected nor intended" is in the nature of an exclusion even though it is contained in the definition of a term in the Insuring Agreement, the insurer bears the burden of proof on the issue. The apparent change in the burden of proof in the revised CGL therefore may appear to be more significant than it actually is.

4. *Combatting Adverse Selection.* If you were Admiral, why might you conclude in retrospect that you had been the victim of adverse selection? If the definition of an insured occurrence adopted in *Honeycomb* is standard, what could you do in the future to guard against this problem?

2. The Number of Occurrences

TRANSPORT INSURANCE COMPANY v. LEE WAY MOTOR FREIGHT, INC.

United States District Court, N.D. Texas, 1980.
487 F.Supp. 1325.

OPINION AND ORDER

SANDERS, District Judge.

Plaintiff Transport Insurance Company ("Transport") sues its insured, Defendant Lee Way Motor Freight, Inc. ("Lee Way"), for declaratory judgment pursuant to Title 28, United States Code § 2201 in order to determine the extent of Transport's liability under excess umbrella insurance policies that provide coverage for damages that Lee Way must pay on account of discrimination.

In a previous suit, *United States v. Lee Way,* Lee Way was found to have engaged in a pattern and practice of race discrimination and ordered to pay over $1.8 million in damages to individual discriminatees. In the present case Transport asks this Court to determine (1) whether the liability imposed upon Lee Way in the previous suit resulted from a single occurrence, a separate occurrence as to each of the four terminal locations involved, or a separate occurrence as to each of the individual discriminatees. * * *

The Court finds and concludes (1) that the pattern and practice of discrimination found by the court in *United States v. Lee Way* constitutes "one occurrence" as that term is used in the insurance policies. * * *

I. Background

A. *United States v. Lee Way*

In June of 1972, the United States filed suit against Lee Way and two labor unions, alleging that they had engaged in and were engaging in a pattern and practice of discrimination in employment. *United States v. Lee Way Motor Freight, Inc., et al.,* W.D.Okla., Civil Action No. 72–445. Following several months of trial, the district court issued its findings and conclusions December 27, 1973, in which it found and concluded that Lee Way had engaged in a pattern and practice of employment discrimination. The court determined that Lee Way had discriminated on the grounds of race in its hiring practices and in its promotion and transfer policies, all of which operated to restrict black employees to the poorest paying and least desirable jobs.[1] The court noted that certain practices, although neutral on their face, operated to freeze the status quo of prior discriminatory practices and thus could not be lawfully maintained.

After referring the case to a special master for determination of individual entitlement to relief, the trial court entered its final judgment October 11, 1977, wherein it ordered Lee Way to pay the sum of $1,818,191.33, as damages in the form of forty-seven individual back-pay awards, ranging from $3,000 to $138,000. The judgment was appealed, and in September 1979, the Tenth Circuit Court of Appeals affirmed the district court's judgment but remanded the case for consideration of additional damages.

---

1. The Court found that Lee Way discriminated against blacks in hiring and job placement and specifically found that Lee Way's no-transfer policy which was neutral on its face operated discriminatorily. (Findings 34–37 and Conclusions 9–11). It was company policy that no employee would transfer between job classifications covered by different bargaining units. The policy's effect "froze" blacks into menial and lower-paying positions which they traditionally had held and prevented placement in more desirable higher-paying jobs. Even though this policy had been found to be unlawful in *Jones v. Lee Way Motor Freight, Inc.,* 431 F.2d 245 (10th Cir.1970), Lee Way had continued to enforce a similar policy which provided that anyone who transferred could not carry over his seniority for bidding and lay-off purposes. It, too, was found to be unlawful by the district court (Conclusion 10).

B.　*The Insurance Policies*

For many years prior to the filing of *United States v. Lee Way,* Lee Way had purchased all its insurance coverage from Transport. In January 1967, Lee Way purchased from Transport additional insurance in the form of a series of eight excess umbrella insurance policies which afforded substantially higher limits of liability and broader coverages than the underlying Transport policies. This excess umbrella coverage (in the form of annually renewed policies) was in effect from January 1, 1967, through early 1978. The first five policies (those in effect from January 1, 1967, until mid–1972) expressly provided coverage for discrimination. However, in late August or early September 1972, Transport rewrote the umbrella policy then in effect with an endorsement excluding any future coverage for discrimination. Consequently, in this action the Court is only concerned with the five umbrella policies which were in effect from January 1, 1967, through late August or early September, 1972.

The parties have stipulated that a specimen policy (admitted into evidence) contains the language relevant to all the policies in question. The general coverage provision says that Transport will indemnify Lee Way

> "for all sums which [Lee Way] shall be obligated to pay by reason of the liability imposed upon [Lee Way] by law * * * for damages, * * * on account of personal injuries * * * caused by or arising out of each occurrence happening anywhere in the world."

The term "personal injuries" is separately defined and includes discrimination as one kind of personal injury. Also defined is "occurrence":

> The term "occurrence" means an accident or a happening or event or a continuous or repeated exposure to conditions which unexpectedly and unintentionally results in personal injury, property damage or advertising liability during the policy period. All such exposure to substantially the same general conditions existing at or emanating from one premises location shall be deemed one occurrence.

The declarations of the policies in question provide for a deductible amount to be borne by Lee Way of $25,000 *per occurrence.*

Thus, if Lee Way's discriminatory conduct constituted one occurrence, then Lee Way bears only one $25,000 deductible amount. If Lee Way's conduct as to each individual discriminatee constituted a separate occurrence as to each, then Lee Way must bear the first $25,000 of each back-pay award.

II.　*Single vs. Multiple Occurrence*

The Court is unable to find another case that has addressed this precise issue. The question of what constitutes a single "accident" or "occurrence," as the terms are used within liability policies to limit an insurer's liability to a specified amount, has been addressed in numerous cases and is the subject of one annotation. 55 A.L.R.2d 1300; *see also*, 8 Appleman's *Insurance Law and Practice* § 4891 and Long, *The Law of Liability Insurance* §§ 2.12–2.14. The cases indicate that a court should "examine the policies in light of the business purposes sought to be achieved by the parties and the plain meaning of the words chosen by them to effect those purposes." *Champion International Corp. v. Continental Casualty Co.*, 546 F.2d 502, 505 (2nd Cir.1976); *see also, Union Carbide Corp. v. Travelers Indemnity Co.*, 399 F.Supp. 12, 17 (W.D.Pa.1975). The district court in *Union Carbide v. Travelers, supra*, explained that a term such as "occurrence" should be construed in the light of the hazard insured against. *Id.*

In this case the hazard insured against is discrimination. In the prior litigation, Lee Way was found to have engaged in a "pattern and practice" of discrimination. "Pattern and practice" actions have the following characteristics:

1. A pattern and practice of discrimination exists only where the defendant routinely follows generalized policies, procedures or practices which have a discriminatory effect. Individual instances of discrimination are not a pattern and practice. *See Teamsters v. United States*, 431 U.S. 324, 336, 97 S.Ct. 1843, 1855, 52 L.Ed.2d 531 (1977); *United States v. Mayton*, 335 F.2d 153 (5th Cir.1964); *United States v. Dillon*, 429 F.2d 800, 804 (4th Cir.1970); *United States v. Ironworkers*, 443 F.2d 544, 551–552 (9th Cir.1971); *United States v. Jacksonville Terminal Co.*, 451 F.2d 418, 441 (5th Cir.1971); *United States v. T.I.M.E.—D.C.*, 517 F.2d 299, 319 (5th Cir.1975); and *United States v. City of Buffalo*, 457 F.Supp. 612, 620 (W.D.N.Y.1978).

2. A pattern and practice of discrimination is ordinarily proven through the use of statistics and other evidence of a general nature. Proof of individual instances of discrimination alone is not proof of a pattern and practice. *See, Teamsters v. United States, supra*, 431 U.S. at 339 n. 20, 97 S.Ct. at 1856; *United States v. Mayton, supra; United States v. Dillon, supra*, at 804; *United States v. Ironworkers, supra*, at 550–551; *United States v. T.I.M.E.—D.C., supra*, at 311–313; *United States v. City of Buffalo, supra*, at 620, 621–622.

3. In a pattern and practice case, the cause of action belongs to the Government and not to the individuals affected. However, once the defendant's liability is established, the Government can obtain equitable relief (including back pay) for those specific individuals found to have been affected by the pattern and practice. *See, Teamsters v. United States, supra*, 431 U.S. at 360, 97 S.Ct. at 1867; *United States v. Mayton, supra* at 158; and *United States v. Georgia Power Company*, 474 F.2d 906 at 920–921 (5th Cir.1973).

4. Intent to discriminate is irrelevant in a pattern and practice case. Instead, the Government must merely show that the defendant's policies, procedures or practices were not accidental or inadvertent. *See,*

Griggs v. Duke Power Co., 401 U.S. 424, 432, 91 S.Ct. 849, 854, 28 L.Ed. 2d 158 (1971); *Teamsters v. United States, supra,* 431 U.S. at 349, 97 S.Ct. at 1861; and *United States v. Jacksonville Terminal Co., supra,* at 438, 442–443.

5. In a pattern and practice case, the defendant's policies, procedures and practices need not themselves be discriminatory. Rather, if they are facially neutral but have the effect of perpetuating past discrimination, the defendant is nevertheless liable. *See, Griggs v. Duke Power Co., supra,* 401 U.S. at 430, 91 S.Ct. at 853; *Teamsters v. United States, supra,* 431 U.S. at 349; *United States v. Dillon, supra* at 804; *United States v. Jacksonville Terminal, supra* at 938; and *United States v. City of Buffalo, supra* at 618.

The findings and conclusions of the district court in *United States v. Lee Way* indicate that these same characteristics existed at Lee Way. The court concluded that Lee Way discriminated on a "system-wide basis" (Conclusion 6) which was found to be "corporate policy" (Finding 34). The government presented statistical evidence establishing a prima facie showing of discrimination as well as evidence of individual instances serving as "examples" which "confirmed" the Court's findings of system-wide discrimination (Finding 49 and Conclusion 8). Furthermore, the court found that evidence of the company's discriminatory reputation was relevant and admissible in proving a pattern or practice of racial discrimination (Conclusion 19). The judgment established clearly that the discrimination suffered by Lee Way's minority employees resulted from a uniform, system-wide policy.[2]

When the language of the Transport policies is construed in light of the particular hazard insured against (see authorities cited *supra*), the inevitable conclusion is that the discrimination suffered by Lee Way's employees constituted a single "occurrence" as that term is used in the policies.

The definition of "occurrence" is broad in its scope:

> The term "occurrence" means an accident or a happening or event or a *continuous or repeated exposure to conditions* which * * * result in personal injury * * * during the policy period. *All such exposure to substantially the same general conditions existing at or emanating from one premises location shall be deemed one occurrence.* (emphasis added)

The first sentence of the definition standing alone indicates that the discrimination here constituted one "occurrence." Lee Way's employees were subject to a "continuous or repeated exposure to conditions," viz., company-wide discriminatory policies and practices, which

---

2. Having established Lee Way's liability for a pattern and practice of discrimination, the court then considered each individual discriminatee's entitlement to relief. Not until the relief phase of the trial did the court delve deeply into individual claims. At that stage, individual employees were not required to prove specific acts of discrimination; the burden shifted to Lee Way to prove in each instance that an individual was not affected by the pattern and practice of discrimination, and, if Lee Way failed, the individual would be deemed entitled to relief. (Tenth Circuit Slip Opinion at 32–33).

resulted in "personal injury," *i.e.* discrimination. The prior judgment (as well as relevant case law) shows that the pattern and practice of discrimination found to have occurred consisted of generalized discriminatory policies routinely followed. Minority employees suffered a "continuous or repeated exposure" to such discriminatory conditions and thus there was only "one occurrence."

The last sentence of the quoted definition establishes clearly that the pattern and practice of discrimination constituted "one occurrence." It states, that all exposure "to substantially the same general conditions" shall be deemed "one occurrence." The individual discriminatees were exposed to the same system-wide corporate policy of discrimination, albeit at different times and places. Yet, the language is clear in its intent that *all* exposure to the same conditions is deemed *one* occurrence. These words must be given their plain meaning and not construed in a technical or limited sense. *National Aviation Underwriters, Inc. v. Altus Flying Service, Inc.*, 555 F.2d 778 (10th Cir. 1977); *Wylie v. Travelers Insurance Co.*, 534 P.2d 1293 (Okla.1974). It follows that all exposure to the pattern and practice of discrimination (*i.e.*, "substantially the same general conditions") must be deemed "one occurrence."

The fact that Lee Way operated four separate trucking terminals (Oklahoma City, Los Angeles, Houston, and San Antonio) is no reason for dividing Lee Way's liability into four separate occurrences—one occurrence at each of the four terminal locations. Exposure to the same general conditions "existing at or *emanating from* one premises location" constitutes a single "occurrence." (emphasis added) The court in *United States v. Lee Way* concluded that the pattern and practice of discrimination was a continuous company-wide policy traceable to the decisions and procedures made at Lee Way's headquarter's terminal in Oklahoma City. Lee Way's discriminatory policies originated in Oklahoma City and emanated from its headquarters there; the discriminatory policies thus emanated from one location; it would gild the lily to say more.

The fact that the parties provided for a "per occurrence" deductible, as opposed to a "per claim" deductible, is further indication that the parties intended that Lee Way's discriminatory practices would be deemed a single occurrence. The $25,000 deductible "per occurrence" suggests that the policy was not intended to define coverage on the basis of individual instances of discrimination. In a case involving very similar policy language, the Second Circuit affirmed a district court's holding that the continuous and repeated distribution of defective products constituted but a single "occurrence," even though there were 1400 different claims arising from individual ultimate users. *Champion International Corp. v. Continental Casualty Co.*, 546 F.2d 502, *supra*. The appellate court considered the insured's selection of a "per occurrence" deductible to be important in interpreting "occurrence." *Id.* at 505. It regarded the insured's distribution of defective vinyl-covered paneling as one "occurrence" out of which 1400 "claims" arose. *Id.* at

506. In the instant case, each individual award of back pay should be regarded as a different "claim" arising out of but one "occurrence," viz., the continuous and repeated exposure to discriminatory employment conditions.

Transport could have limited the meaning and scope of discrimination to single, individual acts of discrimination and excluded from coverage a pattern and practice of discrimination; it did not do so. Discrimination is included without qualification in the definition of "personal injury," and "personal injury" is used in the expansive definition of "occurrence." In any event, any doubt regarding the extent of "discrimination" covered, must be resolved against *Transport. Hardberger and Smylie v. Employers Mut. Liability Ins. Co.,* 444 F.2d 1318 (10th Cir.1971) (applying Oklahoma law).

Finally, although the plain language of the policy alone supports the Court's "single occurrence" conclusion, the analogous case law also upholds this result. The rationale underlying the various decisions which have held that particular events constituted but a single occurrence has been that courts generally look to the *cause* as opposed to the *effect* of such events. The great majority of courts have adopted a "cause" analysis, *American Casualty Co. v. Heary,* 432 F.Supp. 995, 997 (E.D.Va.1977), holding that where a single event, process or condition results in injuries, it will be deemed a single occurrence even though the injuries may be widespread in both time and place and may affect a multitude of individuals. *See generally* 55 A.L.R.2d at 1303; *see also, St. Paul–Mercury Indemnity Co. v. Rutland,* 225 F.2d 689 (5th Cir.1955) (derailment resulting in injury to sixteen freight cars—single occurrence); *Haerens v. Commercial Cas. Ins. Co.,* 279 P.2d 211 (Cal.App. 1955) (several panes of glass broken while working on house—single occurrence); *Barrett v. Iowa National Mut. Ins. Co.,* 264 F.2d 224 (9th Cir.1959) (fire damage to contents of different apartments—single occurrence); *Weissblum v. Glens Falls Ins. Co.,* 31 Misc.2d 132, 219 N.Y.S.2d 711, *rev'd on other grounds,* 40 Misc.2d 964, 244 N.Y.S.2d 689 (1961) (numerous lights broken at different times by different persons during construction work—single occurrence); *Wilkinson & Son, Inc. v. Providence,* 124 N.J.Super. 466, 307 A.2d 639 (1973) (contractor damaged several apartments by tracking paint on carpets—single occurrence); *Union Carbide Corp. v. Travelers Indem. Co.,* 399 F.Supp. 12 (W.D.Pa.1975) (defective chemical product caused widespread damage to a variety of ultimate users—single occurrence); *Champion Intl. Corp. v. Continental Cas. Co.,* 546 F.2d 502 (2nd Cir.1976) (defective vinyl-covered paneling caused widespread damage to a variety of ultimate users—single occurrence); *Southern Intl. Corp. v. Polyurethane Ind., Inc.,* 353 So.2d 646 (Fla.App.1977) (contractor damaged several different condominiums while applying sealant to each roof—single occurrence); *American Cas. Co. v. Heary,* 432 F.Supp. 995 (E.D.Va.1977) (automobile accident caused chain reaction of accidents—single occurrence); *Michaels v. Mutual Marine Office, Inc.,* 472 F.Supp. 26 (S.D.N.Y.1979) (ship's deck damaged over period of days by repeated dropping of "drag buckets"—single occurrence). *But see Elston–Richards Storage Co. v. Indemnity Ins. Co. of North America,* 194 F.Supp. 673 (W.D.Mich.1960), *aff'd* 291 F.2d 627 (6th Cir.1961). The judgment in *United States v. Lee Way* clearly establishes that the individual discriminatees were harmed by a single, continuous cause: company-wide discriminatory employment policies.

The Court could not find any decisions of the Oklahoma appellate courts on this subject, i.e., the construction of "occurrence" in a liability policy. The Court believes, however, that Oklahoma would apply the prevailing view. According to that view, the particular events involved here should be regarded as a single occurrence.[3]

MICHIGAN CHEMICAL CORPORATION v. AMERICAN HOME ASSURANCE COMPANY

United States Court of Appeals, Sixth Circuit, 1984.
728 F.2d 374.

CONTIE, Circuit Judge.

The defendants, American Home Assurance Company (American Home), Aetna Casualty and Surety Company (Aetna) and Insurance Company of North America (INA) have filed an interlocutory appeal in response to a partial summary judgment granted by the district court in favor of the plaintiffs, Michigan Chemical Corporation (MCC) and American Mutual Reinsurance Company (Amreco). Since the district court's order involves a controlling question of law upon which there is substantial ground for difference of opinion, and since an immediate appeal will materially advance the ultimate termination of this litigation, this court has jurisdiction pursuant to 28 U.S.C. § 1292(b). We reverse and remand for further proceedings consistent with this opinion.

I.

MCC filed a declaratory judgment action in the district court in order to determine how much insurance coverage was available to pay farmers who had sustained property damage resulting from the distribution of contaminated livestock feed throughout Michigan. The record reflects that in early 1973, MCC produced and distributed both a magnesium oxide livestock feed supplement and a flame retardant which contained the toxin polybrominated biphenyl (PBB). These

---

3. The insurance industry has been broadening the definition of occurrence. An October 1972 F.C. & S. Bulletin, published by the National Underwriters Co., stated at page A–3 that the "continuous or repeated exposure to conditions" language in the definition of occurrence was intended to avoid the application of multiple occurrences. This language represented a change from previous wording that had been interpreted less expansively. The Federation of Insurance Counsel published an article in its Spring, 1975, F.I.C. Quarterly analyzing the same definition of occurrence as used in the Transport policies. The article explains at page 245 that the definition is intended to result in only a single application of the occurrence limit in repeated exposure cases. Clearly the insurance industry has intended to broaden, rather than shrink, the definition of occurrence.

substances were packaged in nearly identical brown fifty-pound bags. The sole difference between the magnesium oxide and PBB bags was the stenciled trade names of the respective products, "Nutrimaster" and "Firemaster."

The district court found that MCC accidentally shipped PBB rather than magnesium oxide to Farm Bureau Services on May 2, 1973. The court did not determine whether any other accidental shipments occurred. Farm Bureau Services then mixed the PBB with regular feed and sold the resulting product to dairy farmers. In October of 1973, the farmers began complaining that some animals were rejecting the feed and that ingestion caused decreased milk production. After Farm Bureau Services and state authorities discovered that the feed was contaminated, 28,679 cattle, 4,612 swine, 1,399 sheep and over 6,000 chickens and other farm animals were destroyed. Their owners filed hundreds of claims against MCC and Farm Bureau Services.

MCC possessed five liability indemnity insurance policies during 1973–74, the time period in which the property damage took place. Travelers Indemnity Company (Travelers) provided the primary coverage of $1 million per "occurrence," subject to an annual aggregate limit of $1 million. If losses exceeded these limits, excess layers of insurance provided further coverage. Lloyd's of London (Lloyd's) contracted to pay the next $2 million per occurrence, subject to an annual aggregate limit of $2 million. American Home provided an additional $15 million of coverage per occurrence with an annual aggregate limit of $15 million. Midland Insurance Company reinsured some of American Home's potential liability. Amreco reinsured Midland. Finally, Aetna and INA agreed to share equally any further MCC liability up to $10 million per occurrence, subject to an annual aggregate limit of $10 million. The American Home and Aetna policies tracked the other terms and conditions of the Lloyd's policy; the INA policy adopted those of the Travelers' policy. MCC's total liability coverage for property damage during the relevant time period therefore was $28 million per occurrence.

MCC and Amreco have contended throughout this litigation that each claim filed against MCC constitutes an "occurrence" within the meaning of the insurance policies. They argue that there can be no occurrence until injury takes place because an indemnifiable event stems not from an insured's abstract act of negligence, but arises only when damage is suffered. The plaintiffs therefore assert that the five insurers are liable for $28 million per filed claim, subject to the $28 million aggregate annual limit of all the policies combined. Since all of the property damage took place in 1973 and 1974, the plaintiffs argue that MCC's total liability coverage is $56 million.

Conversely, American Home, Aetna and INA contend that the only "occurrence" was the May 2, 1973 accidental shipment of PBB. Although injury must be suffered before the insured becomes liable, the timing of the injury only determines the policy year to which that injury is assigned. The *number of occurrences* is said to be governed by the cause of the accident rather than its effects. Since the cause of the property damage in this case allegedly was a single misshipment of PBB, the defendants conclude that MCC's maximum coverage is $28 million.

To date, MCC and Farm Bureau Services have paid over $45 million in claims. The five insurers have acknowledged that one occurrence took place and have contributed $28 million to the settlement of these claims. In consideration for being dismissed from this suit, Travelers has paid an additional $1 million and Lloyd's has paid an additional $2 million. Travelers has received a refund of over $960,000 in deductibles. Lloyd's will not receive such a refund.

* * *

The district court found the definitions of "occurrence" in the insurance policies to be ambiguous and therefore construed the policies against the defendants. Hence, MCC's argument that the number of occurrences equals the number of claims was held to be reasonable.

* * *

III.

This interlocutory appeal presents the question of what constitutes a separate "occurrence" under each of the five insurance policies. The Lloyd's policy, which controls the liability of defendants American Home and Aetna, contains the following definition:

> The term "Occurrence" wherever used herein shall mean *an accident or a happening or event* or a continuous or repeated exposure to conditions *which unexpectedly and unintentionally results in* personal injury, *property damage* or advertising liability *during the policy period.* All such exposure to substantially the same general conditions existing at or emanating from one premises location shall be deemed one occurrence. [Emphasis supplied.]

The Travelers' policy, which governs the liability of INA, contains a similar definition:

> "Occurrence" means as *respects property damage* 1) *an accident* or 2) continuous or repeated exposure to conditions *which results in injury to or destruction of tangible property,* including consequential loss resulting therefrom, *while this agreement is in effect.* All damages arising out of such exposure to substantially the same general conditions shall be considered as arising out of one occurrence. [Emphasis supplied.]

The parties agree that the minor differences in the wording of these provisions are immaterial. Although the terms "event" and "happening" in the Lloyd's policy may potentially be broader in scope than the term "accident," the district court found and the parties do not dispute, that the term "accident" encompasses the incidents which transpired here. 530 F.Supp. at 150 n. 2. Accordingly, we need not discuss whether the Lloyd's policy provides wider liability coverage for property damage than does the Travelers' policy. Second, the defendants have argued that the distribution of contaminated feed throughout Michigan was a continuous or repeated exposure to a general condition and that all such exposure constitutes one occurrence under the second sentence of both definitions.[1] The district court agreed and held that the farm animals were exposed to a product rather than to a general condition. The latter term was said to include only such things as the conditions within a manufacturing plant or the continuous emanation of pollution or other nuisance from such a plant. In light of our interpretation of the concept of an accident which results in property damage during the policy period, it is not necessary to reach the defendants' alternative argument.

A.

The vast majority of courts (including two courts which have interpreted the precise language of the definition of occurrence in the Lloyd's policy) have concluded that although injury must be suffered before an insured can be held liable, the number of occurrences for purposes of applying coverage limitations is determined by referring to the cause or causes of the damage and not to the number of injuries or claims. *See Appalachian Insurance Co. v. Liberty Mutual Insurance Co.*, 676 F.2d 56, 61 (3d Cir.1982) (Lloyd's policy language); *Maurice Pincoffs Co. v. St. Paul Fire and Marine Insurance Co.*, 447 F.2d 204, 206–07 (5th Cir.1971); *Barrett v. Iowa National Mutual Insurance Co.*, 264 F.2d 224 (9th Cir.1959); *St. Paul–Mercury Indemnity Co. v. Rutland*, 225 F.2d 689 (5th Cir.1955); *Bartholomew v. Insurance Company of North America*, 502 F.Supp. 246, 251 (D.R.I.1980), *aff'd sub. nom. Bartholomew v. Appalachian Insurance Co.*, 655 F.2d 27 (1st Cir.1981); *Transport Insurance Co. v. Lee Way Motor Freight, Inc.*, 487 F.Supp. 1325, 1330 (N.D.Tex.1980) (Lloyd's policy language); *E.B. Michaels v. Mutual Marine Office, Inc.*, 472 F.Supp. 26, 29 (S.D.N.Y.1979); *American Casualty Co. v. Heary*, 432 F.Supp. 995, 997 (E.D.Va.1977); *Union Carbide Corp. v. Travelers Indemnity Co.*, 399 F.Supp. 12, 15–18 (W.D. Pa.1975).[2] The number and timing of injuries is relevant in addressing the distinct question of the policy period to which each injury will be assigned. *See Appalachian Insurance*, 676 F.2d at 61–62.

The definition of "occurrence" in the present insurance policies reflects this approach. First, these provisions in essence refer to an

---

1. The parties have labelled this sentence the "unifying directive."

2. The prevailing rule was best summarized in the *Appalachian Insurance* case:

The general rule is that an occurrence is determined by the cause or causes of the resulting injury. * * * Using this analysis, the court asks if there was but one proximate, uninterrupted, and continuing cause which resulted in all of the injuries and damages.

676 F.2d at 61. In the present case, the cause of the property damage was the mis-shipment or mis-shipments of PBB.

"accident" which results in injury during the policy period. The language makes the accident constituting the occurrence logically distinct from the injuries which later take place. Second, the insurance policies under review afford coverage on an "occurrence" rather than on a "claim" basis. The use of the former term "indicates that the polic[ies were] not intended to gauge coverage on the basis of individual accidents giving rise to claims, but rather on the underlying circumstances which resulted in the claim[s] for damages." *Champion International Corp. v. Continental Casualty Co.,* 546 F.2d 502, 505–06 (2d Cir. 1976), *cert. denied,* 434 U.S. 819, 98 S.Ct. 59, 54 L.Ed.2d 75; *see also Lee Way,* 487 F.Supp. at 1329. We hold that where the courts over such an extended period of time have reached virtually a uniform result in interpreting the term "occurrence" (including two courts which have interpreted the exact language of the Lloyd's policy), and where the policy language reflects this approach, the policy terms admit of only one reasonable interpretation. The terms therefore are unambiguous and require no further construction.

We are aware of only one case which calculated the number of occurrences by referring to the number of injuries rather than to the cause or causes of those injuries. *See Elston–Richards Storage Co. v. Indemnity Insurance Co. of North America,* 194 F.Supp. 673, 678–82 (W.D.Mich.1960), *aff'd.,* 291 F.2d 627 (6th Cir.1961). Although this court decided *Elston–Richards,* the holding is not binding because the current litigation involves Illinois law. We are persuaded that if the Illinois courts were presented with the current case, they would follow the overwhelming majority of decisions which have held that the number of occurrences is determined by examining the cause or causes of the damage.

B.

The plaintiffs attempt to distinguish the cases upon which the defendants rely by arguing that in most of the cited cases, injuries or damages were suffered immediately after the causal event took place. This scenario contrasts with the present situation in which several months elapsed between the mis-shipment or mis-shipments of PBB and the resulting property damage. One commentator has suggested that if a single cause and numerous injuries are closely linked in time and space, then there has been one occurrence, but if a cause and its effects are temporally removed, then each injury constitutes an occurrence. *See* Annot., 55 A.L.R.2d 1300, 1304 (1957). This argument, however, was considered and rejected by the Third Circuit in the *Appalachian Insurance* case: [3]

3. As has been indicated, the definitions of "occurrence" found in the Lloyd's and in the Appalachian Insurance Company's policies are identical. The plaintiffs, however, assert that a footnote in *Appalachian Insurance* renders the case inapposite. 676 F.2d at 62 n. 14. We disagree. This footnote is connected with a discussion of *when* an occurrence takes place for purposes of determining the policy period into which a particular injury falls rather than with a discussion of the *number* of occurrences. The court's opinion was dealing at that point with the relative merits of the manifestation and

The fact that there were multiple injuries and that they were of different magnitudes *and that injuries extended over a period of time* does not alter our conclusion that there was a single occurrence. * * * Indeed, the definition of the term "occurrence" in the Appalachian policy contemplates that one occurrence may have multiple and disparate impacts on individuals *and that injuries may extend over a period of time.* [Emphasis supplied.]

676 F.2d at 61. *See also Lee Way,* 487 F.Supp. at 1330. In addition, the fact patterns of the *Champion, Pincoffs* and *Union Carbide* cases demonstrate that the number of injuries or claims, even if temporally removed from their causes, are irrelevant when determining the number of occurrences.[4]

* * *

IV.

The plaintiffs also argue that if the number of occurrences is calculated by examining the cause or causes of injury, then the definitions of products liability contained in the policies under review make no sense. If the plaintiffs are correct, then our interpretation of the contract violates the general rule that an agreement is to be construed as a whole in order to effectuate all of its provisions. *See, e.g., Joseph,* 106 Ill.App.3d at 991, 62 Ill.Dec. 637, 436 N.E.2d 663. The Lloyd's policy defines the term "Products Liability" as:

Liability arising out of goods or products manufactured, sold, handled or distributed by the Assured * * * if the occurrence occurs after possession of such goods or products has been

exposure theories. The footnote merely indicated that the court's preference for the manifestation theory under the facts of that case would not necessarily be applied to other situations involving different kinds of injuries. Since the district court in the present case expressly reserved the question of which theory would apply, that portion of *Appalachian Insurance* which discussed the manifestation and exposure theories is completely irrelevant to the problem at hand.

4. The district court distinguished the *Champion, Lee Way* and *Michaels* decisions on the ground that the courts in those cases limited the number of occurrences so that the insured parties would not have to pay multiple per occurrence deductibles. The district court implied that this approach was consistent with the Illinois rule that an ambiguous insurance contract is to be construed against the insurer who drafted it. In the present case, however, applying those cases to limit the number of occurrences would disadvantage the insured party.

The problem with this argument is that once courts establish a legal rule, such as how the number of occurrences is to be determined, any party is entitled to rely upon that rule in future litigation. Our jurisprudence is not so result oriented that it will permit court holdings to be relied upon only if such holdings benefit a particular party. Of course, the Illinois rule that an insurance contract will be construed against the insurer remains operative provided that an ambiguity exists. No ambiguity is present, however, where numerous courts, including two courts which have interpreted identical language, have held that the number of occurrences is to be calculated in a particular manner.

The district court also distinguished the *Pincoffs* and *Union Carbide* cases on the ground that the courts did not rely upon the strict construction rule in those cases. Nevertheless, the courts in those cases adopted the cause theory in determining the number of occurrences. The defendants therefore are entitled to rely upon those cases.

relinquished to others by the Assured * * * and if such occurrence occurs away from premises owned, rented or controlled by the Assured. * * *

The Travelers' policy contains the following language:

"Products Hazard" means goods or products manufactured, sold, handled or distributed by the Named Insured or by others trading under his name, if the bodily injury or property damage takes place after possession of such goods or products has been relinquished to others by the Named Insured or others trading under his name and if such injury or damage takes place away from premises owned, rented or controlled by the Named Insured.

The plaintiffs contend that under these definitions, an "occurrence" must take place: (1) after the insured has relinquished control of the product and (2) away from the latter's premises. They argue that under the cause theory, however, occurrences such as mis-shipments or defects in construction and design normally will happen at the insured's facility. The plaintiffs therefore conclude that if this court adopts the cause theory, then the products liability coverage provided in the policies will be nullified.

We disagree. First, the defendants have admitted in their briefs and during oral argument that the present case involves products liability under the provisions of the policies in question. Second, the products liability definitions stipulate *when* and *where* an occurrence must take place for products liability coverage to exist. The cause standard, however, governs only the *number* of occurrences; it is irrelevant in determining when and where an occurrence happens. *See, Appalachian Insurance,* 676 F.2d at 61–62. Consequently, using the cause test in order to calculate the number of occurrences is perfectly consistent with looking to the time and place of injury in order to decide when and where an occurrence or occurrences takes place for purposes of either applying a products liability provision or assigning a claim to a particular policy period.

Third, the definition of "Product Hazard" in the Travelers' policy does not use the word "occurrence." A comparison of the two definitions under consideration reveals that the term "occurrence" in the Lloyd's policy serves the same function as the phrase "bodily injury or property damage" in the Travelers' policy. Therefore it is obvious that the Lloyd's policy uses the term "occurrence" in the products liability definition with reference to "the event of unexpected loss or hurt apart from its cause" rather than with respect to the cause itself. *Union Carbide,* 399 F.Supp. at 16. To state that injury or damage must happen at a particular time and place for liability to arise is not inconsistent with determining the number of occurrences by looking to the cause of such claims. In fact, the question of whether any injury or damage has taken place must be decided in the affirmative before the issue of the number of occurrences need even be considered.

V.

Since the relevant language of the insurance policies is plain and unambiguous, this court may not resort to parol evidence [5] or to the rule of strict construction against the insurer in order to ascertain the parties' intent. We hold that under the language of these contracts, the number of occurrences must be determined by examining the cause of the property damage, *i.e.,* the mis-shipment or mis-shipments of PBB.

As has been indicated, the district court did not decide whether only one mis-shipment of PBB occurred. We nevertheless emphasize that each shipment would constitute a separate occurrence under these policies. In the *Pincoffs* case, the insured made sales of contaminated birdseed to eight dealers who in turn sold the seed to pet owners. Many birds died after eating the seed. One insurer contended that the sole "occurrence" was the contamination of the seed. The court rejected this argument and held that each of the eight sales constituted an occurrence because the sales, rather than the mere possession of contaminated seed, created the exposure to liability. *Id.,* 447 F.2d at 206–07.

The present case is highly analogous. So long as MCC retained possession of the PBB, no liability could result. The shipment of the substance constituted the act from which liability arose. Other shipments, if any took place, created additional exposure to liability and therefore were separate occurrences. In such a situation, there would not have been one uninterrupted and continuing cause, *Appalachian Insurance,* 676 F.2d at 61, but several distinct acts from which liability would have resulted.[6]

The district court therefore is instructed to determine how many shipments of PBB occurred. * * * The judgment of the district court is REVERSED and the case is REMANDED for further proceedings consistent with this opinion. The appellants shall recover costs on appeal, except for those costs associated with the inclusion in the appendix of materials which we have previously held to be unnecessary.

KEITH, Circuit Judge, dissenting.

I dissent from the majority's holding that the number of occurrences for purposes of applying coverage limitations is determined by referring to the cause of the damage. In my view, the district court was correct to construe an occurrence as taking place at the time that damage resulted.

5. This court may not, for instance, take into account various memos prepared by employees or representatives of the insurance companies when preparing for this litigation.

6. The facts of the *Champion* case are not persuasive on this point. The insured in that case sold defective vinyl to twenty-six recreational vehicle manufacturers who in turn used the vinyl in 1,400 vehicles. The court held that one occurrence, not 1,400, had taken place. 546 F.2d at 505–06. The *Pincoffs* court, however, would have ruled that 26 occurrences had happened. We follow the *Pincoffs* approach because the court in *Champion* did not advert to the possibility that 26 occurrences had taken place.

The occurrence definition in the insurance policies is composed of one sentence containing two conjunctive elements. The first element is an "accident," "happening" or "event" or a "continuous or repeated exposure to conditions." The second element is "property damage resulting during the policy period." Thus, the sentence reads that an accident does not take place until it results in damage or injury. The majority's interpretation, which makes these two elements distinct, contravenes both insurance and tort law and is contrary to a plain reading of the sentence. It is well established that liability does not result until harm occurs. In *Steinheider & Sons, Inc. v. Iowa Kemper Ins. Co.*, 204 Neb. 156, 281 N.W.2d 539 (1979), a case relied upon by the district court and involving an incident of negligent misdelivery, the court said "there could be no indemnifiable occurrence if a truck delivering a wrong chemical had simply turned over before it got to the customer, the negligent act must have resulted in damage." 281 N.W.2d at 543–44. Thus an indemnifiable event does not arise at the time of some abstract act of negligence, but rather at the time it results in injury or harm.

The district court's interpretation of occurrence also finds support in *Elston–Richards Storage Co. v. Indemnity Ins. Co. of North America*, 194 F.Supp. 673, 678–82 (W.D.Mich.1960), *aff'd.*, 291 F.2d 627 (6th Cir. 1961). This Court in *Elston–Richards* was presented with the identical insurance policy construction issue now before it: whether the term "occurrence" in an indemnity insurance policy is defined by reference to the negligent act of the insured, or by actual events which inflict injury that follow the initial negligent act. Our Court affirmed the trial judge's holding that each separate incident of damage constituted a separate "occurrence."

Although the majority acknowledged the holding in *Elston–Richards*, it found the case to be inapposite because it involved Michigan law and the current litigation involves questions governed by Illinois law. At 380. This ground for distinction is woefully inadequate since the majority relies upon a multitude of cases which are not governed by the law of Illinois.

I find particularly troubling the majority's reliance in this case upon *Appalachian Ins. Co. v. Liberty Mutual Ins. Co.*, 676 F.2d 56 (3d Cir.1982) and *Transport Ins. Co. v. Lee Way Motor Freight, Inc.*, 487 F.Supp. 1325 (N.D.Tex.1980) because neither case involved products liability but instead concerned issues of employment discrimination. In fact, a footnote in the *Appalachian* opinion indicates that the case may be inapplicable in the products liability arena. The footnote reads: "[T]his is not a case where an insured commits a tortious act and then after a lapse of time a claimant is injured by the act." The majority's attempt to discount this footnote on grounds that it concerned a discussion of when an occurrence takes place as opposed to the number of occurrences is wholly unconvincing. The footnote makes no bright line distinction between "when" and "how many" and in any event the principles underlying an analysis of when an occurrence takes place would be instructive in a determination of how many occurrences took place.

Finally, the majority's opinion fails to recognize the time honored principle that an insurance policy is interpreted in such a way that it makes sense as a whole. 3A Corbin, Contracts § 549 (Supp.1971). An examination of the definition of products liability in the instant policy makes it apparent that the majority's interpretation of occurrence runs contrary to this principle. Indeed, the majority's interpretation deprives the policy's products liability section of any reasonable meaning. This section provides:

> The term "Products Liability" means * * * liability arising out of goods or products manufactured, sold, handled or distributed by the Assured * * * if the occurrence occurs after possession of such goods or products has been relinquished to others by the Assured * * * and if such occurrence occurs away from premises owned, rented or controlled by the Assured.

Thus, products liability coverage only applies to occurrences which occur away from the insured's premises and after the goods have been transferred. Yet, if occurrence means the misshipment or cause of injury, then there could not be liability in this case because neither occurred away from the plant. In contrast, the district court's interpretation gives reasonable meaning to this section. As the district court stated, "if an occurrence occurs when damage appears during the policy period, then almost all products liability actions are covered by the products liability portion of the insurance policy which is presumably what the drafters intended." 530 F.Supp. at 152.

At most, an examination of the policy language and consideration of arguments as to its intended merits lead to a conclusion that occurrence should be construed as taking place at the time injury results. At the very least, one must find the terms ambiguous. Illinois' law as do most states, recognizes that an ambiguous contract should be construed against the insurer who drafted it. Therefore, the district court's decision, interpreting the contract in favor of the insured, was not clearly erroneous and I would affirm.

Notes and Questions

1. *Cause or Effect?* Issues of both definition and application must be resolved in determining the number of insured occurrences under a liability policy. In most single-injury cases, of course, there is only one occurrence almost by definition. In continuous exposure or multiple injury cases, however, definition and application can be critically important. As *Lee Way* and *MCC* make clear, the *cause test* is dominant. The principal rational for the test is that the number of occurrences should be determined from the standpoint of the insured, not its victims. An *effects test,* adopted by a few courts, vastly expands coverage in most, but not all, multiple injury cases. Suppose you

represented the insured in a case like *Lee Way,* but your policy contained a per occurrence deductible of $20,000. How would you decide whether to argue in favor of a cause or an effects test for determining how many occurrences there had been?

2. *Dual Limits of Liability.* Many older policies contain only a per occurrence limit of liability; newer policies, including the Sample Policy in Section A, also contain an aggregate limit. The latter places a ceiling on the total coverage provided during the policy period, regardless of how many occurrences have taken place. In certain situations the inclusion of an aggregate limit renders debate about how many occurrences there have been irrelevant; in others the issue remains despite the aggregate limit. Can you provide examples of the two situations?

3. *The Unifying Directive.* Even after a cause test is adopted it is not always self-applying, because there is often room for debate about how many causes lie behind the injuries that have occurred. For example, why was each shipment in *MCC* a separate cause of the losses that followed? The provision the *MCC* court termed the "unifying directive" seems intended to eliminate causation debates in at least some situations in which they would otherwise arise. The directive states in substance, "All damages arising out of exposure to substantially the same general conditions shall be considered one occurrence." The directive is a common but by no means universal provision in CGL and other liability policies. Would *Lee Way* or *MCC* have been decided differently if there had not been a unifying directive in the policies they interpreted? If not, what does the directive add? Is there more than one occurrence in the following situations when the relevant policy contains a unifying directive? When it does not?

a. The pattern and practice of discrimination in question takes place over a period of thirty years, involves a series of labor agreements with different unions, and affects employees in very different time periods.

b. The insured maintains a hazardous waste disposal site for ten years, receiving waste in fifty-five gallon drums on a monthly basis from hundreds of different companies. The drums corrode, the waste leaches into the soil, and it contaminates a municipal water supply. The municipality sues the insured.

c. The facts are the same as in the preceding paragraph, but the plaintiffs are neighbors whose well-water has been contaminated. Cf. *Township of Jackson v. American Home Assurance Company,* 1984 Chemical and Waste Litigation Reports 646 (N.J.Super.Ct.Law Div. 1984). There the court determined, in the absence of a unifying directive, that the number of occurrences could be based on the number of wells contaminated or on each of ten separately identifiable causes of contamination, including negligent siting and negligent inspection of the landfill at which wastes had been deposited.

d. The insured is a manufacturer which has deposited waste on its own property for several decades. That waste is now contaminating the wells of nearby residents. Investigation by current management discloses that some of the now-leaking waste was spilled during accidents, and some was deliberately buried on the site. There are at least six different locations on the twenty-acre site where the accidents took place or the material was buried.

e. Massive rains cause flood damage to dozens of properties as a result of the insured city's negligence in planning, constructing, maintaining, and operating a surface water drainage system. Property owners sue the city. See *Home Indemnity Company v. City of Mobile,* 749 F.2d 659 (11th Cir.1984).

3. The Meaning of "Damages"

The following case concerns the liability of a CGL insurer for the costs incurred by its insured in connection with the cleanup of improperly disposed of hazardous waste. The opinion describes a small part of a national cleanup program that is being pursued mainly under the Comprehensive Environmental Response, Compensation, and Liability Act of 1980, abbreviated "CERCLA" and often nicknamed the "Superfund" Act. See 42 U.S.C. § 9601 et seq., as amended by the Superfund Amendments and Reauthorization Act of 1986 (SARA). CERCLA has been interpreted to provide that the generators of hazardous waste, those who transport it, and those who own or operate sites where waste is disposed of are retroactively, strictly, and jointly and severally liable for the costs of cleaning up sites where there is a release or a substantial threat of a release of hazardous substances into the environment. See CERCLA § 107, 42 U.S.C. 9607. Estimates of the total cost that will have to be incurred to remedy hazardous conditions at waste disposal sites across the United States vary, but virtually all put the figure at $100 billion or more. Thus, whether and to what extent the cost of such remedial action is insured under pre-existing CGL policies is a matter of extraordinary importance to the insurance industry and to CGL policyholders.

CONTINENTAL INSURANCE COMPANIES v. NORTHEASTERN PHARMACEUTICAL AND CHEMICAL COMPANY, INC.

United States Court of Appeals, Eighth Circuit, En Banc, 1988.
842 F.2d 977.

McMILLIAN, Circuit Judge.   *   *   *

From 1970 to 1972 the Northeastern Pharmaceutical & Chemical Co. (NEPACCO) manufactured hexaclorophene in a factory in Verona, Missouri. (NEPACCO effectively ceased doing business sometime in 1974.) The manufacturing process produced a variety of hazardous wastes, including the highly toxic chemical, dioxin. In July 1971

NEPACCO disposed of about eighty-five 55–gallon drums of hazardous wastes by burying them in a trench on a farm near Verona (hereafter the Denney farm site). Many of the drums had deteriorated and were in poor condition at the time of disposal; many broke open when they were dumped into the trench. A strong chemical odor persisted in the immediate area of the Denney farm site for several months thereafter.

In 1971 or 1972 NEPACCO hired Independent Petrochemical Corp. (IPC) to dispose of more hazardous wastes containing dioxin. IPC in turn hired Russell Bliss to actually dispose of NEPACCO's hazardous wastes. In 1971–1973 Bliss allegedly transported and sprayed the hazardous wastes, mixed with waste oil, as a dust suppressant on the grounds of the Bubbling Springs Stables in Fenton, Missouri, and on the roads of Times Beach, Missouri. In 1974 an individual named Minker bought dirt contaminated with NEPACCO hazardous wastes from the Bubbling Springs Stables to use as landfill on his property located in nearby Imperial, Missouri (the Minker/Stout/Romaine Creek site).

From 1970–1972 NEPACCO was insured under three standard-form CGL insurance policies issued by Continental. The first policy was in effect from August 5, 1970, to August 5, 1971, the second policy from August 5, 1971, to August 5, 1972, and the third policy from August 5, 1972, to November 17, 1972, when it was cancelled. Each policy was slightly different, but each provided that Continental would

> pay on behalf of the insured all sums which the insured shall become legally obligated to pay as damages because of * * * property damage to which this insurance applies caused by an occurrence, and [Continental] shall have the right and duty to defend any suit against the insured seeking damages on account of such * * * property damage.

The policies defined "property damage" as

> (1) Physical injury or destruction of tangible property which occurs during the policy period, including the loss of use thereof at anytime resulting therefrom,

> (2) Loss of use of tangible property which has not been physically injured or destroyed provided such loss of use is caused by an occurrence during the policy period. * * *

In 1980 the Environmental Protection Agency (EPA) investigated the Denney farm site. The EPA took soil and water samples and found "alarming[ly] high concentrations of dioxin" and other toxic chemicals. *EPA,* 579 F.Supp. at 831. The EPA secured and then "cleaned up" the Denney farm site. In August 1980 the federal government filed a lawsuit (the *EPA* lawsuit) against NEPACCO and others, seeking abatement costs, pursuant to § 7003(a) of the Resource Conservation and Recovery Act of 1976 (RCRA) (also known as the Solid Waste Disposal Act), as amended, 42 U.S.C. § 6973(a). In August 1982 the federal government filed an amended complaint adding claims for injunctive relief and reimbursement of its response costs pursuant to §§ 104, 106,

107 of the Comprehensive Environmental Response, Compensation, and Liability Act of 1980 (CERCLA) (commonly known as Superfund), 42 U.S.C. §§ 9604, 9606, 9607 (reauthorized and amended in part by the Superfund Amendments and Reauthorization Act of 1986, Pub.L. No. 99–499, 100 Stat. 1613 (1986) (effective Oct. 17, 1986)). We will use the descriptive term "cleanup costs" to refer to both "abatement costs" under RCRA and "response costs" under CERCLA.

In January 1984 the district court held NEPACCO and several other defendants, jointly and severally, strictly liable for cleanup costs under CERCLA, but not RCRA. *EPA*, 579 F.Supp. at 834–37, 839–52. On appeal, a panel of this court affirmed in part, reversed in part and remanded the case to the district court for further proceedings. 810 F.2d at 749–50. The majority held that the federal government could recover cleanup costs under both RCRA and CERCLA. *Id.* at 732–46. The dissent did not agree that past non-negligent off-site generators or transporters of hazardous waste could be held liable for cleanup costs under the 1984 RCRA amendments or that the corporate officer defendants could be held liable for cleanup costs under RCRA as generators and transporters. *Id.* at 750–51 (J.R. Gibson, J., dissenting in part).

The *EPA* lawsuit prompted the filing of several other related lawsuits, including the present case.

In March 1983 several former residents of the communities of Times Beach and Imperial filed an action in Missouri state court against NEPACCO and other defendants, seeking damages for present and future personal injury and property damage allegedly caused by the transportation and spreading of hazardous wastes and dirt, contaminated by dioxin and other toxic chemicals produced by NEPACCO, on the roads of Times Beach and at the Minker/Stout/Romaine Creek site. NEPACCO and the other defendants failed to enter an appearance or file an answer. As noted earlier, in 1974 NEPACCO had ceased operations; its corporate assets had been liquidated and the proceeds distributed to its shareholders. Thus, by 1984 NEPACCO had been "defunct" for ten years. In November 1984 Continental moved for summary judgment.

[The court then described the disposition of this and other motions in the District Court and before a single panel of the Court of Appeals.]

* * *

REHEARING EN BANC

Both Continental and the state filed petitions for rehearing en banc. Both petitions for rehearing en banc were granted, and the parties, and several amici curiae, including the federal government, several "hazardous waste generators," the AIA, and several other insurers, filed supplemental briefs.

For reversal the state argues that * * * (2) the plain meaning of the policy term "damages" includes "equitable" monetary relief such as cleanup costs or, alternatively, the policy term "damages" is ambiguous and should be construed against the insurer to include payment of cleanup costs; (3) cleanup costs are merely a measurement of "damages" for "property damage," and the characterization of cleanup costs as equitable for purposes of seventh amendment analysis is inapplicable to questions involving insurance coverage; and (4) finally, the public interest in mitigating environmental pollution and cleaning up hazardous waste sites strongly supports imposing liability for the cleanup costs on the polluters and their insurers. * * *

Continental argues that * * * (2) cleanup costs are equitable costs, not legal "damages," and thus are not recoverable under the CGL policies; and (3) cleanup costs constitute economic losses, not "property damage," and thus are not recoverable under the CGL policies. * * *

The "damages" issue is properly before the court en banc. It was expressly raised by the AIA in its initial amicus brief, and the state responded to the AIA's argument in its reply brief. The "damages" issue was considered and discussed at length by the panel majority, 811 F.2d at 1187–89, and the panel dissent, *id.* at 1193–95, and in fact was the only point of significant disagreement between the majority and dissenting opinions. Moreover, the broad issue of the availability of liability insurance coverage under standard-form CGL policies for the costs of cleaning up hazardous waste sites is a question of substantial importance not only to liability insurers and their insureds, but to the public as well.

This case involves the construction of standard-form CGL insurance policies. "An insuring obligation is a contract, and coverage exists only if assumed by the terms of the policy." *Aetna Casualty & Surety Co. v. Hanna,* 224 F.2d 499, 503 (5th Cir.1955) (*Hanna*). The district court correctly applied the law of Missouri, the forum state. *See Klaxon Co. v. Stentor Electric Manufacturing Co.,* 313 U.S. 487, 61 S.Ct. 1020, 85 L.Ed. 1477 (1941). Missouri has adopted the most significant relationship test set forth in the Restatement (Second) Conflict of Laws § 188 (1971). *See American Institute of Marketing Systems, Inc. v. Brooks,* 469 S.W.2d 932 (Mo.Ct.App.1971) (contracts), and is the state with the most significant contacts with the parties and the CGL policies. *See, e.g., Havenfield Corp. v. H & R Block, Inc.,* 509 F.2d 1263, 1267–68 (8th Cir.), *cert. denied,* 421 U.S. 999, 95 S.Ct. 2395, 44 L.Ed.2d 665 (1975).

Under Missouri law

[t]he rules of construction applicable to insurance contracts require that the language used be given its plain meaning. If the language is unambiguous the policy must be enforced according to such language. If the language is ambiguous it will be construed against the insurer. Language is ambiguous if it is reasonably open to different constructions; and language used will be viewed in light of "the meaning that would ordinarily be understood by the lay[person] who bought and paid for the policy."

Robin v. Blue Cross Hospital Service, Inc., 637 S.W.2d 695, 698 (Mo. 1982) (banc) (citations omitted); *see also Pearce v. General American Life Insurance Co.*, 637 F.2d 536, 539 (8th Cir.1980) (Missouri law); *Bellamy v. Pacific Mutual Life Insurance Co.*, 651 S.W.2d 490, 495–96 (Mo.1983) (banc).

Case law on this issue is sharply divided. *Compare Maryland Casualty Co. v. Armco, Inc.*, 822 F.2d at 1352–55 (under Maryland law, holding "damages" does not cover cleanup costs; citing cases), *with New Castle County v. Hartford Accident & Indemnity Co.*, 673 F.Supp. 1359, 1365–67 (D.Del.1987) (under Delaware law, holding "damages" covers cleanup costs; citing cases). For the reasons discussed below, we hold that the term "damages" is not ambiguous in the insurance context and that the plain meaning of the term "damages" used in the CGL policies refers to legal damages and does not cover cleanup costs.

Viewed outside the insurance context, the term "damages" is ambiguous: it is reasonably open to different constructions. Webster's Third New International Dictionary 571 (1971) defines "damages" as "the estimated reparation in money for detriment or injury sustained: compensation or satisfaction imposed by law for wrong or injury caused by a violation of a legal right." The dictionary definition does not distinguish between legal damages and equitable monetary relief. *E.g., New Castle County v. Hartford Accident & Indemnity Co.*, at 1366. Thus, from the viewpoint of the lay insured, the term "damages" could reasonably include all monetary claims, whether such claims are described as damages, expenses, costs, or losses.

In the insurance context, however, the term "damages" is not ambiguous, and the plain meaning of the term "damages" as used in the insurance context refers to legal damages and does not include equitable monetary relief. *See Maryland Casualty Co. v. Armco, Inc.*, 822 F.2d at 1352. The CGL policies require Continental to "pay on behalf of the insured all sums which the insured shall become legally obligated to pay as damages because of * * * property damage to which this insurance applies caused by an occurrence." "The obligation of the insurer to pay is limited to 'damages,' a word which has an accepted technical meaning in law." *Hanna*, 224 F.2d at 503. Although not defined in the CGL policies, "[t]he word 'damages' is not ambiguous in the insurance context. Black letter insurance law holds that claims for equitable relief are not claims for 'damages' under liability insurance contracts." *Maryland Casualty Co. v. Armco, Inc.*, 643 F.Supp. at 432, *citing Haines v. St. Paul Fire & Marine Insurance Co.*, 428 F.Supp. 435, 439–41 (D.Md.1977) (applying Maryland law), *Hanna*, 224 F.2d at 503–04, *and Desrochers v. New York Casualty Co.*, 99 N.H. 129, 106 A.2d 196, 198–99 (1954). *But see, e.g., New Castle County v. Hartford Accident & Indemnity Co.*, at 1365–67 (applying Delaware law; citing cases); *United States Aviex Co. v. Travelers Insurance Co.*, 125 Mich.App. 579, 336 N.W.2d 838, 843 (1983); *Broadwell Realty Services, Inc. v. Fidelity & Casualty Co.*, 218 N.J.Super. 516, 528 A.2d 76, 82–83 (App.Div.1987) (citing cases).

This limited construction of the term "damages" is consistent with the provision defining the insurer's obligation as a whole. Continental did not agree to pay "*all sums* which the insured shall become legally obligated to pay." Continental agreed to pay "all sums which the insured shall become legally obligated to pay *as damages.*" The expansive reading of the term "damages" urged by the state would render the term "all sums" virtually meaningless. "If the term 'damages' is given the broad, boundless connotations sought by the [insured], then the term 'damages' in the contract * * * would become mere surplusage, because any obligation to pay would be covered. The limitation implied by employment of the phrase 'to pay as damages' would be obliterated." *Maryland Casualty Co. v. Armco, Inc.,* 822 F.2d at 1352.

Such a limited construction of the term "damages" is also consistent with the distinction drawn in insurance law between money damages and injunctive relief. "Traditionally, courts have found no insurance coverage for the costs of complying with an injunction even in cases where the suits could have been brought for damages." *Maryland Casualty Co. v. Armco, Inc.,* 643 F.Supp. at 434. *See also Hanna,* 224 F.2d at 503–04; *Garden Sanctuary, Inc. v. Insurance Co. of North America,* 292 So.2d 75, 77–78 (Fla.Ct.App.1974); *Ladd Construction Co. v. Insurance Co. of North America,* 73 Ill.App.3d 43, 29 Ill.Dec. 305, 307–08, 391 N.E.2d 568, 570–73 (1979).

The limited construction of the term "damages" is also consistent with the statutory scheme of CERCLA § 107(a)(4), 42 U.S.C. § 9607(a)(4), which differentiates between cleanup costs and damages. Under CERCLA cleanup costs are not substantially equivalent to compensatory damages for injury to or destruction of the environment. Some cases have overlooked the difference between recovery of cleanup costs under CERCLA § 107(a)(4)(A) (by governments), (B) (by "any other person"), 42 U.S.C. § 9607(a)(4)(A), (B), and recovery of damages for injury, destruction or loss of natural resources under CERCLA § 107(a)(4)(C), 42 U.S.C. § 9607(a)(4)(C). For example, in *United States Aviex Co. v. Travelers Insurance Co.,* 336 N.W.2d at 843 (citations omitted), the court was persuaded that the distinction between recovery of cleanup costs and recovery of damages for damage to natural resources was "merely fortuitous from the standpoint of either [the insured] or [the insurer]." The court reasoned that whether the government chooses to clean up the pollution itself and then sue to recover its cleanup costs, or sues to recover damages for the damage to natural resources, "[t]he damage to the natural resources is simply measured in the cost to restore the [environment] to its original state," and rejected the argument that the term "damages" should be limited to legal damages and should not include equitable costs. *Id.*

Moreover, the distinction between recovery of cleanup costs and recovery of damages is not "merely fortuitous" to either the insured as a CERCLA and RCRA defendant or to the insurer. The cost of cleaning up a hazardous waste site often exceeds its original value. On the other hand, some natural resources are of exceptional value and their destruction could greatly exceed the cost of cleaning up any hazardous waste contamination. A significant difference between the measurement of liability for cleanup costs and for damage to natural resources could determine whether the government sues for cleanup costs or for the damages. *See Maryland Casualty Co. v. Armco, Inc.,* 822 F.2d at 1353, *citing Peevyhouse v. Garland Coal & Mining Co.,* 382 P.2d 109 (Okla.1962) (restoration of strip-mined land cost four times its potential value), *cert. denied,* 375 U.S. 906, 84 S.Ct. 196, 11 L.Ed.2d 145 (1963); *cf. Jack L. Baker Cos. v. Pasley Manufacturing & Distributing Co.,* 413 S.W.2d 268, 273–74 (Mo.1967) (under Missouri law, measure of damages to real property is lesser of either difference in value before and after injury or cost of restoring property to original condition).

Whether the government seeks recovery of cleanup costs, damages for destruction or loss of natural resources, or both, may make little difference to the insured as a CERCLA or RCRA defendant. As noted above, there may be little difference between the *dollar amount* the insured may have to pay as cleanup costs under CERCLA § 107(a)(4)(A), 42 U.S.C. § 9607(a)(4)(A), and the *dollar amount* the insured may have to pay as damages under CERCLA § 107(a)(4)(C), 42 U.S.C. § 9607(a)(4)(C). Nonetheless, the type of relief sought is critical to the insured and the insurer, because under the CGL policies the insurer is liable only for legal damages, not for equitable monetary relief, such as cleanup costs. "The insurance contract, which controls the obligations between the parties and therefore centers the focus of this court, is written in terms of the relief sought. * * *" *Maryland Casualty Co. v. Armco, Inc.,* 822 F.2d at 1352. Here, the federal and state governments seek recovery of cleanup costs under CERCLA § 107(a)(4)(A), 42 U.S.C. § 9607(a)(4)(A) (costs of removal or remedial action), and RCRA § 7003(a), 42 U.S.C. § 6973(a) (abatement costs). These lawsuits are essentially equitable actions for monetary relief in the form of restitution or reimbursement of costs. *See Maryland Casualty Co. v. Armco, Inc.,* 822 F.2d at 1352–53; *cf. EPA,* 810 F.2d at 749 (for purposes of determining seventh amendment jury trial issue, cases cited). The federal and state governments have not sought recovery of "damages for injury to, destruction of, or loss of natural resources," pursuant to CERCLA § 107(a)(4)(C), 42 U.S.C. § 9607(a)(4)(C).

Accordingly, we hold that the federal and state governments' claims for cleanup costs under CERCLA § 107(a)(4)(A), 42 U.S.C. § 9607(a)(4)(A), and RCRA § 7003(a), 42 U.S.C. § 6973(a), are not claims for "damages" under these CGL policies. * * *

The order of the district court is affirmed.

Notes and Questions

1. *Division of Authority.* The issue addressed in *NEPACCO* is among the most difficult insurance coverage questions associated with the massive federal and state programs for cleaning up hazardous waste disposal sites. Case law on the issue has been divided. For

example, compare *Maryland Casualty Company v. Armco,* 822 F.2d 1348 (4th Cir.1987) holding that cleanup costs are not "damages," with *United States Aviex Company v. Travelers Insurance Company,* 125 Mich.App. 579, 336 N.W.2d 838 (1983), holding that they are.

2. *Forms of CERCLA Liability.* There are three separate situations under CERCLA in which the "damages" issue may arise: potentially responsible parties (PRPs, in the argot of the trade) may decide to clean up a site in anticipation of government action; the government may order PRPs to take action; or the government may cleanup and sue PRPs for recovery of cleanup costs.

a. Is an insured who undertakes voluntary cleanup in anticipation of governmental investigation or action "legally obligated" to incur cleanup costs within the meaning of the CGL insuring agreement? See *Port of Portland v. Water Quality Insurance Syndicate,* 796 F.2d 1188 (9th Cir.1986), which at least presupposes an affirmative answer. Does the correct answer depend on whether the insured would be committing an unlawful act by failing to correct conditions at the site? Note that CERCLA itself does not make it unlawful to create or maintain hazardous conditions requiring remedial action; it merely permits the government to undertake cleanup itself or to order cleanup under specified circumstances, and creates a set of liabilities for the costs of cleanup.

b. Sometimes the state or federal government seeks a mandatory injunction directing the insured to remedy a threat to the environment posed by conditions at a site. See CERCLA § 106, 42 U.S.C. § 9606. The obvious question here is whether the insured has incurred "damages" when an injunction does not order the payment of any money to a third party, but simply requires the insured to take remedial action or to assure that it is taken. The "traditional" rule described in *NEPAC-CO* is that the costs of complying with an injunctive order are not insured by a general liability policy. But in fact the rule is derived from only two major cases. See *Aetna Casualty & Surety Company v. Hanna,* 224 F.2d 499 (5th Cir.1955); *Desrochers v. New York Casualty Company,* 99 N.H. 129, 106 A.2d 196 (1954). Since both these decisions pre-date the enactment of CERCLA, it is unclear how much bearing they have on the unique liability regime CERCLA employs. Some courts suggest that the difference between an injunctive remedy under CERCLA or an analogous state statute and governmental cleanup followed by a cost recovery action is inconsequential for insurance purposes. See, e.g., *Broadwell Realty Services, Inc. v. The Fidelity and Casualty Company of New York,* 218 N.J.Super. 516, 528 A.2d 76 (1987); *New Castle County v. Hartford Accident and Indemnity Company,* 673 F.Supp. 1359 (D.Del.1987).

c. The third remedy available under CERCLA involves cleanup by one or more agencies of government (and in some cases, by third parties) followed by an action to recover the costs of cleanup under CERCLA § 107, 42 U.S.C. § 9607. This is the approach that most resembles an action for traditional civil damages: it involves a loss incurred by another party, followed by an action to recover for the loss. In the most general sense, therefore, it is an action for damages. If the costs for which the government seeks reimbursement in a § 107 action constitute damages, would a holding that costs incurred by the insured under either of the first two approaches are not "damages" within the meaning of the CGL insuring agreement create excessive moral hazard? How?

3. *The Merits.* Setting aside the difference between CERCLA remedies, was the *NEPACCO* court correct in holding that even the insured's liability in a governmental cost-recovery action does not constitute a legal obligation to pay money "as damages?" How would you assess the following arguments for and against the different strands of the decision?

a. **Point:** Since CERCLA is a statutory rather than a judicially-created liability regime, it makes no sense to distinguish between coverage for equitable as opposed to legal remedies. In any event, the CGL insuring agreement does not distinguish between damages paid in equitable and legal actions. Therefore, it should not matter whether a CERCLA cost-recovery action sounds in equity rather than law.

Counterpoint: The CGL refers to liability incurred "as damages." The use of the term "as" clearly suggests that not all liabilities—and indeed not all obligations to pay money—fall within coverage. The distinction between legal and equitable relief is what inclusion of this term is getting at.

b. **Point:** The *NEPACCO* court characterized liability for cleanup costs as "essentially equitable actions for monetary relief in the form of restitution * * *". The hallmark of restitution, however, is that it involves the relinquishment of a defendant's ill-gotten gains. In contrast, in actions for damages, liability is measured by the loss the plaintiff suffered, not the magnitude of the defendant's gain. The remedy in CERCLA cost recovery actions—imposition of liability for the costs incurred by the plaintiff to clean up—much more closely resembles recovery of a loss than restitution of a wrongful gain.

Counterpoint: Restitution involves reimbursement, whereas the awarding of damages compensates for injury or loss. In CERCLA cost-recovery actions the government seeks reimbursement for its costs, not compensation for any injury it has suffered, since it has suffered none. Moreover, when a PRP has failed in the past to take steps that would have prevented discharge of hazardous waste or remedied an existing discharge, it has unjustifiably saved the costs of prevention or cleanup that are later incurred by the government. The government's cost of cleanup is therefore precisely a measure of the PRP's ill-gotten gains— the hallmark of restitution.

c. **Point:** The court in *NEPACCO* mistakenly thought that the availability of what CERCLA explicitly refers to as "damages" for injury to natural resources as a category separate from cleanup costs supported the view that the latter do not constitute "damages" under the CGL insuring agreement. Cleanup costs, however, are simply a measure of what it costs to avoid natural resource damages. These costs are therefore insured under the rule that the costs of avoiding or mitigating harm that would be even greater and would be insured are impliedly covered by liability insurance policies. See, e.g., *Bankers Trust Company v. Hartford Accident and Indemnity Company*, 518 F.Supp. 371 (S.D.N.Y.1981).

Counterpoint: The statutory distinction between recovery of cleanup *costs* and recovery of natural resources *damages* means exactly what it suggests: that because the former are costs, not damages, only the latter constitute "damages" under a CGL insuring agreement. Moreover, the occasionally-invoked *Bankers Trust* rule only makes sense, if at all, when mitigation expenses are designed to avoid a greater loss that would definitely occur and for which the insurer would definitely be liable in the absence of mitigation. Under CERCLA, however, hazardous waste sites are cleaned up in order to avoid hypothetical future personal injury or property damage; cleanups do not involve avoidance of the kind of imminent and certain harm—destruction of a nearby building by fire, for example—that are contemplated by *Bankers Trust*.

d. **Point:** The *NEPACCO* court seemed to think that because the costs of cleanup sometimes exceed the value of the property involved, these costs are not damages, since the standard measure of property damage in tort is the lesser of the cost of repair or the diminution in value caused by the tortious activity. This argument, however, confuses the *measure* of recovery and the *nature* of the recovery. The nature of a CERCLA recovery is damages; CERCLA has simply changed the measure of damages used in awarding the plaintiff compensation for its loss.

Counterpoint: The significance of the fact that cleanup costs often exceed property value is twofold. First, cleanup costs are heavily within the control of the insured and they are likely to benefit the insured, at least when the insured is owner of the property to be cleaned up. Thus, holding that cleanup costs in excess of property value are "damages" creates severe moral hazard. Second, once cleanup costs exceed property value, the insurer loses the anchor of predictability that such traditional tort rules as the nonrecoverability of economic loss in the absence of personal injury or property damage assure. The same aim should be achieved by limiting the term "damages" in the manner of *NEPACCO*.

4. *Property Damage*. In a passage omitted from the *NEPACCO* opinion, the court conceded that the contamination of property caused by the discharge of hazardous waste constitutes "property damage" within the meaning of the CGL insuring agreement. Most courts agree in general. See, e.g., *United States Fidelity & Guaranty Company v. Thomas Solvent Company*, 683 F.Supp. 1139 (W.D.Mich.1988). But see, *Mraz v. Canadian Universal Insurance Company*, 804 F.2d 1325 (4th

Cir.1986) (response costs under CERCLA "are not themselves property damages" but economic loss). Suppose, however, that a portion (sometimes a large portion) of cleanup costs at a site are incurred to prevent damage to neighboring property. Are these costs "because of * * * property damage" under a CGL policy? At first glance the inclusion of the phrase "because of" suggests that property damage need not have occurred in order for damages to be because of property damage—i.e., to prevent property damage. If the relevant policy applies only to property damage that occurs "during the policy period," either by so stating in the insuring agreement or in a definition of an insured occurrence, however, should it be necessary to separate the insured costs of repairing existing damage from the uninsured costs of measures taken to prevent future property damage? For discussion of analogous problems of apportionment, see *Broadwell Realty Services, Inc. v. The Fidelity & Casualty Company of New York*, 218 N.J.Super. 516, 528 A.2d 76 (1987).

C. EXCLUSIONS AND CONDITIONS

Standard personal and commercial general liability insurance policies contain a series of exclusions and conditions. A review of the Sample CGL Policy set out in Section A will yield an overall idea of their nature. A key to understanding the different purposes of these provisions is to recognize that there is a tension between the desire of ordinary individuals and businesses to purchase general-purpose liability protection in a single policy, and the need for insurers to segregate from the pool of such insureds those whose activities pose special risks. One method of achieving this aim is simply to price general liability insurance in accordance with the different levels of risk posed by different insureds. See generally Schwartz, The Ethics and Economics of Tort Liability Insurance, 75 Cornell Law Review ____ (1990). Another method, however, is to exclude coverage of certain special risks from general liability policies, leaving those who pose special risks to purchase separate coverage targeted at and priced in accordance with these risks. The material that follows addresses some of the exclusions and conditions that figure most prominently in insurance planning for this and certain other contingencies by potential policyholders, and in the litigation that ensues when this planning process turns out to have been less than perfect.

1. The Owned–Property Exclusion

DIAMOND SHAMROCK CHEMICALS COMPANY v. AETNA CASUALTY AND SURETY COMPANY

Superior Court of New Jersey, Appellate Division, 1989.
231 N.J.Super. 1, 554 A.2d 1342.

BROCHIN, J.S.C. (temporarily assigned).

Plaintiff Diamond Shamrock Chemicals Company is a large corporation engaged in the business of manufacturing chemical products for home and industrial use. The defendants are Aetna Casualty and

Surety Company and other primary and excess insurers which insured Diamond under comprehensive general liability policies issued between 1951 and 1984. Diamond's complaint seeks a declaration that by virtue of these policies, it is entitled to indemnification from its insurers for the costs of remedying the consequences of dioxin contamination which has resulted from its manufacturing operations on its property at 80 Lister Avenue, Newark, New Jersey.

The defendants' answers deny liability and assert affirmative defenses based on the language of the relevant policies, including exclusion clauses, which define their coverage. In order to test these affirmative defenses, the parties made various motions for partial summary judgment. Leave was sought to appeal to this court from several of the trial court's orders on these motions, but leave was granted for an appeal only from an order which ruled that the clauses of the policies which exclude claims for damages to the insured's own property are "inapplicable" to bar the indemnification which Diamond seeks.

The basic insuring agreement contained in Diamond's comprehensive general liability policies reads as follows:

> The company will pay on behalf of the insured all sums which the insured shall become liable to pay as damages because of bodily injury or property damage to which this insurance applies, caused by an occurrence. * * *

The relevant exclusion clauses state:

> This policy does not apply:
>
> (i) to property damage to
>
> > (1) property owned or occupied by or rented to the insured,
> >
> > (2) property used by the insured, or
> >
> > (3) property in the care, custody or control of the insured or as to which the insured is for any purpose exercising physical control;
>
> (j) to property damage to premises alienated by the named insured arising out of such premises or any part thereof.

(In this opinion we refer to clause "i" as the "owned property" exclusion and clause "j" as the "alienated property" exclusion.)

The court's ruling that these provisions are "inapplicable" was incorporated in an order enacted February 4, 1988, which reads as follows:

> ORDERED that the motions of defendants Aetna Casualty and Surety Company * * * joined by the defendants listed * * * for summary judgment to exclude coverage for property damage to the insured's property, and/or to exclude coverage for property damage to property in the care, custody or control of the insured, and/or to exclude coverage for property

damage to premises alienated by the insured are denied, and *that Diamond's cross-motion to declare the aforesaid exclusions inapplicable is granted, all as more particularly set forth in the Court's oral statement * * * on December 11, 1987 * * ** [Emphasis added.]

The only issues now before us are those raised by defendants' appeal from the underlined portion of this order. We reverse and remand, holding only that the exclusions are potentially applicable and that a final decision as to their applicability should be made on the basis of a fully developed record.

Diamond acquired the manufacturing facility at 80 Lister Avenue, Newark, in 1951 and sold it in 1971. It reacquired the site and adjacent property in 1984 and 1986 to facilitate the clean up or containment of the dioxin contamination which was ordered by the DEP.

From 1951 until early 1969, Diamond manufactured a chemical at its 80 Lister Avenue facility which it used in the production of various herbicides. Dioxin, a chemical which has proven highly toxic to laboratory animals was a by-product of that manufacturing process.

On June 2, 1983, Governor Thomas Kean issued an Executive Order which recited that 80 Lister Avenue "may be contaminated with potentially high levels of * * * dioxin," that dioxin is "a substance known to be highly toxic to humans" and that a "potential hazard exists to the public health because of the possibility of transportation of contaminated substances off the above described premises into immediately surrounding areas." The Order invoked the Governor's emergency powers and directed the Commissioner of the Department of Environmental Protection to take the necessary steps to abate those conditions. Pursuant to that Executive Order, the DEP issued an administrative order on June 13, 1983, which directed Diamond to:

install a suitable ground cover over all exposed portions of this Lister Avenue site, utilizing a contractor approved by this Department and EPA, such that wind blown spread of dust from said premises is minimized to the maximum extent practicable [and to] take other measures during and subsequent to the installation of the aforesaid ground cover as directed by the DEP's on scene coordinator to prevent further off-site migration of dioxin.

Diamond was also ordered to construct a fence around the perimeter of the property in order to bar access to the site.

On March 13, 1984, an Administrative Consent Order was executed which required Diamond to obtain a site evaluation plan and a feasibility study at its own expense which would evaluate all remedial action potentially appropriate for the site, and to submit them to the DEP. Diamond states that it has completed the process of gathering data for the study and has submitted it to the DEP. The study recommends the demolition of all buildings on the property, the construction of a slurry wall around its perimeter, the compaction of all contaminated material into a mound which would then be covered by a layered cap, and the installation of a ground water recovery and treatment system.

According to Diamond, the only remedial measures thus far implemented are the installation of a tarpaulin-like ground cover and the construction of the peripheral fence. Implementation of additional remedial measures is awaiting the DEP's approval of the remedial plan. The estimated cost for implementing the plan advocated by Diamond is approximately $8,000,000, plus annual operating and maintenance expenses of $261,000. The estimated cost of the most expensive remediation plan considered by the study, an off-site thermal treatment option, is said to be $248,000,000 plus $62,000 annually for operating and maintenance expenses. Although the costs incurred thus far, for the study and for the tarpaulin and fence, are no doubt more than negligible, presumably they are small in comparison with the potential aggregate costs.

For purposes of the motion for summary judgment which resulted in the February 4, 1988, order from which this appeal has been taken, the foregoing facts are not disputed. However, Diamond denies that "all of the costs at issue in the motion for summary judgment arise from cleanup measures taken within the boundary of the Lister Avenue plant property." It asserts that:

> The motions and cross-motion for summary judgment addressed not the recoverability of particular costs but the sufficiency as defenses of particular exclusions. What may ultimately be involved in the remediation on or off the Newark site for which Diamond is responsible is not presently knowable, and it is for that reason that Diamond seeks a decree declaring and enforcing the obligations of the defendants.

In support of Diamond's assertions that off-site remediation measures may ultimately be required, it relies upon language in Governor Kean's June 2, 1983, Executive Order which declared that the New Jersey Department of Environmental Protection had reached the "preliminary conclusion" that the 80 Lister Avenue site "may be contaminated with potentially high levels of * * * dioxin * * * and, accordingly, * * * that a potential hazard exists to the public health because of the possibility of transportation of contaminated substances * * * into immediately surrounding areas," and upon language in the DEP's orders expressing concern that the dioxin contaminating the site will adversely affect the public health and the environment, presumably by migrating off the site. Diamond does not refer to any findings contained in its newly completed comprehensive investigation of the site to show that dioxin has moved off of its property or presents an imminent threat of doing so. In any event, whether the remediation efforts are expended on or off of Diamond's property was, in the view of the trial court and, for somewhat different reasons, in our view also, immaterial to Diamond's right to indemnification.

As previously noted, the issue which is now before us on appeal is the trial court's ruling that, as a matter of law, Diamond's claims are not barred by the policy exclusions for "property damage to ✳ ✳ ✳ property owned or occupied by ✳ ✳ ✳ or ✳ ✳ ✳ in the care, custody or control of ✳ ✳ ✳ or ✳ ✳ ✳ alienated by the named insured arising out of such premises or any part thereof." After that ruling had been issued, this court rendered its decision in *CPS Chemical Co. v. Continental Insurance Co.,* 222 N.J.Super. 175, 536 A.2d 311 (App.Div.1988). On the basis of that decision, the insurers moved for reconsideration of the trial court's ruling that the "owned property" and "alienated premises" exclusions were "inapplicable" to the present case. They pointed out that in *CPS* we said:

> As we stressed in *Broadwell,* "[t]o the extent that all or a portion of the response expenses pertain solely to damage to the [insured's property] and not to prevent off-site contamination, ✳ ✳ ✳ such damage is not within the coverage provided." [quoting *Broadwell Realty Services, Inc. v. Fidelity & Cas.,* 218 N.J.Super. 516, 528–529 [528 A.2d 76] (App.Div.1987)] We emphasize that the obligation undertaken by [CPS's insurers] relates solely to the cost of preventive measures designed to abate the continued migration of hazardous wastes into the Prickett's Brook watershed and the Runyon well field. It does not encompass damage to the CPS site itself or the cost of alterations designed to improve CPS's property or operations. [*Id.* at 187, 536 A.2d 311]

On the basis of our *CPS* decision, the insurers argued that the summary judgment holding the "owned property" and "alienated premises" exclusions inapplicable should not have been granted, and that the liability of the insurers should have awaited proof at trial showing what part of Diamond's expenditures pertained solely to damage to its own property and what to the cost of preventive measures to prevent off-site contamination.

The trial judge granted the motion for reconsideration, but adhered to his ruling. He distinguished *CPS* and *Broadwell* on the ground that in those cases the property owners were continuing to utilize the property for productive purposes while in the present case Diamond had reacquired the property solely to facilitate the cleanup, and he held that whether all or any part of Diamond's expenditures were being used to clean up its own property or the property of others was immaterial because the remediation measures were not being undertaken for the benefit of Diamond, but solely to comply with the demands of the government.

In their appeal to this court, the insurers (and the amicus curiae) argue, first, that the fact that Diamond was compelled by DEP to spend money for the cleanup of its property did not make the "owned property" and "alienated premises" exclusions inapplicable. Secondly, they contend that *Broadwell* and *CPS* were wrongly decided, but that since the trial court was obligated to follow them, it should have held a trial to distinguish expenses of cleaning up Diamond's own property from those incurred to prevent the imminent spread of pollution; only the latter costs, they argue, are compensable, even under *Broadwell* and *CPS.* Thirdly, one group of insurers argues that the trial court committed error in construing the language of the policies strongly against the insurers (*contra proferentem*) on a motion for summary judgment; rather, these insurers contend, the court should afford them the opportunity to prove at trial that Diamond itself has interpreted the policies in a way which would bar its present claims.

We return to our decisions in *Broadwell Realty Services, Inc. v. Fidelity & Casualty Co.,* 218 N.J.Super. 516, 528 A.2d 76 (App.Div.1987), and *CPS Chemical Co. v. Continental Insurance Co.,* 222 N.J.Super. 175, 536 A.2d 311 (App.Div.1988).

Strictly speaking, *CPS,* as presented to the court, did not involve the "owned property" and "alienated premises" exclusions whose interpretation is the sole issue before us. Our opinion in that case states, "Both carriers [for the polluter] denied liability on the basis that the sum of money for which *CPS* was adjudged liable did not constitute pecuniary damages and thus did not fall within the policy coverage." The relevant provisions of the policy which were quoted verbatim did not include the exclusion provisions at issue here. *CPS Chemical Co. v. Continental Insurance Co.,* 222 N.J.Super. at 181, 536 A.2d 311. Nonetheless, our opinion stated:

> We emphasize that the obligation undertaken by [the insurers] relates solely to the cost of preventive measures designed to abate the continued migration of hazardous wastes into the Prickett's Brook watershed and the Runyon well field. It does not encompass damage to the CPS site itself or the cost of alterations designed to improve CPS's property or operations.
>
> *   *   *
>
> *   *   * we hold that the obligation of the insurers is limited to indemnifying CPS for the monetary amounts awarded to the DEP for the latter's use in attempting to eradicate the effects of the present or past pollution for which the insured has been adjudged liable. At the time of the judgment in the underlying litigation, the migration of contaminants was continuing and ongoing. As in *Broadwell Realty v. Fidelity & Cas., supra,* 218 N.J.Super. at 528 [528 A.2d 76], "[f]urther peril was both imminent and immediate." To that extent, the insurers' obligation is to pay the cost of abating the polluting effects of prior discharges. [*Id.* at 187–188, 536 A.2d 311]

Broadwell squarely holds that an insurer under a general public liability policy like those at issue in the present case which contain the "owned property" and "alienated premises" exclusions, is not liable for "elements of the claim which relate to remedies for damage confined to" the insured's property and that "[t]o the extent that all or a portion of the response expenses pertain solely to damage to the [insured's] site itself and not to prevent off-site contamination, the owned-property exclusion clearly applies, and such damage is not within the coverage provided." *Broadwell Realty Services, Inc. v. Fidelity & Cas.*, 218 N.J. Super. 516, 528, 528 A.2d 76 (App.Div.1987).

More recently, in *Summit Associates, Inc. v. Liberty Mutual Fire Insurance Company*, 229 N.J.Super. 56, 550 A.2d 1235 (App.Div.1988), a suit in which an insured under a general public liability policy sought indemnification from its insurer for the money which the government required it to spend to remove hazardous pollutants which it discovered when it excavated its newly purchased property, we remanded the case to the trial court to determine whether the pollution "damaged or threatened damage to third party property." *Id.* at 65, 550 A.2d 1235. The trial judge was instructed as follows:

> If he decides that no such damage occurred or was threatened, that will be the end of the inquiry because, as a matter of fact, the owned property exclusion will be applicable. If, on the other hand, he decides that the opening of the sludge pit threatened damage to third party property, he must then apply the traditional principles of insurance contract interpretation we reaffirmed in *Broadwell* including whether application or non-application of the owned property exclusion would best carry out the reasonable expectations of the parties. [*Ibid.*]

In *CPS* and *Broadwell,* pollutants had escaped from the property of the insured and had already caused injury to the property of third parties. In *CPS,* those pollutants had infiltrated Perth Amboy's well field, contaminating its water supply. Perth Amboy asserted a conventional damage claim for injury to its property. The Department of Environmental Protection, which was a co-plaintiff, sought and obtained a judgment compelling the defendants to pay money which would be used to remedy injuries to property of parties other than the insured and to protect their property from further injury. We stated, "The critical fact is that *CPS* has been compelled in a court action to pay money to others for harm caused by its tortious conduct." *CPS,* 222 N.J.Super. at 187, 536 A.2d 311.

> We again emphasize the unrefuted evidence contained in the record that contaminants were discharging into a nearby stream and into two New Jersey Bell cable vaults and that this destructive process was ongoing. Under the *parens patriae* doctrine, the State had a colorable claim for damage to the stream. New Jersey Bell also had a right to be compensated for whatever damage was caused by release of the gasoline from the underground storage tanks situated on Broadwell's property. [*Id.* 218 N.J.Super. at 528, 528 A.2d 76]

Insofar as the "owned property" and "alienated premises" exclusions are concerned, the claims asserted against the insureds in both *CPS* and *Broadwell* fell squarely within the coverage of the policies.

Each insured had become liable to pay money as damages because of property damage to property which it did not own and had never alienated. In *CPS* the damaged property was Perth Amboy's well fields; in *Broadwell,* New Jersey Bell's cable vaults and a stream in which the public, represented by the State, had an interest.

In both *Broadwell* and *CPS* this court held that the insured was entitled to be indemnified for, among other things, sums expended on measures to prevent further, imminently impending, injury to property owned by someone other than the insured. There is no novelty to the proposition that in a conventional tort action, once some present injury has been proved, the plaintiff's damages may include the cost of measures intended to prevent future injury. *See Associates Metals Corp. v. Dixon Chemical,* 82 N.J.Super. 281, 315, 197 A.2d 569 (App.Div. 1964), certif. den. 42 N.J. 501, 201 A.2d 580 (Metal dealer's damages for injury to steel inventory from acid dust included the cost of tarpaulin, oil, equipment and labor to protect the steel against further damage.); *Barbari v. Bochinsky,* 43 N.J.Super. 186, 128 A.2d 1 (App.Div.1956) (Damages for continuing trespass by an encroaching wall include costs of removing the wall to abate future trespass.); *Annotation,* "Expense incurred by injured party in remedying temporary nuisance or in preventing injury as element of damages recoverable," 41 A.L.R.2d 1064 (1955). *Cf. Ayers v. Jackson Township,* 106 N.J. 557, 525 A.2d 287 (1987) (Damages for toxic tort include costs of future medical surveillance.). Furthermore, the critical question in *Broadwell* and *CPS* was not whether the measures for which reimbursement was sought had been taken on the insured's own property or on property of a third party. The "owned property" exclusion does not purport to exclude claims because they are for sums expended for work performed within the premises owned by the insured. It excludes claims for sums which the insured is obligated to pay for "property damage to * * * property owned * * * by * * * the insured." Claims arising out of injury to property of others for which the insured is responsible are covered by the terms of the policies even if the insured's damages are measured in part by the cost of remedial work which has to be performed on the insured's own property. The critical question, therefore, was, as we described it in *Broadwell,* whether expenditures were "attributable to correcting damage to Broadwell's property, which are not recoverable," or whether they were "attributable to abatement of damage to adjacent lands, which are." *Broadwell,* supra, 218 N.J.Super. at 529, 528 A.2d 76. Both *CPS* and *Broadwell* were remanded for trial to determine the amount of expenditures in the recoverable category.

We agree that those cases are factually distinguishable from the present case on the ground stated by the trial court, that the property owners in *CPS* and *Broadwell,* unlike Diamond, were continuing to utilize their properties and would benefit directly from some part of the expenditures for which they were seeking indemnification. In our opinion, however, the fact that Diamond's expenditures for remediation have been and will be made only because of governmental compulsion does not establish that the "owned property" and "alienated premises" exclusions are "inapplicable" to a determination of the scope of the insurers' obligations. Suppose for example that a building has been destroyed by fire. Suppose that the building was located in a municipality whose ordinance required that it be rebuilt or totally razed within a stated period of time.[1] Despite governmental compulsion on the owner to comply with such an ordinance, he could not reasonably expect his comprehensive general liability insurer to indemnify him for the costs of rebuilding or demolition. Rather, *CPS* and *Broadwell* establish that under the language of a public liability policy like those upon which Diamond's rights rest, it is a claim against the insured for damage to property of someone other than the insured which triggers the insurers' obligation to indemnify, not merely a coercive claim by the government. In the present case, there has been no showing, certainly no showing beyond genuine dispute, that anyone else besides Diamond has yet been injured in his person or property by the dioxin on Diamond's site.

Summit Associates, Inc. v. Liberty Mutual Fire Insurance Company, supra, raises the possibility of going one step further than *CPS* or *Broadwell.* In *Summit,* unlike either of the other two cases, when the insured spent money to clean up its own property in compliance with the orders of a governmental agency, the pollution on its property had not injured anyone else's person or property. *Summit* holds that if the pollution neither damaged nor threatened to damage the property of someone other than the insured, the insurer is not responsible for the clean up costs. However, our opinion goes on to tell the trial judge that if the pollution on Summit's property did threaten injury to the property of a third party, "he must then apply the traditional principles of contract interpretation we reaffirmed in *Broadwell* including whether application or non-application of the owned property exclusion would best carry out the reasonable expectations of the parties." *Summit Associates, Inc., supra,* 229 N.J.Super. at 65, 550 A.2d 1235. Presumably even if there was threatened injury to the property of a third party, the insurer would be liable in *Summit* only if, applying those principles, the phrase "property damage * * * caused by an occurrence" in the insuring agreement is construed to include "threatened damage." Insofar as appears from the reported opinion in that case, there has been no occasion to decide whether such a construction would be appropriate and that question has not been decided.

Conceivably, the evidence in the present case may ultimately show that the dioxin contamination of Diamond's property itself poses an imminent threat to someone else's property interest. If so, the trial court

---

1. *E.g. Newark Building Construction Code* (as amended to 1985) § 7A:5–7(a) (All buildings or structures that shall become unsafe, or unsanitary, or which contain deficient or blocked exit-way facilities, or which constitute a fire hazard or are otherwise dangerous to human life or the public welfare or which by reason of illegal or improper use or occupancy, shall be deemed unsafe buildings or structures, shall be taken down and removed or made safe and secure. *See Lane v. City of Mount Vernon,* 38 N.Y.2d 344, 379 N.Y.S.2d 798, 342 N.E.2d 571 (1976). (City may assess cost of removing a hazardous, burned out building against a transferee of the property.)

may have to decide whether the costs of abating that threat should be considered "sums which the insured shall become liable to pay as damages because of * * * property damage" other than "property damage to * * * property owned or * * * to premises alienated by the named insured." Perhaps there will be proof that the money which Diamond is called upon to pay is required because of the threat of imminent injury to the State's *parens patriae* interest in land and air. If so, the question may be presented whether such expenditures should be viewed as damages for injury to the property of another just as expenditures to protect the State's interest in a stream were in *Broadwell.* But for purposes of a motion for summary judgment, the record does not demonstrate beyond any genuine dispute of material fact that the damages which Diamond has been compelled to pay are damages for which it is liable because of injury to someone else's person or property, however broadly a court may construe the meaning of "property" and of "damage * * * caused by an occurrence" as those terms are used in the insuring agreements between Diamond and its insurers.

Whether the State's *parens patriae* interest in our air, land and water is "property" within the meaning of a standard comprehensive general liability policy and whether, or under what circumstances, money which an insured is compelled to pay for the abatement of a still unrealized threat of injury to the health or property of others is recoverable under such a policy implicate "highly significant policy considerations" and, for this reason, are best decided on a full record developed at trial. *Jackson v. Muhlenberg Hospital,* 53 N.J. 138, 142, 249 A.2d 65 (1969). As we wrote in *McGowan v. Borough of Eatontown,* 151 N.J.Super. 440, 376 A.2d 1327 (App.Div.1977), by reversing the summary judgment entered in the trial court we do not imply that a plenary trial must necessarily result in a material question of fact.

> We only indicate the necessity in this case of a judge making the legal determinations on which the parties' rights hinge on a full and complete record. If, on a plenary hearing, the judge finds no factual issue present or finds a moving party is entitled to judgment as a matter of law, then judgment should be entered accordingly. [*Id.* at 446, 376 A.2d 1327]

The portion of the trial court's order of February 4, 1988, from which this appeal was taken is therefore reversed and the matter is remanded for a plenary hearing. In response to the argument of some of the defendants that the court should not have sought to interpret the insurance policies without considering evidence of Diamond's conduct to show how it interpreted them, we add that if competent evidence is proffered at that hearing which is material to any of the issues before the trial court, including interpretation of the contracts between the parties, we are confident that it will be received and appropriately considered. *See Michaels v. Brookchester,* 26 N.J. 379, 388, 140 A.2d 199 (1958). ("Where ambiguity exists, the subsequent conduct of the parties in the performance of the agreement may serve to reveal their original understanding."); *Joseph Hilton & Associates, Inc. v. Evans,* 201 N.J.Super. 156, 171, 492 A.2d 1062 (App.Div.1985) (Same).

We reverse and remand for further proceedings in accordance with this opinion.

Notes and Questions

1. *The Language of the Exclusion.* What does the owned-property exclusion mean when it says that the insurance provided by the CGL does not "apply" to property damage to owned property? Is use of the term "apply" instead of "cover" significant? Some policies provide that they do not apply to "property damages" to owned property. Is use of the term "property damages" rather than "property damage" merely a mistake, or is it intended to imply something different from the singular usage?

2. *Allocation and Measurement.* On remand, who will bear the burden of proof on the issue of how to allocate the expenses of cleanup as between protection of owned and non-owned property? On what basis is the allocation of expenses to be made? One possible measure is the comparative benefit each property receives. Aside from actions that clearly benefit only the owned property, however, does this measure require estimating the damage that would have occurred to neighboring property if cleanup had not occurred? Suppose the neighboring property is a lake used for recreation by thousands of people each year, and the owned property's value doubles as a result of the cleanup. How are the two benefits to be compared? Is any other measure of the costs to be allocated between owned and non-owned property available?

3. *The Bottom–Line Issue.* Would a governmental agency ever bother to order an insured to conduct a cleanup in order to assure that the insured protected his own property? If not, can it be argued that all cleanup costs incurred in response to a governmental order are designed to protect the property or health of third-parties? If this argument can be made, does the requirement that the property damage because of which damages are imposed occur "during the policy period" preclude coverage of the costs of preventing imminent (as distinct from already accomplished) harm to other property? Should the *Bankers Trust* rule described in the Notes following *NEPACCO,* supra, apply under such circumstances?

2. The Business Risk Exclusions

WEEDO v. STONE–E–BRICK, INC.

Supreme Court of New Jersey, 1979.
81 N.J. 233, 405 A.2d 788.

CLIFFORD, J.

We granted certification, 75 N.J. 615, 384 A.2d 845 (1978), to review the Appellate Division's determination that the appellant insurance carrier was obliged to defend two claims brought against its assureds. *Weedo v. Stone–E–Brick, Inc.*, 155 N.J.Super. 474, 382 A.2d 1152 (1977). Resolution of both cases, argued here together, calls for construction of the same comprehensive general liability provisions of a policy issued to a masonry contracting concern. Specifically, the question is whether that policy indemnifies the insured against damages in an action for breach of contract and faulty workmanship on a project, where the damages claimed are the cost of correcting the work itself. The Appellate Division held that certain exclusions of the policy, when read together, were ambiguous and hence had to be resolved against the insurer. We reverse.

I

Pennsylvania National Mutual Insurance Company (hereinafter Pennsylvania National) issued a general automobile liability policy to Stone–E–Brick, Inc., a corporation engaged in masonry contracting. As part of the policy there was included Comprehensive General Liability Coverage (hereinafter CGL). During the term of the policy Calvin and Janice Weedo contracted with Stone–E–Brick to pour a concrete flooring on a veranda and to apply stucco masonry to the exterior of their home. The completed job revealed cracks in the stucco and other signs of faulty workmanship, such that the Weedos had to remove the stucco and replace it with a proper material. Thereupon the Weedos instituted suit against Stone–E–Brick and its principal, defendant Romano, alleging in pertinent part that

> [a]s a result of the defective and unworkmanlike manner in which the defendants applied the said stucco, plaintiffs were compelled to and did cause the defects existing therein to be remedied, where possible, and the omissions to be supplied, and, in general, were *compelled to and did furnish all the work, labor, services and materials necessary to complete the application of the said stucco in accordance with the contract and were compelled to and did expend large sums of money for that purpose in excess of the price which plaintiffs agreed to pay defendants for the application of said stucco, all of which was to plaintiffs' damage.* [Emphasis supplied.]

While the same CGL policy was in effect, Stone–E–Brick performed roofing and gutter work on a house being constructed for plaintiff Gellas, under a sub-contract agreement with the general contractor, defendant Vivino. After completion of the home the Gellases brought suit against Vivino based on breach of contract due to defects in workmanship and seeking recovery of costs "in connection with the repair and/or replacement of material necessary to correct the * * * defects in construction." Vivino in turn sought indemnification from Stone–E–Brick by way of third-party complaint, contending that plaintiffs' damages were the result of Stone–E–Brick's "faulty workmanship, materials or construction * * *."

Thereafter Stone–E–Brick requested that Pennsylvania National take over the defense and indemnify it in regard to both complaints. The carrier refused, asserting that the policy of insurance did not furnish coverage for the claims made or, in the alternative, that exclusionary clauses specifically precluded coverage. By way of third-party complaint in the Weedo case and fourth-party complaint in the Gellas suit, Stone–E–Brick demanded judgment against Pennsylvania National for all sums found due as against the insured and in favor of the respective plaintiffs. Cross-motions for summary judgment in each case produced contrary results, namely, an order dismissing Stone–E–Brick's third party complaint against the carrier in the Weedo case and an order in favor of the insured compelling coverage in the Gellas suit. On appeal the Appellate Division, as already noted, found coverage in both instances.

II

Under the CGL provisions of the policy in question Pennsylvania National agreed to pay "on behalf of the insured all sums which the insured shall become legally obligated to pay as damages because of * * * bodily injury * * * or *property damage to which this insurance applies,* caused by an occurrence * * *." (Emphasis supplied). This is the standard language found in the great majority of CGLs written in this country. These provisions, developed by casualty rating bureaus over a period of nearly fifty years, have become an established norm of underwriting policy. Tinker, "Comprehensive General Liability Insurance—Perspective and Overview," 25 *Feder.Ins.Coun.Q.* 217, 218–21 (1975); Henderson, "Insurance Protection for Products Liability and Completed Operations—What Every Lawyer Should Know," 50 *Neb.L.Rev.* 415, 418 (1971).[2]

These agreements set forth, in fundamental terms, the general outlines of coverage, e.g., "for property damage to which this insurance applies." The qualifying phrase, "to which this insurance applies" underscores the basic notion that the premium paid by the insured does not buy coverage for all property damage but only for that type of damage provided for in the policy. The limitations on coverage are set forth in the exclusion clauses of the policy, whose function it is to restrict and shape the coverage otherwise afforded.[3] *Capece v. Allstate Ins. Co.,* 88 N.J.Super. 535, 541, 212 A.2d 863 (Law Div.1965); Tinker, *op. cit., supra,* 25 *Feder.Ins.Coun.Q.* at 264. For example, a tavern-owners' liability coverage under the CGL is limited by force of the

2. The standard provisions of the CGL have undergone four principal revisions—in 1943, 1955, 1966 and 1973—since their initial promulgation in 1940. Tinker, op. cit., supra, 25 Feder.Ins.Coun.Q. at 221. The terms pertinent to the present case have not been altered in a manner relevant to the issues before the Court since the 1966 revision.

3. Pennsylvania National conceded at oral argument before us, as apparently it did before the Appellate Division, see 155 N.J.Super. at 479, 382 A.2d 1152, that but for the exclusions in the policy, coverage would obtain. Hence we need not address the validity of one of the carrier's initially-offered grounds of non-coverage, namely, that the policy did not extend coverage for the claims made even absent the exclusions.

"dram shop" exclusion, where personal injury or property damage results from service of intoxicants to an incapacitated patron. See generally *Mt. Hope Inn v. Travelers Indemnity Company,*157 N.J.Super. 431, 436–38, 384 A.2d 1159 (Law Div.1978).

We set forth these basic principles simply to emphasize that, semantical rules of construction aside, contracts of insurance do contain relevant language (frequently developed, as here, see *n. 1, supra,* over the years after experience with different terms of expression) which serves to define the risks underwritten. In the present instance Pennsylvania National's policy undertook to furnish certain coverage to Stone–E–Brick as a concern engaged in masonry contracting. In order to determine whether the claims of plaintiffs fall within the coverage provided, we start with an examination of the insured's business relationships with its customers.

In the usual course of its business Stone–E–Brick negotiates with homeowners to provide masonry work. As part of the bargaining process the insured may extend an express warranty that its stone, concrete and stucco products and services will be provided in a reasonably workmanlike fashion. See, e.g., *Henningsen v. Bloomfield Motors, Inc.,* 32 N.J. 358, 370, 161 A.2d 69 (1960). Regardless of the existence of express warranties, the insured's provision of stucco and stone "generally carries with it an implied warranty of merchantability and often an implied warranty of fitness for a particular purpose." *McDonald v. Mianecki,* 79 N.J. 275, 284, 398 A.2d 1283, 1288 (1979); see also *Hodgson v. Chin,* 168 N.J.Super. 549, 403 A.2d 942 (App.Div.1979). These warranties arise by operation of law and recognize that, under common circumstances, the insured-contractor holds himself out as having the capacity to apply the stonework in a workmanlike manner, and further, that the homeowner relies upon the representation and anticipates suitable goods and services. *McDonald v. Mianecki, supra,* 79 N.J. at 289–90, 398 A.2d 1283.

Where the work performed by the insured-contractor is faulty, either express or implied warranties, or both, are breached. As a matter of contract law the customer did not obtain that for which he bargained. The dissatisfied customer can, upon repair or replacement of the faulty work, recover the cost thereof from the insured-contractor as the standard measure of damages for breach of warranties. *Id.* at 282 n. 1, 398 A.2d 1283; *525 Main Street Corp. v. Eagle Roofing Co. Inc.,* 34 N.J. 251, 255, 168 A.2d 33 (1961).

As explained in *McDonald v. Mianecki, supra,* a principal justification for imposing warranties by operation of law on contractors is that these parties are often "in a better position to prevent the occurrence of major problems" in the course of constructing a home than is the homeowner. 79 N.J. at 288–89, 398 A.2d at 1289. The insured-contractor can take pains to control the quality of the goods and services supplied. At the same time he undertakes the risk that he may fail in this endeavor and thereby incur contractual liability whether express or implied. The consequence of not performing well is part of every business venture; the replacement or repair of faulty goods and works is a business expense, to be borne by the insured-contractor in order to satisfy customers. See Tinker, *op. cit. supra*, 25 *Feder.Ins. Coun.Q.* at 224; Henderson, *op. cit., supra*, 50 *Neb.L.Rev.* at 441.

There exists another form of risk in the insured-contractor's line of work, that is, injury to people and damage to property caused by faulty workmanship. Unlike business risks of the sort described above, where the tradesman commonly absorbs the cost attendant upon the repair of his faulty work, the accidental injury to property or persons substantially caused by his unworkmanlike performance exposes the contractor to almost limitless liabilities. While it may be true that the same neglectful craftsmanship can be the cause of both a business expense of repair and a loss represented by damage to persons and property, the two consequences are vastly different in relation to sharing the cost of such risks as a matter of insurance underwriting.

In this regard Dean Henderson has remarked:

> The risk intended to be insured is the possibility that the goods, products or work of the insured, once relinquished or completed, will cause bodily injury or damage to property other than to the product or completed work itself, and for which the insured may be found liable. The insured, as a source of goods or services, may be liable as a matter of contract law to make good on products or work which is defective or otherwise unsuitable because it is lacking in some capacity. This may even extend to an obligation to completely replace or rebuild the deficient product or work. This liability, however, is not what the coverages in question are designed to protect against. The coverage is for tort liability for physical damages to others and not for contractual liability of the insured for economic loss because the product or completed work is not that for which the damaged person bargained. [Henderson, *op. cit., supra*, 50 *Neb.L.Rev.* at 441.]

An illustration of this fundamental point may serve to mark the boundaries between "business risks" and occurrences giving rise to insurable liability. When a craftsman applies stucco to an exterior wall of a home in a faulty manner and discoloration, peeling and chipping result, the poorly-performed work will perforce have to be replaced or repaired by the tradesman or by a surety. On the other hand, should the stucco peel and fall from the wall, and thereby cause injury to the homeowner or his neighbor standing below or to a passing automobile, an occurrence of harm arises which is the proper subject of risk-sharing as provided by the type of policy before us in this case. The happenstance and extent of the latter liability is entirely unpredictable—the neighbor could suffer a scratched arm or a fatal blow to the skull from the peeling stonework. Whether the liability of the businessman is predicated upon warranty theory or, preferably and more accurately, upon tort concepts, injury to persons and damage to other property constitute the risks intended to be covered under the CGL.

The standardized provisions in the CGL intended to convey this concept include, *inter alia,* the very exclusion clauses at issue herein. Tinker, *op, cit., supra,* 25 *Feder.Ins.Coun.Q.* at 244–45. These exclusions—"insured products" (exclusion "(n)") and "work performed" (exclusion "(o)")—are as follows:

> * * * This insurance does not apply (n) to property damage to the named insured's products arising out of such products or any part of such products;
>
> (o) to property damage to work performed by or on behalf of the named insured arising out of the work or any portion thereof, or out of materials, parts or equipment furnished in connection therewith.

We agree with Pennsylvania National that, given the precise and limited form of damages which form the basis of the claims against the insured, either exclusion is, or both are, applicable to exclude coverage. In short, the indemnity sought is not for "property damage to which this insurance applies." Tinker, *op. cit., supra,* 25 *Feder.Ins.Coun.Q.* at 233; see also, *Adams Tree Service Inc. v. Hawaiian Insurance & Guaranty Co. Ltd.,* 117 Ariz. 385, 573 P.2d 76, 80 (Ct.App.1977).

Our view is consistent with the treatment of the "insured's products" and "work performed" exclusions in the great majority of courts elsewhere. Because of the factual similarity and the uniform wording of the exclusionary clauses, the reasoning in these decisions is thoroughly persuasive.[4] *Biebel Bros., Inc. v. United States Fidelity & Guar. Co.,* 522 F.2d 1207 (8th Cir.1975), is illustrative. In *Biebel,* a roofing contractor instituted an action against its liability insurer to recover the costs of removing defective roofing and the additional expense of supplying adequate roofing thereafter—work which was called for by the contract with the dissatisfied customer. Not unlike the instant case, the insured's faulty work was not alleged to have caused any property damage to property other than the work product of or materials supplied by the insured. *Id.,* at 1209.

The trial court granted summary judgment in favor of the insured. On appeal the insurer contended that the clear meaning of the exclusion clauses contained in its CGL policy was that the subject insurance did not apply to damage to the insured's work. Exclusion "(m)", identical to exclusion "(o)" in the instant case, was deemed controlling by the Circuit Court of Appeals. In reversing, the court observed:

---

4. The "insured's products" and the "work performed" exclusions, denominated "(n)" and "(o)" in the present standard CGL, appeared as exclusions "(1)" and "(m)" in policies written before the last decade. The literal wording of the exclusions, however denominated, has remained constant for some fifteen years.

The language of the exclusion is broad, unambiguous and all-inclusive. It clearly provides that the insurance does not apply to property damage to work performed by or on behalf of appellee arising out of either the work or any portion thereof, or out of material, parts or equipment furnished in connection therewith. Beyond question, the application of the initial and subsequent coats of asphalt, the placement of the fiberglass insulation and the asphalt-coated base sheets, and the placement of the two layers of saturated roofing felts [and] asphalt was work performed by or on behalf of appellee arising out of its contract. Furthermore, all the materials—not just the asphalt alone—were furnished by appellee in connection with the work project. The entire defective product, consisting of appellee's work and materials, was directly removed by it. If exclusion (m) does not apply to the facts before us, it is completely meaningless. [522 F.2d at 1211.]

The court also concluded that the "insured's product" exclusion (a literal analogue to exclusion "(n)" in the instant matter) applied inasmuch as the damages claimed arose out of the faulty asphalt supplied by the insured. Id. at 1211. Numerous cases construe the pertinent exclusions in similar fashion to exclude coverage in factual circumstances related to those in this case. *Ross Island Sand & Gravel Co. v. General Insurance Co. of America*, 315 F.Supp. 402 (D.Or.1970), affd., 472 F.2d 750 (9th Cir.1973); *B.A. Green Const. Co. v. Liberty Mutual Insurance Co.*, 213 Kan. 393, 517 P.2d 563, 656–67 (1973); *Adams Tree Service, Inc. v. Hawaiian Insurance & Guar. Co., Ltd., supra*, 573 P.2d at 79–80; *Engine Service, Inc. v. Reliable Insurance Co.*, 487 P.2d 474, 475–76 (Wyo.1977); *Timberline Equipment Co., Inc. v. St. Paul Fire and Marine Insurance Co.*, 281 Or. 639, 576 P.2d 1244, 1247–48 (1978); *Overson v. United States Fidelity & Guar. Co.*, 587 P.2d 149, 150–51 (Utah 1978).[5]

In addition to these decisions, which treat the very same "business risk" clauses as the exclusions in issue in this case, there exists another body of case-law pertaining to the "business risk" exclusion as it read

---

5. This case does not involve any claim that the "insured's products" or "work performed" by the insured, because improper when applied to other property, resulted in "property damage" in the form of loss of use of the other property during repair or diminution in value of that other property, especially realty. See *Hauenstein v. St. Paul–Mercury Indem. Co.*, 242 Minn. 354, 65 N.W.2d 122, 125 (1954) (unworkmanlike application of plaster on a building resulting in "property damage" not excluded because it was claimed that presence of faulty stucco reduced value of building containing faulty bricks); *Stone & Webster Engineering Corp. v. American Motorist Insurance Co.*, 458 F.Supp. 792, 794–95 (E.D.Va.1978) ("property damage" exists, notwithstanding the exclusions, on the basis of an insured's supplying a faulty component which, when incorporated into a product, causes damage to the whole); *Yakima Cement Products Co. v. Great American Insurance Co.*, 22 Wash.App. 536, 590 P.2d 371, 376 (Ct.App.1979) (insured's supply of defective panels resulting in "property damage" not excluded because building wherein faulty paneling was placed suffered reduction in value). To the extent that these decisions are at odds with the underlying rationale of our determination today, we specifically disapprove them. Coverage which is not otherwise provided under a CGL cannot be created simply by a change in the form of words by which the damage claim is expressed.

prior to the development of the present standardized wording.[6] The reasoning behind these decisions giving full effect to the "business risk" exclusion further underscores the result we have reached in this case. See, *e.g., Volf v. Ocean Accident & Guar. Corp.,* 50 Cal.2d 373, 325 P.2d 987 (1958) ＊ ＊ ＊.[7]

III

Our review of twenty years' worth of judicial treatment of the "business risk" exclusion demonstrates that, if nothing else, the underwriting policy sought to be articulated by clauses "n" and "o" has been widely recognized as a valid limitation upon standard, readily-available liability insurance coverage. Indeed, several courts have remarked in ruling upon the impact of these clauses that the terms used to convey the "business risk" exclusions are straightforward and without ambiguity. ＊ ＊ ＊

The clarity and effect of the "business risk" exclusion clauses is called into question only under a curious reading of the standard CGL. The court below indulged this reading of the policy when it accepted Stone–E–Brick's argument that an ambiguity existed in the policy when the exclusions for "business risk" were read correlatively with another exclusion clause. This latter clause, denominated exclusion "(a)" in the policy, reads:

6. The "business risk" exclusion contained in policies prepared before 1966 was worded as follows:

This policy does not apply:

＊ ＊ ＊

(h) under Coverage D, to injury or destruction of:

＊ ＊ ＊

(4) any goods, products, or containers thereof manufactured, sold, handled or distributed by the Insured, or work completed by or for the Insured, out of which the accident arises, nor to costs of repair or replacement thereof. [Exclusion "h(4)", quoted in *S.L. Rowland Const. Co. v. St. Paul Fire & Marine Insurance Co.,* 72 Wash.2d 682, 434 P.2d 725, 728 (Wash.1967).]

7. "Business risk" clauses have been given the same exclusionary effect in other contexts of insurance as that contained in the cited cases treating the exclusions in CGLs. For example, "business risk" exclusions are contained in the standard contractual liability policy of insurance, where an insured obtains coverage for liability assumed under written contract limited by, among other things, the terms of the familiar "insured's products" and "work performed" exclusions. The application of these exclusions in cases involving the coverage provided under the contractual liability policy is, once again, virtually unanimous where the damages claimed relate only to the insured's products or work. See, *e.g., Southwest Forest Ind., Inc. v. Pole Buildings, Inc.,* 478 F.2d 185, 187–88 (9th Cir.1973); *Eulich v. Home Indem. Co.,* 503 S.W.2d 846, 849 (Tex.Civ.App. 1973); *Carboline Company v. Home Indem. Co.,* 522 F.2d 363, 366 (7th Cir.1975). A variation of the current "business risk" exclusion clause wording, prepared as part of an optional "Broad Form Property Damage Endorsement" available as an alternative to standard CGL coverage, has also been upheld in its effect of excluding coverage for property damage to the insured's products or work. See, *e.g., Rafeiro v. American Employer's Insurance Co.,* 5 Cal.App.3d 799, 85 Cal.Rptr. 701, 708 (Ct.App.1970); *St. Paul Fire & Marine Insurance Co. v. Coss,* 80 Cal.App.3d 888, 145 Cal.Rptr. 836, 840 (Ct.App. 1978).

This insurance does not apply:

(a) to liability assumed by the insured under any contract or agreement except an incidental contract; but this exclusion does not apply to a warranty of fitness or quality of the named insured's products or a warranty that work performed by or on behalf of the named insured will be done in a workmanlike manner; * * *

On the basis of three decisions which considered the proposed ambiguity between "(a)" and the "business risk" clauses discussed earlier, the Appellate Division found that the "co-existence" of the provisions "creates, at the very least, an ambiguity which must be resolved in favor of the insured so as to provide coverage." 155 N.J.Super. at 486, 382 A.2d at 1159. The import of the "business risk" exclusions is thereby rendered nugatory.

Because we are of the view that exclusion "(a)" cannot serve to becloud the clear import of the "business risk" exclusions, we necessarily disagree that an ambiguity exists in the policy before us. We have only recently reaffirmed the view that only genuine ambiguities engage the so-called "doctrine of ambiguity," see *DiOrio v. New Jersey Manufacturers Insurance Co.,* 79 N.J. 257, 269, 398 A.2d 1274 (1979); and without intending in any wise to undercut the salutary effects of this "doctrine," we observe that it is, and indeed always has been, one of construction, simply an aid to the proper interpretation of terms devised by the professional underwriter. As Chief Justice Weintraub suggested in another context, such an aid "usually serves to describe a result rather than to assist in reaching it." *Reilly v. Ozzard,* 33 N.J. 529, 539, 166 A.2d 360, 365 (1960).

We conceive a genuine ambiguity to arise where the phrasing of the policy is so confusing that the average policyholder cannot make out the boundaries of coverage. In that instance, application of the test of the objectively reasonable expectation of the insured often will result in benefits of coverage never intended from the insurer's point of view. The benefits granted, however, will pertain to the same landscape of risk as contemplated by the policy in issue, that is, the "doctrine of ambiguity" works to effectuate the consumer's expectation that the policy purchased extended greater coverage in the particular underwriting area. The rule of construction embraces ambiguities which are artificial, however, when the reading of coverage urged by the insured affords indemnity in an area of insurance completely distinct from that to which the policy applies in the first instance. To use an extreme example, no amount of semantical ingenuity can be brought to bear on a fire insurance policy so as to afford coverage for an intersection collision. Such an interpretation of a fire policy would hardly be based on any "objectively reasonable" expectation. See *DiOrio, supra,* 79 N.J. at 269, 398 A.2d 1274.

In this case Stone–E–Brick's interpretation of the policy would result in coverage for repair and replacement of its own faulty workmanship. This interpretation relies on the supposition that the exception to exclusion "(a)"—"but this exclusion does not apply to a warranty that work performed by or on behalf of the named insured will be done in a workmanlike manner"—*grants* coverage for claims based on the warranty described. Not so. The contention runs directly counter to the basic principle that exclusion clauses *subtract* from coverage rather than grant it. Precisely this point was made by the Supreme Court of South Dakota, in construing the very clauses we have before us:

> * * * Exclusion (a) does not extend or grant coverage. To the contrary it is a limitation or restriction on the insuring clause. The exception to exclusion (a) merely removes breach of implied warranty of fitness, quality or workmanship from the specific exclusion relating to contractual liability. The exception [to clause (a)] remains subject to and limited by all other related exclusions contained in the policy. When considered with exclusion (m) [(o) in the instant case] it clearly appears that property damage claims of third persons resulting from the insured's breach of an implied warranty are covered unless the claimed loss is confined to the insured's work or work product. [*Haugan v. Home Indem. Co., supra,* 197 N.W.2d at 22.]

To the same effect, see *St. Paul Fire & Marine Insurance Co. v. Coss, supra,* 145 Cal.Rptr. at 841.

As a variant of its argument that exclusion "(a)" grants the coverage it seeks, Stone–E–Brick contends that this exception, when read in conjunction with the "business risk" exceptions, is confusing in that coverage "granted" by the former clause is taken away by the latter two. 155 N.J.Super. at 486, 382 A.2d 1152. But this argument too ignores the principle that

> [e]ach exclusion is meant to be read with the insuring agreement, independently of every other exclusion. The exclusions should be read seriatim, not cumulatively. If any one exclusion applies there should be no coverage, regardless of inferences that might be argued on the basis of exceptions or qualifications contained in other exclusions. There is no instance in which an exclusion can properly be regarded as inconsistent with another exclusion, since they bear no relationship with one another. [Tinker, *op. cit., supra.,* 25 *Feder. Ins.Couns.Q.* at 223.]

When presented with an identical claim of ambiguity as arising out of comparison of exclusions "(a) and the "business risk" clauses, the court in *Biebel Bros., Inc. v. United States F. & G. Co., supra,* stated flatly that the language of the exception in "(a) * * * has no application whatsoever to exclusions (l)[n] or (m)[o] * * *." 522 F.2d at 1212. We agree, and accordingly do not perceive any ambiguity in the instant policy.

We note in passing that each of the four decisions which has found an ambiguity in this standard CGL based upon the interpretation offered by Stone–E–Brick suffers from the same misconception that the exception to "(a)" grants coverage which must be viewed in conjunction with the exclusions in the "business risk" clauses. See *Fountainebleau Hotel Corp. v. United Filigree Corp.,* 298 So.2d 455, 459–60 (Fla.App. 1974); *Federal Insurance Co. v. P.A.T. Homes, Inc.,* 113 Ariz. 136, 547 P.2d 1050, 1053 (Sup.Ct.1976); *Custom Roofing Co., Inc. v. Transamerican Insurance Co.,* 120 Ariz. 196, 584 P.2d 1187, 1189–90 (Ariz.App. 1978); *Commercial Union Assurance Co. v. Gollan,* 394 A.2d 839, 841–42 (N.H.1978). The court below fell into error in relying entirely upon the reasoning of the first two cited cases.

But what does exclusion "(a)" mean and what is its function? As we have endeavored to make clear, the policy in question does not cover an accident of faulty workmanship but rather faulty workmanship which causes an accident. See *Hamilton Die Cast, Inc. v. United States F. & G. Co.,* 508 F.2d 417, 420 (7th Cir.1975); *Dreis & Krump Mfg. Co. v. Phoenix Insurance Co.,* 548 F.2d 681, 689 (7th Cir.1977). Within this structure, contractual liability is excluded under the terms of exclusion "(a)". The exception to this exclusion insures, however, that claims premised upon quasi-contract or contract by implication, such as warranty actions, will be covered. Such claims must nevertheless be otherwise cognizable under the general grant of coverage in the first instance in order to constitute a claim "to which this insurance applies." This analysis of the import of the "(a)" exclusion accords with the generally-held view of other courts, see *e.g., Carboline Co. v. Home Indem. Co.,* 522 F.2d 363, 366 (7th Cir.1975) (same construction given to similar clause in contractual liability policy); *Biebel Bros., Inc. v. United States F. & G. Co., supra,* 522 F.2d at 1212; *Haugan v. Home Indem. Co., supra,* 197 N.W.2d at 22; *Aetna Insurance Co. v. Pete Wilson Roofing & Heating Co., Inc.,* 289 Ala. 719, 272 So.2d 232, 234–35 (1973) (contractual liability policy construed), and at the same time saves the clear import of the exclusions for "business risks."

IV

The judgments under review are reversed and the matters remanded to the respective trial courts for entry there of judgments in favor of Pennsylvania National. No costs.

Notes and Questions

1. *The Rationale of the Decision.* What was the rationale for the court's decision: that the exclusions mean what they say, that the parties did not intend to cover the kind of liability at issue, or that because it would not make sense to insure against that kind of liability, the exclusions preclude such coverage?

2. *Faulty Work versus Property Damage.* Distinguishing damage to the insured's work or product from damage to other property is not

always a simple exercise. For example, suppose that a manufacturer of building materials containing asbestos is sued by a Board of Education for the cost of removing and replacing the materials in the schools under the Board's jurisdiction. Do the business risk exclusions insulate the manufacturer's CGL insurer from liability? See *Dayton Independent School District v. National Gypsum Company*, 682 F.Supp. 1403 (E.D.Tex.1988) holding that the exclusions do not bar coverage. In any event, was the court's argument that it would not make sense to insure against liability for the cost of repairing faulty work persuasive? One strand in this argument is that a party purchasing such work does not get what she bargained for. Is that not also true of faulty work that causes bodily injury or damages other property, liability for which is covered? In addition, because the same faulty work causes the harm at issue, whether the claim is for the cost of repair or for damage to other property or personal injury, an argument based on moral hazard cannot explain why coverage against liability for faulty work is excluded, but coverage for injury or damage caused by the faulty work is not.

3. *An Alternative Explanation.* Consider an alternative way of explaining the function of the business risk exclusions: The CGL contains these exclusions because faulty work appears with enough frequency and involves average losses that are low enough that even small businesses can safely self-insure against them. Consequently, it would not be worth paying the cost of transferring these risks to an insurance company, given the moral hazard and adverse selection that would raise the cost of market insurance against liability for faulty work far above its expected value for any individual business. In contrast, liability for bodily injury or damage to other property is sufficiently infrequent and the average cost of such liability sufficiently high that self-insuring against this kind of liability would be too risky for most small and medium-sized businesses. The business risk exclusions therefore do not pertain to this kind of liability.

4. *The Relation between Exclusions.* Were you comfortable with the court's conclusions about the absence of any relationship between exclusion (a) and the business risk exclusions? Is the rule that ambiguities are construed against the insurer consistent with the rule that the exclusions in a liability insurance policy are to be read as having no relation to each other?

5. *Business Risks in the New CGL Policy.* How has the revised CGL treated business risks? See especially exclusions (k) through (n) in the Sample CGL Policy.

3. Harm Expected or Intended

UNIGARD MUTUAL INSURANCE COMPANY v. ARGONAUT INSURANCE COMPANY

Court of Appeals of Washington, 1978.
20 Wash.App. 261, 579 P.2d 1015.

McINTURFF, Associate Justice.

The insurers of School District No. 81 appeal from a declaratory judgment that Unigard Mutual Insurance Co. (Unigard) is not obligated to defend or indemnify its insureds, William Winkler and Mr. and Mrs. Charles Hensley, in an action by the school district against them for $250,000 in fire damage to Wilson Elementary School in Spokane.

This action arises from a suit brought by the school district in August 1974 alleging that William Winkler carelessly and negligently caused the fire and that his parents, the Hensleys, having knowledge of his propensities, negligently failed to supervise and control him. Unigard filed this action for declaratory judgment in November 1974 seeking to avoid any liability to any of the parties covered by its policy.

The policy in question was issued by Unigard to Ruth Winkler Hensley as the named insured in December 1972. It establishes the duty to defend and indemnify in the following manner:

> This Company agrees to pay on behalf of *the Insured* all sums which *the Insured* shall become legally obligated to pay as damages because of bodily injury or property damage, to which this insurance applies, caused by an occurrence. This Company shall have the right and duty, at its own expense, to defend any suit against the Insured seeking damages on account of such bodily injury or property damage, even if any of the allegations of the suit are groundless, false or fraudulent, but may make such investigation and settlement of any claim or suit as it deems expedient.

(Italics ours.)

The policy defined "occurrence" as "an accident, including injurious exposure to conditions, which results, during the endorsement term, in bodily injury or property damage." And, the following exclusionary provision was included, "This policy does not apply * * * to bodily injury or property damage which is either expected or intended from the standpoint of *the insured*." (Italics ours.) There is no dispute that both William Winkler and the parents are "insureds" within the meaning of the policy.[1]

The record reveals the following facts. On July 8, 1973, William Winkler, who was then 11 years old, broke into the school building and

---

1. The policy provides: "1. 'Insured' means "a. the Named Insured stated in the Declarations of this endorsement; b. if residents of the Named Insured's household, his spouse, the relatives of either, and any other perosn under the age of twenty-one in the care of any insured; * * *"

set fire to the contents of a trash can. He watched the fire burn for a short while, then ran to a nearby drinking fountain for water with which to douse the blaze. It was not working though, so he returned to the fire, became frightened and ran out of the building. He did not notify anyone of the blaze. The fire spread, causing extensive damage to the building and its contents.

He testified he did not intend or expect to cause damage to the school building but that he did intend to light the fire. At the time of the blaze he knew that fire could spread, and he had previously been involved in a fire-starting venture between two neighborhood garages.

The court concluded the school building fire was not an insurable "occurrence" under the policy because it was not an "accident." Instead, the court found the fire damage resulted from the deliberate acts of the boy. The court reasoned that since there was not an insurable "occurrence," Unigard did not have a duty to defend or indemnify either the boy or his parents.

Error is first assigned to the court's conclusion that the fire damage did not result from an insurable "occurrence." The school district's insurers offer two arguments: (1) the term "accident" within the policy is ambiguous in that it is not clear whether the insured's act or the results of his act must be accidental so as to provide coverage; and (2) since the boy neither expected nor intended the fire damage to the school, the exclusionary clause is inapplicable.

The argument that the term "accident" is ambiguous is not well taken. In a long line of cases our courts have said that an accident is never present when a deliberate act is performed unless some additional unexpected, independent and unforeseen happening occurs which produces or brings about the result of injury or death. The means as well as the result must be unforeseen, involuntary, unexpected and unusual. The intentional and deliberate act of William Winkler in starting the fire which caused the school building blaze cannot be said to be involuntary. Therefore, as to William Winkler, the damage to the school was not caused by accidental means nor can it be considered, under the policy definitions, an insurable "occurrence."

Nonetheless, the school district insurers argue that the policy is applicable because in order to exclude the intentional acts of the insured from coverage, the damage must be expected or intended from the standpoint of the insured. There is a definite split of authority as to whether the intentional injury exclusion clause which exempts expected or intended damage requires specific intent on the part of the insured to cause the resultant damage.[2] Here, though, there is substantial evidence from which the court could have found that the

---

2. See cases collected in Annot., *Liability Insurance: Specific Exclusion of Liability for Injury Intentionally Caused by Insured*, 2 A.L.R.3d 1238, 1241 (1965). There the author states:

The courts have generally held that injury or damage is "caused intentionally" within the meaning of an "intentional injury exclusion clause" if the insured has acted with the specific intent to cause harm to a third party, with the result that the insurer will not be

damage to the school building was expected or intended on the part of the boy despite his in-court declarations to the contrary. Thus, as to William Winkler, the fire damage to the building was the expected or intended result of a clearly intentional act. Therefore, Unigard has no duty to defend the youth or indemnify him for any sums he may become legally obligated to pay as a result of the school district action against him.

Error is next assigned to the court's conclusion that since the fire damage was not caused by an "accident" within the terms of the policy, Unigard does not have a duty to defend or indemnify the boy's parents in the action brought against them by the school district. Essentially, the school district's insurers argue that the intentional act of one insured cannot be imputed to other insureds so as to exclude insurance coverage for all; that the liability of the Hensleys, if any, is grounded in their negligent failure to supervise the boy which is not an excluded intentional act. Unigard maintains there was no evidence of negligence on the part of the Hensleys and that the policy of excluding intentional acts from liability insurance coverage would be seriously undermined if coverage was provided to the parents of minors who have committed intentional acts.

We agree with Unigard that public policy prevents an insured from benefitting from his wrongful acts; but here, as in other cases which have considered the question, it is not the intentional act of the parents which has caused the damage. Precedent and the language of the Unigard insurance policy require coverage for Mr. and Mrs. Hensley.

The policy extends defense and indemnification to "the Insured," and it excludes from coverage intentional acts resulting in injury or damage "expected or intended from the standpoint of the insured." The parties concede the boy and the Hensleys are all "insureds" under the policy. In such instances, where coverage and exclusion is defined in terms of "the insured," the courts have uniformly considered the contract between the insurer and several insureds to be separable, rather than joint, i.e., there are separate contracts with each of the insureds. The result is that an excluded act of one insured does not bar coverage for additional insureds who have not engaged in the excluded conduct.

The judgment of the Superior Court is affirmed insofar as it denies coverage to William Winkler and reversed insofar as it denies coverage to the Hensleys.

Notes and Questions

1. *The Scope of Homeowners Coverage.* Homeowners policies typically include two Sections: Property Insurance (the fire and extended coverage addressed in Chapter Four) and Liability Insurance. Was it surprising that the Unigard insuring agreement contained no provision

relieved of its obligations under a liability policy containing such an exclusion unless the insured has acted with such specific intent.

limiting coverage to liability arising out of the use of the property insured under Section One of the policy? Such a limitation is rarely included. Instead, the liability insurance portions of the policy are structured to provide general liability coverage, subject to a long list of exclusions—liability for business operations, liability arising out of the ownership, maintenance or use of automobiles, watercraft, and aircraft, and liability for defamation, among others. When these exclusions are combined with the exclusion of coverage against liability for harm expected or intended, the apparently unlimited liability insurance provided by a homeowners policy turns out to be (roughly) against liability for non-motor vehicle related negligence in one's personal life that causes bodily injury or property damage.

2. *Expected or Intended.* Some courts hold that the terms "expected" and "intended" in homeowners and CGL policies are synoymous. See, e.g., *Patrons–Oxford Mutual Insurance Company v. Dodge,* 426 A.2d 888 (Me.1981). This interpretation conflicts with the principle that each word or phrase in a legal document should be interpreted so that it has a separate meaning. Other courts hold that actions taken where the insured knows that there is a very high probability of damage, even when there is no intention to cause damage, fall within the exclusion. In *Unigard,* did William Winkler expect property damage, intend property damage, or both?

3. *Type of Harm Expected.* For the exclusion to apply, should the harm that is expected or intended be precisely the harm for which liability is imposed, or need it only be harm of the same general sort? In *State Farm Fire & Casualty Company v. Muth,* 190 Neb. 248, 207 N.W.2d 364 (1973), the insured was a minor who shot a B–B gun out of a moving automobile and injured a friend. The insured testified that he intended "to scare somebody," and, on redirect examination, that he did not think he was taking a chance of hitting the friend. The court upheld a finding by the trial judge that the exclusion was inapplicable. Suppose that the insured had shot the friend in the eye, and testified that he intended only to cause temporary discomfort with a grazing shot to the leg, but that his aim was disturbed when the car hit a bump in the road? Suppose that a manufacturer of asbestos knows that exposure to asbestos doses higher than those to which insulation workers normally are exposed causes lung disease, and conspires with other manufacturers to suppress evidence of this effect. Is the exclusion of liability for harm expected or intended applicable when it turns out that exposure at doses lower than expected also causes lung disease? Cf. *Asbestos Insurance Coverage Cases,* No. 1072 (Superior Court of Calif., City and County of San Francisco, May 29, 1987), Tentative Decision on Phase III Issues 74, holding that "so long as an injury was willed, intended, or maliciously sought, it is immaterial that an injury of a different nature or magnitude occurred from that actually contemplated." The cases involved suits by a number of asbestos manufacturers against a number of CGL insurers. For one version of the history of the asbestos crisis, discussing what manufac-

turers of asbestos knew and when they knew it, see P. Brodeur, Outrageous Misconduct (1985).

4. *Moral Hazard?* Is a decision such as *Unigard* likely to increase the moral hazard associated with homeowners liability insurance, or is that a needless concern?

4. The Pollution Exclusion

BROADWELL REALTY SERVICES, INC. v. THE FIDELITY & CASUALTY COMPANY OF NEW YORK

Superior Court of New Jersey, Appellate Division, 1987.
218 N.J.Super. 516, 528 A.2d 76.

BAIME, J.A.D.

This appeal presents difficult questions concerning the construction of language contained in a comprehensive general liability insurance policy. Under the policy, the insurer's obligation is limited to indemnification of the insured for damage to the property of third persons. Coverage does not include damage to the insured's own property. The policy contains additional language which excludes from coverage losses caused by pollution except where the discharge, dispersal, release or escape of the contaminant is sudden and accidental. * * *

The salient facts are not in dispute. On August 24, 1983, plaintiff Broadwell Realty Services, Inc. (Broadwell) received a "directive letter" from the Department of Environmental Protection (DEP) advising it that an "undetermined amount of a hazardous substance" had escaped from several underground storage tanks on its premises and had migrated on to adjacent lands. Although the property was owned by Broadwell, it had been leased to Globe Petroleum, Inc. (Globe), which operated a Citgo Service Station franchise on the premises.

The record reflects that the DEP had received several complaints concerning the presence of gasoline in two New Jersey Bell cable vaults located immediately adjacent to Broadwell's property. Based upon those reports, the DEP had retained private hydrologists whose investigation revealed that gasoline was leaking from Broadwell's property into the cable vaults and was "also discharging into a nearby stream." * * *

At the time that the gasoline leakage was discovered, Globe was insured under a comprehensive general liability policy issued by defendant Fidelity & Casualty Company of New York (Fidelity). Broadwell was named as an additional insured under the policy. The focus of the present dispute is whether expenses incurred by Broadwell in its effort to comply with the DEP's cleanup directive fell within the policy coverage. Because resolution of the issues presented by this appeal hinges upon our interpretation of language contained in the policy, we recite the relevant provisions *verbatim* [The court then quoted the standard CGL insuring agreement]. * * *

The pollution exclusion to which we referred previously reads as follows:

> This insurance does not apply * * * to bodily injury or property damage arising out of the discharge, dispersal, release or escape of smoke, vapors, soot, fumes, acids, alkalis, toxic chemicals, liquids or gases, waste materials or other irritants, contaminants or pollutants into or upon land, the atmosphere or any water course or body of water; but this exclusion does not apply if such discharge, dispersal, release or escape is sudden and accidental.

Broadwell instituted this action seeking monetary damages and counsel fees based upon Fidelity's alleged breach of the insurance agreement. Cross-motions for summary judgment were filed.* * * The judge * * * rejected Fidelity's argument that it had no duty to indemnify Broadwell because the loss or damage fell within the purview of the pollution exclusion. The judge found that the escape of the gasoline from the underground storage tanks was unexpected and unforeseen and was thus covered by the "sudden and accidental" exception to the exclusionary clause. Summary judgment in favor of Broadwell was accordingly entered and this appeal followed.

I

Before turning to the arguments advanced, we find it necessary to make these prefatory comments. We stated at the outset of our opinion, and we emphasize here, that the questions presented are purely ones of contractual interpretation. We stress what might otherwise appear to be obvious because all counsel, to a greater or lesser extent, have relied upon competing public policy arguments in support of their respective positions.

Of course, we recognize that resolution of the issues raised will undoubtedly have serious impact upon both the insurance industry and the consumer public. The past two decades have witnessed an explosion of litigation seeking compensation for damage to the environment and injuries arising from environmental contamination. *See generally,* R. Odell. *Environmental Awakening,* 241–251 (1st ed. 1980); Hourihan, "Insurance Coverage for Environmental Damage Claims," 15 *Forum* 551, 552 (1980); Soderstrom, "The Role of Insurance in Environmental Litigation," 11 *Forum* 762 (1976); Comment, "Compensating Hazardous Waste Victims: RCRA Insurance Regulations and a Not So 'Super' Fund Act," 11 *Envtl.L.* 689, 690–694 (1981); Note, "The Pollution Exclusion Clause Through the Looking Glass," 74 *Geo.L.J.* 1237, 1238 (1986). This new breed of lawsuit has spawned collateral litigation to compel insurers to defend and indemnify polluters. Note, "The Pollution Exclusion Clause Through the Looking Glass," *supra,* 74 *Geo.L.J.* at 1239. The potential liability of defendants and their insurers is enormous.

Having said this, we underscore the limited nature of our inquiry. Whatever the relative merits of the competing public policies identified and advanced by the parties, we perceive no legal principle which would permit us to circumvent what the contract says. So it throws no light to inveigh against the " 'collapse' of the pollution insurance market" allegedly caused by "judicially imposed costs of cleaning up the environment," *id.* at 1278–1279, or, on the other hand, to argue that protection of "blameless victims" is best served by seeking to spread the financial risk. *Id.* at 1237. Our role is merely to interpret the language of the insurance contract.

We are aided in that inquiry by certain well-settled principles. We are confronted here with questions pertaining to the interpretation of language contained in an extensive and complex insurance agreement. In that context, our Supreme Court has stated that while insurance policies are contractual in nature, they are not ordinary agreements but "contracts of adhesion between parties who are not equally situated." *Meier v. New Jersey Life Ins. Co.,* 101 N.J. 597, 611, 503 A.2d 862 (1986). It has been said that "[c]ourts apply the adhesion doctrine because of the unequal bargaining power of the parties." *Id.* at 611–612, 503 A.2d 862. Insurance contracts have thus been described as "unipartite in character." *Mazzilli v. Acc. & Cas. Ins. Co. of Winterthur,* 35 N.J. 1, 7, 170 A.2d 800 (1961). Such contracts "are prepared by the company's experts [people] learned in the law of insurance," *ibid.,* and therefore it is not unfair that the insurer "bear the burden of any resulting confusion." *Gaunt v. John Hancock Mut. Life Ins. Co.,* 160 F.2d 599, 602 (2 Cir.1947), *cert. den.* 331 U.S. 849, 67 S.Ct. 1736, 91 L.Ed. 1858 (1947). These circumstances long ago fathered the principle that doubts as to the existence or extent of coverage must generally be resolved in favor of the insured. * * *

Our courts "have adopted the principle giving effect to the 'objectively reasonable expectations' of the insured for the purpose of rendering a 'fair interpretation' of the boundaries of insurance coverage." * * * The insured "justifiably places heavy reliance on the knowledge and good faith of the [insurer] and its representatives and they, in turn, are under correspondingly heavy responsibility to [it]." *Allen v. Metropolitan Life Ins. Co., supra,* 44 N.J. at 305, 208 A.2d 638. Its reasonable expectations in the transaction "may not justly be frustrated and courts have properly molded their governing interpretative principles with that uppermost in mind." *Ibid.* Although this principle is merely one of construction, "simply an aid to the proper interpretation of terms devised by the professional underwriter," *Weedo v. Stone–E–Brick, Inc.,* 81 N.J. 233, 246, 405 A.2d 788 (1979), and only genuine interpretational difficulties engage the doctrine of ambiguity, *American White Cross v. Continental Ins. Co.,* 202 N.J.Super. 372, 381, 495 A.2d 152 (App.Div.1985), "we have consistently construed policy [language] strictly against the insurer and where several interpretations were permissible, we have chosen the one most favorable to the [insured]." *Allen v. Metropolitan Life Ins. Co., supra,* 44 N.J. at 305, 208 A.2d 638. * * *

III

We next turn to the argument advanced by Fidelity that the dispersal of gasoline from Broadwell's underground storage tanks on to adjacent properties was not "sudden and accidental" and thus came within the pollution exclusion. The principal thrust of its contention is that the word "sudden" has a temporal meaning and that the exclusionary clause thereby bars recovery for losses caused by pollution except where the damage is the result of an unexpected and instantaneous catastrophe.

We disagree. The identical argument has been considered and rejected in several reported New Jersey decisions. *See Lansco, Inc. v. Dept. of Environmental Protection,* 138 N.J.Super. 275, 282, 350 A.2d 520 (Ch.Div.1975), aff'd 145 N.J.Super. 433, 368 A.2d 363 (App.Div. 1976), certif. den. 73 N.J. 57, 372 A.2d 322 (1977); *CPS Chem. Co., Inc. v. Continental Ins. Co.,* 199 N.J.Super. 558, 569, 489 A.2d 1265 (Law Div. 1984), rev'd on other grounds 203 N.J.Super. 15, 495 A.2d 886 (App.Div. 1985); *Jackson Tp. Etc. v. Hartford Acc. & Indemn. Co.,* 186 N.J.Super. 156, 161, 451 A.2d 990 (Law Div.1982). In these cases, our courts have construed the word "sudden" in terms of an "unexpected," "unforeseen" or "fortuitous" event. This definition is consistent with the common meaning of the word in everyday parlance. *See Webster's New International Dictionary* (2d ed. unabridged 1954). *See also Black's Law Dictionary* (4 ed. 1968). * * *

Through our research, we have traced the history of the "occurrence" policy definition and the pollution exclusion to the industry-wide revisions of standard general liability insurance provisions in 1966 and again in 1973. Before 1966, the standard policy covered only property damage and personal injury "caused by accident." *See* Hourihan, "Insurance Coverage for Environmental Damage Claims," *supra,* 15 *Forum* at 552, quoting DRI Monograph, *The New Comprehensive General Liability—A Coverage Analysis* 6 (Nov. 1966). Note, "The Pollution Exclusion Clause Through the Looking Glass," *supra,* 74 Geo.L.J. at 1241. The policy did not define the word "accident," leaving that task to the courts. The courts generally defined "accident" as "an unexpected happening without intention or design." *Beacon Textiles Corp. v. Employers Mut. Liab. Ins. Co.,* 355 Mass. 643, 645, 246 N.E.2d 671, 673 (Sup.Jud.Ct.1969). *See also Spindler v. Universal Chain Corp.,* 11 N.J. 34, 38, 93 A.2d 171 (1952); *Neylon v. Ford Motor Company,* 8 N.J. 586, 588, 86 A.2d 577 (1952), aff'd on reargument 10 N.J. 325, 91 A.2d 569 (1952). Under this test, a volitional act by the insured nevertheless qualified as an "accident" if the insured did not specifically "intend to cause the resulting harm or [was] not substantially certain that such harm w[ould] occur." *Quincy Mut. Fire Ins. Co. v. Abernathy,* 393 Mass. 81, 84, 469 N.E.2d 797, 799 (Sup.Jud.Ct.1984).

In the 1966 revision, the insurance industry switched universally to "occurrence-based coverage." Note, "The Pollution Exclusion Clause Through the Looking Glass," *supra,* 74 Geo.L.J. at 1246. This change was "in response to consumer demands for broader liability protection and in acquiescence to the judicial trend toward a more expansive reading of the term accident. * * *" Tyler and Wilcox, "Pollution Exclusion Clauses: Problems in Interpretation and Application Under the Comprehensive General Liability Policy," 17 Idaho L.Rev. 497, 499 (1981). The standard occurrence-based policy defined an "occurrence" as "an accident, including continuous or repeated exposure to conditions, which results in bodily injury or property damage neither expected nor intended from the standpoint of the insured." 3 Long, *The Law of Liability Insurance,* App.–53 (1966). This definition was designed to "make it clear that occurrence embraces not only the usual accident, but also exposure to conditions which may continue for an unmeasured period of time." *Ibid.*

The pollution exclusion was added by the 1973 revision. Under this exclusion, only pollution-related losses that arose from occurrences both "sudden" and "accidental" were to be covered. According to various commentators, the exclusion was designed to decrease claims for losses caused by pollution by providing an incentive to industry to improve its manufacturing and disposal processes. Soderstrom, "The Role of Insurance in Environmental Litigation," 11 *Forum* 762, 767–768 (1976). In other words, the insured could not "seek protection from his liability insurer if he knowingly pollute[d]" the environment. *Id.* at 768. Although it has been argued that the sole object of this clause was to limit coverage to accidents distinct in time and place, Note, "The Pollution Exclusion Through the Looking Glass," *supra,* 74 Geo.L.J. at 1242, the more reasonable conclusion is that the exclusion was designed to "eliminate coverage for damages arising out of pollution or contamination, where such damages appear to be expected or intended on the part of the insured and hence are excluded by definition of 'occurrence.'" 3 Long, *The Law of Liability Insurance, supra,* App.–58. *See also Niagara Cty. v. Utica Mut. Ins. Co., supra,* 103 Misc.2d at 818, 427 N.Y.S.2d at 174; *Union Pacific Ins. v. Van's Westlake Union, supra,* 34 Wash.App. at 714, 664 P.2d at 1266.

There is substantial authority supporting the thesis that the pollution exclusion was intended to be coextensive with the scope of the definition of occurrence. *See, e.g.,* Hurwitz and Kohane, "The Love Canal—Insurance Coverage for Environmental Accidents," 50 Ins. Couns.J. 378, 379 (1983); 3 Long, *The Law of Liability Insurance, supra,* App.–58; Newman, *Liability Insurance Coverage Principles,* 133 (rev. ed. 1983). Citing statements made by the Insurance Service Office,[1]

1. The Insurance Rating Board stated:

Coverage for pollution or contamination is not provided in most cases under present policies because the damages can be said to be expected or intended and thus are excluded by the definition of occurrence. The above exclusion clarifies this situation so as to avoid any questions of intent. Coverage is *continued for pollution or*

limitation only to intentional polluter

commentators have argued that "the limitation of coverage was intended to apply only to the *intentional polluter*. The pollution exclusion is [thus considered] an intentional polluter's exclusion, and, as such, [is] inapplicable to entities which neither expect nor intend their conduct to result in bodily injury or property damage." Hurwitz and Kohane, "The Love Canal—Insurance Coverage for Environmental Accidents," *supra*, 50 Ins.Couns.J. at 378. (Emphasis in original). Although this argument has its detractors, *see, e.g.*, Hickman, *The Pollution Exclusion Clause: A Hazardous Wasteland*, in Insurance Law Conference: The Most Important Topics of the '80s B–18 (CGL Reporter's Seminar, Apr. 25–26 (1985)), most commentators "view the [policy limitation] as only a typical exclusion for intentionally caused damage by industrial or commercial dumpers. * * *" Joest, "Will Insurance Companies Clean the Augean Stables?—Insurance Coverage for the Landfill Operator," 50 Ins.Couns.J. 258, 259 (1983).

Against this backdrop, decisional law in New Jersey and elsewhere has tended to interpret the pollution exclusion and, more particularly, the "sudden and accidental" exception, as "simply a restatement of the definition of 'occurrence'—that is, that the policy will cover claims where the injury was 'neither expected nor intended.'" *Jackson Tp. Etc. v. Hartford Acc. & Indemn. Co.*, *supra*, 186 N.J.Super. at 164, 451 A.2d 990. *See also Shapiro v. Public Service Mut. Ins. Co.*, *supra*, 19 Mass.App. at 653, 477 N.E.2d at 150; *Niagara Cty. v. Utica Mut. Ins. Co.*, *supra*, 103 Misc.2d at 818, 427 N.Y.S.2d at 174; *United Pacific Ins. v. Van's Westlake Union*, *supra*, 34 Wash.App. at 714, 664 P.2d at 1266. It is a reaffirmation that coverage will not be provided for expected and hence avoidable results.

We agree with this analysis. In our view, the pollution exclusion focuses upon the intention, expectation and foresight of the insured. If an insured knows that liability incurred by a foreseeable polluting event is covered by his policy, he is tempted to diminish his precautions and relax his vigilance. Conversely, we perceive no sound basis anchored in the policy language which requires prescience or clairvoyance on the part of the insured. Where the insured has taken reasonable precautions against contaminating the environment and the dispersal of pollutants is both accidental and unforeseen, we are of the view that the "sudden and accidental" exception to the exclusion is applicable and the loss is thereby covered by the policy.

Our construction of the exclusionary language has several benefits. By defining the word "sudden" as meaning unexpected and unintended, we avoid the question whether the focus of the exclusion is upon the release of the contaminant or the resulting permeation and damage to the environment. This issue has generated substantial debate in those jurisdictions which have construed the word "sudden" in temporal

> *contamination caused injuries where the pollution or contamination results from an accident. * * ***
>
> Hurwitz and Kohane, "The Love Canal—Insurance Coverage for Environmental Accidents," *supra*, 50 Ins.Couns.J. at 379. (Emphasis in original).

terms. *Compare Waste Management v. Peerless Ins. Co., supra,* 315 N.C.
at 697, 340 S.E.2d at 381, *with Travelers Indem. Co. v. Dingwell, supra,*
414 A.2d at 224. In other words, does the word "sudden" refer to "the
time necessary for the ultimate loss to manifest itself fully," *see* Note,
"The Pollution Exclusion Through the Looking Glass," *supra,* 74 Geo.
L.J. at 1296, or does it refer to the actual release, escape or discharge of
the pollutant? If the word "sudden" is defined as "rapid" or "instantaneous," how is the exclusion to be applied to the abrupt escape of a
pollutant from a fissure in a tank caused by a gradual corrosive
process? Mere recitation of these issues discloses the investigative and
evidentiary problems which would inexorably flow from adoption of the
arguments advanced by Fidelity.

More important, our interpretation of the exclusionary language
best advances the objectively reasonable expectations of the insured.
As we have pointed out, the pollution exclusion had its genesis in the
1973 industry-wide revision. Even when considered within the context
of our litigious society, it can fairly be said that the exclusion has
generated an extraordinary number of lawsuits. We have alluded
previously to the disarray in the decisional treatment of this issue.
The question continues to confound scholars and commentators. The
critical circumstance is that the ambiguity and confusion was caused by
language selected by the insurer. We necessarily consider the fact that
"alternative or more precise" wording, if used, "would have put the
matter beyond reasonable question." *Mazzilli v. Acc. & Cas. Ins. Co. of
Winterthur, supra,* 35 N.J. at 7, 170 A.2d 800. The ambiguity thus
created must be resolved against the insurer.

We thus construe the word "sudden" as meaning unexpected and
unintended. Based upon our review of the meager record, we are
persuaded that substantial factual questions exist as to whether the
pollution exclusion, as construed, bars recovery. In our view, summary
judgment should not have been granted. * * *

Accordingly, the summary judgment in favor of Broadwell is reversed and the matter is remanded for further proceedings consistent
with this opinion. We do not retain jurisdiction.

CLAUSSEN v. AETNA CASUALTY & SURETY COMPANY

United States District Court, S.D. Georgia, 1987.
676 F.Supp. 1571.

EDENFIELD, District Judge.

I. *Background*

In one way or another, all of the motions pending in this case
relate to the Court's construction of the "pollution exclusion clause."
The pollution exclusion clause is a standard provision in general
comprehensive liability policies, and has been since 1970. The clause
denies coverage for pollution-related bodily injury or property damage.

It contains an exception which states that the pollution exclusion does not apply where a release, dispersal, or escape of pollutants is "sudden and accidental."

Plaintiff, Henry H. Claussen, brought this action to obtain a declaration that he is covered under various insurance policies for pollution-related liability incurred as a result of the gradual release, over a period of years, of hazardous wastes from land owned by him near Jacksonville, Florida. Plaintiff's land, known as the Picketville landfill (Picketville), has been used by the City of Jacksonville, pursuant to a contract, for the disposal of wastes.

By Order dated August 11, 1987,[1] summary judgment was granted in favor of Aetna, American Home, and Harbor on the ground that liability incurred as a result of the release of hazardous wastes from Picketville fell within the pollution exclusion and, because the hazardous wastes were released gradually over a period of years, did not fall within the exception to the pollution exclusion for "*sudden* and accidental" releases.

Before the pollution exclusion was inserted into insurance policies, coverage of pollution-related liability depended on whether the pollution giving rise to liability fell within the definition of "occurrence." Liability arising from "occurrences" was covered and included "unintended and unexpected" pollution; intentional and expected pollution was not covered. *See generally,* Note, *The Pollution Exclusion Through the Looking Glass,* 74 Geo.L.J. 1237, 1246–51 (1986). Courts generally held that pollution-related damage occurring gradually over the years could constitute an occurrence as long as the damage was unintended and unexpected. *Id.*

The pollution-exclusion clause, as construed by the Court in its Order of August 11, worked a sharp change in coverage for pollution-related liability. By excluding coverage for pollution-related damages unless the release of pollutants is "sudden and accidental," the clause eliminated from coverage a significant category of risk: pollution-related damages which are unexpected and unintended but which result from pollution released gradually over the years. This is just the sort of risk for which plaintiff seeks coverage in this case. In its prior Order, the Court gave effect to the commonly understood meaning of the word "sudden" and affirmed the insurance companies' denial of coverage.

Plaintiff has submitted to the Court certain documents which he hopes will move the Court to reconsider its construction of the pollution-exclusion clause. These documents show that, at the time the pollution exclusion clause was first inserted into insurance policies (1970), the Insurance Rating Board (which represents the insurance industry and on which defendant Aetna participated) represented to the Georgia Insurance Department that "the impact of the [pollution exclusion clause] on the vast majority of risks would be no change. It is

---

1. The Court's Order of August 11 is attached to this Order as Appendix A.

rather a situation of clarification * * * Coverage for expected or intended pollution and contamination is not now present as it is excluded by the definition of occurrence. Coverage for accidental mishaps is continued. * * *" *See* Letter from R. Stanley Smith, Manager of the Insurance Rating Board, to the Georgia Insurance Department dated June 10, 1970 (attached as Appendix B). This statement clearly understates the substantial change in coverage worked by the pollution exclusion clause. On the basis of this statement, and others like it, plaintiff would have the Court reconsider its construction of the pollution exclusion. Plaintiff asserts that the insurance companies should be estopped from contradicting the representations made to the Georgia Insurance Department as to the effect of the pollution exclusion clause.

II. *Analysis*

The Court does not wish to condone the conduct of the insurance industry that plaintiff has exposed. The statements made by the Insurance Rating Board to the Georgia Insurance Department, if not fraudulent, certainly were not straightforward. The Rating Board downplayed the substantial effect the pollution exclusion clause would have on existing coverage in an effort to obtain approval for the clause's insertion into insurance policies.[2] For several reasons, however, the Court is not persuaded that its prior decision should be disturbed.

First, and most importantly, under Georgia law the Court is not to look beyond the language of a contract to ascertain its meaning when the language is clear and unambiguous. *Southern Federal Savings & Loan Ass'n v. Lyle,* 249 Ga. 284, 287, 290 S.E.2d 455 (1982); *Reuss v. Time Insurance Co.,* 177 Ga.App. 672, 673, 340 S.E.2d 625 (1986). Further, words in contracts are to be construed according to their ordinary meaning. *Stinchcomb v. Clayton County Water Auth.,* 177 Ga. App. 558, 561, 340 S.E.2d 217 (1986); O.C.G.A. § 13–2–2(2). As commonly understood, the word "sudden" in the pollution exclusion clause connotes abruptness. The gradual leaching of hazardous wastes into the ground water and soil surrounding Picketville cannot honestly be characterized as sudden. These principles lie at the heart of the Court's analysis in its August 11 Order, and demand the same result today. Accordingly, the Court reaffirms the grant of summary judgment to Aetna, Harbor, and American Home.

2. Plaintiff's view is that the statements made in 1970 by the Insurance Rating Board were honest and prove that the pollution exclusion clause was not intended to eliminate coverage for risks such as plaintiff seeks coverage for in this action. In other words, plaintiff finds dishonesty in the insurance companies' position in this action rather than in the representations made to the Georgia Insurance Department. The Court differs, and believes that the construction urged by the insurance companies in this action, and adopted by the Court, is the one that was originally intended. The Court finds dishonesty in the representation made to the Georgia Insurance Department in 1970 that the pollution exclusion clause would have little effect on preexisting coverage.

Additionally, the Insurance Rating Board's representations to the Georgia Insurance Department, viewed in historical perspective, were not as devious as they appear at first glance. As noted above, prior to the insertion of the pollution exclusion clause into insurance policies, pollution-related damage was covered only if it fell within the definition of "occurrence." Occurrence, in turn, was defined as "an accident, including continuous or repeated exposure to conditions, which results in bodily injury or property damage neither expected nor intended from the standpoint of the insured." [3] *See* Note, *The Pollution Exclusion Clause Through The Looking Glass,* 74 Geo.L.J. 1237, 1246–47 (1986). The insurance industry anticipated that the definition of occurrence would preclude coverage for most pollution-related damage because of the requirement that damage be unintended and unexpected to be covered. *Id.* at 1248. The insurance industry miscalculated: (1) courts interpreted occurrence broadly, holding pollution-related damage to be unintended (and therefore covered) even when an insured knowingly discharged pollutants into the environment, as long as the specific damage giving rise to liability was unintended; (2) public awareness of environmental contamination grew and was accompanied by a sharp increase in pollution liability litigation. *Id.* at 1246–53. In this context, the representations made by the Insurance Rating Board were, to a degree, accurate; the insurance industry was merely trying, through the pollution exclusion clause, to prevent courts from extending coverage to risks that were not calculated into premiums under occurrence-based policies, and were not anticipated when the definition of occurrence was drafted. *Id.; See also* Developments in the Law—Toxic Waste Litigation, 99 Harv.L.Rev. 1458, 1575 (1986) ("the sharp increase in environmental litigation and the courts' broad construction of insurance policies have combined to shock the insurance industry."). Thus, in 1970, the Insurance Rating Board's representation that the pollution exclusion clause was designed to maintain the status quo was, from the standpoint of insurance companies, true.

Still, the Insurance Rating Board did fail to reveal to the Georgia Insurance Department the change in coverage worked by the suddenness requirement. This clearly worked a sharp change in prior coverage because "occurrence" expressly included "continuous or repeated exposure to conditions." *See supra,* note 3 and accompanying text. However, it is not clear whether the significance of this change was fully understood in 1970; environmental disasters such as Love Canal and Pickettville, which are the result of gradual contamination, are a relatively recent phenomenon.

Thus, the hands of the insurance companies, while not immaculate, are not as dirty as plaintiff contends. The insurance companies have not, as plaintiff suggests, perpetrated a fraud on the Court by arguing in favor of a construction which enforces the clear and unambiguous language of their policies.

---

3. This definition continues in present policies. *See* Appendix A at 1577, n. 2.

Defendant Highlands Insurance Co.'s motion for summary judgment is based on the fact that its insurance policy contains a pollution-exclusion clause that does not differ in any material respect from the clauses which entitled Aetna, Harbor and American Home to summary judgment. Accordingly, Highlands Insurance Co.'s motion for summary judgment is GRANTED. * * *

APPENDIX A

* * * At the center of the case *sub judice* is the Pickettville landfill [Picketville], a tract of approximately fifty-two acres of land, located on the outskirts of Jacksonville, Florida. For approximately eighteen years, plaintiff Claussen has had various substantial ownership interests in Pickettville.

In May 1966, Properties & Securities, Inc. [P & S], a corporation of which plaintiff was the principal stockholder, acquired the Pickettville tract. Another company controlled by the plaintiff exploited the property, excavating sand from the site for use in the construction of runways at the Jacksonville Airport. As sand was removed from the property, the area excavated filled with water. Sand removal continued with the use of a dredge. At the conclusion of the removal process, there existed on the property a rather large and deep "lake."

In 1968, P & S and the City of Jacksonville negotiated an agreement whereby the City would acquire the right to use Pickettville as a landfill free of charge. It was Claussen's hope that the filling of the Pickettville site by the City would increase the value of the land and render it suitable for profitable resale or for development. That the water-filled sand pit on the property constituted a liability risk was also a factor taken into account by Claussen. The property was used as a landfill by the City from 1968 until approximately July 1977.

During the negotiations leading to the agreement between the City and Claussen, the City had directed plaintiff's attorney to impress upon his client that the City needed authorization to dump "anything" at Pickettville. Thus, in granting written permission to the City to utilize the property, plaintiff stated that the City would have the right to dump "garbage and other debris and material in accordance with [the City's] waste disposal needs." Whether plaintiff intended this language to allow for the dumping of toxic materials is a disputed question. It is clear, however, that over the years a substantial quantity of hazardous waste did in fact find its way into the property. * * *

The type of *damage* allegedly caused in the instant case was exactly the type of damage with respect to which the parties agreed that there would be no coverage, notwithstanding the happening of an occurrence, except under certain specified circumstances. The circumstances under which coverage would be available are specified by the exception to the pollution exclusion. Only where the release, escape or dispersal of contaminants is "sudden and accidental" would the insurance policies issued by Aetna apply.

In the instant case, if the *dumping* of hazardous wastes at Pickettville is considered the contractually relevant release, escape or dispersal of materials, clearly this dumping was not sudden; trucks were pouring toxic waste into Pickettville for approximately nine years. From a highly technical viewpoint, of course, it might be argued that the dumping was "accidental" in that it allegedly resulted in property damage unintended by Claussen. In any event, the dumping was not sudden within the meaning of the Aetna policies.[4] The same holds true if one considers the *leaching* of contaminants into the groundwater and soil surrounding the landfill as the relevant release, escape or dispersal: this leaching certainly was not sudden, even if it, too, could be said to be accidental. Either way, Aetna is under no duty to defend or indemnify. Moreover, while the foregoing indicates that policy concerns need not be taken into consideration in reaching the conclusion that the Aetna policies provide no coverage, it certainly does no disservice to public policy to hold that plaintiff's alleged ignorance with respect to the dumping or leaching of hazardous wastes at Pickettville or of the property damage resulting therefrom is irrelevant. Plaintiff owned the land in question, and a finding that a defense or coverage should be afforded where an owner disclaims knowledge with respect to the unconscionable use of his property would "pay[ ] the insured to keep his head in the sand." *Waste Management, supra,* 340 S.E.2d at 381.

At any rate, in drafting the pollution exclusion clause, the insurance industry clearly intended to limit coverage for pollution-related damages to situations where such damages are caused by sudden pollution incidents involving equipment malfunctions, explosions and the like. The word sudden was intended by the industry to have its usual temporal meaning, *see* Note, *The Pollution Exclusion Through the Looking Glass,* 74 Geo.L.J. 1237, 1252–53 & n. 79 (1986); Hendrick & Wiezel, *The New Commercial General Liability Forms—An Introduc-*

---

4. The Court sees no reason to conclude that the word sudden in an insurance policy means anything different from that which it means in any other context. Nor does the reasoning of those courts that have held to the contrary appear to be especially persuasive. *See, e.g., Allstate Ins. Co. v. Klock Oil Co.,* 73 A.D.2d 486, 426 N.Y.S.2d 603, 605 (1980):

The term "sudden and accidental" must be construed in its relevant context. The relevant context to be considered is the fact that it is a term employed by an insurer in the contract and should be given the construction most favorable to the insured. Thus, regardless of the initial intent or lack thereof as it relates to causation, or the period of time involved, if the resulting damage could be viewed as unintended by the factfinder, the total situation could be found to constitute an accident. *Id.* 426 N.Y.S.2d at 605.

See also National Grange Mutual Ins. Co. v. Continental Casualty Ins. Co., 650 F.Supp. 1404 (S.D.N.Y.1986); *Independent Petrochemical Corp. v. Aetna Casualty and Surety Co.,* 654 F.Supp. 1334 (D.D.C.1986); *Payne v. United States Fidelity and Guaranty Co.,* 625 F.Supp. 1189 (S.D.Fla.1985); *Shapiro v. Public Service Mutual Ins. Co.,* 19 Mass.App. 648, 477 N.E.2d 146 (1985); *Buckeye Union Ins. Co. v. Liberty Solvents and Chemicals Co., Inc.,* 17 Ohio App.3d 127, 477 N.E.2d 1227, 1235 (1984); *Lansco, Inc. v. Department of Environmental Protection,* 138 N.J.Super. 275, 350 A.2d 520, 524 (1975) ("since the oil spill was neither expected nor intended by [the insured], it follows that the spill was sudden and accidental under the exclusion clause even if caused by the deliberate act of a third party.").

tion and Critique, 1986 Fed.Ins. & Corp.Couns.Q. 319, 343–46, and a reasonable insured with any degree of common sense would assume the word to have that usual meaning. *See generally, Greer v. IDS Life Ins. Co.,* 149 Ga.App. 61, 253 S.E.2d 408 (1979). Only in the minds of hypercreative lawyers could the word "sudden" be stripped of its essential temporal attributes. While not all courts have agreed in this regard, recent decisions have recognized, with increasing frequency, that the pollution exclusion does mean just what it says.[5] *See, e.g., Waste Management, supra; Techalloy Co. v. Reliance Ins. Co.,* 338 Pa. Super. 1, 487 A.2d 820, 826–27 (1984); *see generally Great Lakes Container Corp. v. National Union Fire Ins. Cos.,* 727 F.2d 30 (1st Cir. 1984). * * *

In reliance on the clear wording of the contract between plaintiff and defendant Aetna, and in the hope that an unfortunate judicial trend can indeed be reversed, the motion for summary judgment of defendant Aetna shall be granted, and that of the plaintiff shall be denied. * * *

Notes and Questions

1. *The Meaning of "Sudden."* The courts are divided regarding the meaning of the pollution exclusion. *Broadwell Realty* and *Claussen* are representative of the character of this division. Do the courts that follow *Broadwell Realty* interpret the phrase "sudden and accidental" in the exception to the exclusion to mean "sudden or accidental," or is the interpretation based on a meaning of the word "sudden" that

---

5. The Court acknowledges that the word "accidental," included in the exception to the pollution exclusion, is redundant, in that it needlessly reiterates that portion of the definition of "occurrence" which affords recovery only for "accidents * * * result[ing] * * * in bodily injury or property damage neither expected nor intended from the standpoint of the insured." Nevertheless, it strains logic to find ambiguity in the word sudden, and this latter word is clearly an essential element of the exception to the exclusion. Thus, the *entire* clause is certainly *not* redundant. *See generally, Transamerica Ins. Co. v. Sunnes,* 77 Or.App. 136, 711 P.2d 212 (1985), *review denied,* 301 Or. 76, 717 P.2d 631 (1986). It should be borne in mind, moreover, that a basic rule of contract construction directs courts to "avoid a construction that does not give all portions of the policy meaning and effect," *First Nat'l Bank of Midland v. Protective Life Ins. Co.,* 511 F.2d 731, 734 (5th Cir.1975). *See also Martindale Lumber Co. v. Bituminous Casualty Co.,* 625 F.2d 618 (5th Cir.1980).

As to the fact that one author does indeed find the entire clause to be a restatement of the occurrence definition, *see* 3 R. Long, *Law of Liability Insurance* App–58 (1973), this Court observes, first, that it seems unwise to rely too heavily on what may well have been a hastily prepared supplement to an otherwise respected and reliable treatise and, second, that no matter how many courts have accepted the interpretation suggested by the cited work, thus finding the pollution exclusion clause to be confusing or mere surplusage, *see* cases cited *supra* note 3; *see generally, United Pacific Ins. Co. v. Van's Westlake Union, Inc.,* 34 Wash.App. 708, 664 P.2d 1262, 1265 (1983), it is sometimes appropriate politely to point out that the emperor has no clothes. The pollution exclusion clause is unambiguous under most circumstances, *cf. A–1 Sandblasting v. Baiden,* 53 Or.App. 890, 632 P.2d 1377 (1981), aff'd 293 Or. 17, 643 P.2d 1260 (1982) (term liquid in pollution clause does not apply to paint spilled by workmen while painting bridge), and it would seem that judicial determinations will be perceived as more credible when this fact is generally recognized.

contains no temporal element? Absent a temporal element, what does "sudden" mean?

2. *Estoppel by Lobbying?* Was the court in *Claussen* correct in its interpretation of the significance of the representations made to the Georgia Insurance Department when the pollution exclusion was adopted? Even if the insured's contentions about the significance of these representations were correct, are such representations relevant to a policy's meaning?

3. *The Unexcluded Middle.* Why would the insurance industry have felt the need to reiterate in a separate exclusion that coverage against pollution liability was precluded if the damage caused was either expected or intended? Is it plausible that the industry simply did not contemplate that there might be claims for damage caused by pollution which was accidental but not sudden, and which resulted in harm that was neither expected nor intended?

4. *Is the Pollution Exclusion a Means to Another End?* If the pollution exclusion has a meaning that is independent of the requirement that damage be neither expected nor intended from the standpoint of the insured, what is its function? One argument is that the pollution exclusion, together with the "sudden and accidental" exception was a way of avoiding the moral hazard that would otherwise result because of the insurer's difficulty of proving the insured's failure to mitigate damage caused by gradual discharge of pollutants once a continuing discharge is discovered. See Abraham, Environmental Liability and the Limits of Insurance, 88 Colum.L.Rev. 942, 961–66 (1988). Compare the scope of the exclusion at issue in *Broadwell Realty* and *Claussen* with Exclusion (f) in the new CGL policy. In light of the breadth of this new exclusion, do you think that the courts have done policyholders a favor in cases such as *Broadwell Realty?*

5. Notice Conditions

MIGHTY MIDGETS, INC. v. CENTENNIAL INSURANCE COMPANY

Court of Appeals of New York, 1979.
47 N.Y.2d 12, 416 N.Y.S.2d 559, 389 N.E.2d 1080.

FUCHSBERG, Judge.

Applying an objectively stanced reasonable person standard, in the facts and circumstances of this case we hold that it could be found that written notification of the occurrence of an accident approximately seven and a half months after the assured learned of the event met a liability policy's requirement that the insurer be given notice "as soon as practicable". On a subsidiary issue, we also hold that the insurer is not liable for attorneys' fees and disbursements necessarily incurred in the policyholder's successful prosecution of the action it brought to compel the insurer to comply with its policy obligations.

Plaintiff, Mighty Midgets, Inc., is a nonprofit corporation organized to encourage, manage and otherwise lend support to boys' football teams in Orangetown, Rockland County. On this appeal, its liability carrier, Centennial Insurance Company, challenges so much of an order of the Appellate Division as affirmed a judgment declaring that Centennial was required to defend and, within the limits of the applicable coverage, indemnify the Midgets against liability asserted in a suit arising out of an occurrence in which nine-year-old Glenn De Temple suffered serious personal injuries. The Midgets cross-appeal from so much of the order as deleted an award to cover its attorneys' fees and expenses in the present litigation.

The accident to Glenn, then a member of a Midgets-sponsored team, took place on October 18, 1970, when, immediately after the completion of a game in which he had participated, a large pot of boiling water which rested on the counter of an improvised frankfurter stand the Midgets operated as a fund-raising activity was caused to pour over him. Robert Halle, the unpaid volunteer president of the Midgets, was not present. But, learning of the misadventure before the day was out, he was the one who thereafter acted for his organization in a sequence of communications which, as found by the Trial Judge and later affirmed by the Appellate Division, provide the factual backdrop for the central legal issues confronting us today.

The first communication took the form of a telephone call to the Dunn & Fowler, Division of Frank B. Hall & Company (Dunn), to whom Halle gave oral notice of the event and made inquiry as to the procedure to be followed in presenting a claim. It was no accident that it was Dunn that Halle called. Both the Centennial liability policy and a second one providing accident and health protection with the Hartford Accident & Indemnity Company had been secured for the Midgets at the instance of Dunn, a leading specialist in athletic team insurance and apparently the organization upon which the more than 2,500 teams enrolled in the national program of which the Midgets were a part would rely for guidance in insurance matters. Dunn's role went far beyond that of solicitor of the liability policy. It collected the premiums, issued the policy and was designated by the policy as "agent or broker". Moreover, this disjunctive phraseology was not at odds with the *modus operandi* Dunn and Centennial had in fact adopted. Their established practice was for Dunn, who wrote most if not all of its athletic team business with Centennial, to be entrusted with large batches of policies executed by Centennial's authorized signatories in blank, leaving it to Dunn rather than Centennial to fill in such things as policy numbers, names of assureds it procured and the premiums to be charged. When Dunn was ready to do so, it required no further authorization from Centennial to decide, as indeed it did in the case of the Midgets, if and when a policy was to go into effect.

Returning to Halle's initial telephone call, his testimony, fully credited by the courts below, is that, upon identifying himself, describing the De Temple incident and asking whether he should "put it under a medical or [a] liability claim", the Dunn representative to whom he reported instructed him the appropriate one was under the Hartford accident and health policy. There was not the slightest suggestion that notice to Centennial would also be in order. The result was that the 21-year-old Halle, whose limited personal and vocational backgrounds were totally alien to either the world of insurance or that of the law, and who, as Dunn and Centennial presumably would know, until then had no previous experience in the processing of a liability claim, filed a claim only on a Hartford form supplied him by Dunn.

Thereafter, so far as the Midgets knew, things proceeded uneventfully until April 7, 1971, when Hartford for the first time notified the Midgets that its policy did not cover the accident because it had transpired after the game in which Glenn had participated was over. In the intervening months, Glenn's father, an avid supporter of the Midgets, had never indicated the slightest intention of pursuing any claim other than the one filed against the Hartford. Nor does that possibility appear to have ever entered Halle's mind. But Hartford's refusal to pay the medical claim apparently roused the De Temples from their quiescence sufficiently for them to consult counsel, who, on May 25, sent a letter informing the Midgets that a liability suit on behalf of their clients was in the offing. Still reflecting his belief that communicating with Dunn was the same as communicating with Centennial, Halle forwarded this letter to Centennial care of Dunn and reminded this insurer that the facts of the accident had been reported previously, an obvious reference to his original telephone call to Dunn.[1] This was the Midgets' first written notice to Centennial.[2]

It was on this record that Trial Term, sitting without a jury, found as fact (1) that Dunn's handling of the communications from Halle was negligent,[3] (2) that, "under the circumstances", including Halle's "limited * * * understanding of insurance matters" and the relationship between Dunn and Centennial, the Midgets acted reasonably in that they did all that they "could do" until the arrival of the letter on May 25 first disabused them of the misinformation Dunn had imparted; and (3) that the letter transmitting the De Temple lawyer's liability claim letter constituted written notice given "as soon as practicable" after the claim was made. Though the subsequent affirmance by the Appellate Division was by a vote of three to two, there was no division among its

1. Though Dunn received copies of the documents and correspondence exchanged between the senior De Temple and Hartford and, eventually, of the latter's rejection of the claim, it did not advise the Midgets of these developments.

2. Because of the grounds on which we decide this case, it becomes unnecessary to describe subsequent events, although we note that Centennial's own delay in disclaiming coverage was an alternate ground on which Trial Term premised the insurer's obligation to defend and indemnify the Midgets.

3. A separate suit, brought by the Midgets against Dunn to recover damages for the latter's negligence was consolidated with the declaratory action and the two cases tried together on the same evidence; having decided that Dunn was negligent, the trial court, to avoid duplication, ordered the assessment of damages held in abeyance until after the declaratory and personal injury suits will have been concluded. The personal injury suit has been awaiting the outcome of the one before us now.

members either over the operative facts or over the deletion of the award for fees and expenses. However, the dissenters would have held the Midgets' written notice untimely. For the reasons which follow, we, in turn, now affirm.

At the outset, we draw attention to the two provisions of the Centennial policy about which the controversy revolves. One tells us that, in the event of an occurrence resulting in personal injury or property damage, "written notice * * * shall be given by or for the INSURED to the company or any of its authorized agents as soon as practicable". The other reads: "Notice to any agent * * * shall not effect a waiver or a change in any part of this policy or estop the company from asserting any right under the terms of this policy; nor shall the terms of this policy be waived or changed, except by endorsement issued to form a part of this policy, signed by a duly authorized representative of the company."

It is well settled that the phrase "as soon as practicable" is an elastic one, not to be defined in a vacuum. By no means does it connote an ironbound requirement that notice be "immediate" or even "prompt", relative as even those concepts often are; "soon", a term close to each of these in common parlance, is expressly qualified in the policy here by the word "practicable". Nor was compliance with the insurance policy's temporal requirement to be measured simply by how long it was before written notification came forth. More crucial was the reason it took the time it did. So, the provision that notice be given "as soon as practicable" called for a determination of what was within a reasonable time in the light of the facts and circumstances of the case at hand. * * *

Of course, there is no inflexible test of reasonableness. As with most questions whose answers are heavily dependent on the factual contexts in which they arise, rules of general application are hard to come by (see, e.g., *Chinn v. Butchers' Mut. Cas. Co. of N.Y.*, 190 Misc. 117, 71 N.Y.S.2d 70 [failure to foresee that an insurance claim would eventuate]; *Melcher v. Ocean Acc. & Guar. Corp.*, 226 N.Y. 51, 123 N.E. 81 [failure to foresee that an insurance claim would eventuate]; *Padavan v. Clemente*, 43 A.D.2d 729, 350 N.Y.S.2d 694 [justifiable lack of knowledge of insurance coverage]). Most pertinent to the case now before us, the conduct and representations of Centennial or its agent may be considered in determining whether notice has been unduly delayed.

Measured by these criteria, the contention that the Midgets' delay in providing written notice was unreasonable as a matter of law is untenable. True, approximately seven and a half months elapsed between the date of the accident and the time when Halle, via Dunn, now found to have been Centennial's agent for the receipt of written notice of claim (cf. Insurance Law, § 167, subd. 1, par. [c]), concededly delivered such notice. But, the Trial Judge found that the reason for so long a passage of time was the Midgets' genuine, if misguided, belief that all the insurance notice necessary to protect the Midgets' interests under any policies it carried for the De Temple accident had been furnished. There is nothing to indicate that it had a motive for not complying or that it did not stand ready to provide any information in any form that was required.

These factors could be weighted in the balance in determining whether the eventual written notice was given "as soon as practicable". The dealings between Dunn and the Midgets could bear directly on that issue. Specifically, to that end the conduct of Dunn on the occasion of the original telephone call and thereafter, though ineffectual to legitimatize the oral notice given in the first instance, was relevant and material insofar as it affected the time the Midgets took before meeting the mandate for written notice.

Is the unsophisticated Halle then to be deemed not to have acted "as soon as practicable" as a matter of law because, on his initial experience in the reporting of an accident under the liability policy, he sought direction from Dunn, which had sold the Midgets both policies? To the contrary, even absent the close relationship which the undisputed evidence shows Centennial and Dunn enjoyed, the former, as an insurer, can hardly have failed to appreciate how common it is for policyholders to rely almost exclusively on the advice of intermediaries, be they agents or brokers (cf. *Drennan v. Sun Ind. Co.,* 271 N.Y. 182, 2 N.E.2d 534; *Quinlan v. Providence Washington Ins. Co.,* 133 N.Y. 356, 31 N.E. 31).

Nor did Halle necessarily have to abandon his reliance on the correctness of Dunn's original advice when, in April, he learned that Hartford had taken the position that its health and accident coverage did not apply. Notification that Hartford was denying coverage did not have to dissipate Halle's erroneous belief that Centennial never was in the picture. It could be found, as the Trial Judge did, that, once the sense of security into which Halle had been lulled by Dunn's and Centennial's continued silence was dispelled by the receipt of the De Temple claim letter, he acted posthaste in forwarding it to Centennial's agent.

In sum, under these circumstances there was enough evidence from which it could be found that the Midgets' failure to notify the insurer before it did was not unreasonable and that, consequently, Centennial was not entitled to disclaim. Since our review is limited to determining whether the conclusion of the fact-finding courts finds support in the evidence, we must uphold their determination (*Estate of Canale v. Binghamton Amusement Co.,* 37 N.Y.2d 875, 378 N.Y.S.2d 362, 340 N.E.2d 729). * * *

For all these reasons, the order of the Appellate Division should be affirmed, but without costs.

Notes and Questions

1. *Waiver.* Did the court in *Mighty Midgets* dispense with the requirement that notice of an occurrence be given "as soon as practicable," hold that the agent had waived this requirement, or hold that jury could find that the requirement had been satisfied? Can an agent effectively waive a policy provision stating that the company's agents cannot waive notice requirements?

2. *Reasonable Delay.* Most courts hold that even policy provisions requiring immediate notice are complied with when notice is given within a reasonable time. Moreover, the majority rule is that even an unreasonable delay does not breach the policy so long as the insurer suffers no prejudice as a result of the delay. Some courts also require, however, that the delay be in "good faith." See, e.g., *Great American Insurance Company v. C.G. Tate Construction Company,* 303 N.C. 387, 279 S.E.2d 769 (1981). In light of this judicial inclination to interpret notice requirements flexibly, are apparently liberal provisions such as that at issue in *Mighty Midgets* and that in the Sample CGL Policy (requiring notice "promptly") actually efforts to require a little more promptness by insureds than the courts would otherwise require, instead of creating notice requirements that the courts will automatically ignore?

3. *Prejudice.* The chief issue in most notice cases, apart from whether delay was reasonable, is whether the insurer suffered prejudice because of the delay. But see *Security Mutual Insurance Company v. Acker–Fitzsimons Corp.,* 31 N.Y.2d 436, 340 N.Y.S.2d 902, 293 N.E.2d 76 (1972), holding that the insurer need not show prejudice before it can assert a defense of non-compliance with the notice-of-occurrence requirement. In most jurisdictions other than New York, prejudice to the insurer is required. Here the burden of proof is critically important, for often it is impossible to pinpoint any prejudice that has occurred. For example, sometimes it will simply be unclear whether potentially beneficial evidence disappeared, or whether the case is substantially more difficult to defend for other reasons as a result of the delay in providing notice. The courts are split on the question of who bears the burden of proof, though the majority seem to place it on the insurer. Compare *Weaver Brothers, Inc. v. Chappel,* 684 P.2d 123 (Alaska 1984) (burden on insurer to show that a six-year delay caused prejudice), with *Miller v. Dilts,* 463 N.E.2d 257 (Ind.1984) (burden on insured to show the absence of prejudice).

4. *"As Soon as Practicable."* In addition to the obligation to provide notice of an occurrence, liability insurance policies also contain provisions requiring notice to the insurer that a claim has been made against the insured. The insured almost always knows that a claim has been made, because he has received written notice or has been served with a complaint. In *Mighty Midgets* the court seemed to assume that the insured knew there had been an "occurrence" within

the meaning of the provision governing notice of such an event. Was such an assumption accurate, in light of the fact that Halle did not know whether an accident or liability insurance claim was the appropriate one to file? Suppose that there has been gradual and undiscovered pollution of the sort at issue in *Broadwell Realty?* Would the provision of notice twenty years after the first occurrence be sufficient if the pollution was not discovered until the twentieth year after it had commenced?

D. CLAIMS–MADE COVERAGE

SPARKS v. ST. PAUL INSURANCE COMPANY
Supreme Court of New Jersey, 1985,
100 N.J. 325, 495 A.2d 406.

STEIN, J.

In this case, as in *Zuckerman v. National Union Fire Ins. Co.,* 100 N.J. 304, 495 A.2d 395 (1985), which the Court also decides today, we consider the enforceability of certain coverage limitations contained in a "claims made" professional liability insurance policy issued by appellant St. Paul Insurance Company (St. Paul). The trial court and the Appellate Division refused to enforce the policy provision limiting coverage to claims and potential claims reported to St. Paul during the policy period. We granted the insurance company's petition for certification, 99 N.J. 211, 491 A.2d 706 (1984), in order to resolve the apparent conflict between the unreported Appellate Division decision in this case and the Appellate Division decision in *Zuckerman, supra,* 194 N.J. Super. 206, 476 A.2d 820 (1984), enforcing a similar provision in the "claims made" policy at issue in that case.

I

The material facts are not in dispute. In November, 1978, respondents, John and Carolyn Sparks, retained A. Raymond Guarriello, a New Jersey attorney, to represent them in connection with the sale of their residence. That transaction resulted in litigation between respondents and the prospective purchasers. In the course of that litigation, apparently due to Guarriello's negligence, Mr. and Mrs. Sparks failed to answer interrogatories. This resulted in an order entered in mid-October, 1979, suppressing the Sparks' answer and counterclaim. A default judgment for specific performance was entered against Mr. and Mrs. Sparks in February, 1980, and a money judgment for $18,899.08 was entered against them in May, 1981. It is not disputed that Guarriello's negligence was the proximate cause of the judgments against Mr. and Mrs. Sparks.

On November 6, 1976, appellant, St. Paul, issued Guarriello a one-year professional malpractice policy that was renewed for successive one-year periods, terminating on November 6, 1979. On September 27,

1979, St. Paul issued a substitute policy for one additional year that was to take effect on November 6, 1979. Guarriello failed to pay the premium and appellant sent Guarriello a notice cancelling the substitute policy, effective January 21, 1980. Between June and August of 1980, substituted counsel for respondents notified St. Paul of the underlying facts and demanded that the insurance company provide malpractice coverage with respect to Guarriello's negligence.

The policy issued to Guarriello in 1976 was denominated a "claims made" policy. A "Schedule" attached to the declaration page of the policy bore the following notice:

TO OUR POLICYHOLDERS

This is a "claims made" Coverage Form. It only covers claims arising from the performance of professional services *subsequent to the retroactive date indicated* and then only to claims first made within the provisions of the Policy while this Coverage Form is in force. No coverage is afforded for claims first made after the termination of this insurance unless and to the extent that Reporting Endorsements are purchased in accordance with Condition 3 of this Coverage Form. Please review the Policy carefully. [Emphasis added.]

The retroactive date set forth in the policy was November 6, 1976, the same date as the effective date of coverage. Therefore, unlike the standard "claims made" policy that was involved in our decision in *Zuckerman, supra,* 100 N.J. at 307–309, 495 A.2d 395, St. Paul's policy provided no retroactive coverage whatsoever during its first year. In that year, the coverage provided by the policy applied only to errors and omissions that occurred during the policy year and were reported to the company within the policy year. During the two renewal years beginning November 6, 1977 and November 6, 1978, the policy afforded "retroactive" coverage for negligence that occurred subsequent to November 6, 1976.

In April, 1981, St. Paul rejected respondent's demand that it provide coverage for Guarriello's malpractice since the company received notice of the claim after the termination of the second renewal policy in November, 1979 and after the January, 1980 cancellation of the replacement policy for nonpayment of the premium.[1] In June, 1981, Mr. and Mrs. Sparks obtained a $42,968.08 judgment against Guarriello based upon his malpractice.

The present action commenced in October, 1981. Mr. and Mrs. Sparks sought a declaratory judgment that the liability insurance policy issued by St. Paul was valid and enforceable to pay the judgment obtained against Guarriello. In August, 1983, St. Paul's motion for

1. Although St. Paul's Notice of Cancellation stated that it would be effective January 21, 1980, the insurance company now maintains that its effect was to cancel the replacement policy *ab initio* as of November 6, 1979. As discussed *infra* at 415–416 & n. 5, the effective date of the cancellation is not material.

summary judgment was denied and in September, 1983, summary judgment was granted in favor of Mr. and Mrs. Sparks. That judgment was affirmed by the Appellate Division, which held "claims made" policies to be unenforceable as violative of public policy.

II

In our decision in *Zuckerman, supra,* 100 N.J. at 309–313, 495 A.2d at 398–400, we summarized the origins of "claims made" or "discovery" liability policies and emphasized the distinction between such policies and the more traditional "occurrence" policies. That distinction warrants reiteration in view of the unusual provisions of the policy issued to Guarriello by St. Paul:

> [T]here are two types of Errors and Omissions Policies: the "discovery" policy and the "occurrence" policy. In a discovery policy the coverage is effective if the negligent or omitted act is discovered and brought to the attention of the insurance company during the period of the policy, no matter when the act occurred. In an occurrence policy the coverage is effective if the negligent or omitted act occurred during the period of the policy, whatever the date of discovery. [*Samuel N. Zarpas, Inc. v. Morrow,* 215 F.Supp. 887, 888 (D.N.J.1963).]

Another court characterized "claims made" policies as "provid[ing] unlimited retroactive coverage and no prospective coverage at all," as distinguished from "occurrence" policies which "provide unlimited prospective coverage and no retroactive coverage at all." *Brander v. Nabors,* 443 F.Supp. 764, 767 (N.D.Miss.), aff'd, 579 F.2d 888 (5th Cir. 1978).

The distinction between the two types of policies has also been described in terms of the peril insured:

> In the "occurrence" policy, the peril insured is the "occurrence" itself. Once the "occurrence" takes place, coverage attaches even though the claim may not be made for some time thereafter. While in the "claims made" policy, it is the making of the claim which is the event and peril being insured and, subject to policy language, regardless of when the occurrence took place. [S. Kroll, "The Professional Liability Policy 'Claims Made,'" 13 *Forum* 842, 843 (1978).]

In *Zuckerman, supra,* 100 N.J. at 311–313, 495 A.2d at 399, we discussed in detail the significant social utility of the "claims made" policy that has led to its supplanting the occurrence policy in the professional liability field. We noted that since the insurance company that issues an "occurrence" policy is exposed to a "tail"—that is, the lapse of time between the occurrence and the date on which the claim is made—there is considerable difficulty in accurately calculating underwriting risks and premiums with respect to perils that typically lead to long tail exposure. Moreover, claims asserted in the fields of professional malpractice, products liability, and environmental law often present the added difficulty of determining precisely when the actuating event "occurred" for the purpose of defining coverage. From the standpoint of the insured, there is the danger of inadequate coverage in cases in which claims are asserted long after the error or omission occurred, because inflationary factors lead to judgments that are higher than those originally contemplated when coverage was purchased years earlier. *Id.,* 100 N.J. at 311–313, 495 A.2d at 399.

From the insurer's perspective, the clear advantage derived from a "claims made" policy is the limitation of liability to claims asserted during the policy period. This limitation enables insurers to calculate risks and premiums with greater precision. Although "claims made" policies provide coverage for errors and omissions occurring prior to the policy's inception, the elimination of exposure to claims filed after the policy expiration date enables companies to issue these policies at reduced premiums. *Zuckerman, supra,* 100 N.J. at 312–313, 495 A.2d at 399–400; J. Parker, "The Untimely Demise of the 'Claims Made' Insurance Form? A Critique of *Stine v. Continental Casualty Co.,*" 1983 *Det.C.L.Rev.* 25, 73.

In *Zuckerman,* we observed that Courts throughout the country have upheld the validity of "claims made" policies. 100 N.J. at 313–314, 495 A.2d at 400. Although "claims made" policies have regularly been challenged on public policy grounds, the vast majority of courts that have considered these challenges have enforced the policies as written. *See, e.g., Brander v. Nabors, supra,* 443 F.Supp. 764; *Gulf Ins. Co. v. Dolan, Fertig & Curtis,* 433 So.2d 512 (Fla.1983); *Livingston Parish School Bd. v. Fireman's Fund Am. Ins. Co.,* 282 So.2d 478 (La. 1973); *Stine v. Continental Cas. Co.,* 419 Mich. 89, 349 N.W.2d 127 (1984).[2]

The courts that have declined to enforce "claims made" policies have based their decisions on special factual circumstances. *J.G. Link & Co. v. Continental Cas. Co.,* 470 F.2d 1133 (9th Cir.1972), *cert. denied,* 414 U.S. 829, 94 S.Ct. 55, 38 L.Ed.2d 63 (1973) (policy covered claims made during policy period but due to certain ambiguities in policy language, court could not determine if policy was intended to provide "occurrence" or "claims made" coverage); *Gyler v. Mission Ins. Co.,* 10 Cal.3d 216, 514 P.2d 1219, 110 Cal.Rptr. 139 (1973) (policy insuring against "claims which *may* be made" during the policy period found to be too ambiguous to allow enforcement of "claims made" coverage limitation) (emphasis added); *see Zuckerman, supra,* 100 N.J. at 317, 495 A.2d 395.

We also reviewed in *Zuckerman, supra,* the commercial utility of "claims made" policies and scrutinized the terms of the policy at issue in that case. 100 N.J. at 311–313, 319, 495 A.2d at 399, 403. We concluded that there were "no considerations of public policy that would inhibit ＊ ＊ ＊ enforcement of the 'claims made' policy issued to

2. For a more complete list of cases enforcing "claims made" policies, see *Zuckerman, supra,* 100 N.J. 313–314, 495 A.2d at 400.

appellant [Zuckerman]." *Id.* at 321, 495 A.2d at 404. Similarly, we would not hesitate to enforce St. Paul's policy in this case if it comported with the generally accepted expectations of "claims made" insurance. The coverage provided by St. Paul's policy, however, materially diverges from customary "claims made" coverage in terms of its retroactive protection. It provides neither the prospective coverage typical of an "occurrence" policy, nor the retroactive coverage typical of a "claims made" policy. During the first policy year, coverage was limited to acts of malpractice that occurred, were discovered, and were reported to the insurance company during the same year. Although there was slight retroactive coverage during the second and third renewal years of the policy, the retroactive coverage was significantly more limited than that contemplated in the standard "claims made" policy. *See* S. Kroll, *supra,* 13 *Forum* at 843, 850, 854 (1978); D. Shand, " 'Claims Made' vs 'Occurrence,' " 27 *Int'l Ins. Monitor* 269, 270, 273 (1974); D. Shand, "Is Your Policy on a 'Claims Made' Basis?," *The Weekly Underwriter,* Sept. 15, 1973, at 8; J. Parker, *supra,* 1983 *Det. C.L.Rev.* 25, 27 & n. 3.

III

Jones v. Continental Cas. Co., 123 N.J.Super. 353, 303 A.2d 91 (Ch. Div.1973), is the only reported case in which a "claims made" policy was invalidated because of its lack of retroactive coverage. Jones was a professional engineer who was insured against errors and omissions under a policy that took effect in February, 1965, and was renewed annually until its termination in April, 1970. In August, 1971, a contractor sued Jones for malpractice based upon engineering services he had performed during the policy period. Jones' insurance carrier declined coverage because it did not receive notification of the claim during the policy period. Jones, seeking to compel coverage, sued the carrier. *Id.* at 354–56, 303 A.2d 91.

The retroactive coverage provided for in Jones' policy was unusual in that it was limited "to errors, omissions or negligent acts which occur[red] * * * prior to the effective date of this policy if * * * *insured by this Company under [a] prior policy.*" *Id.* at 356, 303 A.2d 91 (emphasis added). The court concluded that this retroactive coverage impermissibly inhibited plaintiff's freedom of contract because he would be deprived of coverage if he did not continue to renew his policy with the same insurance company. *Id.* at 359, 303 A.2d 91. The court also held that the total absence of prospective coverage violated this State's public policy in favor of extending time for making a claim or bringing suit for latent injuries. *Id.* at 361–63, 303 A.2d 91. Accordingly, the court declined to enforce the coverage limitations in defendant's policy, concluding, on public policy grounds, that such limitations were inconsistent with the plaintiff's "reasonable expectations" of coverage and that plaintiff's notice to defendant was sufficiently timely to invoke coverage under the policy. *Id.* at 359–63, 303 A.2d 91.

Other state and federal courts confronted with "claims made" policies providing limited or no retroactive coverage have declined to follow *Jones*. *Brander v. Nabors, supra,* 443 F.Supp. 764 (applying Mississippi law); *Livingston Parish School Bd. v. Fireman's Fund Am. Ins. Co.,* 282 So.2d 478 (La.1973); *Stine v. Continental Cas. Co.,* 419 Mich. 89, 349 N.W.2d 127 (1984); *Gereboff v. Home Indemnity Co.,* 119 R.I. 814, 383 A.2d 1024 (1978).[3] But at least one proponent of "claims made" policies has acknowledged the unique limitations of the coverage afforded by the "claims made" policy in *Jones:*

> Indeed, the *Jones* [sic] policy was peculiarly narrow in its coverage; it required the insured to have been covered by prior policies issued *only* by the insurer as a condition precedent to being covered for errors and omissions accruing prior to the effective date of the policy.
>
> * * * Consequently, because the insured did not have prior policies with CNA, the *Jones* policy afforded the insured coverage only for acts occurring during the term of insurance and then only if the policy was maintained; in effect, it only provided "occurrence" coverage without the prospective benefits of the same. [J. Parker, *supra,* 1983 *Det.C.L.Rev.* at 36 n. 38.]

Similarly, in *Brander v. Nabors, supra,* 443 F.Supp. 764, a federal district court in Mississippi considered a "claims made" policy that provided no retroactive coverage but afforded prospective coverage for a three-year period beyond the policy expiration date. Although, in the context of that policy, the court found no necessity for retroactive protection, it conceded that a more significant problem would be presented by a policy affording neither prospective nor retroactive coverage:

> We would be confronted with a more serious question of public policy if a "claims made" policy with neither a period of retroactive coverage nor a period of prospective coverage, but requiring notice to the insured within the policy period, were involved; in that event, the insurance coverage would be effective only for the time premiums are paid, and during which notice of the claim would have to be given to the insurer. Such a policy would necessitate closer scrutiny from the standpoint of what period of coverage is reasonable

---

3. The cases rejecting *Jones* reasoned that because unambiguous provisions of the policies clearly restricted retroactive coverage, and premiums were presumably reduced to reflect the limited protection, there was no basis on which to invalidate the limitations on coverage. Other cases have enforced "claims made" policies that afforded significantly limited or no retroactive coverage without expressly discussing that issue. *See, e.g., Scarborough v. Travelers Ins. Co.,* 718 F.2d 702 (5th Cir.1983); *James & Hackworth v. Continental Cas. Co.,* 522 F.Supp. 785 (N.D.Ala.1980); *Mission Ins. Co. v. Nethers,* 119 Ariz. 405, 581 P.2d 250 (Ct.App.1978); *Gulf Ins. Co. v. Dolan, Fertig & Curtis,* 433 So.2d 512 (Fla.1983); *Graman v. Continental Cas. Co.,* 87 Ill.App.3d 896, 42 Ill.Dec. 772, 409 N.E.2d 387 (App.Ct.1980); *Troy & Stalder Co. v. Continental Cas. Co.,* 206 Neb. 28, 290 N.W.2d 809 (1980).

in light of public policy. That precise issue is, however, not
before us, and we express no opinion as to the validity of a
policy structured on such narrow grounds. [*Id.*, 443 F.Supp.
at 773.]

IV

Although it is a well-established principle that insurance contracts will not be enforced if they violate public policy, *Rotwein v.
General Accident Group*, 103 N.J.Super. 406, 416, 247 A.2d 370 (Law
Div.1968); *Jorgenson v. Metropolitan Life Ins. Co.*, 136 N.J.L. 148,
152–54, 55 A.2d 2 (Sup.Ct.1947); *see Allen v. Commercial Cas. Ins.
Co.*, 131 N.J.L. 475, 37 A.2d 37 (E. & A. 1944); 6B *Appleman,
Insurance Law and Practice* § 4254, at 28 & n. 28 (1979), the
application of that principle has been limited in order that freedom
of contract is not impaired unreasonably:

"[P]ublic policy" is that principle of law which holds that "no
person can lawfully do that which has a tendency to be
injurious to the public or against public good * * *" even
though "no actual injury" may have resulted therefrom in a
particular case "to the public." It is a question of law which
the court must decide in light of the particular circumstances
of each case.

* * *

* * * Men of "full age and competent understanding" have the
"utmost liberty of contracting." Contracts so freely and voluntarily
made, in the absence of express or implied prohibition, are sacred and
are enforced by courts of justice. And courts do "not lightly interfere
with this freedom of contract." Lord Jessel, in *Printing Registering Co.
v. Sampson*, 19 Eq. 462, 465; 21 E.R.Co. 696, 699 (cited in *Driver v.
Smith, supra* ([89 N.J.Eq.] at p. 359 [104 A. 717]). Or in the words of
the late Mr. Justice Butler, "The principle that contracts in contravention of public policy are not enforceable should be applied with caution
and only in cases plainly within the reasons on which the doctrine
rests." *Twin City Pipe Line Co. v. Harding Glass Co., supra*, 283 U.S.
353 (at p. 356 [51 S.Ct. 476, at p. 477, 75 L.Ed. 1112 (1931)]); 75 L.Ed.
1116. [*Allen v. Commercial Cas. Ins. Co., supra*, 131 N.J.L. at 477–478,
37 A.2d 37.]

The doctrine that courts do not lightly interfere with freedom of
contract must be applied cautiously and realistically with regard to
complex contracts of insurance, since such contracts are highly
technical, extremely difficult to understand, and not subject to
bargaining over the terms. They are contracts of adhesion, prepared unilaterally by the insurer, and have always been subjected to
careful judicial scrutiny to avoid injury to the public. *DiOrio v.
New Jersey Mfrs. Ins. Co.*, 79 N.J. 257, 269, 398 A.2d 1274 (1979);
Allen v. Metropolitan Life Ins. Co., 44 N.J. 294, 305–06, 208 A.2d 638
(1965). * * *

We find that the contract of insurance sold by St. Paul to Guarriello does not conform to the objectively reasonable expectations of the insured and is violative of the public policy of this State. Although we held today in *Zuckerman v. National Union Fire Ins. Co., supra,* 100 N.J. 304, 495 A.2d 395 (1985), that a "claims made" policy that fulfills the reasonable expectations of the insured with respect to the scope of coverage is valid and enforceable, the policy at issue here is substantially different from the standard "claims made" policy. Indeed, St. Paul's policy combines the worst features of "occurrence" and "claims made" policies and the best of neither. It provides neither the prospective coverage typical of an "occurrence" policy, nor the "retroactive" coverage typical of a "claims made" policy. During the first year that the policy was in force, it provided no retroactive coverage for occurrences prior to the effective date of the policy. Thus, it afforded the insured only minimal protection against professional liability claims. Only claims asserted during the policy year, based on negligence that occurred during the policy year, and that were subsequently communicated to the company during the policy year were under the umbrella of coverage.

The realities of professional malpractice, however, suggest that it would be the rare instance in which an error occurred and was discovered with sufficient time to report it to the insurance company, all within a twelve-month period. The victims of professional malpractice are frequently unaware of any negligence until their injury becomes manifest long after the error or omission was committed.

Our review of the use of "claims made" policies in the professional liability field demonstrates that a policy that defines the scope of coverage so narrowly is incompatible with the objectively reasonable expectations of purchasers of professional liability coverage. We assume that there are vast numbers of professionals covered by "claims made" policies who are unaware of the basic distinction between their policies and the traditional "occurrence" policy. *See Middle Dep't Inspection Agency v. Home Ins. Co.,* 154 N.J.Super. 49, 55–56, 380 A.2d 1165 (App.Div.1977), certif. denied, 76 N.J. 234, 386 A.2d 858 (1978). However, those professionals covered by "claims made" policies who do understand how their policies differ from "occurrence" policies would expect that in return for the loss of prospective coverage provided by "occurrence" policies, they would be afforded reasonable retroactive coverage by their "claims made" policies. A leading proponent of "claims made" coverage has characterized this *quid pro quo*—the relinquishment of prospective coverage in return for retroactive coverage—as "*the essential* trade-off inherent in the concept of 'claims-made' insurance." S. Kroll, *supra,* 13 *Forum* at 854 (emphasis added); *see* J. Parker, *supra,* 1983 *Det.C.L.Rev.* at 27 & n. 3.

We do not decide in this case the precise standard by which the reasonableness of retroactive coverage is to be measured. We hold, however, that where there has been no proof of factual circumstances that would render such limited retroactive coverage both reasonable and expected,[4] a "claims made" policy that affords no retroactive coverage whatsoever during its initial year of issuance does not accord with the objectively reasonable expectations of the purchasers of professional liability insurance. The fact that subsequent renewals of that policy provide minimal retroactive coverage, *i.e.,* to the effective date of the original policy, does not cure the significant deficiency inherent in the underlying policy.

To enforce policies that provide such unrealistically narrow coverage to professionals, and, derivatively, to the public they serve, would in our view cause the kind of broad injury to the public at large contemplated by the doctrine that precludes the enforcement of contracts that violate public policy. *See Allen v. Commercial Cas. Ins. Co., supra,* 131 N.J.L. at 477–78, 37 A.2d 37. Put another way, were we to uphold the validity of St. Paul's policy in this case, the likely result would be the perpetuation in the professional liability insurance market of "claims made" policies offering comparably limited coverage. Because insurance contracts are contracts of adhesion, the terms of which are not customarily bargained for, courts have a special responsibility to prevent the marketing of policies that provide unrealistic and inadequate coverage.

Because in our view the policy sold by respondent is not a true "claims made" policy, we hold that the provisions in the policy that limit coverage to claims asserted only during the policy period are unenforceable. In view of its peculiar, absolute limitations on retroactive coverage, we construe the policy, despite its denomination, as one analogous to an "occurrence" policy. We therefore impute into the policy's provisions a right of prospective notification in order that the policy, as construed by us, provide a scope of coverage commensurate with the reasonable expectations of the insured as to "occurrence" policy coverage. Thus construed, we hold that the actual notice afforded to St. Paul by the attorneys for respondents between June and August, 1980, was furnished as soon as possible under the circumstances.[5] We follow in this limited and special factual setting the doctrine of *Cooper v. Government Employees Ins. Co.,* 51 N.J. 86, 237 A.2d 870 (1968), and find that there is no necessity to consider whether

4. "Claims made" policies with no retroactive coverage might be appropriate in certain contexts. For example, such policies might properly be offered at a reduced premium to the professional in his very first year of practice, or to the professional who changes from "occurrence" to "claims made" protection. Nothing in the record before us suggests that this is such a case.

5. New attorneys for Mr. and Mrs. Sparks were substituted in place of Guarriello on April 8, 1980. They provided St. Paul with official notice of the claim against Guarriello between June and August, 1980. Under the circumstances, we cannot say that the timing of such notice was unreasonable.

We are cognizant that had St. Paul's policy contained adequate retroactive coverage, Mr. and Mrs. Sparks would not have been afforded coverage. See *Zuckerman, supra,* 100 N.J. 304, 495 A.2d 395. An alternative construction of the policy would impute into it reasonable retroactive coverage and sustain the enforceability of the notice requirement. We reject this approach. It would be inequitable to hold an insurance policy void as against public policy and yet, when deciding between two plausible constructions of that policy, adopt the construction that is favorable to the drafter of the offensive document.

the insurance company is exposed to prejudice if the notice has been provided within a reasonable time. We emphasize, as we noted in *Zuckerman, supra,* 100 N.J. at 323–324, 495 A.2d at 405–406, the total inapplicability of the *Cooper* doctrine to a true "claims made" policy, but we apply its principle here because of our conclusion that this policy should be construed as a traditional "occurrence" form rather than as a "claims made" policy.

Accordingly, we hold that under these circumstances, the claim asserted by respondents against Guarriello, to the extent that it is based upon negligence that occurred during the policy period, is within the coverage afforded by appellant's policy. The notice to appellant between June and August, 1980, is sufficient to invoke that coverage. Accordingly, we modify and affirm the judgment of the Appellate Division and remand the matter to the trial court to consider, in accordance with the principles set forth in this opinion, any unresolved issues with respect to the specific coverage afforded by St. Paul's policy for the money judgment recovered against Guarriello.[6] We do not retain jurisdiction.

Notes and Questions

1. *Covering the Tail.* Claims-made policies were introduced in professional liability lines in the mid–1970's, when concern over the difficulty of predicting the scope of long-tail liabilities became pronounced. In the mid–1980's there was also an effort to shift from occurrence to claims-made commercial general liability insurance. This was the same effort that is part of the subject of *In re Insurance Antitrust Litigation,* excerpted in Chapter Three. In contrast to claims-made professional liability insurance, however, claims-made CGL's have met with very little success, both because many commercial purchasers have not been attracted to claims-made coverage and because some state regulators have refused to approve the policies providing it. The advantage of claims-made coverage, of course, is that premiums for this form of coverage can be set much more reliably than for occurrence coverage. This advantage is to a large extent achieved on the backs of insureds, however, who bear a much greater portion of

6. This Court has not ruled previously that "claims made" policies without adequate retroactive coverage are contrary to the public policy of this State. In note 4, *supra,* we referred to the narrow circumstances in which such policies might be appropriate and valid. Accordingly, on remand the trial court should not be precluded from considering evidence tending to prove that the terms of this policy were specifically understood and bargained for by Guarriello and that, although a policy with adequate retroactive coverage was available to him from St. Paul, he specifically elected to purchase this policy with no retroactive coverage in the first year. Our holding is based on the record before us and on the assumption that, had any such evidence existed, it would have been offered in opposition to the motion for summary judgment.

If such evidence is offered, and the trial court concludes that the evidence is sufficient to prove that although insurance contracts are normally contracts of adhesion, good faith bargaining in this instance took place between the parties; that the terms of this policy were specifically bargained for and understood by Guarriello; and that the policy was purchased by him in preference to a policy with adequate retroactive coverage, the trial court would then be justified in enforcing the policy as written.

the risk of an uncertain liability future under claims-made than under occurrence policies. In addition, for insureds who are retiring, some method of protecting against liability for claims that will be made in the future (but arising out of past activities) must be obtained. Typically claims-made insurers address this need by giving their insureds an option to purchase an *Extended Reporting Endorsement* which, for a multiple of the premium paid for the last claims-made policy the insured had purchased, provides coverage against liability for the "tail" of claims that may be made against the insured in the future.

2. *Covering the Nose.* The problem addressed in *Sparks,* however, is not the tail on claims, but (to continue the anatomical metaphor) the "nose" on claims. Why would an insured need coverage against claims resulting from actions taken prior to the date her first policy claims-made policy took effect? How persuasive is the following argument? Either she is just starting to do business or entering professional practice, in which case she has no need for such coverage, or she is shifting from occurrence to claims-made coverage, in which case her earlier occurrence policies fill the gap by providing coverage for liabilities arising out of past acts. The court in *Sparks* seemed to dismiss this argument in footnote 4 of its opinion.

If an insured shifts from one claims-made insurer to another, however, the retroactive-date problem with which the court was concerned may arise. But is there reason to believe that a different claims-made insurer would not sell coverage with a retroactive date that completely covers the insured? That is, was the *Sparks* court worried that claims-made insurers will desert insureds once claims against them begin to be filed, thus leaving them with no coverage for claims yet to be filed arising out of past actions? Is this a threat associated with the setting of a retroactive date, or with the more general possibility under claims-made that coverage will not be perpetually renewed? In any case, should a decision such as *Sparks* be made without consideration of the factors that prompted the state's Insurance Commissioner to approve the marketing of the policy?

3. *Let the Market Beware.* The court in *Sparks* expressed deep skepticism about the capacity of the insurance market to give its customers what they want: " * * * were we to uphold the validity of St. Paul's policy in this case, the likely result would be the perpetuation in the professional liability insurance market of 'claims made' policies offering comparably limited coverage." If the limitations on coverage contained in claims-made policies are not hidden from insureds, why should this be so, unless insureds are simply unwilling to pay the additional cost of fully retroactive coverage? Given that consumers of legal malpractice insurance are attorneys, are matters such as the date when coverage begins likely to be hidden from them? Since other professionals tend to buy group insurance sponsored by or sold under the auspices of professional associations that are in a position to protect their members' interests, was the court's concern groundless in these contexts as well?

4. *Was the Tail Wagging the Dog?* What was the logic behind the court's holding that because Guarriello's policy did not cover him for liability arising out of events occurring *before he purchased his first policy,* he was covered against a claim arising out of events reported *after expiration of the last policy?* Did footnote 5 provide a satisfactory explanation?

5. *Claims-made and Reported?* Most claims-made policies not only require that a claim be made during the policy period to be covered; they also required that the claim be reported to the insurer during the policy period. In light of the very flexible approach taken by courts interpreting notice conditions in occurrence policies, why not import a proof-of-prejudice requirement into the notice conditions of claims-made policies? See, e.g., *Brown–Spaulding & Associates, Inc. v. International Surplus Lines Insurance Company,* 206 Cal.App.3d 1441, 254 Cal.Rptr. 192 (1988).

Chapter Seven

LIABILITY INSURANCE: DEFENSE AND SETTLEMENT

A. THE DUTY TO DEFEND AND THE CONSEQUENCES OF BREACH

Almost all liability insurance policies not only provide indemnity to the insured; they also provide the right to a defense of all claims alleging liability that would be covered by the policy if the allegations were true. Older policies indicated that this duty to defend existed even if the allegations are "groundless, false, or fraudulent." In the drive for plain language, newer policies seem to have dropped this clarification, although it seems likely that the courts will continue to interpret policies as though they contained this clarification. In any event, it is clear that in general the duty to defend is broader than the duty to indemnify. Obviously, however, the duty to defend is not without limits. This Section examines the scope of the duty and the conflicts of interest that may arise in implementing it.

1. The Scope of the Duty

BECKWITH MACHINERY COMPANY v. TRAVELERS INDEMNITY COMPANY

United States District Court, W.D. Pennsylvania, 1986.
638 F.Supp. 1179.

COHILL, Chief Judge.

Presently before us are the Plaintiff's and Defendant's Motions for Summary Judgment.[1] Beckwith Machinery Company ("Beckwith") filed the instant action against Travelers Indemnity Company ("Travelers") alleging a breach of contract when Travelers withdrew its defense of Beckwith in an underlying lawsuit brought by Trumbull Corporation ("Trumbull") against Beckwith and Caterpillar Tractor Company ("Caterpillar"). The issues presented by the cross-motions are . . . whether Travelers, as insurer, had a duty to defend Beckwith, as insured, in the prior Trumbull litigation. For the reasons which follow, we will grant summary judgment in favor of Beckwith.

FACTS

Travelers contracted with Beckwith to provide Beckwith with comprehensive general liability insurance pursuant to manuscript insurance policy number TR–NSL–103T891–6–74, which is the controlling

1. Citations to pleadings and stipulations omitted. [ed.]

policy in this dispute. Travelers agreed to pay all sums which Beckwith became obligated to pay by reason of liability imposed by law, or assumed by Beckwith under any contract, "for damages because of bodily injury, personal injury or property damage to which the policy applied." Further, the policy provided that Travelers "agreed to defend any suit brought against Plaintiff within the United States, even if any of the allegations of the suit were groundless, if said suit alleged bodily injury, personal injury or property damage."

In 1973, Beckwith recommended, and eventually sold, various Caterpillar tractor scrapers and earthmoving equipment to Trumbull, which utilized some of this equipment at a construction job site in the southern part of Florida. This project, which began on or around March 1, 1974, required Trumbull to excavate a reservoir and build a "soil cement" (a mixture of sand and cement) dike to hold water to be used for cooling a power plant, and other related construction. * * *

However, as early as April, 1975, the tractor scrapers supplied by Beckwith broke down from time to time due to engine and transmission problems; thus, hampering the progress of Trumbull's Florida construction project. Consequently, warranty, maintenance and other repairs were performed on the tractor scrapers by a local Caterpillar dealer as well as by representatives of Caterpillar and Beckwith. Counsel for Trumbull formally notified Beckwith by a letter dated September 27, 1976, of its claim that the Caterpillar tractor scrapers were defective and that their failure to perform caused Trumbull to suffer damages in excess of three million dollars ($3,000,000). * * *

On March 17, 1976, prior to Trumbull's written notification to Beckwith that it intended to file a claim, Beckwith had informed Johnson & Higgins, its insurance broker, which then informed Travelers, of the possibility of a claim by Trumbull.

On or about April 15, 1977, Trumbull initiated a lawsuit against Beckwith and Caterpillar in the Court of Common Pleas of Allegheny County, GD 76–22608 (hereinafter the "Trumbull" case). The Trumbull case included claims against Beckwith for breach of warranties and misrepresentation of quality (i.e., failure to inform Trumbull of design defects) in thirteen (13) earth moving tractor scrapers that were manufactured by Caterpillar and sold or rented to Trumbull by Beckwith.

In its complaint, Trumbull alleged *inter alia* that it incurred substantial damages caused by the allegedly defective Caterpillar 651 and 657 tractor scrapers, which included excessive down time, a decrease in their market value and substantial damages in the performance of certain contractual obligations of Trumbull, including, but not limited to, increased project costs for labor, increased machinery down time, impact costs and overall job extension and costs.

Travelers, through the law firm of Stein & Winters, assumed the defense of the Trumbull case from the initiation of the lawsuit with respect to all claims except those pertaining to punitive damages. Based on Stein & Winters' advice that punitive damages might not be covered under the insurance policy, Travelers notified Beckwith in a letter dated June 9, 1977, that it would not provide coverage for the punitive damages claimed by Trumbull and suggested that Beckwith engage counsel to pursue that aspect of its case. At the time, Travelers did not advise Beckwith that any other claims made by Trumbull might not be covered or defended. Thereafter, in response to Travelers' refusal to provide a defense for the claim for punitive damages, Beckwith retained the law firm of Thorp, Reed and Armstrong, which notified Travelers that Beckwith was holding Travelers responsible for coverage and defense of Trumbull's punitive damages claim.

The parties have stipulated that the Trumbull Complaint stated claims of property damage which were potentially within the coverage afforded by the policy. In fact, in its "Claim Experience Review Form" dated September 20, 1977, Travelers stated that the Trumbull Complaint included:

> Multiple allegations against our insured re sale of equipment to contractor for Florida project. Complaint contains many areas of covered and noncovered counts. We will have to get into discovery before we will be in a position to make a final determination.

Moreover, in an internal memorandum authored by Associate Manager Charles E. Michaux, and dated April 10, 1978, Travelers noted the possibility that Beckwith, as a joint tortfeasor, could be liable for as much as 50% of the Trumbull claims. Referring to an opinion from outside counsel, Mr. Michaux stated his belief that Travelers was estopped from withdrawing its defense and coverage at this point. Several other internal memoranda and/or letters were circulated among Travelers' personnel, which reflected the insurer's vacillation and confusion over potential coverage of the Trumbull claims.

Despite the existing differences among Travelers' employees over what course of action to take regarding the Trumbull claims, by letter dated May 19, 1978, thirteen months after the initiation of the Trumbull lawsuit and Travelers' defense of Beckwith for all compensatory damage claims, Travelers suddenly denied coverage and withdrew its defense of Beckwith. In its letter to Beckwith, Travelers stated that it "can no longer afford you defense for any of the causes of action sued upon."

Subsequent to its denial of a defense on the Trumbull claims, Travelers pondered drafting a reservation of rights letter or filing a declaratory action to resolve the coverage issue. In a memorandum dated July 14, 1978 Travelers' Regional Assistant, James R. Murphy, acknowledged that the "initial investigation was lacking and we must now pick up the ball and put this file in a good defense posture." At one point, Travelers proposed to resume the defense of the Trumbull case without providing coverage, if Beckwith, in turn, would waive its claim of "prejudice" against Travelers. Beckwith rejected this offer, believing it was owed both defense and coverage.

On July 24, 1978, Thorp, Reed and Armstrong notified Travelers that Beckwith had instructed them to take over the entire defense of the Trumbull case. Subsequently, in October of 1978, Stein & Winters petitioned and received leave of this Court to withdraw as Beckwith's counsel. Moreover, Travelers was put on notice that Beckwith intended to proceed against Travelers for all costs and expenses it incurred in the defense of the Trumbull lawsuit.

The record discloses that after continued discovery and defense by Beckwith's counsel, the Trumbull case was eventually settled on November 12, 1982, with Beckwith's portion of the settlement payment to Trumbull being $100,000.00. The instant lawsuit followed. * * *

Duty to Defend

The law of Pennsylvania is well settled regarding an insurer's duty to defend its insured. In consideration for the insured's payment of premiums, the insurer becomes contractually obliged to defend its insured. *American Contract Bridge v. Nationwide Mutual Fire Insurance Co.,* 752 F.2d 71, 75 (3d Cir.1985). This obligation arises whenever allegations against the insured state a claim which is *potentially* within the scope of the policy's coverage, even if such allegations are "groundless, false or fraudulent." *Gedeon v. State Farm Mutual Automobile Insurance Co.,* 410 Pa. 55, 58, 188 A.2d 320, 321 (1963); *Zeitz v. Zurich General Accident Liability Insurance Co.,* 165 Pa.Super. 295, 67 A.2d 742 (1949). There were two obligations undertaken by Travelers: the obligation to indemnify Beckwith against Trumbull's damages and the separate duty to defend a lawsuit covered by the policies. It is well settled that an insurer's obligation to defend is separate and distinct from its duty to indemnify; the insurer's duty to defend is broader than its obligation to indemnify the insured. *Liberty Mutual Insurance Co. v. Pacific Indemnity Co.,* 557 F.Supp. 986, 989 (W.D.Pa.1983); *Gedeon,* 410 Pa. at 58–59, 188 A.2d at 322; 7C J. Appleman, Insurance Law and Practice, § 4682 (Berdal ed. 1979) (hereinafter "Appleman").

However, once a third party has raised allegations against an insured which potentially fall within the coverage period, the insurer is obligated to defend its insured fully until it can confine the possibility of recovery to claims outside the coverage of the policy. *Lee v. Aetna Casualty & Surety Co.,* 178 F.2d 750, 753 (2d Cir.1949); *Cadwallader v. New Amsterdam Casualty Co.,* 396 Pa. 582, 152 A.2d 484 (1959). *See also Commercial Union Insurance Co. v. Pittsburgh Corning Corp.,* 789 F.2d at 218; *Bituminous Insurance Co. v. Pennsylvania Manufacturers' Association Insurance Co.,* 427 F.Supp. 539, 555 (E.D.Pa.1976). Therefore, it is clear that where a claim potentially may become one which is within the scope of the policy the insurer's refusal to defend at the outset of the dispute is a decision it makes at its own peril. *American Contract Bridge League,* 752 F.2d at 76; *Pittsburgh Plate Glass Co.,* 752 F.2d at 76; *Pittsburgh Plate Glass Co.,* 281 F.2d at 540; *Cadwallader,* 396 Pa. at 589, 152 A.2d at 488.

Conversely, "[t]here is no principle of Pennsylvania law that the duty to defend automatically 'attaches at the outset of the litigation and cannot afterwards terminate." *Commercial Union Insurance Co.,* 789 F.2d at 218. Pennsylvania courts have held that an insurance company is under no obligation to defend when the suit against its insured is based on a cause of action excluded from the policy's coverage. *See Wilson v. Maryland Casualty Co.,* 377 Pa. 588, 594, 105 A.2d 304, 307 (1954); *Seaboard Industries, Inc. v. Monaco,* 258 Pa.Super. 170, 179, 392 A.2d 738, 743 (1978). "However, if coverage (indemnification) depends upon the existence or nonexistence of facts outside of the complaint that have yet to be determined, the insurer must provide a defense until such time as the facts are determined, and the claim is narrowed to one patently outside of coverage." *C. Raymond Davis & Sons, Inc. v. Liberty Mutual Insurance Co.,* 467 F.Supp. 17, 19 (E.D.Pa. 1979).

In *Aetna Life and Casualty Co. v. McCabe,* 556 F.Supp. 1342, 1354 (E.D.Pa.1983), the court stated "that 'a liability insurer, by assuming the defense of an action against the insured, is thereafter estopped to claim that the loss resulting to the insured from an adverse judgment [or settlement] in such action is not within the coverage of the policy, or to assert against the insured some other defense existing at the time of the accident.'" *Id.* (quoting Annot., 38 A.L.R.2d 1148, 1150 (1954)). *See Jones v. Robbins,* 258 F.Supp. 585, 588 (E.D.Pa.1966), *aff'd,* 374 F.2d 1002 (3d Cir.1967); *Perkoski v. Wilson,* 371 Pa. 553, 92 A.2d 189 (1952).

When the insurance company believes a claim is not covered, it may protect itself by a timely reservation of rights under the policy which fairly informs the insured of its position. *Aetna Life and Casualty Co. v. McCabe,* 556 F.Supp. at 1354–55. Insurers who contemplate refusing to indemnify a claim must inform their insureds so as to allow them to protect their interests and avoid detrimental reliance on indemnity. *Nichols v. American Casualty Co.,* 423 Pa. 480, 225 A.2d 80 (1966). If an insurer undertakes to defend a claim under a reservation of rights it is not precluded from denying coverage. *Brugnoli v. United National Insurance Co.,* 284 Pa.Super. 511, 426 A.2d 164 (1981). Under Pennsylvania law, "reservation of rights" letters do not require the assent of the insured and are given the same effect as a nonwaiver agreement. *See Draft Systems, Inc. v. Alspach,* 756 F.2d 293, 296 (3d Cir.1985) for a cogent review of the feasibility and utilization of nonwaiver agreements and reservation of rights letters.

It is hornbook law that if an insurer assumes the insured's defense without sending the insured a reservation of rights letter or bringing a declaratory relief action, the insurer will later be precluded from denying coverage. *See generally,* 7C Appleman, at §§ 4689, 4694. Moreover, in *Alspach,* the court stated that if the insurer affords representation without some understanding with its insured, the carrier may later be estopped from asserting an otherwise valid coverage defense. *Id.* at 296.

We now apply the above principles of law to the facts before us.

The Trumbull complaint, while not as specific in its allegations of damages as it might have been, contained sufficient information to put Travelers on notice that a claim of property damage, potentially covered by its policy, was being raised against Beckwith, its insured. As noted previously, the parties stipulated that the Trumbull complaint stated claims that were potentially within the scope of coverage, and this is buttressed by the internal memoranda of Travelers' personnel plus the Hill Report. Obviously, Travelers had a duty to defend any potential claims that were within the scope of the policy's coverage. *Gedeon, supra; Cadwallader, supra; Zeitz, supra.*

Alternatively, even if Travelers had a legitimate coverage defense regarding the Trumbull claims of property damage, it assumed the defense of the *Trumbull* case without reserving its rights as to indemnification. The record reveals that Travelers' denial letter of May 19, 1978, only informed Plaintiff that Trumbull's claim for punitive damages was not covered. In no way can this be construed as a denial of coverage as to the compensatory damages claims at issue here.

While some of Travelers' personnel considered filing a reservation of rights letter and/or a declaratory relief action to protect the carrier from having to indemnify Plaintiff, the record discloses that neither course of action was taken by Travelers, Beckwith's Appendix PXZ 3, 5, 6, 9, 11. Without any subsequent revelations excluding coverage and without conducting a proper investigation into the facts supporting the Trumbull claims, Travelers abruptly denied coverage on May 19, 1978, after Beckwith had relied on it for coverage for thirteen months. Based on this obdurate and contumacious conduct on the part of Travelers, we hold that it has waived and is estopped from raising any valid coverage defenses. *Aetna Life and Casualty Co. v. McCabe,* 556 F.Supp. at 1354. *See also Jones v. Robbins,* 258 F.Supp. 585 (E.D.Pa. 1966), *aff'd,* 374 F.2d 1002 (3d Cir.1967) (disclaimer of coverage more than two years after notice of claim); *New Amsterdam Casualty Co. v. Kelly,* 57 F.Supp. 209 (E.D.Pa.1944) (disclaimer of coverage nine months after notice of claim).

Here, Travelers had virtual carte blanche over the defense of the Trumbull case for a period of over two years, and Beckwith justifiably relied on Travelers for indemnification of all claims except the claim for punitive damages.

While Travelers denied coverage of the punitive damages claim, it still had a duty to defend that ancillary claim because, as we stated earlier, the duty to defend is broader than the duty to indemnify, and some of the claims for compensatory damages were potentially covered by the policy. *Gedeon, supra.* However, since the payment of punitive damages by the insurer is invalid and against public policy in Pennsylvania, *see D'Ambrosio v. Pennsylvania National Mutual Casualty Insurance Co.,* 494 Pa. 501, 431 A.2d 966 (1981), we need not address that issue further.

Because of its reliance on Travelers to defend the compensatory damages claims, Beckwith was deprived of the opportunity to itself investigate and defend the Trumbull claims. The record in the case before us reveals that Travelers failed to conduct a proper investigation or a thorough discovery, and at one point, fearful of losing Plaintiff as a "valued account," offered to reassume the defense of the Trumbull claims if Plaintiff would drop its claim that it was prejudiced by Defendant's mishandling of the Trumbull case. Beckwith's Appendix PX 10, 14.

Travelers asserted in the policy the right and duty to "defend any suit against the insured ＊ ＊ ＊ and make such investigation, negotiation and settlement ＊ ＊ ＊ as it deems expedient." An insurer who asserts such a right stands in a fiduciary relationship toward the insured and is obligated to act in good faith and with due care in representing the insured's interests. *Gray v. National Mutual Insurance Co.*, 422 Pa. 500, 223 A.2d 8 (1966). In the instant case, Travelers failed to refrain from exhibiting a greater concern for its own interests than for those of its insured.

In conclusion, we find that: 1) the Trumbull complaint stated claims that were potentially covered by the insurance policy issued by Travelers to Beckwith; 2) Travelers breached its duty to defend Beckwith in the underlying Trumbull case; 3) Travelers failed to reserve its rights to contest indemnity regarding the compensatory damage claims raised in the Trumbull case; and 4) Travelers is estopped from denying coverage because Beckwith detrimentally relied on Travelers' policy for indemnification.

Accordingly, because there are not genuine issues of material fact, we will grant Plaintiff's motion for summary judgment on Counts One, Two and Three. ＊ ＊ ＊

Damages

The law of Pennsylvania clearly recognizes that when an insurer breaches its duty to defend, the appropriate measure of damages is the cost of hiring substitute counsel and other defense costs. *American Contract Bridge League*, 752 F.2d at 76; *Gedeon*, 410 Pa. at 60, 188 A.2d at 322. Consequently, Beckwith is entitled to recover its attorneys' fees and defense costs in the Trumbull case.

In addition, we find that Beckwith is also entitled to recover the $100,000.00 it paid to settle the Trumbull claims on the theory that Travelers, by its defense of these claims for some thirteen months without any reservation of rights, was estopped to claim that the loss resulting to Beckwith (i.e., the $100,000.00 settlement payment) was not within the policy's coverage. *Aetna Life and Casualty v. McCabe*, 556 F.Supp. at 1354. By asserting in its policy the right to handle all claims against the insured, including the right to "settlement of any such suit defended by the company as it deems expedient," Travelers, by its failure to act in good faith and with due care in representing the interests of Beckwith, is liable for the $100,000.00 suit. *Gray,* 422 Pa. at 504, 223 A.2d at 9–10; *Gedeon,* 410 Pa. at 59–60, 188 A.2d at 322. *See also Oliver B. Cannon & Son v. Fidelity and Casualty Co. of New York,* 484 F.Supp. 1375, 1385–87 (D.Del.1980) (applying Pennsylvania law); Keeton, *Liability Insurance and Responsibility for Settlement,* 67 Harv.L.Rev. 1136 (1954).

Moreover, in *Pacific Indemnity Co. v. Linn,* the United States Court of Appeals for the Third Circuit affirmed the district court's rationale that where settlement renders it impossible to determine factually and with exactitude what claims were actually covered, the duty to indemnify must follow the duty to defend. *Id.* at 766. Thus, Plaintiff is entitled to recover the $100,000.00 it paid to settle the Trumbull case.

A less settled question confronts us as to whether Beckwith can recover its attorneys' fees for bringing the instant action. Traditionally, American courts have required the parties to litigation to bear their own attorneys' fees in the absence of statutory or contractual requirements. *Alyeska Pipeline Service Co. v. Wilderness Society,* 421 U.S. 240, 247, 95 S.Ct. 1612, 1616, 44 L.Ed.2d 141, 147 (1975); *Chatham Communications, Inc. v. General Press Corp.,* 463 Pa. 292, 300–01, 344 A.2d 837, 842 (1975). However, when an insurance company wrongfully, unreasonably and in bad faith refuses to provide a defense to its insured in an underlying action brought by a third party, both Pennsylvania and federal courts applying Pennsylvania law have awarded attorneys' fees and costs incurred by the insured in bringing an action to establish the duties to defend and/or indemnify. *Pacific Indemnity Co. v. Linn,* 766 F.2d at 769; *Montgomery Ward & Co. v. Pacific Indemnity Co.,* 557 F.2d 51, 59–60 (3d Cir.1977); *Kelmo Enterprises Inc. v. Commercial Union Insurance Co.,* 285 Pa.Super. 13, 24, 426 A.2d 680, 685 (1981), *impliedly overruled on other grounds, see Standard Venetian Blind Co. v. American Empire Insurance Co.,* 503 Pa. 300, 469 A.2d 563 (1983).

As the Superior Court of Pennsylvania stated in *Kelmo:* "We agree that it would be anomalous to allow an insured attorneys' fees expended in defense of the underlying tort action but to deny the fees in an action brought to vindicate the contractual duty to defend." *Id.* 285 Pa. Super. at 21, 426 A.2d at 684. In support of this result, the *Kelmo* Court stated the following section of 7C Appleman, § 4691 at 283:

> [The general rule, that a litigant is to bear his own attorneys' fees] still appears to be unfair to the insured. After all, the insurer had contracted to defend the insured, and it failed to do so. It guessed wrong as to its duty, and should be compelled to bear the consequences thereof. If the [general] rule * * * should be followed * * *, it would actually amount to permitting the insurer to do by indirection that which it could not do directly. That is, the insured has a contract right to have actions against him defended by the insurer, at its expense. If the insurer can force him into a declaratory judgment proceeding and, even though it loses in such action, compel him to

bear the expense of such litigation, the insured is actually no better off financially than if he had never had the contract right mentioned above. * * *

Id. Another commentator has stated that "[w]here the insurer has wrongfully refused to defend, it may become liable not only for attorneys' fees in the one action in which the insured is sued, but for fees in all other actions involving the insured as a result of its breach." S. Speiser, Attorneys' Fees, § 13.8 (1973) (footnotes omitted).

Defendant argues that attorneys' fees should not be awarded to Plaintiff in the instant action, which is not a declaratory action, since all of the cases relied on by Plaintiff to recover attorneys' fees in this case sought declaratory relief. We disagree and find no rational reason to draw a distinction between a declaratory action brought by insured and the present one, since both actions culminate from the insurer's breach of contract.

In addition, Travelers contends that there is no basis for a finding of bad faith to support an award of attorneys' fees since Count Four, which raised a "bad faith" action for punitive damages, was dismissed by a prior Order of this Court. We cannot agree with this contention and emphasize that Count Four did not seek attorneys' fees for the prosecution of this action; therefore its dismissal has no bearing on this matter.

In the present case, there is ample support in the factual record to substantiate a finding that Travelers' persistent refusal to defend "can only be characterized as unreasonable and lacking in the good faith required of an insurer with respect to its insured." *Pacific Indemnity Co. v. Linn*, 590 F.Supp. 643, 655 (E.D.Pa.1984), *aff'd*, 766 F.2d 754 (3d Cir.1985). Moreover, Travelers has failed to adduce any valid reasons for its vacillation and procrastination. Here, the obdurate conduct of the Defendant, as deduced from a review of the facts, illustrates a general lack of good faith dealing by Travelers, which, after all, had a fiduciary duty to protect the interests of its insured. *Gray, supra; Gedeon, supra.*

In conclusion, we hold that Beckwith is entitled to recover whatever expenses it was compelled to incur in exercising its rights, including reasonable attorneys' fees and defense costs expended in this action since they were incurred as a direct loss incident to the breach of contract. 7C Appleman, § 4691 at 283. We do not adopt this as a general principle, but believe that the ends of justice require its application under this set of facts. * * *

Notes and Questions

1. *Touchstones of the Duty.* It is hornbook law that the insurer must defend any suit whose allegations would fall within coverage if the allegations were proved to be true. See R. Jerry, Understanding Insurance Law 563–64 (1987). In addition to this "four corners of the complaint" or "pleadings" rule, it is almost equally clear that the

insurer must defend even when the complaint does not allege facts within coverage, if the insurer possesses extrinsic information that the claim probably does fall within coverage. See id; *Waste Management of Carolinas, Inc. v. Peerless Insurance Company,* 315 N.C. 688, 340 S.E.2d 374 (1986).

2. *Defense Under Reservation.* It does not follow from the duty to defend under these rules, however, that the insurer will have to indemnify the insured if the underlying suit is successful. A claim the insurer defends may turn out not to be covered. The accepted methods of assuring that by providing a defense the insurer is not later estopped to deny coverage are by presenting the insured with a *Reservation of Rights* or by requesting the insured to execute a *Non–Waiver Agreement.* Each of these documents informs the insured that the insurer's provision of a defense does not constitute waiver of the right to deny coverage later. In some jurisdictions the presentation of a unilateral Reservation of Rights is sufficient to avoid waiver or estoppel; in others, the insurer must obtain the insured's consent to continued representation, through a Non–Waiver Agreement, in order to achieve this protection. Apparently the insurer's mistake in *Beckwith* was the failure to reserve its rights immediately upon undertaking a defense, or as soon as it became aware of facts which created doubt about its coverage obligations. Does the approach the court took recommend in effect that insurers routinely present insureds with Reservations of Rights before undertaking a defense? Is that a sensible rule?

3. *Damages.* Under what theory was Travelers liable for the $100,000 Beckwith paid in settlement? Consider the following possibilities and their implications for the nature of the duty to defend:

a. Had Beckwith defended itself from the outset, it would have paid less, or nothing.

b. Had Travelers defended under a Reservation of Rights throughout the case, it would have paid less, or nothing.

c. The policy covered all the losses for which Beckwith settled.

d. Travelers' breach of the duty to defend made it impossible to determine whether the losses for which Beckwith settled were covered by the policy.

e. Requiring the insurer to indemnify the insured for all reasonable settlements by the insured after a breach of the duty to defend discourages such breaches.

4. *Terminating the Duty to Defend.* Suppose that the insurer defends a suit alleging damages that fall within coverage, but learns in the course of the defense that the claim, even if proved, would not fall within coverage. It is said to have been settled at least since Judge Learned Hand's decision in *Lee v. Aetna Casualty & Surety Company,* 178 F.2d 750 (2d Cir.1949), that the insurer may then withdraw. See, e.g., B. Ostrager and T. Newman, Handbook on Insurance Coverage Disputes 111 (1988). In *Lee,* Hand wrote as follows:

> [I]f the plaintiff's complaint against the insured alleged facts which would have supported a recovery covered by the policy, it was the duty of the defendant to undertake the defence, until it could confine the claim to a recovery that the policy did not cover.

178 F.2d at 753. Does this rule accord with the concerns the *Beckwith* court expressed regarding detrimental reliance by the insured on the insurer's provision of a defense?

A second situation in which the duty to defend may terminate arises after the insurer has paid or offered to pay the full limits of its liability. Whether the duty terminated under such circumstances was a perennial issue until revision of standard liability policies in 1966. In that year a provision that the duty ceased once the limits of liability have been exhausted by payment of a judgment or by settlement was added to standard policies. Thus, the insurer can no longer attempt to escape the duty to defend merely by "tendering" its policy limits; the duty persists until that tender is accepted. When policy provisions provide specifically for termination of the duty to defend, however, they are likely to be enforced. For example, in *Zurich Insurance Company v. Northbrook Excess and Surplus Insurance Company,* 145 Ill.App.3d 175, 98 Ill.Dec. 512, 494 N.E.2d 634 (1986), a pre–1966 policy provided that the undertakings in the Insuring Agreement were "subject to the limits of liability, exclusions, conditions and other terms of this policy." The court held that this phrase rendered the duty to defend subject to the policy's indemnity limits.

An alternative is to provide for an aggregate limit of liability which includes some or all of the costs of defense. A few CGL policies issued after 1986 adopt this "defense within limits" approach. As defense costs are incurred, the policy limits are reduced. When the Insurance Services Office proposed making "defense within limits" a standard CGL provision, it was met with strong regulatory opposition. As an Insurance Commissioner, what kinds of consumer protection concerns would you have in deciding whether to approve such a provision? For discussion of these concerns, see American Bar Association, Report of the Commission to Improve the Liability Insurance System 155–63 (1989).

5. *A Duty to Appeal?* Although the insurer is not automatically obliged to appeal adverse judgments against the insured, a number of courts hold that such an obligation may exist under certain circumstances. What should those circumstances be? See, e.g., *Guarantee Abstract & Title Company, Inc. v. Interstate Fire and Casualty Company, Inc.,* 228 Kan. 532, 618 P.2d 1195 (1980) (good-faith test applied); *Chrestman v. United States Fidelity & Guaranty Company,* 511 F.2d 129 (5th Cir.1975) (duty to appeal where reasonable grounds for doing so exist).

2. Resolving Conflicts of Interest Over Defense

BURD v. SUSSEX MUTUAL INSURANCE COMPANY

Supreme Court of New Jersey, 1970.
56 N.J. 383, 267 A.2d 7.

WEINTRAUB, C.J.

The defendant carrier issued a Home Owner's Policy to plaintiff, Burd, providing him with "Comprehensive Personal Liability Coverage." The ultimate issue is whether the policy covers the liability incurred by Burd when he inflicted shotgun wounds upon August D'Agostino.

The shooting incident led to the conviction of Burd for atrocious assault and battery. Thereafter D'Agostino sued Burd for damages. His complaint contained two counts. The first count charged that Burd "did maliciously and intentionally fire a loaded gun at the plaintiff" and as a proximate result "of said negligence," D'Agostino was injured. The second count charged that Burd "did negligently fire a loaded gun at the plaintiff." Burd called upon the carrier to defend the suit but the carrier refused on the ground that the policy expressly excluded coverage of "bodily injury or property damage caused intentionally by or at the direction of the Insured." Burd defended through his own counsel. There was a general verdict for D'Agostino in the sum of $8,500.

Burd then brought the present action against the carrier to recover the amount of D'Agostino's judgment and also the costs incurred in defending that action. D'Agostino was named a party defendant but no relief was sought against him, and he is not a party to the present appeal. Burd and the carrier both moved for summary judgment. Burd prevailed. We certified the carrier's appeal before argument in the Appellate Division.

Burd and the carrier each contended the other was bound by the judgment in a prior proceeding. The carrier urged that Burd was bound by the finding in the criminal case that he intentionally wounded D'Agostino, while Burd contended the carrier had to defend the civil action, and having refused to do so, may not challenge the allegation therein that the injuries were "negligently" inflicted. The trial court held the carrier was thus precluded, and hence did not reach the question whether, if the carrier were free to dispute coverage, Burd would be foreclosed by the criminal conviction from questioning the carrier's position that D'Agostino was intentionally injured within the meaning of the policy exclusion from coverage.

I.

The judgment against the carrier rests upon the premise that the carrier was obligated to defend the suit D'Agostino brought against the insured because the second count of the complaint alleged only "negligence" and thus on its face was beyond the clause excluding coverage for intentional injury. Hence, the insured argues, the carrier, having foregone the opportunity to defend, is estopped to assert the injuries were intentionally caused.

The policy reads:

> LIABILITY: To pay on behalf of the Insured all sums which the Insured shall become legally obligated to pay as damages because of bodily injury or property damage, and the company shall defend any suit against the Insured alleging such bodily injury or property damage and seeking damages which are payable under the terms of this policy, even if any of the allegations of the suit are groundless, false or fraudulent; but the company may make such investigation and settlement of any claim or suit as it deems expedient.

As already stated, the policy provided, under "Special Exclusions," that this coverage did not apply "to bodily injury or property damage caused intentionally by or at the direction of the insured."

The insured says the carrier is obligated to defend an action whenever the complaint alleges a basis of liability within the covenant to pay. That is the general approach. *Ohio Casualty Ins. Co. v. Flanagin,* 44 N.J. 504, 514, 210 A.2d 221 (1965); *Danek v. Hommer,* 28 N.J.Super. 68, 77, 100 A.2d 198 (App.Div.1953), aff'd o.b., 15 N.J. 573, 105 A.2d 677 (1954). But when coverage, *i.e.,* the duty to pay, depends upon a factual issue which will not be resolved by the trial of the third party's suit against the insured, the duty to defend may depend upon the actual facts and not upon the allegations in the complaint. So, for example, if a policy covered a Ford but not a Chevrolet also owned by the insured, the carrier would not be obligated to defend a third party's complaint against the insured which alleged the automobile involved was the Ford when in fact the car involved was the Chevrolet. The identity of the car, upon which coverage depends, would be irrelevant to the trial of the negligence action.

The sense of the covenant is to defend suits involving claims which the carrier would have to pay if the claimant prevailed in the action. The covenant to defend is thus identified with the covenant to pay. That is the basis of the rule that ordinarily a carrier who defends unsuccessfully may not later deny coverage, absent an express agreement with the insured reserving a right to deny coverage. *Merchants Indemnity Corp. v. Eggleston,* 37 N.J. 114, 127, 179 A.2d 505 (1962). The obligation to defend "groundless, false or fraudulent" claims does not mean that the carrier will defend claims which would be beyond the covenant to pay if the claimant prevailed. It means only that a carrier may not refuse to defend a suit on the ground that the claim asserted against the insured cannot possibly succeed because either in law or in fact there is no basis for a plaintiff's judgment. So in *Danek v. Hommer, supra,* 28 N.J.Super. 68, 100 A.2d 198, it was held that where a *per quod* action brought by the husband of an injured employee against the employer would be covered by the policy if the husband prevailed, the carrier could not refuse to defend merely because it believed, and correctly, that the husband's claim had no foundation in law. In short, the carrier's promise is to defeat or to pay a claim within the policy coverage. As the court said in *Danek,* 28 N.J.Super. at 80, 100 A.2d 198 at 205, "The stipulation for defense of actions, even if groundless, would be of little value if that obligation did not arise when a claim is stated in the pleadings, which, if sustained, would be within the protection afforded by the policy."

Here the obligation to pay a judgment obtained by the injured party depended upon whether the injuries were intentionally inflicted within the meaning of the exclusionary clause. There may be cases in which the interests of the carrier and the insured coincide so that the carrier can defend such an action with complete devotion to the insured's interest. But if the trial will leave the question of coverage unresolved so that the insured may later be called upon to pay, or if the case may be so defended by a carrier as to prejudice the insured thereafter upon the issue of coverage, the carrier should not be permitted to control the defense. That was the situation in the case at hand. Although both the insurer and the insured would want D'Agostino to fail, yet if D'Agostino should succeed, as it was likely he would, the insured would want the basis to be negligence whereas the carrier would profit if the basis was an intentional injury within the policy exclusion. If plaintiff pressed his claim of negligence, the coverage issue would remain open, for the carrier could hardly insist the injuries were intentionally inflicted. Willfulness is not a defense to a charge of negligence. And if plaintiff sought a judgment for intentional hurt, the carrier could not be expected to resist that basis of liability with the fervor or fidelity of an advocate selected by the insured.

In such circumstances the carrier should not be estopped from disputing coverage because it refused to defend. On the contrary the carrier should not be permitted to assume the defense if it intends to dispute its obligation to pay a plaintiff's judgment, unless of course the insured expressly agrees to that reservation. This is not to free the carrier from its covenant to defend, but rather to translate its obligation into one to reimburse the insured if it is later adjudged that the claim was one within the policy covenant to pay. See *Satterwhite v. Stolz,* 79 N.M. 320, 442 P.2d 810 (Ct.App.1968).

We think the case comes within *Williams v. Bituminous Casualty Corp.,* 51 N.J. 146, 238 A.2d 177 (1968). There a workmen's compensation petition alleged the accident occurred on a date which was within the period of the policy coverage. The carrier refused to defend because it contended the accident occurred on another day, outside the period of coverage. After the employee obtained an award, the insured sued the carrier. The carrier did not dispute its insured's liability to the third-party claimant as established in the compensation proceeding, but insisted that the liability so established was beyond its coverage notwithstanding that the award in favor of the employee found the accident occurred on a date within the period of policy coverage. In holding the carrier was not precluded by the award, we said, 51 N.J. at 149, 238 A.2d 177, at 179:

> Thus the coverage question does not depend upon an issue material to the litigation between the employee and the employer. The resolution of the employee's claim against the employer would not have settled the coverage problem. More than that, if the Division of Workmen's Compensation somehow accepted the issue in the trial of the employee's claim against the employer, the carrier could not have asserted its position in the employer's name, for a carrier may not so defend an insured as to leave him liable and uncovered. An attorney, engaged by the carrier to defend in the insured's name, could not ethically seek such a result. See *Szabo v. Standard Commercial Body Corp.*, 221 App.Div. 722, 225 N.Y.S. 332 (3d Dept.1927). That would have been the case here since, if the carrier succeeded in its position that the critical date was the 6th, the employer would have been left with an uninsured compensation liability.

> A carrier's contractual right to defend presupposes that if the defense fails, the carrier will pay. *Merchants Indemnity Corp. v. Eggleston*, 37 N.J. 114, 127, 179 A.2d 505 (1962). Hence it is settled that a carrier is estopped to deny coverage of an action it undertakes to defend. This being so, it would be arbitrary to say also that a carrier which declines to incur an estoppel by defending is equally barred from a hearing as to coverage because of a finding made in the suit it could not safely defend. Elementary fairness demands a proceeding in which the differences between the insurer and the insured may be tried. Ideally the injured claimant should be there as well, so that he may also be heard and concluded upon the issue of the carrier's liability.

Whenever the carrier's position so diverges from the insured's that the carrier cannot defend the action with complete fidelity to the insured, there must be a proceeding in which the carrier and the insured, represented by counsel of their choice, may fight out their differences. That action may, as here, follow the trial of the third party's suit against the insured. Or, unless for special reasons it would be unfair to do so, a declaratory judgment proceeding may be brought in advance of that trial by the carrier or the insured, to the end that the third-party suit may be defended by the party ultimately liable. *Ohio Casualty Insurance Co. v. Flanagin, supra,* 44 N.J. at 511–513, 210 A.2d 221.

In this connection, the insured urges the carrier should be required to seek a declaration of its duty before the trial of the injured party's suit against the insured. But that proposition could lead to unnecessary litigation, for it would compel a lawsuit whenever coverage is denied even though the insured may silently agree with the carrier's position. We think the better course is to leave it to the contenders to decide for themselves if and when to sue. See *Condenser Service & Engineering Co., Inc. v. American Mutual Liability Ins. Co.*, 45 N.J.Super. 31, 131 A.2d 409 (App.Div.1957).

The insured cites *Gray v. Zurich Ins. Co.*, 65 Cal.2d 263, 54 Cal. Rptr. 104, 419 P.2d 168 (1966), which the trial court apparently followed. *Gray* also involved a charge of intentional injury. There the insured claimed self-defense but the carrier refused to defend because the policy excluded intentional injuries from coverage. The insured defended the case, unsuccessfully. He thereupon sued for both the amount of the judgment against him and the cost of defense.

The California court held, as one ground for its decision, that the carrier was obligated to defend because under modern pleading an allegation of intentional wrong carries inherently the "potential" of a recovery upon the lesser thesis of a negligent injury. Hence, the court held, the charge on its face came within the policy coverage notwithstanding that ultimately it might be found the injury was intentionally inflicted within the meaning of the express exclusion from coverage. Thus, under *Gray* the carrier must defend every such complaint, whether it be in terms of negligence or of an intentional injury, notwithstanding that in truth the claim, and a plaintiff's judgment thereon, will be beyond the covenant to pay.

The carrier in *Gray* argued that it could not properly have defended the insured since their interests were irreconcilable. The court resolved that problem by holding that in a later action between the carrier and the insured, neither the carrier nor the insured would be bound by the findings in the action against the insured. On that basis the court concluded the carrier could safely have sought the most favorable result for its insured even though its own interests ran the other way, provided, however, that the carrier had properly reserved its right to dispute coverage. On that approach, of course, the carrier was liable for the cost of defense, whatever the outcome of the coverage issue. The court went further, and held that although the carrier could have litigated the issue of coverage in the policy suit (provided it had defended under a reservation of rights), it could not do so because it breached the covenant to defend and therefore must pay also the amount of the judgment against the insured. The approach taken by *Gray* of course differs basically from the approach adopted by our decisions already cited.

It is not clear whether the thesis of *Gray* would be applied by the California court to all coverage problems or whether it is confined to one involving an exclusion of intentional injury. The exclusion of intentional injury is somewhat unique with respect to the problem of coverage. The usual coverage issue depends upon status, time, place, identity of the instrumentality, and the like. But in the case of the exclusion of intentional injuries, the injuries, which otherwise are within the coverage, are excepted therefrom because of a state of mind, and indeed a state of mind which the injured claimant may but need not allege or prove, to prevail against the insured. Since a claimant who charges intentional injury may thus recover even though the intent to injure is not proved, his complaint, on its face, is simultaneously within both the basic covenant to pay and the intentional-injury exclusion from that coverage.

This being so, it follows that if an action charging intentional injury is wholly defeated, the insured can well argue the claim thus found to be "groundless, false or fraudulent" was for bodily injury or property damage within the covenant to pay and did not cease to be such a claim merely because the claimant added the further "groundless, false or fraudulent" allegation of an intent to injure. In that situation the carrier may fairly be required to reimburse the insured for the cost of the successful defense even though the carrier would not have had to pay the judgment if the case had gone against the insured on a finding of intentional injury. * * *

A judgment in favor of the injured party is the eventuality which presents the difficult problem as to whether the carrier should be precluded because it refused to defend a suit it believed to be within the intentional-injury exclusion. But we see no significant difference between that problem and the problem in *Williams v. Bituminous Casualty Corp., supra.* The carrier's obligation to pay will probably not be resolved by a factual determination in the action brought by the injured claimant against the insured, and if perchance that factual determination is made in that suit against the insured, he will not have been represented by counsel of his own choice upon that critical question. And if the coverage issue is not thus decided in the tort action, or if a finding upon it is held not to be binding in the later litigation over coverage, still the carrier's control over preparation and trial of the tort action may well cast the die against the insured. Hence we prefer to apply the approach of *Williams, i.e.,* that if a carrier defends an action in the face of a coverage issue, the carrier must pay the judgment (unless the insured expressly agreed to a reservation of that issue), and if the carrier does not defend the tort claim because a plaintiff's verdict will not resolve the coverage problem in the insured's favor or because the carrier cannot defend with complete fidelity to the insured's sole interest, then the carrier may be heard upon the coverage issue in a proceeding upon the policy. And of course if the carrier does not defend, it will have to reimburse the insured for the cost of defense if the tort judgment is held to be within the covenant to pay. * * *

The carrier in the case before us was therefore entitled to try the issue whether in truth the injuries inflicted upon D'Agostino were within the exclusion and hence beyond the policy coverage. The summary judgment against the carrier must be reversed. * * *

Notes and Questions

1. *Sources of Conflict.* The court in *Burd* seemed to think that the conflict of interest between the insurer and the insured had to do with the possibility that a finding of liability in the tort suit against Burd could have an affect on the question whether he was covered for such liability by the Sussex Mutual policy. The court in *Gray v. Zurich Mutual,* cited by the court, solved that problem by holding that there could be no such collateral estoppel effect. If Burd had so held, would any conflict of interest have remained?

For example, suppose that during the course of trial preparation, the insured admitted to counsel supplied by the insurer that he had intended to injure the plaintiff. Could this admission be used directly against the insured in the later suit to determine whether he was covered? If not, could knowledge of this admission nonetheless lead an insurer considering whether to deny coverage to investigate its possible defenses against a claim of coverage more carefully than it might in the absence of such knowledge? Would an insured being defended by counsel selected by the insurer be more reluctant to be candid under such circumstances than with counsel independently obtained? Similarly, would an insurer defending under circumstances where it doubted its ultimate duty to indemnify be inclined to defend less vigorously, and therefore to risk incurring a larger judgment—for all of which the insured might later turn out to be liable? Which of these possibilities creates a conflict for the insurer, which creates a conflict for the attorney the insurer retains to represent the insured, and which creates a conflict for both? For discussion of whether conflicts created for the attorney can be adequately handled by the Code of Professional Responsibility, see *Parsons v. Continental National American Group,* which follows these Notes.

2. *Rhetoric versus Reality.* How realistic an option did *Burd* create for most insureds? The insured who is presented with a proposed Reservation of Rights (in effect, a Non–Waiver Agreement) may reject it, select his own attorney, and upon later proof that his policy provided coverage, be reimbursed for his costs of defense. If he is unsuccessful in proving that he was covered or was entitled to a defense, however, he bears these costs himself. On the other hand, if he accepts a defense subject to the insurer's proposed reservation, he avoids the costs of defense even if it later turns out that the policy does not provide coverage. Few insureds will be in a position to take the risks entailed in rejecting a defense provided by the insurer. In light of this fact of life, how far does *Burd* go in eliminating conflicts?

3. *When Should the Coverage Issue Be Resolved?* The conflict of interest in cases such as *Burd* disappears once the coverage issue is resolved. Either there is coverage, in which case there is no conflict, or there is no coverage, in which case there is no defense. Under *Burd,* however, the issue apparently is not resolved until after the underlying

tort action against the insured is completed. In contrast, under the approach in *Gray,* the insurer must always defend if there is a chance that there might be coverage, or it loses the right to deny coverage later. The insured thus sometimes obtains a defense even when it turns out (later) that the claim against him did not fall within coverage. The opinion in *Burd* seems to reject this approach, thus holding that the insurer may refuse to defend with impunity—reimbursing the insured the costs of defense only upon later proof that there was coverage.

In such situations, should there be a firm rule about when to resolve the underlying coverage dispute, or should the sequencing be left to the parties? A declaratory judgment action at the outset would resolve the issue, and thereby also determine whether the insurer has a duty to defend. But such an action would be unnecessary if the insured or the insurer later defeated the tort action against the insured, and the insured (in the meantime) would have incurred the cost of litigating the declaratory judgment action. Should the rule that the insurer is not liable for the costs incurred by the insured (including counsel fees) in proving that there is coverage be reversed in order to encourage resolution of the coverage question? Conversely, determination of the underlying coverage question could await resolution of the tort action against the insured. Such an approach would avoid unnecessary expenditures in declaratory judgment actions preceding tort suits, but would preserve the conflict of interest problems addressed by the rules in *Burd* and *Gray.* Is there reason to think that one approach will be systematically preferable to the other?

THE *CUMIS* CONTROVERSY.

Gray is not the last word in California, which has tended to be a lodestar in these matters. In *San Diego Navy Federal Credit Union v. Cumis Insurance Society, Inc.,* 162 Cal.App.3d 358, 208 Cal.Rptr. 494 (1984), an intermediate appellate court held that the *Gray* rule does not afford the insured sufficient protection when there are potential conflicts of interest between the insurer and the insured. The court first approved the trial court's statement of the problem:

> The reasoning of *Gray,* "[s]ince * * * the court in the third party suit does not adjudicate the issue of coverage the insurer's argument (as to a conflict of interest) collapses," just does not stand scrutiny. What the defense attorney in the third party case does impacts the coverage case, in that, the questions of coverage depends [sic] on the development of facts in the third party case and their proper development is left to the attorney paid for by the Carrier. *Gray* recognized that a finding in the third party action would effect the issues of coverage in a subsequent case but analyzed the question from the point of view of the carrier. *Gray* recognized a possible conflict from the point of view of the insured in footnote 18,

where it stated: "In rare cases the issue of punitive damages or a special verdict might present a conflict of interest, but such possibility does not outweigh the advantages of the general rule. Even in such cases, however, the insurer will still be bound ethically and legally, to litigate in the interests of the insured." * * *

The court then explained:

The Carrier is required to hire independent counsel because an attorney in actual trial would be tempted to develop the facts to help his real client, the Carrier Company, as opposed to the Insured, for whom he will never likely work again. In such a case as this, the Insured is placed in an impossible position; on the one hand the Carrier says it will happily defend him and on the other it says it may dispute paying any judgment, but trust us. The dictum in *Gray* flies in the face of the reality of insurance defense work. Insurance companies hire relatively few lawyers and concentrate their business. A lawyer who does not look out for the Carrier's best interest might soon find himself out of work.

The court in *Cumis* therefore held that unless the insured in a situation of potential conflict gives his informed consent to being represented by counsel selected by the insurer, he has a right to select independent counsel himself, to be paid by the insurer. Does *Cumis* simply recognize that *Burd*, not *Gray*, had the correct view of the conflict problem, but that the remedy prescribed by *Burd* was insufficient to give the insured realistic protection against conflicts? *Cumis* gives the insured the money to pay for independent counsel plus a free defense of certain claims that turn out later not to be covered under the policy, both of which are lacking under *Burd*. Could it be argued that providing only the former, but not the latter, would be the appropriate solution? Is there any way to achieve this?

In 1987, the California legislature responded with a limitation on but substantial acceptance of *Cumis*. The California Civil Code, § 2860 now provides as follows:

OBLIGATION TO DEFEND ACTION

§ **2860.** (a) If the provisions of a policy of insurance impose a duty to defend upon an insurer and a conflict of interest arises which creates a duty on the part of the insurer to provide independent counsel to the insured, the insurer shall provide such counsel to represent the insured unless, at the time the insured is informed that a possible conflict may arise or does exist, the insured expressly waives, in writing, the right to such counsel. An insurance contract may contain a provision which sets forth the method of selecting such counsel consistent with this section.

(b) For purposes of this section, a conflict of interest does not exist as to allegations or facts in the litigation for which the insurer denies coverage; however, when an insurer reserves its rights on a given issue and the outcome of that coverage issue can be controlled by counsel first retained by the insurer for the defense of the claim, a conflict of interest may exist. No conflict of interest shall be deemed to exist as to allegations of punitive damages or be deemed to exist solely because an insured is sued for an amount in excess of the insurance policy limits.

(c) When the insured has selected independent counsel to represent him or her, the insurer may exercise its right to require that the counsel selected by the insured possess certain minimum qualifications which may include that the selected counsel have (1) at least five years of tort litigation practice which includes substantial defense experience in the subject at issue in the litigation, and (2) errors and omissions coverage. The insurer's obligation to pay fees to such independent counsel selected by the insured is limited to the rates which are actually paid by the insurer to attorneys retained by it in the ordinary course of business in the defense of similar actions in the community course of business in the defense of similar actions in the community where the claim arose or is being defended. The provisions of this subdivision shall not invalidate other different or additional policy provisions pertaining to attorney's fees or providing for methods of settlement of disputes concerning those fees. Any dispute concerning attorney's fees not resolved by these methods shall be resolved by final and binding arbitration by a single neutral arbitrator selected by the parties to the dispute.

(d) When independent counsel has been selected by the insured, it shall be the duty of such counsel and the insured to disclose to the insurer all information concerning the action except privileged materials relevant to coverage disputes, and timely to inform and consult with the insurer on all matters relating to the action. Any claim of privilege asserted is subject to in camera review in the appropriate law and motion department of the superior court. Any information disclosed by the insured or by independent counsel is not a waiver of the privilege as to any other party.

(e) The insured may waive its right to select independent counsel by signing the following statement:

"I have been advised and informed of my right to select independent counsel to represent me in this lawsuit. I have considered this matter fully and freely waive my right to select independent counsel at this time. I authorize my insurer to select a defense attorney to represent me in this lawsuit."

(f) Where the insured selects independent counsel pursuant to the provisions of this section, both the counsel provided by the insurer and independent counsel selected by the insured shall be allowed to participate in all aspects of the litigation. Counsel shall cooperate fully in the exchange of information that is consistent with each counsel's ethical and legal obligation to the insured. Nothing in this section shall relieve the insured of his or her duty to cooperate with the insurer under the terms of the insurance contract.

As an Insurance Commissioner in another state, what factors would you take into account in responding to a consumer organization's demand that all liability insurance policies issued in your state contain provisions adopting in substance the terms of California Civil Code § 2860?

PARSONS v. CONTINENTAL NATIONAL AMERICAN GROUP

Supreme Court of Arizona, En Banc, 1976.
113 Ariz. 223, 550 P.2d 94.

GORDON, Justice:

Appellants Ruth, Dawn and Gail Parsons obtained a judgment against appellant Michael Smithey, and then had issued and served a writ of garnishment on appellee, Continental National American Group (hereinafter referred to as CNA). The Superior Court of Pima County entered judgment in favor of the garnishee, CNA and from this judgment appellants appealed. The Court of Appeals, Division Two, reversed the judgment of the Superior Court, 23 Ariz.App. 597, 535 P.2d 17 (1975). Opinion of the Court of Appeals vacated and judgment of the Superior Court of Pima County reversed, and it is ordered that the judgment be entered in favor of appellants in the sum of $50,000.

We accepted this petition for review because of the importance of the question presented. We are asked to determine whether an insurance carrier in a garnishment action is estopped from denying coverage under its policy when its defense in that action is based upon confidential information obtained by the carrier's attorney from an insured as a result of representing him in the original tort action.

Appellant, Michael Smithey, age 14, brutally assaulted his neighbors, appellants Ruth, Dawn and Gail Parsons, on the night of March 26, 1967.

During April, 1967, Frank Candelaria, CNA claims representative, began an investigation of the incident. On June 6, 1967, he wrote to Howard Watt, the private counsel retained by the Smitheys, advising him that CNA was "now in the final stages of our investigation," and to contact the Parsons' attorney to ascertain what type of settlement they would accept. Watt did contact the Parsons' attorney and requested that a formal demand settlement be tendered and the medical bills be forwarded to Candelaria. On August 11, 1967, Candelaria wrote a detailed letter to his company on his investigation of Michael's background in regards to his school experiences. He concluded the letter with the following:

"In view of this information gathered and in discussion with the boy's father's attorney, Mr. Howard Watts, and with the boy's parents, I am reasonably convinced that the boy was not in control of his senses at the time of this incident.

"It is, therefore, my suggestion that, and unless instructed otherwise, I will proceed to commence settlement negotiations with the claimant's attorney so that this matter may be disposed of as soon as possible."

Prior to the following dates: August 15, 1967, August 28, 1967, and October 23, 1967, Candelaria tried to settle with the Parsons for the medical expenses and was unsuccessful.

On October 13, 1967, the Parsons filed a complaint alleging that Michael Smithey assaulted the Parsons and that Michael's parents were negligent in their failure to restrain Michael and obtain the necessary medical and psychological attention for him. At the time that the Parsons filed suit they tendered a demand settlement offer of $22,500 which was refused by CNA as "completely unrealistic."

CNA's retained counsel undertook the Smithey's defense and also continued to communicate with CNA and advised him on November 10, 1967:

"I have secured a rather complete and confidential file on the minor insured who is now in the Paso Robles School for Boys, a maximum-security institution with facilities for psychiatric treatment, and he will be kept there indefinitely and certainly for at least six months * * *.

"The above referred-to confidential file shows that the boy is fully aware of his acts and that he knew what he was doing was wrong. It follows, therefore, that the assaults he committed on claimants can only be a deliberate act on his part."

After CNA had been so advised they sent a reservation of rights letter to the Smitheys stating that the insurance company, as a courtesy to the insureds, would investigate and defend the Parsons' claim, but would do so without waiving any of the rights under the policy. The letter further stated that it was possible the act involved might be found to be an intentional act, and that the policy specifically excludes liability for bodily injury caused by an intentional act. This letter was addressed only to the parents and not to Michael.

In preparing for trial the CNA attorney retained to undertake the defense of the Smitheys interviewed Michael and received a narrative statement from him in regards to the events of March 26, 1967, and then wrote to CNA: "His own story makes it obvious that his acts were willful and criminal."

CNA also requested an evaluation of the tort case and the same attorney advised CNA: "Assuming liability and coverage, the injury is worth the full amount of the policy or $25,000.00."

On the issue of liability the trial court directed a verdict for Michael's parents on the grounds that there was no evidence of the parents being negligent. This Court affirmed, *Parsons v. Smithey,* 109 Ariz. 49, 504 P.2d 1271 (1973). On the question of Michael's liability the trial court granted plaintiff's motion for a directed verdict after the defense presented no evidence and there was no opposition to the motion. Judgment was entered against Michael in the amount of $50,000.

The Parsons then garnished CNA, and moved for a guardian ad litem to be appointed for Michael which was granted by the trial court. On November 23, 1970, appellee Parsons offered to settle with CNA in the amount of its policy limits, $25,000. This offer was not accepted.

CNA successfully defended the garnishment action by claiming that the intentional act exclusion applied. The same law firm and attorney that had previously represented Michael represented the carrier in the garnishment action.

Appellants contend that CNA should be estopped to deny coverage and have waived the intentional act exclusion because the company took advantage of the fiduciary relationship between its agent (the attorney) and Michael Smithey. We agree.

The attorneys, retained by CNA, represented Michael Smithey at the personal liability trial and, as a result, obtained privileged and confidential information from Michael's confidential file at the Paso Robles School for Boys, during the discovery process and, more importantly, from the attorney-client relationship. Both the A.B.A. Committee on Ethics and Professional Responsibility and the State Bar of Arizona, Committee on Rules of Professional Conduct have held that an attorney that represented the insured at the request of the insurer owes undivided fidelity to the insured, and, therefore, may not reveal any information or conclusions derived therefrom to the insurer that may be detrimental to the insured in any subsequent action. The A.B.A. Committee on Ethics and Professional Responsibility in Informal Opinion Number 949 stated:

> "If the firm does represent the insured in the personal injury action, to subsequently reveal to the insurer any information received from the insured for possible use by the insurer in defense of a garnishment proceeding by the injured person, would be a clear violation of both Canon 6 and Canon 37 regarding confidences of a client. A successful defense of the garnishment proceeding by the insurer would be contrary to the interests of the insured, because if the insurer is not obligated to pay the judgment, execution against the insured can be expected. The result would not be different in practical

effect from a suit directly against the insured to escape liability under the policy.

"If the firm does not defend the insured in the personal injury action, the firm cannot reasonably expect the attorney who does represent the insured to furnish either to the firm or to the insurer, for use in a garnishment action by the injured person against the insurer, information that attorney learns during the course of defending the insured, since that attorney should not be expected to breach his professional obligations by furnishing information Canons 6 and 37 prohibit him from furnishing." August 8, 1966.

The Arizona Ethics Opinion No. 261 adopted November 15, 1968 stated:

"A.B.A. Informal Opinion C728 makes it very clear that the inquiring attorney is the attorney for the insured, B, even though the attorney would be paid by G Insurance Company. The undivided fidelity owed by the attorney, then, is to B and not to G Insurance Company.

" * * * it was unethical for the inquiring attorney to represent the insurance company in an action against the insured, after judgment against the insured, to declare that the policy did not provide coverage. A full reading of that opinion and in particular the last paragraph thereof, lead us to this conclusion. That opinion ended as follows:

'Is it now ethical for you to represent the company in an action against the insured to declare that the policy does not cover? We believe that to do so without full disclosure and full consent on the part of the insured would be a violation of Canon 6. Your connection with the case on behalf of the insured no doubt has resulted in the development of confidences of a nature that should in good conscience require you to decline representation of the company in a case so intimately tied to your original litigation. This is particularly true when one of the ideas involved is not only to be fair but to give all appearances of fairness.' * * *."

The State Bar Committee in its Arizona Ethics Opinion No. 282 adopted May 21, 1969 stated:

"No better statement of the basis for our position on this question occurs to us than the following quotation from the Blakslee article cited above (55 A.B.A.Jour. at p. 263):

'Although the opinions of the Committee state that the lawyer represents both the insurer and insured, *it is clear that his highest duty is to the insured and that the lawyer cannot be used as an agent of the company to supply information detrimental to the insured.* The lawyer is a professional retained pursuant to the terms of a contract between the insurer and insured. The company has a right to expect that the issue of liability for injury and damages will be effectively and forcefully presented by the lawyer it has chosen. It has agreed, by its contract, to pay damages once they are determined.

'The client, on the other hand, in order to obtain an insurance policy, has given up the right to direct the incidents of the trial by agreeing that the company shall have the right to choose the attorney. This also is fair since it is the company that will ultimately pay the judgment. *But counsel should not be expected to communicate information received in confidence or to betray confidences lodged in them by trusting clients.* To do so would not only destroy public confidence in the legal profession, but also would make defense attorneys investigators for carriers. That the company has not satisfied itself concerning coverage by its other, independent methods, is no compelling reason why defense counsel should be asked to betray the trust reposed in him by the insured. The fact that the company may be required to pay a monetary judgment does not alter the situation, since the company voluntarily has assumed this contractual obligation by virtue of its existence as an insurer. Its contractual obligation, voluntarily assumed, should not be permitted to be used as the basis for converting the defense counsel into something beyond a lawyer defending a client." (Emphasis supplied.)

The attorney who represents an insured owed him "undeviating and single allegiance" whether the attorney is compensated by the insurer or the insured. *Newcomb v. Meiss,* 263 Minn. 315, 116 N.W.2d 593 (1962).

The attorney in the instant case should have notified CNA that he could no longer represent them when he obtained any information (as a result of his attorney-client relationship with Michael) that could possibly be detrimental to Michael's interests under the coverage of the policy.

The attorney representing Michael Smithey in the personal injury suit instituted by the Parsons had to be sure at all times that the fact that he was compensated by the insurance company did not "adversely affect his judgment on behalf of or dilute his loyalty to [his] client, [Michael Smithey]." Ethical consideration 5–14. Where an attorney is representing the insured in a personal injury suit, and, at the same time advising the insurer on the question of liability under the policy it is difficult to see how that attorney could give individual loyalty to the insured-clients. "The standards of the legal profession require undeviating fidelity of the lawyer to his client. No exceptions can be tolerated." *Van Dyke v. White,* 55 Wash.2d 601, 349 P.2d 430 (1960). This standard is in accord with Ethical Consideration 5–1.

"EC 5–1. The professional judgment of a lawyer should be exercised, within the bounds of the law, solely for the benefit of his client and free of compromising influences and loyalties.

> Neither his personal interests, the interests of other clients, nor the desires of third persons should be permitted to dilute his loyalty to his client."

The attorney in the present case continued to act as Michael's attorney while he was actively working against Michael's interests. When an attorney who is an insurance company's agent uses the confidential relationship between an attorney and a client to gather information so as to deny the insured coverage under the policy in the garnishment proceeding we hold that such conduct constitutes a waiver of any policy defense, and is so contrary to public policy that the insurance company is estopped as a matter of law from disclaiming liability under an exclusionary clause in the policy. *Employers Casualty Company v. Tilley,* 496 S.W.2d 552 (Tex.1973). In the *Tilley* case the Texas Supreme Court also noted that such conduct on the part of an attorney and insurance carrier has been the subject of litigation in other jurisdictions especially in regards to the situation where an attorney representing the carrier does not fully and completely disclose to the insured the specific conflict of interest involved.

> "Conduct in violation of the above principles by the insurer through the attorney selected by it to represent the insured has been condemned by the highest courts of several other jurisdictions. In *Perkoski v. Wilson,* 371 Pa. 553, 92 A.2d 189 (1952); *Tiedtke v. Fidelity & Casualty Company of New York,* 222 So.2d 206 (Fla.1969); *Bogle v. Conway,* 199 Kan. 707, 433 P.2d 407 (1967); *Crum v. Anchor Casualty Company,* 264 Minn. 378, 119 N.W.2d 703 (1963); *Merchants Indemnity Corp. v. Eggleston,* 37 N.J. 114, 179 A.2d 505 (1962); and *Van Dyke v. White,* 55 Wash.2d 601, 349 P.2d 430 (1960), analogous conduct in violation of such principles was held to preclude or estop the insurer from denying coverage or liability. See also general criticisms and consequences of such conduct discussed in *Meirthew v. Last,* 376 Mich. 33, 135 N.W.2d 353 (1965); and *Newcomb v. Meiss,* 263 Minn. 315, 116 N.W.2d 593 (1962)." *Employers Casualty Company v. Tilley,* 496 S.W.2d at 559.

Appellee urges that the personal liability matter was defended under a reservation of rights agreement and this agreement had the effect of allowing the insurance company to investigate and defend the claim and still not waive any defenses. We hold that the reservation of rights agreement is not material to this case because the same attorney was representing conflicting clients. Appellee further urges that the procedure followed in the instant case is provided for by statute in Arizona. A.R.S. § 20–1130 states inter alia:

> "Without limitation of any right of defense of an insurer otherwise, none of the following acts by or on behalf of an insurer shall be deemed to constitute a waiver of any provision of a policy or of any defense of the insurer thereunder:

*   *   *

> "3. Investigating any loss or claim under any policy or engaging in negotiations looking toward a possible settlement of any such loss or claim."

Appellee misconstrues the protection offered to the carrier under A.R.S. § 20–1130. This statute does not grant to a carrier the right to engage an attorney to act on behalf of the insured to defend a claim against the insured while at the same time build a defense against the insured on behalf of the insurer. This conflict of interest constitutes a source of prejudice upon which the insured may invoke the doctrine of estoppel. See *Pacific Indemnity Co. v. Acel Delivery Service, Inc.*, 485 F.2d 1169 (1973), *cert. den.*, 415 U.S. 921, 94 S.Ct. 1422, 39 L.Ed.2d 476 (1974). * * *

Notes and Questions

1. *An Inevitable Conflict?* In theory it is relatively easy for an attorney to avoid deliberately entering into a situation in which there is a conflict between his interests and those of his client. When the attorney has multiple clients, however, or a single client whose interests conflict with those of others with whom the attorney also has relations—such as the insurance company that pays his fees—practical problems are not so easy to avoid. The ABA Code of Ethical Considerations 5–1 reads:

> The professional judgment of a lawyer should be exercised, within the bounds of the new law, solely for the benefit of his client and free of compromising influences and loyalties. Neither his personal interests, the interests of other clients, nor the desires of third persons should be permitted to dilute his loyalty to his client.

Should the attorney who consents to represent an insured and be paid by the insurer recognize that he is automatically in a position of potential conflict? Is there not always a possibility in an ordinary negligence action that the attorney's factual investigation will reveal information relevant to the insurer's possible coverage defense, as it did in *Parsons?*

2. *An Exclusive Duty to the Insured?* One solution would be to adopt the *Cumis* approach in all cases. This would assure that the attorney's loyalty is to the insured alone. That solution is massive and expensive overkill, however, since actual conflicts probably arise in only a small percentage of claims. Another is to hold, as in *Parsons*, that the insurer retains the right to select the defense attorney, but that the attorney owes an exclusive duty of loyalty to the insured. In an important opinion, The ABA Committee on Ethics and Professional Responsibility agreed with the latter approach, holding that an attorney who comes into possession of information relevant to the insurer's coverage defense in the course of defending the insured may not reveal that information to the insurer without the insured's consent. See Informal Opinion Number 1476 (1981).

The opinion constitutes an interpretation of DR 4–101(B), providing that a lawyer shall not knowingly reveal a confidence of his client, or use it to the disadvantage of the client. The Committee considered information gained from a third-party to fall within this rule. One exception to the rule would seem to be information that fraud is being committed by the client. DR 7–102(B) requires the attorney to reveal such fraud to the party or tribunal affected, except when the information is protected as a privileged communication. Suppose the attorney discovers from information provided by a third-party that his client is lying about facts which, if known, would provide the insurer with a coverage defense. Must the attorney reveal these facts to the insurer?

3. *Withdraw From the Case?* One reason conflicts problems in this field are so troubling is that the attorney's standard response to a conflict—withdrawal from the case—is often an unrealistic solution. For example, what kind of message would the attorney's withdrawal and subsequent silence in a case like *Parsons* have sent to the insurer in a case like *Parsons* about how vigorously to investigate possible coverage defenses? Does the ABA Committee approach—say nothing to the insurer, continue to represent the client, and feel free in the future to be retained by the insurer on other matters—deal satisfactorily with the attorney's fear that if the insurer independently discovers the information the attorney did not reveal, that the insurer will never again hire the attorney?

4. *Damages.* Notice that the court in *Parsons* awarded not only the policy limits of $25,000, but the full amount of the $50,000 judgment against the insured. What theory explains this excess-of-policy-limits award?

B. SETTLEMENT

Although standard liability insurance policies create a *duty of defense*, they purport to give the insurer a *privilege to settle* or not as it desires. See, for example, the Sample CGL Policy in Chapter Six, Section I— Coverages: " * * * We may investigate and settle any claim or 'suit' at our discretion * * *". Such provisions impliedly deny the insured the right to refuse to have a case settled; their language also seems to deny the insured the corresponding right to require that a case be settled. The judicial treatment of the privilege to settle, however, has drained some of the insurer's discretion from these provisions.

CRISCI v. THE SECURITY INSURANCE COMPANY OF NEW HAVEN, CONNECTICUT

Supreme Court of California, 1967.
66 Cal.2d 425, 58 Cal.Rptr. 13, 426 P.2d 173.

PETERS, Justice.

In an action against The Security Insurance Company of New Haven, Connecticut, the trial court awarded Rosina Crisci $91,000 (plus interest) because she suffered a judgment in a personal injury action after Security, her insurer, refused to settle the claim. Mrs. Crisci was also awarded $25,000 for mental suffering. Security has appealed.

June DiMare and her husband were tenants in an apartment building owned by Rosina Crisci. Mrs. DiMare was descending the apartment's outside wooden staircase when a tread gave way. She fell through the resulting opening up to her waist and was left hanging 15 feet above the ground. Mrs. DiMare suffered physical injuries and developed a very severe psychosis. In a suit brought against Mrs. Crisci the DiMares alleged that the step broke because Mrs. Crisci was negligent in inspecting and maintaining the stairs. They contended that Mrs. DiMare's mental condition was caused by the accident, and they asked for $400,000 as compensation for physical and mental injuries and medical expenses.

Mrs. Crisci had $10,000 of insurance coverage under a general liability policy issued by Security. The policy obligated Security to defend the suit against Mrs. Crisci and authorized the company to make any settlement it deemed expedient.[1] Security hired an experienced lawyer, Mr. Healy, to handle the case. Both he and defendant's claims manager believed that unless evidence was discovered showing that Mrs. DiMare had a prior mental illness, a jury would probably find that the accident precipitated Mrs. DiMare's psychosis. And both men believed that if the jury felt that the fall triggered the psychosis, a verdict of not less than $100,000 would be returned.

An extensive search turned up no evidence that Mrs. DiMare had any prior mental abnormality. As a teenager Mrs. DiMare had been in a Washington mental hospital, but only to have an abortion. Both Mrs. DiMare and Mrs. Crisci found psychiatrists who would testify that the accident caused Mrs. DiMare's illness, and the insurance company knew of this testimony. Among those who felt the psychosis was not related to the accident were the doctors at the state mental hospital where Mrs. DiMare had been committed following the accident. All the psychiatrists agreed, however, that a psychosis could be triggered by a sudden fear of falling to one's death.

The exact chronology of settlement offers is not established by the record. However, by the time the DiMares' attorney reduced his settlement demands to $10,000, Security had doctors prepared to support its position and was only willing to pay $3,000 for Mrs. DiMare's physical injuries. Security was unwilling to pay one cent for the possibility of a plaintiff's verdict on the mental illness issue. This conclusion was based on the assumption that the jury would believe all of the defendant's psychiatric evidence and none of the plaintiff's. Security also rejected a $9,000 settlement demand at a time when Mrs. Crisci offered to pay $2,500 of the settlement.

1. Mrs. Crisci's own attorney, Mr. Pardini, was consulted by the counsel for the insurance company, but Mr. Pardini did not direct or control either settlement negotiations or the defense of Mrs. DiMare's suit.

A jury awarded Mrs. DiMare $100,000 and her husband $1,000. After an appeal (*DiMare v. Cresci*,[2] 58 Cal.2d 292, 23 Cal.Rptr. 772, 373 P.2d 860) the insurance company paid $10,000 of this amount, the amount of its policy. The DiMares then sought to collect the balance from Mrs. Crisci. A settlement was arranged by which the DiMares received $22,000, a 40 percent interest in Mrs. Crisci's claim to a particular piece of property, and an assignment of Mrs. Crisci's cause of action against Security. Mrs. Crisci, an immigrant widow of 70, became indigent. She worked as a babysitter, and her grandchildren paid her rent. The change in her financial condition was accompanied by a decline in physical health, hysteria, and suicide attempts. Mrs. Crisci then brought this action).

The liability of an insurer in excess of its policy limits for failure to accept a settlement offer within those limits was considered by this court in *Comunale v. Traders & General Ins. Co.*, 50 Cal.2d 654, 328 P.2d 198, 68 A.L.R.2d 883. It was there reasoned that in every contract, including policies of insurance, there is an implied covenant of good faith and fair dealing that neither party will do anything which will injure the right of the other to receive the benefits of the agreement; that it is common knowledge that one of the usual methods by which an insured receives protection under a liability insurance policy is by settlement of claims without litigation; that the implied obligation of good faith and fair dealing requires the insurer to settle in an appropriate case although the express terms of the policy do not impose the duty; that in determining whether to settle the insurer must give the interests of the insured at least as much consideration as it gives to its own interests; and that when "there is great risk of a recovery beyond the policy limits so that the most reasonable manner of disposing of the claim is a settlement which can be made within those limits, a consideration in good faith of the insured's interest requires the insurer to settle the claim." (50 Cal.2d at p. 659, 328 P.2d at p. 201).

In determining whether an insurer has given consideration to the interests of the insured, the test is whether a prudent insurer without policy limits would have accepted the settlement offer.

Several cases, in considering the liability of the insurer, contain language to the effect that bad faith is the equivalent of dishonesty, fraud, and concealment. (See *Critz v. Farmers Ins. Group*, supra, 230 Cal.App.2d 788, 796, 41 Cal.Rptr. 401; *Palmer v. Financial Indem. Co.*, 215 Cal.App.2d 419, 429, 30 Cal.Rptr. 204; *Davy v. Public National Ins. Co.*, supra, 181 Cal.App.2d 387, 396, 5 Cal.Rptr. 488). Obviously a showing that the insurer has been guilty of actual dishonesty, fraud, or concealment is relevant to the determination whether it has given consideration to the insured's interest in considering a settlement offer within the policy limits. The language used in the cases, however, should not be understood as meaning that in the absence of evidence establishing actual dishonesty, fraud, or concealment no recovery may

2. In the prior litigation plaintiff was sued as "Rosina Cresci."

be had for a judgment in excess of the policy limits. *Comunale v. Traders & General Ins. Co.,* supra, 50 Cal.2d 654, 658–659, 328 P.2d 198, makes it clear that liability based on an implied covenant exists whenever the insurer refuses to settle in an appropriate case and that liability may exist when the insurer unwarrantedly refuses an offered settlement where the most reasonable manner of disposing of the claim is by accepting the settlement. Liability is imposed not for a bad faith breach of the contract but for failure to meet the duty to accept reasonable settlements, a duty included within the implied covenant of good faith and fair dealing. Moreover, examination of the balance of the *Palmer, Critz,* and *Davy* opinions makes it abundantly clear that recovery may be based on unwarranted rejection of a reasonable settlement offer and that the absence of evidence, circumstantial or direct, showing actual dishonesty, fraud, or concealment is not fatal to the cause of action.

Amicus curiae argues that, whenever an insurer receives an offer to settle within the policy limits and rejects it, the insurer should be liable in every case for the amount of any final judgment whether or not within the policy limits. As we have seen, the duty of the insurer to consider the insured's interest in settlement offers within the policy limits arises from an implied covenant in the contract, and ordinarily contract duties are strictly enforced and not subject to a standard of reasonableness. Obviously, it will always be in the insured's interest to settle within the policy limits when there is any danger, however slight, of a judgment in excess of those limits. Accordingly the rejection of a settlement within the limits where there is any danger of a judgment in excess of the limits can be justified, if at all, only on the basis of interests of the insurer, and, in light of the common knowledge that settlement is one of the usual methods by which an insured receives protection under a liability policy, it may not be unreasonable for an insured who purchases a policy with limits to believe that a sum of money equal to the limits is available and will be used so as to avoid liability on his part with regard to any covered accident. In view of such expectation an insurer should not be permitted to further its own interests by rejecting opportunities to settle within the policy limits unless it is also willing to absorb losses which may result from its failure to settle.

The proposed rule is a simple one to apply and avoids the burdens of a determination whether a settlement offer within the policy limits was reasonable. The proposed rule would also eliminate the danger that an insurer, faced with a settlement offer at or near the policy limits, will reject it and gamble with the insured's money to further its own interests. Moreover, it is not entirely clear that the proposed rule would place a burden on insurers substantially greater than that which is present under existing law. The size of the judgment recovered in the personal injury action when it exceeds the policy limits, although not conclusive, furnishes an inference that the value of the claim is the equivalent of the amount of the judgment and that acceptance of an offer within those limits was the most reasonable method of dealing with the claim.

Finally, and most importantly, there is more than a small amount of elementary justice in a rule that would require that, in this situation where the insurer's and insured's interests necessarily conflict, the insurer, which may reap the benefits of its determination not to settle, should also suffer the detriments of its decision. On the basis of these and other considerations, a number of commentators have urged that the insurer should be liable for any resulting judgment where it refuses to settle within the policy limits. (Note (1966) 18 Stan.L.Rev. 475, 482–485; Note (1951) 60 Yale L.J. 1037, 1041–1042; Comment (1949) 48 Mich.L.Rev. 95, 102; Note (1945) 13 U.Chi.L.Rev. 105, 109.)

We need not, however, here determine whether there might be some countervailing considerations precluding adoption of the proposed rule because, under *Comunale v. Traders & General Ins. Co.,* supra, 50 Cal.2d 654, 328 P.2d 198, and the cases following it, the evidence is clearly sufficient to support the determination that Security breached its duty to consider the interests of Mrs. Crisci in proposed settlements. Both Security's attorney and its claim manager agreed that if Mrs. DiMare won an award for her psychosis, that award would be at least $100,000. Security attempts to justify its rejection of a settlement by contending that it believed Mrs. DiMare had no chance of winning on the mental suffering issue. That belief in the circumstances present could be found to be unreasonable. Security was putting blind faith in the power of its psychiatrists to convince the jury when it knew that the accident could have caused the psychosis, that its agents had told it that without evidence of prior mental defects a jury was likely to believe the fall precipitated the psychosis, and that Mrs. DiMare had reputable psychiatrists on her side. Further, the company had been told by a psychiatrist that in a group of 24 psychiatrists, 12 could be found to support each side.

The trial court found that defendant "knew that there was a considerable risk of substantial recovery beyond said policy limits" and that "the defendant did not give as much consideration to the financial interests of its said insured as it gave to its own interests." That is all that was required. The award of $91,000 must therefore be affirmed.

We must next determine the propriety of the award to Mrs. Crisci of $25,000 for her mental suffering. In *Comunale v. Traders & General Ins. Co.,* supra, 50 Cal.2d 654, 663, 328 P.2d 198, 203, it was held that an action of the type involved here sounds in both contract and tort and that "where a case sounds both in contract and tort the plaintiff will ordinarily have freedom of election between an action of tort and one of contract. *Eads v. Marks,* 39 Cal.2d 807, 811, 249 P.2d 257. An exception to this rule is made in suits for personal injury caused by negligence, where the tort character of the action is considered to prevail [citations], but no such exception is applied in cases, like the present one, which relate to financial damage [citations]."[3] Although this rule was applied in *Comunale* with regard to a statute of limitations, the rule is also applicable in determining liability. * * * Insofar as language in *Critz v. Farmers Ins. Group,* supra, 230 Cal.App. 2d 788, 799, 41 Cal.Rptr. 401, might be interpreted as providing that the action for wrongful refusal to settle sounds solely in contract, it is disapproved.

Fundamental in our jurisprudence is the principle that for every wrong there is a remedy and that an injured party should be compensated for all damage proximately caused by the wrongdoer. Although we recognize exceptions from these fundamental principles, no departure should be sanctioned unless there is a strong necessity therefor.

The general rule of damages in tort is that the injured party may recover for all detriment caused whether it could have been anticipated or not. (Civ.Code, § 3333; see *Hunt Bros. Co. v. San Lorenzo etc. Co.,* 150 Cal. 51, 56, 87 P. 1093, 7 L.R.A., N.S., 913.) In accordance with the general rule, it is settled in this state that mental suffering constitutes an aggravation of damages when it naturally ensues from the act complained of, and in this connection mental suffering includes nervousness, grief, anxiety, worry, shock, humiliation and indignity as well as physical pain. The commonest example of the award of damages for mental suffering in addition to other damages is probably where the plaintiff suffers personal injuries in addition to mental distress as a result of either negligent or intentional misconduct by the defendant. (*DiMare v. Cresci,* supra, 58 Cal.2d 292, 300–301, 23 Cal.Rptr. 772, 373 P.2d 860; *Deevy v. Tassi,* 21 Cal.2d 109, 120, 130 P.2d 389; *Dryden v. Continental Banking Co.,* 11 Cal.2d 33, 39–40, 77 P.2d 833.) Such awards are not confined to cases where the mental suffering award was in addition to an award for personal injuries; damages for mental distress have also been awarded in cases where the tortious conduct was an interference with property rights without any personal injuries apart from the mental distress. * * *

We are satisfied that a plaintiff who as a result of a defendant's tortious conduct loses his property and suffers mental distress may recover not only for the pecuniary loss but also for his mental distress. No substantial reason exists to distinguish the cases which have permitted recovery for mental distress in actions for invasion of property rights. The principal reason for limiting recovery of damages for mental distress is that to permit recovery of such damages would open the door to fictitious claims, to recovery for mere bad manners, and to litigation in the field of trivialities. (Prosser, Torts (3d ed. 1964) § 11,

3. *Comunale v. Traders & General Ins. Co.,* supra, 50 Cal.2d 654, 328 P.2d 198, was mainly concerned with the contract aspect of the action. This may be due to the facts that the tort duty is ordinarily based on the insurer's assumption of the defense and of settlement negotiations (see Keeton, Liability Insurance and Responsibility for Settlement (1954) 67 Harv.L.Rev. 1136, 1138–1139; Note (1966), supra 18 Stan.L.Rev. 475), and that in *Comunale* the insurer did not undertake defense or settlement but denied coverage. In any event *Comunale* expressly recognizes that "wrongful refusal to settle has generally been treated as a tort." (50 Cal.2d at p. 663, 328 P.2d at p. 203.)

p. 43.) Obviously, where, as here, the claim is actionable and has resulted in substantial damages apart from those due to mental distress, the danger of fictitious claims is reduced, and we are not here concerned with mere bad manners or trivialities but tortious conduct resulting in substantial invasions of clearly protected interests.[4]

Recovery of damages for mental suffering in the instant case does not mean that in every case of breach of contract the injured party may recover such damages. Here the breach also constitutes a tort. Moreover, plaintiff did not seek by the contract involved here to obtain a commercial advantage but to protect herself against the risks of accidental losses, including the mental distress which might follow from the losses. Among the considerations in purchasing liability insurance, as insurers are well aware, is the peace of mind and security it will provide in the event of an accidental loss, and recovery of damages for mental suffering has been permitted for breach of contracts which directly concern the comfort, happiness or personal esteem of one of the parties. (*Chelini v. Nieri*, 32 Cal.2d 480, 482, 196 P.2d 915.)

It is not claimed that plaintiff's mental distress was not caused by defendant's refusal to settle or that the damages awarded were excessive in the light of plaintiff's substantial suffering.

The judgment is affirmed.

MOWRY v. BADGER STATE MUTUAL CASUALTY COMPANY

Supreme Court of Wisconsin, 1986.
129 Wis.2d 496, 385 N.W.2d 171.

CECI, Justice.

This is a review of the circuit court's decision and judgment against Badger State Mutual Casualty Company (Badger State) in the amount of $159,000. In a decision filed on May 23, 1984, the circuit court for Waukesha county, Robert T. McGraw, circuit judge, held that Badger State breached its contract and committed bad faith in refusing to defend its insured and in refusing to settle the third-party claim of victim Bradley Mowry within the liability limits of an insurance policy. We reverse the judgment of the circuit court. * * *

The issue is whether the circuit court erred in holding that Badger State breached its contract with its insured and committed the tort of bad faith in refusing to defend its insured and in refusing to negotiate a settlement within policy limits when Badger State had sought a separate trial on the issue of coverage, under section 803.04(2)(b). We address whether an insurer who receives and loses a separate trial on the issue of coverage and then immediately offers the policy limits

---

4. Nor are we here concerned with the problem whether invasion of the plaintiff's right to be free from emotional disturbance is actionable where there is no injury to person or property rights in addition to the inflicted mental distress. (Cf. *Amaya v. Home Ice, Fuel & Supply Co.*, 59 Cal.2d 295, 29 Cal.Rptr. 33, 379 P.2d 513.)

under an insurance contract may be held liable for damages adjudged against its insured which exceed the liability limits of the insurance policy. We determine that, under the facts of this case, Badger State should not be held responsible for the excess judgment entered against its insured. The trial court erred in holding that Badger State breached its contractual duty to defend and that it committed bad faith in refusing to settle Mowry's claim within its insured's policy limits.

The historical facts of this case are undisputed. On May 3, 1975, Bradley Mowry, then age 19, was injured in an automobile accident and suffered serious bodily injury, including the amputation of part of one foot. He was a passenger in an automobile driven by Steven McCarthy. The vehicle left a roadway and collided with a bridge abutment. McCarthy's parents were insured by Badger State and had policy limits of $15,000 for damages to any one person and medical coverage up to $1,000.

Upon being notified of the accident, Badger State began to investigate the circumstances surrounding the accident. The claims manager for Badger State, John Graeber, concluded after reading the police report and interviewing all of the automobile's occupants that the case was one of probable liability on McCarthy's part. He also determined that the case would probably involve damages to Mowry in excess of the $16,000 policy limits.

Badger State's investigations indicated to it, however, that a question of policy coverage existed. The question revolved around the ownership of the vehicle which McCarthy was driving at the time of the accident. The insurer believed that it was unclear whether McCarthy or his parents were the true owners of the automobile involved in the accident. Its investigation disclosed that the car was titled in McCarthy's mother's name, but that McCarthy had paid for the car with his own money, did not need permission to drive the car, and had told several people at the scene of the accident that he owned the vehicle and that it was uninsured. Given these circumstances, Graeber concluded that the issue of ownership was debatable and that serious question of coverage had arisen.

In March, 1976, ten months after the accident, Mowry filed suit against McCarthy, McCarthy's parents, Badger State, and an insurance agent. In its answer dated March 2, 1977, Badger State denied any coverage under the policy for the automobile driven by McCarthy on the date of the accident, based on its belief that the automobile was not owned by its insureds, McCarthy's parents.

On September 13, 1977, Mowry issued a formal demand of settlement for the full amount of the liability insurance coverage, $15,000. Badger State's attorney, Kurt Frauen, responded that Badger State had denied coverage under the policy, but that he would inform Badger State of the offer. Badger State did not accept the offer.

At a pretrial conference on September 26, 1977, Attorney Frauen requested that Mowry's counsel and other parties present agree to a bifurcated trial in which a determination on coverage would precede any trial on the issue of liability. In relating the events of the pretrial conference to Badger State, Attorney Frauen wrote, "Everyone seemed to feel that if the coverage issue were resolved, the rest of the case would not have to be tried." Mowry's counsel reiterated Mowry's offer of settlement on September 26, 1977, but Badger State again refused to accept it.

A subsequent stipulation and order set April 4, 1979, as the commencement date for the trial on the issue of coverage; the issues of liability and damages were to be held in abeyance until the resolution of the coverage issue. On March 12, 1979, approximately three weeks before the coverage trial, Mowry once more demanded that Badger State pay the limits of McCarthy's liability insurance policy plus $1,000 under the medical payments coverage; he set a March 23, 1979, deadline for its acceptance. Badger State's counsel in correspondence to Mowry's counsel, stated that he felt the settlement demand was contrary to the stipulation and order separating the coverage issue from the liability and damages issues: "The court has in fact bifurcated the trial * * * to resolve the coverage dispute before proceeding with the plaintiff's case." Mowry's counsel responded that he believed that stipulating to a bifurcation of issues "should not in any way be construed as barring plaintiff from attempting to negotiate settlement of his entire claim."

Badger State refused Mowry's March 12 settlement offer. On April 4, 1979, the coverage issue was tried before a jury. The jury returned a verdict the next day which found that McCarthy's parents owned the vehicle in question at the time of the accident. Coverage was thereby afforded Steven McCarthy under the policy.

On April 6, 1979, Badger State offered the limits on its liability policy and medical payments coverage. On January 10, 1980, Badger State's counsel informed McCarthy that it would assume McCarthy's defense in the action. Following negotiations between counsel for Mowry and Badger State, the parties entered into a stipulation of judgment in October, 1980, thereby rendering a trial on the liability and damages issues unnecessary. The judgment was in favor of Mowry and against Badger State for $16,000 and against Steven McCarthy for $175,000. The stipulation further called for McCarthy to assign to Mowry any and all causes of action which McCarthy might have against Badger State, in satisfaction of Mowry's judgment against McCarthy. Following that stipulation and entry of judgment, Mowry, suing under McCarthy's assignment of rights, brought the present action against Badger State for bad faith and breach of contract.

The circuit court, in holding that Badger State breached its contract in refusing to defend and that it committed bad faith in refusing to negotiate a settlement, was indignant that an insurer would delay settlement negotiations until the coverage issue has been judicially determined, particularly when liability and excess damages are undisputed. The court felt that Badger State's posture of not negotiating a settlement until the determination of the coverage issue placed all the risk of an excess judgment on the insured. It found that an insurance company who refuses to defend and refused to negotiate may not protect itself from a claim for damages in excess of policy limits by tendering the policy limits only upon losing the coverage issue of a bifurcated trial. Citing *Luke v. American Family Mut. Ins. Co.*, 476 F.2d 1015 (8th Cir.1973), Judge McGraw stated that the proper rule should be " 'when an offer of settlement within the policy limits has been made and ignored, a good faith refusal to defend is not a valid defense to a claim in excess of the policy limits. * * *' " *Luke*, 476 F.2d at 1021. The court then awarded Mowry damages in the amount of $159,000, representing the stipulated amount of liquidated for which Badger State would be liable in any action brought by Mowry as assignee against Badger State.

Badger State appealed. The court of appeals, in its certification memorandum, framed the issue to be whether an insurance carrier "should be held liable for damages in excess of its policy coverage where its belief that there was no coverage led it to reject" an earlier offer of settlement within the policy limits. The court noted that this particular scenario presents an unaddressed area of insurance law in this state.

The parties assert the same arguments here as they did below. Mowry states that, in refusing to negotiate a settlement and in refusing to defend McCarthy, Badger State breached contractual and fiduciary duties it owed to McCarthy. Badger State argues that it committed no bad faith in pursuing a fairly debatable coverage question within the framework of a bifurcated trial. In effect, it argues that any duty to negotiate a settlement is suspended when a bifurcated trial has been granted on a threshold issue of coverage. If it breached its contractual duty to defend, Badger State believes that damages should be limited to the liability limits of the policy. Because we hold that Badger State did not act in bad faith, nor did it breach its contractual duties owed to McCarthy, we do not reach the matter of calculation of damages.

We note the competing interests on each side of this case. When an insurer is certain of its insured's liability for an accident and where damages to the victim exceed policy limits, the insurer would normally be responsible for indemnifying its insured to the extent of its policy limits. The insurer, however, experiences a conflict of interests whenever an offer of settlement within policy limits is received where a legitimate question of coverage under the policy also exists. *See,* Keeton, *Liability Insurance and Responsibility for Settlement,* 67 Harv. L.Rev. 1136 (1954). *See also, Hilker v. Western Automobile Ins. Co.,* 204 Wis. 1, 14, 235 N.W. 413 (1931) (on rehearing). The insurer will be reluctant to settle within policy limits if there is a likelihood that coverage does not exist. On the other hand, an insurer's failure to settle a victim's claim within policy limits may subject an insured to a judgment in excess of his policy limits. This case presents a good example of these conflicting interests.

BAD FAITH CLAIM

An insurer owes a general duty to its insured to settle or compromise a claim made against the insured. *Hilker,* 204 Wis. at 13, 235 N.W. 413. This duty does not arise out of an express contractual provision; rather, it is implied from the terms of the contract which give the insurer the absolute control of the defense of the action against the insured. *Id.* at 13–14, 235 N.W. 413.

The insurer has the right to exercise its own judgment in determining whether a claim should be settled or contested. But "exercise of this right should be accompanied by considerations of good faith." *Id.* at 14, 235 N.W. 413. In order to be made in good faith, a decision not to settle a claim must be based on a thorough evaluation of the underlying circumstances of the claim and on informed interaction with the insured. This gives rise to several obligations on the part of the insurer. First, the insurer must exercise reasonable diligence in ascertaining facts upon which a good-faith decision to settle or not settle must be based. Second, where a likelihood of liability in excess of policy limits exists, the insurer must so inform the insured so that the insured might properly protect himself. *Id.* at 15–16, 235 N.W. 413. Third, the insurer must keep the insured timely abreast of any settlement offers received from the victim and of the progress of settlement negotiations. *Baker v. Northwestern Nat. Casualty Co.,* 22 Wis.2d 77, 83, 125 N.W.2d 370 (1963).

These three obligations arise as a result of the insurer's general duty owed to its insured to settle a claim. The duty to settle, in turn, emanates from the contractual terms giving the insurer the absolute control of the defense of the victim's action against the insured. Because the insured has given up something of value to the insurer— namely, the right to defend and settle a claim—the insurer has been said to be in the position of a fiduciary with respect to an insured's interests in settlement of a claim. *See, Alt v. American Family Mut. Ins. Co.,* 71 Wis.2d 340, 348, 237 N.W.2d 706 (1976). Whenever a question of policy coverage exists, however, as insurer's duty to settle under the contract is in doubt. Its duty to settle is dependent upon whether the policy extends coverage for the circumstances underlying the harm sustained. Mowry argues that the insurer's mistaken decision about the nonexistence of coverage should render Badger State liable for the excess judgment entered against the insured. He does not assert that Badger State breached any of the three traditional obligations arising out of the general duty to settle. Rather, he asserts that Badger State acted in bad faith in deciding to disclaim coverage where it was convinced that no real issue as to liability or damages existed. Moreover, he argues that Badger State's liability for damages caused by its refusal to settle an excess liability claim is not excused by a good-faith failure to defend.

To support his argument, Mowry cites cases from other jurisdictions which ostensibly are on point. In *Luke*, 476 F.2d 1015, the court held that an insurer who denied coverage to its insured because the insurer doubted that coverage existed under the contract was liable to the insured's assignees for the entire excess judgment for the breach of its duty to settle. Like the instant case, the insurer in *Luke* believed that an issue as to automobile ownership had arisen. The insurer denied coverage on that basis. It also received several offers of settlement within policy limits. However, the offers were ignored. In addition, the insurance company refused to consider a declaratory action concerning the coverage issue. Despite this conduct, the lower court held that the insurer exercised good faith in refusing to provide coverage. *Id.* at 1018–20.

The Eighth Circuit Court of Appeals found that the insurer refused to settle *and* refused to defend and, therefore, had breached its contract with the insured. Good faith, the court found, is irrelevant to a breach of contract action. "When an insurer refused to defend and, additionally, refused to accept a reasonable settlement within the policy limits, the company's liability for damages may be measured as well by its rejection of the offer to settle and may thus exceed the policy limits." *Id.* at 1020.

We do not find *Luke* to be persuasive in the present situation. First, in this case there was no breach of contract for failure to defend (for reasons which will be discussed below) as there was in *Luke*. Good faith, although of no importance in breach of contract actions, is a consideration in actions claiming a breach of the duty to settle, which arises out of fiduciary principles. *Alt*, 71 Wis.2d at 348, 237 N.W.2d 706. *Johnson v. American Family Mut. Ins. Co.*, 93 Wis.2d 633, 646, 287 N.W.2d 729 (1980). Second, the insurer in *Luke* refused the plaintiff's offer to hold the suits in abeyance in order to give the insurer an opportunity to file a declaratory judgment suit. Here, Badger State sought out an agreement based on a statutory provision whereby the coverage issue could be judicially determined prior to any liability and damages issues. It did not simply ignore the victim's claim, as the insurer in *Luke* apparently did.

Mowry also cites *Comunale v. Traders & General Ins. Co.*, 50 Cal.2d 654, 328 P.2d 198 (1958). *Comunale* involves another "refusal to defend" case. The insurer, believing that the insurance contract did not provide coverage for the victim's injury, refused to defend its insured. The trial proceeded to judgment against the insured, which included an award to the victim in excess of the insured's policy limits. Under assignment, the victim sued the insurer. The Supreme Court of California stated,

"When there is a great risk of recovery beyond the policy limits so that the most reasonable manner of disposing of the claim is a settlement which can be made within those limits, a consideration in good faith of the insured's interest requires the insurer to settle the claim. Its unwarranted refusal to do so constitutes a breach of the implied covenant of good faith and fair dealing." 50 Cal.2d at 659, 328 P.2d at 201.

That court then held the insurer liable for the excess judgment entered against the insured, representing the insured's damages for breach of the duty to settle.

The *Comunale* rule, in effect, renders an insurer strictly liable for any decision not to settle within policy limits, whether or not made in good faith, when a subsequent judgment against the insured exceeds policy limits:

> " 'An insurer who denies coverage does so at its own risk, and, although its position may not have been entirely groundless, if the denial is found to be wrongful it is liable for the full amount which will compensate the insured for all the detriment caused by the insurer's breach of the express and implied obligations of the contract. 50 Cal.2d at 660, 328 P.2d at 202.' " *Johansen v. California State Auto. Assn. Inter–Ins. Bureau,* 15 Cal.3d 9, 15, 123 Cal.Rptr. 288, 538 P.2d 744, (1975).

In *Johansen,* the California court further explained the upshot of its strict liability approach:

> "[T]he only permissible consideration in evaluating the reasonableness of the settlement offer becomes whether, in light of the victim's injuries and the probable liability of the insured, the ultimate judgment is likely to exceed the amount of the settlement offer. Such factors as the limits imposed by the policy, a desire to reduce the amount of future settlements, or a belief that the policy does not provide coverage, should not affect a decision as to whether the settlement offer in question is a reasonable one." 15 Cal.3d at 16, 123 Cal.Rptr. at 292–93, 538 P.2d at 748–49.

Although we acknowledge the apparent goal of the California approach—to protect the insured from liability for an excess judgment by placing the risk of an erroneous decision not to settle on an insurer—we decline to accept that strict approach for this jurisdiction. Such a policy is unduly oppressive on insurance companies and would force them to settle claims where coverage may be dubious. The California approach is particularly unseemly in a jurisdiction such as our own, where an insurer may seek judicial determination of coverage issues prior to litigating liability and damages issues. *See,* section 803.04(2)(b), Stats. The California approach is unrealistic if only to the extent that an insurer's belief that an insurance policy does or does not provide coverage must necessarily "affect a decision as to whether the settlement offer in question is a reasonable one." *Johansen,* 15 Cal.3d at 16, 123 Cal.Rptr. at 293, 538 P.2d at 749.

We have held that an insurer has a right to exercise its own judgment in deciding whether to settle or contest a claim, within parameters of good faith considerations. *Hilker,* 204 Wis. at 14, 235 N.W. 413. An insurer need not accept every offer of settlement within policy limits under sanction of liability for an excess judgment against its insured. *See, Johnson,* 93 Wis.2d at 645–46, 287 N.W.2d 729. The *Hilker* and *Johnson* cases did not involve an issue of coverage as a basis for denial of settlement offers. Whether an insurer who rejects an offer to settle within policy limits because of a coverage question shall be liable for some measure of damages upon a determination of coverage depends upon whether the insurer acted in bad faith in determining that a coverage question existed. The tort of bad faith is "the knowing failure to exercise an honest and informed judgment." *Anderson v. Continental Ins. Co.,* 85 Wis.2d 675, 692, 271 N.W.2d 368 (1978). To hold that Badger State breached its duty to settle requires a finding that it committed the tort of bad faith.[1] Badger State asks this court to adopt the standard set forth in *Anderson.*

Bad faith in deciding to litigate rather than settle a claim involves more than a mere finding of negligence on the part of the insurer. *Warren v. American Family Mut. Ins. Co.,* 122 Wis.2d 381, 385, 361 N.W.2d 724 (Ct.App.1984). Where there is no bad faith, an insured (or an insured's assignee) may not "surcharge an overage against his insurance company merely because of" any possible negligence on the insurer's part in deciding to litigate rather than to settle. *Baker v. Northwestern Nat. Casualty Co.,* 26 Wis.2d 306, 314–15, 132 N.W.2d 493 (1965).

In *Anderson,* a first-party claim case, this court held that an insurance company may challenge claims which are fairly debatable. 85 Wis.2d at 693, 271 N.W.2d 368. We said,

> "To show a claim for bad faith, a plaintiff must show the absence of a reasonable basis for denying benefits of the policy and the defendant's knowledge or reckless disregard of the lack of a reasonable basis for denying the claim." *Id.* at 691, 271 N.W.2d 368.

An insurer will have committed the tort of bad faith only when it has denied a claim without a reasonable basis for doing so, that is, when the claim is not fairly debatable.

This court has held that in third-party claim situations, it is not bad faith for an insurer to refuse to settle a victim's claim "under the bona fide belief that the insurer might defeat the action. * * *" *Johnson,* 93 Wis.2d at 646, 287 N.W.2d 729. *See also, Maroney v. Allstate Ins. Co.,* 12 Wis.2d 197, 200–01, 107 N.W.2d 261 (1961). Although the "bona fide belief" language applies to a third party's action

---

1. We reiterate that Mowry does not assert that Badger State failed to meet any of the obligations arising out of the duty to settle. *See, Baker,* 22 Wis.2d at 82–83, 125 N.W.2d 370. An insurer must exercise reasonable diligence in the undertaking of these obligations. *Hilker,* 204 Wis. at 15, 235 N.W. 413.

against the insured, we similarly hold that it is not bad faith for an insurer to refuse to settle an injured's claim within the policy limits when the question of policy coverage is fairly debatable and when the grounds for the refusal, if determined in the insurer's favor, would wholly defeat the indemnity responsibility of the insurer to its insured.

We hold that the circuit court erred in finding in this case that Badger State committed bad faith by refusing to settle and negotiate a settlement within policy limits. A finding of bad faith must not be measured solely against a backdrop that coverage was ultimately found to exist under the policy. Bad faith should be found in this case only if there was no fairly debatable coverage question. However, the circuit court, sitting without a jury, did not use this standard to reach its bad faith conclusion. The court concluded that Badger State's posture of waiting to defend the action and to negotiate a settlement until the coverage issue was determined itself constituted bad faith. Because the circuit court did not rely on appropriate and applicable law in making its bad faith determination, its holding is an abuse of discretion and, as such, is erroneous. *See, Hartung v. Hartung,* 102 Wis.2d 58, 66, 306 N.W.2d 16 (1981).

The upshot of the trial court's holding would be to require the insurer to accept an offer within policy limits even where a fairly debatable coverage question exists. We have, however, rejected the California approach, which would make an insurer strictly liable for an offer of settlement within policy limits.

Although this court might otherwise remand a matter to the circuit court for further consideration where the appropriate law has not been applied, we choose to decide the bad faith issue as a matter of law.

Bad faith is a determination to be made by the trier of fact. *Baker,* 26 Wis.2d at 315, 132 N.W.2d 493. Like negligence, whether certain conduct constitutes bad faith raises a mixed question of fact and law. *See, Millonig v. Bakken,* 112 Wis.2d 445, 450, 334 N.W.2d 80 (1983). First a question is raised with respect to what the party allegedly in bad faith did or failed to do. The second inquiry is whether a reasonable insurer would have denied policy coverage under the facts and circumstances of the particular case. *See, Anderson,* 85 Wis.2d at 692, 271 N.W.2d 368. In instances in which such a matter is tried to a jury, and when the facts are undisputed and the evidence permits only one reasonable inference or conclusion, then the issue of bad faith is to be decided by the court as a matter of law, rather than by the fact finder as a question of fact. *See, Millonig,* 112 Wis.2d at 450–51, 334 N.W.2d 80. In this case the issue of bad faith was tried to the court, not to a jury. With respect to the court's findings in such an instance,

> "[w]hen the principal facts in a case are undisputed and the controversy centers on what has been called ultimate conclusions of fact, or conclusions of law, this court has indicated it will not be bound by the findings of the trial court." *Chicago,*

Milwaukee, St. Paul & Pacific R.R. Co. v. Milwaukee, 47 Wis. 2d 88, 96, 176 N.W.2d 580 (1970).

Here, because the principal facts underlying the bad faith claim are undisputed and because there is only one reasonable inference, we may review the matter of bad faith as a question of law without deference to the trial court or court of appeals.

Badger State's grounds for refusing the settlement offers within policy limits were that it did not believe that the car involved in the accident was owned by its insureds, McCarthy's parents. Badger State, therefore, concluded that the policy did not extend coverage to McCarthy through his parents. Mowry disputes Badger State's conclusion that the coverage question was fairly debatable. He notes that whether a matter is fairly debatable "implicates the question whether the facts necessary to evaluate the claim are properly investigated and developed or recklessly ignored and disregarded." *Anderson,* 85 Wis.2d at 691, 271 N.W.2d 368. He asserts in his brief that Badger State recklessly ignored the fact that the automobile in question was registered in the name of Mildred McCarthy (who is one of the policy's two named insureds and Steven McCarthy's mother), that McCarthy's father contributed to the purchase price of the car, and that Mildred had driven the car as well as Steven, among other relevant facts.

Badger State responds that McCarthy did not need parental permission to operate the car, that McCarthy said at the accident site that the car was uninsured, and that McCarthy's father told McCarthy to obtain insurance on the car. In addition, Mowry's counsel conceded during the underlying bad faith trial before Judge McGraw that evidence existed which presented a jury issue on coverage. Mowry's counsel stated:

> "I'm willing to stipulate as I have always been that there was a jury issue on the question of coverage[,] period. As attempting to cloak it in the terms of the wise men to the west as being fairly debatable and so on, I object to, but your Honor, there is no question but what there was evidence which presented a jury issue on coverage."

Significantly, the original trial court bifurcated the liability and damages issues from the coverage issue and ordered that the issues of liability and damages be held in abeyance until the determination of the coverage issue. The court of appeals in its certification memorandum stated that the evidence for and against coverage "was at least somewhat balanced."

We hold that Badger State did not act in bad faith in initially denying coverage to McCarthy. The record establishes a reasonable basis for Badger State's denial of coverage. Although the vehicle was registered in Mildred McCarthy's name, other items within the record suggest Steven McCarthy's ownership of the vehicle. Eugene McCarthy, Steven's father, stated that Steven paid for the car with money from Steven's own checking account, but that Eugene also "gave him some money." McCarthy apparently had approached his father about the idea of "buy[ing] the car" from a third party. Steven, according to the elder McCarthy, paid $150 for the car, but Mildred McCarthy's name appeared on the title. McCarthy never had to ask his father or mother for permission to use the car. Eugene McCarthy suggested that his son obtain insurance on the vehicle. In a statement made to a Badger State representative, McCarthy claimed that his mother owned the car on the date of the accident but that he had paid for it. One of the vehicle's occupants on the date of the accident stated that McCarthy said at the accident scene that he owned the car and that it was uninsured.

Although the record itself does not conclusively establish that the vehicle in question was covered under the elder McCarthy's insurance policy (that task was undertaken and resolved by the jury in the coverage trial), the record sufficiently establishes that Badger State was presented with a fairly debatable coverage issue. There is no absence of a reasonable basis for Badger State's denial of coverage. The record gives no indication that Badger State failed to properly investigate the claim, or that important facts were recklessly ignored and disregarded. Badger State did not commit bad faith in failing to settle Mowry's claim within policy limits even though McCarthy's liability for the accident was probable and damages were concededly in excess of policy limits. The question of coverage under the policy was fairly debatable.

Badger State could have protected both its interests and its insured's interests by settling under a reservation of rights agreement, Mowry and the circuit court assert. The record reflects that Badger State's counsel and its claims manager considered such an option, but ultimately decided to pursue the bifurcation procedure. A reservation of rights agreement would result in a settlement of the injured's claims, while preserving the insurer's rights to litigate the coverage issue. The insured benefits from this procedure because it is protected from excess judgment. Badger State argues, however, that the reservation of rights procedure will rarely result in the insurer's recouping the payments it made to the victim from the insured where coverage is found not to exist under the policy, because the insured may be judgment-proof.

An insurer is always at liberty to seek a reservation of its rights in settling a claim. But Badger State's failure to seek such a reservation in this case does not, by itself, constitute bad faith. Badger State merely sought a statutory mechanism to bifurcate the coverage issue from the liability and damages issues. To require an insurer to enter into a reservation of rights agreement in addition to proceeding within a separation framework would run contrary to the bifurcation allowed by section 803.04(2)(b), Stats. Even though Badger State's determination that coverage did not exist was wrong, its mistake does not mean that it acted in bad faith in refusing to settle if the issue of coverage was fairly debatable. Although the mere ordering of a separate trial on the coverage issue is not conclusive that the coverage issue was fairly debatable, we cannot conclude that failure to enter into a reservation of rights agreement when a bifurcated trial has been granted is bad faith. We note that none of the cases cited by Mowry (e.g., *Luke, Comunale,* and *Johansen*) dealt with situations where the insurer sought and was granted a statutory separation procedure similar to section 803.04(2)(b).

Mowry argues that it is inherently unfair for McCarthy to be liable for a judgment in excess of policy limits when the judgment could have been wholly avoided had Badger State settled within policy limits when it had the opportunity to do so. But to require an insurer to settle any claim within policy limits where the insured's liability and the victim's damages in excess of policy limits are relatively certain, without consideration as to whether coverage exists, may result in extortionate lawsuits against the insurer. *See, Anderson,* 85 Wis.2d at 693, 271 N.W.2d 368. Section 803.04(2)(b), Stats., provides some measure of protection against pressure settlement situations in which an insurer might find itself. We cannot penalize an insurer merely for utilizing such a mechanism. The bad faith standard, moreover, strikes an acceptable balance between the insurer's and insured's competing interests concerning settlement offers within policy limits where liability and damages in excess of policy limits are apparent. * * *

When the insured's liability for an accident is undisputed and damage clearly exceeds policy limits and yet the insurer seeks a separate trial on a coverage issue, the insurer and insured may still interact to avoid an excess judgment against the insured. For example, Mowry's counsel extended several settlement offers to Badger State after a stipulation had been reached and after a separation order had been granted. Although Badger State's acceptance of any of Mowry's offers would have been contrary to its decision to litigate the coverage issue—to be sure, a requirement that Badger State accept any such offers under penalty of bad faith would emasculate any benefit of the statutory separation procedure—Badger State still had the obligation to inform its insured of settlement offers and negotiations. Once an insurer has rejected an offer, the insured should then have the opportunity to settle for the proffered amount. In this case, McCarthy may have wished to accept Mowry's $16,000 offer, thereby limiting his liability for Mowry's damages. If the coverage trial results in a finding of coverage, then the insurer would assume responsibility for its insured's indemnification. If coverage does not exist, then the insured will at least have limited its liability in what was concededly an excess liability case, rather than exposing itself to extensive liability. The victim should be willing to extend the same offer to the insured which it would extend to the insurer; if the victim is unwilling, the insurer and the insured might reasonably conclude that the offer was frivolous. An insurer may ignore a frivolous offer. *Baker,* 26 Wis.2d at 313, 132 N.W.2d 493.

Because the trial court held that Badger State committed bad faith in refusing to negotiate or settle a claim within its policy limits and did not apply the fairly debatable standard to the coverage question, the trial court erred as a matter of law. We hold that when a coverage issue is fairly debatable, an insurer will not have acted in bad faith in refusing to settle within policy limits, even when the insured's liability for the incident is undisputed and when the victim's damages appear to exceed policy limits. Because no determination was made that the coverage issue was fairly debatable, the circuit court abused its discretion in holding that Badger State acted in bad faith and in holding it liable for McCarthy's excess judgment. * * *

Notes and Questions

1. *The Reasonable–Offer Test.* The *Crisci* rule is standard law now in most jurisdictions. Under the reasonable offer test the question is whether an insurer under a policy without limits would accept the offer. An earlier test for excess liability was whether the insurer gave the insured's interests "equal consideration." Under the reasonable offer test, however, truly equal consideration is not the norm. Rather, in certain cases the insurer's interests quite properly receive greater consideration, while in other cases the insured's interests carry more weight. Can you see why?

2. *The Insurer's Strict Liability for Excess Judgments?* No court has squarely adopted the strict liability test described in *Crisci*, notwithstanding the *Mowry* court's interpretation of the state of California law. For a time there was discussion of adopting strict liability in New Jersey, but the move to this standard never took place. See *Rova Farms Resort, Inc. v. Investors Insurance Company of America,* 65 N.J. 474, 323 A.2d 495 (1974). In theory, such a test should create precisely the same incentives as the *Crisci* test; the only difference would be that insurers also would bear liability for excess judgments which it was reasonable for them to reject. In practice, however, proving that offers close to the line of reasonableness should have been accepted might be difficult and expensive—consider what would be involved in such proof. A strict liability test might therefore cause insurers to accept offers they would reject under a reasonable offer test, because of the difficulties of proof that insureds would encounter in attempting to show that an offer which the insurer rejected was in fact reasonable. See K. Abraham, Distributing Risk: Insurance, Legal Theory, and Public Policy 193–95 (1986).

3. *The Measure of Damages.* *Crisci* is a distinct minority in allowing recovery of noneconomic damages for the failure to settle. From a deterrence standpoint, is there any need to award such damages if the reasonable offer rule works properly? Should the availability of noneconomic damages be used to counterbalance the under-enforcement problems described in the preceding paragraph?

4. *The Johansen Alternative.* Is the result in *Mowry* fair to insureds, or should a rule similar to that in *Crisci* be applied? For example, what advantages would be entailed in a rule requiring the insurer to weigh settlement offers in cases where coverage is in doubt

as though the insurer would be liable without limit if there were coverage? The Supreme Court of California adopted this requirement in *Johansen v. California State Automobile Association Inter–Insurance Bureau,* 15 Cal.3d 9, 123 Cal.Rptr. 288, 538 P.2d 744 (1975). Under the *Johansen* rule presumably insurers do not always accept such offers merely because they are liable for the consequences of rejecting them. Rather, insurers take into account the probability that an ensuing judgment will not exceed the policy limit if the offer is rejected, and the probability that a later resolution of the coverage dispute will determine that the policy does not cover the loss in question.

The argument for the *Johansen* approach is that it requires insurers to internalize not only the benefits of rejecting offers, but the costs of doing so as well. The result is avoidance of unnecessary litigation, at least in cases where the insured simply cannot produce the funds necessary to accept the claimant's offer of settlement. On this view, is *Mowry's* emphasis on the absence of bad faith appropriate? On the other hand, is it possible that *Crisci* and *Johansen* generate strategic behavior that also is wasteful? For example, claimants may offer to settle for more than they think the insurer will pay in cases where coverage is questionable, in the hope that the offer will be rejected, an above-limits judgment returned, and a later finding that the policy provides coverage reached. *Mowry* avoids at least some such behavior.

5. *Recoupment.* Would a better rule be that the insurer has the duty imposed in *Johansen,* but that if it later prevails in the coverage dispute it is entitled to recoup the amount of any settlement from the insured? Under what circumstances would the right to recoup be of value?

BAD FAITH LIABILITY TO A THIRD–PARTY: THE *ROYAL GLOBE* ISSUE

Does a liability insurer owe a duty to accept reasonable settlements not only to its own insured, but to the party who sues the insured? In a few states, at least for a time, the surprising answer may have been in the affirmative. The most celebrated case so holding is *Royal Globe Insurance Company v. Superior Court,* 23 Cal.3d 880, 592 P.2d 329, 153 Cal.Rptr. 842 (1979). See also *Jenkins v. J.C. Penney Casualty Insurance Company,* 167 W.Va. 597, 280 S.E.2d 252 (1981). The source of this duty in *Royal Globe* was a statute adopted in substantially the same form in a number of states, known as the Unfair Insurance Practices Act.

The Acts tend to make it an unfair practice, among other things, to engage in a "general business practice" of "Not attempting in good faith to effectuate prompt, fair, and equitable settlements of claims in which liability has become reasonably clear." See, e.g., California Insurance Code § 790.03. Violations are subject to the issuance of cease and desist orders by the Insurance Commissioner. In *Royal*

Globe the Supreme Court of California held that a plaintiff in a liability action also had a private right of action against the defendant's insurer for violation of this and other provisions of the Act on a single occasion. The decision required that the plaintiff prevail in the trial of his action against the insured in order to bring a bad-faith claim against the insurer. In light of this requirement, what damages would a plaintiff be entitled to recover in the bad-faith action?

The case created a firestorm of controversy at the time, perhaps out of fear that the fire itself would spread to other states. See, e.g., Mecherle & Overton, A New Extra Contractual Cloud Upon the Horizon: Do Unfair Claim Settlement Acts Create a Private Cause of Action? 50 Ins. Counsel J. 262 (1983). The storm did not spread, however, and nine years later was extinguished at its source. In 1988 the Supreme Court of California—with three members appointed after the electoral defeat of three who had participated in *Royal Globe* and other controversial cases—overruled *Royal Globe,* in *Moradi–Shalal v. Fireman's Fund Insurance Companies,* 46 Cal.App.3d 287, 250 Cal.Rptr. 116, 758 P.2d 58 (1988). Although there still are remnants of the private cause of action in a few other states, it now appears to be a development whose time has passed.

C. RELATIONS BETWEEN PRIMARY AND EXCESS INSURERS

1. The Duty to Settle

COMMERCIAL UNION ASSURANCE COMPANIES v. SAFEWAY STORES, INC.

Supreme Court of California, 1980.
164 Cal.Rptr. 709, 610 P.2d 1038.

By the Court:

We granted a hearing herein in order to resolve a conflict between Court of Appeal opinions in this case and the earlier case of *Transit Casualty Co. v. Spink Corp.* (1979) 94 Cal.App.3d 124, 156 Cal.Rptr. 360. After an independent study of the issue, we have concluded that the thoughtful opinion of Justice Sabraw (assigned) for the Court of Appeal, First Appellate District, 158 Cal.Rptr. 97, in this case correctly treats the issues, and that we should adopt it as our own opinion. That opinion, with appropriate deletions and additions,* is as follows:

This case presents the question of whether an insured owes a duty [   ] to its excess liability insurance carrier which would require it to accept a settlement offer below the thresh-

---

* Brackets together, in this manner [   ], are used to indicate deletions from the opinion of the Court of Appeal; brackets enclosing material (other than the editor's parallel citations) are, unless otherwise indicated, used to denote insertions or additions by this court. (*Estate of McDill* (1975) 14 Cal.3d 831, 834, 122 Cal.Rptr. 754, 537 P.2d 874.)

old figure of the excess carrier's exposure where there is a substantial probability of liability in excess of that figure.

Facts:

At all times relevant herein Safeway Stores, Incorporated (hereafter Safeway) had liability insurance coverage as follows:

(a) Travelers Insurance Company and Travelers Indemnity Company (hereafter Travelers) insured Safeway for the first $50,000 of liability.

(b) Safeway insured itself for liability between the sums of $50,000 and $100,000.

(c) Commercial Union Assurance Companies and Mission Insurance Company (hereafter conjunctively referred to as Commercial) provided insurance coverage for Safeway's liability in excess of $100,000 to $20 million.

One Hazel Callies brought an action against Safeway in San Francisco Superior Court and recovered judgment for the sum of $125,000. Thereafter, Commercial was required to pay $25,000 of said judgment in order to discharge its liability under the excess insurance policy.

Commercial, as excess liability carrier, brought the instant action against its insured Safeway and Safeway's primary insurance carrier, Travelers, to recover the $25,000 which it had expended. Commercial alleged that Safeway and Travelers had an opportunity to settle the case for $60,000, or possibly even $50,000, and knew or should have known that there was a possible and probable liability in excess of $100,000. It was further alleged that said defendants had a duty to settle the claim for a sum less than $100,000 when they had an opportunity to do so. Commercial's complaint attempts to state two causes of action against Safeway and Travelers, one in negligence and another for breach of the duty of good faith and fair dealing.

Safeway demurred to the complaint on the grounds of failure to state a cause of action. The court sustained the demurrer with 20 days' leave to amend. When Commercial failed to amend its complaint, the complaint was dismissed as to Safeway. Commercial now appeals from the judgment of dismissal.[ ]

The present case is unusual in that the policyholder, Safeway, was self-insured for liability in an amount below Commercial's initial exposure. While this status may explain Safeway's reluctance to settle, it remains to be determined if the insured owes an independent duty to his excess carrier to accept a reasonable settlement offer so as to avoid exposing the latter to pecuniary harm. [Both of Commercial's theories of recovery, negligence and breach of good faith, depend upon the existence of such a duty.]

It is now well established that an insurer may be held liable for a judgment against the insured in excess of its policy limits where it has breached its implied covenant of good faith and fair dealing by unreasonably refusing to accept a settlement offer within the policy limits (*Crisci v. Security Ins. Co.*, 66 Cal.2d 425, 429 [58 Cal.Rptr. 13, 426 P.2d 173]; *Comunale v. Traders & General Ins. Co.* (1958) 50 Cal.2d 654, 661 [328 P.2d 198, 68 A.L.R.2d 883]). The insurer's duty of good faith requires it to "settle within policy limits when there is substantial likelihood of recovery in excess of those limits." (*Murphy v. Allstate Ins. Co.* (1976) 17 Cal.3d 937, 941 [132 Cal.Rptr. 424, 426, 553 P.2d 584, 586].)

Although an insurance policy normally only carries an express statement of a duty to defend, an insurer's duty to settle is derived from the implied covenant of good faith and fair dealing which is part of any contract (see 4 Witkin, Summary of Cal.Law (8th ed., 1974) § 754, p. 3050, and cases collected therein). This duty was first recognized in *Comunale v. Traders & General Ins. Co.*, supra, 50 Cal.2d 654, 328 P.2d 198. The rationale for the "*Comunale* duty" was articulated by [ ] [us] at page 659, 328 P.2d at page 201: "It is common knowledge that a large percentage of the claims covered by insurance are settled without litigation and that this is one of the usual methods by which the insured receives protection. (See *Douglas v. United States Fidelity & Guaranty Co.*, 81 N.H. 371 [127 A. 708, 712]; *Hilker v. Western Automobile Ins. Co.* [204 Wis. 1, 231 N.W.2d 257] supra.) * * *

"The insurer, in deciding whether a claim should be compromised, must take into account the interest of the insured and give it at least as much consideration as it does to its own interest. (See *Ivy v. Pacific Automobile Ins. Co.*, 156 Cal.App.2d 652, 659 [320 P.2d 140].) When there is great risk of a recovery beyond the policy limits so that the most reasonable manner of disposing of the claim is a settlement which can be made within those limits, a consideration in good faith of the insured's interest requires the insurer to settle the claim. Its unwarranted refusal to do so constitutes a breach of the implied covenant of good faith and fair dealing."

It has been held in California and other jurisdictions that the excess carrier may maintain an action against the primary carrier for [ ] [wrongful] refusal to settle within the latter's policy limits (*Northwestern Mut. Ins. Co. v. Farmer's Ins. Group* (1978) 76 Cal.App.3d 1031 [143 Cal.Rptr. 415]; *Valentine v. Aetna Ins. Co.*, 564 F.2d 292; *Estate of Penn v. Amalgamated General Agencies* (1977) 148 N.J.Super. 419 [372 A.2d 1124]). This rule, however, is based on the theory of equitable subrogation: Since the insured would have been able to recover from the primary carrier for a judgment in excess of policy limits caused by the carrier's wrongful refusal to settle, the excess carrier, who discharged the insured's liability as a result of this tort, stands in the shoes of the insured and should be permitted to assert all claims against the primary carrier which the insured himself could have asserted (see *Northwestern Mut. Ins. Co. v. Farmer's Ins. Group*, supra, 76 Cal.App.3d at pp. 1040, 1049–1050, 143 Cal.Rptr. 415). Hence, the rule does not rest upon the finding of any separate duty owed to an excess insurance carrier.

Commercial argues that the implied covenant of good faith and fair dealing is reciprocal, binding the policyholder as well as the carrier (see *Liberty Mut. Ins. Co. v. Altfillisch Constr. Co.* (1977) 70 Cal.App.3d 789, 797 [139 Cal.Rptr. 91]). It is further contended, in effect, that turnabout is fair play: that the implied covenant of good faith and fair dealing applies to the insured as well as the insurer, and thus the policyholder owes a duty to his excess carrier not to unreasonably refuse an offer of settlement below the amount of excess coverage where a judgment of liability above that amount is substantially likely to occur.

This theory, while possessing superficial plausibility and exquisite simplicity, cannot withstand closer analysis. We have no quarrel with the proposition that a duty of good faith and fair dealing in an insurance policy is a two-way street, running from the insured to his insurer as well as vice versa (*Liberty Mut. Ins. Co. v. Altfillisch Constr. Co.,* supra, 70 Cal.App.3d at p. 797, 139 Cal.Rptr. 91; *Crisci v. Security Ins. Co.,* supra, 66 Cal.2d at p. 429, 58 Cal.Rptr. 13, 426 P.2d 173). However, what that duty embraces is dependent upon the nature of the bargain struck between the insurer and the insured and the legitimate expectations of the parties which arise from the contract.

The essence of the implied covenant of good faith in insurance policies is that " 'neither party will do anything which injures the right of the other to receive the benefits of the agreement' " (*Murphy v. Allstate Ins. Co.,* supra, 17 Cal.3d at p. 940, 132 Cal.Rptr. at p. 426, 553 P.2d at p. 586, quoting from *Brown v. Superior Court* (1949) 34 Cal.2d 559, 564 [212 P.2d 878]). One of the most important benefits of a maximum limit insurance policy is the assurance that the company will provide the insured with defense and indemnification for the purpose of protecting him from liability. Accordingly, the insured has the legitimate right to expect that the method of settlement within policy limits will be employed in order to give him such protection.

No such expectations can be said to reasonably flow from an excess insurer to its insured. The object of the excess insurance policy is to provide additional resources should the insured's liability surpass a specified sum. The insured owes no duty to defend or indemnify the excess carrier; hence, the carrier can possess no reasonable expectation that the insured will accept a settlement offer as a means of "protecting" the carrier from exposure. The protection of the insurer's pecuniary interests is simply not the object of the bargain.

As[ ] [we have] stated: "The duty to settle is implied in law to protect the insured from exposure to liability in excess of coverage as a result of the insurer's gamble—on which only the insured might lose." *Murphy v. Allstate Ins. Co.,* supra, 17 Cal.3d at p. 941, 132 Cal.Rptr. at p. 426, 553 P.2d at p. 586.) Similar considerations do not apply where the situation is reversed: where the insured is fully covered by primary insurance, the primary insurer is entitled to take control of the settlement negotiations and the insured is precluded from interfering therewith (see *Shapero v. Allstate Ins. Co.* (1971) 14 Cal.App.3d 433, 437–438 [92 Cal.Rptr. 244], quoting from *Ivy v. Pacific Automobile Ins. Co.* (1958) 156 Cal.App.2d 652, 659–660 [320 P.2d 140]). Where, as here, the policyholder is self-insured for an amount below the beginning of the excess insurance coverage, he is gambling as much with his own money as with that of the carrier. The crucial point is that the excess carrier has no legitimate expectation that the insured will " 'give at least as much consideration to the financial well-being' " of the insurance company as he does to his " 'own interests' " (*Shapero,* supra, 14 Cal. App.3d at p. 438, 92 Cal.Rptr. at p. 247), in considering whether to settle for an amount below the excess policy coverage. In fact, the primary reason excess insurance is purchased is to provide an available pool of money in the event that the decision is made to take the gamble of litigating.

With these principles in mind, it becomes clear that the case of *Liberty Mut. Ins. Co. v. Altfillisch Constr. Co.,* supra, 70 Cal.App.3d 789, 139 Cal.Rptr. 91, upon which Commercial bases its argument, is easily distinguishable.

In *Liberty,* the insurance policy contained the standard clauses giving the company the right of subrogation against third parties, plus a provision which expressly prohibited the insured from doing anything which would prejudice such right (*id.,* at p. 796, 139 Cal.Rptr. 91). The insured leased the equipment covered in the policy to a third party under a contract which effectively released that party from liability for damage, thus cutting off the company's right of subrogation. The court held that the reciprocal covenant of good faith and fair dealing in the insurance policy was breached by the insured, since its act had destroyed "Liberty's expectation of opportunities to subrogate in the event of payment of a loss caused by the negligence of a third party." (P. 797, 139 Cal.Rptr. p. 95.)

In the instant case, whether Commercial could harbor any legitimate expectation that its insured would settle a claim for less than the threshold amount of the policy coverage must be determined in the light of what the parties bargained for. The complaint makes no reference to any language in the policy which would give rise to such expectation. We must therefore ask the question: Did Safeway, when it purchased excess coverage, impliedly promise that it would take all reasonable steps to settle a claim below the limits of Commercial's coverage so as to protect Commercial from possible exposure? Further, did Commercial extend excess coverage with the understanding and expectation that it would receive such favorable treatment from Safeway under the policy? We think not.

At this point, two recent appellate decisions which bear upon this issue, deserve mention.

First, in the case of *Kaiser Foundation Hospitals v. North Star Reinsurance Corp.* (1979) 90 Cal.App.3d 786 [153 Cal.Rptr. 678], the Court of Appeal for the Second District, Division Five, concluded that the relationship between an insured and primary carrier vis-a-vis the excess carrier was governed by an implied covenant of good faith and fair dealing p. 792, 153 Cal.Rptr. 678). That decision, however, dealt with a situation where the insured and its primary carrier acted in collusion to wrongfully allocate certain dates of loss so as to maximize the liability of the excess carrier. It appears that the aggravated conduct on the part of the insured and the primary carrier in taking advantage of the excess carrier prompted the Court of Appeal to invoke the basic principles of good faith and fair dealing in order to give proper redress to the excess carrier. It is to be noted that the opinion takes careful pains to emphasize that in speaking of a good faith and fair dealing duty owed by the insured to the excess carrier under these circumstances, it was expressly not amplifying on the nature of such duty: "[W]e make no attempt to define precisely what rights and duties that entails in a case such as this. Such questions are best decided in the light of concrete facts * * *" (p. 794, 153 Cal.Rptr. p. 683).

We acknowledge that equity requires fair dealing between the parties to an insurance contract. We view the *Kaiser* and *Liberty* cases as pointing up a recognition in the law that the insured status as such is not a license for the insured to engage in unconscionable acts which would subvert the legitimate rights and expectations of the excess insurance carrier.

However, we are unable to derive from this sound principle, the precipitous conclusion that the covenant of good faith and fair dealing should be extended to include a *"Comunale duty"*—that is, a duty which would require an insured contemplating settlement to put the excess carrier's financial interests on at least an equal footing with his own. Such a duty cannot reasonably be found from the mere existence of the contractual relationship between insured and excess carrier in the absence of express language in the contract so providing.

We observe that an apparently contrary conclusion has been reached by the Third District in the recent case of *Transit Casualty Co. v. Spink Corp.* [ ] [supra] 94 Cal.App.3d 124, 156 Cal.Rptr. 360. [ ] [We disapprove that case] insofar as it holds that an insured's duty of good faith and fair dealing to his excess carrier compels him to accept a settlement offer or proceed at his peril where there is a substantial likelihood that an adverse judgment will bring excess insurance coverage into play.

In conclusion, we hold that a policy providing for excess insurance coverage imposes no implied duty upon the insured to accept a settlement offer which would avoid exposing the insurer to liability. Moreover such a duty cannot be predicated upon an insured's implied covenant of good faith and fair dealing. If an excess carrier wishes to insulate itself from liability for an insured's failure to accept what it deems to be a reasonable settlement offer, it may do so by appropriate language in the policy. We hesitate, however, to read into the policy obligations which are neither sought after nor contemplated by the parties. (End of Court of Appeal opinion.)

The judgment is affirmed.

Notes and Questions

1. *Layers of Coverage.* Businesses with large liability exposures tend to purchase coverage in layers. The first layer—often subject to a retained deductible—is termed the primary layer. Other layers are said to be "excess" over the primary or retained layers. Large businesses may have a number of layers of coverage provided by different insurers, which taken together constitute an "excess program." In the principal case Safeway may have retained a layer of liability between its primary and excess coverage because it was unable to locate suitable excess coverage over a primary layer of anything less than $100,000.

2. *The Two Types of "Excess" Liability Insurance.* Excess liability insurance falls into two major categories: *follow-form* and *umbrella* coverage. The former provides insurance above the primary limits according to the same terms as the primary policy. The latter not only provides excess liability insurance, but also provides some primary insurance that fills gaps in the coverage provided by the primary policy. The excess policy at issue in the case that follows these notes contained both follow-form and umbrella coverage provisions.

3. *The Source of the Primary Insurer's Duty.* It is generally accepted that the primary insurer owes a duty to the excess insurer to accept reasonable offers of settlement. See, e.g., *Vencill v. Continental Casualty Company,* 433 F.Supp. 1371 (S.D.W.Va.1977); *Continental Casualty Company v. Reserve Insurance Company,* 307 Minn. 5, 238 N.W.2d 862 (1976). The *Safeway* court's explanation of the duty that runs from the primary to the excess insurer as arising from equitable subrogation virtually decided the case for it. If the source of that duty is the insured's right against the primary insurer, then the duty obviously cannot create rights in an excess insurer against the insured. Thus, if the insured and the primary jointly agree to reject a settlement offer, the excess insurer has no ground for avoiding liability for a judgment in excess of the primary limits of liability, even if the settlement offer would be considered "reasonable" (and therefore improper to reject) in the primary insurer/insured setting. See *Puritan Insurance Company v. Canadian Universal Insurance Company Ltd.,* 775 F.2d 76 (3d Cir. 1985).

Is there any ground, however, for arguing that the source of the duty running from primary to excess insurers lies elsewhere? Certainly the source is not contract, for the two insurers have no contractual relations with each other. Suppose that the primary retains an attorney to defend the insured, and the judgment returned exceeds the primary's policy limits. Some courts hold that the excess insurer is liable for a pro-rata share of the costs of defense. See, e.g., *Jostens, Inc. v. Mission Insurance Company,* 387 N.W.2d 161 (Minn.1986); *Aetna*

Casualty & Surety Company v. Certain Underwriters at Lloyds of London, 56 Cal.App.3d 791, 129 Cal.Rptr. 47 (1976). Can this liability be explained in terms of subrogation, or must its source be some sort of equitable right that runs directly from the primary to the excess insurer?

2. Drop–Down Liability

MISSION NATIONAL INSURANCE COMPANY v. DUKE TRANSPORTATION COMPANY

United States Court of Appeals, Fifth Circuit, 1986.
792 F.2d 550.

ROBERT MADDEN HILL, Circuit Judge:

In this Louisiana diversity case, Duke Transportation Company (Duke) appeals from the district court's grant of a motion for summary judgment in favor of Mission National Insurance Company (Mission). The district court held that Mission, an excess insurance carrier, was not required to provide primary coverage to or to defend its insured, Duke, after the primary insurance carrier, Northwest Insurance Company (Northwest), became insolvent. Finding the district court's ruling entirely correct, we affirm.

I.

Neither party contests the facts of this case. Duke purchased primary insurance coverage from Northwest for general liability, automobile, and worker's compensation claims. The Northwest policy provided for general liability coverage up to a maximum amount of $300,000 for an injury to one person. Duke also purchased umbrella or excess insurance coverage from Mission. The Mission policy provided for individual occurrence and aggregate annual maximum liability coverage in the amount of $5,000,000, subject to the following limitations:

The Company shall only be liable for ultimate net loss the excess of either

(a) the limits of the underlying insurance as set out in the attached schedule [$300,000] in respect of each occurrence *covered* by said underlying insurance, or

(b) the amount as set out in item 2(c) of the Declarations [$10,000] ultimate net loss in respect of each occurrence *not covered* by said underlying insurance, (hereinafter called the "underlying limits"),

and then only up to a further sum as stated in item 2(a) of the Declarations [$5,000,000] in all in respect of each occurrence— subject to a limit as stated in item 2(b) of the Declarations [$5,000,000] in the aggregate for each annual period during the currency of this Policy separately in respect of Products Liability and in respect of Personal Injury (fatal or non-fatal) by Occupational Disease sustained by any employees of the Insured.

In the event of reduction or exhaustion of the aggregate limits of liability under said underlying insurance by reason of losses paid thereunder, this policy subject to all the terms, conditions and definitions hereof shall

(1) in the event of reduction pay the excess of the reduced underlying limit

(2) in the event of exhaustion continue in force as underlying insurance.

(emphasis added). The Mission policy also contained the following limited obligation to defend:

As respects occurrences *covered* under this policy, but *not covered* under the underlying insurances as set out in the attached schedule or under any other collectible insurance, the Company shall

(a) defend in his name and behalf any suit against the Insured alleging liability insured under the provisions of this policy and seeking damages on account thereof, even if such suit is groundless, false or fraudulent, but the Company shall have the right to make such investigation, negotiation and settlement of any claim or suit as may be deemed expedient by the company.

(b) pay all premiums on bonds to release attachments for an amount not in excess of the limit of liability of this policy, all premiums on appeal bonds required in any such defended suit but without any obligations to apply for or furnish such bonds, all costs taxed against the insured in any such suit, all expenses incurred by the Company and all interest accruing after the entry of judgment until the company has paid, tendered or deposited in court that part of such judgment as does not exceed the limit of the Company's liability thereon.

(c) reimburse the Insured for all reasonable expenses, other than loss of earnings incurred at the Company's request

(emphasis added).

When it became apparent that due to insolvency Northwest would be unable to fulfill its obligations of primary coverage and defense and would be placed in liquidation, Duke requested that Mission provide Duke with primary coverage and defense for suits arising during the period covered by the Northwest policy. After Mission refused the request to provide primary coverage and to defend the pending suits, Duke brought a declaratory judgment action in Louisiana state court, requesting that the court require Mission to provide primary coverage and to defend Duke. Mission removed the case to federal district court and also filed a declaratory judgment action asking the district court to declare that Mission owed no primary insurance coverage or duty to defend to Duke; the district court consolidated the two cases. On cross-motions for summary judgment the district court granted Mission's motion. The district court stated that:

> Under the plain language of Mission's policy there is no obligation to pay for any loss which is within the limits of the Northwest policy, that is, until the loss exceeds $300,000. The occurrences involved in these cases were *covered* by the underlying insurance. Further reduction or exhaustion of the limits of the underlying insurance can only be accomplished under the terms of umbrella policy *by payment of losses under the underlying insurance and not by the insolvency of Northwest.* See, *Molina v. U.S. Fire Ins. Co.,* 574 F.2d 1176, 1178 (4th Cir. 1978).
>
> The provision of the insurance agreement containing Mission's obligation to defend provides that Mission shall defend every case not covered by the underlying coverage *or,* by other collectible insurance. Since it is undisputed that the claims involved herein were covered under the Northwest policy, there is no duty to defend by Mission.

(emphasis in original). This appeal followed.

II.

A.

Duke argues that the district court erred in its interpretation of the insurance contract. Duke reads the limitation of liability section as limiting Mission's liability to amounts over the primary coverage only when the primary coverage remains collectible. In the case where the primary insurer collapses, Duke reads the policy as providing "drop down" coverage, i.e., the excess insurer drops down and assumes the primary insurer's responsibilities.

Duke bases its argument on its interpretation of the words "covered" and "not covered" in subsections (a) and (b) of the limitation of liability section of the Mission policy. Duke interprets "covered" to mean covered by the coverage terms of an underlying policy on which the insured can collect. Mission, and the district court, interpret "covered" to mean covered by an underlying policy without regard to whether the insured can collect from the primary insurer.

While our research has not uncovered, nor have the parties cited to us, any Louisiana cases or any other state's cases interpreting the words "covered" and "not covered," we are confident in predicting that a Louisiana court would hold that the use of the words "covered" and "not covered" in the Mission policy does not result in drop down coverage in favor of Duke. Recently, in a case arising out of the collapse of the same primary insurance carrier, we held that the following policy provision did not provide drop down coverage:

> The company shall be liable only for ultimate net loss resulting from any one occurrence in excess of * * * if the insurance afforded by such underlying insurance is inapplicable to the occurrence, the amount stated in the declarations as the retained limit.

Continental Marble & Granite v. Canal Insurance Co., 785 F.2d 1258, 1259 (5th Cir.1986) (construing Louisiana law). In *Continental Marble* the insured argued that the primary insurer's insolvency rendered the underlying insurance "inapplicable" and that, therefore, the excess liability policy dropped down to become the primary policy. We rejected the insured's contention. *Id.*

We believe the term "covered" provides at least as narrow, if not narrower, excess coverage than does the term "inapplicable." Just as the primary insurance coverage in *Continental Marble* remained applicable to the insured so too does the primary insurance coverage in the instant case cover the occurrences Duke claims that Mission should provide primary coverage for and defend Duke against. The terms of the Northwest policy specifically provide coverage for all of the claims that Duke asserts Mission should provide primary coverage for and defend Duke against.

The cases from outside Louisiana also support this interpretation. The only cases where the courts have found that the excess insurer drops down involve policies where the excess insurer used the terms "inapplicable," "collectible," or "recoverable." *E.g. Reserve Insurance Co. v. Pisciotta*, 30 Cal.3d 800, 180 Cal.Rptr. 628, 640 P.2d 764, 772 (1982) ("recoverable"); *Gros v. Houston Fire & Casualty Insurance Co.*, 195 So.2d 674, 676 (La.Ct.App.1967) ("collectible"); *Macalco, Inc. v. Gulf Insurance Co.*, 550 S.W.2d 883, 896 (Mo.Ct.App.1977) ("inapplicable"). Of course, our ruling in *Continental Marble* establishes, at least until the Louisiana courts advise us otherwise, the interpretation to be given to the term "inapplicable." And the terms "collectible" and "recoverable" are clearly distinguishable from the term "covered." When an excess insurer uses the term "collectible" or "recoverable" it is agreeing to drop down in the event the primary coverage becomes uncollectible or unrecoverable; on the other hand, when an excess insurer uses the term "covered" or "not covered," it is agreeing to drop down only in the event that the terms of the underlying policy do not provide coverage for the occurrence or occurrences in question.

B.

Duke also proffers as a reason for its contention that Mission should have to assume Northwest's obligation to provide primary coverage to and defend Duke that the limits of the underlying policy have been exhausted and that, therefore, under the terms of the Mission policy, Mission's policy continues in force as the underlying insurance.

We disagree. The policy provides that: "In the event of reduction or exhaustion of the aggregate limits of liability under said underlying insurance by reason of losses paid thereunder, this policy *   *   * shall *   *   * in the event of exhaustion continue in force as underlying insurance." Duke's argument ignores the phrase "by reason of losses paid thereunder." Duke argues that the underlying policy is exhausted because Northwest is unable to pay any claim under the policy; however, the policy specifically provides that it functions as the underlying insurance only when the exhaustion occurs by reason of losses paid under the policy. Since Duke is not claiming exhaustion due to losses paid under the policy, its argument must fail. *See Molina v. United States Fire Insurance Co.,* 574 F.2d 1176, 1178 (4th Cir.1978); *St. Vincent's Hospital & Medical Center v. Insurance Co. of North America,* 117 Misc.2d 665, 457 N.Y.S.2d 670, 672 (N.Y.Sup.Ct.1982).

C.

Duke's last argument for its contention that Mission should have to assume Northwest's obligation to provide primary coverage to and defend Duke is based on the language of the policy in the section defining "ultimate net loss:"

> Except as provided in insuring Agreement II, the term "Ultimate Net Loss" shall mean the total sum which the insured, or his *Underlying Insurers as scheduled,* or both, become obligated to pay by reason of personal injuries, property damage or advertising liability claims, either through adjudication or compromise, and shall also include hospital, medical and funeral charges and all sums paid as salaries, wages, compensation, fees, charges and law costs, premiums on attachment or appeal bonds, interest, expenses for doctors, lawyers, nurses and investigators and other persons, and for litigation, settlement, adjustment and investigation of claims and suits which are paid as a consequence of any occurrence covered hereunder.

> The Company shall not be liable for expenses as aforesaid when such expenses are included in *other valid and collectible insurance.*

(emphasis added). Duke contends that, because the policy refers to "other valid and collectible insurance," there is an implication that any insurance which might apply to limit Mission's liability must be collectible. Again, we must disagree. When the entire section is read in context, it is clear that the phrase "other valid and collectible insurance" refers to any insurance Duke carried in addition to the underlying insurance listed in the schedule contained in the Mission policy, i.e., the Northwest policy. The Mission policy clearly provides that Mission's liability is excess both to occurrences covered by the Northwest policy and to expenses included in any other valid and collectible insurance. Thus, the use of the term "collectible" in no way refers to the Northwest policy, and Duke's last argument is therefore without merit.

None of the arguments offered by Duke support its contention that Mission's excess liability policy drops down to become the primary policy. We therefore affirm the judgment of the district court.

AFFIRMED.

Notes and Questions

1. *"Covered" versus "Recoverable".* The issue in *Duke* is increasingly litigated. The answer tends to turn, as did *Duke,* on the language the excess policy employs in obligating the insured to maintain primary coverage under the excess layer. Subtle differences produce divergent results. For example, in *Reserve Insurance Company v. Pisciotta,* 30 Cal.3d 800, 180 Cal.Rptr. 628, 640 P.2d 764 (1982), the excess liability policy required the insured to maintain a specified layer of primary coverage. But it also indicated that the excess insurer would be liable for the insured's "ultimate net loss in excess of * * * the amount *recoverable* under the underlying insurance * * *" [emphasis added]. The Supreme Court of California held the provision ambiguous, construed it in favor of the insured, and imposed a drop-down obligation on the excess insurer. Was this provision really ambiguous, or did it instead suggest unambiguously that there was a drop-down obligation in the event of the primary insurer's insolvency?

2. *Allocating the Incentive to Monitor Solvency.* The policy language in *Duke* created an incentive for the insured to monitor the primary insurer's solvency, whereas the policy language in *Pisciotta* created a similar incentive for the excess insurer. Is there reason to prefer one approach to the other? If you were an Insurance Commissioner, would you consider requiring that all excess policies contain the same language?

Chapter Eight

AUTOMOBILE INSURANCE

This Chapter examines a range of issues associated with automobile insurance coverage. A reading of the Sample Policy in the next Section will reveal that many of its provisions run parallel to those in standard personal and commercial general liability policies. This Chapter focuses on the issues that are characteristic of automobile insurance alone, for two reasons. First, and most obviously, they are issues with which any student of insurance law should be familiar. In addition, however, it is important to recognize that the law governing general liability insurance and other special-purpose forms of coverage should not be used as a model for automobile insurance law. Automobile insurance coverage issues have so predominant an impact on ordinary individuals and account for so large a portion of the personal injury law suits brought in the United States that the field is necessarily special. The result is that consumer-protection and victim-protection concerns appear to operate even more strongly in this area of insurance than others.

We begin, as before, with a sample insurance policy, and follow the policy with cases and materials on the four kinds of coverage provided by automobile insurance policies: liability, medical payments or broader personal injury protection, uninsured motorists, and property damage coverage.

A. SAMPLE PERSONAL AUTOMOBILE INSURANCE POLICY

PERSONAL AUTO POLICY | DECLARATIONS

Policy Number

1 Named Insured and mailing address	2 Policy period	The premium stated in the Declarations is the initial premium for this policy. On each renewal, continuation or anniversary of the effective date of this policy the premium shall be computed by us in accordance with our manual then in use.
	From	
	To	
	12:01 a.m. standard time	
The Auto(s) or Trailer(s) described in this policy is principally garaged at the above address unless otherwise stated:	Agent/Broker	

Insured's occupation

3 Description of auto(s) or trailer(s)								
Auto	Year	Trade name	Model	Body type	Vehicle identification number	Actual cost when purchased	Purchased Mo. Yr.	New or used

Auto	Driven to or from work yes/no mi. one way	Car pool	Use	Annual mileage	Sym-bol	Inspection	Classification	Territory liability phy. dam.	Credits (see below)

4 Coverages, Limits of liability and Premiums. Coverage is provided only where a premium or limit of liability is shown for the coverage.

Auto	A-Liability—in thousands	B-Medical payments each person	C-Uninsured motorists in thousands	D-Damage to your auto Actual cash value minus deductible 1-Collision loss 2-Other than collision loss	Towing and labor per disablement
	$	$		$ $	$

Auto	Cov. A	Cov. B	Cov. C	Cov. D-1	Cov. D-2	Towing	Supp. Cov.*	Auto Total
	$ $ $ $							

*Any supplementary coverage premium stated above is for the endorsements indicated here:

Auto	Endorsement no.	Premium $	Auto	Endorsement no.	Premium $	Auto	Endorsement no.	Premium $	Total premium
									$

Endorsements made part of this policy at time of issue:

Loss payee

Countersigned at	Countersignature of licensed resident agent

Premium credits
(not all credits available in every state)

1 Two or more cars
2 Driver training
3 Compact car
4 Good grades saving
5 Good student
6 Bumper discount
7 Accident prevention course
A Passive restraint discount
B Anti-theft device discount

[F3864]

4K3004 36M 7-82-3

PERSONAL AUTO POLICY

AGREEMENT

In return for payment of the premium and subject to all the terms of this policy, we agree with you as follows:

DEFINITIONS

A. Throughout this policy, "you" and "your" refer to:

    1. The "named insured" shown in the Declarations; and

    2. The spouse if a resident of the same household.

B. "We", "us" and "our" refer to the Company providing this insurance.

C. For purposes of this policy, a private passenger type auto shall be deemed to be owned by a person if leased:

    1. Under a written agreement to that person; and

    2. For a continuous period of at least 6 months.

Other words and phrases are defined. They are in quotation marks when used.

D. "Bodily injury" means bodily harm, sickness or disease, including death that results.

E. "Business" includes trade, profession or occupation.

F. "Family member" means a person related to you by blood, marriage or adoption who is a resident of your household. This includes a ward or foster child.

G. "Occupying" means in, upon, getting in, on, out or off.

H. "Property damage" means physical injury to, destruction of or loss of use of tangible property.

I. "Trailer" means a vehicle designed to be pulled by a:

    1. Private passenger auto; or

    2. Pickup or van.

It also means a farm wagon or farm implement while towed by a vehicle listed in 1. or 2. above.

J. "Your covered auto" means:

    1. Any vehicle shown in the Declarations.

    2. Any of the following types of vehicles on the date you become the owner:

      a. a private passenger auto; or

      b. a pickup or van.

    This provision (J.2.) applies only if:

      a. you acquire the vehicle during the policy period;

      b. you ask us to insure it within 30 days after you become the owner; and

      c. with respect to a pickup or van, no other insurance policy provides coverage for that vehicle.

    If the vehicle you acquire replaces one shown in the Declarations, it will have the same coverage as the vehicle it replaced. You must ask us to insure a replacement vehicle within 30 days only if:

      a. you wish to add or continue Coverage for Damage to Your Auto; or

      b. it is a pickup or van used in any "business" other than farming or ranching.

    If the vehicle you acquire is in addition to any shown in the Declarations, it will have the broadest coverage we now provide for any vehicle shown in the Declarations.

    3. Any "trailer" you own.

    4. Any auto or "trailer" you do not own while used as a temporary substitute for any other vehicle described in this definition which is out of normal use because of its:

      a. breakdown;   d. loss; or

      b. repair;   e. destruction.

      c. servicing;

PART A—LIABILITY COVERAGE

INSURING AGREEMENT

A. We will pay damages for "bodily injury" or "property damage" for which any "insured" becomes legally responsible because of an auto accident. Damages include pre-judgment interest awarded against the "insured." We will settle or defend, as we consider appropriate, any claim or suit asking for these damages. In addition to our limit of liability, we will pay all defense costs we incur. Our duty to settle or defend ends when our limit of liability for this coverage has been exhausted. We have no duty to defend any suit or settle any claim for "bodily injury" or "property damage" not covered under this policy.

B. "Insured" as used in this Part means:

1. You or any "family member" for the ownership, maintenance or use of any auto or "trailer."

2. Any person using "your covered auto."

3. For "your covered auto," any person or organization but only with respect to legal responsibility for acts or omissions of a person for whom coverage is afforded under this Part.

4. For any auto or "trailer," other than "your covered auto," any other person or organization but only with respect to legal responsibility for acts or omissions of you or any "family member" for whom coverage is afforded under this Part. This provision (B.4.) applies only if the person or organization does not own or hire the auto or "trailer."

SUPPLEMENTARY PAYMENTS

In addition to our limit of liability, we will pay on behalf of an "insured:"

1. Up to $250 for the cost of bail bonds required because of an accident, including related traffic law violations. The accident must result in "bodily injury" or "property damage" covered under this policy.

2. Premiums on appeal bonds and bonds to release attachments in any suit we defend.

3. Interest accruing after a judgment is entered in any suit we defend. Our duty to pay interest ends when we offer to pay that part of the judgment which does not exceed our limit of liability for this coverage.

4. Up to $50 a day for loss of earnings, but not other income, because of attendance at hearings or trials at our request.

5. Other reasonable expenses incurred at our request.

EXCLUSIONS

A. We do not provide Liability Coverage for any person:

1. Who intentionally causes "bodily injury" or "property damage."

2. For damage to property owned or being transported by that person.

3. For damage to property:

   a. rented to;

   b. used by; or

   c. in the care of;

   that person.

   This exclusion (A.3.) does not apply to damage to a residence or private garage.

4. For "bodily injury" to an employee of that person during the course of employment. This exclusion (A.4.) does not apply to "bodily injury" to a domestic employee unless workers' compensation benefits are required or available for that domestic employee.

5. For that person's liability arising out of the ownership or operation of a vehicle while it is being used to carry persons or property for a fee. This exclusion (A.5.) does not apply to a share-the-expense car pool.

6. While employed or otherwise engaged in the "business" of:

   a. selling;   d. storing; or
   b. repairing;   e. parking;
   c. servicing;

   vehicles designed for use mainly on public highways. This includes road testing and delivery. This exclusion (A.6.) does not apply to the ownership, maintenance or use of "your covered auto" by:

   a. you;

   b. any "family member;" or

   c. any partner, agent or employee of you or any "family member."

7. Maintaining or using any vehicle while that person is employed or otherwise engaged in any "business" (other than farming or ranching) not described in Exclusion A.6. This exclusion (A.7.) does not apply to the maintenance or use of a:

EXCLUSIONS (Continued)

    a.   private passenger auto;

    b.   pickup or van that you own; or

    c.   "trailer" used with a vehicle described in a. or b. above.

8.   Using a vehicle without a reasonable belief that that person is entitled to do so.

9.   For "bodily injury" or "property damage" for which that person:

    a.   is an insured under a nuclear energy liability policy; or

    b.   would be an insured under a nuclear energy liability policy but for its termination upon exhaustion of its limit of liability.

A nuclear energy liability policy is a policy issued by any of the following or their successors:

    a.   American Nuclear Insurers;

    b.   Mutual Atomic Energy Liability Underwriters; or

    c.   Nuclear Insurance Association of Canada.

B.   We do not provide Liability Coverage for the ownership, maintenance or use of:

1.   Any motorized vehicle having fewer than four wheels.

2.   Any vehicle, other than "your covered auto," which is:

    a.   owned by you; or

    b.   furnished or available for your regular use.

3.   Any vehicle, other than "your covered auto," which is:

    a.   owned by any "family member;" or

    b.   furnished or available for the regular use of any "family member."

However, this exclusion (B.3.) does not apply to your maintenance or use of any vehicle which is:

    a.   owned by a "family member;" or

    b.   furnished or available for the regular use of a "family member."

LIMIT OF LIABILITY

A.   The limit of liability shown in the Declarations for this coverage is our maximum limit of liability for all damages resulting from any one auto accident. This is the most we will pay regardless of the number of:

1.   "Insureds;"

2.   Claims made;

3.   Vehicles or premiums shown in the Declarations; or

4.   Vehicles involved in the auto accident.

B.   We will apply the limit of liability to provide any separate limits required by law for bodily injury and property damage liability. However, this provision (B.) will not change our total limit of liability.

OUT OF STATE COVERAGE

If an auto accident to which this policy applies occurs in any state or province other than the one in which "your covered auto" is principally garaged, we will interpret your policy for that accident as follows:

A.   If the state or province has:

1.   A financial responsibility or similar law specifying limits of liability for "bodily injury" or "property damage" higher than the limit shown in the Declarations, your policy will provide the higher specified limit.

2.   A compulsory insurance or similar law requiring a nonresident to maintain insurance whenever the nonresident uses a vehicle in that state or province, your policy will provide at least the required minimum amounts and types of coverage.

B.   No one will be entitled to duplicate payments for the same elements of loss.

FINANCIAL RESPONSIBILITY

When this policy is certified as future proof of financial responsibility, this policy shall comply with the law to the extent required.

OTHER INSURANCE

If there is other applicable liability insurance we will pay only our share of the loss. Our share is the proportion that our limit of liability bears to the total of all applicable limits. However, any insurance we provide for a vehicle you do not own shall be excess over any other collectible insurance.

PART B—MEDICAL PAYMENTS COVERAGE

INSURING AGREEMENT

A. We will pay reasonable expenses incurred for necessary medical and funeral services because of "bodily injury:"

1. Caused by accident; and

2. Sustained by an "insured."

We will pay only those expenses incurred within 3 years from the date of the accident.

B. "Insured" as used in this Part means:

1. You or any "family member:"

   a. while "occupying;" or

   b. as a pedestrian when struck by;

   a motor vehicle designed for use mainly on public roads or a trailer of any type.

2. Any other person while "occupying" "your covered auto."

EXCLUSIONS

We do not provide Medical Payments Coverage for any person for "bodily injury:"

1. Sustained while "occupying" any motorized vehicle having fewer than four wheels.

2. Sustained while "occupying" "your covered auto" when it is being used to carry persons or property for a fee. This exclusion (2.) does not apply to a share-the-expense car pool.

3. Sustained while "occupying" any vehicle located for use as a residence or premises.

4. Occurring during the course of employment if workers' compensation benefits are required or available for the "bodily injury."

5. Sustained while "occupying," or when struck by, any vehicle (other than "your covered auto") which is:

   a. owned by you; or

   b. furnished or available for your regular use.

6. Sustained while "occupying," or when struck by, any vehicle (other than "your covered auto") which is:

   a. owned by any "family member;" or

   b. furnished or available for the regular use of any "family member."

   However, this exclusion (6.) does not apply to you.

7. Sustained while "occupying" a vehicle without a reasonable belief that that person is entitled to do so.

8. Sustained while "occupying" a vehicle when it is being used in the "business" of an "insured." This exclusion (8.) does not apply to "bodily injury" sustained while "occupying" a:

   a. private passenger auto;

   b. pickup or van that you own; or

   c. "trailer" used with a vehicle described in a. or b. above.

9. Caused by or as a consequence of:

   a. discharge of a nuclear weapon (even if accidental);

   b. war (declared or undeclared);

   c. civil war;

   d. insurrection; or

   e. rebellion or revolution.

10. From or as a consequence of the following, whether controlled or uncontrolled or however caused:

    a. nuclear reaction;

    b. radiation; or

    c. radioactive contamination.

LIMIT OF LIABILITY

A. The limit of liability shown in the Declarations for this coverage is our maximum limit of liability for each person injured in any one accident. This is the most we will pay regardless of the number of:

1. "Insureds;"

2. Claims made;

3. Vehicles or premiums shown in the Declarations; or

4. Vehicles involved in the accident.

B. Any amounts otherwise payable for expenses under this coverage shall be reduced by any amounts paid or payable for the same expenses under Part A or Part C.

C. No payment will be made unless the injured person or that person's legal representative agrees in writing that any payment shall be applied toward any settlement or judgment that person receives under Part A or Part C.

OTHER INSURANCE

If there is other applicable auto medical payments insurance we will pay only our share of the loss. Our share is the proportion that our limit of liability bears to the total of all applicable limits. However, any insurance we provide with respect to a vehicle you do not own shall be excess over any other collectible auto insurance providing payments for medical or funeral expenses.

PART C—UNINSURED MOTORISTS COVERAGE

INSURING AGREEMENT

A. We will pay damages which an "insured" is legally entitled to recover from the owner or operator of an "uninsured motor vehicle" because of "bodily injury:"

1. Sustained by an "insured;" and
2. Caused by an accident.

The owner's or operator's liability for these damages must arise out of the ownership, maintenance or use of the "uninsured motor vehicle."

Any judgment for damages arising out of a suit brought without our written consent is not binding on us.

B. "Insured" as used in this Part means:

1. You or any "family member."
2. Any other person "occupying" "your covered auto."
3. Any person for damages that person is entitled to recover because of "bodily injury" to which this coverage applies sustained by a person described in **1.** or **2.** above.

C. "Uninsured motor vehicle" means a land motor vehicle or trailer of any type:

1. To which no bodily injury liability bond or policy applies at the time of the accident.
2. To which a bodily injury liability bond or policy applies at the time of the accident. In this case its limit for bodily injury liability must be less than the minimum limit for bodily injury liability specified by the financial responsibility law of the state in which "your covered auto" is principally garaged.
3. Which is a hit and run vehicle whose operator or owner cannot be identified and which hits:

   a. you or any "family member;"
   b. a vehicle which you or any "family member" are "occupying;" or
   c. "your covered auto."
4. To which a bodily injury liability bond or policy applies at the time of the accident but the bonding or insuring company;

   a. denies coverage; or
   b. is or becomes insolvent.

However, "uninsured motor vehicle" does not include any vehicle or equipment:

1. Owned by or furnished or available for the regular use of you or any "family member."
2. Owned or operated by a self-insurer under any applicable motor vehicle law.
3. Owned by any governmental unit or agency.
4. Operated on rails or crawler treads.
5. Designed mainly for use off public roads while not on public roads.
6. While located for use as a residence or premises.

EXCLUSIONS

A. We do not provide Uninsured Motorists Coverage for "bodily injury" sustained by any person:

1. While "occupying," or when struck by, any motor vehicle owned by you or any "family member" which is not insured for this coverage under this policy. This includes a trailer of any type used with that vehicle.
2. If that person or the legal representative settles the "bodily injury" claim without our consent.
3. While "occupying" "your covered auto" when it is being used to carry persons or property for a fee. This exclusion (A.3.) does not apply to a share-the-expense car pool.
4. Using a vehicle without a reasonable belief that that person is entitled to do so.

B. This coverage shall not apply directly or indirectly to benefit any insurer or self-insurer under any of the following or similar law:

1. workers' compensation law; or
2. disability benefits law.

LIMIT OF LIABILITY

A. The limit of liability shown in the Declarations for this coverage is our maximum limit of liability for all damages resulting from any one accident. This is the most we will pay regardless of the number of:

1. "Insureds;"
2. Claims made;
3. Vehicles or premiums shown in the Declarations; or
4. Vehicles involved in the accident.

B. Any amounts otherwise payable for damages under this coverage shall be reduced by all sums:

1. Paid because of the "bodily injury" by or on behalf of persons or organizations who may be legally responsible. This includes all sums paid under Part A; and
2. Paid or payable because of the "bodily injury" under any of the following or similar law:

   a. workers' compensation law; or
   b. disability benefits law.

C. Any payment under this coverage will reduce any amount that person is entitled to recover for the same damages under Part A.

OTHER INSURANCE

If there is other applicable similar insurance we will pay only our share of the loss. Our share is the proportion that our limit of liability bears to the total of all applicable limits. However, any insurance we provide with respect to a vehicle you do not own shall be excess over any other collectible insurance.

ARBITRATION

A. If we and an "insured" do not agree:

1. Whether that person is legally entitled to recover damages under this Part; or

2. As to the amount of damages;

either party may make a written demand for arbitration. In this event, each party will select an arbitrator. The two arbitrators will select a third. If they cannot agree within 30 days, either may request that selection be made by a judge of a court having jurisdiction.

B. Each party will:

1. Pay the expenses it incurs; and

2. Bear the expenses of the third arbitrator equally.

C. Unless both parties agree otherwise, arbitration will take place in the county in which the "insured" lives. Local rules of law as to procedure and evidence will apply. A decision agreed to by two of the arbitrators will be binding as to:

1. Whether the "insured" is legally entitled to recover damages; and

2. The amount of damages. This applies only if the amount does not exceed the minimum limit for bodily injury liability specified by the financial responsibility law of the state in which "your covered auto" is principally garaged. If the amount exceeds that limit, either party may demand the right to a trial. This demand must be made within 60 days of the arbitrators' decision. If this demand is not made, the amount of damages agreed to by the arbitrators will be binding.

PART D—COVERAGE FOR DAMAGE TO YOUR AUTO

INSURING AGREEMENT

A. We will pay for direct and accidental loss to "your covered auto" or any "non-owned auto," including their equipment, minus any applicable deductible shown in the Declarations. We will pay for loss to "your covered auto" caused by:

1. Other than "collision" only if the Declarations indicate that Other Than Collision Coverage is provided for that auto.

2. "Collision" only if the Declarations indicate that Collision Coverage is provided for that auto.

If there is a loss to a "non-owned auto," we will provide the broadest coverage applicable to any "your covered auto" shown in the Declarations.

B. "Collision" means the upset of "your covered auto" or its impact with another vehicle or object.

Loss caused by the following is considered other than "collision:"

1. Missiles or falling objects;
2. Fire;
3. Theft or larceny;
4. Explosion or earthquake;
5. Windstorm;
6. Hail, water or flood;
7. Malicious mischief or vandalism;
8. Riot or civil commotion;
9. Contact with bird or animal; or
10. Breakage of glass.

If breakage of glass is caused by a "collision," you may elect to have it considered a loss caused by "collision."

C. "Non-owned auto" means any private passenger auto, pickup, van or "trailer" not owned by or furnished or available for the regular use of you or any "family member" while in the custody of or being operated by you or any "family member." However, "non-owned auto" does not include any vehicle used as a temporary substitute for a vehicle you own which is out of normal use because of its:

1. Breakdown;
2. Repair;
3. Servicing;
4. Loss; or
5. Destruction.

TRANSPORTATION EXPENSES

In addition, we will pay up to $10 per day, to a maximum of $300, for transportation expenses incurred by you. This applies only in the event of the total theft of "your covered auto." We will pay only transportation expenses incurred during the period:

1. Beginning 48 hours after the theft; and

2. Ending when "your covered auto" is returned to use or we pay for its loss

EXCLUSIONS

We will not pay for:

1. Loss to "your covered auto" which occurs while it is used to carry persons or property for a fee. This exclusion (1.) does not apply to a share-the-expense car pool.

2. Damage due and confined to:
   a. wear and tear;
   b. freezing;
   c. mechanical or electrical breakdown or failure; or
   d. road damage to tires.

   This exclusion (2.) does not apply if the damage results from the total theft of "your covered auto."

3. Loss due to or as a consequence of:
   a. radioactive contamination;
   b. discharge of any nuclear weapon (even if accidental);
   c. war (declared or undeclared);
   d. civil war;
   e. insurrection; or
   f. rebellion or revolution.

4. Loss to equipment designed for the reproduction of sound. This exclusion (4.) does not apply if the equipment is permanently installed in "your covered auto " or any "non-owned auto"

5. Loss to tapes, records or other devices for use with equipment designed for the reproduction of sound.

6. Loss to a camper body or "trailer" you own which is not shown in the Declarations. This exclusion (6.) does not apply to a camper body or "trailer" you:
   a. acquire during the policy period; and
   b. ask us to insure within 30 days after you become the owner.

7. Loss to any "non-owned auto" or any vehicle used as a temporary substitute for a vehicle you own, when used by you or any "family member" without a reasonable belief that you or that "family member" are entitled to do so.

8. Loss to:
   a. TV antennas;
   b. awnings or cabanas; or
   c. equipment designed to create additional living facilities.

9. Loss to any of the following or their accessories:
   a. citizens band radio;
   b. two-way mobile radio;
   c. telephone; or
   d. scanning monitor receiver.

   This exclusion (9.) does not apply if the equipment is permanently installed in the opening of the dash or console of "your covered auto" or any "non-owned auto". This opening must be normally used by the auto manufacturer for the installation of a radio.

10. Loss to any custom furnishings or equipment in or upon any pickup or van. Custom furnishings or equipment include but are not limited to:
    a. special carpeting and insulation, furniture, bars or television receivers;
    b. facilities for cooking and sleeping;
    c. height-extending roofs; or
    d. custom murals, paintings or other decals or graphics.

11. Loss to equipment designed or used for the detection or location of radar.

12. Loss to any "non-owned auto" being maintained or used by any person while employed or otherwise engaged in the "business" of:
    a. selling;   d. storing; or
    b. repairing;   e. parking;
    c. servicing;

    vehicles designed for use on public highways. This includes road testing and delivery.

13. Loss to any "non-owned auto" being maintained or used by any person while employed or otherwise engaged in any "business" not described in exclusion 12. This exclusion (13.) does not apply to the maintenance or use by you or any "family member" of a "non-owned auto" which is a private passenger auto or "trailer".

LIMIT OF LIABILITY

A. Our limit of liability for loss will be the lesser of the:

1. Actual cash value of the stolen or damaged property; or

2. Amount necessary to repair or replace the property.

   However, the most we will pay for loss to any "non-owned auto" which is a "trailer" is $500.

B. An adjustment for depreciation and physical condition will be made in determining actual cash value at the time of loss.

PAYMENT OF LOSS

We may pay for loss in money or repair or replace the damaged or stolen property. We may, at our expense, return any stolen property to:

1. You; or

2. The address shown in this policy.

If we return stolen property we will pay for any damage resulting from the theft. We may keep all or part of the property at an agreed or appraised value.

NO BENEFIT TO BAILEE

This insurance shall not directly or indirectly benefit any carrier or other bailee for hire.

OTHER INSURANCE

If other insurance also covers the loss we will pay only our share of the loss. Our share is the proportion that our limit of liability bears to the total of all applicable limits. However, any insurance we provide with respect to a "non-owned auto" or any vehicle used as a temporary substitute for a vehicle you own shall be excess over any other collectible insurance.

APPRAISAL

A. If we and you do not agree on the amount of loss, either may demand an appraisal of the loss. In this event, each party will select a competent ap-praiser. The two appraisers will select an umpire. The appraisers will state separately the actual cash value and the amount of loss. If they fail to agree, they will submit their differences to the umpire. A decision agreed to by any two will be binding. Each party will:

1. Pay its chosen appraiser; and

2. Bear the expenses of the appraisal and umpire equally.

B. We do not waive any of our rights under this policy by agreeing to an appraisal.

PART E—DUTIES AFTER AN ACCIDENT OR LOSS

A. We must be notified promptly of how, when and where the accident or loss happened. Notice should also include the names and addresses of any injured persons and of any witnesses.

B. A person seeking any coverage must:

1. Cooperate with us in the investigation, settlement or defense of any claim or suit.

2. Promptly send us copies of any notices or legal papers received in connection with the accident or loss.

3. Submit, as often as we reasonably require:

   a. to physical exams by physicians we select. We will pay for these exams.

   b. to examination under oath and subscribe the same.

4. Authorize us to obtain:

   a. medical reports; and

   b. other pertinent records.

5. Submit a proof of loss when required by us.

C. A person seeking Uninsured Motorists Coverage must also:

1. Promptly notify the police if a hit and run driver is involved.

2. Promptly send us copies of the legal papers if a suit is brought.

D. A person seeking Coverage for Damage to Your Auto must also:

1. Take reasonable steps after loss to protect "your covered auto" and its equipment from further loss. We will pay reasonable expenses incurred to do this.

2. Promptly notify the police if "your covered auto" is stolen.

3. Permit us to inspect and appraise the damaged property before its repair or disposal.

PART F—GENERAL PROVISIONS

BANKRUPTCY

Bankruptcy or insolvency of the "insured" shall not relieve us of any obligations under this policy.

CHANGES

This policy contains all the agreements between you and us. Its terms may not be changed or waived except by endorsement issued by us. If a change requires a premium adjustment, we will adjust the premium as of the effective date of change.

We may revise this policy form to provide more coverage without additional premium charge. If we do this your policy will automatically provide the additional coverage as of the date the revision is effective in your state.

FRAUD

We do not provide coverage for any "insured" who has made fraudulent statements or engaged in fraudulent conduct in connection with any accident or loss for which coverage is sought under this policy.

LEGAL ACTION AGAINST US

A. No legal action may be brought against us until there has been full compliance with all the terms of this policy. In addition, under Part A, no legal action may be brought against us until:

1. We agree in writing that the "insured" has an obligation to pay; or

2. The amount of that obligation has been finally determined by judgment after trial.

B. No person or organization has any right under this policy to bring us into any action to determine the liability of an "insured."

OUR RIGHT TO RECOVER PAYMENT

A. If we make a payment under this policy and the person to or for whom payment was made has a right to recover damages from another we shall be subrogated to that right. That person shall do:

1. Whatever is necessary to enable us to exercise our rights; and

2. Nothing after loss to prejudice them.

However, our rights in this paragraph (A.) do not apply under Part D, against any person using "your covered auto" with a reasonable belief that that person is entitled to do so.

B. If we make a payment under this policy and the person to or for whom payment is made recovers damages from another, that person shall:

1. Hold in trust for us the proceeds of the recovery, and

2. Reimburse us to the extent of our payment.

POLICY PERIOD AND TERRITORY

A. This policy applies only to accidents and losses which occur:

1. During the policy period as shown in the Declarations; and

2. Within the policy territory.

B. The policy territory is:

1. The United States of America, its territories or possessions;

2. Puerto Rico; or

3. Canada.

This policy also applies to loss to, or accidents involving, "your covered auto" while being transported between their ports.

TERMINATION

A. Cancellation. This policy may be cancelled during the policy period as follows:

1. The named insured shown in the Declarations may cancel by:

   a. returning this policy to us; or

   b. giving us advance written notice of the date cancellation is to take effect.

2. We may cancel by mailing to the named insured shown in the Declarations at the address shown in this policy:

   a. at least 10 days notice:

      (1) if cancellation is for nonpayment of premium; or

      (2) if notice is mailed during the first 60 days this policy is in effect and this is not a renewal or continuation policy; or

   b. at least 20 days notice in all other cases.

3. After this policy is in effect for 60 days, or if this is a renewal or continuation policy, we will cancel only:

   a. for nonpayment of premium; or

   b. if your driver's license or that of:

      (1) any driver who lives with you; or

      (2) any driver who customarily uses "your covered auto;"

   has been suspended or revoked. This must have occurred:

      (1) during the policy period; or

      (2) since the last anniversary of the original effective date if the policy period is other than 1 year; or

   c. if the policy was obtained through material misrepresentation.

B. Nonrenewal. If we decide not to renew or continue this policy, we will mail notice to the named insured shown in the Declarations at the address shown in this policy. Notice will be mailed at least 20 days before the end of the policy period. If the policy period is other than 1 year, we will have the right not to renew or continue it only at each anniversary of its original effective date.

C. Automatic Termination. If we offer to renew or continue and you or your representative do not accept, this policy will automatically terminate at the end of the current policy period. Failure to pay the required renewal or continuation premium when due shall mean that you have not accepted our offer.

If you obtain other insurance on "your covered auto," any similar insurance provided by this policy will terminate as to that auto on the effective date of the other insurance.

D. Other Termination Provisions.

1. If the law in effect in your state at the time this policy is issued, renewed or continued:

   a. requires a longer notice period;

   b. requires a special form of or procedure for giving notice; or

   c. modifies any of the stated termination reasons;

   we will comply with those requirements.

2. We may deliver any notice instead of mailing it. Proof of mailing of any notice shall be sufficient proof of notice.

3. If this policy is cancelled, you may be entitled to a premium refund. If so, we will send you the refund. The premium refund, if any, will be computed according to our manuals. However, making or offering to make the refund is not a condition of cancellation.

4. The effective date of cancellation stated in the notice shall become the end of the policy period.

TRANSFER OF YOUR INTEREST IN THIS POLICY

A. Your rights and duties under this policy may not be assigned without our written consent. However, if a named insured shown in the Declarations dies, coverage will be provided for:

   1. The surviving spouse if resident in the same household at the time of death. Coverage applies to the spouse as if a named insured shown in the Declarations; and

2. The legal representative of the deceased person as if a named insured shown in the Declarations. This applies only with respect to the representative's legal responsibility to maintain or use "your covered auto."

B. Coverage will only be provided until the end of the policy period.

TWO OR MORE AUTO POLICIES

If this policy and any other auto insurance policy issued to you by us apply to the same accident, the maximum limit of our liability under all the policies shall not exceed the highest applicable limit of liability under any one policy.

B. LIABILITY INSURANCE

1. Compulsory Insurance Requirements

STATE FARM FIRE & CASUALTY COMPANY
v. TRINGALI

United States Court of Appeals, Ninth Circuit, 1982.
686 F.2d 821.

DUNIWAY, Circuit Judge:

This is an appeal from a summary judgment for the insured in an action for a declaration of rights and liabilities under a compulsory automobile liability insurance policy. We affirm.

I. *Facts.*

Glenn K. Makua intentionally drove his car against a stationary motorcycle on which Matthew S. Tringali was a passenger. Tringali brought a diversity action for personal injuries against Makua in the federal district court. Makua had automobile liability insurance with State Farm Fire & Casualty Company. The policy required State Farm "to pay all sums which the insured shall become legally obligated to pay as damages because of (A) bodily injury sustained by other persons * * * *caused by accident* arising out of the * * * use, * * * of the owned motor vehicle; and to defend * * * any suit against the insured alleging such bodily injury * * * and seeking damages which are payable hereunder. * * *" (emphasis supplied). State Farm filed the present action for a declaratory judgment that it has no obligation either to defend or to indemnify Makua, because the injuries to Tringali were not "caused by accident." Makua made no appearance. State Farm and Tringali each moved for summary judgment.

The district judge entered a summary judgment for Tringali without reaching questions of intent. He found that "the law of Hawaii is that an insurer of a motor vehicle involved in an accident must provide coverage for damages which the driver of the motor vehicle becomes obligated to pay, up to the limit of the policy, even if the accident may have been caused intentionally by the driver of the motor vehicle." He also found that "an insurer is liable regardless of the mental state of the insured." The judgment was entered as a final judgment under F.R.Civ.P. 54(b). State Farm appeals.

II. *The Hawaii Statutes.*

Automobile insurance in Hawaii is regulated by various statutes. One is the Motor Vehicle Safety Responsibility Act, Hawaii Revised Statutes, chapter 287. This provides that a driver or owner who has an accident must post security unless certain conditions are met. H.R.S. § 287–5. One way to avoid posting security is to have an automobile liability policy with a certain minimum coverage. H.R.S. § 287–7. The Act also provides that a driver guilty of certain offenses, under certain conditions, may be required to provide proof of financial responsibility as a condition of retaining a driver's license. H.R.S. § 287–20. One acceptable form of proof is a certificate of insurance showing that the driver has a "motor vehicle policy" with a certain minimum coverage and an "omnibus clause," covering those who use the car with express or implied permission. H.R.S. § 287–25. This Motor Vehicle Safety Responsibility Act is still in effect insofar as it is consistent with the later enacted Chapter 294, Motor Vehicle Accident Reparations.

H.R.S., Chapter 294, makes insurance compulsory for all who own or drive a car in Hawaii. Those who do must have insurance that satisfies certain specified conditions. H.R.S. § 294–8(a)(1). There must be provision for "no-fault benefits for *accidental harm*." H.R.S. § 294–4 (emphasis supplied). These benefits compensate for such expenses as doctors' fees and hospital charges and loss of earnings, and are subject to a maximum limit of $15,000 per person. H.R.S. § 294–2, 3. There must also be provision for "sums which the owner or operator may legally be obligated to pay for injury * * * which arises out of * * * use of the motor vehicle: (1) Liability coverage of not less than $25,000 for all damages arising out of *accidental harm* sustained by any one person as the result of any one *accident* applicable to each person sustaining *accidental harm* arising out of * * * use, * * * of the insured vehicle. * * *" H.R.S. § 294–10(a) (emphasis supplied). This statute also abolishes tort liability except in some circumstances, but it retains tort liability in cases of death or certain serious injuries, cases where expenses exceed the no-fault benefits, and cases where a person intentionally causes injury to another. H.R.S. § 294–6.

The insurance policy in the present case was not certified under the provisions of Chapter 287. Tringali and State Farm agree that the policy was issued under Chapter 294, not Chapter 287. It is clear that Makua and State Farm, the parties to the contract for insurance, intended that it be interpreted so as to provide the "not less than $25,000" coverage for "accidental harm sustained by any one person" that is required by H.R.S. § 294–10(a). Thus, in the present case, we are concerned with compulsory liability insurance rather than with no-fault insurance, even though Hawaii uses the label "no-fault insurance" for the whole package of insurance required by Chapter 294.

III. *Compulsory Insurance and Intent.*

We have found no relevant decision by the Supreme Court of Hawaii, and the parties cite none. We delayed submission of this case in the hope that the question would be decided in *State Farm Mutual Automobile Insurance Co. v. Fernandez*, Civil No. 54527 (May 21, 1982). However, that case was decided on other grounds, so we must ourselves address a question of first impression in the law of Hawaii.

In *Hartford Accident and Indemnity Co. v. Wolbarst*, 1948, 95 N.H. 40, 57 A.2d 151, the Supreme Court of New Hampshire held that a policy which provided that it complied with "the provision of the Motor Vehicle Financial Responsibility Law of any state" covered injuries where a collision was intended by the insured. The relevant law was that of New Hampshire, and it spoke of "bodily injuries * * * *accidentally sustained*" (emphasis supplied). *Id.*, 57 A.2d at 152–53. Other courts have refused to follow this decision, saying that a state legislature, when it enacted a financial responsibility law, intended only to make compulsory for proven bad risks the usual insurance coverage against accidental harm and not to require them to have broader coverage. *Utica Mutual Insurance Co. v. Travelers' Indemnity Co.*, 1982, 223 Va. 145, 286 S.E.2d 225; *Snyder v. Nelson*, 1977, 278 Or. 409, 564 P.2d 681. However, these cases did not involve compulsory insurance.

In *Wheeler v. O'Connell*, 1937, 297 Mass. 549, 9 N.E.2d 544, the Supreme Judicial Court of Massachusetts interpreted a statutory requirement of insurance for "bodily injuries * * * arising out of the ownership, operation, maintenance, control or use upon the ways of the commonwealth of [a] motor vehicle. * * * " A policeman who stopped a car was pushed off its running board and won a civil suit against the driver for "wilful wanton and reckless behavior" where there was not "negligence or gross negligence." The court found that the driver's insurer was liable. It said that the words of the statute must be read broadly, and continued:

> The purpose of the compulsory motor vehicle insurance law is not, like ordinary insurance, to protect the owner or operator alone from loss, but rather is to provide compensation to persons injured through the operation of the automobile insured by the owner. * * * And it has been pointed out by this court in many cases that the protection of the traveller on the public ways is the fundamental basis of the statute. * * * [I]f the purpose of the statute is to compensate the injured party rather than to save the operator of the vehicle from loss it is difficult to see why an injured person's rights should be affected by the fact that the operator's conduct was wilful, * * * as distinguished from negligent. The evil intended to be remedied is as certainly present in the one case as in the other.

9 N.E.2d at 546. The court acknowledged that there was a rule of public policy in insurance law that makes void a policy indemnifying an insured against a liability for his wilful wrong, but held that the rule did not apply to compulsory automobile liability insurance. "The statute itself is declaratory of public policy applicable to compulsory insurance and supersedes any rule of public policy which obtains in ordinary insurance law." *Id.*, 9 N.E.2d at 547.

It is true that the section of Massachusetts law construed in *Wheeler* did not use the term "accident" or "accidental." However, the court did say that "if the policy under consideration had contained an express exception against liability for injuries caused by the wilful conduct of the operator, such a policy would be in violation of [a further section of Massachusetts insurance law], as containing an exception or exclusion 'as to specified accidents or injuries or causes thereof.'" *Id.* Here the term "accident" is used, and apparently includes wilful acts.

In *Nationwide Mutual Insurance Co. v. Roberts,* 1964, 261 N.C. 285, 134 S.E.2d 654, the Supreme Court of North Carolina interpreted a statute that did contain the word "accident" in the description of compulsory insurance. The insured had deliberately run down a person with whom he had previously had an argument. The law required insurance for damages "arising out of the ownership, maintenance or use of [a] motor vehicle * * * subject to limits * * * as follows: five thousand dollars * * * because of bodily injury to one person *in any one accident. * * **" *Id.,* 134 S.E.2d at 659 (emphasis supplied). The court said this: "The primary purpose of compulsory motor vehicle liability insurance is to compensate innocent victims who have been injured by the negligence of financially irresponsible motorists. Its purpose is not, like that of ordinary insurance, to save harmless the tortfeasor himself. Therefore, there is no reason why the victim's right to recover from the insurance carrier should depend upon whether the conduct of its insured was intentional or negligent. * * * The victim's rights against the insurer are not derived through the insured as in the case of voluntary insurance." *Id.* It added: "[W]e hold that injuries intentionally inflicted by the use of an automobile are within the coverage of a motor vehicle liability policy as defined by [the North Carolina statute]. The word *accident* as used in that section with reference to compulsory insurance is used in the popular sense and means any unfortunate occurrence causing injury for which the insured is liable." *Id.* at 660 (emphasis in original).

State Farm has not drawn our attention to any cases where intentionally caused injuries were found to be outside the scope of a compulsory automobile insurance scheme. We are persuaded that the adoption of a compulsory scheme of automobile liability insurance very strongly suggests a legislative intent that there be no exclusion of intentional acts of the insured. Compulsory automobile insurance is adopted for the protection of the victims. From the viewpoint of the victim, the mental state of the insured is irrelevant. The common objection to insuring one's self against liability for deliberately wrongful acts has little force in this context. Where compulsory automobile liability insurance statutes use the terms "accident" or "accidental" we should, if possible, read those terms in a way that does not exclude intentional acts of, or even intentional wrongs done by, the insured. An event is accidental if it is neither expected nor intended from the viewpoint of the person who is injured. *Tomlin v. State Farm Mutual Automobile Liability Insurance Co.,* 1980, 95 Wis.2d 215, 290 N.W.2d

285, 289 (policy worded the same as that in the present case); *Nation-wide Mutual Insurance Co. v. Roberts, supra.*

"Accidental harm" is defined in the statute of Hawaii as "bodily injury, death, sickness or disease caused by a motor vehicle accident to a person." H.R.S. § 294–2(1). There is nothing to suggest a restrictive reading of the term "motor vehicle accident." It can and should be read to include deliberately caused collisions and deliberate attempts to injure through a collision. The terms "accident" and "accidental" are used throughout Chapter 294, including those parts of the statute that describe no-fault benefits, H.R.S. § 294–3 to –5. We are convinced that the legislature of Hawaii could not have intended no-fault benefits to depend upon a determination of the state of mind of the drivers of automobiles. That would have been inconsistent with the no-fault concept. The words should be read in the same way throughout the statute.

State Farm intended that the policy issued to Makua should satisfy the requirements of Chapter 294. The policy speaks of injury "caused by accident." It gives no definition of "accident." In particular it does not give a definition of the sort now suggested by State Farm: "an unexpected happening without intention or design" or something "neither expected nor intended from the viewpoint of the insured." Nor does the policy contain any clause that expressly excludes from coverage intentional injuries or injuries caused by intentional acts.

State Farm quotes from the debate in the Hawaiian Legislature when the House adopted the report of the Conference Committee:

Representative O'Connor responded:

"＊ ＊ ＊ In this State today, punitive or exemplary damages are recovered against one who operates a motor vehicle in a wanton and reckless manner with gross negligence; for example, the drag racer who loses control of his car on one of our streets or something of that nature.

For that reason, from time immemorial, there has been no insurance protection for that type of action. Even under our bankruptcy law, such a judgment cannot be wiped out by bankruptcy. These are damages which are given in punishment against the driver who acts in that fashion. For that reason, they fall outside the scope of any insurance plan and that is why they are exempted in this plan.

I would suggest that the comments made by the prior speaker that they return the whole area of tort under a simple negligence scheme of this State is entirely erroneous."

Representative Wong then inquired where this particular individual would get his relief.

Representative O'Connor replied that they would get it from the pocketbook of he who acts wantonly, recklessly or negligently on our streets with his motor vehicle and not from his insurance coverage.

House Journal, 1973 Regular Session, Seventh Legislature of Hawaii, p. 702.

It is possible to read these remarks to support State Farm's position. However, it would be wrong to do so, for two reasons. First, the parties agree that Representative O'Connor was answering a question about what is now H.R.S. § 294–6(d), a section that retains the tort system for actions against one who "intentionally causes injury." The point to be answered seems to have been that the section restricted the no-fault system too much. Those who opposed the bill in the House demanded a pure no-fault system rather than the hybrid favored by the majority. Representative O'Connor's remarks are to be read as an explanation that a tort action for intentional wrongs must be preserved because the no-fault system did not provide punitive damages. Second, whether or not that interpretation is correct, Representative O'Connor can be understood as asserting that the bill did not change the traditional rule that insurance will not indemnify against punitive damages, and not as asserting that it did not change the other traditional rule that insurance will not indemnify any claim arising from injuries intended by the insured. We do not decide the question of whether the law of Hawaii requires an automobile liability insurer to indemnify its insured against punitive damages. * * *

Affirmed.

Notes and Questions

1. *Liability Insurance Requirements.* Every state has enacted some form of statutory requirement regarding automobile insurance. In some states, *Financial Responsibility Statutes* require any party who is held liable for damages arising out of an auto accident to show proof of financial responsibility as a prerequisite to continued licensure. Such proof typically is in the form of liability insurance in specified minimum amounts. In many other states the requirement is imposed from the outset, i.e., before the driver's first accident. There are also variations on these two themes. For example, drivers may have to show either that they have the required minimum liability coverage *or* that they have contributed to a state fund designed to compensate the victims of uninsured drivers. For more detailed discussion, see R. Jerry, Understanding Insurance Law 647 (1987).

2. *Victim Protection or Driver Insurance?* The decision in *Tringali* illustrates the strength of the public policy underlying compulsory insurance legislation: the primary purpose of such legislation has been to assure compensation of victims. The moral hazard created by decisions such as *Tringali* is sometimes tolerated in order to help achieve this purpose. Are the courts correct in concluding that the policy behind these statutes is strong enough to override the moral hazard created by insuring liability for intentional harm? Legislatures

adopting compulsory insurance statutes obviously contemplate that large numbers of victims of non-negligent driving (or of their own negligence) will not receive compensation via another driver's liability insurance. In light of this recognition, is it not possible that these legislatures contemplated that victims of intentional wrongdoing might also be denied such compensation? If there had been evidence in the record in *Tringali* that the State Farm policy had been approved by the state Insurance Commissioner and contained a provision excluding coverage of liability for damage that is "either expected or intended from the standpoint of the insured," would the result in *Tringali* have been different? Should it be different under these circumstances?

3. *Reimbursement of the Insurer.* Some states have resolved this dilemma by permitting insurers to make provision in their policies for reimbursement from the insured in situations such as *Tringali*. Thus, in relation to the victim, the tortfeasor is insured; in relation to the tortfeasor's own insurer, however, he is merely a debtor whose obligation has been paid by a guarantor. Does this approach violate the rule that an insurer cannot have subrogation against its own insured? Does it matter?

4. *The Household Exclusion.* Another issue whose resolution is influenced by the purposes underlying compulsory automobile liability insurance legislation is the validity of policy provisions excluding coverage of liability to persons residing in the insured's own home. This *household exclusion* (sometimes termed the *family exclusion*) is designed to eliminate the possibility of fraudulent suits within the family that arises once intra-family tort immunity is abolished, as it has been in many states. A typical compulsory liability insurance statute requires the purchase of insurance in specified amounts against liability for bodily injury or property damage "to any person." Most courts interpreting such statutory provisions have held the household exclusion to be inconsistent with the requirement and invalidated it. See, e.g., *Mutual of Enumclaw Insurance Company v. Wiscomb*, 97 Wash.2d 203, 643 P.2d 441 (1982).

Some courts explain this result by saying that the exclusion is against public policy. This is little more than a tautology if what they mean is that insurance policy provisions that violate statutes violate public policy. If this is not all that these courts mean—that is, if there is more to their reasoning than mere application of a statutory prohibition—what is going on in such decisions? For example, suppose that a son sues his father (who is a member of the same household) for negligence in the operation of the insured auto, and the jury awards the son $100,000. The father has auto liability insurance covering him against liability to any single person in the amount of $100,000, and the state has a compulsory liability insurance statute requiring the purchase of at least $20,000 of such insurance. The father's policy contains the following provision:

> We do not provide Liability Coverage for any person for bodily injury to you or any family member to the extent that the limits of liability for this coverage exceed the limits of liability required by the state Compulsory Insurance Act.

Is the father entitled to $100,000 or $20,000 of coverage? Cf. *Farmers Insurance Exchange v. Call,* 712 P.2d 231 (Utah 1985) (household exclusion void as to minimum amount of coverage required by Utah financial responsibility statute).

2. The Omnibus Clause

CURTIS v. STATE FARM MUTUAL AUTOMOBILE INSURANCE COMPANY

United States Court of Appeals, Tenth Circuit, 1979.
591 F.2d 572.

HOLLOWAY, Circuit Judge.

Defendant State Farm Mutual Automobile Insurance Company appeals from a declaratory judgment, entered on a jury verdict, declaring that a liability insurance policy issued by State Farm to Robert E. Ahrens and JoAnn Ahrens extended coverage to one Joseph Wallace, the driver of the Ahrens vehicle at the time of the accident involved herein. Jurisdiction is founded upon diversity. The primary question before us is whether Wallace comes within the definition of "insured" contained in the policy's omnibus clause as "any * * * *person* while using the *owned motor vehicle,* PROVIDED THE OPERATION AND THE ACTUAL USE OF SUCH VEHICLE ARE WITH THE PERMISSION OF THE NAMED INSURED * * * AND ARE WITHIN THE SCOPE OF SUCH PERMISSION * * *." [1]

The Ahrens family had three cars—an Oldsmobile, a Volkswagen owned by Mr. and Mrs. Ahrens, and a pickup. The older Ahrens girls,

---

1. The omnibus clause constitutes only one part of the five-part definition of "insured" contained in the policy. The definition as a whole states that the unqualified word "insured" includes:

(1) the named insured, and

(2) if the named insured is a *person or persons,* also includes his or their spouse(s), if a *resident* of the same household, and

(3) if *residents* of the same household, the relatives of the first *person* named in the declarations, or of his spouse, and

(4) any other *person* while using the *owned motor vehicle,* PROVIDED THE OPERATION AND THE ACTUAL USE OF SUCH VEHICLE ARE WITH THE PERMISSION OF THE NAMED INSURED OR SUCH SPOUSE AND ARE WITHIN THE SCOPE OF SUCH PERMISSION, and

(5) under coverages A and B any other *person* or organization, but only with respect to his or its liability for the use of such *owned motor vehicle* by an *insured* as defined in the four subsections above.

(Plaintiff's Ex. No. 1). It is evident that Wallace can fit—if at all—only within the omnibus clause (4), since he is unrelated to the named insureds, Robert E. Ahrens and JoAnn Ahrens. (II R. 166).

Beth and Shawnna, mainly used the Oldsmobile and Volkswagen, and Mr. Ahrens used the pickup to drive to work.

The accident in question occurred in the early morning of July 5, 1973, outside of Cheyenne, Wyoming. During the previous afternoon, Deborah Ahrens, the 14–year–old daughter of Robert and JoAnn Ahrens, had made arrangements with her friend Helen Curtis and with Brian Tottenhoff and Joseph Wallace to meet at the local ballpark between 1:00 and 2:00 a.m. to shoot off some fireworks. (II R. 40). Helen was spending the night of July 4 with Deborah at her home. Sometime between 1:30 and 2:00 a.m., Deborah and Helen left the Ahrens home—after Deborah's parents had gone to bed—and proceeded to drive the family Volkswagen to the chosen meeting place.

Deborah was not licensed to drive. She had taken the car keys from their customary location on top of the television set without her parents' knowledge. (Id. 33, 45–46, 141). On their way out of the Ahrens' neighborhood, the girls encountered Deborah's older sister, Beth, driving home in the family Oldsmobile. The two sisters stopped and talked for five or ten minutes, but Deborah's use of the Volkswagen was never discussed. (Id. 47). Before she left home, Deborah had also told Shawnna what they were going to do that night; Shawnna knew the girls were going out and made no comment either to forbid or consent to their going. However, Deborah did not tell Beth or Shawnna that she and Helen were going to pick up the boys. (Id. 48–49, 52–53, 54).

Deborah and Helen picked up the boys and went to shoot off the fireworks. The four then started home around 3:30 a.m. Deborah had been driving all along, but at this point Joe Wallace asked if he could drive, and she agreed. (Id. 49). Wallace, like Deborah, was unlicensed. According to Deborah, the accident occurred about five minutes after Wallace took the wheel: "He was going too fast, and he went airbound with the car, and it went over on to the embankment." (Id. 51).

Helen Curtis suffered extensive injuries in the accident, and her father incurred about $15,000 in medical expenses for her treatment. When State Farm disclaimed coverage as to Wallace, Helen's father brought this suit on her behalf for a determination that the defendant State Farm was obligated to defend and indemnify Wallace under the company's policy issued to Mr. and Mrs. Ahrens. As noted, a verdict and declaratory judgment adverse to the company resulted. This appeal followed.

I

The company's primary contention on appeal is that the evidence is clear that Wallace did not have permission to drive the vehicle under the terms of the omnibus clause of the policy, so that coverage did not extend to him. The company says that the district court therefore erred in its denial of a motion for a directed verdict made at the conclusion of plaintiff's case and again at the end of defendant's case, as well as in its denial of a motion for judgment n.o.v.

Wallace was not covered by the policy unless his operation and actual use of the Volkswagen were with the permission of a named insured. The district court instructed the jury that Robert Ahrens and his wife JoAnn were the named insureds under the policy and that neither named insured gave Wallace actual permission to drive the car. (II R. 166). Thus, the controlling question is whether Wallace had implied permission for use of the car so as to bring him within the coverage of the policy.

In *United Services Automobile Association v. Preferred Accident Insurance Co.*, 190 F.2d 404, 406 (10th Cir.), we stated that:

> The necessary permission may be in the form of implied affirmative consent. It may result by implication from the relationship of the parties and their course of conduct in which they mutually acquiesced. And it may arise from a course of conduct pursued with knowledge of the facts for such time and in such manner as to signify clearly and convincingly an understanding consent which amounts in law to a grant of the privilege involved.

The question of implied permission is thus one of fact. *Phoenix Assurance Co. v. Latta*, 373 P.2d 146, 149 (Wyo.). Plaintiff points to much in the record which, it is said, supports the jury's implicit finding of implied permission. In view of such evidence, plaintiff argues that it would have been improper for the trial court to direct a verdict or grant judgment n.o.v. for defendant, because the evidence did not point "all one way" in favor of the moving party. *Bertot v. School District No. 1*, 522 F.2d 1171, 1178 (10th Cir.).

The foundation for a finding of implied permission, plaintiff argues, is the fact that JoAnn Ahrens, Deborah's mother and one of the named insureds, has been blind due to the effects of diabetes since before 1973. Because of this tragic fact, Mrs. Ahrens has had to rely on her three daughters to "take care of everything" around the house. (II R. 14). In July 1973, the two older daughters, Beth (then age 17) and Shawnna (age 16), were licensed drivers and had free use of the family cars, both for carrying out family-related responsibilities such as grocery shopping and for going to and from their part-time jobs. (Id. 16, 26). As noted, the family custom was to keep the car keys on top of the television set; anyone who had used the car would lay the keys down on the set and anyone who wanted to use the car would take the keys off the set. (Id. 19).

Around that time Beth also often took one of the cars out of town on recreational trips to Steamboat Springs and similar places, staying two or three days. Mrs. Ahrens knew that on such trips friends of Beth's went with her and drove the car. There was testimony that Beth's friends McCue and Fleming would sometimes drive the car on such trips and that, while neither JoAnn nor Robert Ahrens gave express permission to them to drive, both parents knew about such driving and neither objected to it. (Id. 20, 29, 143, 145). Also, Shawnna was allowed to take the family cars around town frequently and drove one of the cars to work sometimes. (Id. 18).

Thus, Beth and Shawnna were allowed to drive the cars "as they needed or liked" (Id. 26)—except when their father was using them. They bought gas "when they had money and they were out and they needed it"—though customarily their father would maintain the automobiles in working condition. (Id. 35–36). And with Beth at least, there was precedent for allowing other persons to drive the family automobiles without express permission from either parent.

With respect to Deborah, there was testimony that Mr. Ahrens had signed a statement that he had never given Deborah any restrictions as to her use of the car and that there had been no express prohibition to its use. The statement also said, however, that "Debbie was not supposed to drive this vehicle." (Id. 80–82). Mr. Ahrens testified that he thought his wife had been asked during the taking of earlier statements whether the parents had ever specifically told Deborah she could not take the car, that he had said they never specified she could not take it, but that it was "understood on down the line, that I think it probably started with Beth and then Shawnna and then Debbie." (Id. 146). Both Mr. and Mrs. Ahrens testified that they had not given Deborah permission to use the car on the night of the accident and did not know that she had taken the car until they were notified about the accident. (Id. 26–27, 34, 140, 142).

Deborah testified that one time she had driven a family car with her father to a friends' house. She also said that once about a month before the accident she had driven the car without her father. (Id. 38–39). However, her parents both testified they had not known that Deborah had taken the Volkswagen out on any occasion before the accident. (Id. 23, 140).

Plaintiff argues that because of the unusual circumstances relating to the blindness of Mrs. Ahrens, the mother and father had permitted the two older daughters to operate the family vehicles as if they had actually been owners, and that when the older daughters were aware of Deborah's going for the ride in the Volkswagen on the night of July 4, they had unqualified permission to allow Deborah to operate the car. (Brief of Appellee, 4). From Beth and Shawnna's implied consent that Deborah drive the car, and from Deborah's actual consent for Wallace to drive, plaintiff says there was implied consent by Mr. and Mrs. Ahrens that Wallace drive the Volkswagen at the time of the accident.[2]

We must hold that, on this record, the judgment in favor of coverage cannot stand. Plaintiff had the burden of proof to establish

2. There is no evidence which would support an inference that Deborah had direct permission to drive the Volkswagen from her parents. For this reason it cannot be said that Wallace had implied permission from Mr. and Mrs. Ahrens as the named insureds merely because he had Deborah's actual permission to drive. See *Travelers Insurance Co. v. Weatherford,* 520 S.W.2d 726 (Tenn.); *State Farm Mutual Automobile Insurance Co. v. Strang,* 27 Utah 2d 362, 496 P.2d 707; *Bilsten v. Porter,* 547 P.2d 255 (Colo.Ct.App.).

coverage. See *Chronister v. State Farm Mutual Automobile Insurance Co.,* 72 N.M. 159, 381 P.2d 673, 675; 46 C.J.S. Insurance § 1641. Under the terms of the omnibus clause, permission of the named insureds, Mr. and Mrs. Ahrens, to the operation and actual use of the Volkswagen was required for coverage to apply. The only plausible theory in this case is that permission flowed from the parents to Beth and Shawnna, from them to Deborah, and from Deborah then to Wallace, the driver at the time of the accident. As noted, however, Beth and Shawnna were not told by Deborah that Wallace would even be accompanying Deborah and Helen the night of the accident and, of course, the parents did not even know that Deborah was going to use the car.

In view of the broad permission given by the parents to Beth and Shawnna for use of the family cars, an inference might be drawn that the older daughters as first permittees could permit Deborah to use the Volkswagen. See *Gillen v. Globe Indemnity Co.,* 377 F.2d 328, 331 (8th Cir.); *Krebsbach v. Miller,* 22 Wis.2d 171, 125 N.W.2d 408, 411; *Baesler v. Globe Indemnity Co.,* 33 N.J. 148, 162 A.2d 854, 857; *Government Employees Insurance Co. v. Lammert,* 483 S.W.2d 652 (Mo.Ct.App.). The trial judge apparently accepted such a view as valid under Wyoming law since he charged the jury that "the named insured's permission to a second permittee need not be express, *but may be implied from the broad nature of scope of the initial permission,* or from the conduct of the parties and from the attendant facts and circumstances." (II R. 167) (emphasis added).

The difficulty, however, is that here it is not the driving of Deborah as a second permittee which is in question, but that of Wallace as a *third* permittee. We note again that neither of the first permittees, Beth and Shawnna, were told by Deborah that Wallace was to be in the car with Deborah and Helen. We are convinced that implied permission cannot be stretched so far as to include the driving of Wallace on the night of the accident. See *West v. McNamara,* 159 Ohio St. 187, 111 N.E.2d 909; *Bailey v. General Insurance Co.,* 265 N.C. 675, 144 S.E.2d 898; *Novo v. Employers' Liability Assurance Corp.,* 295 Mass. 232, 3 N.E.2d 737, denying coverage as to third permittees.[3] A scintilla of evidence, such as the remote permission of the parents given to Beth and Shawnna to drive the family cars, was not enough to raise a jury

---

3. We find only one case holding that a third permittee was covered under an omnibus clause and it is easily distinguished from this case, as well as from *West, Bailey* and *Novo.* In *Boyer v. Massachusetts Bonding & Insurance Co.,* 277 Mass. 359, 178 N.E. 523, the named insured lent the vehicle to his son (the first permittee) who in turn permitted one Chester Carter (the second permittee) to take the car to Massachusetts and have use of it, and then leave it with his family to be sold. Chester Carter left the car with his father, who permitted Chester's brother Lloyd to use the car, and Lloyd's use resulted in the accident. It was found that the insured's son (the first permittee) had been given full use and custody of the car and that his acts were within his authority.

On appeal, the Massachusetts Court referred to the fact that the insured "knew what his son had done, and [that] it could be found that he assented to the use of the vehicle by the Carters, although the details of that use were not specifically authorized." Thus, *Boyer* is unlike the instant case where the named insureds had no knowledge that either Deborah or Wallace would use the car.

question of implied permission for Wallace to drive the Volkswagen. We are convinced that the evidence points only one way and is not susceptible of a reasonable inference that Wallace had any implied permission of the parents to drive their car. *Bertot v. School District No. 1, supra,* 522 F.2d 1171, 1175–76.

We find two Wyoming cases dealing with omnibus clauses, *Wyoming Farm Bureau Mutual Insurance Co. v. May,* 434 P.2d 507 (Wyo.), and *Phoenix Assurance Co. v. Latta,* 373 P.2d 146 (Wyo.). These cases do not support the plaintiff's theory for extending implied permission as far as Deborah's friend Wallace, and we feel they indicate that the Wyoming courts would not go that far.[4] We are mindful that the views of a resident district judge on the unsettled law of his state are persuasive and ordinarily accepted. *Sade v. Northern Natural Gas Co.,* 483 F.2d 230, 234 (10th Cir.). However, regardless of whether some such expression of views on state law was made here by the trial court's rulings and charge,[5] or whether the court merely treated the issue as one for the jury, we feel it was clearly error on this record to enter judgment affording coverage to Wallace.[6] The evidence simply does not stretch far enough to support any reasonable inference that Wallace had implied permission from the named insureds, Mr. and Mrs. Ahrens, for coverage under the omnibus clause as written.

II

As another basis for sustaining the judgment, plaintiff argues that the facts did not even involve a primary-secondary permission situation, that this was rather a situation where the two older daughters became the named insureds because of the mother's blindness, and that since there was no way in which JoAnn Ahrens could have operated

---

4. Thus, in *Phoenix Assurance Co. v. Latta, supra,* 373 P.2d at 150, although holding that coverage applied, the court stated that initial permission to use an automobile would not suffice in all cases to bring the use of the vehicle within coverage of an omnibus clause, contrary to the liberal view adopted by some authorities. Likewise, in *Wyoming Farm Bureau Mutual Insurance Co. v. May, supra,* 434 P.2d at 510–11, the court cited cases in support of a no-coverage holding, several of which express the view that general permission by a named insured to another is not as such sufficient to imply like permission to a second, unknown permittee. See *e.g., General Casualty Co. v. Woodby,* 238 F.2d 452, 455 (6th Cir.); *Aetna Casualty & Surety Co. v. De Maison,* 213 F.2d 826, 830–31, 834 (3d Cir.); *Howell v. Accident & Casualty Insurance Co.,* 32 Tenn.App. 83, 221 S.W.2d 901, 905.

5. As noted, the trial judge referred in the charge to implied permission to a *second* permittee only, and he apparently found some basis for treating Wallace as a second permittee. On this record we do not, however, find any basis for so treating Wallace. There was no proof that Deborah was a *first* permittee of the parents; her permission to use the car can only be premised on implied permission coming to her through her sisters. Thus Deborah was at best a *second* permittee and Wallace a *third* permittee—too remote to have implied permission of the parents to use the car.

6. Plaintiff relies, *inter alia,* on *State Farm Mutual Automobile Insurance Co. v. Cook,* 186 Va. 658, 43 S.E.2d 863 and *Baesler v. Globe Indemnity Co.,* 33 N.J. 148, 162 A.2d 854. The holding in *Cook* and the dictum in *Baesler* would merely uphold coverage as to a *second* permittee given permission to drive by a first permittee having general use of the vehicle. The cases in no way support extension of coverage as far as a third permittee like Wallace, whose use of the vehicle had not been disclosed by Deborah to the named insureds or to the first permittees, Beth and Shawnna.

the vehicle herself, her designation as a "named insured" was only a technicality. (Brief of Appellee, 4). Thus, the argument seems to be that Deborah was a *first* permitted authorized to drive by Beth and Shawnna as named insureds, that Wallace was admittedly authorized by Deborah to drive, and that the reasoning of cases rejecting coverage of third permittees as too remote is therefore not applicable.

We cannot agree with the position that Beth and Shawnna should be treated as named insureds. It is clear that by the terms of the policy the "named insureds" were defined as Robert and JoAnn Ahrens.[7] That term carries special meaning in such policies affecting the rights and obligations of the parties. We cannot "rewrite the policy," *American Casualty Co. v. Myrick,* 304 F.2d 179, 184 (5th Cir.), because of the unusual circumstances in the family. See *Alm v. Hartford Fire Insurance Co.,* 369 P.2d 216, 217 (Wyo.). The family circumstances are relevant, as we have recognized, in connection with the factual issue relating to implied permission for use of the family cars. However, nothing in the facts here demonstrates a change in the agreement of the policyholders with the company, as was the case in *Unigard Insurance Co. v. Studer,* 536 F.2d 1337 (10th Cir.), where an endorsement to the policy effected a change naming an additional insured. The insurer has a right to assume that the risk undertaken will not be enlarged beyond the agreement. See *Travelers Insurance Co. v. Weatherford,* 520 S.W.2d 726, 728 (Tenn.). We therefore feel there is no warrant for varying from the terms of the policy definition of the "named insured."

Plaintiff Curtis further contends that if the company were to prevail here, then an undesirable situation would result, contrary to the public's understanding about insurance coverage. The argument is that if any children were riding in a vehicle driven and operated by a child of the owner, and that child were to permit another child to drive, then according to the company there would be no coverage, contrary to the public's expectation. This policy argument does not persuade us. We cannot impose liability contrary to the terms of the agreement and without justification in the facts of record. As the Supreme Court of Wyoming stated in *Wyoming Farm Bureau Mutual Insurance Co. v. May, supra,* 434 P.2d at 511–12, in rejecting a similar public policy argument:

> Granting that the need for better regulation of use of highways is a meritorious and even a necessary objective, to argue that liability coverage of one person should be extended to cover another simply because it is desirable that all drivers of motor vehicles should be covered, is whimsical and unsupported either in reason or by law. This contention is without merit.

---

7. While plaintiff's exhibit 1, a copy of the policy, does not contain the declarations portion of the policy, it is common ground between the parties that the named insureds, at least as stated in the policy, were Robert and JoAnn Ahrens. The trial judge so instructed the jury (II R. 166), and there is no contention to the contrary by either party.

For these reasons we conclude that the verdict and judgment cannot stand and that the defendant was entitled to judgment notwithstanding the verdict. Accordingly, the judgment is reversed and the cause is remanded for entry of judgment in accordance with this opinion.

Notes and Questions

1. *The Relation Between the Omnibus and DOC Clauses.* The omnibus clause—usually as a definition of the term "insured"—is universally included in auto liability policies. In addition, most policies contain "drive other cars," or "DOC" coverage, providing insurance for the named insured against liability arising out of the permitted use of a non-owned vehicle. Many plain-language policies have omitted some or all of the language in the omnibus and DOC clauses, apparently relying on precedent to fill in the gaps. See, e.g., the Sample Personal Auto Policy in Section A. Once the DOC clause became common, the need for an omnibus clause in every policy declined, although it did not disappear. But the two clauses must still be coordinated by the "other insurance" provisions in the two policies (the driver's and the owner's) that potentially provide coverage when a permittee is sued. See id., Part A, "Other Insurance." For more discussion of coordination under "other insurance" clauses, see Chapter Nine.

2. *The Meaning of "Permission".* Most state statutes contain language suggesting that an omnibus clause must be included in auto liability policies. The purpose of such statutes often figures in the interpretation of omnibus clauses, sometimes prompting rulings that "public policy" requires that the term "permission" in the clause be given an expansive interpretation. But even absent a statutory requirement, concern for the compensation of victims—and for not bankrupting drivers who are not thieves—seems to influence some courts' interpretations. The threefold breakdown of judicial approaches to interpretation of the permission provisions in omnibus and DOC clauses generally distinguishes among the liberal, minor-deviation, and conservative approaches.

a. Under the *liberal rule*, once the named insured gives permission to another to drive the insured vehicle, that driver and all others in the chain of permission have full authority to grant further permission, and full authority to make use of the vehicle, regardless of any restrictions on the scope of use contained in the original permission. As a consequence there is coverage, so to speak, all the way down. See, e.g., *Odolecki v. Hartford Accident & Indemnity Company*, 55 N.J. 542, 264 A.2d 38 (1970). This statement of the liberal rule may well employ a bit more caricature than characterization, for all courts would probably draw the line short of this pure approach. Nonetheless, some courts would hold that whether there was permission on the facts in cases like *Curtis* is a question for the jury.

b. The *minor deviation* approach is by far the most predominant. The issue for most courts is the degree of the deviation from the owner's permission, and the question—as it was in *Curtis* at the trial court level—becomes one of fact and degree. Probably *Curtis* itself should be placed in this category. If the minor deviation rule relies on juries for its application, are insurers likely to be much comforted when it rather than the liberal rule prevails?

c. The *conservative rule* simply goes one step further, holding that deviations from the scope of the original grant of permission take the use of the vehicle outside the scope of coverage. Would the issue be as critical as the division between these rules suggests if DOC coverage were available regardless of actual permission, so long as the driver in question reasonably believed he had permission? Would such an approach have been helpful in *Curtis*?

How would you classify the manner in which the Sample Policy handles the problem in Part A, Exclusion (8)?

3. "Use" of the Vehicle

ALLSTATE INSURANCE COMPANY v. GILLESPIE

District Court of Appeal of Florida, 1984.
455 So.2d 617.

RYDER, Chief Judge.

In the recent case of *Government Employees Insurance Co. v. Novak,* 453 So.2d 1116 (Fla.1984), our supreme court addressed the question of an automobile insurer's liability for injuries "arising out of the ownership, maintenance, or use of a motor vehicle." *Novak* held that when a driver was attacked and shot while sitting in a car by a person to whom she refused entry, she was entitled to personal injury protection benefits under the insurance policy covering the automobile. The court found a sufficient causal connection between the use of the automobile and the driver's injuries. We are today confronted with yet another factual variation of a claim for injuries allegedly arising from the use of an automobile.

Although the parties disputed what happened, there is substantial evidence in the record to support the trial judge's findings that the testimony of appellee, John J. Stewart, Jr., and of an uninterested witness, Ronald Collmeyer, was credible and that the testimony of appellee/cross-appellant Robert Gillespie, was not credible. *Strawgate v. Turner,* 339 So.2d 1112 (Fla.1976). Stewart testified that he was in his automobile stopped at a red traffic light when Gillespie approached him on foot and began assaulting him. Gillespie testified that although Stewart had cut off his vehicle in traffic, when he initially approached Stewart's vehicle he was merely offering aid to Stewart whom he thought to be a disabled motorist. However, Mr. Collmeyer testified he observed the acts of the parties and overheard their voices during the Gillespie–Stewart confrontation. Mr. Collmeyer related that Gillespie was shouting at Stewart calling him a "son-of-a-bitch" and other "names." Gillespie, according to Collmeyer, ordered Stewart to get out of the car and fight like a man. During this time, Gillespie attempted to hit Stewart through an open door window. Collmeyer further testified that Stewart also attempted to drive his car through the traffic light but was blocked by cross traffic. Stewart then moved over in the seat to avoid Gillespie and raised the window. Thereafter, Gillespie further attempted to strike Stewart taking advantage of an open sun roof. Stewart was unsuccessfully attempting to repel the attack when he took a revolver from the car's glove compartment and, during a struggle over the gun, fired it several times, injuring Gillespie. Stewart testified that he fired the gun to frighten Gillespie rather than harm him.

Gillespie sued Stewart for damages stemming from his injuries. In a separate action, now before this court, Allstate Insurance Company, Stewart's automobile liability insurer, asked the court to declare whether its policy provided coverage in connection with the incident. The policy covered "claims for accidents arising out of the ownership, maintenance or use, loading or unloading" of the insured automobile. The policy also promised to defend the insured if sued.

After a nonjury trial, the trial judge ruled that the use of Stewart's automobile was inexorably tied to the incident at issue, that Stewart was covered under Allstate's policy, and that he was entitled to a defense by Allstate. Allstate appeals from that ruling.

Allstate argues, relying on *Florida Farm Bureau Insurance Co. v. Shaffer,* 391 So.2d 216 (Fla.4th DCA 1980), *petition for review denied,* 402 So.2d 613 (Fla.1981), that the incident did not arise out of the use of Stewart's automobile, therefore, Stewart is not covered under the policy. It is well established that for the insurance coverage to apply it is not necessary that the use of automobile proximately cause the injury but rather that there be a nexus between the automobile and the injury. *Novak; Government Employees Insurance Co. v. Batchelder,* 421 So.2d 59 (Fla.1st DCA 1982); *Auto–Owners Insurance Co. v. Pridgen,* 339 So.2d 1164 (Fla.2d DCA 1976). The inquiry should be whether the attack arose out of, or flowed from, the use of the vehicle. *Novak* (quoting *Novak v. Government Employees Insurance Co.,* 424 So.2d 178, 180 (Fla.4th DCA 1983)).

Being mindful of the rule that the phrase "arising out of the use of a motor vehicle" should be liberally construed to effect broad coverage, *Novak; Valdes v. Smalley,* 303 So.2d 342 (Fla.3d DCA 1974), *cert. dismissed,* 341 So.2d 975 (Fla.1976), we agree with the trial judge that the incident was, indeed, inexorably tied to Stewart's use of his automobile. Gillespie became enraged because of the manner in which Stewart drove his car, which precipitated and led to Gillespie's attack on Stewart. Surely, this is certainly sufficient nexus between the car and the injury.

Although the Fourth District's decision in *Shaffer* gives us pause, *Shaffer* relied on foreign law. *Nationwide Mutual Insurance Co. v. Knight,* 34 N.C.App. 96, 237 S.E.2d 341 (1977), while we are guided by our supreme court's teachings in *Novak.* We also note that the *Shaffer* court denied coverage when the insured was the aggressor. In the case *sub judice,* however, as in *Novak,* the insured was the non-aggressor and victim of an attack. * * *

In summary, we affirm in all respects the lower court's judgment, holding that there is competent, substantial evidence in the record and law to support it. We hold that, under these facts, Allstate's policy provides coverage to Stewart and Allstate has the duty to defend Stewart in the action brought by Gillespie and any other actions stemming from the incident in question. * * *

AFFIRMED.

Notes and Questions

1. *Plain–Language Terminology.* The Allstate policy contained detailed language, referring to "ownership, maintenance or use, loading or unloading" of the insured vehicle. Should plain-language policies that simply refer to liability for "automobile accidents" or "use" of the vehicle be interpreted any differently?

2. *I Know It When I See It?* Can the kind of problem addressed in *Gillespie* be resolved on a principled basis without depriving victims of compensation in sympathetic situations? What "rule," if any, can you derive from the proper resolution of the following situations? Would use of a proximate cause test advance the inquiry?

a. Suppose that Gillespie had broken Stewart's arm in attempting to avoid being shot. Would Gillespie have been covered by his liability policy, or would his behavior fall outside the "use" requirement?

b. The insured throws a firecracker out the back of a station wagon parked at an outdoor party and is sued by a woman whom the explosion injures. *Farm Bureau Mutual Insurance Company, Inc. v. Evans,* 7 Kan.App.2d 60, 637 P.2d 491 (1981).

c. The insured's dog bites a passenger while the passenger is opening the car door to exit the vehicle. *Hartford Accident & Indemnity Company v. Civil Service Employees Insurance Company,* 33 Cal.App. 3d 26, 108 Cal.Rptr. 737 (1973).

4. Notice and Cooperation Conditions

All automobile insurance policies provide that the insured must provide the insurer with notice of any claim or suit, and cooperate in the investigation or defense of such claims or suits. The issues surrounding the obligation to provide notice parallel those already surveyed in connection with general liability insurance. The scope of the insured's duty to cooperate and the effect of any breach of that duty, however, are common issues in auto liability insurance litigation.

STATE FARM MUTUAL AUTOMOBILE
INSURANCE COMPANY v. DAVIES

Supreme Court of Virginia, 1983.
226 Va. 310, 310 S.E.2d 167.

CARRICO, Chief Justice.

This appeal in a declaratory judgment proceeding involves the conceded breach of the cooperation clause of an automobile liability insurance policy and presents the question whether the breach prejudiced the insurance carrier in its defense of an action for damages. The question is presented against the following background:

On August 2, 1974, Dixie K. Davies was injured when the vehicle she was driving collided with an automobile operated by Patricia Ann Turner. At the time, Turner was an insured under a policy issued by State Farm Mutual Automobile Insurance Company (State Farm), containing the usual cooperation clause, and Davies was an insured under a policy issued by Government Employees Insurance Company (GEICO), with standard provisions for uninsured motorist coverage.

Davies filed a personal injury action against Turner, who delivered the suit papers to State Farm. When the case came on for trial, Turner failed to appear, and State Farm defended the action under a reservation of rights.

The trial resulted in a verdict and judgment in favor of Davies for $10,725.00. Thereafter, the judgment remaining unpaid, Davies brought this declaratory judgment proceeding to determine which of the two insurance companies was liable to her. State Farm disclaimed liability on the ground that Turner's failure to appear at trial constituted a material and prejudicial breach of the cooperation clause of the State Farm policy. GEICO defended on the basis that State Farm's disclaimer of liability was ineffective and, hence, that Turner was not an uninsured motorist.

After a hearing, the trial court ruled that State Farm had not been prejudiced by Turner's failure to appear at trial. Accordingly, the court entered judgment in favor of Davies against State Farm and dismissed GEICO. Because we believe these actions were erroneous, we will reverse.

Under the terms of State Farm's policy, Turner was required to "cooperate with the company and to * * * attend hearings and trials and assist in securing and giving evidence and obtaining the attendance of witnesses." Pursuant to Code § 38.1–381(a1), however, an insurance carrier cannot escape liability on the ground of noncooperation unless the failure to cooperate "prejudices the insurer in the defense of an action for damages."

The parties stipulated below that Turner failed to cooperate as required and that State Farm had not waived its right to rely upon the defense of noncooperation. The only issue for determination, therefore, the parties agreed, was whether Turner's failure to cooperate prejudiced State Farm in the defense of Davies' personal injury action.

On this issue, the trial court properly held that State Farm had the burden of proving prejudice. *See Shipp v. Connecticut Indem. Co.*, 194 Va. 249, 258, 72 S.E.2d 343, 348 (1952). The court found, however, that the "evidence of liability [in the personal injury action] was rather overwhelming and it would stretch the imagination to believe that a different result would have been obtained."

GEICO argues that the importance of this finding of fact "cannot be overemphasized" and that the finding may not be set aside since it is supported by credible evidence. The difficulty with GEICO's argument is that the so-called "finding of fact" contains a built-in rule of law imposing upon State Farm the burden of proving that Turner's appearance and testimony at trial *would* have produced a different result. We believe this was an improper burden, and we think one of our prior decisions demonstrates the error in the trial court's holding. For this reason, we need not consider the several out-of-state decisions cited by GEICO.

In *Cooper v. Insurance Company*, 199 Va. 908, 103 S.E.2d 210 (1958), Traynham, an insured under a policy issued by Employers Mutual Automobile Insurance Company, was involved in an accident with Cooper. Traynham notified the insurance company of the accident and gave it a signed statement concerning the details of the incident. Thereafter, Traynham disappeared and failed to cooperate further with the company. Cooper obtained a judgment against Traynham in a personal injury action which the company defended under a reservation of rights. When Cooper brought an action on the policy, the company defended on the ground of Traynham's noncooperation. Affirming the trial court's finding in favor of the company, we said:

> [Traynham] did not assist in any manner in the preparation for trial nor did he appear at the trial. These facts and circumstances constituted a wilful lack of cooperation with the company and such lack of cooperation was substantial and material and was prejudicial to [the company]. His failure to assist in the preparation for trial and to attend the trial unquestionably prejudiced his case, especially in view of the fact that his report of the accident * * * indicated a defense to the action.

Id. at 915, 103 S.E.2d at 215.

GEICO dismisses *Cooper* on the ground that the language concerning prejudice quoted above "is unquestionably dictum." Prejudice was not an issue in *Cooper*, GEICO says, because the case predated a 1966 amendment adding to Code § 38.1–381 new subsection (a1), which included the prejudice requirement, and, as this court was careful to point out, it was not necessary at the time of *Cooper* for the insurer "to show prejudice in order to prevail in the defense of non-cooperation." 199 Va. at 915–16, 103 S.E.2d at 215.

It is true, of course, that subsection (a1) had not been added to Code § 38.1–381 at the time *Cooper* was decided. And we did make clear in *Cooper* that a showing of prejudice was not essential at that time to the establishment of a noncooperation defense, the insurer's burden then consisting of proof that a breach was material. 199 Va. at 914, 915, 103 S.E.2d at 214, 215. But it does not follow that the language concerning prejudice in the above-quoted excerpt is dictum.

We noted in *Cooper* that the issue in the case was whether the evidence showed that Traynham willfully failed to comply with the terms of the policy "in some substantial and material respect." *Id.* at 913, 103 S.E.2d at 214. And, quoting from *Shipp*, we said that " 'the absence of prejudice * * * is a circumstance to be considered on the question of * * * materiality.' " *Id.* at 914, 103 S.E.2d at 214. Then, rationalizing conversely, we found that Traynham's failure to cooperate was material because prejudicial to the insurer in the defense of the personal injury action. Hence, the language concerning prejudice was essential to the rationale of the *Cooper* decision and was not dictum.

GEICO argues that in view of the 1966 amendment to Code § 38.1–381, *Cooper* would be decided differently today. We disagree. So far as its impact upon *Cooper* is concerned, what the 1966 amendment accomplished was to require a showing of prejudice as the dispositive factor in a failure-to-cooperate case, rather than as a mere circumstance to be considered in determining materiality. *See State Farm v. Porter*, 221 Va. 592, 597–98, 272 S.E.2d 196, 199 (1980). But prejudice is prejudice, whether found as a dispositive factor or as a circumstance demonstrating materiality; therefore, the precedential value of *Cooper* is unaffected by the 1966 amendment.

GEICO maintains, however, that *Cooper* is not entitled to weight because this Court did not discuss what constitutes prejudice in the noncooperation context. We should disregard *Cooper*, GEICO says, and also eschew State Farm's invitation to follow a rule that would make "the absence of an insured from trial prejudice *per se*." Instead, GEICO submits, we should affirm the judgment below, thus sanctioning the rule followed by the trial court requiring an insurer to prove prejudice by showing that the insured's appearance at trial would have produced a different result. Alternatively, GEICO asserts, we should adopt a rule requiring the insurer to show "substantial likelihood that the trier of fact would have found in the insured's favor" or, at a minimum, a rule requiring the insurer to show "some likelihood that the result would have been different."

Admittedly, *Cooper* does not discuss the nature of the evidence that is required to establish prejudice. It is clear from the opinion, however, that where the insured's willful absence from trial deprives the insurer of evidence sufficient to establish a defense to the original claim, then prejudice results. And we believe it is implicit that evidence necessary to establish a defense means evidence of sufficient quality and weight to take the issue of the insured's conduct to the jury and to support a verdict in his or her favor.

It follows that we favor neither a *per se* rule that would permit an insurer to show merely that its insured failed to appear at trial nor a rule that would require an insurer to show that, had its insured appeared, the result would have been in his or her favor. Instead, we believe that the proper rule lies midway between these two extremes and emanates from the rationale of *Cooper*: in an action on the policy, when the insurer shows that the insured's willful failure to appear at the original trial deprived the insurer of evidence which would have made a jury issue of the insured's liability and supported a verdict in his or her favor, the insurer has established a reasonable likelihood the result would have been favorable to the insured and has carried its burden of proving prejudice under Code § 38.1–381(a).

To determine whether State Farm carried its burden of proving prejudice, we turn now to the evidence adduced in the present proceeding. This evidence, most of which was stipulated, shows that the accident in question occurred on a rainy afternoon in early August, 1974, at the intersection of City Park Avenue and Park Manor Road in the City of Portsmouth. A traffic island is located on Park Manor Road at the intersection, and traffic turning left from City Park Avenue onto Park Manor Road passes to the left of the island. Davies, who had been proceeding northward on City Park Avenue, was in the process of turning left onto Park Manor Road. Turner was travelling eastward on Park Manor Road intending to turn right onto City Park Avenue. The two vehicles collided left side to left side.

Turner reported the accident to State Farm and signed an "Automobile Claim Report" setting forth her version of the incident, which indicated she had a defense. State Farm made a prompt and full investigation. As part of the investigation, a State Farm claims representative interviewed Turner some four months after the accident. Repeating her version of the accident, Turner stated in the interview that she was approaching the intersection about five miles per hour when Davies, travelling around fifteen miles per hour, "turned too short" onto Park Manor Road and proceeded toward Turner on Davies' wrong side of the road. Turner pulled to her right "in the dirt off of the road" but was hit on her left front fender by Davies, and the impact "spun [Turner's] car around." When police officers arrived, they did not issue any summons or indicate who was at fault in the accident.

Jimmy Smith, Turner's brother, was a passenger in her car at the time of the accident. He was also interviewed by the State Farm claims representative, and he corroborated Turner's version of the accident.

Following the filing of Davies' personal injury action on August 2, 1976, Turner was served with process, and she turned the suit papers over to State Farm. George Gray, an attorney, was designated by State

Farm to defend the action and he filed defensive pleadings on Turner's behalf.

Trial of the personal injury action was set for February 22, 1977. Gray notified Turner of the trial date and requested that she contact him to arrange a pretrial interview. She telephoned his office to make an appointment but, following this call, she moved from her local address and never again contacted Gray or anyone else connected with State Farm. Because of her absence, the case was continued several times during a period of more than two years. Despite "every reasonable effort" made by State Farm, she could not be found.

Jimmy Smith did cooperate with State Farm in the early stages of the case, and he indicated to Gray he would give testimony favorable to Turner. In late 1978, however, after Smith had joined the Army and left the state, Gray attempted to take his deposition, but Smith did not appear at the scheduled time. Gray talked with him on the phone later, and he was "an entirely different person." He told Gray that he remembered "little, if anything, about the accident," and that he did not wish to be deposed. Gray made no further attempt to depose Smith.

The personal injury action was finally heard on August 3, 1979, in the absence of both Turner and her brother. The testimony presented at trial was stipulated into the present record. According to Davies' version of the accident, as she was making her left turn from City Park Avenue onto Park Manor Road, she saw Turner approaching in the middle of Park Manor Road at a speed of thirty-five miles per hour in a twenty-five mile zone. Davies moved to her right and had come to a stop partially on the traffic island when the left side of her vehicle was struck by the left side of Turner's automobile.

Park Ranger Caviness was the first police officer to arrive on the scene. He observed both vehicles on Davies' side of the road, with a portion of Davies' vehicle on the traffic island. Davies' husband, who was also a police officer, and Officer Burke later arrived on the scene. They corroborated Caviness' statements concerning the positions of the vehicles. All three police officers and Mrs. Davies heard Turner admit fault for the accident.

There was no evidence presented in the personal injury trial supporting Turner's version of the accident. Specifically, there was no testimony that Davies "cut the corner short," that Turner turned to her right in an attempt to avoid the accident, or that the impact occurred on Turner's side of the road.

Testifying in the present proceeding as a witness for State Farm, Gray said Turner and her brother were the "only [possible] witnesses * * * who [could] provide a defense in the case." Gray said further that the statements Turner and her brother made in their interviews with State Farm's claims representative "indicated, to [Gray], that [he] did have a defense * * * which [he] could classify as substantial"; by "substantial defense," he meant "evidence which can be presented to a jury which, if believed, would result in a verdict for [the defendant]."

Gray testified further that when Turner and her brother failed to appear at the personal injury trial, he "lost every chance of any defense on the issue of liability"; he was unable through cross-examination or otherwise to develop any "evidence or testimony [he] could put on to defend." Gray conceded he had advised State Farm some time prior to the personal injury trial that there was "apparent liability" in the case. Gray insisted, however, that this advice to State Farm did not "mean that [he had] backed off from what [he thought was] a substantial defense."

We believe the evidence in this case compels the conclusion that had Turner appeared at the personal injury trial and testified as State Farm had the right to assume she would testify, that is, by reciting the same version of the accident she gave in her interview with State Farm's claims representative, then a jury issue of her liability would have been established. A jury issue exists " '[i]f there is conflict of the testimony on a material point, or if reasonably fair-minded [persons] may differ as to the conclusions of fact to be drawn from the evidence, or if the conclusion is dependent on the weight to be given the testimony.' " *Hoover v. Neff & Son,* 183 Va. 56, 62, 31 S.E.2d 265, 268 (1944) (quoting M. Burkes, *Pleading and Practice* 543 (3d ed. 1934)).

While these are alternative criteria and all three exist in the present case, we need only point out that, had Turner repeated at the personal injury trial her version of the accident, her testimony would have been in direct conflict with Davies' evidence. Turner's version was not inherently incredible, and the question then would have become one of credibility for the jury. Had the jury accepted Turner's version and returned a verdict in her favor, the verdict would have been supported by evidence. Yet, by willfully failing to attend and testify at the personal injury trial and by failing to assist in securing her brother's testimony, Turner deprived State Farm of the very evidence necessary to make a jury issue of her liability. These failures, concededly in breach of the cooperation clause, clearly prejudiced State Farm in its defense of the personal injury action.

Accordingly, the judgment of the trial court will be reversed. The parties have stipulated that if it is determined Turner's breach of the cooperation clause prejudiced State Farm in the defense of the personal injury action, "then [GEICO] owes [Davies] the amount of the said previous judgment, plus interest and the Court costs of this [declaratory judgment] action." Pursuant to this stipulation, we will dismiss State Farm and enter final judgment in favor of Davies against GEICO in the amounts indicated.

Reversed and final judgment.

Notes and Questions

1. *Forms of Non–cooperation.* The behavior that constitutes breach of the insured's duty to cooperate often involves the failure to appear at trial, or the repeated failure to appear for depositions or

interviews. On this issue, in addition to *Davies,* see *MFA Mutual Insurance Company v. Sailors,* 180 Neb. 201, 141 N.W.2d 846 (1966). To the extent that the insurer has made special efforts to assist or assure cooperation, its case is strengthened. Conversely, an insurer that does nothing to encourage cooperation has a much weaker—indeed, in some instances empty—claim to be relieved of its obligations. For example, suppose the insurer persists in sending communications in English to a Spanish–speaking insured or in scheduling depositions during working hours without taking affirmative steps to facilitate the insured's appearance. When the insured does not reply to communications or appear as requested, and the insurer claims non-cooperation, who prevails? A number of other forms of non-cooperation also appear in the cases; the most common is lying or giving false testimony. See, e.g., *Employers Mutual Casualty Company v. Nelson,* 109 N.H. 6, 241 A.2d 207 (1968).

2. *Forms of Prejudice.* Determining what kind of behavior constitutes non-cooperation is only the first step in applying the cooperation clause. Prejudice to the insurer, or at least materiality of breach, is almost everywhere required before breach of the notice and cooperation clause voids coverage. The court in *Davies* staked out a middle ground between a requirement that there be proof that but for the insured's failure to cooperate the claim would have failed, and the requirement that the insured's failure to cooperate merely have some effect on the insurer's prospect of defeating the claim. Most courts seem to adopt a *substantial impact test* in fact, if not in name, that makes predicting results difficult. In many cases there can be no real evidence—short of trying a hypothetical case in which cooperation *is* provided—regarding the effect of non-cooperation. The court can either estimate based on its own experience and judgment what impact cooperation by the insured might have had on the outcome of the case, or throw up its hands in despair of estimating that impact based on the meager evidence available. The *Davies* test avoids both alternatives.

The key question in many cases, therefore, is not so much the character of the test to be applied, but the party bearing the burden of proof. If the insurer bears the burden of proving prejudice, it is likely to lose all but the clearest cases of prejudice. If the insured bears that burden, he is likely to prevail only occasionally. Most jurisdictions place the burden of proof on the insurer. See, e.g., *Home Indemnity Company v. Reed Equipment Company,* 381 So.2d 45 (Ala.1980). But see *Western Mutual Insurance Company v. Baldwin,* 258 Iowa 460, 137 N.W.2d 918 (1965).

3. *Shortsighted Strategy?* Why was GEICO, a high-volume auto insurer, pressing so hard for a rule that would make it more difficult for auto insurers to avoid liability when the insured has breached the cooperation condition of an auto policy? If you were general counsel for GEICO, would you have advised GEICO to try to settle the case before appeal?

5. Restrictions on Suits Against the Insurer

In automobile as well as in general liability insurance, the liability insurer's obligations arise when the insured is made the defendant in a law suit or a similar proceeding. If the plaintiff prevails in that suit and the insurer's obligation to indemnify is triggered, then the insured has a contract right to that indemnity. All this takes place without any rights against the defendant's liability insurer being vested in the party to whom the insured may be liable. Two sources of law, however, may vest rights in this party as well. The first setting in which the insurer may be subjected to a suit brought directly by a third-party/ plaintiff is found in those few states which actually permit a direct action against insurers, under certain circumstances, prior to the entry of judgment against an insured. Louisiana and Wisconsin are the most notable. See, e.g., L.S.A.Rev.Stat. 22:655, 22:983; Wis.Rev.Stat. 632.24, 632.34, 803.04. Not only do these statutes make it possible to vindicate a claim even when it is not possible to obtain service of process on the insured; they also have the potential for provoking the jury reaction that rules in other states making mere mention of liability insurance grounds for a mistrial are directed at avoiding. On the other hand, in an age of nearly universal automobile liability coverage, is such a jury reaction in an auto negligence case likely to occur anyway?

The second situation arises in states without "direct action" statutes. Most automobile policies contain a "No–Action" clause, providing that no legal action may be brought against the insurer until the amount of the insured's liability has been finally determined by settlement or judgment. See the Sample Personal Auto Policy, Part F. Thus, the plaintiff in a tort claim against an auto liability insured is precluded by such a clause from joining the insurer in the suit in order to assure that there is a finding of coverage, or from instituting an action in advance of the tort suit to determine whether there would be coverage if the suit were successful. After a judgment against the insured is entered, however, the successful plaintiff is in effect a third-party beneficiary of the insured's policy, and can bring an action against the insurer to recover the amount owed. In this action the coverage question usually can be resolved. That may be impossible when the insured files for bankruptcy, however, in the absence of the kind of judicial assistance that was provided in the following case.

IN RE HONOSKY

United States Bankruptcy Court, S.D. West Virginia, 1980.
6 B.R. 667.

Edwin F. Flowers, Bankruptcy Judge.

The Plaintiff seeks a lifting of the automatic stay imposed by 11 U.S.C. § 362(a) so that she may prosecute a lawsuit now pending in the Circuit Court of McDowell County against the Debtor. The suit was instituted on January 21, 1980, to recover damages allegedly incurred when the Debtor's coal truck struck the Plaintiff's automobile. The

Debtor subsequently filed his bankruptcy petition on July 10, 1980, and the automatic stay of 11 U.S.C. § 362(a) was invoked.

A hearing on the complaint to lift the stay was held on September 19, 1980, at which time the parties presented evidence to support their positions. The hearing was regarded as the final hearing upon the representation by counsel that they had no further evidence to present at any future time.

The Plaintiff presented evidence establishing that Nationwide Mutual Insurance Company, the Debtor's insurer, hired counsel to represent the Debtor in the circuit court suit and that the Debtor's insurance coverage for bodily injury is $100,000/$300,000. The Plaintiff asserts that the stay should be lifted to permit her to proceed in the circuit court against the Debtor to the extent of the liability insurance coverage. She contends that the Debtor's bankruptcy estate will not be damaged in the event of an adverse judgment against the Debtor because of the insurance coverage and, since the insurance company is required to defend the Debtor, the estate will not be subject to claims for attorney fees.

Conversely, the Debtor objects to a lifting of the stay since there has been no allegation of grounds in the circuit court suit or claim in Bankruptcy Court that this debt is excepted from discharge. If not excepted from discharge, then the injunctive force of section 524(a)(2) of the Bankruptcy Code will bar all further action on the debt. * * *

Even though the Plaintiff is barred from seeking a determination of the nondischargeable character of the debt, that is not the relief which the Plaintiff here seeks. She asks not that the debt survive the bankruptcy as a continuing personal liability of the Debtor, but only that she be permitted to have the liability judicially determined without cost to the Debtor or threat to the Debtor's discharge.

Section 362(a), unless modified by this Court, prevents such a judicial determination in the circuit court. It provides:

> Except as provided in subsection (b) of this section, a petition filed under section 301, 302, or 303 of this title operates as a stay, applicable to all entities, of—
>
> 　(1) the commencement or continuation, * * * of a judicial * * * or other proceeding against the debtor. * * *

The scope of the stay, without doubt, covers the circuit court suit. Congress explained that:

> The scope of the paragraph [subsection (a)] is broad. All proceedings are stayed, including * * * judicial proceedings. Proceeding in this sense encompasses *civil actions* as well, and all proceedings even if they are not before governmental tribunals. [H.R.Rep. No. 95–595, 95th Cong., 1st Sess. 340 (1977), U.S.Code Cong. & Admin.News 1978, p. 5787] [Emphasis added].

However, Congress recognized that in some instances the stay against judicial proceedings should be lifted:

> [I]t will often be more appropriate to permit proceedings to continue in their place of origin, when no great prejudice to the bankruptcy estate would result, in order to leave the parties to their chosen forum and to relieve the bankruptcy court from many duties that may be handled elsewhere. [*Id.* at 341; S.Rep. 989, 95th Cong., 2d Sess. 50 (1978), U.S.Code Cong. & Admin.News 1978 at 5836].

The Plaintiff's evidence, unrefuted by the Debtor, discloses that the Debtor has liability insurance coverage of $100,000/$300,000, and that the insurance company has hired counsel to represent the Debtor. The Debtor did not refute the Plaintiff's assertion that the insurance company would absorb the costs of his defense against the civil suit. The Debtor has produced no showing that the continuation of the civil suit would result in great prejudice to either the bankruptcy estate or to himself. In a case decided under the Bankruptcy Act, the burden of proving prejudice to the estate was placed on the debtor and the trustee. In the absence of such a showing the debtor was not entitled to an injunction against the civil suit. *See Foust v. Munson Steamship Lines,* 299 U.S. 77, 57 S.Ct. 90, 81 L.Ed. 49 (1936).

Collier on Bankruptcy proposes that a debtor's insurance coverage can affect the decision to lift or modify the automatic stay:

> Lack of adequate protection and lack of equity are not the sole grounds for relief from the stay. * * * Where the claim is one covered by insurance or indemnity, continuation of the [civil] action should be permitted since hardship to the debtor is likely to be outweighed by hardship to the plaintiff. [2 *Collier on Bankruptcy* § 362.07[3] at 362–49 (15th ed. 1979)].

Collier cites several cases decided upon the Bankruptcy Act, including *Foust v. Munson Steamship Lines, supra,* which considered the effect of insurance coverage on decisions to permit civil suits to proceed outside the bankruptcy court. *In re Adolf Gobel, Inc.,* 89 F.2d 171, 172 (2d Cir. 1937), contains the following language:

> [W]e are convinced that the exercise of sound discretion required permitting the appellant to liquidate his claim in his pending action at law since that will preserve the added assurance afforded by the debtor's liability insurance that the claim will be paid if established by judgment and there is no good reason to believe that by so doing any unreasonable hindrance or delay will result. * * *

Similarly, *In re Gerstenzang,* 52 F.2d 863 (S.D.N.Y.1931), contains the following statement: "Where a creditor's rights against a surety are contingent upon recovery of a judgment against the bankrupt, permission to prosecute suit in the state courts to this extent is frequently given." 52 F.2d at 864. This is especially significant in jurisdictions which do not permit suit directly against the insurer. West Virginia is such a state. *United Dispatch v. Albrecht Co.,* 135 W.Va. 34, 62 S.E.2d 289 (1950); *Criss v. United States Fidelity & Guaranty Co.,* 105 W.Va. 380, 142 S.E. 849 (1928).

Thus, were this Court not to lift the stay to permit the Plaintiff to proceed against the Debtor, she would be effectively precluded from any recovery for her alleged injuries. The choice is between lifting the stay to permit the civil action to proceed or to simply allow the unliquidated claim to be discharged. The court is not convinced that the Bankruptcy Code was intended to bestow such a benefit upon insurance companies. The cases referred to above, although decided under the Bankruptcy Act, demonstrate judicial recognition of the equity of permitting a civil suit to proceed against one covered by insurance where the bankruptcy estate is in no way harmed.

The injunctive provisions of the Code which enforce the discharge seem to accommodate this result. Section 524(a) provides:

A discharge in a case under this title—(2) operates as an injunction against the commencement or continuation of an action * * * to collect, recover or offset any such debt *as a personal liability of the debtor, or from property of the debtor* * * * [Emphasis added].

No property of the Debtor will be put in jeopardy. If there is a liability of the Debtor, it is "personal" only to the extent necessary to sustain the recovery against the insurer.

Thus, though the liability to the Plaintiff is dischargeable in bankruptcy, the automatic stay will be modified to permit the Plaintiff to proceed with her suit in the Circuit Court of McDowell County to the extent of the Debtor's insurance coverage. The Plaintiff may not take any step toward collecting any judgment personally from the Debtor, however, nor may the issue of dischargeability be raised in another court. An order so modifying the stay will be entered.

Notes and Questions

1. *The Purpose of the Suit.* The plaintiff sought an exception to the automatic stay provisions of the Bankruptcy Act in order to obtain a judgment against the debtor that would make the No–Action clause of the debtor's auto liability insurance policy inapplicable. There are surprisingly few cases lifting such automatic stays. For discussions of the issue, see *Cissell v. American Home Assurance Company,* 521 F.2d 790 (6th Cir.1975); *Lane v. State Farm Mutual Auto Insurance Company,* 209 Neb. 396, 308 N.W.2d 503 (1981).

2. *The Alternative.* The alternative to the *Honosky* approach might have been to allow the plaintiff to prove her claim in the Bankruptcy Court. Presumably, however, she would then become only a general creditor. Would the amount of her judgment then be paid into the debtor's estate by Nationwide and distributed pro-rata among the plaintiff and the other general creditors? The court seemed to

assume instead that if it did not act, her claim would simply be discharged without payment and that Nationwide would pay nothing to anyone. Which of the three alternatives makes more sense: the implication of *Honosky* that the debtor's insurance coverage is exclusively an asset of a single judgment creditor, the notion that this coverage should be considered an asset of all the debtor's creditors, or leaving both the plaintiff and other general creditors without any payment by Nationwide?

C. COLLISION AND COMPREHENSIVE COVERAGE

Most purchasers of auto liability insurance elect to purchase coverage against damage to their own vehicles as well. This is first-party property insurance, much like the fire and homeowners coverage discussed in Chapter Four, but limited to the insured vehicle and other vehicles driven by the insured with the permission of the owner. The insurance is payable in the event that damage to the insured vehicle resulting from specified causes occurs, regardless of whether the cause is negligence by any third-party and regardless of any negligence by the insured or other operator of the vehicle.

Automobile property insurance comes in two forms. *Collision coverage* insures against damage to the insured vehicle caused by the upset of the vehicle or by its impact with another vehicle or object. The term "collision" also tends to be defined by reference to a set of causes which the policy specifies do not constitute collision—including fire, theft, and windstorm. The principal legal issue that arises in connection with collision coverage is whether this definition, which has the effect of excluding coverage of damage caused by certain kinds of collisions, creates a conclusive or a merely inconclusive exclusion for purposes of determining the cause of damage. For example, suppose that a windstorm upsets the vehicle, or a fire burns out the brakes while the vehicle is moving, and it collides with a tree: is collision coverage excluded?

By contrast, *comprehensive* coverage insures against loss resulting from many of the causes excluded from the definition of collision: fire, windstorm, theft, breakage of glass, vandalism, and flood, among others. For the full list, see the Sample Personal Auto Policy, Part D, where comprehensive coverage is denominated "other than collision." The obvious intent of this approach is that collision and comprehensive coverage should dovetail, but not overlap. When a driver is covered by one form of coverage but not the other, however, it is not surprising that some courts interpret provisions in the driver's policy to cover certain losses that the other form of coverage also would have covered.

ALLISON v. IOWA MUTUAL INSURANCE COMPANY

Court of Appeals of North Carolina, 1979.
43 N.C.App. 200, 258 S.E.2d 489.

This is a civil action wherein plaintiff seeks to recover $8,500.00 under a "general automobile liability" insurance policy for damages resulting to his dump truck when the bridge upon which the truck was traveling collapsed. Defendant answered, admitting that the policy was in effect on the date of the accident, but denying that it provided coverage for the type of accident that occurred. A stipulation entered into between the parties, except where quoted, is summarized as follows:

Defendant issued an insurance policy, numbered G2075509, to plaintiff on 10 February 1975, which provided comprehensive insurance coverage on certain personal property owned by plaintiff, but did not extend collision coverage. On 31 October 1975 the plaintiff was the owner of a 1970 white, two-ton dump truck, Serial No. 735485, which was included in the personal property covered by the policy, and which was "being operated across the South Mills River Bridge No. 185 on Highlander Camp Road * * * transporting a load of gravel." As the truck was being driven across the bridge, "said bridge collapsed and the plaintiff's truck slid into the river or creek running under said bridge and turned on its right side, therein damaging said vehicle." The truck was subsequently repaired at a cost of $8,500.00. Plaintiff in due time submitted a claim to defendant for the total repair of the truck, but, except for paying $111.00 to repair the windshield, defendant "has refused to pay said claim taking the position that said damage was caused by collision and was not covered under * * * the aforesaid policy. * * *"

After considering the above stipulation, the trial judge made findings of fact in accordance therewith, drew separate conclusions of law, and entered judgment for plaintiff in the amount of $8,500.00. Defendant appealed. * * *

HEDRICK, Judge.

Defendant's exceptions to each of the trial judge's conclusions of law present for review the single question of whether the court erred in entering judgment for plaintiff. The question is not whether plaintiff's truck was covered under the policy. It was. Rather, the question is whether the event which gave rise to the damage is excluded from the kind of loss for which the policy provides protection.

Defendant argues that the collapse of the bridge resulting in damage to plaintiff's truck was an accident by collision and that the occurrence was therefore excluded from coverage since the plaintiff had not insured this vehicle against loss by collision. Plaintiff, on the other hand, contends that the collapse of the bridge did not constitute a collision and asserts that the policy includes such an occurrence under its provisions for comprehensive coverage. The relevant inquiry for this Court is thus refined into determining whether the trial judge erred in concluding that the accident occasioned by the collapse of the bridge was not a "collision" within the meaning of the policy which provides in pertinent part as follows:

1. The company will pay for loss to covered automobiles: COVERAGE O—COMPREHENSIVE—*from any cause except collisions;* but, for the purpose of this coverage, breakage of glass and loss caused by missiles, falling objects, fire, theft or larceny, windstorm, hail, earthquake, explosion, riot or civil commotion, malicious mischief or vandalism, water, flood, or (as to a covered automobile of the private passenger type) colliding with a bird or animal, shall not be deemed loss caused by collisions. * * * [Emphasis added.]

Elsewhere the policy defines "collision" to mean "(i) collision of a covered automobile with another object or with a vehicle to which it is attached, or (ii) upset of such covered automobile. * * * "

The principles of law with respect to the interpretation and construction of insurance policies are firmly established. As with any contract, the ultimate goal is to divine the parties' intentions at the time the policy was issued. *Woods v. Nationwide Mutual Insurance Co.,* 295 N.C. 500, 246 S.E.2d 773 (1978). Where the policy defines a term, that definition must be used. Conversely, nontechnical words which are not defined "are to be given the same meaning they usually receive in ordinary speech, unless the context requires otherwise." *Grant v. Emmco Insurance Co.,* 295 N.C. 39, 42, 243 S.E.2d 894, 897 (1978) [citing *Trust Co. v. Insurance Co.,* 276 N.C. 348, 354, 172 S.E.2d 518 (1970); *Insurance Co. v. Shaffer,* 250 N.C. 45, 108 S.E.2d 49 (1959); *Powers v. Insurance Co.,* 186 N.C. 336, 119 S.E. 481 (1923)]. Moreover, if the meaning of language "or *the effect of provisions* is uncertain or capable of several reasonable interpretations," *Woods v. Nationwide Mutual Insurance Co.,* 295 N.C. at 506, 246 S.E.2d at 777 [emphasis added], such ambiguity will be resolved in favor of the insured and against the insurance company since, as it is said, the company chose the language. *Grant v. Emmco Insurance Co., supra.*

In the instant case, although the policy sets out three types of occurrences that are deemed to constitute a collision, the term itself is not defined. The word is popularly understood, however, to mean a striking together of two objects. "The term denotes the act of colliding; striking together; violent contact. * * * [It] implies an impact or sudden contact of a moving body with an obstruction in its line of motion, whether both bodies are in motion or one stationary. * * * " Black's Law Dictionary 330 (4th ed. 1968). *See also Morton v. Blue Ridge Insurance Co.,* 255 N.C. 360, 121 S.E.2d 716 (1961).

In 7 Am.Jur.2d, *Automobile Insurance* § 65 (1963), it is said:

While the ground of a highway is considered an "object" within the meaning of a collision insurance policy, it is generally held that contact of an automobile with the roadbed itself does not constitute a "collision" with an object within the meaning of the term as used in a collision insurance policy.

Furthermore, in a case which presents strikingly similar facts to the case at bar, the Florida Supreme Court held that the giving way of the roadbed over which the plaintiff's car was traveling, resulting in the car's sliding down into the soft sand under the road and getting stuck, was not a collision within the popular and usual meaning of the term. *Aetna Casualty & Surety Co. v. Cartmel,* 87 Fla. 495, 100 So. 802 (1924).

With reference to defendant's contention that the event giving rise to the damage in this case was a "collision", we have carefully considered each case upon which defendant purports to rely and find only one of them to be worthy of comment. Our Supreme Court held, in *Morton v. Blue Ridge Insurance Co., supra,* that a collision, within the meaning of that term as used in the policy being construed there, resulted when the plaintiff's automobile suddenly rolled backwards into a canal. The car had been backed down a launching ramp to launch a boat from a trailer hooked to the rear of the car. While the driver and passengers were lowering the boat into the water, the unattended and previously stationary car suddenly rolled into the water. When the insurance company refused to honor his claim, plaintiff brought suit, and the Court held that the car's striking of the water in the canal and of the bottom of the canal was a collision, entitling plaintiff to recover under the collision provisions of the policy.

We find this case to be readily distinguishable on its facts. The impetus of the accident in *Morton* was obviously occasioned by the manner in which the vehicle was being used. Although there was no evidence regarding what caused the car to suddenly roll backwards, the driver had driven it onto and parked it on the ramp, thereby initiating the chain of events that culminated in the collision of his car with the bottom of the canal. Conversely, in the present case, there is plainly no element of driver control. Nothing the operator of the truck did can be said to have set in force the succeeding events. The collapse of the bridge, and that occurrence only, engendered the consequent accident and damage. We think the cases are clearly distinguishable and find the *Morton* case to be inapposite.

In the case at bar, we hold that the collapse of the bridge upon which plaintiff's truck was being operated, resulting in the truck's sliding down into the river or creek underneath the bridge and thereby being damaged, was not a "collision" either within the usual meaning of the term or as contemplated by the policy and the parties. Since it is not disputed that the policy provides coverage for losses arising from all causes except collision, it follows that the losses suffered under the circumstances here are covered, and the company is liable on plaintiff's claim. Thus, in the conclusions and judgment of the trial judge, we find no error.

Affirmed.

RODEMICH v. STATE FARM MUTUAL AUTOMOBILE INSURANCE COMPANY

Court of Appeals of Arizona, 1981.
130 Ariz. 538, 637 P.2d 748.

EUBANK, Judge.

The main issue to be decided on this appeal is whether the trial court erred in directing a verdict in favor of the appellees on the issue of comprehensive insurance coverage.

The appellees, Mr. and Mrs. Rodemich, were owners of a 1973 Winnebago motor home. On May 7, 1975, Mr. Rodemich was driving the motor home at approximately 15–20 m.p.h. on a paved two-lane road in Alamo State Park, Arizona. According to Mr. Rodemich, a gray four-legged animal, approximately four feet high, suddenly appeared in the roadway. Mr. Rodemich swerved to avoid hitting the animal, causing the motor home to go off the road where it rolled over and was severely damaged. Neither the animal nor any of its hair or blood were found on or near the motor home.

At the time of the accident, the appellees had allowed their collision policy to lapse and retained only comprehensive coverage on the Winnebago. That coverage afforded the appellees the following protection:

COVERAGE D—COMPREHENSIVE

(1) The Owned Motor Vehicle. To pay for loss to the owned motor vehicle EXCEPT LOSS CAUSED BY COLLISION but only for the amount of each such loss in excess of the deductible amount, if any, stated in the declarations as applicable thereto. The deductible amount shall not apply to loss caused by a fire or by a theft of the entire vehicle. Breakage of glass, or loss caused by missiles, falling objects, fire, theft, larceny, explosion, earthquake, windstorm, hail, water, flood, malicious mischief or vandalism, riot or civil commotion or colliding with birds or animals shall not be deemed to be loss caused by collision.

(underlined in the policy—indicating defined terms).

Appellees filed a claim under this provision eight months after the rollover incident occurred. Appellant insurance carrier repudiated any liability under the policy except for glass breakage. Appellees then commenced this action on July 29, 1976, asserting coverage under the comprehensive provision (Coverage D, *supra*) and seeking damages for the damaged Winnebago.

The matter was tried to a jury. After the plaintiffs-appellees rested their case, appellant moved for a directed verdict on the grounds that there existed no competent evidence of any actual contact between the Winnebago and an animal, and that since no contact occurred, no comprehensive coverage under the policy could exist. The trial court denied this motion. The trial continued and at the close of all the evidence, appellees moved for a directed verdict on the coverage issue and the court granted this motion. In granting it the trial judge stated that a "swerving to miss an animal was covered by the policy." He further stated that whether or not an animal was present at the time to cause the accident was a fact question for the jury. Thus the issue of the presence or nonpresence of an animal went to the jury. The jury found in favor of the appellees and assessed damages against the defendant in the amount of $10,000. Judgment was entered pursuant to the verdict. Appellant then filed a motion for new trial and/or judgment notwithstanding the verdict, which was denied. This appeal followed.

Appellant first contends that the trial court erred in directing a verdict in appellees' favor because the court equated a "near miss" with a "collision" thereby withdrawing the coverage issue from the jury's consideration. Appellees, on the other hand, take the position that "as a matter of law, in interpreting an insurance contract, there is no difference between an actual collision with an animal and a near collision with an animal which the insured successfully avoids when in both situations the collision or avoidance results in a subsequent collision or upset." * * *

In the case *sub judice,* the comprehensive provision protected appellees against loss to the motor home except loss caused by collision. The term "collision" is defined in Section II of the policy as follows:

Collision—means collision of a motor vehicle covered by this policy *with another object* or with a vehicle to which it is attached or *upset of such motor vehicle.* (Emphasis added).

However, a "loss caused by * * * *colliding* with birds or animals shall not be deemed to be loss caused by collision." (Emphasis added). Hence, Coverage D. provides that a loss caused by *colliding* with an animal would be within the comprehensive coverage. We believe that the policy's use of the term "colliding," rather than the term "collision" which was specifically defined in the policy, indicates that, "collision" and "colliding" are not the same thing under the policy. "Collision" is defined to include "upsets" of the covered vehicle, regardless of the cause, and therefore does not require any contact between the vehicle and any other object. Because the policy used the different term "colliding" in excluding from the definition of "collision" any "loss caused by * * * colliding with birds or animals," we believe that the terms of the policy indicate that the parties intended "colliding with * * * animals" to be read in its ordinary dictionary sense and thus to require an actual striking, clashing, or coming together of the motor home and an animal. Therefore, unless the motor home actually struck the animal, there was no "loss caused by * * * colliding with * * * animals." Instead, the motor home suffered an upset, within the definition of "collision" excluded from the comprehensive coverage.

Appellees, however, contend that coverage exists in this fact situation "where imminent collision with an animal precipitates evasive action all of which directly and proximately results in a collision or upset." Appellees acknowledge that there are no cases directly on point relating to this fact situation, but cite a number of cases and authorities holding and stating that where a risk insured against operates to subject the insured property to a risk not insured against, the loss is covered. *Rust Tractor Co. v. Consolidated Constructors, Inc.*, 86 N.M. 658, 526 P.2d 800 (1974); Annot. 160 A.L.R. 946 (1946); 5 Appleman, *Insurance Law and Practice*, § 3803 (1970). The simple answer to this contention is that the policy *sub judice* did not insure appellees against the risk of collision and therefore the cited authorities are not particularly helpful. We find that the language of the policy governs the coverage here, and that unless the motor home actually struck the animal, the loss caused by the upset of the motor home was within the policy's exclusion for loss caused by "collision." Therefore we find as a matter of law that appellees' loss is not covered under the comprehensive coverage of the policy unless in fact the motor home struck an animal, as appellees allege.

A directed verdict is justified only where the evidence is insufficient to support a contrary verdict or so weak that the court would feel constrained to set aside the verdict. *Pruett v. Precision Plumbing*, 27 Ariz.App. 288, 554 P.2d 655 (1976). At the trial, appellee stated that he heard a "thump," presumably caused by his motor home striking the animal, directly before the wheels of the motor home went off the pavement. On the other hand, no blood or hair was found on the motor home or on the highway. We believe that reasonable minds could differ as to whether this evidence showed that appellees' motor home actually struck an animal. Because coverage in this case depends on whether the motor home actually struck an animal, we hold that the trial court erred in granting a directed verdict to appellees on the issue of coverage where that proper fact issue was not presented and determined by the jury.

The remaining issues raised in the brief were waived at oral argument by appellant and will not be discussed.

Since the trial court erred in determining the coverage under the policy, and in instructing the jury, the matter is reversed and remanded for a new trial.

Notes and Questions

1. *The Boundary between Collision and Comprehensive.* Several methods of distinguishing collision from comprehensive coverage are available. One is simply to construe the term "collision" according to ordinary usage. Another is to apply collision coverage to operational risks and comprehensive to non-operational risks. A third is to distinguish between the application of force to the vehicle independently of the vehicle's momentum and the application of force in which the

vehicle's momentum is also a substantial contributing cause. How satisfactory are these tests?

2. *Colliding with an Animal.* Does *Rodemich* hold that under comprehensive coverage, colliding with an animal does not constitute a collision, but that the results of avoiding a collision with an animal can constitute a collision? Is this a sensible way to structure the two forms of coverage?

3. *The Purpose of the Coverage.* Collision coverage is generally sold subject to a deductible; often comprehensive coverage is not—it is "first-dollar" coverage. Does this difference imply anything about the kinds of losses the two forms of insurance are intended to cover? For example, could it be argued that because drivers normally do not want to repair small dents, they purchase collision coverage subject to a deductible, but that the kinds of losses covered by comprehensive coverage—broken windshields, flooded radiators, stolen radios—always need repair or replacement? Is this distinction powerful enough to resolve disputes that are not clearly resolved by the language in policies affording collision and comprehensive coverage?

D. AUTO NO–FAULT

Notwithstanding the effort of state legislatures and the courts to close the automobile-injury compensation gap, that gap cannot be closed completely. Some drivers (in violation of law) do not purchase coverage, and some cause injuries under circumstances where the stretching and pulling of coverage still will not close the gap. In addition, injury and damage caused by certain kinds of auto accidents simply cannot be compensated by liability insurance, because no one is liable for it. Automobile tort law, after all, is predicated on an act of negligence by one party that injures another party. Some accidents result even when no one has been negligent, and some are single-party accidents involving only the party injured.

Concern for the uncompensated victim during the 1950's prompted the development of *medical payments coverage* in the standard personal auto policy. Essentially insurance against health care costs resulting from injuries incurred in auto accidents, medical payments coverage is first-party no-fault insurance: proof of negligence by another party is not required, and negligence by the injured party does not preclude recovery. Typically such coverage was and is subject to relatively low-limits—$2000 is a representative limit. But as a method of assuring the victims of all but very severe accidents a ready source of coverage for medical expenses without the need to bring a tort action, such coverage is a simple method of closing at least part of the compensation gap that still remains even after liability insurance becomes nearly universal. In many states liability insurers are required to offer such coverage to all purchasers of liability insurance. The scope of such coverage is set out in the Sample Personal Auto Policy, Part B. No-fault automobile insurance systems build on the medical payments coverage model, by expanding the limits of medical coverage, providing insurance against wage-loss as well, and requiring that both be purchased. This form of coverage is generally termed "personal injury protection," or PIP coverage.

The states adopting no-fault then link their requirement that PIP coverage be purchased by all drivers with a limited abolition of the right to bring an action in tort, in ways described below. First proposed in full-blown form by Robert Keeton and Jeffrey O'Connell in Basic Protection for the Traffic Victim (1965), the no-fault idea caught hold in the 1970's, by the end of which roughly twenty states had adopted it, the precise number depending on how one defines the no-fault concept. There followed in many states debate about the constitutionality of no-fault systems. Although detailed examination of the constitutionality of these systems is beyond the scope of this book, it is appropriate here to survey the issues raised by challenges to no-fault and to sketch the scope of the expanded insurance protection that is at the heart of all auto no-fault systems.

MONTGOMERY v. DANIELS

Court of Appeals of New York, 1975.
38 N.Y.2d 41, 378 N.Y.S.2d 1, 340 N.E.2d 444.

Jones, Judge.

We hold that the New York no-fault automobile accident compensation law is not unconstitutional. This case comes to us on direct appeal . . . from a judgment at Special Term which, on cross motions for summary judgment, declared article 18 of the Insurance Law in violation of the due process and equal protection clauses of the Federal and State Constitutions and a denial of the right to trial by jury guaranteed by our State Constitution.

The New York No–Fault Act

We first describe this insurance program.

Under the title, "Comprehensive Automobile Insurance Reparations Act," article 18 of the Insurance Law (as added by L. 1973, ch. 13, in full effect Feb. 1, 1974) provides a plan for compensating victims of automobile accidents without regard to fault. In essence, it is a two-pronged, partial modification of the pre-existing system of reparation for personal injuries suffered in automobile accidents under which system liability was grounded in negligence under classic principles of tort law. One prong deals with compensation; the other with limitation of tort actions.

The first prong lays down the requirement that every owner of a motor vehicle provide himself, members of his household, operators, occupants and pedestrians with compensation for "basic economic loss" resulting from injuries occasioned by the use or operation of that vehicle in this State, regardless of fault (§ 672, subd. 1). "Motor vehicle" is defined to exclude motorcycles from the act's coverage (§ 671, subd. 6). "Basic economic loss," subject to a maximum of $50,000 per person, is defined to include:

(a) Treatment Expense—All "reasonable and necessary expenses" for medical, hospital, surgical, nursing, dental, ambulance, X ray, prescription drug and prosthetic services, as well as for psychiatric care, other professional health services, and any nonmedical remedial care rendered in accordance with a religious method of healing recognized by the laws of this State, all without limitation as to time, provided that, within one year after the date of the accident causing injury, it is ascertainable that further expenses may be incurred as a result of the injury (§ 671, subd. 1, par. [a]);

(b) Lost Earnings—Loss of earnings and expenses incurred in obtaining substitute services up to $1,000 per month for not more than three years from the date of the accident (§ 671, subd. 1, par. [c]).

Compensation for basic economic loss is payable as "first party benefits" after reducing the gross amount of such loss by deducting (a) 20% of "lost earnings (§ 671, subd. 2, par. [a]), (b) all amounts recoverable under State or Federal laws providing social security disability benefits or workmen's compensation benefits (§ 671, subd. 2, par. [b]), and (c) amounts deductible under the applicable insurance policy" (§ 671, subd. 2, par. [c]). "First party benefits" become due and payable "as the loss is incurred" and "are overdue if not paid within thirty days after the claimant supplies proof of the fact and amount of loss sustained" (§ 675, subd. 1). Any dispute with the insurer as to benefits may be resolved expeditiously by submission to binding arbitration at the option of the claimant (§ 675, subd. 2).

The right to first-party benefits accrues to the injured person *who gets benefits* regardless of fault or negligence on the part of the covered person, except that the insurer may exclude from coverage a person who intentionally causes his own injury, is injured as a result of operating a motor vehicle while in an intoxicated condition or while his ability to operate such vehicle is impaired by the use of a drug, or is injured while committing an act which would constitute a felony, seeking to avoid lawful apprehension or arrest, participating in a race or speed test, or operating or occupying a vehicle he knows to be stolen (§ 672, subd. 2).

The second prong of the act imposes two limitations on tort recovery for personal injuries, applicable, however, only to actions between "covered persons" (as defined in § 671, subd. 10): (1) there can be no duplicate tort compensation for "basic economic loss" (§ 673, subd. 1); and (2) damages for noneconomic loss (i.e., pain and suffering) are not recoverable in tort unless the plaintiff can establish that he has suffered a "serious injury" (§ 673, subd. 1). Serious injury is defined in subdivision 4 of section 671 as a personal injury:

"(a) which results in death, dismemberment; significant disfigurement; a compound or comminuted fracture; or permanent loss of use of a body organ, member, function, or system; or

"(b) if the reasonable and customary charges for medical, hospital, surgical, nursing, dental, ambulance, x-ray, prescription drug and prosthetic services necessarily performed as a result of the injury would exceed five hundred dollars."

Thus, an injured party may bring a third-party tort action and may recover therein for economic loss over $50,000, for treatment expenses not ascertainable within one year of injury, for lost earnings which exceed $1,000 per month or continue beyond three years, and for other reasonable and necessary expenses which exceed $25 per day or continue after one year. Damages for pain and suffering may likewise still be recovered in a tort action if there was a "serious injury." Finally, article 18 erects no bar whatever to tort actions seeking recovery for personal injury against noncovered persons or for property damage against covered or noncovered persons.

Plaintiffs' Claims

Plaintiffs, each of whom was injured in a separate automobile accident occurring after February 1, 1974, the effective date of article 18, joined together in this action against their respective alleged tortfeasors and insurers seeking a declaration that article 18 is unconstitutional and void in its entirety. Plaintiffs allege in each case that because the reasonable and customary charges for medical treatment for their respective injuries will not exceed $500, they are barred under the challenged law from commencing an action for their injuries and particularly for the pain and suffering allegedly occasioned thereby. Plaintiffs' constitutional attack on article 18 is multifaceted and can be summarized as follows:

(1) Article 18 is in contravention of the due process clauses of the Federal and State Constitutions because it is without rational relationship to its purported purposes, because it abolishes plaintiffs' common-law tort remedies as motor vehicle accident victims without providing a reasonable substitute remedy, and because the phrase "significant disfigurement" as used to define a "serious injury" (§ 671, subd. 4, par. [a]) is void for vagueness;

(2) Article 18 violates the equal protection clauses of the Federal and State Constitutions because, in declaring who shall and who shall not be precluded from maintaining a tort action for noneconomic losses (pain and suffering), the statute establishes arbitrary and irrational classifications between persons injured by covered persons and those injured by noncovered persons (§ 671, subd. 10; § 673), between those persons whose treatment expenses exceed $500 and those whose expenses fall below that threshold amount (§ 671, subd. 4, par. [b]; § 673), and between injuries defined as "serious" and those excluded from that definition (§ 671, subd. 4, par. [a]; § 673); and

(3) Article 18 violates the trial by jury provision of the New York State Constitution (art. I, § 2).

Plaintiffs' assertions of unconstitutionality focus, of course, on the details of article 18. We note, however, that to a very large extent the methodology of their assault would be equally applicable (or as we hold inapplicable) to any no-fault plan whatever its specifics. The techniques of their attack are those which are always available to challenge any statute in which lines of demarcation must be laid down—contentions predicated, at least implicitly, on the assumption that to draw any line involves an element of the arbitrary, that wherever the line is drawn instances can be suggested which appear to involve inequitable inclusion or exclusion (*see, infra,* p. 64, 378 N.Y.S.2d 20–21, 340 N.E.2d 458). The ineluctable projection of plaintiffs' arguments is that our Legislature does not have authority to adopt any no-fault plan.

Prepassage Studies and Proceedings

Before turning to an analysis of the constitutional claims advanced, it will be helpful to review some of the studies and proceedings which preceded enactment of article 18.

Debate over the efficacy of the tort system of compensating automobile accident victims has raged for over 40 years.[1] Our Legislature in 1973 thus had available to it a staggering number of reports and studies which provided analysis of the concept of a no-fault system of reparations and to which our attention is now drawn by both plaintiffs and defendants on this appeal.[2] These studies identify at least four basic infirmities or defects in the common-law fault system of automobile accident reparation for personal injuries. For the purposes of this appeal, we recognize these four infirmities or defects as predicates for the Legislature's enactment of article 18.[3]

The first infirmity was the acknowledged fact that exposure to the risk of tort liability did not function as a significant factor in motivating drivers to operate their vehicles carefully or prudently. (DOT

1. For a brief history of the development of the concept of no-fault insurance see Shermer, Automobile Liability Insurance—No Fault Insurance, Uninsured Motorists, Compulsory Coverage (§ 1.01).

2. We find three such studies particularly helpful in their marshaling of statistical evidence: the oft-cited study prepared by Professors Keeton and O'Connell in 1965 in which was proposed a scheme encompassing no-fault protection in conjunction with the preservation of tort liability for major injuries (Keeton and O'Connell, Basic Protection for the Traffic Victim [Keeton and O'Connell]); a report by the New York State Department of Insurance published in 1970 and entitled, Automobile Insurance ∗ ∗ ∗ For Whose Benefit? [Insurance Department Report]; a 1971 report by the United States Department of Transportation prepared at the request of Congress and entitled, Motor Vehicle Crash Losses and Their Compensation in the United States [DOT Report]).

We, of course, express no judicial view as to the conclusions reached by any of these studies for, in determining whether or not the Legislature's response to this issue was constitutionally permissible, it is not within the judiciary's province to pass on the wisdom, propriety or even correctness of that legislative response. ∗ ∗ ∗

3. See, generally, then Governor Rockefeller's Memorandum approving the act, N.Y. Legis.Ann., 1973, p. 298.

Report, at pp. 53–57; Insurance Department Report, at pp. 12–13;[4] Keeton and O'Connell, at pp. 247–249.) Nothing in the new no-fault act seeks to remedy this infirmity; indeed the new law apparently proceeds on the assumption that threat of economic disadvantage, by way either of increased insurance premiums or of excess recoveries, is no effective deterrent to bad driving.

Secondly it was urged that the tort system was excessively and needlessly expensive and inefficient. Keeton and O'Connell (at p. 70, n. 190) and the DOT Report (at p. 51) both concluded that half or perhaps less than half of the automobile liability insurance premium dollar was paid in actual compensation to accident victims. The Insurance Department Report stated (at p. 35) that only 44 cents of the premium dollar reached the injured claimants.

Thirdly it was urged that the distribution of compensation among accident victims under the tort system of reparation was unfair and inequitable for a number of reasons. The most revealing statistic reported was that one quarter of the persons who sustained bodily injury in auto accidents in New York received no compensation whatsoever (Insurance Department Report, at p. 18). Where the tort system did provide recompense, the statistics further revealed that minor injuries were often overcompensated (at least in terms of readily ascertainable medical expenses) while those suffering serious injuries were being underpaid.[5] Moreover it was concluded in all reports that the tort system was plagued by long delays in claim payment.[6]

4. The Insurance Department Report added (at p. 48, n. 96): "Now we can fully appreciate the absurdity of the notion that the fault insurance system is a 'deterrent' to bad driving. Earlier we saw that, taken just as a theoretical proposition, the notion of insured civil liability as a deterrent to unsafe conduct was not plausible * * * and all that is possibly left of the 'deterrence' argument under the fault insurance system is that insurance company underwriting and rating practices will cause the bad drivers to be denied insurance, to have their insurance cancelled or to have their rates go up. Even in this attenuated form the argument is without substance. It has, in effect, been overwhelmed by the very steps society has taken to expand compensation to victims, or to protect consumers against harsh actions by insurers. Insurers cannot cancel policies for accident involvement, even if the policyholder was adjudged at fault. People who cannot get insurance in the normal market can obtain it through the assigned risk plan, again without regard to fault. Rate differentials, being matters of prediction and not recoupment, vary according to many factors (such as place of residence, age and car use) that have nothing to do with the individual policyholder's driving record."

5. It was concluded in the Insurance Department Report (at p. 27) that 33% of the victims with small economic losses recovered one and one half of their economic losses, and only 18% did not receive as much as three quarters of their economic losses. On the other hand, of those victims studied who incurred the largest economic losses, not one received three quarters of his economic loss and 71% recovered one quarter or less of such loss.

The DOT Report (at pp. 94–95) found: "For those whose economic losses were more than $25,000, only about a third was usually recovered. Those with relatively small economic losses, by contrast, fared much better; if they recovered from tort and had losses less than $500, their recovery averaged four and a half times actual economic loss."

6. The Insurance Department Report (at pp. 19–20) found that the average claim-to-payment interval for automobile personal injury was 15.8 months, or 10 times as long as the interval for automobile collision, homeowners or burglary insurance and 40 times as long as the interval for accident and health insurance. In addition, 17% of total claims

As a fourth major inadequacy of the fault system of reparation, it was argued that the system placed an inordinate strain on the State's court systems and judicial resources. (See, generally, Insurance Department Report, at pp. 19–24; DOT Report, at pp. 70–79; and Keeton and O'Connell, at pp. 13–15.)

In March, 1970 the Governor sent the first proposed legislation for implementing no-fault concepts in this State to the Legislature accompanied by a special message (reprinted in 111th Annual Report of the Superintendent of Insurance to the Legislature for 1969 [1970], at pp. 329–331). Public hearings were held on the proposed bill, but no action was taken that year. In 1971 the Governor followed a similar procedure (see 112th Annual Report of the Superintendent of Insurance to the Legislature for 1970 [1971], at pp. 155–157) and more hearings were held, but again no action was taken on any of the at least five bills before the Legislature. In 1972 even more extensive hearings were held at which some 90 witnesses testified including the Governor, Superintendent of Insurance and Federal Insurance Administrator, but again no legislative action was taken. In 1973, however, the act which is here under scrutiny was passed and signed into law as chapter 13. This synopsis of article 18's legislative history is presented to demonstrate that the Legislature acted only after unusually extensive study and investigation and on what must be accepted for purposes of judicial review as an uncommonly sturdy legislative basis.

It is additionally worth noting that prior to February 1, 1974, the effective date of article 18, 13 other jurisdictions had enacted various forms of no-fault insurance laws. In those jurisdictions where the courts of last resort have passed on the constitutionality of the no-fault plans enacted by their respective Legislatures, all but one have sustained the legislation.[7]

It remains here only to add that we recognize that other studies and data can be cited which tend to refute the conclusions on which our Legislature predicated its enactment of article 18. The judiciary, however, is not called on to weigh the relative worth of data or arguments which may be marshaled on either side as to the wisdom of determinations made by the Legislature in the realm of policy. "Whether the enactment is wise or unwise, whether it is based on

which remained unpaid after two years represented 45% of the total dollar loss. (And see DOT Report, at pp. 41–42; Keeton and O'Connell, at pp. 46–49.)

7. In the following cases, in what must be recognized as at least partially distinguishable legal contexts, the legislation was sustained in its entirety: *Pinnick v. Cleary,* 360 Mass. 1, 271 N.E.2d 592; *Opinion of The Justices,* 113 N.H. 205, 304 A.2d 881; *Manzanares v. Bell,* 214 Kan. 589, 522 P.2d 1291; *Singer v. Sheppard,* Pa., 346 A.2d 897 (1975); *Gentile v. Altermatt,* Conn. (August 6, 1975). In *Lasky v. State Farm Ins. Co.,* 296 So.2d 9 [Fla.1974], the Supreme Court of Florida, while finding portions of the no-fault statute before it unconstitutional, severed such portions and found the bulk of the statute constitutional. The Illinois Supreme Court is the only State court of last resort to invalidate in its entirety a no-fault law. (*Grace v. Howlett,* 51 Ill.2d 478, 283 N.E.2d 474.) That case is entirely distinguishable from the case here under consideration both as to the Illinois statute under review and as to the controlling provisions of the Illinois State Constitution.

sound economic theory, whether it is the best means to achieve the desired result, whether, in short, the legislative discretion within its prescribed limits should be exercised in a particular manner, are matters for the judgment of the legislature, and the earnest conflict of serious opinion does not suffice to bring them within the range of judicial cognizance." * * *

In this instance, perhaps more than in most, in the light of the exhaustive and vigorous public discussion of no-fault insurance in this State and elsewhere and the extended legislative consideration which preceded adoption of article 18, it would be a demonstration of judicial arrogation and highly inept and inapt to express any opinion as to the factual predicate for this legislation, its philosophical justification or the ultimate wisdom of its enactment. It is not our office to rejoice or to lament. A fair regard for the basic policy of separation of powers dictates judicial respect for the proper role of the legislative branch, and pride in the uniquely and essentially neutral role of the judicial branch. That judicial role is both a privilege and a limitation. * * *

Due Process Issues

We turn then to consideration of the several arguments advanced to support the contention that article 18 is unconstitutional.

We conclude that the partial abolition here of an accident victim's right to sue for damages caused by another's negligent action does not deprive the victim of a right or interest protected by the due process clause of either our State or the Federal Constitution.

In *West Coast Hotel Co. v. Parrish,* 300 U.S. 379, 391, 57 S.Ct. 578, 581, 81 L.Ed. 703 the United States Supreme Court stated that "regulation which is reasonable in relation to its subject and is adopted in the interests of the community is due process." Thus where a statute is challenged on nonprocedural grounds as violative of due process of law we have consistently asked the question whether there is "some fair, just and reasonable connection 'between it and the promotion of the health, comfort, safety and welfare of society.'" * * *

[W]e reject plaintiffs' argument that there is no reasonable basis between reform as undertaken in article 18 and the objective of remedying the defects perceived by the Legislature to inhere in the fault-based tort system for compensating automobile accident personal injury claimants. On the contrary we conclude that, by eliminating recovery for pain and suffering in relatively minor cases and by simultaneously guaranteeing prompt and full compensation for economic losses up to $50,000 without the necessity of recourse to the courts, the Legislature acted reasonably to eliminate much of the wasted expenditures of premium dollars on expenses extraneous to treatment of injury (e.g., legal and investigative costs involved in determining fault and in establishing the value of the alleged pain and suffering). Such action may further be viewed as reasonably related to guaranteeing full and fair recovery to all victims by reducing pressure on a seriously injured person to compromise down his claims in order to obtain funds for treatment while at the same time eliminating pressure on insurers to compromise up claims by persons suffering minor injuries in order to avoid the expense of investigating and defending against such minor claims. Finally, it cannot be said that by partially obviating recourse to the courts the statute was unreasonable in relation to its purpose to reduce the long delays in the payment of claims experienced under judicial procedures and to lessen the burden on our State courts and judicial resources.

In so holding it is not necessary for us to conclude that article 18 represents the only or necessarily the wisest response which the Legislature could have taken to accomplish the objectives sought. "Assuming that there were other effective methods by which to accomplish the same end, this court should not substitute its judgment for that of the Legislature in determining the particular method to meet a given need." (*Matter of Taylor v. Sise,* 33 N.Y.2d 357, 365, 352 N.Y.S.2d 924, 930, 308 N.E.2d 442, 447, *supra.*) Nor is it necessary to conclude that article 18 will surely accomplish the ends sought to be achieved, for "only time will tell whether the course pursued will prove effective or will fail" (*People v. Broadie,* 37 N.Y.2d 100, 118, 371 N.Y.S.2d 471, 482, 332 N.E.2d 338, 346, *supra*). We hold only that article 18 is reasonably related to the promotion of the public welfare and thus represents a legitimate exercise of our State's police power. * * *

Finally under the due process heading, we find no merit in plaintiffs' additional claim that the term "significant disfigurement," as used in section 671 (subd. 4, par. [a]) to define a "serious injury," is unconstitutionally vague. While it is true that civil as well as penal statutes can be tested for vagueness under the due process clause (*Giaccio v. Pennsylvania,* 382 U.S. 399, 402, 86 S.Ct. 518, 15 L.Ed.2d 447), we find the words "significant disfigurement" well within that test. "While these are abstract words, they have through daily use acquired a content that conveys to any interested person a sufficiently accurate concept." (*Kovacs v. Cooper,* 336 U.S. 77, 79, 69 S.Ct. 448, 449, 93 L.Ed. 513.) The challenged phrase is no less vague than that found in our State's Workmen's Compensation Law (§ 15, subd. 3, par. t, cl. 1) which provides that the "board may award proper and equitable compensation for serious facial and head disfigurement"—a provision which has been interpreted and applied without constitutional difficulty. * * *

Equal Protection Claims

* * *

Plaintiffs first contend that the operation of section 673 creates an arbitrary and capricious classification as between covered and noncovered persons. Subdivision 1 of that section bars a suit in tort in actions between covered persons unless the injured party sustains a serious injury or incurs expenses in excess of basic economic loss. Under subdivision 2 of that section, however, no such bar attaches where a noncovered person is a party to the suit. Noncovered person under article 18 include: (1) an owner, operator or passenger on a motorcycle (§ 671, subd. 6, par. [b]); (2) the owner, operator or occupant of an uninsured motor vehicle (§ 671, subds. 9, 10); and (3) the owner or operator of an out-of-State motor vehicle whose insurance policy does not include no-fault coverage for New York operation (§ 676). Plaintiffs claim that there can be no rational basis for a scheme which determines whether a right to recover in tort exists by reference to the identity of the motorist involved. Such a claim does not withstand analysis.

There was a rational basis for the exclusion of motorcycles from the definition of motor vehicle. The Legislature had before it evidence that the premium cost to motorcyclists, should they have been required to purchase first-party coverage under the no-fault plan, would have been prohibitively high. * * * As one of the legislative purposes in enacting a no-fault plan was to reduce the cost of premium insurance, exclusion of motorcycles was certainly rationally related to that purpose.[8] Additionally, we note that in enacting reform, the Legislature is entitled to proceed "one step at a time, addressing itself to the phase of the problem which seems most acute to the legislative mind." (*Williamson v. Lee Opt. Co.*, 348 U.S. 483, 489, 75 S.Ct. 461, 465, 99 L.Ed. 563; *Silver v. Silver*, 280 U.S. 117, 123, 50 S.Ct. 57, 74 L.Ed. 221, *supra*.)

Similarly it was not unreasonable for the Legislature to have excluded persons operating uninsured vehicles from coverage under article 18. Such persons operate their vehicles in violation of the law of our State (Vehicle and Traffic Law, arts. 6, 8) and further make no contribution to the automobile injury compensation system designed to spread the risk of loss among all who drive.

Finally with respect to this contention, we find no infirmity in the exclusion from coverage of an out-of-State motor vehicle whose insurance policy does not include no-fault coverage for operation in our State. Certainly the Legislature cannot be faulted for not extending the requirement of coverage to those over whom the Legislature had no power to act.[9] Rather than representing an arbitrary and capricious exercise of legislative power, this exclusion merely recognizes the

---

8. At least three other State courts of last resort have sustained the exclusion of motorcycles from no-fault coverage (*Lasky v. State Farm Ins. Co.*, 296 So.2d 9 [Fla.], *supra; Manzanares v. Bell*, 214 Kan. 589, 522 P.2d 1291, *supra; Singer v. Sheppard*, Pa., 346 A.2d 897 [1975], *supra*).

9. To the extent of its power, the Legislature acted to guarantee that nonresident motorists do not fall within the noncovered class. Articles 6 and 8 of the Vehicle and Traffic Law require that nonresident motorists carry no-fault coverage for their excursions into New York. Furthermore section 676 of the Insurance Law requires all insurers (i) licensed in New York, (ii) controlled by an insurer licensed in New York, or (iii) controlled by a holding company affiliated with a New York licensed insurer, to provide New York no-fault coverage when a vehicle they cover happens to be driven in New York. In addition, the Insurance Department requested insurers not licensed in New York voluntarily to provide New York no-fault coverage to their policyholders. Of the 524 such insurers contacted over 85% had agreed to do so as of May, 1974. (New York Insurance Department, 115 Annual Report of the Superintendent of Insurance to the New York State Legislature for 1973, at p. 19.)

realities of the situation. Additionally we note that the number of persons excluded from coverage under section 676 is minuscule.[10] The classification having a reasonable basis, "it does not offend the Constitution simply because [it] 'is not made with mathematical nicety or because in practice it results in some inequality.'" (*Dandridge v. Williams*, 397 U.S. 471, 485, 90 S.Ct. 1153, 1161, 25 L.Ed.2d 491, *supra*.)

Still urging their claim of denial of equal protection plaintiffs next challenge the legislative definition of "serious injury" (§ 671, subd. 4) by which it is determined whether or not a party shall or shall not have a right to sue for pain and suffering (§ 673), as creating an arbitrary and capricious classification. Serious injury is defined to mean a personal injury:

"(a) which results in death; dismemberment; significant disfigurement; a compound or comminuted fracture; or permanent loss of use of a body organ, member, function, or system; or

"(b) if the reasonable and customary charges for medical, hospital, surgical, nursing, dental, ambulance, x-ray, prescription drug and prosthetic services necessarily performed as a result of the injury would exceed five hundred dollars."

Plaintiffs argue that certain injuries such as a simple fracture to the skull or vertebrae, while not included within the statutory list of serious injuries, are capable of producing pain and suffering to a far greater degree than other injuries such as comminuted fractures to the little fingers which the Legislature did include in the list. Plaintiffs further argue that the $500 threshold amount is not related to any rational basis.[11]

We have already expressed our views as to the reasonableness of the Legislature's conclusion that the tort system of recovery for nonserious injuries resulting in minimal economic losses was beset with deficiencies and inequities which were within the Legislature's power to address. Having therefore decided to limit tort recovery to pain and suffering associated with serious injury, the Legislature was confronted with the problem of establishing a line of demarcation between serious

10. The Attorney–General has provided the following pertinent statistics: The 69 insurers having no contact with New York who "either declined to provide no-fault coverage for their insureds while driving in this State or neglected to respond to the State Insurance Department's request [see n. 9, *supra*] ∗ ∗ ∗ write less than 1% of total United States and Canadian automobile premiums of over 12 billion dollars. Moreover, fewer than 5% of all New York auto personal injuries involve out-of-state drivers (State Dept. of Motor V., 1973 Annual Rpt. at 21). Hence, the possibility that any accident *may* involve such a non-covered person is less than ¹/₂₀ of 1%. This minuscule probability is diluted further, since the 69 small carriers (save four in Quebec and Ontario) are located in noncontiguous states."

11. It is notable that all of the State courts of last resort have upheld monetary thresholds computed with respect to medical or treatment expenses (*Gentile v. Altermatt*, Conn. (August 6, 1975), *supra* [$400]; *Lasky v. State Farm Ins. Co.*, 296 So.2d 9 [Fla.], *supra* [$1,000]; *Manzanares v. Bell*, 214 Kan. 589, 522 P.2d 1291 (1974); *Fann v. McGuffey*, Ky. (June 27, 1975), *supra* [$1,000]; *Pinnick v. Cleary*, 360 Mass. 1, 271 N.E.2d 592, *supra* [$500]; *Opinion of the Justices*, 113 N.H. 205, 304 A.2d 881, *supra* [$1,000]; *Singer v. Sheppard*, Pa., 346 A.2d 897 [1975], *supra* [$750]).

and nonserious injury and between large and small claims—a line which would be marked by rules easily and readily applied to avoid the expenditure of time and money in investigation and determination on which side of the line each particular claim would fall.

We find the classifications created by the Legislature to be reasonably related to the end of establishing a rational line of distinction and of eliminating the evils which that body perceived to exist. True it may be that certain injuries not listed might well have been included within the class of serious injuries or that the threshold amount might more wisely have been set at $400 or $600. But such decisions are not of determinative concern to this court. "[E]very line drawn by a legislature leaves out some that might well have been included. That exercise of discretion, however, is a legislative, not a judicial, function." (*Village of Belle Terre v. Boraas*, 416 U.S. 1, 8, 94 S.Ct. 1536, 1540, 39 L.Ed.2d 797 * * *). * * *

Nor can we accept plaintiffs' contention that it was irrational to base the computation of the $500 amount on treatment expenses alone rather than on "basic economic cost." To have utilized the latter standard would clearly have been to favor those in higher earned income brackets.

Plaintiffs' attack on the $500 threshold amount on the grounds that particular charges for medical services vary from one locality to another and in operation might discriminate against the poor is not persuasive.[12] Section 671 (subd. 4, par. [b]) provides that the threshold requirement is met when it is determined that "reasonable and customary" charges would exceed $500. We note the difference in diction employed by the Legislature in different provisions of article 18. The standard for proof of a claimant's basic economic loss is "*all reasonable and necessary* expenses incurred," i.e., an individualized standard related to the expenses in fact incurred by the particular plaintiff (§ 671, subd. 1, par. [a]). The standard for determination of the threshold amount, by contrast, is "*the reasonable and customary* charges for * * * services necessarily performed" (§ 671, subd. 4, par. [b]; italics supplied), a general standard in the application of which payments actually made by the particular claimant will not be determinative. The argument that an absolute $500 threshold will work a denial of equal protection because medical and hospital charges are relative, varying from community to community (an argument equally applicable to any dollar amount which our Legislature might have fixed) proceeds on the fallacious assumption again that the legislative stan-

---

12. We note in passing that there were findings before the Legislature that the tort system worked particularly to the disadvantage of people who were poor and uneducated. The United States Department of Transportation found that where family income was $10,000 or more accident victims recovered 61% of their economic loss, but where it was below $5,000 they recovered only 38% of their economic loss. (U.S. Dept. of Transportation, Economic Consequences of Automobile Accident Injuries, p. 54 [1970].) Likewise it was shown that seriously injured victims with postgraduate education recovered 73% of their economic loss while those with only five to eight years of formal education recovered only 27% of their economic loss. (*Id.*, at p. 52).

dard must be made with "mathematical nicety" and in practice result in no "inequity" (*Dandridge v. Williams,* 397 U.S. 471, 485 *supra*). Dispute as to what is "reasonable and customary" is a question of fact not dissimilar to many issues of damages which can be and are effectively determined by a jury or Judge without a jury. (See, e.g., *Morell v. Vargas,* 83 Misc.2d 30, 371 N.Y.S.2d 828, wherein a complaint was dismissed on a jury finding that the plaintiff had not incurred "reasonable and customary charges" over $500 despite uncontradicted proof of actual medical expenditure of $927.)

Right to a Jury Trial

Finally plaintiffs argue that article 18, in limiting their right to recover in tort, infringes on their right to trial by jury, protected by section 2 of article I of our State Constitution.[13] This argument is similar to the claim discussed (*supra,* p. 60, 378 N.Y.S.2d p. 17, 340 N.E.2d p. 455) that article 18 infringes on plaintiffs' right of "access to the courts." The argument is no more tenable in its new guise.[14]

Article 18 does not replace the jury as trier of fact with some other trier of fact. Rather it modifies the substantive law and redefines the rights of those personally injured in automobile accidents. The Constitution guarantees the right to trial by jury if the plaintiff has a claim to assert. If, as here, the Legislature otherwise properly abrogates the claim in part, to that extent there remains nothing to which the right to trial by jury may attach. (Cf. *Hanfgarn v. Mark,* 274 N.Y. 22, 26, 8 N.E.2d 47, 48.) * * *

The judgment of Supreme Court should be reversed, summary judgment granted to defendants, and the case remitted to Supreme Court for a declaration consistent with the views expressed in this opinion.

Notes and Questions

1. *The Two Prongs of No-Fault.* No state has adopted pure no-fault—that is, a statute that completely abolishes the cause of action for negligence in the operation of an automobile and substitutes mandatory PIP coverage. In addition, some states that mandate the purchase of PIP coverage have not limited the cause of action in tort at all. Rather, they have simply added a requirement that all drivers purchase PIP coverage. Thus the distinction between *no-fault states* (those that both require PIP coverage and limit, but do not abolish the right to sue in tort) and *add-on states* (those that merely require PIP

13. Section 2 of article I provides in pertinent part: "trial by jury in all cases in which it has heretofore been guaranteed by constitutional provision shall remain inviolate forever."

14. In distinguishable contexts, the highest courts of other States have rejected similar denial-of-right-to-trial-by-jury challenges to no-fault plans (*Gentile v. Altermatt,* Conn. (August 6, 1975), *supra; Lasky v. State Farm Ins. Co.,* 296 So.2d 9 [Fla.], *supra; Manzanares v. Bell,* 214 Kan. 589, 616, 522 P.2d 1291, *supra; Pinnick v. Cleary,* 360 Mass. 1, 271 N.E.2d 592, *supra; Opinion of the Justices,* 113 N.H. 205, 211, 304 A.2d 881, *supra*).

coverage). As of 1989, there were 14 no-fault states and 10 add-on states.

2. *Thresholds and Benefit Levels.* The contours of a no-fault system are defined by two concepts: the *threshold* that must be passed for the injured party to bring a tort action, and the minimum *benefit levels* to be provided by the PIP coverage that the statute requires be purchased.

a. *Thresholds.* Most no-fault states have both verbal and monetary thresholds; a few have only verbal thresholds. New York, for example, has abolished its monetary threshold. See N.Y.Ins.Law §§ 5102, 5104. The result of a low monetary threshold—several hundred dollars of medical expenses, for example—is that few if any victims are legally precluded from suing in tort. Nonetheless, most statutes also repeal the collateral source rule as applied to PIP benefits. Where PIP benefit levels are high, the fact that these benefits are not recoverable in a tort action probably acts as a disincentive to most suits that could be brought, except where the victim has suffered out-of-pocket expenses beyond these benefits or very serious pain and suffering. In contrast, some states have relatively high monetary thresholds. The threshold for entry into the tort system in the District of Columbia, for example, is $5000 in medical expenses. See D.C. Code § 35.2105. Presumably the design behind such statutes is to preclude all but the very severely injured victim from suing in tort.

b. *Benefit Levels.* The other important feature of any no-fault system is the level of PIP benefits that must be purchased. When Massachusetts enacted the first such statute, the required minimum benefit level was $2000. See R. Keeton and A. Widiss, Insurance Law 418 (2d ed. 1988). The concern of statutes that require such minimal benefit levels obviously is to move cases involving only minor or moderate injuries out of the courts and into the insurance system. States with much higher benefit levels, such as New York's $50,000—or the few states that require unlimited benefits—would seem to have other objectives as well. How would you distinguish the objectives of low benefit-level and high benefit-level states? For a wonderfully insightful and analytical discussion of this and related issues, see Blum and Kalven, Ceilings, Costs, and Compulsion in Auto Compensation Legislation, 1973 Utah L.Rev. 341.

3. *The Cost of No–Fault.* Notwithstanding the entry of auto no-fault into middle age (at least as statutes go), debate about whether no-fault or fault-based insurance is less expensive continues. For data on the performance of the two systems, see U.S. Dep't. of Transportation, Compensating Accident Victims: A Follow–Up Report on No–Fault Auto Insurance Experiences (1985). For an analysis of this issue and a proposal for creating an option for motorists to select the system they prefer and to purchase the appropriate form of insurance for that selection, see O'Connell and Joost, Giving Motorists a Choice Between Fault and No–Fault Insurance, 72 Va.L.Rev. 61 (1986).

E. UNINSURED MOTORISTS COVERAGE

ALLSTATE INSURANCE v. BOYNTON

Supreme Court of Florida, 1986.
486 So.2d 552.

EHRLICH, Justice.

In this uninsured motorist case, Allstate Insurance Company seeks review of the decision of the District Court of Appeal, Fifth District, in *Boynton v. Allstate Insurance Co.,* 443 So.2d 427 (Fla. 5th DCA 1984). Acknowledging conflict with *Centennial Insurance Co. v. Wallace,* 330 So.2d 815 (Fla. 3d DCA), *cert. denied,* 341 So.2d 1087 (Fla.1976), the district court reversed a summary judgment that had been entered in favor of the uninsured motorist insurance carrier. * * *

We quash the district court's decision. We agree with the district court that a vehicle may be an "uninsured motor vehicle" under section 627.727(1), Florida Statutes (Supp.1978),[1] even when it is covered by a liability insurance policy, if that policy does not provide coverage for the particular occurrence that caused plaintiff's damages. However, we also hold that the phrase "legally entitled to recover" in the context of section 627.727(1) does not encompass claims where the uninsured tortfeasor is immune from liability because of the Workers' Compensation Law, chapter 440; Florida Statutes.

In this case, the plaintiff, Richard Boynton, was employed by Sears, Roebuck & Company as an auto mechanic. While on the job, Boynton was struck and injured by a car on which his co-employee, James Luke, was working. The car was leased to Xerox Corporation and was left at the Sears Auto Center for repairs. Boynton first brought suit against Sears, Xerox, and their insurance carriers. He voluntarily dismissed his suit against Sears and its insurer because Sears was immune from tort suit under section 440.11, Florida Statutes.[2] The trial court granted summary judgment in favor of Xerox and its insurer based on *Castillo v. Bickley,* 363 So.2d 792 (Fla.1978). That case held that an automobile owner, absent his own negligence, is not liable for the

---

1. Section 627.727(1) provides in pertinent part:

(1) No automobile liability insurance covering liability arising out of the ownership, maintenance, or use of any motor vehicle shall be delivered or issued for delivery in this state with respect to any motor vehicle registered or principally garaged in this state unless coverage is provided therein or supplemental thereto for the protection of persons insured thereunder who are *legally entitled to recover damages from owners or operators of uninsured motor vehicles* because of bodily injury, sickness, or disease, including death, resulting therefrom. However, the coverage required under this section shall not be applicable when, or to the extent that, any insured named in the policy shall reject the coverage. (Emphasis added.)

2. 440.11 Exclusiveness of liability.—

(1) The liability of an employer prescribed in s. 440.10 [for workers' compensation benefits] shall be exclusive and in place of all other liability of such employer to any third-party tortfeasor and to the employee; legal representative thereof, husband or wife.

negligent operation of a vehicle left at a repair shop. Boynton then
sought to recover damages from Luke's automobile liability insurance
carrier, but that carrier denied coverage because of a provision in
Luke's policy excluding injuries occurring during the pursuit of a
business.

Boynton then amended his complaint to allege that Luke was an
uninsured motorist and sought to recover under his own uninsured
motorist policy with Allstate.[3] The trial court entered summary judgment in favor of Allstate. On appeal from this judgment, Boynton
raised two issues:

> (1) Is a vehicle an uninsured vehicle when a policy of
> liability insurance covers it, but the policy does not provide
> coverage for the particular occurrence?

> (2) Is the insured "legally entitled to recover" from the
> operator of an insured motor vehicle when there is a statutory
> bar to an action against the operator, but for which bar,
> recovery would lie?

The Fifth District reversed. It held that in the context of the Florida
uninsured motorist statute, a vehicle is an "uninsured vehicle" when a
policy of liability insurance covers it, but the policy does not provide
coverage for the particular occurrence and that an insured is "legally
entitled to recover" from the operator of an insured motor vehicle when
there is a statutory bar to an action against the operator, but for which
bar, recovery would lie.

First Issue

Allstate asserts that the vehicle in question was not "uninsured"
because Xerox had a liability insurance policy that would have provided coverage if Boynton had had a cause of action against Xerox. We
reject this argument. The fact that an owner or operator of a motor
vehicle has a liability insurance policy does not always mean that the
vehicle is insured in the context of section 627.727(1). A vehicle is
insured in this context only when the insurance in question is available
to the injured plaintiff. It is undisputed that Xerox was without fault
as a matter of law and that it could not be held responsible for Luke's
negligence. That being the case, Xerox's liability insurance was not
available to Boynton. In the context of Boynton's uninsured motorist
claim, it cannot be said that this was an insured motor vehicle just
because Xerox had liability insurance coverage.

Allstate next asserts that the vehicle in question was not "uninsured" because Luke also had a liability insurance policy. We likewise
reject this contention. Luke's policy specifically excluded injuries oc-

---

3. In Boynton's uninsured motorist policy, Allstate agreed that:

We will pay damages for bodily injury, sickness, death or disease which you are
legally entitled to recover from the owner or operator of an uninsured auto. Injury
must be caused by accident and arise out of the ownership, maintenance or use of an
uninsured or underinsured auto. (Emphasis added.)

curring in the pursuit of a business. This exclusion is applicable to the facts of this case. Luke's policy, therefore, did not provide coverage for this particular occurrence.

An analogous situation is found in *American Fire & Casualty Co. v. Boyd,* 357 So.2d 768 (Fla. 1st DCA 1978). In that case, Boyd was injured in an automobile accident caused by the negligence of Hansen. Hansen had a liability policy which excluded coverage while traveling on military orders, which is what he was doing at the time of the accident. The district court correctly found that Hansen's automobile was "uninsured" in the context of Boyd's uninsured motorist policy and permitted him to recover motorist benefits. The district court reasoned:

> Although Hansen had procured a policy of insurance, that policy afforded no coverage because of the exclusionary clause; and the mere fact that Hansen was in such a position as to cause to be invoked by his negligence the provisions of the Federal Tort Claims Act does not mean that he is thereby "insured" within the meaning of the statute.

Id. at 769. The availability of a collateral remedy, the Federal Tort Claims Act in *Hansen,* workers' compensation in this case, likewise does not render a vehicle "insured."

In the present case, we hold that in the context of Boynton's uninsured motorist policy, the motor vehicle which injured him was "uninsured." Xerox's policy afforded no coverage because Xerox was without fault as a matter of law. Luke's liability policy afforded no coverage because of the policy exclusion.[4]

Second Issue

Although the vehicle was technically uninsured as to respondents, section 627.727(1) and the policy endorsement still require the policyholder be "legally entitled to recover" from the owner or operator of the uninsured vehicle. The plain meaning of the requirement would appear to be that the insured must have a claim against the tortfeasor which could be reduced to judgment in a court of law. The district court, however, construes the phrase in more limited fashion:

> The majority of courts which have construed the words "legally entitled to recover" have construed them to mean simply that the insured must be able to establish fault on the part of the uninsured motorist which gives rise to the damages and to prove the extent of the damages. See, *e.g., Winner v.*

4. Allstate, citing *Reid v. State Farm Fire & Casualty Co.,* 352 So.2d 1172 (Fla.1977), asserts in its brief that a valid exclusion in a liability policy does not make a vehicle uninsured for uninsured motorist purpose. In *Reid* we held that a vehicle cannot be both an insured and uninsured vehicle under the *same* policy. The present case is distinguishable because it involves separate policies. *Reid* is inapplicable.

Also, denial of coverage of Luke's carrier renders the vehicle uninsured within the express terms of Boynton's Allstate policy, which provides: "An uninsured auto is * * * [a] motor vehicle for which the insurer denies coverage. * * *."

> *Ratzlaff,* 211 Kan. 59, 505 P.2d 606 (1973), and cases cited in
> Anno., 73 A.L.R.3d 632, 649. Recovery may be had under this
> coverage when the claimant shows conduct on the part of the
> tortfeasor which would entitle the claimant to recover dam-
> ages, even though a defense available to the tortfeasor would
> defeat actual recovery.

Boynton v. Allstate, 443 So.2d 427, 430 (Fla. 5th DCA 1984). However,
none of the cases cited in support of this interpretation were decided in
the context of a statutory bar by a workers' compensation law.

For instance, in *Winner v. Ratzlaff* the issue was not even whether
some statutory bar to recovery against the tortfeasor prevented recovery from the insurer, but rather whether the insured could sustain a
direct action against his insurer. The insured had originally sued only
the tortfeasor, but after discovery revealed the defendant was uninsured, the insured added his UM carrier as a defendant. He then
sought to dismiss the tortfeasor from the suit. The Kansas Supreme
Court held it was error for the trial judge to refuse to dismiss the
tortfeasor. The court reasoned that the Kansas uninsured motorist law
had been enacted, in part, to avoid any requirement that a judgment be
had against the tortfeasor before liability would arise against the UM
carrier. In reaching this conclusion, the court discussed the phrase at
issue here.

> We construe the words "legally entitled to recover as
> damages" to mean simply that the insured must be able to
> establish fault on the part of the uninsured motorist which
> gives rise to the damages and to prove the extent of those
> damages. This would mean in a direct action against the
> insurer the insured has the burden of proving that the other
> motorist was uninsured, that the other motorist is legally
> liable for damage to the insured, and the amount of this
> liability. *In resisting the claim the insurer would have availa-
> ble to it, in addition to policy defenses compatible with the
> statute, the substantive defenses that would have been available
> to the uninsured motorist such as contributory negligence, etc.*

211 Kan. at 64, 505 P.2d at 610 (citation omitted, emphasis added). The
district court was correct in noting that the insured need only show
fault and damages, but neglected to note the qualification that the
insurer has available all substantive defenses the tortfeasor could have
raised.

The *Winner* court looked to the cogent observations of a commentator on UM law in reaching its conclusion. His explanation of the
origins of UM coverage sheds light on the problem before us.

> The antecedent of the uninsured motorist endorsement
> * * * can be found in the unsatisfied judgment insurance
> first offered in about 1925 by the Utilities Indemnity Ex-
> change. This insurance provided indemnification when the
> insured showed both (1) that he had reduced a claim to judg-

ment and (2) that he was unable to collect the judgment from the negligent party. Such insurance was available from several companies during the years from 1925 and 1956. When the uninsured motorist coverage became generally available, the unsatisfied judgment insurance was abandoned. *It should be noted that the uninsured motorist endorsement—as proposed and subsequently issued—differed significantly from its predecessor in that it eliminated the requirement that the insured obtain a judgment against the uninsured motorist prior to recovering under his policy.* A. Widiss, *A Guide to Uninsured Motorist Coverage* § 1.9 (1969) (emphasis added) (hereinafter cited as *Widiss*).

Uninsured motorist coverage therefore arose in the context of providing a less cumbersome method for an insured to receive payment from the party with the ultimate financial responsibility, the insurer. UM coverage, with its normal procedure of settling disputes through arbitration, would save both the insured and insurer the time and expense of a trial against the uninsured motorist, and would also help the insurer avoid the complications inherent in a trial where the interests of the tortfeasor and the insurer may not necessarily coincide.

None of this suggests that UM coverage was developed to expand the coverage previously provided by unsatisfied judgment insurance. Indeed, *Widiss* notes that "[t]he insurance industry conceived and developed the uninsured motorist endorsement in an attempt to forestall the enactment of state legislation directed at either creating compulsory insurance requirements or otherwise altering the character of the then-existing insurance market in order to deal with the hazard created by [financially irresponsible] uninsured motorists." *Widiss* at § 1.12. It seems unlikely that the companies would deliberately relinquish valid substantive defenses when it was wholly unnecessary to do so to achieve the goal of protecting against financially irresponsible motorists. Widiss also observes that in most states where UM coverage has been made mandatory subsequent to its development, the legislation has merely required a UM endorsement. While Florida's section 627.727 does go into some detail regarding UM coverage, the first sentence of the statute, containing the language at issue here, merely defines UM coverage in terms sufficient to identify it as such. This does not suggest any legislative intent to expand UM coverage beyond that contemplated by the insurance-industry-developed endorsement.

The legislature wisely enacted a scheme whereby a motorist may obtain a limited form of insurance coverage for the uninsured motorist, by requiring that every insurer doing business in this state offer and make available to its automobile liability policyholders UM coverage in an amount equal to the policyholder's automobile liability insurance. The policyholder pays an additional premium for such coverage. The uninsured motorist statute provides that coverage is "for the protection of persons insured thereunder who are legally entitled to recover damages from owners or operators of uninsured motor vehicles because of bodily injury." § 627.727(1). The UM coverage, in purpose and effect, provides a limited form of insurance coverage up to the applicable policy limits for the uninsured motorist. The carrier effectually stands in the uninsured motorist's shoes and can raise and assert any defense that the uninsured motorist could urge. In other words, UM coverage is a limited form of third party coverage inuring to the limited benefit of the tortfeasor to provide a source of financial responsibility if the policyholder is entitled under the law to recover from the tortfeasor. It is not first party coverage even though the policyholder pays for it. In first party coverage, such as medical, collision or theft insurance, fault is not an element. The insurance carrier pays even though the policyholder is totally at fault. With UM coverage, the carrier pays only if the tortfeasor would have to pay, if the claim were made directly against the tortfeasor.

One involved in an accident with an uninsured motorist can bring a common law action against the uninsured motorist, if he so desires. The uninsured motorist can of course defend and interpose any defense available to him at law including contributory negligence and the exclusiveness of worker's compensation. If the injured party recovers a judgment, he may endeavor to satisfy his judgment from the tortfeasor's assets. However, the insured motorist may opt to make claim against his UM carrier instead of suing the tortfeasor. In so doing he has a policy prerequisite, namely, proof that the tortfeasor is uninsured. The tortfeasor may be financially responsible, but if he is without insurance or has not complied with the self-insurance provisions of the statutes, the injured party may make claim against his UM carrier. The insurer is subrogated to any sum that it pays the policyholder under the UM coverage and may bring suit against the uninsured motorist to recover all sums it has paid its insured under the UM policy. The subrogation right would be frustrated if the insurer were forced to pay claims when it would be barred by a substantive defense from winning a judgment against a tortfeasor.

The district court and respondent dispute the argument that the case is controlled by the proposition that the insurer stands in the shoes of the tortfeasor. The court relied in part on *Sahloff v. Western Casualty & Surety Co.*, 45 Wis.2d 60, 171 N.W.2d 914 (1969), which held that the expiration of the statute of limitations which would bar an action against the tortfeasor did not bar an action against the insurer when the suit was brought before expiration of the statute of limitations for contract actions. From the portion of *Sahloff* quoted by the district court, it is clear the Wisconsin court relied heavily on the notion that the relationship between insurer and insured arises in contract, not tort. *See also Mendlein v. United States Fidelity & Guaranty Co.*, 277 So.2d 538 (Fla.3d DCA 1973) (the district court did not dispute the assumption of all parties that the contract statute of limitations controlled the UM claim at issue). Also, while substantive defenses are available to the insurer, *Winner,* a procedural defense such as a statute of limitations is not necessarily also available. However, the statute of limitations issue is not before us, and we reserve a decision on this for a later day. It is enough that we here find that the insurer has the tortfeasor's substantive defenses available, and we need not decide whether this is to the exclusion of some or all procedural defenses.

There is another reason for our decision here. Widiss writes, in the context of whether the insurer should be able to claim the protection of the tortfeasor's tort immunities:

> The issue raised by such immunities is whether, for purposes of the uninsured motorist coverage, the claimant is "legally entitled to recover" as contemplated in the endorsement. * * *
>
> Professor Prosser states that "such immunity does not mean that conduct which would amount to a tort on the part of other defendants is not equally tortious in character, but merely that for protection of the particular defendant or interests which he represents, he is given absolution from liability." [W. Prosser, *Law of Torts* 996 (3d ed. 1964).] Professor Prosser's language seems to suggest that the insured party *is* legally entitled to recover, but that the immunity involved absolves the defendant from liability. * * *
>
> Attempting to resolve this issue as a problem in semantics—that is, over whether the claimant is "legally entitled"— is not especially productive. * * * To the extent that there is a strong interest in protecting the insurance company's right of subrogation following the payment of a claim, there is a persuasive reason why the existence of an immunity from liability should mean that the insurer will not be liable under the policy. On the other hand, to the extent that the objective of providing indemnification is a stronger policy in this context, the technicality of whether the tortfeasor is immune from litigation assumes a much smaller degree of importance. It seems probable that in those states where the trend is to assure that a source of indemnification is available, the courts are likely to reject an argument as to the applicability of such tort immunities. However, it may not be appropriate to attempt to speak of all these immunities as an undivided group. For example, in a jurisdiction which affirms the importance of the interspousal immunity, the court might well be inclined to distinguish this type of case on the basis that the policy and goals underlying the establishment of this type of immunity are sufficiently important to warrant separate consideration and treatment.

Widiss at § 2.27 (footnotes deleted, emphasis in original). In Florida a source of indemnification for a worker injured by a co-worker driving an uninsured vehicle is already available, i.e. the benefits of the Workers' Compensation Law. Society's goal of protecting the worker under this circumstance has been achieved. We do not need to torture the meaning of a statute aimed at curing another ill entirely to provide a remedy where one has already been provided.

In addition, the immunity offered through workers' compensation exists not only to protect the employer in exchange for his provision of immediate, guaranteed benefits, but also to protect society by limiting the impact of a work-related injury to the remedy offered. Expanding UM coverage to cover the circumstance before us here would, as Judge Upchurch noted in his dissent in the district court, 443 So.2d at 433, create a large class of uninsured vehicles. The ensuing litigation would roil the waters in an area where the legislature has attempted to calm the seas. Absent a clear statement of intent from the legislature that it considers the benefits of broader UM coverage to outweigh the detriment, we will not disturb its clear and unambiguous statement that coverage exists only when the insured is legally entitled to recover from the tortfeasor.

Accordingly, the decision of the district court is quashed and remanded for further proceedings in accord herewith.

It is so ordered.

Notes and Questions

1. *Forms of UM Coverage.* In some states the purchase of UM coverage is mandatory; in certain others, purchase is not mandatory, but insurers are required to offer such coverage to any purchaser of liability insurance. In recent years a supplement to UM coverage, "underinsured motorist coverage," has developed to fill the gap between the amount of liability insurance covering the defendant and the amount of UM coverage the insured has purchased. See generally A. Widiss, Uninsured and Underinsured Motorist Insurance (1985). Since the insured in *Boynton* was already covered by workers compensation and would not be entitled to duplicate recovery of his medical expenses or lost wages, why did he care whether he was also covered by his uninsured motorists insurance?

2. *Subrogation as a Test.* To what extent did the district court's decision in *Boynton* in effect convert UM coverage into no-fault insurance? How much point would there be in purchasing UM coverage if its availability depended on whether the UM insurer could vindicate its subrogation rights after making payment to its insured?

3. *Arbitration of UM Disputes.* Suppose that the insured and insurer agree that the party who injured the insured was driving an uninsured vehicle, but disagree about whether the insured is "legally entitled to recover" from that driver. For example, there may be a dispute about whether that driver was negligent. Standard UM policies provide that such disputes will be arbitrated. See Sample Personal Auto Policy, Part C. What advantages are there to this approach for each party? If you were an attorney for the insured, would you prefer arbitration or trial? Some states have prohibited or invalidated policy

provisions requiring arbitration of UM disputes. See, e.g., Ga.Code Ann. § 33–7–11(g); Md.Ann.Code art. 48A, § 541(c)(2).

4. *Plain–Language UM Coverage.* How would the first issue the court in *Boynton* addressed be resolved under the definition of an uninsured motor vehicle contained in Part C of the Sample Personal Auto Policy in Section A of this Chapter: " * * * a land motor vehicle or trailer of any type * * * to which no bodily injury liability bond or policy applies at the time of the accident."? Is the term "applies" in this definition ambiguous?

SIMPSON v. FARMERS INSURANCE COMPANY, INC.

Supreme Court of Kansas, 1979.
225 Kan. 508, 592 P.2d 445.

PRAGER, Justice.

This is an action brought by the plaintiff-appellant Yvonne Joanne Simpson, against the defendant-appellee, Farmers Insurance Company, Inc., seeking a declaratory judgment concerning the coverage and rights of the plaintiff under the uninsured motorist endorsement to an automobile insurance policy issued by the defendant to the plaintiff. The basic issue presented for determination is one of law and, simply stated, is as follows: Is the "physical contact" requirement in the "hit and run" clause in the uninsured motorist provision of an automobile insurance policy void and unenforceable as contrary to the public policy and legislative intent of the Kansas Uninsured Motorist Statute (K.S.A. 40–284)? The district court answered this question in the negative. We have concluded that it should be answered in the affirmative and, accordingly, we reverse.

For the purposes of this appeal, the facts in the case are assumed to be as follows: On December 12, 1976, the plaintiff, Simpson, was forced to drive her automobile into a ditch in order to avoid a collision with another vehicle at 34th and Steele Road in Kansas City, Kansas. After it left the highway, the automobile struck a utility pole, causing plaintiff to suffer personal injuries. The unidentified vehicle immediately fled from the scene and the identity of the driver or owner of that vehicle remains unknown. There was no actual physical contact between the unidentified vehicle and the vehicle driven by Mrs. Simpson.

Following the accident, plaintiff sought to recover under the uninsured motorist provision of her automobile insurance policy. The defendant, Farmers Insurance Company, refused to pay the claim on the basis that the insurance policy required that a recovery under that section be limited to those instances where the unidentified vehicle came into physical contact with the insured vehicle. Mrs. Simpson then brought this action for a declaratory judgment to determine whether her injuries fell within the uninsured motorist coverage of her Farmers policy. The insurance company filed a motion for summary judgment, contending that the plaintiff was not entitled to recover under the terms of the policy, because, admittedly, there was no physical contact between the unknown vehicle and the insured's vehicle. The trial court sustained the motion and granted summary judgment to the defendant. The plaintiff appealed to this court.

We should first examine the pertinent sections of the insurance policy. The policy contains the standard policy provisions relating to uninsured motorist coverage:

> "Coverage J—Uninsured Motorists (Damages for Bodily Injury) to pay all sums which the insured or his legal representatives shall be legally entitled to recover as damages *from the owner or operator of an uninsured automobile because of bodily injury, * * * caused by accident and arising out of the ownership, maintenance or use of such uninsured automobile * * *"* Emphasis supplied.)

Under the definition section, an uninsured automobile is defined to include a "hit and run" automobile. A "hit and run" automobile is then defined as follows:

> "Hit and run motor vehicle means a motor vehicle which causes bodily injury *arising out of physical contact* of such motor vehicle with the insured or with the automobile which the insured is occupying at the time of the accident, provided (a) there cannot be ascertained the identity of either the operator or the owner of such 'hit and run motor vehicle,' * * *." (Emphasis supplied.)

Since, admittedly, there was no physical contact between the insured's vehicle and the "hit and run" vehicle, there would be no coverage afforded by the policy if the "physical contact" requirement is a valid and enforceable provision.

We should now consider the Kansas Uninsured Motorist Statute (K.S.A. 40–284) which provides as follows:

> "40–284. Coverage relating to injury or death caused by uninsured motorist; rejection; renewal policies; effect of prior policies. No automobile liability insurance policy covering liability arising out of the ownership, maintenance, or use of any motor vehicle shall be delivered or issued for delivery in this state with respect to any motor vehicle registered or principally garaged in this state, unless the policy contains or has endorsed thereon, a provision with coverage limits not less than the limits for bodily injury or death set forth in K.S.A. 1967 Supp. 8–729, providing for payment of part or all sums which the insured or his legal representative shall be legally entitled to recover as damages from the uninsured owner or operator of the motor vehicle because of bodily injury, sickness or disease, including death, resulting therefrom sustained by the insured, caused by accident and arising out of ownership, maintenance or use of such motor vehicle, or providing for

such payment irrespective of legal liability of the insured or any other person or organization. *Provided,* That the coverage required under this section shall not be applicable where any insured named in the policy shall reject the coverage in writing: *Provided further,* That unless the insured named in the policy requests such coverage in writing, such coverage need not be provided in or supplemental to a renewal policy where the named insured had rejected the coverage in connection with a policy previously issued him by the same insurer. Provisions affording such insurance protection against uninsured motorists issued in this state prior to the effective date of this act shall, when afforded by any authorized insurer, be deemed, subject to the limits prescribed in this section, to satisfy the requirements of this section."

The primary question is whether the legislature, by the enactment of the uninsured motorist statute (K.S.A. 40–284), intended to include within the term "uninsured motorist" all hit and run drivers. In order to answer this question, we must consider the uninsured motorist statute from a historical perspective.

K.S.A. 40–284 was enacted in 1968 and has not been amended. In *Winner v. Ratzlaff,* 211 Kan. 59, 505 P.2d 606 (1973), this court determined the legislative purpose in enacting the statute to be as follows:

> "The purpose of legislation mandating the offer of uninsured motorist coverage is to fill the gap inherent in motor vehicle financial responsibility and compulsory insurance legislation and this coverage is intended to provide recompense to innocent persons who are damaged through the wrongful conduct of motorists who, because they are uninsured and not financially responsible, cannot be made to respond in damages." (Syl. ¶ 1.)

In *Winner,* the court also stated that, as remedial legislation, the statute should be liberally construed to provide the intended protection. The legislative purpose was again recognized in *Forrester v. State Farm Mutual Automobile Ins. Co.,* 213 Kan. 442, 517 P.2d 173 (1973). In *Forrester,* this court further stated in regard to the legislative intent:

> "The intent of the legislature in requiring the mandatory offering of uninsured motorist coverage was to insure that those insured under the contract of insurance would be protected generally against injuries caused by motorists who are uninsured and that such protection would complement the liability coverage." (Syl. ¶ 3.)

The court, in addition, stated that K.S.A. 40–284 becomes a part of the policy of insurance to which it is applicable to the same effect as if the provisions thereof were written out in full in the policy itself.

After the uninsured motorist statute was enacted, some insurance companies attempted to dilute the broad coverage contemplated by

K.S.A. 40–284. In *Clayton v. Alliance Mutual Casualty Co.,* 212 Kan. 640, 512 P.2d 507 (1973), the insurance policy contained clauses described as the "consent to sue" clause, the "arbitration" clause, the "other insurance" clause, the "proof of loss" clause, the "medical authorization" clause, and the "furnishing of medical reports" clause. All of them placed certain restrictions on the right of the insured to bring an action against the insurance company under the uninsured motorist coverage. This court held that all of the clauses were an attempt to place requirements on the insured which constituted a condition precedent to the commencement of an action to recover damages under an uninsured motorist endorsement and were void and of no effect as an attempt to condition, limit, or dilute the statutory mandate of uninsured motorist coverage under K.S.A. 40–284.

A similar problem was before the court in *Van Hoozer v. Farmers Insurance Exchange,* 219 Kan. 595, 549 P.2d 1354 (1976). The policy involved in that case contained a provision that, in substance, stated that any loss payable under the uninsured motorist coverage should be reduced by any amount paid or payable to the insured under any workmen's compensation law, disability benefits law, or any similar law. It was held that the trial court was correct in striking down that provision since it was void and of no effect as an attempt to limit or dilute the statutory mandate of uninsured motorist coverage. The policy also contained a provision which prohibited the stacking of policies owned by the insured. This provision was also held to be invalid as being contrary to the provisions of the statute. The policy in *Van Hoozer* contained another provision which sought to define the word "insured" under the uninsured motorist coverage in such a way as to eliminate some of the coverage contemplated by the statute. This was likewise held to be invalid. *Van Hoozer,* like *Clayton,* is important to the resolution of the case now before us because it supports the rule that insurance policy provisions which purport to condition, limit, or dilute the broad, unqualified uninsured motorist coverage mandated by K.S.A. 40–284, are void and unenforceable.

In all of the cases just discussed, this court has made it crystal clear that the uninsured motorist statute is remedial in nature and should be liberally construed to provide a broad protection to the insured against all damages resulting from bodily injuries sustained by the insured, caused by an automobile accident, and arising out of the ownership, maintenance, or use of the insured motor vehicle, where those damages are caused by the acts of an uninsured motorist. A provision placed in the policy by an insurance company which denies protection to an insured for damages and injuries caused by a "hit and run" vehicle unless there is actual physical contact between the vehicles, like the various policy restrictions discussed in *Clayton* and *Van Hoozer,* is an attempt to limit or dilute the unqualified uninsured motorist coverage mandated by K.S.A. 40–284 and is therefore void and unenforceable. The rationale of *Clayton* and *Van Hoozer* is clearly applicable to such a restrictive provision.

Although, as noted above, the question is one of first impression in Kansas, the issue of the validity of the "physical contact" requirement in an insurance policy has been faced by courts of other states for quite a long period of time. See the annotation at 25 A.L.R.3d 1299 and the supplement. In most states there is a general statute requiring insurance companies to offer uninsured or unknown motorist coverage. There is, however, usually no specific statutory requirement to include coverage for "hit and run" drivers, nor a requirement that physical contact must have occurred before an insured can recover for damages due to a "hit and run" vehicle. The courts of those states have been almost unanimous in holding that the operator of a "hit and run" vehicle is an uninsured or unknown motorist. As to the physical contact issue, there is definitely a split of authority among the various states.

A number of jurisdictions hold that it is reasonable to require physical contact between a "hit and run" vehicle and the insured vehicle before coverage is allowed under the uninsured or unknown motorist provisions. * * * The rationale of those cases is based on the premise that requiring physical contact will prevent fraud upon the insurance company and will prevent recovery of damages in those cases where the insured's injuries are actually the result of his own negligence, without the intervention of any other vehicle, but the insured falsely claims that the accident was caused by an unidentified vehicle which subsequently left the scene of the accident.

The other line of authority, which now appears to be the majority rule, holds that the physical contact requirement is an impermissible limitation on the uninsured or unknown motorist statute, is contrary to public and legislative policy, and is, thus, invalid. * * *

It should be noted that in a few states the uninsured motorist statute specifically provides that, where recovery is sought for injuries caused by a hit and run vehicle, the claimant must show that there was physical contact with the unidentified vehicle. * * *

Those cases which hold the physical contact requirement to be invalid have stated a variety of reasons for its invalidity. However, the common theme of all the cases is that the uninsured or unknown motorist statute was adopted, and the clear legislative intent was, to expand insurance protection to the public who use the streets and highways. The public was to be protected from damage or injury caused by other motorists who were not insured and who could not make the injured party whole. The public was no longer to be faced with the financial calamity often caused by negligent and insolvent drivers. These cases have recognized the possibility of fraud by an insured who claims injury due to an unidentified "hit and run" driver, when, in fact, there was no such driver. A criticism of the "physical contact" requirement as an anti-fraud measure has been expressed by A. Widiss, *A Guide To Uninsured Motorist Coverage* (1969), which is quoted in *Montoya v. Dairyland Insurance Company,* 394 F.Supp. at 1340. It states:

> " 'It seems unreasonable to establish a rule under which recovery is possible if there is a minute scratch on the insured's car, but no impartial witnesses—and to deny all rights where there was no contact, even though there are many witnesses and there is no reason to suspect collusion or fraud. Some standard assuring adequate evidence in support of a claim that the injuries (for which indemnification is sought) are the result of an evasive action executed to avoid a collision with an unidentified negligent driver is certainly warranted. It is suggested that the claimant should bear the burden of persuasion, leaving to the judge, jury or arbitrator the determination of whether the claimant has sustained the requisite burden of proof, and providing an opportunity for the insurance company to raise fraud or collusion as a defense to such a claim.' "

* * *

We agree with the rationale of those cases which hold that the physical contact requirement violates the public policy of those uninsured or unknown motorist statutes which provide a broad and unrestricted protection for damage and injury caused by an uninsured motorist. We hold, therefore, that the "physical contact" requirement in the "hit and run" provisions of the automobile liability policy under consideration in this case is in derogation of the Kansas Uninsured Motorist Statute, and is therefore, void as against public policy.

The judgment of the district court sustaining the defendant's motion for summary judgment is reversed. The case is remanded to the district court with instructions to proceed to ascertain any issues remaining in the case and to determine the rights of the parties under the facts and the law.

Notes and Questions

1. *The Statutory Policy.* Was the policy of the Kansas legislature favoring the provision of UM coverage sufficiently precise to yield the *Simpson* decision? Did this legislative policy, as described, prohibit every limitation on recovery in a UM policy?

2. *Phantom Headlights.* The physical contact requirement is very common in UM policies. Among other purposes, it is designed to avoid the "phantom headlight" problem—possibly fraudulent claims by the insured that an oncoming vehicle came into his lane at night and that the insured swerved off the road (and into a tree or ditch) to avoid a collision. Did the Kansas statute mandate that UM policies cover accidents involving unidentifiable drivers at all? If not, then why was the failure of the Simpson policy to cover losses caused by all such drivers held to be a violation of the statute?

Chapter Nine

COORDINATING MULTIPLE COVERAGES

We have already encountered problems of coordination in connection with the coordination of benefits provisions in health insurance policies examined in Chapter Five. This Chapter examines several important coordination issues that arise when multiple liability or auto policies are potentially applicable to the same suit or loss.

A. THE TRIGGER OF COVERAGE

AMERICAN HOME PRODUCTS CORPORATION v. LIBERTY MUTUAL INSURANCE COMPANY

United States District Court, S.D. New York, 1983.
565 F.Supp. 1485.

SOFAER, District Judge.

Plaintiff American Home Products Corporation ("AHP"), a diversified company manufacturing drugs, foods, and household products, is the defendant in fifty-four products-liability suits arising from AHP's manufacture and sale of six pharmaceuticals: Ovral and L/Ovral (oral contraceptives), DES (Diethylstilbestrol), Mysoline, Atromid–S, Premarin, and Anacin. Defendant Liberty Mutual Insurance Company ("Liberty"), which provided AHP with insurance from 1944 until 1976, has refused to assume AHP's burden of defense or to indemnify AHP in those lawsuits, because in each case physical harm did not become manifest until after termination of the insurance policies. In this action AHP seeks a judgment declaring that Liberty is obliged to defend and to indemnify AHP in the underlying lawsuits because, regardless of when physical harm became manifest, exposure to the alleged agents of harm occurred during the policy periods, thereby triggering coverage.

Jurisdiction is based on diversity of citizenship, 28 U.S.C. § 1332 (1976), and New York law controls. AHP contends there are no disputed issues of material fact, and has moved for summary judgment awarding the declaration it seeks. Liberty opposes this motion, and has itself moved for partial summary judgment on the basis of a provision in the AHP policies which Liberty argues excludes coverage for all claims involving exposures to allegedly harmful substances after termination of Liberty's coverage on November 1, 1976.

Several courts have recently ruled on the scope of insurance policies covering liability for insidious diseases, which are illnesses that

677

become manifest long after initial exposure to the substances believed to cause them. The policy provisions at issue in these cases were all variants of the Comprehensive General Liability Policy ("CGL"), a standard-form policy for liability coverage drafted during the 1960's by representatives of the insurance industry to deal with the problem of liability for injuries caused over a period of time. Instead of covering only "accidents", a word that connotes an event causing immediate or contemporaneous injury, the CGL was written to cover "occurrences", defined to include "an accident, including injurious exposure to conditions, which results, during the policy period, in bodily injury * * * neither expected nor intended from the standpoint of the insured." CGL, Pl.Ex. 22 at 12. This change in terminology made clear the intent of insurers to provide coverage for insidious diseases. But the new language provided no definition of "bodily injury" other than the words themselves, thereby creating a basis for disputes as to the trigger of coverage.

AHP's insurance policies with Liberty were "manuscript" policies written specifically for AHP. Like the 1966 version of the CGL, however, AHP's policies throughout the period relevant to this litigation provided liability coverage for "occurrences" that result in "personal injury, sickness or disease including death resulting therefrom * * * sustained by any person." An occurrence is defined by inference from Article IV: "This policy applies only to (1) personal injury, sickness or disease including death resulting therefrom * * * which occurs during the policy period." Pl.Ex. 20 at 3. The ultimate question under both the CGL language and the AHP policies at issue here is therefore the same: when does "injury, sickness or disease" occur? Under both policies, coverage exists only for injuries occurring during the policy period. Moreover, both the CGL and AHP's policies require the insurer to defend any suit against the insured that seeks damages for an injury alleged to have occurred under the policy, even if the suit is groundless or fraudulent. *See* CGL, Pl.Ex. 22 at 1; AHP Policy, Pl. Ex. 20 at 1.

One provision in AHP's policies after 1968 differs from anything in the CGL, however. The provision Liberty relies on in its motion for partial summary judgment states:

> The policy does not apply to such injury, death or destruction caused by such continuous or repeated exposure any part of which occurs after the termination of the policy.

Liberty contends that this provision renders these policies inapplicable to twenty-eight specified cases. *See* Urmston Aff't, Ex. 1.

For the reasons that follow the policies in this case are construed as they are written—to require a showing of actual injury, sickness or disease occurring during the policy period, based upon the facts proved in each particular case. Thus, an occurrence of "personal injury, sickness, or disease" is read to mean any point in time at which a finder of fact determines that the effects of exposure to a drug actually resulted in a diagnosable and compensable injury. Depending upon the facts of each case, the drug involved, the period and intensity of exposure, and the person affected, an injury may occur in this sense upon exposure, at some point in time after exposure but before manifestation of the injury, and at manifestation. This construction is supported by the policy's language and background, the intentions and expectations of the parties, and considerations of practicability and fairness. It provides liberal protection to the insured, without doing violence to the principle—long a part of the law of New York—that insurance policies are contracts under which insureds obtain all the protection for which they may reasonably be said to have paid, but not more.

I. *Meaning of The Policy Language*

Whether the contract between AHP and Liberty is ambiguous is of central importance to this case, and particularly to the disposition of this motion. AHP argues that the policies supply an ambiguous definition of "occurrence" that is susceptible to at least two plausible constructions. Under one construction coverage would be triggered by every exposure to a harmful substance that could ultimately result in bodily injury. Another construction would trigger coverage only when injury became manifest, which has been defined to mean when the injury was diagnosed or when it produced symptoms that placed or should have placed the injured person on notice. Relying on these alleged ambiguities, AHP invokes the well established rule that resolves ambiguities in insurance contracts in favor of the insured and against the insurer. *See, e.g., Breed v. Insurance Co. of North America,* 46 N.Y.2d 351, 353, 385 N.E.2d 1280, 1282, 413 N.Y.S.2d 352, 354 (1978). AHP argues that, in this case, the governing rule of construction requires application of the exposure theory, which favors manufacturers, or perhaps an even broader construction providing coverage at any point from exposure to manifestation. An exposure theory makes sense, AHP contends, because it recognizes that manufacturers intend to protect themselves against the long-term risk of claims associated with insidious diseases; "personal injury, sickness or disease" should therefore be read to cover every potentially injurious exposure during the policy period that results at any future time in a claim for injury. If an exposure theory were applied, Liberty would be responsible to pay any liability AHP incurs in any suit against AHP where the plaintiff ingested the harmful product during the policy period, irrespective of how long after termination a diagnosable injury, sickness, or disease developed, or manifested itself.

Several courts have construed the CGL terms to provide coverage upon exposure. The Sixth Circuit, in *Insurance Co. of North America v. Forty–Eight Insulations, Inc.,* 633 F.2d 1212, 1222 (6th Cir.1980), *reh'g granted in part and denied in part,* 657 F.2d 814 (1981), *cert. denied,* 454 U.S. 1109, 102 S.Ct. 686, 70 L.Ed.2d 650 (1981), found the terms "bodily injury" and "occurrence" inherently ambiguous as applied in the "progressive disease context." The Court, faced with determining an asbestos manufacturer's coverage under a CGL-derived policy, relied on that ambiguity, on medical testimony of the progressive nature of diseases caused by prolonged exposure to asbestos, and on the presumed intent of the parties, to read the contract as providing coverage for all potentially injurious exposures. *See also Porter v. American Optical Corp.*, 641 F.2d 1128 (5th Cir.), *cert. denied*, 454 U.S. 1109, 102 S.Ct. 686, 70 L.Ed.2d 650 (1981). In *Keene v. Insurance Co. of North America*, 667 F.2d 1034 (D.C.Cir.1981), *cert. denied*, 455 U.S. 1007, 102 S.Ct. 1644, 71 L.Ed.2d 875 (1982), the District of Columbia Circuit also found that exposure to asbestos triggered coverage under the "ambiguous" CGL terms. It concluded that an exposure theory most closely approximated the reasonable expectation of manufacturers, who purchase insurance in order to gain certainty and be free from all risk of liability arising out of products-liability suits. To protect this alleged expectation, the Court held that insurance coverage was triggered not only by every exposure, but by "exposure in residence," when asbestos fibers were present in the body and causing further injury, and by every manifestation of an injury, sickness, or disease. 667 F.2d at 1048.[1]

Liberty counters with the claim that the relevant policy provisions unambiguously define manifestation as the trigger of insurance coverage. The average person, Liberty argues, would understand the terms

1. AHP argues that *Keene* collaterally estops Liberty from denying liability to indemnify or to defend. *Keene* construed the "occurrence" clause of the 1966 CGL to be triggered if any part of a latent-disease process, including any exposure or "exposure in residence," occurred during the policy period. The insurance policies are different here, however, from those involved in *Keene*, and the parties' course of dealing is different because the parties are different. None of the policies in *Keene* contained a clause expressly exempting Liberty from liability for injuries resulting from exposure any part of which occurred after termination of the policy, and AHP's involvement in negotiating its "manuscript" policies requires that they be treated as contracts treated at arms length, not contracts of adhesion. Moreover, the agents of harm and the alleged harms in this case differ from those at issue in *Keene*. While the Court of Appeals there insisted that the etiology of diseases caused by the ingestion of asbestos fibers was irrelevant, 667 F.2d at 1038 n. 3, it placed weight at other points on the special effects of asbestos ingestion, 667 F.2d at 1041–42. The products at issue here are claimed by all to operate very differently from asbestos. Thus the issues are not the same in both actions, making collateral estoppel inapplicable. *See, e.g., Hardy v. Johns–Manville Sales Corp.*, 681 F.2d 334 (5th Cir.1982).

To give *Keene* binding force here would also be unfair and inappropriate. Other courts have considered the scope of coverage afforded by contracts issued by Liberty, and have reached results that vary markedly from the results reached in *Keene*. *See Eagle–Picher Ind., Inc. v. Liberty Mutual Ins. Co.*, 682 F.2d 12 (1st Cir.1982); *Porter v. American Optical Corp.*, 641 F.2d 1128 (5th Cir.1981); *Insurance Company of North America v. Forty–Eight Insulations, Inc.*, 633 F.2d 1212 (6th Cir.1980). Furthermore, the degree of respect to be accorded *Keene* is made doubtful by the Court's failure to apply the law of New York (or for that matter the law of any other state). While the decision states at one point that no material differences exist among the legal rules of the four states to which the Court could arguably have turned for guidance under *Erie v. Tompkins*, 304 U.S. 64, 58 S.Ct. 817, 82 L.Ed.2d 1188 (1938), *see* 667 F.2d at 1041 n. 10, the applicable law from any of those jurisdictions is nowhere described or applied, and hence the Court was free to adopt its novel approach without explaining how its ruling could be justified. *Compare, e.g., American Motorists Ins. Co. v. E.R. Squibb & Sons, Inc.*, 95 Misc.2d 222, 406 N.Y.S.2d 658 (1st Dep't 1978). This circumstance alone makes it appropriate to relitigate the issues. Restatement (Second) of Judgments § 88(7) & Comment I (Tent.Draft No. 2, 1975).

"injury" and "disease" to mean an "abnormal condition" that "occurs" when it becomes manifest and is or should be discovered by the claimant. Thus Liberty argues that, under the policy, it incurs no duty to defend unless the claimant seeks recovery for an injury, sickness, or disease that allegedly became manifest while the policy was in effect, and that it has no duty to pay AHP sums for which AHP becomes liable unless the alleged injury became manifest during coverage.

Some courts have indeed rejected the exposure theory and found that, properly construed, the CGL provisions support a manifestation theory. *See, e.g., Eagle–Picher Industries, Inc. v. Liberty Mutual Insurance Co.,* 523 F.Supp. 110 (D.Mass.1981), *modified,* 682 F.2d 12 (1st Cir. 1982); *American Motorists Insurance Co. v. E.R. Squibb & Sons, Inc.,* 95 Misc.2d 222, 406 N.Y.S.2d 658 (N.Y.Sup.Ct.1978). They reason that manufacturers and insurance companies intend to cover only risks that ripen into claims, and that "bodily injury" in the CGL cannot logically be read to mean injurious exposures that are not themselves injuries. Thus, District Judge Zobel, addressing policy coverage for asbestos related diseases, cogently reasoned:

> All policies except the later group of those written by Liberty Mutual define occurrence as "an accident or a continuous or repeated exposure to conditions which results, during the policy period, in personal injury. * * *" This definition is broad and inclusive. Each "occurrence" is made up of two components, initial exposure or accident and resulting injury; neither one without the other would be sufficient. There can be no question but that the aspect of the occurrence which must take place within the policy period, however, is the "result", that is, the time when the accident of injurious exposure produces personal injury. The time-limiting phrase "during the policy period" always follows the words "results" and frequently is set off by commas, so that it can modify only the preceding verb "results". Thus, the definitional language explicitly focuses on the result rather than the cause as the component to which coverage is linked.

Eagle–Picher Industries, 523 F.Supp. at 114. On appeal, the First Circuit agreed that "[t]he policies clearly distinguish between the event which causes injury—the accident or exposure—and the resulting injury or disease. Yet * * * it is the resulting injury, *not* the exposure, which must take place 'during the policy period' in order to trigger coverage. * * *" *Eagle–Picher Industries,* 682 F.2d at 17 (emphasis in original). Liberty relies on these cases in seeking denial of AHP's motion for summary judgment; it argues for partial summary judgment, moreover, based on the special limiting clause in its policies after 1968, which it claims incontrovertibly excludes coverage for several of the claims referred to in this action.

Insofar as AHP and Liberty attack each other's construction, both sides are correct: neither the exposure nor the manifestation theory can be wholly justified by the policy language.

A. *Governing Legal Principles*

AHP correctly argues that insurance contracts must be liberally construed, with ambiguities in the policy language resolved in favor of the insured. *See Pan American World Airways, Inc. v. Aetna Casualty & Surety Co.,* 505 F.2d 989, 999 (2d Cir.1974); *Breed v. Insurance Co. of North America,* 46 N.Y.2d 351, 353, 385 N.E.2d 1280, 1282, 413 N.Y.S.2d 352, 354 (1978). This rule of construction, in fact, appears to be the single factor that unifies the discordant opinions applying the CGL and its derivatives to insidious diseases. Whether or not explicitly finding ambiguities, and irrespective of the construction adopted, every court construing these provisions has reached the result that extended coverage to the insured. *See, e.g., Eagle–Picher Industries,* 682 F.2d at 17 (manifestation); *Keene,* 667 F.2d at 1041 (manifestation and exposure); *Forty–Eight Insulations,* 663 F.2d at 1223 (exposure). ＊ ＊ ＊

B. *Proposed Constructions of the Parties*

Neither construction proffered by the parties is supported by the plain meaning of the terms employed.

1. *The Exposure Theory.* An exposure theory is inconsistent with the policies' plain meaning, and AHP has offered no evidence or explanation to demonstrate how an "occurrence" could logically include every exposure to the substances it manufactures. The policies require that the resulting injury and not the exposure occur "during the policy period." Moreover, the policies were designed to protect against liability from law suits brought because of compensable injuries. To that end they cover "occurrences" wherein both exposure and an injury take place.

The only New York case on point also rejected the exposure theory as unsupported by the language of a policy that covered "[a]n accident or injurious exposure to conditions which results, during the policy period, in bodily injury. ＊ ＊ ＊" The injured plaintiffs, who had sued the insured, were the daughters of women who had ingested DES while pregnant with the plaintiffs in 1952, 1953, and 1961 respectively; the plaintiffs thereafter developed cervical cancers that were discovered in 1970, 1971, and 1975. Justice Greenfield concentrated on the policy language:

> A reading of the policy language would appear to indicate that coverage is predicated not on the act which might give rise to ultimate liability, but upon the result. It would be a strained interpretation to construe the occurrence clause as though it covered "exposure during the policy period which results in bodily injury." It is the *result* which is keyed to the policy period, and not the accident or exposure.

American Motorists Ins. v. E.R. Squibb & Sons, 95 Misc.2d 222, 406 N.Y.S.2d 658, 659–60 (N.Y.Sup.Ct.1978) (emphasis in original).

A limited version of the exposure theory, adopted in some litigations, is at least linguistically respectable. Some courts, relying on medical evidence, have found that, on exposure, asbestos particles enter the body and cause discrete injuries to lung and other tissue, and that these injuries are sufficient to establish coverage under the CGL language, even though they must aggregate over time to cause diseases and sicknesses such as asbestosis, carcinoma, and mesothelioma. *Keene*, 667 F.2d at 1044; *Insurance Co. of North America v. Forty–Eight Insulations, Inc.*, 451 F.Supp. 1230, 1239 (E.D.Mich.1978), *modified*, 633 F.2d 1212, 1222–23 (6th Cir.1980), *cert. denied*, 454 U.S. 1109, 102 S.Ct. 686, 70 L.Ed.2d 650 (1981). *But see, e.g., Eagle–Picher*, 523 F.Supp. at 115 & 682 F.2d at 17 (medical evidence establishes that (1) not every exposure to asbestos results in injury of any sort, since body's natural mechanisms often remove fibers before they become embedded; and (2) even when discrete injuries are caused, they frequently fail to lead to any compensable injury).

AHP cannot rely on the rationale of cases that have found immediate injury from the ingestion of asbestos fibers, because the drugs at issue in this case differ markedly from asbestos in the manner in which they are alleged to injure humans. AHP has failed to submit any proof with respect to the effects of any of the drugs involved, and has not claimed that any of them injures upon every exposure. The record establishes without material dispute, moreover, that at least two of the drugs at issue (Ovral and DES) do not injure upon every exposure. Flessa Aff'd, Def.Ex. 35 (Feb. 14, 1982) (Ovral); Mattingly Aff't, Def.Ex. 36 (Feb. 10, 1982) (DES). As discussed below, a particular plaintiff might be able to establish, despite this evidence, that a particular exposure to one of the drugs at issue constituted an actual and compensable injury. No evidence has been presented, however, that could support a general declaration that every exposure to any of the drugs at issue in this case causes injury, and therefore triggers coverage, under the AHP policies. * * *

Finally, the exposure theory is made particularly untenable in this case by the special limitation added to the AHP–Liberty policies since at least 1968, which excludes coverage for injuries "caused by continuous or repeated exposure, any part of which occurred after termination of the policy." If every exposure were an occurrence under the policies, the limitation would have no meaning; it can have meaning only if the occurrences insured against are the injuries, diseases, or sicknesses caused by exposures, and not the exposures themselves.

2. *The Manifestation Theory.* Liberty contends that the policy words "injury", and "disease" or "sickness" are ordinary words which the average person would understand respectively to mean "damage" and an "abnormal condition," and that the average person would think of these consequences as having occurred when they take place or are discovered. The First Circuit accepted this view in extending coverage to the claims at issue in *Eagle–Picher:*

[W]e agree with the district court that the common, ordinary meaning of the policy language supports the manifestation theory. An individual with tiny subclinical insults to her lungs would not say that she had any injury or disease, given one expert's testimony that "over 90% of all urban city dwellers have asbestos-related scarring." Rather, she would say that a disease resulted when she had symptoms which impaired her sense of well-being, or when a doctor was able to detect sufficient scarring to make a prognosis that the onset of manifested disease was inevitable. "Injury" is defined by Webster as "hurt, damage, or loss sustained"; it is a broad term which covers the "result of inflicting on a person or thing something that causes loss, pain, distress, or impairment." As sweeping as this definition is, it is difficult to consider subclinical insults to the lung to constitute an "injury" when these insults do not cause "loss, pain, distress, or impairment" until, if ever, they accumulate to become clinically evident or manifest.

682 F.2d at 19 (footnote omitted).

The "manifestation" theory adopted in *Eagle–Picher,* and now advanced by Liberty, is in part a departure from what has conventionally been understood as the manifestation approach. The meaning of manifestation proposed in prior cases is that an injury, sickness, or disease becomes manifest only when symptoms become noticeable or a diagnosis is made. "The manifestation theorists contend that the date of manifestation is 'the date on which the condition became known or should have become known to plaintiff or the date on which plaintiff's condition was medically diagnosed, whichever comes first.'" Wrubel, *supra,* 48 Fordham L.Rev. at 668 n. 58 (quoting *Forty–Eight Insulations,* 451 F.Supp. at 1238). Thus stated, the manifestation theory refuses to recognize that any bodily injury may have existed prior to the appearance of symptoms or an actual diagnosis. Under this construction, the manifestation theory would be convenient to apply, but it is inconsistent with the policy language.

The ordinary person may construe an "occurrence" of injury to mean manifestation in the sense of discovery. Discovery of an injury or disease is a truly significant event which makes the victim aware of what had theretofore been only a latent, medical problem without conscious significance. The plain meaning of the policy language is not measured, however, by the understanding of a lay person, but by the understanding of a person engaged in the insured's course of business. *See Champion International Corp. v. Continental Casualty Co.,* 546 F.2d 502, 505–06 (2d Cir.1976); *McGrail v. Equitable Life Assurance Society,* 292 N.Y. 419, 424–25, 55 N.E.2d 483, 486 (1944); *Loblaw, Inc. v. Employers' Liability Assurance Corp.,* 85 A.D.2d 880, 446 N.Y.S.2d 743, 745 (4th Dep't 1981). From the point of view of a drug manufacturer, familiar with the potential development of insidious diseases from its products, and seeking to insure against liability for harm, an injury, sickness, or disease would include any compensable, medical condition that is fully developed, even though dormant.

For example, a particular drug may cause a heart attack in some women long after they ingest it. Under the manifestation theory, liability for the heart attack would be covered by a CGL-type policy in effect when the injury occurs. But the manufacturer would also expect that a latent, undiscovered disease caused by the same drug prior to the heart attack would be covered by a policy in effect at the time it arose, regardless of when the disease was discovered or the heart attack or some other manifestation occurred. The CGL policy language covers *all* injuries, sicknesses, or diseases that occur during coverage, not merely those that become manifest.

The restriction imposed on the policy language by the manifestation approach is, moreover, inconsistent with insurance law principles. If the policy language were deemed ambiguous enough to permit reading in a manifestation requirement, the process of doing so would be unacceptable in New York because that reading is not "the only construction which may fairly be placed on" the policy's words, *Filor, Bullard & Smyth v. Insurance Co. of North America*, 605 F.2d 598, 602 (2d Cir.1978), *cert. denied*, 440 U.S. 962, 99 S.Ct. 1506, 59 L.Ed.2d 776 (1979) (emphasis omitted) (citing *Lachs v. Fidelity & Casualty Co.*, 306 N.Y. 357, 365–66, 118 N.E.2d 555, 559 (1954)), and because the construction proposed would be more restrictive than one that treated as "occurrences" all injuries, diseases, and sicknesses, whether manifest or merely discoverable, *see Thomas J. Lipton, Inc. v. Liberty Mutual Insurance Co.*, 34 N.Y.2d 356, 361, 314 N.E.2d 37, 357 N.Y.S.2d 705, 708 (1974); *National Screen Service Corp. v. United States Fidelity & Guaranty Co.*, 364 F.2d 275, 277 (2d Cir.1966); *Vargas v. Insurance Co. of North America*, 651 F.2d 838, 839–40 (2d Cir.1981). Significantly, courts that have accepted the manifestation theory have invariably done so in extending, rather than restricting, the coverage of an ambiguous policy.   *   *   *

C. *Plain Meaning of the Policy Provisions.*

1. *The Occurrence Clause.* The plain meaning of the "occurrence" clause is no secret to the parties. Courts and writers have recognized that "occurrence" is most logically construed to include only those injuries, sicknesses, or diseases that are proved to have existed during coverage. For example, in *Forty–Eight Insulations* the Sixth Circuit stated:

> In each case where a plaintiff sues an asbestos manufacturer, a hearing could be held to determine at what point the build-up of asbestos in the plaintiff's lungs resulted in the body's defenses being overwhelmed. At that point, asbestosis could truly be said to "occur". From then on, all companies which insured the manufacturer would be treated as being "on the risk".

633 F.2d at 1217 (footnote omitted); *see also Schering Corp. v. Home Insurance Co.*, 544 F.Supp. 613, 616 (E.D.N.Y.1982). *See generally*

Wrubel, *supra*. Indeed, while Liberty has advanced its position as based on a manifestation theory requiring knowledge or actual diagnosis, Liberty at times defines "manifestation" to include the unknown presence of diagnosable and compensable disease. *See, e.g.,* Portmann Dep., Pl.Ex. 3 at 136, 138; Stevens Dep., Pl.Ex. 8 at 113–17.

This straight-forward interpretation has been rejected, however, as impractical and unfair. According to critics, to require the courts and the parties to CGL-type contracts to determine coverage in the many thousands of pending and anticipated latent-injury claims on a case-by-case basis would be impossible, *e.g., Forty–Eight Insulations,* 633 F.2d at 1218, and also inconsistent with the reasonable expectations of the insured, and with developing tort-law doctrine in the latent-disease area, *e.g., Keene,* 667 F.2d at 1044 n. 20; *Forty–Eight Insulations,* 633 F.2d at 1219. These practical and ethical concerns are shown below to be unpersuasive. Before addressing them, however, a full appraisal of the policy's plain meaning is in order to demonstrate why, linguistically at least, the injury-in-fact approach is plainly the proper construction.

The most basic demand of the policy language is that to establish Liberty's liability the insured must prove that an "occurrence"—injury, sickness, or disease—arose during the policy period. The plain language demands that the insured prove the cause of the occurrence (accident or exposure), and that the result occurred during the policy period. An exposure that does not result in injury during coverage would not satisfy the policy's terms. On the other hand, a real but undiscovered injury, proved in retrospect to have existed at the relevant time, would establish coverage, irrespective of the time the injury became manifest.

This approach is faithful to the policy language because it gives separate meaning to the three concepts of exposure, injury, and discovery. The policy expressly gives separate significance to the first two concepts, and its provisions strongly suggest that an occurrence means something different—and more expansive—than manifestation or discovery. On the other hand, nothing in the policy language precludes a finding that a single exposure, or a single period of exposures, immediately injured a person to a compensable extent; similarly the policy language also permits courts or juries to find that injury, sickness, or disease, occurred in a particular case at the time it became manifest. So long as the insured is held liable for an identifiable and compensable injury, sickness, or disease that is shown to have existed during coverage, that liability will be insured against whether or not the injury coincides with exposure or manifestation. * * *

2. *The Limitation Provision.* The special limitation, appearing first in the AHP–Liberty policy for 1964 and made effective in 1968, provides strong support for this reading of the plain language.[2] Liberty

2. The policies agreed to by AHP and Liberty between 1964 and 1965 contained this limiting provision, but an endorsement negotiated by the parties for each of the policies for those years appears to negate this limiting language. *See* Pl.Ex. 17–20, endorsement 14. The 1968–76 policies retain the limitation without amendment.

argues correctly that the provision is unambiguous, but its meaning is not the one Liberty suggests. Rather, on its face the provision removes from coverage only injury, death, or destruction that is caused by continuous or repeated exposure occurring in part after November 1, 1976, the date AHP terminated the policy. It does not remove from coverage harm caused wholly by exposure occurring prior to November 1, 1976. Nothing in the language of the provision takes such harm out of the policy simply because exposure to the same products continued after November 1, 1976, or indeed because further harm may have occurred from such continued exposure. If, in a particular case, pre-November 1, 1976 exposure is found to have caused a particular harm, no exposure after November 1, 1976 would be a cause of that particular harm; such harm is not "caused by * * * exposure any part of which" occurred after November 1, 1976, because all of that harm-causing exposure occurred before that date. * * *

IV. Conclusion

The policies at issue in this case explicitly cover liability for injuries, sicknesses, or diseases that occur during each period of coverage. They were intended to cover no more and no less. Coverage is triggered by neither exposure nor manifestation, except when those events constitute in themselves an injury, sickness, or disease for which an injured may be held liable. The policies also expressly require Liberty to bear the costs of defending AHP in all suits, however meritless, that can be read to permit proof that an injury, sickness, or disease occurred during a period of coverage. No considerations of practicability or fairness justify ignoring the plain meaning and purposes of these policies.

The parties will submit within twenty days a declaratory order encompassing these rulings.

SO ORDERED.

Notes and Questions

1. *Practical Problems of Proof.* Is the injury-in-fact trigger of coverage an ideal that cannot be implemented in practice? The Sixth Circuit Court of Appeals thought so, at least in asbestos cases:

> The only problem with this Solomonian interpretation is that no one wants it. The principal reason is cost. If medical testimony as to asbestosis' origin would have to be taken in each of the thousands of asbestosis cases, the cost of litigation would be prohibitive. This appears to be especially true since many of the asbestosis cases are settled before trial. In addition, it is almost impossible for a doctor to look back and testify with any precision as to when the development of asbestosis "crossed the line" and became a disease. The only thing on which all parties agree is that there is a need for us to arrive at an administratively manageable interpretation of the insur-

ance policies—one that can be applied with minimal need for litigation. Reaching such a beneficial result is certainly desirable, but it greatly complicates our task. In the real world, there are few Solomonian possibilities. And, as we have just seen, those that do exist are often impractical.

Insurance Company of North America v. Forty–Eight Insulations, Inc., 633 F.2d 1212, 1218 (6th Cir.1980), cert. denied, 454 U.S. 1109, 102 S.Ct. 686, 70 L.Ed.2d 650 (1981). Was the court overlooking the practical problems posed by the exposure test that it adopted? For example, could it be argued that in cases in which the exposure occurred several decades before suit was brought, pinpointing the year or years of exposure will often be just as difficult as pinpointing the year of injury?

2. *The Other Triggers.* Few courts have adopted manifestation as the exclusive trigger of coverage. In the one leading case that did adopt this trigger, the result was to enable the insured to call upon the only coverage potentially available to it. See *Eagle–Picher Industries, Inc. v. Liberty Mutual Insurance Co.,* 523 F.Supp. 110 (D.Mass.1981), modified, 682 F.2d 12 (1st Cir.1982). If you had been counsel for a liability insurer in 1975, when cascades of asbestos suits began to be filed, and the manifestation trigger already had been widely adopted in other long-latency disease cases, what would you have advised your client to do about renewing liability insurance policies that would expire shortly? Does your answer help to explain the unpopularity of the manifestation trigger?

In contrast, the disadvantage of an exposure trigger in long-latency cases is that the limits of liability afforded by the older policies that are triggered by exposure tend to be unduly low in light of the magnitude of modern awards. Liability policies purchased even in the 1950's, for example, often provided only $50,000 or $100,000 of coverage. Of course, the continuous trigger adopted in *Keene Corporation v. Insurance Company of North America,* 667 F.2d 1034 (D.C.Cir.1981), cert. denied, 455 U.S. 1007, 102 S.Ct. 1644, 71 L.Ed.2d 875 (1982), avoids at least some of the problems associated with triggers based exclusively on manifestation or exposure. But the plausibility of this trigger depends on proof that there was a "continuing" injury from exposure through manifestation—proof that may be available in some kinds of long-latency disease or property damage cases, but not in others.

3. *The Trigger of Coverage in Hazardous Waste Cases.* Although it can be argued that the injury-in-fact trigger may be difficult to apply to asbestos or drug-injury cases in practice, it is at least theoretically sound. On the other hand, is such a trigger even coherent when it is applied to a third major setting in which trigger of coverage issues arise: liability for disposal of hazardous waste? Consider how to apply an injury-in-fact or an exposure trigger to the following cases.

a. Waste in 55 gallon drums is deposited on a site in 1959. As the drums begin to corrode, minute quantities of the waste leak out onto the soil, but it is impossible to reconstruct the first year in which such leakage occurred. Sometime after the drums begin to leak, waste contacts the groundwater (underground water, in the language of hydrology) under the site, but it is impossible to determine the first year when such contact was made. Sometime after the first year when waste contacted the groundwater, the waste flowed beyond the border of the property and contaminated water under neighboring property. Again, determining the exact year when this occurred is not possible. Finally, during 1983, nearby residents became aware that their well-water had been contaminated by waste traceable to the site. The residents sue the site-owner and waste generators for property damage; EPA cleans up the site and sues to recover its costs.

b. Waste is poured directly into a holding pond on a site beginning in 1959. At some point between 1959 and 1983, the pond begins to leak. Other facts are the same as in the preceding paragraph.

c. Waste generated by different companies is deposited at a site over a period of 20 years. The waste leaks from different drums at different times, and mixes together on the surface of the site before leaching into the soil and into the groundwater, in the manner described in paragraph a. A CERCLA action seeks to hold each company jointly and severally liable for cleanup costs.

4. *Apportionment Among Different Years.* Even after surmounting the problems of determining which policy or policies are triggered in hazardous waste liability actions, other obstacles to coordination remain. One is how to apportion liability among triggered policies when more than one policy is triggered. For example, it is easy to see how an exposure, injury-in-fact or continuous trigger would create obligations on the part of insurers issuing policies in more than one year in any of the preceding hypothetical cases. But triggering a policy is only a first step; the amount of its liability then must be determined.

Would it be correct to say that each policy is liable only for the damage caused by the waste which first caused injury during the period the policy was in force? That approach would most closely track the language of the pre–1986 standard CGL, which insures, in effect, against liability for damages because of bodily injury or property damage that occurs during the policy period. Thus, as long as some injury first occurred during a given policy period, the policy in effect during that period would be liable for all the injury ultimately resulting from *that* waste, even if some injury also occurred later. This, after all, is the approach that liability policies apply to ordinary injuries: an insured who injures a victim in an auto accident in 1989 is covered by his 1989 liability insurance policy for all damages resulting, even if the victim suffers pain and incurs medical expenses in 1989, 1990, 1991 and 1992. Any other approach would be chaotic.

Could such a trigger be effectively applied, however, in the hazardous waste setting? Waste may leak from a single drum or group of drums for several years; or waste may be dumped directly onto the ground over several years. Once this material mixes together and begins to cause damage, the portion of damage caused by each separate discharge or discharges in each year normally cannot be disaggregated from the total damage at the site. In the absence of the proof required, is each policy immune from liability, or is each policy liable jointly and severally for all the damage? The latter approach entitles the insured to "stack" the limits of liability available from all triggered policies— possibly underburdening some policies and overburdening others. There is very little law directly on point. For discussions of the problem, see *Uniroyal, Inc. v. The Home Insurance Company,* 707 F.Supp. 1368 (E.D.N.Y.1988); *Dayton Independent School District v. National Gypsum Company,* 682 F.Supp. 1403 (E.D.Tex.1988).

An alternative approach, apparently adopted in bodily injury cases by the celebrated *Keene* decision cited in Note 2 is to hold that there has been only one continuous occurrence, and to allow the insured to pick any of the triggered policies to provide coverage, but only for that policy's limits of liability. Thus, this version of the continuous trigger makes many policies available, but by precluding stacking of the limits of all triggered policies, may produce less actual coverage. See also *Consolidated Asbestos Coverage Cases,* No. 1072 (Superior Ct. of Calif., City and County of San Francisco, May 29, 1987), Tentative Decision on Phase III Issues 43. Which approach seems more consistent with the nature of the damage that occurs in asbestos and hazardous waste cases?

5. *The Problem of Uninsured Years.* Sometimes the insured cannot prove that it had any coverage during certain years when a policy would be triggered if it existed. The cause of the gap in coverage varies. The gap may result from the insured's decision not to purchase coverage for a given year; often the explanation is that the insured's thirty or forty-year old records have disappeared and it simply does not know which company, if any, provided coverage for years long past; a policy may have been in force but a court may find that it provides no coverage for that year because of the insured's breach of a condition of coverage; or liability may arise out of very old occurrences that antedate the first year when the insured purchased liability insurance of any sort. Consultants specializing in tracking down old coverage (insurance "archeologists") now offer their services to putative policyholders searching for old policies. For discussion of methods of proving the existence of coverage without introducing lost policies into evidence, see *Emons Industries, Inc. v. Liberty Mutual Fire Insurance Company,* 545 F.Supp. 185 (S.D.N.Y.1982).

Whatever the reason for an insured's failure to prove coverage in a particular year, what is to be done about uninsured years? The court in *Keene* declined (for not entirely explicable reasons) to allocate any coverage responsibility to uninsured years. But does the logic behind most theories of trigger and apportionment suggest that the insured should bear that portion of the liability allocable to injury (or exposure, or manifestation, depending on the trigger theory in force) occurring during uninsured years? Some method of allocation is then required.

Normally, allocation among multiple triggered insurance policies is achieved by pro-rating in proportion to policy limits. This allocates coverage responsibility based on the magnitude of the risk each insurer agreed to take. This approach will not work in allocating to uninsured years, however, because there were no policy limits during an uninsured year. An alternative is to allocate by years alone—if the insured was covered for nine of ten triggered years, then it bears 10 percent of the total liability involved. But this approach can produce results that may seem peculiar. Suppose that an insured faces a total liability of $1 million, and had coverage of $200,000 for each of eight years plus coverage of $1 million in a ninth year. A total of $2,600,000 in coverage is triggered to cover $1 million of liability, yet the insured nonetheless bears $200,000 of liability itself. Is this method of allocation appropriate?

6. *Solutions Under the Newer CGL Policy.* The Sample CGL Policy set out in Chapter 6 was drafted after the insurance industry became aware of the problems associated with defining and applying a trigger of coverage to long-latency liability claims. How satisfactorily does the new CGL resolve the issues that the old policy seems to have left open?

B. "OTHER INSURANCE" CLAUSES

JONES v. MEDOX, INC.

District of Columbia Court of Appeals, 1981.
430 A.2d 488.

GALLAGHER, Associate Judge, Retired.

The question presented is one of first impression in this jurisdiction and requires this court to scrutinize the "other insurance" clauses [1] of two insurance policies in order to determine how two insurance companies, insuring the same risk, should apportion liability. Specifically, this court must determine whether the pro rata clause in the policy issued by Globe Insurance and the excess clause in the policy issued by the Insurance Company of North America can be reconciled and interpreted to give effect to the intent of the contracting parties, or

1. There are three basic types of "other insurance" provisions: the pro rata clause, the excess clause, and the escape clause. The pro rata clause provides that the insurer will pay its pro rata share of the loss, usually in the proportion that the limit of its policy bears to the aggregate limits of all valid and collectible insurance. The excess clause generally provides that the insurer's liability is limited to the amount by which the loss exceeds the coverage provided by all other valid and collectible insurance, up to the limits of the excess policy. The policy with the escape clause attempts to avoid all liability for the loss when there is other valid and collectible insurance. Frequently, where several insurance policies cover the same insurable risk, the courts are left to interpret and reconcile various "other insurance" clauses. For a good discussion of the judicial treatment of these clauses, see Comment, *Is There a Solution to the Circular Riddle? The Effect of "Other Insurance" Clauses on the Public, the Courts, and the Insurance Industry,* 25 So.Dak.L.Rev. 37 (1980) [hereinafter cited as *Is There a Solution to the Circular Riddle?*].

whether the clauses are irreconcilable and require that this court sweep away the contractual language of the parties and impose a pro rata share of the loss upon each insurance company.

Although this issue has never been addressed and resolved by this court, many other jurisdictions have grappled with this problem and two distinct lines of authority have emerged. Courts adopting the majority view have reconciled the pro rata clause and the excess clause by interpreting the policy containing the excess clause as secondary coverage where there is another insurance policy covering the same risk. The result, under this view, is that the excess insurer is generally liable for the loss only to the extent that the insured's claim exceeds the policy limits of the insurance policy containing the pro rata clause.

Appellant urges this court to reject the majority rule and instead to adopt the minority rule. Courts adopting the minority rule view the pro rata clause and the excess clause as conflicting and automatically require that each insurance company shoulder a pro rata share of the claim. We do not view such clauses as being irreconcilable and choose not to adopt a rule that requires this court automatically to sweep away the contractual language and, perhaps, the negotiated intent of the parties. We therefore decline to adopt the minority rule and affirm the decision of the trial court.

This case originated in a malpractice action initiated by the plaintiff below who sustained injuries allegedly resulting from an injection administered by Nancy Jones, a nurse at Doctors Hospital. Defendants in the action were Ms. Jones, the hospital, and Ms. Jones' employer, Medox, Inc., a corporation which provides temporary medical personnel to local doctors and hospitals. The case was settled for $100,000 pursuant to a settlement agreement which provided that the insurance companies representing all defendants would litigate separately their respective liabilities. In the event that this litigation was not concluded by March 1, 1978, the agreement provided further that Ms. Jones' insurer, Globe Indemnity Co., would pay the full amount of the settlement with no prejudice to its rights.

The insurers' liabilities were not adjudicated by the agreed date. Globe therefore paid the full amount of the settlement. Globe and Mrs. Jones then brought an action against the hospital and its insurer, Hartford Insurance Co., and Medox and its insurer, Insurance Company of North America (INA). The trial court granted summary judgment to the hospital, Hartford Insurance Co., Medox, and INA, and dismissed the claim of Ms. Jones and Globe, thus ruling that Globe should bear the entire cost of the settlement. Ms. Jones and Globe have appealed the dismissal of their claim and the denial of their motions for summary judgment against Medox and INA.

The central dispute in this case is between INA and Globe and concerns the proper interpretation and application of two "other insurance" clauses, one in the INA policy and the other in the Globe policy. The "other insurance" clauses in both policies were designed to limit liability and to apply in situations where the insured event was also covered by another insurance company. At the time of the injection, Ms. Jones was the sole insured under the Globe policy. This policy had a $1,000,000 limit of liability and contained a pro rata "other insurance" clause which provided:

> If the insured has other insurance against a loss covered by this policy * * * the company shall not be liable under this policy for a greater proportion of such loss than the applicable limit of liability * * * bears to the total applicable limit of liability of all valid and collectible insurance against such loss.

Ms. Jones was also covered under a provision of Medox's INA policy by which INA contracted with Medox to pay liabilities incurred under stated circumstances by Medox's employees and contractors. The applicable limit of liability in the INA policy was also $1,000,000 and the policy contained an excess "other insurance" clause which provided:

> The insurance afforded [by this policy] shall be excess insurance over any other valid and collectible insurance. [Hereinafter INA's blanket excess clause.][2]

We begin our discussion of the issue in this case by recognizing the confusion that pervades the entire realm of "other insurance" clauses. The problems created by "other insurance" provisions have been covered extensively in numerous articles in legal periodicals written during the past thirty years.[3] Some commentators have urged that the insurance industry solve these problems by adopting uniform pro rata clauses in all insurance policies or that, in the alternative, a legislative solution be devised.[4] Because the insurance industry continues to

---

2. INA's policy contained another excess "other insurance" clause which stated that the benefits of the policy were intended to be in excess of other insurance available to "the insured." The policy defined "the insured" as Medox or certain of its principals. Both the trial court and the parties on appeal devoted a great deal of attention to the question of whether Ms. Jones was "the insured" for the purpose of applying the excess provisions of this "other insurance" clause. Ms. Jones and Globe argued that Ms. Jones was not "the insured" for the purpose of applying this excess clause and that, therefore, the Globe insurance policy was not "other valid and collectible insurance" that triggered the excess clause in the INA policy. The broadly worded blanket excess clause, however, overrides these provisions, and makes the resolution of this problem unnecessary. Apparently INA did not rely on its blanket excess clause at trial, although it is in the record.

3. *E.g., Is There a Solution to the Circular Riddle? supra* note 1; Comment, *"Other Insurance" Clauses: The Lamb–Weston Doctrine,* 47 Or.L.Rev. 430 (1968) [hereinafter cited as *"Other Insurance" Clauses*]; Watson, *The "Other Insurance" Dilemma,* 16 Fed'n Ins.Counsel Q. 47 (1966); Comment, *Concurrent Coverage in Automobile Liability Insurance,* 65 Colum.L.Rev. 319 (1965); Snow, *Other Insurance Clauses—Multiple Coverage,* 40 Den.L.Center J. 259 (1963); Russ, *The Double Insurance Problem—A Proposal,* 13 Hastings L.J. 183 (1961); Note, *Automobile Insurance—Effect of Double Coverage and "Other Insurance" Clauses,* 38 Minn.L.Rev. 838 (1954); Comment, *"Other Insurance" Clauses Conflict,* 5 Stan.L.Rev. 147 (1952); Gorton, *A Further Study of the Effect of the "Other Insurance" Provision Upon Automobile Liability Insurance,* 16 Ins.Counsel J. 190 (1949).

4. One commentator has presented a set of model rules aimed at solving problems related to "other insurance" provisions and has urged that these rules be adopted by the insurance industry or by direct legislation. Under these rules, escape clauses, which attempt to avoid all liability, would be prohibited as against public policy. Excess clauses would be given effect only where the insurer intends to provide secondary coverage

employ "other insurance" clauses without defining the relationship of these clauses to one another in situations involving multiple insurance policies and because no legislative action has been taken, courts are sometimes forced "into a game that ought not, and need not, be played." *Schoenecker v. Haines,* 88 Wis.2d 665, 674, 277 N.W.2d 782, 786 (1979).

We turn now to analyze the majority and the minority rules and to confront the specific problem presented by the pro rata clause contained in the Globe policy and the excess clause contained in the INA policy. Most courts attempt to reconcile dissimilar "other insurance" clauses by giving effect to the intent of the parties through an examination of the language of the clauses whenever possible.[5] In order to reconcile a pro rata clause and an excess clause and to interpret the clauses so as to give effect to the intent of the parties, these courts reason that

> [W]here an excess clause is inserted in a typical ✱ ✱ ✱ liability insurance policy the usual intent of the insurer is that the policy will afford only *secondary* coverage when the loss is covered by "other insurance." On the other hand, a provision that limits a policy to only pro rata liability in the event of concurrent coverage usually is intended to become effective only when other valid and collectible *primary* insurance is available. [Comment, *Concurrent Coverage in Automobile Insurance,* 65 Colum.L.Rev. 319, 328 (1965) (citations and footnote omitted; emphasis in original).]

Stated another way, these courts assume that the standard phrase "other valid and collectible insurance" means other valid and collectible *primary* insurance. It follows, then, that the policy containing the pro rata clause is other valid and collectible primary insurance that triggers application of the excess clause in the second policy. The excess clause in the second policy therefore is given full effect and that carrier is liable only for the loss after the primary insurer had paid up to its policy limits. The policy containing the excess clause, however, is not considered to be other valid and collectible primary insurance for the purpose of triggering the operation of the pro rata clause, because when a stated contingency occurs, that is, when there is other valid and collectible primary insurance available to the insured, the policy containing the excess clause becomes secondary coverage only.

Critics of this approach to interpretation of insurance contracts have argued that it requires a circularity of reasoning, and that the decision as to which policy constitutes other valid and collectible

exclusively and where the premium paid for such coverage is specifically based upon such limited contingent liability. The general rule urged by this commentator is that, in all cases involving multiple coverage, there shall be proration of liability among all insurers up to the limits of their respective policies. *See Is There a Solution to the Circular Riddle?, supra* note 1, at 52–54.

5. *Is there a Solution to the Circular Riddle?, supra* note 1, at 42; *"Other Insurance" Clauses, supra* note 3, at 433.

insurance triggering the "other insurance" clause of the second policy will depend on which contract is read first. *See, e.g., Oregon Automobile Insurance Co. v. United States Fidelity and Guaranty Co.,* 195 F.2d 958, 960 (9th Cir.1952); *Werley v. United States Automobile Association,* 498 P.2d 112, 117 (Alaska 1972). *See generally* Note, *Automobile Insurance—Effect of Double Coverage and "Other Insurance" Clauses,* 38 Minn.L.Rev. 838, 852 (1954). Disenchanted with the majority approach and with insurance companies' attempts to escape liability, a minority of courts have adopted the *Lamb–Weston* rule. *Lamb–Weston, Inc. v. Oregon Automobile Insurance Co.,* 219 Or. 110, 129, 341 P.2d 110, 119 (1959). Courts applying the *Lamb–Weston* rule abandon all attempts to discern the intent of the contracting parties where there are dissimilar "other insurance" clauses and take the position that all "other insurance" clauses, regardless of their nature, are mutually repugnant, requiring proration of liability.[6]

The *Lamb–Weston* rule presents an appealingly simple and no-nonsense way to deal with the vagaries of insurance policies. A principal concern of courts adopting this rule apparently is that one insurance company is getting "stuck" and that regardless of the intent of the contracting parties as expressed in their "other insurance" clauses, two companies covering the same risk should pay equally. Courts swayed by this concern, however, have failed to recognize that the insurance companies have no contractual relationship with each other, and one company hardly needs to be protected from the other. Neither insurance company is getting "stuck" for anything more than it contracted to provide for its insured. Moreover, courts applying the *Lamb–Weston* rule ignore a basic rule of contracts requiring consideration of all the language in a policy to determine its meaning and intent.[7] By sweeping away the contractual language and, perhaps, the negotiated intent of the parties, these courts effectually are legislating mandatory pro rata clauses for insurance policies having "other insurance" provisions. Courts generally should take such drastic action only when presented with clearly irreconcilable provisions.

Some commentators have noted that there is yet another reason not to adopt the *Lamb–Weston* rule. These commentators have observed that, by sweeping away the contractual language and the negotiated intent of the parties, the *Lamb–Weston* rule will have a substantial impact upon the insurance industry and policy rates. *See, e.g.,* Comment, *Is There a Solution to the Circular Riddle? The Effect on the*

---

6. It should be noted that some courts that have adopted the *Lamb–Weston* rule were not confronted with identical "other insurance" clauses. *See, e.g., Sloviaczek v. Estate of Puckett,* 98 Idaho 371, 377, 565 P.2d 564, 569 (1977); *Werley v. United Serv. Auto. Ass'n, supra.* In *Sloviaczek* and *Werley,* the courts were faced with essentially identical clauses which provided excess coverage only in the amount by which the limit of liability of each exceeded the limit of the other. In such cases, the "other insurance" clauses are virtually always invalidated by the courts. *See* Russ, *supra* note 4, at 191. *See also Is There a Solution to the Circular Riddle?, supra* note 1, at 42.

7. *See* A. Corbin, Contracts §§ 545–554 (one volume ed. 1952); *Is There a Solution to the Circular Riddle?, supra* note 1, at 46.

Public, the Courts, and the Insurance Industry, 25 So.Dak.L.Rev. 37, 47–48 (1980); Comment, *"Other Insurance" Clauses: The Lamb–Weston Doctrine,* 47 Or.L.Rev. 430, 445 (1968).[8] The commentators maintain that the validity of "other insurance" clauses is a factor included in actuarial tables used to determine premiums, and that, when a court adopts a rule that automatically invalidates these provisions, insurance underwriters must confront a new element of uncertainty. This uncertainty results in increased premiums for all policyholders, thus allowing the insurance company to maintain the actuarial soundness of the premium structure. Moreover, the commentators observe that there is a necessary duplication of claim investigation, claim supervision, and settlement and defense costs that result from the application of the *Lamb–Weston* doctrine. This duplication of effort on the part of multiple insurers also may play a role in increasing the cost of each claim and ultimately result in increased premiums to policyholders.

After carefully examining the majority position and the *Lamb–Weston* rule with all its ramifications, we conclude that the majority position is the better approach. We do not view a pro rata clause and an excess clause as being automatically in conflict or mutually repugnant. The interpretation of these clauses under the majority view is, as the highest court in Maryland has recognized, reasonable and fair:

> A construction which will give a fair meaning to both terms, as used in "other insurance" clauses "is that the *excess* provision alone controls in every situation which falls within its terms * * * and that the *prorate [sic]* provision alone governs in * * *, other situations, for example, when more than one [primary] policy has been issued to the same person." *American Auto Insurance Co. v. Republic Indemnity Co.,* 52 Cal.2d 507, 513, 341 P.2d 675, 678 (1959) [*Consolidated Mutual Insurance Co. v. Bankers Insurance Co.,* 244 Md. 392, 399, 223 A.2d 594, 599 (1966) (emphasis in original).]

See also Ryder Truck Rental, Inc. v. Schapiro & Whitehouse, Inc., 259 Md. 354, 269 A.2d 826 (1970).

8. Indeed, the Oregon court itself, subsequent to *Lamb–Weston,* implicitly indicated a similar concern with respect to the effect that the *Lamb–Weston* rule would have on the insurance industry. In *Liberty Mut. Ins. Co. v. Truck Ins. Exch.,* 245 Or. 30, 35, 420 P.2d 66, 69 (1966) the Oregon Court noted that, in some instances, "[p]remiums [are] paid the excess carriers in light of the relatively remote risks so insured," and that applying the *Lamb–Weston* rule would force "excess-insurance carriers to participate in a loss contrary to the terms of their contracts." The court held, *inter alia,* that, where an insurer is an excess insurer only, the excess insurer is not required to pay a portion of the loss until the first layer of coverage is exhausted. The court observed:

> There are decisions to the effect that the policy containing the pro-rata clause should always bear the whole loss when the other policy contains an excess clause. However, when the two contracts are compared in such cases, the other-insurance clauses frequently are not held to be repugnant. But when *repugnancy cannot be resolved by reference to the contracts,* the case is a proper case for the equitable rule set forth in *Lamb–Weston.* [*Liberty Mut. Ins. Co. v. Truck Ins. Exch., supra* at 39, 420 P.2d at 70–71 (citations and footnote omitted; emphasis supplied).]

The Oregon court thus limited the application of the *Lamb–Weston* rule.

The rule in the District of Columbia, then, is that where there are two applicable insurance policies, one policy containing a pro rata clause and the other an excess clause, the provisions of each will be interpreted to give effect to the intent of the contracting parties. Generally speaking, the application of this rule will probably result in the excess clause being given effect. The insurance company including a pro rata clause in its policy will be required to shoulder the loss up to its policy limit. We stress, however, that the determination of what is or is not valid and collectible insurance for the purpose of triggering an "other insurance" clause should not be made in the abstract, but must be based on a consideration of all the contractual terms of both applicable insurance policies. We also note that, by adopting the majority rule with respect to pro rata and excess clauses, we do not rule out the possibility that in some instances this court may find it necessary to affirmatively intervene in order to resolve conflicts between "other insurance" clauses, for in some instances it may be impossible to reconcile the two clauses or to give effect to the intent of the contracting parties. Where, for example, the applicable portions of the two "other insurance" clauses are identical excess clauses, even those courts adopting the majority view almost always require the insurers to apportion the liability. *See, e.g., State Farm Fire and Casualty Co. v. St. Paul Fire and Marine Insurance Co.,* S.D., 268 N.W.2d 147, 149 (1978).[9] Such cases present a true problem of circularity. Each insurer, claiming that the other must pay first, declines to pay at all. A literal interpretation of the policies containing conflicting excess clauses would leave the insured without any coverage where it first appeared that he had double coverage. In these cases, there is no rational reason to give the language of one policy preference over identical language in the other policy. *See generally Is There a Solution to the Circular Riddle?, supra* note 1, at 42. This is not the case before us.

We consider that Globe's pro rata clause and INA's blanket excess clause are not irreconcilable. Globe's provision contemplates contribution from all other valid and collectible insurance. INA is *not* collectible insurance for this purpose because INA's blanket excess clause expressly states that it *will not* pay if the claim is covered by any other valid and collectible insurance and does not exceed the policy limit of that other insurance. Globe is collectible insurance under INA's clause because it states that it will pay the claim in any event, subject to any applicable pro rata contribution. The Globe contract does not foresee the possibility that another insurance policy should constitute only excess coverage and does not provide for this possibility in its other insurance clause. Thus, applied together, the two policies result in

9. *Cf. Employers' Liab. Assurance Corp., Ltd. v. Fireman's Fund Ins. Group,* 104 U.S. App.D.C. 351, 262 F.2d 239 (1958). In *Employers' Liability,* the court was confronted with two excess clauses. After considering the specific clauses and the circumstances of the case, the court held that, under the policies of the lender and the borrower of a substitute automobile, the lender's policy was primary and that the borrower's insurer was not liable for damages unless the claim exceeded the lender's policy limit.

Globe being liable for any claim up to its policy limit, with INA picking up any excess.

It has been observed that "[q]uestions of contribution between coinsurers have caused much trouble to the courts, a large part of which has arisen through efforts to equalize equities outside the contract," and that "[t]his trouble is lessened if the parties are left with their contracts as they themselves have made them." *Grollimund v. Germania Fire Insurance Co.*, 82 N.J.L. 618, 621, 83 A. 1108, 1109 (1912), *quoted in Citizens Mutual Automobile Insurance Co. v. Liberty Mutual Insurance Co.*, 273 F.2d 189, 194 (6th Cir.1969) and in *American Surety Co. v. American Indemnity Co.*, 8 N.J.Super. 343, 345, 72 A.2d 798, 799 (Ch.Div.1950). For this reason, we reject the *Lamb–Weston* rule and adopt the majority view, which focuses on the contractual provisions and the intent of the parties.[10] In this case, INA's excess clause was triggered and the claim did not exceed Globe's policy limit. Thus, INA was exonerated from all liability. We affirm the trial court's decision that Globe must bear the entire cost of the settlement.

Affirmed.

CARRIERS INSURANCE COMPANY v. AMERICAN POLICYHOLDERS' INSURANCE COMPANY

Supreme Judicial Court of Maine, 1979.
404 A.2d 216.

DELAHANTY, Justice.

This action was brought in the Superior Court, Kennebec County, by the plaintiff, Carriers Insurance Company (Carriers), seeking contribution from the defendant, American Policyholders' Insurance Co. (American). The parties joined issue upon whether and to what extent American was required to contribute to a settlement made by the plaintiff. Upon an agreed statement of facts, the presiding Justice found for Carriers, and American has appealed. We deny the appeal.

During April of 1963, Cummings Bros. (Cummings) entered into a contractual agreement with Merrill's Rental Service, Inc. (Merrill's) whereby it leased certain motor vehicles from Merrill's. Pursuant to the lease and for Cummings' benefit, Merrill's agreed to provide insurance coverage—both personal injury and property damage—for its vehicles while they were being operated by Cummings' employees. In 1971, this personal injury liability coverage which Merrill's obtained through Carriers stood at approximately $3,000,000 with $500,000 of property damage coverage. In the meantime, Cummings independently procured $250,000 of liability insurance through the defendant, American.

In March of 1972, one of Cummings' employees, while negligently driving a vehicle leased from Merrill's, collided with a Lincoln Conti-

---

10. At the same time, however, we join the view that the insurance industry should at long last provide the impetus to deal with the recurring problem generated by "other insurance" clauses. *See* note 3 & accompanying text *supra*.

nental killing the driver and extensively damaging his automobile. Carriers, acting in good faith and in the best interests of its insured, settled a wrongful death claim for $200,000 and a property damage claim for approximately $8,000. Both prior and subsequent to the settlement, American refused Carriers' demand for contribution. Thereafter, Carriers instituted the present action and received a judgment against the defendant for approximately $104,000. Both Carriers and American had "other insurance" clauses in their insurance policies. Carriers' contract stated:

OTHER INSURANCE

If there is other insurance against an occurrence covered by this policy the insurance afforded by this policy shall be deemed *excess insurance* over and above the applicable limits of all such other insurance. (emphasis supplied.)

American's policy contained an endorsement specifically covering "hired automobiles" which provided:

OTHER INSURANCE

This insurance shall be excess insurance over any other valid and collectible insurance for Bodily Injury Liability for Property Damage Liability and for Automobile Medical Payments. (emphasis supplied.)

Faced with these competing clauses, the presiding Justice disregarded them as "mutually repugnant." American assigns this as error and insists that its clause should be given preference over Carriers.

I

We begin our discussion by acknowledging the utter confusion that pervades the entire realm of "other insurance" clauses. *See Insurance Company of Texas v. Employers Liability Assurance Corp.,* 163 F.Supp. 143, 145 (S.D.Cal.1958). Originating in the property insurance field, these clauses were designed to prevent fraudulent claims induced by overinsuring. With automobiles, however, the fear of death or injury was in itself sufficient to deter specious accidents. The original purpose of other insurance clauses has little relevance, therefore, to automobile liability insurance other than to limit, reduce, or even avoid an insurer's loss in those cases where there is multiple coverage. *See* Comment, *"Other Insurance" Clauses: The Lamb–Weston Doctrine,* 47 Or.L.Rev. 430 (1968); Note, *Concurrent Coverage in Automobile Liability Insurance,* 65 Colum.L.Rev. 319 (1965). However, these clauses violate no public policy and in the absence of a statute to the contrary they will be given effect, even if the insured is unaware of the existence of the other insurance. 8 D. Blashfield, Automobile Law and Practice § 345.10 (3rd ed. 1966).

There are three basic types of other insurance clauses which regulate how liability is to be divided when multiple coverage exists. The first, a "pro-rata" clause, limits the liability of an insurer to a proportion of the total loss. The second, an "escape" clause, seeks to avoid all liability. The third, an "excess" clause, the provision used in the present case, provides that the insurance will only be excess. *See* 8 J. Appleman, Insurance Law and Practice § 4911 (Cum.Supp.1973); 7 Am.Jur.2d *Automobile Insurance* §§ 200–202 (2d ed. 1963).

No problems arise as long as only one policy contains an other insurance clause since the particular provision can be given effect as written. Complications and conflicts occur where more than one applicable policy contains an other insurance clause. In that situation, the court is faced with a battle of the clauses.

In the case at bar, each policy, in virtually identical language, states that it will be excess over any other valid and collectible insurance. Any attempt at a literal reconciliation of the clauses involves hopeless circular reasoning. One clause cannot be given effect as "excess" unless the other is considered "primary." Since both claim to be excess, neither could operate as primary and hence neither could take effect as excess. Taken to its *reductio ad absurdum* conclusion, even though each insurer concedes that its policy would have covered the loss in the absence of the other, where there is double coverage both would escape liability, a result which neither party advocates. As well stated in *State Farm Mutual Insurance Co. v. Travelers Insurance Co.,* 184 So.2d 750, 753–54 (La.App.1966) (Tate, J., concurring),

> [i]ndeed, there is actually no way by logic or word-sense to reconcile two such clauses, where each policy by itself can apply as a primary insurer, but where the clause in each policy nevertheless attempts to make its own liability secondary to that of any other policy issued by a similar primary insurer: For then the primary and (attempted) secondary liability of each policy chase the other through infinity, something like trying to answer the question: Which came first, the chicken or the egg?

Faced with this logical logjam, a number of different and conflicting methods have at various times been used to determine which policy is primary and hence which should bear the brunt of the loss. Thus, it has been stated that the primary policy is the one: covering the tortfeasor, *Employers Mutual Liability Insurance Company of Wisconsin v. Pacific Indemnity Company,* 167 Cal.App.2d 369, 334 P.2d 658 (1959); issued prior in time, *Automobile Insurance Company of Hartford v. Springfield Dyeing Company,* 109 F.2d 533 (3rd Cir.1940); insuring the vehicle's owner, *Farm Bureau Mut. Automobile Ins. Co. v. Preferred Acc. Ins. Co.,* 78 F.Supp. 561 (W.D.Va.1948); whose policy covered the particular loss more specifically, *Trinity Universal Insurance Co. v. General Accident, Fire & Life Assurance Corp.,* 138 Ohio St. 488, 35 N.E.2d 836 (1941); or whose other insurance clause is written in more general terms, *Zurich General Accident & Liability Insurance Co. v. Clamor,* 124 F.2d 717 (7th Cir.1941).

Seizing on one of these approaches, American argues that Carriers' policy should be construed as primary based upon minute differences in the language of the excess insurance clauses. We prefer not to engage in such semantic microscopy. "It [merely] encourages the continuing draftsmanship battle by which insurers seek still more specific policy terms, and the end is not in sight." Note, *Concurrent Coverage in Automobile Liability Insurance, supra* at 322. Fairly read, each insurer, through its excess clause, seeks to place the initial loss on any other applicable insurance, saving for itself a role as secondary insurer.

As an alternative argument, American asserts that the intent of the underlying parties should be given effect. Merrill's, for valuable consideration, contractually agreed to insure Cummings.[1] Merrill's insurance should therefore be considered primary.

We disagree.

American's argument would be well taken were this suit simply one for breach of contract between Cummings and Merrill's. We fail, however, to see the relevance in this case of the lease agreement to which the insurers were neither parties nor beneficiaries. The only appropriate considerations are the two insurance policies through which the respective insurers and insureds manifested their contractual intent. *See Farm Bureau Mutual Insurance Co. v. Waugh*, 159 Me. 115, 188 A.2d 889 (1963). An examination of the policies issued is the single criteria [sic] for analyzing an insurer's obligations which can neither be enlarged nor diminished beyond the terms employed. *Limberis v. Aetna Casualty & Surety Co.*, Me., 263 A.2d 83 (1970). A determination of the primary insurer must turn, therefore, upon a construction of the insurance contracts and not upon a collateral agreement between an insured and a third party.　*　*　*

We perceive no methodology which is neither arbitrary nor utterly mechanical by which we could rationally resolve the enigma of which policy should be given effect over the other. Both clauses attempt to occupy the same legal status. Any construction this Court renders should attempt to maintain this status quo. This goal can be achieved

---

1. In pertinent part, the lease provided:

F. INSURANCE COVERAGE AND LIABILITY

Subject to the following conditions, MERRILL shall provide, at its expense, insurance coverage for its benefit and the benefit of CUMMINGS and the drivers and/or operator of CUMMINGS.

1. All rental units described in Schedule A including any emergency spares or other vehicles or trailers of MERRILL's used by CUMMINGS under the terms hereof will be covered, for the benefit of CUMMINGS and its operating and driving personnel:

(a). Personal injury, [$2,990,000.00].

(b). Property damage, $500,000.00.

2. CUMMINGS shall not be liable to MERRILL for any damages or injuries sustained to the rental units described in Schedule A while being used by CUMMINGS under the terms hereof if occasioned by:

(a). The negligent operation of CUMMINGS' drivers or operators while operating or driving said rental units in the scope of their employment with CUMMINGS.

only by abandoning the search for the mythical "primary" insurer and insisting instead that both insurers share in the loss. Such an approach best carries out the intent of the insurers which was to reduce or limit their liability.

There are additional benefits to adopting this rule. It would introduce certainty and uniformity into the insurance industry, discourage litigation between insurers, and enable underwriters to predict the losses of the insurers more accurately. Note, *Conflicts Between "Other Insurance" Clauses in Automobile Liability Insurance Policies,* 20 Hastings L.J. 1292, 1304 (1969). We hold that where there are conflicting excess insurance clause provisions they are to be disregarded as mutually repugnant thus rendering applicable the general coverage of each policy. This, we note, is the clear majority rule.[2]

II

Having found that both policies are to be considered "primary," we are brought to the question of how should the liability be prorated where the total loss does not exceed the limits of either policy. American argues that the loss should be prorated according to the policy limits. Because Carriers provided $2,990,000 of coverage compared to only $250,000 for American, appellant contends that Carriers should bear close to ninety percent of the settlement cost. Carriers, on the other hand, argues that the loss should be shared equally between the insurers, the approach adopted by the presiding Justice.

There are three basic methods of proration. The majority rule, the one urged upon by appellant, prorates liability according to the limits contained in each policy.[3] The next, which is seldom followed, prorates on the basis of the premiums paid to each insurer.[4] Finally, there is a minority but growing number of courts which prorate the loss equally up to the limits of the lower policy,[5] the approach adopted by the court below.

Each method is grounded on the premises, often unarticulated, that on equitable principles the loss should be shared among the insurers either on the basis of the risk that they have undertaken or the benefit

2. As stated in 69 A.L.R.2d, *supra* note 1 at 1123–24,

[t]here is a growing tendency in the entire picture to reject the circular reasoning, more prevalent in an earlier day, whereby the restrictive clause of one policy will be given prior effect, or one of two policies affording coverage upon different hypotheses will be deemed "specific," and, therefore, to constitute the "primary" insurance. This rejection has been strongest in cases where the conflict has been between like "other insurance" clauses.   *   *   *

  *   *   *

3. *See, e.g., State Farm Mut. Auto. Ins. Co. v. General Mut. Ins. Co.,* 282 Ala. 212, 210 So.2d 688 (1968); *Buckeye Union Ins. Co. v. State Auto. Mut. Ins. Co., supra* note 2; *Lamb–Weston, Inc. v. Oregon Auto. Ins. Co.,* 219 Or. 110, 346 P.2d 643 (1959); *Pacific Indem. Co. v. Federated Am. Ins. Co.,* 82 Wash.2d 412, 511 P.2d 56 (1973).

4. *Insurance Co. of Tex. v. Employers Liab. Assur. Corp., supra.*

5. *See, e.g., Ruan Transport Corp. v. Truck Rentals, Inc.,* 278 F.Supp. 692 (D.Colo.1968); *Ryder Truck Rental, Inc. v. Schapiro & Whitehouse, Inc.,* 259 Md. 354, 269 A.2d 826 (1970): *Cosmopolitan Mut. Ins. Co. v. Continental Cas. Co., supra* note 2.

they have received. In its clearest expression, the majority rule has been justified on the theory that

> the burden imposed on each insurer is generally proportional to the benefit which he received, since the size of the premium is most always directly related to the size of the policy. *Lamb–Weston, Inc. v. Oregon Automobile Insurance Company, supra* note 3 at 137, 346 P.2d at 647.

On precisely these grounds, the majority rule has been criticized since "[it] is commonly known that the cost of liability insurance does not increase proportionately with the policy limits." *Cosmopolitan Mutual Insurance Company v. Continental Casualty Co., supra* note 4 at 564, 147 A.2d at 534. Once minimum coverage has been obtained, significant supplemental coverage can be provided at only a modest increase in cost.

On the other hand, if the majority rule is less equitable than that minority approach which apportions on the basis of premiums received, it has the advantage of facile application. Unless the multiple policies cover the identical risks, there would be too many variables affecting the premiums to permit them to serve as a benchmark for an equitable adjustment. *Nationwide Mutual Insurance Company v. State Farm Mutual Automobile Insurance Company,* 209 F.Supp. 83 (N.D.W.Va. 1962).

The minority rule adopted by the presiding Justice utilizes the best aspects of both approaches without the limitations. Like the majority rule, it is easy to administer. It would simply require each company to contribute equally until the limits of the smaller policy were exhausted, with any remaining portion of the loss then being paid from the larger policy up to its limits. *Nationwide Mutual Insurance Company v. State Farm Mutual Automobile Insurance Company, supra; Dairyland Insurance Company v. Drum,* 568 P.2d 459, 464 (Colo.1977) (Carrigan, J., dissenting in part).

Unlike the majority rule, this Solomon-like approach comports with a most basic sense of justice. *See* Exodus, ch. 21, par. 35 ("When one man's ox hurts another's ox so badly that it dies, they shall sell the live ox and divide this money as well as the dead animal they shall divide equally between them.") Moreover, the majority rule unfairly discriminates against the larger policy by apportioning the loss in proportion to the respective policy limits, utterly forgetting that both insurers, by their contracts, have in fact agreed to cover a loss up to the limits of the lesser policy. Until that point is reached, the majority rule amounts to no more than an unacceptable subsidy from the high-coverage to the low-coverage carrier. We are in complete accord with the presiding Justice when he adopted the persuasive opinion of Judge Doyle in *Ruan Transport Corp. v. Truck Rentals, Inc., supra* note 5 at 696.

> The majority method of prorating operates inequitably in its differentiating treatment of the high-loss and low-loss insurer.

In return for a greater premium the insurer providing higher coverage has undertaken to protect the insured against accidents involving high losses. Yet because of this undertaking to protect against high loss the larger insurer is in an unfavorable position vis-a-vis the other insurer even in cases of low loss, since under the majority method of prorating the insurer affording the greater maximum coverage pays the greater segment of any loss incurred, regardless of the amount of the loss. This seems inequitable since both insurers have equally undertaken to insure against the low-loss accident.

The majority rule would hardly encourage an insurer from increasing its coverage where it is aware that there is a lesser policy. It would increase the insurer's potential liability not only in the high-risk situation which the additional premiums are presumably meant to recompense, but it would have the untoward effect of increasing liability in the more likely to occur low-risk situation. Carried to its extreme, it would further increase the cost of additional insurance thereby reducing the likelihood that an insured would choose such coverage. *See Dairyland Insurance Company v. Drum, supra,* (Carrigan, J., dissenting in part). The Court would be reluctant to adopt a rule which would seemingly have little social utility.

For all of the aforesaid reasons, the presiding Justice correctly prorated the loss between Carriers and American.

Accordingly, the entry shall be:

Appeal denied.

Judgment affirmed.

Notes and Questions

1. *Predictability of Result.* If the question whether an excess and a pro-rata clause can live together depends partly on the language of the policies, will the decision in *Jones* provide insurers with any more predictability than the *Lamb–Weston* rule?

2. *Principal Coverage or Back–Up Coverage?* Did the court in *Jones* gloss over the difference between an excess "other insurance" clause in a policy designed to be primary most of the time, and an other insurance clause in a primary policy designed largely to be excess, but to provide primary coverage on the rare occasions when the insured does not have other primary coverage? Should more deference be accorded to the intention behind the latter than the former?

3. *Methods of Coordination.* What should be the preferred method of avoiding conflicts between other insurance clauses: regulatory prescriptions regarding their terms, intra-industry cooperation to assure that clauses in different policies are consistent, or judicial interpretation of the clauses on a case-by-case basis? Note that at least in the auto insurance field, the problem has been solved by the adoption of standard policies containing identical "other insurance"

clauses. See, e.g., the Sample Personal Auto Policy in Chapter Eight, which provides (in each of its Parts) that the coverage it provides is pro-rata with respect to the owned vehicle, and excess with respect to non-owned vehicles. Consequently, whenever a permittee is driving another party's car, the owner's policy is primary and the driver's policy is excess. This allocation yields perfect clarity, but should the priorities it adopts be reversed?

4. *Other Insurance Clauses and Rate Regulation.* In a line of insurance subject to careful rate regulation, in theory an insurer would want to argue in advance that its policies contain other insurance clauses that render them primary, but argue in subsequent coverage disputes that the clauses render the policies secondary. What, if anything, prevents insurers from doing this? How difficult would it be for an Insurance Commissioner to estimate the incidence and outcome of "other insurance" conflicts in a given line or subclass of insurance in order to evaluate insurers' arguments on this issue?

5. *Methods of Pro-rating.* Was the court in *Carriers* correct in suggesting that pro-rating in proportion to policy limits is the approach most consistent with the coverage expectations of the insurers that had issued conflicting policies? Can an estimate of these expectations be anything but circular before a rule governing the method by which coverage will be pro-rated when other insurance clauses conflict is adopted?

6. *Toward a System of Coordination.* With the proliferation of different forms and sources of insurance coverage, the possibility that there will be overlapping coverage for a single loss has increased exponentially. Although the court in *Jones* was accurate when it stated that the insurers issuing the policies under scrutiny had no contract relations with or rights against each other, does it make sense to continue to treat separate insurance policies as the product of atomistic contracts? For an argument that there has developed a private insurance *system,* requiring legal intervention that creates legal relations among insurers through rules governing coordination, see K. Abraham, Distributing Risk: Insurance, Legal Theory, and Public Policy 133–72 (1986).

C. "STACKING" UNINSURED MOTORISTS COVERAGE

TAFT v. CERWONKA

Supreme Court of Rhode Island, 1981.
433 A.2d 215.

MURRAY, Justice.

The plaintiffs, Earl W. Taft and his wife, Marian F. Taft, brought this civil action to recover for the alleged wrongful death of their daughter, Beverly A. Taft (Beverly), alleging that the negligence of the defendant Eric A. Cerwonka (Cerwonka) in operating a motor vehicle was the proximate cause of their daughter's death. Because the defendant Cerwonka, and the defendant Richard A. Miller (Miller), the owner of the vehicle, were uninsured at the time of the fatal mishap, the plaintiffs also filed a complaint against their insurer, Allstate Insurance Company (Allstate) under the uninsured-motorist provisions of their policy. Prior to trial, the two suits were consolidated. ＊　＊　＊

Prior to trial, plaintiffs moved for partial summary judgment on the issue of whether they would be able to "stack" the uninsured-motorist coverage provided for each automobile on the one policy underwritten by defendant Allstate. Such motion was granted by a justice of the Superior Court. The matter then proceeded to trial in the Superior Court. After all parties had rested, defendant Allstate moved for a directed verdict, stating "that if there is a verdict for the plaintiff, and I see no reason why at this juncture that the verdict for the plaintiff should not be entered, that the jury be instructed and directed that the verdict should be the minimum verdict of five thousand dollars ＊　＊　＊." The trial justice denied this motion and then gave his instructions to the jury, which returned a verdict in favor of plaintiffs in the sum of $33,000. Subsequently, Allstate moved for a new trial on the issue of damages, and it also moved the court to enter judgment against it in the amount of $10,000, the amount it contended was the limit of its liability under the policy issued to plaintiffs. The trial justice's denial of these motions and his entry of judgment in the amount of $20,000 (the aggregate limits of Allstate's liability) against defendant Allstate forms the basis of its present appeal.

I

In passing upon defendant's contention, we are called upon to determine an issue of first impression in this jurisdiction. That issue is whether plaintiffs should be permitted to "stack" the uninsured-motorist coverage provided for each of the two automobiles insured by Allstate.

Because the fact situations in "stacking" cases tend to be similar and because the Rhode Island uninsured-motorist statute is typical of those in other jurisdictions, decisions of other courts that have confronted this issue merit analysis here. In those jurisdictions where intra-policy stacking has been allowed,[1] courts have advanced one or more of three general theories in support of their decisions. See Comment, *Intra–Policy Stacking of Uninsured Motorist and Medical Payments Coverage: To Be or Not to Be,* 22 S.D.L.Rev. 349 (1977). One theory advanced is the theory that the applicable provisions of the insurance contract are ambiguous and that such ambiguities are to be resolved against the insurer. For example, in *Jeffries v. Stewart,* 159 Ind.App.

---

1. Intra-policy stacking is the aggregation of the limits of liability for uninsured-motorist coverage of each car covered in one policy, whereas inter-policy stacking involves the aggregation of coverage under more than one policy.

701, 309 N.E.2d 448 (1974), the Supreme Court of Indiana found an ambiguity in that the separability clause and the limits-of-liability clause conflicted with each other. The court resolved the ambiguity in favor of the insured and allowed him to stack the limits of liability. *See Id.* at 709, 309 N.E.2d at 453.

Another theory cited in support of stacking is that the particular jurisdiction's uninsured-motorist statute requires such a result. Representative of this class of cases is *Tucker v. Government Employees Insurance Co.*, 288 So.2d 238 (Fla.1974). In that case, the Supreme Court of Florida held that their uninsured-motorist statute, Fla.Stat. Ann. § 627.727 (West 1977) "does not disclose any statutory basis for a 'stacking' exclusion in a policy combining auto liability coverage for two or more automobiles of the named insured with uninsured motorist coverage included." *Id.* at 241.[2] Another court in *Holloway v. Nationwide Mutual Insurance Co.*, 376 So.2d 690 (Ala.1979), held that the jurisdiction's uninsured-motorist statute *mandated* stacking for the primary insured.

A final theory is the double-premiums theory, under which courts have held that the payment of separate premiums for uninsured-motorist coverage for each vehicle covered by the policy entitles the insured to stack the limits of liability for each insured vehicle of the policy. A recent case espousing this view is *Kemp v. Allstate Insurance Co.*, Mont., 601 P.2d 20 (1979).

In the jurisdictions where intra-policy stacking has not been allowed, courts have attempted to discredit each of the above theories. In *Grimes v. Concord General Mutual Insurance Co.*, N.H., 422 A.2d 1312 (1980) the Supreme Court of New Hampshire discarded the double-premium theory, stating:

> "Neither can we agree, with confidence that the plaintiff is paying an extra premium without receiving something in return. When an insured owns two vehicles that are constantly available for use, not only by him, but by members of his family and others, the risk that someone operating one of those vehicles will be involved in an accident with an uninsured motorist is obviously greater than if only one vehicle were available for use. Consequently, an insurance carrier's exposure to that risk may be enhanced. Other courts have recognized that the second premium paid on the second car does afford some extra protection that otherwise would not exist." [Citations omitted.] *Id.* 422 A.2d at 1315.

The court went on to hold that their uninsured-motorist statute did not require intra-policy stacking.[3]

* * *

2. We note here that the legislature in the State of Florida has since passed antistacking legislation. *See* Fla.Stat.Ann. § 627.4132 (West 1977).

3. See N.H.Rev.Stat.Ann. § 268:15–a.

708

COORDINATING MULTIPLE COVERAGES

Ch. 9

It is not disputed that plaintiffs paid two separate premiums for uninsured-motorist coverage; nevertheless, Allstate contends that to allow stacking is to render a "tortured" construction of the policy and of our uninsured-motorist statute. To give credence to Allstate's contentions, however, would defeat the reasonable expectations of a policyholder.

> "It is reasonable to expect the same coverage where comparable premium dollars are paid to insure the same two cars, for convenience, under a single policy. A combination coverage should not be the predicate for an exclusion of coverage. Such a result would allow a simple change in form to defeat the insured's reasonable expectation, as well as the substance of law." [Citation omitted.] *Allstate Insurance Co. v. Maglish,* 94 Nev. 699, 703, 586 P.2d 313, 315 (1978).

Indeed if plaintiffs had insured their automobiles under two separate policies and had paid uninsured-motorist premiums for each car, they would be entitled to $20,000 in uninsured-motorist coverage from Allstate. Under these circumstances we find persuasive the statement of dissenting Justice Douglas of the Supreme Court of New Hampshire in *Grimes v. Concord General Mutual Insurance Co.,* N.H., 422 A.2d at 1317, that

> "[i]t is an anomaly that if the same two premiums were paid to two *different* companies, we would permit *inter*-policy stacking of 'as many uninsured motorist policies as are applicable to him, up to his total damages,' *Courtemanche v. Lumbermens Mut. Cas. Co.,* 118 N.H. 168, 173, 385 A.2d 105, 108 (1978), but because the two different coverages were both purchased from the same insurer, we do not." (Emphasis in original.)

Other cases have reflected the same view, *e.g., Traveler's Insurance Co. v. Pac,* 337 So.2d 397 (Fla.App.1976); *Breaux v. Government Employees Insurance Co.,* 373 So.2d 1335 (La.App.1979); *Allstate Insurance Co. v. Maglish,* 94 Nev. 699, 586 P.2d 313 (1978).

We hold therefore that under the circumstances of this case where plaintiffs have paid two separate premiums providing each vehicle with uninsured-motorist coverage, they are entitled to recover under the uninsured-motorist provisions of the policy sums found legally recoverable up to the aggregate sum of the motor vehicles so insured. *Accord, Kemp v. Allstate Insurance Co.,* Mont., 601 P.2d 20, 24 (1979). We are careful to limit our holding on this issue to cases factually similar to the one at bar, for we foresee and rue the day when our reasoning may be twisted to achieve an absurd result. For example, what is the result to be if a plaintiff was injured while riding in an automobile which was insured as only one of a fleet of cars? We defer decision on this and related issues until a case with the appropriate factual setting presents itself for review.[4] * * *

4. In these circumstances even in those jurisdictions where intra-policy stacking for two or three vehicles is allowed, courts have uniformly denied such an extension of the

Accordingly, the defendant's appeal is denied and dismissed. The judgment appealed from is affirmed, and the case is remanded to the Superior Court.

Notes and Questions

1. *Sources of Authority.* Whether inter-policy stacking is permitted should (presumably) be resolved by the "other insurance" clauses in the two potentially applicable policies. Whether intra-policy stacking is allowed, however, must be resolved by other sources of authority, within or outside the policy. What are these other sources?

2. *Precluding Stacking.* What source of law or contract did the court in *Taft* draw upon to answer the question posed? Should the language of a statute specifying the required scope of UM coverage be consulted? If the fact that two premiums have been paid is relevant, should the language in the policy for which the premiums have been paid also be consulted? Consider the following language from Part C of the Sample Personal Auto Policy in Chapter Eight:

> The Limit of Liability shown in the Declarations for this coverage is our maximum limit of liability for all damages resulting from any one accident. This is the most we will pay regardless of the number of: * * * Vehicles or premiums shown in the Declarations. * * *

Does this provision definitively preclude intra-policy stacking?

stacking theory. *See, e.g. Holloway v. Nationwide Mutual Insurance Co.,* 376 So.2d 690 (Ala.1979); *Ohio Casualty Insurance Co. v. Stanfield,* 581 S.W.2d 555 (Ky.1979); *Linderer v. Royal Globe Insurance Co.,* 597 S.W.2d 656 (Mo.App.1980); *Continental Casualty Co. v. Darch,* 27 Wash.App. 726, 620 P.2d 1005 (1980).

Chapter Ten

THE SECONDARY MARKET

The preceding Chapters have been concerned almost exclusively with what might be called the *primary market* for insurance: lines of primary coverage sold by private insurers licensed to do business in and regulated under the laws of the states in which they sell coverage. This Chapter examines a variety of enterprises and institutions that can be generally characterized as the *secondary market:* assigned risk plans, joint underwriting associations, the surplus lines market, and reinsurance. The theme that links each of these quite disparate forms and sources of coverage together is that they fall outside the authority of conventional regulatory regimes and serve purposes quite distinct from the standard coverages sold in the primary market.

A. RESIDUAL MARKET MECHANISMS

Insurance Services Office,

OVERVIEW: RESIDUAL MARKET MECHANISMS *
(1988).

INTRODUCTION

The residual market provides coverage for risks unable to purchase insurance in the voluntary market. The residual market mechanisms in place today to provide coverage for these risks have developed over the last half-century. In the 1930's, the first automobile residual market plan was developed in response to insurance needs following the enactment of a financial responsibility law. In the 1960's, Fair Access to Insurance Requirements (FAIR) Plans were formed in response to insurance availability problems following property losses of catastrophic proportions from riots and civil disorders. In 1969, the first Beach or Windstorm Plan was formed to alleviate insurance availability problems in areas especially vulnerable to windstorm loss. In the mid–1970's, Joint Underwriting Associations (JUA's) were formed in response to medical malpractice insurance availability problems. And most recently, beginning in 1985, legislation authorizing the formation of Joint Underwriting Associations for certain classes of general liability insurance coverage was enacted. * * *

AUTOMOBILE LINES

Most states provide coverage for the automobile residual market through an Automobile Insurance Plan (AIP). An Automobile Insurance Plan is commonly referred to as an Assigned Risk Plan since, historically, coverage was provided for risks that could not obtain coverage in the voluntary market by assigning them to an insurance company. The Plan would assign applicants to an insurance company in proportion to that company's share of the voluntary market. The insurance company would then issue policies in its own name and perform all services, including paying claims, just as if the company wrote the policy voluntarily. Today, the assigned risk system is applicable in 42 jurisdictions to private passenger non-fleet classes. All jurisdictions provide liability coverage but most jurisdictions provide both liability and physical damage coverage. * * *

Besides the Automobile Insurance Plans, there are a number of different automobile residual market mechanisms currently in effect in various states. The two more common alternative mechanisms are the Joint Underwriting Association (JUA) and the Reinsurance Facility (RF).

A Joint Underwriting Association functions as a pooling mechanism whereby all companies share in the losses as well as the expenses incurred. Several companies agree to act as servicing carriers for the business insured by the JUA. Agents submit the policy applications to these servicing carriers, and the carriers issue and service the policies. All companies writing automobile business in the state are assessed (based on their voluntary market share) for their share of the underwriting losses on the JUA business plus the servicing costs and expenses of operating the JUA.

Under a Reinsurance Facility system, each automobile insurer is required to provide coverage and to service the claims for any applicant (i.e., "take all comers"), but is permitted to cede a percentage of its policies to the Facility. The Reinsurance Facility is considered a pooling mechanism like the JUA, but the key difference is that a JUA has a limited number of servicing carriers that write and service the residual business. As in the JUA, any losses on Facility business are shared equitably among all the automobile insurers in the state. Each company's assessment is based on its voluntary market share and its share of cessions to the Reinsurance Facility.

Last year, ISO released separate personal and commercial automobile circulars displaying information on residual market rate level deficits based on data through December 31, 1985. Where data were available, historical deficits were calculated as ratios to voluntary earned premium and as ratios to total voluntary and residual earned premium. The commercial automobile results have been updated using data through December 31, 1986. The deficits by line on a countrywide basis and for the five states with the greatest volume of AIP business and the highest deficits are shown on the next page. Also shown is the residual market volume as a percentage of the total premium volume.

	Deficit as % of Voluntary Premium	Deficit as % of Total Premium	Resid. Market Volume as % of Total Volume
Personal Automobile Liability			
Rhode Island	5.5%	4.8%	12.2%
New York	4.8	3.9	17.9
Connecticut	4.2	3.7	10.9
Pennsylvania	3.1	2.9	5.1
Delaware	2.8	2.7	5.7
Countrywide *	1.3	1.2	4.2
Commercial Automobile Liability			
New Jersey	10.0	7.4	25.2
New York	5.4	4.4	18.7
California	3.2	2.9	9.8
Rhode Island	2.6	2.2	15.1
Louisiana	1.7	1.4	13.1
Countrywide #	1.7	1.6	10.5

* Includes only states with an Automobile Insurance Plan

Excludes states where data are unavailable—Maryland, Massachusetts, North Carolina, South Carolina, Texas . . .

Several states do allow for recouping residual market deficits or shortfalls through a subsidy or recoupment mechanism. New York and Rhode Island have flat fees which are applicable to all personal automobile risks insured in the voluntary market. In New Jersey, flat fees are charged to commercial private passenger types as well as all personal automobile insureds purchasing uninsured motorists coverage. North Carolina and South Carolina have retrospective recoupments for Reinsurance Facility deficits. Effective July 1, 1988 in North Carolina, a portion of the recoupment is charged to "clean" personal automobile risks. As of July 1, 1988, Reinsurance Facility recoupment charges in South Carolina are allocated to all personal automobile risks on the basis of SDIP points. * * *

PROPERTY LINES

Fair Access to Insurance Requirements (FAIR) Plans were formed as a result of the riots and civil disorders that took place in many metropolitan areas during the 1960's. The FAIR Plans commonly write fire, extended coverage, vandalism or malicious mischief and, in some jurisdictions, crime, sprinkler leakage and homeowners coverage. Arkansas and Mississippi recently set up FAIR Plans that are considered limited territory plans since eligibility is limited to rural dwellings. Counting these limited plans, there are 31 jurisdictions in total that have set up a FAIR Plan.

Beach or Windstorm Plans were formed to provide coverage in designated coastal areas particularly subject to damage caused by hurricanes. There are currently 7 jurisdictions that have Beach Plans—Alabama, Florida, Louisiana, Mississippi, North Carolina, South Carolina and Texas. There is considerable variety among the Plans concerning coverage provided and eligible property. Most jurisdictions provide fire and extended coverage, but some only provide coverage for windstorm or hail. Homeowners coverage is available under one Plan only.

The Property Insurance Plans Service Office (PIPSO), a division of the National Committee on Property Insurance, collects data from the various state property residual market plans, with the exception of the Puerto Rico FAIR Plan. PIPSO prepares quarterly reports that summarize the experience of the FAIR and Beach Plans. A summary of the five year experience through calendar year 1987 of the FAIR and Beach Plans is shown below.

Five Year Totals (Calendar Years 1983–1987)

	Premiums Earned ($000)	Total Loss & LAE ($000)	Loss Ratio	Profit or (Loss) ($000)	Statutory Underwriting Ratio
FAIR Plans*	$1,109,999	$930,911	83.9%	$(144,626)	113.0%
Beach Plans	150,627	243,840	161.9	(153,157)	201.7

*Excludes Arkansas, Mississippi and Puerto Rico

The FAIR Plans that issue the greatest number of policies are Michigan, California, New York, Pennsylvania and New Jersey. The policy count and underwriting results for these Plans are indicated [below], along with comparable information for the 28 jurisdictions in total for which data are available.

	Policies Issued in 1987	5 Year Statutory Underwriting Ratio
Michigan	201,352	162.0%
California	129,205	81.7
New York	101,067	91.3
Pennsylvania	80,219	99.2
New Jersey	62,284	126.7
FAIR Plan Total*	913,041	113.0

*Excludes Arkansas, Mississippi and Puerto Rico. * * *

MEDICAL MALPRACTICE AND GENERAL LIABILITY

There are 13 Medical Malpractice Joint Underwriting Associations (JUA's) currently activated to write coverage in their respective jurisdictions. In addition, there are 3 JUA's that have stopped writing coverage but continue to pay claims—Maine, New Jersey and Ohio. At one time or another, 31 jurisdictions have authorized the operation of JUA's for writing medical malpractice insurance.

Of the 13 current Medical Malpractice JUA's, 3 were activated in 1986—Minnesota, Virginia and Puerto Rico. The remaining 10 Medical Malpractice JUA's—Florida, Kansas, Massachusetts, New Hampshire, New York, Pennsylvania, Rhode Island, South Carolina, Texas and Wisconsin—were activated in 1975 or 1976.

The JUA pooling mechanism concept as applied to medical malpractice insurance is the same as described earlier for the automobile lines. The coverage provided, participation, assessment base, deficit funding mechanism and recoupment provisions vary greatly for each JUA. Some provide coverage only for physicians, but most provide coverage for all health care providers and facilities.

As a deficit funding mechanism, many of the 13 jurisdictions have set up a Stabilization Reserve Fund funded by policyholder surcharges and insurer assessments. In terms of recoupments, some jurisdictions provide for a premium tax offset or credit for a percentage of the amount insurers are assessed, while some jurisdictions allow for prospective policyholder assessments. With the exception of Texas, no Medical Malpractice JUA had funded its deficit by insurer assessment. The Texas JUA has assessed insurers in two of the last three years after policyholder assessments (capped at 100% of current premium) did not raise sufficient funds to cover the deficits.

According to a recent study by the Alliance of American Insurers that was commissioned by the National Coordinating Committee on Medical Malpractice JUA's, 5 of the 10 JUA's activated by states in 1975 or 1976 have insufficient funds to pay all existing claims if operating income is not maintained. The JUA's in Massachusetts, New Hampshire, New York, Rhode Island and South Carolina could collapse due to insufficient funds if premiums or investment income level off. Recent JUA deficits in these states are set forth [below].

	Fiscal 1986 Deficit ($Million)	Fiscal 1985 Deficit ($Million)
Massachusetts	$365.3	$182.3
New York	132.5	4.4
Rhode Island	81.2	78.5
New Hampshire	6.3	10.3
South Carolina	3.5	4.1

The market shares of the Medical Malpractice JUA's are rather large. A comparison of the 1985 and 1986 market shares is shown below. Although the market shares did not change significantly for most states, the JUA's in Florida, New York and Wisconsin almost doubled their market share from 1985 to 1986.

	1986 Market Share	1985 Market Share
Florida	10.5%	5.5%
Kansas	3.1	3.8
Massachusetts	69.0	73.0
New Hampshire	53.2	56.1
New York	21.6	12.5
Pennsylvania	3.4	3.2
Rhode Island	82.6	87.4
South Carolina	47.0	52.4
Texas	13.2	11.8
Wisconsin	34.8	20.7

The data from the JUA's are used in ratemaking for the ISO medical malpractice manual rates. Each JUA makes its own filing and sets its own rate structure.

Many states in the last three years have enacted laws allowing formation of Commercial Liability JUA's for specific classes of business where there have been insurance availability problems. Many were set up to handle problem classes such as day care, nurses-midwives, liquor stores and local governments or municipalities.

To date, 28 states have set up standby authority or activated a Liability JUA. The five activated Liability JUA's and their activation dates are—Maryland (6/9/86), Massachusetts (10/29/85), Minnesota (3/25/86), Oklahoma (5/15/86) and Washington (7/1/86). Two of these five JUA's—Oklahoma and Washington—have no provision addressing deficit funding in the enabling statute. The Maryland JUA allows for surcharges of all commercial liability policyholders to fund any deficits. The Massachusetts JUA allows for policyholder assessments and prospective rate increases, while the Minnesota JUA relies on a Stabilization Reserve Fund as a deficit funding mechanism. * * *

Notes and Questions

1. *The Purpose of Residual Market Mechanisms.* Residual market mechanisms tend to be formed in response to acute shortages of coverage for those whom these mechanisms are designed to serve. The mechanisms then continue to operate or to stand ready to be called upon during the next acute shortage. If one believed that in a properly functioning market coverage will generally be available to any potential purchaser at some price, then residual market mechanisms can be understood in one of two ways. On the one hand, they may constitute an effort to force insurers to offer coverage at prices below what they would charge in the absence of such mechanisms. Thus, if driving is considered such a necessity of life that no one should be forced to pay more than (for example) $2000 per year for minimum limits auto liability insurance, then a ceiling can be placed on the charge for such coverage made by the assigned risk plans that insure high-risk drivers rejected by the primary market. Under this view, it is no surprise that residual market mechanisms show deficits, since in a sense that is precisely what they are designed to do.

On the other hand, the creation of residual market mechanisms might be seen as a response to structural deficiencies in the market— the arbitrariness of auto insurers' risk classification decisions, periodic overcautiousness by companies writing small-volume lines such as medical malpractice, or suspected conspiracy among insurers to make coverage unavailable in order to provoke tort reform. Under this view, residual market mechanisms combat these structural imperfections in the market by forcing insurers to write coverage at a fair price. Deficits must then be interpreted as the product of either excessive regulatory constraints on rates, or improper management of the mechanism by the state or insurer-sponsored entity charged with this responsibility.

2. *Deficit Recoupment.* Deficits can be made up in a variety of ways. In auto insurance, all other risk drivers may be surcharged, directly or indirectly, to correct for the subsidy that runs to those in the assigned-risk pool. In medical malpractice and commercial liability JUA's, participating insurers in many states are permitted to surcharge policyholders in other lines, or to take a credit for their share of any deficit against future premium taxes owed to the state. Which approach seems most appropriate? What does your answer imply about the view you take concerning who should bear the ultimate responsibility for assuring the affordability of each form of coverage?

B. SURPLUS AND EXCESS LINES

In most states a two-tiered private insurance market exists. All insurance companies licensed to do business in the state operate in what is known as the *admitted market*. These companies are subject to state regulation and are authorized to sell coverage under the terms and conditions of that regulatory regime. Alongside stands the *non-admitted market,* composed of surplus and excess line insurers that are not licensed, and are permitted to do business in the state only when a prospective purchaser is unable to obtain coverage from an insurer in the admitted market. Obviously, the purchaser who is relegated to the non-admitted market does not receive the same kinds of protections available when she purchases from a licensed insurer. Rates in the non-admitted market are unregulated; policy provisions are unscrutinized; solvency assurance and guaranty fund protection are unavailable. Of course, unregulated insurance may well be preferable to none at all, which is the alternative in such situations.

Although purchasers in the non-admitted market are not afforded traditional regulatory protections, some minimal effort to provide indirect protection sometimes is made. For example, in New York, where a high volume of insurance is sold and regulated, a typical applicant can purchase coverage from the non-admitted market only through a licensed surplus-lines broker, only if the broker certifies that the coverage cannot be obtained from the admitted market, and even then only from unlicensed insurers on an approved list. See N.Y.Ins.Law § 2118(b)(1)–(3). Direct purchase without a broker is extremely difficult, because unlicensed insurers are prohibited from doing business within the state even by mail from outside it. Thus, in theory the insured would have to travel out of state to purchase coverage directly. As a consequence, the surplus-lines broker becomes a key intermediary in obtaining coverage from the non-admitted market, and may engage in at least some monitoring of the quality and solvency of individual insurers operating in that market.

C. REINSURANCE

Reinsurance is an agreement between two or more insurers, whereby all or part of the risk of loss under an insurance policy or policies sold by one is transferred to the other. The insurer selling the initial policy is termed the *ceding insurer;* the insurer to whom the ceding insurer transfers some or all of the risk assumed under the initial policy is termed the *reinsurer.* Some reinsurers specialize, sometimes exclusively, in reinsurance; these companies are known as *professional reinsurers.* Other reinsurers are primary insurers who sell reinsurance as a more or less minor part of their business.

Reinsurance is a device by which insurance companies diversify their risk. Such diversification may include protection against unexpected frequency of losses, unexpected severity, or both. By diversifying risk through the purchase of reinsurance, an insurer also can increase its underwriting capacity, since the reserves it must maintain to cover potential losses are reduced. Consequently, the proportion of a company's book of business that it reinsures is likely to vary from line to line, depending on the volume of business it does in a given line and the volatility of losses in the line. For example, commercial liability and medical malpractice insurance tend to be more heavily reinsured, other things being equal, than auto property damage insurance. Reinsurers themselves sometimes need to diversify their own risks; the process by which they reinsure is known as *retrocession.* Reinsurance and sometimes several subsequent retrocessions are a means by which the risk undertaken by primary insurers is diversified widely into the global financial markets.

Reinsurance tends to be custom-made; there are no form policies or rates. The varieties of reinsurance therefore are manifold. There are, however, general categories into which different types of reinsurance tend to fall. When coverage is specifically arranged to reinsure a particular risk or policy, it is known as *facultative* reinsurance. When coverage applies to a specified type or portion of a primary insurer's business in advance, it is *treaty* reinsurance. In the latter case (and sometimes the former) the document memorializing the parties' agreement is called a treaty rather than a policy. In both facultative and treaty reinsurance, the risks reinsured may be transferred in a variety of ways: in some specified proportion between the ceding insurer and the reinsurer (*proportional* reinsurance), or above a specified retained limit (*excess-of-loss* reinsurance). For more detailed discussion, see R. Strain (ed.), Reinsurance (1980).

In many ways the rules that govern reinsurance are more lore than law. There are few statutes or judicial decisions governing reinsurance, in part because the duty of *utmost good faith* that is said to run between the parties discourages litigation, and also because any disputes that do occur traditionally have been resolved in binding arbitration. That situation may be changing in the 1990's, however, in part as a result of the entry of non-traditional companies into the reinsurance market a decade earlier. For example, the number of stock reinsurance companies doing business in the United States increased from 62 in 1974 to 147 in 1981. See Stewart, Profit Cycles in Property–Casualty Insurance, in E. Randall (ed.), 2 Issues in Insurance 111, 161 n. 22 (1987). In addition, the huge sums that are at stake once primary layers of coverage for mass toxic tort liability are pierced and excess-of-loss reinsurance comes into play may prompt reinsurers to litigate issues that would have been settled or arbitrated in the past. The cases that follow address some of the more salient issues in reinsurance law.

1. The Duty of Utmost Good Faith

OLD RELIABLE FIRE INSURANCE COMPANY v. CASTLE REINSURANCE COMPANY, LIMITED

United States Court of Appeals, Eighth Circuit, 1981.
665 F.2d 239.

STEPHENSON, Circuit Judge.

Defendant Castle Reinsurance Co., Ltd. (Castle) appeals the judgment of the district court awarding plaintiff Old Reliable Fire Insurance Co. (Old Reliable) $541,311 in its diversity, breach of contract case. The court also denied Castle relief on its third-party complaint against J.H. Minet & Co., Ltd. (Minet). Appellant Castle contends that many of the fact findings concerning Castle's acceptance of a line in Old Reliable's reinsurance treaty are clearly erroneous. Castle also attacks several conclusions of law by arguing that the industry customs and the contractual promises made by Old Reliable support a denial of relief. We affirm the district court.

I. BACKGROUND

Old Reliable, a Missouri corporation with its principal place of business in Webster Groves, Missouri, is an underwriter of property-casualty insurance. In mid–1975, Old Reliable became interested in using a quota share treaty to reinsure a portion of the insurance risks that it had underwritten. The company wanted to retain forty percent and cede sixty percent to reinsurers. Old Reliable contacted Adrian N. Baker Reinsurance, Inc. (Baker Reinsurance) for assistance in placing a quota share treaty. Old Reliable supplied Baker Reinsurance with the underwriting information, documents and exhibits necessary for treaty placement. Old Reliable also informed Baker that it was taking steps to improve underwriting through its objectives of tightening underwriting procedures, using inspection reports to insure to value and having automatic increases in appraised value at renewal.

On September 10, 1975, Baker Reinsurance sent a letter to Minet, a London, England corporation, requesting it to act as a broker for placing the Old Reliable reinsurance treaty in the overseas market. Along with the letter, Baker Reinsurance sent information describing the proposed treaty and copies of relevant sections of Best's Annual Reports. Best's is a private company that does financial ratings on every property and casualty insurance company in the United States.

Minet took an active role in placing the treaty. First, Minet attempted to place the treaty in the Lloyd's market but was unsuccessful. Minet then attempted to place and did, in fact, place portions of the treaty in the London market and with overseas reinsurers.[1]

One of the overseas reinsurers that accepted a line on the treaty was Castle. In the fall of 1975, a Minet broker, Mr. Fettroll, met with Mr. Searle, an underwriter for Indemnity Guarantee Assurance, Ltd. (IGA). IGA is a subsidiary of Castle and Mr. Kaplan, the managing director of Castle, shared office space with IGA. Mr. Searle declined to accept a line on the treaty for IGA but indicated that Mr. Kaplan might be interested in taking a line on the treaty for Castle. Mr. Searle discussed that possibility with Mr. Kaplan and then informed Mr. Fettroll that Castle was interested in a ten percent line, but it wanted a change in the commission procedure. Several days later, Mr. Kaplan agreed to drop Castle's request for a different commission procedure and agreed to a ten percent line of the treaty on behalf of Castle. In a letter to Minet dated November 14, 1975, Castle confirmed its acceptance of a ten percent share.

On July 5, 1976, Mr. Thirkill, Castle's chief underwriter signed the treaty accepting a ten percent line. The treaty was in effect from July 1, 1975, through December 31, 1976.

At the beginning of the treaty, Castle received premium money from its investment. The treaty later became a losing proposition and Castle refused to pay its portion of the losses. On November 22, 1978, Old Reliable instituted this breach of contract action against Castle to recover Castle's portion of the treaty losses. Castle responded by asserting a third-party complaint against Minet and by arguing that Minet and Old Reliable induced Castle to enter into the treaty through false misrepresentations and omissions. Additionally, Castle contended that Old Reliable breached part of its contractual duties and that Minet negligently misrepresented the treaty to Castle.

After a trial to the court, the court ruled that Castle owed Old Reliable $541,322 for breaching the contract. *Old Reliable Fire Insurance Co. v. Castle Reinsurance Co.,* 507 F.Supp. 46, 50 (E.D.Mo.1981). The court determined that the actions of Old Reliable and Minet conformed to the usual practices of the industry and did not amount to fraudulent or negligent misrepresentations or omissions. Also, the court determined that Old Reliable had not breached contractual promises to Castle. *Id.* at 49.

1. Contrary to Castle's arguments, the court's finding that Minet utilized the information supplied by Baker Reinsurance in its discussions of the proposed reinsurance with various underwriters is supported by substantial evidence and is not clearly erroneous.

II.　ANALYSIS

A.　*Describing the Insurance to Be Reinsured*

Castle argues that the district court erred in concluding that "[i]n the insurance industry, and in the London market in particular, automobile physical damage risk is properly described as 'property business.'" *See Old Reliable Fire Insurance Co. v. Castle Reinsurance Co., supra,* 507 F.Supp. at 49. A related claim is Castle's contention that the court erred in stating that "[t]he portfolio to be reinsured by the Treaty was in fact 'approximately 65% property and 35% casualty.'" *Id.*

Our review of the above fact finding is limited by the clearly erroneous rule. Fed.R.Civ.P. 52(a). *See McCluskey v. Board of Education,* 662 F.2d 1263 (1981). Substantial evidence supports both findings of the trial court. The managing director of the North America Treaty Division of Minet in 1975, Mr. Fundell, testified that it is customary to treat automobile physical damage as property insurance. An experienced underwriter with John Poland and Company, Mr. Theobald, testified that automobile physical damage belongs in the property account. Mr. Thorvaldsson, the managing director of Trygging, an Iceland reinsurance company, stated that automobile physical damage should certainly be classified as property. Although two Castle employees testified to the contrary, this court must give due regard "to the opportunity of the trial court to judge the credibility of the witnesses." *Kendrick v. Commission of Zoological Subdistrict,* 565 F.2d 524, 526 (8th Cir.1977). The finding of fact that automobile physical damage is properly described as property is not clearly erroneous. Since Castle's argument regarding the court's finding that the treaty was approximately 65% property and 35% casualty depends upon automobile physical damage being excluded from property, that finding of fact is likewise not clearly erroneous.[2] * * *

C.　*Customs in Placing Reinsurance Treaties*

The district court found that "[b]y custom and practice in the reinsurance industry, and in the London market in particular, the usual and customary practice of underwriters is to ask questions and seek additional information from brokers when they have questions concerning potential business." *Old Reliable Fire Insurance Co. v. Castle Reinsurance Co., supra,* 507 F.Supp. at 49. Although Castle argues that this is erroneous, the finding is supported by the testimony of four different witnesses. Mr. Fettroll testified that it was the custom for brokers to put information about the proposed transaction in summary form. Then the normal procedure was for the underwriters to question the broker and the broker would answer the questions. In

---

2. Castle also challenges the court's fact findings that the telex and the placing slip prepared by Minet outlined the salient terms of the proposed reinsurance. Both documents are summaries of the terms of the treaty, both indicate that the treaty includes automobile business and both cover the significant aspects of the treaty. The court's findings are not clearly erroneous.

a proposed treaty where automobile is listed as part of the business, Mr. Fettroll stated that the underwriter would ask what proportion of the business was automobile if he was interested in knowing that.

Mr. Fundell testified that in the insurance brokering business there are often very extensive oral discussions and that the underwriter would normally ask questions. He pointed out that sometimes the insurance broker has to contact his client to get more information so that the underwriter's questions can be answered. He stated that one would reasonably expect the underwriter to ask questions regarding the treaty lines. For example, if automobile is listed as a line, the underwriter would question whether that involved automobile physical damage or liability or both.

Mr. Theobald, an experienced underwriter, testified that placing reinsurance is a team concept with a broker coming to see the underwriter and presenting his information and the underwriter asking questions so that the two professionals can arrive at a satisfactory conclusion. He further stated that if he saw automobile listed as part of the lines covered, he would want to determine whether it was physical or liability and whether it was commercial or private automobile.

Mr. Searle testified that if a treaty proposal indicated automobile coverage, he would want more details before deciding whether to accept a line so he would check Best's for information and then question the broker to obtain information more current than that contained in Best's. Mr. Searle also stated, after reviewing the telex in this case, that he would have questioned the broker and checked Best's to find out the automobile content of the business.

As indicated by the above testimony, substantial evidence supports the court's finding that the customary practice includes an underwriter asking questions in order to gain additional information regarding the proposed reinsurance business.

Two related conclusions of law challenged by Castle are that "[t]he actions of Mr. Kaplan in accepting the 10% line in the Treaty on behalf of Castle without substantial inquiry past the Telex were not in accordance with the usual and customary practices within the industry" and that "[t]he acts and representations of Minet with respect to the placing of the Treaty with Castle were in conformity with the usual and customary practices within the industry and did not amount to fraudulent or negligent misrepresentations or omissions." See *Old Reliable Fire Insurance Co. v. Castle Reinsurance Co., supra,* 507 F.Supp. at 49. Castle argues that the standard of utmost good faith applicable to brokers required Minet to specifically tell Kaplan the amount of the automobile content in the treaty.

As previously discussed, Minet utilized information from Baker Reinsurance and Old Reliable to prepare, as was customary, a placing slip and a telex which contained all the salient terms of the proposed reinsurance. See n. 2, *supra.* These documents both indicated that automobile was included in the treaty and the telex appropriately characterized automobile physical damage risk as property business therefore stating that the portfolio to be reinsured was approximately sixty-five percent property and thirty-five percent casualty. There is no fraudulent misrepresentation of the portfolio in these documents.

Minet presented the documents to Mr. Kaplan in the usual and customary manner and did not misrepresent the treaty to Mr. Kaplan. Mr. Fettroll, the Minet broker, was available to answer any questions Mr. Kaplan felt were necessary to ask regarding the treaty. Mr. Kaplan testified that Mr. Fettroll answered every question asked but that he did not question Mr. Fettroll about the automobile portion of the treaty. Two experienced underwriters, Mr. Searle and Mr. Theobald, testified that if they had been presented with the same telex, they would have asked questions regarding the automobile portion of the treaty. Further, Mr. Kaplan admitted that according to the assumptions he was relying upon, as much as thirty-five percent of the treaty could have been automobile business. Although Mr. Kaplan's own reinsurance treaty expressly excluded automobile business, he asked no questions regarding the automobile content, did not consult Best's reports and merely "assumed" the automobile content was minimal. He made this assumption despite the fact that he had the entire Minet broking file available to him. We agree with the district court that Mr. Kaplan's actions of accepting a portion of the treaty without substantial inquiry were not in accord with industry customs.

We also agree that Minet's actions do not amount to fraudulent or negligent omissions. The slip and telex are only a summary of the proposal and both clearly state that automobile is a portion of the business. None of the lines of the business listed include a percent figure regarding the proportion of that particular line. In light of the customs of the industry and because these documents are only a summary of the business and they disclose the nature of the business, we cannot agree with Castle that Minet breached its duty of good faith by failing to list the automobile percentage of the business.

D. *Policy Goals*

The district court concluded that "[t]he expressed policy goals of Old Reliable to 1) tighten its underwriting procedures, 2) require policy holders to insure to value, and 3) force policy holders to increase the value of their policies by 30% on renewal did not amount to contractual promises to Castle as part of the quota share Treaty." *Old Reliable Fire Insurance Co. v. Castle Reinsurance Co., supra,* 507 F.Supp. at 49. Castle contends that the above three items, which were set forth in the *telex,* should be deemed binding provisions of the reinsurance treaty.

The president of Old Reliable at the time of this treaty testified that these statements were not promises to the reinsurers but were objectives of the company to improve underwriting in the future. The telex paragraph setting out the goals begins: "In line with general USA trend company is further tightening underwriting procedures with emphasis being placed upon * * *." That language certainly does not indicate any promise on behalf of Old Reliable, but instead describes the areas of underwriting which the company hopes to improve. The court did not err in concluding that the statements regarding underwriting procedures were not contractual promises.

We have examined Castle's other arguments challenging the district court's decision that Castle failed to sustain its affirmative defenses, its counterclaims and third-party complaint and we find them unconvincing. We affirm the district court's judgment awarding Old Reliable $541,322 plus interest against Castle.

Affirmed.

Notes and Questions

1. *The Context of the Transaction.* It is common practice for a reinsurer to accept a "line" on a treaty, i.e., to agree to reinsure a portion of the total package of risks the insurer wishes reinsured. This process, especially when reinsurance is being placed overseas, often necessitates use of a reinsurance broker or brokers, as in *Old Reliable.* The duty of the parties to exercise the "utmost good faith" in dealing with each other is partly a residue of the practices that grew out of Lloyds Coffee House in earlier centuries. One of the key elements of that duty is the obligation to make full disclosure of the character of the risks being transferred. The duty of utmost good faith in reinsurance thus resonates with the strict enforcement of insurance warranties that also prevailed during the period when the duty was evolving.

The duty probably would not have survived into modern times, however, if it had not continued to be useful. With the growth of international reinsurance and the geographical separation of the parties to a reinsurance treaty that accompanied this growth in the twentieth century, the duty may have been an effective method of avoiding the production of cumbersome, detailed contractual agreements at long distances. In light of the facts of *Old Reliable,* did that decision accord the duty of utmost good faith as much importance as the reinsurance community has a right to expect? Should the court have felt as comfortable as it apparently did upholding the trial court's factual findings about customs in London governing situations in which disputes are normally arbitrated by experts who have direct experience with these customs?

2. *Demise of the Duty?* As more and more insurers and reinsurers enter the field, a customary "duty" that can cement relations among a relatively small group of continuously interacting enterprises may lose strength. The increased possibility of nearly instantaneous electronic transfer of lengthy documents across the globe also may tend to obviate the need for such a duty. Should the courts hasten the decline of the duty to exercise the utmost good faith by applying standard misrepre-

sentation law to disputes over customary reinsurance obligations, as the court in *Old Reliable* apparently did?

3. *The Consequences of Breach.* Just as American courts may pay less attention to the duty of utmost good faith than traditional reinsurance practice might require, they may also invoke less stringent remedies when they do find the duty to have been breached. For example, in *Security Mutual Casualty Company v. Century Casualty Company,* 531 F.2d 974 (10th Cir.1976), the court found that the ceding insurer had breached an obligation under a reinsurance treaty to provide the reinsurer with notice of all claims reserved in excess of the ceding insurer's retained liability. But the court went on to hold that because the obligation to provide notice was a mere "covenant" in the reinsurance agreement rather than a condition precedent to coverage, the reinsurer was not entitled to void the treaty, but only to recover any damages it suffered as a result of the breach. To what extent does this holding import what amounts to the contribute-to-loss standard found in some state warranty statutes into reinsurance transactions?

2. "Follow-the-Fortunes" Clauses

AMERICAN INSURANCE COMPANY v. NORTH AMERICAN COMPANY FOR PROPERTY AND CASUALTY INSURANCE

United States Court of Appeals, Second Circuit, 1982.
697 F.2d 79.

NEWMAN, Circuit Judge.

Plaintiff American Insurance Company (AIC) appeals from a March 4, 1982, judgment of the United States District Court for the Southern District of New York (Henry F. Werker, Judge) entered in favor of defendant North American Company for Property and Casualty Insurance (NACPAC). After a bench trial, the District Court found that NACPAC was not required under its agreement with AIC to reimburse AIC for any part of a settlement AIC made on behalf of Dow Chemical Company.

During the 1970's, AIC insured Dow Chemical Company for all damages that Dow became legally obliged to pay. In 1974, NACPAC agreed to reinsure part of AIC's risk and assumed responsibility for a layer of liability between $250,000 and $500,000 per damage award. On July 15, 1977, a Minnesota state court jury awarded $146,970 of compensatory damages and $750,000 of punitive damages against Dow for damages caused by a fire in a building insulated with Styrofoam, a Dow product. While the Minnesota award was on appeal, AIC agreed to settle a number of Styrofoam cases, including the Minnesota case, for $1.2 million. Of that settlement, $500,000 was allocated to the Minnesota case. AIC then requested that NACPAC honor its reinsurance policy and reimburse AIC for $250,000 of the Minnesota award. When NACPAC refused, AIC brought this suit.

In the District Court, <u>NACPAC</u> defended on the ground that AIC's <u>insurance policy with Dow (and therefore NACPAC's reinsurance agreement</u> with AIC) did not cover punitive damages assessed to punish <u>corporate officials for intentional misconduct.</u> According to NACPAC, the Minnesota jury had awarded punitive damages against Dow for deliberate corporate misbehavior, and consequently most of AIC's Minnesota settlement had compensated Dow for damages excluded from the insurance and reinsurance policies. <u>NACPAC claimed that the part of the settlement attributable to compensatory damages, which was the only part covered by NACPAC's policy, was less than $250,000; NACPAC therefore had no duty to reimburse AIC for any portion of the</u> settlement. The District Court accepted NACPAC's interpretation of AIC's insurance policy with Dow, and also agreed that NACPAC owed nothing to AIC under the reinsurance agreement.

On this appeal, AIC challenges the District Court's interpretation of the AIC–Dow insurance policy. The District Court had concluded that, although the policy itself was ambiguous, evidence introduced as to the intent of the parties supported NACPAC's view that punitive damages awarded for corporate misconduct were not covered. AIC now claims that the District Court did not give enough weight to evidence suggesting that Dow may have thought the agreement covered these punitive damages.

If our consideration of the matter were confined to the terms of the policy, we might not share the District Court's view that there was sufficient ambiguity concerning the meaning of the term "damages" to permit examination of extrinsic evidence of the intentions of AIC and Dow. Nor would we necessarily think that there was sufficient ambiguity in the phrase of the policy's definition of "occurrence" that refers to "damage not intended from the standpoint of the insured." But however we might view the bare terms of the policy, <u>the record discloses additional circumstances that support the District Court's ultimate conclusion that the punitive damages awarded in the Minnesota litigation were not within the policy's coverage.</u> The parties in this litigation have stipulated that on December 15, 1971, plaintiff issued a memorandum "that, since that date, has governed the circumstances in which plaintiff would be liable to its insureds for punitive damages when the liability policy was itself silent on the question." The stipulation further provides that by the end of 1973 Dow and its insurance broker "agreed that the Dow Policy would contain no reference to insurance of punitive or exemplary damages. Instead, [the broker] accepted, on Dow's behalf, plaintiff's proposal that the Dow Policy be interpreted according to the terms of the [December 15, 1971,] Memorandum." That memorandum makes clear <u>that coverage for punitive damages will be provided, unless prohibited by local public policy, only when the insured is "vicariously assessed with punitive damages but did not itself direct or ratify the offending act"</u> and will not be provided for punitive damages assessed because the insured "has itself performed, directed or ratified the offending act." The record adequately supports Judge Werker's finding that the punitive damages assessed by the Minnesota jury fell within the category of punitive damages for which the AIC–Dow policy, as supplemented by the December 15, 1971, memorandum, did not provide coverage.

AIC also claims that, even if the AIC–Dow policy excluded the Minnesota punitive damage award, the reinsurance agreement's "follow the fortunes" clause obliges NACPAC to reimburse AIC for its settlement on behalf of Dow. That clause provides, "All claims involving this reinsurance, when settled by the company, shall be binding on the reinsurer. * * *" According to AIC, "follow the fortunes" clauses are designed to force reinsurers like NACPAC to reimburse companies like AIC when they decide to enter into a settlement like the $500,000 settlement reached in the Minnesota case. NACPAC claims that "follow the fortune" clauses bind the reinsurer only when the reinsured settles a claim covered by the underlying policy, but not when the reinsurer makes *ex gratia* payments outside the scope of that policy. *See Insurance Co. of North America v. United States Fire Insurance Co.,* 67 Misc.2d 7, 322 N.Y.S.2d 520 (Sup.Ct.1971), *aff'd,* 42 A.D.2d 1056, 348 N.Y.S.2d 122 (1st Dep't 1973); 13A J. Appleman & J. Appleman, *Insurance Law and Practice* § 7698, at 556 (1976) ("despite a 'follow the fortune clause,' the reinsurer is only liable for a loss of the kind reinsured").

This disagreement between AIC and NACPAC reflects the inherent tension between "follow the fortune" clauses and limitations on the liability of reinsurers. In some cases in which there is genuine ambiguity over what a settlement covers, a "follow the fortunes" clause may oblige a reinsurer to contribute to a settlement even though it might encompass excluded items. AIC claims that such an ambiguity exists in this case. It contends that it entered into a settlement not because of the Minnesota jury's award of punitive damages, but for a variety of valid business reasons, including a fear that the compensatory damage award might be increased as a result of the appeal. On the facts of this case, we reject AIC's claim. It is clear that the settlement here was primarily designed to compensate Dow for a punitive damage award that is excluded from the reinsurance policy. As the District Court found, the settlement did not compensate Dow for insured risks in an amount greater than $250,000. Under these circumstances, it would be unfair to NACPAC to hold it liable for damages beyond the scope of its policy. * * *

The judgment of the District Court is affirmed.

Notes and Questions

1. *The Relation Between Duties.* Was the *NACPAC* court's interpretation of the follow-the-fortunes clause in the AIC–NACPAC treaty merely an application of the ceding insurer's duty to exercise the utmost good faith, or something more? For example, suppose that the facts in NACPAC had warranted the conclusion that AIC had indeed

settled the case in order to avoid liability for a larger award of compensatory damages upon retrial. Would the same result have been appropriate?

2. *A Duty to Settle?* Suppose that the plaintiff in the suit against DOW had offered to settle the case before trial for $249,000 compensatory damages, AIC rejected the offer, and the jury brought in a verdict against DOW for $500,000 compensatory damages. Would NACPAC owe AIC $250,000? What more would you want to know in order to answer the question?

3. *Avoiding the Problem.* If you were counsel to AIC in cases like *NACPAC,* would you advise that there be consultation with your reinsurers before settlement of claims covered in whole or in part by a reinsurance treaty, regardless of whether the treaty expressly required such consultation?

3. Insolvency Clauses

AINSWORTH v. GENERAL REINSURANCE CORPORATION

United States Court of Appeals, Eighth Circuit, 1985.
751 F.2d 962.

FAIRCHILD, Senior Circuit Judge.

This is an appeal from a judgment holding a reinsurer (General Reinsurance Corporation) liable to the receiver of an insolvent insurance company (Medallion) for the reinsured amount of insured liability, under a so-called insolvency clause of a reinsurance agreement. Federal court jurisdiction is based on diversity, and the parties agree that the law of Missouri governs substantive questions.

I

On January 1, 1971, General Reinsurance entered into Agreement of Reinsurance No. 4191 with Medallion and its subsidiaries, among them Consolidated Underwriters. In late 1972, Medallion assumed all assets and liabilities of Consolidated Underwriters.

Medallion subsequently experienced financial difficulties. On September 12, 1975, the companies were formally declared insolvent and ordered liquidated by the Circuit Court of Jackson County, Missouri. In the present action Medallion's court appointed Receiver recovered for liability incurred by two companies insured by Consolidated Underwriters: Pittsburgh and New England Trucking Company ("P & NE") and B–K Cattle Company ("B–K"). The liabilities arose out of accidents involving company trucks. The parties agree that these accidents constitute "loss occurrences" covered under Agreement of Reinsurance No. 4191 and the insured liabilities remained unpaid at the time Medallion was declared insolvent.

Article IX of the Agreement of Reinsurance, the insolvency clause, provided as follows:

> In the event of the insolvency of the Company the reinsurance afforded by this Agreement shall be payable by the Reinsurer on the basis of the liability of the Company under the policy or policies reinsured, without diminution because of such insolvency, directly to the Company or its liquidator, receiver or statutory successor. The Reinsurer shall be given written notice of the pendency of each claim or loss which may involve the reinsurance afforded by this Agreement within a reasonable time after such claim or loss is filed in the insolvency proceedings. The Reinsurer shall have the right to investigate each such claim or loss and interpose, at its own expense, in the proceeding where the claim or loss is to be adjudicated, any defense which it may deem available to the Company or its liquidator, receiver or statutory successor. The expense thus incurred by the Reinsurer shall be chargeable subject to Court approval against the insolvent Company as part of the expense of liquidation to the extent of a proportionate share of the benefit which may accrue to the Company solely as a result of the defense undertaken by the Reinsurer.

It is clear that this clause was inserted in response to a Missouri statute, § 375.246 RSMo, requiring, similarly to law in many states, that reinsurance must not be treated as an asset or deduction from liability of an insurance company unless the reinsurance is payable "without diminution because of the insolvency of the ceding company."

A. P & NE Loss

On December 9, 1974, plaintiffs Ernest and Alice Nemeth won a jury verdict and money judgment against P & NE in the amount of $485,000 for personal injuries and damages suffered in an accident in West Virginia. Following notice of the insolvency, P & NE sought payment of the judgment from Medallion's Receiver and General Reinsurance. Attorneys for General Reinsurance responded in a March 12, 1976 letter that:

> The commissioner of claims and the attorney for Medallion Insurance Company has taken the position that the reinsurance assets belong to the receiver for the benefit of general creditors and that my client, General Reinsurance Corporation, cannot legally make payments to any claimant or insurer.

> Because of the position taken by the attorney for the receiver and the commissioner of claims and the agreement of the reinsurance treaty, we are certainly not in a position to make any payment to the plaintiff or to your client in this suit.

The attorneys again wrote P & NE in April 1976 that:

> [I]t appears to General Reinsurance that the agreement does not provide any means, method, nor language which

would warrant payment to you and your client of any sums claimed by your client by reason of judgment or otherwise. The language of the reinsurance agreement seems clear. It would appear that our obligation is solely to the representatives of Medallion Insurance Company, now in receivership.

The position taken in these letters is clearly consistent with Article IX, the insolvency clause, and the underlying statutory requirement. Changing its position, however, General Reinsurance later negotiated and paid the Nemeths and P & NE $25,000 for a release discharging Medallion and its Receiver from all liability arising out of the accident. The Receiver did not participate in the negotiations or settlement of the P & NE case.

The district court concluded that the liability of P & NE to the Nemeths, insured up to policy limits by Consolidated (and Medallion), gave rise to a right of Medallion to proceeds of reinsurance and that such right vested in the Receiver when Medallion was declared insolvent. General Reinsurance was without authority to negotiate a settlement altering that right. In accordance with this holding, the court awarded the Receiver $89,557.53, plus interest from the date of insolvency.[1]

B. B–K Loss

The other loss occurrence concerned a 1972 accident in Texas involving a B–K truck. Plaintiffs in that suit agreed to a court-approved settlement of $85,000 on December 28, 1976. The Texas ancillary receiver of Medallion paid $50,000; B–K contributed $10,000; and B–K's excess insurance carrier contributed $25,000.

General Reinsurance made a payment to the Receiver, apparently on the theory that the settlement determined $50,000 as the amount of insured liability, General's payment represented $50,000, less the amount of retention, and other adjustments not relevant to the issue in this case. Although the Receiver originally contended that the appropriate amount of insured liability was $100,000, the policy limit, he ultimately conceded that the settlement determined liability at $85,000, and claimed that amount less the amount of retention. The district court entered judgment reflecting the latter theory.

II

The insolvency clause appears to require that when the insurer becomes insolvent the reinsurer's obligation with respect to an outstanding liability insured by the insurer becomes an asset of the insolvency estate. The amount of the obligation is not to be diminished because of the insolvency. The central issue in this case is whether the

---

1. Medallion's policy limit on liability to P & NE was $100,000 plus interest. The retention under the reinsurance agreement was $25,000. The award above represents General's $75,000 exposure plus interest and expenses, and the amount was to be disputed before the district court or on appeal.

reinsurer may reduce or eliminate its obligation by making a settlement directly with the insured and those to whom the insured is liable. General Reinsurance would contend that because the direct settlement discharges the liability of the insurer, fully in a case like P & NE or partially in a case like B–K, and obviates any determination of a claim of liability in the insolvency proceeding, General's obligation is similarly discharged. We think the result contended for is inconsistent with the insolvency clause. It seems very clear that the payment has not been made directly to the Receiver, that the reinsurance has been diminished because of the insolvency, and the obligation of the reinsurer has ceased to be an asset of the insolvent estate.

Clearly the reinsurer has a right to defend against a claim on its merits, but is not given a right to reduce its obligation by taking advantage of the willingness of the insured and the insured's obligee to take less because of the insolvency.

We begin with the general principle that the beneficiary of the reinsurance agreement is usually the insurer (the reinsured) and not the insured under Missouri law. "An ordinary contract of reinsurance, in the absence of provisions to the contrary, operates solely as between the reinsurer and the reinsured. It creates no privity between the original insured and the reinsurer." *First National Bank of Kansas City v. Higgins,* 357 S.W.2d 139, 142 (Mo.1962) (quoting *O'Hare v. Pursell,* 329 S.W.2d 614, 620 (Mo.1959)). "[T]he liability of the reinsuring company is solely to the reinsured company, or to its receiver in the event of its insolvency." *Higgins,* 357 S.W.2d at 143. The only exception to this general rule occurs when the reinsurance contract is "drawn in such form and with such provisions so as to create a liability on the part of the reinsurer directly to the original insured." *Higgins,* 357 S.W.2d at 143. Contrary to General Reliance's assertions, this exception is inapplicable to the Agreement of Reinsurance No. 4191. The same agreement of reinsurance has been considered by Chief Judge Oliver of the same district court, and by this court on appeal. In *General Reinsurance Corp. v. Missouri Gen. Ins.,* 458 F.Supp. 1 (W.D.Mo. 1977), there was a claim to reinsurance proceeds upon a theory that a claimant is a third-party beneficiary of the reinsurance agreement. Agreements in some forms have been held in Missouri to create such a right. In rejecting the theory, Judge Oliver emphasized the clarity of the requirement of this agreement that the proceeds are to be paid to the receiver of the insolvent company. 458 F.Supp. at 4. This court affirmed on the basis of the district court opinion, adding our own emphasis on another provision as compelling rejection of a third-party beneficiary theory. *General Reinsurance Corp. v. Mo. General Ins. Co.,* 596 F.2d 330 (8th Cir.1979).

The Missouri Supreme Court held in *Homan v. Employers Reinsurance Corp.,* 345 Mo. 650, 136 S.W.2d 289 (1939), that "upon the insolvency of the insurer, the proceeds of the reinsurance are assets to be distributed generally amongst its creditors." 136 S.W.2d at 296.

The principal argument of General Reinsurance on appeal is that the Receiver has no right to reinsurance proceeds under Agreement No. 4191 until the claim is allowed by the commissioner of claims pursuant to Mo.Ann.Stat. § 375.670 (Vernon's 1968). The P & NE claim was withdrawn after settlement, and apparently no claim was filed with respect to the B–K loss.

We do not think that the portion of the insolvency clause making reference to claims supports General's position. Nor does § 375.670 address the liability of a reinsurer to an insolvent insurer. Further, General's interpretation runs counter to the holding of the Missouri Supreme Court in *Clay v. Independence Mutual Insurance Co.,* 359 S.W.2d 679 (Mo.1962), that the appointment of the Superintendent of Insurance as receiver of an insolvent insurance company was, in effect, "an adjudication of insolvency by which the rights of the receiver became fixed." 359 S.W.2d at 683–84. In *Clay,* the court considered an action by the Superintendent to recover premiums held by an agent of an insolvent insurance company at the time the company was placed in receivership. The agent used the premiums to purchase alternative coverage for the policyholders. The court concluded that to permit the agent to use the premiums "to purchase other insurance for these policyholders would result in refunds in full to the policyholders, thus creating a preference over other insureds and creditors." 359 S.W.2d at 684.

The same concerns that prompted the *Clay* court to fix assets due an insolvent corporation in the hands of agents dictate a limit on General's right to settle claims without the participation of Medallion's Receiver. Indeed, without such a limit the potential exists for reinsurers not only to deny general creditors their acknowledged interest in reinsurance proceeds but also, at the same time, a reinsurer would be able to make cheap settlements with insureds facing the prospect of low dividends on their allowed claims.

Admittedly, where the reinsurer settles directly and obviates the determination of liability and its amount through claims procedure, there will arise questions as to proper valuation of outstanding tort claims. But it is the reinsurer's attempt to take advantage of the insolvency which causes the difficulty. The judgment in the P & NE case pretty solidly determined the liability of Medallion for $100,000. Although the settlement in the B–K case, including the payment by the excess carrier, may not be an exact valuation of Medallion's liability for the B–K loss, it provides the best approximation available.

Accordingly, the judgment of the district court is AFFIRMED.

Notes and Questions

1. *Reinsurance "afforded."* Two propositions are implicit in *Ainsworth.* One is the generally accepted rule that the reinsurer owes no duty to the policyholders of a ceding company. A fundamental principle of reinsurance is that it is a contract of indemnity and that, absent

a provision to the contrary, the reinsurer is not in privity of contract with the insured. In addition to *Ainsworth,* for discussion of this point see *Arrow Trucking Co. v. Continental Insurance Company,* 465 So.2d 691 (La.1985); *Fontenot v. Marquette Casualty Co.,* 258 La. 671, 247 So. 2d 572 (1971). The other proposition is that the insolvency of a ceding insurer does not terminate the reinsurer's obligations under its agreement with that insurer. Beyond that, however, did the *Ainsworth* court properly interpret the insolvency clause in the reinsurance agreement, which referred to "reinsurance afforded by this Agreement"? At least in the B–K case, was there any reinsurance "afforded" if the case was settled without final judgment? Would recourse to the reinsurer's duty of utmost good faith assist in resolving this question?

2. *Cut-through Clauses.* A number of state statutes resemble the Missouri Act in requiring the inclusion of insolvency clauses in reinsurance agreements as a condition of the ceding insurer's accounting for recoverable reinsurance as an asset. This accounting convention increases the insurer's surplus, thereby reducing its premium-to-surplus ratio, which is generally used to set a ceiling on the volume of insurance that regulators will allow the insurer to write. Some state statutes, however, allow an exception to the insolvency clause known as the "cut-through" clause, under which the reinsurer obligates itself directly to the insured under a specified policy, or to all the ceding company's insureds. See, e.g., N.Y.Ins.Law § 1308(2)(B). Suit on a policy may then be brought directly against the reinsurer, and payment may be made on behalf of the insured notwithstanding the ceding insurer's insolvency.

In the absence of a cut-through clause, insureds must seek imaginative methods of reaching the reinsurer's assets, or suffer the consequences of failing to do so. Consider the inventiveness of counsel in *Ott v. All–Star Insurance Corporation,* 99 Wis.2d 635, 299 N.W.2d 839 (1981). All–Star, the ceding insurer, was held liable to its liability insured for an excess-over-policy limits judgment entered after the insurer rejected a reasonable offer of settlement. The insurer then became insolvent. Counsel for the insured then argued successfully, however, that a clause in All–Star's reinsurance agreement with North Star Reinsurance Corporation, affording reinsurance of a portion of judgments entered against All–Star in excess of policy limits, was in fact insurance of the insurer rather than reinsurance. Under the Wisconsin Direct Action statute, this permitted the insured to sue the North Star directly, in its capacity as insurer of All–Star's liability for bad-faith rejection of reasonable settlement offers.

3. *In Support of the Insolvency Clause.* The message of *Ainsworth* is of course that an insolvency clause makes reinsurance proceeds an asset of an insolvent insurer's creditors generally, not an asset of any single insured. One argument in favor of this proposition is that this approach provides *ex ante* reassurance to prospective creditors, including policyholders, which functions like a bond that precludes the creation of preferences for individual creditors. Another argument is

that, even absent the clause, it would not always be clear *which insured* would be entitled to the proceeds of recoverable reinsurance. For example, suppose that a treaty provides that the reinsurer will cover 25 percent of all judgments in medical malpractice cases between $100,000 and $500,000, once the insurer has paid $5,000,000 in judgments in any given year. Which insured would be entitled to recover directly from the reinsurer in the absence of an insolvency clause, once the reinsurer's obligation had been triggered?

4. Set–Offs in Insolvency

O'CONNOR v. INSURANCE COMPANY OF NORTH AMERICA

United States District Court, N.D. Illinois, 1985.
622 F.Supp. 611.

PLUNKETT, District Judge.

Plaintiff, Philip R. O'Connor (the "Liquidator"), brings this diversity action on behalf of Reserve Insurance Company ("Reserve"). Reserve has been found insolvent, pursuant to the provisions of the Illinois Insurance Code ("Insurance Code") and the Final Order of Liquidation entered by the Circuit Court of Cook County in *People ex rel. Mathias v. Reserve Insurance Co.*, 79 Ch. 2828. Defendants include twenty-six insurance companies which acted as reinsurers of Reserve's liability under various reinsurance contracts (sometimes referred to as the "Reinsurers"); American Reserve Insurance Brokers International, Inc. ("ARIB"), which served as the manager under the contracts prior to Reserve's liquidation and shortly thereafter; Montgomery and Collins, Inc. of Texas ("Montgomery"), which purchased ARIB's rights as manager of the contracts after entry of Reserve's order of liquidation; and Petroleum Insurance, Inc. ("Petroleum"), an affiliate of Montgomery, which obtained from Montgomery the right to serve as manager under the contracts.   *   *   *

For the reasons stated below, Defendants' motions for partial summary judgment are granted, and, accordingly, the Liquidator's cross-motion is denied.

Factual Background

The relevant facts as we understand them, although complex, do not appear to be in dispute. On May 29, 1979, an order of liquidation was entered by the Circuit Court of Cook County, naming the Director of Insurance of the State of Illinois the Liquidator of Reserve. The Liquidator has title to Reserve's property and is authorized to deal with the property and business of the company.

For several years prior to the entry of the liquidation order, Reserve was a party to several reinsurance contracts which shared insured property risks in the petroleum and petrochemical industries.

In June 1975, Reserve entered into a "Quota Share Contract of Reinsurance" (the "3100 Treaty") with certain reinsurers whereby a portion of the risk on petroleum and petrochemical insurance policies written by Reserve would be carried by the reinsurers. In July 1976, Reserve entered into a "First Surplus Reinsurance Agreement" (the "P3200 Treaty") which established a reinsurance arrangement for risks written above a certain dollar amount under the 3100 Treaty. ARIB acted as the manager under both the 3100 and the 3200 treaties.

Effective January 1, 1979, the 3100 and 3200 reinsurance contracts were replaced by a new contract of reinsurance between various reinsurers, with ARIB as the manager (the "3400 pool"). Reserve was a party to the 3400 pool both as a reinsurer of risks undertaken by other insurance companies and as a reinsured on its own risks. By an agreement dated June 25, 1979, Montgomery purchased ARIB's interest as manager under the reinsurance contracts, and thereafter Petroleum became the new manager under the agreements. (The Liquidator refers to the three companies collectively as the "Manager").

While a participant in the reinsurance pool, Reserve wrote many insurance policies covering property risks in the petroleum and petrochemical industries and ceded to the reinsurers under the 3100, 3200, and 3400 treaties their share of the risk insured by such policies. Reserve also accepted reinsurance risks on policies written by other insurance companies which were members of the pool. The reinsurance pool was governed by a written contract and operated as follows. ARIB collected the insurance premium from the policyholder. ARIB then used approximately 30% of the premium to pay commissions to the producing agent or broker and the ceding company. ARIB retained the remaining 70% which was credited to the ceding company and the reinsurers in proportion to their assumption of the risk. As losses were incurred, ARIB paid the loss payments to claimants out of those retained funds.

Each quarter ARIB provided the reinsurers with an accounting of net written premiums, losses, loss adjustment expense, salvage, etc. If the net written premiums plus salvage recovered exceeded losses and expenses, ARIB paid out the net amount to the pool participants. If losses and expenses exceeded the net written premiums and salvage recoveries, the participants paid the difference to ARIB as manager. Defendants claim, and the Liquidator does not dispute, that from January 1, 1979 to the date of Reserve's insolvency the losses exceeded the net premiums in the pool and Reserve failed to make the necessary payments during that period.

Sometime after January 1, 1979, ARIB ceased issuing Reserve policies. The Liquidator contends that in April and May 1979, ARIB cancelled a large number of Reserve's policies because ARIB was concerned about Reserve's failing financial condition. During that time, ARIB issued new policies in the name of one of the other ceding companies. The Liquidator asserts that this cancellation and rewriting of policies, prior to Reserve's insolvency, was unauthorized and unlawful.

On the basis of the foregoing facts, the Liquidator alleges that he is entitled to recover, among other things, (1) certain reinsurance proceeds for losses incurred by Reserve's policyholders prior to liquidation but not paid as of the date of the liquidation order (Count I); (2) certain monies which the reinsurers and the manager owe Reserve for claims of policyholders which ARIB paid with Reserve's funds prior to liquidation (Count II); (3) Reserve's proportionate share of premiums written (less losses and other expenses) which Reserve earned under the 3400 reinsurance agreement (Count III); (4) the unearned premiums which the Manager or the reinsurers are holding and which relate to Reserve policies which were cancelled on May 30, 1979 as a result of Reserve's insolvency (Count IV); (5) the unearned premiums on Reserve policies to which the Liquidator would have been entitled had the Manager not cancelled such policies during the months prior to the liquidation order (Count V); and (6) the unearned commissions on policies cancelled by the liquidation order and cancelled by ARIB, allegedly without authority, during the months prior to the liquidation order (Count VI).

Defendants' motions for partial summary judgment request, pursuant to Fed.R.Civ.P.Rules 12(b)(6) and 56: (1) a declaration that the amounts, if any, that the Liquidator may ultimately be entitled to receive under Counts I–IV are to be reduced by the debts of Reserve to the Reinsurers and other Defendants, to the extent the amount of those debts may ultimately be proven. * * *

The Liquidator's cross-motion moves the court, pursuant to Fed.R. Civ.P.Rule 56, for partial summary judgment: (1) adjudging and declaring that the amounts the Liquidator is entitled to recover from Defendants may not be reduced by Reserve's debts, or, in the alternative, adjudging and declaring that the amounts the Liquidator is entitled to recover under Counts, I, IV, V, VI, and VII of the complaint may not be reduced by Reserve's debts. * * *

I. *Set–Offs*

Defendants contend that they are entitled to reduce the amount of any debt they may owe the Liquidator by debts Reserve owes to Defendants under the reinsurance agreements.[1] The Liquidator opposes Defendant's motions, arguing (1) that Defendants may not assert

---

1. Defendants contend that this court should allow a reduction of their amounts owed under the common law doctrine of recoupment. However, the Illinois Insurance Code provides a comprehensive scheme by which insurance companies are to be liquidated, and no provision in the Insurance Code permits a reduction in debt under the recoupment doctrine. Indeed, the careful limitations set forth in the statute would be completely subsumed by the more expansive reach of the recoupment doctrine. While the concept of recoupment makes sense in the context of ordinary contract disputes, it is not applicable in the context of an insolvency, where we must consider the concerns of persons who are not necessarily parties to a contract, but who nonetheless also have claims against assets of the insolvent's estate. We therefore decline Defendants' invitation to base our decision on common law principle and instead rely on the statutory set-off provision of the Insurance Code, Ill.Rev.Stat. ch. 73, § 818 (1983).

their set-off claim in this forum, but only in the liquidation court pursuant to provisions of the Insurance Code and the liquidation order, and (2) that even if Defendants' set-off claims may be considered by this court, certain of those claims do not meet the requirements set out in the statute. *See* Ill.Rev.Stat. ch. 73, § 818 (1983).

1. *The jurisdiction issue*

The heart of the Liquidator's argument is that the Insurance Code provides an exclusive procedure for the filing and determination of claims against an insolvent insurer, and that this procedure encompasses the assertion of set-offs. Furthermore, it is the Liquidator's position that the injunctions contained in the liquidation order pursuant to Ill. Rev.Stat. ch. 73, § 801 (1983) present a bar to Defendants' set-offs in this forum.[2] Thus, the Liquidator argues, Defendants' set-offs must be brought in the liquidation proceedings. Defendants argue that the Insurance Code's provision regarding set-offs mandates that they be entitled to assert set-offs in this proceeding.

To resolve the issue we must examine Ill.Rev.Stat. ch. 73, § 818 (1983) which provides, in relevant part:

> In all cases of mutual debts or mutual credits between the company and another person, such credits and debts shall be set off or counterclaimed and the balance only shall be allowed or paid. * * *

Although the statutory language appears to be mandatory, it has been held that the right of set-off is permissive, not mandatory, and that its application lies within the discretion of the trial court, which exercises such discretion under the general principles of equity. *See* 4 *Collier On Bankruptcy* ¶ 68.02[1] (14th ed. 1978).[3] Even if the statute is

---

2. The applicable provisions of the liquidation order provide as follows:

G. That * * * persons be and are hereby enjoined and restrained from bringing or further prosecuting any action at law or in equity or other proceeding against said RESERVE INSURANCE COMPANY or the Director of Insurance of the State of Illinois, or from interfering in any way with the Director's conduct of the business of RESERVE INSURANCE COMPANY, or from obtaining preferences, judgments, attachments, or liens in the making of any levy against said Company or its property and assets while in possession and control of the Director, or from in any way interfering with the Director of Insurance in his possession or control of or in his title, right and interest to the property, books, records and all other assets of the said RESERVE INSURANCE COMPANY.

H. That all persons be and are hereby enjoined and restrained from asserting any claim against the Liquidator or RESERVE INSURANCE COMPANY except insofar as such claims arise in the liquidation proceedings of RESERVE INSURANCE COMPANY and all persons asserting claims against such policyholders, be and are hereby enjoined from instituting or pursuing any action or proceeding in any court * * * which seeks in any way, directly or indirectly to contest or interfere with the Liquidator's exclusive right, title and interest to funds, recoverable under treaties and agreements of reinsurance heretofore entered into by RESERVE INSURANCE COMPANY as the ceding insurer, or otherwise.

3. The scope of the liquidation court's jurisdiction under the Insurance Code is similar to that granted the bankruptcy courts under the former Bankruptcy Act. *See People ex rel. Gerber v. Central Casualty Co.*, 37 Ill.2d 392, 397, 226 N.E.2d 862 (1967). Accordingly, we refer to bankruptcy cases interpreting the former Act. Similarly, we refer to Collier's

not mandatory, however, there can be little question that Defendants are entitled to assert their set-off claims in this proceeding. It is true, as the Liquidator urges, that the liquidation order in sweeping terms bars the assertion of "claims" against the Liquidator or Reserve, except in the liquidation proceedings; however, the Liquidator's argument that the term "claim" in that order is broad enough to encompass set-offs is unavailing. Such an interpretation of the liquidation court's order would mean that the set-off provision under Illinois law had been effectively overridden by the liquidation order. * * *

Defendants do not seek affirmative relief in this proceeding against assets held by the liquidation court, even though they claim that the set-offs asserted in this proceeding may exceed the amounts owed to the Liquidator, and even though the language of the Illinois statute expressly permitting "counterclaims" might be construed to permit the assertion of claims for affirmative relief. Defendants concede that they must file with the liquidation court their affirmative claims for amounts exceeding that which the Liquidator seeks in this action. All Defendants attempt to do in this action is to show that the Liquidator has no claim or a lesser claim against them. The plain language of the statute gives Defendants that right. * * *

2. The set-off requirements

The Insurance Code states that "mutual debts * * * shall be set off or counterclaimed and the balance only shall be allowed or paid." Ill.Rev.Stat. ch. 73, § 818 (1983). The concept of "mutuality" refers to the idea that:

> claims owed by or to the bankrupt prior to bankruptcy cannot be set off against claims owed by or to the bankrupt's estate (as represented by the receiver of trustee) and arising after bankruptcy. This is because the element of mutuality of obligation is lacking.

4 Collier On Bankruptcy ¶ 68.10[1] (14th ed. 1978) (analyzing the Bankruptcy Act's similar set-off provision). Essentially this means that "pre-liquidation" debts owed by Reserve can only be set-off against "pre-liquidation" debts owed to Reserve, and similarly that "post-liquidation" debts owed by Reserve can only be set-off against "post-liquidation" debts owed to Reserve. The parties do not dispute that mutuality must exist before a set-off can be asserted; however, they disagree as to what constitutes a "pre-liquidation" rather than a "post-liquidation" debt.[4]

The Liquidator contends that even if Defendants' set-offs may be heard by this court, the debts owed to the Liquidator under Counts I, IV, V, VI and VIII, involving reinsurance proceeds and unearned

14th edition, which analyzes the former Act, rather than the more recent 15th edition, which analyzes the new Bankruptcy Code.

4. All parties agree that the debts owed by Reserve under the contracts are pre-liquidation debts.

premiums as a result of the cancellation of the policies upon insolvency, may not be set off because those debts are *post*-liquidation debts while the debts owed by Reserve to Defendants are *pre*-liquidation debts. The Liquidator's position is that since the reinsurance proceeds will not be due until the policyholders' loss claims are allowed or liquidated by the liquidation court, this claim is a post-liquidation claim. Similarly, since unearned premiums do not become due until the cancellation of the policies, there was no obligation to refund those amounts before Reserve's insolvency, and these, too, are post-liquidation debts. Therefore, the Liquidator argues, mutuality does not exist as between these debts and Reserve's pre-liquidation debts, and no set-off may be permitted. Defendants argue that the debts described in Counts I, IV, V, VI, and VIII arise because of provisions in the reinsurance contracts, and that since the contracts had been executed and performed prior to the time of insolvency, the debts in question are all pre-liquidation debts. Mutuality thus exists and set-offs are permitted under the statute.

We agree with defendants. Even if the Liquidator is correct in his assertion that the debts for reinsurance proceeds and unearned premiums were not due at the time of liquidation, that fact has no bearing on whether Defendants may use these debts for set-off purposes. "The right of set-off may be asserted in the bankruptcy proceedings even though at the time the petition is filed one of the debts involved is absolutely owing but not presently due, or where a definite liability has accrued but is as yet unliquidated." 4 *Collier On Bankruptcy* ¶ 68.10[2] (14th ed. 1978). Defendants and Reserve entered into a reinsurance contract which defined all of the parties' rights and obligations. Any liability Defendants may incur to pay reinsurance proceeds or return unearned premiums or ceding commissions arises as a result of provisions in the previously executed reinsurance agreement that require them to make these payments. In *Cunningham v. Commissioner of Banks,* 249 Mass. 401, 144 N.E. 447, 459 (1924), the court stated, "[p]rovable debts under the Bankruptcy Act include all liabilities of the bankrupt founded on contract express or implied which existed at the time of the bankruptcy and either were fixed in amount or susceptible of liquidation." In this case, the reinsurance contract was in existence at the time of Reserve's insolvency. With respect to these insurance proceeds, all the claims giving rise to Defendants' liability were filed prior to Reserve's insolvency. Therefore, although the claims were not paid prior to Reserve's insolvency, they were susceptible of liquidation. The unearned premiums on policies still in existence on the date of insolvency became payable on that date, and the amounts were fixed. Accordingly, we find that Defendants' debts are pre-liquidation debts; therefore, mutuality of obligation exists and a set-off is permitted.

The Liquidator directs our attention to *Melco System v. Receivers of Trans-america Ins. Co.,* 268 Ala. 152, 105 So.2d 43, 53 (1958), in which the Supreme Court of Alabama held that the reinsurer incurred no debt to the reinsured until the reinsured had actually paid the losses. The court noted that it felt to allow the offset would give a preference to the reinsurer over other creditors because the reinsurer would be receiving full payment on its claim while other creditors would receive only fractional payment. 105 So.2d at 53. It is true that the reinsurer would be paid in full if a set-off is permitted, but of course, that is the case *anytime* a set-off is permitted. The whole point of the statutory set-off section is to make clear that such actions are permissible, even though one creditor may be getting paid more than other creditors. Professor Collier explains:

> The object of the statute is to permit a statement of the account between the bankrupt and its creditors with a view to the application of the doctrine of set-off between mutual debts and credits. And it has been pointed out that while the operation of this privilege of set-off has the effect to pay one creditor more than another, it is a provision based upon the generally recognized right of mutual debtors, which has been enacted as part of the Bankruptcy Act. Without such enactment, it would be argued that any attempt to offset mutual debts or credits between the estate and a creditor would amount to a preference * * * and would, therefore, be invalid. But the Act, instead, has recognized the possible injustice which would thus result and which would, for example, compel a creditor to prove his claim in full and accept possible dividends thereon and at the same time pay in full his indebtedness to the estate.

4 *Collier on Bankruptcy* ¶ 68.02[1] (14th ed. 1978). Thus, we respectfully decline to follow the *Melco* court's reasoning in that it seems to ignore the established policy in an area of bankruptcy law quite analogous to the situation with which we are faced. Defendants' debts are pre-liquidation debts, mutuality exists, and a set-off is permissible.

* * *

Conclusion

For all the reasons stated above, Defendants' motions for partial summary judgment are granted. The Liquidator's cross-motion for partial summary judgment is denied.

Notes and Questions

1. *The Impact of Set–Off.* A reinsurer's right of set-off may have a substantial impact on general creditors, since it operates like a preference (or a security interest) that takes priority over the claims of these creditors. Moreover, it is an interest of which the creditors have no direct notice and about which they often have no practical means of obtaining information. On the other hand, as a practical matter, insurers and reinsurers may have hundreds of monthly debits and credits between them which the denial of a right to set-off would make much more cumbersome to clear.

2. *Contractual Set–Off.* The principal case propounds as a finding of law what many reinsurance treaties provide as a matter of contract—a specifically provided for right of set-off. See Semple and Hall, The Reinsurer's Liability in the Event of the Insolvency of A Ceding Property and Casualty Insurer, 21 TIPS J. 407, 419 (1986).

INDEX

References are to Pages

ACCIDENT
See also Accidental-Death Insurance; Intentional Acts; Liability Insurance; Occurrences
Automobile Insurance,
Intentional conduct by insured, 613–618

ACCIDENTAL–DEATH INSURANCE
See also Life Insurance
Accidental means, 341–342
Suicide, 342–344

ACTUAL CASH VALUE
See Coinsurance; Measure of Recovery (Coverage Provided); Property Insurance

ADDITIONAL (OMNIBUS) INSUREDS, 620–628
See also Automobile Insurance

ADMITTED MARKET, 716
See also Insurance Market

ADVERSE SELECTION
See also Misrepresentation; Moral Hazard; Rates and Ratemaking (Method and Regulation)
Aids, 22–24
Defined, 3–4
Discriminatory rates structures, 127–139
Duty to disclose, 24–27
Health and disability insurance exclusions, 407–410
Liability insurance, 455

AGENTS (Intermediaries), 54–72
Authority,
Employers as agents, 65–72
Group insurance, 65–72
Scope of authority generally, 54–60
Direct writers and independent agents, 55
Estoppel (and waiver), 60–65
Indemnity, 60
Reasonable expectations (estoppel), 47
Waiver and estoppel, 60–65

AIDS
See also Adverse Selection; Moral Hazard
Misrepresentation law, 22–24

ALL–RISK INSURANCE
See also Property Insurance
Property insurance, 196

AMBIGUITIES
See *Contra Proferentem;* Drafting Insurance Policies; Misrepresentation; Reasonable Expectations of the Insured; Warranties

ANTITRUST LAWS
See also McCarran-Ferguson Act; Regulation of Insurance
Federal, 91–92, 139–141
State, 181–182

ASBESTOS
See also Liability Insurance; Trigger of Coverage
Expected harm exclusion to liability coverage, 508–509

ASSIGNED RISK PLANS, 710–716
See also Automobile Insurance; Residual Market Mechanisms

ATTORNEY'S MALPRACTICE INSURANCE
See Liability Insurance; Malpractice Insurance

AUTHORITY
See Agents (Intermediaries)

AUTOMOBILE INSURANCE, 601–676
See also Coordination of Multiple Coverages; Duty to Defend; Liability Insurance; No-Fault Insurance; Residual Market Mechanisms; Settlement of Claims; Uninsured Motorists Insurance
Additional insureds, 620–628
Assigned risk plans, 710–716
Automobile insurance plan, 710–716
Causation examined, 627–628
Collision coverage, 642–649
Comprehensive coverage, 642–649
Cooperation conditions, 630–637
Coordination of multiple coverages, 704–705
Direct action statutes, 638
Drive other cars (DOC) coverage, 627
Family exclusion, 619–620
Household exclusion, 619–620

AUTOMOBILE INSURANCE—Cont'd
Liability insurance, 613–642
  Compulsory insurance requirements, 613–620
  Financial responsibility laws, 618
  Moral hazard, 618–619
No-Action clauses, 638–642
No-Fault automobile insurance, 649–662
Notice and cooperation conditions, 630–637
  Prejudice to insurer, 637
Omnibus clause, 620–628
  "Permission" examined, 627–628
Reinsurance facility, 711
Residual market mechanisms, 710–712
Sample policy, 602–612
Underinsured motorists insurance, 670
Uninsured motorists insurance, 663–676
"Use" of the vehicle construed, 628–630

AUTOMOBILE INSURANCE PLANS, 710–716
See also Automobile Insurance; Residual Market Mechanisms

BAD–FAITH BREACH LIABILITY OF INSURER, 411–438
See also Remedies (Against the Insurer)
Compensatory damages, 411–438
ERISA and agents employers, 428–438
Nature of the cause of action, 425–427
Punitive damages discussed, 427

BAILEE'S INSURANCE, 233–240
See also Property Insurance; Limited Interests; Insured

BANKRUPTCY OF INSURER
See Insolvency of Insurers; Reinsurance

BANKRUPTCY DISCHARGE AND FINANCIAL RESPONSIBILITY
Automobile Insurers (No-Action clauses), 638–642

BENEFICIARY (LIFE INSURANCE)
See also Life Insurance
Change of beneficiary or assignment of policies, 311–321
Insurable interest required, 304–311, 318–321
Limitations on recovery, 321–332
  Murder and manslaughter verdicts, 326–332

BINDING RECEIPTS, 299–303
See also Life Insurance

BLUE CROSS/BLUE SHIELD, 357, 361–370
See also Health and Disability Insurance
Coordination of coverage, 372–379

BOYCOTT, COERCION, OR INTIMIDATION, 154–182
See also McCarran-Ferguson Act

BUSINESS INTERRUPTION INSURANCE, 269–278
See also Property Insurance
Due diligence and the duty to mitigate, 277–278

BUSINESS OF INSURANCE
See also Employment Retirement Income Security Act (ERISA); McCarran-Ferguson Act; Regulation of Insurance
Antitrust regulation (McCarran–Ferguson Act), 140–154
ERISA's insurance regulation exception, 430–433, 438

CAUSATION
See also Auto Insurance; Liability Insurance; Property Insurance; Trigger of Coverage
Auto insurance,
  Causation generally, 627–628
  Collision coverage, 248, 642–649
  Comprehensive coverage, 248, 642–649
Property insurance, 241–248
  Conclusive v. Inconclusive exclusions, 241
  Proximate causation, 244–245, 247

CERCLA
See also Hazardous Waste (Liability Insurance); Liability Insurance
"Damages" covered under liability insurance, 473–483

CESTUI QUE VIE, 310
See also Beneficiary; Life Insurance

CLAIMS–MADE COVERAGE
See also Liability Insurance; Malpractice Insurance
Coverage in the 1980's, 167–179
Liability insurance, 528–539
Medical malpractice insurance, 156–167
Underwriting cycle rate crises, 155–156

CLASSIFICATION OF INSUREDS
See Adverse Selection; Exclusions and Conditions; Moral Hazard; Rates and Ratemaking

COINSURANCE, 267–269
See also Property Insurance

COLLISION INSURANCE (Automobile), 642–649
See also Automobile Insurance

COMPLETED–OPERATIONS EXCLUSION, 43–45

COMPREHENSIVE ENVIRONMENTAL RESPONSE, COMPENSATION, AND LIABILITY ACT OF 1980
See CERCLA; Liability Insurance

COMPREHENSIVE INSURANCE (Automobile), 642–649
See also Automobile Insurance

COMPULSORY INSURANCE
Automobile insurance, 613–620
Financial responsibility statutes, 618

CONDITIONAL RECEIPTS AND TEMPORARY INSURANCE, 299–303
See also Life Insurance

CONDITIONS
See Evidentiary Conditions; Exclusions and Conditions; Warranties

CONFLICTS OF INTEREST
See Duty to Defend; Settlement of Claims

CONSEQUENTIAL DAMAGES
See Bad-Faith Breach Liability of Insurer; Measure of Recovery; Punitive Damages; Remedies (Against the Insurer)

CONSTRUCTION
See *Contra Proferentem;* Drafting Insurance Policies; Misrepresentation; Plain Language Policies; Reasonable Expectations of the Insured; Warranties

CONTRA PROFERENTEM
Defined, 33–42
Health insurance ("Medically Necessary"), 361–370
Plain language—tension, 38
Reasonable expectations, 41, 42–54

CONTRACT TO INSURE FOR ANOTHER
See also Property Insurance
Open mortgage clauses, 215–216
Standard (or union) mortgage clauses, 209–210

CONTRACTUAL SUBROGATION
See Subrogation

COORDINATION OF MULTIPLE COVERAGES, 381–382
See also Excess Liability Insurance; Health and Disability Insurance; Liability Insurance; Occurrences; Trigger of Coverage
Disability insurance, 371, 381–387
Health insurance, 371–381, 387–394
Liability and automobile insurance, 677–709
Exposure Trigger Theory, 682–683, 688
Hazardous waste, 688–690
Lamb-Weston Doctrine, 694–698
Manifestation Trigger Theory, 683–685, 688
Methods of coordination of multiple coverages, 704–705
"Occurrence" clauses construed, 685–687

COORDINATION OF MULTIPLE COVERAGES—Cont'd
"Other Insurance" clauses, 691–705
Proration of multiple coverages, 698–704, 705
Rate regulation, 705
Trigger of coverage, 677–691
"Stacking" uninsured motorist insurance, 705–709

CQV
See Beneficiary; *Cestui Que Vie;* Life Insurance

CUT-THROUGH CLAUSES, 732
See also Insolvency of Insurers; Insolvency clauses

DOC COVERAGE
See Automobile Insurance; Drive Other Cars (DOC) Coverage

DAMAGES
See Bad-Faith Breach Liability of the Insurer; Measure of Recovery (Coverage Provided); Punitive Damages; Remedies (Against the Insurer)

DEFENSE OBLIGATION
See Duty to Defend

DIRECT–ACTION STATUTES, 638

DIRECT WRITERS
See Agents (Intermediaries)

DISABILITY INSURANCE
See also Health and Disability Insurance
Coordination of coverage, 371, 381–387
"Disability" defined, 394–407
Exclusion due to preexisting conditions, 407–410
Market for disability insurance, 386
Mitigation (insured's implied duty to mitigate), 406–407
Moral hazard (conduct clauses), 398
Partial coverage, 386–387
Partial disability problem, 397
Preexisting conditions exclusions, 407–410
Public policy, 382–386
Total disability, 394–397, 398, 398–407
Unconscionability, 385–386, 387

DISCRIMINATION BY SEX, 127–139
See also Rates and Ratemaking

DOCTRINE OF REASONABLE EXPECTATIONS
See *Contra Proferentem;* Reasonable Expectations

DIVORCE (and Separation Agreements)
See also Life Insurance
Beneficiary change, 312–317

DRAFTING INSURANCE POLICIES
See also Plain Language Policies
Insurance services office, 29–33
Standardized forms, 28–33
Uniformity in drafting, 31–33
   Antitrust challenges, 154–182

DRIVE OTHER CARS (DOC) COVERAGE,
  627
See also Automobile Insurance

DROP–DOWN LIABILITY, 595–600
See also Liability Insurance

DUPLICATIVE RECOVERIES
See Coordination of Multiple Coverages

DUTY OF CARE (Insurer's Duty of Care)
Life insurance, 344–356

DUTY OF UTMOST GOOD FAITH, 717–724
See also Reinsurance

DUTY TO DEFEND, 540–568
   See also Auto Insurance; Liability Insurance; Settlement of Claims
Conflicts of interest, 551–567
Duty to appeal, 550
Non-Waiver agreement, 549
Reservation of rights notice, 544–549
Scope of the duty to defend, 540–550
Settlement of claims, 568–587
Terminating the duty to defend, 549–550

DUTY TO DISCLOSE, 24–27
See also Misrepresentation

ERISA
See Employment Retirement Income Security Act

EQUITABLE SUBROGATION
See Subrogation

EMPLOYEE BENEFITS
See Employment Retirement Income Security Act

EMPLOYMENT RETIREMENT INCOME SECURITY ACT (ERISA)
   See also Bad-Faith Breach Liability of Insurer; Group Insurance; Health and Disability Insurance
Scope of the act,
  Bad-Faith actions against insurer agents/insurers, 428–438
  Disability insurance, 372–528
  McCarran-Ferguson Act ("Business of Insurance") test applied, 430–433, 438
Text of the act (and the insurance exception), 375

ENTIRE CONTRACT STATUTES, 22

ESTOPPEL AGAINST INSURER
  See also Agents (Intermediaries)
Agent's actions, 60–65
Lobbying activities of insurers, 522
Reasonable expectations, 43–47

EVIDENTIARY CONDITIONS, 52
  See also Exclusions and Conditions
Disability insurance conduct clauses, 398
Forcible entry requirement, 47–52

EXCESS LIABILITY INSURANCE, 462–471,
  588–600
   See also Automobile Insurance; Coordination of Multiple Coverages; Liability Insurance
Follow-Form coverage, 594
Relationship of primary and excess insurers, 588–600
  Drop-Down liability, 595–600
  Duty to settle, 588–595
Umbrella coverage, 594

EXCESS LINES, 716
See also Insurance Market Residual Markets Mechanisms

EXCLUSIONS AND CONDITIONS (to Coverage)
   See also Hazardous Waste (Liability Insurance); Insurable Interest; Liability Insurance; "Other Insurance" Clauses; Pollution Liability; Warranties
Automobile Insurance,
  Cooperation conditions, 630–637
  Family exclusion, 619–620
  Household exclusion, 619–620
  No-Action clauses, 638–642
  Notice and cooperation conditions, 630–637
  Prejudice to insurer, 637
Disability Insurance,
  Conduct clauses, 398
  Preexisting conditions exclusion, 407–410
Health Insurance,
  Preexisting conditions exclusion, 407–410
Liability Insurance, 483–528
  Business risk exclusion, 493–504
  Completed-Operations exclusion, 43–45
  Expected or intended harm, 505–509
  Notice condition, 522–528
  Owned-Property exclusion, 483–493
  Pollution exclusion, 509–522
Life Insurance,
  Approval of the insurer, 299–303
  Conditional receipts and temporary coverage, 299–303
  Incontestability, 332–344
  Insurable interest of beneficiary, 304–311, 318–321
Property Insurance, 240–257

EXCLUSIONS AND CONDITIONS (to Coverage)—Cont'd
Causation, 241–248
Forcible entry requirement, 47–52
Increase-of-Hazard exclusions, 248–257
Vacancy exclusions, 252–257
Warranties through exclusion, 256

EXEMPLARY DAMAGES
See also Measure of Recovery (Coverage Provided); Punitive Damages; Remedies (Against the Insurer)
Bad-Faith breach by the insurer, 411–438

EXPOSURE THEORY
See Trigger of Coverage

EXTENDED COVERAGE, 196
See also Property Insurance

FAIR ACCESS TO INSURANCE REQUIREMENTS PLANS
See Fair Plans

FAIR PLANS, 712–713

FAMILY EXCLUSION TO AUTO LIABILITY INSURANCE, 619–620
See also Automobile Insurance

FEDERALISM
See McCarran-Ferguson Act

FINANCIAL RESPONSIBILITY LAWS, 618
See also Automobile Insurance; Compulsory Insurance

FIRE INSURANCE
See Property Insurance

FIRST–DOLLAR COVERAGE, 649
See also Automobile Insurance; Comprehensive Coverage

FIRST–PARTY INSURANCE, 183
See also Automobile Insurance; Disability Insurance; Health Insurance; Property Insurance

FOLLOW–FORM COVERAGE, 594
See also Excess Insurance; Liability Insurance

"FOLLOW–THE–FORTUNES" CLAUSES, 724–727
See also Reinsurance

FORCIBLE ENTRY REQUIREMENT, 47–52

FORMS USED
See Sample Policies

FRAUDULENT INDUCEMENT, 22
See also Misrepresentation

FUNCTIONS OF INSURANCE, 2–3

GENDER
See also Rates and Ratemaking (Method and Regulation)
Rate classification, 127–139

GOVERNMENT–SPONSORED INSURANCE
National health insurance, 356–361

GROUP INSURANCE
See also Agents (Intermediaries); Disability Insurance; Health and Disability Insurance; Incontestability; Life Insurance
Employers as agents, 65–72

HAZARDOUS WASTE (Liability Insurance)
See also CERCLA; Liability Insurance; Occurrences; Pollution Liability; Trigger of Coverage
Coordination of multiple coverages, 688–691
Coverage for cleanup costs, 473–493
Owned-Property exclusion, 483–493

HEALTH AND DISABILITY INSURANCE, 356–410
See also Bad-Faith Breach Liability of Insurer; Coordination of Multiple Coverages; Disability Insurance
Disability insurance,
Coordination of coverage, 371, 381–387
"Disability" defined, 394–407
Market for disability insurance, 386
Mitigation (insured's implied duty to mitigate), 406–407
Moral hazard (conduct clauses), 398
Partial coverage, 386–387
Preexisting conditions exclusions, 407–410
Public policy, 382–386
Unconscionability, 385–386, 387
Health insurance,
Coordination of coverage, 371–382, 387–394
Cost control, 360–361
Forms of coverage, 360
Health insurance in the U.S. (nature and scope), 356–361
Moral hazard, 360–371
National health insurance, 356–361
"Necessary" or "Reasonable" services, 361–371
Preadmission review, 370–371
Preexisting conditions exclusions, 407–410
Prepaid medical services, 370
Public policy, 371, 385–386
Regulation of health insurance, 359–360
Settlement, 393–394
Time Limitations on claims, 83–89
Tort recovery by subrogation, 387–394
Uncompensated care, 361

HOMEOWNERS INSURANCE
See Property Insurance

HOMICIDE
See Life Insurance; Beneficiaries

HOUSEHOLD EXCLUSION TO AUTO LIA-BILITY COVERAGE, 619–620

IMPERFECT INFORMATION
See Adverse Selection; Moral Hazard

INCONTESTABILITY, 332–344
  See also Life Insurance
Employment as a condition of group coverage, 333–337
Limitations of risk, 338–344

INCREASE OF HAZARD (Exclusions), 248–257
See also Property Insurance; Warranties

INDEMNITY
  See also Insurable Interest; Measure of Recovery (Coverage Provided); Property Insurance
Economic conception v. functional conception, 265–266
Indemnity explained, 60
Insurable interest, 200
Subrogation, 202

INDEPENDENT AGENTS
See Agents (Intermediaries)

INSOLVENCY OF INSURERS
  See also Regulation of Insurance; State; Reinsurance
Cut-through clauses, 732
Guaranty funds, 93–99
Insolvency clauses, 727–733
Reinsurer's right of set-off, 733–740

INSURABLE INTEREST
  See also Beneficiary; Indemnity; Moral Hazard
Indemnity principle, 200
Life insurance, 304–311, 317–321
  Cestui que vie (CQV) insured, 310
  Creditor's insurable interest, 309–310
Property insurance, 196–201

INSURANCE MARKET
Claims-Made liability coverage, 538
Reinsurance, 717–740
Residual market mechanisms, 710–716
Secondary markets, 710–740
  Automobile insurance, 710–712
  Liability insurance, 713–715
  Malpractice insurance, 713–715
  Property insurance, 712–713
  Reinsurance, 717–740
Surplus and excess lines, 716

INSURANCE SERVICES OFFICE (ISO), 29–33
See also Drafting Insurance Policies

INSURED EVENT
See Exclusions and Conditions (to Coverage); Occurrences

INSURING AGREEMENT, 449–483
Damages covered, 473–483
Number of occurrences, 455–473
"Occurrence" defined, 449–455

INTENTIONAL ACTS
  See also Automobile Insurance; Occurrences; Public Policy and Insurance
Automobile insurance, 613–618
Coverage generally denied, 72–75, 81–83
Liability insurance,
  Intended harms exclusion, 505–509
  "Occurrences" (Not expected), 449–455

INTERMEDIARIES
See Agents (Intermediaries)

INTERPRETATION
See *Contra Proferentem;* Drafting Insurance Policies; Misrepresentation; Plain Language Policies; Reasonable Expectations of Insured; Warranties

ISO
See Insurance Services Office

JOINT UNDERWRITING ASSOCIATIONS, 711–716

LAMB–WESTON DOCTRINE, 694–698
See also Coordination of Multiple Coverages

LEASES AND INSURANCE
  See also Property Insurance
Lessees as implied co-insureds, 216–221

LIABILITY INSURANCE, 439–600
  See also Coordination of Multiple Coverages; Duty to Defend; Excess Liability Insurance; Insuring Agreement; Occurrences; Pollution Liability; Settlement of Claims; Trigger of Coverage
Automobile liability insurance, 613–642
CERCLA, 473–483
Claims-made coverage, 528–539
Coordination of multiple coverages, 677–709
"Damages" covered, 473–483
Drop-down liability, 595–600
Duty to defend, 540–588
  Conflicts of interest, 551–567
  Duty to appeal, 550
  Scope of the duty to defend, 540–550
  Settlement of claims, 568–587
  Terminating the duty to defend, 549–550

LIABILITY INSURANCE—Cont'd
Excess insurance, 462–471, 588–600
  Follow-form coverage, 594
  Relationship of primary and excess insurers, 588–600
  Umbrella coverage, 594
Exclusions and conditions of coverage, 483–528
  Business risk exclusions, 493–504
  Completed-operations exclusion, 43–45
  Expected or intended harm, 505–509
  Notice conditions to coverage, 522–528
  Owned-property exclusion, 483–493
  Pollution exclusion, 509–522
Hazardous waste, 473–483
Insuring agreement (coverage provided), 449–483
  Damages covered, 473–483
  Number of occurrences, 455–473
  "Occurrence" defined, 449–455
Products liability, 462–472
Punitive damages coverage prohibited, 75–83
Sample CGL policy, 439–449
Settlement of claims, 568–588
  Bad-faith in settlement, 574–588
  Duty of settlement, 568–574, 588–595
Trigger of coverage, 677–691
  Exposure theory, 682–683, 688
  Hazardous waste cases, 688–690
  Manifestation theory, 683–685, 688
  "Occurrence" clauses construed, 685–687
Unifying directive, 472–473

LIFE ESTATES (and Immediate Death of the Insured), 229–232
See also Property Insurance

LIFE INSURANCE
  See also Accidental-Death Insurance; Beneficiary (Life Insurance)
Application (temporary coverage), 299–303
Assignment of policies, 311–321
Beneficiaries,
  Change of beneficiary or assignment of policies, 311–321
  Insurable interest required, 304–311, 318–321
  Limitations on recovery, 321–332
  Murder or manslaughter, 326–332
Binder or binding receipts, 303
Conditional receipts, 303
Conversion to present cash value, 318–321
Insurable interest requirement, 304–311
  Cestui Que Vie (CQV) insured, 310
  Creditor's insurable interest, 309
  Standing to question in court, 310
  Time of interest, 310–311
Incontestability, 332–344
  Conditions of coverage (become incontestable), 332–338
Insuring the life of another (owner not the insured), 310

LIFE INSURANCE—Cont'd
Limitations of risk (never incontestable), 338–344
Negligence actions against the insurer, 344–356
Retroactive coverage upon approval, 299–303
Sample policy, 279–298
Temporary coverage upon application, 303–304
Term v. Whole Life insurance, 279

LIMITED INTERESTS, 209–240
  See also Property Insurance
Bailees, 233–240
Leaseholds (Lessee as co-insured), 216–221
Life estates (and immediate death of the insured), 229–232
Mortgagees, 209–216
  Open-mortgage clauses, 215–216
  Standard (or union) mortgage clauses, 209–210
Real estate sales (mismatched or double insurance), 221–228

LORD MANSFIELD'S RULE
See Warranties

LOSS RATIOS, 99–104
See also Rates and Ratemaking

MALPRACTICE INSURANCE, 156–179
  See also Liability Insurance; Medical Malpractice Insurance
Claims-made coverage, 528–539

MANIFESTATION THEORY, 683–685, 688
See also Liability Insurance; Trigger of Coverage

MARKET
See Insurance Market

MASS–MARKETED INSURANCE, 47

McCARRAN–FERGUSON ACT, 91–92, 139–141
  See also Regulation of Insurance
"Boycott, Coercion, or Intimidation", 154–181
  Medical malpractice insurance crises, 156–167
  Underwriting cycle/premium explosion, 155–156
"Business of Insurance", 140–154
ERISA's insurance regulation exception, 430–433, 438
"Regulation" defined, 154
State regulation, 92–139
  State antitrust provisions, 181–182
Text of the statute, 91–92

MEASURE OF RECOVERY (Coverage Provided)
See also Bad-Faith Breach, Liability of Insurer; CERCLA; Coordination of Multiple Coverages; Hazardous Waste (Liability Insurance); Liability Insurance; Occurrences; Public Policy and Insurance; Remedies (Against the Insurer); Trigger of Coverage
Actual cash value, 259–265
CERCLA (hazardous waste clean-up), 473–483
Coinsurance, 267–269
Liability insurance for punitive damages, 75–83
Replacement–Cost coverage, 266
Valued policies, 266–267

MEDICAL MALPRACTICE INSURANCE
See also Claims-Made Coverage
Coordination of multiple coverages, 691–698
Crisis in the 1970's, 156–167
Crisis in the 1980's (Claims-made coverage), 167–179
Joint underwriting associations, 713–715

"MISMATCHED" INSURANCE, 221–228
See also Property Insurance

MISREPRESENTATION
Affirmative misrepresentation, 14–15
Agents—as intermediaries, 17–22
AIDS, 22–24
Concealment, 15–16
Duty to disclose, 24–27
Fraudulent inducement, 22
Health and disability insurance, 410

MORAL HAZARD
See also Indemnity; Insurable Interest
Automobile insurance,
  Liability insurance, 618–619
  Uninsured motorists insurance, 676
Disability insurance conduct clauses, 398
Discriminatory by sex, 127–139
Evidentiary conditions, 52–54
Health insurance, 360–371
Liability insurance,
  Business risk exclusions, 504
  Expected or intended harms not covered, 505
  Pollution exclusion, 522
Moral hazard defined, 4–5

MORTGAGEE'S INSURANCE, 209–216
See also Property Insurance
Open-mortgage clauses, 215–216
Standard (or union) mortgage clauses, 209–210

MULTIPLE COVERAGES
See Coordination of Multiple Coverages; Excess Liability Insurance

MURDER OR MANSLAUGHTER (Life Insurance), 326–332

MUTUAL INSURANCE COMPANIES, 1

NATIONAL HEALTH INSURANCE, 356–361
See also Health and Disability Insurance

NEGLIGENCE ACTIONS AGAINST INSURERS
See also Duty of Care (Insurer's Duty to Care)
Life insurers, 344–356

NEGLIGENT SUPERVISION OF CHILDREN, 505–509

NO–ACTION CLAUSES, 638–642
See also Automobile Insurance

NO–FAULT INSURANCE, 649–662
See also Automobile Insurance
Benefit levels, 662
Due process issues, 656–657
Empirical analyses, 653–656, 662
Equal protection concerns, 657–660
Thresholds and benefit levels, 662

NON–ADMITTED MARKET, 716
See also Insurance Market; Residual Market Mechanisms; Surplus Lines (Insurance)

NONDISCLOSURE
See Misrepresentation

NON–WAIVER AGREEMENTS, 549
See also Duty to Defend

NOTICE TO INSURER
See also Automobile Insurance; Liability Insurance
Notice conditions in automobile insurance, 630–637
  Prejudice to insurer, 637
Notice conditions in liability insurance, 522–528
  Prejudice to insurer, 527
  Waiver by insurer, 527

OCCURRENCE COVERAGE, 155–156
See also Claims-Made Coverage; Liability Insurance

OCCURRENCES
See also Coordination of Multiple Coverages; Intentional Acts; Liability Insurance; Trigger of Coverage
Number of occurrences, 455–473
"Occurrence" defined, 449–455
Trigger of coverage, 677–691

OMNIBUS CLAUSE, 620–628

OPEN–MORTGAGE CLAUSES, 215–216
See also Property Insurance

"OTHER INSURANCE" CLAUSES, 691–705
See also Coordination of Multiple Coverages

PERSONAL INJURY PROTECTION (PIP), 650–662

PLAIN LANGUAGE POLICIES
See also *Contra Proferentem;* Drafting Insurance Policies; Reasonable Expectations
Automobile insurance, 630
Uninsured motorist coverage, 671

POLLUTION LIABILITY
See also CERCLA; Hazardous Waste (Liability Insurance); Liability Insurance
Pollution exclusion from liability coverage, 509–522

PREJUDICE TO INSURER
See also Automobile Insurance; Liability Insurance
Automobile insurance, 637
Liability insurance, 527

PREMIUM RATES
See Rates and Ratemaking (Method and Regulation)

PRIMARY INSURERS
See Excess Liability Insurance

PRODUCTS LIABILITY
See also Coordination of Multiple Coverages; Liability Insurance; Occurrences; Trigger of Coverage
Coordination of multiple coverages, 677–687
Number of occurrences insured, 462–472

PROFESSIONAL LIABILITY INSURANCE
See Liability Insurance; Malpractice Insurance; Medical Malpractice Insurance

PROPERTY INSURANCE
See also Insurable Interest; Limited Interests
All-risk coverage vs. specified risk coverage, 196
Business interruption insurance, 269–278
Causation, 241–248
Exclusions and exceptions, 240–257
Causation, 241–248
Increased risk exclusions, 248–257
Vacancy exclusions, 252–257
Extended coverage, 196
FAIR plans, 712–713

PROPERTY INSURANCE—Cont'd
Fire coverage vs. fire-and-extended coverage, 196
Insurable interest requirement, 196
Limited interests insured, 209–240
Bailees, 233–240
Leaseholds (lessee as co-insured), 216–221
Life estates (and immediate death of the insured), 229–232
Mortgagees, 209–216
Real estate sales (mismatched or double insurance), 221–228
Measure of recovery, 257–269
Actual cash value, 259–265
Coinsurance, 267–269
Replacement-cost coverage, 266
Valued policies, 266–267
Proximate cause, 244–245, 247
Residual market mechanisms, 712–713
Sample homeowners policy, 184–195
Subrogation, 201–209

PROPOSITION, 103, 114–127

PUBLIC POLICY AND INSURANCE, 72–89
Automobile insurance,
Household or family exclusion, 619–620
General discussion, 72, 83–89
Health and disability insurance, 371, 385–386
Intentional acts coverage, 72–75, 81–83
Punitive damages coverage, 75–83
Time limits on accident/dismemberment claims, 83–89

PUNITIVE DAMAGES
See also Bad-Faith Breach Liability of the Insurer; Public Policy; Remedies (Against the Insurer)
Bad-faith actions against the insurer, 427
Liability insurance for punitive damages, 75–83

RATES AND RATEMAKING
See also Adverse Selection; Claims-Made Coverage; Drafting Insurance Policies; Regulation of Insurance; Underwriting Cycle
Collective ratemaking,
Antitrust challenges, 154–182
Coordination of multiple coverages, 705
Discrimination by sex, 127–139
Actuarial unfairness, 132–138
Causality, 137
Federal law, 138–139
Remedies, 139
Forms of rate regulation, 104–105
Insurer profitability and ratemaking, 99–104, 107–112
Hypothetical case, 103–104
Standard of review, 106–107, 112–114
Trending and development considered, 105–112

RATES AND RATEMAKING—Cont'd
Rate rollbacks, 114–127
Standard of review, 106–107, 112–114
Underwriting cycle, 155–156

REAL ESTATE SALES (Mismatched or Double Insurance), 221–228
See also Property Insurance

REASONABLE EXPECTATIONS OF THE INSURED, 42–54
See also Agents (Intermediaries); *Contra Proferentem;* Waiver
Estoppel rationale, 43–47

RECOVERY OF CLAIMS
See Coinsurance; Measure of Recovery (Coverage Provided)

REGULATION OF INSURANCE
See also McCarran-Ferguson Act; Rates and Ratemaking (Method and Regulation)
Federal regulation,
Antitrust regulation, 91–92, 140–181
Discriminatory rate classification, 138–139
Health insurance, 359–360
Interstate commerce power, 90–91
McCarran–Ferguson Act, 91–92, 140–181
State guaranty funds, 94–99
State Regulation of Insurance, 92–141
Antitrust law (state regulation), 181–182
Health insurance, 359–360
Rates and ratemaking, 99–139
Solvency assured, 93–99

REINSURANCE, 717–740
See also Assigned Risk Plans; Joint Underwriting Associations; Residual Market Mechanisms
Duty of utmost good faith, 717–724
"Follow-the-fortunes" clauses, 724–727
Insolvency of insurers,
Cut-through clauses, 732
Insolvency clauses, 727–733
Reinsurer's right of set-off, 733–740
Reinsurance facility, 711

RELIANCE
See Agents (Intermediaries); Estoppel against Insurer

REMEDIES (Against the Insurer)
See also Bad-Faith Breach Liability of the Insurer; Measure of Recovery; Punitive Damages
Bad-Faith breach, 411–438
Compensatory damages, 411–438
Punitive damages, 427

REPRESENTATION
See Misrepresentation

RESERVATION OF RIGHTS NOTICE, 544–549
See also Duty to Defend

RESIDUAL MARKET MECHANISMS, 710–716
See also Automobile Insurance; Liability Insurance; Property Insurance
Automobile insurance, 710–712
Liability insurance, 713–715
Malpractice insurance, 713–715
Property insurance, 712–713

RETIREMENT–BENEFIT PLANS
See ERISA

RISK, 2–3
Risk allocation, 2–3
Risk pooling, 2
Risk transfer, 2

SALE OF LAND
See Real Estate Sales (Mismatched or Double Insurance)

SAMPLE POLICIES
Automobile insurance, 602–612
Homeowners insurance, 184–195
Liability insurance, 439–449
Life insurance, 279–298
Property insurance, 184–195

SECONDARY MARKET FOR INSURANCE
See Insurance Market

SEPARATION AGREEMENTS
See Divorce (and Separation Agreements)

SETTLEMENT OF CLAIMS, 568–588
See also Automobile Insurance; Duty to Defend; Excess Insurance; Liability Insurance; Reinsurance
Bad-Faith in settlement, 574–588
Duty of settlement, 568–574, 588–595
Duty of excess insurers to primary insurers, 588–595
Duty owed to insureds, 568–574
Duty owed to reinsurers, 727

SEX
See also Rates and Ratemaking (Method and Regulation)
Rate classification, 127–139

SHERMAN ACT
See McCarran-Ferguson Act

SIMPLIFIED POLICIES
See Drafting Insurance Policies; Plain Language Policies

SOLVENCY OF INSURERS
See Insolvency of Insurers; Regulation of Insurance, State

SPECIMEN POLICIES
See Sample Policies

"STACKING" UNINSURED MOTORIST COVERAGE, 705–709
See also Coordination of Multiple Coverages; Uninsured Motorist Insurance

STANDARD FIRE INSURANCE POLICY
See Property Insurance

STANDARD MORTGAGEE CLAUSE, 209–210
See also Mortgagees Insurance; Property Insurance

STANDARDIZED FORMS
See Drafting Insurance Policies

STOCK INSURANCE COMPANIES, 1

SUBROGATION, 201–203, 392
Equitable and contractual subrogation, 201–202, 392
Equitable subrogation and the duty to settle, 588–595
Health insurance and tort recovery by subrogation, 387–394
Property insurance, 201–209
Uninsured motorists insurance, 671

SUPERFUND
See CERCLA; Hazardous Waste (Liability Insurance)

SURPLUS LINES (Insurance), 716

TENANTS AS IMPLIED CO–INSUREDS, 216–221
See also Property Insurance

TERM INSURANCE
See Life Insurance

THEFT LOSS
See Property Insurance
Forcible entry requirement, 47–52

THIRD PARTY BENEFICIARY
See Insurable Interest; Life Insurance

THIRD PARTY INSURANCE, 183
See also Automobile Insurance; Liability Insurance

TIME LIMITS ON ACCIDENTAL INJURY CLAIMS, 83–89
See also Public Policy and Insurance

TIME OF OCCURRENCE
See Claims-Made Coverage; Occurrence; Trigger of Coverage

TITLE VII
Discriminatory rate classification, 138–139

TOXIC WASTE
See Hazardous Waste (Liability Insurance)

TRIGGER OF COVERAGE, 677–691
See also Coordination of Multiple Coverages
Exposure theory, 682–683, 688
Hazardous waste cases, 688–690
Manifestation theory, 683–685, 688
Occurrence clauses construed, 685–687

TYPES OF INSURANCE
See Automobile Insurance; Claims-Made Coverage; Liability Insurance; Life Insurance; Malpractice Insurance; No-Fault Insurance; Property Insurance; Uninsured Motorists Insurance

UMBRELLA COVERAGE, 594
See also Excess Insurance; Liability Insurance

UNCONSCIONABILITY
Disability insurance, 385–386

UNDERWRITING CYCLE, 155–156

UNIFYING DIRECTIVE, 472–473
See also Liability Insurance

UNINSURED MOTORISTS INSURANCE, 663–676, 705–709
See also Automobile Insurance; Coordination of Multiple Coverages
Arbitration, 670–671
Contact requirement, 671–676
Contra Proferentem, 38–42
Forms of coverage, 670
Moral hazard, 676
Multiple coverages, 705–709
Plain-language UM coverage, 671
"Stacking" coverage, 705–709
Statutory requirement, 671–676
Subrogation, 670
Underinsured motorists insurance, 670

USE OF VEHICLE, 628–630
See also Automobile Insurance

VACANCY EXCLUSIONS, 252–257
See also Property Insurance

VALUED POLICIES, 266–267
See also Measure of Recovery (Coverage Provided)

VENDOR–VENDEE PROBLEMS
See also Property Insurance
Mismatched and double insurance, 221–228

WAIVER, 60–65
See also Agents (Intermediaries); *Contra Proferentem;* Estoppel against Insurer

WARRANTIES
  See also Adverse Selection; Exclusions
    and Conditions (to Coverage); Prop-
    erty Insurance, Exclusions and Ex-
    ceptions; Reasonable Expectations
    of the Insured
Breach of warranty, 5–14
Exclusions (a modern approach to warran-
  ty law), 256

WARRANTIES—Cont'd
History of warranties, 10–11
Lord Mansfield's Rule, 10–11
Materiality of breach, 11–12
Regulation of warranties, 12–13

WHOLE LIFE COVERAGE
See Life Insurance

†